George Eaton Simpson / *J. Milton Yinger*

OBERLIN COLLEGE

RACIAL AND CULTURAL MINORITIES: An Analysis of Prejudice and Discrimination

FOURTH EDITION

Harper & Row, Publishers
New York / Evanston / San Francisco / London

To E. B. S. and W. M. Y

CONTENTS

PREFACE
TO THE FOURTH
EDITION

The General Assembly of the United Nations proclaimed 1971 as the "International Year to Fight Against Racism and Racial Discrimination." We hope that 1972 and the years to follow will be thought of, if not proclaimed, in the same way. This book is our expression of that hope.

In this new edition we have not shifted from our basically analytical perspective. Our aim is to contribute to the understanding of problems associated with intergroup relations, not to name the villains and heroes. This perspective is more difficult to maintain today than it was a few years ago. Commentaries on racial and cultural relations have become heavily politicized. This is scarcely surprising during a period when the problems associated with discordant intergroup relations have been opened fully to public view. Indeed, it is probably essential. It is equally essential, however, that we try to understand where we are and what forces are creating the existing situation. Proclamations that mankind suffers from racism will not cure him.

At a time when mankind seems even more prone than usual to use declarations and condemnations of the other man's prejudice as a substitute for an investigation of its causes, we are reminded of the pilot who tried to calm his passengers during a severe storm. The plane was pitching and jumping wildly, but he assured them that it could withstand the stress. Then one of the engines went out, but he told them that the three remaining engines furnished adequate power. When the radio went dead and the compass failed, the pilot himself was alarmed. But he reassured the passengers, after describing all the difficulties and hazards that confronted them, in these words: "We are not certain precisely where we are, and with the compass out, we're not certain just where we're going. But you'll be glad to know that we're making very good time."

We, too, want to make good time, provided it is toward the destination of reduced intergroup hostility. To that end, this book is an effort to fix the compass and repair the radio.

Books, monographs, and articles dealing with prejudice and discrimination and with the place of racial and cultural minorities in a social structure are now very numerous. Many of them are of excellent quality, and the scope of their coverage is so wide that no single volume can even hope to indicate the range of materials. Our aim is not simply to sample these materials in order to assess the present status of the science of majority-minority relations. We hope also to contribute to two essential tasks. First, the very quantity of present studies increases the problem of synthesis—of relating the various analyses to each other and to a systematic group of principles that underlie them all. Many of the studies are highly specialized, with reference both to the groups that they examine and to the concepts and explanatory principles that they employ. Only by bringing them into a common framework of analysis can the valid observations be separated from the errors and exaggerations and the omissions be pointed up. We have not given full attention to the many excellent studies of racial and cultural relations outside of the United States because pressures of space make an adequate worldwide comparative statement impossible within the framework of this volume. It is our hope, however, that the principles stated and illustrated here can be profitably used in the study of intergroup relations in other parts of the world. If this hope is realized, the reader interested in an intensive study of a majority-minority situation not dealt with in this volume will have been furnished some guiding concepts for his own work. He may be less likely to adopt an oversimplified, one-factor view and less likely to study one situation in isolation from the total society of which it is a part.

The second question that seemed to us to demand further attention in the literature on majority-minority relations is the connection between studies in this field and the whole range of the sciences of human behavior. This is an important area of study, in fact, not only because it takes us into the human arena, with its pathos and tragedy—and glory, but also because it involves us in most of the major social scientific questions. In this edition we have sought again to stress this relationship to larger questions of the theory of human behavior. We have consistently tried to write from the point of view that the material we were discussing was simply one manifestation of the total complex of human life, not to be understood as an isolated or unique phenomenon. Every proposition concerning intergroup relations should be harmonious with, in fact a part of, the general principles being developed in the sciences of human behavior. If we have succeeded in any measure in achieving this aim, the careful student should gain from this volume not only some understanding of prejudice and of the place of minorities in the social structure, but also some knowledge of the nature of personality, the types of social interaction, the functions of institutions, and the meaning of culture. It is also our hope that he will be alerted to some of the problems of methodology faced by social scientists today. A fairly large share of the writings in the field of majority-minority relations are quite uncritical of the sources of their material—the objectivity of the reporting, the extent to which it is typical, the usefulness of the concepts employed, and the kinds of causal inference that are justified. To take account of these methodological and logical problems requires more tentative statements, the addition of qualifying phrases, and the recognition of the need for more carefully controlled studies on which one can place more reliance. This caution makes the analysis less clear-cut and sharp; but to fail to take into account methodological problems is to give an impression of finality that no science, and particularly no science of human behavior, can accept.

Although there are few major social scientific concepts that do not arise in the study of intergroup relations, stratification theory is particularly involved. Human societies everywhere—or almost everywhere—have developed patterns that distribute income, power, and prestige unequally. These patterns vary widely, from those that are heavily reinforced by culture, social structure, and individual tendencies to those that are relatively open, with extensive changes in individual placement and structural support. Majority-minority systems, as we shall use that concept, are in the middle of this range. This volume is an effort to understand societies where such structures are predominant. Majority-minority systems, as contrasted with class or caste systems, are extremely volatile. They are also very common—the frequent product of our kind of world. No topic is more important to the contemporary student of human societies and behavior.

In examining the dramatic events of the last decade, we have been struck by the fact that the changes in race relations have depended scarcely at all on reduction of individual prejudices. Changes in the structure of society—economic, political, demographic, educational—have shattered earlier patterns of accommodation and required the formation of new relationships, almost regardless of individual attitudes. We have tried, in this fourth edition, not to exaggerate this fact; we have thoroughly reviewed the new research on prejudice, but events before us have demanded that we give major attention to the transformation of institutional patterns.

The vital role now being played by minority-group members themselves in the reformulation of race relations also shifts attention away from the prejudices of the majority. This does not, of course, eliminate the need for attention to the personality level. It calls, in fact, for renewed attention to questions of continuity and change in the personalities of minority-group members, as well as for continuing attention to the conditions under which attitudes of the majority are crucial to the course of events.

The flood of events during the last several years, and the flood of commentary and analysis of those events, have demanded that we rework every chapter thoroughly. Some have been almost completely rewritten. In the division of labor, Simpson has taken major responsibility for Chapters 2, 11 through 16, and 18 through 20; Yinger for Chapters 1, 3 through 10, 17, 21, and 22. The work throughout, however, is the product of years of collaborative effort. References in footnotes and bibliography can only inadequately express our indebtedness to the hundreds of scholars on whose work we have drawn in this process. In addition, many persons have responded, in conversation and letter, to our request for information. We are grateful to them for their generous help. In particular we would like to thank Mrs. Arlene Hall, and Mrs. Betty Berman and her staff for their skillful, prompt, and good-humored help in preparing the final copy.

George Eaton Simpson
J. Milton Yinger

LIST
OF ABBREVIATIONS

Because of the frequency with which several organizations and periodicals are referred to, they are abbreviated as follows:

AA	*American Anthropologist*
AAUP	*American Association of University Professors Bulletin*
ACE	American Council on Education
ADL	Anti-Defamation League of B'nai B'rith
AJS	*American Journal of Sociology*
Annals	*Annals of the American Academy of Political and Social Science*
ASR	*American Sociological Review*
CA	*Current Anthropology*
CD	*Child Development*
GPO	Government Printing Office
HER	*Harvard Educational Review*
HEW	Department of Health, Education and Welfare
HR	*Human Relations*
HUD	Department of Housing and Urban Development
IE	*Integrated Education*
JASP	*Journal of Abnormal and Social Psychology*
JCR	*Journal of Conflict Resolution*
JIR	*Journal of Intergroup Relations*
JNE	*Journal of Negro Education*
JP	*Journal of Psychology*
JPSP	*Journal of Personality and Social Psychology*
JSI	*Journal of Social Issues*
JSP	*Journal of Social Psychology*
JSSR	*Journal for the Scientific Study of Religion*
MFL	*Marriage and Family Living*
MH	*Mental Hygiene*
NAACP	National Association for the Advancement of Colored People
POQ	*Public Opinion Quarterly*
RRLS	*Race Relations Law Survey*
SA	*Social Action*
SER	*Southern Educational Reporter*
SERS	*Southern Educational Reporting Service*
SF	*Social Forces*
SP	*Social Problems*
SRC	The Southern Regional Council
SSN	*Southern School News*
SSRC	The Social Science Research Council
USCCR	United States Commission on Civil Rights

Part 1 / CAUSES AND CONSEQUENCES
OF PREJUDICE
AND DISCRIMINATION

Chapter 1 / TYPES OF MAJORITY-MINORITY SITUATIONS

Wherever one looks in these dramatic times, the puzzling phenomena of intergroup relations leap to attention. Civil rights, freedom marches, desegregation, discrimination, cultural pluralism, genocide, apartheid, Black Power–Red Power–Brown Power—these are terms the student of contemporary life must learn to use. England, with a steady migration of persons from India, Pakistan, Africa, and the West Indies, finds herself faced with problems of a color bar, and passes an unprecedented law limiting immigration; pressures against persons of Indian descent in the nations of East Africa not only reshape intergroup relations in those lands, but influence Britain's restrictive immigration policy; throughout most of Southeast Asia, the status of the "overseas Chinese" is being redefined in the face of nationalistic movements; the South African government boldly proclaims a policy of apartheid but keeps stumbling over the problem of economic interdependence; the United States, rapidly becoming a thoroughly urbanized society, discovers that desegregation is a national question; Russia, faced with difficult problems at home and a vast restlessness among her satellites, reverts again to anti-Semitism. How shall we seek to understand these developments? To what system of concepts shall we turn?

Man has always struggled to understand the world, to predict the sequence of events, and to achieve some control over the world around him. In the last few centuries, the method of inquiry that we call science has occupied a more and more important place in this struggle. Slowly we have begun to grasp the meaning of some of the complicated interactions of the natural world. Only recently, however, have the efforts to understand through science been turned toward man himself. Other methods of inquiry, to be sure, contribute to our understanding of man. Some of these methods are not sharply distinct from science. They often involve careful observation and an acute understanding of the variables influencing a given situation. The work of the historian, the philosopher, the artist demands our careful attention. The particular role of the scientist is to contribute to knowledge by isolating, one by one, each of the many variables that are involved in every situation and then studying the effects of their interaction. Either through laboratory manipulation or by the analysis of comparative situations, the scientist measures the influence of each factor alone and in interaction with other variables.

This book is an attempt to study one aspect of man's behavior from the point of view of contemporary science—particularly from the point of view of sociology, anthropology, and social psychology. For decades men have been studying and observing the puzzling phenomena of intergroup relations; but recently these studies have begun to turn from description to analysis, from isolated observation to controlled observation that begins to place the study of intergroup relations within the framework of the social sciences. Good will and a high interest are no longer sufficient to understand the complicated problems of "race relations" (as this area of human behavior is frequently called). We must use the methods of science and the total body of information that makes up the emerging knowledge of the sciences of man.

There is a tendency in most books on this subject—including perhaps this one—to speak of heroes and villains rather than of the human condition. We shall try to avoid that tendency. Even when our value positions are clearly apparent—for this is not a question of having or not having a point of view—our aim will be to specify the conditions under which various events occur. The vocabulary of praise and blame is inappropriate to our task. Deep-seated prejudices are natural events which we shall try to understand. Insofar as one's aim is to remove prejudices, he will be successful to the degree that the reader understands their causes rather than in proportion to the vigor of his condemnation of their carriers.

In the last several years it has become increasingly difficult to avoid politicizing the study of race relations, to steer between special pleading and indifference. Throughout this book we shall attempt to avoid special pleading precisely because we are *not* indifferent.

One need make no lengthy defense of the importance of the study of minority-majority relations, for it is a matter of daily observation. Pick up the daily paper or read the record of an international debate or watch the actions of a crowd: prejudice is there, sometimes unrecognized, but more often today defended or attacked—for we are becoming self-conscious about our prejudices.

Kuala Lumpur, Malaysia: The Government of this eight-year-old nation is on the verge of amending its Constitution to make it a crime to talk about racial issues.

The idea is that if everyone, especially the politicians and the press, stops talking about certain "sensitive issues"—namely, the serious racial problems here—the country would be a lot better off.

The amendments would make it an act of sedition, punishable by fine and imprisonment, to discuss any subject deemed "likely to arouse racial feelings and endanger racial peace in the country." This applies to discussions in the two chambers of Parliament.[1]

If you come across a Punjabi and a snake, kill the Punjabi first. (Old Bengali saying.)

A special grand jury reported yesterday that Chicago police had grossly exaggerated Black Panthers' resistance in a shooting incident last Dec. 4 in which two of the militants were killed and four others were wounded. The panel said police had riddled the Panthers' apartment with at least 83 shots, while only one shot apparently was fired from inside.

But the grand jury said it could not find evidence upon which to indict the men for violations of the victims' civil rights.

In a 250-page report, the grand jury said that

its hands were tied because the Black Panthers who survived the shooting refused to testify, claiming that they would talk only to a "peer group."[2]

In Belfast, Unyielding Men are Divided by History and Hate: Belfast lies awake at night listening for explosions. The city waits for the morning to learn what further bomb attacks— or murders—have occurred.

The Rev. Ian Paisley . . . a Member of Parliament and champion of Northern Ireland's Protestant right wing . . . demands strong measures to crush the underground Irish Republican Army.

At the Starry Plough Inn in the Roman Catholic New Lodge district, a thin young man talks softly and swiftly among the beer kegs in the back room. He brags of his part in terrorist bombings. . . .

Belfast thus appears irretrievably divided. The two communities are segregated by residential areas, schools (church-supported vs. state-supported) and social customs. Catholics like Gaelic football, curling and Irish folk dancing, while the Protestants tend to soccer and rugby and show little interest in Irish culture. There are Catholic pubs and Protestant pubs.[3]

In Nürnberg's warm, well-lighted courtroom, the lawyers tried to get the point across—these Nazis had killed 6,000,000 Jews. . . . This was no report from a refugee agency. Here it was, right out of the Nazi files. The Gestapo chief Jew catcher, Adolf Eichmann said that 4,000,000 died in concentration camps and 2,000,000 were killed by extermination squads. Fat, brutal Hans Frank counted 3,500,000 Jews in Western Poland in 1941, "perhaps 100,000" in 1944. If the untellable crime could ever be told, Nürnberg's evidence, as clear and specific as last week's robbery, had told it. But its immense inhumanity made it almost immune to translation into human terms.[4]

I charge the white man with being the greatest liar on earth! I charge the white man with being the greatest drunkard on earth. . . . I charge the white man with being the greatest gambler on earth. I charge the white man, ladies and gentlemen of the jury, with being the greatest peace-breaker on earth. I charge the white man with being the greatest adulterer on earth. I charge the white man with being the greatest deceiver on earth. I charge the white man with

[1] *The New York Times*, March 2, 1971, p. 7.

[2] *The Plain Dealer*, May 16, 1970, p. 1.
[3] *The New York Times*, April 10, 1971, p. 2.
[4] *Time*, Dec. 24, 1945, p. 29.

being the greatest trouble-maker on earth. So, therefore, ladies and gentlemen of the jury, I ask you, bring back a verdict of guilty as charged.[5]

Augusta, Georgia: Six Negro men killed in rioting last Monday night were shot in the back with buckshot, autopsies showed yesterday.[6]

Tel Aviv: Numerically, they were insignificant —an extremist group of perhaps 50 youths who sprang from the anonymous squalor of Jerusalem's slums to clash with the Israeli police in the capital's Zion square. Yet last week the group's name—the Black Panthers—was on everyone's lips and Israel was undergoing an extraordinary bout of soul-searching.

Who are the Israeli Black Panthers and what did they do to disturb the National Conscience? The organization was formed only two months ago by a dozen young Jews of North African extraction to combat what they regarded as "discrimination" against the country's Oriental Jewish community. . . .

Israelis, long preoccupied with external issues, were forced to turn their attention inward. They were made to recognize that a country founded and headed by Socialist revolutionaries had produced a large group of disillusioned, frustrated, bitter youth. . . .

While 70 percent of the children who start elementary school are of Oriental extraction, Oriental Jews account for only 14 percent of the student population in the universities. . . .

Many Israelis believe that the appearance of the Black Panther movement has thus served a useful purpose. A danger signal has been lit. Last Tuesday night, virtually the whole country watched a three-hour television program on the Black Panthers. Interviewed on the program, the mother of one of the young men screamed at the camera, "Aren't you ashamed, all of you people there?"

Isreal Kats, director of the National Security Service, summed up the mood of a troubled nation when he answered her, "I am proud of the things we have done. I am ashamed of that which we have not done."[7]

Men on whom the somber shadow of the synagogue falls are diverted from public activity and turn aside from all great deeds achieved by the Soviet people. Jewish clerks attempted to sow poisoned seeds of Chauvinism in the

consciousness of believers and to chain their thoughts and feelings to the promised land of Palestine.

These poisoned people often become the victims of various religious dealers, feathering comfortable nests under synagogue vaults.[8]

A children's picture book about the marriage of a white rabbit and a black rabbit has been removed from the open shelves of Alabama public libraries because of criticism by segregationists. . . . The black rabbit is male; the white, female. . . . [The] director of the Alabama Public Library service division said in Montgomery that the book had not been entirely removed from circulation. "That would not be morally right," she said. "We have put it on the reserve shelf where the public can get it by request only."[9]

Thus the stories range, from whimsical censorship to vicious mass murders. Our task is to try to understand such phenomena. Do they have anything in common? What are the factors in individual personality and group conflict that account for these expressions of prejudice and discrimination? What various forms do prejudice and discrimination take?

It would be a mistake to assume from these incidents that prejudice is universal or that there is no evidence on the other side. There are many variations in time and space; opposition to discrimination and the absence of categorizing prejudices are also newsworthy items in the contemporary scene. In the United States, for example:

The number of blacks attending school at both ends of the educational cycle increased sharply during the late nineteen-sixties, according to a new Census Bureau study.

The number in college more than doubled between 1964 and 1969. The number aged 3 to 4 in nursery schools almost doubled. The number of blacks in college jumped from 234,000 in 1964 to 492,000 last year . . . an increase of 111 percent. White college enrollment, involving much larger numbers, increased 58 percent in the same period.[10]

Police Chief Herbert T. Jenkins of Atlanta, who said he used to be a firm segregationist, reported with some satisfaction to a law-enforce-

---

[5] From a radio drama presented by the Black Muslims, quoted in C. Eric Lincoln, *The Black Muslims*, Beacon, 1961, pp. 3–4.

[6] *The Plain Dealer*, May 16, 1970, p. 1.

[7] *The New York Times*, May 30, 1971, p. 2–E.

[8] Byelorussian *Zviazda*, Oct. 6, 1960, as translated by the *New York Herald Tribune* News Service.

[9] *Seattle Times*, May 22, 1959.

[10] *The New York Times*, Oct. 11, 1970, p. 81.

ment conference at the University of California that he has fifty Negroes on his 750-man force, and that they are authorized to arrest both white and colored offenders. "My thinking in recent years had to be changed," the chief explained. "The time has come . . . when an individual cannot be denied any public or official right or privilege because he is a Negro." To a heckler who asked, "Would you like your wife to be arrested by a Negro Policeman?" Mr. Jenkins retorted, "Hell, no! Not by a white one either."[11]

Since World War II, Australian immigration policy has undergone basic changes. . . . The rule barring "non-Europeans" from citizenship was removed in 1956. Ten years later the residence time required before naturalization was reduced from 15 years to 5. A test for language qualification, easily rigged against an unwanted entrant, was abolished in 1958. . . . By the time of the 1966 Census . . . the number of permanent residents of Asian descent had more than quadrupled [since 1947] to 101,387, while the total population of about 11.5 million represented an increase of 62.5 percent in the same period.[12]

Every Dutchman seems to know that more than 300,000 nonwhite colonials from Holland's crumbled East Indian empire have moved in among the canals and windmills. Few seem to give it a second thought.[13]

Three Negroes from districts where blacks are in the minority were elected to the House of Representatives in Tuesday's election. They will become the only Negro House members to represent constituencies that are not mostly black.

By retaining the seats they already held, Negroes won a total of 12 House contests. Counting Senator Edward W. Brooke, Republican of Massachusetts, who was not up for reelection this year, there will be 13 Negroes in the 92d Congress, the most since reconstruction.[14]

This month George Wallace returned to the Alabama statehouse—and in Greene County, a new probate judge, a new sheriff, a county clerk, and two school board members—all black— also took office, joining six other blacks elected 18 months ago. This leaves the county with only two white officials, who weren't up for reelection in 1970. . . . The emergence of black power in

Greene, a direct outgrowth of the Voting Rights Act of 1965, may foreshadow similar developments in many of the 80 Southern counties in which blacks form a majority.[15]

Today, education is perhaps the most important function of state and local governments. . . . It is the very foundation of good citizenship. Today, it is a principal instrument in awakening the child to cultural values, in preparing him for later professional training, and in helping him to adjust normally to his environment. . . .

Does segregation of children in public schools solely on the basis of race, even though the physical facilities and other "tangible" factors may be equal, deprive the children of the minority group of equal educational opportunities? We believe that it does. . . . To separate them from others of similar age and qualifications solely because of their race generates a feeling of inferiority as to their status in the community that may affect their hearts and minds in a way unlikely ever to be undone. . . .

We conclude that in the field of public education the doctrine of "separate but equal" has no place. Separate educational facilities are inherently unequal. Therefore, we hold that the plaintiffs and others similarly situated for whom the actions have been brought are, by reason of the segregation complained of, deprived of the equal protection of the laws guaranteed by the Fourteenth Amendment.[16]

THE RAPIDLY CHANGING CONTEMPORARY SCENE

The student of race relations is confronted with a rapidly changing situation, both as to the facts of prejudice and discrimination and as to our knowledge of their meaning. In the enormous international struggles of our time, with their power and ideological aspects, the role of minority groups inevitably became tremendously important. How maintain national unity? How win or preserve the cooperation of colonial or former colonial peoples? How adjust to the rising literacy, power, and demands of minority groups everywhere? How preserve and extend a democratic ideology in the face of its obvious violations in almost every land? Such questions might, perhaps,

[11] *The Reporter*, Oct. 25, 1962, p. 20.
[12] *The New York Times*, Feb. 22, 1970, p. 24.
[13] *The New York Times*, Dec. 7, 1969, p. 23.
[14] *The New York Times*, Nov. 5, 1970, p. 28.

[15] *The New Republic*, Jan. 17, 1971, p. 11.
[16] Brown v. Board of Education of Topeka, 347 U.S. 483 (1954).

have been treated casually a generation ago; they have leaped, now, to the forefront of international attention and cannot be disregarded. The result is a ferment in minority-majority relations of greater importance than the modern world has witnessed before.

In the United States, the national compromise over the "Negro question" that lasted for two generations has been broken by changes in the nature of American society and is being intensely re-examined. Crucial Supreme Court decisions, changes in the practices of labor unions, the migration and industrialization of an important part of the Negro labor force, the demands made by our position on the international scene—these and many other factors are forcing us to work out a new and more effective adjustment among the races.

More than 500 American groups are working to reduce discrimination. The industrialization of the South has been speeded up enormously since 1940. Tens of thousands of new industrial concerns have been added to its economy, increasing its income by several billions, shifting its population toward the cities, breaking the status patterns of Jim Crow that depended on the social structure of the plantation. The North and West have had a rapid increase in their Negro populations. Sharp disputes and conflicts as well as gains have accompanied these changes. But as Blumer says: ". . . Race relations cannot avoid being incorporated to the full in the unsettling and dynamic changes that are part and parcel of the industrialized and urbanized mass society that is emerging in the world today."[17]

During World War I many people were made aware of the problem of minorities by the discovery here, in times of crisis, of partially assimilated national groups. They were shocked at the failure of the "melting-pot" idea. One reaction was antiforeignism, a demand for tightened immigration restrictions. Some few, however, began to wonder whether the melting-pot idea might not itself be inadequate, demanding, as it did, Americanization on quite narrow terms. Many of our immigrants, as Randolph Bourne points out, are not

simply those who missed the *Mayflower* and came over on a later boat; when they did come they took a *Maiblume*, a *Fleur de Mai*, a *Fior di Maggio*, or a *Majblomst*. There were national, cultural, religious, and lingual differences to be accommodated. In a world of international tension and publicity, insistent "Americanization" of our national minorities, with the strong implication that their ways of doing things are queer, foolish, and unacceptable, is unlikely to be a successful procedure. Myrdal says that ". . . the Negro problem is not only America's greatest failure but also America's incomparably great opportunity for the future."[18] And in the same vein, Bourne declares: "To seek no other goal than the weary old nationalism, belligerent, exclusive, inbreeding . . . is to make patriotism a hollow sham. . . . The failure of the melting-pot, far from closing the great American democratic experiment, means that it has only just begun. . . . In a world which has dreamed of internationalism, we find that we have all unawares been building up the first international nation."[19]

Other facets of majority-minority relations are appearing rapidly in the contemporary world. Imperialistic domination of "native" peoples is running into self-contradictions and costs that have greatly weakened it. The 400-year period of colonial domination, at least by the West, is passing. (Russian domination of Eastern Europe and parts of Asia, involving the more open use of force, more frequent manipulation of local political movements, and exploitation of an international ideology, shares some aspects of the old pattern. It adds, however, surveillance and control over the total life of the people that makes it in important ways a new phenomenon. Its survival seems to rest upon the possibility of a continuing monopolization of power.) After World War II the western nations found that the practical advantages of colonialism had sharply declined just at the time when the costs of maintaining the old pattern had in-

[17] Herbert Blumer, in A. W. Lind (ed.), *Race Relations in World Perspective*, Univ. of Hawaii Press, 1955, p. 17.

[18] Gunnar Myrdal, *An American Dilemma*, Harper & Row, 1944, p. 1021.
[19] Quoted in Alain Locke and B. J. Stern (eds.), *When Peoples Meet*, Hinds, Hayden and Eldredge, 1946, pp. 730–731.

creased vastly. Indigenous labor was no longer so cheap and tractable; local political movements could be stopped only by costly suppression; the defense of colonies against rivals was difficult and expensive. During the period of domination there had been a diffusion of western ideas of nationalism, democracy, and freedom that armed the colonies against their overlords. Meanwhile, the growth of democratic movements in the mother countries themselves weakened the colonial system. Many people came to the conviction that lack of democracy anywhere endangers world peace.[20]

These forces, and others, are bringing important changes to the colonial world. Japan's effort to extend her imperial domination was completely broken. China freed herself from the extraterritorial privileges that many western nations demanded and held. (Protests against these privileges may be one of the factors in the rise of contemporary counterimperialism in China; she may have learned her lessons from the West too well.) Scores of new nations have been formed since 1945 from former colonies in Africa, Asia, and Oceania.

Many of the new and renewed nations of the world are inhabited primarily by "colored" persons. Thus "race relations" increasingly takes on the pattern of contact between sovereign peoples. This shift is important, not only in international affairs, but in the internal processes of many nations.

All of this does not mean that domination across national boundaries has decreased, but only that the pattern is changing. Major powers continue to attempt to seat and unseat those governments that they consider essential to their interests. Nor does it indicate the growth of democracy, for the decline of imperialism is not necessarily a gain for the majority of human beings; it may represent only a shift in power from an external to an internal ruling class. J. H. Boeke describes this situation well: ". . . There is abundant evidence that often new national governments, behind the screen of nationalism, fight colonialism by

taking over its policy. But it is no longer colonialism since foreign capitalists have been eliminated. The small villager and the poor consumer who are the victims of this game of puss in the corner have every reason to remember the Dutch proverb that it is all the same whether one is bitten by a she-cat or a he-cat."[21]

Policies concerning industrialization, landholding, imports, granting of credit, and the like, may be primarily in the interests of the new internal elite, as Boeke points out, the masses being paid in slogans of nationalism and anticolonialism.

We cannot describe other aspects of contemporary minority-majority relations here. Tribal conflicts within African nations and discrimination against residents—and often citizens—of Asian or European descent have become severe. Rhodesia has joined South Africa in an effort to develop a strictly segregated society, with superior status for Whites. Merely to mention Pakistan, Ireland, or Malaysia is to recall instances of severe intergroup conflict. Eastern Europe is going through a new phase in its struggles with the question of the dozens of national and cultural minorities living there. The Zionist movement and the founding of Israel have added a new dimension to the question of the status of Jews in many lands. Wherever we look, new adjustments to the age-old problems of group interaction are being tried.

There are at least modest success stories in Mexico, Brazil, Nigeria (since 1970), Holland, Yugoslavia, the United States, and elsewhere; but mainly what we see is that mankind has yet to find ways to achieve full equality for diverse racial and ethnic groups within a pluralistic society. Nevertheless, such a time of change can yield valued insights into the nature of the subject with which we are concerned in this book. Fixed notions of causes and cures are obviously inadequate today. Equipped with tentativeness and modesty we can, with the knowledge available, begin to grasp the basic nature of intergroup relations, of prejudice and discrimination, of hierarchies of power within and between societies.

[20] Raymond Kennedy, "The Colonial Crisis and the Future," in Ralph Linton (ed.), *The Science of Man in the World Crisis*, Columbia, 1945, pp. 338–346.

[21] In Lind (ed.), *op. cit.*, p. 73.

THE CHANGING SCIENTIFIC VIEW OF INTERGROUP RELATIONS

The speed with which majority-minority relations are changing in the contemporary world is matched by the development of scientific theories in the field. The concepts and beliefs of competent scholars only a few decades ago are now looked upon as entirely inadequate; and many of the writings that were most widely read are seen today as scarcely more than elaborate rationalizations for existing stereotypes and prejudices. (This rapid change in our conceptions should encourage us to hold present hypotheses and theories—including those advanced in this book—tentatively. They may prove to be inadequate to account for tomorrow's evidence.)

We shall not undertake here a history of "race" theories; but a brief statement may indicate the recency of scientific views and help to show the relationship between theories in this field and the total intellectual and power aspects of the environment. Our reference here is to persons who were primarily scholars; but they cannot be distinguished sharply from various publicists who wrote about race relations. At various points in the chapters that follow we shall refer to the work of such well-known propagandists as Count de Gobineau, Houston Stewart Chamberlain, Lothrop Stoddard, and Madison Grant. For two or three generations their type of analysis of "race relations" was widely circulated among the literate group and helped to reinforce the traditional views of millions who had never heard of these authors.[22] The work of such

writers was intellectually respectable only a few decades ago. Their contemporary successors, however, have no such standing. Even the "popular" intellectual supports of prejudice are crumbling.

Meanwhile, professional students of human behavior have also been struggling with the questions of majority-minority relations, and their various concepts have reflected their general theoretical and value orientations. Lester F. Ward, often thought of as the founder of American sociology, was an environmentalist and a firm believer in the value of social science in directing social change. Consequently he minimized the biological factors in race differences and did not believe that the existing patterns of race relations were inevitably fixed in the mores. In his enthusiasm for the use of social science to reduce the world's ills, he tended to underestimate the tenacity of prejudice. A more influential writer at the turn of the century, William Graham Sumner, emphasized the stability of patterns of intergroup relations. They were often embedded in the mores. Mores change when the conditions of life and the interests of men change, and they can be modified by conscious decision; but they do not change quickly, and attempts at conscious modifications—as by law—are limited by existing norms.[23] In the contemporary view, Sumner tended to overestimate the stability of custom and to underestimate the power of law to shape "ritual" (prescribed acts) in heterogeneous, urban societies, although evidence for the view that change can be initiated by rational plan can also be found in his writings.

Before World War I, sociological writing about race relations often reflected ". . . not only outmoded conceptions concerning primitive people but all the current popular prejudices concerning the Negro." One author, later to become a well-known scholar ". . . assumed that the Negro has a 'racial' temperament and that his 'shiftlessness and sensuality' are partly due to heredity and that he is inferior in his adaptiveness to a complex civilization. The infiltration of white blood is re-

---

[22] For two recent interpretations of such writers see Charles Alexander, "Prophet of American Racism: Madison Grant and the Nordic Myth," *Phylon*, Spring, 1962, pp. 73–90; and James Gregor, "Nordicism Revisited," *Phylon*, Winter, 1961, pp. 351–360. Gregor discusses the work of the German "Nordicist" Hans Guenther who, over a period of forty years, has described the "Nordic features" and "Nordic spiritual traits" in every person or thing he finds admirable. Recently the American periodical *Northern World* has reprinted lengthy selections from Guenther, without any identification of authorship. The selections are from his 1927 book *Rassenkunde Europas* (translated as *The Racial Elements of European History*). See *ibid.*, pp. 352–353. See also Richard Hofstadter, *Social Darwinism in American Thought*, Braziller, rev. ed., 1959, especially chap. 9, "Racism and Imperialism."

[23] See Harry V. Ball, George E. Simpson, and Kiyoshi Ikeda, "Law and Social Change: Sumner Reconsidered," *AJS*, Mar., 1962, pp. 532–540.

sponsible for ambition and superiority on the one hand and vice and immorality on the other."[24]

During World War I and for a few years thereafter some of the psychologists working with intelligence test scores were so convinced of their validity—as measures of inherited intelligence, unaffected by experience—that they accepted them as definite proof of racial differences. Negroes made much lower scores on these tests on the average; so did American Indians, Mexicans, Italians, and members of other groups. We shall discuss the validity of intelligence test scores in the next chapter; here we only need to say that virtually all psychologists today insist that comparisons are meaningless except within a group that has very similar background, experience, and status.

These brief references to earlier writers may serve to indicate that theories of majority-minority relations, as those dealing with other aspects of human behavior, are strongly influenced by the surrounding intellectual and moral environment. There are several ways in which this influence on particular theorists—the authors included—is expressed. The following are particularly notable: (1) the availability or lack of various kinds of empirical research; (2) the focusing of attention by dramatic events; (3) disciplinary perspectives; (4) various "style" aspects of all theoretical work; (5) the moral-political concerns with which the study of majority-minority relations is connected; (6) research methodologies available, and those deemed sufficiently powerful to be worthy of use.[25]

Such influences not only shape theoretical perspectives, but also affect the choice of problems on which those perspectives will be focused. Today, group conflict is the most visible fact and is receiving a great deal of attention. This is connected with the study of cultural variation, the types, the limits, and the consequences of cultural pluralism. This topic is readily attached to an interest in stratification systems. And in a day of world-wide communication and travel, comparative studies that seek to identify analytic variables in race relations, variables that are of shared significance in what appear on the surface to be widely variant systems, gain in importance. Substantial attention is still paid to the roots of individual prejudice and to the experience of individual minority-group members; but these themes are not so dominant as they were a decade ago.

We will not attempt, here, to give a condensed version of our own theoretical perspective. It will unfold as we explore particular topics. Here we only stress the fact that there is no special theory of "race relations." There is only a theory of human behavior, on which the study of race relations and majority-minority relations generally must draw, and to which it can contribute importantly. Nor can the material be handled adequately, in our judgment, from the perspective of any one discipline. We shall be using the research—and hopefully employing the insights—of several disciplines, particularly anthropology, psychology, and sociology. And it is our aim to use them in a unified, "field theoretical" way, not to treat them independently.

We shall not undertake an explication of other theoretical works and texts that deal with racial and cultural minorities or related theoretical issues. In the last several years a number of writers have focused on the need for

[24] E. Franklin Frazier, "Sociological Theory and Race Relations," *ASR*, June, 1947, p. 267. See also E. B. Reuter, "Racial Theory," *AJS*, May, 1945, pp. 452–461.

[25] For illustrative discussion of the ways in which theories of race and of race relations are influenced by these various contextual factors, see John S. Haller, Jr., "The Species Problem: Nineteenth-Century Concepts of Racial Inferiority in the Origin of Man Controversy," *AA*, Dec., 1970, pp. 1319–1329; Leonard Lieberman, "The Debate over Race: A Study in the Sociology of Knowledge," *Phylon*, Summer, 1968, pp. 127–141; William Petersen "The Classification of Subnations in Hawaii: An Essay in the Sociology of Knowledge," *ASR*, Dec., 1969, pp. 863–877. Some of the influences of the present context sustain or renew various emphases on biological

and racialist explanations of behavior. We will comment on this at several points in the chapters that follow. See, for example, Robert Ardrey, *Territorial Imperative*, Atheneum, 1966; Konrad Lorenz, *On Aggression*, Harcourt Brace Jovanovich, 1960; I. A. Newby, *Challenge to the Court: Social Scientists and the Defense of Segregation, 1954–1966*, Louisiana State Univ. Press, 1967; Isabella Black, "Race and Unreason: Anti-Negro Opinion in Professional and Scientific Literature Since 1954," *Phylon*, Spring, 1965, pp. 65–79.

more explicit and unified theoretical work, and we shall be discussing their points of view in connection with various topics in the chapters that follow. These works do not escape the influences we have specified above; a few of them tend to be somewhat argumentative and "schoolish"—and thus perhaps reduce their contributions to a cumulative and fully synthesized theory of majority-minority relations. Nevertheless they represent valuable steps toward a unified theory.[26] If we cannot speak yet of a mature science of intergroup relations, thoroughly integrated with a systematic science of man, we do have fundamental parts of such a discipline and valuable approaches to it. We can profit greatly by studying them with care.

DEFINITIONS AND TYPES OF MINORITIES

One of our first tasks is to delimit our area of inquiry, separating it from closely related but distinctive neighboring fields. We need also to define several basic concepts carefully.

There are many definitions of the primary terms in the study of intergroup relations. Sharp disagreements have frequently resulted from differences in definition, partly because of a misunderstanding of the nature of definitions. Definitions do not reveal what the data in question "really are." The phenomena of the world are not divided into neat, mutually exclusive types which, if we study hard enough, we can discover. They flow endlessly one into another, by minute gradations, and

any definition which tries to draw a sharp line is bound to be arbitrary to some degree. The phenomena included within the definition are not exactly alike, but only more or less alike; some phenomena excluded are also alike—but presumably less rather than more. In defining relations as complicated as those with which we are dealing in this study, with so many variables involved, one is bound to run into disagreement over what is more and what is less.

Yet definitions are necessary for communication. We must remember simply that they are, to some degree, empirically arbitrary.

The most important concept throughout the book is *minority*. From its definition one can derive its reciprocal, *majority*. Some counties of Mississippi have three times as many black citizens as white. Negroes make up an even higher proportion of the population of South Africa. For two centuries a handful of British dominated hundreds of millions of Indians. Yet we frequently refer to these situations as majority-minority situations—clearly meaning a pattern of relationship, the distribution of power, and not numbers. According to Louis Wirth: "We may define a minority as a group of people who, because of their physical or cultural characteristics, are singled out from the others in the society in which they live for differential and unequal treatment, and who therefore regard themselves as objects of collective discrimination. The existence of a minority in a society implies the existence of a corresponding dominant group with higher social status and greater privileges. Minority status carries with it the exclusion from full participation in the life of the society."[27]

From the perspective of the individual minority-group member, his status is character-

[26] See, for example, Michael Banton, *Race Relations*, Basic Books, 1967; H. M. Blalock, Jr., *Toward a Theory of Minority-Group Relations*, Wiley, 1967; Philip Mason, *Race Relations*, Oxford, 1970; John Rex, *Race Relations in Sociological Theory*, Weidenfeld and Nicolson, 1970; Richard A. Schermerhorn, *Comparative Ethnic Relations: A Framework for Theory and Research*, Random House, 1970; Tamotsu Shibutani and Kian M. Kwan, *Ethnic Stratification: A Comparative Approach*, Macmillan, 1965; Pierre van den Berghe, *Race and Ethnicity*, Basic Books, 1970; Pierre van den Berghe, *Race and Racism*, Wiley, 1967. More general studies of stratification are also of value; see, for example, Gerhard Lenski, *Power and Privilege*, McGraw-Hill, 1966; Edward O. Laumann (ed.), *Social Stratification: Research and Theory for the 1970s*, Bobbs-Merrill, 1970.

[27] In Linton (ed.), *op. cit.*, p. 347. Schermerhorn takes account of the numerical connotation of minority by separating two types of "Subordinate Groups": "mass subjects," who are low in power, but the numerical majority; and "minority groups," who are low in power and also the numerical minority. Although this has some value, it tends, in our judgment, to stress differences in number and to minimize sociological similarities. Ought two counties in Mississippi, one with slightly fewer than 50 percent Blacks, the other with slightly more than 50 percent, be classified separately by the student of race relations? See Schermerhorn, *op. cit.*, p. 13.

ized primarily by its categorical nature; he cannot resign or escape by merit. Whatever his unique characteristics, he is treated, in the defining case, simply as one unit of a group by those of dominant status.

Minorities, however, are not all alike. They differ in the symbols that set them apart, in the nature of their relationship to the dominant group, and in their reactions to the situation. It was once thought that the difference in symbols was most important—that the study of racial minorities was different from the study of groups set apart by religion, nationality, or culture. While recognizing that symbolic differences do affect the nature of the interaction, we must see that it is the pattern of relationship that is crucial. Several variables affect the pattern, as Wirth pointed out. A situation in which there is only one minority will be different from one in which there are several. A single minority has to absorb all the anxieties and frustration of the dominant group and become the object of all its power manipulations. Where there are several minorities, as in the United States, some may escape relatively easily; a hierarchy develops among them. The majority will play one minority off against another—and this maneuver will affect the way in which minorities respond to one another.

The degree of difference in culture, language, and race is another variable. The sharper the differences, the more the status pattern tends to persist.

Analysis of majority-minority interaction must also pay attention to the different effects of various types of social structure. John Blue notes that race relations, for example, develop differently in colonial, imperial, reservation, segregated, and equalitarian or quasi-segregated social systems.[28] Van den Berghe contrasts the kinds of race relations that develop in a competitive system (typically an urban, industrial setting where the dominant group is numerically larger, is itself stratified into many classes, and motivated by the ideology of an open, liberal, democratic society) with those that appear in a paternalistic system (where the dominant group is often numerically small, the economy largely agricultural, and the division of labor strictly along racial lines).[29] Lieberson points out that race relations develop differently in societies where a migrant population has imposed its order from the way they develop in situations where the indigenous population is dominant.[30]

In Europe, the term minority is typically applied ". . . to a group of people living on soil which they have occupied from time immemorial, but who, through change of boundaries, have become politically subordinate."[31] Such minorities are "cultural nationalities" deprived of political independence. This conception is found in the definition used by the United Nations Subcommission on Prevention and Protection of Minorities: Minorities are ". . . those nondominant groups in a population which possess and wish to preserve stable ethnic, religious or linguistic traditions or characteristics markedly different from those of the rest of the population."[32]

Recognizing the complexity of the empirical world—the extent to which the phenomena of our interest shade off into related but distinctive phenomena—how shall we specify the primary defining properties of "minority"? Wagley and Harris suggest five characteristics: (1) minorities are subordinate segments of complex state societies; (2) minorities have special physical or cultural traits that are held in low esteem by the dominant segments of the society; (3) minorities are self-conscious units bound together by the special traits that their members share and by the special disabilities which these bring; (4) membership in a minority is transmitted by a rule of descent which is capable of affiliating succeeding generations even in the absence of readily apparent special cultural or physical traits; (5) mi-

[28] John Blue, Jr., "Patterns of Racial Stratification: A Categoric Typology," *Phylon*, Winter, 1959, pp. 364–371.

[29] Van den Berghe, *Race and Ethnicity*, pp. 21–41.

[30] Stanley Lieberson, "A Societal Theory of Race and Ethnic Relations," *ASR*, Dec., 1961, pp. 902–910.

[31] Richard Schermerhorn, "Minorities: European and American," *Phylon*, Summer, 1959, p. 179.

[32] *Yearbook on Human Rights for 1950*, UN, 1952, p. 490.

Figure 1 / *Relationships Among Caste, Minority, and Class*

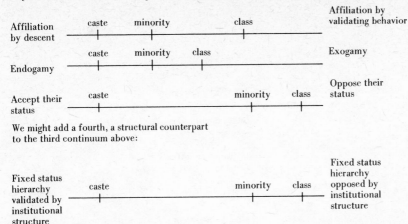

We might add a fourth, a structural counterpart
to the third continuum above:

nority peoples, by choice or necessity, tend to
marry within the group.[33]

Three Types of Stratification Systems

The value of these criteria is increased when
one uses them in making distinctions between
"minority" and closely related terms. Harris
compares minority with "caste" and "class,"
and in doing so notes the need for at least one
additional variable. The three terms share
many connotations; caste and minority, particularly, are often used interchangeably. Do
we need all three terms? Harris believes that
we do, if we are to make refined distinctions;
and argues his point by suggesting three con-
tinua by which groups can be classified.[34] We
might put these into quasi-scales, as in Figure 1.

These are subtle distinctions. But we are
dealing with complicated phenomena and we
need as powerful a vocabulary as we can create. It is well to note that, on two of the scales,
caste and minority are placed close together
while on the other two, minority and class are
close.

We must be careful not to place a given system of social relationships in one of these categories and then overlook changing patterns
that require reclassification. In India, for example, there is good evidence that "acceptance
of status" has been reduced for lower "castes."

This means that they have become more "mi-
nority-like." There is some tendency in the
United States to respond to Negroes more in
terms of their individual behavior, somewhat
less in terms of descent,[35] moving them, to that
degree, from the category of minority toward
that of class.

Perhaps these variations around the meaning of caste, minority, and class can be made
clearer by scaling the four variables in a somewhat different way. In Figure 2 we have designated possible "profiles" from among many
that might be drawn.

Such a chart may help us to avoid using
only a few nouns that cannot do justice to the
full range of facts; and it may facilitate the
recognition of change. Rather than state what
a society "really is" in its stratification system
in terms of a few types, we need to locate it
along the scale.

Our concern in this book is with minority-
majority systems, not with all varieties of
stratification. Clearly, however, we will need
to make comparative references, at many
points, to caste systems, on the one hand, and
to class systems on the other.

Varieties of Minority Aims. Having distinguished minorities from related types of
groups, we must still note that minorities vary
widely among themselves. Perhaps they can be
most usefully classified on the basis of their

[33] Charles Wagley and Marvin Harris, *Minorities
in the New World*, Columbia, 1958, p. 10.

[34] Marvin Harris, "Caste, Class, and Minority,"
SF, March, 1959, pp. 248–254.

[35] See Frank Westie, "Negro-White Status Differentials and Social Distance," *ASR*, Oct., 1952, pp.
550–558; Frank Westie and Margaret Westie, "The
Social Distance Pyramid," *AJS*, Sept., 1957, pp. 190–
196.

Figure 2 / Types of Stratification Systems Using Four Criteria

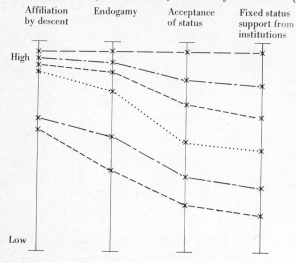

ultimate objectives, using Louis Wirth's classic distinction among four types:[36]

1. Pluralistic: a minority desiring peaceful existence side by side with the majority and other minorities. Pluralism is often a precondition of a dynamic civilization, for it allows mutual exchange and stimulation. It usually takes the form of a desire for basic political and economic unity along with toleration of cultural, lingual, and religious diversity. Many American Negroes, as we shall see, have become more pluralistic in recent years. The awakening of the ethnic minorities of Eastern Europe in the late eighteenth century was first of all a cultural renaissance, a change from feelings of inferiority to pride in their distinctness. Where economic and political equality have been achieved or granted, this awakening has continued to be pluralistic. When cultural diversity has been suppressed, the minorities have tended to become secessionistic.

The concept of pluralism varies from setting to setting. In some societies it implies toleration but little active cooperation among cultural groups; political and economic unity, but little exchange and common participation in other matters. This pattern has often been dominant in eastern Europe. Cultural pluralism may imply, however, a more active kind

of unity among diverse groups, a reaching out toward common goals, a sharing of their different heritages. This has frequently been the response of ethnic groups in the United States. After they have become thoroughly established in this country, pride in their cultural heritage becomes less defensive and protective. The last shreds of secessionism are gone, but a desire to contribute to the full range of American life out of their earlier experience remains.

2. Assimilationist: a minority desiring absorption into the larger society and treatment simply as individuals. Assimilation is likely to occur only when the majority accepts the idea; but it may prevail as a goal even in the face of majority opposition. Assimilationism is a common tendency among minorities in the United States. Yet a group may be divided on the question of the relative desirability of pluralism and assimilationism. Jews whose families have been in the United States for several generations, for example, are more likely to be assimilationists; more recent Jewish immigrants are likely to be pluralistic. Many Negroes are assimilationists, desirous of full participation in American society, thinking of themselves as sharing the common culture. Some take a pluralistic position, however; still others are secessionist or militant.[37]

[36] Varieties of minority aims cannot be thoroughly discussed without reference to majority aims and larger questions of social structure, a topic we shall examine below.

[37] Techniques for measuring assimilation are not highly developed. For an interesting attempt to design measurements, see Stanley L. M. Fong, "Assimilation of Chinese in America," *AJS*, Nov., 1965, pp. 265–273.

3. Secessionist: a minority that seeks both cultural and political independence. When a friendly plural existence or assimilation is frustrated, a minority may develop a movement dedicated to complete independence. They become discontented with cultural pluralism and antagonistic to assimilation. Such a movement most often occurs among a minority that has once had political independence—for example, Zionism. There may be some tendencies in this direction among other minorities, however, as illustrated by the Garveyite movement for a separate nation among American Negroes, and the separatist tendencies of the Black Muslims.

4. Militant: a minority that goes beyond the desire for equality to a desire for domination—the total reversal of statuses. It becomes convinced of its own superiority. When Hitler overran Czechoslovakia, the Sudeten Germans sought domination over the Czechs and Slovaks. When Britain withdrew from Palestine, both Arabs and Jews attempted to establish a dominant status. With the forming of new nations in Asia and Africa there have been many reversals of status.[38]

What we have described are abstract types, not empirical groups or explicitly formulated policies. Although groups might be compared as more or less supportive of a particular aim, we would be better served by information that permitted us to describe profiles. We need to think in terms of the proportionate share of support for these different aims, both within individuals (for many are ambivalent) and among them. If we are to avoid stereotypy, we need also to recognize change. Each minority can best be studied in terms of a sequence

[38] See Louis Wirth, "The Problem of Minority Groups," in Ralph Linton (ed.), *The Science of Man in the World Crisis*, Columbia, 1945, pp. 354–363. See also Shibutani and Kwan, *op. cit.*, esp. chaps. 17 and 18; Schermerhorn, *op. cit.*, chap. 4; Banton, *op. cit.*, chap. 11; van den Berghe, *Race and Racism*, chap. 7; Horace M. Kallen, *Cultural Pluralism and the American Idea*, Univ. of Pennsylvania Press, 1956; Joshua Fishman, "Childhood Indoctrination for Minority-Group Membership," *Daedalus*, Spring, 1961, pp. 329–349; Nathan Glazer and Daniel P. Moynihan, *Beyond the Melting Pot: The Negroes, Puerto Ricans, Jews, Italians, and Irish of New York City*, M.I.T. and Harvard, 1963; Milton Gordon, *Assimilation in American Life*, Oxford Univ. Press, 1964.

of profiles, indicating varying aims in response to changing circumstances. Lacking precise information, we can only make an estimate, but the "aim profile" of American Negroes might have been characterized by Line A, in the chart below, in 1940, and by Line B in 1970.

Figure 3 / Estimate of Combinations of Aims Among American Negroes

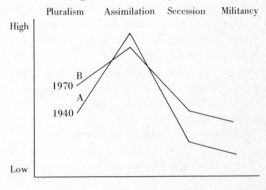

THE ORIGIN OF MINORITIES

There are unique elements in the history of every minority, but a few general principles are involved. Since a minority is a group of people that can be distinguished by physical or social characteristics, it follows that anything which makes a population more heterogeneous may create a minority situation. The kind of heterogeneity that will be noticed, of course, depends upon national, cultural, religious, and racial ideologies—in other words, on the characteristics of the majority, those with the greatest power and highest status. Migration, cultural contact, conquering armies bring diverse peoples together. This process has doubtless been accelerated by modern technology and transportation. "The genesis of minorities must therefore be sought in the fact that territory, political authority, people, and culture rarely coincide."[39] Whether or not a minority situation would develop in a stable, isolated society, starting from an original homogeneity, one can only guess. It is possible that the internal struggle for the values of that society

[39] Wirth, *op. cit.*, p. 365.

would result in some categorical system of rights and privileges. The evidence of anthropology, however, seems to show that homogeneous societies have little group prejudice. There are conflict and hostility but they are focused on individuals, not on supposed categories of people. It is the modern, mobile, heterogeneous society that is most likely to face a minority situation.

The development of the nation-state system has been the central fact in the origin of minorities. Both the spread of dominance over formerly separate groups and the common desire to create a homogeneous nation (leading to attempts to repress cultural variation) have created the minority-majority situation. Wagley and Harris view this development against the background of tribal societies:

An individual's world in primitive societies is . . . populated largely by "relatives," all of whom speak the same language, practice the same customs, and belong to the same physical stock. . . . Primitive social organization thus contains no provisions for incorporating into a single social unit groups of individuals who are not related by descent or by marriage, who follow different customs, who stress distinctive values, and who, in sum, are an alien people.

Only with the development of the state did human societies become equipped with a form of social organization which could bind masses of culturally and physically heterogeneous "strangers" into a single social entity. . . .

Yet the growth of the state form of organization did not entirely replace the principles by which unity is achieved among primitive peoples. On the contrary, if a thoroughgoing replacement had indeed taken place, minorities, as we know them today, would not exist.[40]

Many people, even in modern urban and heterogeneous societies, continue to view the world from a "tribal" perspective. The dominant groups particularly ". . . have tended to act as if the state society to which they belong ideally ought to consist of their own physical and cultural type. . . ."[41] We need now to examine the various ways in which they have acted on this conviction.

TYPES OF MAJORITY POLICY

Majority-minority situations are doubtless ancient. It was with the coming of the era of nationalism, however, with the Renaissance, the rise of trade, and increasing secularization, that the problem of minorities became very important. Merchants and kings were demanding national unity at the same time that minorities were becoming more self-conscious. The theories of national sovereignty and the divine right of kings were manufactured to oppose the universalist claims of the papacy on the one hand and the decentralization of power of feudalism on the other. In the process of national centralization, institutions were modeled after those of the majority, and the minorities were required, with varying degrees of rigidity, to bring their customs into line. When nationalism began to come to the more diverse peoples of Central and Eastern Europe, with their histories of imperial domination, the cultural minorities had a strong feeling of unity that resisted the larger nationalism. As Macartney points out, the Serb had never been a true part of the Ottoman Empire, but he knew that he was a Serb. Centuries of domination had produced a secessionist feeling that would not easily be worn away.[42]

Along with the growth of nationalism, new minority problems were developing as a result of imperialism and a fresh wave of conquests. Even greater diversity—of culture, of religion, of race—was brought into one political framework by the expansion of European power. The dominant groups were faced with new questions of policy with regard to minority groups. Extermination, subjugation, toleration, assimilation—each of these was tried at various times and places, as "external" minorities (the "colonies") were added to "internal" minorities (those within the mother country). England had scarcely worked out a peaceful *modus vivendi* with Scotland and Wales and was still fighting bitterly with Ireland when she was faced with the problems of policy in dealing with American Indians, Asiatic Indians, Arabs, Africans, Malayans, and a host of other peoples. Czarist Russia crossed

---

[40] Wagley and Harris, *op. cit.*, pp. 241–242.
[41] *Ibid.*, p. 242.

[42] C. A. Macartney, *National States and National Minorities*, Oxford, 1934.

mountains and plains, rather than oceans, but she absorbed an equally diverse group of minorities, as did many other nations.

With this brief sketch of the rise of internal and external minorities in mind, we may ask: What major types of policies have the dominant groups developed? Six varieties may be seen, sometimes paralleling, sometimes opposing the aims of minorities:

1. Assimilation
   a. Forced
   b. Permitted
2. Pluralism
3. Legal protection of minorities
4. Population transfer
   a. Peaceful transfer
   b. Forced migration
5. Continued subjugation
6. Extermination.

A brief discussion of these types of policies will indicate the wide range of responses that dominant groups may make to majority-minority situations.

1. Assimilation

One way to "solve" the problem is to eliminate the minority—as a minority. We have noted that this is the aim of some minorities, but their approach to assimilation is often very different. Dominant groups have frequently adopted an extreme ethnocentrism that refused minorities the right to practice their own religion, speak their own language, follow their own customs. The czarist regime went through periods of vigorous Russification during which the only alternatives available to minorities who wished to preserve their identity were rigid segregation, expulsion, or extermination. Perhaps the most extreme manifestation of forced assimilation was the Nazi regime, with its ideology of a monocultural, monolingual, monoracial people ruled by an authoritarian state. The Nazi policy went beyond forced assimilation, of course, for its doctrine of race superiority claimed that some groups were unassimilable. For them, forced population transfers and extermination were the policies adopted.

Oscar Janowsky points out that the basis of Nazi policy lies in the old conception that the best nation is a homogeneous one:

The savagery of Nazism does not derive exclusively from the distorted mind of a Hitler or a Goebbels. The deliberate and cold-blooded manner in which several million Jews, Poles, Russians, and others have been done to death in Nazi concentration camps . . . must not be ascribed solely to the frenzy of the hooligans, maddened by the prospect of defeat. The roots of that depravity lie deeply imbedded in the teachings of respectable *Junkers* like Bismarck and von Bülow. It stems from the belief that "members of different nationalities, with different languages and customs," cannot possibly live side by side in one and the same state; that when fate has cast two peoples upon the same territory, one must inevitably be "the hammer and the other the anvil"; that the suppression of the language and culture of the weaker nationality is a legitimate state policy: in a word, that the relentless pursuit of national-cultural uniformity is a law of historical development.[43]

Thus forced assimilation is an extreme manifestation of ethnocentrism developed into an active policy for the supposed benefit of a national state.

Peaceful assimilation is in marked contrast. It is a long-run policy of cultural and sometimes racial unity; but it permits minorities to absorb the dominant patterns in their own way and at their own speed, and it envisages reciprocal assimilation, a blending of the diverse group, not a one-way adjustment. Brazil has an ideology that looks with favor on the eventual blending of diverse racial types into a Brazilian stock. Gunnar Myrdal declares that the assimilation of many of her minorities is part of the value creed of the United States, although the creed does not have a strong reciprocal emphasis (minorities are to give up their differences) and it tends to exclude racial minorities. The supposed unassimilability of the Negro and other racial groups in the United States adds a dimension that must be taken into account in any analysis of the American situation.

Gordon uses the term "Anglo-conformity" to refer to what he considers the most prevalent form of American assimilationism. Although the term covers a variety of interpretations, they all assume "the desirability of

[43] Oscar Janowsky, *Nationalities and National Minorities*, Macmillan, 1945, pp. 30–31.

maintaining English institutions (as modified by the American Revolution), the English language, and English-oriented cultural patterns as dominant and standard in American life."[44] This conception has sometimes been related to notions of "Nordic" or "Aryan" superiority, to strong opposition to non-British immigration, and to vigorous Americanization campaigns. There has also been a moderate variant, however, which eschews ideas of racial superiority and accepts immigration from diverse sources, demanding only a fairly rapid adoption of "Anglo-Saxon" culture patterns.

This moderate "Anglo-conformity" view shades off into the "melting-pot" view of assimilation. Conditions in America were different in many ways from those in England; the population was drawn from many nations. "Was it not possible, then, to think of the evolving American society not simply as a slightly modified England but rather as a totally new blend, culturally and biologically, in which the stocks and folkways of Europe were, figuratively speaking, indiscriminantly mixed in the political pot of the emerging nation and

[44] Gordon, op. cit., p. 88.

melted together by the fires of American influence and interaction into a distinctly new type?"[45] This thesis has perhaps been more prominent in America as ideology than as policy; yet for 150 years our immigration laws were based, in part, on it, and the melting-pot idea probably affects, to some degree, the way in which most Americans view their society.

Conceptualization and measurement of assimilation are not far advanced, so that one cannot easily compare two groups on the extent of their assimilation. It is one thing to see it as a majority policy, however widely shared, and something else to see it as a societal condition, involving the interaction of majority and minority.[46] Seen in the latter way, assimilation undoubtedly has several dimensions, which require some separate investigation. Gordon has contributed to our understanding by specifying what he calls "the assimilation variables," as indicated in the following table.

[45] Ibid., p. 115.
[46] See George E. Simpson, "Assimilation," International Encyclopedia of the Social Sciences, Macmillan, 1968, Vol. 1, pp. 438–444.

The Assimilation Variables

Subprocess or Condition	Type or Stage of Assimilation	Special Term
Change of cultural patterns to those of host society	Cultural or behavioral assimilation	Acculturation
Large-scale entrance into cliques, clubs and institutions of host society, on primary group level	Structural assimilation	None
Large-scale intermarriage	Marital assimilation	Amalgamation
Development of sense of peoplehood based exclusively on host society	Identificational assimilation	None
Absence of prejudice	Attitude receptional assimilation	None
Absence of discrimination	Behavior receptional assimilation	None
Absence of value and power conflict	Civic assimilation	None

Source: Adapted from Milton Gordon, *Assimilation in American Life*, Oxford Univ. Press, 1964, p. 71.

This is a helpful statement, as it alerts us to the complexity of assimilation and shows how it involves both majority and minority, when thought of as a social process. It is not, however, entirely satisfactory in our judgment. The last three conditions are not specifically associated with assimilation. They are conditions that promote it, but they could also promote pluralism. Large-scale intermarriage can also be seen more as an index of assimilation, an indication that it has occurred to a substantial degree. We are left, then, with three primary dimensions: cultural, structural, and characterological. Gordon's assessment seems correct that, from the point of view of social process, structural assimilation is the critical condition, or the most decisive indicator. There can be extensive acculturation and probably even identification, without absorption into the dominant society. Structural assimilation, however, cannot occur without a major influence on the other conditions.[47]

2. Pluralism

Some minorities do not want to be assimilated, to lose their separate identity, whether it be unilaterally or bilaterally. And parallel to the pluralistic aims of such groups is the willingness on the part of some dominant groups to permit cultural variability within the range still consonant with national unity and security. This is frequently the immediate policy of an ultimate assimilationist approach. The Soviet Union sought, and apparently won, the support of scores of cultural and national minorities who had bitterly resented the czarist policy of suppression. In 1917 the Communists appealed to the various minorities by defending the right of cultural autonomy: "Mohammedans of Russia . . . Tartars of the Volga and Crimea; Kirghiz and Sartes of Siberia and Turkestan; Turks and Tartars of Transcaucasia, your beliefs and customs, your national institutions and culture, are hereafter free and inviolable."[48] Stalin, himself a member of a small nationality, was made People's Commissar for Nationalities and was impor-

tant in the policy that separated statehood from cultural nationality and race. Native languages and arts were not only permitted but encouraged, and the political organization of the Soviet Union reflects, to some degree, cultural units of the population. The Soviet policy was not, however, thoroughly pluralistic, and it has become less so. It opposed the extraterritorial pluralism of the Zionists; religious autonomy was systematically undermined by antireligious propaganda; vigorous insistence upon political and economic orthodoxy reduced the significance of cultural autonomy; and, since the beginning of World War II, a resurgent Russian nationalism has brought some return of the Russification policy of the czars. During that war, some Soviet minorities were forcefully broken up and dispersed; Jews and others have been attacked, in recent years, for being "cosmopolites"; and the theory of the Great Russian as the "elder brother" of the other groups in the Soviet Union implies at best an Orwellian equality, the Russian being "more equal than others."[49]

Janowsky, referring to the nations of east central Europe, believes that pluralism is the only way to reduce the internal dissension that has characterized those nations:

The core of the minorities problem, as envisaged in this book, can be grasped in a few sentences. The states of east-central Europe are not homogeneous in language or culture. A considerable proportion of the citizens of a state speak distinctive languages and cherish diverse historical memories or usages. Therefore national uniformity, which is symbolized by a single countrywide language and a single national culture, is unattainable except through the suppression or elimination of the minorities. Such efforts inevitably engender strife which in turn endangers the peace of the world. If oppression and conflict are to give way to harmony and contentment, the way must be found to recognize cultural differences within a framework of political and economic unity. The multi-national state provides the principle for sanctioning differences, and national federalism furnishes the means of integrating minori-

[47] Gordon, *op. cit.*, p. 81.
[48] Quoted by Sidney Webb and Beatrice Webb, in Locke and Stern (eds.), *op. cit.*, p. 673.

[49] W. J. Kolarz in Lind (ed.), *op. cit.*, chap. 9. For discussions of Soviet policy see chap. 9, below, and Geoffrey Wheeler, *Racial Problems in Soviet Muslim Asia*, Oxford, 1962.

ties, along with their institutions and customs in the life of the larger community.[50]

Switzerland is probably the outstanding example of a thoroughgoing use of the policy of pluralism. Her experience demonstrates the fact, however, that where pluralism is thoroughly accepted by all the groups involved, one no longer has a minority-majority society, but simply a culturally differentiated society. Only a careful measurement of levels of discrimination can indicate where these varieties of pluralism prevail. For several centuries the French and Italian Swiss have not been minorities, in our sense of the term, nor have they given up lingual and cultural differences from the German Swiss, who make up three-fourths of the population. A strong political and economic unity overrides the cultural differences. Geographical location, the presence nearby of large supporting nations for each of the three major groups in the Swiss confederation, a democratic ideology, and other factors have contributed to this development.

There are several dimensions to pluralism, as there are to assimilation. Seen from the perspective of the dominant group, one can envisage situations in which cultural pluralism, but not structural, is permitted. This is to some degree true in South Africa, which permits black Africans some cultural identity, but strongly inhibits the development of separate structures. Some societies insist on structural separation, but discourage cultural variation. Or a society may permit rather wide variation in individual beliefs and values, perhaps in the name of civil liberty, provided these do not accumulate into groups that are sharply distinct in culture and structure.[51]

Whatever the pattern of pluralism in a so-ciety, there comes a point at which the variation is constrained. The critical line may be language; it may be religion. In the modern nation-state it tends to be politico-economic. Loyalty is defined in terms of allegiance to the dominant political and economic structures and values. Setting the limits of legitimate opposition is one of the critical tasks of a complex society. The prevailing theory tries to reconcile two somewhat opposing views of the consequences of pluralism:

On the one hand, well-organized groups with which individuals feel closely identified are regarded as the best means of maximizing freedom, creating channels for the expression of interests, preventing alienation, and achieving some flexibility in the system. On the other hand, cross-cutting memberships that prevent the piling up of differences are considered necessary to safeguard society from splitting into such distinctive units that mobility, political compromise, and national action would be prevented.[52]

The United States has followed a complex and somewhat contradictory course with regard to pluralism. She is sometimes described as basically assimilationist, not only permitting, but demanding conformity to a rather narrow range of options. There is substantial evidence for this description. On the other hand, religious pluralism is now nearly fully the fact as well as the ideal; the country has followed a "hands-off" policy toward the private associations and foreign-language newspapers of many immigrant groups; Blacks, Chicanos, Indians, Orientals, and others assert their separate identities with some approval and even support from the majority; and pluralism is widely accepted as a value.[53] If America has never been so even-handed in her treatment of different groups as her ideology would imply, neither has she been so utterly indifferent to the range of cultures and peoples as her most severe critics have declared.

---

[50] Janowsky, *op. cit.*, p. xiii.

[51] See van den Berghe, *Race and Racism*, pp. 142–143, for a systematic examination of some of pluralism's dimensions. His usage, however, is somewhat different from the one developed here. He sees some varieties of pluralism as containing a high potential for separation and conflict; thus he includes types of intergroup relations that we discuss under different headings—"continued subjugation," when referring to majority policy, "secessionist" or "militant" when referring to minorities. The use of several terms seems preferable to broadening the meaning of pluralism, and then developing subtypes.

[52] J. Milton Yinger, *The Scientific Study of Religion*, Macmillan, 1970, p. 244. See pp. 239–244 and 425–430 for a discussion of the various theoretical issues involved in the study of pluralism.

[53] One interesting recent expression of this support is the Bilingual Education Act of 1967. For a comment on some of its effects, see *The New York Times*, March 17, 1971, p. 39.

3. *Legal Protection of Minorities*

Closely related to pluralism, or a subdivision of it, is the policy of protecting minorities by legal, constitutional, and diplomatic means. This is often official pluralism, but the emphasis on legal protection implies that there are important groups involved that do not accept the pattern. After World War I, for example, the constitutions of Bulgaria and Turkey guaranteed rights of autonomy for minorities. The Thirteenth, Fourteenth, and Fifteenth Amendments to the United States Constitution, although not pluralistic in aim, sought to protect the equal rights of minorities, primarily Negroes, in a situation that had been unfavorable to that aim. Recent fair-employment practices legislation has similar objectives.

Another variety of legal protection involves international action. This again implies that there are important groups who do not accept the principle of equal rights for minorities and that therefore some coercive legal force is necessary. The Genocide Convention of the United Nations is perhaps more moral than legal in its implications, but it seeks to establish a clear-cut international law against the kind of mass extermination of peoples that was part of Nazi policy. The Versailles Treaty was also concerned with minorities—particularly in the countries of the old Austro-Hungarian Empire, where so many conflicts had originated. One "solution," involved in Woodrow Wilson's famous Fourteen Points, was the "self-determination of peoples." Had this been carried out it would have eliminated "national" minorities by making it possible for each minority to form itself into a nation. It was based on the assumption that a monocultural, monolingual state was most likely to be successful; but it minimized the important economic forces that demanded multigroup unity. It tended to encourage small cultural group self-consciousness rather than large multigroup cooperation. Moreover, it was virtually impossible to carry out, without enormous migrations, for many of the minorities were scattered in small "islands" throughout the area. Nevertheless, the fact that the rights of minorities were given careful consideration represented a significant change in peacemaking. And when the "self-determination" principle was disregarded, as it often was, an additional treaty provision for pluralism within nations was invoked.

Civil and religious liberties, the right of citizenship, language rights, and special attention to the rights of Jews—who had been the most disadvantaged minority in most of these nations—were among the provisions in the treaties.

The United Nations has not followed the lead of the League of Nations in regard to the minorities question, for a number of reasons. The League had applied legal protection clauses mainly to the defeated nations and new nations of eastern Europe. The United Nations, with more attention to world-wide problems, inevitably becomes entangled with questions of diplomacy and international conflict. The United States, eager to hold Latin-American support, has emphasized nonintervention in internal affairs by the United Nations, and thus can scarcely support strenuous international efforts to protect minorities within a state. The Soviet Union will not accept international surveillance over states that she wants under her control. Nations which found that some members of their national minorities had been disloyal during World War II—Czechoslovakia, for example—are entirely unwilling to think in terms of their international protection. If the spotlight shifts to South Africa and her treatment of Indian and Bantu groups, she virtually withdraws from the United Nations. Nor do the Soviet Union and the United States respond favorably to debate in the United Nations concerning their minority policies. The result of such forces as these has been a de-internationalization of the minorities problem since the days of the League of Nations.[54]

This does not mean that the United Nations is unconcerned with minorities. There has been a shift in emphasis toward human rights—the rights of all individuals as individuals, not as members of groups. And as we shall see below, the United Nations has given attention to the process of population transfer. Active efforts to protect minorities by international legal means, following the pattern of the League of Nations, have, however, been weak.

[54] Inis L. Claude, Jr., *National Minorities*, Harvard, 1955.

The effectiveness of legal action as a way of protecting minorities is a subject of great complexity that we shall not discuss here. Some aspects of this question will be dealt with in Part III. Certainly the policy established in the Versailles Treaty was not carried out with great success, except perhaps in Czechoslovakia. But how much of this weakness was a reflection of the general weakness of the League of Nations and the sharp conflicts of the period between the wars and how much was a reflection of the inability to protect minorities by international legal action can scarcely be decided on the basis of this limited experience. The United Nations, through many of its agencies, is interested in the question of minorities and may well develop more effective techniques (indirect approaches that reduce the causes of discrimination).

4. Population Transfer

Majorities have sometimes adopted a policy of population transfer to attempt to reduce minorities' problems. This matches the secessionist aim of some minorities—both hoping for a reduction of tension through physical separation. In a few instances population transfer has been a peaceful process, with some concern for the rights and desires of individual minority-group members and a general interest in improving their situation. More often it has been a thoroughly discriminatory policy aimed at "solving" the problem by driving minority-group members out of an area.

In the early 1920s a fairly successful exchange was made among Greece, Turkey, and Bulgaria. There are many obstacles, however, to the widespread use of this policy. When the transfer is on an exchange basis, many will not want to move. Are they to be compelled to? The minorities may be of unequal size and trained for different occupations. Can they, under such conditions, be absorbed into the new lands? The basic difficulty is that this policy assumes that a homogeneous population will be a more peaceful one, although transfer of minorities does little to reduce the primary causes of conflict. These causes will be discussed in later chapters.

Some Americans have felt that the way to solve the "Negro problem" was to recolonize Negroes in Africa or segregate them in a separate state. Many thousands of Negroes did, in fact, return to Africa during the nineteenth century. The separate state idea is often the manifestation of a vigorous prejudice. It is sometimes, paradoxically, part of a Communist policy, presumably designed to benefit a minority. And it is sometimes given well-meaning support by persons of relatively mild prejudice mixed with good intentions. When Paul Robeson was graduated from college, wealthy alumni of his school proposed that he cooperate with them, as a leader, in helping to establish a separate geographical area for Negroes in the United States. The response of Robeson was one of strong disagreement. Most Negroes repudiate such a plan. Why, they ask, should we, any more than any other group of individuals, be separated from the total community? Negroes are very old Americans; they are thoroughly identified with America's society. Even the separatist views of the Black Muslims are more oriented to the transfer of the white than of the Negro population.

If population transfer sometimes has good intentions, it far more often expresses only hostility and discrimination as a policy of the majority. The transfer can be of two types—direct and indirect. In the former, the minority involved is specifically required and forced to leave. Many nations and cities drove out Jews in the late medieval period; the United States drove the Indians out of area after area; the British kept the Irish beyond the Pale; the Soviet Union deported millions of her citizens, members of religious and national minorities, during World War II; and Nazi Germany followed a relentless policy, aimed at a homogeneous nation, by forcibly transferring large numbers of persons of many minorities. The indirect policy is to make life so unbearable for members of the minority that they "choose" to migrate. Thus czarist Russia drove out millions of Jews. This was also part of Germany's policy.[55]

[55] Petersen uses this distinction between direct and indirect (which he labels forced and impelled) in his general typology of migration. By adding an ad-

After World War II, efforts to reduce minority problems in Europe by population transfer received a great deal of support. During the war, some German groups had been brought back to the *Vaterland*; and after the war, others were expelled. The desire in Eastern Europe to drive out a "disloyal minority" showed a great deal of categorical prejudice, because there was little effort to distinguish between loyal and disloyal members of the national minorities. (This was paralleled in some measure in the United States, where those of Japanese ancestry, the vast majority of whom were loyal to the United States, were "driven out" of the West into relocation camps.)

Population transfer may be effective in a few marginal cases, but in the modern world it can scarcely solve, or in most cases even reduce, the minorities problems. It is based on the monocultural ideal, which in a day of mobility and international communication, is progressively less meaningful. To be effective, it would have to block later population movement, despite labor demands or other economic changes, an action that contradicts the growing internationalization of the economy. Even when carried out in a humane way, it violates many of the most basic rights of individuals.[56]

5. Continued Subjugation

The policies just discussed have sought either to incorporate the minorities into a society or to drive them out. Often, however, the dominant group wants neither of these results; it wants the minority groups around, but it wants them kept "in their place," subservient and exploitable. There may be some ultimate

ditional variable referring to function (to be rid of migrants or to use migrants' labor), he designs a helpful paradigm of the varieties of coerced migration. The very listing of these varieties emphasizes the frequency with which coerced migration has been involved in human affairs:

Function	Impelled	Forced
To be rid of migrants	Flight	Displacement
To use migrant's labor	Coolie trade	Slave trade

William Petersen, "A General Typology of Migration," *ASR*, June, 1958, pp. 261–263.

[56] Claude, *op. cit.*, especially chaps. 8, 10.

promise of equality, but often not even that. The average white South African cannot conceive of the time when the black man will be his equal. Yet he would be dismayed at the thought of a nation without the Negro. Who would do all the hard work?

Many persons in the United States have supported large-scale immigration in the expectation that it would bring cheap labor. Today it is difficult to enforce laws regarding the migration of Mexicans into the United States because many powerful people in the Southwest and elsewhere want an exploitable minority. Were the "wetbacks" not a subjugated minority, were they able to command wages equal to those of American citizens, it would be far less difficult to enforce immigration laws. Much of this volume will be concerned with the subjugation policy employed by majorities.

6. Extermination

Conflict between groups sometimes becomes so severe that physical destruction of one by the other becomes an accepted goal. This may have been true of some ancient tribal contacts; modern history gives many examples. The United States destroyed perhaps two-thirds of the Indian population before her policy changed.[57] The small Tasmanian population was completely wiped out by the British (and by the civilized diseases that they brought to the island). The Boers of South Africa looked upon the Hottentots as scarcely more than animals of the jungle and hunted them ruthlessly. And Germany, between 1933 and 1945, murdered six million Jews.

These six policies of dominant groups are not, of course, mutually exclusive; many may be practiced simultaneously. Some are conscious long-run plans; some are *ad hoc* adjustments to specific situations; some are the by-products (perhaps unintended) of other policies. In some instances they are the official

[57] For a general discussion of genocide and specific comments on American Indians, see Louise G. Howton, "Genocide and the American Indians," in Bernard Rosenberg, Israel Gerver, and F. William Howton (eds.), *Mass Society in Crisis*, Macmillan, 2nd ed., 1971, pp. 144–150.

actions of majority-group leaders; in others they are the day-by-day responses of individual members of the dominant group. In this book we shall see many of the policies in operation—from complete acceptance, to toleration, to subjugation, to extermination.

WHAT IS PREJUDICE?

Our reference, up to this point, has been primarily to the group dimensions of intergroup relations. There are individual dimensions that, although closely connected, require separate definition.

For our purposes, we shall define prejudice as an emotional, rigid attitude (a *predisposition* to respond to a certain stimulus in a certain way) toward a group of people. They may be a group only in the mind of the prejudiced person; that is, he categorizes them together, although they may have little similarity or interaction. Prejudices are thus attitudes, but not all attitudes are prejudices. They both contain the element of prejudgment, but prejudiced attitudes have an affective or emotional quality that not all attitudes possess.

Prejudice leads one to select facts for emphasis, blinding one to other facts. It causes one to look upon all members of a "group" as if they were alike. New experiences are fitted into the old categories by selecting only those cues that harmonize with the prejudgment or stereotype. Prejudiced attitudes, because of their emotional quality, have a relative unmodifiability that is not characteristic of all attitudes. Many people have attitudes toward various kinds of automobiles (predispositions to respond favorably or unfavorably). These may be defended with a good deal of emotion, but far more often they are subject to change. An unfavorable attitude toward a given make may shift quite readily when one has a series of favorable experiences—or a gift from one's father-in-law—that bring new facts into the situation.

The unmodifiability of prejudices should not be exaggerated. They are, after all, anchored in life experiences that are subject to drastic reorganization. At many points in this book we will discuss change as well as sta-

bility of prejudice, and here note only that the socialization and communication processes by which modification occurs are not well understood. To many groups, the "unthinkable" of a decade ago has become thinkable, perhaps ". . . through the socialization of the young into a new pattern by parents who have been forced to regard the previously unthinkable as the commonplace of the future that their children will be facing."[58]

Most studies of socialization deal with a model of a stable society. Only gradually are we learning how parents respond to the overwhelming likelihood that their children will live in a significantly different world. There is some evidence that prejudiced parents ". . . may well maintain their own prejudices and yet prepare their children for a world they know is coming but do not welcome."[59]

Are all attitudes that are heavily laden with emotion to be considered prejudices? Is belief in democracy or the value of the scientific method a prejudice? Certainly they involve *predispositions to respond to these stimuli in a particular way. Something is to be gained by seeing the similarities between value stands and tastes and what we are calling prejudices. There are sufficient differences, however, to make it seem wise to the present writers to classify such attitudes in a different category. By prejudice we shall mean a rigid, emotional attitude toward a human group.

Prejudice involves not only prejudgment but, as Vickery and Opler point out, misjudgment as well. It is categorical thinking that systematically misinterprets the facts. Again, not all misjudgment is prejudice. Prejudice is misjudgment of the members of a supposed human group; it is socially oriented action. One may misjudge the speed of an approaching car, but one is anxious to correct the error. Prejudice is a misjudgment that one defends.[60] When a pre-existing attitude is so strong and inflexible that it seriously distorts perception and judgment, one has a prejudice.

[58] Herbert Hyman in Irwin Katz and Patricia Gurin (eds.), *Race and the Social Sciences*, Basic Books, 1969, p. 6.

[59] *Ibid.*

[60] William Vickery and Morris Opler, "A Redefinition of Prejudice for Purposes of Social Science Research," *HR*, 1948, pp. 419–428.

In discussing the emotional and rigid quality of prejudice, we do not want to give the impression that no cognitive or even rational elements are involved. From one perspective, prejudice can be seen as an effort to give some coherence and order to a puzzling and complex situation, or as an effort to defend some value. Facts and experience may play some part, adding strength to the inflexibility of a prejudgment. We would only emphasize that these cognitive and rational elements are used in the service of attitudes that are primarily emotional.[61]

The limitation of the meaning of the term "prejudice" to human interaction has some etymological justification. As Kimball Young points out, the word comes from the Latin *prejudicum*—a preceding judgment. "The word took on special meaning when it came to refer to judicial examination in Rome held prior to a trial as a way of determining the social status of the would-be litigants. . . . This status-defining function of prejudice has never been lost.[62] Prejudice puts an individual "in his place."

Many writers have worked on refinements of the term in order to isolate what seems to be a more homogeneous group of phenomena for inclusion. Communication is made more accurate by limiting a term to homogeneous elements. If I say, "Will you bring me that piece of furniture from the next room," I may get anything from a footstool to a grand piano. If I ask for a small chair, I'm quite likely to get what I want. Prejudice is a "furniture" kind of word. As it is normally used, it includes a wide variety of phenomena. Efforts to make it more precise are very useful, provided their arbitrary quality is recognized and one does not quarrel with a person who makes a different limitation based on different criteria.

In isolating homogeneous phenomena, one can either talk about types of prejudice (prejudice$_1$, prejudice$_2$, prejudice$_3$) or find different terms to assign to the related, yet different phenomena (prejudice for one type, intolerance for another, stereotypy for a third, for example).

Robin Williams, Jr., distinguishes between prejudices based on functional differences in the social order or real differences in value, on the one hand, and those that emphasize stereotypes centered on some symbol, such as skin color, that has no functional significance, on the other. Thus for a democrat to be prejudiced against communists or fascists is different from his being prejudiced against Japanese—not entirely different, to be sure, but sufficiently so to require separation in our vocabularies (prejudice$_1$ and prejudice$_2$). It is the latter type that is the subject of this book.

Even in this narrower meaning prejudice is a blanket concept, covering a variety of concrete phenomena. The prejudice may be mild or violent. There is a contrast between prejudice manifested against groups with whom one has had no personal contact, and against those with whom contact is intensive and continuous. There is the prejudice of the provincial—to anything strange, different, "foreign"—and the rather different prejudice of the dweller in cosmopolitan centers. . . . There is prejudice based on conformity to the social customs of a group as against the prejudice, anchored in deep aggressive needs in the personality, which may persist even in the face of group pressure. There is the prejudice of economic or political opportunism, often calculating and impersonal, in contrast to the fanaticism of the religious or cultural zealot. There is the prejudice manifest in a specific idée fixe concerning a particular group, on the one hand, and the prejudice expressive of generalized antipathy to outgroups, on the other. Even the prejudice which arises primarily out of individual psychological needs appears in many forms; it may serve, for example, as a projection of repressed hatreds and other "antisocial" urges of the individual, a prop for ego-level or sense of self-esteem, a defense against repressed sexual drives, or a method of winning group approval.[63]

[61] We shall discuss this question in Chapter 3, in connection with the study of the individual functions of prejudice. There is a great need to identify the possible rational element in prejudice and to study its interactions with other elements. See Howard Schuman and John Harding, "Prejudice and the Norm of Rationality," *Sociometry*, Sept., 1964, pp. 353–371; Henri Tajfel, "Cognitive Aspects of Prejudice," *JSI*, Autumn, 1969, pp. 79–97.

[62] Kimball Young, *Social Psychology*, 3rd ed., Appleton-Century-Crofts, 1956, p. 502.

[63] Robin Williams, Jr., *The Reduction of Intergroup Tensions*, SSRC, 1947, pp. 37–38.

Most of the distinctions that Williams draws are based on analysis of the causes and functions of prejudice—a subject with which we shall be concerned in several chapters. Recognition of the diversity of the phenomena with which we are dealing, in terms of causes and functions, is essential to understanding and control. Our analysis and our vocabulary must reflect that diversity.

Some writers prefer to distinguish among the varieties of related phenomena by using different terms, rather than by prescribing types and degrees of "prejudice." Ackerman and Jahoda, for example, distinguish between prejudice and stereotypy:

Prejudice . . . is a term applied to categorical generalizations based on inadequate data and without sufficient regard for individual differences. . . . But inherent in the process of forming prejudgments is the danger of stereotyped thinking. The stereotype is distinguished from the prejudgment only by a greater degree of rigidity. Prejudgment occurs where facts are not available. But stereotypy is a process which shows little concern for facts even when they are available.

Prejudice in its narrowest sense is distinct from prejudgment and stereotypy. It is a subcategory of prejudgment and it uses stereotypy but it is not identical with either. In the psychological context . . . , *prejudice is a pattern of hostility in interpersonal relations which is directed against an entire group, or against its individual members; it fulfills a specific irrational function for its bearer.*[64]

It is the last phrase of this quotation that requires attention. It limits the term "prejudice" more sharply than most definitions—to irrational personality factors. This is quite legitimate, provided other terms are indicated for *closely related* phenomena. Ackerman and Jahoda's study is concerned primarily with anti-Semitism. They write:

If a person alleges that Jews are economically powerful, he is employing stereotyped thinking. He may be right or wrong; if sufficient facts are presented to him, he may change the content of his stereotype to saying: Jews are not

powerful economically. But neither of these two statements is in itself a sufficient indication of prejudice. Only when there is evidence that his stereotypes are used as rationalizations for an irrational hostility rooted in his own personality are we talking of prejudice. That anti-Semitism in the cases here investigated is a prejudice in the sense of this definition, and not just a prejudgment or a manifestation of stereotyped thinking, is the main hypothesis of this investigation.[65]

This statement shows an awareness of the arbitrary quality of a definition; but it also reflects a belief on the part of the authors, shown throughout their book, that they are analyzing the "basic" or "fundamental" cause of anti-Semitism when they study personality factors. If their definition of prejudice is used, one must be alert to the other forces causing anti-Semitism. It is prejudice—plus. The fact that they have taken over what is doubtless the primary term—prejudice—to refer to the phenomena with which they are mainly concerned seems to reflect a theoretical limitation.

The tendency for definitions to reflect theoretical positions is shown clearly by the very different interpretation of the relationship between prejudice and anti-Semitism that Oliver Cox makes. He believes that *economic* forces are the fundamental ones in determining the patterns of intergroup relations that we are discussing. He is also concerned primarily with race relations. He therefore uses the basic term "prejudice" to refer to attitudes that facilitate economic exploitation of racial minorities. Unlike Ackerman and Jahoda, Cox declares that anti-Semitism is *not* prejudice, but intolerance:

Anti-Semitism, to begin with, is clearly a form of social intolerance, which attitude may be defined as an unwillingness on the part of a dominant group to tolerate the beliefs or practices of a subordinate group because it considers these beliefs and practices to be either inimical to group solidarity or a threat to the continuity of the status quo. Race prejudice, on the other hand, is a social attitude propagated among the public by an exploiting class for the purpose of stigmatizing some group as inferior so that the exploitation of either the group itself or its

[64] Nathan Ackerman and Marie Jahoda, *Anti-Semitism and Emotional Disorder*, Harper & Row, 1950, pp. 3–4.

[65] *Ibid.*, p. 4.

resources or both may be justified. Persecution and exploitation are the behavior aspects of intolerance and race prejudice respectively. In other words, race prejudice is the socio-attitudinal facilitation of a particular type of labor exploitation, while social intolerance is a reactionary attitude supporting the action of a society in purging itself of contrary cultural groups.[66]

That economic exploitation is importantly involved in majority-minority relations no one can doubt. That the term "prejudice" may be used to refer only to the attitudes that facilitate economic exploitation is also legitimate. But Cox, in his enthusiasm for the economic interpretation of human behavior, obscures the similarities between the various types of majority-minority relations and oversimplifies the causal complex. Thus he is led to such inaccurate and oversimplified statements as these:

Anti-Semitism is an attitude directed against the Jews because they are Jews, while race prejudice is an attitude directed against Negroes because they want to be something other than Negroes.

Probably the clearest distinction between intolerance and race prejudice is that the intolerant group welcomes conversion and assimilation, while the race-prejudiced group is antagonized by attempts to assimilate. . . .

Religious persecution and racial domination are categorically different social facts.[67]

It is wise to emphasize the variety of types of majority-minority relations, to isolate separate causes, and to develop a terminology based on these distinctions. But if this procedure leads to the claim that related phenomena are "categorically different social facts," it will block our ability to see interconnections. Science must search not only for differences that lie behind superficial similarities, but also for similarities that may be disguised by superficial differences.

It is the contention of the present authors that the causes of antipathy between groups are *cumulative* and *interactive*. They prefer,

in order to emphasize this relatedness, to use the term "prejudice" to refer to the total complex involved in the rigid prejudgment and misjudgment of groups. The discussion, then, must give full attention to the differences in types and variations in degree of prejudice. We shall be concerned with that problem in Chapters 3, 4, and 5.

WHAT IS DISCRIMINATION?

Prejudice is an attitude, a *tendency* to respond or a symbolic response. It may never involve overt action toward members of the minority group, either because no situation presents itself or, in situations where one might show antipathy, because other attitudes inhibit open expressions of hostility. You may have a strong prejudice against the residents of southwest Euthanasia, but since you have never met one of them, you have had no opportunity to express your attitude. A black man may have a vigorous prejudice against white men, but disguise his feelings or give them indirect expression.

Thus prejudice must not be equated with discrimination although they are closely related.

In a neutral sense, discrimination means simply "to draw a distinction," but this can be done, as the dictionary meanings show, by showing a "faculty for nicely distinguishing," according to generally accepted standards, or by drawing "an unfair or injurious distinction." It is the latter with which we are concerned, that is, the drawing of distinctions in such a way that widely accepted values and procedures are violated. It is apparent from such a definition that a given act can be labelled discriminatory only when particular values or a particular labelling group is specified.

Petersen and Matza point out that to discriminate against a group because of what it is and wants to be is different from discriminating against a group because of what others believe it to be or because of what it is despite its own plans or desires. The first is cultural or subcultural conflict (e.g., opposition to Mormon polygamy), the latter is discrimina-

[66] Oliver C. Cox, *Caste, Class and Race*, Doubleday, 1948, p. 393.

[67] *Ibid.*, pp. 394, 481.

tion (e.g., opposition to a Negro of similar values and style of life moving into my neighborhood). The first is value judgment—because of what they are or want to be; the latter is prejudgment—regardless of what they are or want to be. Problems of definition arise because the empirical situation is often mixed. Moreover, we should be careful to note that this distinction is not a moral one that labels value conflicts good and discrimination bad. It is a logical distinction. Independent moral criteria must be specified before the issue can be transposed into a moral one.[68]

The essence of social discrimination is that there are some who say: we are "nicely distinguishing"; while others reply: no, you are drawing "an unfair and injurious distinction." That is, discrimination tends to be supported by secondary, if not by primary, norms, and by significant subgroups in a society, thus making it the subject of intergroup, and not simply interindividual conflict.[69] In Robin Williams well-known definition: "Discrimination may be said to exist to the degree that individuals of a given group who are otherwise formally qualified are not treated in conformity with these nominally universal institutionalized codes."[70]

Antonovsky uses a similar definition. "Discrimination may be defined as the effective injurious treatment of persons on grounds rationally irrelevant to the situation."[71] He notes that discrimination is a "system of social relations," not an isolated individual act. It involves such social forces as tradition, role playing, social sanctions, ideological support, and the responses of those who are attacked. Because discrimination "vitiates the power and knowledge of its victims," their behavior feeds back into and reenforces the system, a point we shall discuss at length in Chapter 5.

[68] William Petersen and David Matza (eds.), *Social Controversy*, Wadsworth, 1963, pp. 156–157.
[69] See J. Milton Yinger, "Prejudice: Social Discrimination," *International Encyclopedia of the Social Sciences*, Macmillan, 1968, Vol. 12, pp. 448–451.
[70] Williams, *op. cit.*, p. 39. See Ernest Works, "Types of Racial Discrimination," *Phylon*, Fall, 1969, pp. 223–233, for a study of the conditions under which discrimination is likely to occur, particularly variation in role relations.
[71] Aaron Antonovsky, "The Social Meaning of Discrimination," *Phylon*, Spring, 1960, p. 81.

THE RELATION OF DISCRIMINATION TO PREJUDICE

To say that prejudice and discrimination are distinct phenomena is not to say that they are empirically separate. One might discriminate against a member of a minority group without feeling any prejudice; but almost certainly it would be because he believes other persons hold a prejudice. A businessman, for example, might refuse to accept clients from a minority group, despite his own lack of prejudice, because he thinks that their presence would injure his business. Ordinarily, however, discrimination is the overt expression of prejudice.

Warner and Dennis have designed an interesting field study to investigate the conditions under which the various possible relationships between prejudice and discrimination prevail. Eight items measuring prejudice against Negroes were scattered through a much longer questionnaire given to 731 freshmen college students. Two months later, 537 of these subjects were asked to check whether they would engage in various interracial activities under each of the possible combinations of high and low social distance from the Negro participants and high and low social constraint (degree of visibility of the action to others).

Both those high in prejudice and those low were inconsistent under some conditions. Briefly, those low in prejudice did not seem to be influenced by the level of constraint, but they were more likely to discriminate if they perceived the Negro involved in an interaction as lower in status. Those high in prejudice, on the other hand, were more affected by the conditions of social constraint: high constraint maximized the likelihood that they would discriminate. Knowing individual attitudes alone, then, would have been insufficient to predict behavior.[72]

The distinction between a tendency to act and overt action between prejudice and discrimination, has been emphasized strongly by a number of writers in recent years. It has played a particularly important part in the

[72] See Lyle G. Warner and Rutledge M. Dennis, "Prejudice Versus Discrimination: An Empirical Example and Theoretical Extensions," *SF*, June, 1970, pp. 473–484.

analyses of those who are working to reduce intergroup hostility. They have pointed out that it is frequently possible to prevent discrimination—by making it unprofitable, painful, or simply unusual—without reducing prejudice directly. We shall examine this problem in Part III.

Analysis of the relationship between prejudice and discrimination can also prevent an easy assumption of a particular causal connection between them. Behind many of the studies of "the prejudiced personality" is the hypothesis that personal needs and insecurities, expressing themselves in prejudices, are the primary cause of discrimination. (It would follow that any important reduction in discrimination requires large-scale reduction of personal insecurity.) There is good evidence, however, that prejudice is in part the *result of discrimination*—a way of rationalizing and getting rid of guilt feelings that arise when one has treated an individual unfairly, according to one's own definition. By emphasizing that conflicts over power and gain and traditional factors, as well as personal insecurities, are involved in prejudice, we can more readily understand the interaction between prejudice and discrimination.

McWilliams believes that our understanding of minority-majority relations is being reduced by excessive attention to prejudice:

Race relations are not based on prejudice; prejudice is a by-product of race relations—as influenced by other factors. Current psychological theories of race relations, however, are almost exclusively concerned with prejudice, which is discussed as though it were the cause of discrimination. . . . To make a theory of the function of prejudice in the psychic economy of the individual do double duty as a theory of group discrimination is to confuse different, if related, levels of meaning. Case histories of every German would have failed to explain what happened to the Jews in Germany between 1918 and 1939. The clearest delineation of the personality types most susceptible to anti-Semitism will not explain why Jewish dentists find it almost impossible to practice dentistry in certain Western states. In the same way, concepts of social psychology are relevant to an understanding of race relations, but they do not explain the strategies by which

certain groups maintain their dominance over other groups.[73]

In recent years, with the struggle over civil rights bringing the forms of discrimination vividly to public attention, the emphasis on prejudice characteristic of the 1950s has been modified. Many social scientists have underlined the point made by McWilliams that a theory of prejudice cannot do double duty as a theory of discrimination.[74] This writing is a valuable corrective to an excessively psychologistic approach to race relations. We would only note the equal need for avoiding an excessively sociologistic approach. In technical terms, the task is to discover how much of the variance in prejudice and discrimination can be explained by attention to personality variables, how much by social structural variables, and how much by their interaction.

No one expression of the relationship between prejudice and discrimination is adequate:

1. There can be prejudice without discrimination.
2. There can be discrimination without prejudice.
3. Discrimination can be among the causes of prejudice.
4. Prejudice can be among the causes of discrimination.
5. Probably most frequently there are mutually reinforcing.

The need is for careful specification of the personal and structural conditions under which these various relationships prevail.

[73] Carey McWilliams, *Brothers Under the Skin*, rev. ed., Little, Brown, 1951, pp. 315–317.
[74] See, for example, Arnold Rose, "Intergroup Relations vs. Prejudice," *SP*, Oct., 1956, pp. 173–176; Dietrich Reitzes, "Institutional Structure and Race Relations," *Phylon*, Spring, 1959, pp. 48–66; Edwin H. Rhyne, "Racial Prejudice and Personality Scales: An Alternative Approach," *SF*, Oct., 1962, pp. 44–53; Anthony Richmond, "Sociological and Psychological Explanations of Racial Prejudice: Some Light on the Controversy from Recent Researches in Britain," *Pacific Sociological Review*, 1961, pp. 63–68; Aaron Antonovsky, *op. cit.*, pp. 81–95; and Herbert Blumer, "Race Prejudice as a Sense of Group Position," in J. Masouka and Preston Valien (eds.), *Race Relations, Problems and Theory*, Univ. of North Carolina Press, 1961, pp. 217–228.

GROUP CONFLICT AND TENSION

In a majority-minority social system, prejudice and discrimination are almost always accompanied by tension and often by conflict. Yet each of these can exist independently of the others. In his comment on group conflict, Williams writes: "Although often closely connected in life situations, these elements have a considerable range of independent variation."[75] There can be a great deal of prejudice and discrimination—for example, in a caste system—with relatively little open conflict. Attempts to reduce discrimination, on the other hand, may lead, at least in the short run, to *increased* conflict; and efforts to avoid conflict may take the form of accepting patterns of discrimination. On the whole, however, group conflict is an outgrowth of widespread prejudice and discrimination. It is particularly likely to occur in an open-class society, where the suppressed groups have some hope of improving their status and the dominant group has some fear that the minorities may advance (and perhaps ambivalent feelings about whether they ought to advance).

The relationship of prejudice and discrimination to conflict is affected by other attitudes of the participants ("law should be obeyed," for example, or "outsiders have no right to tell us what to do"), by the availability of alternative opportunities for action (prejudices of those who feel trapped by circumstances around them are likely to be expressed in discrimination), and by the strength or weakness of the external control system. Grimshaw has recently shown the usefulness of conceptualizing social conflict (or one manifestation of it in which he is interested—violence) separately from prejudice and discrimination. "Social violence—attacks upon individuals or their property solely or primarily because of their membership in social groups or categories"[76]—is not the inevitable concomitant of prejudice and discrimination. Grimshaw notes that violence is not even a necessary manifestation of social tension, which he suggests as a fourth variable. Although he does not define the term, social tension might be thought of as a high level of shared fear of social conflict and status loss among members of the dominant group and a high level of shared status frustration and of fear of social conflict among minorities. Four such variables can logically be combined in numerous ways, but the empirical possibilities are fewer. (See Figure 4.)[77]

There are, of course, many other possibilities. In particular we would note that prejudice may not be the starting point. A cycle of interaction may well start with discrimination that leads, in turn, both to prejudice and to social tension. Note also that violence, or the absence thereof, which is here seen as the end of a process, is also the beginning of new processes of interaction.

In our discussion, in sum, we must be alert both to the distinctions among prejudice, discrimination, tension, and conflict and to their important interconnections. We shall sometimes use the term "prejudice" alone as an abbreviated reference to the whole pattern of intergroup antipathy when we are referring to situations where several forms occur together.

CONCLUSION

This chapter has been primarily concerned with some basic terms. We have seen that they can be defined in many ways, but we have tried to develop a meaning that will be useful in the study of the relationships with which we are concerned. One term, "race," is of such importance that it will be dealt with separately in the next chapter. This book is not limited to the study of "race relations"; but because that phrase is so frequently used to refer to the larger field of majority-minority relations, and because "race" is used so broadly and vaguely by many people, we need to develop clear-cut definitions.

It is the thesis of this book that relations among races have a great deal in common with relations among groups that think of themselves as different on other grounds—culture, nationality, religion. Race differences are primarily important for what people believe them to be. Some writers object to this approach. They declare that race prejudice,

[75] Williams, *op. cit.*, p. 36.

[76] Allen Grimshaw, "Relationships among Prejudice, Discrimination, Social Tension, and Social Violence," *JIR, Autumn*, 1961, p. 303.

[77] *Ibid.*, p. 305.

Figure 4 / Relationships Among Prejudice, Discrimination,
Tension, and Violence

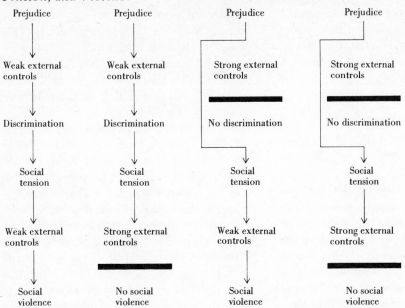

Source: Allen Grinshaw, "Relationships Among Prejudice, Social Discrimination, Social Tension,
Social Violence," *Journal of Intergroup Relations*, Autumn, 1961, p. 303. Reprinted with
permission.

or religious prejudice, or some other variety, is fundamentally different. Insofar as they are pointing out that there are unique elements in the employment of any symbol, that each has some historically distinct roots, the present writers agree. But insofar as they obscure the similarities that underlie the use of different symbols of group differentiation, disregarding the common pattern of causes and functions, we disagree.

The study of "race" alone will yield little understanding of the nature of group conflict, prejudice, and discrimination. But seeing race as a symbol that is *used* to set people apart for differential treatment will cause our understanding to grow. This analysis needs also to be enlarged to include the use of other symbols by means of which "minorities" are designated, which expansion will lead to the study of all phases of majority-minority relations, the search for patterns of relationship, for causes and functions, for trends. Even this, however, does not complete our task. If our analysis is to be valid, it must rest upon the foundation of contemporary social science. Prejudice and discrimination can be understood only as manifestations of larger situations, not as isolated phenomena. We must

understand the nature of individual and group behavior. Our analysis of majority-minority relations must be thoroughly in harmony with the broader principles of all human relations. It must draw its fundamental concepts from the sciences of man.

Figure 5 / The Multi-Leveled Approach
to the Study of Race

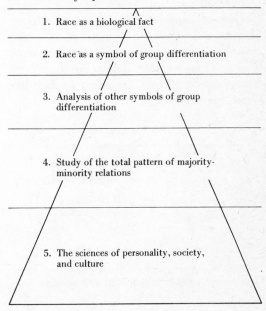

1. Race as a biological fact

2. Race as a symbol of group differentiation

3. Analysis of other symbols of group differentiation

4. Study of the total pattern of majority-minority relations

5. The sciences of personality, society, and culture

Our approach might be charted as a pyramid (see above). Our primary concern will be with levels 1 to 4 of this pyramid, but we shall draw continually on principles that derive from level 5—from the sciences of sociology, cultural anthropology, and social psychology particularly.

Let us turn now to an analysis of race.

A NOTE ON THE USE OF GROUP NAMES

Questions of personal identity, courtesy, accuracy, and fashion are found in the use of group names. Pejorative terms, of course, are symbols and indeed weapons of group conflict. But even in scholarly discourse, one faces difficult problems of communication, because of the wide range of connotations that become associated with different group terms. If one adopts a short-cut and refers to "Mexicans" when he has "Americans-of-Mexican-descent" in mind, he runs the risk of seeming to grant them less than full citizenship. Should one speak of Indians (who, as someone has said, didn't even know they were Indians until Columbus told them), or native Americans, or pre-Columbian Americans?

The sharpest controversy over name in America today surrounds the question of the appropriate term for Americans-of-African-or-part-African-descent. When *Newsweek* asked a random sample of Americans of African descent which name they liked most, which name they liked least, four names received 87 percent of the positive choices. But those same four names received 78 percent of the "like least" choices:

	Like most	Like least
	(in percent)	
Negro	38	11
Colored People	20	31
Blacks	19	25
Afro-Americans	10	11

Source: Newsweek, June 30, 1969, p. 12. Copyright, Newsweek, Inc., 1969. Reprinted with permission.

The controversy over names rages, as Lerone Bennett notes, with religious intensity. In his careful review of the historical shifts, he records the swings of usage and the variations in attitudes with which they were associated. He notes W. E. B. Du Bois' reply to a student who criticized the use of the term Negro in *Crisis:* "Do not at the outset of your career make the all too common error of mistaking names for things. Names are only conventional signs for identifying things. Things are the reality that counts. If a thing is despised, either because of ignorance or because it is despicable, you will not alter matters by changing the names. If men despise Negroes, they will not despise them less if Negroes are called 'colored' or 'Afro-Americans.' "[78]

Du Bois' comment will displease as many as it pleases. His opponents would say that words prefigure and control experience to some degree; they are not simply innocent labels. If someone says that "Negro" is a slave-oriented epithet and should be replaced by "Black," he will find it irrelevant that Negro is derived from the Portuguese and Spanish words for black.[79] The irony of the situation is pointed up sharply by Jules Feiffer's series of six identical black faces, with the following commentary: "As a matter of racial pride we want to be called 'Blacks'—which has replaced the term 'Afro-American'—which replaced 'Negroes'—which replaced 'Colored People'—which replaced 'Darkies'—which replaced 'Blacks.' "[80]

We cannot resolve the problems associated with racial and ethnic labels. Since there are persons within any group who prefer different group titles, any single choice will cause some discomfort. We shall use Black, Negro, and Afro-American interchangeably when referring to persons of African background.[81] When quoting or drawing directly

[78] Quoted by Lerone Bennett, Jr., "What's in a Name," in Peter I. Rose (ed.), *Americans from Africa: Old Memories, New Moods,* Atherton, 1970, p. 379. The article first appeared in *Ebony,* Nov., 1967, pp. 46–52, 54.

[79] See Bennett's valuable discussion of these matters, *op. cit.*

[80] Oberlin College *Review,* Nov., 1969.

[81] This raises a question about spelling, which also has its political-moral aspects. We shall capital-

on another source, we will employ the term of the original author. We trust that the tone of this work will convey our sense of the shared dignity of all mankind. We only hope that this book gets into print before some new "most preferred choice" that we have neglected entirely appears.

---

ize White, Black, Chicano, and the like when they are used as nouns, as group names. When they are used adjectivally, we shall use lower case.

Race is one of the most misunderstood concepts in modern vocabularies. Formal and informal definitions of this word run into the thousands, but we shall consider three broad approaches to this term.

THE MYSTICAL CONCEPTION OF RACE

The first conception we shall label "mystical," although it would be almost as appropriate to call it "romantic," or "literary," or "political." This viewpoint has been the stock in trade in the chicanery of rabble rousers, fanatics, demagogues, adventurers, and charlatans (rational or psychopathic). It has been a convenient rationalization for reactionaries in opposing social change. It has provided a crutch for lesser artists in the stereotyping of characters in their mediocre products. And it has been immeasurably useful to the mass populations of the modern world whose members are largely unaware of the nature of prejudices, their sources, and their functions.

During the Middle Ages and for centuries later, the nobility of Europe considered itself of better ancestry than the common people. In France, for example, Count de Boulainvilliers declared that there were two races: the nobles, who were descended from the Germanic conquerors, and the masses, who were the descendants of the subject Celts and Romans. In this manner he sought to defend the privileges of the nobles. After the French Revolution Count de Gobineau brought out his famous *Essay on the Inequality of the Human Races.* Gobineau hated democracy and admitted that his purpose was to strike at liberal ideas. His racial theory, a new version of the old defense of feudalism, was popular among the slaveowners of the Old South in the years preceding the Civil War.[1]

[1] Banton says that some American sociologists, acquainted with racism in its modern forms, work

H. S. Chamberlain, an Englishman who took a German wife and became a Germanophile, utilized a "racial" approach in his influential work, *The Foundations of the Nineteenth Century.* According to Chamberlain: "Whoever reveals himself German by his acts, whatever his genealogical tree, is a German." T. L. Stoddard's *Rising Tide of Color* included the thesis that there are higher races and lower races, that intermixture produces a race that reverts to the lower type, and that the downfall of the great civilizations has been due to the crossing of higher and lower races. Madison Grant's *The Passing of a Great Race* developed the theme that the United States was founded by Anglo-Saxon Protestants with democratic ideals and that this country should be reserved for their kind.

Perhaps the most repercussive racial dogma was set forth by Adolf Hitler in *Mein Kampf,* in which the author stated: "If we divide the human race into three categories—founders, maintainers, and destroyers of culture—the Aryan stock alone can be considered as representing the first category."

About 40 years ago a Southern statesman declared:

No statutory law, no organic law, no military law, supercedes the law of racial necessity and social identity.

backwards and view earlier statements about race from a modern standpoint instead of setting them in the intellectual context of the time in which they were made. He is correct in saying that Simpson and Yinger (*Racial and Cultural Minorities,* 1965) imply that the nineteenth-century theorists were wrong about race because they "adopted the wrong outlook, instead of locating the errors within a historical pattern of discovery." In discussing the "mystical" conception of race, however, we cite also the following twentieth century writers: Lothrop Stoddard, Madison Grant, Adolf Hitler, Samuel J. Green, Carleton Putnam, Henry E. Garrett, Wesley C. George, Robert Gayre, and R. R. Gates. See Michael Banton, "What Do We Mean By 'Racism'?," *New Society,* (April 10, 1969), p. 552.

Why apologize or evade? We have been very careful to obey the letter of the Federal Constitution—but we have been very diligent and astute in violating the spirit of such amendments and such statutes as would lead the Negro to believe himself the equal of a white man. And we shall continue to conduct ourselves in that way.[2]

For the most part, racial apologies from the South in the 1940s were ineptly expressed. A succinct example is the comment of Grand Dragon Dr. Samuel J. Green of the Ku Klux Klan when a Negro journalist, Roi Ottley, told Green that scientific thought and world opinion ran counter to the theory of Negro inferiority. Green insisted: "I'm still livin' in Georgia, no matter what the world and science thinks."[3]

More recently the doctrine of the innate inferiority of the Negro has been worked over and widely disseminated by Mr. Carleton Putnam and his associates. Among the organizations promoting Putnam's tracts are: the National Putnam Letters Committee; the Citizens' Councils of America, of Jackson, Mississippi; and the North-South Council of Washington, D.C.

According to Putnam, such scientists as Boas, Herskovits, Klineberg, and Montagu (racists get a special anti-Semitic bonus from Putnam) are "slippery," "clever," "prolix," and "insidious," and their "fruitless efforts at proof of unprovable theories" are "sound without the substance." Their conclusions are so ridiculous that Mr. and Mrs. Putnam found themselves "laughing out loud." Mr. Putnam claims to have found "professional scientists aplenty" trembling with fear, afraid to expose the fraudulent scientists because the universities, museums, and foundations are all controlled or intimidated by "equalitarians." One scientist even confided that he was "being checked by mulattoes at his lectures."

Putnam's booklet *Race and Reason* appeared in 1961. Although he has had no training in anthropology, the Louisiana State Board of Education called him "an eminent American anthropologist and scholar," and said that he had written "a book that exposes the flagrant distortion and perversion of scientific truth by so-called anthropologists and socialistically oriented sociologists." The Board made the volume required reading for "selected college personnel, including (1) all deans, professors, and other instrumental personnel, (2) all students enrolled in courses in anthropology, sociology, and psychology, and (3) all students enrolled in the required course in Americanism vs. Communism." Also, the booklet is required reading for high school students specially selected on the basis of "maturity, sincerity, and dependability."[4] Governor Ross Barnett issued a proclamation designating a Race and Reason Day, and Mr. Putnam addressed 500 "patriots" at a Carleton Putnam dinner in Jackson, Mississippi. He delivered a similar address at a rally of the New Orleans Citizens Council. An issue of *The Citizen,* official journal of The Citizens' Councils of America was devoted to Carleton Putnam and *Race and Reason.*

Putnam found four men with scientific training and academic backgrounds who were willing to endorse his tract on race. Two are retired professors, Henry E. Garrett[5] and Wesley C. George, whose early enculturation in the South has stayed with them throughout their lifetimes. The others are Robert Gayre, formerly a professor of Anthropo-Geography at the University of Saugor, India, and later editor of *Mankind Quarterly,* and the late R. R. Gates, an English geneticist.[6]

[2] *Liberty Magazine,* Apr. 21, 1928, p. 10.
[3] *Time,* July 11, 1949, p. 38.

[4] *Science,* Dec. 8, 1961, vol. 134, p. 1868.
[5] Some idea of Garrett's point of view may be gained from his comments on Juan Comas' paper on " 'Scientific' Racism Again?" Samples follow:

"I do think that the Negro's relative immaturity and childishness predispose him to emotionally-motivated crimes; and that his much better record in the South than in the North represents the southern lawman's knowledge and understanding of this immaturity."
"He [Comas] asks, 'Does he class all 15 new Negro nations as unhappy examples of self-government?' The answer to this one is a resounding YES—and contemporary history as revealed in the daily newspapers fully corroborates this judgment."
"Should American Whites under the emotional goading of various pressure groups become convinced that it is their 'duty' to absorb the Negroes now living in this country, our culture would inevitably deteriorate intellectually, morally, and materially." In *CA,* 1961, pp. 319–320.

[6] Putnam continued his crusade on "the Negro question" by publishing *Race and Reality,* a sequel

ADMINISTRATIVE AND SOCIAL CONCEPTIONS OF RACE

The administrative conception of race frequently is related closely to mystical viewpoints. It is an official conception and has far-reaching consequences in the lives of large numbers of human beings. Either by legislative act or by bureaucratic practice, certain "racial" categories are established and governmental actions are based on them. Examples include the Nazi dichotomy of Aryan and non-Aryan, the enumeration of Negroes by the United States Bureau of the Census, and the distinction between "native" and "colored" in South Africa. Such definitions can be used as racial weapons. In Hitler's Germany to be classified as "non-Aryan" meant dismissal from civil service and university positions, severe restrictions in the practice of medicine, law, dentistry, and journalism, special identity cards, the adoption of Jewish first names for all Jews, business and property restrictions and confiscations, deprivation of the rights of citizenship, and the prohibition of marriage to an "Aryan."

In taking the United States Census, usually a person who has any Negro ancestry has been recorded as "Negro," even though he is indistinguishable in appearance from "white" Americans.[7] The practical consequences of such a practice on the part of the federal, state, and local governments ramify to some extent into church membership, schools and colleges attended south of the Mason-Dixon line (with a sizable number of exceptions in recent years), marriage, voting and office-holding, certain aspects of the administration

of criminal justice, and the administration of relief. A person who is regarded by the community in which he lives as "Indian" has been recorded in the Census as "Indian." Although the effects of this definition have not been as marked as in the case previously cited, some official policies have been laid down on this "racial" line, notably school attendance and marriage.

In Latin America, a social conception of race among the members of local populations is quite common.[8] In a Mexican community, Lasker found that

practically the whole range of physical types occurs both in individuals whose parents are described as Indians and in those whose parents are considered to be Mestizos or Spanish. It is clear therefore that the physical appearance of the people cannot enter appreciably into their categorization of themselves. This supplements direct evidence that the ethnic identification is considered a cultural and linguistic matter and eliminates the possibility that considerations based on biological race significantly enter into the judgments.[9]

Generally, in the Latin American countries, "recognized Indians" are not considered members of the national society or culture. However, they can become accepted if they learn to speak the national language (Spanish or Portuguese) fluently, adopt European-type clothing, and move from a recognized Indian community to a city or town regarded as national in culture.[10] Gillin estimates that there are approximately ten million recognized Indi-

in the form of a "midnight soliloquy" to *Race and Reason.* According to the National Putnam Letters Committee, this book "throws light on the world's deepening racial crisis." Putnam reiterates his earlier finding that innate racial differences, rather than the Negro's surroundings and education, are the "cause of his comparative performance." Dismissing modern anthropology as taught in Anglo-American schools and colleges as "the result of a political ideology," he says that the people who developed it were "almost all partisan and passionate crusaders for socialism." Carleton Putnam, *Race and Reality*, Public Affairs Press, 1967, p. 14. For a review of sporadic instances of "scientific" racism during the past twenty years, see Juan Comas, *op. cit.*, pp. 303–340, and "More on 'Scientific' Racism," *CA*, 1962, pp. 284 ff.

[7] See "Postscript on Legal and U.S.A. Census Definitions of Race" at the end of this chapter.

[8] Ralph Beals, "Indian-Mestizo-White Relations in Spanish America," in A. W. Lind (ed.), *Race Relations in World Perspective*, Univ. of Hawaii Press, 1955, chap. 18; Donald Pierson, "Race Relations in Portuguese America," *ibid.*, chap. 19; Charles Wagley (ed.), *Race and Class in Brazil*, UNESCO, 1952; and Charles Wagley, "On the Concept of Social Race in the Americas," in D. B. Heath and R. N. Adams (eds.), *Contemporary Cultures and Societies of Latin America*, Random House, 1965, pp. 542–543.

[9] Gabriel W. Lasker, "Ethnic Identification in an Indian Mestizo Community," *Phylon*, Second Quarter, 1953, p. 190.

[10] George E. Simpson, "Ethnic Groups, Social Mobility, and Power in Latin America," in Anthony Leeds (ed.), "Social Structure, Stratification, and Mobility," Pan American Union, *Studies and Monographs*, VIII, 1967, pp. 272–273.

ans in Latin America's total population of 180 million.[11]

Pierson reports an interesting example of situational influences on the specification of color categories in the Brazilian village of Cruz das Almas. In the vital statistics of the community, the categories used are: *branco* (white), *preto* (black), and *pardo* (intermediate). Pierson says:

. . . the listing of a given individual reflects the relation to him of the person who is making the listing. If the registrar is a particular friend of the person in question, or of his family, an obvious black in all likelihood will be listed as a *pardo* and an obvious *pardo* as a 'white.' This may also occur if . . . the person doing the listing happens to be in an especially friendly mood or otherwise to be more than usually well-disposed toward the person being listed. The tendency to 'grade-up' individuals in the color scale, especially under conditions of primary contact, is marked."[12]

BIOLOGICAL VIEWPOINTS ON RACE

The Traditional Physical Anthropological Approach to Race

The first endeavors along this line began with more or less crude observations of obvious physical differences, and was followed later by careful measurement of external physical traits. In recent years the approach broadened to take account of several physiological tests. Among the most widely used characteristics are skin color, nasal index, hair texture, head form, lip form, hair and eye color, facial index, and stature. Brief reference will be made to each of these traits.

Skin color has been called the most obvious racial feature; certainly it is, sociologically, the most important one. However, it is one of the most unreliable traits if taken singly, because of the great variation within the major divisions of mankind, because of the overlapping from one group to another, and because

of environmental influences. Extreme types can, of course, be identified by inspection without the use of refined techniques. Thus the ordinary person has no difficulty in distinguishing a Swede from a north Chinese or a Bantu, or, to add two other "colors," a Crow Indian from a Samoan. But man's great proclivities for travel and interbreeding have mixed human genes to such an extent that it is by no means easy to tell racial background by glancing at skin surfaces. The technique of spectrophotometry permits accurate and more objective measurement of skin colors. As Hooton pointed out, the sources of skin color are five pigments, the main ones being melanin and carotene, and an effect known as scattering.[13]

By nasal index is meant the relationship between the width of the nose, measured between the wings, and the length of the nose from the juncture of the nasal bones and the frontal bone to the juncture of the septum with the upper lip. If the percentage of the width relative to the length is less than 70, the index is called leptorrhine (narrow-nosed); if it is 84 or over, the indexes are known as platyrrhine or chamaerrhine (broad-nosed); intermediate indexes are mesorrhine (medium-nosed). Generally speaking, these nasal forms are characteristic of Caucasoids, Negroids, and Mongoloids, respectively.

Hair form, one of the most reliable criteria of race, falls into three main categories: ulotrichy (oval, tightly curled strands), leiotrichy (straight, round in cross section), and cymotrichy (wavy, intermediate in cross-section shape). Typically, these three types of hair form are found in Negroes, Mongoloids, and Whites.

One of the most widely known racial indexes is head form, although it is less useful in racial classification, except in the establishment of subracial categories, than a number of other physical traits. The cephalic index is obtained by dividing the maximum transverse head breadth by the maximum glabello-occipital length. A percentage of less than 75 indicates dolichocephaly (long-headedness), one of 75–80 mesocephaly (medium-headed-

---

[11] John P. Gillin, "Some Signposts for Policy," in Council on Foreign Relations, *Social Change in Latin America Today*, Harper & Row, 1960, pp. 19–20.

[12] Donald Pierson, *Cruz das Almas: a Brazilian Village*, Smithsonian Institution, Institute of Social Anthropology Publication No. 12, 1951, p. 190.

[13] E. A. Hooton, *Up from the Ape*, Macmillan, rev. ed., 1946, p. 456.

ness), and over 80 brachycephaly (broad-headedness, or short-headedness).

Lip form refers to lip thickness, which ranges from the thin, inverted anthropoidal lips of Caucasoids through the intermediate structures of Mongoloids to the wide, everted, highly evolved Negroid lips. According to Hooton, lip form is significant in racial classification chiefly when there is a Negro strain in the group under study.

Hair color and eye color in human beings is an exceedingly complex and technical subject, and details concerning them cannot be presented here. Hooton stated that "the commonest hair pigment is granular, brown or black pigment identical with that in the skin" although "a diffuse and soluble red-gold pigment is sometimes present in the hair." Eye color is determined mainly by the pigment in the iris, and seems to be due more to quantitative than to qualitative differences in pigment. An overwhelming majority of the world's population has black hair. Blonds are numerically insignificant. When eyes are classified on the basis of primary or background color and secondary detailed hue, there are four main types: "light," "pale mixed," "mixed," and "dark." In general, light and dark coloration in hair and eyes are associated although there are differences in these associations between the sexes, and dark hair-blue eye combinations occur frequently where there has been a crossing of ethnic stocks.[14]

Even less useful in racial classification than the cephalic index is the facial index. This criterion is obtained by dividing the length of the face from the root of the nose to the bottom of the chin by the maximum breadth across the malars. When the percentages are 88 or over the index is called leptoprosopic or narrow-faced; indexes of less than 84 are euryprosopic or broad-faced; and those between 85 and 88 are mesoprosopic or medium-faced. Broad-headed persons usually have broad faces and narrow-headed individuals are usually narrow-faced, although notable exceptions include some unmixed Negroes who have long heads and broad faces and some Armenoids who have relatively broad

heads and narrow faces. Pronounced prognathism (protrusion of the jaws) is found mainly among Australoids and Negroids, but facial protrusion tends to be recessive and so most Negro-white mixtures in the United States have little prognathism.

Coon's comments on facial contours, which are not susceptible of exact measurement, are interesting. He refers to the extreme cragginess and ruggedness of the facial features, including the forehead, the brow ridges, the cheekbones, the jaws, and the nose, associated with the "western marginal fringe area (of Europe), and especially with the region of largest heads and maximum Palaeolithic survival." Nordics and Mediterraneans are said to display a maximum of facial relief without the appearance of bony massiveness. "Facial flatness" typifies the Mongoloids but is also characteristic of eastern Europe, Poland, Finland, and Hungary. The "maximum nasality" of Near-Eastern peoples is accompanied by a convexity of the nose as a whole, the depression of the tip of the nose, and eyebrows over the nose.[15]

Stature or bodily height is one of the least satisfactory criteria of race because of the great range found within each major human grouping. There is also the question of the extent to which stature may be regarded as a heredity character. Numerous studies have attempted to show that height is affected by such environmental factors as diet, sickness, occupation, and social class.

Data concerning such physiological differences as internal and external body temperature, pulse rate, basal metabolism, and perspiration lost under certain conditions, in terms of work loads, temperature, humidity, and altitude are not extensive, but physiologists have found some racial differences. According to Coon and Hunt: "Negroes are superior to whites in keeping cool in wet heat. Australian aborigines and nomadic Lapps have one kind of cold adaptation—heat transfer between blood vessels in the extremities—and Mongoloids have another—a combination of fat insulation and increased peripheral blood flow with high basal metabolism. Other

---

[14] On hair and eye color, see *ibid.*, especially pp. 469, 477–478, 480.

[15] C. S. Coon, *The Races of Europe*, Macmillan, 1939, p. 279.

(non-Lapp) Caucasoids do not have any of these. Furthermore, for various reasons, subcutaneous fat protects Negroes less from cold than it does whites. Whites with tanned skins do better on hot deserts than unclothed Negroes of the same height and weight. Only Mongoloids have acquired successful adaptation to the thin air of the Andes and Tibet."[16]

It must not be thought that the traits considered here are the only sorting criteria used in the traditional anthropological approach to race, or that all are utilized by every classifier. In classification of this type much depends on the selection of criteria and how the characteristics are defined. There is, of course, much variation with respect to a single trait within a given race, but usually the classifications are based on combinations of three or more characteristics. Once the measurements have been taken on the selected racial traits, averages are found for a given group. From the averages hypothetical "ideal types" are established, although it is clear that no individual will exemplify in himself the precise set of averages for the racial type. In this procedure races become statistical abstractions, artificial mental constructs to be used as measuring sticks in identifying the world's peoples. Regardless of the terminology used for the main physical groupings (divisions, stocks, races, subspecies) and for the smaller physical sections (subraces, sub-subraces, breed, ethnic groups, etc.), there is an impressive underlying consensus.

Montagu's Major and Ethnic Groups of Man. On the basis of certain external characters, M. F. Ashley Montagu, the physical anthropologist who has taken the strongest stand against the fixity of racial differences and racial categories, has classified the "major and ethnic groups of man." An ethnic group is defined as one of a number of populations within the species *Homo sapiens* that maintains "certain differences by means of isolating mechanisms such as geographical and social barriers. If the barriers are high, such isolates tend to remain distinct; where they are low, neighboring isolates hybridize with

one another." A major group is defined as "a number of ethnic groups classified together on the basis of their possession of certain common characters which serve to distinguish that major group from others." Montagu regards his classification as a tentative and temporary convenience, saying, that a major or ethnic group is, in most cases, an abstraction that exists only in the minds of classifiers. He points out that since the same types of physical characters may have different origins, their origin can be traced only by tracing the distribution of the genes determining them.[17] He lists "The Major and Ethnic Groups of Man" as follows:[18]

Major Group: Negroid

African Negroes
Ethnic Group:
  a. The True Negro: West Africa, Cameroons and Congo.
  b. The Half-Hamites: East Africa and East Central Africa.
  c. Forest Negro: Equatorial and Tropical Africa.
  d. "Bantu-Speaking Negroids": Central and Southern Africa.
  e. Nilotic Negro: Eastern Sudan and Upper Nile Valley.
  f. Bushman: Southern Angola and North-West Africa.
  g. Hottentot: South Africa.

Oceanic Negroids
Ethnic Group:
  a. Papuans: New Guinea.
  b. Melanesians: Melanesia.

African Pygmies or Negrillos
Ethnic Group:
  a. African Pygmies or Negrillos: Equatorial Africa.

Asiatic Pygmies or Negritos
Ethnic Group:
  a. Andamanese: Andaman Islands.
  b. Semang: Central region of Malay Peninsula, and East Sumatra.
  c. Philippine Negritos: Philippine Islands.

Oceanic Pygmies or Negritos
Ethnic Group:
  a. New Guinea Pygmies: New Guinea.

[16] C. S. Coon, with E. E. Hunt, Jr., *The Living Races of Man*, Knopf, 1965, pp. 16–17.

[17] M. F. Ashley Montagu, *Introduction to Physical Anthropology*, Thomas, 3rd ed., 1960, pp. 409, 410, 417, 419.

[18] *Ibid.*, pp. 470–471.

Major Group: Caucasoid

Ethnic Group:
a. Basic Mediterranean: Borderlands of the Mediterranean Basin.
b. Atlanto-Mediterranean: Middle East, eastern Balkans, East Africa, Portugal, Spain, British Isles.
c. Irano-Afghan Mediterranean: Iran, Afghanistan, parts of India, Arabia, and North Africa.
d. Nordic: Central Europe, Scandinavia and neighboring regions.
e. East Baltic: East Baltic regions.
f. Lapps: Northern Scandinavia, Kola Peninsula.
g. Alpine: France along the Alps to Russia.
h. Dinaric: Eastern Alps from Switzerland to Albania, Asia Minor, and Syria.
i. Armenoids: Asia Minor.
j. Hamites: North and East Africa.
k. Indo-Dravidians: India and Ceylon.
l. Polynesians: Polynesia (Central Pacific).

Sub-Division: Australoid or Archaic Caucasoid
Ethnic Group:
a. Australian: Australia.
b. Veddah: Ceylon.
c. Pre-Dravidian: India.
d. Ainu: Japan, Hokkaido (Yezo) and Sakhalin Islands.

Major Group: Mongoloid

Classical Mongoloids
Ethnic Group:
a. An undetermined number of ethnic groups in the older populations of Tibet, Mongolia, China, Korea, Japan, and Siberia, including such tribes as the Buriats east and west of Lake Baikal, the Koryak of northern Siberia, the Gilyak of northernmost Sakhalin and the mainland north of the Amur estuary (who appear to have mixed with the Ainu), and the Goldi on the Lower Amur and Ussuri.

Arctic Mongoloids
Ethnic Group:
a. Eskimo: Extreme northeast of Asia, Arctic coast of North America, Greenland. This type includes the Aleuts of the Aleutian Islands, and the Reindeer and coastal Chukchee of northeastern Siberia.

b. Evenki or true Tungus (Americanoids): Mongolia, Siberia, Asiatic highlands north of the Himalayas.
c. Kamchadales: Kamchatka.
d. Samoyedes: Kola Peninsula, White Sea and Yenisei regions.

The Mongoloids of the extreme north-east of the Asiatic continent are distinguished as the *Paleoasiatics*. These are considered to be the complex of ancient populations of Asia who early migrated to this extreme peripheral region. The populations believed to have migrated later into the northeast of the Asiatic continent are known as the *Neoasiatics*.

Paleoasiatics: Chuckchee, Koryak, Kamchadale, Gilyak, Eskimo, Aleut, Yukaghir, Chuvantzi, Ostyak of Yenisei, Ainu.

Neoasiatics: Finnic tribes, Samoyedic tribes, Turkic including Yakut, Mongolic, Tungusic.

American Indians
Ethnic Group:
a. An undetermined number of ethnic groups of North, Middle, Central, and South America.

Indo-Malay
Ethnic Group:
a. Indonesian: Southern China, Indo-China, Burma, Thailand, interior of Malay Archipelago.
b. Malay: In addition to Indonesian distribution, Malay Peninsula, Dutch East Indies, Philippines, Okinawa, and adjacent islands.

Anthropometric and Blood Group Data. Cavalli-Sforza and Edwards selected fifteen populations representing various geographical regions and constructed a dichotomous tree representing phylogenetic relationships between many anthropometric characters and the frequencies of a number of blood group genes. Although there were some striking discrepancies, the patterns of relationship were similar and both "were fairly consistent with orthodox schemes of classification reached by less precise methods."[19]

[19] L. L. Cavalli-Sforza and A. W. F. Edwards, "Analysis of Human Evolution," *Proceedings of the International Congress of Genetics*, 1964. Quoted in Nigel A. Barnicot, "Taxonomy and Variation in Modern Man," in M. F. Ashley Montagu (ed.), *The Concept of Race*, Collier Books, 1969, pp. 204–205.

GENETICS AND RACE

The main shortcoming of the traditional physical anthropological method is its inability to indicate the frequencies within different breeding populations of the genes associated with physical characters. Head form, hair form, skin color, and other morphological characteristics are determined by the interaction of a number of genes, the influence of the physical environment, and local customs. Those who are interested in the evolution of human populations have turned to the study of those differences in gene frequencies that can be ascertained. With this approach, races are defined as populations which have different frequencies of variable genes.

Racial differences in the proportions of the ABO blood groups were first observed in 1914–1915, and the method has since been applied to peoples in various countries and to other genes, mainly those for sickling, *thalassemia,* taste blindness, and color blindness.[20] Humans can now be described in terms of at least 20 blood group systems and types including ABO, MN, P, Rh, Kell, Duffy, Lewis, Lutheran, Kidd, and secretor. Some of these groups and types are responsible for many different phenotypes (what the individual looks like or tests like) because of the number of allelic alterations found in some of the genes.[21] Boyd notes that in the Rh system "the twelve or more phenotypes distinguishable with the usual serums depend upon the action of more than eight genes. . . ."[22]

Differences in blood group and blood type gene frequencies characterize a number of human populations, and with further research on these and other traits, the differences may stand out more clearly. Several examples of distinctions known at present may be cited. First, American Indians lack the allele B, the Rh-negative allele r, the Kell allele, and, probably, the nonsecretor allele, but have high frequencies of M. The Diego positive allele, found elsewhere only in Asia, has been found in variable proportions in the few American Indian populations that have been studied in this respect. Second, northwestern European populations have relatively high percentages of A, but the gene frequency of B is only 10 percent. The proportion of A_2 is higher than in Africa (A_2 is lacking in most of the rest of the world), and the Duffy gene Fy^a is about 40 percent. Except for the Basques, these populations have the world's highest percentage of the Rh negative gene. M has only slightly higher frequency than N. Third, the Lapps have the highest proportion of N in Europe, a high percentage of Fy^a, a very low frequency of B, and A_2 frequencies three times as high as any other population in the world. Unlike the northwest Europeans, the Rh-negative gene r is relatively low in the Lapps, but R^1 is somewhat higher than in other European groups, and R^2 is high. Fourth, the aborigines of Australia lack the B allele, the S allele of the MNS system, and the Rh-negative allele, but have a very high percentage of N and of A. Fifth, Asia, although less completely studied than other areas, includes the regions with the highest percentages of the allele B; the Rh-negative is rare or absent, and, in the few groups that have been tested, the Diego factor is present. Sixth, African Negroes have very high frequencies of R^o (50 to 90 percent); this gene is frequent in populations of African origin in other parts of the world, but its percentages are very low in other populations. A new factor (V) in the Rh system is common among Negroes but rare in Whites, and Fy has a frequency of 80 percent in Negroes but is almost unknown in Europeans.[23]

In 1910, deformed red cells, some of them sickle-shaped, were found in the blood of a West Indian Negro ill with anemia. The sickle-cell trait has been shown to be inherited, and, according to Dunn, the three phenotypes produced by matings between sickle-cell persons correspond to the following three genotypes (genic descriptions of individuals) in the usual Mendelian proportions: $1/4$ si/si (homo-

[20] See L. C. Dunn, *Heredity and Evolution in Human Populations,* Harvard, 1960, pp. 90, 93; W. C. Boyd, *Genetics and the Races of Man,* Little, Brown, 1950, p. 202; and L. C. Dunn and Th. Dobzhansky, *Heredity, Race and Society,* Penguin, 1952, p. 118.

[21] A summary of basic concepts in genetics is not included here. For an excellent review of these concepts, see Dunn, *op. cit.,* chaps. 1 and 2.

[22] W. C. Boyd, *Genetics and the Races of Man,* Boston Univ. Press, 1958, p. 9.

[23] Boyd, *op. cit.,* pp. 8, 9, 11; Dunn, *op. cit.,* pp. 95–98.

zygotes—normal people), ½ Si/si (heterozygotes—those with the sickle-cell trait), and ¼ Si/Si (homozygotes—persons with sickle-cell anemia.[24] The significance of the presence of one or the other or both of the alleles (forms) of this gene are revealed in the experience of the populations in which they are found. The highest frequencies of this gene are found in Africa south of the Sahara and north of the Zambesi river, with noteworthy frequencies in Sicily, Greece, Turkey, southern Arabia, India, and among New World Negroes. Dunn points out that there is considerable variation in its frequency among persons of the same racial group, but that in general it is highest (up to 45 percent) in regions where malicious malaria is prevalent.[25] Although the question of increased resistance of sicklers to malaria is complicated by the possibility that immunity may be acquired by early exposure to malaria, it appears that malaria is lower in persons heterozygous for the sickle gene. Allison estimated that heterozygotes may have an advantage of 25 percent over normal homozygotes. Thus, in malarial areas, the death of homozygotes from sickle-cell anemia is balanced "by increase due to the larger number of children produced by the protected heterozygotes." If malaria is eradicated in other parts of the world, as it has been in recent years in Europe and the United States, it is predicted that the incidence of the sickle gene will decline after a number of generations until the only cases of sickle-cell anemia will be due to the appearance of new mutations.[26]

Formerly it was believed that the blood groups were nonadaptive traits, that is, that they were less subject to the action of natural selection than were other traits. It has now been shown that some half dozen diseases have some association with blood groups belonging to the ABO systems. Persons in group O are slightly more susceptible to duodenal ulcer and pituitary adenoma (benign tumor) than are those of groups A, B, or AB. People with type A blood are slightly more likely to get pernicious anemia or hip fractures than are other people. As Lehrman points out, however, the selective value of a gene is not a fixed quantity. Studies have shown that the type O blood group gene also provides strong protection against syphilis. Whether the influence of this gene is salutary or not depends then upon whether the person possessing it is exposed to the germ of syphilis.[27]

There is no indication in any of the diseases studied thus far that blood-group heterozygotes have an advantage as is the case with the hemoglobin heterozygotes in relation to malaria. An important discovery shows that women of group O married to men of A or B have fewer living children than A or B women married to O men. Also, incompatibility of mother and fetus in the ABO group is a cause of hemolytic disease of the newborn. Dunn says: "Deaths of unborn children, if selective in respect of genotype, would, of course, be the most potent of all effects in changing the gene frequency in subsequent generations." Mourant has pointed out that while ABO frequencies are relatively stable for periods of about 2000 years, it cannot be assumed that these blood groups are completely stable. Epidemic disease is a possible cause of sudden large frequency changes. A recent study of the micro-organisms that cause plague and smallpox has shown an antigen like that of blood group A in the smallpox virus, and an antigen similar to the blood-group substance H (most abundant in O cells) in the plague bacillus. On the assumption that an individual will have difficulty in developing an antibody to an organism antigenically similar to any of his own blood-group substances, it is suggested that group A persons are especially susceptible to smallpox and group O persons to plague. A comparison of the world distribution of smallpox and plague epidemics and ABO blood groups shows that the hypothesis that such epidemics have importantly affected blood-group distribution merits further study.[28]

Geneticists have contributed to our understanding of human variation by mapping, for

[24] Dunn, *op. cit.*, p. 93.
[25] *Ibid.*, pp. 52–53.
[26] *Ibid.*, pp. 55–58.

[27] R. L. Lehrman, *Race, Evolution, and Mankind*, Basic Books, 1966, pp. 69, 121–122.
[28] A. E. Mourant, "Evolution, Genetics and Anthropology," *The Journal of the Royal Anthropology Institute of Great Britain and Ireland*, 1961, pp. 159–160; Dunn, *op. cit.*, pp. 78–80; Boyd, *op. cit.*, p. 14.

a substantial part of the earth, the global gene frequencies for more than 20 traits inherited as alleles (alternative genes on single chromosomal sites). Four achievements of the genetical method in physical anthropology stated by Boyd are:

1. showing that the blood groups of some Hungarian Gypsies agreed quite well with those of the Indian soldiers tested and differed significantly from those of the Hungarians.
2. determining that the amount of white mixture in the North American Negro is 30.565 percent.
3. indicating that the Lapps are Europeans, that they are not even partly of Mongoloid origin.
4. showing that the Pacific pygmies (Papuan and Andaman Negritos) are not derived from African gene contributions.[29]

Information concerning the frequencies of a number of genes has been combined in a number of studies, but the results so far about the relationships between populations have been rather disappointing. Lehrman says: "Either we need a great deal more information in order to arrive at an answer, or selection is changing the gene frequencies much faster than anyone now believes possible."[30]

Marvin Harris, Gloria Marshall, and others have shown that the genetical approach to the study of race in the United States has serious limitations. According to Harris, the rule of hypodescent assigns individuals whose parents belong to different "races" to the one that is politically subordinate.[31] Marshall criticizes scholars whose works imply that the "white race" and the "Negro race" are genetically defined. She sees race as a biopolitical concept rather than a purely statistical one.[32] Margaret Mead's summary is incisive: "Negro Americans do constitute a partial Mendelian population because of preferential mating with one another, but this is enormously different from

the state of an isolated group of Eskimo, African desert dwellers, or inhabitants of isolated Pacific islands."[33]

Race Formation

Mutation permanently alters the nature of a particular gene and occasions a change in a trait that can be inherited. Most mutations are deleterious, but some have been advantageous in certain environments. In addition to gene recombinations, mutations provide the raw materials for natural selection. It is impossible to delineate all or even most of the physical traits that have had the highest survival value under specific conditions, in the history of mankind. The relations between climate and skin color that hold for lower animals seem also to apply to man. (The most depigmented people today are those whose ancestry goes back to the zone where human survival depended on the use of clothing for a longer period of time than anywhere else in the world.)[34] Narrow noses and wide noses may have had some selective advantage in different physical environments. Recent research relates the distribution of big noses to the areas where people have had to live with either extreme dryness or extreme cold and finds that short low noses tend to occur among peoples of the humid tropics.[35] Body weight and linear development of the limbs are correlated with mean temperature.[36] The blood groups no longer seem to be neutral adaptive factors. According to Lehrman, except for those genes that produce gross defects, most genes may be either good or bad, depending on other factors.[37] Montagu points out that the association between blood groups and disease does not imply a causal relationship, but that the blood groups may be indicators of other factors with

[29] W. C. Boyd, "Four Achievements of the Genetical Method in Physical Anthropology," *AA*, 1963, Vol. 65, pp. 243–252.

[30] Lehrman, *op. cit.*, p. 176.

[31] M. Harris, *Patterns of Race in the Americas*, Walker, 1964, p. 56.

[32] G. Marshall, "Racial Classifications, Popular and Scientific," in M. Mead, *et al.* (eds.), *Science and the Concept of Race*, Columbia, 1968, pp. 155–156, 161.

[33] Mead, *ibid.*, pp. 173–174.

[34] Montagu, *Introduction to Physical Anthropology*, p. 390; C. L. Brace and A. Montagu, *Man's Evolution*, Macmillan, 1965, p. 286.

[35] Montagu, *Introduction to Physical Anthropology*, pp. 390–391; Brace and Montagu, *op. cit.*, pp. 307–308.

[36] Montagu, *Introduction to Physical Anthropology*, pp. 591–592; Brace and Montagu, *op. cit.*, pp. 310–311; T. Dobzhansky, *Mankind Evolving*, Yale, 1962, 271–278.

[37] Lehrman, *op. cit.*, pp. 121–122.

which they are associated and which are more directly related to susceptibility to certain diseases.[38] Dunn says:

Connections between blood-group genes and diseases of maturity like gastric caricinoma or duodenal ulcer, interesting and important as they are, do not in themselves provide decisive evolutionary effects. The fact that most large and successful populations, like those of Europe, Africa, and Asia, contain all four groups indicates that no one is clearly superior under all conditions. The very widespread occurrence of polymorphism in this and in most other blood-group systems indicates that it is some kind of balance which is adaptive in particular circumstances. It is probably balance not only within but between different blood-group systems which is important.[39]

As a result of geographic or social isolation of small groups, inbreeding tends to fix any mutations that occur. It is also true that in small, isolated populations a mutant gene may be completely lost and the mutation may disappear. Such accidental increase or decrease of mutant genes, and the resultant random variations in gene frequencies, is called genetic drift. Another illustration of genetic drift is that of a small group of migrants who leave a population where only a small proportion of the people are of one of the four ABO blood groups. The probability is high that there will be no person of this blood group among those who leave. In this case, the new community will never contain this blood group unless it appears later as a new mutation.

Dunn's study of Roman Jews demonstrates the possibilities of analyzing the relation of such factors as isolation and genetic drift to gene frequency. Seven hundred isolated, in-marrying persons in the Roman Jewish population of 4000 (the other 8000 Jews in Rome are of non-Roman origin) were given blood, saliva, and urine tests to determine genotypes. The proportion of individuals of blood group B (27 percent) was more than twice as high as in the Italian Catholic population (up to 10 or 11 percent). Such a great difference indicates that very little mixture between the

small community and Italian Catholics has occurred. The proportion of persons of blood group B is high in comparison with other Jewish communities, probably due mainly to random genetic drift but the selective factor may also have been involved. Another characteristic of the Roman Jewish community is the frequency of more than 5 percent of r' (a form of Rh-negative). This allele, rare in Europe, is much higher in the Roman Jewish population than in Italy generally or in any Jewish population thus far tested. The high frequency of r' cannot be attributed to mixture with a population with a much higher frequency of this allele because no such population is known.[40]

Hybridization modifies the distinctness between populations and, when followed by isolation, leads to the establishment of a new pattern of genes. The Australian aborigines may represent a relationship with both Mongoloid and Caucasoid peoples. The distribution of eight Rh types in this population is similar to that of Mongoloids, but, with the exception of the absence of rh, their gene pattern is even closer to that of Caucasoids. Also, the Australian aborigines are very low while Negroids are very high in Rh_o. These data are of interest because the Australian aborigines have often been grouped with the Archaic Caucasoid stock, presumably a people of Asiatic origin.[41] It has been hypothesized that some of the characteristics of the western European populations (low percentages of B, high percentages of Rh-negative) may have resulted from mixture of a population with little or no B and relatively high proportions of Rh-negative with immigrants from the East with a higher frequency of B and low or no Rh-negative. The Basques of today have the lowest proportion of B in Europe and the highest Rh-negative in the world. In addition, as Dunn points out, they speak a non-Indo-European language and have skeletal features similar to Western Europeans of the late Palaeolithic. Perhaps the Basques are descended from an ancient European race that has been incorporated elsewhere into a mixture. Such hypothesizing does not explain

---

[38] Montagu, *Introduction to Physical Anthropology*, p. 379.
[39] Dunn, *op. cit.*, pp. 103–104.

[40] *Ibid.*, pp. 112–114.
[41] Montagu, *Introduction to Physical Anthropology*, p. 353.

what caused the differences in gene frequencies in the earlier groups.[42]

The study of smaller populations has revealed that gene frequencies are related to physical distance. For example, the frequency of O decreases from north to south in Britain, and A increases from north to south in Australia. Such gradual transitions in gene frequencies are called "clines." These gradients indicate the possibility of mixture ("gene flow") and some differences in the environment from one locality to the next, e.g., the cline in the frequency of thalassemia with increasing altitude.

Additional aspects of the process of race formation are sexual selection, or the selection by high-ranking males of women possessing what are regarded as the most desirable traits, and social selection, or the regulation of mating by arbitrarily established social standards.

From a genetical point of view, then, race formation is a process of diversification of complexes of genes, beginning with the appearance of mutations. Variants are acted on by selective forces and a balance compatible with environmental conditions is produced. The complexes so produced may be protected for some time by relative isolation, physical or social, but sooner or later these complexes of genes are modified by migration and mixture. To these evolutionary factors must be added another of great importance: culture.

Number of Races

From time to time, Montagu and others have advocated the elimination of the term "race" in scientific discussions because it has been employed to refer to "fixed clear-cut differences." In 1962, Montagu said he preferred the term "genogroup" to refer to a "breeding population which differs from other breeding populations of the species in the frequency of one or more genes."[43] A number of scientists favor substituting the term "population" for "race." As Brace and Montagu point out, this suggestion is not entirely satisfactory because the assumption "that there is something significant in the association of traits in a single group of people obscures the factors influencing the occurrence and distribution of any single trait." They add that "the most important requirement is the appreciation of the selective pressures which have operated to influence the expression of each trait separately."[44]

We have pointed out above that, in the United States, Negro Americans constitute only a partial Mendelian population.

Mayr recognizes that there are races, but concludes that drawing the line between them is impossible.[45] Stanley Garn names nine major geographical races: Amerindian, Polynesian, Micronesian, Melanesia-Papuan, Australian, Asiatic, Indian, European, and African, and 32 local races (breeding populations).[46] Dobzhansky combines the Coon, Garn, Birdsell classification of 30 races[47] with Garn's list to form a classification of 34 races, a classification based on gene frequencies and all observable physical traits.[48] He points out that the Coon-Garn-Birdsell classification differs from previous classifications because it recognizes that races are Mendelian populations that will change in time. Four of the 34 races listed by Dobzhansky have arisen within the last 400 years. He follows the Coon-Garn-Birdsell position that races are of different kinds.

Murrayians, Ainus, Negritos, Bushman, Carpentarians, and perhaps some others are relics of ancient populations, which were more widely distributed in the past than they are at present. Some of them are being submerged and assimilated by intermarriage with their neighbors or becoming extinct. The new races are still in formative stages; their gene pools, not clearly separated from those of their neighbors, are still without internal coherence. For example, Ladinos are in reality a social class in some Latin American countries, and in different countries they constitute genetically different populations, which have few or no genetic ties be-

[42] Dunn, *op. cit.*, p. 102.

[43] M. F. Ashley Montagu, "The Concept of Race," *AA*, Oct., 1962, p. 925.

[44] Brace and Montagu, *op. cit.*, p. 270.

[45] E. Mayr, "Discussion," in Mead *et al.*, *op. cit.*, p. 103.

[46] S. Garn, *Human Races*, Thomas, 1961, pp. 127–132.

[47] C. S. Coon, S. M. Garn, and J. B. Birdsell, *Races*, Thomas, 1950.

[48] T. Dobzhansky, *op. cit.*, pp. 263–265.

tween them. Hindus are a complex mosaic of caste populations which scarcely interbreed. North Chinese, Classic Mongoloids, and Southeast Asiatics are huge masses of humanity forming numerous geographically separated Mendelian populations which could as well as be treated as different races or placed in a single race. The same is true of the populations of Europe, which are on the way to fusion into a single race.[49]

Boyd's racial classification, based on genetical method, includes seven geographical groups (European, African, Asian, Indo-Dravidian, American, Pacific, and Australian) and thirteen races (North Africans seem to be included with the Mediterraneans).

European
  1. Early European
  2. Lapps
  3. Northwest Europeans
  4. East and Central Europeans
  5. Mediterraneans

African
  6. African

Asian
  7. Asian
  8. Indo-Dravidian

American
  9. American Indian

Pacific
  10. Indonesian
  11. Melanesian
  12. Polynesian
  13. Australian[50]

Perhaps the most judicious position on the number of human races is that taken by S. L. Washburn:

Since races are open systems which are intergrading, the number of races will depend on the purpose of the classification. . . . If we are classifying races in order to understand human history, there aren't many human races, and there is very substantial agreement as to what they are. There are from six to nine races, and this difference in number is very largely a mat-

ter of definition. These races occupied the major separate geographical areas of the Old World.[51]

Race isn't very important biologically. It should be remembered that races are products of the past. As human culture develops, special adaptations are no longer needed. In Washburn's words, races "are relics of times and conditions which have long ceased to exist."[52] Racial groups are not fixed entities, but populations with distinctive gene frequencies tend to persist longer than social groups, including political groups, and thus give an illusion of permanence.[53] The races are disappearing, but at present rates the process will require thousands of years.[54] In the meantime, color and racial diversity will continue to have great and, possibly, increasing social and political significance.

Coon's Theory of the Origin of Races

In 1962, Carleton S. Coon published a theory of the origin of races that derives the five living races of mankind from five *Homo erectus* ancestral lines. According to this theory, the Mongoloids stem from *Sinanthropus*, the Caucasoids from early Neanderthals, the Australoids from *Pithecanthropus, Solo,* and *Wadjak,* and the Capoids (Bushmen and Hottentots) from the *Ternefine-Tangier* line of North Africa. The latter line is said to bear a similarity both to the *Australopithicines* and to *Pithecanthropus* and *Sinanthropus,* especially the latter. Coon says that "the origin of the African Negroes and of the Pygmies is the greatest unsolved mystery in the field of racial study." Because the oldest *sapiens* (Coon's definition) remains found thus far in sub-Saharan Africa appear to be less than 50,000 years old, Congoids (Negroes and Pygmies) are said to have crossed the sapient line some 200,000 years later than Caucasoids.

Coon sets the boundary between *Homo erectus* and *Homo sapiens* "on the basis of brain size, the degrees of curvature of the

[49] *Ibid.,* p. 266. Murrayians and Carpentarians are aboriginal populations of Australia.

[50] W. C. Boyd, "Genetics and Human Races," *Science,* 1963, pp. 1057–1065.

[51] S. L. Washburn, "The Study of Race," *AA,* 1963, p. 524.

[52] *Ibid.,* p. 531. See also Lehrman, *op. cit.,* p. 103.

[53] F. S. Hulse, "Race as an Evolutionary Episode," *AA,* 1962, vol. 64, p. 943.

[54] Bentley Glass, "The Genetic Basis of Human Races," in Mead *et al, op. cit.,* p. 92.

bones composing the cranial vault, and, to a lesser extent, on teeth size, particularly as tooth size is related to brain size."[55] His category of *Homo erectus* is based on only 19 adult fossil skulls spaced over a period of more than a half-million years: three *Pithecanthropus* specimens from Java; six *Solo* skulls from Java; six *Sinanthropus* skulls; one skull found in Tze-Yang, China in 1951; the *Chellian-3* skull found in Olduvai Gorge, Tanzania in 1960; the *Saldanha Bay* skullcap found in South Africa in 1953; and Broken Hill (Rhodesian) man.

One objection to Coon's theory is his decision as to the point in time when each of his subspecies of *erectus* became *sapiens*. Garn says that the problem of taxonomic criteria and the tremendous gaps in the fossil record make it impossible for him to say when *erectus* ended and *sapiens* began.[56] Also, to many biological scientists, the evidence for a transition to *Homo sapiens* five different times seems extremely weak. The view that Congoids crossed the *sapiens* line only 20,000 years ago, whereas the Caucasoids became *sapiens* 600,-000 years earlier has been challenged. One biologist says that the independent evolution over a period of half a million years of two genetic systems that then became interfertile would be a biological miracle.[57] According to most authorities, man evolved only once, and the physical differences appeared after—rather than before—the *sapiens* state.[58]

THE BIOLOGICAL EFFECTS OF RACE MIXTURE

Much emotion has been generated over the question of race mixture. Rationalizations are constantly developed to justify opposition to interbreeding; legislation and terrorism are employed to discourage it; and the offspring of racial crosses are often stigmatized. We shall give some of the accumulated evidence concerning the biological effects of race crossing.[59]

The descendants of nine mutineers from the English warship *Bounty* and Tahitian women are vigorous, long-lived, and alert people. Members of this group have interbred for five generations, and according to Shapiro, they equal or exceed in physical exuberance either parent stock. In Hawaii there has been much crossing between Polynesians, Whites of many nationalities, Filipinos, Japanese, Chinese, Koreans, and others. The mixed population produced by these crosses seems to be made up of very satisfactory physical and mental types. Further evidence of successful race crossing in Polynesia is found in New Zealand where Maori-white mixture has produced healthy and capable hybrids.

The thesis that the crossing of quite different racial stocks results more frequently in physical disharmonies than is normally the case has been sharply questioned in recent years. If such results were to be expected anywhere, the most logical place would be South Africa. Fischer's study of the descendants of Hottentots and Boers in South-West Africa does not reveal a disproportionate number of disharmonious types. These hybrids, known as Bastaards, are taller than their parental stocks, show a high vitality, and are very fertile.

Negro-white crossing in the United States has produced a group of hybrids that has survived, increased, and prospered in spite of tremendous social and economic obstacles.

A number of studies of Indian-white mixture in the United States, Canada, and Mexico show that the mixed offspring are taller and more fertile than the original parental stocks.

Mongoloid-white crosses have not been studied extensively, but there is an interesting report concerning Dutch soldiers and the women of Kisar, an island in the Indo-Malayan Archipelago. Rodenwald found that the

[55] C. S. Coon, *The Origin of Races*, Knopf, 1962, p. 369.

[56] Stanley M. Garn, Review of Coon, *ibid.*, *ASR*, Aug., 1963, pp. 637–638.

[57] Lehrman, *op. cit.*, p. 246.

[58] M. F. Ashley Montagu, *The Idea of Race*, Univ. of Nebraska Press, 1965, p. 53.

[59] See M. F. Ashley Montagu, *Man's Most Dangerous Myth: The Fallacy of Race*, 4th ed., World, 1964, pp. 185–223; *An Introduction to Physical Anthropology*, pp. 476–478; Juan Comas, "Racial Myths," in UNESCO, *The Race Question in Modern Science*, William Morrow, 1956, pp. 17–24; H. L. Shapiro, "Race Mixture," *ibid.*, pp. 348–373; Lehrman, *op. cit.*, pp. 211 ff.

hybrids born of these unions were quite satisfactory physical types.

Although social conditions have been most unfavorable for the hybrids resulting from the matings of Whites and Australian aborigines, the offspring are said to be excellent physical specimens. Their reproductive and survival rates are probably higher than for Whites, and in other respects they compare favorably with Whites of comparable socioeconomic backgrounds.

The weight of present opinion seems to regard race mixture as biologically advantageous. Ehrlich and Holm state that there is "some reason to believe that progeny of parents drawn from two different human populations would be, on the average, more fit in the sense of the population geneticist than the offspring of individuals from the same population."[60]

The older viewpoints concerning physical disharmonies, defectiveness, and constitutional unbalance are not supported by recent investigations. Genetic opinion holds that, "at the present time, human populations do not represent coadapted genetic combinations which are disrupted by outcrossing."[61] Unfavorable characteristics in hybrids are no longer thought to be the results of crossing *per se*, but are considered due to defective genes carried recessively by particular individuals. In fact, it is now thought that the chances are greater for matching such genes within a group than in matings between members of different groups. On this point Montagu says:

. . . It must be remembered that gene distributions are not so much a matter of the distribution of the genes of individuals as of the distribution of genes within populations. It is not, therefore, a matter of speaking in terms of two individuals who, characterized by either a superior or a mediocre assortment of genes, transmit them to their offspring, but of the continuous interchange and shuffling and reshuffling of every kind of gene within a population to yield a very large number of gene combinations. Some of these will be superior to others; in fact, there will be every possible form of variation within the limits set by the genetic equipment of the population. This is true of all populations. No population has a monopoly of good genes, and no population has a monopoly of bad genes; normal and defective genes are found in all populations of all human beings. Furthermore, it is most unlikely that the kind of defective genes distributed in one population will be found to occur in anything like as great a frequency, if at all, in another population or ethnic group.[62]

The dire claims and the dismal forecasts of those who oppose race mixing on biological grounds are not supported by the achievements of nations where crossing has occurred. The ancient Egyptians were a mixture of Mediterranean, Negroid, Armenoid, and possibly other elements. The ancient Greeks were a hybridized people of Mediterranean, Armenoid, Alpine, Nordic, and possibly other lines of descent. The ancient Romans were by no means a "pure" race. The great civilizational developments in recent times in Western Europe and the United States have occurred where "mongrelization" has been exceedingly common. Geographical position, historical events, natural resources, contacts with neighbors and strangers, and other factors, as well as hybridization, must be taken into consideration in explaining "the blossoming of culture," but it cannot be demonstrated that race mixture *per se* causes cultural blight. In fact, the hybrid members of racial minorities have frequently showed capacities for leadership in many lines of endeavor, probably not so much because of biological facts as such (although there is some evidence that mixed offspring may be biologically superior to both parent stocks) as because of stimulating culture contact situations and the influences of marginal social status.

[60] P. R. Ehrlich and R. W. Holm, "A Biographical View of Race," in Montagu (ed.), *The Concept of Race, op. cit.* p. 176. According to Ashley Montagu, the gene differences between contemporary human populations do not appear to be significant enough to produce hybrid vigor, although the offspring produced are biologically healthy in every way. Montagu, *Introduction to Physical Anthropology, op. cit.,* p. 400.

[61] N. E. Morton, C. S. Chung, and M. Mi, *Genetics of Interracial Crosses in Hawaii,* S. Karger, 1967, p. 148.

[62] Montagu, *Man's Most Dangerous Myth: The Fallacy of Race,* pp. 219–220.

The biological consequences of race mixture may be summed up in these statements:

1. Race mixture does not produce biologically or mentally inferior offspring.

2. Race mixture tends to produce offspring that equal or exceed their parental groups in vitality, stature, and fertility.

3. Radical crosses between races in the United States, and in certain places outside this country, may occasion serious personal problems for parents and children in the 1970s. The hybrid may be treated as an outcast and discriminated against. Race mixture has its social disadvantages, and these will be discussed later, but the evidence does not indicate that such mixing is biologically inadvisable.

DO THE JEWS CONSTITUTE A RACE?

The answer to this question depends upon the existence of a combination of physical traits that would distinguish Jews from others. No such grouping of traits has been discovered by a reputable scientist. In every country Jews tend to approximate the local gentile type because of the intermixture that has invariably occurred. Usually a considerable part of a given Jewish population is physically indistinguishable from the Christian or Moslem inhabitants of the area.

Whether there is a quality of "looking Jewish" is a controversial matter. Coon maintains that this quality is undeniable, although he states that the deciding factor may not be so much physical as social and psychological. According to Coon,

It is possible that the feature which confirms the tentative identification of a person as a Jew, aside from clothing, speech, and other external cultural phenomena, is a characteristic facial expression centered about the eyes, nose, and mouth; this seems to be a socially induced element of behavior. . . . Not all Jews . . . have it. . . . The Jewish look may be seen occasionally upon members of other ethnic groups. . . .[63]

[63] Coon, *The Races of Europe*, p. 441. See also Coon's "Have the Jews a Racial Identity?" in Isacque Graeber and S. H. Britt (eds.), *Jews in a Gentile World*, Macmillan, 1942, pp. 20–37; and Melville Jacobs, "Jewish Blood and Culture," in *ibid.*, pp. 38–55.

Herskovits pointed out that "nasality" was regarded for many years as an identifying trait of the Jew, but that Fishberg's analysis (1905) of Topinard's conception of the "hooked," or aquiline, nose as Jewish showed the following percentages for nasal profile in Jews of European origin living in New York City:

	Males (Percent)	Females (Percent)
Straight	58	59
Hooked, aquiline	14	13
Retrousse (snub)	22	14
Flat and broad	6	14

Herskovits added, "The aspects of the trait that figure in the stereotype may, of course, be other than profile—Fishberg himself felt that it might be a matter of 'nostrility.' But to date no device for measuring this exists, so that, on the basis of other studies, and until data to the contrary are presented, it can be regarded as a stereotypical rather than typical 'Jewish' characteristic."[64] On the question of the "Jewish look" Herskovits remarked:

Is the "Jewish look" contained in the gestures the Jew employs when he talks? That Jews "talk with their hands" is a fundamental element in the Jewish stereotype, and one that is not easily susceptible of objective analysis. The study made by Efron (1941) does, however, throw considerable light on the matter. With the aid of an artist and using motion pictures, he analyzed the gestures of Italians and Jews, dividing each group into "assimilated" and "traditional" categories. The findings demonstrate how little validity there is in the assumption that the Jewish type is to be described in terms of patterns of gesturing. Both from the standpoint of number of people gesturing and of frequency and manner of gesticulation in those people who do gesture, the assimilated Eastern Jews and the assimilated Southern Italians in New York City (a) appear to differ

[64] M. J. Herskovits, "Who Are the Jews?" in Louis Finkelstein (ed.), *The Jews, Their History, Culture, and Religion*, Harper & Row, 3rd ed., vol. 27, 1960, p. 1505.

greatly from their respective traditional group, and (b) appear to resemble each other.[65]

The present writers agree with Montagu's statement that, from the viewpoint of physical anthropology, there is "no such thing as a Jewish physical type, and there is not, nor was there ever, anything even remotely resembling a Jewish 'race' . . ."[66] The Jews are a mixed people derived originally from Caucasoid stocks in the eastern Mediterranean area. Insofar as the original stock remains the basis of their inheritance, they can sometimes be identified as eastern Mediterranean peoples, but not as Jews. Since there are very few eastern Mediterranean peoples in the United States except Jews, their identification with this wider stock is not usually made.[67]

If the Jews do not constitute a race, how should they be designated? Kroeber regarded the Jews as "a social quasi-caste based originally and mainly on a religion that of course is voluntary, not enforced. Their social segregation is markedly stronger than their cultural distinctiveness, though the latter is not absolutely lacking."[68] Lowie wrote that the Jews under Hitler became "a degraded caste" comparable to the untouchables of India.[69] Montagu prefers to call the Jews a "quasi-national" group, saying that "it is by virtue of the traits of this quasi-Jewish national culture that a Jewish community may be said to exist and that any person exhibiting these traits may be recognized as a Jew, whether he is an adherent of the Jewish religion or not. Such traits . . . are conditioned by culture alone."[70]

FIVE UNPROVED RACIAL BELIEFS

Among the commonly held notions about race are the following: Some races are mentally

[65] *Ibid.*, p. 1505.
[66] Montagu, *Man's Most Dangerous Myth*, 4th ed., p. 327.
[67] On this point, see M. F. Ashley Montagu, *Statement on Race*, Henry Schuman, 1951, p. 65.
[68] A. L. Kroeber, *Anthropology*, Harcourt Brace Jovanovich, 1948, p. 279.
[69] R. H. Lowie, *Social Organization*, Holt, Rinehart & Winston, 1948, p. 276.
[70] Montagu, *Man's Most Dangerous Myth*, 4th ed., pp. 337–338.

superior to others; race and temperament are closely related; definite relationships exist between race and biological endowment; race and culture are correlated; some races outrank others in morality.

The Doctrine of Mentally Superior and Mentally Inferior Races

The belief that some groups have greater innate intellectual capacity than others goes back at least as far as Aristotle, who justified slavery on the ground that nature intends some men to rule and some to serve. We have referred earlier to the dogmas of Boulainvilliers, Gobineau, Chamberlain, Stoddard, Grant, and Hitler. Although he changed his position late in life, Lucien Lévy-Bruhl contended for many years that the primitive mind is prelogical. In his earlier writings Lévy-Bruhl said that primitives are unable to separate ideas or objects from the sentiments and emotions engendered by them. Primitives were adjudged by him to be emotional and mystical in contrast to civilized men, who are supposedly logical. In *The Mind of Primitive Man,* Boas showed that the reasoning processes of nonliterate peoples are perfectly logical. The fact that such peoples, lacking the storehouse of modern knowledge, start from different premises and arrive at different conclusions has nothing to do with their basic intellectual processes. The Italian sociologist Vilfredo Pareto amply demonstrated the importance of nonlogical behavior in recent and contemporary civilized affairs. C. S. Myers, professor of experimental psychology at the University of Cambridge, concluded after many years' study of local populations in Australia and Africa "that the mental features of the rural populations in Europe correspond essentially to those observed in primitive peoples, and that differences, where they occur, must be ascribed to environmental influences."

The development of mental testing seemed to many to offer possibilities for determining the relative abilities of racial groups. Numerous mental measurements were taken on United States racial and cultural groups in the period 1915 to 1935, and, while the conclusions of the testers vary, "the results show that groups like the English, Scotch, Germans, Jews, Chinese, and Japanese [test] close to the norm (white American); and American Negroes, Indians, Italians, Portuguese, and Mexicans [test] definitely below the norm."[71]

A number of questions arise in connection with the interpretation of intelligence testing of racial and cultural groups. One of the most important problems is *sampling*, that is, finding test groups that are truly representative of the total groups. Different studies have shown considerable differences in median I.Q. for groups within the same race. An example is the comparison of southern Negroes and northern Negroes during World War I. In the army study of nearly 15,000 southern Negroes and 8000 northern Negroes in 1918, the northern Negroes were clearly superior to the southern Negroes. This study also revealed the interesting fact that although northern Negroes ranked below northern Whites, the median I.Q.'s for Negroes from Ohio, Illinois, New York, and Pennsylvania were higher than the median I.Q.'s for Whites from Mississippi, Kentucky, Arkansas, and Georgia. A later study by Peterson and Lanier showed white children in Nashville markedly superior to Nashville Negro children, Chicago Whites slightly superior to the Chicago Negroes (only three ingenuity tests were used in this part of the study), but no significant differences in New York City. These authors suggested that their results might have been due to (1) a highly selected group of Negro children in the New York sample, (2) the superior environmental opportunities of these subjects, and (3) the possibility that the white group was an inferior sample. Klineberg points out that the third suggestion is inapplicable when the scores are compared with norms obtained by Yerkes. His own investigation of selective migration creates great doubt concerning the first interpretation of Peterson and Lanier. Klineberg examined the school marks obtained by the northern migrants as compared with the nonmigrants and investigated school records in Birmingham, Nashville, and Charleston. There was no evidence in the 562

cases studied to indicate that the migrants constituted a superior group. In further studies Klineberg found that the lowest average scores in a sample of Harlem school children were made by the groups which had arrived most recently from the South,[72] thus showing the effects of opportunity on I.Q.

Another factor that merits consideration in racial testing is *socioeconomic background*. An investigation of this factor by Arlitt showed that when the Stanford-Binet was administered to 341 native white, Negro, and Italian children in the primary grades, each of a single school, the variation in results was greater in groups separated according to Taussig's classification of social classes than when the comparison was made on the basis of race. When *all* the native white children were compared with *all* the Italian and *all* the Negro children, the I.Q. averages were 106.5, 85, and 83.4; but when the lower-class native whites were compared with the lower-class Italian and Negro children, the results were 92, 85, and 83.4. The undifferentiated figure measured class more than race. By controlling one variable, the investigator eliminated two-thirds of the difference. In H. G. Canady's study of West Virginia State College freshmen the rank order by occupational groups of median scores on the American Council Psychological Examination was professional, commercial, artisan, skilled labor, and unskilled labor. Similar results have been found in comparable studies of white students. Obviously the task of matching individuals of two or more racial or cultural groups socioeconomically is an extremely difficult one.

Recent studies have shown the effects of specific factors associated with poverty on intellectual development. Mental development in slum children, black and white, is affected by the amount of toxemia of pregnancy in the mothers before the child is born. Many of these mothers have no prenatal care and toxemic conditions are not detected. Studies have shown that poor nutrition, both in the pregnant mother and the young child inhibit men-

[71] Otto Klineberg (ed.), *Characteristics of the American Negro*, Harper & Row, 1944, p. 35.

[72] *Ibid.*, Part II, chaps. 1–3, and, also by Klineberg, "Race and Psychology," in UNESCO, *The Race Question in Modern Science*, pp. 66–67.

tal development.[73] Another mediator of mental development is premature births. Regardless of race, premature children show a greater incidence of neurologic abnormalities, a greater susceptibility to disease, and a larger percentage of mental defectives.[74] Still another organic factor in intelligence is brain injury in the newborn. Both of these conditions have higher incidences among Negroes because they are found more frequently in the lowest economic groups of the population.[75] A further factor influencing mental development is severe restriction in activity and stimulation or its opposite. Recent sensory-deprivation experiments reveal the extreme effects that can result from an impoverished environment. These studies show that normal people respond with marked psychological disturbances when they are severely restricted. According to Pettigrew, typically they experience "temporal and spatial distortions and pronounced hallucinations; and they evidence sharply impaired thinking and reasoning both during and after their isolation."[76]

The importance of the *language factor* has been demonstrated in many studies of European immigrant groups, Chinese, Japanese, American Indians, and Mexicans. In all of these cases the average I.Q. obtained on performance tests is higher than that obtained on tests calling for language facility. Klineberg

points out that the language handicap of the American Negro is more indirect than in the other cases. It is obvious that the Negro, particularly the southern Negro, does not have the same language facility as the average White, and this difference may have some influence on the scores made on linguistic tests.[77]

An important factor in racial testing is *schooling.* While intelligence tests were designed originally to measure innate ability, evidence has accumulated to show that results are affected by educational opportunities. This factor is particularly important in the case of Negro-white testing since predominantly Negro schools, especially in the South, have often been substandard. Only when educational conditions have been equalized can racial testing be taken seriously, and even then other factors influencing scores must be carefully scrutinized.

Other factors to be considered in this type of testing are *motivation, rapport* and *speed.* It cannot be assumed that all racial and cultural groups are equally interested in making the best possible showing in the tests. Many testers have reported that their Negro subjects were indifferent, inattentive, or suspicious as to the value of the test. Investigators who have worked with American Indian children report cultural factors that are tied up with motivation, including the interesting refusal of Hopi children to compete against one another.[78] *Rapport,* or the relation between the investigator and the subject, may be a significant factor in test scores. That distrust, embarrassment, and uneasiness may enter into the results has been shown by studies like those of Canady, who found a variation of six points in the I.Q., both for Negro and for white college students, when the students were tested on different occasions by a Negro and a white psychologist. Dreger and Miller cite studies showing that the color of the investigator may

---

[73] Lehrman, *op. cit.,* p. 181. Pettigrew reports:

One study found that dietary supplementation by vitamins supplied during the last half of pregnancy had directly beneficial effects on I.Q. scores of the children later. In a sample of mothers from the lowest socio-economic level, 80 percent of whom were Negro, the group fortified with iron and vitamin B complex had children whose mean I.Q. at three years of age averaged five full points above the children of the unfortified control group, 103.4 to 98.4. One year later, the mean difference had enlarged to eight points, 101.7 to 93.6. The same researchers failed to find a similar effect among white mothers and their children from a mountain area. Presumably, the largely Negro sample was even poorer and more malnourished than the white sample from the mountains. Dire poverty, through the mother's inadequate diet, can thus impair intelligence before the lower-class Negro child is born.
T. F. Pettigrew, *A Profile of the Negro American,* Van Nostrand Reinhold, 1964, p. 111.

[74] *Ibid.,* p. 111.
[75] *Ibid.,* p. 111.
[76] *Ibid.,* pp. 110–111.

[77] A study of "verbal destitution" in the South indicated that those Negro students who were most retarded in a reading clinic came from small, segregated high schools and showed language patterns typical of the only adult models they had known—poorly educated parents, teachers, and ministers. *Ibid.,* p. 112.
[78] On this point, as well as others mentioned in this section, see Klineberg, *Characteristics of the American Negro,* Part II, chap. 3.

influence performance, and say that this may be related to deterioration of intellectual performance under anxiety-provoking conditions.[79] The attitude toward *speed* needs to be taken into account, even in tests like the Binet where speed is less important than in some other tests. In the tests used by Peterson, Lanier, and Walker in a study of ingenuity and speed in white and Negro children where speed and accuracy were measured separately, the accuracy scores showed little or no difference between the two groups. Other investigations of Negro children, of American Indian children, and of Australian subjects have revealed a relative indifference to speed.

Another problem that arises in racial testing is *race mixture*. This is especially important in the mixed American Negro population, where an estimated three-fourths have some white ancestry.[80] The results of tests administered to Negro samples, subdivided according to the amount of white ancestry by means of general impression, anthropometric measurements, and genealogies, are inconclusive. Studies of this type have not been numerous, and in most of them the number of subjects has been small. In no case has the investigator shown that the parent groups which have entered into the mixture are not either relatively superior or relatively inferior and therefore not representative samples of the total populations. Even if it could be shown that those with a higher percentage of white ancestry in groups such as the American Negro or the American Indian did stand higher on the intelligence tests, it would be necessary to determine whether differentials in educational and socioeconomic opportunities existed on the basis of amount of intermixture.

The widely publicized assertions of three psychologists (McGurk; Shuey; Jensen) that intelligence tests reveal innate differences between Negroes and Whites require some comment. F. C. J. McGurk, of Villanova Univer-

sity, says that intelligence tests prove that "Negroes are below Whites in capacity for education" and that "improvement of Negroes' social and economic status does not reduce this difference."[81]

Howard H. Long questions McGurk's attempts at controlling the social-cultural variable. He points out that McGurk reports no evidence to support his assumption that Negroes have made vastly more welfare progress, relatively, since 1920 than Whites. He criticizes the attempt to partial out experimentally the influence of the social-cultural variable by matching subjects by means of the Sims Score Card of Socio-Economic Status or by attempting to separate test items into "cultural" and "noncultural" categories. According to Long, it would be necessary to control the following conditions before it would be possible to conclude that native mental differences exist:

1. There must be equal *opportunities* for the individuals of both groups to become assimilated to the culture in terms of schooling, work, and the like, and to participate freely in the other prevailing currents of benefit and progress of the large community to which the groups belong.
2. There must be similar *incentives* to master learnings, significant for the real life of the individuals of the group whose expected sequel is similar *motivations*.
3. There must be similar group *expectancy* and opportunities for *goal-setting* in the home and community.[82]

Concerning McGurk's work and conclusions, Dreger and Miller say: ". . . we do not see how the issue [comparative intelligence of Negroes and Whites] can be resolved by any number of ingenious methods of equating for social and economic variables. The various indices of socioeconomic status already devised or those at present conceivable on the same principles are intended to distinguish social *classes* from one another. How they can be employed to compare individuals in different

[79] R. M. Dreger and Kent S. Miller, "Comparative Psychological Studies of Negroes and Whites in the United States," *Psychological Bulletin*, Sept., 1960, pp. 366–367.

[80] Boyd, "Four Achievements of the Genetical Method in Physical Anthropology," p. 247. Boyd gives the amount of white mixture in the American Negro population as 31 percent.

[81] F. C. J. McGurk, in *U.S. News and World Report*, Sept. 21, 1956, p. 92.

[82] Howard H. Long, "The Relative Learning Capacities of Negroes and Whites," *JNE*, Spring, 1957, p. 126.

castes, except very roughly, is difficult to see."[83]

Deutsch also criticizes studies that confuse social with racial status:

To avoid confounding social with racial status, a number of studies attempted to equate middle-class Negroes with similar white groups. It is doubtful if such an equation can be validly made. The results of the present study, and of other studies, delineate some of the negative psychological attributes associated with self-awareness of Negro status, or any racial status deviating from the valued white norm. But even if this could be controlled for, middle-class identification is more than simply socio-economic position. The great majority of Negro middle-class members is at most one or two generations removed from lower-class status, and in order to achieve truly comparable populations for social psychological research, comparable class stability is essential.[84]

In a review of the literature, Audrey M. Shuey, Randolph-Macon Woman's College, concluded in 1958 that the studies "all point to the presence of some native differences between Negroes and whites as determined by intelligence tests."[85] She lumped together various studies of racial testing, ignoring interpretations of individual testers and arriving at her own interpretations of the results. Using the same format and essentially the same chapter titles, but including more studies, Shuey arrived at the same conclusions in 1966 (A. M. Shuey, 1966). An example of the slight differences in her later as compared with her earlier conclusions is seen in her discussion of selective migration. In 1958 she wrote:

If our estimate is correct that about 9 points separate the average IQ of northern and southern Negroes, then about half or possibly two thirds of this difference would be accounted for by environmental factors and the remainder presumably by selective migration. (1958, p. 306)

In 1966 she wrote:

Our best single estimate was that approximately seven points separate the average IQ of Southern colored children from Northern children of their race. If this is correct, a little more than half of this difference may be accounted for by environmental factors and the remainder by selective migration. (1966. p. 490)

Apparently Shuey is unaware of B. Glass and C. C. Li's conclusion, based on a study of the frequencies of seven genes, that the amount of white mixture in the North American Negro population is 30.5 percent.[86] Shuey cites only D. F. Roberts' provisional estimate of "the amount of accumulated white admixture in the American Negro population" as 20 percent. (Shuey, 1966, p. 3)

In the foreword to the second edition of Shuey's book (p. vii), Henry E. Garrett makes two quite remarkable comments concerning what he regards as the major difficulties that arise when Negroes and Whites are compared in mental test performance in the United States. Granting that the American Negro is generally below the White in social and economic status and that his work opportunities are more limited, Garrett remarks that "many of these inequalities have been exaggerated." Ignoring the complexities and subtleties of the racial situation in the United States, he states that "fair comparisons can be and have been made by a careful equating of background variables." Even more revealing is his assertion that extensive racial mixture "should cause Negro-white differences, if found, to be even more significant. *For then racial differences would probably be much greater if American whites and African Negroes were compared.*" (Emphasis ours) Garrett is convinced that the tests "strongly suggest a genetic basis for the differences." (Shuey, 1966, p. viii)

Shuey reached essentially the same conclusion in 1958 and in 1966, namely, that the test results "inevitably point to the presence of native differences between Negroes and whites

[83] Dreger and Miller, *op. cit.,* pp. 366–367.

[84] Martin Deutsch, "Minority Group and Class Status as Related to Social and Personality Factors in Scholastic Achievement," *Society for Applied Anthropology,* monograph no. 2, 1960, p. 26.

[85] Audrey M. Shuey, *The Testing of Negro Intelligence,* J. P. Bell, 1958, p. 318.

[86] B. Glass and C. C. Li, "The Dynamics of Racial Intermixture—An Analysis of the American Negro," *American Journal of Human Genetics,* 1953, pp. 1–20. Cited in Boyd, "Four Achievements of the Genetical Method," p. 247.

as determined by intelligence tests." (1966, p. 521)

In a recent study, Arthur R. Jensen, University of California, Berkeley, psychologist, concludes that the heritability of intelligence is quite high. He thinks that it is "a not unreasonable hypothesis that genetic factors are strongly implicated in the average Negrowhite intelligence difference." In the reports known to Jensen, especially large upward shifts in I.Q. explicitly associated with environmental factors have involved quite young children, "whose initial social environment was deplorable to a greater extreme than can be found among any children who are free to interact with other persons or to run about out-of-doors." Jensen says that environmental means, including compensatory education programs, can affect school achievement through their influence on motivation, values, and other conditioned habits. He doubts that such means can have any marked effect on I.Q. except in the case of children who have been severely isolated socially. Jensen cites findings of the Coleman study (1966) that a dozen environmental variables and socioeconomic indices correlated—in the expected direction—with scholastic performance within each of the racial and ethnic groups studied. Jensen adds that the American Indians are "by far the most environmentally disadvantaged groups," but that their ability and achievement tests average about half a standard deviation higher than the scores of Negroes.[87]

Friedenberg stresses the difficulties involved in inferring that Negroes do less well on abstract reasoning as determined by the demands made by I.Q. tests in a society as racist as ours.

Jensen has thoroughly and conscientiously attempted to 'control-out' as much of this kind of variation [environmental effects] as possible, but a great deal of it cannot be eliminated, especially from data like his that were gathered by other investigators for quite different purposes, rather than designed to test the issues under consideration. Controlled comparison is, in any case, a much less effective way of accounting for irrelevant sources of variation than it is usually supposed to be; the characteristics that can be controlled in studying a social problem are never subtle enough, and if they were they would reduce the sample size so much that statistical inference would be meaningless.[88]

Jencks reminds us of the relatively modest role that I.Q. plays in determining a person's life chances: "After school the importance of IQ diminishes even further. Men's IQ account for only about a fifth of the variation in their occupational status and a tenth of the variation in their incomes. . . . Among men with the same amount of schooling, those with high IQ's are hardly more successful than those with low IQ's."[89] Jencks says that even if I.Q. differences have a genetic as well as an environmental basis, such differences have little to do with the ways in which blacks and whites are treated in the United States. Low I.Q.'s, he says, "are not the cause of America's racial problems and higher IQ's would not solve these problems."

Four outstanding scientists (Henry C. Dyer, Vice President, Educational Testing Service, Princeton, New Jersey; Silvan Tomkins, Professor of Psychology, Princeton University; Ralph H. Turner, Professor of Sociology, University of California, Los Angeles; and Sherwood L. Washburn, Professor of Anthropology, University of California, Berkeley) are in substantial agreement that the claims advanced by Shuey, Putnam, and Garrett cannot be supported by scientific evidence. This panel concluded that "any future claims regarding innate differences between Negroes and Whites with regard to intelligence cannot be substantiated unless three conditions are met:

(1) The distinctive *genetic*, or "racial," homogeneity of the Negro group being tested, as well as that of the white group being tested, must be *demonstrated*, not assumed.

(2) The social and cultural backgrounds of

---

[87] Arthur R. Jensen, "How Much Can We Boost IQ and Scholastic Achievement?", in *Environment, Heredity, and Intelligence*, Harvard Educational Review Reprint Series No. 2, 1969, pp. 59–60, 82, 85–86.

[88] Edgar Z. Friedenberg, "What Are Our Schools Trying to Do?," *The New York Times Book Review*, Sept. 14, 1969, p. 57.

[89] Christopher Jencks, "I.Q. and Race," *South Today*, Oct., 1969, p. 3 (reprinted from *The New Republic*, 1969).

the Negroes and whites being tested or otherwise being measured must be fully equal.

(3) Adequate tests of native intelligence and other mental and psychological capacities, with proven reliability and validity, will have to be used."

Melvin M. Tumin adds that, to date, none of these conditions has been met.[90]

In conclusion, the most recent, as well as the most comprehensive and most competent reviews of comparative studies of the intelligence of Negroes and Whites make the following crucial points:

1. Groups of Negroes consistently make lower average test scores than do groups of Whites.
2. The lowered scores do not reflect racial difference, but are related to forces more subject to change. [Dreger and Miller say: "The search for a culture-free test is illusory." *Op. cit.*, p. 368.]
3. To the extent that the Negro has to respond to the demands of a white middle-class environment, on the average he is less well equipped to meet these demands than is the White.
4. Approximately 25 percent of the Negroes tested make scores that are higher than those of the average white person tested, and many make high scores.
5. That Negro children earn I.Q.s of 160 or above. . . even as high as 200 . . . on tests standardized on Whites is a remarkable phenomenon.
6. Anyone who has tested Negro children has probably been impressed with the fact that a Negro child whom the examiner knows to be functioning as a normal, not a retarded child, may receive a score that automatically would classify him in the retarded range if scores only were regarded. *Roughly speaking, the Negro child seems to operate in everyday life situations in a way expected of a white child about 10 I.Q. points above.* (Emphasis ours.) With the curve of measured Negro intelligence displaced downward it is thus a surprise to find any Negro children scoring among the highest levels on white-standardized tests.
7. Much talent among this [Negro] group is

currently being wasted or lost because of social and economic restrictions.[91]

The Belief That Races Are Temperamentally Different

Folk beliefs concerning innate racial and national temperaments have persisted through the centuries and provide the basis for widely held stereotypes. Dozens of scientific studies have been made in attempts to verify or refute these popular beliefs, but they have yielded few definite conclusions.[92] According to Klineberg, there is a suggestion, from the use of the Bernreuter Personality Inventory and the Rorschach test, of greater extroversion in Negroes. Also, Negroes seem more suggestible, but the problems of the relation of subject to investigator has not been adequately explored. Tests of Negro musical ability appear to indicate that the Negro is inferior except in rhythm, but the tests and their interpretation are under criticism. Results on handwriting tests are negative, and color preference tests have produced no significant conclusions. Work habits are said to show no special Negro characteristics, and gesture seems to be a matter of response to cultural environment.

Carleton Coon finds that "human beings vary in temperament. It is a common observation among anthropologists who have worked in many parts of the world in intimate contact with people of different races that racial differences in temperament also exist and can be predicted." Ashley Montagu remarks that this will be news to many anthropologists who have found that beneath the surface of superficial differences the peoples of the world apper to be fundamentally alike.[93]

Until more adequate tests of temperamental characteristics have been constructed and the groups studied are equated on the basis of class and other background factors, no objec-

[90] M. M. Tumin (ed.), *Race and Intelligence: A Scientific Evaluation*, Anti-Defamation League of B'nai B'rith, 1963, p. 9.

[91] Kent S. Miller, "Psychological Characteristics of the Negro," in *The Negro in American Society*, Florida State Univ. Studies, no. 28, 1958, pp. 22–23; Dreger and Miller, *op. cit.*, p. 369.

[92] Klineberg, *Characteristics of the American Negro*, Part III, chap. 3.

[93] Montagu, *Man's Most Dangerous Myth*, 4th ed., p. 88.

tive generalizations can be made on the question of race and temperament.[94]

The Notion of Biologically Superior and Biologically Inferior Races

Proof of the biological inferiority of nonwhite peoples in the United States has been seen by some in certain differential mortality and morbidity rates. In 1960, the total death rate for Whites was 9.5 per 1000; for nonwhites it was 10.1. In 1967, this rate was the same (9.4) for Whites, Negroes, and other races. The mortality rate from tuberculosis has been greatly reduced in recent decades, but the rate for Nonwhites is still considerably higher than it is for Whites. The mortality rate for syphilis was twice as high for Nonwhites as for Whites in 1967. The infant mortality rate for Whites is 55 percent of the nonwhite rate.[95]

Psychosis rates are higher for Negroes than they are for Whites, but the ratio of Negro to white neuroses is less than for the psychoses.[96] With respect to social mobility, Parker and Kleiner found the highest rates of mental illness in the urban Negro community at the low end of the status hierarchy and among the upwardly mobile at the high end of the scale. Also, their study linked mental disorder with the status inconsistency profile of relatively high education and low occupation.[97] Whereas the Negro suffers from psychosis relatively more than he does from neurosis, Jews in the United States have fairly low psychosis rates but especially high neurosis rates.[98]

Although the fatal complications of communicable childhood diseases, such as whooping cough, meningitis, measles, diphtheria, and scarlet fever, can be reduced by modern medicine, Negro death rates from them are at least twice as high as for Whites.[99] Improved medical services are needed also to reduce the high death rates among adult Negroes for nephritis, influenza, and pneumonia.

It is expected that pulmonary tuberculosis death rates for both races will continue to decline as treatment and environmental conditions improve. Reported mortality rates due to syphilis and gonorrhea are notoriously unreliable, but available data indicate high Negro rates for these diseases and their complications. Differences in group rates are attributable largely to differences in income, education, housing, availability of medical care, and provision of control measures.[100]

Reported Negro deaths for cardiovascular diseases are higher than for Whites, but a breakdown by type is important. Hypertension and hypertensive heart disease, with Negro death rates three times as high as those of whites, are contributed to by psychosocial influences such as anxiety and the repression of hostility. White males constitute the most vulnerable group to arteriosclerotic disease (hardening of the arteries). Negroes have higher mortality rates from cardiovascular diseases stemming from infections, reflecting differential infection rates (for example, tuberculosis). Whites seem to be more suscep-

[94] Dreger and Miller write of the sparsity of data concerning racial differences in temperament and conclude that "so-called 'personality tests' may be inappropriate for testing most Negroes who are different from whites in socioeconomic status . . . and caste. In this area intensive studies of whites and Negroes need to be performed by scientists who understand both psychodynamics, sociodynamics, and adequate scientific procedure." *Op. cit.*, p. 381.

[95] The total death rate for the United States in 1933 was 10.3 for Whites and 14.1 for Nonwhites. For the death registration states in 1900 this rate was 17.0 for Whites and 25.0 for Nonwhites. The actual death rate for tuberculosis for Whites was 5.1 per 100,000 and 13.2 for Nonwhites in 1960. For syphilis the rates were 1.3 per 100,000 for Whites and 4.5 for Nonwhites. U.S. Department of Health, Education, and Welfare, *Vital Statistics of the United States 1960*, vol. II, sec. 1, pp. 1–18 and 1–26. Infant mortality rates for the United States in 1960 per 1000 live births were: Whites, 22.9; Nonwhites, 43.2. For the period 1915–1919, these rates were: Whites, 92.8; Nonwhites, 149.7. *Ibid.*, sec. 3, pp. 3–4. In 1967, the death rate for tuberculosis for Whites was 0.2 per 100,000 and 1.1 for Nonwhites. For syphilis the rates were 1.1 for Whites and 2.2 for Nonwhites in 1967. The infant mortality rate for Whites in 1967 was 19.7 per 1,000 live births and 35.9 for Nonwhites. U.S. Department of HEW, *Vital Statistics of the United States* 1967, Vol. II, "Mortality," Part A, pp. 1–8.

[96] Pettigrew, *op. cit.*, pp. 76–77 (Ann Pettigrew, M.D., is co-author of Chapter 4, "Negro American Health").

[97] Seymour Parker and Robert J. Kleiner, *Mental Illness in the Urban Negro Community*, Free Press, 1966, pp. 340–341.

[98] Pettigrew, *op. cit.*, p. 81.

[99] *Ibid.*, p. 88.

[100] *Ibid.*, pp. 86–87.

tible to rheumatic fever and rheumatic heart disease.[101] A recent survey of 2310 Detroiters, half white, half black, half poor, half middle class, and half men and half women, directed by Ernest Harburg, University of Michigan, showed that in high-stress areas 19 percent of the Negro women have high blood pressure, while the rate for white women residing in similar areas is 9 percent. In low-stress areas the percentages were: Negro 10, white 5. Among men, high blood pressure was found in 20 percent of Negroes and in 14 percent of Whites. Further study in this survey will focus on the degree to which this difference is due to genetic factors and how much results from ghetto living.[102]

Negroes have a lower incidence of skin cancer, cancer of the gall bladder, and of the lower lip. Leukemia is twice as prevalent in Whites. Most other cancers show comparable rates for both races. Since Negro females have slightly higher rates than do white females, there is a sex difference in total cancer mortality rates. When Negro and white women of the same socioeconomic backgrounds are considered, the incidence is essentially the same.[103]

What Pettigrew calls "the birth processes" bring further disparities in Negro-white health standards. Perinatal mortality and maternal mortality are still considerably higher for Negroes, and premature births are about 50 percent more frequent among Negroes. As Pettigrew points out, prenatal, perinatal, and postnatal morbidity are not adequately revealed by mortality figures. Increased infection, anoxia, and birth trauma may retard Negro children for life. These conditions are found among the poor of all races and are the results of the lack of prenatal care, poor health education, inadequate diet, and inexpert delivery.[104]

Although the percentage gain in life expectancy for Negroes has been twice as great as it has been for Whites, there remains a difference of approximately seven years. On the basis of data now available, this difference can be accounted for in terms of diseases that can be prevented or treated. At the end of the last century some scholars thought the Negro would eventually disappear in this country because of general biological inferiority. He was not considered rugged enough to survive the fast tempo of life in a temperate climate. The record of the past seven decades shows how mistaken these views were.

The Myth of Racial Cultures

There is no correlation between race and culture. One looks in vain for a "Negro" culture, or a "Mongoloid" or a "Caucasoid" culture. There is considerable variation in government, family institutions, religious beliefs, economic practices, artistic traditions, and other aspects of culture from one section of Africa to another and even from tribe to tribe in the same area. The same is true for pre-Columbian America, and for Europe, Asia, and Oceania. Before the age of discovery and exploration, a number of inventions were made independently by racially unlike and geographically remote peoples. Since the development of rapid means of communication and transportation, the inventions and beliefs of diverse peoples have been transplanted to all habitable regions of the earth. The young children of any race have no difficulty absorbing any set of cultural norms provided they are constantly exposed to it. One of the best examples of the lack of relationship between race and culture is seen in the American Negro population. Relatively few African cultural traits have been retained in the United States. Close and continuous contact has given Caucasoids and Negroids the same basic Western European type of culture. Such differences in behavior as are observed between individual Whites and Negroes in this country seem to be attributable, mainly, to (1) class, educational, occupational, and other nonracial factors and (2) the somewhat different "social world" in which the Negro lives because of racial segregation and discrimination.

The Dogma of Racial Morality

A widespread belief exists that there are strong connections between skin color (and

[101] *Ibid.*, pp. 95–96.
[102] *The Plain Dealer*, Feb. 8, 1970.
[103] Pettigrew, *op. cit.*, pp. 93–95.
[104] *Ibid.*, p. 97.

other physical characteristics) and ethical standards. Deviations from genteel middle- or upper-class norms on the part of members of racial or cultural minorities are often credited to the "wild blood" of the recently domesticated savages or to the "low-grade blood" of peasant hordes. Back of these explanations is the notion that nonliterate peoples are untamed men controlled by personal whim and feeling rather than by self-restraint and laws for the general good. This idea is worthy of somewhat more careful examination.

The practices usually cited to show the brutality and undeveloped moral sense of non-white, nonwestern Europeans include infanticide, the abandonment of disabled kin, cannibalism, polygyny, incest, and premarital sexual intercourse. All of these customs occur in specific cultural contexts. They are not random forms of behavior, nor are they race-linked. Infanticide is found under special conditions such as poverty or a belief that twins or triplets will bring misfortune. Moreover, this practice is not unknown to Caucasoid populations, as, for example, in ancient Sparta, ancient Egypt, and ancient Rome. Abandonment of disabled kin is not brutal, callous behavior since it is often initiated by the sick, crippled, or aged person himself and may involve a return for the deserted one if the hunting party succeeds in replenishing its supplies. Cannibalism seems not to have been widespread in primitive society. It occurs for different reasons, including magical beliefs, revenge, and near-starvation, and cannot be attributed to group bestiality. Polygyny can seldom, if ever, be explained on the basis of masculine lechery. A long period of lactation, running to two or three years in certain societies, during which marital intercourse is prohibited seems to have been a factor in the emergence of polygyny in some groups. In others, polygyny appears to have been a consequence of an unbalanced sex ratio. Elsewhere, several wives have been desired because of their economic and prestige values. Polygyny has had social approval in a number of Caucasian groups, including the ancient Egyptians, the ancient Babylonians, the ancient Hebrews, the early followers of Mohammed in Arabia, the ancient Slavs, Teutons, and

Irish. Every human society has rules against incest, although the definition of incest varies. According to Malinowski, premarital freedom in nonliterate societies tends to reduce the importance of the erotic element in courtship, thus allowing nonsexual considerations to exert more influence in matrimonial choice.

Western civilization is notable mainly for technological and economic developments and the corresponding growth of order. As Hobhouse, Wheeler, and Ginsburg point out, economic development "does not imply greater considerateness or a keener sense of justice, and may in some ways be held even adverse to them." When comparative morality is under discussion, it is well to keep in mind current crime and delinquency rates, divorce rates, gangsterism, political corruption, vigilantism, civil disorders, unemployment, and mental disease in the United States.

Regardless of ever present discrepancies between ideals and performances, the basic morality of literate and nonliterate groups is much the same. Lowie wrote: ". . . Notwithstanding undeniable differences in outward manifestations, savagery and civilization display the same sentiments with reference to the basic human relations. Not unbridled self-indulgence, but restraint; not brutality, but kindness; not neglect of one's neighbors, but regard for them, are prescribed as proper goals of social conduct. What differs is essentially the extent of the group to which these sentiments are applied."[105]

SUMMARY AND CONCLUSION

In spite of (1) the lack of full genetic data on human beings, (2) a great amount of race mixture, and (3) the modifiability of races, race is not just a figment of the imagination. Scientists can identify major categories of mankind and there is fairly general agreement on smaller groupings.

Students of intergroup relations need to acquaint themselves with the techniques and

[105] R. H. Lowie, "Intellectual and Cultural Achievements of Human Races," in H. S. Jennings, *et al.*, *Scientific Aspects of the Race Problem*, Longmans, 1941, p. 233.

problems of race from the standpoint of physical anthropology. If there are no final answers as to what constitutes a race, the physical anthropologist can at least dispel common misconceptions about human physical differences. Physical anthropology has value for the study of race relations, even if the value is largely negative.

The student of intergroup relations cannot stop with physical anthropology. It is only the beginning for him because he has to deal with the attitudes and behaviors of the scientifically uninitiated. He must operate primarily in the fields of sociology and social psychology for the simple reason that, while most people use the term "race" inaccurately, it means something definite to them and they have strong feelings about it. The man in the street can see that men differ in physical appearance and he is certain that the differences are more than skin deep. Sociologically, race is a real thing to him. Perhaps he "knows" that physical traits are linked with intelligence, temperament, character, morality, and so forth. Perhaps he "knows" that Jews constitute a "race," and he may be convinced of racial superiorities and inferiorities. He may believe that races differ inwardly as well as outwardly, or he may be one of those who, in recent years, regards the issue of race as part of a power struggle. Banton concludes that in the United States, as well as in the United Kingdom and in southern Africa, "policies implying the unequal treatment of ethnic groups are more and more defended on political and cultural rather than on pseudo-biological grounds." He refers to such doctrines as new varieties of "ethnic nationalism."[106] In any case, the "average man" treats those who differ from himself in special ways. He may behave "as if" men with other traits were a different species of the genus Homo or he may simply feel threatened by their demands and act accordingly.

Where a racial or ethnic ideology does exist, it has, as Nash points out, a number of important functions. Such an ideology

1. provides a moral rationale for systematic disprivilege.

2. allows the members of the dominant group to reconcile their values with their activities.
3. aims to discourage the subordinate group from making claims on the society.
4. rallies the adherents to political action in a "just" cause.
5. defends the existing division of labor as eternal.

We agree with Nash when he says that the development of a racial ideology is not a function of the state of knowledge about racial differences, but is, rather, the response to social conflict and crisis.[107] In turn, such an ideology determines invidious distinctions and action programs. Empirical findings on racial differences are utilized in the ideology where they fit and ignored if they do not fit.[108]

This book is concerned mainly with the special conceptions that the members of one racial or cultural group have of other groups, and the believed-to-be-proper treatment of the others in certain historical associations.

POSTSCRIPT ON LEGAL AND U.S. CENSUS DEFINITIONS OF RACE

An authoritative treatment of the legal definitions of race in the United States is found in *Race Relations Law Reporter*, June, 1958, pp. 571–588. On the bases of definition:

Statutory definitions of race are generally based on the individual's blood, ancestry, appearances, or a combination of these factors. Moreover, the factor of blood is further subdivided into the so-called proportion or percentage test and the ascertainable trace test. The statutes may provide that a person is a member of the racial group either if he has a stated percent of the blood of that group in his veins or if he has any ascertainable trace of the blood of that group. Definitions which utilize ancestry as the basic factor generally provide that a person will be deemed a member of the racial group affected if he has an ancestor who was a member of that group within a specified number of generations removed. The appearances test has been generally restricted to segregation of public transporta-

[106] Banton, *op. cit.*, pp. 553–554.

[107] Manning Nash, "Race and the Ideology of Race," *CA*, 1962, pp. 286–288.
[108] *Ibid.*, pp. 287–288.

tion facilities or some other circumstance in which the racial classification must be made quickly and without investigation. This test is generally referred to as the visible and distinct admixture test. (p. 573)

The 1960 Census gave the following definitions of race:

Color. The term "color" refers to the division of the population into two groups, white and nonwhite. Persons of Mexican birth or ancestry who are not definitely of Indian or other nonwhite race are classified as white. . . .

Negro. In addition to persons of Negro and of mixed Negro and white descent, this classification, according to instructions to enumerators, includes persons of mixed American Indian and Negro descent, unless the Indian ancestry very definitely predominates or unless the individual is regarded as an Indian in the community.

American Indian. In addition to fullblooded American Indians, persons of mixed white and Indian blood are included in this category if they are enrolled on an Indian tribal or agency roll or if they are regarded as Indians in the community. A common requirement for such enrollment is that the proportion of Indian blood should be at least one-fourth.

Japanese, Chinese, Filipinos, and residual "all other" races. Separate statistics are given in this report for Japanese, Chinese, Filipinos, and a residual "all other" races category. This residual category includes Hawaiians, Eskimos, Aleuts, Koreans, Asian Indians, Malayans, etc. . . .

Mixed parentage. Persons of mixed racial parentage are classified according to the race of the nonwhite parent, and mixtures of nonwhite races are classified according to the father, with the special exceptions noted above.

Since the 1960 Census was the first in which some respondents had an opportunity to classify themselves with respect to race—in previous censuses the racial classification was made for the most part by the enumerator on the basis of observation—it was expected that the character of the racial data in 1960 might differ from that of previous censuses. In terms of the final results, however, there is little evidence of such a change for the major categories. . . . The use of self-enumeration may have added to the accuracy of the 1960 count of the Indian population.

Studies of the adequacy of this count in the last several censuses have led to the conclusion that it was incomplete largely as the result of the failure of enumerators to identify off-reservation Indians. Also, some Indians may have been motivated to report their race correctly as a basis for establishing claims to possible future tribal benefits. . . .[109]

In 1970, the concept of race as used by the Census Bureau

does not denote clear-cut scientific definitions of biological stock. Rather it reflects self-identification by respondents. Since the 1970 census obtained the information on race principally through self-enumeration, the data represent essentially self-classification by people according to the race with which they identify themselves. For persons of mixed parentage who are in doubt as to their classification, the race of the person's father is used. Persons of Mexican or Puerto Rican birth or ancestry who do not identify themselves as of a race other than white (e.g., American Indian, Negro, etc.), are classified as white. In the 3-category grouping shown in this report, the 'other' category consists of all races except white or Negro, i.e., American Indian, Japanese, Chinese, Filipino. Korean, Eskimo, etc.[110]

In 1969, the Bureau of the Budget issued an instruction to eliminate inconsistencies in the treatment of race or color in statistical presentations. Included in this statement are the following acceptable race and color designations to be used in statistical publications of the federal government:

The designation "nonwhite" will no longer be acceptable for use in presenting federal statistics.

The designations "Negro and other races," or "all other races," or "all other" as collective descriptions of minority races are acceptable for use in the publication of federal government statistics in those cases when the most summary distinction between the majority and minority races is appropriate.

[109] U.S. Census of Population: 1960, Final Report PC (1)-1B, *United States Summary, General Population Characteristics*, p. xi.

[110] U.S. Census of Population; Hawaii, 1970, Advance Report, PC (V2)-13, *General Population Characteristics*, p. 2.

The designations "Negro" and "other races" are acceptable for use in the publication of federal government statistics when the distinction among the majority race, the principal minority race, and other races is appropriate.

When the primary focus of a statistical report is on a particular minority race or particular minority races, it is acceptable to present data pertaining to the particular minority race, or races separately, and to include "white" with "other races" if such a collective description is appropriate for the purpose of the report.[111]

In the 1970 census, the questions listed under "Color or Race" are: White, Negro or Black, Indian (American), Japanese, Chinese, Filipino, Hawaiian, Korean, and Other. For Alaska, the racial categories Aleut and Eskimo are substituted for Hawaiian and Korean.[112]

[111] *Statistical Reporter*, No. 70-3 (Sept., 1969), pp. 37–38.

[112] U.S. Department of Commerce, Bureau of the Census, *Data Access Description*, No. 14, Mar., 1970, p. 7.

Chapter 3 / THE PERSONALITY FUNCTIONS OF PREJUDICE AND DISCRIMINATION

A THEORY OF PREJUDICE[1]

In the early studies of prejudice and majority-minority relations two elements blocked an adequate explanation: prejudice was seen as a distinct and separate item of behavior, to be studied by itself; and its explanation was sought in some simple, one-factor analysis. In contemporary studies the explanations for prejudice are sought in the general body of systematic sociological and psychological theory about human behavior. One cannot be a student of majority-minority relations without, at the same time, being a student of personality and of the whole pattern of intergroup adjustments. In the development of our knowledge in this field the relationship has been reciprocal; the study of prejudice has been a fruitful approach to many problems of general sociology and social psychology. At the same time, the advances in the sciences of human behavior have made possible, and imperative, the reformulation of our explanations of prejudice. One-factor explanations clearly could not survive such a shift in approach. To say simply that there is an "instinct" or natural tendency toward prejudice, or that there is an inevitable "dislike of the unlike," or that so-called prejudice against minority groups is a natural reaction to their factual inferiority—explanations that abound in the early literature—is to fail to bring the study of prejudice into the framework of contemporary theory of human behavior.

An effective way to begin the search for the explanations of prejudice is to ask ourselves a group of questions:

Do groups differ in the direction and amount of prejudice that they exhibit? If so, why?

Do individuals differ in the direction and amount of prejudice that they exhibit? If so, why?

Is there change, through time and space, in the groups, and kinds of groups, toward which prejudice is directed?

What is the process by which an individual acquires prejudice?

What forces, in the lives of individuals and of groups, operate to sustain, and to reduce, prejudice?

To answer such questions as these we must turn to a social science that deals adequately both with the process of individual personality development and with the dynamics of group interaction.

While studies of prejudice still stress a large number of separate forces—and there are many specialists who try to reduce the explanation to what they call the one "ultimate" or basic cause—a comprehensive theory is developing around three highly interactive—but analytically distinct—factors, each the convergence of several lines of theory and evidence.

Prejudice may be partly understood as a manifestation of the "needs" of individuals —needs that are an amalgam of constitutional and learned forces that are, to some degree, unique but in part shared by fellow group members. On this level we need give little attention to the characteristics of the groups against whom prejudice and discrimination are directed; the attention, rather, must be given to the prejudiced person himself, the process by which he was "socialized," the nature of his self-regard, the values instilled in him by his society, and the degree to which he is able to satisfy those values. We need to be especially alert to any factors that help to differentiate the more prejudiced from the less prejudiced, because these factors may well be important in helping to explain the origins of prejudice.

[1] Note again that the term prejudice will often be used as shorthand for the prejudice-discrimination complex. At some points we shall call attention to the need for clear distinction between the two processes.

The second level of explanation of prejudice looks for evidence not in the individual personality, but in the structure of society. It is particularly concerned with the power arrangements. It seeks to find out who makes the key economic, political, educational, and religious decisions, and to what degree they employ prejudice against minority groups in order to make those decisions as favorable to themselves as possible. Such use of prejudice is seldom rational and conscious; it is hidden, as we shall see, by many protective beliefs. The task of the social scientist is to uncover the power relationships that are thus disguised, to show how prejudice is, in part, simply one manifestation of intergroup conflict and competition. This is an area where one-factor explanations abound. It is easy to say that prejudice is nothing but a way of getting an economic advantage, that it is forced on the great majority by the propaganda of a small ruling group who profit mightily from it. The exaggerations of the proponents of such a view, however, must not blind us to the accumulated evidence that prejudice *is* an economic and political weapon. We shall examine that evidence in Chapter 4.

The distinction between the personal and the social factors in prejudice is, of course, an analytical one. Since Cooley, it has been impossible for the careful student to reify society as separate from individual members; also—what is perhaps more often forgotten—it is impossible to interpret individual behavior adequately without careful attention to the social dimension. The behaving individual will carry within his personality the social norms and processes that permit the use of prejudice as a power device; and, oppositely, the individual personality, with its "need" for prejudice, will to some degree influence and interpret the social processes and norms to which it has been socialized. However, bearing carefully in mind the nature of our abstraction, we can analyze prejudice more effectively by seeing it as a manifestation both of the "needs" of individual personalities and of group conflicts.

The third basic cause of prejudice is culture itself. In almost every society, if not in all, each new generation is taught appropriate beliefs and practices regarding other groups. Prejudices are, in part, simply a portion of the cultural heritage; they are among the folkways. We learn these cultural responses in the same way that we acquire other attitudes and behavior patterns. Belief in the superiority of "their group" is as natural to the dominant members of many societies as belief in the rightness of their marriage custom or their political structures. The speech and action of those around him, his observation of status differentials among the races, the jokes he hears, the histories he reads, the rewards and punishments he receives for various actions toward members of minority groups all teach him the correct behavior as it is defined by his society. He does not have to have any individual experience with members of minority groups; he will often be equipped with ready-made responses in advance of any such experience, or even in the complete absence of contact. In many instances the correct referent in this type of analysis will be to subsocieties, for norms may vary by region or occupation or ethnic group. Under those conditions we can speak of the subcultural factor in prejudice.

On this level of explanation we need not refer to personality needs or to group conflicts. A person can be prejudiced even when he has a minimum of the frustrations for which prejudice is an outlet and even when his economic or political interests, far from being served by the attitude, are actually injured by it as we shall see later. To be sure, the prejudice may not be so deeply rooted when it is acquired simply as a culture norm and is unsustained by personality and group needs. But for purposes of scientific understanding of the causes of prejudice and for any kind of effective action in its reduction, the analytic separation of the cultural factor from the others is very important. This "culture norm" theory does not explain the origin of a prejudice as part of a group's culture. One can understand how an attitude toward minority groups can be passed along as tradition, but to explain the origin of that tradition, and perhaps its continuing vitality, one must refer to the personality and group functions. Similarly, one can understand the "need" for prejudice without seeing why specific groups should be used for the supposed satisfaction of that need. The selection of certain groups as targets can be understood only by analysis of the traditions of the society. Thus the three factors interact. Any specific individual, in his pattern of prejudice, almost certainly reflects all of the causes. The importance of the various causes, however, will vary from person to person. Prejudice will be most intense, and least subject to change, when all three factors are concentrated in the same individual. A person brought up in a culture that is rich with traditions of prejudice, who identifies himself with groups that stand to gain, or think they do, from discriminatory actions, and who is insecure and frustrated will have a high probability for prejudice.

We can say that the *probability* is high that such a person will have a deep prejudice, but not that he positively will have it. Several closely related factors require this qualification. Other influences doubtless tend to produce prejudice that are unmentioned and unmeasured; since they are unmeasured, we cannot know to what degree they act upon this individual. Moreover, every person is influenced also by many unique experiences that make him something different from a perfectly typical representative of the groups to which he belongs. One may be a member of a group that believes it profits from an exclusionist policy; but he may have had experiences that cause him to doubt or deny this. Finally, a culture that is rich in traditions of prejudice may also be rich—or at least not lacking—in traditions of nonprejudice. If one has experienced this aspect of his culture in more than normal amount, the traditions of prejudice may be offset or counteracted.

Thus in its attempt to predict the likelihood of prejudice by study of its causes, social science must speak in terms of probabilities. So it must in every other phase of its work, and so must science in general, to the degree that it is not dealing with homogeneous units, and to the degree that it does not control or measure the effects of all the variables influencing a given interaction. Our belief is that the systematic study of these three clusters of factors, with the refinements in observation and measurement that are being made, will yield scientifically useful results. This picture of the roots of prejudice is tentative, of course. It will have to be refined both by the breakdown of these major factors into analytically more precise elements and by the isolation of new variables as yet unaccounted for.[2]

Many readers may wonder why no mention has been made of the targets of prejudice in this outline of causes. Are their characteristics not involved? If one asks a prejudiced person why he believes as he does or acts as he does toward the members of a minority group, he will cite *their* characteristics, not his own, as the cause. Is this a wholly irrational response? We think not. Any complete analysis of prejudice will have to take fully into account the influence of minority-group behavior, as we shall do in Chapters 6 and 7 and elsewhere. A good case could be made for identifying the response of minority-group members to their disprivileged positions as a fourth major cause of prejudice. The key word in this sentence, however, is "response." Although the targets of prejudice and hostility may develop tendencies that feed back into the system of causes which created them, thus re-enforcing those causes, in the first instance the tendencies are the effects of prejudice and discrimination. A person deprived of opportunity may be lazy, deprived of schools may be ignorant, deprived of hope may be careless —and the depriving majority may then accuse him of the very characteristics they have brought about. And the "facts" support their claim in many instances. We shall have to give full attention to this process whereby effects become re-enforcing causes. But to

[2] For a similar outline of the multiple causes of prejudice see Gordon Allport, "Prejudice: A Problem in Psychological and Social Causation," *JSI*, supplement series, Nov., 1950. And for a valuable review of recent research, see John Harding, Harold Proshansky, Bernard Kutner, and Isidor Chein, "Prejudice and Ethnic Relations," in Gardner Lindzey and Elliot Aronson (eds.), *The Handbook of Social Psychology*, Addison-Wesley, 2nd. ed., vol. 5, 1969, pp. 1–77.

list them as a primary cause would be to obscure the sequence of events and to mistake the roots of prejudice for its fruit. At this point we need say only that the fruit may furnish the seed for further growth. In the organic life of man and his societies—and elsewhere in nature—the cycle of causes is of profound importance.

A THEORY OF PERSONALITY

In recent years, evidence from cultural anthropology, psychiatry, psychology, social psychology, and sociology, has made possible the emergence of a theory of personality that is of great value in the analysis of prejudice. In this study we can only sketch its major outlines, while urging the reader to refresh and extend his information in the field by reference to the extensive literature available.[3] The theory is new and tentative, and only part of it has direct application to the study of prejudice and minority-majority relations. Its key concepts must be stated, however, for they furnish the context in which our analysis of the personality functions of prejudice is carried on.

It is too early to speak of a unified theory, combining the several levels of analysis on which various students have worked. There is, however, a growing awareness of the need for taking a series of factors into account. The heredity versus environment controversy has been dismissed as meaningless. The effort now is to find out what the range of biological *potentialities* is, and then to study which of those potentialities result from a particular series of experiences in the physical, social, and cultural environments. One of the most important ideas is that personality is best conceived as *process*, not as a collection of fixed traits. As process, it can be understood only by analysis of the flow of behavior that comes from the interaction of the individual with the situation. An individual does not exist or behave in a vacuum, but always in some situation. Which tendencies —from among the numerous and often contradictory tendencies of which we all are capable—will be set in motion cannot be predicted from knowledge of the individual alone. With what "reference groups" is he most closely identified at the moment? Which of his various potentialities are being encouraged by the existing situation, which are being blocked? How do the structured aspects of his "role" channel his behavior? Role is a cultural concept designating the expected behavior of a person in a given social relationship. The process of carrying out the functions of "shop steward" in a union, "superintendent of schools," or "courteous customer" does not allow full individual variation to come into play. The roles themselves have some compulsions that influence which of various tendencies the individual will express. Thus personality thought of as process is "field" determined.

This does not mean that we can disregard individual differences. Knowledge of the groups within which one develops and within which behavior occurs is vital. Frequently knowledge of group values and role requirements alone will yield good predictive power concerning individual behavior. Under other circumstances, however, such knowledge is inadequate. The individual is never completely socialized. Innate motivations may to some degree contradict his socialized motives, the unique elements in his genetic make-up and, in his experience, give him some unique needs, and every cluster of group experience develops some mutually contradictory needs.

An adequate theory of personality, therefore, whether used with reference to prejudice or to some other aspect of life, must be concerned with the study both of tendencies and of the situations in which they are ex-

[3] See J. Milton Yinger, *Toward A Field Theory of Behavior*, McGraw-Hill, 1965; see also Norman Cameron, *Psychology of Behavior Disorders: A Bio-Social Interpretation*, Houghton Mifflin, 1947; Walter Coutu, *Emergent Human Nature*, Knopf, 1949; Abram Kardiner, *Psychological Frontiers of Society*, Columbia, 1945; Clyde Kluckhohn, H. A. Murray, and David Schneider (eds.), *Personality in Nature, Culture, and Society*, Knopf, rev. ed., 1953; Kurt Lewin, *A Dynamic Theory of Personality*, McGraw-Hill, 1935; Ralph Linton, *The Cultural Background of Personality*, Appleton-Century-Crofts, 1945; Gardner Murphy, *Personality*, Harper & Row, 1947; Alex Inkeles, "Personality and Social Structure," in Robert Merton, Leonard Broom, and Leonard Cottrell (eds.), *Sociology Today*, Basic Books, 1959.

pressed.[4] In this chapter we shall describe some of the processes involved in the generation of hostile tendencies, but will also note the way in which their expression is affected by the situation.

PREJUDICE AS A PRODUCT OF FRUSTRATION

One of the most frequent applications of modern social psychological theory to prejudice is found in the frustration-aggression hypothesis and a group of concepts related to it. Every person is a cluster of propelling forces—original organic forces that have been shaped, coerced, and heavily supplemented by sociocultural forces—pointed toward goals. But no human being moves smoothly toward all the goals that have become part of him. Major and minor frustrations are a continuing part of everyone's life. Achievement of these goals may be blocked by other people, by natural forces (illness, for example), by one's own lack of skill or some other personal tendency. We may have mutually contradictory goals, one of which inevitably must be denied.

There is much evidence to indicate that the blocking of goal-directed behavior frequently creates hostile impulses in the individual. In many instances this hostility cannot be directed toward the source of the frustration; there may be no human agent, or the agent may be unknown, or too powerful to strike. The frustration may result from self-contradictory tendencies in the individual. A pattern of beliefs may define the agent as an in-group member, a friend, a protector, so that it is impossible to recognize him, consciously, as a source of frustration. He may be a task leader, necessary for the attainment of desired goals, yet demanding sacrifices or undertaking actions beyond the level of legitimacy granted him.[5] One may be tied

to him in an ambivalent relationship of both love and hostility—as is the child to the parent. The hostility under such circumstances may be stored up, or it may be directed toward oneself or toward some substitute target that is more accessible or less able to strike back. In other words, a "free-floating," undirected hostility may result from frustration when the actual frustrating agent cannot be attacked; and the social context often favors displacement of this hostility onto minority-group members.

The newly directed attack does not take place, however, without some emotional and intellectual strains; the irrationality and injustice of such hostility, from the point of view of the prejudiced person himself, cannot be completely ignored, although it may not be consciously recognized. The substitute target is, after all, a substitute. In order to make himself seem reasonable and moral, according to his own standards, the person who has shown prejudice or discrimination toward a scapegoat looks for justifications. He creates or accepts convincing reasons for hating or discriminating against members of the minority group. He discovers and believes many kinds of evidence that "prove" that the members of that group thoroughly deserve the treatment he gives them. In a strange, but common, perversion of the facts he even projects onto the scapegoat some of the evil traits (again according to his own definition) which characterize his own behavior, in an attempt to get rid of the feeling of guilt that is too heavy for his ego to bear. Finally, to get rid of any sense of doubt and to give an absolute quality to his beliefs, the prejudiced person categorizes all the individual members of the minority group by stereotypes, usually furnished by society, which help him to rationalize his prejudice toward the whole group, despite the variations that characterize any human group.[6]

---

[4] For a development of these ideas in relationship to prejudice and discrimination, see Yinger, *op. cit.*, chap. 11.

[5] See Peter Burke, "Scapegoating: An Alternative to Role Differentiation," *Sociometry*, June, 1969, pp. 159–168. Burke's evidence comes from the small group laboratory. If the principle applies to larger,

natural groups, current lower levels of legitimacy granted political, educational, and occupational task leaders may be a source, not only of opposition to those leaders but, in some contexts, increased scapegoating as well.

[6] Cf. Bohdan Zawadski, "Limitations of the Scapegoat Theory of Prejudice," *JASP*, Apr., 1948, pp. 127–141.

In this process, the theory goes on to state, the prejudiced person is not wholly successful in reducing his feelings of hostility. Attacks on a scapegoat, after all, are of little use in reducing the actual source of frustrations. They may, in fact, protect the frustrating agent, because attention is diverted in the wrong direction, permitting the person or the social situation that is causing the frustration to continue its activities or even to intensify them. Thus, for example, if the true cause of the frustrations of unemployment of an industrial worker is automation or a group of attitudes held by management and/or his fellow workers, but he thinks that he is unemployed because of competition from Negro workmen he may displace his hostility onto the Negro while the true cause of his frustrations continues unaffected. There is another reason for the ineffectiveness of this frustration-hostility-displacement (or projection) cycle in reducing hostility. The displacement of hostility on a substitute may well be accompanied by some doubts concerning its effectiveness and justice; and projection of one's own failings onto others almost certainly leaves, at least unconsciously, a sense of guilt and a fear of retaliation. These doubts and feelings of guilt create further anxiety and hostility—the more so because they cannot be consciously recognized—and lead to even further displacement and projection. Such a vicious circle helps to explain the tenacity with which prejudice, once started, survives attempts to reduce it by appeal to reason.

It is clear that this theory of prejudice owes much to Freudian doctrines. Some of the writers who support it continue to interpret the process in "classic" Freudian terms. Almost any social norm is looked upon as a frustrating restriction of the "natural" organic man. Frustration and hostility are thus not only widespread and inevitable but basic to the very process of socialization. Non-Freudians contend that the needs of the socialized human being are scarcely to be understood solely by reference to original tendencies. The *channeling* of behavior by culture is not necessarily the *inhibiting* of behavior, for learned patterns are just as natural as biological needs, and they may be much more urgent. Whatever the balance between innate and acquired needs—the present authors incline toward an emphasis of the latter—it is clear that we all face frustrations of those needs. And out of that frustration may grow prejudice and discrimination.

Prejudice and Displacement

Having stated the "personality approach" in general terms, let us examine some of the evidence for it, looking first at the process of displacement. We must keep in mind that this is only a partial explanation; some of its weaknesses will be discussed in later sections of this chapter.

Displacement is the tendency to direct hostility toward a target that cannot realistically be shown to be the cause of one's difficulties. In a study by Miller and Bugelski, boys at a camp were compelled, as part of a testing program, to take a long, dull exam composed of questions that were, on the whole, too difficult for them to answer. At first relatively unaware of what was in store for them, the boys presently realized that the tests were running overtime and that they would be unable to attend bank night at the local theater —an event to which they looked forward all week. The authors used this situation to give the boys brief attitude tests before and after the examination with its attendant frustrations. Before the exam, half were asked to rate Japanese and half were asked to rate Mexicans; afterward, those who had rated the Japanese rated the Mexicans, and vice versa. In both instances unfavorable attitudes increased.[7] Whether the increase in prejudice was a temporary verbal response or a more lasting attitude would be important to know. If we grant that the boys were more prejudice-prone after the exam, did the fact that they were furnished groups upon whom to displace their hostility at just that time help to fixate an attitude toward those groups? The study does not provide an answer to this question.

The authors of *Frustration and Aggression*

[7] John Dollard, Neal Miller, Leonard Doob, *Frustration and Aggression*, Yale, 1939, pp. 43–44.

connect the many frustrations of the Germans from 1914 to 1933 with the ease with which they adopted overt anti-Semitism. Defeated in war, their prestige destroyed, forced to accept the Treaty of Versailles and to relinquish their colonies and other territory, they came to the peace only to face depression, a ruinous inflation (which virtually destroyed a middle class that had sought security through frugality), and finally a world-wide economic collapse that deepened their own depression. Direct aggression against the Allies was impossible, but various kinds of displaced aggression appeared. Many joined the Social Democratic and Communist parties to fight the old order, some joined youth movements, and an increasingly large number gave support to Hitler's anti-Semitism and other aggressive moves.[8]

In a test of college students, 32 men and 32 women were asked to express their attitudes on a scale that measured their tendencies toward authoritarianism, general anti-minority feelings, anti-Negro responses, and patriotism. There followed a mild frustration: they were given two puzzles which were not solvable in the time allowed and the experimenter was unsupporting and unbelieving that they could not finish. They were then given a matched scale for the remeasurement of their attitudes. Anti-Negro scores went up significantly,[9] especially for the males. Since changes in other parts of the scale were not significant, there seemed to be a "targeting" of the Negro as a scapegoat.[10]

Such a finding indicates that scapegoating is not sheer displacement, with the target selected at random. One must explore not only the hostility leading to displacement but also the "stimulus qualities of the scapegoat."[11] Some are attacked but not others. White and Lippitt note that in the boys' groups that they studied, scapegoating was never against the weakest persons. They interpret this to mean that the attacks were an attempt to recover self-esteem. This required that one attack someone strong and dangerous, yet not too threatening.[12] Under other circumstances, with scapegoating performing different functions, weaker or stronger persons may be the targets.

Berkowitz and Green sought by experiment to discover the extent to which hostility was a function of frustration or a function of the perceived qualities of the targets. They made it possible for a person to give small electric shocks to "partners" under conditions that had been made frustrating. Some of the partners were liked and others were not, again as a result of experimenter manipulation. They found that the disliked partners were the primary victims of the resentment caused by the frustrations created in the experiment.[13]

Thus in the interpretation of displacement, one must take account not only of tendencies of the displacer (his level of frustration or hostility), but also of the perceived qualities of potential targets. Among other variables one must also note the influence of the kind of frustration or threat that is involved. Feshbach and Singer observed that, contrary to their expectations, discussion of atomic attack and dangers of cancer did not increase the prejudice scores of their respondents but actually decreased them. The anxiety generated did not get focused on minority-group targets. Perhaps the effects of a shared threat are different from those of a personal threat. To test this possibility, they randomly assigned

[8] *Ibid.*, pp. 153–156.
[9] Occasionally we shall refer to such statistical terms as "critical ratio," "significant difference," "standard error," or "level of significance." For those unfamiliar with these terms, this brief explanation may be of value. A statistically significant difference (as, in this case, between the scores before and the scores after the frustration) is a difference too large to be accounted for by chance, by the accidents of sampling. The difference may be stated in terms of critical ratio or standard error (2.0 generally being regarded as significant—a figure which indicates that not more often than once in 20 times could the result have been produced by chance) or in terms of a percent level of significance (a "p" or probability of .05 indicating again the one-in-twenty chance).
[10] Emory Cowen, Judah Landes, and Donald Shaet, "The Effects of Mild Frustration on the Expression of Prejudiced Attitudes," *JASP*, Jan., 1959, pp. 33–38.

[11] Leonard Berkowitz and James Green, "The Stimulus Qualities of the Scapegoat," *JASP*, Apr., 1962, pp. 293–301.
[12] Ralph White and Ronald Lippitt, *Autocracy and Democracy: An Experimental Inquiry*, Harper & Row, 1960, chap. 11.
[13] *Op. cit.*, pp. 293–301.

the members of introductory psychology classes to six groups: a control group, three personal threat groups (risks in attaining a happy marriage, dangers of fire, and problems of mental illness), and two shared threat groups (dangers of flood and atomic war). Attitudes of the students toward Negroes were measured and about four weeks later the groups were given mimeographed statements about one of the five threats (the control group received no statement) and were asked to discuss these statements. No student saw more than one. After their discussions, attitudes toward Negroes were measured again and, as predicted, all three of the personal threat groups gained significantly in prejudice beyond the change in the control group (at the .05 and .06 levels of significance). The flood threat group lost significantly (at the .02 level). Far from producing a scapegoating expression against Negroes, there was an expression of reduced prejudice, perhaps as a result of the sense of a shared fate. The atomic-war threat group, however, gained prejudice, although not significantly. This may indicate that references to Russia in the discussion (as contrasted with the impersonal flood threat) led to aggressive targeting that was to some degree generalized to other groups.[14]

Such studies indicate the complexity of the displacement process and should alert us to the fact that it cannot be explained by reference to the individual's tendencies in isolation from the setting in which they are expressed. It is especially important to know what alternative ways of reducing threat or struggling for status are available. Even when the level of personality dynamics alone is considered, the interactions of several forces are complicated. Frenkel-Brunswik measured the explicit ethnic prejudices of 250 sixth- to eighth-grade pupils, and then found, by sociometric tests, that the more highly prejudiced tended to be less often mentioned as best friends, were less popular, more seeking of attention, more unwilling to be bossed, more frustrated and complaining, less trust-

worthy and helpful.[15] We must carefully avoid assuming that such a study, even if its measurements are considered reliable and valid, proves that the observed personality tendencies *cause* the prejudice, that, perhaps, the prejudice is an attempt to get rid of hostility. It may be simply that the kinds of experiences—family training, for example—that produce untrustworthy, attention-seeking, frustrated individuals are also the kinds of experiences that are likely to furnish them prejudices. The causal sequence may even be the opposite from that inferred. Children who are taught to be prejudiced may thereby be trained in rigidity of mind, lack of ability to adjust to reality, and other tendencies that produce the inclinations the study found. It is perhaps most likely that all of these possibilities are involved in a complicated interaction.

Prejudice and Projection

Closely associated with the hypothesis that free-floating hostility may be important in prejudice through the process of displacement is the conception that prejudice may be an attempt to help individuals accept the rigid inhibitions that culture imposes on them or to rationalize violations of those inhibitions when they do occur. This idea has been suggested at various points above but now needs explicit formulation. The "reasoning" of the prejudiced person might be stated briefly in this way: "I must not do that" (show uninhibited aggressive or sexual acts, for example), "but there is no great loss— only inferior people do that anyway." Or "I should not have done that" (joined in mob violence against a member of a minority group or violated the sex code), "but these people are inferior, so I have not really done anything bad." The unity of a society is maintained by interdependence, by the suppression of in-group aggressions, and by defensive-aggressive actions against outgroups. Hostility toward the in-group is generated in the process of transmitting its pat-

---

[14] Seymour Feshbach and Robert Singer, "The Effects of Personal and Shared Threats upon Social Prejudice," *JASP*, May, 1957, pp. 411–416.

[15] Else Frenkel-Brunswik, "Studies of Social Discrimination in Children," *American Psychologist*, Oct., 1946, p. 456.

terns of behavior to each member, but society suppresses such hostility by many sanctions and rewards. For the most part, individuals find that such hostile moves are either useless or dangerous and abandon them as overt responses. No one is perfectly socialized, however; each is the record of a battle in which frustration, hostility, and fear have played roles. The hostility toward in-group members and norms that is built up in the process of socialization and that continues as a result of the controls on adult behavior is often underestimated. Control over it is one of the chief problems of social life. No society requires the complete renunciation of in-group aggression, of course. There are standardized, culturally defined channels for aggression. In modern American society, economic competition and sports, for example, may serve this function. Moreover, aggression can be suppressed to some degree—one of man's most useful capacities from the point of view of adjustment to society. Seldom, however, does a society rechannel aggressions effectively enough to permit sufficient aggression to drain off all hostility. In-group members live in a constant state of readiness for aggressive responses.

As was stated earlier, the degree to which frustration and hostility are the *inevitable* result of *any* socialization (the position of the doctrinaire Freudian) is a question on which the evidence is as yet incomplete. Anthropological evidence seems to indicate that human beings can be socialized to widely different cultural standards, including some highly restrictive practices, without having their hostility raised to the point where social cohesion is endangered. Doubtless it is a matter in part of the restrictiveness of the cultural norms and in part of the way in which those norms are transferred to the maturing individual. More hostility may be aroused by the inhibitions imposed on the aspiring middle-class American or the maturing boy among the Manus of New Guinea than results from socialization in a Latin-American culture or in aboriginal Samoa. But more serious hostility arises when cultural norms, whatever they are, are brought to conscious attention and scrutiny by culture

contact, by social and technological change. Then the weight of the inhibitions imposed by society begins to be felt.

Whatever the degree of truth in the Freudian contention that social norms inevitably lead to hostility, it is clear that many societies, including modern American society, do have individuals who carry within themselves both propelling needs and inhibitions against the satisfaction of those needs. Such individuals must block overt response to these tendencies in order to avoid social pressure and guilt feelings (to the degree that they have taken the cultural standards into their own personalities); but the tendencies continue to work on them. This situation is favorable to the development of prejudice. The inhibition seems more bearable if it is only inferior people who behave that way anyway; or the violation of a norm is less of a blow at one's self-respect and conscience if the violation has been aimed at a member of a "lower" group. Here the familiar process of projection comes into use.[16] Many studies have shown, for example, that a ruling group which has exhibited violent aggression against a minority and has exploited it sexually is likely to be firmly convinced that members of the minority are uniformly violent and sexually unrestrained. MacCrone states that the sexual life of the "natives" has a perennial fascination for the South African whites. There is a widespread belief that native men are more potent sexually and native women more voluptuous. This is combined with morbid fear of miscegenation and great emotional fear of rape[17]—a strange combination of beliefs since virtually all sexual contact has been initiated by white men, despite intense social disapproval. This prejudice against black Africans—we have described only a part of the whole cluster of attitudes that defines them as inferior and evil—seems to be a clear case of projection. The picture of the Blacks as vicious and violent can be interpreted in the same way, since

[16] For a helpful review, but somewhat controversial interpretation, see B. I. Murstein and R. S. Pryer, "The Concept of Projection: A Review," *Psychological Bulletin*, 1959, pp. 353–374.

[17] I. D. MacCrone, *Race Attitudes in South Africa*, Oxford, 1937, pp. 294–310.

the Whites have often been ruthless in their use of violent suppression. Having ignored their own standards regarding the use of violence and the control of the sex impulse, the ruling Whites find the strains on their consciences too heavy to bear. They attempt to reduce the tension by projecting the traits of violence and sexuality onto the native group. As already noted, this attempt to reduce strain may not work, for it may be accompanied by a sense of guilt that leads to further anxiety, more hostility, the need for even more projection—and thus a vicious circle which can be broken only by a change of action or of conscience on the part of the projecting person.

Dollard described much the same combination of beliefs and actions in "Southerntown" a generation ago. There has probably been more change in these patterns in the American South than in South Africa—projection, of course, has not disappeared—but they well illustrate the process of projection. Most of the sex contacts between Negroes and Whites were initiated by white men, most of the violence was used by Whites against the Negroes; yet there was an emotionally vivid belief in the violent and sexually aggressive nature of the Negro. This belief was needed not only to rid many white people of a sense of guilt for having violated their own standards, but to help them resist the impulses toward violation. The Negro, a designated inferior group, symbolized the repressed impulses that one must not admit are still motivating him. In "Southerntown" the white male was torn by a group of contradictory desires and accompanying beliefs: to maintain "race purity," to live up to the dominant moral code with regard to sex, and yet to take advantage of the relatively defenseless status of the Negro population for wider sexual contact. He saw that preventing contact of Negroes with Whites would help to satisfy the first desire; but he forgot that if Whites initiate such contacts, the results are not different. His belief in the inferiority of the Negro helped him to satisfy the second desire or to rationalize its violation: if the inferior Negro is sexually promiscuous, I must not be; or if I make advances toward a

Negro woman, it isn't really a violation of the code. This same concept of the inferiority of the Negro and belief in the strong sex urges and easy virtue of Negro women helped him to satisfy the third desire. Race prejudice is a natural outcome of such a complex of mutually contradictory desires, feelings of guilt, and repressions interacting with the other factors we shall be examining.[18]

One need not assume, in this discussion, that the claims of prejudiced persons that "inferior" groups are violent and sexually uninhibited are entirely false. Such characteristics are not uncommon among groups discriminated against—the American Negro in the South, for example. The partial truth of the stereotype of the minority group upon whom a dominant group has projected its faults helps to reinforce the prejudice, to make it seem reasonable. The personality functions served by the prejudice are thereby carried on more effectively, unmindful of several complications: actual errors in the picture of the minority group, with gross exaggeration of most other traits; assumption that the traits are innate; categorization of the whole group, without attention to wide individual variations; and an emotional defense of the total picture which shows how important it is to the prejudiced person that the issue not be examined.

Nor should we assume that projection characterizes only majority-group members. Norman Podhoretz has vividly reminded us that if, as James Baldwin makes tragically clear, Negroes are often faceless to Whites, his experience as a white child in New York was that he was faceless to Negroes. He suggests that if Whites hate Negroes because they project onto them their own wild impulses, Negroes may hate Whites because they project onto them their own tendencies toward submission to authority, discipline, and the desire for achievement—impulses that must be repressed because they can lead only to frustration. He speaks of his own fearful admiration for the toughness and the utter

[18] Cf. John Dollard, *Caste and Class in a Southern Town*, Yale, 1937, pp. 363–388.

freedom of the Negro boys which led him to believe that it was surely he, not they who was underprivileged.[19]

From this discussion it should be apparent that the concept of projection, "the attribution of internal characteristics to some external person or objects,"[20] is a complicated one. A full inquiry must ask: Who projects what self-alienating tendencies onto whom in what circumstances? Knowledge of the guilt and anxiety of the projecting individual by itself is insufficient to answer this question. The groups to which one belongs may furnish some targets and prohibit the use of others. Because it aids the process of repression of our guilt those whom we have harmed are likely to be the focus of our hostility. By accusing them of the very tendencies we have shown in our dealings with them, we seek to allay our anxieties.

The use of projection onto minority-group targets, and also of displacement, is often shown in extreme form among those who are mentally ill. Sadists and paranoiacs, for example, may use prejudice to rationalize and "explain" their deviant behavior. There is a bit of evidence in the study of Frenkel-Brunswik and Sanford that persons scoring high in anti-Semitism have more than average paranoid tendencies. They agree significantly more often to the statement: "To a greater extent than most people realize, our lives are governed by plots hatched in secret by politicians."[21] Although strongly conventional in their attitudes toward sex, they seem to exhibit a repressed striving that sometimes takes on sadistic connotations—a great willingness, for example, to agree with the statement that persons who commit sex crimes deserve not mere punishment, but a public whipping. The tensions of the mentally ill often have no specific referent. In a given culture, they may have learned, as many normal people have, that some racial or other minority group is an appropriate object for attack. The paranoiac, who lives in a world of groundless suspicions (groundless from the point of view of the outsider), who attributes sinister motives to every act, may feel that his own actions are explained and justified by his "information" about a minority group. Such persons are doubtless few in number; but if the intensity of their prejudice is high, they may become the leaders of antiracial mobs or movements, drawing in others who are less highly motivated to act in a discriminatory way. Their propelling need for aggression may be so strong that they seek out and create incidents, rather than merely wait for them.[22] Dustin and Davis compared 20 undergraduate men who had scored high in authoritarian tendencies with 20 who had scored low. In a laboratory experiment, they were permitted to reward or punish a series of "followers" for their performances. The more authoritarian subjects significantly more often used negative sanctions (monetary penalties or negative evaluations); the less authoritarian significantly more often used no sanctions.[23]

Nathan Ackerman and Marie Jahoda have explored the relationship between anti-Semitism and emotional disorder. Their data are drawn from intensive analyses of patients who had sought the help of psychoanalysts. The difficulties of the patients ranged from

[19] Norman Podhoretz, "My Negro Problem—and Ours," *Commentary*, Feb., 1963, pp. 93–101. The depth of the need for projection, growing from the strength of the hostility and fear, are often unknown to middle- and upper-class whites who have seldom experienced its power in race relations. Although Podhoretz and Baldwin both speak too easily of a presumed universal hostility between Negro and white, they capture much of the feel of it, particularly for urban children in the lower classes. See James Baldwin, *Notes of a Native Son*, Beacon, 1955, *Nobody Knows My Name*, Dell, 1961, and *The Fire Next Time*, Dial, 1963.

For a poignant story of affection and hostility, see Bernard Malamud, "Black is My Favorite Color," *Reporter*, July 18, 1963, pp. 43–48. In all of these it is clear that we are not viewing race relations in any special sense, but are seeing, through the eyes of these writers, the lives of blocked and frustrated persons for whom, in their struggles, race symbols have become important.

[20] Philip Chase, "A Note on Projection," *Psychological Bulletin*, July, 1960, p. 289.

[21] Else Frenkel-Brunswik and R. N. Sanford, "Some Personality Factors in Anti-Semitism," *JP*, Oct., 1945, p. 283.

[22] David Krech and Richard Crutchfield, *Theory and Problems of Social Psychology*, McGraw-Hill, 1948, pp. 448–449.

[23] David Dustin and Henry Davis, "Authoritarianism and Sanctioning Behavior," *JPSP*, 1967, pp. 222–224.

fairly mild personality disturbances to serious mental illness—degrees of disorder that require some separate analysis. We may see among the patients, however, certain common problems that frequently were associated, in a functional way, with anti-Semitism:

Each of these individuals is plagued by pervasive anxiety. Deeply confused in his own self-image, he derives no strength from his personal identity with which to face a menacing world. His personal relationships are shallow and unsatisfying. His group relations are characterized by an exaggerated surface conformity beneath which lurks a primitive, untamed hostility. Within his group the slightest indication of nonconformity appears as a threat. Outside his group, differences are exaggerated. Lacking a basis of genuine identification, he tends in a compensatory way to define his group status by reference to qualities he does not actually possess. He achieves only a partial adaptation to reality, and is unable to develop spontaneous and genuine personal relationships. His conscience is underdeveloped and unreliable, his repressions incomplete and inefficient, thereby necessitating recourse to the laborious tasks of conscious suppression.[24]

The authors then relate this kind of personality instability to the life experiences of the patients and to anti-Semitism as a mechanism of "adjustment." For example:

Common to every case of anti-Semitism collected for this study is the strikingly similar psychological atmosphere into which the patient was born. There is not a single example of a permanently well-adjusted marital relationship between the parents. . . .

Generally a sharp contrast characterized the parents as individuals. They were at cross-purposes on every possible occasion. In temperament, ethical values, sexual attitudes, and social interests, father and mother seemed to represent different worlds. Even when such basic differences were not understood by the children, the fundamental hostility between the parents was inescapable. . . .

Both open rejection and narcissistic exploitation damage considerably the self-esteem and self-confidence of the child, who, consequently, feels unwanted, unloved, and unworthy. . . .

To find a semblance of balance in spite of their frustrations, they mobilize against their anxiety and self-hate a variety of defense mechanisms. In the interlocking pattern of these defenses anti-Semitism seems to fulfill a functionally well-defined role. It represents an effort to displace the self-destroying trends in the personality. At the psychic level, anti-Semitic hostility can be viewed as a profound though irrational and futile defensive effort to restore a crippled self. At the social level, it can be regarded as a device for achieving secondary emotional and material gain.[25]

Evidence of the kind represented by this study scarcely permits one to say that emotional disorder "causes" prejudice in general or anti-Semitism in particular. The data concern a relatively small number of people in the New York area who had sought help from psychoanalysts and whose cases, in turn, had been arbitrarily selected by the psychoanalysts willing to cooperate in the study. The problems of sampling and the chances for bias are clear. Nor can we assume that even for the type of person studied a clear causal sequence is indicated. As Ackerman and Jahoda point out: "The syndrome of emotional predispositions and character tendencies that we have described cannot of course be considered unique in the anti-Semite. It exists in many persons and there is no reason to believe that all who share such characteristics will necessarily manifest anti-Semitic attitudes."[26] Many people are prejudiced, moreover, who are not troubled with emotional disorder. And one major type of personality disturbance, depression, was not found among the cases. The sample is too small for statistical test, but probably the guilt and self-destructive features of a depression psychosis are incompatible with the tendency to blame outside forces for all of one's difficulties that characterizes prejudice.

Nevertheless, the study demonstrates in a valuable way the manner in which anti-Semitism may be used, in a society that furnishes this prejudice, by some persons suffering from emotional disorder.

To conclude our discussion of displacement

[24] Nathan Ackerman and Marie Jahoda, *Anti-Semitism and Emotional Disorder*, Harper & Row, 1950, pp. 39–40.

[25] *Ibid.*, pp. 43–55.
[26] *Ibid.*, p. 55.

and projection, we must be careful to note that this "scapegoat theory" of prejudice is by no means adequate by itself. There seems to be good evidence that frustration does not always lead to aggression and hostile acts. The theory does not explain how the hostile *impulses* become transformed into hostile *attitudes*—persistent, patterned hostility toward an individual or a group—rather than selecting some new and unique target each time.[27] And it does not explain why this patterning takes the form of prejudice against specific groups. One may say correctly that frustration may well make a person more susceptible to prejudice, that it is one of the forces found where prejudice is most common; but the many other factors involved must be taken into account. Persons in whom the frustrations and guilt feelings we have discussed are at a minimum are, nevertheless, often prejudiced because of the other factors that we shall discuss later. Although the scapegoat theory helps to explain some of the force behind prejudice, the "need" for it, it does not explain the direction that prejudice takes.

We shall be concerned with that question in Chapter 5, but a brief comment here will help us to avoid misunderstanding. Zawadski holds that extreme proponents of the scapegoat theory are reacting against the earlier racist doctrines that explained prejudice simply by reference to the supposed traits of the minority groups: We are prejudiced against them only because of their "well-earned reputation" for evil acts and inferior abilities. Such an explanation pays attention only to the groups against which prejudice is directed; but the scapegoat theory pays attention only to the tendencies of the prejudiced persons. It is not adequate to explain why a given group, or groups, have been selected for the role of scapegoats. Part of the explanation, says Zawadski, may lie in the characteristics of the minority groups that make them particularly vulnerable. In the process of disproving that the traits which typify a group are not innate or inevitable, contemporary students have sometimes de-

nied the possibility of distinguishing at all among groups on the basis of average differences in tendencies toward certain kinds of behavior. This error is perhaps as likely to prevent an adequate social psychology of prejudice as the error that it supplants. It would be remarkable indeed if the members of minority groups, experiencing as they do significantly different influences throughout the course of their lives, did not develop some personality tendencies by which, to some degree, they can be distinguished. Having said that, one must then, in any complete theory of prejudice, seek to isolate such distinctive tendencies, measure them, and explain them. Here the interaction of the various factors in prejudice becomes clear, because one of the key explanations of these minority-group characteristics lies in prejudice and discrimination themselves. To begin with, the tendencies are responses, at least in large measure, to the treatment received from the majority.[28] But within a specific interacting field they are, however caused, among the forces to be studied. Thus we must state again that the study of prejudice from the point of view of analysis of prejudiced persons is a scientific abstraction —necessary for research, but eventually requiring synthesis with the total interacting field.

Personality, Uncertainty, and Status Needs

In many instances writers examining the personality of the prejudiced individual have limited themselves to the discussion of frustration, repression, and closely related topics. There are, however, a number of other "needs," which in only a very general sense can be brought into this kind of explanation, that are also important in helping us to understand how prejudice reflects the personality.[29] Prejudice may be an attempt to bring meaning into a confusing and ambiguous crisis situation. Few of us like the feeling that we do not understand an important situation close to us; yet there are many situations that we cannot understand. If the

[27] Cf. Theodore M. Newcomb, "Autistic Hostility and Social Reality," *HR*, 1947, pp. 69–86.

[28] Cf. Zawadski, *op. cit.*
[29] Cf. Krech and Crutchfield, *op. cit.*, pp. 443–498.

content of our culture includes prejudices, or if, in a new situation, the media of communication offer prejudices, we may adopt them to "explain" the crisis. If a businessman or worker is suddenly confronted with an economic crisis, his vague ideas and beliefs about the economy of the country may not be able to explain the depression and his personal problems. If there is available the "explanation" of the international Jew, with monopoly power and shady business practices, he may adopt it. On this level, prejudice is an attempt to find meaning, to explain; it may be the search for a reason, not an alibi. Seldom, if ever, would such a factor be the only one operative in a given situation, but in a society as complex as our own it may play an important part. Lacking true explanations, we rely on comforting pseudo explanations.

This cognitive element in prejudice has often been forgotten in favor of exclusive attention to unconscious motives.[30] In recent years, in fact, there may have been increased neglect of the study of man's search for meaning, his attempts to bring some order into his confusing and rapidly changing situation. It has somehow ". . . been taken for granted that inferences can be made directly from motivation and the evolutionary past of the species to complex intergroup behavior without paying much attention to the flimsy cognitive byproducts thrown out, as if at random, by the subterranean springs of emotion and 'instinct.' "[31]

To say that there is a cognitive element in prejudice is not to say that it is reasonable or rational, but only that it is, in part, an effort to comprehend a complex and often threatening world. "It is hardly startling to say that the best way to predict whether a man will harbor hostile attitudes toward a particular group and what will be the content of these attitudes is to find out how he understands the intergroup situation. And it is hardly any more startling to say that this understanding will in turn affect his behavior. This does not mean, of course, that emotional and motivational factors are unimportant."[32] Tajfel seems to overstate the case. Whether knowing how a person understands an intergroup situation is the best way to predict hostile attitudes remains problematic. What will yield best prediction for one person in a given situation may be less valuable in different contexts. There is little doubt, however, that man's search for meaning is involved in his prejudices. He categorizes, as Tajfel notes, in an effort to simplify the complicated world to which he must respond; he assimilates the views of those around him, including prejudices, as part of the process of becoming a group member; he searches for coherence in a changing intergroup setting by imposing a structure on it, often in a way that justifies various advantages for him. We shall be studying these processes with care in Chapters 4 and 5, with particular reference to their group dimensions. Here we emphasize them as part of the complex of causes out of which individual prejudice grows.

Prejudice may be an attempt to enhance one's self-esteem or to remove a threat to self-esteem. [In a culture that stresses the opportunities each person has for success but prevents success (by its own definition) for a great many people, a shadowy image of success is created by the dominant group's placing itself categorically, above all members of "inferior" groups.] Success may be blocked by personal incapacity or ill fortune, by membership in a disadvantaged group, or simply by the fact that, by definition, only a few can attain success. Whatever the cause, many will feel failure as a blow to self-esteem. The white "failure" may get some small comfort from the belief that he is better than Ralph Bunche, James Baldwin, and Willie Mays all rolled into one. The

[30] See, however, Henri Tajfel, "Cognitive Aspects of Prejudice," *JSI*, Autumn, 1969, pp. 79–97; Howard Schuman and John Harding, "Prejudice and the Norm of Rationality," *Sociometry*, Sept., 1964, pp. 353–371; and Krech and Crutchfield, *op. cit.*, pp. 454–455.

[31] Tajfel, *op. cit.*, p. 80. In this day of violence and mass behavior, it has been easy for the public to accept such inferences, as found, for example, in Robert Ardrey, *Territorial Imperative*, Atheneum, 1966; and in Konrad Lorenz, *On Aggression*, Harcourt Brace Jovanovich, 1960.

[32] Tajfel, *op. cit.*, p. 81.

sense of failure may be temporary—a result, perhaps, of loss of job. If the prejudice is available, one may then accept the belief that unscrupulous Jews caused the loss of job. "His pride has been saved, but an anti-Semite has been created."[33]

A "genteel" kind of prejudice may be sustained simply by the need for social acceptance in one's group. "Nice" people have no social contact with Negroes. They wish them no harm; there is little projection or displacement involved; the individuals are well adjusted. Nevertheless, prejudice directs their activities, and the polite "gentlemen's agreements" of various kinds furnish the context in which more vigorous prejudices thrive.

IS THERE A PREJUDICED "PERSONALITY TYPE"?

Some of the research in the field of the social psychology of prejudice has sought to discover the degree to which an attitude of prejudice should be interpreted as a more or less independent "trait" and the degree to which it should be seen as simply one manifestation of a total personality. The question might be put in this way: Are there certain kinds of total personality integrations that have prejudice as a natural expression, or is prejudice a specific response to specific stimuli, likely to be associated with almost any kind of personality? This problem is closely related to our discussion of personality "needs," but can be given separate attention profitably. Social psychology has gone through a long controversy over the question of the generality and the specificity of personality attributes—a controversy that has not yet been closed by the evidence. There have been rather drastic swings from the position that supposed "traits," such as intelligence or honesty, were general—expressed themselves in any situation where they applied—to the opposite position that personality was simply a loosely joined bundle of specific responses to specific stimuli. We need not examine that controversy here,

[33] Krech and Crutchfield, *op. cit.*, p. 456.

except to note the contemporary point of view: Neither extreme should be asserted in a doctrinaire way; specific studies should attempt to measure the degree of generality or specificity; and tendencies should be studied in the context of the situations with which they interact.

For us the question becomes: Is there a "prejudiced personality" that is different from the unprejudiced in major ways, or is prejudice a specific response to a specific stimulus? In recent years the impact of psychiatry and cultural anthropology has encouraged greatly increased attention to the matter of personality integration. In the process of acquiring the responses characteristic of his culture, particularly in the intimate contacts within the family during his earliest years, the individual has built a basic "ego structure." This is a fundamental attitude toward himself and toward others which, once established, reacts upon objective experiences and strongly influences their meaning for the individual. A person, for example, who in his earliest experiences acquires an attitude of superiority and a tendency toward domination may continue to hold that attitude when the objective situation contradicts it. He may fail in a certain endeavor according to the judgments of others, but he can find for himself reasons that prove that he did not "really" fail; luck was against him, or the other party was dishonest or had some undue advantage, or the referee was blind—at least he won a moral victory.

The Authoritarian Personality

In the last several years there has been a great deal of research to test the hypothesis that prejudice is part of a complicated personality "syndrome." According to this thesis, prejudice is one manifestation of a basically insecure person, one who is "ego alien"—that is, has repressed many of his own impulses—one who looks upon life as capricious and threatening, and one who looks upon all human relationships in competitive power terms. Prejudice, moreover, is tied in a functional way to many other personality trends, to particular style of politics, religion, and sex behavior. The authors of *The Authoritarian Personality* write:

The most crucial result of the present study, as it seems to the authors, is the demonstration of close correspondence in the type of approach and outlook a subject is likely to have in a great variety of areas, ranging from the most intimate features of family and sex adjustment through relationships to other people in general, to religion and to social and political philosophy. Thus a basically hierarchical, authoritarian, exploitive parent-child relationship is apt to carry over into a power-oriented, exploitively dependent attitude toward one's sex partner and one's God and may well culminate in a political philosophy and social outlook which has no room for anything but a desperate clinging to what appears to be strong and a disdainful rejection of whatever is relegated to the bottom.[34]

In one of the studies that preceded and led up to *The Authoritarian Personality*, Frenkel-Brunswik and Sanford analyzed the deep-seated personality functions of prejudice. The authors applied an anonymous scale on anti-Semitism to 24 University of California men and 76 women. The scale measured the tendency to accept or reject anti-Semitic statements and attitudes, allowing several steps for agreement or disagreement. There were also questions on politics, group membership, and public issues, to see if anti-Semitism was part of a complex of attitudes. There were 'projective" items to find the subjects' goals, fears, identifications: Whom do you most admire? If you had six months to live, and could do what you wished, what would you do? The eight women who scored highest in anti-Semitism and the eight who scored lowest were then interviewed at length and given Rorschach and Thematic Apperception Tests. With this evidence, the questionnaire was revised, with added items on conventionality, aggression, superstition, attitudes toward family, and others; and the revised scale was given to 140 University of California women.

The girls who were high in anti-Semitism were, on the average, well groomed, of higher than average income, greatly interested in social standing, conservative, from socially mobile families, ethnocentric. All of them said they liked their parents and subscribed to statements that indicate obedience to authority. The girls low in anti-Semitism were more nondescript in appearance, less at ease socially, more willing to talk about themselves and to make critical appraisals of their parents. An analysis of responses to the pictures in the Thematic Apperception Tests indicates, moreover, some other differences. Girls high in anti-Semitism responded to one picture with ideas of violence, death, murder, and aggression. The same picture shown to the girls low in anti-Semitism elicited little aggression and no reference to death. One picture showed an older woman with a younger one; violence and suspicion came out in the responses of the girls high in anti-Semitism. "The mother starts a racket," says one; "the mother has the daughter mingle with the rich and sort of act as bait. . . . The mother is a very clever woman and always manages to have all her schemes work."[35] The girls low in anti-Semitism saw little conflict between the young and the old woman. The pattern of human relations as seen by the "highs" is fundamentally a struggle between dominance and submission. They interpret a picture of a hypnotist as a story of the misuse of "superhuman" powers for evil or queer deeds. The "lows" describe it as an "experiment," a "demonstration in class."

Those high on the anti-Semitic scale show a great deal of "social anxiety." They draw a sharp line between nice people and bad people. They are more prone to think in terms of fate. Among the 140 who took the revised questionnaire, the one-fourth at the top of the anti-Semitic scale were much more likely to agree with the following statement than the one-fourth at the bottom: "Although many people may scoff, it may yet be shown that astrology can explain a lot of things."[36]

[34] T. W. Adorno, Else Frenkel-Brunswik, D. J. Levinson, and R. N. Sanford, *The Authoritarian Personality*, Harper & Row, 1950, p. 971.

[35] Frenkel-Brunswik and Sanford, *op. cit.*, p. 283.
[36] *Ibid.*, p. 278.

The difference between the two groups was statistically significant, with a critical ratio of 4.4. The "highs" deny overtly what the tests reveal to be strong covert tendencies. They praise self-sacrifice and kindness but have many underlying aggressive feelings; they are reluctant to express such strong drives as aggression and sex but project them onto out-groups. "Inferior" and "lower" people are seen as aggressive and uninhibited sexually.

These tendencies cannot be understood, of course, except in the light of the social and cultural situations in which these persons developed. The authors note that insecure times cause the parents anxiety and encourage the excessively rigid teaching of standards in the attempt to cling to status.

In a study of social attitudes, Hartley throws a great deal of light on the way in which prejudice is related to a whole complex of personal tendencies. He asked several groups of college students to mark, on a standard social-distance scale, their attitudes toward a large number of racial, religious, national, and economic groups. The scale permitted a differentiation of response ranging from 'Would admit to close kinship by marriage" to "Would exclude from my country," with five intervening steps at least roughly scalable. Among the 35 groups, Hartley included the names of three nonexistent groups —Danireans, Pireneans, and Wallonians. Some students may have associated the names with some existent groups—thinking the Pireneans to be people who live in the Pyrenees, for example—but they almost certainly knew nothing about these groups, even when thus identified; and the very fact that they tended to find an existent group for the label in order to express an attitude, is itself significant. Since in reality there are no such groups, one can explain the attributes assigned to them only by studying the individual who makes the judgment. If his response to the nonexistent groups is very similar to his response to the existent and partially known groups, one is perhaps justified in speaking in terms of generalized prejudice or nonprejudice. "Our hypothesis is that such tolerance represents to a significant

extent a function of the persons responding rather than of the groups responded to."[37] To test this hypothesis, Hartley correlated the average tolerance for the 32 existing groups with the expressed attitude toward the three "nonesuch" groups. The Pearsonian product-moment coefficients of correlation, computed separately for the students from the five schools who took the test, ranged from .78 to .85, a strong confirmation of the hypothesis.

Such studies support the hypothesis that prejudice is frequently a symptom of a basic personality organization, and not simply an isolated and independent attitude. There is not just one type of prejudiced personality, to be sure. (Adorno identifies six types from the evidence in these studies),[38] but many tendencies seem to occur frequently among all the varieties. On the basis of interview materials, Frenkel-Brunswik states that those with high scores on prejudice tests exhibit, among other tendencies, rigidity of outlook (inaccessibility to new experience), intolerance of ambiguity (they want to know the answers), pseudoscientific or antiscientific attitudes (more superstition, reliance on accidents as explanations, attribution of behavior to heredity), suggestibility and gullibility, and autistic thinking in goal behavior (unrealistic views of what will achieve the desired goals). Those low in prejudice, on the other hand, show more flexibility of judgment, greater tolerance of ambiguity, a more scientific-naturalistic explanation of events, greater autonomy and self-reliance, and realistic thinking about goal behavior.[39]

Scores of studies in the last ten years have sought to test and refine, and more recently to qualify, the thesis that prejudice is to an important degree the expression of an insecure personality. They converge on such concepts as self-rejection, repression, a strong concern for power in human relationships, a general "threat orientation," as Newcomb

[37] Eugene Hartley, *Problems in Prejudice*, King's Crown, 1946, p. 26.
[38] Adorno, Frenkel-Brunswik, Levinson, and Sanford, *op. cit.*, pp. 753 ff.
[39] *Ibid.*, p. 461. For further comparisons of those high and low in prejudice, see James G. Martin, *The Tolerant Personality*, Wayne State Univ. Press, 1964.

calls it.[40] Many of these studies have introduced new variables and some, as we shall see in the next section, have required extensive modifications of the thesis of *The Authoritarian Personality*. Those that are concerned with general descriptions of individuals high in prejudice substantially agree with this summary of the studies by Gough:

anti-intellectuality, a pervading sense of pessimism and lack of hope and confidence in the future; feelings of cynicism, distrust, doubt, and suspicion; a diffuse misanthropy and querulousness; a hostile and bitter outlook which verged on destructiveness; a grumbling and discontented evaluation of their current status; a rigid, somewhat dogmatic style of thinking; a lack of poise and self-assurance; and an underlying perplexity related to a feeling that something dreadful is about to happen.[41]

A CRITIQUE OF "THE AUTHORITARIAN PERSONALITY"

The scales developed in the Berkeley studies of the authoritarian personality were immediately put to use in replications and modifications of the original research. The methodology and theoretical perspective of the book

---

[40] For valuable bibliographies and summaries of the literature see John P. Kirscht and Ronald C. Dillehay, *Dimensions of Authoritarianism: A Review of Research And Theory*, Univ. of Kentucky Press, 1967; and Richard Christie and Peggy Cook, "A Guide to Published Literature Relating to the Authoritarian Personality Through 1956," *JP, Apr.*, 1958, pp. 171–199. See also Donn Byrne and Terry Wong, "Racial Prejudice, Interpersonal Attraction, and Assumed Dissimilarity of Attitudes," *JASP*, Oct., 1962, pp. 246–253; Loren Chapman and Donald Campbell, "The Effect of Acquiescence Response-Set upon Relationships among the F Scale, Ethnocentrism, and Intelligence, *Sociometry*, June, 1959, pp. 153–161; Richard Christie, Joan Havel, and Bernard Seidenberg, "Is the F Scale Irreversible?," *JASP*, Mar. 1958, pp. 143–159; Milton Rokeach, *The Open and Closed Mind*, Basic Books, 1960; and Ivan Steiner and Homer Johnson, "Authoritarianism and Conformity," *Sociometry*, Mar., 1963, pp. 21–34.

[41] Richard Christie, in Richard Christie and Marie Jahoda (eds.), *Studies in the Scope and Method of "The Authoritarian Personality,"* Free Press, 1954, p. 159.

---

have been carefully analyzed. A brief examination of this process of testing and criticism can be of value as a lesson in the way in which science grows, as well as a source of knowledge concerning the personality factors in prejudice.

Broadly speaking, there have been three types of commentary and interpretation: comments on the methodology of the original study, further research that has sought to refine the measurement of the variables used and to discover other variables that affect the extent of prejudice, and discussion of the adequacy of the theoretical assumptions. These approaches cannot be sharply distinguished, but they can be discussed separately.

SOME QUESTIONS OF METHOD

Confidence in the findings of *The Authoritarian Personality* is increased by the wide variety of research instruments used by the authors. The effort to measure several different levels of personality also strengthens the study. There were, however, serious methodological weaknesses. The authors paid little attention to questions of sampling; hence the extent to which their findings could be generalized to a wider group was unknown. Memories of childhood, which they obtained from many interviewees, are not necessarily accurate records of past events. Failure to control such variables as education and group membership sometimes led to unwarranted interpretations of the findings. If a person high on a scale of prejudice (ethnocentrism) admires generals and political figures and one low in prejudice admires scientists and writers, this is not necessarily evidence of a different outlook on life. If a prejudice scale is negatively correlated with education (as many studies have shown), the difference in selection of admired persons may be a function of the educational differences, not of the attitudes toward minorities. The study also faced serious problems in coding qualitative material. One respondent said: "Very, very fine man—intelligent, and understanding, excellent father, in every way." Is this to be classed as "conventionalized idealization" or "positive effect"?[42]

Studies of human behavior based on verbal responses often face serious problems of reliability; today's answer may not be tomorrow's answer, and one is not certain whether the difference represents a change in attitude or the crudity of the measuring device. Kendall reports, for example, the following shift on answers to one of *The Authoritarian Personality* "F-Scale" items ("Prison is too good for sex criminals; they should be publicly whipped or worse") :[43]

| May Interview | November Interview | | |
	Agree	Disagree	Total
Agree	155	58	213
Disagree	63	161	224
Total	218	219	437

If 28 percent give different answers after a six months interval, it is difficult to know what their "true" attitudes are.

A number of studies have indicated that the F scale is not unidimensional; it measures several things at the same time, which is to say that it does not measure any of them very well. If the compound of conventionality, rigidity of mind, cynicism, tendencies toward aggression and projection, and the like, is not stable—if the separate parts can vary independently of one another—one cannot measure them by a single scale nor think of them as a single personality characteristic. Factor analyses of the F scale have tended to show that six or seven distinct tendencies are represented.[44] A general fac-

tor may underlie them all; or there may be subtypes of authoritarianism. But more careful work on the measuring device is needed before we can speak with confidence.

Despite the seriousness of such methodological problems, they do not refute, in the judgment of most observers, the significance of personality research for the student of prejudice. They do alert us, however, to the need for tentativeness and for further research with more careful methods. Fortunately, a great deal of work is being done along this line. A sampling of the studies that have been made will indicate the way in which new variables have been introduced and the analysis of others refined.

VARIABLES RELATED TO AUTHORITARIANISM AND PREJUDICE

There are rather consistent findings with respect to the influence of age, intelligence, and education. Using an abbreviated scale based on *The Authoritarian Personality*, Mac-Kinnon and Center found, in general, in a sample of 460 drawn from Los Angeles County census tracts, that agreement with authoritarian items went up as age went up. One should not assume, however, that age *per se* is the central fact, or that age can be interpreted without reference to the social setting in which it is experienced. Persons of similar ages may share a view of the world based on common cultural norms; they may have experienced a decisive experience—war or depression—at a critical time in their lives. Moreover, MacKinnon and Centers found that their respondents under 30 had a higher proportion authoritarian in tendency (50 percent) than those between 30 and 40 (35 percent), with the proportion rising steadily thereafter (to 75 percent for those over 70). The somewhat less secure status of the youngest age group may be involved in their attitudes.[45]

[42] *Ibid.*, especially the chapter by H. H. Hyman and P. B. Sheatsley. Race of the investigator can also influence the results. See Gene F. Summers and Andre D. Hammonds, "Effect of Racial Characteristics of Investigator on Self-Enumerated Responses to a Negro Prejudice Scale," *SF*, June, 1966, pp. 515–518.

[43] Patricia Kendall, *Conflict and Mood*, The Free Press, 1954, pp. 6 ff.

[44] Santo Camilleri, "A Factor Analysis of the F-Scale," *SF*, May, 1959, pp. 316–323; Robert Krug, "An Analysis of the F Scale: I. Item Factor Analysis," and Robert Krug and K. E. Moyer, "An Analy-

sis of the F Scale: II. Relationship to Standardized Personality Inventories," *JSP*, Apr., 1961, pp. 285–291 and 293–301.

[45] William MacKinnon and Richard Centers, "Authoritarianism and Urban Stratification," *AJS*, May,

Numerous studies have indicated that authoritarian tendencies fall as intelligence goes up. Simple correlations are usually of the order of −.50 to −.60, falling to perhaps −.20 when education is held constant.[46] In early studies this relationship between the measures of intelligence and of authoritarianism was often disregarded. Since authoritarianism was believed to involve many cognitive aspects (rigidity, stereotypy, superstition), the disregard was unfortunate. One could not be certain whether the scores obtained were a result of the level of intelligence or of presumed authoritarian tendencies. Any measure of authoritarianism by such devices as the F scale must control for intelligence (compare only those persons with similar intelligence scores).[47] Even when this is done, one cannot know without developmental knowledge of the persons involved what the time sequence of the variables is. Childhood experiences that promote an authoritarian view of the world may repress intelligence (as measured by I.Q. tests), or low intelligence may predispose one to an authoritarian view of the world, or both.

The same need for control is strong in the study of the relationship of education to authoritarian tendencies. The evidence for a simple correlation is clear: as education goes up, authoritarianism goes down. One cannot draw from this fact, however, the easy conclusion that education reduces prejudice and promotes tolerance. MacKinnon and Centers found, for example, that 88 percent of those with the least education were in the top half on measures of authoritarianism, but only 20 percent of college graduates were in the top half.[48] This relationship may reflect the intelligence variable, or class, or selectivity. There is some evidence that those with

authoritarian inclinations are less likely to attend college[49] or to stay in college.[50] Even when controls are applied, however, by factor analysis or partial correlation, the relationship between education and tolerance holds up,[51] lending strong support to Angell's statement: "One could say that the well educated are active participants in a world broadened by modern communication, and that they are relatively secure in that world. It neither frightens or frustrates them. In contrast, those with little schooling are parochially oriented but not secure in their parochialism. They are vaguely aware of larger forces that they do not understand but which may bode them ill."[52]

Are authoritarian attitudes related to personal maladjustment? Evidence on this question is somewhat contradictory, varying with the measures of maladjustment being used. Mild neurotic tendencies seem to be only slightly or not at all related to prejudice.[53] More severe personality disturbances, however, as we have noted above, may be functionally related to intolerance. This does not mean that persons who are mentally ill necessarily exhibit authoritarian tendencies; but it may mean, as Jensen has observed, that those with extreme authoritarian tendencies are psychologically maladjusted. "The impression is that prejudiced, authoritarian persons have less well developed ego defenses and are thus more exposed and vulnerable to psychological stress, in the face of which they develop toward pessimism, cynicism, low morale . . . , and psychological isolation

---

1956, pp. 612–614; see also Robert Angell, "Preferences for Moral Norms in Three Problem Areas, *AJS*, May, 1962, pp. 650–660.

[46] Christie and Cook, *op. cit.*, p. 176.

[47] Frank Jacobson and Salomon Rettig, "Authoritarianism and Intelligence," *JSP*, Sept., 1959, pp. 213–219.

[48] MacKinnon and Centers, *op. cit.*, p. 615; see also C. H. Stember, *Education and Attitude Change*, Institute of Human Relations Press, 1961.

[49] Herbert Greenberg, C. Marvin, and B. Bivens, "Authoritarianism as a Variable in Motivation to Attend College," *JSP*, Feb., 1959, pp. 81–85.

[50] G. C. Stern, M. I. Stein, and B. S. Bloom, *Methods in Personality Assessment*, Free Press, 1956.

[51] Edward McDill, "Anomie, Authoritarianism, Prejudice, and Socio-Economic Status: An Attempt at Clarification," *SF*, Mar., 1961, pp. 239–245; John Photiadis and Jeanne Biggar, "Religiosity, Education, and Social Distance," *AJS*, May, 1962, pp. 666–672; and Angell, *op. cit.*

[52] Angell, *op. cit.*, p. 660.

[53] Mervin Freedman, Harold Webster and Nevitt Sanford, "A Study of Authoritarianism and Psychopathology," *JP*, Apr., 1956, pp. 315–322; and Norman Prentice, "Ethnic Attitudes, Neuroticism, and Culture," *JSP*, June, 1961 pp. 75–82.

. . . along with more primitive defenses of a compulsive, ritualistic, and schizoid nature. . . ."[54]

The origins of these functionally related tendencies are often sought in early family experiences. Harsh, restrictive, unloving parent-child relations are believed by many researchers to be the source of both intolerance and maladjustment. In tests and interviews with 126 young, middle-class mothers, Hart found a consistent relationship between authoritarian tendencies and the use of harsh training methods.[55] He did not, however, show how this pattern affected the children. Other studies have measured the relationship between the level of prejudice among students and the training methods of mothers, either as seen by the students[56] or as reported by the mothers themselves.[57] Although the results were not entirely consistent, there were several significant relationships between prejudice on the part of children and high scores by the mothers on dominance, possessiveness, and ignoring scales (as measured by the Shoben Parent Attitude Survey).

Such evidence, however, is scarcely conclusive. We shall discuss below the need for taking group membership into account. Perhaps parents who treat their children harshly also teach them prejudices—both results being the expression of group norms and not demonstrations of a functional connection between childtraining and prejudice. There is, moreover, direct evidence that intolerance is not necessarily linked to childhood experiences. In a longitudinal study of 63 working-class men, McCord, McCord, and Howard found no significant relationships between level of

tolerance and 11 measures of early family experiences.[58] In this lower-class sample, prejudice seems to be more closely related to group norms, to frustrating adult experiences, to level of education, or to contact with minorities than it is to punitive, harsh, and inconsistent childhood experiences. It would be foolish to overlook the effects of early training on tendencies toward authoritarianism; but it is equally foolish to exaggerate its importance or to fail to study it in the context of group variations in norms and of adult experiences.

A promising line of inquiry is the study of the interpersonal behavior of those high and those low in authoritarian tendencies. In a study of 234 students, Canning and Baker found that those who had rated high on an authoritarian measure were significantly more influenced by group pressure than those who measured low. The experiment involved the autokinetic effect—judgment of the stability or movement of a light (actually perfectly stationary) in a darkened room. When the small groups, not including those individuals being rated, were instructed to say that the light had moved, the mean estimate of movement increased more than 100 percent for the less authoritarian and more than 500 percent for the more authoritarian.[59] Martin Deutsch used a two-person game designed to discover how much a subject trusted his partner and how trustworthy the subject was. The game was designed to yield maximum gain when a trusting and an untrustworthy response were combined. Those subjects with high F scale scores were least trusting and least trustworthy, while those with low F scale scores tended to be trusting and trustworthy.[60] When Haythorn and his associates put persons of high authoritarian tendencies in small groups (to write a script for a brief movie scene), their pattern of in-

[54] A. R. Jensen, "Authoritarian Attitudes and Personality Maladjustment," *JASP*, May, 1957, p. 310.

[55] I. Hart, "Maternal Child-Rearing Practices and Authoritarian Ideology," *JASP*, Sept., 1957, pp. 232–237.

[56] S. L. Kates and L. N. Diab, "Authoritarian Ideology and Attitudes on Parent-Child Relationships," *JASP*, July, 1955, pp. 13–16.

[57] Sarah Dickens and Charles Hobart, "Paternal Dominance and Offspring Ethnocentrism," *JSP*, May, 1959, pp. 297–303. See also Ralph Epstein and S. S. Komorita, "Childhood Prejudice as a Function of Parental Ethnocentrism, Punitiveness and Outgroup Characteristics," *JPSP*, 1966, pp. 259–264.

[58] William McCord, Joan McCord, and Alan Howard, "Early Familial Experiences and Bigotry," *ASR*, Oct., 1960, pp. 717–722.

[59] Ray Canning and James Baker, "Effect of the Group on Authoritarian and Non-Authoritarian Persons," *AJS*, May, 1959, pp. 579–581.

[60] Martin Deutsch, "Trust, Trustworthiness, and the F Scale," *JASP*, 1960, pp. 138–141.

teraction, their leadership styles, their satisfaction with the experience were in many ways different from those in groups made up of persons low in authoritarianism. They conclude that the group "cultures" were to some degree shaped by the traits of the members.[61] This conclusion must be held lightly, however, because there was no control of social class and other variables. The results may come from lower-class and middle-class subcultures that have the effect of producing differences in both the authoritarian scores and in expected group-response patterns.[62]

THE STUDY OF NEW VARIABLES RELATED TO AUTHORITARIANISM

Although the original thesis of *The Authoritarian Personality* has received substantial support, it has been continuously qualified by the study of additional variables. Our interest is particularly in the search for variables that may explain the relationship between authoritarianism and prejudice better than (or along with) the presumed functional connection between them. Taking 29 items from the Berkeley prejudice scales, Sullivan and Adelson rewrote them to refer to "people" or "most people," instead of to Jews, Negroes, or other specific groups. Thus "Jews seem to prefer the most luxurious, extravagant, and sensual way of living," becomes "People seem to prefer the most luxurious, extravagant, and sensual way of living." Two hundred and twenty-one students at a midwestern university were given this revised M (for misanthropy) scale, along with a 20-

item E (ethnocentrism) scale. There was a correlation of .53 between the two. Thus prejudice is correlated, in these data, with a general misanthropy. It appears that for the antidemocratic person ". . . there may be no in-group other than the self."[63] How far this finding applies to persons other than the college students involved is not yet known, but the study suggests a need for further exploration.

Response Set as a Factor in Authoritarianism. Several writers have suggested that "response set" or a tendency toward acquiescence can account for part of what appears to be a strong relationship between an authoritarian outlook on life and prejudice. In the original F scale, all items were "agree" items. To get a low "authoritarian" score on an item, one needed to disagree with the statement. Bass reversed 28 statements on the original F scale to make what he labeled a G scale. Thus, "People can be divided into two distinct classes, the weak and the strong," became, "People cannot be divided into two distinct classes, the weak and the strong." Half of the F items and half of the G were then put into one test, and the remainder into another. Sixty-three students were given form 1, then form 2 two weeks later. Twenty-one students were given form 2 first and then form 1. By factor analysis, Bass found that one-fourth of the variance of the F scale could be accounted for by acquiescence. That is, the tendency to accept a positively stated item (however that tendency may be explained) accounted for a large part of the relationship between authoritarianism and prejudice.[64] A number of studies have replicated this finding[65] at levels of strength ranging from one-

---

[61] William Haythorn, Arthur Couch, Donald Haefner, Peter Langham, and L. F. Carter, "The Behavior of Authoritarian and Equalitarian Personalities in Groups," *HR*, 1956, pp. 57–74.

[62] For further studies of interpersonal judgments and behavior see Christie and Cook, *op. cit.*; Alan Roberts and Richard Jessor, "Authoritarianism, Punitiveness, and Perceived Social Status," *JASP*, May, 1958, pp. 311–314; John Thibaut and Henry Riecken, "Authoritarianism, Status, and the Communication of Aggression," *HR*, 1955, pp. 95–120; Herbert Schulberg, "Authoritarianism, Tendency to Agree, and Interpersonal Perception," *JASP*, July, 1961, pp. 101–108; Frederick Koenig and Morton King, Jr., "Cognitive Simplicity and Prejudice," *SF*, Mar., 1962, pp. 220–222.

[63] Patrick L. Sullivan and Joseph Adelson, "Ethnocentrism and Misanthropy," *JASP*, Apr., 1954, pp. 246–250.

[64] See Bernard Bass, "Authoritarianism or Acquiescence," *JASP*, Nov., 1955, pp. 616–623. In this publication, the amount of variance to be accounted for by acquiescence is noted to be .59 rather than .25. Samuel Messick and Douglas Jackson, however, have indicated an error in Bass's calculations. See "Authoritarianism or Acquiescence in Bass's Data," *JASP*, May, 1957, pp. 424–427. There is a reply by Bass.

[65] See Chapman and Campbell, *op. cit.*; also their "Response Set in the F Scale," *JASP*, Jan., 1957, pp.

quarter to three-quarters. When all items on a test of authoritarianism are worded positively, these studies suggest, a substantial part of the presumed authoritarian score derives from acquiescence—the tendency to say "I agree" to all questions, even opposites.

The interpretation of this finding, however, is difficult. The subjects are usually college students, with low to medium authoritarian scores and perhaps with less decisive opinions than they will have later. Some writers argue that acquiescence is part of authoritarianism in any event,[66] because both are associated with low ego-strength and conformity. In a valuable review of this problem, Christie, Havel, and Seidenberg note the great difficulty in producing a true reversal of the original questions in both a logical and a psychological sense. Are "familiarity does not breed contempt" or "we are bound to admire and respect a person if we get to know him well" true reversals of the common saying? On the basis of the study of eight samples they conclude that, although acquiescence plays some part in determining the scores on tests when questions are all stated in one way, acquiescence is not identical with authoritarianism.[67]

Attempts to eliminate the problem of ac-

quiescence from measures of authoritarianism are inadequate if the reverse items are not similar in content and if the tendency toward "yeasaying" is not balanced by the tendency toward "naysaying"—for there is a negative as well as a positive response set. These criteria are seldom met, however, so that combining positively and negatively worded items has not produced a thoroughly reliable and valid scale.[68] Berkowitz and Wolkon have attempted to reduce these difficulties by combining a positive and negative statement *within* each item. All answers, in such an arrangement, involve agreement, hence the problem of response set is eliminated. Respondents are asked, for example, to check one of the six positions with regard to a pair of items:

A. Astrology will never explain anything.
B. Some day it will probably be shown that astrology can explain a lot of things.
___I agree a great deal more with A than B.
___I agree somewhat more with A than B.
___I agree slightly more with A than B.
___I agree slightly more with B than A.
___I agree somewhat more with B than A.
___I agree a great deal more with B than A.[69]

This controls for the problem of acquiescence, but as the authors note the "forced choice" pattern may be affected by the fact that in half the pairs the negative item is given first, in the other half, the positive is given first. Order does seem to influence the results, since correlation between the two scores obtained by the different patterns vary from .24 to .54 in different versions and samples. And the larger problem of validity remains: Having measured re-

129–132; Marvin Shaw, "Some Correlates of Social Acquiescence," *JSP*, Oct., 1961, pp. 133–141; Marvin Zuckerman and James Norton, "Response Set and Content Factors in the California F Scale and the Parental Attitude Research Instrument," *JSP*, Apr., 1961, pp. 199–210; Eugene Gaier and Bernard Bass, "Regional Differences in Interrelations among Authoritarianism, Acquiescence, and Ethnocentrism," *JSP*, Feb., 1959, pp. 47–51; Dean Peabody, "Attitude Content and Agreement Set in Scales of Authoritarianism, Dogmatism, Anti-Semitism, and Economic Conservatism," *JASP*, July, 1961, pp. 1–11; Arthur Couch and Kenneth Keniston, "Yeasayers and Naysayers: Agreeing Response Set as a Personality Variable," *JASP*, Mar., 1960, pp. 151–174; and Dean Peabody, "Authoritarian Scales and Response Bias," *Psychological Bulletin*, 1966, pp. 11–23. Leslie G. Carr, "The Srole Items and Acquiescence," *ASR*, April, 1971, pp. 287–293) documents response set among Negro respondents also.

[66] N. L. Gage, George Leavitt, and George Stone, "The Psychological Meaning of Acquiescence Set for Authoritarianism," *JASP*, July, 1957, pp. 98–103.

[67] Christie, Havel, and Seidenberg, *op. cit.*; see also L. G. Rorer, "The Great Response-Style Myth," *Psychological Bulletin*, 1965, pp. 129–156, in which a generally critical approach is taken to studies of response bias.

[68] See Loren J. Chapman and R. Darrell Bock, "Components of Variance Due to Acquiescence and Content in the F Scale Measure of Authoritarianism," *Psychological Bulletin*, Sept., 1958, pp. 328–333; Robert Mogar, "Three Versions of the F Scale and Performance on the Semantic Differential," *JASP*, Mar., 1960, pp. 262–265; Norman Berkowitz and George Wolkon, "A Forced Choice Form of the F Scale—Free of Acquiescence Response Set," *Sociometry*, March, 1964, pp. 54–65; and Jonathan Cloud and Graham Vaughan, "Using Balanced Scales to Control Acquiescence," *Sociometry*, June, 1970, pp. 193–202.

[69] Berkowitz and Wolkon, *op. cit.*, p. 58.

sponses to these items, what does one know about the attitude universe from which they are drawn? Or, to apply an even more severe test of validity: What predictions to behavior can be made from measures obtained by a given scale?[70] In our view, such predictions will always be rough, regardless of the internal validity of a scale, until equivalent information about situations is introduced into the formulation.

Mental Rigidity as a Factor in Authoritarianism. One of the presumed characteristics of the prejudiced person is a general mental rigidity, an inflexibility of mind. In a well-known study closely associated with the Authoritarian Personality research, Rokeach tried to discover if the tendency toward ethnocentrism (categorical judgments in favor of one's own group) was associated with a general rigidity of mind. Having separated a group of University of California students into high and low ethnocentric groups on the basis of a standardized test, he asked them to do a series of "puzzles," in order to determine the degree to which they would rigidly pursue a complicated method that had been used in illustration, rather than adopt a simple solution. The puzzles were of the familiar variety: If you have 3 jars that hold, respectively, 31, 61, and 4 quarts, how can you measure out 22 quarts? Some of the puzzles could be solved only by a fairly complicated method, others could be solved by a simple procedure. When puzzles requiring complicated solutions were followed by several that could be done simply, Rokeach found that ethnocentric persons tended rigidly to continue to use the complicated method. The difference between those high and those low in ethnocentrism was statistically significant, seeming to demonstrate that ethnocentric individuals are more rigid in their approach to nonsocial as well as to social problems.[71]

Several recent studies, however, have shown that the relationship between rigidity and ethnocentrism is not a simple one. Jackson, Messick, and Solley found that rigidity in the jar test was correlated with score on a reverse F as well as on the original F scale (and also that there was a correlation of .35 between scores on the F and reverse-F scales). This study is not strictly comparable with Rokeach's, for the latter employed the E scale of the California research, but it indicates the need for studying "response set" and "acquiescence," as well as authoritarian tendencies, as variables related to rigidity. A person who gets a high reverse-F score is presumably low in authoritarianism. If he rigidly pursues complicated methods of solving the jar tests, this cannot be part of a syndrome which includes authoritarianism (in which he scores low), but shows a tendency to persist in an established way of doing things.[72]

Not finding the same relationship between rigidity and authoritarianism described by Rokeach, Brown looked for refinements in the meaning of rigid. With hundreds of subjects he had always failed to get a significant correlation between rigidity and authoritarianism (as measured by the California F scale). Were the differences in results due to differences in the atmosphere of the testing situation? Rokeach had made his test in a large lecture class; problems were given as a "test" in bluebooks. Brown had made his measurements in small laboratory groups. He suspected that the former situation created a strong ego-involving atmosphere and that the rigidity was ". . . a defensive, situationally dependent rigidity . . . ," not a generalized trait. To test this possibility, Brown gave the jar test to two matched groups. For the first group he created an ego-involving atmosphere, stressing the test as a measure of intelligence and motivation, cautioning the subjects repeatedly against looking at the test ahead of time. The experimenter was aloof; he dressed quite formally. The subjects wrote their names before they took the test. For the

[70] *Ibid.*, p. 65.

[71] Milton Rokeach, "Generalized Mental Rigidity as a Factor in Ethnocentrism," *JASP*, July, 1948, pp. 259–278.

[72] D. N. Jackson, S. J. Messick, and C. M. Solley, "How 'Rigid,' Is the 'Authoritarian,'" *JASP*, Jan., 1957, pp. 137–140.

Likelihood of Mental Rigidity As Measured by the Jar Test

Experimental Conditions	Tendencies		Studies
	Authoritarian	Nonauthoritarian	
Relaxed	no	no	Brown
Ego-involving	yes	no	Rokeach, Brown
Anxiety-producing	yes	yes	Maher

second group the experimenter created a relaxed atmosphere. He was dressed in sports clothes, treated the test casually, showed little interest in the results, and asked for the names of the subjects only at the end. The results confirmed his hypothesis. The correlation between the F scale (authoritarian) score and the jar test score was significantly higher for the ego-involved group than for the casual group. This does not indicate a lack of difference in rigidity between those high and those low in authoritarianism. But it does indicate the need for careful definition of rigidity and the recognition that results are affected by the situation, not simply by the personalities involved. Rokeach had defined rigidity as ". . . inability to restructure a field in which there are alternative solutions to a problem in order to solve the problem more efficiently." Brown prefers this definition, ". . . inability to restructure a field when a familiar structuring is perceived as warding off personal failure." Rigidity is not sluggishness of the nervous system; it is very sensitive to situational factors. When the authoritarian is in a relaxed setting, he solves the problems as easily as the equalitarian; when he senses a threat he clings to security.[73] Supporting this situational view, Maher found that he could promote rigidity of response in persons with equalitarian as well as authoritarian tendencies by creating a situation more laden with anxiety than Brown had designed. Where Brown created

a formal or austere atmosphere, Maher set up a punishment-reward situation by relating performance to marks in a course. Thus, he suggests, some anxiety may make those with authoritarian tendencies more rigid and much anxiety may make most or all persons more rigid.[74]

Such diverse findings must give us pause, not only about the presumed mental rigidity of those with authoritarian tendencies, but about the range of situational influences.[75] By putting some of the studies into a crude tendency-situation field model, we can emphasize the interactions involved (see table).

Knowledge of tendency or of condition alone could not have predicted the observed results. Their interaction was crucial.

Authoritarianism and Politics. Are certain kinds of political views and actions the logical and necessary expression of authoritarian tendencies? We think that the answer clearly is no. Psychodynamic and motivational influences are doubtless involved in the complex of causes leading to particular political beliefs and activities; but the same individual tendencies can lead to widely different political expressions, depending upon the setting; and persons whose tendencies are quite different can support the same political process.

The importance of combining measures of character with measures of situational influence has been emphasized in recent years by

[73] See R. W. Brown, *op. cit.*; see also E. E. Levitt and S. L. Zelen, "The Validity of the Einstellung Test as a Measure of Rigidity," *JASP*, Oct., 1953, pp. 573–580; and Nora C. Forster, W. E. Vinacke, and J. M. Digman, "Flexibility and Rigidity in a Variety of Problem Situations," *JASP*, Mar., 1955, pp. 211–216.

[74] Brendan Maher, "Personality, Problem Solving, and the Einstellung Effect," *JASP*, Jan., 1957, pp. 70–74; see also Theodore Million, "Authoritarianism, Intolerance of Ambiguity, and Rigidity under Ego- and Task-Involving Conditions," *JASP*, July, 1957, pp. 29–33.
[75] For a detailed methodological critique, see E. Levitt and M. Zuckerman, "The Water Jar Test Revisited: The Replication of a Review," *Psychological Reports*, 1959, pp. 365–380.

research in political science. As political science has become more "behavioral" in its approach, it has tended to recapitulate some of the theoretical stages exhibited by psychology and sociology in dealing with related issues. Much of the early work was strongly Freudian: political behavior expressed unconscious hostilities and hidden ambivalences of individuals,[76] ". . . private motives are displaced onto a public object and rationalized in terms of public interest."[77] This is basically the approach of the authors of *The Authoritarian Personality* when they deal with politics and of McClosky, in his study of the sources of conservatism.[78] Few would deny the importance of traditional training, of interests, of location in the social structure. These factors are sometimes treated quite lightly, however, while childhood sexual conflicts, inner drives and unclear self-images, love of life versus attraction to the mechanical and dead—factors we have seen referred to recently—are given major attention.[79]

We have no doubt that individual tendencies, including unconscious motivations, are involved in the creation of authoritarian or nonauthoritarian politics. There is now substantial literature dealing with "political socialization" that examines many of the sources of these tendencies.[80] The necessary next stage, however, is to explore the way in which these tendencies combine with various environments to produce the observed political outcomes. The need for such

a combination is now widely recognized and is beginning to be reflected in research.[81] We can no longer be content with formulations that affirm a direct and unqualified relationship between authoritarianism and certain kinds of political behavior. Assuming valid measures of authoritarian tendencies and reliable measures of correlation with particular political outcomes, we must elaborate the relationship, in the sense in which Lazarsfeld uses the term, by introducing numerous other test variables. Various simple forms of elaboration might be sketched in the following ways:

Authoritarianism $\longrightarrow$ Politics $\times$ (.70)

(Read this to mean: A high level of authoritarianism is strongly correlated [.70] with a given political belief or activity.)
If this pattern were "specified" it might read:

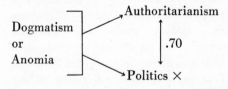

Or the relationship could be "explained" by introducing a preceding variable:

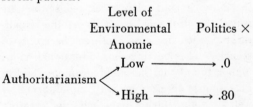

"Interpretation" might produce still a different pattern:

$$\begin{array}{c} \text{Level of} \\ \text{Environmental} \quad \text{Politics} \times \\ \text{Anomie} \end{array}$$

Authoritarianism $\Big\langle$
Low $\longrightarrow$ .0
High $\longrightarrow$ .80

---

[76] See Harold Lasswell, *Psychopathology and Politics,* Univ. of Chicago Press, 1930.

[77] M. Brewster Smith, "Opinions, Personality, and Political Behavior," *American Political Science Review,*" Mar. 1958, p. 3.

[78] Herbert McClosky, "Conservatism and Personality," *American Political Science Review,* Mar., 1968, pp. 27–45. See also Herbert McClosky and John H. Schaar, "Psychological Dimensions of Anomy," *ASR,* Feb., 1965, pp. 14–40.

[79] See *The New York Times,* July 14, 1968, p. 51; *Newsweek,* Sept. 15, 1969, pp. 25–26.

[80] See, for example, Richard Dawson and Kenneth Prewitt, *Aspects of Political Socialization,* Little, Brown, 1969; Robert Lane, "Fathers and Sons: Foundations of Political Belief," *ASR,* Aug., 1959, pp. 502–511; Herbert Hyman, *Political Socialization: A Study in the Psychology of Political Behavior,* Free Press, 1959; Kenneth Langton, *Political Socialization,* Oxford, 1969.

[81] See, for example, David Easton, *A System Analysis of Political Life,* Wiley, 1965; Fred Greenstein, "Personality and Political Socialization: The Theories of Authoritarian and Democratic Character," *Annals,* 1965, pp. 81–95; Fred Greenstein, "The Impact of Personality on Politics; An Attempt to Clear Away Underbrush," *American Political Science Review,* Sept., 1967, pp. 629–641; M. Brewster Smith, "A Map for the Analysis of Personality and Politics," *JSI,* July, 1968, pp. 15–28.

Dogmatism vs. Authoritarianism. One of the most persistent criticisms of *The Authoritarian Personality* has dealt with its tendency to equate political authoritarian tendencies with a right-wing political philosophy and to assume that a person with a general threat-orientation to the world expressed this characteristic by racial and ethnic prejudices. Are there not left-wing authoritarians? Might not the person who believes the world is hostile and threatening demonstrate this in ways other than prejudice? There are two ways one can attempt to answer these questions: One can look for a different personality tendency, probably a more general one, than authoritarianism to explain the range of observations that the original thesis could not explain. Or one can introduce group and situational factors to seek to discover how they affect behavior, as we shall do below. In a major series of studies Rokeach has undertaken the former approach. He holds that authoritarianism as described by the Berkeley studies is a subspecies of a more general personality syndrome, which he labels dogmatism. Although he introduces more situational and field influences than did the authors of *The Authoritarian Personality*,[82] his theory is still primarily concerned with the personality level.

Dogmatism, in Rokeach's formulation is "(a) a relatively closed cognitive organization of beliefs and disbeliefs about reality, (b) organized around a central set of beliefs about absolute authority which, in turn, (c) provide a framework for patterns of intolerance and qualified tolerance toward others."[83] Thus Rokeach starts with a person's belief system as a central fact. His "dogmatism scale" is an attempt to devise a measuring instrument on which bigots of the left, center, and right will get the same score. This is an expression of his contention that the *structure* of a belief system (a rigid, closed structure, for example) is distinct from its *content*. One could, presumably, be dogmatically prejudiced against other races or dogmatically tolerant. The rigid structure does not imply a specific content. Rokeach seeks further to study the *function* of dogmatic belief systems (and all belief systems), proposing that they are defenses against threat and attempts to satisfy the need to know the world one lives in. Dogmatism is correlated with authoritarianism, as measured by the F scale, but is factorially discriminable.[84]

A major result of this approach to dogmatism is the proposition that the dogmatic person is much more likely to reject the person who disagrees with him than he is to reject persons because of their group identities—their race or ethnic group, for example. In an ingenious series of studies, Rokeach and others have sought to put this proposition to the test. They have presented evidence to show that when persons are confronted with a choice between a person of different race or ethnic group who agrees with them on a major belief and a person of their own race or ethnic group who disagrees with them on a major belief, a large majority will feel more friendly toward the former.[85] Prejudice against Negroes, according to this view, is importantly based for most people, not on categorical racial views, but on the perception of the Negro as one who disagrees with or threatens one's belief system.

A study of 630 ninth-graders in a New England suburb mainly supports Rokeach's theory. Stein found similarity or dissimilarity of beliefs to be primary determinants of attitudes of white gentiles toward Negroes and Jews.[86] Race difference also influenced

[82] See *The Open and Closed Mind*, chaps. 10 and 12; and also his *Beliefs, Attitudes and Values*, Jossey-Bass, 1967, chap. 3.

[83] Milton Rokeach, "Political and Religious Dogmatism: An Alternative to the Authoritarian Personality," *Psychological Monographs*, 1956, p. 3.

[84] Fred Kerlinger and Milton Rokeach, "The Factorial Nature of the F and D Scales, *JPSP*, Oct., 1966, pp. 391–399. For short forms of the Dogmatism scale, see V. C. Troldahl and F. A. Powell, "A Short-Form Dogmatism Scale for Use in Field Studies," *SF*, Dec., 1965, pp. 211–214.

[85] See, for example, Chap. 7 of *The Open and Closed Mind*.

[86] David Stein, "The Influence of Belief Systems on Inter-personal Preference: A Validation of Rokeach's Theory of Prejudice," *Psychological Monographs: General and Applied*, No. 8, 1966, pp. 1–29.

the results, but explained less of the variance than did belief. If knowledge of the beliefs of others, however, is not fully available, assumptions regarding the beliefs of one's own group, institutional patterns, and individual tendencies other than belief will strongly affect the results. Belief congruence, in other words, requires support. "If people of different races encounter one another under conditions favoring the perception of belief congruence (as, for example, in equal-status contacts) then racial prejudice should be substantially reduced."[87]

Additional studies of belief congruence have helped to specify the conditions under which it is strong or weak in its influence on prejudice. Whether or not the perception that a person of another race holds the same beliefs will govern one's attitudes towards that person depends upon the issue involved (interactions of a more personal or intimate source may be more affected by race than belief), other individual perceptions and attitudes (some persons are more sensitive to race than others), the responses of others to the situation (regional differences indicating greater or lesser support for attitudes based on belief congruence), and doubtless other variables. Reference to a few of the many studies of this question will illustrate the interplay of belief and other factors. Smith, Williams, and Willis found that belief congruence was more important than race among five northern and border groups that they studied, but race was somewhat more important with a sample from Louisiana. To say that race was more important is not to say that belief was unimportant: even in the group for which race was a powerful symbol, belief congruence significantly influenced the results.[88] There was one interaction effect between race and belief: Among the three Negro samples, friendship choices for other Negroes who disagreed in belief

were consistently lower than choices for Whites who disagreed. Although Triandis and his associates have, in a series of papers, supported the idea that perceived racial similarity or difference governs response more than perceived belief similarity or difference, they have not denied the importance of the belief factor, and have recently suggested that belief may be the more influencial in nonintimate circumstances.[89]

One would expect, from theories of Heider, Newcomb, and others, that most persons would be attracted to those who hold similar values and attitudes and, in the absence of knowledge of strangers' values and attitudes, would attribute one's own to strangers who belong to preferred groups and conflicting values and attitudes to those belonging to disliked groups.[90] Byrne and Wong found support for this view in a study of 54 University of Texas students. They were divided into high and low categories on a desegregation scale and then asked, several weeks later by a different experimenter, to judge the attitudes of several strangers (shown in pictures) on such topics as politics, religion, and sexual norms. Prejudiced judges believed Negroes were more dissimilar from themselves than were white strangers. Prejudiced judges believed Negroes were more dissimilar than did the nonprejudiced judges.[91] What happens if the strangers are identified with certain attitudes? Classifying 120 students into high and low categories on the Desegregation scale, Byrne and Wong found that on a "Work Partner scale" (how would you like

---

[87] David Stein, Jane Smith, and M. Brewster Smith, "Race and Belief: An Open and Shut Case," *JPSP*, Apr., 1965, p. 289.

[88] Carole Smith, Lev Williams, and Richard Willis, "Race, Sex, and Belief as Determinants of Friendship Acceptance," *JPSP*, Feb., 1967, pp. 127–137.

[89] See Harry Triandis and Earl Davis, "Race and Belief as Determinants of Behavioral Intentions," *JPSP*, Nov., 1965, pp. 715–725. See also Harry Triandis and W. D. Loh, "Race, Status, Quality of Spoken English, and Opinions about Civil Rights as Determinants of Interpersonal Attitudes," *JPSP*, Apr., 1966, pp. 468–472; and Harry Triandis, Earl Davis, and Shin-Ichi Takezawa, "Some Determinants of Social Distance Among American, German, and Japanese Students," *JPSP*, Oct., 1965, pp. 540–551.

[90] Although not for our purposes here, in most contexts, the distinction between values and attitudes is important. See Milton Rokeach, "The Role of Values in Public Opinion Research, *POQ*, Winter, 1968–1969, pp. 547–559; and his *Beliefs, Attitudes, and Values, op. cit.*

[91] Byrne and Wong, *op. cit.*, pp. 246–248.

to work with this student in an experiment?) prejudiced persons rated agreeing Whites higher than agreeing Negroes, but they rated disagreeing Whites lower than disagreeing Negroes. Moreover, the rating of agreeing Negroes, while lower than that of Whites, was still on the positive side of the scale.[92] Thus their work lends support to Rokeach's emphasis on the importance of shared belief.

This is an important avenue of research; but it requires careful examination. The problem of validity looms large, as Rokeach notes. If a southerner says, "I like Negroes who know their place" (i.e., I have nothing against their race so long as they share my belief), is this not part of a verbal culture that may tell us little about other kinds of behavior than verbal? At the least there is something paradoxical about the idea that a person is belief oriented, not race oriented, if he responds favorably to a Negro who accepts his prejudices against Negroes. There is no reason to doubt that belief orientation plays an important part in the behavior of most persons, that race is the definitive criterion in all situations for few, that many "prejudiced" persons will nevertheless prefer a Negro Christian or American to a white atheist or Communist. But the salience of the choices is strongly affected by the wording of questions;[93] and perhaps by response-set (on his Dogmatism scale, Rokeach wrote all questions in such a way that an affirmative answer yielded a high dogmatism score).[94] What we need now are careful observations of behavior outside the laboratory and beyond the pencil-and-paper test that will indicate for whom, and under what conditions, belief systems will override the influence of categorical judgement of groups. Under what conditions, for example, does a white businessman see a Negro businessman as a businessman? To answer such a question requires the introduction of the kind of situational and group variables that we shall comment on below. *Anomie, Anomia, and Prejudice.* Another line of research explores a factor that was implied—but not explicitly developed—in earlier studies of the highly prejudiced person. Drawing on a long interest in sociology in the concept of "anomie" or normlessness, Srole hypothesized that this well might be related to the tendency toward prejudice and the rejection of out-groups. There is a vast literature relating anomie, which is a sign of lack of consensus in society, to a personal sense of isolation, to political movements, of both right and left, to many of the developments in modern religions—in fact to almost every aspect of life today.[95] Many different responses may be seen as functionally alternative ways of attempting to deal with "the breakdown of the individual's sense of attachment to society" (to use MacIver's phrase). May not our knowledge of prejudice be increased by studying it in this same context? A sample of 401 white, native-born adults in an eastern city were interviewed and asked questions from three different scales. Five questions and their spontaneous comments measured the degree of racial and religious prejudice; five questions, in revised form, were drawn from the Berkeley F scale to measure authoritarian tendencies; and five question were devised to measure feelings of anomia or isolation from others (thought of as the individual counterpart of anomie as a group fact).

[92] *Ibid.*, pp. 248–252.

[93] See Harry Triandis, "A Note on Rokeach's Theory of Prejudice" and Milton Rokeach, "Belief versus Race as Determinants of Social Distance," *JASP*, Jan. 1961, pp. 184–186 and 187–188.

[94] For Rokeach's explanation, see *The Open and Closed Mind*, pp. 405–417; for a critique, see Edward Lichtenstein, Robert Quinn, and Gerald Hover, "Dogmatism and Acquiescent Response Set," *JASP*, Nov., 1961, pp. 636–638.

[95] Unfortunately, key terms are used in widely different ways in this literature. Unless we are quoting, we shall always use "anomie" as a term to refer to a group property, either a gap between the cultural norms and the structured opportunities for fulfilling those norms, as in Merton's definition, or as a quality of a social situation in which there is a low level of agreement on means and ends. Anomia, on the other hand, or more satisfactorily alienation, is a quality of individuals. It has several facets that are beginning to be identified. For an attempt to clarify these individual and group dimensions, see Yinger, *op. cit.*, chap. 9. See also Robert Merton, *Social Theory and Social Structure*, Free Press, rev. ed., 1957, chaps. 4 and 5; and Melvin Seeman, "On the Meaning of Alienation," *ASR*, 1959, pp. 783–791.

The degree of anomia was measured by asking respondents the extent to which they agreed with such statements as these: "There's little use writing to public officials because often they aren't really interested in the problems of the average man." "These days a person doesn't really know whom he can count on." There was a significant correlation between both authoritarianism and anomia and the scores on the prejudice scale. By means of partial correlation, Srole was able to discover the degree to which each of the former was *independently* correlated with the prejudice score, that is, the degree to which authoritarianism was correlated with prejudice when the effect of anomia was held constant, and the degree to which anomia was correlated with prejudice when the effect of authoritarianism was held constant. The partial correlation of anomia and prejudice was .35; that of authoritarianism and prejudice, .12. For the sample studied and with the scales used, it appears that the sense of isolation was more closely associated with antiminority views than was authoritarianism.[96]

Using the same five-item anomia and authoritarianism scales and a ten-item ethnocentrism scale from the Berkeley studies, Roberts and Rokeach obtained somewhat different results than Srole did. With a sample of 86 adults, they found a correlation of .53 between authoritarianism and ethnocentrism when anomia was held constant, and a correlation of .37 between anomia and ethnocentrism when authoritarianism was held constant. Since this study is not an exact replication of Srole's, we cannot know the degree to which differences in samples, in the scales used, in the scoring methods, or other factors affected the results. Nevertheless together they establish the tentative thesis that the prejudiced person is likely to be one who feels isolated and alone.[97]

In the last few years a number of additional studies have sought to measure the extent of anomia in various groups and to measure its relationship to prejudice and authoritarianism. Unhappily, their results are not wholly consistent. McDill, in a study of samples drawn from three census tracts in Nashville (n = 266) found that the correlation between anomia and prejudice was .35 when authoritarianism was controlled and the correlation between authoritarianism and prejudice was .38 when anomia was controlled—a situation midway between those found by Srole and Roberts and Rokeach. Factor analysis revealed that these three tendencies were quite closely interrelated, designating, in McDill's judgment, an underlying dimension that can be thought of as a negative *Weltanschauung*: Persons who have strong feelings of anomia, of isolation and powerlessness, are likely also to hold strong intergroup prejudices and respond to others in a hostile and power-oriented way.[98] This interpretation is close to that of the authors of *The Authoritarian Personality*.

Hamblin secured somewhat different results in a factor analysis of the responses of a quota sample of 100 white adults in the St. Louis metropolitan area. Although most of the nine variables that he measured showed substantial relationship with the tendency to discriminate when measured by simple correlation, only three variables proved to be important when analyzed by multiple-regression correlation: fear of equal-status competition, family pressures to discriminate, and friends' pressures to discriminate together explained 65 percent of the variance. If one knew these three things about a person he could predict quite accurately his discrimination score. The other six variables added little. Even a little improvement, however, is desirable; and

[96] Leo Srole, "Social Integration and Certain Corollaries: "An Exploratory Study," *ASR*, Dec., 1956, pp. 709–716.

[97] A. H. Roberts and Milton Rokeach, "Anomie, Authoritarianism, and Prejudice: A Replication," *AJS*, Jan., 1956, pp. 355–358; see also letters to the editor by Srole and Rokeach, indicating differences of interpretation, *AJS*, July, 1956, pp. 63–67. A more recent study, using a sample of college and university students, supports the Roberts-Rokeach findings; but the authors note methodological problems in this whole line of research. See Kenneth Lutterman and Russell Middleton, "Authoritarianism, Anomia, and Prejudice," *SF*, June, 1970, pp. 485–492.

[98] McDill, *op. cit.*

Hamblin found that knowledge of anomia scores and authoritarian scores aided prediction. If the full sample is divided into three groups—those low, medium, and high in anomia—the relationship between discrimination and parental discrimination goes up (from .68 to .73 to .83). Perhaps for those persons who feel highly anomic, parental pressure is particularly important. Somewhat strangely there is a tendency toward the opposite relationship with friends' pressure: the more anomic individuals are less likely to show a close correlation between discrimination and pressure from friends. Authoritarianism also affects the relationship between the three primary variables indicated above and the tendency to discriminate. Those low in authoritarianism, for example, resist friends' pressure more than do those high in authoritarianism.[99]

What do such diverse facts mean? Are variations in result due to different samples, different measuring instruments, different variables controlled? One must speak with caution, but these points seem valid: There is some tendency for feelings of anomia and authoritarianism to be found together; they are probably functionally interconnected in the life of a person. Both are often related to prejudice and the tendency to discriminate, *but in an indirect way*. Their influence is mediated through the interpretations of family and friends and doubtless other group definitions. To try to measure the influence of anomia and authoritarianism as personal tendencies without reference to the situation in which they are expressed and the groups to which one belongs (as several of the studies reported above tried to do) is to leave important determining variables uncontrolled. Simple or multiple correlations yield good prediction only if these other variables remain constant. Since they do not, in fact, remain constant, outside influences must be brought into the analysis.

This requires a major restatement of the thesis of *The Authoritarian Personality* and the follow-up studies that qualified and refined its interpretation. To that restatement we now turn.

SITUATIONAL AND GROUP INFLUENCES ON PREJUDICE

By way of summary of our examination of the "personality" approach to prejudice and our theoretical criticism of *The Authoritarian Personality*, we shall discuss three related ideas: (1) The approach would benefit from the use of the concept of "functional alternatives." (2) It is insufficiently aware of subcultural and group factors in prejudice. (3) It fails to give adequate attention to situational influences which affect the likelihood that prejudice will be translated into discrimination. These weaknesses stem from what, in our view, is an inadequate theory of personality—a theory that emphasizes traits, not process and interaction, a theory that isolates the individual as the unit of analysis, when what is needed is a series of concepts that functionally interrelate the individual and the situation of which he is a part.

(1) The person who is "ego alien," insecure, suffering from feelings of anomia and powerlessness may, as the authors of *The Authoritarian Personality* indicate, express hostility and prejudice toward minority groups and support fascistic types of totalitarian political movements. They may, however, express their insecurities and seek to resolve their doubts in other ways. What the functional alternatives are for a given individual depends upon his total situation. Shils has well argued that in certain circumstances the "authoritarian" may support the "radical left" not the "reactionary right"—indeed, the whole picture of a simple right-left continuum is inadequate, for the two extremes share a great deal in common. The Fascist who says that Jews control everything and the Communist who contends that big business has absolute power express views that are concretely very different.

[99] Robert Hamblin, "The Dynamics of Racial Discrimination," *SP*, Fall, 1962, pp. 103–121. For other studies making use of the concept of anomia see Photiadis and Biggar, *op. cit.*; Angell, *op. cit.*, Lewis Killian and Charles Grigg, "Urbanism, Race, and Anomia," *AJS*, May, 1962, pp. 661–665.

"Yet looked at from another point of view, they are strikingly similar. Both aver that a small group has with doubtful legitimacy concentrated the power of the country in their hands."[100] They may also share an extreme hostility toward out-groups, submissiveness in in-groups, the tendency toward all-or-none judgments, the vision of the world as a realm of conflict.[101] Some religious movements may be interpreted in part in these same terms. Even some aspects of anti-authoritarian sentiments and organizations can be interpreted as manifestations of hostility and ego alienation. Which expressions of the inner insecurity will be made depends upon the whole range of values and motives of the individual and on the surrounding social situation.

(2) Before one can explain antiminority feelings in terms of a harsh, capricious, and unloving childhood, he needs to be aware of group structure and of variation in values among the "subcultures" of a society. We shall examine the social and cultural aspects of prejudice in detail in the next two chapters, but a brief statement here may help us to see more accurately the way in which personality tendencies interact with other influences. If residents of Mississippi have a higher anti-Negro score than those of Minnesota, this does not prove that they are more "authoritarian"—more intolerant of ambiguity, more cynical, more rigid, less self-accepting. It may be that they simply express different cultural influences. Allen Williams found that authoritarian scores were highest in the South, as were scores on a measure of discriminatory attitudes. Without independent evidence on individual psychodynamic qualities, however, it seems reasonable to conclude from his data that the authoritarianism being measured was, to an important degree, the expression of regional or subcultural values.[102]

Differences in agreement with the idea that there are two different kinds of people in the world, the weak and the strong, may simply indicate differences in actual experience. As Christie says:

Anyone familiar with lower socio-economic groupings can scarcely be unaware of the fact that there is realistic justification for their view that the world is indeed jungle-like and capricious. They have no relatives or friends with the power to intercede successfully when they are rightly or wrongly accused of legal offenses. . . . The acceptance of an item referring to people prying into personal affairs may reflect paranoid tendencies among middle-class respondents; it may be reality based among lower-class individuals who are the first to be questioned by police, social workers, and other functionaries of the social structure.[103]

Before one draws personality conclusions from the tendency of one person to select General MacArthur as a hero, another to choose Bertrand Russell, he should be aware of any educational differences in the respondents. MacKinnon and Centers found that authoritarianism varied with age, with social status, with income, with education.[104] Differences in the realities of the situation, in cultural values, in role, in the ways different groups use language and respond to the testing process, and other variables are involved. All of this is not to say that deeply-lying personal insecurity, frustration, guilt, and diffuse hostility are not involved in the origins of prejudice. It is to say that before the extent of these personality factors can be measured, other variables must be controlled. To disregard group membership is to permit all sorts of spurious factors to obscure the actual relationships on the personality level. One might sketch the research needs in an overly simplified way, using only a few variables and dichotomizing those for purposes of brevity; such a scheme is shown in the accompanying tabulation (Figure 6).

With this scheme the research task would be to compare the eight subgroups under A with their matching subgroups under B.

---

[100] E. A. Shils, in Christie and Jahoda, *op. cit.*, p. 32.

[101] *Ibid.*, pp. 24–29; and Eric Hoffer, *The True Believer*, Harper & Row, 1951.

[102] J. Allen Williams, Jr., "Regional Differences in Authoritarianism," *SF*, Dec., 1966, pp. 273–277.

[103] Richard Christie in Christie and Jahoda (eds.), *op. cit.*, p. 175.

[104] MacKinnon and Centers, *op. cit.*

Figure 6 / Design for a Four-Variable Study

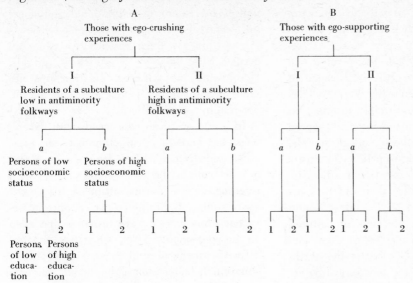

Since they would be "alike" in subculture, socioeconomic status, and educational level, any differences that continued between A and B could more confidently (but not, of course, in this limited design, with great confidence) be attributed to the personality-forming conditions that were the focus of the study. Lacking this, we must hold tentatively to any generalizations concerning personality factors in prejudice.

Stewart and Hoult have made the interesting suggestion that the level of authoritarianism expressed by an individual is negatively correlated with the number of social roles he has mastered. They note that many studies have found high levels of authoritarianism among (1) the less well educated, (2) the aged, (3) the rural, (4) members of disadvantaged minorities, (5) the more dogmatic religious organizations, (6) lower socio-economic strata, (7) social isolates, and (8) those who have been reared in an authoritarian family environment.[105] They believe that a scientifically more parsimonious explanation of the similarity among such diverse groups than the psychoanalytic emphasis on early

family environment, on which these groups vary widely, is an emphasis on their common poverty in role-taking ability. Their perspectives are limited by this fact; when they meet new situations they are confronted with interpersonal failure and thus tend to cling to the familiar; poorly trained in "taking the role of the other," they cannot well understand or sympathize with members of other groups.[106] Until this proposition is submitted to formal test, we can only say that it suggests a promising line of inquiry. We would add that it seems to pose an unnecessarily sharp conflict with the personality approach to authoritarianism, for the level of role-playing skill can be a function of early conditioning, of self-confidence and anxiety, as well as of structural conditions shared by the members of groups.

In the last several years scores of studies have documented the variations in levels of prejudice and authoritarianism by group membership and social category. It is essential that one take account of nationality, region, social class, religion, and other groups, with their varying norms, before one tries to assess the influence of personality dynamics. The F-scale scores of Arab students in the United States are high,

[105] Don Stewart and Thomas Hoult, "A Social-Psychological Theory of the Authoritarian Personality," *AJS*, Nov., p. 277.

[106] *Ibid.*, pp. 274–279.

by American standards;[107] levels of prejudice in South Africa vary by group membership;[108] regional differences in the United
States are large;[109] prejudice varies by religion;[110] and by class.[111] Evidence of group
variation does not refute the importance of
personality dynamics in affecting the level
of prejudice, but it calls forcibly to attention
the influence of group norms and shared
experience. For a southern college sample,
Rhyne found that "a rigorously sociologistic
approach" led to better prediction of variation in levels of prejudice than did the personality approach.[112] And Pettigrew found
that ". . . females, the 'carriers of culture,'
are significantly more anti-Negro than men
in the southern sample but *not* in the northern sample,"[113] a finding more readily accounted for by a cultural than a personality
explanation.

In citing these facts we do not intend to
dismiss the thesis that individuals vary in
their tendencies toward prejudice and discrimination. Once group facts are taken into
account, the range of tendencies within
groups requires careful attention.

Interactions of Situation and Tendency. We
have already, at various points, introduced
the third element in our evaluation of the
personality approach to prejudice; but here
we shall focus more explicitly on it. Group
norms and individual tendencies are not behavior. We can indicate their importance

to a larger theory of prejudice and discrimination by examining situational influences
on behavior. Thinking of personality as
process, not as fixed essence, we are concerned with the way in which it unfolds.
Here again the self-other relationships are
vital to a theory of personality and an understanding of prejudice.

In part, we are concerned with re-em-
phasizing here the distinction between prejudice and discrimination. How a person will
behave cannot be understood solely with
reference to his internal attitudes, his verbal
expressions of prejudice or nonprejudice.
In part, however, we are insisting that even
on the personality level, when one is concerned with the prejudices of the individual,
situational factors must be taken into account. There is now widespread if not universal agreement that collective behavior in
intergroup relations cannot be explained by
what is "in" individuals. Men are role-playing creatures; they act in structured situations; to an important degree they behave
in terms of their obligations and group-
defined interests. As Shils emphasizes, only
by ability to inhibit many tendencies can
men live in societies. We shall cite some of
the evidence for this point of view below.
There is less agreement—yet we think the
point is vital—that personality itself may be
thought of in interactional terms. A person
"is" what he "does." To hypothesize some
"essence" previous to the doing is to compli-
cate analysis and make prediction of behavior more difficult.

This point of view does not make the individual a wholly malleable agent of the situation. It is equally inappropriate to
hypothesize some fixed structure for the
situation (patterns of roles, norms, group
interests) as the determining factor in behavior. Situations must also be defined "in
process."

Some of these problems are illustrated
in this statement by Adorno and his associates:

Although personality is a product of the social
environment of the past, it is not, once it has
developed, a mere object of the contemporary

[107] Lutfy Diab, "Authoritarianism and Prejudice in
Near-Eastern Students Attending American Universities," *JSP*, Sept., 1959, pp. 175–187.

[108] Thomas Pettigrew, "Personality and Sociocultural Factors in Intergroup Attitudes: A Cross-National Comparison," *JCR*, Mar., 1958, pp. 29–42.

[109] Thomas Pettigrew, "Regional Differences in
Anti-Negro Prejudice," *JASP*, July, 1959, pp. 28–36;
Herbert Greenberg and Don Fare, "An Investigation
of Several Variables as Determinants of Authoritarianism," *JSP*, Feb., 1959, pp. 105–111.

[110] See Chap. 17.

[111] See Chap. 4; for other studies of group variation, see J. G. Kelly, J. E. Ferson, and W. H.
Holtzman, "The Measurement of Attitudes Toward
the Negro in the South," *JSP*, Nov., 1958, pp. 305–
317; and Edwin H. Rhyne, "Racial Prejudice and
Personality Scales: An Alternative Approach," *SF*,
Oct., 1962, pp. 44–53.

[112] *Ibid.*

[113] Pettigrew, "Personality and Sociocultural Factors in Intergroup Conflict," p. 38.

environment. What has developed is a *structure* within the individual, something which is capable of self-initiated action upon the social environment and of selection with respect to varied impinging stimuli, something which though always modifiable is frequently very resistant to fundamental change. This conception is necessary to explain consistency of behavior in widely varying situations, to explain the persistence of ideological trends in the face of contradicting facts and radically altered social conditions, to explain why people in the same sociological situation have different or even conflicting views on social issues, and why it is that people whose behavior has been changed through psychological manipulation lapse into their old ways as soon as the agencies of manipulation are removed.[114]

Insofar as this statement emphasizes the need for taking account of personal tendency, it is helpful. It fails to note, however, that we must explain inconsistency as well as consistency (being tolerant of Negroes in one's union but not in one's neighborhood); that an adequate theory must account for changes in ideological trends as well as persistence (many navy officers dedicated to segregation have reversed their judgment on an integrated ship); that one must note that persons in the same sociological situation often *do* have similar views (and what appears to be the "same" situation often proves, on close study, to be different constellations of group influences); and finally, that people do not always lapse into their old ways when influencing agencies are removed, and if they do, it may well be because they return to the old pattern of situations.

In our use of the concept, personality is what personality does; and the doing varies with how a situation is defined, the reference group with which one identifies at the moment, the sanctions and rewards in a given setting, the roles into which one is cast, and the range of tendencies brought by the individual. Many of the problems connected with the development of an adequate theory to deal with tendency, situation, and be-

havior are revealed in discussions of the concept "attitude." We shall not review the extensive literature dealing with the concept, but will develop here, in a series of statements for our own usage, a way of summarizing this chapter:[115]

1. Attitudes are individual predispositions to respond to a given event, person, or situation in a given way.

2. Attitudes vary in intensity, as measured by the ease with which they become involved in behavior. Some people will pay a higher price or will require a lower inducement from a situation to act on an attitude than will others.

3. A person generally has several attitudes that relate to a given attitude-object. Within his attitude repertoire there are multiple possibilities for action. These possibilities may, indeed, contain mutually contradictory attitudes, whether of equal or unequal intensity.[116]

4. Situations furnish cues and opportunities that call up or activate attitudes. In any given situation, most attitudes of the participants are latent. When Fendrich asked a group of respondents whether they would commit themselves to various interracial activities before he asked them to express their attitudes, he found a higher association between attitudes and behavior and between

---

[114] *The Authoritarian Personality*, p. 6.

[115] For important statements relevant to a theory of minority-majority relations, and the implications of attitudes for behavior, see Allan Wicker, "Attitudes versus Actions: The Relationship of Verbal and Overt Behavioral Responses to Attitude Objects," *JSI*, Autumn, 1969, pp. 41–78; Donald Campbell, "Social Attitudes and Other Acquired Behavioral Dispositions," in Sigmund Koch (ed.), *Psychology: A Study of a Science*, vol. 6, *Investigations of Man as Socius: Their Place in Psychology and the Social Sciences*, McGraw-Hill, 1963; Melvin DeFleur and Frank Westie, "Attitudes as a Scientific Concept," *SF*, Oct., 1963, pp. 17–31; L. G. Warner and Melvin DeFleur, "Attitude as an Interactional Concept: Social Constraints and Social Distance as Intervening Variables between Attitudes and Action," *ASR*, Apr., 1969, pp. 153–169; Milton Rokeach, "Attitude Change and Behavior Change," *POQ*, Winter 1966–1967, pp. 529–550; Howard Ehrlich, "Attitudes, Behavior, and the Intervening Variables," *The American Sociologist*, Feb., 1969, pp. 29–34; James Fendrich, "Perceived Reference Group Support: Racial Attitudes and Overt Behavior," *ASR*, Dec., 1967, pp. 960–970.

[116] On the "principle of multiple possibilities," see Yinger, *op. cit.*, pp. 42–45, 250–254.

commitment and behavior than among those who expressed their attitudes first. Different values and attitudes apparently assumed priority in the two situations.[117]

5. An attitude-relevant situation is one that has reward and punishment potential for an individual, either directly, because he perceives that potential, or indirectly, because others who influence him perceive it.

6. A situation generally carries several possible patterns of rewards and punishments, whether of equal or unequal strength. Thus there are multiple possibilities for behavior. (E.g., a white child in a recently integrated school may have a wide range of rewards and sanctions from teachers, parents, white children, black children, and others in the school situation.)

7. Behavior is a *product* of the interaction of attitudes (and other individual influences) and situations. If there are no attitudes or tendencies (expressed symbolically by a zero) or no relevant stimuli from the environment, behavior related to the issue being studied will not occur, for the product of the interaction will be zero. An attitude, no matter what its strength, remains latent if no relevant situation is encountered. A situation also remains latent for any individuals who have no attitudes relevant to it.

Perhaps this sequence of observations can be put into numerical form to illustrate that behavior is a product of the interaction of individuals, with certain tendencies, and situations, with certain potentials for action. A given person may have a weak tendency in one direction, for example, toward friendliness to persons of other races (we shall give that tendency a "score" of 2 on an imaginary 10-point scale) and a strong tendency to discriminate (with a score of 6). Other persons and situational forces, however, set the costs and opportunities for acting out these attitudes. Suppose the supports for friendliness are strong (8) and those for discrimination weak (2). Then

behavior will be nondiscriminatory (2×8) even though the stronger attitude supports discrimination (6×2). In another context, however, supports for friendliness may be medium (5) and supports for discrimination, although weaker (3), are not absent. Here we may expect discrimination from the person involved even though the situation seems supportive of friendliness $(2 \times 5$ vs. $6 \times 3)$.

All of this is to say that efforts to discover whether individuals are "consistent" in their attitudes or whether situations govern behavior seem, to us, to formulate the problem in an inadequate way. Behavior is always the result of a transaction between individuals and situations, each having multiple latent possibilities. Which possibilities will become manifest cannot be determined for either individuals or situations without knowledge of the range and intensity of the possibilities in the other.

A substantial amount of research documents and measures the interactions between attitudes and situations, the multiplicity of attitudes, and the range of behavior in majority-minority relations. Lohman and Reitzes report that a group of industrial workers supported and applauded a racially integrated union, yet lived in a segregated neighborhood that they defended against "invasion."[118] A number of studies have introduced situational variables into their attempts to discover whether or not those with authoritarian tendencies were "conformists." These studies show that it is better to ask: Under what conditions do those with authoritarian and nonauthoritarian tendencies conform.[119] Laboratory studies that have con-

[117] James Fendrich, "A Study of the Association among Verbal Attitudes, Commitment, and Overt Behavior in Different Experimental Situations," *SF*, Mar., 1967, pp. 347–355.

[118] J. D. Lohman and D. C. Reitzes, "Note on Race Relations in Mass Society," *AJS*, Nov., 1952, pp. 240–246; also their "Deliberately Organized Groups and Racial Behavior," *ASR*, June, 1954, pp. 342–344; see also Lewis M. Killian, "The Effects of Southern White Workers on Race Relations in Northern Plants," *ASR*, June, 1952, pp. 327–331; and Pettigrew, *op. cit.*

[119] See, for example, Homer Johnson, James Torcivia, and Mary Ann Poprick, "Effects of Source Credibility on the Relationship between Authoritarianism and Attitude Change," *JPSP*, June, 1968, pp. 179–183; Ivan Steiner and J. Vannoy, "Personality Correlates of Two Types of Conformity Behavior, *JPSP*, Sept., 1966, pp. 307–315; G. Vaughan and

fronted the former with unanimous judgments against their own senses have often found them ready to conform. Outside the laboratory, however, as Steiner and Johnson observe, they are seldom confronted with such unanimous pressure. When they instructed two accomplices to give unanimous —often false—answers to a series of questions, those individuals in the group with them who were high on the F scale significantly more often conformed than did those who had low scores. But when the accomplices were instructed to disagree a moderate number of times, those high in authoritarianism more often than those low, conformed equally to the two others. When the accomplices disagreed many times, authoritarian subjects rejected one and conformed to the other.[120]

In a variation on this problem, Malof and Lott selected 30 students high on the Berkeley E scale (measuring minority-group prejudice) and 30 students with low scores. Those with high scores significantly more often conformed to the incorrect judgments of the other group members (concerning the comparative length of two lines). Out of 12 judgments, those with high E scores conformed from 0 to 12 times, those with low scores from 0 to 4 times. When those with high scores were given a partner, however, white or Negro, their conformity scores dropped significantly (p = .01).[121] Although there are doubtless individual differences in tendency to conform, ". . . it seems inappropriate to regard the authoritarian as a person with a 'conformist personality,' for, like the nonauthoritarian, he conforms in some situations but not in others. Moreover, given certain situations he may conform to some people but not to others."[122] The per-

son with strong authoritarian tendencies may conform over a wider range of situations, but knowledge of the specific situation is necessary for prediction.

An interesting test of situational influences on prejudice and discrimination was made in a fashionable suburb in the Northeast. Two white young women went into a restaurant and were seated; a Negro young woman then entered, asked for her party, and was seated. This was repeated in ten different places and in each instance they were all served without incident. In two places the party attracted some attention. Two weeks later, the management of each restaurant was sent a letter requesting a reservation for an interracial party. In 17 days not one of the letters was answered. The managers were then phoned, with a variety of results. Eight denied having received the letter; five finally gave tentative approval to the party, although each acceptance was qualified in some way. The next day each restaurant was called to request reservations without any mention of the race issue. Ten accepted the reservation and the eleventh indicated that no reservation was necessary.[123] Here we have a series of responses to interracial situations: acceptance (the original situation), avoidance (no responses to the letter), and a variety of improvisations (to the telephone call). Which represents the "true" attitudes? They all do; they all represent potentialities of the individuals involved in certain kinds of situations with a variety of influences at work.[124] Sometimes it is assumed that the

K. White, "Conformity and Authoritarianism Re-Examined," *JPSP*, March, 1966, pp. 363–366; Irwin Katz and L. Benjamin, "Effects of White Authoritarianism in Biracial Work Group," *JASP*, Nov., 1960, pp. 448–456.

[120] Steiner and Johnson, *op. cit.*

[121] Milton Malof and Albert Lott, "Ethnocentrism and the Acceptance of Negro Support in a Group Situation," *JASP*, Oct., 1962, pp. 254–258. The authors note that this lends support to Rokeach's thesis as well as to a situational explanation.

[122] Steiner and Johnson, *op. cit.*, p. 34.

[123] See Bernard Kutner, Carol Wilkins, and P. R. Yarrow, "Verbal Attitudes and Overt Behavior Involving Racial Prejudice," *JASP*, July, 1952, pp. 649–652. For further examination of situational influences, see Muzafer Sherif and Carolyn Sherif, *Groups in Harmony and Tension*, Harper & Row, 1953; Wilbur Brookover and John Holland, "An Inquiry into the Meaning of Minority Group Attitude Expressions," *ASR*, Apr., 1952, pp. 196–202; Alvin Winder, "White Attitudes Toward Negro-White Interaction in a Number of Community Situations," *JSP*, Aug., 1956, pp. 15–32; Muzafer Sherif, *In Common Predicament: Social Psychology of Intergroup Conflict and Cooperation*, Houghton, Mifflin, 1966; and Robin M. Williams, Jr., *Strangers Next Door: Ethnic Relations in American Communities*, Prentice-Hall, 1964, esp. pp. 28–36 and chap. 9.

[124] Arnold Rose has a valuable discussion of the complexity, indeed the inconsistency of attitudes in

"true" attitudes, somehow unaffected by a situation, are expressed in paper-and-pencil tests or interview situations in which persons are asked to express their feelings toward minority groups. If behavior in another setting deviates from the verbal description, it is often assumed that the "true" attitude has been blocked and that the individual will "return to normal" under more usual circumstances. We prefer to state that the verbalized attitudes are also behavior in a situation—the situation of a paper-and-pencil test or an interview. They express the tendencies of the person that are set in motion in that particular set of conditions. Other sets of conditions facilitate the expression of different tendencies. They all are part of the personality, they all can be understood only by studying process, by searching for "the conditions under which" an individual acts in various ways.

In a recent study, Warner and DeFleur have combined attitudinal and situational variables in a valuable way. Attitudes toward Negroes were measured by a 16-item scale, including both positively and negatively worded items, that was included in a longer "public opinion" study given to 731 university students. Several weeks later, the respondents were asked by letter to sign a pledge to engage in several kinds of activity with Negroes, and to mail the pledge back to the "Henry Clay Club," which had been created for the research. Some of the activities implied the reduction of social distance (dating, petitioning a restaurant to admit Negro guests), others did not (donating a small sum to a Negro charity organization). In addition, the authors indicated to half the respondents that their responses would be anonymous and to the other half that their pledges would be disclosed to the campus through the newspaper and other media. To control for the possible influence of other factors, students within each quartile on the attitude scale were matched on nine social and demographic variables. This process of

matching reduced the group from 731 to 537.

Warner and DeFleur predicted that attitudes, level of social constraint (as determined by anonymity or publicity), and maintenance or reduction of social distance would each influence behavior. These predictions were generally borne out by the pattern of responses. Since only about one-fourth of the matched sample returned the inquiry, one must be cautious about interpretations, but among those who responded, it is clear that willingness or unwillingness to participate in the various interracial activities was influenced by their attitudes, as previously measured, the degree of social distance maintained by the activity, and the presence or absence of constraint (public observability). Where all three of the variables were negative (high initial prejudice, high social constraint, reduction of social distance), many more refused to comply with the request than complied. Giving the former a negative sign, the difference was −87.5. In the three combinations where one support was positive and two negative, the average percentage difference between those refusing and those complying was −23.6. In the three combinations where two supports were positive and one negative, the average percentage difference was +19.6 (more complied than refused). And when all three supports were positive, the percentage difference between those complying and those refusing was +38.5.[125]

There are many interesting interaction effects among the variables, but since the sample size is small, reliability of the Warner and DeFleur findings may not be high. We shall mention one interaction because of its theoretical interest: Among those with high prejudice scores, sensitivity to the reduction of social distance was strong only under conditions of high social constraint—when their readiness to engage in these interracial activities was going to be publicly recorded. There was a different compounding or "multiplier" effect among those with low initial prejudice: They were not much

race relations. See "Inconsistencies in Attitudes Toward Negro Housing," *SP*, Spring, 1961, pp. 287–292.

[125] Warner and DeFleur, *op. cit.*

influenced by social constraint—by the public quality of the activity—so long as social distance was maintained. Those high in prejudice said, in effect: We don't mind if you reduce social distance, if you don't make the situation public. Those low in prejudice said, in effect: We don't mind if you make our willingness to engage in interracial activities public, if they don't imply reduction of social distance.

From such studies as these it is becoming clear that efforts to predict discriminatory behavior cannot rest on measures of individual prejudices alone. Behavior is "field" determined.

These findings may express sensitivity to different reference groups. Fendrich found that readiness to participate in interracial activity was more closely associated with his respondents' perceptions of the attitudes of friends, parents, roommates, and respected older persons than it was with the respondents' own attitudes, although the latter were also of some effect.[126] In another study involving college students, Linn found no significant relationship between attitudes and interracial behavior. He concluded that involvement with the surrounding liberal environment was a powerful influence—indicating again the need for taking reference groups and other situational forces into account.[127]

CONCLUSION

Gradually emerging out of the type of material discussed above is a theory of the personality functions of prejudice that is in harmony with contemporary social psychology. The interpretation is still too eclectic—it puts separate concepts side by side in a mechanical way—because we lack a truly integrated theory of personality. But the latter is being built by the combined efforts of several social sciences, and with it the scattered and sometimes contradictory concepts relating to prejudice can be coordinated. Much of our knowledge, however, is still on the descriptive level. We can expect systematic effort in the years ahead to explain the meaning of several relationships that have been observed but not yet adequately explained. The evidence to date indicates that certain types of personality are prejudice-prone; that a wide variety of needs may, in appropriate social settings, be served by prejudice; that a person's relationships with those around him may strongly influence his attitudes and behavior toward the members of minority groups. These explanations must come into any total theory of prejudice. We must be alert, however, to the weaknesses of this approach.

By most measures, prejudice in the United States has declined quite sharply in the last generation. There is no equivalent evidence that the proportion of persons who are insecure, ego-alien, or alienated has also declined. When asked whether they thought white students and Negro students should go to the same schools or to separate schools, the percentage of national samples answering "the same schools" rose from 30 in 1942 to 48 in 1956 to 60 in 1968. "If a Negro with the same income and education as you moved into your block, would it make any difference to you?" In 1942, 35 percent said no; in 1956, 51 percent; and in 1968, 65 percent. Such data do not mean, of course, that prejudice has disappeared or that discrimination is declining. It is quite possible, in fact, for the nation to experience rising discrimination at the same time it sees declining prejudice. As we have seen, the verbal and attitudinal world is not identical with the behavioral world. The limits to a purely individual approach operate in both directions: There may be relatively equalitarian behavior despite prejudice, or there

[126] Fendrich, *op. cit.* For another study of interaction effects between attitudes and reference group influence, see Gordon DeFriese and Scott Ford, "Verbal Attitudes, Overt Acts, and the Influence of Social Constraint in Interracial Behavior," *Social Problems,* Spring, 1969, pp. 493–505.

[127] Lawrence Linn, "Verbal Attitudes and Overt Behavior: A Study of Racial Discrimination," *SF,* Mar., 1965, pp. 353–364. See also Donald Tarter, "Toward Prediction of Attitude-Action Discrepancy," *SF,* June, 1969, pp. 398–405; and James Fendrich, "A Study of the Association among Verbal Attitudes, Commitment and Overt Behavior in Different Experimental Situations," *SF,* Mar., 1967, pp. 347–355.

may be discrimination despite reduced prejudice.

There has been a tendency on the part of many writers to interpret prejudice as if it served *only* the need for ridding oneself of fear, guilt, and hostility. We require a more systematic study of its use in the service of other needs—for "explaining" a complex situation, making it seem simple, and for giving one a sense of belonging, for example. Some authors have assumed not only that frustration can lead to prejudice, but that frustration is always present when there is prejudice. The authors of *Frustration and Aggression* declare: "For race prejudice to occur, *not only must there be frustration and ensuing aggression,* not only must there be permission to be aggressive but there must also be a way of identifying the people to be hated."[128] They do not hold that frustration is a sufficient cause of prejudice but do contend that it is a necessary

[128] Dollard, Miller, Doob, *et. al., op. cit.,* pp. 152–153. Italics ours.

cause, a force that is always present where prejudice is found. There seems to be little evidence for this, unless one defines frustration so broadly that the term is meaningless.

Writers who have been strongly influenced by psychoanalysis tend to *assume,* in advance of the evidence, that the "basic" cause of prejudice, as of virtually all other aspects of personality, is reaction to the coercions of early training. Other forces may be used in the total explanation, but in a secondary way. In our view, however, prejudice is a complicated phenomenon compounded of social and cultural elements as well as individual personality elements. The various specialties in research, while abstracting one influence from the total, must avoid the error of reductionism—explaining the total by the abstracted part. Keeping in mind the important evidence concerning the personality factors involved in prejudice, we now turn to a study of the social and cultural influences.

Chapter 4 / PREJUDICE AND DISCRIMINATION AS WEAPONS IN GROUP CONFLICT

We have reviewed the evidence that prejudice and discrimination stem, in part, from the tendencies of individuals. Most research on this theme explores the ways in which intergroup hostility expresses motives and needs that have no direct relationship to minority groups. These motives and needs, many of them unconscious, are deflected onto minority groups in an attempt by insecure persons to bring some greater sense of control over their own lives, to reduce their anxieties, and to handle their guilts and fears.

As we have tried to show, however, this is not the whole story. There are realistic conflicts and scarcity-based competitions that can support prejudice and discrimination. Interpretations of, and responses to, conflictful and competitive situations are often the product of groups, that is, of interacting individuals who share significant life conditions. When people come together in groups a new influence begins to operate on their behavior, an influence that cannot be explained by analysis of their individual tendencies, studied separately. Emergent qualities of the group situation, the product of the *interaction* of individuals, are influences that can occur only when individuals come into communication with one another. The situation is analogous to that in chemistry where the most complete analysis of the properties of the gases hydrogen and oxygen cannot explain the properties of the liquid water, which is a result of their interaction. This distinction between individual and group influences is analytic, of course; there is continuous mutual conditioning of the one by the other. The way in which an individual will respond to group influences is in part a function of his tendencies, and those tendencies are in part a result of the group influences he has experienced. Understanding any given situation will require the examination of both sets of influences. For purposes of scientific analysis, however, they must be studied separately.

The study of the influences on behavior that arise from groups, from human interaction, is usually considered the heart of the science of sociology. Like all other abstract sciences, its explanations are of the "if and when" variety: If individuals with certain tendencies are involved, and when certain group influences are operative, then the results of a given interaction can be predicted. The explanation of any existing situation, in contrast with the explanation of abstract situations where variables have been controlled, requires the examination of all the "ifs and whens" that may be involved. In terms of our problem, the analysis of the group influences in prejudice will be insufficient to explain existing manifestations of prejudice until the kind of forces examined in Chapter 3 are also taken into account. Similarly, analysis of the individual functions of prejudice is not sufficient to explain actual cases of prejudice, for they almost certainly involve group influences as well.

In recent years the flood of research and commentary on the individual aspects of prejudice and discrimination has sometimes obscured the social and cultural aspects. In Chapter 3 we have sought to interpret the personality dimension as part of a larger system of causes. The key to this interpretation is the word "tendency": To isolate an authoritarian predisposition or a prejudice is not to describe behavior but only to indicate one of the forces at work. Among other things we need also to ask: What other tendencies furnish different possibilities? Most persons have complex, even contradictory attitudes. What is the relative salience of the diverse values and attitudes held by an individual? What role is he playing? The concept of role implies that he is bound into a network of interacting persons who are governed, to an important degree, by shared expectations. What is the system of rewards and sanctions in the situation? Without knowledge of potential gains and costs for an individual we cannot predict which of his various tendencies will be brought into play. How are the groups of which he is a member helping to define the situation for him? What kinds of cues are being furnished by leaders?

Such questions are of special importance in understanding prejudice and discrimination in a mobile, heterogeneous society. As Reitzes has excellently shown, in such a society we interact more in the framework of specialized organizations wherein we are engaged not as total persons but as role players. Many contacts in the modern world have limited and specific objectives. Relationships tend to be "contractual," thus allowing fewer individual tendencies to come into play. Large groups with explicit organizational objectives and policies govern our actions in more and more ways. Since these groups often bring together individuals with widely differing personal tendencies, any policy will contradict some of the personal inclinations.[1] Thus labor unions may discriminate in an effort to protect a limited job market despite a low level of prejudice among many of their members. Or unions may develop a nondiscriminatory policy in order to present a united front despite a high level of prejudice among many of their members.

Even in situations that are poorly structured by groups or norms, individuals do not simply "express themselves." They look for clues, for a "definition of the situation" that can guide them in their interaction with others.[2] If there are leaders taking a definite stand, their clues may well be followed; but in the absence of leaders the tentative actions of others may furnish the direction (and this response, in turn, may support the first person's tentative move, thus promoting a *group* cycle of causation).

Although the sociological approach is interested in the origin, the salience, and the group supports for prejudice, it directs its attention more fully toward discrimination. A large part of the resistance to desegregation, for example, can be explained by attention to certain demographic and structural facts without any attention to individual prejudices and attitudes. Breed notes, in illustration, that the Deep South is our least "pluralistic," open, and competing region. There are fewer associations, less political and economic controversy (in the relative absence of diverse parties, vigorous labor unions, organized ethnic groups, and religious variety), lower political participation, structural supports for segregation in most institutions, and few organizations for opposing it.[3] On this level of analysis, knowledge of the extent to which people are ego-alien, threat-oriented, or authoritarian is of little value.

It is important to remember, of course, that the social and cultural forces that we shall discuss in this chapter and the next are brought to bear on persons with various inclinations and potentialities. Man is a role-playing creature, but he invests something of his own interpretation into the playing. He looks to the situation—to leaders and the behavior of others—for definitions, but others, including leaders, also look to him.

---

[1] Dietrich Reitzes, "Institutional Structure and Race Relations," *Phylon*, Spring, 1959, pp. 48–66.

[2] M. L. Kohn and Robin Williams, Jr., "Situational Patterning in Intergroup Relations," *ASR*, Apr., 1956, pp. 164–174. See also Isidor Chein, Morton Deutsch, Herbert Hyman, and Marie Jahoda (issue eds.), "Consistency and Inconsistency in Intergroup Relations," *JSI*, 1949.

[3] Warren Breed, "Group Structure and Resistance to Desegregation in the Deep South," *SP*, Summer, 1962, pp. 84–94. In recent years it has become fashionable to refer to this group-based source of discrimination by the phrase "institutional racism." Insofar as this calls attention to the structured sources of discrimination, it can contribute to our understanding. We have sought to give emphasis to those sources in this as in previous editions of this book. There is some danger, however, that "institutional racism," or simply "racism," will be used as an explanatory term when, in fact, it designates a mode of behavior which itself requires explanation. This chapter and the next and most of Part II are concerned with such an explanation. For an illustration of the use of the term, see Louis L. Knowles and Kenneth Prewitt, *Institutional Racism in America*, Prentice-Hall, 1969.

He has inconsistent tendencies, but they are not of equal salience for him. A full understanding requires maximum information on all of the levels—and not simply in the sense that we add them together: We must be aware of their interaction.

When human beings come together, they tend both to unite for common purposes and to oppose each other. There is cooperation and accommodation, but there is also competition and conflict; and the cooperating members of one group are often united for purposes of opposition toward another group. Thus the two processes of association and dissociation are opposite sides of the same interaction. The study of prejudice can perhaps best be made from the side of dissociation—of conflict and competition. Many of the things that human beings desire— prestige, power, income—come in scarce quantity; and much of the social process, both of association and of dissociation, can be understood as an attempt to hold on to or to increase one's share of these scarce values. We cooperate with some in order to compete more effectively with others.[4]

One of the widespread and probably universal results of this process is the stratification of human societies into many ranks, sharing differently in the distribution of prestige, power, and income. These ranks may be defined in the folkways, buttressed by tradition, and are often maintained by force. But the distribution of values is not permanent; human beings are constantly widening or narrowing their claims. Technological change, culture contact, and new systems of belief continually bring new forces into the "moving equilibrium" that makes up a social order. The entrance of these factors is obviously more rapid in some situations than in others, but they can

scarcely be entirely lacking in any human society. To protect their established positions or to improve upon them, human groups are quick to invent or to accept systems of belief and attitudes that justify and explain what they are trying to do. The explanation may be "religious"—the infidel, the barbarian, the pagan deserves no better—or cultural, or national, or based on class distinctions. In our time it is frequently racial, or pseudoracial. In the following pages we shall examine some attempts to use these distinctions as bases for maintaining or improving a group's position in the struggle for prestige, power, and income.

One must avoid exaggerating, as many writers have done, the role of conflict and competition in human life. There are those who think of conflict as "the father of all things" and those who, especially since Darwin's day (despite Darwin, one might add), think of it in moral terms—conflict is good, and without it life would lack both zest and progress. Our position here is simply that conflict and competition are important social processes, natural to human society (as is cooperation) and probably inevitable. That is *not* to say, however, that any specific mode of conflict is inevitable or that any particular group alignment is natural. History is filled with evidence of the shifting pattern of groups among whom conflict occurs and of the wide range of modes of conflict, from violence to rational argument, that characterize human interaction.

The scientific study of social stratification and of the struggle for power has been one of the key jobs of social scientists for a century. But its full import for the understanding of human behavior, including such specific manifestations of behavior as prejudice, has been recognized slowly by the average American and by a number of the scientists themselves. Many of the facts of American life, particularly in its early years, and almost all of the beliefs and traditions with which Americans interpret their society have prevented an adequate study and understanding of the role of power and of group conflict as expressions of human interaction. It is commonly thought that the

[4] There is a rich literature on the place of conflict in societies. See, for example, Georg Simmel, *Conflict*, Free Press, 1955; Ralf Dahrendorf, *Class and Class Conflict in Industrial Society*, Stanford, 1959; Lewis Coser, *The Functions of Social Conflict*, Free Press, 1954; Lewis Coser, *Continuities in the Study of Social Conflict*, Free Press, 1967; Raymond Mack and Richard Snyder, "The Analysis of Social Conflict—Toward an Overview and Synthesis," *Journal of Conflict Resolution*, June, 1957, pp. 212–248.

United States has no class structure, no ruling class, for such concepts violate our ideas of individualism and democracy. To be sure, our behavior—particularly that of the middle and upper classes—is not so lacking in realism. As Charles A. Beard once said: "We talk like Thomas Jefferson and act like Alexander Hamilton." Our beliefs may, in fact, serve the function, among other things, of obscuring the class alignment and the pattern of conflict. However that may be, Americans have been slow to understand the facts of social stratification and the nature of group conflict. This circumstance has left a gap in our explanation of prejudice. We shall now turn to the evidence for the theory that prejudice is, in part, a manifestation of group conflict and a rationalization for discrimination.

PREJUDICE IN THE STRUGGLE FOR POWER, PRESTIGE, AND INCOME

Qualified statements and even exaggerated assertions of the role of economic factors in prejudice are not difficult to find, but well-tested evidence is less common. In this field, even more than in the material discussed in Chapter 3, the theory of prejudice is based on observation of historical relationships, not of controlled experimental situations, so that the precise role of political and economic factors, analytically separate from other factors, is not easy to demonstrate. Nevertheless, the great fund of evidence indicates clearly, if not with precision, the importance of group prejudice in the struggles within and between societies.

The fundamental attitude underlying the use of prejudice as a group weapon is ethnocentrism—belief in the unique value and "rightness" of one's own group. This nearly universal tendency was explained at first by the theory that there was a natural aversion to difference. Having been socialized to the behavior and beliefs of his own society, seeing them as "natural," each individual inevitably judged other behavior and beliefs as unnatural. The very standards by which one judges the value or desirability

of any action are part of the culture that the growing individual absorbs; therefore he cannot avoid ethnocentrism. While this explanation is still regarded as valid, another element which relates it to the topic of this chapter has been added. Ethnocentrism is functional; it serves the group in its struggles for power and wealth. (We noted in Chapter 3 that it also serves the individual in his attempt to find personal security.) It flourishes best in conflict situations. In the eighteenth century an East Indian, traveling in England, was received as an honored guest; there was also a general admiration for the Chinese. With the growth of conflicts of power between Britain and the East, however, this attitude faded; there was a loss of appreciation for the civilizations of the eastern lands; ethnocentrism and prejudice grew.[5]

To say that ethnocentrism is "functional" is not to say that it is good. We mean only that it contributes to the stability of a social system in a given situation. One may abhor the system thus stabilized. Or the situation may change in such a way that gains from in-group cohesion are outweighed by the losses from intergroup conflict. Catton points out that ". . . ethnocentrism may have contributed to the futility of many well-meant attempts by statesmen to use the conference table as a functional alternative to war."[6] An attitude of superiority within a society may contribute to a group's dominance at one time but add inflexibility and blindness that weakens their position in a changed situation.

If ethnocentrism is functional in group conflict, as well as a result of the limitations

[5] Arnold J. Toynbee, *A Study of History*, Oxford, 1934, vol. 1.

[6] William Catton, Jr., "The Functions and Dysfunctions of Ethnocentrism: A Theory," *SP*, Winter, 1960–1961, pp. 201–211. For other useful discussions see Donald Campbell and Robert LeVine, "A Proposal for Cooperative Cross-Cultural Research on Ethnocentrism," *JCR*, Mar., 1961, pp. 82–108; Marc Swartz, "Negative Ethnocentrism," *JCR*, Mar., 1961, pp. 75–81; Paul Rosenblatt, "Origins and Effects of Group Ethnocentrism," *JCR*, June, 1964, pp. 131–146. For a useful experimental study of ethnocentric processes, see Daniel Druckman, "Ethnocentrism in the Inter-Nation Simulation," *JCR*, Mar., 1968, pp. 45–68.

in perspective that come from the process of socialization, it is an expression of the "needs" of the powerful people as a ruling group, not simply a reflection of the frustrations of powerless individuals. This is also true of group prejudices within a society; the designation of inferior groups comes from those on top—an expression of their right to rule—as well as from frustrated persons often near the bottom, as an expression of their need for security. In the former case, those in power may use prejudice in a "rational" and objective way without necessarily sharing the attitude; in the latter case, one could not possibly use prejudice without believing it, at least on the conscious level. In the one case, prejudice is used to manipulate other persons, and hence can be outside oneself; but in the other case, prejudice is an attempt to govern oneself— to reduce tensions and hostilities—hence must be believed, to be effective. This is an analytic distinction, of course. Usually the "outside" and "inside" uses of prejudice would be blended and mutually reinforcing.

Sherif has stated clearly the theory that prejudice is functional in the power struggle:

The scale of hierarchy of prejudice in settled and stable times, flows from the politically, economically, and socially strong and eminent down to lower hierarchies of the established order. The time to look for the greatest and most impregnable hierarchies of social distance is in the mightiest periods of the empires. A glance at the Greek, Roman, Turkish, British, or French empire, for example, shows convincingly that the periods of highly observed social distances and their psychological correlates were the "golden ages" of those empires. The caste system in India, which is disintegrating now, was not the idea of the ignorant and frustrated "untouchables." It was the philosophical Brahmins and the British masters of the local Indian princes and rulers who were interested in keeping these delineations intact. . . . The most elaborate "race" superiority doctrines are products of already existing organizations of superiority-inferiority relationships and exploitations. The superiority doctrines have been the deliberate or unconscious standardizations of the powerful and prosperous groups at the top and not the ideas of the frustrated and deprived majority at the bottom.[7]

In examining the usefulness of this theory in helping us to account for prejudice, we must be careful not to limit the study to prejudices with which we happen to be familiar. Although race prejudice is doubtless most important in our time, it has not always been, nor will it necessarily continue to be. A few centuries ago it was easier to designate "inferior" groups by religious than by racial lines of division. In Europe there was relatively little contact with the members of non-Caucasian races, for instance. Differences in religious belief, however, frequently reflected different status positions; social changes and conflicts were accompanied by religious differentiation. At a time when the religious view of life was extremely powerful, it was easy to believe that a religiously different group was inferior.

Subsidiary beliefs (subsidiary from the point of view of a theory of prejudice) helped to account for the use of *religious* prejudice in *secular* group conflicts. The medieval world believed that life on earth was a brief second, that eternal salvation was the most important thing. Was it not common humanity to kill any Antichrist who might lead thousands to eternal damnation?[8] An examination of the setting in which this religious prejudice flourished, however, shows that a strictly "religious" explanation of the conflict is insufficient. Involved in the Inquisition of the thirteenth century, for example, were many power gains for the inquisitor—confiscation of property, political gains, weakening the hold of emerging new ruling groups, avoiding attention to the role of the church in the secular power structure. "Heresy hunting was profitable, and all those who sought riches and power eagerly took advantage of the opportunity, masking their satisfactions behind the dogma that the heretics were guilty of treason against the Almighty."[9]

[7] Muzafer Sherif, *An Outline of Social Psychology*, Harper & Row, 1948, p. 343.

[8] See Ruth Benedict, *Race: Science and Politics*, Modern Age Books, 1940, pp. 220–223 ff.

[9] *Ibid.*, p. 225.

From Religious to Racial Prejudice

In our time, religious lines of demarcation are less useful in group conflict. Religious cleavages coincide less well with political and economic divisions. If there had been as many Huguenots among the aristocracy and peasantry of France as there were among the middle class, it would have been impossible for the government of Louis XIV to attack the growing power of the bourgeoisie under the claim of religious heresy. To be sure, there are cleavages in modern society where religious differentiation and political-economic differentiation coincide, with something of the same results as were found in the "religious wars" of medieval Europe. Northern Ireland suffers severe conflict because the economic and political interests of Catholics only partly coincide with those of Protestants. In the United States and other predominantly capitalist societies, most Communists are antireligious as well as being opposed to the political and economic structure of capitalism. Those who fight Communists, therefore, can oppose them for their irreligion as well as their secular ideas—and it is not always easy to know when, or to what degree, the opposition is on religious grounds and when it is on secular grounds.

Strictly religious differentiation, however, is less often used for group conflict in modern society because the religious frame of reference is less crucial today. In a large measure, racial differentiation, or supposed racial differentiation, has come to take its place. We now fight our economic and political opponents not by claiming that they believe the wrong things in religion but by claiming that they are natively inferior. Even modern anti-Semitism, as we shall see, is in only a small measure dependent upon religious differentiation. Prejudice against the Jews has been assimilated into the standard "racial" frame of reference.

It was not difficult to make the transition from the religious to the racial line of demarcation. Europe's first extensive contacts with Negroes and Orientals occurred when religious differences were still regarded as vitally important. The relative tolerance in religious matters had not yet developed. The members of other races were, in most cases, not only racially different but also religiously different. If, at first, the white European did not condemn the Negro because he was a Negro, he could condemn him because he was a pagan. But what if the black pagan were converted to Christianity? When there were only a few such persons, the adjustment was not difficult; they could be given a higher status or even admitted to the dominant group. MacCrone states that the earliest practice in South Africa was to free slaves who had been baptized. But in time this threatened to become a costly economic burden and a challenge to the whole status structure. In 1792 the Church Council of Capetown explicitly stated that "neither the law of the land nor the law of the church" required the freeing of converted slaves.[10] Even earlier the same decision had been made in Britain's American colonies. "A series of laws enacted between 1667 and 1671 had systematically removed any lingering doubts whether conversion to Christianity should make a difference in status: henceforth it made none."[11] Thus a line of cleavage originally symbolized in part by religion came to be symbolized wholly by race.

Racial reasons for persecution are convenient in modern life, as Benedict pointed out, because of the greatly increased contact among the members of different races and because of the racial heterogeneity of many societies. Emerging science, with its efforts to measure physical differences and its studies of racial origins, drew attention to race, and its data were distorted to justify the use of race differences in economic con-

[10] I. D. MacCrone, *Race Attitudes in South Africa*, Oxford, 1937, p. 135.

[11] Stanley Elkins, *Slavery: A Problem in American Institutional and Intellectual Life*, Univ. of Chicago Press, 1959, p. 50. In Catholic countries the situation was somewhat different. Conversion did not bring freedom, but as we shall see below, the whole slave system was milder, manumission more common, and the overpowering economic considerations that were dominant in the United States were softened by various legal, familial, and religious considerations.

flict. The racial line of cleavage had the additional advantage, as a weapon, of relative permanence. Poverty, or occupation, or language, or religion can set a group apart as sharply as skin color or head shape, but the line of distinction may be more difficult for the dominant group to maintain.[12] George Bernard Shaw has caricatured this difficulty in *Pygmalion* by having a speech expert transform a servant girl into a "duchess" by giving her an Oxford accent. The transformation was not complete, to be sure, for it proved harder to control what she said than to change how she said it. After six months of training she seldom slipped back into cockney accent when she said "the rain in Spain falls mainly in the plain"; but it was a bit disconcerting to her teacher to see how often the weather conditions of southwestern Europe came into her conversation. Nevertheless she could "pass" relatively successfully. Had her skin been black, the most perfect Oxford accent and all the appropriate ideas to go with it would not have sufficed. It might be well to add that even the racial line is far from permanent, for wherever races have come into contact, miscegenation has produced a mixed group. The "line" between the dominant and subordinate races may then be drawn at one of several places, depending on the power needs of the dominant group.

In the study of this shift from a religious to a racial mark of distinction, it is apparent that to understand race conflict in the modern world one must understand conflict, not race.

Persecution was an old, old story before racism was thought of. Social change is inevitable, and it is always fought by those whose ties are to the old order. . . . Those who have these ties will consciously or unconsciously ferret out reasons for believing that their group is supremely valuable and that the new claimants threaten the achievements of civilization. They will raise a cry of rights of inheritance or divine right of kings or religious orthodoxy or racial purity or manifest destiny. These cries

[12] Cf. Benedict, *op. cit.*, pp. 233–236.

reflect the temporary conditions of the moment, and all the efforts of the slogan-makers need not convince us that any one of them is based on eternal verities.[13]

Once race differences had become established as symbols of superiority-inferiority, they were used as weapons in many group conflicts. Until the French Revolution there had been little racial prejudice; but by that time the slave trade had become a big business. The nominally Christian slave trader found belief in the inferiority and even nonhuman nature of the Negro a very convenient idea. When the British first established economic interests in India, they encouraged intermarriage with the native population. When, however, the mixed-bloods threatened to outnumber the whites and began to offer competition for positions—particularly minor managerial and administrative jobs—the racial policy changed and a pattern of acute racial discrimination appeared. As Charles Johnson said: "The Indians and mixed bloods were relegated to a fixed economic subordination, and their consequent poverty and degredation were used to justify the judgment of an inherent degeneracy and shiftlessness and unfitness for the society of the English."[14]

Race prejudice was not only a weapon of imperialism, as in Africa and India, but a weapon of class conflict within many nations. In the eighteenth century the Count de Boulainvilliers, an admirer of feudalism, tried to oppose not only the peasantry but Louis XIV as well by claiming that the nobles, who were losing their autonomous power to the absolute monarch, were of superior "Teuton" blood. To attack their power was to destroy the racial leadership of France. It was not until the nineteenth century, however, that this idea was widely used. In *The Inequality of Human Races*, de Gobineau declared that the hope of the world was the fair-haired Teutons—

[13] *Ibid.*, pp. 230–231.
[14] Charles S. Johnson, "Race Relations and Social Change," in E. T. Thompson (ed.), *Race Relations and the Race Problem*, Duke, 1939, pp. 275–276.

"Aryans." All the countries of Europe had been swamped by "Gallo-Romans" while the racial aristocrats were being destroyed. The revolutionary movements of 1848 were, to de Gobineau, an uprising of racial trash. Since the masses were innately inferior, the democracy and liberalism for which they fought were impossible. Thus he fought a class battle with racism.[15]

Anti-Semitism will be studied in detail in Chapters 9 and 10, but here we must indicate that out of the political and economic struggles of Europe in the latter half of the nineteenth century there emerged an anti-Semitic program that demonstrates clearly the role of prejudice in group conflict. Overt expressions of anti-Semitism had gradually subsided in western Europe during the eighteenth and first half of the nineteenth centuries. The merchant and industrial middle class had fought its way to power under the banner of democracy and liberalism; it had sought, and won, the support of many Jews. Legal and political discriminations against Jews were generally abolished. By the middle of the nineteenth century, however, the central political-economic battle was no longer between the new middle class and the old feudal aristocracy, but had become a struggle between the now powerful middle class and a rising proletarian movement (of many types). Whereas democracy and liberalism had been appropriate ideologies for the earlier struggle, they were embarrassing and difficult concepts for the middle class to use in its conflicts with the proletariat. In this setting anti-Semitism began to revive. In Germany, where the conflicts were sharpest, there was no time between 1870 and 1945 when there was not a frankly anti-Semitic political party. Bismarck, although probably personally disdainful of the intellectual "supports" to anti-Semitism, nevertheless began to use it to fight the liberal movement. Since several Jews or persons of Jewish parentage had been prominent in his government, it was not religious or cultural

difference that led to the new attacks, but the usefulness of Jews as symbols. "It was a political maneuver which found the Jews useful ammunition, but had no interest in them as Jews."[16] Finding it difficult to get a positive political program behind which they could unite a sufficiently large following, the conservatives discovered that they could achieve a kind of negative unity by the use of anti-Semitism.

It mattered nothing to the conservatives that the reason for Stoecker's [leader of the Christian Socialists] semi-socialistic antisemitism was that the Jews were capitalists, for Stoecker himself sat in Parliament with the conservatives; and it did not disturb Stoecker that the conservatives supported him because they felt that his tepid socialism would be an insurance against the more violent or "Jewish" form of the disease, represented by Marx and Lassalle. It was an adequate bond of union to regard Jews as the enemy. Antisemitism also helped to bring the second group whose support Bismarck desired to cultivate, the Roman Catholic center, into alliance with the Protestant conservatives. For the Kulturkampf could now be represented as the work of Jewish-led liberal secularists. . . . It was altogether a most curious alliance. . . . Its real point of union was hostility not to Jewry but to the progressive ideas of liberalism; it mattered little to Bismarck from which gun-site the enemy was discomfited.[17]

Since the 1870s many other struggles between the political left and right, including some in the United States, have involved anti-Semitism. Gradually the attacks on Jews shifted from a religious and cultural base to a "racial" one. As late as 1899 Chamberlain, in his *Foundations of the Nineteenth Century*, declared that Jews were enemies, not because of biological differences but because of their special ways of thinking and acting. "One can very soon become a Jew." By the time of Hitler, however, anti-Semitism had become thoroughly biologized. Jews were held to be innately inferior and vicious, the destroyers of civilization. Throughout this period anti-

[15] Arthur de Gobineau, *The Inequality of Human Races*, Putnam, 1915; see also Benedict, *op. cit.*, pp. 173–179.

[16] James W. Parkes, *An Enemy of the People: Antisemitism*, Penguin, 1946, p. 10.
[17] *Ibid.*, pp. 10–11.

Semitism, whether rationalized on cultural or "racial" grounds, was a clear example of the use of prejudice for political and economic purposes.

Interlaced with the use of race prejudice in class conflict was its employment for national purposes. If you can condemn your economic opponent on the grounds that he is racially inferior, why not condemn your national enemy for his biological inferiority? We shall not try to examine here[18] the rather extensive literature upholding this policy. It is only necessary to state that the attempt to define a nation as a homogeneous racial group, to "prove" the superiority of that group over others, and to explain history in terms of inherited differences does such violence to the facts that it can be understood only as a weapon in a conflict situation. Hitler and his "intelligentsia" made the issue clear by the extremes to which they went. Only the "Aryan" can be a leader, a builder of civilization (although some other "racial" group may be sustainers). Wherever genius has been shown, there the presence of Aryan blood has been proved. Leonardo da Vinci and Dante become Aryans; the Japanese share in the biological guarantee of leadership (were they not allies of the Germans?) because of a small admixture of Aryan blood. But their leadership is precarious; it would be bound to fade if they lost contact with the creative Aryan peoples. Said Hitler: ". . . If, starting today, all further Aryan influence upon Japan should stop . . . , Japan's present advance in science and technology could take place for a little while longer, but in the time of a few years the source would dry out, Japanese life would gain, but its culture would stiffen and fall back into the sleep out of which it was startled seven decades ago by the Aryan wave of culture."[19]

Such racism stems from politics, not science. It is not only Germans who have used it thus. Before World War I Carlyle claimed that the German tribes were ancestors of the British, but by 1914 many British discovered that Germans were the barbarians who had fought their ancestors and had destroyed Roman civilization. Germans were the Huns and Mongols. Since the use of racism in this manner stems from political needs, it can be expected to change widely and rapidly. These changes can be understood only by study of the functions that such prejudice serves.[20]

PREJUDICE AS A WEAPON IN THE UNITED STATES

Most of the preceding material has referred to prejudice as a weapon in the struggles of Europe. No less convincing a demonstration of its role in group conflict can be found in the history of the United States, which was being settled at the very time that racial lines of cleavage were beginning to be drawn. Several factors in American history encouraged the use and elaboration of race prejudice. As the colonists became numerous and began to press deeper into the Indians' lands, sharp conflicts inevitably arose. Few of the settlers seriously considered that the Indians might have some rights to the land. It was easier to develop a picture of the lying, thieving, murdering savage, pagan in religion, racially stupid except for a kind of animal cunning. Such a person has no rights; the only good Indian is a dead Indian. This picture was frequently not held by the trappers and traders who moved individually among the Indians. They gained by friendly contact and therefore tended to judge the Indian differently. But the prejudice of the farmer-settler prevailed. There were qualifications and exceptions and ambivalent feeling of course. These were never strong enough, however, to prevent the continuing seizure of Indian lands with a minimum of compensation, the decimation of the Indian population to scarcely more than one-third its original size, and the development of a rationalizing prejudice that moved with the white man

[18] Benedict, *op. cit.*, pp. 199–218.
[19] Adolf Hitler, *Mein Kampf*, Reynal and Hitchcock, 1940, p. 399.

[20] Benedict, *op. cit.*, pp. 215–218.

across the continent. In recent decades categorical race prejudice against the Indian has sharply declined—and so has the economic function which that prejudice formerly served.[21]

The Slave System in the United States

The development and entrenchment of prejudice against the Negro are also made more meaningful by an examination of the economic situation in which it throve. The situation before the American Revolution had potentialities for several different attitudes, and economic factors were important in helping to select the one that finally became dominant. Many of the Negroes who came to America first were indentu 1 servants, not slaves; there were also white indentured servants. From this situation it was possible that both Negro and white bondsmen would move toward freedom as the settlements became more stable, or that both would sink into a permanent status of inferiority (whether of slavery or some other legal form), or that one group would break out of servitude while the other was kept in. Before the Revolution the first possibility seemed most likely. In the seventeenth century a Virginia court had upheld the right of one Negro to claim the perpetual service of another Negro—showing that no categorical race line had yet been drawn. With the failure of tobacco, rice, and indigo to support the plantation economy, the settlers became lukewarm toward slavery.

In Granville County, North Carolina, a full-blooded Negro, John Chavis, educated at Princeton, conducted a private school for white children, and was a licentiate under the local Presbytery, preaching to white congregations in the state. One of his pupils became Governor of North Carolina, another was the state's Whig Senator. Two were sons of the Chief Justice of North Carolina. He was not stopped until the Denmark Vesey uprising in South Carolina (the first state to show promise of economic prosperity through the cotton industry) threatened the whole structure of slavery.[22]

Myrdal states that in the first two decades of the nineteenth century the abolitionist movement was as strong in the South as in the North, if not stronger.[23]

Despite these signs of contradictory tendencies in the South, the legal and institutional structure of slavery had developed, since the late seventeenth century, into a system of great clarity and consistency focused primarily on one goal: the maximization of profit. No matter how harsh or beneficent might be the personal relationship of master to slave, in the last analysis the slave was property, without personal rights, without family rights, without religious rights.

How did a system of such unmitigated power develop? This question has been examined by many American social scientists, particularly by historians; it continues to be a question of great interest and importance over 100 years after the end of slavery. Interpretations vary, with regard to the harshness of the system as well as to the basic supports for it in the American social, economic, and political structure. U. B. Phillips, who powerfully influenced the study of slavery for many decades, saw it as a relatively natural product of environmental conditions that supported a plantation system and sharp status contrast. If his interpretations today seem insensitive to the cruelties of slavery and his examination of the feelings and attitudes of black men superficial, we may yet learn something from his careful historical research. This has been extended and improved upon by Kenneth Stampp, who is perhaps the most

[21] For a sweeping review of Indian-white contact in the Southwest, see Edward Spicer, *Cycles of Conquest: The Impact of Spain, Mexico, and the United States on Indians of the Southwest, 1553–1960*, Univ. of Arizona, 1962. See also Jack D. Forbes, (ed.), *The Indian in America's Past*, Prentice-Hall, 1964; William Brophy and Sophie Aberle (eds.), *The Indian: America's Unfinished Business*, The Fund for the Republic, 1966; Stan Steiner, *The New Indians*, Dell, 1968; Stuart Levine and Nancy Lurie (eds.), *The American Indian Today*, Everett Edwards, 1968.

[22] Johnson, *op. cit.*, pp. 280–281.
[23] Gunnar Myrdal, *An American Dilemma*, Harper & Row, 1944, p. 86.

successful of contemporary writers in excluding ideological factors from his historical studies of slavery. Stanley Elkins skillfully blends structural and psychological
interpretations of the sources and consequences of slavery. Eugene Genovese has
effectively stated a Marxian view that
slavery is fundamentally a class system, and
that the Civil War was the final expression
of a reactionary elite attempting to protect
its status against major changes in the nation.[24]

We shall not examine this valuable historical literature, but will note briefly that
the nature of a slave system and the direction of its development were closely tied to
the larger social structure of which it was a
part. In a brilliant interpretation, Elkins
shows how slavery was established in a society without prior traditional institutions.
The slave was not protected by the feudal
immunities that aided even the lowliest of
the medieval peasants; the crown was primarily concerned with revenue; competing
churches could not command moral leadership. In this open society the road to success
was to create a plantation; and for the slave
there was little "to prevent unmitigated
capitalism from becoming unmitigated slavery." ". . . the drive of the law—unem-
barrassed by the perplexities of competing
interests—was to clarify beyond all question, to rationalize, to simplify, and to make

more logical and symmetrical the slave's
status in society."[25] The relationship to
England was crucial. "Virginia was settled
during the very key period in which the
English middle class forcibly reduced, by
revolution, the power of those standing
institutions—the church and the crown—
that most directly symbolized society's traditional limitations upon personal success and
mobility."[26]

In Latin America significantly different
forces were at work. Economic conditions
for the slave were no better—and perhaps
worse; and he may have been treated with
less personal kindliness than in North
America. But this misses the main point:
"In one case we would be dealing with the
cruelty of man to man, and, in the other,
with the care, maintenance, and indulgence
of men toward creatures who were legally
and morally *not* men—not in the sense that
Christendom had traditionally defined man's
nature."[27] Because Spain and Portugal remained basically feudal, with crown and
church the dominant institutions, unmitigated pursuit of profit did not develop
in their colonies. In sharp contrast to the
legal situation in North America, slaves in
Latin America could buy their own freedom;
they could hold property and work for
themselves (in some places on Sundays and
holidays, in others for two hours a day).
The Catholic Church, while fully implicated in the slave system, sought nevertheless to temper it, to hold it within its own
system of morality, to maintain religious
supervision over the life of the slave. A slave
might be freed by an officer of the crown if
he had performed some meritorious service
or had been severely mistreated; or he might
be freed to celebrate an anniversary or marriage in the planter's family.[28] In such a

[24] See U. B. Phillips, *American Negro Slavery*,
Appleton-Century-Crofts, 1918; U. B. Phillips, *Life
and Labor in the Old South*, Little, Brown, 1929;
Kenneth M. Stampp, *The Peculiar Institution: Slavery in the Ante-Bellum South*, Knopf, 1956; Elkins,
op. cit.; Eugene D. Genovese, *The Political Economy
of Slavery*, Pantheon, 1965; Euguene D. Genovese,
The World the Slaveholders Made, Pantheon, 1969.
For other valuable studies of slavery and some of its
consequences, see August Meier and Elliott M. Rudwick, *From Plantation to Ghetto*, Hill and Wang,
1966; and Peter I. Rose (ed.), *Americans from Africa: Slavery and Its Aftermath*, Atherton, 1970. For
an interesting study of the treatment of slavery in
American school books, see Mark M. Krug, "Freedom and Racial Equality: A Study of "Revised High
School Texts," *School Review*, May, 1970, pp. 297–
354. Krug discovers more candor and depth in the
way texts treat slavery, but sees the need still for
major improvement. In particular, the texts seem
bland; they smooth over conflict, perhaps in an effort
to be more salable.

[25] Elkins, *op. cit.*, p. 52.
[26] *Ibid.*, pp. 43–44. For a perceptive account of effects of this situation on southern culture and on the
white "failure" as well as plantation owner, see W. J.
Cash, *The Mind of the South*, Knopf, 1941.
[27] Elkins, *op. cit.*, p. 78.
[28] On all this see *ibid.*; see also Gilberto Freyre,
The Masters and the Slaves, Knopf, 1946; Gilberto
Freyre, *The Mansions and the Shanties*, Knopf, 1963;
Frank Tannenbaum, *Slave and Citizen: The Negro in
the Americas*, Knopf, 1947.

context, the legal abolition of slavery was a relatively smooth process—the extension of traditions and practices, not their abrupt reversal.

If the legal clarity of an unmitigated slave system in the United States was not fully matched by practice in the seventeenth and eighteenth centuries, in the first half of the nineteenth century almost all the ambiguities were eliminated. Economic forces were of great importance in this development. The invention of the cotton gin and other mechanical devices for the processing of cotton cloth began to make cotton agriculture profitable. In 1793, 500,000 pounds of cotton were exported to Europe. The cotton gin was patented in 1794, and the next year six million pounds were exported. By a decade later, 1805, the amount had grown to 40 million pounds, and by 1850 to over one billion pounds.[29] The effects of this increase were soon felt. The price of cotton rose, the value of slaves doubled, and land values increased sharply; "and with every increase in value the difficulty of breaking the status of Negro slavery increased."[30] The belief in slavery, which had been on the decline for a century or more, began to revive in the South. After 1830 an extensive literature to justify slavery appeared. It attempted to show that slavery was contrary neither to nature nor to religion, and that since the Negro was inferior and subhuman, it was even harmonious with democracy. Occasionally a writer would recognize the economic foundation of these beliefs. In *Sociology for the South,* 1854, George Fitzhugh wrote, "Our Southern patriots at the time of the Revolution, finding Negroes expensive and useless, became warm antislavery men. We, their wiser sons, having learned to make cotton and sugar, find slavery very useful and profitable, and think it a most excellent institution. We of the South advocate slavery, no doubt, from just as selfish motives as induce the Yankees and English to deprecate it."[31] But Fitzhugh

hastened to add, "We have, however, almost all human and divine authority on our side of the argument. The Bible nowhere condemns, and throughout recognizes slavery."[32]

IMMIGRATION INTO THE UNITED STATES

That racial distinctions by themselves are unimportant in explaining prejudice in group conflict is shown in a study of the changing attitude toward immigrants in the United States. Since many of the same arguments and beliefs are involved in the treatment of white and of colored immigrants, one must conclude that something other than "race difference" lies behind the situation. This conclusion is also supported by the fact that an immigrant group that is accepted and even welcomed in one circumstance, despite a racial difference, may be condemned and attacked in another situation "because" of its race. It is obviously impossible to explain the changing amount of prejudice by the racial constant.

The belief is rather widespread that there was no "immigrant problem," no prejudice against the newcomers to America, until the late nineteenth century. A careful study of early American history will show this to be false. It is easy today to assume that the early immigrants were readily accepted because of their passion for liberty, their thrift, their industry. Their contemporaries, however, were as likely to complain of the immigrants' foreign ways, criminality, and filth. The agitation of the Know-Nothing Order was directed against the Irish and Germans. The supposed contrast between the "new" immigration (from southern and eastern Europe) and the "old" immigration (from northern Europe) that was drawn so sharply by many writers in the early twentieth century is interestingly paralleled by a writer comparing the "new" and the "old" of 1835: "Then our accessions of immigration were real accessions of strength from

---

[29] W. D. Weatherford and Charles S. Johnson, *Race Relations,* Heath, 1934, p. 136.

[30] Johnson, *op. cit.,* p. 282.

[31] Quoted by Myrdal, *op. cit.,* p. 1188.

[32] *Ibid.*

the ranks of the learned and the good, from the enlightened mechanic and artisan and intelligent husbandman. Now, immigration is the accession of weakness, from the ignorant and vicious, or the priest ridden slaves of Ireland and Germany, or the outcast tenants of the poorhouses and prisons of Europe."[33] Compare that with the writers of 1910–1920 who were exalting the quality of the early immigrants in order to condemn the newcomers. Lothrop Stoddard, for example, wrote:

. . . . The white race divides into three main sub-species—the Nordics, the Alpines, and the Mediterraneans. All three are good stocks, ranking in genetic worth well above the various colored races. However, there seems to be no question that the Nordic is far and away the most valuable type. . . . Our country, originally settled almost exclusively by Nordics, was toward the close of the nineteenth century invaded by hordes of immigrant Alpines and Mediterraneans, not to mention Asiatic elements like Levantines and Jews. As a result, the Nordic native American has been crowded out with amazing rapidity by the swarming, prolific aliens. . . .[34]

It is easy to see from such statements that things are not as good as they used to be— and perhaps they never were.[35]

Racial differences or supposed differences, national, religious, cultural differences, or simply a general "inferiority" are the reasons ordinarily given to explain opposition to immigrants. Do these "explanations" hide, perhaps even from the person who uses them, economic and political conflicts that are the more basic causes of the attitude? Two cautions are necessary before we examine this question. One need not assume that all opposition to immigration is a result of prejudice, as we are using that term. We have not called the defense of values prejudice, unless that defense is tied up categorically with attitudes toward whole groups of people. If one says that he is opposed to immigration because it leads to a higher rate of criminality or because it makes more difficult the functioning of a political democracy, he has not necessarily expressed a prejudice; he may be giving a judgment on the consequences of cultural heretogeneity. The social scientist asks at this point: Is this judgment correct? *Does* immigration lead to greater criminality or a weakened political democracy? What are the other effects on social structure and process? These are complicated questions we shall not deal with here. When, however, one says that he is opposed to immigration because it leads to more crime and weakens democracy, *and* that this is true because of the categorical inferiority of the immigrant group, he has then taken a value stand of that special type which we have called group prejudice.

The second caution is that we must not assume all categorical opposition to immigrants to be a result of economic and political interests. Part of it is simply a matter of tradition, as we shall see in the next chapter. Many people are opposed to alien groups not because they have, or think they have, any economic interest in such opposition but simply because they have been taught that "keep Australia white" or "America for the Americans" is a proper attitude if they are to feel at home in their group. It is also clear that opposition to immigrants may serve all the personality functions dealt with in the preceding chapter. Newcomers to a country, because they can be easily identified by their differences and because they are relatively powerless, are convenient targets for random aggressions.

Nevertheless, the evidence seems to indi-

---

[33] Quoted by Isaac A. Hourwich, *Immigration and Labor*, Putnam, 1912. For other valuable historical studies of immigration, see Oscar Handlin, *The Uprooted*, Little, Brown, 1951; and Maldwyn Jones, *American Immigration*, Univ. of Chicago Press, 1960. Technical treatment of immigrant statistics and absorption can be found in E. P. Hutchinson, *Immigrants and Their Children, 1850–1950*, Wiley, 1956; and E. P. Hutchinson, "Notes on Immigration Statistics of the United States," *Journal of The American Statistical Association*, Dec., 1958, pp. 963–1025.

[34] Lothrop Stoddard, *The Rising Tide of Color Against White World-Supremacy*, Scribner, 1920, pp. 162–165.

[35] For an interesting discussion of the "old" and "new" immigration into Australia see Stanley Lieberson, "The Old-New Distinction and Immigrants in Australia," *ASR*, Aug., 1963, pp. 550–565. For the most part, Lieberson found that rates of adaptation and assimilation in Australia were similar for South and North Europeans.

cate clearly a tradition of opposition to immigrants, who are accepted targets for aggression partly because of economic and political conflicts. There seems to be a direct correlation between the peaks of "nativist" activity and the valleys of economic depression. The Native American party of the 1830s, the Know-Nothing Order of the 1850s, the American Protective Association in the last two decades of the nineteenth century, and the scores of anti-alien, one-hundred-percent-American groups in the 1930s—these all show the tendency to try to bolster a shaky economic situation by prejudice against recent immigrant groups.[36] This correlation between prejudice and economic insecurity is low because many other variables influence the strength of prejudice, and they may operate strongly in different circumstances from those that encourage the use of prejudice as an economic weapon. Anti-Semitic activities may increase in the United States because of political factors in Germany that have reverberations here. Such activities may have no direct relation to economic stresses in the United States, except as those stresses create a favorable setting for the borrowing of the German pattern. It should also be noted that economic forces may encourage prejudice in "good times" (and among the economically powerful), hope of gain rather than fear of loss being the underlying motive. In a multiple-factor situation, such as prejudice, it is important not to assume that because the course of events does not follow the pattern indicated by one factor (economic crisis, for example) the factor in question isn't operative. Its influence may simply be canceled out by other factors that obscure its effects.

RESTRICTIVE LEGISLATION

The story of legislation that gradually controlled and restricted immigration into the United States after 1882 is a useful case study of the ways in which anti-immigrant

prejudice reflects, in part, economic forces.[37] Many people who had no economic interest in this legislation, supported it nevertheless —probably, in fact, in opposition to their long-run economic interest. But some of the strongest proponents of restriction were groups who could see immediate economic advantage in weakening or getting rid of immigrant competitors. The arguments used were partly racial or biological—continued immigration means "blood pollution" or "mongrelization;" they were partly religious and cultural—"our capacity to maintain our cherished institutions stands diluted by a stream of alien blood." But the economic factor was occasionally stated in undisguised fashion. "The Chinaman is here because his presence pays, and he will remain and continue to increase so long as there is money in him. When the time comes that he is no longer profitable *that* generation will take care of him and will send him back."[38]

Changing American Policy Toward Chinese Immigration. Vigorous exclusionist sentiments developed first on the West Coast, where a visible racial minority with a unifying cultural tradition came into economic competition with some of the "native" whites, who in exploiting the resources of a new area were accustomed to a conflict pattern and a vigilante tradition. When unskilled workers were needed to build railroads and to begin the development of the resources of the West, many Chinese were imported and welcomed. Agitation against the Chinese began, perhaps, in the 1860s. During this decade the Central Pacific Railroad was completed, so that competition for jobs among the unskilled was intensified. The gold boom began to fade and unemployment to rise. Serious economic crises in the 1870s, accompanied by extensive migration of unemployed persons from the East,

[36] See Donald Young, *Research Memorandum on Minority Groups in the Depression*, SSRC, 1937.

[37] There are interesting comparisons and contrasts in the experience of Great Britain since World War II. See Sheila Patterson, *Immigrants in Industry*, Oxford, 1968.

[38] Quoted from the Sacramento *Record Union*, Jan. 10, 1879. Oliver C. Cox, *Caste, Class and Race*, Doubleday, 1948, p. 413.

brought sharper and sharper demands from the white workers that the continuing Chinese immigration be stopped. In 1876 both major parties in California had anti-Chinese planks in their platforms, and a statewide vote in 1879 was overwhelmingly for exclusion.[39]

The changing economic situation was accompanied by a shifting stereotype of the Chinese. From worthy, industrious, sober, lawabiding citizens they rather suddenly developed into unassimilable, deceitful, servile people smuggling opium.

There were no new personal experiences to account for the contrast. There was no increase in native aggressiveness on the part of the White group. There was no heightening of an instinctive consciousness of kind. There was, however, a change in the economic conditions in California which made it to the advantage of the Whites to eliminate the Chinese as a factor in competition, and the attitude toward them was an effect of this situation.[40]

In 1882 Congress passed a law that suspended all immigration of Chinese labor for ten years. The legislation was renewed from time to time and in 1904 the time limit was removed. The act of 1924 assigned Asiatic countries no quota from the total amount of immigration to be permitted. Even the alien wives of citizens of Oriental ancestry were barred by the clause which stated that "no alien ineligible for citizenship shall be admitted to the United States." Some Chinese were able to enter under various nonquota provisions of the law. Ninety-three thousand, in fact, emigrated to the United States during the first half of the twentieth century (compared with 309,000 during the last half of the nineteenth century), most of them before the 1924 law went into effect.[41] But the failure to grant any quota under the regular immigration procedures was a decisive proclamation of racism. That this exclusion of Chinese and other Asiatics was an expression of a purely traditional race prejudice, by 1924 almost completely independent of its economic origins, seems clear from the fact that, had China been assigned a quota according to the formula contained in the act of 1924, she would have been granted approximately 100 immigrants per year. During World War II, in fact, the United States made this gesture to her Chinese ally by giving her a quota of 105 per year.

To bring this story up to date it should be noted that various provisions of the 1952 and 1965 immigration laws have made it possible for additional Chinese to emigrate to the United States, thus significantly changing the picture. Spouses and dependent children of American citizens are admitted. Persons born in China may now be naturalized. And by provisions of the 1965 act, up to 20,000 per year may enter the United States from China (until now, basically Taiwan). Between 1951 and 1969 there were 39,000 immigrants from China; and in 1970 alone there were over 16,000.[42]
Changing American Policy Toward Japanese Immigration. Responses to Japanese immigrants have followed much the same pattern as those to Chinese immigration. At first they were welcomed; but by 1900 there were demands that the Japanese be excluded, and these grew more and more insistent. On March 1, 1905, the California legislature, by a vote of 28–0 and 70–0 in the two houses, passed a resolution urging Congress to exclude Japanese from the country.[43] In 1906 the San Francisco school board passed a resolution that barred Japanese children from white schools. This was repealed, under pressure from the federal government, but continued agitation finally led to the "gentlemen's agreement" of 1907 in which the Japanese government agreed to issue no more passports to skilled or unskilled workers, except those who had previously resided in the United States or their

[39] See B. Schreike, *Alien Americans*, Viking, 1936, pp. 3–22.

[40] Otto Klineberg, *Social Psychology*, Holt, Rinehart & Winston, 1940, pp. 385–386.

[41] *Report of the Commissioner of Immigration and Naturalization*, Government Printing Office, 1969.

[42] *Ibid.*, and *The New York Times*, Aug. 31, 1970, p. 37.

[43] Carey McWilliams, *Prejudice—Japanese-Americans: Symbol of Racial Intolerance*, Little, Brown, 1944, p. 19.

wives or their children under 21 years of age. The immigration of women to become the wives of Japanese already in the United States was permitted until 1920, when Japan agreed to refuse emigration to the "picture brides." The act of 1924 stopped all immigration from Japan.

Anti-Japanese activity had not stopped with the virtual cutting off of immigration by the gentlemen's agreement. Newspaper headlines and editorials, nativist organizations such as the Native Sons of the Golden West, mob action, political oratory, and legal enactments all continued to show the extent of the prejudice, particularly in California. Gradually the federal government became involved after having tried for several decades to restrain California's anti-Japanese expressions because of the difficulties they created in international diplomacy. By the Immigration Act of 1924, and by the resettlement policy of 1942, the federal government expressed agreement with the racial sentiments involved.

It is our concern to ask at this point: Who profited, or thought they profited, from such moves? Perhaps the most tangible and continuous gains accrued to men running for office or in office, who, by striking out at the Japanese, could create in-group feeling, could sponsor a cause, could exploit the tensions of the average voter, and could avoid reference to any of the critical issues which might have two opposing sides that were difficult to occupy simultaneously. Many California politicians during the first half of the twentieth century, made use of prejudice against the Japanese to win an election. If the existing fund of prejudice was not enough to make the tactic effective, their supporting newspapers could manufacture enough to help. Before World War II there was a strong correlation between the waves of anti-Japanese agitation and election years. Since the Japanese group was small and politically and economically weak, candidates could attack it almost without fear of reprisals; it was as politically safe to be against the Japanese as to be against sin. Even Woodrow Wilson, speaking in California during the presidential election

of 1912, declared: "The whole question is one of assimilation of diverse races. We cannot make a homogeneous population of a people who do not blend with the Caucasian race." McWilliams reports that the Democratic party distributed over 100,000 copies of this declaration around the state.

There were doubtless economic as well as political motives involved in the anti-Japanese activities on the West Coast after 1900. At various times trade unions and small landowners took part in these agitations, but organized opposition stemmed most directly from the owners of the huge estates that characterize parts of California. These men certainly did not fear the competition of the few Japanese farmers with their relatively small holdings. What they did fear was the opposition of the small white landowners who found it difficult to compete with the estates, the struggles for improvement of their very badly paid field hands, the traditions in favor of family-sized farms and homesteads, and federal legislation that prevented them from monopolizing the water supplied through governmentally sponsored irrigation projects. If they could divert attention from their own control of the land by attacking the Japanese farmer as the cause of everybody's difficulties, they might funnel off some of the hostility to which they were vulnerable and get political support for laws favorable to them.

These factors may help to explain their support of the nativist associations and their backing of alien land laws that in actuality had little effect on the control of the land— but which made many people *think* that the land problem was solved. If the farm laborers, working at low wages and often under very poor working conditions, could be persuaded that the Japanese farmers were the cause of their difficulties, they might show less hostility toward the owners of the large estates. Out of this situation came the Alien Land Acts of 1913 and 1920 in California, and similar bills in other states. (These statutes, 16 in all, were voided by the Walter-McCarran Act of 1952 which removed barriers to citizenship.) The

1920 act was passed as an initiative measure, and approved by a majority of three to one. These two bills did not change the actual landholding situation much, for they could not dispossess alien Japanese of land they already held nor could they apply to the increasing number of second-generation Japanese who were American citizens. To be sure, by 1940 the acreage controlled by Japanese had fallen to 226,094 from 361,-275 in 1920 (a tiny fraction of the agricultural land in the state in either year), and the average farm had been reduced from 80.1 acres to 44. But the total value of the produce from these farms increased during the period. It seems likely that few people were interested in enforcing the law anyway, for Japanese "managers" rather than "tenants" appeared, and title to land was transferred to American- or Hawaiian-born Japanese—with little objection from officials.[44] The chief gains to economic and political groups came not from the provisions of the bill, but from the controversy, the pseudoconflict situation, that was built up in the process of passing the bill. Actually, most of those who voted for the 1920 act, insofar as it was effective at all, suffered from the legislation—the landowner by lower rentals (he had been able to charge the Japanese tenant high rents) and the consumer by higher prices. But the powerful few found the anti-Japanese agitation very useful in their diversionary tactics.

The economic motives involved in prejudice are almost always alloyed with other motives and may be explicitly denied. Lothrop Stoddard, writing during the anti-immigration period at the close of World War I, built his attack against immigration around a "racial purity" argument; he criticized those who supported immigration on economic grounds:

There is no more damning indictment of our lopsided, materialistic civilization than the way in which, throughout the nineteenth century, immigration was almost universally regarded, not from the social, but from the material point of view, the immigrant being viewed not as a creator of race-values, but as a mere vocal tool for the production of material wealth.[45]

Yet a few pages later in the book he writes that the Asiatic

. . . is perfectly justified in trying to win broader opportunities in white lands. But we whites are equally justified in keeping these opportunities for ourselves and our children. The hard facts are that there is not enough for both; that when the enormous outward thrust of colored population-pressure bursts into a white land *it cannot let live*, but automatically crushes the white man out—first the white laborer, then the white merchant, lastly the white aristocrat; until every vestige of white has gone from that land forever.[46]

Relocation of Americans of Japanese Ancestry. Economic factors in the prejudice against the Japanese continued to operate in the period of their "relocation" from the West Coast during World War II. After Pearl Harbor the groups that had long agitated against the Japanese lost no time in telling Washington that the presence of 110,000 Japanese on the west coast, including about 40,000 "enemy aliens" (those born in Japan were ineligible for citizenship), was a grave threat to the safety of the country. There were, of course, many motives involved in the order to evacuate all persons of Japanese ancestry to relocation camps away from the West Coast; but the climate of opinion that had been built up by those who saw economic and political gain in anti-Japanese agitation was important in the complex of causes. Persons of Japanese descent who might have been a military danger were already known to the FBI and were taken into custody within a few days. That all the rest, including 70,000 American citizens, should be treated as military threats was an act of unprecedented official racism in the United States.

Judgments differ concerning the importance of various influences that led to the relocation order. The direct pressure of

---

[44] *Ibid.*, pp. 64–65.

[45] Stoddard, *op. cit.*, p. 252.
[46] *Ibid.*, p. 274.

interested economic groups was probably relatively unimportant, although they had helped to create the atmosphere in which such an order was accepted with little protest. TenBroek, Barnhart, and Matson argue cogently that the direct responsibility must be shared by many groups—the general public, particularly in the West; the military leaders; President Roosevelt and his staff, who concurred with the military decision; the Congress, which reinforced the process with legislation; and finally the courts, especially the Supreme Court, which gave the relocation order what now seems to many students a dubious constitutional sanction. All of these acted out of fear and, in our opinion, bad judgment. But behind the fear and the error stood prejudice, distorting the ability to deal rationally with the situation. Definitive support for the relocation came from the Supreme Court:

The Japanese American cases—*Hirabayashi, Korematsu,* and *Endo*— . . . represent a constitutional yielding to the awe inspired in all men by total war and the new weapons of warfare. They disclose a judicial unwillingness to interfere with—or even to look upon—the actions of the military taken in time of global war, even to the extent of determining whether those actions are substantially or somehow connected with the prosecution of the war. . . . In these cases, the historically established balance between the military and the civil—constitutionally sanctified in the United States by the classic majority opinion in *Ex parte Milligan*—has been shifted dangerously to the side of the military by the known and unknown terrors of total war and by a quiescent and irresolute judiciary. In them, the *Milligan* rule of subordination of the military to the Constitution except in battlefield conditions is abandoned. Instead, the national war powers, though explicitly conferred by the Constitution and not exempted from its limitations, are founded on and circumscribed by a military estimate of military necessity. Citizens, on a mass basis, were allowed to be uprooted, removed and imprisoned by the military without trial, without attribution of guilt, without the institutional or individual procedural guarantees of Article Three and Amendments Five and Six, and without regard to the individual

guarantees of Amendments One, Four, Five, and others.[47]

Whatever the role of economic factors in causing the evacuation of Americans of Japanese descent, the economic results were clearcut and severe for the people involved. They suffered a loss variously estimated from 350 to 500 million dollars, with losses averaging nearly $10,000 per family.[48] Some of this loss resulted in no gain for anyone else; property deterioration, inefficient and incomplete use of skills, costs of property transfer and storage, etc., profited no one. Some of the losses to the Japanese-Americans, however, were direct gains to others; property sold in desperation at a fraction of its worth or abandoned completely, vandalism of goods that had to be stored for several years, further monopolization of job and business opportunities by Whites—these gave economic incentive to prejudice, to the few who thus profited. The costs to the whole nation were scarcely noticed.

This brief reference to the wartime relocation of Americans of Japanese descent would be incomplete without some mention of the current situation. Gradually, from 1943 on, residents of the relocation centers were allowed to leave, to attend college, to accept jobs, and to enter the armed services, where they achieved outstanding records. After the war, 80 percent of the Japanese-Americans returned to the West Coast, with

[47] Jacobus tenBroek, Edward N. Barnhart, and Floyd W. Matson, *Prejudice, War, and the Constitution,* Univ. of California Press, 1954, p. 259. Of the existensive literature on the relocation question, see also Leonard Bloom and Ruth Riemer, *Removal and Return: The Socio-Economic Effects of the War on Japanese Americans,* Univ. of California Press, 1949; Morton Grodzins, *Americans Betrayed,* Univ. of Chicago Press, 1949; Alexander Leighton, *The Governing of Men,* Princeton, 1945; McWilliams, *op. cit.*; Dorothy S. Thomas, *The Salvage,* Univ. of California Press, 1952; Dorothy S. Thomas and Richard S. Nishimoto, *The Spoilage,* Univ. of California Press, 1946; Edward H. Spicer, *et al., Impounded People: Japanese-Americans in the Relocation Centers,* Univ. of Arizona Press, 1969.

[48] See Bloom and Riemer, *op. cit.,* chap. 5; see also E. V. Rostow, "Our Worst Wartime Mistake," *Harper's Magazine,* Sept. 1945, pp. 193–201.

three-fourths of these going to California. Slowly their claims for property losses received legislative and judicial attention. With the help of the Japanese-American Citizens League and other groups, 24,000 claims totaling 130 million dollars were filed. Congress passed legislation permitting claims up to $100,000 to be settled administratively, without court litigation.[49] It is not yet clear what proportion of the actual losses may ultimately be recovered; it will doubtless be a small fraction, but some restitution at least is under way ($36,000,-000 having been paid by 1962).

The Japanese-Americans who did not return to the West Coast have been absorbed into many cities with relatively little prejudice and at fairly high job levels.[50] The Walter-McCarran Act of 1952 brought Japan into the American immigration quota system (185 Japanese were permitted to migrate per year, in addition to spouses of American citizens and unmarried minor children) and made foreign-born Japanese eligible for citizenship. Over 50,000 Japanese have been naturalized since 1952. By 1959 over 90 percent of the 5766 Nisei (Americans of Japanese ancestry) who had renounced their American citizenship during the wartime "relocation" had had their citizenship rights restored. And with the addition of Hawaii as a state, the status and influence of Americans of Japanese descent further improved. They constitute nearly one-third of the population of Hawaii and are important in its political and economic life. These developments all represent a substantial change from the prewar and wartime situation.

In the country as a whole citizens of Japanese descent increased significantly in number by the addition of an estimated 50,000

brides of American servicemen, brought in by special legal provision outside the quota. This explains the entrance of most of the 66,000 who came to the United States from 1951–1965. The quota during this whole period was less than 3,000. Under the 1965 Immigration Act, which we shall describe later, it is now possible for Japan to send 20,000 immigrants per year. In fact, however, the total during the 1965–1970 period was less than 20,000.[51] The population of Japanese descent in the United States in 1970 was approximately one-half million.

Recent Trends in Immigration

We shall not undertake an analysis of the political and economic setting out of which American immigration policy has grown. There is general agreement that the Quota Act of 1924, the culmination of decades of agitation to restrict immigration, was partly the product of economic and political forces related to the closing of our frontier, the ideological and power aspects of "manifest destiny" imperialism at the turn of the century, and the postwar tensions and economic difficulties of the early 1920s. In a rather strange combination of forces: industrialists, unionists, and farmers, exuberant nationalists, racists, and many intellectuals combined to produce the pressure for legislation.[52] The 1924 law not only restricted the number to approximately 150,000 a year, but sought to determine the national origin of future immigrants. Immigration from Asia was barred; no quantitative restrictions were placed on migration from the western hemisphere; and the 150,000 was divided among other nations in proportion to their supposed representation in our population in 1920. The result was to assign 68.9 percent of the quota to Great Britain, Ireland, and Germany. Immigra-

[49] *The New York Times*, Aug. 12, 1956, p. 38.
[50] See William Caudill and George DeVos, "Achievement, Culture and Personality: The Case of the Japanese Americans," *AA*, Dec., 1956, pp. 1102–1126; Alan Jacobson and Lee Rainwater, "A Study of Management Representative Evaluations of Nisei Workers," *SF*, Oct., 1953, pp. 35–41; Harry H. L. Kitano, *Japanese Americans: The Evolution of a Subculture*, Prentice-Hall, 1969.

[51] See *Report of the Commissioner of Immigration and Naturalization*, 1969.
[52] For a valuable account of the developments leading up to the 1924 law, see Barbara Solomon, *Ancestors and Immigrants*, Harvard, 1956.

tion from southern and eastern Europe was drastically curtailed.

There is no doubt that immigration from the countries affected was sharply reduced. Migration from the countries under the quota averaged well over 500,000 a year during the first quarter of the twentieth century; in the second quarter of the century the average was scarcely 100,000 per year. Great Britain, with over 40 percent of the quota, seldom used more than a fraction of her assignment, whereas many countries with small quotas had waiting lists for years to come.

In 1952, our immigration legislation was slightly revised by the Walter-McCarran Immigration and Naturalization Act. The quota system and the quantitative limit were essentially retained, except that Asiatic countries were now assigned their "appropriate" quota, in most instances the minimum number of 100 per year. The total number was raised to approximately 155,000; and resident aliens from the Orient, formerly ineligible for citizenship, were granted naturalization rights. Racial distinctions continued to be drawn, however, not only by the differences in quotas, but by the mode of defining country of origin. A person of German descent, born and living in Brazil, for example, was Brazilian; but a person of Chinese descent, born and living in Brazil, was Chinese. He could immigrate to the United States only by obtaining one of the 105 places annually allotted to the Chinese.

The changes in the law slightly reduced the national and racist prejudices it contained—but only slightly. The whole quota system made sense only if one assumes that there are racial and national differences in desirability, that is, that desirability can be determined by one's race and national origin, not by individual characteristics.

Chicanos in the United States. The abrupt reduction of immigration and its redirection by the 1924 and 1952 laws had a number of unanticipated effects. It produced serious diplomatic strains, particularly with the nations of the East. Many economists hold that it sped the approach of the depression of the

1930s and made it worse. It increased the northward migration of white and Negro workers from the South (thereby probably speeding desegregation). And it greatly increased the number of migrants from the western hemisphere, particularly from Mexico. Only Canada exceeds Mexico as a source of immigrants during the last 20 years. Of approximately 10 million persons of Spanish-speaking background in the United States, half are of Mexican descent. A substantial proportion of these have entered since 1924 or are the children of migrants. Their experience has matched that of earlier migrants; economic exploitation, political powerlessness, educational handicaps, the sting of prejudice and of stereotypes.

Some of the Mexican-American immigration is illegal. Migrant workers—wetbacks—cross the Rio Grande to fill the tremendous demand for temporary workers to harvest the crops. Conflicting interests in the United States make their status very uncertain. They are deported or allowed to stay—until the crops are in—depending upon a delicate balance of forces in American politics. Some desire low-paid, tractable laborers; others try to keep out "undesirables" or workers who depress the wage scale. In either event, the migrant feels the full weight of discrimination and prejudice.

Several factors encourage the heavy rate of migration from Mexico. The country's high rate of population increase, contact of Mexican workers with the United States as a result of the "bracero program" for the importation of temporary workers, and the continuing campaign to expel the wetbacks—most of them eager to re-enter legally—have resulted in the heavy rate of applications. Total legal immigration from Mexico from 1951–1970 (20-year period), was 750,000.

Native Americans of Mexican descent, permanent immigrants from Mexico, and wetbacks share many burdens. Although there is now a substantial middle class, the continued deprivation of many Mexican-Americans is reinforced by a series of interacting factors. Many of the Mexican-

Americans work in homogeneous gangs, with few contacts with non-Mexicans; the kind of casual labor that they usually find means migration, unemployment, isolation in labor camps; the language barrier reinforces the other problems; the cleavage between generations means that Mexican youth have inadequate adult models, a problem that is often associated with the formation of gangs that block integration still further.[53] A contrast of cultural values may make it difficult for persons trained to the more present-oriented, group controlled, and particularistic Mexican culture to enter fully or quickly into the future-oriented, individualistic, and universalistic patterns more characteristic of American culture.[54] This is not, however, a determining and unchanging influence. Among the more acculturated persons, and in situations where there are opportunities for advancement, Americans of Mexican descent are quite similar to Anglos in work attitudes and performance.[55]

Prejudice and segregation have helped to keep the Chicanos on the bottom rungs of the ladder, but there are important signs of improving status. Their segregation in schools has sharply diminished; contract conditions and distribution centers for migrant workers have been improved, partly under pressure from both governments; more are finding industrial jobs, although still largely at the unskilled and semiskilled levels, and are getting the support of labor unions; at least 250,000 have served in the armed forces, thus breaking the patterns of isolation; there has been an increase in group pride, with cries of "Viva La Raza" being heard, with something of the range of meanings carried by "Black Power;" they are beginning to get political representation, including many local and state offices and congressmen from California, New Mexico, and Texas; and, since World War II, various state, regional, and national civil rights and defense organizations have been founded. These include the Political Association of Spanish-Speaking Organizations, Mexican-American Political Association, League of United Latin American Citizens, G. I. Forum, Community Service Organization, La Raza Unida, National Mexican-American Anti-Defamation Committee, and United Farm Workers Organizing Committee. If these have not yet attained the experience, range, and community support of Negro organizations, they at least represent important beginnings of community action. At the same time, scholarly studies of Americans of Mexican descent have now begun to appear in significant numbers, indicating that the relative neglect of this group, by scholars as well as by policy makers, is being overcome.[56]

[53] Leonard Broom and Eshref Shevky, "Mexicans in the United States, A Problem in Social Differentiation," *Sociology and Social Research*, Jan.–Feb., 1952, pp. 150–158.

[54] See Florence Kluckhohn, "Dominant and Variant Value Orientations," in Clyde Kluckhohn and Henry A. Miller (eds.), *Personality in Nature, Society, and Culture*, Knopf, rev. ed., 1953, pp. 342–357; and Louis A. Zurcher, Arnold Meadow, and Susan L. Zurcher, "Value Orientation, Role Conflict, and Alienation from Work: A Cross-Cultural Study, *ASR*, Aug., 1965, pp. 539–548.

[55] See Charles Weaver and Norval Glenn, "The Job Performance of Mexican-Americans," *Sociology and Social Research*, July, 1970, pp. 477–494; and Fernando Penalosa and Edward McDonagh, "Social Mobility in a Mexican-American Community," *SF*, June, 1966, pp. 498–505.

[56] See, for example, Peter Matthiessen, *Sal Si Puedes: Cesar Chavez and the New American Revolution*, Random House, 1970; John H. Burma (ed.), *Mexican-Americans in the United States*, Schenkman, 1970; Leo Grebler, Joan Moore, and Ralph Guzman, *The Mexican American People*, Free Press, 1970; June Helm (ed.), *Spanish Speaking People in the United States*, Univ. of Washington Press, 1969; Joan W. Moore, "Colonialism: The Case of the Mexican Americans," *SP*, Spring, 1970, pp. 463–472; Fred Schmidt, *Spanish Surnamed American Employment in the Southwest*, Government Printing Office, 1970; Elson Snyder and Joseph Perry, Jr., "Farm Employer Attitudes toward Mexican-American Migrant Workers," *Rural Sociology*, June, 1970, pp. 244–252; Stan Steiner, *La Raza: The Mexican Americans*, Harper & Row, 1970; Inter-Agency Committee on Mexican-American Affairs, *The Mexican American: A New Focus on Opportunity*, Government Printing Office, 1969; Arthur J. Rubel *Across the Tracks: Mexican-Americans in a Texas City*, Texas, 1966; Julian Samora and Richard Lamanna, *Mexican-Americans in a Midwest Metropolis*, Univ. of California Press, 1967; Celia Heller, *Mexican American Youth*, Random House, 1966; Center for Latin American Studies, Stanford Univ., *The Mexican American: A Selected and Annotated Bibliography*, Stanford, 1969.

Puerto Rican Migration. With the reduction of immigration that began with the 1924 law, the number of Puerto Ricans entering the country has increased. This is not, strictly speaking, immigration, since Puerto Ricans are American citizens. But they have shared in the prejudice and discrimination so frequently directed toward the newcomer. In 1970 there were approximately one-and-one-half million persons of Puerto Rican birth or Puerto Rican descent living in the United States, about half of these in New York City. The rate of migration was particularly heavy in the 1945–1960 period. Since then, as a result of an improved economic situation on the island and of unemployment and discrimination on the mainland, there has been, in some years, a net emigration back to Puerto Rico. On balance, however, the mainland population of Puerto Rican descent has grown significantly.

The migration has been welcomed and aided by employers. The total experience of the newcomers, however, has been difficult. Their jobs are largely at the lower skill levels, they live in the least desirable sections of the cities, landlords and loansharks exploit them, their crimes become "crime waves," and they are caught, quite unprepared, in "the Negro problem," for many of them who are "white" in Puerto Rico are "colored" by mainland standards. In general, as Clarence Senior puts it, all sorts of conditions "of which the newcomer is a victim are laid at his door."[57]

The Puerto Rican migrant may experience a somewhat briefer period of exploitation and prejudice than have some earlier groups. The fact that he is a citizen, the greater appreciation today of the nature of culture contact and conflict, the serious efforts being made in New York City and elsewhere to strengthen education for Puerto Ricans, and other factors are hopeful aspects of the situation. There is good evidence that movement up the educational ladder and into middle-class occupations is proceeding at a rapid pace among Puerto Ricans. In November, 1970, Mr. Herman Badillo became the nation's first congressman of Puerto Rican descent. He was elected from the 21st district of New York.[58]

Current Immigration Policy in the United States. In 1965 American immigration law was revised again, this time more thoroughly. In an era of greater sensitivity to international perspectives and in the context of a vigorous civil rights movement at home, existing legislation seemed more and more anachronistic. National quotas were eliminated and replaced by two international quotas: 170,000 per year for the Eastern Hemisphere, with a maximum of 20,000 from any one country; and 120,000 for the Western Hemisphere, without specific national limitations. Preference is given to relatives of United States citizens or of resident aliens and to persons with occupational skills. A few persons in addition to the 290,000 in the two quotas are admitted by provisions of the law dealing with dependent children, husbands, wives, and parents of American citizens. In 1969, the first year of full operation for the new law, 359,000 new immigrants came to the United States.

Although some advantage still remains with persons from Canada and Latin America who wish to migrate to the United States, the 1965 law sharply reduces the national and racial preferences that were so prominent in the 1924 and 1952 laws. Results of the new law have been to increase the number of immigrants slightly and to revise drastically the pattern of national origins. These effects are shown in a comparison of the number of immigrants from selected countries at two different time periods:

---

[57] Clarence Senior, in Joseph Gittler (ed.), *Understanding Minority Groups*, Wiley, 1956, p. 110; see also C. W. Mills, Clarence Senior, and R. K. Goldsen, *The Puerto Rican Journey*, Harper & Row, 1950.

[58] For accounts of the mixture of discrimination and progress, see Patricia C. Sexton, *Spanish Harlem*, Harper & Row, 1969; Eva E. Sandis (ed.), *The Puerto Rican Experience*, Selected Academic Readings, 1970; Oscar Lewis, *La Vida: A Puerto Rican Family in the Culture of Poverty—San Juan and New York*, Random House, 1966; Clarence Senior, "Strangers—Then Neighbors," *ADL*, 1961; "The Puerto Rican Experience on the United States Mainland," *International Migration Review*, Spring, 1968, whole issue. For bibliography, see *IRCD* Bulletin, Jan., 1968.

Immigration into the United States before and after the 1965 Immigration Act

	1961-1965 (000)	1966-1970 (000)
Canada	243	155
Mexico	226	224
Germany	119	71
Great Britain	110	99
	698	549
Italy	79	131
Cuba	77	180
Greece	19	68
Philippines	16	80
Portugal	14	62
China	8	36
	213	557

Not all of the change illustrated by the shifts among these ten countries can, of course, be accounted for by the immigration law; but it was a substantial factor, particularly among those countries that increased the number sent from the earlier period to the later. Doubtless there will be further modifications of laws dealing with immigration to the United States. It was hoped that the 1965 law would eliminate the long waiting lists produced, for some countries, by earlier laws. But after the first five years, at any rate, applications for visas from both hemispheres had created backlogs larger than a year's quota. The law lacks flexibility in dealing with refugees. Its occupational criteria contribute to a "brain drain" from nations already lacking in skilled personnel. Nevertheless, the law represents, in our judgment, a significant improvement over earlier statutes.

Despite this improvement, it can scarcely be said that American immigration law represents the culmination of a carefully worked-out policy. To be sure, one cannot argue on sociological grounds that unlimited and undirected immigration strengthens a society. Starting from the premise that a nation's immigration policy will be an attempt to serve its economic, political, and social interests, we believe that both number and direction of flow must necessarily be taken into account. Present American laws, however, do not explicitly control the number of immigrants nor attempt to specify in rational terms the number who might be absorbed effectively in a given period of time. Between 1951 and 1960, the number of immigrants to the United States averaged over 250,000 a year; between 1961 and 1970 the average was over 325,000. This represents approximately one-seventh of one percent of the total population each year. For the 20-year period, total immigration was nearly six million.

Considerations of health, economic placement, and supposed cultural suitability enter into the immigration laws of most countries.[59] These considerations are likely to be of particular importance in the case of refugees seeking asylum. And in the last several decades a large proportion of international migrants have been refugees from political, economic, and religious oppression. The movement across national lines has been characterized by the extreme cruelty of the propelling forces, the difficulty in escaping, the reluctance of many nations to grant asylum, the creation of a great deal of statelessness.[60] An incomplete list of countries or areas from which large numbers of refugees have fled includes China, North Korea, Southeast Asia, Pakistan, India, Israel (Palestine), the Congo, most of the nations of Central and Eastern Europe, Cuba, and Chile. Perhaps 40 million persons have been uprooted from their homes since World War I. The United States Committee for Refugees lists over 17 million refugees in "temporary asylum" in 1969.[61] Three-and-one-half million were being aided by the UN in 1967.[62] It is not possible to estimate the

[59] See W. D. Borrie *et al.*, *The Cultural Integration of Immigrants*, UNESCO, 1959.

[60] Maurice R. Davie, *Refugees in America*, Harper & Row, 1947.

[61] See United States Commission for Refugees, *World Refugee Report*, 1970. In addition, perhaps nine million fled East Pakistan into India in the early months of 1971. Many of these had returned to their homes (now Bangladesh) by 1972.

[62] *The New York Times*, Dec. 3, 1967, p. 167.

proportion of immigration to the United States that is of refugee origin; but American laws have generally kept such immigration down.

ECONOMIC AND POLITICAL BELIEFS IN SUPPORT OF PREJUDICE

The situations we have described give credence to the theory that prejudice is often used, consciously or unconsciously, to help a group win or maintain a larger share of life's values. Whether or not prejudice is an effective weapon for this purpose we shall discuss in Chapter 8 and elsewhere; but it is often so used. The power function of prejudice is seldom explicitly recognized, however, for the American tradition—and that of many other lands—does not allow the open use of inequality and discrimination as legitimate economic and political weapons. Most Americans are quite heavily saturated, on the speech-reaction level, with democratic and Judaic-Christian ideals that can be reconciled with the constant factual contradictions in the treatment of minorities only by a group of rationalizing beliefs. The nature and functions of stereotypes will be taken up in the next chapter, but it may be well at this point to indicate some of the specifically economic beliefs that make it easier for the American to use prejudice as an economic weapon. That there may be some truth in these beliefs should not cause us to lose sight of their function. This function is especially difficult to recognize when it is formulated into an institutional pattern, into law and custom, because then the individual can place all responsibility on the institution.

In *Religion and the Rise of Capitalism*, R. H. Tawney has pointed out the ease with which the wealthy classes accepted the idea of predestination. They were naturally disposed, he said, to regard the poor as damned in the next world, because that was a fine justification for making their life a hell in this world. Similarly, belief in the "predestined" inferiority or viciousness of minority groups makes discriminatory treatment of them seem reasonable, or, as Dollard says, at least inevitable. If the American Negro is shiftless, lazy, unable to master the skills necessary for handling modern machinery, and especially if these traits are innate, then it is not prejudice that limits him to the most tedious, least desirable unskilled work; it is his own lack of capacity. Interestingly enough, with regard to the widespread belief that the Negro is naturally unable to acquire mechanical skills, one of the most vigorous protests against him in the decades following the Civil War was precisely that he monopolized the skilled crafts, because of the protected training he had received under slavery. Rationalizing beliefs for conflict situations do not need to be mutually consistent; they are *ad hoc* creations for specific battles. Slaveowners did not find it difficult to believe that slaves were inferior, unable to absorb civilization, suitable only for menial tasks, and yet at the same time to train them to do the most of the skilled work around the plantation. The picture of the Jew as an international banker and, simultaneously, as a Communist organizer doesn't strain the logical capacity of many people.

One of the most elaborate rationalizations of a power position was built up around the dominations of modern empires. The European nations, we discover, were in Africa or the East Indies to rescue the natives from barbarism, to convert them to Christianity, to bring them the benefits of civilization. It is unfortunate that the natives were incapable of self-government, not yet ready for independence, unable to manage the machinery of modern technology—they were the white man's burden. We do not mean to imply that no other motives than economic and political were involved in the relations between modern states and their empires. We are simply indicating that the power motives, while very important, are seldom explicitly stated.

During the last quarter of a century direct colonialism has been sharply reduced; but even in the recent instances in which powerful nations have "voluntarily freed" a subject people, economic and political considerations have not been unimportant. American sugar interests, for example, wanted Philippine sugar outside the tariff walls, and Britain knew that the balance of shipments, which, for over a century before 1931, had sent more goods from India to Britain than from Britain to India, had since 1931 been continuously the other way around. A large part of the white man's burden has been the burden of carrying Indian cotton and steel, Javanese rubber and tin, and Philippine sugar and gold back to the empires' homelands. That some benefits have been carried in the other direction and that the difference between what he receives and what he gives is obscured for the white man by his comforting beliefs are testimony to the fact that the dominators have a conscience that cannot be completely disregarded. They are also evidence of the presence of some bargaining power in the hands of the colonists.

Rationalizing economic beliefs may originate in a group that profits by the situation which it disguises, but these beliefs may be accepted by people who have nothing to gain —and perhaps much to lose—from that situation. They may be accepted even by persons who do not *believe* they profit from the situation. This circumstance should prevent us from making an oversimplified economic interpretation of these beliefs. Many people on the West Coast have believed that the Japanese farmer was a menace to "the American standard of living," that the long hours he worked and the degree to which the Japanese father used his own family as cheap labor made it impossible for the white farmer to compete. The white man's income was lowered, his ability to buy goods from other producers (who in turn were injured) was curtailed, and thus out went the injury in an ever-widening circle until the whole economy, presumably including the original Japanese farmer, was harmed. This type of reasoning was popular over a century ago when Henry Clay fought political battles with his "American system." That most economists think it false has not prevented it from becoming a part of the system of economic beliefs of a great many Americans.

The economist is more likely to say: The Japanese farmer, by his efficiency, forces other farmers to be more efficient, and by the lower prices that he makes possible he leaves extra dollars in the purses of West Coast housewives. Those extra dollars, in turn, permit them to buy other goods, which they otherwise would not have been able to afford, make other businesses more prosperous, put more wages in circulation, so that further production is encouraged, until, presumably, even the white farmer who was immediately injured by the competition of the Japanese farmer may be compensated, at least in part. We are not trying to argue the economics of the case but to indicate that people often hold economic beliefs that qualified experts consider false. The function of those beliefs is not changed; a gun that backfires is still intended to shoot the other way.

ECONOMIC CONFLICT AND THE ORIGINS OF JIM CROW

We have surveyed some of the evidence for the theory that prejudice can be understood partly as an expression of the economic, political, and other interests of groups. In their attempts to maintain or increase their share of income, prestige, and power, groups find it easy to invent or accept the idea that other groups are inferior and thus less deserving of life's values. The idea can be put briefly. Prejudice exists because someone gains by it. Some writers lean upon this interpretation so heavily that they make it *the* theory of prejudice. Just as the doctrinaire Freudian insists that the "fundamental" cause of prejudice is the frustrations and anxieties of individuals, so the doctrinaire Marxian insists that the "fundamental" cause of prejudice is class conflict. Some people contend that racial stereotypes are consciously created by the ruling class as weapons to fight minority groups and the lower classes of their own race.

Race prejudice in the United States is the socio-attitudinal matrix supporting a calculated and determined effort of a white ruling class to keep some people or peoples of color and their resources exploitable.[63]

The Negro people are oppressed because the rulers of our society find it highly profitable to oppress them. In terms of fundamental motivations, the explanation of the Negro question is as simple as that. . . . If there is anything which the history and contemporary life of America clearly reveal about the Negro question, it is the stark material, profit-seeking core from which all of the varied forms of anti-Negro discrimination and oppression emerge.[64]

This theory of prejudice has received especially intense examination since the publication of Gunnar Myrdal's well-known study, *An American Dilemma*. Because it is not only a descriptive account of the American Negro but attempts also a theoretical explanation of the prejudice against the Negro, this research has stimulated a great deal of further study. Myrdal develops a multiple-factor theory of prejudice in which he gives a relatively unimportant place to the economic and political forces discussed above. His formulations have been accepted widely (and sometimes uncritically), but they have also been sharply attacked by some writers.

We can perhaps approach an understanding of the actual role of the forces of group conflict by examining this controversy. Compare, for example, the very different interpretations of the factors involved in the continued subjugation of the Negro in the United States after 1865. There is general agreement that after the Civil War anti-Negro prejudice continued to serve—or seemed to serve—functions for several groups of Whites. There is a great deal of dispute, however, regarding the roles of the various classes of Whites in reaffirming the inferior status of the Negro that had been legally broken by emancipation. Left-wing writers claim, and not without some historical evidence in their favor, that the poor Whites and Negroes recognized their common problems even before the war to some degree, but

very explicitly afterward, and set about, in 1865, to establish a political and economic structure that would serve the majority. The Reconstruction legislatures of several of the southern states had written, by 1875, some of the most liberal state constitutions in the country—constitutions which, if put into effect even today, would radically change economic, political, and educational practices in the South.[65] These legislatures were composed largely of "poor whites" (not from the former slave-holding group), Negroes, and abolitionists and carpetbaggers from the North. The contention is that the breaking, for the moment, of the dominance of the planter class, their demoralization and loss of prestige, allowed the poor Whites and Negroes to see their common economic and political interests and to act upon them together. Here the economic force was working in the direction of nonprejudice. This theory goes on to state, however, that the confusions of the postwar period, the continued economic power of the planters through their control of the land, and the clumsiness, if not the outright collusion, of the federal government permitted the old southern aristocracy to come back into power. By 1900 most of the new constitutions had been repealed or rewritten; the Negroes' claim for equality was pushed farther and farther back by disfranchisement, segregation statutes (passed in every southern state by 1907), and economic barriers.

It was not difficult for the ruling group to draw the masses of white workers back into the circle of prejudice. One of the first places where economic conflict occurred was among the artisan group. Many of the former slaves were skilled carpenters, bricklayers, and blacksmiths. Under slavery they were protected from direct attack of the white workers who felt that their economic opportunities were blocked by the work of the artisan slaves. After 1865, however, there was nothing to prevent the white worker from striking out at his black competitor.

---

[63] Cox, *op. cit.*, p. 475.

[64] Doxey Wilkerson, in the introduction to Herbert Aptheker, *The Negro People in America*, International Publishers, 1946, pp. 8–10.

[65] Cf. James S. Allen, *Reconstruction, the Battle for Democracy*, International Publishers, 1937; and John Hope Franklin, *From Slavery to Freedom*, Knopf, 1947, pp. 293–338.

Each successive census shows the decline in proportion of skilled workers who are Negro.

Even the poorest of Whites was convinced rather easily that he had more to gain by keeping the Negro down than by uniting with him against the upper-class Whites. His own deprivations were made somewhat more bearable by the continuous sight of even more serious deprivations among the Negroes. Though he was actually injured by a system that rested upon the exploitation of cheap labor, he was not perceptive enough to recognize the true source of his difficulty. Moreover, as Dollard has shown, he received some prestige and sexual gains over the Negro which made it easier for him to acquiesce in the system. The more doctrinaire Marxists assume that the upper-class Whites understood all this and by conscious decision "used" prejudice as a weapon, implanting it in the poor whites by propaganda, by control over the schools, churches, and newspapers, as well as by control of job opportunities. The process was doubtless far less rational than this assumption would have it appear; prejudice simply seemed "right" to the upper class, for it is always easy to believe that which harmonizes with one's class interest. And it also seemed right to the lower-class White because he did not understand the true causes of his economic difficulties. On the surface the Negro was obviously his direct competitor, and the white worker felt that he received some gains from restricting active competitors for jobs. In any event he was highly frustrated and in need of easily accessible outlets for his hostility.

It should not be forgotten, however, that *there were some tendencies* for the lower-class White to join with the Negro in political and economic action. They would doubtless have been stronger but for the systematic opposition to that development from the upper class. Even the powerful interests of the North, after having finished a war against the southern planters, found it to be in their interest to permit the South to develop its own pattern of race relations. Attempts to interpret the Fourteenth and Fifteenth Amendments in radical equalitarian fashion were blocked by the Supreme Court. Northern banking, industrial, and insurance interests, with large holdings in the South, found the cheap-labor system to their liking. Even when the Republican party, strictly a northern party, was at the height of its power, there was virtually no attempt to achieve full civil rights for the Negro—one of the aims for which, presumably, they had led the North during the Civil War. The cooperation of northern and southern upper classes is a political commonplace even today, although it is complicated by the pull of other forces in their respective environments.

Woodward reminds us of the "forgotten alternatives" that were being debated in the South between 1865 and 1895. His account of the ways in which all of these alternatives were pushed aside one by one, except for the victorious pattern of segregation and discrimination against the Negro, indicates well the way in which economic and political factors were involved. Before the doctrines of the extreme racists were adopted, conservatives, liberals, and radical populists also sought to establish their point of view. "All three of these alternative philosophies rejected the doctrines of extreme racism and all three were indigenously and thoroughly Southern in origin."[66] The period during which these alternatives contested for supremacy was not, of course, a peaceful period in race relations. Lynching and violent intimidation of Negroes were at their worst in the 1880s and 1890s. Yet in 1897, a Charleston, South Carolina, newspaper wrote: "The common sense and proper arrangement, in our opinion, is to provide first-class cars for first-class passengers, white and colored. . . . To speak plainly, we need, as everybody knows, separate cars or apartments for rowdy or drunken white passengers far more than Jim Crow cars for colored passengers."[67]

The liberal alternative was probably least well represented during this period. Yet a

[66] C. Vann Woodward, *The Strange Career of Jim Crow*, Oxford, 1955, p. 27.

[67] *Ibid.*, quoted on pp. 30–31.

few, such as George Washington Cable, spoke for equality in every sphere of life and fought discrimination and segregation. The conservatives thought in terms of a stratified society, with Negroes in a subordinate role; but they opposed the idea that Negroes should be segregated and humiliated. Radical populism sought to join with the freed Negroes to achieve agrarian reform. Over a period of a generation of debate, however, these alternatives failed. The pattern of extreme segregation and discrimination that was to prevail for half a century won out. What political and economic forces were involved in this outcome? Woodward discusses a number of interacting factors.

Beginning with the compromise of 1877, northern liberal opinion progressively disregarded the race issue and left the South to its own pattern. This was in part due to the fact that sectional reconciliation, healing the wounds of the Civil War, was a clear liberal cause. Since many persons in the North shared the racial attitudes of most Southerners, sectional reconciliation was easily put ahead of racial equality. The Supreme Court reflected, if it did not lead, this development by a series of decisions between 1873 and 1896 that progressively limited the privileges and immunities of Negroes and sanctioned discrimination. Then into this scene came America's imperialist adventures in the Caribbean and the Pacific. In view of the white supremacy mystique with which European and American imperialism was being justified, racial arguments in the South could not be answered. "Senator Ben Tillman, the most impudent racist in the South, could now gloat over his Republican colleagues from the Yankee North and defy them to do anything about the Counterrevolution then taking place in the South."[68]

While the North was relaxing its opposition to extreme racism, southern restraints also were greatly weakened, primarily as a result of the economic and political struggles going on. The conservative forces had at first joined with the anti-Negro Whites to win power from the carpetbaggers. Then, as Woodward shows, they sought to conciliate the Negro freedman by opposing the extremists and offering him small political plums. This stage, however, was a casualty of the political weakness of the conservatives. Their sympathy with the political and economic views of northern conservatives was in sharp opposition to the money policies and agrarian reforms supported by poorer Southerners. To save themselves politically in face of the challenge of the populists, they turned to the anti-Negro views that had helped them defeat the carpetbaggers. "The same means of fraud, intimidation, bribery, violence, and terror were used against the one that had been used against the other. 'I told them to go to it, boys, count them out,' admitted the conservative Governor William C. Oates of Alabama. 'We had to do it. Unfortunately, I say it was a necessity. We could not help ourselves.' "[69]

Thus Negroes were "counted out" by the conservatives. This tactic helped to split the populists, who had continued their precarious effort to unify white and Negro voters. Weakened by the serious depressions of the 1890s, seeing some of their members pulled away by the racist views of the opposition, receiving "permissions to hate" from the Supreme Court and northern intellectuals, the populists saw their biracial policy "dissolve in frustration and bitterness."

Having served as the national scapegoat in the reconciliation and reunion of North and South, the Negro was now pressed into service as a sectional scapegoat in the reconciliation of estranged white classes and the reunion of the Solid South. . . . The only formula powerful enough to accomplish that was the magical formula of white supremacy, applied without stint and without any of the old conservative reservations of paternalism, without deference to any lingering resistance to Northern liberalism, or any fear of further check from a defunct Southern Populism.[70]

---

[68] William G. Carleton, in the introduction to H. D. Price, *The Negro and Southern Politics. A Chapter of Florida History*, New York Univ. Press, 1957, p. xii.

[69] Woodward, *op. cit.*, p. 61.

[70] *Ibid.*, pp. 65–66. For supporting historical material see Charles Wynes, *Race Relations in Virginia, 1890–1902*, Univ. of Virginia Press, 1961.

Thus economic and political conflicts played a vital role in determining which of the various alternative ways of dealing with the freedmen would predominate. By the end of the nineteenth century, disfranchisement, segregation, and relegation to second-class citizenship had won out.

There are also alternatives on the race relations scene today. Which ones will be forgotten in half a century is not clear. Some are stridently racist, continuing to use prejudice as a weapon to protect or win economic and political advantages. Economic coercion and political pressure are also being used in an effort to prevent desegregation. There are other alternatives, however; and if in a day of race conflict, opposition to school integration, and continuing economic discrimination they seem obscured, they may nevertheless be the ones likely to win out. There are now powerful economic, political, and other forces supporting desegregation and the full enfranchisement of Negro Americans. Throughout Part II of this volume we will give the evidence that leads us to the conclusion that this time segregation will be the "forgotten alternative."

SOCIAL CLASS, PREJUDICE, AND DISCRIMINATION

The interpretation holding that the continued subjection of Negroes after emancipation was, to an important degree, the result of economic and political conflict among Whites is sharply challenged by Myrdal and others. They contend that the upper-class white man in the South, far from being one of the key sources of prejudice and the segregation system, is the Negroes' best friend. Louis Wirth wrote: "It has been repeatedly found by students of Negro-White relations in the South that the so-called white aristocracy shows less racial prejudice than do the 'poor whites' whose own position is relatively insecure and who must compete with Negroes for jobs, for property, for social position, and for power. Only those who themselves are insecure feel impelled to press their claims for superiority over

others. . . ."[71] Myrdal contends that it was impossible that the Negro and lower-class white should have joined hands after 1865 to get land reform. When the feedbox is empty, says a Swedish proverb, the horses will bite each other. Lower classes are not naturally radical, or even liberal; they do not readily take a favorable attitude toward disadvantaged groups.

In recent years there have been numerous efforts to test this proposition, to discover, by comparative study, the extent of prejudice among persons on various class levels. Using the methods of attitude research, a number of writers have established that in the United States persons in the lower socioeconomic strata are more authoritarian, are less supportive of civil liberties, express prejudice toward more groups. Dividing their respondents into five income classes, MacKinnon and Centers found the following percentages in the upper half on authoritarian scores: 40, 33, 46, 68, and 85. Thus the three higher income groups were underrepresented and the two lower ones were overrepresented among the authoritarians.[72] Lipset reviewed the evidence from many countries and found a consistent pattern of intolerance and prejudice among those of low status. The causes, he suggests, are numerous. "A number of elements in the typical social situation of lower-class individuals may be singled out as contributing to authoritarian predispositions: low education, low participation in political organizations or in voluntary organizations of any type, little reading, isolated occupations, economic insecurity, and authoritarian family patterns."[73] The intolerance should not be identified with a general conservative outlook. Lower status groups often take liberal positions on economic issues—welfare state measures, graduated income taxes, and the like. The reference here is to their intolerance toward

[71] Louis Wirth, "Race and Public Policy," *Scientific Monthly*, Apr., 1944, p. 304.
[72] William MacKinnon and Richard Centers, "Authoritarianism and Urban Stratification," *AJS*, May, 1956, p. 616.
[73] Seymour Lipset, "Democracy and Working-Class Authoritarianism," *ASR*, Aug., 1959, p. 489.

unpopular political groups and racial and ethnic minorities.

Other research supports this finding. Stouffer, in an extensive study of a national sample of 5000 Americans, found that intolerance went up as position on the status ladder (measured by occupation) went down.[74] In interviews with 2600 male heads of households in three northern California counties, Cohen and Hodges discovered that intolerance was highest among the lowest strata. With reference to the most disprivileged person, the lower lower-class member, they report that ". . . it was above all toward the ethnic minority group that he directed his animosity."[75] They agree with Lipset that this expresses in part the need among unsophisticated and poorly trained persons to simplify their world. In political matters they choose the least complex alternative; in intergroup relations they divide the world sharply into "we" and "they" groups. In addition to that, however, Cohen and Hodges suggest that the prejudiced responses of the lower-lower class are not only a denial of the "American Creed" of equality but also a result of it. When they apply the creed to themselves they measure up so poorly that they are strongly motivated to look for other bases of evaluation; ascriptive group membership is readily seized upon.[76]

SPECIFYING THE CLASS-PREJUDICE RELATIONSHIP

There are strong evidences for class differentials in prejudice. A number of qualifications must be noted, however, if we are to interpret these evidences correctly. There are measurement problems involved, particularly when prejudice is determined by verbal tests: measures of authoritarianism may tap their realistic experiences of deprivation and hostility, rather than or in addition to their attitudes; when education is controlled, class differences in levels of prejudice may be sharply reduced or eliminated.[77] Miller and Riessman argue, in fact, that many qualities of lower-class life and subculture promote democratic tendencies—support for the underdog, more egalitarian values, perhaps a stronger sense of group solidarity.[78]

Westie and Westie differentiate the general observation of a relationship between class and prejudice by noting that the class of the persons being responded to is also involved. Lower-class Whites express the greatest feelings of social distance from Negroes, but they make some distinctions among lower-middle- and upper-class Negroes. Middle- and upper-class Whites indicate less prejudice and draw larger distinctions among various classes of Negroes.[79]

Since class is, to some degree, related to authoritarianism, it is well to note that those scoring high on authoritarian measures are more likely to change attitudes in the direction of a message attributed to a high status source than are those low in authoritarianism.[80]

In some measure it is not objective class status but the fact of having *fallen into* a lower class status that is the decisive fact.[81] Greenblum and Pearlin, in a study of a sample from Elmira, New York, found that

[74] Samuel Stouffer, *Communism, Conformity, and Civil Liberties*, Doubleday, 1955.

[75] Albert Cohen and Harold Hodges, Jr., "Characteristics of the Lower-Blue-Collar-Class," *SP*, Spring, 1963, p. 321.

[76] *Ibid.*, pp. 321–322.

[77] See Lewis Lipsitz, "Working-Class Authoritarianism: A Re-Evaluation," *ASR*, Feb., 1965, pp. 103–109. From three national samples, Lipsitz found that education accounts for most class differentials. He emphasizes the need for differentiation among various aspects of authoritarianism.

[78] S. M. Miller and Frank Riessman, "Working-Class Authoritarianism: A Critique of Lipset," *British Journal of Sociology*, Sept., 1961, pp. 263–276.

[79] Frank Westie and Margaret Westie, "The Social-Distance Pyramid: Relationships Between Caste and Class," *AJS*, Sept., 1957, pp. 190–196. H. M. Blalock has examined the relationships among status differences and prejudice in a valuable way. See his *Toward a Theory of Minority-Group Relations*, Wiley, 1967, esp. pp. 61–70, 199–203.

[80] See O. J. Harvey and G. Beverly, "Some Personality Correlates of Concept Change Through Role Playing," *JASP*, July, 1961, pp. 125–130.

[81] See the discussion of the findings of Bettelheim and Janowitz, chapter 10, below. For a valuable discussion of political effects of downward mobility, see Harold Wilensky and Hugh Edwards, "The Skidders: Ideological Adjustments of Downward Mobile Workers," *ASR*, Apr., 1959, pp. 215–231.

downward mobility was associated with greater prejudice. They noted in addition, however, that upward mobility was equally or perhaps even more likely to be associated with prejudice, a fact that they interpret as a manifestation of an effort to enhance or secure hard-won prestige.[82]

In a re-examination of this study, however, and an addition of material from a national sample of the adult white population of the United States, Hodge and Treiman arrive at a different interpretation: for both upwardly mobile and downwardly mobile persons, pro-integration sentiments were in between what one would expect from a knowledge of their class origins and a knowledge of their present class. Thus those who move into the middle class may be more prejudiced than stable members of the middle class, not because of the experience of mobility, but because they carry some of the values and attitudes of their earlier class with them. And those who fall into the lower class may be more prejudiced than the middle class that they have left, not because of the impact of mobility, but because of the influence of the new class situation in which they are found. Levels of prejudice seem to be intermediary between class of origin and present class.[83]

Light is thrown on these somewhat ambiguous findings by the introduction of another variable. Silberstein and Seeman found that it was not downward mobility by itself that was associated with prejudice but downward mobility of those who were strongly "mobility oriented," who were highly sensitive to status considerations. Such persons were significantly more anti-Semitic and anti-Negro than stationary worker- or middle-class persons or downwardly-mobile persons who were not status-seeking. Middle-class persons showed somewhat less prejudice than did those from the working-class; and

those who had climbed into the middle class showed the least of all. Even those climbers who were mobility oriented exhibited, contrary to the Greenblum and Pearlin sample, lower levels of prejudice than did the stable middle class.[84] In a further observation on mobility, Pettigrew found that the downwardly mobile in four small northern towns were more prejudiced than the stationary or upwardly mobile, but in four small southern towns downward social mobility was associated with less prejudice.[85] This suggests that loss of status cuts a person off from the norms of the surrounding community, whatever they are. In the case of the southern sample the result was some alienation from norms of prejudice. Thus the effects of mobility on prejudice are complex, depending on the setting, other attitudes of the individual, and doubtless other variables.

We must qualify further by noting that not all the evidence supports the observed relationship between lower-class status and prejudice. In a sample from the Detroit area, Angell found that lower-class Protestants (with a large number of persons raised in the South) were more prejudiced than higher-class Protestants; but the reverse was true among Catholics.[86] It is not easy to interpret these facts without controls for education, ethnic group, and other factors, but at least they indicate that higher-class standing is not automatically associated with lower prejudice. In two nationwide samples taken by the Survey Research Center, in fact, highest authoritarian scores, measured by a modified F Scale, were found among the lower-middle-class, especially among those with low levels of education.[87]

Methodological considerations require a

---

[82] Joseph Greenblum and L. I. Pearlin, "Vertical Mobility and Prejudice," in Reinhard Bendix and Seymour Lipset (eds.), *Class, Status, and Power*, Free Press, 1953, pp. 480–491.

[83] Robert Hodge and Donald Treiman, "Occupational Mobility and Attitudes Toward Negroes," *ASR*, Feb., 1966, pp. 93–102.

[84] F. B. Silberstein and Melvin Seeman, "Social Mobility and Prejudice," *AJS*, Nov., 1959, pp. 258–264. Their data are based on interviews of a random sample of 665 persons in the metropolitan area of Morgantown, West Virginia.

[85] Thomas Pettigrew, "Personality and Socio-cultural Factors in Intergroup Attitudes: A Cross-National Comparison," *JCR*, Mar., 1958, pp. 38–39.

[86] Robert Angell, "Preference for Moral Norms in Three Problem Areas," *AJS*, May, 1962, pp. 658–659.

[87] Morris Janowitz and Dwaine Marvick, "Authoritarianism and Political Behavior," *POQ*, Summer, 1953, pp. 185–201.

further qualification. Most measures of prejudice have been developed and standardized against middle- and upper-class groups; their reliability in measuring the attitudes of lower-class persons, with different vocabularies, different styles of response to written documents or to strangers, different skills in interpersonal relations has not been established. When a cross section of Detroiters were asked to give their opinions of two mutually contradictory propositions, widely separated in the interview, nearly eight percent agreed with both. Whether this is the result of a norm of deference toward the interviewer, as Lenski and Leggett suggest, or "response set," in the sense in which we have discussed that term in Chapter 3, is not crucial here. What is interesting is that the mutually contradictory responses were most characteristic of those with lower-class standing or with low education. They may get high scores on some measures of prejudice just because they say "yes" to a stranger interviewing them (and on most scales a yes answer means prejudice). On one question measuring "anomia," for example, the contrast between white collar and blue collar was 4 percent to 15 percent. When those who agreed to an opposite statement were removed, however, the numbers agreeing fell to 2 and 5 percent. When the same comparison is made for white and Negro respondents, the percentages fall from 8 and 25 to 3 and 6, respectively.[88] Such data should encourage us to be cautious in our interpretation of statements of comparative levels of prejudice among classes that are based on the measurement of verbal attitudes.

Assessment of the influence of class location on prejudice is further complicated by status inconsistency: many persons are higher by some measures of status than by others; their placement, therefore, is problematic—a fact that influences their attitudes and opinions and the responses of others to them. A person of high education may have a modest income; or a person belonging to

the dominant ethnic group may work at a low-status job.

There is now substantial literature dealing with status inconsistency, much of it concerned with its effects on political attitudes and behavior.[89] Only a few studies have dealt with the implications of status inconsistency for prejudice, and the results have not been entirely compatible.[90] On balance, however, it appears that prejudice is supported by a combination of dominant ethnic status with low income, education, and occupational attainment.

A final qualification is perhaps of greatest importance: We need to keep fully in mind the distinction between discrimination and prejudice. It is one thing to note that lower-class Whites get a higher prejudice score on verbal tests. It is another to discover what class of Whites is most discriminatory. Middle- and upper-class people may have more skillful rationalizations and verbal disguises. They may recite the American creed more spontaneously. They may have a great need to seem reasonable and tolerant. Hence their prejudice score may be low. These tendencies, however, could be accompanied by vigorous discrimination against minority-group members—low wages paid to them, high rents charged for slum dwellings, exclusion from business and professional or-

[89] We cannot examine that literature here, but much of it, even when not concerned with race relations, has indirect relevance for the student of prejudice. In particular, the analysis of the varieties of status inconsistency that promote right-wing extremism on one hand and liberal views on the other are of value. See, for example, Gerhard Lenski, "Status Crystallization: A Non-Vertical Dimension of Social Status," *ASR*, Aug., 1954, pp. 405–413; Martin Hyman, "Determining the Effects of Status Inconsistency," *POQ*, Spring, 1966, pp. 120–129, and the Comment by H. M. Blalock, pp. 130–132; James Geschwender, "Continuities in Theories of Status Consistency and Cognitive Dissonance," *SF*, Dec., 1967, pp. 160–171; G. B. Rush, "Status Consistency and Right-Wing Extremism," *ASR*, Feb., 1967, pp. 86–92; Stanley Eitzen, "Status Inconsistency and Wallace Supporters in a Midwestern City," *SF*, June, 1970, pp. 493–498; D. R. Segal, "Status Inconsistency, Cross Pressures, and American Political Behavior," *ASR*, June, 1969, pp. 352–359.

[90] See Donald Treiman, "Status Discrepancy and Prejudice," *AJS*, May, 1966, pp. 651–666; and James Geshwender, "Status Discrepancy and Prejudice Reconsidered," *AJS*, Mar. 1970, pp. 863–865.

[88] Gerhard Lenski and J. C. Leggett, "Caste, Class, and Deference in the Research Interview," *AJS*, Mar., 1960, pp. 463–467.

ganizations, refusal to rent or sell property to them, ambitious programs to prevent them from voting. If it is true that the powerful, upper-class Whites are the chief defenders —not without exceptions, of course—of the whole institutional structure by which the minority group is exploited, then their more polite verbal behavior may be of relatively little importance. On the other hand, the verbal world is an important world. Inhibitions against the expression of deep prejudice may help to create a situation in which change toward more tolerant action is easier for middle- and upper-class Whites. The way in which prejudices are expressed also strongly affects the responses of minority-group members and thus the whole cycle of interaction.

In discussing class differences in discrimination it is well to note that in one situation the economic or political interests of the upper classes may be served by discrimination, but in another situation they may be served by equality of treatment. As employers, for example, they could profit from free choice among all members of the labor force on the basis of skill. Similarly, the interests of lower-class members may in one instance be served by discrimination while in another they demand equalitarianism and solidarity.

In terms of discrimination, then, if not of prejudice, different social classes present a complex picture. Vander Zanden found that most of the participants in a revised Ku Klux Klan in the late 1950s were ". . . in the upper rungs of the working class and the lower rungs of the middle class."[91] Citizens Councils are drawn largely from the newly rich and the threatened old plantation élite,[92] aided and abetted by those seeking or holding public office. On the state level, the Councils are organized like a modern business, with skilled secretaries, public relations committees, and substantial budgets. Theirs is not the work of either authoritarian

personalities or of insecure and unsophisticated members of the lower class. The complexity of the class-prejudice picture is nicely shown by Campbell when he writes:

Who were the people with the brickbats forming the crowd in front of Central High School in Little Rock, screaming and crying, "They're in. They're in. The niggers are in," on September 23, 1957? They were the rural and lower class urban riffraff. But who were the people who built a new high school on the western edge of the city and planned to keep its attendance area lily-white, by this act securing a private public school for their kind and releasing Central High School to the residents of the city's inner zones? This was the urban middle class, the Southern moderate. Understanding community processes, and controlling the mechanisms of decision, they had no need to resort to violence; they had alternative methods of securing their ends.[93]

To indicate the complexity of the relationship we must add that it has often been the businessmen and industrialists who have taken the lead, as in Atlanta and Dallas, in the desegregation process.[94]

On the basis of these several qualifications, let us return to Myrdal's observations concerning the relationship of class and prejudice. He writes:

Our hypothesis is that in a society where there are broad social classes, and in addition, more minute distinctions and splits in the lower strata, *the lower class groups will, to a great extent, take care of keeping each other subdued,* thus relieving, to that extent, the higher classes of this otherwise painful task necessary to the

---

[91] James Vander Zanden, "The Klan Revival," *AJS*, Mar., 1960, p. 458.

[92] James Vander Zanden, "Desegregation and Social Strains in the South," *JSI*, Fourth Quarter, 1959, pp. 53–60.

[93] Ernest Campbell, "On Desegregation and Matters Sociological," *Phylon*, Summer, 1961, p. 137. One should add, however, that the suburban Hall High School and all other junior and senior high schools in Little Rock were desegregated during the next three or four years. On the place of the moderate, see also Richard Cramer, "School Desegregation and New Industry: The Southern Community Leaders' Viewpoint," *SF*, May, 1963, pp. 384–389.

[94] This is not to suggest that the lead is very decisive or dramatic. There is good evidence that the southern "moderate" goes into action only when faced with threat of loss, and then moves only minimally. See Campbell, *op. cit.*; Cramer, *op. cit.*; and Thomas Pettigrew, "The Myth of the Moderates," *The Christian Century*, May 24, 1961.

monopolization of the power and the advantages.

It will be observed that this hypothesis is contrary to the Marxian theory of class society. . . . The Marxian scheme assumes that there is an actual solidarity between the several lower class groups against the higher classes, or, in any case, a potential solidarity which as a matter of natural development is bound to emerge. . . .

A solidarity between poor whites and Negroes has been said to be "natural" and the conflicts to be due to "illusions." . . . Everything we know about human frustration and aggression, and the displacement of aggression speaks against it.[95]

Myrdal has made two mistakes in this statement that render his conflict with the "Marxian" interpretation unnecessarily sharp. When he says that "everything we know about human frustration and aggression" points to vigorous conflict between various divisions within the lower class, he overlooks the fact that some, and in some instances much, of the aggression of lower-class people is directed against the upper classes. As we shall see in Chapter 7, the *apparent* nonaggressiveness of many Negroes toward the dominant Whites hides a great deal of subtle attack. His second error is in dismissing completely the fact that to some degree the lower-class Negroes and Whites *did* join forces after the Civil War and are joining forces today. This situation shows two forces at work that give opposite encouragement to prejudice and discrimination. Myrdal has emphasized one, and left-wing writers such as Cox and Aptheker have emphasized the other. Each has then been quick to point up the errors of his opponent without seeing his own omissions. Myrdal is right in noting that a great deal (not all) of the frustrations of the lower-class White and Negro tend to keep them apart, to encourage prejudice between them. Not all the hostility is displaced, however. Lower-class Whites often feel a bitter resentment against upper-class Whites, and in some instances this is accompanied by a feeling of common fate with lower-class Negroes—even though there is a simultaneous attitude of prejudice.

These various forces are expressed in the fragile but visible political coalitions between working-class Whites and Blacks. A story in *The New York Times* illustrates the situation:

When Maynard Jackson ran for the United States Senate in Georgia against Senator Herman Talmadge in 1968, he received a call one evening from a white man in southern Georgia who said he represented a group of small farmers.

"I know you're colored," the man said, "but I have to admire someone who can rise above his station."

When Mr. Jackson tells the story he says, "Before he even realized he had insulted me and before I had time to respond appropriately, he said, 'We're going to vote for you because Herman has turned his back on us.' "

Last year when Mr. Jackson was elected vice mayor of Atlanta, he received 18 per cent of the vote in working-class white precincts.

Mr. Jackson's experience is one of several developments that have kindled tentative, qualified hope among some Southern blacks and white liberals for a new populist coalition in the South that would bring low-income whites and blacks together to work for programs of common benefit.[96]

In examining the question of the balance of class solidarity versus racial antagonisms, moreover, one must be careful not to use data about the distribution of prejudice against one minority to generalize about attitudes toward other minorities. Members of the lower class may verbalize more prejudice against one minority, and middle- or upper-class members may express more prejudice against another.

Many Negroes *believe* that upper-class Whites are less prejudiced. This conviction may indicate that prejudice is defined in terms of day-to-day contacts, not on the basis

---

[95] Myrdal, *op. cit.*, p. 68.

[96] *The New York Times*, Oct. 10, 1970, p. 69.

of the underlying discriminatory pattern that the upper classes may be most important in defending. It may show also that Negroes share the status values—belief in the marks of superiority—that define the upper classes. It reflects in part, of course, the effects of the leadership that some upper-class Whites furnish to movements for the improvement of the Negro's position.

Some Negroes, particularly those in the middle class, contend that middle-class Whites are their chief opponents. Dollard reports that in Southerntown many of his informants believed that the upper classes are too secure to need much prejudice and the lower-class Whites feel some sympathy for Negroes because of similar difficulties, whereas the middle classes, not certain of their status and anxious to improve it, draw a sharp line of prejudice. Negroes often call them "strainers," a term that corresponds well with the position of the middle class.[97]

Altogether it seems clear that we dare not assume, as Myrdal tends to do, a clear-cut relationship between class position and the likelihood of prejudice.

The Marxian theory is correct in pointing out that prejudice brings more gains to the upper classes of the dominant group than to the lower, that sometimes the ruling class consciously manipulates prejudice as a power device, that in some situations lower-class Whites will turn away from race prejudice in order to work together with a minority group against the upper class. The theory is one-sided, however, in failing to note that some of the forces encourage nonprejudice among the upper class (greater personal security, a feeling of *noblesse oblige*, and probably their long-run economic interests). Oppositely, the theory is weak in failing to indicate the forces that encourage prejudice among lower-class Whites (greater personal insecurity, a richer tradition with regard to violence and aggression, and direct immediate economic competition with minority-

group members). The Marxian analysis is too rationalistic; the dominant group does not often create and exploit prejudice to its own advantage. It simply finds an attitude that justifies its position very easy to accept.

Many contradictory forces are at work in any given expression of prejudice. Which one will predominate depends upon their relative strengths and the setting in which they work. The "economic" element in prejudice is *least* likely to predominate where traditional definitions of roles are most stable, where economic classes are least self-conscious and organized, where the "intellectual climate" encourages the interpretation of individual frustrations in terms of personal opponents. The "economic" element in prejudice is *most* likely to predominate where traditional definitions of roles are being challenged, where large-scale organizations along class lines are most highly developed, and where group differentiation tends to correspond with differences in economic functions. The careful student will not accept a blanket statement of the *general* role of group conflict in prejudice, whether it be a statement that stresses or one that minimizes the role. He will rather seek to find the role of group conflict in *specific* situations as it interacts with the other forces at work in those situations. Group conflict from one point of view, moreover, works in favor of nonprejudice, for it establishes attitudes favorable to members of the in-group with which one has identified himself. A white union member may feel more solidarity with fellow members, of whatever race, than with the white race, per se. He may, of course, seek to maintain solidarity with both the union and the white race by a segregated union. Contemporary experiences are demonstrating, however, that when other factors combine to make a segregated union impossible or undesirable, race prejudice, or at least discrimination, among the members of highly integrated unions drops rapidly. In other words, though prejudice may be one of the manifestations of group conflict, a particular kind of prejudice is not inevitable. Racial or religious prejudice may be used as

[97] John Dollard, *Caste and Class in a Southern Town*, Yale, 1937, pp. 77–78.

an economic weapon: but in another setting the racial and religious lines may be obscured and the class line emphasized. The degree to which group conflict is involved in prejudice and the targets of that prejudice both vary widely.

Do prejudice and discrimination actually pay off, in a narrowly economic sense? There is little doubt that Blacks, Chicanos, Indians, and other minority-group Americans are hurt by discrimination; but it is possible that group conflict over scarce values generates—and is generated by—prejudice and discrimination without anyone profiting thereby. It is also possible that discriminators believe that they profit without that, in fact, being true. It seems most likely, however, that a system of prejudice and discrimination will survive over a long period only if it yields to some an advantage, whether it be absolute or only comparative. We will be discussing this topic in several other chapters, and refer to it here only to connect it with our general theory.[98] Discrimination is not simply an individual eccentricity; it is tied into social structures and privilege systems. It cannot be removed by paying attention to individual attitudes alone. Change will require significant revision of occupational structures, of access to training, of presently protected economic opportunity channels. Discrimination is a "tough" system in which individual anxiety and group advantage support each other. Out of their interaction, moreover, there comes a shared attitude of prejudice that, once launched, becomes in some measure a force on its own, able to continue, at least for a time, without the support of group conflict or personal insecurity. The discussion of this aspect of a theory of prejudice and discrimination—the cultural—will occupy the next chapter.

[98] See Lester Thurow, *Poverty and Discrimination*, The Brookings Institution, 1969; and Beverly Duncan and O. D. Duncan, "Minorities and the Process of Stratification," *ASR*, June, 1968, pp. 356–364.

Chapter 5 / THE CULTURAL FACTOR IN PREJUDICE AND DISCRIMINATION

The last two chapters have shown how prejudice can be understood in part as an attempt to satisfy certain individual and group needs; it is functional in the life of the individual and of the group and must be studied as part of the dynamic process of human interaction. Even the most complete analysis of the personality and socioeconomic functions of prejudice, however, does not explain why any particular group should be selected as the object of prejudice. Nor does it explain why prejudice should continue even among individuals and groups who are in virtually no way served by it. There is nothing intrinsic about group conflict or personality insecurity that requires that certain specific groups should be the objects of hostility. A group must be socially visible, recognizably distinct from the majority, to be subject to discrimination; but visibility is a function of attention. Blond hair could be as useful as brown skin in setting a person apart for prejudicial treatment. Why has modern America selected the latter? And why will a stable and secure person exhibit prejudice against the brown skin when he has a low amount of hostility, has never known a Negro, and has no conceivable economic or political interest to be served? In this chapter we shall attempt to answer these two related questions. We shall see that, in addition to the functions of prejudice already discussed, other sociological and historical factors must be taken into account in any complete analysis.

An attitude toward a minority group can be seen, from one point of view, as simply one of the folkways, one of the learned ways of responding that are part of the standard cultural equipment. A person is taught to be prejudiced against certain groups just as he is taught to dislike certain foods that people in other societies consider great delicacies. He may be equipped with a number of culturally learned responses to minority groups that he is never called upon to use. These responses scarcely can be called functional, except in the general sense of representing the cohesiveness of a culture group. They survive, however, as group-patterned ways of thinking, ready to influence one's responses if an occasion arises. A brief statement concerning the origin and nature of cultural definitions may be of help in the study of this cultural root of prejudice.

Many, perhaps most, of the ways of behaving that are agreed upon by members of a society had their origin in an attempt to meet a specific need. The attempt was not necessarily rational or objectively valid, though it may have been, but somehow it came to be accepted as the appropriate way to meet a certain situation. Individuals could not possibly bear the strain that would come from trying to decide, for each of the hundreds of actions they perform each day, what the best response might be. For this and other reasons they accept the cultural norm. Not to do so not only would put them in the intolerable position of having constantly to make decisions but would also tend to cut them off from groups with which they identify—thus producing a sense of isolation that few human beings can accept. Some of these folkways designated by culture perform their functions as well as any alternative form would, for the action is symbolic. So long as everybody accepts the symbol it "works," even though its meaning may have changed. Shaking hands may originally have been a way of saying, "See, my hand is not on my sword; it is outstretched; I am a friend." Having lost some of its original meaning, it can still serve as the symbol of greeting. Other folkways, however, are not symbolic, but adjustments to actual circumstances. If they are used outside the situation in which they developed, therefore, they may serve the functions for which they are intended very badly. Wearing a coat of mail may help one survive the thrusts of the spear of an enemy, but its modern survival, the stiff shirt of formal clothing for men, is hardly adequate to protect one against the barbed remarks or the arrows of love that he may encounter in gatherings to which the dress suit is appropriate.

The things that are important about cultural norms, from our point of view, are their tendency to continue beyond the situation in which they were devised and their coercive power over individuals. These traits were probably overemphasized by the early students of culture, who drew much of their material from primitive, isolated societies and tried to apply their conclusions unmodified to a complex, mobile, urban society. This exaggeration should not cause us, however, to go to the opposite extreme that overemphasizes the speed with which new patterns of thought and behavior are created in the modern world. It is reported that George III of England suffered from a goiter which he felt was disfiguring. His tailor came up with the brilliant thought one day that the goiter could be hid by a piece of brightly colored silk wrapped around the king's neck. The men of the court, anxious to show the king that they admired his taste, were soon copying the pattern. So today uncomfortable males in many lands wear ties because George III had a goiter.

Folkways change, of course, and today they doubtless change more rapidly than they did formerly; but in varying degrees they continue to coerce individual behavior and to furnish guides to thought and action. They may have outlived their original meaning, they may even bring pain and discomfort to those who follow them, they may seem absurd to the outsider, but they seldom die out abruptly. To contradict the folkways of one's group is to set oneself apart, to subject oneself to the charges of heresy and eccentricity with which the group tries to maintain its unity. It may be that each member of a group, as an individual, would gladly dispense with a given pattern of behavior, but none can take the first step.

PREJUDICE AS CULTURE

If this view of one aspect of culture is correct, it may help us to understand prejudice. Attitudes toward minority groups have been started by various circumstances doubtless related to the personality and group conflict functions, have become fixed as part of the culture—embodied in its lore, developed in its literature, built into its institutions—and have continued even when the original circumstances were drastically changed. The institutional formulation of the folkways of prejudice is especially effective in preserving them for a number of reasons. The basic institutions are so important in the socialization of the individual that they can build into him the very standards by which they themselves are judged. Institutions are the chief symbol of group cohesion; they are surrounded with ritual and an elaborate system of protective beliefs. And the functionaries of institutions, and others who profit most from their pattern of control, are diligent in defense of the institutional framework.

To some degree, the reasons for the development of prejudice in a culture are unique for each minority; but to some degree they are generic. Once members of a different race, for example, have been set apart by a given group of historical circumstances as legitimate objects of discrimination, it is likely that other minority races will also be set apart, even though the particular sociological and historical forces involved are different. We cannot analyze the reasons for the selection of all, even of the largest, American minorities. We can only suggest some kinds of factors, particularly those that are common to a group of minorities, and encourage the reader to look for the specific elements in other minorities in whom he is interested.

Early theorists tried to explain the origin of a tradition of prejudice by reference to a supposed natural tendency to "dislike the unlike." Giddings coined the famous phrase "consciousness of kind" to describe what he thought of as the basis of unity in a group. Some writers have added a kind of narcissism to the explanation—we admire ourselves and dislike the different. This theory suffers from two weaknesses. It does not take sufficient account of the fact that most people are interested in the novel, as well as the familiar, and desire new experience as well as repetition of the old. Nor does it explain why certain differences are emphasized while others are completely disregarded in drawing the line between in-group and out-group. It is not difference *per se* that is related to prejudice, but certain kinds of differences that, in a given situation, prove to be useful to the individual or group making the distinction. That is why small children don't have the prejudices proper for their group—they have to be taught which differences are supposed to place others beyond the pale. Middle-class children, for example, may be tempted at first to admire the aggressive youngster who has the nerve to strike back at inhibiting adults or to lead them in excitingly forbidden activities; or they may admire the junkman because of all the fascinating objects he carries on his truck. It is only after some little effort that the parents are able to teach the child whom it is proper for him to admire and whom he should dislike or shun. Finally, if the process of socialization is carried on with reasonable skill, the child will be equipped with the appropriate prejudices. That "dislike of the unlike" is not a very useful theory by itself is also shown by the fact that what is considered sufficiently "unlike" to justify prejudice varies in time and place, as we have seen in Chapter 4. Day before yesterday many Americans liked the Japanese because "they are the most Western of all Oriental peoples." Yesterday we disliked them because of their "Asiatic mentality." Today we like them again "because" they share many traits in common with us. The Japanese haven't changed with such speed, but the usefulness of certain lines of distinction can vary rapidly.

We are not trying to say that group differences are not involved in the establishment of traditions of prejudice—for a group has to be different, has to be set apart some way in order to be discriminated against—but only that the kinds of differences chosen are accidental by-products of a given situation, not intrinsically important in themselves. In each situation the question is: Why were these particular differences seized upon as legitimate ones for marking a group off as inferior? There are two basic factors that help to answer this question. First, those differences that help to distinguish a group whose exploitation will be profitable (in terms of all the gains discussed in Chapters 3 and 4) for the dominant group will be used. Second, each group has a hierarchy of values, a system of beliefs that it carries into conflict situations. It will most readily set apart another group that differs from it in a high-order value. As the system of values and standardized beliefs changes, so will the pattern of prejudice tend to change.

We have already analyzed some of the factors involved in setting in motion the tradition of anti-Negro prejudice. At the time of first continuous contact between Negro and White, religious symbols had a high place in the hierarchy of values, making it relatively easy for the Whites to differentiate the Negro as heathen. This combined with the felt "need" for seizing the Negroes' land and its resources or for seizing the African himself, to transport him to the New World to use his muscles and skill to develop a plantation economy. In time, slavery itself became part of the traditional pattern. Contemporary Whites still react to the Negro in a given way, to a certain extent because he once was a slave. Attitudes were then formed that have become part of the culture, to some degree living an independent and autonomous life and to some degree continually reinforced by the actual present status of the Negro, which is partly a result of those very attitudes.

Where this historical background was different a different pattern of relationship has become fixed in the traditions and passed on to contemporary people. The differences between attitudes toward race lines in North and South America, for example, have been explained by Frank Tannenbaum as a result of legal differences that were involved in the early contact. Gilberto Freyre believes that the relative lack of race prejudice in Brazil can be understood in a measure by analysis of the earlier contacts between Portuguese and Moors, by the nature of the early migration to Brazil (a large proportion of unattached men), and by the fact that slavery was abolished without a war to cause resentment. Similarly, Romanzo Adams accounts for the attitude toward Orientals in Hawaii, as contrasted with California, by reference to the nature of the earliest contacts between white and nonwhite. Some of the white men who served as advisers to the court of the king of Hawaii were honored by permission to marry ladies of the king's court. As Klineberg remarks,

This set a pattern of racial friendliness which was later extended to other racial groups as well. It soon became impossible to set up any hard and fast racial line since for so many white families it had become a sign of honor to have intermarried with members of a nonwhite group. In this case historical factors can be shown to have had an effect which continues long after the situation has changed; without knowledge of this history, adequate understanding of this difference in attitudes between Hawaii and California is not possible.[1]

THE AMERICAN PATTERN OF SOCIAL DISTANCE

We have given only a sketchy outline of some of the possible origins of attitudes toward other races. The point here is that *however started* and *to some degree independent* of contemporary functions, such attitudes continue to affect behavior by persistence in tradition. Individuals for whom prejudice is highly functional today will doubtless be more likely to express a tradition of prejudice or to act in a discriminatory way. One of the factors involved in the prejudice of a great many people, however, is the traditional way of looking at things that most members of a group absorb.

The evidence for this theory is the similar pattern of prejudice, as measured by social-

distance scales, that is found across the country. This pattern varies to some degree with income, region, occupation, and education. Yet even minority groups accept it—rejecting only that part of it that applies to them, and partially accepting even that. There is little or no correlation between the amount and type of prejudice and the degree of contact with members of a minority group or extent of information about them. A large number of studies in the last 40 years have tried to describe the American pattern of prejudice. Before indicating the major conclusions of these studies, we should note a number of qualifications: Almost all the evidence has been in the form of verbal responses to paper-and-pencil tests. Insofar as these tests are valid, they show that most Americans share a verbal tradition. They do not indicate, for the most part, the degree to which this verbal behavior might be correlated with other behavior, nor do they indicate whether there are important differences among individuals in the ease with which the verbal behavior might be changed. If the analysis in the preceding two chapters is correct, individuals who express similar verbal opinions about a minority group may vary widely in the extent to which their prejudice reaches into the core of their personalities, in the degree to which the prejudice functions for them. One person may express the "proper" opinions, may sincerely "believe" them, but may act in a way that shows the prejudices have little functional significance for him. Another person may have not only the same traditional prejudices, but a strong contemporary need for their defense. This will influence the vigor with which he holds to his attitudes and acts upon them. Finally, it should be emphasized that stereotypes are to some degree anchored to particular societal conditions. They are fairly persistent, as are other elements of culture, but they are not permanent. When major social changes remake the conditions of intergroup relations —as is happening in many parts of the world—old stereotypes are broken up. This is a significant part of the cultural dimension of social change. We need to be alert to the

[1] Otto Klineberg, *Tensions Affecting International Understanding*, SSRC, 1950, p. 192.

conditions under which stereotypes persist and the conditions under which they are revised or discarded.

The Importance of Traditional Prejudices

The existence of wide contrasts between verbal behavior and nonsymbolic behavior should make us cautious in our study of the role of tradition in a theory of prejudice. A study of intergroup hostility that limited itself to the traditional verbalizations, unmindful of the contemporary personality and group functions involved, would certainly be inadequate. Equally inadequate, however, would be dismissal of the traditional element in prejudice as a "mere survival." It is very much a part of the contemporary process. A traditional prejudice can produce complacence, acquiescence, and a fertile area for the cultivation, by interested groups, of more vigorous prejudices. Even the relatively innocuous statement or acceptance of a verbal tradition of prejudice can set in motion a chain of events that is highly significant in the relationship between majority- and minority-group members.

1. Acceptance of the tradition by those who are only mildly served by it helps to reinforce the prejudice of those who use it to satisfy more fundamental needs. It is easy to say, "I can scarcely be accused of being prejudiced because of self-interest when those people who obviously have no self-interest express the same prejudice." In other words, anyone who accepts a tradition of prejudice helps to sharpen the sword for those who want to use it.

2. The mild verbal prejudice may govern a person's actions in one of those either-or decisions that have a watershed effect on many subsequent events. Shall the community accept or oppose a segregated school that is gradually appearing because of housing shifts? One with the traditional prejudice may easily assume that segregation is pretty normal and natural. He has nothing in particular to gain or lose by it, but it seems right. Once fixed as a pattern, however, the segregated school has a long sequence of effects on the personalities of the black and white students, on comparative educational and economic opportunities, on the extent and nature of interracial contacts, on the whole life of the community. An action that came about as the logical result of a mild, verbal, traditional prejudice may have effects as significant in race relations as actions which result from more deeply rooted prejudice.

3. Finally, traditional attitudes keep alive a mind-set that, when crisis situations arrive, will be strengthened and attached to contemporary needs. Having survived as tradition, the prejudice takes on renewed life as a weapon. Had the traditional prejudice not been available, some other adjustment to the situation might have occurred—an adjustment conceivably more in harmony with the realities of the situation and thus more in the interest of the prejudiced person as well as the target of his hostility. For long periods, anti-Semitism has lingered as tradition, functional in the lives of only a small proportion of those who believed it. But when conflict situations and frustrations have arisen, it has been asserted with a renewed force, blocking adjustments that were more in line with the actual problems.

For these reasons the social scientist must study the traditional factor in prejudice. The fact that it is "only verbal," "skin-deep," and relatively nonfunctional should not be allowed to obscure the basic role it often plays. In any complete analysis of prejudice one cannot ignore the casual, verbal, "proper" prejudices of the average person, for they are involved in this important interactional way with the other factors in prejudice. They are not simply survivals or cultural lags that are gradually disappearing and meanwhile have little significance for social interaction. They are part of the total process by which prejudice is sustained and through which it functions.

Descriptions of the American Pattern of Prejudice

Many studies have sought to describe the pattern of prejudice in the United States.

In a pioneer study Bogardus devised a "social-distance scale" with which he secured the responses of nearly 2000 Americans to forty racial, national, and religious groups. The respondents were asked to which step on the following scale they would admit the members of each group:

1. to close kinship by marriage
2. to my club as personal chums
3. to my street as neighbors
4. to employment in my occupation
5. to citizenship in my country
6. as visitors only to my country
7. would exclude from my country

These steps were assumed to be on a quantitative scale that ranged from most favorable to least favorable. It is unlikely that all the respondents would regard the questions in this way or would agree entirely on the amount of social distance expressed by each question, but the instrument is certainly of sufficient precision to give an approximate preference ranking of the forty groups.[2] Near the top were British, native white Americans, and Canadians; then come French, Germans, Norwegians, Swedes, and other north Europeans; then Spaniards, Italians, south and east Europeans, and Jews; and near the bottom Negroes, Japanese, Chinese, Hindus, and Turks.[3]

This pattern appeared, with only minor fluctuations, in several of the early studies. It is interesting to compare the rankings obtained when Bogardus asked 110 businessmen and schoolteachers on the West Coast the degree of social intimacy to which they were willing to admit various ethnic groups with the rankings that Thurstone found in studying the likes and dislikes of 239 midwestern college students.[4] Referring only to those groups that appear in both studies, five

have identical ranking; nine differ by only one rank; four by two ranks; the largest disagreement is three ranks, which occurs only once. In 1928 Guilford found that the students in seven widely separated colleges had the same pattern of prejudice. Those from New York University, which has a high proportion of students from minority groups, showed correlations ranging from .84 to .89 with the rankings of the other schools; the correlations among the other six universities ranged from .975 to .99.[5] Hartley discovered that the girls in Bennington College, Vermont, had the same attitudes toward minority groups as did the Negro students of Howard University, Washington, D.C. In general he found the same pattern in 1946 that Bogardus had found in 1928, and concluded that ". . . this pattern of prejudice is practically an American institution."[6]

Minority groups themselves tended to share this tradition, although with some variations. Zeligs and Hendrickson found a correlation of .87 between the rankings of Jewish and non-Jewish children.[7] Compare the rankings that Bogardus obtained from 202 American Negroes and 178 native-born Jews with those found in the study of the businessmen and schoolteachers noted above. (We have eliminated groups that were not found in all three studies, so the comparisons should be taken as a rough indication of the degree of similarity in attitudes.)[8]

Evidence of some degree of national culture and continuity comes from the rankings given to many of these same groups by a sample of 491 underclassmen at the University of Hawaii in 1961. Although over 75

[2] For valuable commentary and critique of "social distance" research, see Michael Banton, "Social Distance: A New Appreciation," *The Sociological Review*, Dec., 1960; and Sidney Siegel and Irma Lee Shepherd, "An Ordered Metric Measure of Social Distance," *Sociometry*, Dec., 1959, pp. 336–342.

[3] See Emory S. Bogardus, *Immigration and Race Attitudes*, Heath, 1928, pp. 13–29 ff.

[4] See Theodore M. Newcomb and E. L. Hartley (eds.), *Readings in Social Psychology*, Holt, Rinehart & Winston, 1947, p. 204.

[5] J. P. Guilford, "Racial Preferences of a Thousand American University Students," *JSP*, May, 1931, pp. 179–204.

[6] See Eugene Hartley, *Problems in Prejudice*, King's Crown, 1946.

[7] R. Zeligs and G. Hendrickson, "Racial Attitudes of 200 Sixth Grade Children," *Sociology and Social Research*, Sept.–Oct., 1933, pp. 26–36.

[8] Adapted from Bogardus, *op. cit.* In a later study of Negroes, Robert Derbyshire and Eugene Brody found several changes in rank order, but the 1964 list was, if anything, even closer to the earlier ranking obtained from white respondents. See their "Social Distance and Identity Conflict in Negro College Students," *Sociology and Social Research*, Apr. 1964, pp. 301–314.

Native White Businessmen and Schoolteachers	American Negroes	Native-Born Jews
1. English	1. Negro	1. Jewish
2. French	2. French	2. English
3. German	3. Spanish	3. French
4. Spanish	4. English	4. German
5. Italian	5. Mexican	5. Spanish
6. Jewish	6. Hindu	6. Italian
7. Greek	7. Japanese	7. Mexican
8. Mexican	8. German	8. Japanese
9. Chinese	9. Italian	9. Turkish
10. Japanese	10. Chinese	10. Greek
11. Negro	11. Jewish	11. Chinese
12. Hindu	12. Greek	12. Hindu
13. Turkish	13. Turkish	13. Negro

percent of the students are of Oriental ancestry (primarily Japanese) and have had little contact with mainland United States, their rankings of the groups on a social distance scale is identical with that of businessmen and school teachers 33 years earlier, except that Japanese and Chinese are raised to the top of the list.[9]

Social distance scales have been applied to other societies,[10] and in time we may be able to specify the conditions under which social distance attitudes are widely shared in a society and to examine the conditions under which they change.

We shall discuss below various efforts to refine the measurement of social distance; but before examining these developments, it may be well to comment briefly on a closely related mode of research designed to assess the cultural dimension in prejudice. Built into the cultures of many societies are guidelines that tell their members not only whom to like and to dislike, but why these attitudes are appropriate. In the process of growing up, individuals learn, by various direct and indirect means, what the qualities of the members of ethnic, racial, religious, and other groups presumably are. This line of research has frequently been used in the United States. Katz and Braly asked 25 students to list all the traits they thought typical of Germans, Italians, Irish, English, Negroes, Jews, Americans, Chinese, Japanese, Turks. This list was supplemented by other traits commonly found in the literature. One hundred Princeton students were then asked to select, from the 84 characteristics listed, the five traits that were typical of each of the ten groups. If there had been no patterning in the pictures that the students had of these groups, 42 (half) of the traits would have received 50 percent of the votes. Oppositely, if the students had agreed perfectly on the five traits that were typical of a group, 2.5 traits would have received 50 percent of the votes. The degree of uniformity in attitude is shown by the fact that only 4.6 traits were needed to include half of all selections referring to Negroes; only 5.0 to include half the selection of traits referring to Germans; and for the Turks, about whom there was least agreement, only 15.9 traits were required, compared with the 42 that would have occurred on a chance basis. With 84 characteristics to select among, over half the designations were to only five that supposedly typify the Negro: He was seen as superstitious, lazy, happy-go-lucky, ignorant, and musical. Just half of all the traits listed for Germans were selected from five: they were scientifically-minded, industrious, stolid, intelligent, and methodical. Over half of all listings for Jews were chosen from six traits: They were shrewd, mercenary, industrious, grasping, intelligent, and ambitious.[11] When it is seen that even these few traits are often virtual synonyms (superstitious and ignorant, scientifically-minded and intelligent, mercenary and grasping), the limited picture that the students had of these groups is emphasized. The pictures can scarcely be a description of reality, for the students had had relatively little contact with

---

[9] From "Interethnic Attitudes in Hawaii," unpublished manuscript by J. Milton Yinger. The two lists of groups are not identical. Spanish, Greek, Mexican, Hindu, and Turkish were not used in the Hawaii study. Reference is to the eight groups found on both lists.

[10] For example, see P. A. U. Opara, "Social Distance Attitude of Nigerian Students," *Phylon*, Spring, 1968, pp. 13–18; Harry Triandis and Leigh Triandis, "A Cross-Culture Study of Social Distance," *Psychological Monographs*, Vol. 76, 1962 (whole issue).

[11] See David Katz and Kenneth Braly, "Racial Stereotypes of One Hundred College Students," *JASP*, Oct.–Dec., 1933, pp. 280–290.

some of these groups, and probably no contact with a few. That did not prevent them from "knowing" what they were like, for they were the heirs of a tradition that informed them.

In 1941 Bayton discovered that 100 Negro students at the Virginia State College had nearly the same picture *of the Negro* that the Princeton students had, although they added a few more favorable traits (e.g., progressive) to the list.[12]

Two decades later the pictures of Jews and Negroes held by students at two midwestern universities again indicated the stability, under some conditions, of group stereotypes. They were asked to indicate which of 47 unfavorable statements applied to Jews, to Negroes, to both, or to neither. Nine items were assigned to Jews, giving a picture of a "distinctive, cohesive economic élite, exclusive and ethnocentric, and aggressive and exploitative in his relations with others."[13] Seven unfavorable terms were assigned to Negroes, giving a picture of the "classic primitive"—irresponsible, lazy, and ignorant. Eight unfavorable terms were assigned to both. These negative aspects were qualified by the assignment of three of the 24 favorable statements to each group and nine to both.[14]

Change and Variation in Stereotypes. Despite the evidence of persistence, we need to remember that these are the rankings of particular times and places. Although there is stability in traditions of social distance, there is also change. In a study of Negro college students, for example, Prothro and Jensen found that the tendency to share the ratings of Whites which had been found in most prewar studies was not duplicated in the postwar situation. In this study, Negroes rated Whites no higher than Whites rated Negroes. Both rated Jews higher than most prewar studies had shown, again indicating

that patterns of social distance change.[15] By the 1960s, forces that sustained a "black is beautiful" theme were furnishing an in-group frame of reference for America's black population more strongly than in the past. With increasing political and economic power and awareness among Negroes, dependence on white men for standards of self-appraisal has sharply declined. In 1969, *Newsweek* asked a national sample of Negroes: "Do you think that most Negroes agree that 'black is beautiful'?" Seventy-four percent answered yes.[16] In another national sample, only 17 percent of the black respondents agreed with the statement that "generally speaking, Negroes are lazy and don't like to work hard."[17] Derbyshire and Brody found that black stereotypes were largely rejected by a group of Negro college students.[18]

There have been similar shifts in the stereotypes held by Whites. In a follow-up study in 1950, Gilbert found that Princeton students checked many of the same "traits" that Katz and Braly had measured in 1932. There were, however, some important differences. Students were more resistent to stereotyping in 1950; although the traits put at the top of the list for various national and racial groups tended to be the same, they were checked by fewer students.[19] By 1967, Karlins, Coffman, and Walters found, in a replication of the earlier studies, that these trends were accentuated. There was still a measurable tendency for judgments to cluster around a few adjectives. Students often pro-

---

[12] J. A. Bayton, "The Racial Stereotypes of Negro College Students," *JASP*, Jan., 1941, pp. 97–102.

[13] Howard Ehrlich, "Stereotyping and Negro-Jewish Stereotypes," *SF*, Dec., 1962, p. 174.

[14] *Ibid.*, pp. 171–176.

[15] E. T. Prothro and J. A. Jensen, "Comparison of Some Ethnic and Religious Attitudes of Negro and White College Students in the Deep South," *SF*, May, 1952, pp. 426–428.

[16] *Newsweek*, June 30, 1969, p. 14.

[17] Gary Marx, *Protestant and Prejudice*, Harper & Row, 1967. p. 89. At about the same time, 40 percent of a national sample of whites agreed with the statement. See Gertrude Selznick and Stephen Steinberg, *The Tenacity of Prejudice*, Harper & Row, 1969, p. 171.

[18] Robert Derbyshire and Eugene Brody, "Identity and Ethnocentrism in American Negro College Students," *Mental Hygene*, Apr., 1964, pp. 202–208.

[19] See G. M. Gilbert, "Stereotype Persistence and Change Among College Students," *JASP*, Apr., 1951, pp. 245–254.

Characteristics Assigned to Negroes by
Princeton Students (in percentages)

	1933	1951	1967
Superstitious	84	41	13
Lazy	75	31	26
Happy-go-lucky	38	17	27
Ignorant	38	24	11
Musical	26	33	47

tested the process of measurement, however, and there were major changes in content, particularly with the addition of favorable characteristics to the stereotype. Four of the five traits most frequently assigned to Negroes by the 1933 students were much less likely to be selected in 1967.[20]

Another way to describe trends in stereotyping, as measured by adjective check lists, is to record the changes in the number of traits needed to get half of the votes. From a sample of 84 adjectives, if selection were random, 42 adjectives would be needed to get half the votes. The average number went up, in the studies reported above, from 8.5 in 1933 to 15.3 in 1951, but fell to 10.9 in 1967. This indicates some return to a shared stereotype for many groups, but with the

Adjectives Needed for One-Half of the
Selections to Describe Various Groups

	1933	1951	1967
Americans	8.8	13.6	9.6
Chinese	12.0	14.5	10.8
English	7.0	9.2	8.0
Germans	5.0	6.3	6.3
Japanese	10.9	26.0	9.4
Jews	5.5	10.0	7.7
Negroes	4.6	12.0	12.3
Turks	15.9	32.0	25.6

Source: Adapted from Marvin Karlins, Thomas Coffman, and Gary Walters, "On the Fading of Social Stereotypes: Studies in Three Generations of College Students," JPSP, Sept., 1969, p. 9.

[20] Marvin Karlins, Thomas Coffman, and Gary Walters, "On the Fading of Social Stereotypes: Studies in Three Generations of College Students," JPSP, Sept., 1969, pp. 4–5.

addition of favorable characteristics in many instances.

One additional way to view these stereotypes is to measure the favorableness of the adjectives chosen. Although stereotypes are sometimes regarded as inherently negative, this is not the picture that emerges from the method being described here. Using a scale ranging from +2 to −2, Karlins, Coffman and Walters found a generally positive shift in the content of stereotypes of minorities.

Favorableness of Adjectives Chosen by
Princeton Students to Describe Various Groups

	1933	1951	1967
Americans	.99	.86	.49
Chinese	−.12	.25	.46
English	.63	.59	.51
German	.89	.57	.77
Japanese	.66	−.14	.84
Jews	.24	.45	.66
Negroes	−.70	−.37	.07
Turks	−.98	−1.03	−.62
Mean for all groups	.22	.16	.33

Source: Adapted from Marvin Karlins, Thomas Coffman, and Gary Walters, "On the Fading of Social Stereotypes: Studies in Three Generations of College Students," JPSP, Sept., 1969, p. 11.

These are average evaluations of the 1967 students, and, therefore, the interpretation is somewhat problematic. Adjectival meanings may have shifted since 1933; and the individuals using an adjective may not give it the degree of favorableness or unfavorableness represented by the mean.

It seems probable that there has been some reduction in stereotyping in the United States and a shift toward a more favorable image for many groups. Why the change? Referring to his 1950 college sample, Gilbert suggests that the trends reflect in part a changed student body (more persons from the lower classes), the growing influence of social science, a reduction in stereotypes in the entertainment media, but perhaps, also,

Occupational Distribution of Negroes and Whites in Advertisements of Six General Magazines

Occupational Category	% Negro		% White	
	1949–50	1967–68	1949–50	1967–68
Above Skilled Labor				
Entertainment	3.3	28.4	7.0	2.6
Sports	1.4	7.8	7.0	2.6
Professional, business, student	0	16.8	9.9	32.1
Idle	1.4	14.2	64.8	57.8
Clerical	0	4.1	4.7	2.2
Total above skilled labor	6.1	71.3	93.4	97.3
Below Skilled Labor				
Maid, cook, servant	21.1	2.2	.5	.4
Waiter, porter, butler, chauffeur	54.5	5.6	.5	.4
Cowboy, farmer, soldier	.5	1.1	5.6	1.5
African or Island laborer	17.8	19.8	0	.4
Total below skilled labor	93.9	28.7	6.6	2.7

Source: Keith Cox, "Changes in Stereotyping of Negroes and Whites in Magazine Advertisements," *POQ*, Winter, 1969–1970, p. 605. Reprinted with permission.

simply a change in verbal conventions.[21] Each of these factors seems operative today. In a content analysis of 42 recent works of fiction for children, for example, Gast discovered little negative stereotyping. Negroes were frequently portrayed as the group most likely to be seeking higher education, and they were not cast in occupational stereotypes, although some other groups were.[22] Something of this same picture is found in advertising in the United States. Negroes are appearing more often, and in a more favorable light. Comparing the ads in *Life, Look, The Saturday Evening Post, Time, The New Yorker,* and *Ladies' Home Journal* for 1949–1950 and 1967–1968, Cox found that, of those ads having identifiable adults, only .57 percent had Negroes in the earlier period, while 2.17 percent of the 1967–1968 ads contained Negroes. More importantly, there was a shift in the occupations portrayed.

Most whites in the ads could not be identified by occupation (they are classified as "idle" in the table above), but most Negroes could be assigned an occupation by the theme of the ad.

Actual changes in the class and occupational distribution of a group, and not simply its portrayal in the media, are important, because racial stereotypes are influenced by the class of the person responded to. When explicitly asked to characterize upper-class Negroes, white college students used none of the traits that have appeared in general stereotypes, but they did use several of those traits to characterize lower-class white persons. Although there were racial differences, the class of persons responded to was more important than his race in determining the stereotypes.[23]

Research dealing with stereotypes is developing in various new directions. More comparative work is being undertaken; new instruments, for example the semantic differ-

[21] Gilbert, *op. cit.*
[22] See D. Gast, "Minority Americans in Children's Literature," *Elementary English,* Jan., 1967, pp. 12–23. Cited by Herbert Hyman in Irwin Katz and Patricia Gurin (eds.), *Race and the Social Sciences,* Basic Books, 1969, pp. 8–9.

[23] J. A. Bayton, L. B. McAllister, and J. Hamer, "Race-Class Stereotypes," *Journal of Negro Education,* Vol. 25, 1956, pp. 75–78.

ential, are being employed; comparisons of attitudes toward peoples and toward governments are being developed; questions of validity are being explored; and the relationships between tendencies to stereotype and other qualities—ease in interracial contacts, for example, or acquaintanceship with and liking for a group—are being studied.[24] From all of this it is clear that, although members of a society still share beliefs about what various groups are supposed to be like, the process of stereotyping is more complicated than it was formerly thought to be, and is subject to rather continuous change.

Studies of stereotypes are probably of less value in times of rapid change and among groups—whether on those doing the judging or on those being judged—that are heterogeneous. One person may offer a stereotype as his estimate of how those around him view a group; another may be stating his own view. One person may be thinking of an average or a "modal" member of the stereotyped group, leaving rather wide room for variation; another may think that the description fits most of those in a group. This latter view becomes less likely when a minority group becomes highly diversified by occupation, class, educational level, region, religion, and the like. Such diversity tends to break up the cultural element in prejudice, although it may support, or even enhance, prejudice based on economic conflict or status anxiety.[25]

The qualifications and refinements we have indicated in connection with research on stereotypes also characterize the continuing studies of social distance. Following his studies of 1926 and 1946, Bogardus obtained data from widely scattered groups of college students and adults in 1956. Although this is not a sample of national opinion (the 2053 persons studied were mostly under 35 and almost entirely drawn from higher educational levels), it compares with the groups studied by Bogardus earlier. Groups in the upper third of social nearness (largely North European) remained the same, although with somewhat higher scores, due probably to greater social distance expressed toward them by Blacks. Although Jews remained in the middle of the range of groups being ranked and Japanese and Negroes near the bottom, less social distance was expressed toward each of them. On a seven-step scale, the greatest social distance score fell from 3.91 (1926) to 3.61 (1946) to 2.83 (1956), and the average score fell from 2.14 to 2.12 to 2.09.[26]

In the literature on "social distance" more attention is being given to variations within societies. Educational, regional, and class differences have been measured.[27] In his 1956 research Bogardus found that women expressed greater social distance than men toward 29 of the 30 groups listed; their average score was 2.17 (on the seven-step scale) compared with 1.97 for men.[28] He also found significant regional variations, with the following average scores recorded:

[24] See Richard Willis, "Ethnic and National Images: Peoples vs. Nations," *POQ*, Summer, 1968, pp. 186–201; F. Kenneth Berrien, "Stereotype Similarities and Contracts," *JSP*, Aug., 1969, pp. 173–183; Mario Abate and F. Kenneth Berrien, "Validation of Stereotypes: Japanese versus American Students," *JPSP*, Dec., 1967, pp. 435–438; Howard Schuman, "Social Change and the Validity of Regional Stereotypes in East Pakistan," *Sociometry*, Dec., 1966, pp. 428–440; Stuart Cook and J. J. Woodmanse, "Dimensions of Verbal Racial Attitudes: Their Identification and Measurement," *JPSP*, Nov., 1967, pp. 240–250; Howard Ehrlich and G. Norman Van Tubergen, "Exploring the Structure and Salience of Stereotypes," *JSP*, vol. 83, 1971, pp. 113–127.

[25] See Herbert Hyman, *op. cit.*, p. 12.

[26] Emory Bogardus, "Racial Distance Changes in the United States During the Past Thirty Years," *Sociology and Social Research*, Nov.–Dec., 1958, pp. 127–135.

[27] See Richard Christie and John Garcia, "Subcultural Variation in Authoritarian Personality," *JASP*, Oct., 1951, pp. 457–469; E. T. Prothro and O. K. Miles, "Comparison of Ethnic Attitudes of College Students and Middle Class Adults from the Same State," *JSP*, Aug., 1952, pp. 53–58; Frank R. Westie, "Negro-White Status Differentials and Social Distance," *ASR*, Oct., 1952, pp. 550–558; Charles U. Smith and James W. Prothro, "Ethnic Differences in Authoritarian Personality," *SF*, May, 1957, pp. 334–338; T. F. Pettigrew, "Desegregation and Its Chances for Success: Northern and Southern Views," *SF*, May, 1957, pp. 339–344.

[28] Emory Bogardus, "Race Reactions by Sex," *Sociology and Social Research*, July–Aug., 1959, pp. 439–441.

Northeast, 2.06; South, 2.40; North Middle-west, 1.96; and Pacific West, 1.97.[29] Un-happily these are undifferentiated scores (with many Negroes in the southern sample, for example), but their significance is enhanced by the pattern that emerges: the regions tend to fall into the same order on each group that they do on average score.

Most studies of social distance ask respondents to think of an average or standard member of a group in making their judgment. It is doubtless significant that many persons find little difficulty in doing this. Yet we need to know how they might respond to a differentiated picture of a minority group. Westie attacked this problem by measuring the differences in responses of white persons to Negroes in various occupations. Sixty lower-class, 56 middle-class, and 58 upper-class Whites, chosen by random sample blocks in Indianapolis, were interviewed in their homes. The degree of "social distance" that they felt toward Negroes was measured by a series of four scales which referred to various kinds of interpersonal contact. Lower-class Whites made very little distinction among Negroes in various occupations, whether the Negroes were doctors, bankers, machine operators, or ditch diggers. With a score of 24 representing the maximum social distance, lower-class Whites averaged from 14.03 to 15.10 for the eight occupations listed in the study, a range of only 1.07 scale points. The scores of the middle-class Whites were from 10.91 to 13.09, indicating both less social distance and the willingness to distinguish more sharply among Negroes in various occupational groups. The range for upper-class Whites was from 9.38 to 12.52, again indicating a lower amount of social distance and a greater willingness to differentiate among Negroes of different occupations.[30] Since the white respondents were not classified by education, region of birth, or other variables, we cannot know how much their class standing per se influenced the results. But the study indicates the need

for measuring the variations in social distance as well as the nationally shared traditions.

In Chapter 3 we discussed Rokeach's analysis of the effects of perceived difference in belief on prejudice. If Whites and Blacks feel distant from one another (to state the issue in terms of our problem here), this is so, to an important degree, according to the Rokeach thesis, because they see each other as holding different beliefs. Following this same logic Triandis and his associates have asked: Do not perceived differences or similarities other than belief also enhance or reduce the effects of race difference on feelings of social distance? In a series of studies they have measured the comparative importance of race, class, religion, and nationality in determining social distance attitudes. Eighty-six undergraduate students were asked to note to which persons each of 15 statements would apply, the statements having been assigned scale values by the Thurstone method. The statements ranged from "I would accept this person as an intimate friend" (scale value 11.11) to "I would be willing to participate in the lynching of this person" (scale value 97.20). Sixteen types of persons were then designated by combining the four variables in all possible ways. Thus they were asked to respond to "Swedish, physician, white, same religion," and "Negro, American, same religion, physician." By analysis of variance the authors found that for this sample, race explained 77 percent of the distance that whites felt toward Negroes; class explained 16.6 percent.[31]

In a comparative study, Triandis, Davis, and Takizawa introduced these same four variables to see if they influenced feelings of social distance differently in different contexts. Among German students, occupation was the most important characteristic, followed by religion, race, and nationality; among the Japanese the order was occupation, race, nationality, and religion; and among the students from Illinois, the order

[29] Emory Bogardus, "Racial Reactions by Regions," *Sociology and Social Research*, Mar.–Apr., 1959, pp. 286–290.

[30] Westie, *op. cit.*

[31] Harry Triandis and Leigh Triandis, "Race, Social Class, Religion, and Nationality as Determinants of Social Distance," *JASP*, July, 1960, pp. 110–118.

was race, occupation, religion, and nationality.[32]

It is clear that race must be treated as one variable among many in determining stereotypes and feelings of social distance. Its importance varies through time and among different groups. As Negroes diffuse through the class and occupational structure, present perceptions of them by Whites will be further differentiated. Hyman judiciously summarizes the possible consequences and the need for further study of this process.

These studies, if they may be taken as substantial evidence, bode well for the future. The apprehension about closer contact and social relations will diminish as perception of the rising education and class position of American Negroes grows among whites. The relevance of such studies urges me to suggest that their obvious deficiency be remedied by further research. They are all small in scope and on highly selected populations; most of them are out of date. None of them provides any descriptive evidence on the perceptions that prevail among whites as to the class characteristics of the Negro population. Studies should be projected on a large scale through attaching appropriate questions to national surveys. Measures of feelings of status anxiety and competitive threat, and status consciousness and status loss, should also be included. Thereby this alternative body of theory will be subject to empirical test, and the possible negative as well as positive effects that may flow from the rising status of Negroes can be estimated.[33]

Within every society there are some individuals who for a number of reasons turn out to be atypical. They may have acquired a system of beliefs and values from some other frame of references (a different culture, a

thoroughgoing belief in science, or the teachings of religion taken seriously), or they may be simply maladjusted as individuals, with no integrated system of beliefs. From the point of view of the majority, they are heretics, radicals, and eccentrics. They do not share the dominant values of the society, and they frequently do not share its prejudices. No statement of the traditional factors in prejudice should disregard these exceptions. Several studies have documented, for example, the extent of "readiness to desegregate" among southern Whites. They are in strong agreement that the small number who approve or are ready to accept the process (variously estimated to range from 15 to 30 percent) are mostly to be found among the younger and better-educated persons. A key fact in their atypicality is the degree to which national standards, not simply the norms of the region, have become important to them.[34]

There are, of course, traditions of non-prejudice as well; for example, what Myrdal calls the American creed contains traditions of democracy and equality. One cannot say, therefore, that the reduction of the hold of tradition on an individual will, other things being equal, make him less prejudiced. We need to know, further, whether or not the atypical person has experienced an emotional reaction against all cultural norms; we need to know why he is atypical; we need to know what part of the culture he does accept. The Nazis, while building upon many traditional ideas, were at the same time flaunters of tradition.

Finally, it must be remembered that each society has its own scale of social distances, its own traditions of prejudice, reflecting its past experiences and the present social structure. Our analysis has been concerned with the American pattern. It is well known that race is considered to be a relatively unimportant line of cleavage in Brazil, that France

---

[32] Harry Triandis, Earl Davis, and Shin-Ichi Takizawa, "Some Determinants of Social Distance among American, German, and Japanese Students," *JPSP*, Oct., 1965, pp. 540–551. The samples, it should be noted, were small and not necessarily representative. For studies of other variables that influence social distance attitudes, see R. Epstein and S. S. Komorita, "Parental Discipline, Stimulus Characteristics of Outgroups, and Social Distance in Children," *JPSP*, Sept., 1965, pp. 416–420; Harry Triandis and W. D. Loh, "Race, Status, Quality of Spoken English, and Opinions about Civil Rights as Determinants of Interpersonal Attitudes," *JPSP*, Apr., 1966, pp. 468–472.

[33] Hyman in Katz and Gurin, *op. cit.*, p. 15.

[34] See, for example, Lewis Killian and John Haer, "Variables Related to Attitudes Regarding School Desegregation among White Southerners," *Sociometry*, June, 1958, pp. 159–164; Thomas Pettigrew, "The Demography of Desegregation," *JSI*, 1959, Fourth Quarter, pp. 61–71; Melvin Tumin, *Desegregation: Resistance and Readiness*, Princeton, 1958.

shows little prejudice against the Negro, that many black American soldiers were reluctant to leave Italy because they found so little discrimination there.[35] Race prejudice is a fundamental part of the culture of the white people of South Africa (and probably also, reciprocally, of the non-whites),[36] no more easily to be escaped by the great majority of the population than belief in other major aspects of culture.

Problems of Reliability and Validity in the Measurement of Stereotypes. In addition to questions of change and subcultural variation, we need to be alert to problems of reliability and validity in the measurement of stereotypes. The many risks that inhere in efforts to record attitudes on fairly objective and simple verbal scales require that we hold the evidences recorded above lightly. In recent years a number of studies have shown how responses may be affected by the measuring process. Diab asked 50 Arab-Moslem students at the American University in Beirut to select adjectives that characterized 13 groups from a list of 99 adjectives. Fifty other students were asked to make their selection with reference to only seven groups (five of them being found also on the first list). Although some of the pictures were similar, there were also important changes. Americans, for example, were characterized by the first 50 students as superficial, rich, materialistic, industrial, and selfish. When several of the low-ranking groups were removed from this list for the second test, Americans tended to be contrasted more specifically with the Russians and, on the whole, were seen in a more favorable light. The five adjectives most selected by the second group were: rich, democratic, materialistic, industrial, and sociable.[37]

In his descriptions of the attitudes of Africans in Ghana toward Europeans, Jahoda notes that there are many contradictions. At least three different images emerge, one of the European of daily contact, one the idealized picture of the democratic Englishman, and one of the "scheming imperialist."[38] It is just such ambivalent attitudinal clusters that are peculiarly sensitive to the measuring process—to the form of questions and the interview situation.

Weiss asked 65 students to select, from 40 adjectives, the five that would best describe Negroes to a person who had never heard of them. The list was not unlike those chosen by other groups: flashy, musical, God-fearing, superstitious, and happy-go-lucky. But only four students selected all five of these adjectives, 14 selected four of them and 18 chose three; that is, 55 percent agree on three or more, but 45 percent chose two (17 students), one (9) or none (3) of the five adjectives. This is not, as Weiss notes, a very tight configuration for a stereotype. Moreover, when he asked another group of students to rank-order the 40 adjectives in terms of their importance in influencing opinions and responses to a person, the five selected as characterizing Negroes by the first group were given a very low rank. When he added three other descriptions (more friendly, more pleasure-loving, less ambitious) to the original five and asked the second group of students how they would respond to a person thus characterized, 55 percent said that they would like such a person "somewhat" or "very much"; 26 percent were neutral.[39] Thus the meaning of the stereotype for behavior is strongly qualified.

The question of validity suggested by Weiss' research is raised more directly by DeFleur and Westie. Can behavior be predicted from expressed attitudes? They compare 23 persons with high scores of verbal rejection of Negroes with 23 persons with low scores, having matched them first on age, religion, sex, and other variables. They had been shown a series of slides of inter-

[35] This is not to suggest, of course, that there are no lines of stratification in these societies. Class standing or demonstration of the mastery of language and culture may be decisive marks of distinction only slightly less rigid, and often correlated with race.

[36] See Thomas Pettigrew, "Social Distance Attitudes," *SF*, May, 1960, pp. 246–253.

[37] Lutfy Diab, "Factors Affecting Studies of National Stereotypes," *JSP*, Feb., 1963, pp. 29–40.

[38] Gustav Jahoda, *White Man: A Study of the Attitudes of Africans to Europeans in Ghana before Independence*, Oxford, 1961.

[39] Walter Weiss, "An Examination of Attitude Toward Negroes," *JSP*, Oct., 1961, pp. 3–21.

racial groups and then were told that there was a need for more such slides. Would they pose, they were asked, with a Negro of the opposite sex? If so, to what use would they permit the slides to be put? The suggested uses ranged from laboratory use by professional sociologists to a nationwide program advocating integration. Those high in prejudice were significantly different from the lows in their readiness to sign a "photograph release agreement," and in the kinds of uses to which they were willing to have the slides put. That is, attitudes predicted readiness for behavior (although not, in this instance, behavior). Some of the highs, however, would accept the most extensive use of the slides. Predictions of behavior from their scores would have been in error.[40]

A related line of investigation employs factor analysis to see whether "social distance" is a unitary attitude or whether it is comprised of several components. Evidence is accumulating that the latter is true, which means that a general measure of social distance is likely to obscure the way one person will respond to another in a particular social situation. If there are several aspects to the phenomenon "social distance," we can use the concept with precision only when we get further research specifying its dimensions and indicating the conditions under which various forms of social distance are operative.[41]

STEREOTYPES AS THE EMBODIMENT OF A TRADITION OF PREJUDICE

In the preceding section we noted that a tradition of prejudice not only tells the members of a group what the proper scale of social distance is but assigns to each group

a list of characteristics that are supposed to typify it. These characteristics are not wholly imaginary, as we shall see, but they are such a compound of error, exaggeration, omission, and half-truth that they tell more about the people who believe them, the needs of the group in which they circulate, than about the group to which they are supposed to refer. One of the most important aspects of a tradition of prejudice is the stereotyped pictures it contains. These are to some degree explicitly functional, as we have seen in Chapters 3 and 4, but to some degree simply traditional, part of the mental equipment that an individual receives as a member of a culture. Once fixed in the culture, they react back upon it, guiding the interaction of the groups involved.[42]

Stereotypes of the majority group also abound in the thinking of minorities, so that interaction is, in part, not among individuals as they are, but among individuals as they are thought to be. The beliefs about the majority are perhaps less important to the student of prejudice for two reasons. Minority-group members are frequently in a better position to know the true characteristics of the majority than the other way around; a servant knows his master better than a master knows his servant. The servant may be more highly motivated to know what the master is really like, for he can scarcely afford the luxury of the errors involved in a stereotype. In spite of oversimplification and distortion in the picture of the dominant group held by the dominated, it contains a larger share of truth. Secondly, even though there are many errors in the stereotypes held by the minority, the consequences of these errors are less important, because the minority group does not have as much power to make reality out of its beliefs.

Whether held by the majority- or minority-group member, stereotypes are easy ways of explaining things. They take less effort and give an appearance of order without the difficult work that understanding the true order of things demands. They are a way of

[40] Melvin DeFleur and Frank Westie, "Verbal Attitudes and Overt Acts: An Experiment on the Salience of Attitudes," *ASR*, Dec., 1958, pp. 667–673.

[41] For valuable work on this question, see Harry Triandis, "Toward an Analysis of the Components of Interpersonal Attitudes," in Carolyn and Muzafer Sherif (eds.), *Attitude, Ego-Involvement, and Change*, Wiley, 1967, pp. 227–270; and Howard Ehrlich and G. Norman Van Tubergen, "Social Distance as Behavioral Intentions: A Replication, a Failure, and a New Proposal," *Psychological Reports*, Apr., 1969, pp. 627–634.

[42] For a discussion of the many different meanings and uses of stereotyping, see Joshua A. Fishman, "An Examination of the Process and Function of Social Stereotyping," *JSP*, Feb., 1956, pp. 27–64.

classifying, which in itself is a necessary process for any kind of thinking. The word "chair" is an abstraction that leaves out a large number of specific traits of specific chairs in favor of general characteristics. A scientific abstraction, however, differs from a stereotype in including *all* important traits, and in selecting those traits on purely rational grounds. The traits assigned to a stereotype are selected for their ability to produce some desired effect or on the basis of an emotional predisposition. Classification and typing are justified, and necessary, even in the study of human beings; but science insists that the process follow all the rules of logic and be based on all possible evidence.

There is doubtless some truth in many stereotypes, but the commonplace application of them as descriptive of the behavior of all the members of a group is in error in several ways:

1. The stereotype gives a highly exaggerated picture of the importance of some few characteristics—whether they be favorable or unfavorable.

2. It invents some supposed traits out of whole cloth, making them seem reasonable by association with other tendencies that may have a kernel of truth.

3. In a negative stereotype, personality tendencies that are favorable, that would have to be mentioned to give a complete picture, are either omitted entirely or insufficiently stressed.

4. The stereotype fails to show how the majority, or other groups, share the same tendencies or have other undesirable characteristics.

5. It fails to give any attention to the cause of the tendencies of the minority group—particularly to the place of the majority itself, and its stereotypes, in creating the very characteristics being condemned. They are thought of rather as intrinsic or even self-willed traits of the minority.

6. It leaves little room for change; there is a lag in keeping up with the tendencies that actually typify many members of a group.

7. It leaves little room for individual variation, which is always wide in human groups. One does not deal with a group average, but with specific individuals. One of the functions of stereotypes is shown by this failure to adjust to individual differences—to do so would be to destroy the discriminatory value of the stereotype. We shall see shortly how easy it is for the human mind to overlook completely or to treat as unimportant exceptions the evidence that contradicts a well-established belief.

These logical and factual weaknesses of the stereotype do not prevent it from occupying an important role in the pattern of prejudice. One does not readily challenge the definitions passed on to him by his culture. Moreover, they are useful; they are effective weapons. We seldom see them in that light, but our actions may reveal an unconscious appreciation of their functional importance.

The stereotyped pictures of the minority groups held by members of dominant groups are not all alike. They differ both because of the various historical circumstances out of which they grew and also because they are related to different kinds of conflict situations. But even stereotypes can be classified. One often can discern a great similarity between the stereotyped pictures of two minority groups who are related in about the same way to a dominant group. One group of stereotypes seems aimed especially at *keeping* a group down, another at *pushing* a group down that has achieved some degree of competitive power. Thus the picture of the American Negro as lazy, shiftless, irresponsible, unable to acquire a skill, and unable to appreciate a higher standard of living is matched by the stereotype of similarly disadvantaged groups in other settings. ". . . One could not distinguish the stereotype of the Polish worker which developed in Germany in the latter part of the last century from the stereotype of the Negro which exists in the United States today."[43] The same picture was drawn of the migrants to California from Oklahoma and Arkansas during the 1930s, despite the fact that they were overwhelmingly white Protestant Anglo-Saxons.[44]

There is another pattern to the stereotypes

[43] Carey McWilliams, *A Mask for Privilege: Anti-Semitism in America*, Little, Brown, 1948, p. 163.
[44] *Ibid.*

of groups that have been somewhat more successful in competing with the dominant group. It would be too great a distortion of the fact to label them lazy or unintelligent, so they are pictured as too ambitious, and with a crafty kind of self-interested intelligence. In various settings this picture has arisen in connection with Jews, Greeks, Syrians, Armenians, the American Japanese, Chinese in the Philippines, and other groups. Such stereotypes indicate the skill that human beings have in interpreting almost any phenomenon so that it reinforces their established beliefs. The stereotype of "the Jew" shows particularly clearly that it is not what the out-group does or fails to do that causes prejudice. "Superficial appearances notwithstanding, prejudice and discrimination aimed at the out-group are not a result of what the out-group does, but are rooted deep in the structure of our society and the social psychology of its members."[45] It is a simple matter for most of us to make what we consider virtues in ourselves into vices when they are found in the behavior of a minority-group member. Merton puts the matter sharply:

. . . The very same behavior undergoes a complete change of evaluation in its transition from the in-group Abe Lincoln to the out-group Abe Cohen or Abe Kurokawa. . . . Did Lincoln work far into the night? This testifies that he was industrious, resolute, perseverant, and eager to realize his capacities to the full. Do the out-group Jews or Japanese keep these same hours? This only bears witness to their sweatshop mentality, their ruthless undercutting of American standards, their unfair competitive practices. Is the in-group hero frugal, thrifty, and sparing? Then the out-group villain is stingy, miserly, and penny-pinching. All honor is due the in-group Abe for his having been smart, shrewd, and intelligent, and, by the same token, all contempt is owing the out-group Abes for their being sharp, cunning, crafty, and too clever by far.[46]

Whether we are dealing with a stereotype that attacks a minority group for failing to

[45] Robert K. Merton, *Social Theory and Social Structure*, Free Press, rev. ed., 1957, p. 428.

[46] *Ibid.*, pp. 428–429. For another commentary on the "double standard" involved in stereotypy, see Robert Sommer and Lewis Killian, "Areas of Value Difference: I. A Method for Investigation. II. Negro-White Relations," *JSP*, May, 1954, pp. 227–244.

be like the majority or with one that accuses the minority group of having virtues—but in excess—the important thing to keep in mind is that these categorical judgments are part of the stream of culture. They are transferred to children in the process of socialization. They are not dormant traditional items but active ingredients in human interaction, helping to shape experience, to color observations, and finally, as we shall see in the next section, to create the very tendencies with which they were in the first instance justified.

"FACTS" AS THE EMBODIMENT AND SUPPORT OF A TRADITION OF PREJUDICE

Having noted the important place of essentially false stereotypes in our judgments of minority groups, must we conclude that there are no important differences among human groups? Are our observations so completely distorted by the "pictures in our heads" that reality disappears? Apparently when majority-group members look around for confirmation of the "inferiority" of minority groups, they do not look entirely in vain. This point needs careful study, for it has been the subject of much misunderstanding. One likes to think of himself as rational. He would probably not accept a tradition of prejudice as readily as he does if he could not, in his daily experiences, find support—or what seems to be support—for the validity (granted certain premises) of the tradition. Stereotypes, as we have seen, lend a kind of support; the beliefs and verbalizations of other people, the definitions of roles found in the culture—these are taken by most people as "evidence" of the inferiority of some groups. And for many people this is all the evidence they ever have, for they lack contact with the minority groups themselves.

Some majority-group members, however, see for themselves. And what do they see? Negroes, on the average, for example, live in poorer houses than Whites; they perform more menial tasks; they are more often illiterate and poorly educated; their sexual behavior more often violates the dominant mores; they probably break the letter of the law more often. Are these signs of inferiority? The scientist makes no such judgment, for his job is to describe, not to evaluate. When we state that minority groups are inferior, we refer to the fact that they can be differentiated frequently from the majority group in terms of the dominant standards of a society. From this value stand, the characteristics of minorities can be made to seem a confirmation of the tradition of prejudice; minority-group members are given an inferior status because that is the only one they deserve or can fill. In other words, these "facts" are the basis of a theory of prejudice. The traits of a minority group are the cause of its low status, not the result of that status.

That this is an inadequate theory our whole discussion to this point should demonstrate. The word "cause," however, is a slippery concept. Many scientists and philosophers have stopped using it entirely because of the misunderstandings that result from its naïve application. Only the use of the concept of many "levels of causation" can prevent the attempt to explain a phenomenon by one surface relationship. Behind each cause is another cause, and behind that another, and the third may, in turn, affect the first. Science is not interested in finding the "ultimate" cause but in describing the total group of interacting forces that occur in connection with the phenomenon being studied. Some forces, to be sure, may be more important than others. This is determined by a simple criterion: How consistently does the force occur in connection with the phenomenon, when other forces are controlled? How well can one predict the occurrence of the phenomenon by analysis of the "cause"?

The Principle of Cumulation

From this point of view, the attempt to explain prejudice as a result of the inferiority of minority-group members is very inadequate. There can be inferiority without prejudice; and there can be prejudice without inferiority. Even when the two occur together the likelihood is that the majority group assumes a *post hoc, ergo propter hoc* relationship that is not justified. It is reported that during the London blitz rescue workers were tunneling into a demolished house when

they discovered a frightened but unhurt old man sitting in a bathtub. He was shaking his head, looking very puzzled, and mumbling: "I can't understand it! I can't understand it! I pulled out the plug and the house blew up." Majority-group members are less modest. They declare: "We do understand it. We grew up observing the factual inferiority of the Negro, and our attitudes toward him are simply a result of that fact." Our anology here is not perfect, for presumably the bathtub plug was not a booby trap; it was completely uninvolved in the cycle of forces that led to the demolition of the house. The "inferiority" of the Negro, however, is a booby trap; it helps to explode discriminatory activities. To be sure, that inferiority is in part the product of prejudice and discrimination in the first place; but *once established*, it becomes a part of the cycle of interaction. This is the interaction that Myrdal has described as "the vicious circle," or, if one's value premises are different, "the beneficent circle." If a group of forces (associated with slavery, for example) have created an inferior status for a minority, there will appear, both as rationalization of the discrimination shown and as a result of the fact of observation of that inferior status, an attitude of prejudice toward the minority group. Such prejudice will block members of the "inferior" group from the life chances necessary to advancement. By limiting the opportunities of a minority group, by segregating it, by putting it at every competitive disadvantage, the prejudice helps to create the very inferiority by which it seems "justified" in the minds of the dominant group. Start out by saying that the black man is inferior; use this as the reason for giving him poor schools, poor jobs, poor opportunities for advancement; and one soon proves himself correct by creating and enforcing that very inferiority. This in turn, will deepen the prejudice, which, again, will further restrict the opportunities of the minority person.[47]

MacIver and Merton have shown how the idea of the "vicious circle" in race relations

[47] Gunnar Myrdal, *An American Dilemma*, Harper & Row, 1944, pp. 75–78.

Figure 7 / The Field Context of Discrimination

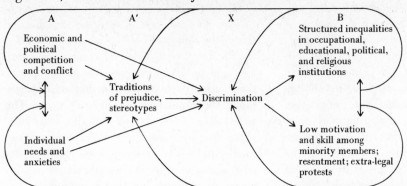

can be seen as one manifestation of a general principle, "the self-fulfilling prophecy."[48] Men respond not only to the objective features of a situation, but to their own definition of that situation—to the meaning it has for them. Even though the original definition of the situation is false, it may, by becoming part of the interacting forces, help to make itself true. A rumor (a false definition) spreads that the local bank is insolvent; a run on the bank starts; and, since no bank can immediately honor all claims upon it, the bank has to close. "The rumor is self-confirming." This self-fulfilling postulate is not completely circular, since the original state does not recur, but it illustrates how a belief —and actions based upon it—can produce the very situation with which it is supposed to have started. In other situations the interaction is circular. ". . . The process of international armament may run as follows:

armament in country A→fear in country B →armament in country B→fear in country A→armament in country A, and so on *ad infinitum*—or *ad bellum*."[49]

This kind of sequence in race relations would move from discrimination to conditions confirmed or imposed by discrimination back to discrimination.

The various forces with which we have been concerned can be brought within a general field theoretical statement. What we see

is a "feedback system" of human events, with primary processes being influenced, and often reenforced, by their own consequences.

Several observations are required to interpret this system. The forces listed in A and the results listed in B can have consequences other than those noted here. We disregard those other consequences to focus on the discrimination cycle. The rigidity or continuity implied in the system we have described becomes problematic when that system is seen as part of a larger pattern. The discrimination cycle in the United States is part of a larger system containing various tensions —religious and political norms and values opposed to discrimination, for example. When these are strengthened, a formerly fairly stable smaller system of discrimination tends to break up. Yet it is a "tough" system; it has homeostatic properties that bring it back to "normal" unless the disrupting outer pressures are continuous and strong. Some of those who regret what they see as a "conservative bias" in this kind of functional analysis (mistaking the judgment that systems have self-sustaining qualities for approval of such systems) are also quick to lament the "conservative toughness" of the system of discrimination. In our judgment, field theoretical interpretations of functional systems need not have any conservative bias. Carefully stated, they identify the conditions under which various cycles of causation are continued and when they are broken up.[50]

If we may accept this approach that the

[48] R. M. MacIver, *The More Perfect Union*, Macmillan, 1948, pp. 52–81; and Merton, *op. cit.*, pp. 421–436.

[49] MacIver, *op. cit.*, p. 63.

[50] For a more general statement of this perspective, see J. Milton Yinger, *The Scientific Study of Religion*, Macmillan, 1970, chaps. 5 and 6.

characteristics of the members of minority groups are involved in the *process* of prejudice (note again that they are a "cause" of prejudice in only the most superficial sense), what "traits" are used to make the discrimination possible? Krech and Crutchfield have observed that there are physical, psychological, and sociological "cues" for designating the "inferior" groups. Racial differences may furnish a fairly clear line of demarcation physically; the dominant group defines its particular combination of physical traits as good or beautiful, whereas the traits of the minority race are bad or ugly. In some instances the minority will accept the dominant standards, will try to match the physical appearance of the ruling group, and perhaps will be itself internally stratified, partly on the basis of the differences in approaching these standards. This practice has, to some degree, been characteristic of the American Negro. On the other hand, a highly integrated minority, more anxious to be independent of the ruling group than to be assimilated, may counter with its own standards of beauty, and thus differentiate itself from the majority. For the American Indian, "pale face," "flop ears," and "crooked feet" were terms of contempt for the ugly appearance of the white man. In recent years these have been matched by derogatory terms used by Negroes to refer to Whites, such as "honky" and "whitey"—often used in contrast with a "black is beautiful" theme.

Obviously physical cues alone are not sufficient to designate the inferior group. They are too unpredictable and, in most societies where race mixture has been fairly common, too vague to draw a sharp line. Psychological cues are used universally as an explanation for discriminatory behavior: We are not prejudiced against them but are simply assigning them to the status that they deserve owing to lack of intelligence or certain personality traits. Is there any evidence to support this conception of group differences? In Chapter 2 we examined the question of differences in average native intelligence among racial groups. Although one must speak cautiously, because of the great difficulty in equating the variables involved, it is certainly

accurate to say that there is a great deal of overlapping in the distribution of native capacity among the races. And the fact that the more the cultural variables are controlled the smaller become the differences in group averages points in the direction of the theory that native capacity is distributed in pretty much the same way through all races. The wide differences in opportunity, however, make for significant differences in average intellectual *ability* among human groups—at least according to the standards of intelligence as defined by the dominant group. Many persons do not make a scientific interpretation of those differences but take them as evidence of inherited differences, as facts which prove that their attitude toward the members of the minority group is not a prejudice.

The "facts" concerning other differences in personality are subject to the same interpretation. These are almost entirely, if not entirely, due to different experiences. The Negro, seeing little to be achieved by effort, may, on the average, be less responsible than the White; the Jew, having been barred from association with others on the basis of individual choice, may, on the average, be more "clannish." To the naive observer, however, these are simply "facts" that make the traditional prejudices he has been taught seem to be based on experience.

Often correlated with these physical and psychological cues that point out the "inferior" persons are a large number of sociological cues which are learned by the member of the dominant group as he is growing up, simply as facts of the environment. The minority group is segregated; its share of societal values is almost always inferior, as we shall see in detail in later chapters. If one starts with a prejudice, these again are confirming facts of the inferiority of the members of the group involved. Sociological distinctions are most likely to be used to support a tradition of prejudice against a group that is already in a disadvantaged position and is to be *kept* there—for contrast will be sharpest with them. Psychological distinctions are more likely to be used to support a tradition of prejudice against a group that the ruling group is trying to *push* down. Altogether, the sociological facts are probably the most persistent support to prejudice because they are the easiest to perceive and the least ambiguous. They are often built into legal, religious, educational, and military institutions, thus being given, for many people, a cultural sanction that makes them acceptable. Moreover, in many societies one's occupation, residence, and class are considered especially important, carrying definite implications concerning one's ability, character, and personality.[51]

These physical, psychological, and sociological differences among groups mean that a tradition of prejudice is constantly being reinforced by reference to observed facts. It is thus made far more complicated (and far more difficult to uproot) than it would be if it were based completely on error and bias. To be sure, the causal sequence may be very different from what most persons believe, but pragmatically the prejudice "works," it explains, and not many are interested in testing the scientific logic involved in the explanation. Partial observation and crude logic satisfy most of us, particularly if the resulting conclusion is useful for our individual and group needs. A primitive medicine man may cure an infection by hiding a stone in his mouth, sucking on the wound, and then pulling the stone out of his mouth with the statement that it was causing the infection. It is unlikely that in a stable society where this practice was used a person would have much success in getting the people to drop it by appeal to John Stuart Mill's second canon of causation. Their belief in the practice would be based on some observation: Most infections treated in this way cleared up; and perhaps even more cleared up under this treatment than under other known practices. As long as it works, why doubt it, why take a chance? It explains things pretty well to everybody but the doubter who wants to control a few variables—and there are not many such. You could even silence some of them, if you could show that 95 percent of all infections treated in this way were healed,

whereas only 90 percent of those treated solely by dancing and incantation were healed. Here is evidence, facts. Who is left to say that the stone had nothing to do with the infection, that it was the sucking, the greater blood circulation, the opening up of the wound that was the true "cause" of the cure?

Prejudice, too, is based on facts. That these facts happen simply to correlate with other phenomena (including the prejudice itself) and are not the true cause of the prejudice is a sophisticated observation that most of us are not able—or willing—to make. MacIver says:

Prejudice is not a simple thing. It is not a mere expression of human blindness and bias. Prejudice, so to speak, is not altogether prejudice. It has a rational element with an irrational one. The irrational element is often sustained by a response to observed behavior that might be accounted fair and proper if the observation were not so selective or if the observed behavior were the whole evidence. The proportion of the two ingredients, the rational and the irrational, will vary according to the kind and degree of prejudice.[52]

In studying the way in which a culture transmits attitudes of prejudice, therefore, we must take into account the support given the tradition by the facts of group differences. Many theories in recent years have failed to consider this relationship, probably because of equalitarian and democratic value premises. The present authors happen to share those premises, but they also believe that such values will be served best by a scientifically adequate theory of prejudice, a theory that does not avoid a body of evidence because, on the surface, it seems to be "undemocratic."[53] The theory of the vicious circle is, to be sure, only one part of a complex explanation of prejudice. The vicious circle sustains prejudice but does not create it. That the support of "facts" is not essential to prejudice is shown by the elaborate cultural

---

[51] Krech and Crutchfield, *op. cit.*, pp. 461–467.

[52] MacIver, *op. cit.*, p. 77.

[53] For a valuable account of self-fulfilling prophecies in housing, see Eleanor Wolf, "The Invasion-Succession Sequence as a Self-Fulfilling Prophecy," *JSI*, Fourth Quarter 1957, pp. 7–20. As she notes, it is not easy to disprove a "myth" that comes true before one's eyes.

equipment for prejudice that most Americans share even when they know no facts, when they have had no contact with the people to whom the prejudice refers. Nor could appeal to the "facts" justify the categorical nature of prejudice—for the facts are very uncategorical; Negroes may have lower I.Q.'s on the average than Whites, but there are Negroes with I.Q.'s of 200. The "facts" help to sustain prejudice only because of man's capacity for partial observations, rigid ideas, and poor logic.

It should be stated again that, in saying the facts of group differences support prejudice, we have taken the point of view of the prejudiced person: *to him* they are a proof of the reasonableness of his attitudes. That he is in error, from the point of view of the scientist, does not prevent his attitude from being a factor in prejudice. We have already noted some of the errors involved in the reasoning that uses the facts of group differences to support prejudice, but it may be well to summarize them.

1. The minority groups are not inferior in any absolute sense, but only relative to the standards of the dominant group. The "proof" that the prejudice is justified, therefore, is convincing only to a person who accepts the values of the dominant group as absolutely valid.

2. Reality is taken *as is* by the prejudiced person. He is scarcely interested in *why* minority groups are "inferior"; or his explanation is likely to be very simple—it is their nature. MacIver calls this the vicious-circle argument:

Its peculiar property is that it takes the existence of one link in the circle as independently given, as a fact of nature or even as ordained by God, and concludes from that premise that the next link, the behavior predicated on the earlier link, is not prejudicial or discriminatory but a rational and proper response to the inferior capacities or qualities of the group subjected to it. Those who put forward the argument wilfully or blindly ignore the sector of the circle that lies on the other side of the evidences to which they appeal. They refuse to recognize that the conditions on which they base their argument arise out of, or are themselves sustained by, a prior process of discrimination.[54]

This kind of "logic" or use of evidence is doubtless encouraged by the fact that it comes out with the "right" answer—the answer that profits the individual or group using it or corresponds to their established notions. It may be due in part, however, to a cultural pattern of thought. We are gradually discovering that the forms of logic and the kinds of evidences that one will accept are to some degree cultural. The kind of thinking that "explains" prejudice by the "nature" of minority groups is the *substantive mode of mentality*, ". . . the tendency to account for or describe events (social and otherwise) in terms of the 'essence' of things instead of in terms of related processes."[55] This is an easy kind of thinking; it gives the answer by an examination of surface relationships without concern for the complicated chains of events that preceded those relationships. Why are the roles and statuses of men and women different in the United States? Because they are different by nature. Very simple, isn't it? And very inadequate; for we know that the roles and statuses of men and women vary widely in time and space, whereas their "natures" presumably are quite constant.

More and more people are accepting the *process mode of mentality*[56] in dealing with the physical world. If something goes wrong with one's car, he is not likely to say that it is the "nature" of cars to behave that way; he looks, or has an expert look for a disturbance in the usual process. Gradually that way of looking at things is being applied to human behavior. It is less commonly said today than formerly that children behave in a particular way "because it is the nature of children." We are beginning to be interested in the sequence of events that leads to certain behavior. At least a few people are beginning to study criminal behavior and abnormal behavior in the same way. To say that a per-

54 MacIver, *op. cit.*, p. 65.
55 Sherif, *op. cit.*, p. 361.
56 *Ibid.*, pp. 359–361.

son commits a crime because he is criminal by nature is as useless a statement as to say that a person or group is in an inferior status because he or it is inferior by nature. To some degree, this kind of explanation is simply part of our cultural equipment; but there seems to be a trend—however slow in its reference to human behavior—toward the process mode of mentality. Meanwhile "facts" support prejudice.

3. Another error in the assumption that prejudice is simply a description of reality is the use of incomplete and distorted pictures of reality. The truth, the whole truth, and nothing but the truth would support prejudice far less effectively than the part-truth, the half-truth, and error with the truth. Human events are almost always ambiguous, and our preconceived notions assign them the proper interpretation. What is thrifty, businesslike behavior in our gentile neighbor may be stingy, unfair competition from our Jewish competitor. Under such circumstances it is difficult to know what "facts" are justifying prejudice. The "sampling errors of experience" give us only a one-sided view of the "facts." We know the Negro janitor, but not the Negro author; the Mexican field hand, but not the Mexican doctor.[57]

Thus the facts of group differences are a reinforcement to prejudice only for the superficial and biased observer. Since a high proportion of us are superficial and biased observers, however, an adequate theory of prejudice must take account of this factor.

HOW DOES THE INDIVIDUAL ACQUIRE THE TRADITIONS OF PREJUDICE?

We have discussed the traditional element in prejudice—its place as part of culture, embodied in stereotypes and supported by selective observation of facts. Now comes the question: How is this tradition transferred to the maturing individuals of a new generation? One of the most important areas of modern sociology is the study of *how* an

[57] Krech and Crutchfield, *op. cit.*, pp. 466–467.

individual is inducted into his social groups, how he learns—or fails to learn—their values, how he acquires his various roles. This is the study of the process of socialization. Reference to it can help us understand the mechanisms by which a tradition of prejudice is passed on.

It is now universally agreed among scientists that there are no innate antipathies toward the members of different racial, national, religious, or other groups. We have to learn whom to dislike just as we learn other group norms. The baby is an iconoclast, with no respect for even the most cherished beliefs of his elders. He is dependent, however, on adults for the satisfaction of most of his needs; they are likely to reward and punish according to his orthodoxy. Sometimes a child will take quite a bit of punishment before he acquires the proper prejudices. Negro and white boys, for example, may have a common interest in a game or sport that for some time brings enough pleasure, is a strong enough drive, to outweigh the requests, threats, or punishments that the white parents bring upon their children. Prejudice is usually acquired less painfully than that. The very acquisition of language may start a child off with a mind-set favorable to the absorption of the traditions of prejudice. Some things are "white and clean," others are "dirty and black." He will hear his parents say: "That is white of you," or "He tried to jew me down." The more serious conversations of adults that he overhears may refer to the inferiority or undesirable traits of several minority groups. They will be associated with observations of the social segregation of those groups, which, to the child, seems a confirmation of their inferiority.

These influences will be joined, even in the young child, with several of the needs discussed in Chapter 3. The need for "belonging," for feeling secure in relation to the groups with which one is most closely identified, will be served by accepting the values of those groups. The need for aggression is strong in most children. It arises from conflict with parental discipline, from sibling rivalry, from clashes on the playground.

This, of course, does not directly produce prejudice, for the child may strike back at the parent, sibling, or playmate. If these channels are blocked, however, as they frequently are, both by the outside forces and from within (by the felt need for belonging), and the child has simultaneously learned that Negroes are inferior or that he is not to play with the children of the immigrant Italian family across the street, and that aggressions against these children are less severely punished, he easily learns to accept prejudice.

The development of prejudice begins very early. Horowitz found that most of the boys in a kindergarten, children barely five years of age, had acquired anti-Negro attitudes. In one test he asked them to select from a group of pictures the ones they liked best; in another test he asked them to show him the pictures of the boys they would like to sit next to on the streetcar, or play ball with, or swim with; and in a third test he asked them to select from pictures of various social situations (some containing only white boys, others containing both white and Negro boys) which ones they would like to join. The tests produced somewhat different results, but they all revealed a prejudice among the five-year-olds, and an increasing prejudice to the age of fourteen, which was the oldest age group studied.[58]

A person is not likely to be aware of his own categorical prejudice at an early age. Allport and Kramer asked their respondents to estimate the time when they became prejudiced. The average estimate was 12.6 years for anti-Negro and 13.7 for anti-Jewish attitudes. The great majority estimated that their prejudice began in elementary or junior high school, especially the latter; and there were some new recruits even to age 22.[59] These estimates doubtless reflect the stronger and stronger pressures toward prejudice that are brought to bear on children as they grow older. With the approach of adolescence and the beginning of "dating" the line between proper and improper associates is likely to be drawn sharply and categorically by the adult society, whereas a somewhat more tolerant attitude is usually shown toward interracial or other intergroup activities of small children.

The prejudice of small children is likely to be "inconsistent"—the hierarchy of attitudes has not become well established, so that one cannot predict which value will come to the fore in a specific instance. A small child may have been taught to dislike Negroes but to like curly hair. She may then show an "inconsistency" in her prejudice by expressing liking for a curly-haired Negro.[60] Gradually the child learns which kinds of attitudes take precedence in his social group. At first he will explain his negative responses on the basis of differences between himself and the disliked person. The older child, however, will increasingly recognize the role of social pressure. If asked why he dislikes the members of a minority group, he will recite the reasons taught him by his culture, by the adults around him—always assuming, of course, that they are strictly his own reasons and that they are the true reasons. He has forgotten the punishment, the threats, the stories and jokes that have given him the prejudice. The cultural norm is now his norm; he is socialized.

We do not mean to imply by this discussion that prejudice is the inevitable product of socialization. Tolerance and attitudes of intergroup harmony are also taught. It is interesting and unfortunate, however, that less is known about the development of attitudes of nonprejudice.

CONCLUSION

In this chapter we have examined the role of tradition in sustaining and passing along a prejudice. The analysis of personality needs and group conflicts can go a long way toward answering the question, "Why prejudice?" but it cannot explain "Why prejudice toward this group?" The choice of a target

[58] Eugene L. Horowitz, in Newcomb and Hartley (eds.) *op. cit.*, pp. 507–517.

[59] See Gordon Allport and B. M. Kramer, "Some Roots of Prejudice," *JP*, July, 1946, pp. 21–22.

[60] See Ruth Horowitz, "Racial Aspects of Self-Identification in Nursery School Children," *JP*, Jan., 1939, pp. 91–99.

for group hostility frequently rests upon historical conflicts that have been fixed in tradition. There can also be traditions of nonprejudice, of course, that emerge out of one group of circumstances but survive to affect others. Part of what Myrdal calls "the American creed" is a product of the French and American revolutions—times when concepts of equality were effective weapons for rallying the support of the masses to the middle class. Equality was a useful idea then. Once lodged in the democratic societies, it became fixed in tradition, supported by some institutional structures, and passed on to later generations. Many have found it an embarrassing idea that runs counter to their group or individual interests. Yet they cannot escape all of its influence over them. Some of the most extreme prejudices—belief in the subhuman nature of another race, for example—are in part a sign of an equalitarian tradition that the persons involved are having a difficult time forgetting. Such traditions are likely to be largely verbal in their influence if they are not sustained by contemporary functions, but they have some power to react back upon the society that carries them.

We have used the term "functional" to describe the sustaining force of prejudice in group conflict situations and in the service of personality needs. The term "traditional," on the other hand, carries the connotation of lacking in contemporary functions. That implication is not strictly true, for the traditional is certainly functional in the general sense of contributing to group solidarity; and it is functional for the individual to accept and act upon a tradition that will help him to identify with his group. Tradition cannot be regarded as an unimportant and powerless survival from the past, for it is thoroughly involved in the interactions of the present. One might say that personality and group needs furnish the motive power of prejudice, and that tradition is the steering wheel. But tradition is even more important than that: it is in part a motor. It may sustain prejudice as a mode of adjustment when its absence might have permitted a more satisfactory adjustment to be made.

In examining the three clusters of factors involved in prejudice, we have noted that the distinctions drawn were analytic. In virtually every case the several elements are interactive and mutually reinforcing. The use of prejudice as an economic weapon strengthens the tradition, and the presence of the tradition makes it easier to employ prejudice in economic conflict. A stereotype facilitates projection; and having projected one's faults onto a minority group, one's belief in the stereotype is strengthened. Moreover, every prejudicial activity tends to affect the members of the minority group involved in such a way as to create superficial justification for the original activity. The often baffling tenacity of prejudice, in the face of emotional and rational appeals, moral arguments, and proof that it is against obvious self-interest, can be understood only by an appreciation of the interaction of the many forces involved and their consequent strength. Myrdal exaggerates the ease with which prejudice can be changed when he says that a change in any one segment of the interacting circle will have effects on all other segments. The impulse toward change may be temporary and local; it may be submerged by the cumulative force of the continuing factors in prejudice. A wartime labor shortage, for example, may temporarily obscure the economic element in discrimination against minority groups in industry, but it will not necessarily produce a long-run reduction in prejudice. An organism is not killed by one wound; and unless the blow that produced the wound is dealt over and over again, the organism will not be any weaker after recovery. The mutually interlocking and sustaining forces of prejudice give it power of recovery. We do not mean that prejudice as a cultural element cannot be reduced, but only that it has a strength that one-factor analyses are likely to minimize.

Hence we must revise the proposition that an upward change anywhere in the lower caste complex will tend to raise all the other conditions within it. Instead we should say that *a favorable change in any one of the distinctive conditions will, if it can be held constant long enough, tend to raise the other conditions and to bring about a readjustment of the whole system in conformity with the favorable change.* By "long enough" we denote the period within which the requisite habituations and reconditionings, the responses of the group to the altered condition, are formed and established. Thus the receipt of high wages must last long enough to be translated into a higher standard of living and to evoke the attitudes and expectations congenial to it. When we say that the advance must be "held constant" we mean that the forces that brought it into being must continue in operation, aided by whatever new forces the change may evoke, in sufficient strength to resist the assaults of resurgent opposing forces. Such assaults are indirect as well as direct. If, for example, a new statute against discrimination has been set up there is the danger that it will be evaded or even nullified even though it is most unlikely that it will be actually repealed.[61]

In the light of the evidence cited in this chapter, MacIver's last point needs careful attention. A person may experience a vigorous attack on his prejudice—a scientific course of study or close acquaintance with atypical (from his point of view) members of a minority group. A slight reshuffling of

[61] MacIver, *op. cit.*, p. 71.

some of the surface manifestations of his prejudice may be required, some new rationalizations, the granting of a few more "exceptions"; *but these very changes may be a way of protecting the core of the prejudice unaltered.*

Prejudice is a deep-rooted part of American culture, a vital part of the adjustment systems of most individuals, a weapon in economic and political conflict, a significant part of the stream of tradition that brings the influences of the past into the present and puts them to use in contemporary conflicts. As we turn to the study of the manifestations of prejudice—its effects—we must keep steadily in mind the complex and interlocked forces that sustain it.

The next three chapters will examine some of the consequences of prejudice, first for those against whom it is directed and then for those who use it. It is too simple to designate these consequences as effects only, with the factors we have discussed being regarded as the causes. Once established, these consequences become part of the total interaction by which prejudice is sustained, part of the total causal complex.

Chapter 6 / THE CONSEQUEN[...] AND DISCRIMINATION: THE [...] OF MINORITY-GROUP MEMB[...]

At several points in the preceding cha[...] we noted the impossibility of distingui[...] sharply between the "causes" of pre[...] and discriminatory activity and the "e[...] that follow from them. In a comp[...] interactive process an "effect," once [...] may significantly influence the situ[...] which it is found. However, there a[...] ences among the various factors in the primacy of their influence. One would weaken both his scientific understanding and his moral effectiveness if he failed to see that certain behavioral aspects of prejudice and discrimination are primarily consequences, and only secondarily causes. This distinction is especially true of the behavior of minority-group members, but the same can be said for majority-group members as well, as we shall see in Chapter 8. In this chapter and the next two, therefore, we shall deal with the aspects of behavior that are primarily the results of having received, or having used, prejudice and discrimination. It must be kept clearly in mind, however, that these responses, once set in motion, become a part of the total interaction. In an important way they affect the maintenance, the increase, or the decrease of the original "causes."

There are two closely related but distinguishable consequences of prejudice for minority-group members: the effects on the personality tendencies of the individuals involved and the effects on the structures and processes of the groups that are formed as a result of the prejudice. Our concern here is not directly with the details of the social institutions and groups that have grown up to serve minority-group members; these will receive a great deal of attention in Part II. We shall be largely concerned in this chapter and the next with the general principles of personality formation and, to a small degree, with the group processes and structures that underlie the specific economic, political,

those of majo[...] ences are often exaggerated b[...] group; it is assumed that they mark th[...] minority group as inferior; and they are usually explained, if at all, by inadequate concepts. These errors should not, however, obscure the significant differences in personality that are bound to result from the important differences in experience. It would be surprising indeed if the whole range of influences at work on the individual who is identified as a member of an "inferior" group did not produce significantly different personality tendencies from those that result from majority-group membership. It must be added, of course, that minority-group members almost always share with the other members of the society of which they are a part a great number of societal and cultural influences. Minority and majority are likely to have many more values and aspirations and behavioral tendencies in common than differences that separate them. But in a study of prejudice it is primarily the differences that count.

Members of the dominant group are likely to take these differences thoroughly for granted, assuming them to be the inevitable signs of superiority-inferiority rankings. If they offer any explanation, it is usually in terms of "natural" or "innate" factors that are simply being reflected in social differentiation. The task of an adequate sociology and social psychology dealing with this problem is to try to answer four questions.

ferences
stion can-
partial and
frequently used
ense observation
t *the* Negro is more
c observer, however,
fferentiation among Ne-
is as useless a concept as
studying criminality he com-
Blacks with all Whites, but
Whites of similar economic, edu-
religious, and familial backgrounds
ention only a few factors). He also
: Does criminality mean the same thing
th reference to the two groups? Does it
mean the number of crimes of each type committed, or the number of arrests, or of convictions, or the number in prison? If it refers
to any of the last three, is there equal chance
of arrest, conviction, and serving a full term
in prison for Black and for White? Until one
knows the answers to these questions, he can
scarcely speak of "personality differences."
The accumulating evidence permits us
to speak tentatively, but with some confidence, about the personality consequences of
membership in a minority group, paying full
attention to the wide range of subgroupings
that differentiate experience. We shall discuss
that evidence later.

2. What personality tendencies of minority-group members are the result of factors
that happen simply to be correlated with
minority-group status but are not the direct
product of that status? It would be clearly a
mistake to try to explain all aspects of the
behavior of Negroes, for example, by reference to the prejudice and discrimination they
experience. In part their behavior tendencies
are the result of influences that act upon all
members of the society, thus reflecting the
general pattern of social organization and
disorganization. There is some tendency to
generalize about black characteristics without
matching studies of Whites, thus leaving
problematic the extent to which race is involved in the situation. It is meaningless, for
example, to speak of a "black matriarchy,"
with the implication that females dominate
black families, without comparative data
from white families. Reviewing various na-

tional studies, Hyman and Reed found, in
fact, that there was little difference between
intact black and white families.[1] Many studies,
of course, have found significant differences.[2]
In each case we need to ask: Are comparable
areas of decision-making being studied; have
families been matched for other characteristics—educational and class levels, for example; and are we dealing with similar
ratios of intact families?

To some degree, the personalities of American Negroes reflect the background of rural
society in which a quarter of them live and
from which a large proportion of the other
three quarters has recently migrated. The
effects of urbanization, entirely apart from
prejudice, would have to be examined in
order to give an accurate picture of many
Negro personalities. Personality tendencies of
Jews will have to be explained partly as a
result of the sharing of a common tradition
(which itself has been influenced by, but not
created by, prejudice), partly by occupational and residential factors and other
influences, *along with* the direct and indirect
effects of prejudice.

⟶Many aspects of behavior are the consequences of class status, not simply of prejudice. They are shared with fellow class members of other races and groups. Lower-class
Negroes, for example, may exhibit a lower
degree of motivation for education; but that
this is not simply a product of their race
status but, in part, a result of their class
status is shown by the similar pattern of
motivation found among lower-class white
children.[3]/Prejudice doubtless increases the

[1] Herbert H. Hyman and John S. Reed, " 'Black
Matriarchy' Reconsidered: Evidence from Secondary
Analysis of Sample Surveys," *POQ*, Fall, 1969, pp.
346–354.

[2] For a recent study, see Richard Centers and
Bertram Raven, "Conjugal Power Structure: A Re-
Examination," *ASR*, Apr., 1971, pp. 264–278.

[3] Richard Bloom, Martin Whiteman, and Martin
Deutsch found that of 11 dependent variables that
they were studying, eight were more closely related
to class than to race. See "Race and Social Class as
Separate Factors Related to Social Environment,"
AJS, Jan., 1965, pp. 471–476; see also Martin
Deutsch, Irwin Katz, and Arthur Jensen (eds.),
Social Class, Race, and Psychological Development,
Holt, Rinehart & Winston, 1968; John Porter, "The
Future of Upward Mobility," *ASR*, Feb., 1968, pp.
5–19; Bernard Rosen, "Race, Ethnicity, and the
Achievement Syndrome," *ASR*, Feb., 1959, pp. 47–60.

likelihood that a Negro will be a member of the lower class, and thus lies behind this tendency; but the class factor *per se* must also be considered. Thus, in our analysis of the tendencies of minority-group members we must not rest the whole explanation on prejudice and discrimination.

3. What value stands are stated or implied in the study of personality? This is an important question, because not only do the members of the dominant group assume that the behavior of the minority group is inferior but most scientific studies, while maintaining objectivity in the explanation of causes of behavior, *assume* the value stand of the dominant group in evaluating the results. It is almost universally assumed that to be thrifty, ambitious for job improvement, interested in formal education, etc., is good, that to lack such attitudes or tendencies is bad. Such a value stand is legitimate, even for the scientist, provided it is made entirely explicit. The danger is that it will be used implicitly as "proof" of the general "inferiority" of minority-group members.

4. The fourth question is the basic one. What are the causes of observed differences in tendencies between members of majority and minority groups? We cannot be content with observing them or taking them for granted. In Chapter 2 we saw that a racial-biological explanation of behavioral differences was virtually useless. Not that biological factors are unimportant in personality differences, but they do not vary in any important way with race. For any differences in behavior that vary from group to group we must look to differences in experience. Explanations that rely on "natural" differences seem fairly good in a stable environment, but under conditions of mobility and culture contact they are seen to be inadequate. Under such conditions the "traits" that are supposed to characterize the members of a given group undergo a great deal of change; the "naturally lazy and ignorant" Negro peasant may become, in a city where he is given the opportunity, a typical occupationally ambitious and thrifty member of the middle class or a dedicated activist promoting drastic change.

We have avoided the term "trait" in our discussion of personality. Unless carefully defined, it is likely to carry the connotation of a fixed and rigid aspect of personality, perhaps of an innate origin and not varying with the situation in which the person is behaving. The attempt to explain an individual's behavior by an analysis of his "traits" fails to give sufficient attention to the fact that what a person "is" cannot be defined independently of the whole situation with which he is interacting. Each person has a great many potentialities for behavior. Which ones will appear depends upon the situation, but none can appear for which there is no potentiality. Level of self-esteem, for example, is not simply an inner quality. It is also a function of the situation. Williams and Byars found that among Negro eleventh-graders, a shift to a desegregated school raised the level of self-esteem, indicating that the level of esteem was partly a reflection of surrounding conditions.[4]

Such a social psychological concept may seem to be far removed from the study of prejudice, but the present authors contend that minority-majority relations can be understood only within the framework of a thoroughly adequate science of human behavior. If we look to the "traits" of members of dominant and minority groups as the "causes" of their behavior, even if we have accounted for them by reference to their differing experiences, we shall add a rigidity to our observations that will block understanding.

Keeping these four questions in mind, we can turn to the study of the personality consequences of prejudice and discrimination. The pioneer work of William James, James M. Baldwin, John Dewey, Jean Piaget, Charles H. Cooley, and George H. Mead has given us a great deal of insight into the way a child acquires basic attitudes toward himself, toward the norms of the groups of which he is a member and the norms of the larger society, and toward those in authority over him. These aspects of personality are the results of his experiences with others,

[4] Robert L. Williams and Harry Byars, "The Effect of Academic Integration on the Self-Esteem of Southern Negro Students," *JSP*, Apr., 1970, pp. 183–188.

the ways they define his roles for him, the ways in which they encourage him (by their behavior toward him) to look at himself—all conditioned, of course, by his particular inherited tendencies and previous experiences. Even the way one looks upon himself is a product of his social experiences. In Cooley's classic phrase, we have a "looking-glass self," compounded of others' reactions to us, our interpretation of those reactions, and a response to the interpretation. Or, as Mead put it, we know ourselves only by "taking the role of the other," by reacting to ourselves as we imagine others react toward us. In time we learn to take the role of the "generalized other"—the norms of society and the groups with which we are associated. We come to see ourselves in the light of these norms.

It is clear that such a process is significantly different for the members of a minority group from what it is for members of a dominant group. In American society a high proportion of non-Caucasian children come to see themselves, at an early age, as somehow different from white children—unable to do certain things, to go certain places, rebuffed by words and violence. From early childhood to death minority-group members are likely to experience a long series of events, from exclusion from play groups and cliques to violence and the threat of violence, that are far less likely to be experienced by the average member of the majority group. Not all the experiences of the low-status person are necessarily "bad" or unfortunate from the point of view of generally accepted values. He may have a more relaxed play environment or, in some situations, less sharply competitive group associations. Moreover, his difficulties may lead to achievement, to a kind of "challenge-response" situation, to use Arnold Toynbee's phrase. Some of the notable contributions of minority-group members, to art, to religion, to science, may have been achieved because of their difficulties, not simply in spite of them. A marginal role can lead to understanding; suffering can produce personal warmth and regard for others. Such results, however, are probably not the most common and most important. The great weight of prejudice and discrimination often cramps and distorts the personality development of the minority-group member. Many of his experiences, varying with several factors that we shall note, put him into disorganizing conflict situations and cause him, to an important degree, to be at odds with himself.

VARIABLES THAT AFFECT THE RESPONSES OF MINORITY-GROUP MEMBERS

Before turning to specific personality consequences of prejudice and discrimination, we must make careful note of the many variables that affect the nature of the experience for a minority-group member. We shall draw chiefly upon studies of the American Negro, for the evidence is more extensive here than, perhaps, for any other minority; but the same need for subclassifying, on the basis of several factors, applies to any minority group. Both the amount and type of prejudice and discrimination and the *meaning* of them for members of the minority groups will vary according to such factors as these: nature of parental advice and training with regard to the dominant group; level of education; income; occupational status,[5] temperament of the individual; amount of minority-group cohesiveness and solidarity (the increased solidarity and pride demonstrated by the contemporary Negro protest movement is creating a significantly different setting for personality formation of Negro children);[6] nature of the minority-majority contact (contrast the experience of the north European immigrant, for example, with that of the American Indian in terms of the kinds of contact they had with the dominant group); region of the country; nature of surrounding group

[5] One of the critical effects of social class is to influence the sense of self direction, on one hand, or conformity to external authority, on the other. See Melvin Kohn and Carmi Schooler, "Class, Occupation, and Orientation," *ASR*, Oct., 1969, pp. 659–678.

[6] Robert Coles, *Children of Crisis*, Dell, 1967.

support or opposition to prejudice and extent of segregation;[7] age;[8] extent of experience with other intergroup patterns (for example, the Jamaica-born Negro in Harlem will see the situation very differently from the way the native born New Yorker sees it, and to both it will look different from the way the migrant from Georgia sees it);[9] color variations *within* the minority group (there is ample evidence that a light-skinned Negro and a dark-skinned Negro have, in many ways, significantly different experiences, although this differentiating factor has become less important).

In our discussion of personality consequences of prejudice we must keep constantly in mind the ways in which these variables, and others, affect the nature of the experience of the minority-group member. We cannot, of course, discuss every possible combination, for even with subdivision on the basis of only five or six variables there would be hundreds of subgroups. Warner, Junker, and Adams, in a study of the effects of minority-group status on the personality development of Negro youth in Chicago, distinguished their group on the basis of three criteria only—yet this led to thirty-two "types." Their basic hypothesis was that systematic subordination of Negroes to whites has a definite effect on the development of the personalities of the Negroes. But corollary hypotheses were that the effect was different for men and for women; that the evaluation of color and other physical traits made by Negroes themselves conditioned the effect; and that

social-class position and occupational status in Negro society affect the nature of the influence. Having differentiated four social-class positions and four color categories, they had 32 types for analysis.[10] Within these types informal refinements were made on the basis of other characteristics—education, birthplace, number of years in Chicago, and others.

Although we shall not, in our discussion, develop a system of "social personality types," we shall make frequent reference to the different effects of prejudice on persons who play different social roles. The following questions will be raised: What are the effects of prejudice in encouraging members of minority groups to accept the dominant pattern of motivation and morality? How does prejudice affect attitudes toward oneself and one's own group? What are the various kinds of responses that can be made to a situation filled with prejudice and discrimination? These questions can be examined best against the background of some illustrative experiences.

In the autobiography of his boyhood, Richard Wright described in vivid terms the intimidation and violence that have been a part of life for many Negroes. He had been given a job at a small firm that manufactured optical instruments. The owner, a native of Illinois who had migrated to Mississippi, had promised him a chance to learn the trade; but the two white men working in the shop had different ideas. Any intimation on Wright's part that he would like to acquire the necessary skill aroused their anger and abuse. He dared not report the problem to Mr. Crane, the owner, for fear of further trouble.

The climax came at noon one summer day. Pease called me to his workbench; to get to him I had to go between two narrow benches and stand with my back against a wall.

"Richard, I want to ask you something," Pease began pleasantly, not looking up from his work.

"Yes, sir."

---

[7] A low sense of personal control over one's life and a high degree of alienation tend to be associated with segregation. See, for example, James S. Coleman, et. al., *Equality of Educational Opportunity*, Government Printing Office, 1966; Bonnie Bullough, "Alienation in the Ghetto," *AJS*, Mar., 1967, pp. 469–478.

[8] At first glance, age seems to be a critical variable, influencing basic attitudes (toward white people, use of violence, integration, for example). When education is controlled, however, the effects of age are sharply reduced. Education itself explains a substantial part of the variance in such attitudes among Negroes. See Ann F. Brunswick, "What Generation Gap?," *SP*, Winter, 1970, pp. 358–371.

[9] See Robert Harrison and Edward Kass, "MMPI Correlates of Negro Acculturation in a Northern City," *JPSP*, Nov., 1968, pp. 262–270.

[10] W. Lloyd Warner, B. H. Junker, and W. A. Adams, *Color and Human Nature, Negro Personality Development in a Northern City*, ACE, 1941, p. 26.

Reynolds came over and stood blocking the narrow passage between the benches; he folded his arms and stared at me solemnly. I looked from one to the other, sensing trouble. Pease looked up and spoke slowly so there would be no possibility of my not understanding.

"Richard, Reynolds here tells me that you called me Pease," he said.

I stiffened. A void opened up in me. I knew that this was the showdown. He meant that I had failed to call him Mr. Pease. I looked at Reynolds; he was gripping a steel bar in his hand. I opened my mouth to speak, to protest, to assure Pease that I had never called him simply Pease, and that I had never had any intention of doing so, when Reynolds grabbed me by the collar, ramming my head against a wall.

"Now, be careful, nigger," snarled Reynolds, baring his teeth. "I heard you call 'im Pease. And if you say you didn't you're calling me a liar, see?" He waved the steel bar threateningly.

If I had said: No sir, Mr. Pease, I never called you Pease, I would by inference have been calling Reynolds a liar; and if I said: Yes sir, Mr. Pease, I called you Pease, I would have been pleading guilty to the worst insult that a Negro can offer to a southern white man. I stood trying to think of a neutral course that would resolve this quickly risen nightmare, but my tongue would not move.

"Richard, I asked you a question!" Pease said. Anger was creeping into his voice.

"I don't remember calling you Pease, Mr. Pease," I said cautiously. "And if I did, I sure didn't mean . . ."

"You black sonofabitch! You called me Pease, then!" he spat, rising and slapping me till I bent sideways over a bench.

Reynolds was up on top of me demanding:

"Didn't you call him Pease? If you say you didn't. I'll rip your gut string loose with this f-k-g bar, you black granny dodger! You can't call a white man a liar and get away with it!"

I wilted. I begged them not to hit me. I knew what they wanted. They wanted me to leave the job.

"I'll leave," I promised. "I'll leave right now!"

They gave me a minute to get out of the factory, and warned me not to show up again or tell the boss. Reynolds loosened his hand on my collar and I ducked out of the room. . . .

For weeks after that I could not believe in my feelings. My personality was numb, reduced to a lumpish, loose, dissolved state. I was a non-man, something that knew vaguely that it was human but felt that it was not. As time separated me from the experience, I could feel no hate for the men who had driven me from the job. They did not seem to be individual men, but part of a huge, implacable, elemental design toward which hate was futile. What I did feel was a longing to attack. But how? And because I knew of no way to grapple with this thing, I felt doubly cast out.

I went to bed tired and got up tired, though I was having no physical exercise. During the day I overreacted to each event, my banked emotions spilling around it. I refused to talk to anyone about my affairs, because I knew that I would only hear a justification of the ways of the white folks and I did not want to hear it. I lived carrying a huge wound, tender, festering, and I shrank when I came near anything that I thought would touch it.[11]

Such clear-cut cases of discrimination are perhaps more the exception than the rule today. Much more common is the continuous flow of small incidents, the segregation, the closed doors and blocked opportunities that give the person to understand that he belongs to an "inferior" group.

The world of the minority-group member is shaped not only by such individual experiences but also by group responses that are passed along in the stream of culture. The experiences of one's parents and grandparents are built into their personalities, shaping their responses to their children and affecting the kinds of advice or unconsciously chosen influences they furnish to the growing generation. Fear and insecurity and hostility are thus to some degree cumulative, as, of course, are pride and courage. A terrifying experience for one Negro affects many others, in different times and places. The personality tendencies of contemporary Jews are affected to some degree by the accumulated experiences of preceding generations.

THE PERSONALITY-FORMING CONDITIONS OF SLAVERY

The impact of discriminatory conditions on personality development is shown with devastating clarity by an examination of slavery. Ideological factors loom large in studies of

[11] Reprinted from *Black Boy*, by Richard Wright, pp. 165–170. Copyright 1937 by Harper & Row.

this topic; and solid evidence is scarce. Yet it seems clear that slavery produced a wide range of responses, from angry protest, to creative adjustment to the power of the master, to docile accommodation.

Genovese suggests that we miss many subtle forms of resistance and effective adaptation when we think in terms of "defenseless slaves."

. . . although any individual at any given moment may be defenseless, a whole people rarely if ever is. A people may be on the defensive and dangerously exposed, but it often finds its own ways to survive and fight back. The trouble is that we keep looking for overt rebellious actions—a strike, a revolt, a murder, arson, tool-breaking—and often fail to realize that in given conditions and at particular times the wisdom of a people and their experience in struggle may dictate a different course, one of keeping together. From this point of view, the most ignorant of the field slaves who followed the conjurer on the plantation was saying no to the boss and seeking a form of cultural autonomy. That the conjurer may in any one case have been a fraud and even a kind of extortionist, and in another case a genuine popular religious leader is, from this point of view, of little importance.[12]

A different part of the range of responses —or perhaps it would be more accurate to say, a different quality within the responses, blended in with other qualities is stressed by Elkins. Even after due allowance is made for exaggeration and caricature, he observes, there is good evidence that the "Sambo" of fable and story is not wholly a figment of the imagination. In North America there were strong elements of docility, irresponsibility, laziness, and childish dependence among the slaves.[13] How is one to account for such tendencies? Certainly not by reference to the African background, for contemporary research has well documented the energy and vitality of West African tribal life.[14] Nor is slavery *per se* the source of

the "Sambo" tendencies, for they are not to be found among the slaves in Latin American societies. In North America, however, the utter dependence of the slave on the master created for him a permanent childlike status. The shock of capture and transport (two-thirds of the fifteen million taken died before reaching the Americas), the annihilation of the social ground for past standards (partly by random purchase and partly by owner design), and most importantly the entrance into a closed system wherein the master had virtually complete power, all combined to force onto the slave a highly constricted mode of adjustment. The master was the overwhelmingly "significant other," on whom all lines of authority converged. He had to be seen by the slave as somehow good, else the world would be unbearably destructive.

Elkins draws an instructive parallel between the utterly closed condition of North American slavery and the life of the concentration camp and notes their similar personality consequences. After a time, most of those who survived in the concentration camps of Hitler's Germany took on many of the values of the guards, who wielded the decision of life or death. The prisoners felt utter depersonalization, the loss of past values and identities; they acquired a childlike dependence; their interests and values became those of children.[15]

By the examination of such extreme conditions we can see in highlighted form the depth of the influence of social experience on personality. Once established, there is some tendency for personality styles to be perpetuated, through the socialization of children by parents and by the operation of self-fulfilling cycles. Thus the Sambo of slave days has something in common with the plantation field hand a century later. Much of this, of course, can be explained by the perpetuation of the conditions of a

[12] Eugene Genovese, "American Slaves and Their History," *The New York Review of Books*, Dec. 3, 1970, p. 35.

[13] Stanley Elkins, *Slavery*, Univ. of Chicago Press, 1959, chap. 3.

[14] For example, see M. J. Herskovits, *The Human Factor in Changing Africa*, Knopf, 1962, chaps. 3 and 4.

[15] For studies of the personality consequences of concentration camps see, for example, Bruno Bettelheim, "Individual and Mass Behavior in Extreme Situations," *JASP*, Oct. 1943, pp. 417–452; E. A. Cohen, *Human Behavior in the Concentration Camp*, Norton, 1953; and Czeslaw Milosz, *The Captive Mind*, Knopf, 1953.

fixed, low status and of overwhelming dependence.

We must also be prepared to explain, however, "abrupt" changes in personality, changes that will be unanticipated if Elkin's points are emphasized too strongly. The current "Negro revolt" represents the welling up of tendencies formerly obscure or deflected, but by no means absent, as Genovese notes. When circumstances change, when the Negro peasant becomes an urban industrial worker, when hope and aspiration and communication rise, formerly blocked or deflected tendencies are brought into play and new tendencies are formed. The "Sambo" type disappears.

RESPONDING TO THE CULTURE OF THE DOMINANT GROUP

How do various social circumstances affect the likelihood that a member of a minority group will become thoroughly assimilated to the dominant culture? Will he take on the pattern of motivation and morality that the majority group considers right? Is that, in fact, a desirable goal to strive for? We have seen that prejudiced persons often justify their attitudes and actions by reference to the inferior behavior and ideals of the members of the minority group. Is that inferiority —in terms of the standards of the dominant group—in a significant way the very product of prejudice and discrimination? Sutherland points out that there are many minority-group members who have never experienced "the American dream." They have never known a society composed largely of respectable, law-abiding, industrious families whose ambition and self-discipline were rewarded by a comfortable house, improved status, or a better job. A child is responsive to the rewards and punishments of his immediate environment, his family, his clique, his community. Behavior patterns that bring social approval and satisfaction from these groups are adopted very early. Only slightly does one strive for patterns of action that are approved by "society in general."[16]

Many white children and youth, of course, are also blocked from effective understanding or sharing of "the American dream"— with many of the same results.

There are many problems of policy and morality, as well as of science, in this issue. The operation and management of more and more complex societies require a sharp increase in the proportion of the population able and willing to undertake strenuous educational programs. Yet the motivation for such undertakings is not automatic, even when opportunities are opened up. Some are asking, as John Porter notes: "Why should working-class children be educated out of their good world [the presumed warm and communal world of the working class] into the hazards, the competitiveness, the impersonality, and the truncated kin groups of upwardly mobile middle-class society?"[17] To change motivational patterns requires drastic revision of the subcultures and structures on which they rest—with risks of an assumption of middle-class superiority or an antipluralism bias. But, as Porter says, ". . . there is also a moral problem in not providing working- and lower-class children with a chance to move up."[18]

IS THERE A "CULTURE OF POVERTY"?

In recent years, one manifestation of the effort to overcome a middle-class bias in the study of value contrasts and behavioral differences has been the use of the concept of the "culture of poverty," or of "lower-class subculture." Although this topic is approached from several different points of view, there is widespread agreement among those who study the question that barriers to social interaction between members of different classes help to maintain fairly well-defined and distinctive life styles. With our interest in minority groups, we need to remember that many of the tendencies of minority-group members are the product of their class status, and not specifically of their race or ethnicity. Prejudice, of course, is often involved in determining a person's

[16] Robert L. Sutherland, *Color, Class, and Personality*, ACE, 1942, pp. 22–23.

[17] Porter, *op. cit.*, p. 18.
[18] *Ibid.*, p. 17.

class status, so the two phenomena are closely related.

There have been two rather distinct phases in the study of class subcultures. Both emphasize the importance of the class structure in creating significantly different learning environments for children in different class locations. The earlier literature, however, tended to view the result as a consequence of isolation and lack of opportunity. More recently there has been an emphasis on the distinctive subculture of the slum or of an impoverished ethnic minority. One might say that the former stressed what was lacking in the experience of a child, the latter emphasized what was present. In an overly-simple contrast, the approaches were structural and cultural.[19] Both groups of authors express opposition to discrimination and seek to increase our understanding of the sources of different patterns of behavior. But the "subculture" school adds some elements of the current widespread dismay over the dominant culture and society. If one is unhappy with the "establishment," contrasting styles and policies take on a positive appearance. This perspective helps to control middle-class biases; it is a good antidote to ethnocentrism; it can help enrich our sympathetic understanding of differences in a pluralistic society. We should not forget, however, that the literature on the culture of poverty comes mainly from the pens of middle- and upper-class persons. They are not free from the danger of romanticizing a life style they do not share, in part as a form of deflected criticism and an expression of disenchantment with the foibles and absurdities of the one they do share. (We share much of this disenchantment, but do not want to let it govern our assessment of the sources of those foibles and absurdities.)

The isolation stressed by the first school could be either geographical or social. Some of the literature emphasizes class location, without much reference to minority-group status, while other studies are concerned

with both.[20] If a Negro from the rural peasantry or the city slums is, from the point of view of the dominant society, careless, without ambition, immoral, or criminal, the causes are to be sought in the personality-forming conditions that he has experienced.

In the customs governing sex behavior, the isolation of Negroes from the general culture is easily observable. It is one thing to know what the accepted standards are and then to violate them—such infringements are not uncommon in any class—but it is quite another thing to have no conception of such standards. In a group of ten boys in Chicago, all separated from their own parents and living a foot-loose existence, the investigator found an almost complete absence of inhibition in their reporting of sex relations. These boys were not "naturally" immoral because they were Negroes, as white judgments so often indicate, they merely had never known other standards. They reported their sex behavior, which a middle-class schoolteacher would condemn as immoral, as freely and unemotionally as they did their employment records or their love of swimming. With them some forms of sex behavior were taboo, and they had received some warnings and instructions from friends, but their sex behavior would indicate that they were thoroughly isolated from accepted middle-class standards.[21]

To "explain" or judge the behavior of the adult without a thorough understanding of the experiences of the child is clearly to miss the basic causes. If the dominant elements in American society—or any other society—isolate a segment of the people from contact with the prevailing norms and prevent them from sharing in any of the

---

[19] This distinction parallels that of Irvin Katz, who contrasts "cultural deprivation" studies with "cultural conflict" studies. See his "A Critique of Personality Approaches to Negro Performance, with Research Suggestions," *JSI*, Summer, 1969, pp. 13–27.

[20] See Allison W. Davis and Robert J. Havighurst, *Father of the Man: How Your Child Gets His Personality*, Houghton, Mifflin, 1947; Martha C. Ericson, "Child-Rearing and Social Status," *AJS*, Nov., 1946, pp. 190–192; Bernard C. Rosen, "The Achievement Syndrome," *ASR*, Apr., 1956, pp. 203–211; Louis Schneider and Sverre Lysgaard, "The Deferred Gratification Pattern," *ASR*, Apr., 1953, pp. 142–149; Melvin Kohn, "Social Class and Parental Values," *AJS*, Jan., 1959, pp. 337–351; Murray Straus, "Deferred Gratification, Social Class, and the Achievement Syndrome," *ASR*, June, 1962, pp. 326–335; Urie Bronfenbrenner, "Socialization and Social Class Through Time and Space, in *Readings in Social Psychology*, Eleanor Maccoby, Theodore Newcomb, and Eugene Hartley (eds.), Holt, Rinehart & Winston, 1958, pp. 400–425; Deutsch, Katz, and Jensen, *op. cit.*

[21] Sutherland, *op. cit.*, pp. 36–37.

rewards that may follow from abiding by those norms, they should not be surprised at the appearance of different standards of conduct and motivations.

The isolation we are referring to is far from complete. A minority group, by definition, cannot be fully isolated from the majority. For persons in a deprived group, in fact, learning how to handle the prejudices of members of a dominant group is an essential lesson. For students of these subtle interactions, it is also necessary to understand the anxieties of the "dominants." Robert Coles emphasizes these points in *Children of Crisis*.

One Negro mother put rather well the feelings I have heard many others express. "I guess we all don't like white people too much deep inside. . . . But if something is inside of you, it doesn't mean it's there alone. We have to live with one another, black with white I mean. I keep on telling that to the children, and if they don't seem to learn it, like everything else I have to punish them to make sure they do. . . . It's like with cars and knives, you have to teach your children to know what's dangerous and how to stay away from it, or else they sure won't live long. White people are a real danger to us until we learn how to live with them. So if you want your kids to live long, they have to grow up scared of whites; and the way they get scared is through us. . . ."[22]

Coles illustrates this with the story of Ruby, a little black girl who was one of the first to enter a "white" school in the South. Though she showed great courage in the face of intense hostility, she began to lose weight and to refuse foods that formerly had been her favorites. Every day she faced threats as she approached school: " 'You little nigger, we'll get you and kill you,' was a commonplace. Some of the language is unprintable. But one comment is both printable and important. Spoken in a high-pitched but determined voice, its words were always the same: 'We're going to poison you until you choke to death.' Its speaker was always the same."[23] This threat, among the many, was particularly disturbing to Ruby, for she was familiar with threats about food from her family—threats of going without food, of

getting indigestion, of choking if she was bad. "Her mother had threatened her often with no supper if she persisted in wrongdoing—hitting her sister too hard, failing to obey a command or request. Now segregationist mobs were telling her she might be hurt, poisoned and killed. One member of that mob, impelled by reasons within her own life, kept telling Ruby of poison in her lunch or supper, forging in the child's mind a link between home and school, between the child's personal conflicts and this public struggle which found her a sudden participant."[24]

After several months, the school situation improved, and Ruby's appetite returned. We would miss much of the significance of the story, however, if we disregarded the woman who was making the threats.

. . . as language went this woman's was mild for a member of the mob that bothered Ruby. Moreover, part of her threat to Ruby was one she hurled at her own children. If they misbehave she threatens to choke them. I have heard her use the expression commonly enough to indicate that for her it has the meaning of a serious spanking. . . .

There is no question that this woman fears and hates Negroes, and there is also no question about her generally suspicious personality. She is poor, now in her very late thirties, with little education (eighth-grade) and perhaps too many children as well as a wayward, fickle, heavily drinking husband. Most of all she is tired. . . .

When she is weary she becomes surly, and underneath it all very sad and very frightened. She is struggling to manage herself and her large family in the face of poverty, ignorance, social isolation . . . and virtual abandonment by her occasionally employed husband . . . Her life is cheated and impoverished, and she feels at times lonely and hard-worked with little hope of an end to either condition. Her feelings emerge in remarks like this: "I have to do the best I can with little help from anyone, and I'll probably die young doing nothing else."[25]

Knowledge of the woman's dreary life does not make her verbal attacks on Ruby any less dismaying. But they are dismaying as a serious illness is dismaying. To treat them as a cause, rather than as a link near

[22] Robert Coles, *op. cit.*, p. 66.
[23] *Ibid.*, p. 78.
[24] *Ibid.*, p. 82.
[25] *Ibid.*, pp. 83–84.

the end of a chain of causes, is to reduce one's understanding and one's effectiveness in producing a change.

When we turn to studies dealing directly with the concept of the "culture of poverty," we find a wide range of interpretations. There are some who see the life style of those in poverty as the cumulative cultural result of the experience of poverty, mingled perhaps with various ethnic elements. "Lower class culture is a distinctive tradition many centuries old with an integrity of its own."[26] Limited opportunities and discrimination play a part, according to this view, but in an indirect sense, as they act upon a traditional life style.

Other writers emphasize the interaction of subcultural elements with the experience of discrimination and the high chance of failure. A complex value system has developed as a way of dealing, both with training in and aspirations to the dominant patterns, and with the realistic chances for failure and frustration. Rodman describes this nicely as a "value stretch." The lower-class person develops an alternative set of values to deal with his difficult situation "without abandoning the general values of the society."[27] This point of view has been expanded in a valuable way in a number of recent studies. Liebow remarks, for example, that family instability among lower-class Negroes does not so much represent a subcultural style

as ". . . the cultural model of the larger society as seen through the prism of repeated failure."[28] Lee Rainwater adds a necessary time dimension to the question by tracing the interaction of subcultural norms with the dominant culture in a particular existential situation:

Norms with their existential concomitants can be regarded as rules for playing a particular game. That game represents one kind of adaptation to the environmental situation in which a group finds itself. . . . If the individual is not allowed in the game (for example, Negro slaves under slavery), or if he cannot obtain the resources to play the game successfully and thus experiences constant failure at it, he is not "conceptual boob" enough to continue knocking his head against a stone wall—he withdraws from the game. Instead, he will try to find another game to play, either one that is already existing and at hand or one that he himself invents. . . .

But what if a good many people cannot play the normative game, are in constant communication with each other, and there is generational continuity among them? In that case, the stage is set for the invention and diffusion of substitute games of a wide variety . . . The substitute adaptations of each generation condition the possibilities subsequent generations have of adapting in terms of the requirements of the normative games.

Nevertheless, in the American context at least it is clear that each generation of Negroes has a strong desire to be able to perform successfully in terms of the norms of the larger society and makes efforts in this direction. The inadequacies of the opportunity structure doom most to failure to achieve in terms of their own desires, and therefore facilitate the adoption of the readily available alternatives.[29]

Still other studies of the "culture of poverty" see it as an excessively rigid concept

[26] Walter B. Miller, "Lower Class Culture as a Generating Milieu of Gang Delinquency," *JSI*, Third Quarter, 1958, p. 18. Something of this same position is taken also by Oscar Lewis in a number of books: *Five Families: Mexican Case Studies in the Culture of Poverty*, Basic Books, 1959; *Children of Sanchez*, Random House, 1961; *La Vida*, Random House, 1966; *A Study of Slum Culture: Backgrounds for La Vida*, Random House, 1968. See also Edward Banfield, *The Moral Basis of a Backward Society*, Free Press, 1958; Edward Banfield, *The Unheavenly City*, Little, Brown, 1968; Albert K. Cohen and Harold M. Hodges, Jr., "Characteristics of the Lower-Blue-Collar-Class," *SP*, Spring, 1963, pp. 303–334. Variation *within* the lower class is explored by some writers. See, for example, Norman J. Johnson and Peggy R. Sanday, "Subcultural Variations in an Urban Poor Population," *AA*, Feb., 1971, pp. 128–143; Lola M. Irelan, Oliver C. Moles, and Robert M. O'Shea, "Ethnicity, Poverty, and Selected Attitudes: A Test of the 'Culture of Poverty' Hypothesis," *SF*, June, 1969, pp. 405–413.

[27] Hyman Rodman, "The Lower-Class Value Stretch," *SF*, Dec., 1963, pp. 205–215.

[28] Elliot Liebow, *Tally's Corner*, Little, Brown, 1967, p. 221.

[29] Lee Rainwater, "The Problem of Lower Class Culture," *JSI*, Spring, 1970, pp. 142–143. For other valuable developments of this perspective, see Seymour Parker and Robert J. Kleiner, "The Culture of Poverty: An Adjustive Dimension," *AA*, June, 1970, pp. 516–527; Wan Sang Han, "Two Conflicting Themes: Common Values versus Class Differential Values," *ASR*, Oct., 1969, pp. 679–690; Raymond T. Smith, "Culture and Social Structure in the Caribbean," *Comparative Studies in Society and History*, Oct., 1963, p. 24–46; Richard Ball, "A Poverty Case: The Analgesic Subculture of the Southern Appalachians," *ASR*, Dec., 1968, pp. 885–895.

that overemphasizes value contrasts among the classes of a society and underemphasizes the situational contrasts that produce different behavior.[30]

As Valentine notes, explanations by "culture," sweepingly defined, have become almost a fad, spreading out from culture of poverty to "lower 'class' culture," "culture of violence," "culture of the uninvolved," etc. Exclusive or major attention to the cultural element can have the effect, as Valentine says, of "blaming poverty on the poor," since it is seen as a natural expression of their values.[31] Thus what started out as support for cultural pluralism and an affirmation of the dignity of the life styles of lower classes and minority groups may end up as support for conditions that perpetuate poverty and discrimination.[32]

In our judgment, these diverse approaches to the concept of a "culture of poverty" can be made consistent—their contradictions removed and their various omissions filled—only by studying them together in a field theoretical system. We think the phrase "subculture of poverty" should be used to refer only to shared normative elements. "Structure of poverty" refers to the lack of power and the low level of opportunity that characterize certain groups. Norms and opportunities, in turn, give rise to, and then are reinforced by, certain individual qualities—attitudes, motives, skill levels. If one seeks to answer the question "Who will be poor?" with reference to these three elements seen separately, or analytically, he would say:

1. those trained to and supported by poverty-oriented norms.
2. those living in low-opportunity areas, whatever their culture.
3. those with certain individual tendencies,

whatever the opportunity system around them or the values emphasized in their communities.

These separate statements, however, are of little value. It is particularly in the interaction of these various elements, in their system quality, that the explanation of both the sources and the consequences of poverty resides. One possible sequence that illustrates the feedback processes among these elements might run as follows: Low opportunity leads to low motivation and skill which, when widely shared, leads to values adapted to poverty that prevent recognition or pursuit of available opportunities.

A correct statement of this problem is peculiarly important, because policies based on a partial statement are bound to be ineffective and often counterproductive. The conservative sees only level 3, the character level. He has no objection to admitting the "poor" into full participation in society, as soon as they acquire the attitudes, skills, and motivations necessary to perform important functions at a sufficiently high level. The conservative doesn't make clear how those who are not allowed in the water are going to learn to swim. The issue is seldom put as baldly as it has been by Eric Hoffer, but his view is probably shared by many:

The 20 million Negroes in America seem to lack the will and the gumption to build and create something impressive—something that would demonstrate to the world what Negro energy, initiative, skill, and guts can do. . . .

They expect Whitey to feed and house them, housebreak and educate their children, and supply them with stores, adequately stocked with liquor and television sets for periodic looting sprees. . . .

There is no reason why the Negroes in America, who breathe the air we breathe and share in the work we do, should not become world pioneers in the overcoming of backwardness.[33]

The radical sees this as "bootstrap thinking." He sees little chance for change in motivation and skill level until those now trapped in poverty are convinced that their

[30] See Charles Valentine, *Culture and Poverty*, Univ. of Chicago Press, 1968; Jack L. Roach and Orville R. Gursslin, "An Evaluation of the Concept 'Culture of Poverty,'" *SF*, Mar., 1967, pp. 383–392; and Lewis A. Coser, "Unanticipated Conservative Consequences of Liberal Theorizing," *SP*, Winter, 1969, pp. 263–272. Kenneth Clark does not use or criticize the concept, but his interpretation is primarily in terms of deprived situations, not culture. See *Dark Ghetto*, Harper & Row, 1965.

[31] Valentine, *op. cit.*, p. 15.

[32] This is the thesis defended by Coser, *op. cit.*

[33] Eric Hoffer, Honolulu *Star-Bulletin*, Sept. 16, 1968, p. A–22.

efforts will be rewarded, that opportunities will be opened. After generations of restricted opportunity, it will not be easy to develop the socialization processes that establish such a conviction. The radical who counts wholly on the need for structural change may give insufficient attention to "character lag."

The liberal, as we have noted, is caught between his desire to avoid ethnocentrism and middle-class bias and the fact that some of the values and norms that emerge out of poverty are, as a result of the very fact of their adaptive power, part of a cycle that keeps individuals in poverty. The need is to support an open-minded pluralism without falling into sentimental approval of a life style that is in some measure a desperate expedient to deal with an extremely difficult situation.[34]

STRIVING TO ACHIEVE THE AMERICAN DREAM

It would be unfortunate if our discussion of the concept of the culture of poverty caused us to overlook the extent of striving for educational and occupational advance among minority-group members. Even in fairly remote rural areas a generation ago there was hope and aspiration.[35] In a recent Gallup Poll Blacks responded more optimistically than Whites to the question: "Do you think, for people like yourself, that the world in ten years' time will be a better place to live in than it is now, not so good, or just about the same?" Fifty-one percent of the Nonwhites (mostly Negroes) responded "better," compared with 37 percent of the Whites.[36]

It is important also to remember the growing numbers of middle- and upper-class persons in American minority groups. The critical questions for them are not so much those of educational and economic opportunity as of marginality and status discrepancies. We shall refer to their responses to the dominant culture below. Most Chicanos, Blacks, Puerto Ricans, and other minorities, however, are fully in touch with the sights and sounds and promises of an affluent society, but denied access to achievement in that society by discrimination and by their own responses. The result, inevitably, is disillusionment and frustration.

The sharp contrast between promise and fulfillment is a highly important factor in the development of personality tendencies of minority-group members (as, indeed, it is to a lesser degree in the development of the great majority of dominant-group members, who are taught to aspire to goals that few will reach).

Contemporary research on the effects of minority status on personality helps us to spell out some of the conditions under which various results occur. On this issue, as on so many of the issues with which we are concerned in this volume, we must be alert to methodological problems. Many personality tests have been standardized on white, and usually middle-class, populations. Their reliability and validity when applied to minority-group members is often subject to doubt. When comparisons are being made it is often difficult to establish adequate scientific controls across major racial or cultural lines. Are a white boy and a Negro boy who have both finished the tenth grade in segregated schools, for example, "equated" for education? In most cases this is doubtless an unwarranted assumption. How should one interpret the different results, in the measurement of attitudes for example, recorded by a Negro interviewer and a white interviewer for a Negro population? Most research is carried on by white scholars, who may get traditional or restrained answers from Negroes; yet it would not be wise to assume that answers to black interviewers are more valid. Only as several lines of independent evidence accumulate can we

[34] The effort to adapt to a frustrating situation, particularly one toward which one feels strong ambivalence, can lead to the affirmation of a contraculture—of norms and values that specifically reverse those of the dominant culture. Contracultures are not traditional subcultures, but arise in situations where there is a high level both of interindividual and intraindividual conflict. See J. Milton Yinger, "Contraculture and Subculture," *ASR*, Oct., 1960, pp. 625–635.

[35] Charles S. Johnson, *Growing Up in the Black Belt*, ACE, 1941, pp. 114–115.

[36] *The New York Times*, Dec. 7, 1969, p. 67.

speak with great confidence. Effects of the race of a researcher differ when different variables are being studied, and there are important interaction effects, for example, between a skill being measured and instructions given to the subjects.[37]

Keeping methodological cautions in mind, we can properly examine some of the evidence concerning the relationship of minority-group members to the dominant society. A great deal of research has been devoted to the sources of "achievement motive"—the readiness to work hard and postpone satisfactions in order to get ahead.[38] Three generalizations seem appropriate on the basis of current evidence: (1) class is more important than race or ethnic group in determining the strength of achievement motive; (2) an important line of demarcation can be drawn between the lower-lower and upper-lower class (a line of special significance among nonwhites); and (3) the desire for achievement is not always accompanied by the values, norms, and goals related to achievement, nor by the expectation of achievement—and their separation is a strategic fact. Stephenson found, for example, that among 1000 ninth-graders whom he studied, Negro lower-class students had aspirations as high as white students from the same class, but their plans—their expectations—were uniformly lower.[39]

On the basis of interview and projective tests given in 62 communities on the East Coast, Rosen found that both class and ethnic group were related to achievement values. On answers to seven questions testing what he called "activistic-passivistic," "individualistic-collectivistic," and "present-future" orientations, he found the following results: Jews, 5.54; Protestants, 5.16; Greeks (persons of Greek background), 5.08; Negroes, 5.03; Italians, 4.17; and French-Canadian, 3.68. When only persons of similar class were compared, ethnicity continued to be related significantly to aspiration, but class proved to be more significant. When mothers were asked how far they intended their sons to go in school, the groups appeared in the same order, ranging from 96 percent of the Jewish mothers down to 56 percent of the French-Canadian mothers expecting their sons to go to college. Negro mothers again were high—83 percent. Negro vocational aspirations, however, were significantly lower than all of the others except the French-Canadian, indicating that the educational hopes of the mothers were unrealistically high or that a step into the lower middle class was already a long step for most of the Negro respondents.[40]

Partly supporting and partly qualifying these findings, Antonovsky and Lerner discovered higher educational and job aspirations among lower-class Negro than among lower-class white boys. Their study was carried out among a sample of 16- to 20-year-olds in an upstate New York city. (Since they reached 88 percent of the Negro sample but only 65 percent of the white sample, some sampling error may have entered in.) Among their interviewees, Negroes were more often in college preparatory courses, fewer had dropped out of school before graduation, and more of them remembered guidance programs in school (although they had had no more such programs). These differences appeared even though the Negro families were of lower economic status, the parents less well-educated, and more of the families were broken. Antonovsky and Lerner account for this rather surprising finding by the closeness Negro boys felt to famous Negro models, by the fact that realistically the high-status professions may be more open to Negroes than skilled jobs or

[37] See the valuable series of studies carried out by Irwin Katz and his colleagues: "The Influence of Race of the Experimenter and Instructions upon the Expression of Hostility by Negro Boys," *JSI*, Apr., 1964, pp. 54–56; "Effects of Task Difficulty, Race of Administrator, and Instructions on Digit-Symbol Performance of Negroes," *JPSP*, July, 1965, pp. 53–59; "Effects of Race of Tester, Approval-Disapproval, and Need on Negro Children's Learning," *JPSP*, Jan., 1968, pp. 38–42.

[38] See especially David McClelland, *The Achieving Society*, Van Nostrand, 1961.

[39] Richard Stephenson, "Mobility Orientation and Stratification of 1,000 Ninth Graders," *ASR*, Apr., 1957, pp. 204–212. See also John Scanzoni, "Socialization, *n* Achievement, and Achievement Values," *ASR*, June, 1967, pp. 449–456; Joseph Kahl, "Some Measurements of Achievement Orientation," *AJS*, May, 1965, pp. 669–681.

[40] See Bernard Rosen, "Race, Ethnicity, and the Achievement Syndrone," *ASR*, Feb., 1959, pp. 47–60.

businesses, by the "negative reference group" furnished by the parents who, in fact, often encouraged them in this by stressing that the children must do better than they had done—an influence found also among many immigrant groups.[41]

Research along this line has been carried forward by a number of writers. Rytina, Form, and Pease, for example, found that Negroes were significantly less likely than Whites to see America as a land of opportunity, or to believe that voting influences governmental action.[42] It should be noted, however, that even among low-income Negroes, a majority shared the beliefs about open opportunity. We are left with questions about the effects of time and place. (The Rytina, Form, and Pease data come from a medium-sized industrial city in Michigan, 1966–1967.)

In a study of Negroes and Whites in Lexington, Kentucky, Garza introduced a measure of "perception of opportunity." With income controlled, Negro mothers were significantly more likely than white mothers to believe that their sons would obtain rewarding jobs.[43] As a variable, "perception of opportunity" is closely related to a number of other concepts that are proving of value in the study of motivation: expectancy of success, sense of powerlessness, and internal versus external control. The last, as described by Rotter, is the contrast between the belief that rewards follow from one's own behavior and the belief that rewards are the result of external forces beyond one's control.[44]

There are valuable concepts that prompt us to pay careful attention to variation in aspiration and motivation; but they have not been thoroughly absorbed into a theory of prejudice and discrimination. The various terms need fuller specification.[45] The sources and the correlates of high aspiration require further study. And the interactions between individual tendencies and the facilitating of inhibiting situations must be examined. Measures of level of achievement motive become more valuable when they are specified by measures of expectancy of success.[46] These two individual tendencies do not necessarily vary together, and the significance of high achievement motive for behavior is quite different for a person with low expectancy of success from what it is for a person with high expectancy of success. These relationships, in turn, are made more meaningful by examining "the social context of ambition"—the context within which achievement motives and feelings of internal or external control are formed.[47]

Seeman has shown that the level of alienation, defined in his study as powerlessness, influences the process of learning of information about parole on the part of inmates in a reformatory. As one would predict from Rotter's theory, those who felt most controlled by chance learned less, those who had higher expectations of control over their lives learned more.[48] In a comment on Seeman's research, James Coleman notes its significance for the student of race relation: "Seeman's results suggest a general

[41] Aaron Antonovsky and Melvin Lerner, "Occupational Aspirations of Lower Class Negro and White Youth," *SP*, Fall, 1959, pp. 132–138.

[42] Joan Huber Rytina, William H. Form, and John Pease, "Income and Stratification Ideology: Beliefs About the American Opportunity Structure," *AJS*, Jan., 1970, pp. 703–716.

[43] Joseph M. Garza, "Race, the Achievement Syndrome, and Perception of Opportunity," *Phylon*, Winter, 1969, pp. 338–354.

[44] See J. B. Rotter, "Generalized Expectancies for Internal versus External Control of Reinforcement," *Psychological Monographs* 80, no. 1, 1966. On powerlessness, see Melvin Seeman, "On the Meaning of Alienation," *ASR*, Dec., 1959, pp. 783–791; and Dwight G. Dean, "Alienation: Its Meaning and Measurement," *ASR*, Oct., 1961, pp. 753–758.

[45] This is done for the internal-external distinction in a valuable way by Patricia Gurin, Gerald Gurin, Rosina Lao, and Muriel Beattie, "Internal-External Control in the Motivational Dynamics of Negro Youth," *JSI*, Summer, 1969, pp. 29–53.

[46] See Patricia Gurin, "Motivation and Aspiration of Southern Negro College Youth," *AJS*, Jan. 1970, pp. 607–631.

[47] There is a large literature on this question that makes no reference to race or minority status, as well as many studies concerned with these variables. The interested student will want to consult both. See, for example, Ralph H. Turner, *The Social Context of Ambition*, Chandler, 1964; William H. Sewell, A. O. Haller, and Alejandro Portes, "The Educational and Early Occupational Attainment Process," *ASR*, Feb., 1969, pp. 82–92; Lee N. Robins, Robin S. Jones, and George E. Murphy, "School Milieu and School Problems of Negro Boys," *SP*, Spring, 1966, pp. 428–436.

[48] Melvin Seeman, "Alienation and Social Learning in a Reformatory," *AJS*, Nov., 1963, pp. 270–284.

phenomenon that a man is sensitive to the cues of his environment only when he believes he can have some effect upon it."[49] Negroes who have migrated from or live in an environment which gives them little sense of control are likely to have a mind set that makes them insensitive to learning cues— a set that will, in part, be transmitted to their children.

To study the influence of a context, moreover, one needs to know what individuals and groups are available as reference groups. Theodore Kemper has noted three types of reference groups that act together to produce achievement striving.[50] One type, the "normative," furnishes norms and espouses values; it not only sets standards but brings pressure to bear on those for whom it is a reference group to secure compliance (e.g., family, church, nation). "Comparison" groups facilitate judgments about how one is doing. "Audience" groups, to which an actor imputes standards, do not sanction the behavior of the individual, as the normative group does, and may not even be aware of him; but he seeks their approval. Motives and performance, Kemper suggests, are strongly affected by the combinations of reference groups available, as well as by their standards. In the optimum case, all three types are available; but there may be comparison and audience groups, for example, without normative ones; or no comparison groups, or no audiences. Although we lack systematic study of the effect of various combinations of reference groups on achievement values and performance of minority-group members, the influences of school desegregation, integrated neighborhoods, and ethnic identity to which we have referred can plausibly be interpreted by use of reference group theory.

It would be a mistake to conclude, from the data in hand, that the aspirations of Negro youth are equivalent to those of white youth in the United States today. When we control for class we should not forget that a vastly larger proportion of Negroes are found in the lower class. And the studies cited refer largely to *upper*-lower-class persons in northern cities. Difficult as their situation is, they have come in touch with the American Dream and have begun to share in at least a few of its promises; their hopes are aroused. There is still a large group, however, for whom even dreams are remote. They stand on the edge of the economy barely sustained by this affluent society; their children go to inferior and segregated, or nearly segregated, schools, whether they live in the North or the South; they are "piled up," sometimes over 50,000 to the square mile, in substandard dwellings in northern cities; or they are cut off by massive segregation from the agencies of hope and improvement in most parts of the South.

Although they do not refer specifically to minority-group members of the lower-lower class, Cohen and Hodges have given us a rich description of its life-situation—the narrow range of experience, the powerlessness, the deprivation, the insecurity. Out of this situation there emerges a cynical and distrustful view of the world, based partly on realistic assessment, but partly also on a moral view rooted in the search for security. "The LL . . . has a relatively small investment in the 'universalistic-achievement' sector of society. It is the sector in which he fares poorly, in which he moves awkwardly, which he can least exploit to his own advantage, and which provides him with little security."[51] He comes to depend on a "morality of particularistic loyalties and reciprocities;" he can trust those close at hand, but all others are strangers in a puzzling and threatening world.

This description is given substance by an account of gang life among lower-class Negroes in New Orleans.[52] Negro women have won some small measure of security by

[49] James S. Coleman, "Implications of the Findings on Alienation," *AJS*, July, 1964, p. 77. See also the commentaries by J. C. Mouledous and E. C. Mouledous and the reply by Seeman, pp. 78–84.

[50] Theodore Kemper, "Reference Groups, Socialization and Achievement," *ASR*, Feb., 1968, pp. 31–45.

[51] Albert Cohen and Harold Hodges, Jr., "Characteristics of the Lower-Blue-Collar-Class," *SP*, Spring, 1963, pp. 303–334.

[52] John H. Rohrer and Munro S. Edmonson (eds.), *The Eighth Generation: Culture and Personalities of New Orleans Negroes*, Harper & Row, 1960.

the development of matriarchal patterns of dominance. But their adjustment to an unstable family situation—part of the heritage of slavery—helps to perpetuate that situation. The adult male is deprived of self-respect; the boy is often raised without contact with his father,[53] or in a context that demonstrates his father's inferiority; and mothers, though they may show affection for their sons, ". . . are clearly convinced that all little boys must inexorably and deplorably become men, with all pathologies of that sex."[54] In this setting, as Rohrer and Edmonson observe, if a defensive and protective male culture were not available, it would have to be invented. But it is available in the gang. This is not necessarily a criminal organization; nor is it a formal group. It is a convergence upon a pattern of life by persons equally in search of self-respect and a meaningful social role.

The psychic economy of the gang demands aggressive independence, a touchy and exaggerated virility, and a deep, protective secrecy. Acceptance by the gang provides almost the only source of security for its members, but such acceptance is conditional upon continual proof that it is merited, and this proof can only be furnished through physical aggressivness, a restless demonstration of sexual prowess, and a symbolic execution of those illegal deeds that a "sissy" would not perform. These activities victimize women, but it would seem that they are not specifically directed toward women. Rather the enemy of the gang is the world of people (especially men) too unmanly for survival in what has often been described as a social jungle.[55]

In all this there is more than a little reaction-formation, more than a little effort to rid one's self of doubt about one's manhood and worth. The result, however, is to create a style of life, perhaps a contraculture, that aids temporary adjustment but cuts the participants off from alternative ways of struggling with their problems.

There is little doubt that the situation is more difficult for most lower-class Negro males than it is for females. In a study of over 500 ninth-graders in New Haven and Harrisburg, Sprey found that fewer Negro boys than girls expected to rise above their parents. This was also true among white ninth-graders, but to a much smaller degree. In these groups children in the lowest parental occupational category (unskilled manual) more often aspired to positions above those of their parents than did those in the skilled manual category. We should not assume that this is evidence against the importance of the distinction between lower-lower and upper-lower without noting that by the ninth grade some of the lower-lower had already left school, and were therefore not in the sample, and that aspiration above parental level for the unskilled manual is almost unavoidable. Yet over one-third of the Negro boys and one-sixth of the white boys from the lower manual class in these schools did not have aspirations above the parents' occupational levels. (This was true of eight percent of the Negro and ten percent of the white girls from the same class.)[56] Probably more significant, however, is the extent to which these aspirations are demonstrated in behavior. Sprey indicates the proportions enrolled in college preparatory courses. Among both Negroes and whites the line between skilled manual and unskilled manual now proves to be important, with about twice as large a proportion of the former enrolled in college preparatory divisions as of the latter. The race line is also important among the boys, with white boys on both class levels more than twice as likely to be in college preparatory divisions. And the sex line is important among Negroes, with almost twice as large a proportion of girls, at both class levels, in the college preparatory courses (while among the white students, boys were somewhat more likely to be enrolled in such courses).[57]

Such data are given biographical substance by Liebow's study of an urban neigh-

---

[53] For an interesting cross-cultural study of the effects of father absence, see Walter Mischel, "Father-Absence and Delay of Gratification: Cross-Cultural Comparisons," *JASP*, July, 1961, pp. 116–124.

[54] Rohrer and Edmonson, *op. cit.*, p. 161.

[55] *Ibid.*, p. 160.

[56] Jetse Sprey, "Sex Differences in Occupational Choice Patterns Among Negro Adolescents," *SP*, Summer, 1962, p. 13.

[57] *Ibid.*, p. 16.

borhood. Low aspirations and lack of plans are not so much the result of "present-orientation" as of bleak prospects.

As for the future, the young streetcorner man has a fairly good picture of it. In Richard or Sea Cat or Arthur he can see himself in his middle twenties; he can look at Tally to see himself at thirty, at Wee Tom to see himself in his middle thirties, and at Budder and Stanton to see himself in his forties. It is a future in which everything is uncertain except the ultimate destruction of his hopes and the eventual realization of his fears. The most he can reasonably look forward to is that these things do not come too soon. Thus, when Richard squanders a week's pay in two days it is not because, like an animal or a child, he is 'present-time oriented,' unaware of or unconcerned with his future. He does so precisely because he is aware of the future and the hopelessness of it all.[58]

Situational Pressures Toward Deviation.
One of the consequences of knowing and sharing but being blocked from full participation in the "American dream" is the ambivalent attitudes that oppressed persons get toward the nation and its laws. It is impossible for them to give full allegiance to a society which itself has not fully accepted them. When Americans of Japanese ancestry were forcibly evacuated from the West Coast in 1942, doubts were inevitably raised in their minds about the sincerity of America's democracy. The Issei (those born in Japan, and therefore unable to become citizens) were particularly disillusioned and frustrated. Leighton says of those who came to Poston (one of the relocation camps): "The Isseis came to Poston with feelings of life's work wasted, bitterness, apathy, and fear, shot through with the conviction that there was no future in America for the Japanese. As for democratic principles and form of government, they thought that had proved a failure."[59] One would scarcely expect the Issei to show unalloyed enthusiasm for a nation that refused them citizenship and dis-

criminated against them so drastically. (Despite their resentment, the great majority of Japanese-Americans supported the United States, and the Nisei, who are citizens, gave the nation unflinching support.)

The responses of Japanese-Americans to relocation illustrate again not only some of the personality-forming conditions for minority-group members, but the general social psychological theory that personality is a function of situations and tendencies in interaction, not of fixed "traits." The evacuation meant financial disaster to most of the Japanese-Americans; self-government in the camps was limited; salary schedules ranged from $12 to $19 a month; the first-generation Japanese were defined as enemy aliens. In this context, in January, 1943, all residents of the relocation centers over 16 years of age were required to declare their loyalty or disloyalty to the United States. Six thousand Japanese-Americans answered "no" to the loyalty question. Grodzins indicates very clearly the ways in which discrimination affected these results. A declaration of disloyalty was a protest: "We have citizenship and still we are . . . treated just like aliens. So what's the use of talking about citizenship and being loyal citizens?" It was also an indication of family loyalty, an expression of the identity of the Nisei with their alien parents who were not permitted to become citizens and had suffered great economic loss. A declaration of disloyalty was an attempt to find security in a situation that was very threatening.[60] It is important to note that there were great differences in the percentage of people in the ten relocation centers who declared themselves disloyal (ranging from 8 to 52 percent of adult males). This range reflects the differences in social situations in the centers—residential conditions, the frequency of change of administration, location of the center, attitudes of governing officials, types of leadership among the Japanese-

[58] Liebow, *op. cit.*, p. 66.
[59] Alexander Leighton, *The Governing of Men,* Princeton, 1945, p. 71.

[60] For a discussion of these and other factors involved in the declarations of disloyalty, see Morton Grodzins, "Making Un-Americans," *AJS*, May, 1955, pp. 570–582; and for a general treatise on the meaning of loyalty, see his *The Loyal and the Disloyal,* Univ. of Chicago Press, 1956.

Americans, etc. Grodzins summarizes the situation well:

Loyalties change as social situation changes and individuals assess previous experience, present plight, and future promise. Loyalty to his nation comes easily if an individual's job and career are secure, if he participates amiably in work and play with colleagues and friends, if he feels accepted and secure, if his relationship to the larger community is not strained. Destroy his career, disrupt his work and play groups, isolate him, persecute him, show your disdain for him, and you plant the seeds of his disaffection. His allegiance will withstand maltreatment. But the multiplication of abuses will weaken his loyalty; and, as abuse continues, loyalty to nation erodes away—the more completely and rapidly if he believes that the government is directly responsible for his difficulties. Loyalty does not thereby disappear. It is transferred to another cause, another group, perhaps another nation.[61]

Discrimination may encourage ambivalence in matters of lawfulness on the part of those who have experienced only inadequate protection by the law. In a society where legal controls are notoriously weak one must be cautious not to assume that such a response is limited to minority-group members. There is evidence, however, that the pressures of an inferior status predispose one to certain forms of illegality. It is known, for example, that some kinds of gambling, particularly the policy or numbers racket, are widespread forms of lawbreaking among disadvantaged Negro slum dwellers. This situation can be understood as the result of a total experience that promises much but gives little. The numbers game has the attraction of large possible returns: one cent brings five dollars. Few win, of course (not more than one in a thousand); but in a large community like Harlem no day passes without somebody winning—and many hear of it and are encouraged to live in hope. Chance-taking and gambling are quite congruent with many aspects of American culture and of many other cultures, and thus occur among a far wider range of people than minority-group members. Among the latter, however, there is the additional stimulus of gambling that

results from losing hope of achieving even a modest success by the more stable methods of hard work and thrift. The prejudice and discrimination that they see all around them cause them to doubt the rewards of "virtue." They turn, rather, to a kind of magic (just as men seem to do everywhere when the odds are heavily against them) in their search for success.[62]

Estimates of the amount spent on the numbers in New York City annually range from $250 million to $1.5 billion—either amount giving substance to the words of Langston Hughes: "You might almost say the numbers is the salvation of Harlem, its Medicare, and its Black Draught, its 666 [two laxatives popular in the South], its little liver pills, its vitamins, its aspirins and its analgesic balm combined."[63] Since New York state has legalized off-track betting, the illegality of numbers is as marginal as the lives of those who play them. Some black legislators, in fact, and the Offtrack Corporation of New York are seeking to "legalize the numbers under community control."[64]

Gary Marx has reported that the frustrations associated with the current civil rights struggle have led a substantial number of Negroes—perhaps as many as 20 percent —into a "depth of estrangement and bitterness unique in American history."[65] Illustrative of the extreme disenchantment are such writings as those of Eldridge Cleaver

---

[61] Grodzins, "Making Un-Americans," p. 582.

[62] See George McCall, "Symbiosis: The Case of Hoodoo and the Numbers Racket," *SP*, Spring, 1963, pp. 361–371.

[63] Quoted in *The New York Times*, Mar. 1, 1971, p. 1.

[64] *Ibid.* This illustrates the problem of defining deviation in a period of change, alienation, and loss of legitimacy. The presumed moral and legal criteria become suspect in some persons' eyes, who say, in effect: deviation is determined by those who have the power to make their definitions stick. We will examine some of the implications of this question in Chapter 22. For valuable commentaries, see Irving L. Horowitz and Martin Liebowitz, "Social Deviance and Political Marginality: Toward a Redefinition of the Relation Between Sociology and Politics," *SP*, Winter, 1968, pp. 280-296; Marvin E. Olsen, "Perceived Legitimacy of Social Protest Actions," *SP*, Winter, 1968, pp. 297–310; Ralph H. Turner, "The Public Perception of Protest," *ASR*, Dec., 1969, pp. 815–831.

[65] See *Protest and Prejudice*, Harper Torchbooks, rev. ed., 1969.

and George Jackson.[66] Jackson describes, for example his loathing for the "Amerikan" system, and remarks that he ". . . was born with terminal cancer." We can set these remarks alongside the fact that at 18 he was sentenced to ten years in Soledad Prison for allegedly stealing $70.

It is extremely difficult to assess how extensively this estrangement and bitterness have been translated into deviant acts. There have been, of course, a highly visible series of destructive riots, with substantial illegality by both blacks and whites, including police officers.[67] A small number of militants have engaged in more focused, violent attack on the existing system of order, including the police. (The attacks have been reciprocal, of course. In a later chapter we will examine the interactions between police and segments of America's black population. We will not find the causes of this deeply unfortunate conflict in the "evil natures" of either police or blacks, but in structural conditions of American society, in our traditions of violence, and in demographic changes in our cities.)[68]

Minorities that are discriminated against are also likely to have higher than average rates of more "traditional" delinquencies and crimes. There are subtle interactions between the absence of legitimate opportunities and the presence of illegitimate ones.[69] When both factors are operative, in a society that promises "liberty and justice for

all," but rations them severely for the black population, deviant responses are not uncommon.

In his well-known essay, "Social Structure and Anomie,"[70] Robert Merton discusses the consequences for behavior of a society that places strong emphasis on the desirability of specific goals without placing a corresponding emphasis upon institutionalized procedures. One type of adjustment that people make to such a situation is to strive for goals they have been taught to desire with little regard for the legitimacy of the means used. Recent analyses of "white-collar crime" show this adjustment to be not uncommon among members of the dominant group; but the pressures toward deviation are probably greater on those who have the least opportunity for success by legitimate means.

"Least opportunity" should probably be read as "least relative opportunity," because perceptions and reference groups play an important part. Lefton found, for example, that ". . . Negro autoworkers who were economically advantaged registered significantly higher anomia scores than those who were considerably less well off in terms of seniority and employment history."[71] Anomia, which we shall regard here as one possible individual manifestation of the experience of anomie, thus expresses, Lefton notes, frustration as well as despair. It is an indication that modest gains may *increase* the gap between expectations and reality.

It would be a mistake, of course, to assume from this discussion that a deviant pattern of motivation and regard for law are the inevitable results of minority-group status in a society or, conversely, that membership in the dominant group is a promise of high motivation and complete honesty.

"Daddy wasn't a numbers runner, Mama wasn't a loose woman, my two brothers were neither pickpockets nor pimps, and I have never seen heroin in my life.

"When I read reviews of current fiction by and about black Americans, I wonder if I

[66] Eldridge Cleaver, *Soul on Ice*, Dell, 1968; George Jackson, *Soledad Brother*, Coward-McCann, 1970.

[67] See the *Report of the National Advisory Commission on Civil Disorders* (the Kerner Report), Government Printing Office, 1968; Vernon Allen (ed.), "Ghetto Riots," *Journal of Social Issues* (whole issue), Winter, 1970.

[68] See William Westley, *Violence and the Police: A Sociological Study of Law, Custom and Morality*, MIT, 1971; David Bayley and Harold Mendelsohn, *Minorities and the Police: Confrontation in America*, Free Press, 1969; James Q. Wilson, *Varieties of Police Behavior*, Harvard, 1968.

[69] See, for example, Erdman Palmore and Philip Hammond, "Interacting Factors in Juvenile Delinquency," *ASR*, Dec., 1964, pp. 848–853; James Short, Ramon Rivera, and Ray Tennyson, "Perceived Opportunities, Gang Membership, and Deliquency," *ASR*, Feb., 1965, pp. 56–67; John P. Hewitt, *Social Stratification and Deviant Behavior*, Random House, 1970.

[70] Robert K. Merton, *Social Theory and Social Structure*, Free Press, rev. ed., 1957, pp. 131–160.

[71] Mark Lefton, "Race, Expectations, and Anomia," *SF*, Mar. 1968, p. 347.

should turn in my membership card, or better still I wonder how I'll ever be able to become a member of the black community."[72]

Selective attention to conflict and deviation, not unaffected by stereotypes, may cause us to overlook such facts as these: Among New York state families on relief rolls, in the "aid to dependent children category," 59 percent of the white families had been involved in desertions, separations, or divorces, compared with 44.4 percent of Negroes and 52.3 percent of Puerto Ricans. The illegitimacy rate among black women, although much higher than the rate among white women, has been declining in recent years (from 101 per 1000 in 1961 to 87 in 1968), while the white rate has been increasing (from 10 to 13, for the same period). In a major northern city, the incidence of Negro crime has gone up sharply, between 1942 and 1965, but the *rate* of Negro crime has gone down.[73]

It is a matter for careful study that most minority-group members, despite the obstacles, continued to strive for improved status and, notwithstanding the unequal protection of the law and resentment against discriminations, are reliable and honest in their relationships with others. The differences in motivation and morality should not be exaggerated, but insofar as they do exist, they can be accounted for by the differential sharing in the rewards and encouragement of society.

THE MARGINAL MAN AND CULTURAL PARTICIPATION

There is an extensive literature dealing with the concept of "the marginal man" that offers a number of valuable hypotheses for the study of the personality development of minority-group members. Most members of minority groups are marginal. They share

the dominant culture to a significant degree, they absorb its aspirations, yet they are blocked from full participation. The consequences of marginality are not limited to minority-group members, of course, for in a rapidly changing society the lack of a stable, continuous, unchallenged set of life definitions makes virtually everyone, to a greater or lesser degree, marginal and likely to exhibit the tendencies characteristic of that condition.[74] But inability to participate fully in the life of society according to one's individual interests and talents complicates this experience for those in low status. Most discussions of the marginal man are somewhat impressionistic, so generalizations must be highly tentative. The consequences vary, moreover, with the height of the barriers to full participation, with the presence or absence of a minority culture to which the marginal man feels attached, and with the degree to which an individual is self-conscious of his status between two groups— part of both, yet belonging to neither.

Discussions of marginality do not always distinguish between measures that are used to define the condition and measures of presumed consequences of it. Our interest is primarily in the latter; but causal connections are not readily ascertained.

We need to note that the experience of marginality may be avoided by opting for

[72] Mary E. Mebane (Liza) in *The New York Times*, Feb. 18, 1971, p. 35.

[73] See *The New York Times*, Mar. 14, 1971, p. 67; *The New York Times*, Apr. 20, 1971, p. 1; Edward Green, "Race, Social Status, and Criminal Arrest," *ASR*, June, 1970, pp. 476–490.

[74] Many of the phenomena characteristic of marginality appear, for example, in a study of lower-class youth in a university made up primarily of high-status youth. See Robert A. Ellis and W. Clayton Lane, "Social Mobility and Social Isolation: A Test of Sorokin's Dissociative Hypothesis," *ASR*, Apr., 1967, pp. 237–253.

There is great need for comparative study that might help us to isolate the critical variables. We are beginning to get the raw materials for such study. See, for example, B. G. Burton-Bradley, *Mixed Race Society in Port Moresby*, New Guinea Research Bulletin, 23, Canberra: The Australian National University, 1968; and Noel P. Gist, "Cultural Versus Social Marginality: The Anglo-Indian Case," *Phylon*, Winter, 1967, pp. 361–375. For other valuable theoretical or empirical work on marginality, see Robert E. Park, "Human Migration and the Marginal Man," *AJS*, May, 1928, pp. 881–893 (perhaps the starting point for this line of inquiry); Alan C. Kerckhoff and Thomas C. McCormick, "Marginal Status and Marginal Personality," *SF*, Oct., 1955, pp. 48–55; Aaron Antonovsky, "Towards a Refinement of the 'Marginal Man' Concept," *SF*, Oct., 1956, pp. 57–62.

one or another identity. This may be achieved, however, only at a cost, if it involves repression of an important part of self or choices that tend to be irreversible. Wiley illustrates this latter situation by use of the concept of "mobility trap." He uses the metaphor of climbing a tree, rather than a social ladder. One can go up, as well as out on a limb, but he reaches a dead-end. To go higher he must climb down the limb to the trunk. "The essence of the mobility trap is this: the means for moving up within a stratum are contrary to those for moving to the next higher stratum."[75] Thus a boy in the slums may advance in a gang by "accumulating tattoos, knife skills and a police record;" but by the very process he will block advance in the larger society. When mobile ethnics climb the ethnic ladder, they may deprive their group of leadership for a more concerted attack on the marginality and discrimination experienced by their followers.

Keeping these qualifications in mind, we can note some of the personality tendencies that seem to be associated with marginal status. There is an ambivalence, a strain of roles, that heightens self-consciousness and attention to oneself. This may take the form of self-hatred (see the discussion of self-attitudes below) and an inferiority complex, or it may express itself in egocentrism, withdrawal, and/or "aggressiveness."[76]

Some writers have emphasized the influence of a marginal role in encouraging a rational instead of a traditional view of life. Robert Park wrote in the introduction to Stonequist's study, "The fate which condemns him to live, at the same time, in two worlds is the same which compels him to assume, in relation to the worlds in which he lives, the role of a cosmopolitan and a stranger. Inevitably he becomes, relatively to his cultural milieu, the individual with the wider horizon, the keener intelligence, the more detached and rational viewpoint."[77] If thinking comes from perplexity and doubt, from problems posed but not solved by established traditional answers, then indeed the marginal man may take a more rational view of life.

Other authors emphasize the personal instability that they believe is likely to characterize persons who lack a strong feeling of identification with one group. It is well established that personality integration is, to an important degree, a function of group experiences. Personal stability is greatly aided by a sense of security in group identifications, by a feeling of belonging. The minority-group member who feels torn between his association with the group in which he is categorically placed by prejudice and his feelings of identification with the dominant society, may well lack some of the security that comes from stable and acceptable group relationships. This generalization must be used with care, however, for, as Wirth and Goldhamer point out, one is very likely to "read into" the behavior of the minority-group member (they were referring specifically to the mulatto) the tendencies that supposedly characterize the marginal man.[78]

The Effects of Status Inconsistency. Marginality is not limited to the experience of racial or cultural minorities. In recent years the kind of marginality associated with inconsistent status placement has been carefully studied. A person may have high educational and occupational achievements, but relatively low income, or high income and low education, or low ethnic group status and high occupational position, or high ethnic status and low income and occupation. As we noted in Chapter 4, such status inconsistencies have been found to influence many attitudes and values. Liberal political views, for example, are often associated with status inconsistency, particularly of the variety that combines high income, education, or occupation with low

[75] Norbert Wiley, "The Ethnic Mobility Trap and Stratification Theory," *SP*, Fall, 1967, p. 149.

[76] See Everett V. Stonequist, *The Marginal Man. A Study in Personality and Culture Conflict*, Scribner, 1937.

[77] *Ibid.*, pp. xvii–xviii.

[78] Louis Wirth and Herbert Goldhamer, "The Hybrid and the Problem of Miscegenation," in Otto Klineberg (ed.), *Characteristics of the American Negro*, Harper & Row, 1944, Part V.

ethnic status.[79] Having won some measure of success on the basis of socially designated criteria, a person occupying inconsistent statuses may feel frustrated and cheated at being denied full acceptance. Their liberal attitudes indicate a desire to modify a system that puts them in an unpleasant ambivalent situation. On the other hand, there is some evidence that persons whose ascribed status is higher than their achieved status are inclined toward conservative, or in some instances "right-wing extremist," views.

Thus status inconsistency can be associated with the protest movements of minority-group members, and also with the prejudices and reactionary views of dominant-group members whose incomes or occupational attainments are modest.

These statements concerning possible outcomes of status inconsistency must be treated with caution, because the evidences are somewhat mixed. Due to the use of different measuring instruments, different status variables, and different populations, the various studies have led to conclusions that are only partly congruent.[80] Gary Marx found, for ex-

ample, that among Negroes with at least some college education, those in high-status occupations were more militant than those in low-status occupations, although he defines the latter as having more discrepant statuses.[81] His data could be interpreted to mean, however, that there is a perceptual element in status inconsistency. When ethnicity is taken into account, well educated black workers, whether in high- or low-status occupations, experience discrepancy. Were extent of awareness of the discrepancy also measured, as Marx, notes, or the effect of available reference groups studied, those in higher-status jobs might be found to be experiencing more inconsistency.

Seen this way, the recent experience of America's mobile and urban black population has led to greater status inconsistency. Although most of them were uniformly low in income, power, education, and other status variables at the beginning of the century, a significant number have climbed one or more of these ladders, thus increasing their inconsistency of status. The civil rights movement and militancy can be read as indicatory of *improvement* in *some* status measures. Whenever this happens to many people in close communication, we have the ingredients for a sharp protest movement or a revolutionary situation.

When one adds more subjective variables, the status inconsistency of many American Negroes is even more readily apparent. Small improvements on the objective scales may lead to soaring hopes and to dreams of dramatic change. A uniformly low-status situation smothers many dreams, as well as repressing motivation; but visible, if modest, improvement releases the imagination. The result may be a split between objective and subjective measures of status— a split as significant as inconsistency among the various objective measures.[82]

Such difficulties of interpretation must

[79] See Gerhard Lenski, "Status Crystallization," *ASR*, Aug., 1954, pp. 405–413; and Everett Hughes, "Dilemmas and Contradictions of Status," *AJS*, 1944, March, pp. 353–357. See also Elton Jackson, "Status Consistency and Symptoms of Stress," *ASR*, Aug., 1962, pp. 469–480.

[80] H. F. Dickie-Clark explicitly connects the concepts of marginality and status inconsistency. See "The Marginal Situation: A Contribution to Marginality Theory," *SF*, Mar., 1966, pp. 363–370. For representative studies of status inconsistency, see also David Segal and Mady Segal, "Status Inconsistency and Self-Evaluation," *Sociometry*, Sept., 1970, pp. 347–357; R. E. Mitchell, "Methodological Notes on a Theory of Status Crystallization," *POQ*, Summer, 1964, pp. 315–330; Thomas S. Smith, "Structural Crystallization, Status Inconsistency and Political Partisanship," *ASR*, Dec., 1969, pp. 907–921; Gary B. Rush, "Status Consistency and Right-Wing Extremism," *ASR*, Feb., 1967, pp. 86–92; Donald Treiman, "Status Discrepancy and Prejudice," *AJS*, May, 1966, pp. 651–666; James Geschwender, "Status Discrepancy and Prejudice Reconsidered," *AJS*, Mar., 1970, pp. 863–865; Martin D. Hyman, "Determining the Effects of Status Inconsistency," *POQ*, Spring, 1966, pp. 120–129; Leonard Broom and F. Lancaster Jones, "Status Consistency and Political Preference: the Australian Case," *ASR*, Dec., 1970, pp. 989–1001; Christopher Bagley, "Race Relations and Theories of Status Consistency," *Race*, Jan., 1970, pp. 267–288.

[81] Gary Marx, *op. cit.*, esp. pp. 57–60. Fifty-seven percent of those in high-status occupations were militant, compared with 26 percent of those in low-status occupations.

[82] See Milton Yinger, *A Minority Group in American Society*, McGraw-Hill, 1965, pp. 10–14.

give us pause in adding the concept of status inconsistency to our examination of the effects of marginality. In our judgment, nevertheless, the concept deserves the careful study of those investigating majority-minority relations.

Illustrations of Marginality. The personality consequences of the marginal role vary greatly from group to group, and the interested student will need to explore carefully the differential effects on the American Indian (this in itself being a highly differentiated group, varying with the type of contact with the dominant white society and the nature of the aboriginal culture), the first-generation immigrant, the second-generation immigrant, etc. Feelings that one's status as a minority-group member is permanent and unchangeable, regardless of one's individual beliefs or behavior, produce different influences than does knowledge or belief that one can in time become a member of the majority group. For example, the Issei, faced before 1952 with the legal impossibility of becoming citizens, were probably more protective of their original culture and less likely to be enthusiastic American nationals than were those immigrants who faced lower barriers to assimilation.

We can develop only a few illustrations of the ways in which marginal status affects personality development, but these may help us to see the principles involved. It is, of course, a mistake to attribute all the consequences of marginal position to prejudice. Individuals who stand between two cultural worlds, influenced by two sets of values, often exhibit strong personality effects even when no prejudice is involved. Frequently, however, the marginal man is not only bicultural but the recipient of prejudice as well. These two factors interlock and increase the impact of his position.

Studies of American Indians furnish a great deal of information on the personality consequences of culture contact. As white men came into contact with the Indians, many treated them with harshness and prejudice, looking upon the indigenous cultures as inferior and demanding either rapid assimilation or segregation. The Indian leaders, often subjected to the authority of the white stranger, lost the respect and confidence of their people. They felt themselves to be in a cultural vacuum, without incentives or objectives. The indigenous religions were generally condemned and efforts were made to force their replacement by Christianity; but faith in the original beliefs was lost long before Christianity was adopted, with resulting personal and social disorganization.[83] This loss of an integrated value system helps to account for the brutality that many settlers claimed was embedded in the very nature of the Indians. The tribes of the Iroquois League, for example, were much less warlike before the white settlers began to seize their lands and undermine their culture. Then the decline of cultural cohesion expressed itself in increased personal aggressiveness and organized violence.

MacGregor has described the disorganizing effects on the American Indians of the reservation policies to which they were subjected in the latter part of the nineteenth century:

Excerpts from the statement of the educational policy for all Indian children at this time are enlightening. The policy was "to civilize," "to humanize," and "to put the children in boarding school where they will learn English" and "not relapse into their former moral and mental stupor." In connection with this statement, the federal superintendent of Indian Schools in 1885 makes one remark which is highly significant in light of this study. "The Indian is the strangest compound of individualism and socialism run to seed. It is this being that we endeavor to make a member of a new social order. . . . To do this we must recreate him, MAKE A NEW PERSONALITY."

Children were virtually kidnaped to force them into government schools, their hair was cut, and their Indian clothes thrown away. They were forbidden to speak in their own language. Life in the school was under military discipline, and rules were enforced by corporal punishment. Those who persisted in clinging to their old ways

---

[83] This was by no means a universal experience. There were also creative religious responses. See Anthony F. C. Wallace, *The Death and Rebirth of the Seneca*, Knopf, 1970.

and those who ran away and were recaptured were thrown into jail. Parents who objected were also jailed. Where possible, children were kept in school year after year to avoid the influence of their families.[84]

This particular expression of the white man's burden continues to have important effects on the personality development of Indian children today. MacGregor found among the Dakota Indian children an anxiety that arises from not knowing "how to behave." "Rebuffed in their contacts with others and unable to find inner satisfactions, they withdraw further into themselves and lack warm and emotional responsiveness and vigor."[85] Stories and fantasies that were given in Thematic Apperception Tests indicated that the Dakota children thought of the world as a dangerous and hostile place. "Characters in the children's stories often have too little to eat and few of the other material things which make life comfortable. Hence they feel deprived and dissatisfied. In their uncomfortable surroundings they often become tired or sick. . . . The characters in the stories, with whom the children identify themselves, are uncertain and suffer many accidents and lose what little security they have."[86] These stories express the confusion and pain of children caught between two cultures.

There are, of course, many different responses possible to the intrusions of a dominant society, and these vary with the nature of the aboriginal culture, the types of contact, and the particular individuals' experience with both worlds.[87] Among American Indians, patterns have varied from complete assimilation to vigorous resistance to "white culture," with many positions in between.

[84] Gordon MacGregor, *Warriors Without Weapons,* Univ. of Chicago Press, 1946, p. 36.

[85] *Ibid.,* p. 204.

[86] *Ibid.,* p. 205.

[87] See Ralph Linton (ed.), *Acculturation in Seven American Indian Tribes,* Appleton-Century-Crofts, 1940. For two excellent accounts of variation in the extent of acculturation among Indians and differences in personality types, see Evon. Z. Vogt, "The Acculturation of American Indians," *Annals,* May, 1957, pp. 137–146; and George D. Spindler and Louise S. Spindler, "American Indian Personality Types and Their Sociocultural Roots," *Annals,* May, 1957, pp. 147–157.

These marginal positions are now the most common. A resurgent interest in Indian identity, "red power" movements, and continued pride in their heritage, on the one hand, are balanced, on the other, by economic pressure on an inadequate land base, by extensive contact with the larger society in schools, the armed forces, and jobs, and by the pull of the dominant culture. Indian students perhaps experience the marginal situation most strongly.

Going down the rough dirt road, from the earthy and easygoing tribal life on the rural reservations to the middle-class upmanship of university life in the cities, these young Indians were like refugees in an unknown country. The university was more than strange. It was foreign and alien.

"Very few of us crossed the gap between the two cultures," Blatchford said [Herbert Blatchford, a Navaho who founded the National Indian Youth Council]. "Those who found it difficult to indulge in the new culture developed into a hybrid group, belonging fully to neither culture."[88]

Indian experience of marginality, to be sure, is somewhat different from that of other minorities, particularly those who find return to the "homeland" costly and unlikely. The picture of marginality as a kind of way station between tribal isolation and complete assimilation now seems especially inadequate to describe American Indians. Their population is growing, and is now twice as large as it was in 1900. It is being dispersed, but at the same time Indian communities are appearing, both in rural areas and in cities. "American Indians are not so much disappearing into—as they are appearing within—the 'larger society' "[89]

Analysis of the experience of marginality is also useful in understanding the problems often faced by immigrants and the children of immigrants in American society. Thomas and Znaniecki, in their classic study, *The Polish Peasant in Europe and America,* describe the demoralizing effect of the transfer from the stable, closely-knit agricultural village in Poland to the rapidly changing,

[88] Stan Steiner, *The New Indians,* Dell, 1968, p. 30.

[89] Elizabeth C. Rosenthal, in Stuart Levine and Nancy O. Lurie (eds.), *The American Indian Today,* Penguin Books, 1968, p. 82.

complex American industrial city. The immigrants' disorganization is increased by the prejudice shown against them. Some of the immigrants and their children were able to make the adjustment without major difficulties, but many others exhibited several forms of demoralization. Thomas and Znaniecki illustrate at length the increase, among adults, of economic dependency, of divorce and desertion, and of murder. They describe the increase of vagabondage and delinquency in boys and sexual immorality among girls.[90]

Since 1924, the communities of European immigrants in America have been shrinking, although they have by no means disappeared. There has been, for many of them, a gradual reduction of "cultural shock" and disorganization. Their place is being taken, however, by a continuing flow of new migrants, primarily from the rural South (both white and black), from Mexico, and from the West Indies. The same pattern of disorganization and of self-contradictory marginal statuses has developed, frequently intensified by race prejudice and rigid demands for segregation on the part of the dominant group.

Five percent of America's population is of Spanish-speaking descent. For many persons in this group, cultural marginality is enhanced by the problems of bilinguality, by job discrimination, and by prejudice.[91] Difficulties associated with marginality, however, are not simply the result of majority-group rigidity. Some serious dilemmas are involved. How pay special attention to differential language background, for example, without producing substantial segregation; or, how support pluralism and subcultural

variation without reinforcing traditions that separate? Efforts to deal with these dilemmas have often leaned toward enforcement of cultural uniformity, but not without some attention to the minority's culture:

On the one hand, there has been the tendency to remove or suppress certain foreign features, often rather crudely. On the other hand, there has been the tendency to build upon the Mexican culture, often equally crudely. The most obvious form that the former takes is the prohibition of behavioral manifestations of foreignness, including the prohibition of the carrier of the minority culture, the Spanish language. Children's names are changed in teacher-student conversation and sometimes in school records: Jesus, in particular, seems disturbing, and is almost invariably changed to Jesse. Dress codes in high school appear to be more elaborate and more strictly enforced in Mexican high schools than in the same district's mixed Anglo schools. In some cities these are directed against particular symbols of peer-group identification, which are often defined as alien to school culture and authority. . . .

On the other hand, even the most restrictive institutions permit and even encourage some symbols of Mexican culture.[92]

In recent years, the dilemmas associated with the marginality of many Americans of Mexican descent, as of other minorities, have at least become more visible. Earlier programs, whether characterized by pressure toward assimilation or segregation, are being replaced by attention to the facts of biculturality, its problems, and its possibilities. Although awareness of dilemmas does not automatically produce resolutions, it is a necessary first step. Thus we have seen some gains in recognition of Spanish as the first language of many Americans, and study of the consequences of different school policies in teaching children of Spanish-speaking descent. These range from attempts to get more Spanish-speaking teachers, to treatment of English as the second language, to more fully reciprocal situations, in which both pupils and teachers, Spanish- and English-speaking, assist one another in learning the

[90] W. I. Thomas and Florian Znaniecki, *The Polish Peasant in Europe and America*, Knopf, vol. 2, 1927, pp. 1647–1827.

[91] See, for example, Philip D. Ortega, "Schools for Mexican Americans: Between Two Cultures," *Saturday Review*, Apr. 17, 1971, p. 62 ff.; Fred Schmidt, *Spanish Surnamed American Employment in the Southwest*, prepared for the U.S. Equal Employment Opportunity Commission, Government Printing Office, 1970; and Leo Grebler, Joan W. Moore, and Ralph C. Guzman, *The Mexican-American People: The Nation's Second Largest Minority*, Free Press, 1970.

[92] Grebler, Moore, and Guzman, *op. cit.*, p. 157.

language and culture of the other group.[93] An important tangible expression of these interests is the Bilingual Education Act, passed by Congress in 1968. Although it was funded, and at a rather modest level, only after strong pressure from President Johnson, the Act represents an important shift in policy toward the education of children for whom English is a second language.

Despite such developments, the United States, with her prejudices, with her patterns of segregation, with her tendencies to permit assimilation of culturally diverse peoples only on the terms of the dominant group, continues the shock of culture transfer. That shock is large, at best, in a society where even the privileged groups are confused by the lack of an integrating system of values. For the "marginal man" it may be severe; and personal demoralization, loss of incentive, feelings of resentment continue to be among the consequences.

Marginality, however, is scarcely an American invention. Groups of outsiders, strangers, or "pariahs," as Weber called them, have appeared frequently in history, often to perform commercial functions in a rigidly stratified society. In such a situation, the illiterate peasantry is unable—and the traditional aristocracy is unwilling—to take on tasks that are essential when social change and economic opportunity call for bankers, money-lenders, merchants, and traders. Howard Becker has documented the frequency of this pattern and the remarkable similarity of the status assigned to the "middleman trading peoples."[94] Greek, Armenian, Turk, Jew, Chinese, Scotsman, Yankee, and others have stepped into the "status gap" at various times and places. Despite the wide cultural differences and the contrasting setting, these marginal trading peoples have tended to resist assimilation, even after many genera-

tions of contact and, reciprocally, to be the targets of prejudice and discrimination. Those on top in the societies where they work exploit their services but deny them full accreditation; those on bottom see them as exploiting outsiders. Despite this scapegoat position, however, these groups are often characterized by high achievement. Rinder remarks that ". . . location in the status gap is more likely to result in the desirable and creative types of marginality than are marginalities having different etiologies."[95] They are not powerless groups, they are literate and mobile, and they typically deal with their problems not as individuals but as collectivities.

In an interesting qualification of this thesis, Stryker points out that prejudice is not an inevitable result of the occupation of a marginal trading position. Comparing Armenian Christians in Turkey, Jews in Germany, and Parsis in India, he notes their similarities as peoples ". . . concentrated in occupations which were, at the same time, functionally important, financially remunerative, conspicuous, and socially despicable."[96] They all tended to be separatist. Yet strong prejudice developed against the first two but not against the Parsis. The difference, Stryker believes, lies in the pressures toward nationalism in Turkey and Germany, the relative lack of such pressures in India (with primary reference to the nineteenth century). In a context of emerging nationalism, identifiable outsiders are easily made the target of random hostilities and the agent of in-group solidarity. Opposition to the Chinese subcommunities in many nations of the Far East, in this day of powerful national movements, lends support to this thesis. It will be important to watch developments in South America—where the Yankee is already subject to much categorical rejection—and in Africa, as Russians, French, English, Americans, Chinese, and others seek commercial and other opportunities in the "status gap."

[93] See, for example, NEA-Tuscon Survey on the Teaching of Spanish to the Spanish-Speaking, *The Invisible Minority*, Department of Rural Education, National Education Association, 1966, pp. 13–17; "Bilingualism," *The Center Forum* (whole issue), Sept., 1969; "Bilingual Schools Flourishing Here," *The New York Times*, Mar. 17, 1971, p. 39.

[94] Howard Becker, *Man in Reciprocity*, Praeger, 1956, chap. 15.

[95] I. D. Rinder, "Strangers in the Land," *SP*, Winter, 1958–1959, p. 259.

[96] Sheldon Stryker, "Social Structure and Prejudice," *SP*, Spring, 1959, p. 351.

Doll Choices Among Negro Children

	Colored Doll (%)	White Doll (%)	Don't Know or No Answer (%)
Give me the doll that you like to play with.	32	67	1
Give me the doll that is a nice doll.	38	59	3
Give me the doll that looks bad.	59	17	24
Give me the doll that is a nice color.	38	60	2

THE EFFECTS OF PREJUDICE AND DISCRIMINATION ON SELF-ATTITUDES

Prejudice and discrimination affect not only the attitudes and behavior of minority-group members toward the standards set by the dominant society but also their responses to themselves and their groups. We have noted that self-regarding attitudes are as much a product of one's social experience as are attitudes toward other persons and toward social norms. The nature of that experience effectively conditions the basic ego structure, the central core of personality. At an early age in an interracial community children develop an awareness of themselves as different, particularly with regard to skin color. This awareness varies with the social definitions of color differences given by the minority and majority groups (important class, regional, and other variables are involved). It is, however, a very widespread experience, embedded even in language—"that was white of you," or "black as the devil,"; but also "black is beautiful" and the "white flag of surrender." These contrasts should remind us not to take these lingual practices too seriously. It is not only Indians who suffer from red tape or confuse an argument with red herrings.

Our analysis will be built largely around the experience of learning that one is of an "inferior" color, but this should be seen as illustrative of the whole experience of learning that one belongs to a minority group. It is in the context of slights, rebuffs, forbidden opportunities, restraints, and often violence that the minority-group member shapes that fundamental aspect of personality—a sense of oneself and of one's place in the total scheme of things.

In a study of 253 Negro children aged three to seven, some from a segregated southern school and some from a mixed school in the North, they found that a high proportion of the children (over 90 percent) were aware of racial differences. Even at these ages, however, there were important differences. When asked to choose, between a white and a Negro doll, "the doll that looks like you," only 20 percent of the lighter-colored children selected the Negro doll, whereas 73 percent of the medium and 81 percent of the dark children identified with the Negro doll. When asked to give their preferences, a majority of the Negro children preferred the white doll.[97]

There are significant differences in the answers when they are analyzed by age groups. A higher proportion of the three-year-old Negro children selected the Negro doll to play with or as one that was a nice doll (still, however, a minority) than did the four-, five-, and six-year-olds. The four-year-olds rejected the Negro doll most often (about three-quarters selected the white, in answer to the first two questions), the seven-year-olds again approximated the proportion of the three-year-olds (about 60 percent).

[97] See Kenneth B. Clark and Mamie P. Clark, "Racial Identification and Preference in Negro Children," in Eleanor Maccoby, Theodore M. Newcomb, and E. L. Hartley (eds.), *Readings in Social Psychology*, Holt, Rinehart & Winston, 3rd ed., 1958, p. 608. Results of a study by Herbert Greenwald and Don Oppenheim were somewhat different, when they gave nursery school children a choice among three dolls—white, light brown, and dark brown. Negro children still made slightly more choices of the white doll, but less commonly than in the Clarks' study. And white children chose one of the brown dolls about one-quarter of the time. See their "Reported Magnitude of Self-Misidentification among Negro Children—an Artifact?" *JPSP*, Jan., 1968, pp. 49–52.

The third question showed an irregular variation, with the seven-year-olds least often indicating that the Negro doll "looks bad;" but even they selected the Negro doll over twice as frequently as the white doll. In answer to the fourth question, the four- and five-year-olds definitely preferred the "nice color" of the white doll (3–1), but preferences of the six- and seven-year-olds turned toward the Negro doll, with just half of the older age group selecting that as the one with the "nice color."[98]

These data suggest that the valuations of the dominant society are known and shared by three-year-old Negro children, that four- and five-year-olds have an even stronger rejection of their own color, and that the six- and seven-year-olds have begun to acquire a group identification to counter the self-devaluating beliefs they had absorbed. This change may not eliminate the earlier beliefs but may represent a greater verbal skill on the part of the older children in disguising feelings that seem, by that time, to be inappropriate. Thus an ambivalence toward oneself is indicated that will continue to have important personality consequences. This is revealed to a degree in the rationalizations that some of the older children felt obliged to offer: "A northern medium six-year-old justified his rejection of the brown doll by stating that 'he looks bad' 'cause he hasn't got a eyelash.' A seven-year-old medium northern child justified his choice of the white doll as the doll with a 'nice color' because 'his feet, hands, ears, elbows, knees, and hair are clean.' "[99] Differences between northern and southern Negro children were not statistically significant, but there was consistently a somewhat higher preference for the white doll among the northern children.

Numerous studies have replicated the Clarks' research or, more precisely, have explored the phenomenon of race awareness and preferences among a variety of groups. Problems of methodology and interpretation are severe, so that we must speak with caution about the possible influence of age, sex, class, region, race of experimenter, group pressure, and other variables on the observed results.[100] There is substantial support, however, for these generalizations: Race awareness begins at an early age, particularly in societies where the race line is important; in the United States, a large majority of both black and white children express preferences for white dolls, puppets, or play-group members; boys may be more likely to favor white than girls; by age seven or eight, the expressed preference of black children for white begins to decline; these patterns have remained quite constant through the last several decades.

This last generalization poses the theoretical problem sharply. (As Asher and Allen note, many of the studies have paid little attention to theoretical issues.) From one point of view, we might expect that black color preferences would increase as a result of the civil rights movement, economic and political gains, and growing feelings of racial pride. In particular, one would expect to find these trends among middle-class children. A "social comparison theory," however, leads to opposite predictions, as Asher and Allen note.[101] Economic progress and social mobility lead to more comparison with

[98] Clark and Clark, *op. cit.*, pp. 602–611.

[99] *Ibid.*, p. 611.

[100] See, for example, Steven Asher and Vernon Allen, "Racial Preference and Social Comparison Processes," *JSI*, Jan., 1969, pp. 157–166; Mary Ellen Goodman, *Race Awareness in Young Children,* Collier Books, rev. ed., 1964; J. Kenneth Morland, "A Comparison of Race Awareness in Northern and Southern Children," *American Journal of Orthopsychiatry,* Jan., 1966, pp. 22–31; J. Kenneth Morland, "Race Awareness Among American and Hong Kong Chinese Children," *AJS,* Nov., 1969, pp. 360–374; Sidney Peck and Sidney Rosen, "The Influence of the Peer Group on the Attitudes of Girls Toward Color Differences," *Phylon,* Spring, 1965, pp. 50–63; Howard Freeman, J. Michael Ross, David Armor, and Thomas Pettigrew, "Color Gradation and Attitudes Among Middle-Income Negroes," *ASR,* June, 1966, pp. 365–374; H. W. Stevenson and E. C. Stewart, "A Developmental Study of Racial Awareness in Young Children," *CD,* Sept., 1958, pp. 399–409. For an account of the background of color evaluations and evidence that in recent years American Negroes respond to their own appearance much less in terms of "white" standards, see Harold Isaacs, *The New World of Negro Americans,* John Day, 1963, pp. 72–96. For an examination of underlying processes in self-evaluation, see Stanley Coopersmith, *The Antecedents of Self-Esteem,* Freeman, 1967.

[101] See Leon Festinger, "A Theory of Social Comparison Processes," *Human Relations,* May, 1954, pp. 117–140.

whites and to greater feelings of inferiority. From this theory, one would predict that ". . . lower-class Negro children will respond more favorably to their own race than middle-class Negro children."[102] The social comparison theory is lent support by the fact that the northern sample in the Clark study showed greater white preference, by Coleman's finding that "academic self-concept" for Negro children was lower in integrated than in segregated schools,[103] despite the higher achievements of the former, and by the data in the Asher-Allen study. If these are accurate descriptions of effects, important issues of theory and practice are raised. Are tendencies toward black self-segregation, on college campuses for example, partly explained by painful social comparisons, despite the reduction of prejudice and discrimination? How do recency of the change, the extent and depth of integration, the competence of the black and white persons involved, and other factors influence the results? Perhaps the social comparison theory more accurately predicts attitudes and behavior in the early stages of an integration process, while an "individual competence" model predicts more accurately at a later stage. Further evidence is needed before we can describe with confidence the effects of recent changes in race relations on self-evaluation.[104]

The evaluations of one's own color are affected both by what he is taught in his own group and by the attitudes of the dominant group. White people in the United States have generally and consistently shown a preference for the lighter shades of brown, insofar as they have made any distinctions among Negroes. This has also been true among Negroes, as indicated by the Clarks' study, but not without some important countercurrents that create a strong ambivalence

of feeling in many Negroes. Under conditions of discrimination, moreover, ambivalence may be a "realistic and adaptive" condition, as Parker and Kleiner argue.[105] In recent years, as self-confidence and group identification have increased among Negroes, there have been some forces to encourage them to take pride in their racial identity and, in a few instances, to assert it as a mark of superiority. Negro parents are less likely, either intentionally or unintentionally, to teach their children that white is superior; and there has been a slow reduction, in many communities, of actions on the part of the dominant Whites that convey this racial preference. The continuing force of a reciprocal prejudice, and often a hatred, against Whites that is the natural product of the experiences of the Negro is also among the factors working against self-devaluation.

"The greatest task in growing up consists of coming to terms with oneself, of learning to know who one is, what one can do, and how one stands in relation to others."[106] It is almost universally agreed among social scientists that this "coming to terms" is made difficult for Negro children by segregation and prejudice. Perhaps too little attention has been paid to the fact that for some Negro children the first five or six years of life may be a period of warm and rewarding family experience, leading to a good start in developing a healthy self-regard. Later, stress situations may be handled with less crushing impact. A sound "ego" can develop a kind of external response system to the outer world of conflict. As Milner points out, the psychologically vulnerable Negro, the person with a heavy load of self-doubt, cannot thus isolate the stresses of the world when they hit him.[107] Insofar as discrimination and segregation invade the personality-forming family situation by the creation of poverty, ill

[102] Asher and Allen, *op. cit.*, p. 158.

[103] James S. Coleman, *et. al.*, *Equality of Opportunity*, Government Printing Office, 1966.

[104] We may find leads in reference group theory. For a valuable empirical study, without reference to race, see James A. Davis, "The Campus as a Frog Pond: An Application of the Theory of Relative Deprivation to Career Decisions of College Men," *AJS*, July, 1966, pp. 17–31.

[105] Seymour Parker and Robert Kleiner, *Mental Illness in the Urban Negro Community*, Free Press, 1966, p. 160.

[106] Group for the Advancement of Psychiatry, *Psychiatric Aspects of School Desegregation*, Report no. 37, 1957, p. 32.

[107] See Esther Milner, "Some Hypotheses Concerning the Influence of Segregation on Negro Personality Development," *Psychiatry*, Aug., 1953, pp. 291–297.

health, frustration of many kinds, they indirectly increase the weak ego defenses that later must deal with a harsh experience. Yet it is wise to recognize the variety of family influences. The families of minority groups have too often been overlooked as "intervening variables" that influence the meaning of prejudice. In his penetrating studies of the psychological meaning of school desegregation, Robert Coles charts the range of support from families.[108] In favorable circumstances they furnish a child with strong defenses. Lee Rainwater sees black families, as, in many instances, highly adaptive to the difficult environment they face. They promote a self-sufficiency and toughness that protect their members from some of the ego-destroying impact of discrimination. These adaptive qualities, however, may stabilize majority-minority interactions, thus making it less likely that the black family will break out of its disprivileged situation.[109] While noting the resources which protect the self-images of minority-group members, we should not forget that the stronger forces are probably on the other side. The Negro, as a member of American society, tends to take on the culture of that society, including its prejudices. He sees that most Negroes *are* "inferior" in occupation, in education, and in general status. "He unconsciously comes to feel that by rejecting Negroes and 'Negro ways' he can escape being a Negro and all the handicaps that involves."[110] Displacement onto oneself and one's group is also involved in the self-attitude of a minority-group member. "When one is abused or insulted and forces oneself to react passively, the hatred that would normally be directed toward the abusing or insulting person is instead turned inward."[111]

Displacement is related to another response that can be understood only against the background of partial belief in one's own inferiority and also great frustration.

This response is envy of fellow minority-group members who improve their status, an unwillingness to assist in, or even to accept, their advance. Even within a family, differences in color can give rise to problems of favoritism, resentment, and invidious comparisons.

The ambivalence of feeling of minority-group members toward themselves sometimes takes the form of extreme expressions of "race pride" or chauvinistic claims. It would be a mistake to interpret these as unambiguous signs of feelings of equality or superiority. As Rose wrote:

Still another phenomenon that is psychologically related to Negro self-hatred, although it appears to be just the opposite, is the blatant, nationalistic claim to the cultural achievements of Negroes with whom there is no cultural contact. For American Negroes to be proud of the achievements of Alexander Dumas, who had some Negro ancestry but whose culture was entirely French, indicates an unconscious assumption on the part of Negroes that race *is* important for achievement (which they usually consciously, and correctly, deny), and a feeling that they are inferior and must hunt far afield for something to be proud of.

This phenomenon is not unimportant. The whole tendency of the Negro History movement —not as history but as propaganda—is to encourage the average Negro to escape the realities—the actual achievements and the actual failures—of the present. Although the movement consciously tends to build race pride, it may also cause Negroes unconsciously to recognize that group pride is built partly on delusion, and therefore may result in a devaluation of themselves for being forced to resort to self-deception.[112]

The Prejudices of Minority-Group Members

Related to minority-group chauvinism are the various prejudices that are often found among those in low status—expressed partly toward other minority groups and partly toward the dominant group. And when minorities become dominant groups, they sometimes turn quickly to discriminations of their own. Thus many African na-

[108] See his *Children of Crisis.*
[109] See Lee Rainwater, "Crucible of Identity: The Negro Lower-Class Family," *Daedalus,* Winter, 1966, pp. 172–216.
[110] Arnold M. Rose, *The Negro's Morale,* Univ. of Minnesota Press, 1949, p. 89.
[111] *Ibid.*

[112] *Ibid.,* pp. 92–93.

tions have experienced sharp inter-tribal conflicts; and "oriental" Jews suffer discrimination in Israel."[113]

Chicanos and Puerto Ricans are often at pains to set themselves apart from blacks. This doubtless reflects, however, not simply their own minority status, but also the influence of the dominant "Anglo" view.[114] Guy Johnson has described the extreme vigor with which the Croatan Indians in North Carolina try to distinguish themselves from the Negroes of the area. The whites tend to class Indians and Negroes together, but the Indians strive for a separate status. The large amount of admixture of Negro blood among the Indians has produced sharp internal cleavages based largely on the amount of Negro ancestry. The ultimate insult to a Croatan is to be mistaken for a "Negro"— a classification somewhat difficult to establish, since many of the Indians clearly have Negro blood. The darker Indians are particularly likely to show this prejudice in an attempt to free themselves from the caste stigma to which their color makes them especially susceptible. "So intense is the feeling on this subject that one can only conclude that there is present in many persons a certain 'sense of guilt' that arises from the observed reality and which calls for constant denial of the reality."[115]

Negro anti-Semitism, not uncommon among urban Negroes, is partly a displaced prejudice, using another minority group as a substitute target for the hostilities felt toward the more powerful white gentiles, and partly a reciprocal prejudice against whites directed at Jews as a group of whites with whom urban Negroes have fairly frequent contact. To some degree it indicates

only that Negroes share an attitude that is quite prevalent in our culture. It is partly an attempt by Negroes to make their own status seem better by expressing prejudice against another minority group. "It is an aspect of his humiliation whittled down to a manageable size and then transferred; it is the best form the Negro has for tabulating vocally his long record of grievances against his native land."[116] Baldwin adds there is an expectation that the Jew should "know better," having suffered so much himself. It should be noted, on the other hand, that many Negroes realize that Jews are probably, on the average, less prejudiced against them than are other Whites; that they are more often willing to trade with them, hire them, rent to them; that they give a great deal of support to organizations dedicated to the reduction of discrimination against all minorities.[117]

A number of studies have shown that some minority-group members rank high in authoritarianism. Keeping in mind the methodological qualifications we have discussed (their mistrust of the world may be realism, not generalized misanthropy; they may be specially prone to response-set if interviewed by majority-group persons; the scales have been standardized on white middle-class groups; and the like) we may find the evidence valuable. MacKinnon and Centers, using an abbreviated F Scale, found that 80 percent of their respondents of Mexican descent and 77 percent of the Negroes were in the upper half on authoritarian scores. This is an undifferentiated score, however, and they note that the result may reflect the preponderance of manual workers in these two groups,[118] only 25 percent of a small number of persons of Oriental descent (16) were in the upper half on authoritarianism. Greenberg found that 49 Negro high school students in Texas had significantly higher F-scale scores than 233 white high school and

[113] See G. H. T. Kimble, "Racialism is an African Sickness, Too," in Milton Barron (ed.), *Minorities in a Changing World*, Knopf, 1967, pp. 69–76; Judith T. Shuval, "Emerging Patterns of Ethnic Strain in Israel," *SF*, May, 1962, pp. 323–330; and Yochanan Peres, "Ethnic Relations in Israel," *AJS*, May, 1971, pp. 1021–1047.

[114] See Grebler, Moore, and Guzman, *op. cit.*, pp. 390–394.

[115] See Guy B. Johnson, "Personality in a White-Indian-Negro Community," *ASP*, Aug., 1939, pp. 516–523. See also Brewton Berry, *Almost White*, Macmillan, 1963.

[116] James Baldwin, *Notes of a Native Son*, Beacon Press, 1955, p. 69.

[117] See *Ibid.*, pp. 129–139. We will discuss Negro anti-Semitism more fully in Chapter 9.

[118] William MacKinnon and Richard Centers, "Authoritarianism and Urban Stratification," *AJS*, May, 1956, p. 615.

860 white college students.[119] And Steckler, in a study of several hundred Negro college students from seven predominantly Negro colleges, recorded F-scale scores that were considerably higher than those reported for most white college samples. These groups tended also to be anti-Negro, indicating identity with the values of the white majority and a feeling that many of their troubles stem from deviant behavior of their own group.[120]

Adelson reports somewhat similar results for 242 Jewish college students. He designed a Jewish authoritarianism score which correlated +.67 with the F scale. Those high on both scales tended to agree with such items as these: "most Jews who meet a great deal of anti-Semitism bring it about by their own obnoxious behavior"; "Jews can combat anti-Semitism by showing Gentiles they can behave like any other people." It is interesting that those students who most fully rejected Jewish identification (with religious or social groups) received the lowest authoritarian scores; and those who most closely identified with such organization received the next lowest scores; the partially identified received the highest scores—perhaps an expression of their effort to handle their own marginality by rejecting fellow group members whose behavior threatened majority-group reprisals.[121]

The reciprocal prejudices of minority-group members toward the dominant group sometimes become as rigid and stereotyped as the attitudes of the majority. This is an important result of prejudice and, in turn, may become a cause of the continuation of prejudice. In a useful study, MacCrone describes the attitudes of a group of educated Bantu in South Africa. They were persons with very different backgrounds, but most of them were teachers, taking training in social work at Johannesburg, and all were quite highly "Europeanized." Their reactions to domination were hostility, hatred, suspicion, and "counter-domination," expressed particularly against the "Boers," the Afrikaans-speaking "Dutch." Despite their differences in background and despite the complexity of the race situation, these educated Bantu had converged on this attitude of hatred for the "Boer." Such a polarization has put other groups—for example, the British—in a more favorable light than the facts might indicate. The lesser of two evils has become a positive good. South Africans of English descent have, in fact, shown less hostility in the past and are more favorably inclined toward the African today; but to many of the Bantu the difference is almost an innate one between the English and the Dutch.

MacCrone believes that the subjects of his study show a "Boer-phobia," not a simple case of resentment against discrimination. The Boer is used as a scapegoat, unrealistically, for displacement, projection, and compensation in a kind of mass neurosis that is unseen because it is so widespread in the group. There is, of course, a great deal of real provocation in the highly discriminatory treatment that the Bantu experience. But a scapegoat is a standing temptation to use autistic thinking and to overlook one's own faults. Out of this situation has come a caricature of the Boer—a quarrelsome, stubborn, brutal person—that is as one-sided and inaccurate as other caricatures. The students resisted MacCrone's suggestion that their picture of the Boer was a caricature, for it was so convenient a vehicle for hostility and an important rallying ground for their unity against a common enemy—two very common functions of scapegoats. Altogether, the frustrations of their drives for equal status have had many devastating effects on the personalities of these Bantu, manifest in pathological states of aggressiveness and sensitivity.[122]

[119] Herbert Greenberg, "The Development of an Integration Attitude Scale," *JSP*, June, 1961, pp. 103–109.

[120] G. A. Steckler, "Authoritarian Ideology in Negro College Students," *JASP*, May, 1957, pp. 396–399.

[121] See Joseph Adelson, "A Study of Minority Group Authoritarianism," in Marshall Sklare, (ed.), *The Jews, Social Patterns of an American Group*, Free Press, 1958, pp. 475–492.

[122] See I. D. MacCrone, "Reactions to Dominations in a Colour-Caste Society: A Preliminary Study of the Race Attitudes of a Dominated Group," *JSP*, Aug., 1947, pp. 69–98.

The various prejudices of the minority-group member—toward himself, toward other minorities, and toward the dominant group—are among the most important results of the discriminatory pattern.

Minority-Group Solidarity

The feelings of inferiority, the self-hatred, and the reciprocal prejudices that may be the product of membership in a group which is the object of prejudice and discrimination are not, however, the only attitudes produced by such experiences. There is a lack of group solidarity, but there is also a group cohesiveness and even an interest in the problems of other minority groups. There are strong tendencies toward self-devaluation but also genuine feelings of pride and self-confidence that come from achievements made in the face of severe handicaps. One aspect of this response is the development of protest groups and social movements that tend to bind the group together, whether for attacks against their status or for escape. A sense of group identification is, in fact, to a greater or lesser degree, an almost universal result of discrimination. Locke and Stern used this concept of group consciousness, forced by the treatment received as members of the group, as the core of their definition of minority group: "A minority group, irrespective of size or constituency, is thus best characterized as a social group whose solidarity is primarily determined by external pressure, which forces it to live in terms of opposition and ostracism."[123]

In other words, Negroes would not think of themselves as Negroes first, but as lower-, middle-, or upper-class persons, as Methodists, Baptists, or Catholics, as farmers, factory workers, or teachers, as Southerners or Northerners, and so on, were they not identified by most members of the dominant community *primarily* as Negroes. There is nothing intrinsically important about sharing the trait of race in common that binds people together into a group. The same principle applies, at varying levels of importance, to other minority groups. Jews, for example, are a heterogeneous people with a vast range in income, occupation, education, interests of various kinds, and, of course, even religion. In a friendly environment they begin to stop thinking of themselves as Jews *first*. (They do not, of course, necessarily stop thinking of themselves as Jews at all, although that is the result with some. Episcopalians think of themselves as Episcopalians, but usually they think of themselves first as Americans, or lawyers, or New Yorkers, or identify themselves primarily by some group association other than religious.)[124]

Group solidarity or morale, as Arnold Rose called it, is thus one of the consequences of prejudice. A feeling of common fate and shared problems exists alongside intragroup conflict and jealousy. Which of the two will predominate in a given situation depends upon the extent and the nature of the prejudice, cultural aspects of the minority group (for example, its family and community patterns), the resources of the group, and the nature of its leadership. In general, a relatively weak group, with disorganized institutions and wide internal differences, will tend toward intragroup conflict and a lack of solidarity in its dealings with the dominant group. A minority with greater resources in income, education, and skill, however, and with well-organized family and community life, is likely to have a strong feeling of group cohesion and identification, at least in the situations that involve contact with the dominant group.[125]

[123] Alain Locke and B. J. Stern (eds.), *When Peoples Meet*, Hinds, Hayden and Eldredge, 1946, p. 465.

[124] For useful discussions of factors involved in group solidarity, see J. T. Borhek, "Ethnic-Group Cohesion," *AJS*, July, 1970, pp. 33–46; Jan E. Dizard, "Black Identity, Social Class, and Black Power," *Psychiatry*, May, 1970, pp. 195–207; and Donald E. Noel, "Group Identification among Negroes: An Empirical Analysis," *JSI*, Apr., 1964, pp. 71–84.

[125] It is ironic that for minority groups with strong cohesiveness, the reduction of prejudice and discrimination may weaken group solidarity. For those most anxious to hold the group together, justice and prosperity are mixed blessings; and they are motivated to record, to publicize, and perhaps to exaggerate incidents and vestiges of discrimination and prejudice.

Americans of Japanese ancestry and Jews are groups that have rather high morale or solidarity. Chicanos and black Americans, on the other hand, illustrate groups that have, until the recent past, lacked a sense of group cohesion. In the last several years, however, each has been moving toward greater and greater solidarity. This is shown both in the organized protests against discrimination and in the growth of group pride.[126]

There is, of course, internal differentiation within a minority group in connection with the degree of group solidarity. In a study of 183 Negro public-school and college students, Grossack suggests a typology of responses among Negroes that may have more general applicability. He distinguishes among the respondents who showed "Nondefensive group pride," "ethnocentric group pride," "ambivalence," "defensive reaction," and "hostility to own group."[127] This list is paralleled in many ways by Antonovsky's comparison of six types of Jewish orientation, which is also based to a large degree on the extent of identification with one's group. He lists these types: "Active Jewish," "Passive Jewish," "Ambivalent," "Dual," "Passive General," "Active General."[128] The task of further research is to describe and measure the variables—in personality tendencies, in group structures, and in the total situation—that determine the extent of group solidarity and group withdrawal.[129]

In recent years, as the educational and economic status of Negroes has improved and their political power grown, cooperative activity has become much more common and

pride in one's group and in one's self has been strengthened. Some of this is perhaps overcompensatory, as we have noted, but some of it is based on genuine accomplishments and a sense of identity with the group. In fact, a growing number of American Blacks are beginning to ask: What is so great about this society that the white man has built? Why should we struggle for middle-class status in a society of shady morality (expense-account living, income-tax evasion, and many forms of official violence), of mediocre artistic standards (witness the normal level of movies, television shows, and literary products), of doubtful ranking of values (bigger cars seem so much more important than better schools or cleaner air, swimming pools and color television for the well-to-do than a basic minimum standard of living for the millions of poor)? Why break our backs, some few are asking, to integrate with that? We can do better.

Even among the most self-confident who take this position there is doubtless some ambivalence. But in the current protest movements of the black population in America, there are also genuine expressions of pride and self-confidence, and a reciprocal dismay at some of our society's foibles. Perhaps we have here a "culture-building process" emerging from a group with a powerful shared experience and now with enough training and energy to use that experience in a creative way. We shall develop some implications of this development in another connection at the end of the next chapter.

The sense of cohesion that comes from sharing the burdens of minority-group status may extend to other minority groups. (This does not, of course, prevent the opposite tendency, projection of one's hostility onto other low-status groups. The two reactions can exist side by side, even in the same individual in different situations.) Jews are among the most vigorous and numerous workers for equality of status for all minorities in the United States—a fact that is sometimes noticed, with complaint, by those who oppose equality of status.

---

[126] See, for example, Stan Steiner, *La Raza: The Mexican-Americans*, Harper & Row, 1969; Stokely Carmichael and Charles Hamilton, *Black Power*, Random House, 1967; and John H. Bracey, Jr., August Meier, and Elliott Rudwick (eds.), *Black Nationalism in America*, Bobbs-Merrill, 1970. This last title documents the fact that group pride and protests among Blacks are by no means new phenomena, but that they have become stronger.

[127] Martin M. Grossack, "Group Belongingness Among Negroes," *JSP*, Feb., 1956, pp. 167–180.

[128] Aaron Antonovsky, "Toward a Refinement of the 'Marginal Man' Concept," *SF*, Oct., 1956, pp. 57–62.

[129] J. Milton Yinger, *Sociology Looks At Religion*, Macmillan, 1963, chap. 4.

Less advantaged minorities are more likely to identify with other oppressed groups abroad, emphasizing their solidarity with them as one form of criticism of the "colonial" power at home. Thus, many American Blacks, since World War II, have expressed their sympathy with independence movements in India, Africa, and Southeast Asia. As they gain strength and resources, we can expect sentiments and actions of mutual support among black, Puerto Rican, chicano, Indian, and other groups at home as well.

OTHER PERSONALITY DIFFERENCES THAT ARE AFFECTED BY MINORITY STATUS

There is scarcely an aspect of personality that has not been held to vary with race or to be differentially associated with various groups. General intelligence; specialized capacities (e.g., music, athletic prowess); tendencies toward aggressiveness, criminal behavior, mental illness; interest and potency in sexual behavior; temperament—all these and other aspects of personality are thought by some to differ from group to group. We saw in Chapter 2 that biological explanations of differences in group averages, with reference to such attributes as those mentioned here, are unlikely. Not that there are no differences, but they are best explained by differences in experience. The experiences we are particularly concerned with here are those that grow out of minority-group status, that reflect the impact of prejudice and discrimination on personality development. In this field there is a lack of carefully controlled studies of an experimental nature. Dozens of paper-and-pencil and performance tests of various kinds have compared the tendencies or behavior of Negroes, or other racial groups, with those of whites. Few of them, however, have even approximately solved the complicated methodological problems involved in such studies, and we must be very careful, therefore, in evaluating the results. Many of the studies assume that they are trying to measure a racial difference *per se*. To do

this, the influence of all other factors would have to be eliminated by matching the groups compared—an almost impossible task in a society where the members of minority races are the objects of prejudice and discrimination. To discover, for example, whether the single fact of being a Negro or a White (independent of any experience or training) is related to the degree of suggestibility, the "power of inhibition," or intelligence, one would have to compare Negroes and Whites who were entirely alike in class status, education, reaction to test situation, motivation, cultural values and goals, and many other factors. Where can one find Negro and white groups whose general experiences have been so similar in all regards that any observed differences in personality can be attributed to the racial difference?

The weaknesses of such studies, however, should not lead one to assume that there are no personality differences. Other studies of differences among racial groups start from the premise that racial difference, unaffected by experience, is unimportant (or at least unmeasurable at the present time), and seek rather to measure the differences that are the result of differing experience. This is safer scientific ground. The question of perfect matching of the groups is far less important in these studies, for the task is to measure the personality consequences precisely when important factors *do* vary. The chief methodological problem in such studies is to know how widely the results may be generalized. How typical is the sample studied? Negro college students are an accessible group for study—but how much may one know of other Negro groups from study of this one? Case studies, interviews, and general observations—many of which we have drawn on in this chapter—are far more common research techniques in this area than are more objective "experimental" devices. Whatever the technique used, we must continually ask: How widely does this result apply?

Minority Status and Mental Illness. Illustrative of research of this type is the attempt to discover whether there are differences in types and amounts of mental illness and whether prejudice and discrimination are among the factors that affect the development of personality disorder. It is difficult to give an adequate appraisal of this question because the data on the incidence of mental illness are seldom comparable. How mental illness is defined and the amount of hospitalization vary greatly from time to time and in different places. In comparing the rates for minority and majority groups there is the additional hazard of assuming that differences are caused by different biological tendencies, without regard to the many differences in experience and pattern of life that make that assumption impossible.

There are further problems of a technical sort that we shall mention here, to indicate the complexity of the situation, but shall not discuss: One must distinguish the prevalence rate (the ratio of any given group that is ill at a particular time) from the incidence rate (the ratio who fall ill in a given time period). Any group that suffers longer neglect, poorer care, or lower community support will have a higher prevalence rate, even if its incidence rate is equal. Diagnostic practices can influence the rates. Physicians may be more likely, for example, to diagnose minority-group or lower-class members as schizophrenic because of the mixture of their symptoms with behavior normal to their situation—greater distrust, suspicion, anger. Groups may vary in the number of alternative ways available to express their anxieties. The wealthy person may be a tolerated eccentric—a luxury that minority-group members cannot afford. Communities may differ, as a result of their subcultures or their resources, in the ways they deal with the illness "role." Mental illness is in part a group fact, with some individuals selected, so to speak, to carry and express the anxieties for a group of interacting persons.

Keeping these difficulties in mind, we may note that contemporary explanations of the causes of mental illness would lead us to expect a higher incidence, at least for many varieties of illness, among an oppressed group. For example, according to the data on Negroes in New York State given by Malzberg (these cannot be generalized to include Negroes in other situations; data with regard to mental illness among Negroes in the South, for instance, are very inadequate), when standardized for age differences, first admissions to all hospitals in New York State, 1929–1931, showed a ratio of 2.3 for Negroes to 1 for whites. When the comparison is made between Negroes and several groups of foreign-born whites, the Negroes still have the higher rates, in a ratio of 1.9 to 1.[130]

These ratios vary with particular diseases. Without citing the data for the various types, we may note that differences in experience account for the variations in rates. For example, Negroes in New York State, 1929–1931, had a rate for general paresis (caused by syphilis) 4.1 times the white rate. The differences in family pattern and sex mores and the great difference in availability of medical facilities explain the difference. Malzberg summarizes his findings by noting that there are no mental disorders that are not shared by Whites and Negroes, that family clustering of illness is found in both groups—a fact as readily explained by environmental as by biological causes, and that the comparative rates of total illness seem best explained by the overwhelmingly more difficult experience of Negroes.[131]

Even this careful study, however, must be interpreted with caution. Not only do the life conditions of Negroes vary significantly from those of whites, but their attitudes toward treatment, the facilities available to them, and the kinds of treatment they receive also vary. Lower-class persons generally are more likely to be ignorant, or suspicious, of psychiatry; their illnesses are likely to be more deeply entrenched before they receive treatment, hence the rate of cure is lower and the length of treatment

[130] See Benjamin Malzberg, "Mental Disease Among American Negroes: A Statistical Analysis," in Klineberg (ed.), *op. cit.*, pp. 382–383.
[131] *Ibid.*, p. 394.

is longer.[132] If they are thrown in jail, as Negro alcoholics are in some areas, their illness may become much more severe, less subject to out-patient treatment, and therefore more likely to appear on hospital records. In his report of the Baltimore Commission on Chronic Illness Study, Pasamanick concludes that the psychosis rate is slightly *lower* for Negroes than for whites, even when age is controlled (an important control, since the white population has a larger proportion reaching the age when senile dementia becomes important). The rate of acute brain syndromes (primarily alcoholism) is much higher for Negroes. Psychoneuroses are about twice as frequent among whites.[133]

These statements summarizing the findings of an intensive study in Baltimore do not correspond with the summary of a wide range of research made by Dreger and Miller. Noting the great difficulties in evaluating the evidence, they conclude:

From these studies we are left wondering whether psychoneurosis actually is more extensive among Negroes [which, contrary to the Baltimore findings, many studies showed] or if standards of judging psychoneurosis differ for whites and Negroes. . . . The picture is clearer when serious mental illness is concerned. . . . Even when allowances are made for the fact that whites are more likely to be able to afford private hospitalization, it seems apparent that the relative incidence of psychoses among Negroes is significantly higher.[134]

From the current evidence we cannot speak with confidence concerning the relationship of race to mental illness. We cannot state categorically that there are no purely racial differences in the amount and types of mental illness; but it seems much more likely that differences in rates are the result of differences in experience. We cannot even state beyond doubt what the comparative incidence rates are, whether of neuroses (which are often thought to be found more often in the middle and upper classes and therefore, by correlation, among the white population) or of psychoses which generally bear more heavily on the lower classes). Any measure of racial difference in rate must control for class before one can isolate the possible psychic burdens imposed by prejudice and discrimination. One must, indeed, study psychosis rates in the context of possible functionally alternative modes of response to extreme stress—rates of suicide, of outward aggression (thinking of mental illness as inner aggression), of low motivation and aspiration (shutting out and devaluing the harsh world). Such alternative responses may be more available, as a result of socialization and subcultural values, to one group than another, thus affecting their rates of mental illness.

That contemporary American race patterns carry a heavy psychic cost we think there is little doubt;[135] that it is measured in higher rates of psychosis for Negroes we think is probable. We need more explicit study of this question, however, before these general statements can be formulated into the kind of differentiated statements that science requires. Fortunately, important steps are being taken by current work in the field of "social psychiatry," which seeks

---

[132] See Jerome Myers and Bertram Roberts, *Family and Class Dynamics in Mental Illness*, Wiley, 1959; and O. R. Gursslin, R. G. Hunt, and J. L. Roach, "Social Class and the Mental Health Movement," *SP*, Winter, 1959–1960, pp. 210–218.

[133] Benjamin Pasamanick, "Some Misconceptions Concerning Differences in the Racial Prevalence of Mental Disease," *American Journal of Orthopsychiatry*, Jan., 1963, pp. 72–86.

[134] R. M. Dreger and K. S. Miller, "Comparative Psychological Studies of Negroes and Whites in the United States," *Psychological Bulletin*, Sept., 1960, pp. 389–390.

[135] Research on this question, unfortunately, is limited. Furthermore, the complexity of the problem requires that we use our sources with particular care. See William Grier and Price Cobbs, *Black Rage*, Basic Books, 1968; Seymour Parker and Robert Kleiner, *Mental Illness in the Urban Negro Community*, Free Press, 1966; Herbert Hendin, *Black Suicide*, Basic Books, 1969; Thomas Pettigrew, *A Profile of the Negro American*, Van Nostrand, 1964, pp. 72–82; Robert Coles, *op. cit.*; Malzberg, *op. cit.*, pp. 373–399; Bertram Karon, *The Negro Personality*, Springer, 1958; Rohrer and Edmonson, *op. cit.*; Abram Kardiner and Lionel Ovesey, *The Mark of Oppression*, Norton, 1951; and Henry J. Myers and Leon Yochelson, "Color Denial in the Negro," *Psychiatry*, Feb., 1948, pp. 39–46.

to isolate the social and cultural factors involved in mental disorder.[136]

Minority Status and Intelligence. In Chapter 2 we discussed the evidence regarding differences in group averages in intelligence test scores. There is no need to repeat that account here; but it may be useful to summarize several points: (1) In every large group there is wide variation in intelligence scores, ranging, in terms of I.Q., from under 50 to over 200. (2) Group means, therefore, are of little significance, since it is individuals who are given or denied opportunities. To oppose higher education or some other opportunity for a Negro with an I.Q. of 140 because "his group" has an average score of 90 compared with an average among whites of 100 or 105 makes no sense. (3) Even those who argue in favor of the thesis that there are important racial differences note the extensive overlap among races, although the interpretation of that overlap is sometimes obscure. A 25 percent overlap between Negroes and whites, for example, means that 25 percent of the Negro scores are above the *median* white score. (4) White groups vary extensively in average scores, and in a way incapable of interpretation on national grounds, unless one cares to argue that the predominantly "Anglo-Saxon" South represents an inferior national stock. (5) Differences by group averages among young children are small,

but they become progressively larger with age, particularly on those tests that rely more heavily on language. (6) Intelligence is strongly influenced by health and nutrition in the earliest years of life. An inadequate supply of protein and other nutriments means, almost literally, a lack of "food for thought." Joaquin Cravioto and Herman Birch have compared the intelligence of 37 children who had been hospitalized for kwashkor [or kwashiorkor] disease, with siblings who had not suffered the disease. The average I.Q. of the former was 68.5; of the latter, 81.5.[137] (7) Intellectual and stimulus deprivation, correlated with but not identical to low socioeconomic status, leads to poor concept development and poor verbal skills; these in turn lead to inadequate school performance, alienation from school, and barriers to environmental stimuli; and these lead to poor test performance. Although we do not yet know a great deal about the what, when, and how of it, reversal of deprivation can reduce the deficits in intellectual performance.[138] (8) Organism-environment interactions in the building of intelligence are very complex. Evidence does not support the idea, most recently advanced by Jensen, that intelligence is primarily a fixed, hereditary capacity, only slightly subject to environmental modification. In his words: "The environment with respect to intelligence is analogous to nutrition with respect to stature."[139] Since good or poor nutrition makes only a few inches difference in stature, by analogy, a stimulating or repressing environment can make only a few points difference in I.Q. As Deutsch observes, were

[136] For valuable work in social psychiatry, which can furnish useful underlying principles to complement more traditional psychiatry, see Thomas Scheff, *Being Mentally Ill*, Aldine, 1966; Bruce Dohrenwend, "Social Status and Psychological Disorder: An Issue of Substance and an Issue of Method," *ASR*, Feb., 1966, pp. 14–34; Edward A. Suchman, "Sociomedical Variations Among Ethnic Groups," *AJS*, Nov., 1964, pp. 319–331; R. D. Laing and A. Esterson, *Sanity, Madness and the Family*, Tavistock, 1964; T. S. Szasz, *The Myth of Mental Illness*, Dell, 1961; Dorothea Leighton, *et. al.*, *The Character of Danger*, Basic Books, 1963; Myers and Roberts, *op. cit.*; A. B. Hollingshead and Frederick C. Redlich, *Social Class and Mental Illness: A Community Study*, Wiley, 1958; Alexander Leighton, John A. Clausen, and Robert N. Wilson, *Explorations in Social Psychiatry*, Basic Books, 1957; Morris K. Opler, *Culture, Psychiatry and Human Values*, Thomas, 1956; and Arnold M. Rose (ed.), *Mental Health and Mental Disorder: A Sociological Approach*, Norton, 1955.

[137] *The New York Times*, Mar. 1, 1970, p. E-11. See also Heinz F. Eichenwald and Peggy Crooke Fry, "Nutrition and Learning," *Science*, Feb. 14, 1969, pp. 644–648; and *IRCD Bulletin*, Sept. 1970, for both commentary and bibliography on nutrition.

[138] See Martin Whiteman and Martin Deutsch, "Social Disadvantage as Related to Intellective and Language Development," in Martin Deutsch, Irwin Katz, and Arthur Jensen (eds.), *Social Class, Race, and Psychological Development*, Holt, Rinehart & Winston, 1968, pp. 86–114.

[139] Arthur Jensen, "How Much Can We Boost IQ and Scholastic Achievement?" *Harvard Educational Review*, Winter, 1969, p. 69.

this true, the "ball game," so far as intelligence is concerned, would already be in the ninth inning at birth.[140] Such a perspective is in sharp contrast with the picture one gets from studies of variation in nutrition, stimulus deprivation, and environmental support. It also contradicts sharply the view of intelligence as an organism-environment transaction—a transaction that affects not simply content and style of thought, but its deepest processes. In Hunt's words: ". . . deprivation may be seen as a failure to provide an opportunity for infants and young children to have the experiences required for adequate development of those semiautonomous central processes demanded for acquiring skill in the use of linguistic and mathematical symbols and for the analysis of causal relationships."[141] (9) Test conditions, including the expectations of testers and of respondents, affect the results.[142] (10) Differences in group averages become progressively smaller as life conditions (income, residence, education, occupation, etc.) become more nearly similar.[143] (11) Full equation of conditions is difficult because equivalent income and education does not protect many minority-group members, Negroes for example, from rebuffs and other ego-crushing conditions that lead to ". . . intellectually defeating personality traits that play a significant role in their ability to score on measures of intelligence."[144] (12) Intelligence defined solely with reference to the usual tests scarcely gives an adequate picture. If intelligence is skillful adaptation to the stresses and possibilities of one's environment—a functional interpretation—Negro responses may measure up well. (13) Tests free of cultural and subcultural influences have yet to be designed—indeed are probably not possible to design.[145]

With such a list of qualifications it is obvious that one must speak with caution, but the evidence to date seems to us to show that, although members of some minority groups do exhibit lower average scores in the abilities that intelligence tests measure, these are more accurately understood as personality consequences of inferior status than as biological causes of inferior status.

Such, then, are the consequences of minority status. The pressures at work on those who are the targets for prejudice and discrimination require that they develop some mechanisms of adjustment and response. These may be looked upon as further personality consequences of the experiences that come from an inferior position. They are the subject matter of the next chapter.

---

[140] Martin Deutsch, "Organizational and Conceptual Barriers to Social Change," *JSI*, Autumn, 1969, p. 11.

[141] J. McVicker Hunt, "Environment, Development, and Scholastic Achievement," in Deutsch, Katz, and Jensen, *op. cit.*, p. 323. For a careful statement of this contemporary picture of the meaning of intelligence, see his whole essay, pp. 293–336.

[142] See, for example, Herbert Smith, Theodore May, and Leon Lebovitz, "Testing Experience of the Examiner and Stanford-Binet Scores," *Journal of Educational Measurement*, Fall, 1966, pp. 229–233; E. Zigler and E. C. Butterfield, "Motivational Aspects of Changes in the IQ Test Performance of Culturally Deprived Nursery School Children," *Child Development*, Mar., 1968, pp. 1–14; Murray Webster, Jr., "Sources of Evaluations and Expectations of Performance," *Sociometry*, Sept., 1969, pp. 243–258; Robert Rosenthal and Lenore Jacobson, *Pygmalion in the Classroom: Teacher Expectations and Pupils' Intellectual Development*, Holt, Rinehart & Winston, 1968; Wallace Kennedy and Manuel Vegas, "Negro Children's Performance on a Discrimination Task as a Function of Examiner Race and Verbal Incentive," *JPSR*, Dec., 1965, pp. 839–843.

[143] See, for example, Steven Tulkin, "Race, Class, Family, and School Achievement," *JPSP*, May, 1968, pp. 31–37.

[144] Sheldon Roen, "Personality and Negro-White Intelligence," *JASP*, July, 1960, p. 150.

[145] See Rosalie Cohen, "Conceptual Styles, Culture Conflict, and Nonverbal Tests of Intelligence," *AA*, Oct., 1969, pp. 828–856; *IRCD* Bulletin, "Education, Ethnicity, Genetics, and Intelligence," Fall, 1969; Kenneth Eells, *et. al.*, *Intelligence and Cultural Differences*, Univ. of Chicago Press, 1951; Dregner and Miller, *op. cit.*; and Otto Klineberg, "Negro-White Differences in Intelligence Test Performance," *American Psychologist*, Apr., 1968, pp. 198–203; Pettigrew, *op. cit.*, pp. 100–135.

Chapter 7 / THE CONSEQUENCES
OF PREJUDICE: TYPES OF ADJUSTMENT
TO PREJUDICE AND DISCRIMINATION

Probably no two persons respond in exactly the same way to the problems they face as members of a minority group. It is possible, however, to classify the patterns of adjustment into broad types, for purposes of analysis, and to point out the kinds of persons who are most likely to adopt each type as the primary mode of response to prejudice and discrimination. Response to the dominant world is not simply a matter of individual trial and error, for the culture of a minority group contains traditional adjustment techniques that are passed on, intentionally and unintentionally, to the oncoming generation. These techniques will vary from group to group; the responses of Jews will be different from those of Japanese-Americans, and both, in turn, different from those of Negroes. There will be many variations, moreover, within each group. To speak simply of "Americans of Mexican descent," for example, is to miss sharp contrasts among them. Both the nature of their problems and the modes of response are quite different for immigrant farm laborers, second-generation urban dwellers, and those families of Mexican ancestry who have roots in the Southwest going back, in some instances, 400 years. As Charles S. Johnson pointed out with respect to Negroes, the response to prejudice varies with the regional and cultural setting, social status, the specific situational factors in a given response, and the basic personality type of the individuals, among other factors.[1]

How one learns the nature of his status and adjusts to it ranges all the way from systematic training by parents to entirely informal and accidental picking up of points of view from small incidents or major crises. Some parents feel it necessary to give their children explicit attitudes concerning their relationship to the dominant world—whether they be attitudes of acceptance or rejection of that relationship. Some may try to teach specific ways of avoiding trouble, or of facing trouble if it comes. Others, however, make no conscious effort to equip their children with attitudes or techniques. These are then acquired informally by observation, by the learning of traditional modes of behavior, by the use of peer-group folkways, and by on-the-spot adjustments to members of the dominant group.

What, then, are the basic types of response to prejudice and discrimination? There are three fundamental varieties:

Avoidance
Aggression
Acceptance

These types of response represent a special application of the outline of types of social interaction employed in sociological analysis: association (acceptance), dissociation (aggression), and the absence of communication (avoidance). To these three types we need, perhaps, to add a fourth, or to note an important sub-type of "acceptance." This type we can call the conciliation, or reform, response. This implies acceptance of many elements of the system, seen as an ideal or model, but not of one's place in it; it implies a need for change, but a belief that change is possible; there is opposition to discrimination, but a readiness to engage in peaceful interaction with majority-group members to reduce that discrimination.

Several qualifications and clarifications are necessary in the use of such typologies: (1) as analytic types, they don't describe particular individuals, who usually express mixed responses; (2) few specific actions are purely of one type or another; (3) these

---

[1] See Charles S. Johnson, *Patterns of Negro Segregation*, Harper & Row, 1943, p. 231.

Discrepancy between ideal and real	Perceived locus of control of means	
	External	Internal
Low	(1) Content fatalism Traditional society Passive behavior	(4) Content activism Stable society Reactive (adjustive) behavior
High	(2) Discontent fatalism Unstable society Expressive behavior	(3) Discontent activism Transitional society Instrumental behavior

Source: Adapted from Thomas J. Crawford and Murray Naditch, "Relative Deprivation, Powerlessness, and Militancy: The Psychology of Social Protest," *Psychiatry*, May, 1970, p. 314. For another useful discussion of minority responses, see Donald L. Noel, "Minority Responses to Intergroup Situations," *Phylon*, Winter, 1969, pp. 367–374.

modes of response are subject to change, often quite rapidly, as situations change; (4) they feed back into the system from which they come, and thus are causes as well as effects; (5) they match the modes of response in areas of human behavior other than those of minority-majority relations—for example, ascetic (avoidance), prophetic (aggressive), and mystical (acceptance) religious sects, or value-oriented, power-oriented, and participation-oriented social movements.[2] (6) They match, to an important degree, the types of minorities discussed in Chapter 1. Types of minorities can be thought of as organized, structured manifestations of *shared* strategies or responses. The kinds of qualifications applicable to a typology of individual responses, of course, must be applied also to types of minorities.

These adjustments to discrimination can be put into a system by noting the various possible combinations of critical variables. Crawford and Naditch, for example, create a paradigm by combining two variables

[2] See J. Milton Yinger, *The Scientific Study of Religion*, Macmillan, 1970, chap. 13; and Ralph H. Turner and Lewis M. Killian, *Collective Behavior*, Prentice-Hall, 1957, part 4.

(dichotomized, for simplicity): discrepancy between the ideal and the real (i.e., the extent of relative deprivation); and the perceived locus of control, internal to one's self, or external. When these variables are combined, one gets the types shown in the above table.

This paradigm is not entirely adequate for our purposes, because it includes only two types of minorities (2 and 3, above). Minorities, by definition, experience discrepancy between their ideal goals and the realities; *all* are discontented. Type 1 describes a caste situation, as we have used that term in Chapter 1, and type 4 an upwardly mobile group in an open-class society. By specifying types 2 and 3 by an additional variable, however, we find four varieties of minorities. That second variable can be stated in the form of a question: Can change be accomplished within the system (column I, below)? Column III indicates the type of minority group corresponding with the type of individual response; and column II refers to the important question of perceived locus of power.

To answer the two questions in the typology in yes-or-no terms is clearly to oversimplify; yet the scheme would get excessively complex if we put them into scales.

Type of Individual and Group Responses to Minority Status

	I Can change be accomplished within the system? Is reform possible?	II Do minority-group members have access to change forces?	III If many agree on the answers, one has a group or social movement of these types:
Types of individual response			
1. Avoidance	no	no	Secessionist
2. Aggression	no	yes	Militant
3. Acceptance	yes	no	Assimilationist
4. Reformist	yes	yes	Pluralistic

To emphasize the full range, nevertheless, we will illustrate the possible subvarieties of type 2, "Aggression," by suggesting a three-step scale for each question (see table below).

Whether or not these guesses are near the mark, they may suggest the complexity of responses to minority status—a complexity that might be obscured by the listing of a few types only. We shall emphasize that complexity further in our discussion of each of the major types, by noting the numerous ways in which each response can be expressed.

AVOIDANCE

If a member of a minority group cannot abolish the status restrictions under which he lives, he can, at least under many circumstances, avoid situations where he must experience prejudice, or he can avoid some aspects of these situations. The avoidance can

Varieties of Aggressive Response to Minority Status

Can change be accomplished within the system?	Do minority group members have access to change forces?		
	Full access	*Substantial* access	*Some* access
Absolutely not	Revolutionary		Militantly alienated. Close to Secessionist groups
Clearly not		Militant activist	
Problably not	Militant but close to Reform groups		Verbally militant, Close to Assimilationist groups

be permanent ("passing" or assimilation) or temporary and partial (simply crossing to the other side of the street to avoid contact, or reticence in speaking to a member of the dominant group). Many motives encourage avoidance: the desire to preserve self-respect, to escape the need for conforming to the role of an "inferior," to gain status, power, and income *within* the minority group, to protect personal safety, etc. Avoidance is more frequently found in—and more readily available to—middle- and upper-class members of a minority group, but it is used to some degree among all classes.

Types of Avoidance

1. The most complete form of avoidance, clearly, is to withdraw entirely from the minority group. Where the color line is drawn as sharply as it is in the United States, this adjustment is open to only a small proportion of mixed-bloods. Estimates of the extent of Negro "passing," which of necessity are very rough, range from a few thousands to tens of thousands per year. Even with national or religious minorities, passing into the dominant group is often restricted by the presence of identifying characteristics: language accents, names, cultural differences, or knowledge, by the dominant community, of the family background can inhibit passing. Obviously these are much less categorical and permanent differences. Extensive assimilation, after three or four generations, has been the rule in the United States and in many other societies, particularly for national minorities.

In some situations, as in eastern Europe, where minorities have not wanted to be assimilated but have worked and fought for cultural and/or national independence, this process has, of course, not taken place. Under such circumstances relatively few members of a minority group have sought to avoid the penalties of that status by joining the majority. They have, far more often, united to try to win independence or at least a protected position within the larger society for the continuation of their group as a distinct

cultural-national population. Having felt a long series of outside imperialisms—Turkish, Austro-Hungarian, German, Russian—most Eastern European minorities have had their group self-consciousness and cohesiveness sharply accentuated. It seems not unreasonable to suppose that the present Russian domination of this area, as well as the highly centralized national domination within the eastern European countries, will face the same kind of group resistance already witnessed, in both external and internal affairs, in Yugoslavia.

Racial passing, particularly, and individual assimilation (e.g., a Jew who gives up his religion and leaves the Jewish community) are not guaranteed to permit the individual to avoid all the consequences of minority-group status. There is the danger of "discovery," which might destroy the whole pattern of adjustment. There is the problem of relationship to one's old friends and community. To break contact completely is sometimes a painful experience. Some persons who pass develop a sense of guilt that they have deserted "their group." They cannot completely break off identification with it. Some members of their former community may look with approval at their decision (happy that they are avoiding some of the hardships of their former status or glad that they are putting something over on the majority group). Others, however, may strongly disapprove and so give those who pass a sense of fear or guilt. A random sample of Detroit area residents were asked: "Suppose someone you knew told you he could 'pass' into white society, and was going to because of the advantages it would give him. How would you feel toward this person?" The results are tabulated according to the race of the interviewer which, however, in this instance had little effect (see table at top of page 209).

Passing is largely limited to urban communities, where one's former status can more readily be hidden.

Despite these difficulties, passing is for a few members of minority groups a decisive way to avoid some of the penalties of their status. Doubtless many more use it tempo-

	To White Interviewers	To Black Interviewers
Approve	17%	19%
Don't care	40	28
Disapprove	40	46
Other	3	7
	100%	100%
	(N = 165)	(N = 330)

Source: Howard Schuman and Jean M. Converse, "The Effects of Black and White Interviewers on Black Responses in 1968," *POQ*, Spring, 1971, p. 53. Reprinted with permission.

rarily for specific purposes, than attempt to cross permanently into the dominant group.

2. Upper-class members of a minority are able to avoid some prejudice and discrimination by sealing themselves off from contact with lower-class members of their group and by insulating themselves from their struggles and problems. They are able to afford well-ordered lives free from contact with the dominant group in large measure, and free from dependence upon it. Under these circumstances, some upper-class persons develop a complacency about "race problems." Having achieved a satisfactory adjustment, they see no reason to endanger it by being identified with the minority group as a whole. (Many upper-class persons, of course, refuse to make this adjustment and instead become aggressive leaders of the minority.) This kind of avoidance is not wholly successful. Even those who have most successfully reduced the necessity for contact with the dominant group run into rigid barriers, especially with regard to finding a good place to live and in economic matters. Some have feelings of guilt which make their "complacency" in the matter somewhat less than whole-hearted.[3]

An interesting aspect of the desire to avoid economic involvement with the dominant community is the effort to persuade the members of a minority group to patronize only business and professional people from

[3] See Robert L. Sutherland, "Color, Class, and Personality," *ACE*, 1942, pp. 44–46.

their own group. Some leaders have developed this into an ideology of a "separate economy" or a "nation within a nation." This ideology, largely found among Negroes in our society, is closely related to the growth of black "nationalism." Its appeal has not been large; but for a minority who see in it a mode of adjustment, it has often led to support of segregation. It is an attempt to derive "advantages from the disadvantages." Some businessmen have appealed to "race pride" to reduce or eliminate competition. A few black teachers have said: If we are going to be discriminated against in mixed schools, why not encourage segregated schools in which all jobs will be opened to us? The effects of lack of competition in the first example or of segregation on the personalities of white and Negro pupils in the second are given little or no attention by those who take such a stand.

With public attention focused on Black Power and racial conflict, it is easy to exaggerate the appeal of such separationist beliefs. In a study of a black neighborhood in Cleveland, Dubey found that from 10 to 16 percent preferred a black to a white person as doctor, nurse, social worker, store owner, and other occupations. From 77 to 84 percent said that race made no difference and from 5 to 11 percent preferred Whites. Only for ministers was there a fairly large vote for a black person, and even then, the majority said that it made no difference (42 percent preferred a Negro; 56 percent thought it made no difference).[4] In a study of "Racial Attitudes in Fifteen American Cities," Angus Campbell and Howard Schuman[5] found that the percentage agreeing with the statement "Stores in Negro neighborhoods should be owned and run by Negroes" varied from 13 to 30, depending on age and education. It is interesting that the only groups with over 20 percent agreeing were young (16–19) with less than nine grades of schooling (22 percent) and the

[4] Sumati Dubey, "Blacks' Preference for Black Professionals, Businessmen, and Religious Leaders," *POQ*, Spring, 1970, pp. 113–116.
[5] *Supplemental Studies for the National Advisory Commission on Civil Disorders*, Government Printing Office, 1968.

young (20–39) who had completed college (30 percent).

It is difficult to generalize from the wide range of questions, samples, and time periods, but we think it is substantially correct to say that from five to twenty percent of American Negroes support various separationist statements. This may underestimate, but probably overestimates the proportion who would engage in extensive separationist activities.[6]

3. The avoidance response is made by a few in the development of communities composed only of minority-group persons—for example, the all-Negro town of Mound Bayou, Mississippi. A more extreme expression of this tendency is the call for a separate nation. The appeal of Zionism among Jews, particularly those in Europe, has been not only positive (the desire to preserve the religio-cultural tradition) but also an avoidance response (the desire to lay down the burden of prejudice and discrimination). Negro "Zionism" in the Americas has relied on remote or even pseudo connections with Africa, as in the Ras Tafari movement in the West Indies,[7] the Garveyite movement in the United States,[8] and more recently the Black Muslims.[9] Since we shall discuss the Muslims in Chapter 17, we need mention here only that their call for a separate nation, their attack on integration, their appeal to the unifying force of a supposed separate black culture are expressions not only of avoidance, but contain also powerful themes of aggression against the system.

Far more common than separate communities of nations—or dreams of them—are the segregated subcommunities in our cities. They are largely forced upon the minority but to some degree are encouraged by the desire to find an island partly free from the prejudice and discrimination of the dominant group. The people of Harlem, a major city in its own right, can avoid some of the daily and even hourly symbols and experiences of "inferiority." The great majority of the residents cannot, however, avoid the fact that the very existence of Harlem as a separate community is largely a result of prejudice. They are still largely dependent upon white employers and white landlords. And even the daily interaction *within* the community is strongly influenced by the fact that it is a segregated area. This fact is always in the background, conditioning the internal status structure, influencing the nature of its leadership, affecting the cohesiveness of the community. Segregated communities have a decided tendency to split into factions—partly because of the intensified internal struggle for status, partly because of disagreements over the best way to deal with the dominant group. They often generate an ultranationalism among some of the members, a movement that is likely to increase the prejudice of the majority.

Thus a forced segregated community is inadequate for avoiding prejudice and discrimination. Immigrant communities, faced with the additional problems of language and cultural assimilation, are not to be understood simply as devices for avoiding the pressures of the dominant group. On the one hand, they serve as stepping stones to the new society; on the other, they serve to slow down the transition by acting as a center for the old culture—with native-language papers, schools, and churches, and a general emphasis on the common background. The balance of these two tendencies varies from community to community, depending upon the size and type of the immigrant group and the attitudes of the larger society. Until about 1924 these communities were often kept intact by the constant influx of newcomers from abroad; but in the second and third generations there has been a progressive loss of functions, including the

---

[6] See Gary Marx, *Protest and Prejudice*, Harper & Row, 1969, pp. 224–229; and Ann F. Brunswick, "What Generation Gap? A Comparison of Some Generational Differences among Blacks and Whites," *SP*, Winter, 1970, pp. 358–371.

[7] George E. Simpson, "Political Cultism in West Kingston, Jamaica," *Social and Economic Studies*, June, 1955, pp. 133–149.

[8] E. D. Cronon, *Black Moses*, Univ. of Wisconsin Press, 1955.

[9] Only one Negro in 20, according to the Campbell-Schuman study (*op. cit.*) and a national CBS poll favors the idea of a separate nation. "Ironically . . . 33 percent of the whites questioned in the CBS poll felt this was a good idea." (Marx, *op. cit.*, p. 226.)

function of avoiding prejudice, as individual members were absorbed into the general community.

Major exceptions to this generalization at the present time are the communities of persons of Spanish-speaking descent and of Jews. In the former case, the size and recency of much of the immigration (whether from Mexico, Puerto Rico, Cuba, or elsewhere), the importance of the Spanish language, and related cultural elements, widespread poverty, discrimination, and doubtless other factors, contribute to the maintenance of fairly distinctive residential areas. The degree of separation, however, varies widely from city to city, and is sharply reduced as income and educational differentials are reduced.[10]

In the United States today, separate Jewish communities are in only small measure the result of enforced segregation. They reflect the desire to avoid prejudice which, although much abated, lives in vivid memory—a memory which, on occasion, can be sharply revived.[11] Most important, however, is the widely shared desire to reenforce a distinctive tradition and group identity. This has led, in recent years, not so much to wholly separate communities as to neighborhoods with a sufficiently large Jewish population to maintain private associations.[12]

4. The desire to escape a highly discriminatory situation has often been a powerful motive in the migration of persons of low status. Religious prejudice was one of the factors in the migration of some of the early settlers to America; discrimination against socialist workers encouraged a great many

[10] See Leo Grebler, Joan Moore, and Ralph Guzman, *The Mexican American People*, Free Press, 1970, chap. 12.

[11] See Boris Weiss, "Reilly and I," *Commentary*, Apr., 1963, pp. 302–311.

[12] See chap. 10, where we will discuss this question more fully. See also Sidney Goldstein and Calvin Goldscheider, *Jewish Americans: Three Generations in a Jewish Community*, Prentice-Hall, 1968; Stuart Rosenberg, *The Search for Jewish Identity in America*, Doubleday, 1965; Benjamin Ringer, *The Edge of Friendliness: A Study of Jewish-Gentile Relations*, Basic Books, 1967; Peter Rose (ed.), *The Ghetto and Beyond*, Random House, 1969; Marshall Sklare and Joseph Greenblum, *Jewish Identity on the Suburban Frontier*, Basic Books, 1967.

to leave Bismarck's Germany; discrimination and violence in Poland and Russia, particularly after 1880, and in Germany after 1933, caused millions of Jews to seek avoidance by emigration; and one of the propelling forces behind the migration of Negroes from South to North has been the hope of escaping from low status. The success of such moves has varied greatly, depending on existing prejudices in the new situation; the ease with which the newcomers could be absorbed economically; the size of the migrating group; the degree to which the migrants desired assimilation or a separate, protected status, etc. One aspect of this kind of avoidance is the belief—based partly on known facts, partly on fervent hope—that the new land is the promised land, where the great problems of discrimination are solved. This has been the attitude of many southern Negroes toward the North.

5. For most people the rather intensive avoidance techniques that we have discussed are either impossible or held to be undesirable. Most members of minority groups have to face frequent contact with prejudiced members of the dominant group. They may try to reduce these by ordering goods from a catalogue or making reservations by telephone or patronizing the business and professional people of their own group. In some situations, particularly in the rural South, Negroes try to avoid contact with whites for fear some violation, or supposed violation, of the etiquette of race relations may endanger their personal safety.

No matter how intensive the efforts to avoid contact with prejudiced persons, however, members of minority groups, particularly those of the lower classes, because of their economic dependence are almost certain to have frequent associations with persons of high status. Their efforts under these circumstances are directed toward avoiding some of the unwanted aspects of the contacts—the blows to self-respect or the dangers to personal safety.

6. Frazier has described a somewhat different type of avoidance response. This is an effort not to avoid punishing or humiliating contact with the dominant group, but to

escape the feelings of inferiority and futility that the discriminations of the dominant group have forced into one's own self-image. Some aspects of this process may have happy results, as judged by the dominant values, whereas other results are unfortunate. There may be strong efforts at self-improvement and an emphasis on education. There may develop, however, a "world of make-believe," as Frazier calls it, in which the members of a minority group struggle with their feelings of inferiority in wholly unrealistic terms. He describes the exaggerations in the Negro press of the economic and cultural achievements of Negroes, and the emphasis on Negro "society" as part of this world of make-believe. More particularly, he describes the search for excitement, glamor, and entertainment among the "black bourgeoisie," the new Negro middle class.

Their escape into a world of make-believe with its sham 'society' leaves them with a feeling of emptiness and futility which causes them to constantly seek an escape in new delusions. . . . However, the majority of the black bourgeoisie who seek an escape from their frustrations in delusions seemingly have not been able to find it in the delusion of wealth or power. They have found it in magic or chance, and in sex and alcohol."[13]

These escape devices doubtless indicate to an important degree "the mark of oppression," inadequate and self-defeating efforts to avoid a world that denies one self-respect. Before we conclude that such responses are wholly the result of prejudice and discrimination, however, we need to measure the extent to which similar patterns are found among "the white bourgeoisie." Negroes certainly have no monopoly on the world of make-believe. In a complex society, most people carry some feelings of inadequacy and inferiority, and many develop awkward ways of responding to those feelings—chauvinism, perhaps, or prejudice; alcoholism or mental illness. Here again the concept of "functional alternatives" can be helpful, for widely different types of responses can partly be understood as alterna-

tive ways of dealing with the same situation. Thus "the return to religion" in some may be matched in others by peer-group identification and "other-directedness," in Riesman's phrase. In *Blackways of Kent*, Hylan Lewis interprets a wide variety of different responses—aggression, heavy drinking, loitering, some aspects of religion—as alternative ways of struggling with a very difficult situation for Negroes in a small southern town. Studies of low-status Whites in the same community indicate that they make many of the same responses.[14] The research task is to discover the conditions under which the various alternative responses occur, and to describe the similarities and differences between members of the majority and minority groups in types of response.

Many avoidance responses carry a strong undertone of aggression, but in a context of accommodation and a sense of powerlessness the aggressive aspect is deflected. Many Negro youth in the slums are keenly aware of the values and criteria for success in the dominant society. They are also highly sensitive to the barriers that separate them from those values. Some strive for achievement in the system; some react by delinquency or random aggression; but others develop a world of make-believe akin, as Finestone points out, to that described by Frazier for the Black Bourgeoisie.[15] They deny the values of the larger society; or perhaps raise to a primary level what are generally regarded as secondary and marginal values.[16] Thus they avoid the sense of failure, at least consciously, by creating a world in which *they* are the successful ones. The squares who work hard, stay in school, and keep within the narrow bounds approved by society are the failures. The Cat rejects work; he seeks for a "hustle" —a way of getting income by the easiest means possible. Life is a search for kicks— any act tabooed by squares—that will heighten the experience of the moment. Thus

[13] E. Franklin Frazier, *Black Bourgeoisie*, Free Press, 1957, pp. 213, 231.

[14] Hylan Lewis, *Blackways of Kent*, Univ. of North Carolina Press, 1955.

[15] Harold Finestone, "Cats, Kicks, and Color," *SP*, July, 1957, pp. 3–13.

[16] David Matza and Gresham Sykes, "Juvenile Delinquency and Subterranean Values," *ASR*, Oct., 1961, pp. 712–719.

the ego-crushing feelings from encounters with the dominant society are turned aside; a private world is built according to one's own plan.[17]

In sum, we see that avoidance as a means of adjustment varies all the way from complete withdrawal to playing a role in a specific incident. The behavior patterns it represents are largely *responses*—the results of the attitudes and behavior of the dominant group; but they also become part of the interaction that affects the dominant group. Seldom is a given action a pure case of avoidance; it more often contains also elements of aggression and protest, and perhaps also of acceptance.

Variables Affecting Types and Extent of Avoidance

At several points we have referred to the fact that avoidance is not equally available to all members of a minority group. Those least dependent on the majority for jobs, housing, protection in the courts, etc., are most able to avoid painful contact. Segregation therefore does little to aid avoidance, because it is most often found precisely in those regions where minorities are most dependent on the dominant group. Other things being equal, the higher the income and occupational status of a minority-group member, the more successfully can he avoid direct contact with prejudice. Avoidance, in fact, may become part of the culture of upper-class members of a minority, as is the case among American Negroes. Even wealthy members of a low-status group, however, cannot avoid all contacts and cannot insulate their children completely from the dominant group. For lower-class members, daily contacts with members of the dominant group in their roles of employer, landlord, merchant, police, etc.,

[17] Finestone, *op. cit.* Like other forms of escape, this one is only minimally successful. If it involves the use of drugs, there is usually a downward spiral of health. It leads easily into illegal activities that, far from helping one avoid the outside world, brings one into painful confrontation with it. And the dismissal of the values of society is often not wholehearted; there is ambivalence, exposed by the intensity of the attack on the world of the squares.

are almost inevitable. They are much less likely to use avoidance as a mode of adjustment, therefore; and when they do use it, the application is of the temporary and partial variety.

AGGRESSION: STRIKING BACK

It seems unlikely that members of minority groups could experience prejudice and discrimination without feeling hostility, a desire to strike back, to attack the source of their frustration or a substitute target. The nature of this aggression varies greatly from person to person and from group to group. Much of it will be unconscious—unrecognized as hostility either by the person using it or by the majority. A great deal will be directed away from the primary source of frustration because of the dangers or difficulties in attacking members of the dominant group. Underlying this diversity of expression, however, will be a common function. As we shall see, some writers go so far as to interpret almost all responses of minority-group members, no matter how unaggressive they may seem on the surface, in terms of hostility. It does not seem possible, at our present level of knowledge, to accept this hypothesis with complete assurance. But the evidence does point to the need for seeing the relationship between outward, more or less obvious, acts of aggression and internal or covert modes of adjustment that seem very different but which, from the point of view of the person using them, serve the same social psychological functions. Majority-group members frequently fail to see the similarity in these different ways of behaving, and consequently seriously misunderstand the behavior of minority-group members with whom they come in contact. In fact, the more completely the modes of aggression have to be disguised—in areas where overt hostility would be most vigorously suppressed and most violently punished by the dominant group—the more likely are people of high status to misinterpret the behavior of people of low status. It is precisely in these areas that the claim "to know" the minority group is most frequently asserted, because outward behavior is usually more uniform and predictable there. A deeper knowledge of personality, of the feelings, the desires, the motives of the persons of low status, however, will probably be lacking under these conditions.

In a valuable essay Hortense Powdermaker noted how modes of aggression change with varying conditions.[18] Even the faithful slave and the "meek, unaggressive" Negro that followed him after the Civil War were not, she asserted, lacking in hostility but were simply forced by circumstances, and taught by their culture, to express their hostility mainly in indirect and hidden ways. The nature of their religion, their internal relationships, even the strong tendency to identify with the master can be interpreted, in part, as modes of aggression. The slave was dependent upon the white man. His security and the avoidance of pain demanded the white man's good will, so that much of the hatred the Negro felt had to be repressed. There were, of course, direct expressions of hostility. Thousands ran away; others committed crimes against Whites despite brutal punishment; there were slave revolts. The great majority, however, were "loyal," and expressed their hostility indirectly.

Powdermaker interpreted even the meekness and deference to Whites not as a lack of aggression but as a form of adaptation containing a great deal of aggression, an aggression whose expression was appropriate to the personalities involved and the nature of the cultural surroundings. Following the sharply modified Freudian view of Theodore Reik, Powdermaker interpreted the self-effacing humbleness of most slaves and the freedmen as an attempt to rescue victory from defeat—one's suffering is only a prelude to ultimate victory and reward; one gets power from his suffering. Meek Negroes, moreover, have feelings of guilt because of their hostile feelings toward the Whites. They have taken the Christian injunctions against hatred seriously, yet they are continuously

[18] Hortense Powdermaker, "The Channeling of Negro Aggression by the Cultural Process," *AJS*, May, 1943, pp. 750–758.

faced with situations that produce hatred. The meekness is a way of appeasing their own guilt feelings. A feeling of superiority is also a part of the pleasure of the "meek" Negro. He gets a sense of Christian virtue and also a feeling that he is fooling the Whites—they don't know his true thoughts.

The nature of this "aggressive meekness" is perhaps best seen in the types of religious expression that have been important in the lives of many Negroes. Christian missionaries of pre-Civil War days emphasized the rewards for humbleness and the glories of the future life. This emphasis stemmed partly from their own doctrines and partly from the insistence of planters that they preach only that kind of religion. In any event it harmonized, considering the status they were caught in, with the needs of the Blacks. The meek shall inherit the earth; the suffering shall be rewarded; and ultimate victory shall be given to the faithful, not the powerful. Not all the rewards were to be postponed to "the sweet by-and-by," but there was a strong other-worldly emphasis. It is also possible to interpret such religious beliefs as a kind of "vicarious avoidance" or escape; they help one to avoid the penalties of low status by devaluing this life, thus making one's sufferings here less important. Almost all of the responses we are discussing represent a combination of two, or all three, of the basic adjustment patterns.

This type of adjustment has certainly diminished. There has been a decline in religious faith, a less sincere belief in the rewards of heaven, and thus a deeper feeling of injury at the deprivations on earth. The reduction of illiteracy has brought more independence to the Negro. Migration to the cities has created a situation in which the meek adjustment is less likely to be successful. Most Negro leaders and institutions are stressing other ways of adaptation and protest. Altogether, more overt modes of aggression have increased and can be expected to increase further as the goals of Negroes become more and more like those of Whites and as the rewards for the humble, unaggressive response decline.

Nevertheless, there may be a strong

cultural continuity between the "aggressive-meekness" of the plantation Negro and the nonviolent resistance movement that appeared in the late 1950s. The relation of Martin Luther King's methods to those of Gandhi has been often remarked. It may be equally or more to the point to note that King was a Christian minister, heir of a tradition which, for all of its ambivalences, has always contained an explosive potential, often expressed in sectarian movements. The nature of the protest is strongly influenced by the hopes of the participants, their educational level and other resources, and the potentialities of the situation. There are, therefore, important differences between the forms of religious "attack" used by an illiterate peasantry and a literate, urban group with strong middle-class leadership. But in observing these differences we should not overlook the continuity.

The strength of the Negro protest movement that developed, arbitrarily we shall say, after the school-desegregation decision of 1954, has involved more people, in more settings, seeking more goals than was thought at all likely when it began. This is testimony, we believe, to the fact that resentment against segregation and discrimination had always been strong, that many earlier forms of response—as Powdermaker noted—were deflected and disguised aggression, that direct protests had been inhibited by powerlessness and fear of reprisals. Now "the lid is off"; attacks on the system are direct, and it seems highly unlikely that they will abate short of substantial change in America's race relations patterns.

Since many of the forms of aggression we shall mention are thought of, by users and targets alike, as efforts to change existing status arrangements, they will be discussed in Part III and in other chapters as well. Here the emphasis will be on aggression as an effect, a response to prejudice and discrimination. The later emphasis will be on the study of aggression and conflict as possible causes of change. But this distinction is purely analytic. In fact, aggression is involved in a sequence of causes and effects, from one perspective being a consequence, from another the precipitating factor in further events.

Turning now to a wider context, we can discuss briefly some of the many ways in which minority-group members express their resentment against their status and attempt to strike back against their oppressors. These vary with the personalities of the people involved and with the environment. The response that is permitted, or likely to be effective, in one place might be dangerous or ineffective in another.

Types of Aggression

1. Some individuals become active and aggressive group leaders, professionally championing the claims of the whole group by editing papers, leading protest groups, organizing boycotts, trying to persuade friends among the dominant group to support them economically and politically. (To a few, this furnishes middle- and upper-class status and thus simultaneously aids them in avoiding some of the hardships of the group they defend.)

During this period of sharp protest against America's race relations patterns, we are rediscovering the works of black leaders who opposed those patterns earlier. The tone of protest and the medium of expression vary widely. But through the generations there have been aggressive black leaders who have fought against discrimination. It is not clear, for example, that Eldridge Cleaver and Stokely Carmichael have, in the last few years, been in sharper opposition to discrimination than Frederick Douglass, in the generation before the Civil War, or W. E. B. DuBois, in a career spanning the first half of the twentieth century and longer.[19]

Forms of protest among American Indians

[19] See, for example, Frederick Douglass, *The Life and Times of Frederick Douglass*, Park, 1882; W. E. B. DuBois, *Black Reconstruction in America*, World, 1962; Stokely Carmichael and Charles V. Hamilton, *Black Power*, Random House, 1967; Eldridge Cleaver, *Soul on Ice*, Dell, 1968. For valuable commentary and documents, see August Meier, *Negro Thought in America: 1889–1915*, Univ. of Michigan Press, 1963; and John H. Bracey, Jr., August Meier, and Elliott Rudwick (eds.), *Black Nationalism in America*, Bobbs-Merrill, 1970.

have also changed, but the leaders of the current "red power" movement are scarcely more vigorous in their opposition to white domination than Wodziwob, Wovoka, and other leaders of the Ghost Dance.[20] There is less historical depth in the work of protest leaders among Americans of Spanish-speaking descent. They have been, perhaps, "the invisible minority," as some have called them. But in recent years, with increasing political organization, with demands for education designed to meet their needs, and with the growth of labor organizations, we have seen the appearance of such aggressive leaders as Cesar Chavez.

A few members of subservient groups express their aggression by proclaiming a racial patriotism or a strong group chauvinism. One phase of the Negro protest movement in the United States is the assertion of the superiority of all things black, shown in the doctrines of Marcus Garvey and Elijah Muhammad. This reaches beyond the range of ethnocentrism in an attempt to turn what seems to be a handicap into an advantage. There is some evidence that both the origin and the survival of the Jewish concept of a "chosen people" are in a measure products of the oppressions the Jews have experienced as a group. Japanese propaganda in the Far East before and during World War II to some degree exploited the feelings of resentment that Asiatics felt toward the race prejudice of the white man by developing a doctrine of the superiority of the darker peoples. (Chauvinistic assertion of the superiority of the white race is also a common form of aggression, as we have seen in Chapter 4.)

2. Direct physical aggression against one's oppressors is not unusual. From the days of slavery some Negroes have expressed their resentment by furtive, individual acts of violence. Organized hostility has been uncommon, largely, perhaps, because of a feeling of inevitable failure, partly because of

the lack of internal solidarity among the oppressed group, particularly with regard to agreement on the appropriate means of dealing with the white man. The police and the courts are especially likely to side with a member of the dominant group in a case of physical aggression (see Chapter 14). The unlawful use of violence by the dominant group has also been common in American history,[21] inviting retaliation, but even more strongly blocking it. The current scene, however, indicates that significant changes may be taking place: Growing power and intensive communication have removed some of the inhibitions against violence in the oppressed groups; the gap between their aspirations and their actual conditions has widened; the lower classes—with stronger subcultural support for violence—have been drawn more fully into the struggle for equality. These forces may combine to increase the frequency with which minority-group members in the United States use physical aggression in attempts to improve their situation. This possibility may be increased by the fact that the traditions of violence are strongest in the South—the cultural homeland if not now the residence of most American Negroes. The slavery and plantation system, the related perpetuation of a "frontier" spirit in the South, and the frustrations of the Civil War nurtured the traditions of violence.[22] Pettigrew and Spier believe that the high Negro homicide rate may well be explained by the triggering effect of rapid social change and social mobility acting upon a severely frustrated group that is largely the product of a region with a violent tradition.[23] Insofar as this thesis is correct, such violent attacks as Negroes may make on the segregation system

[20] See, in particular, James Mooney, *The Ghost-Dance and the Sioux Outbreak of 1890*, Univ. of Chicago Press, 1965. On the current scene, see Stan Steiner, *The New Indians*, Dell, 1968.

[21] See National Commission on the Causes and Prevention of Violence, *To Establish Justice, to Insure Domestic Tranquility*, Government Printing Office, 1970; Allen Grimshaw (ed.), *Racial Violence in the United States*, Aldine, 1969.

[22] See Thomas Pettigrew and Rosalind Spier, "The Ecological Structure of Negro Homicide," *AJS*, May, 1962, pp. 621–629; W. J. Cash, *The Mind of the South*, Knopf, 1941; and John Hope Franklin, *From Slavery to Freedom*, Knopf, 1948.

[23] Pettigrew and Spier, *op. cit.*

are to be explained, ironically, as expressions of their southernness.

This is not the whole story, however. As has often happened, violent aggression has been released by the break-up of a traditional status structure. Hopes have been raised faster than opportunities could be opened up or, if opened, made visible. Bitterness and anger are the result. Only a minority have expressed this bitterness and anger by physical aggression, but the number has grown during the last decade. The aggression has taken several forms: random or spontaneous acts of violence directed mainly against property (most of the people killed during the race riots of the 1960s in the United States were Blacks); more focused and planned, but, as yet, small-scale attacks on "the establishment," particularly the police; and a justifying ideology that acclaims violence as a purification ceremony or an effective strategy.

Since we shall examine conflict as strategy in Chapter 22, we shall deal with it briefly here as an effect, the outcome of certain conditions. The various forms of violence express in common the reduction in legitimacy accorded the political, legal, economic, and social system by a population that is deeply frustrated and angered.[24] Loss of legitimacy is a long-run, step-by-step process, but its sequence can be seen in the impact of particular decisive events. Hofstetter was involved in a study of electoral behavior in central Ohio in April, 1968. As it happened, he had gathered part of his data before April 4, the day of Martin Luther King's murder, and part in the days that followed. There were some sharp changes in the "affect level" with reference to various groups on the part of his Negro respondents. Positive attitudes toward the police, for example, fell from 88.9 percent to 58.6 percent after April 4. (The white percentages were 87.9 and 86.5.) With reference to Whites,

the percentages fell from 70.4 to 51.7, and to national politicians from 55.6 to 34.5.[25]

Data from another study, however, reveal that the effects of King's death were complex. *The Miami Herald* had conducted a survey among a random sample of Miami's Negroes between February 26, 1968, and March 25, 1968, two weeks before King was killed. In the May–July period, Philip Meyer interviewed a subsample of the original 530 respondents, made up of similar proportions of persons low, medium, and high in militancy, and a second sample of persons not seen earlier, to control for the possible effects of being interviewed twice. There was some increase in militancy, by the measures used, with the "high" category increasing from 24.4 percent to 30.6 percent. It was the better educated and more politically aware who were more likely to increase in militancy. There was, however, no corresponding increase in the proportion who advocated violence (11 percent in both cases), although there was a small shift toward the "uncertain" position and away from the "against" position. Pessimism increased, but so also did the sense of political efficacy. Meyer concludes that King's assassination did not have, at least in the area studied in the period immediately after his death, the often predicted effect of increasing support for violence. There was more of a martyr effect, with many white as well as black Americans appreciating King more fully after his death. "Nonviolence is not dead. Indeed, the militant middle may be stronger than ever."[26]

On the national scene, although the evi-

---

[24] For a valuable discussion of the grounds of legitimacy, see Herbert C. Kelman, "A Social-Psychological Model of Political Legitimacy and Its Relevance to Black and White Student Protest Movements," *Psychiatry*, May, 1970, pp. 224–246.

[25] C. Richard Hofstetter, "Political Disengagement and the Death of Martin Luther King," POQ, Summer, 1969, pp. 174–179.

[26] Philip Meyer, "Aftermath of Martyrdom: Negro Militancy and Martin Luther King," *POQ*, Summer, 1969, pp. 160–173. Meyer notes that the seasonal difference (February–March vs. May–July), the death of Robert F. Kennedy, which came near the end of the second round of interviews, or reading about the results of the first survey may have influenced the results. He concludes that only the latter may have played a part, perhaps by encouraging persons to express more militant attitudes, having discovered that they were quite widely shared.

dence is somewhat contradictory, there appears to have been an increased readiness to use or to condone violence in recent years.[27] At the same time, paradoxically, a sense of efficacy may be increasing—the belief by Blacks that they can take effective action to improve their own situation.[28] Up to a point, both sentiments may grow without serious contradictions, within individuals or groups; but it seems likely that, in the last analysis, they indicate different contexts for action. Readiness to use violence represents a reduction of the sense of efficacy; a growth in that sense will restrict the likelihood of violence.

There is now a large literature on the violent aggression of recent years, some of it descriptive, but much of it seeking also to identify the variables that most frequently underlie participation in riots or other violent acts of protest. It is a mixture of several conditions that produces violence: (1) severe discrimination and deprivation, made more visible by the mass media, by rising hopes and even by rising achievements (for *relative* deprivation is the key), by population concentration, and by the general affluence of the society; (2) demographic changes that have brought a higher ratio of young, better educated, more self-confident Blacks into close interaction; (3) a general environment that challenges legitimacy, not only with reference to minorities and race relations, but with reference to national war policies, educational procedures, and many other aspects of national life; (4) a reciprocal readiness to talk and act violently by many Whites, in part a continuation of earlier patterns, in part a change produced by the tensions of the civil rights struggles of the last generation; (5) racial isolation that promotes misperceptions and the spread of

rumors. These various factors are systematically interrelated. It would be too much to say that the severe outbreaks of the 1960s required that all the factors be present in each instance, but the absence of even one of these factors would have significantly reduced the likelihood of violence.[29]

There is less adequate evidence on violent aggression that is more focused and planned than spontaneous rebellion against deprivation. An excessively sharp distinction is often drawn between rioting, which is thought to be spontaneous, and insurrection, which is seen as premeditated attack on the social order. On the one hand, riotous destruction is sometimes quite focused, with merchants, employers, or others who are believed to be particularly discriminatory receiving the major attack. On the other hand, insurrection is sometimes a creation of the news media or the police, who, in an ambiguous situation, find it easy to read the signals in such a way as to confirm their definition of the situation, when in fact an outburst has been

[29] See, for example, Robert H. Connery, "Urban Riots: Violence and Social Change," *Proceedings of the Academy of Political Science*, vol. 29, no. 1, 1968; Vernon L. Allen, issue editor, "Ghetto Riots," *JSI*, Winter, 1970; National Advisory Commission on Civil Disorders, *Report*, Government Printing Office, 1968; Nathan Cohen (ed.), *The Los Angeles Riots: A Socio-Psychological Study*, Praeger, 1970; Martin Oppenheimer, *The Urban Guerrilla*, Quadrangle Books, 1969; David Boesel, "The Liberal Society, Black Youths, and the Ghetto Riots," *Psychiatry*, May, 1970, pp. 265–281; Seymour Spilerman, "The Causes of Racial Disturbances: A Comparison of Alternative Explanations," *ASR*, Aug., 1970, pp. 627–649; H. Edward Ransford, "Isolation, Powerlessness, and Violence: A Study of Attitudes and Participation in the Watts Riot," *AJS*, Mar., 1968, pp. 581–591; Louis H. Masotti and Don R. Bowen (eds.), *Riots and Rebellions: Civil Violence in the Urban Community*, Sage Publications, 1968; David O. Sears and John B. McConahay, "Participation in the Los Angeles Riot," *Social Problems*, Summer, 1969, pp. 3–20; Donald I. Warren, "Neighborhood Structure and Riot Behavior in Detroit: Some Exploratory Findings," *SP*, Spring, 1969, pp. 464–484; James A. Geschwender and Benjamin D. Singer, "Deprivation and the Detroit Riot," *SP*, Spring, 1970, pp. 457–462. For valuable studies of more general theoretical interest, see Henry Bienen, *Violence and Social Change: A Review of Current Literature*, Univ. of Chicago Press, 1968; Ted R. Gurr, *Why Men Rebel*, Princeton Univ. Press, 1970; Hans H. Toch, *Violent Men: An Inquiry into the Psychology of Violence*, Aldine, 1969.

[27] The percentages answering "violence is probably necessary" to win rights, according to polls taken by *Time*, were 22 in 1963, 21 in 1966, and 31 in 1970. (*Time*, Apr. 6, 1970, p. 29.)

[28] See Campbell and Schuman, *op. cit.*; and T. M. Tomlinson, "Determinants of Black Politics: Riots and the Growth of Militancy," *Psychiatry*, May, 1970, pp. 247–264; John R. Forward and Jay R. Williams, "Internal-External Control and Black Militancy," *JSI*, Winter, 1970, pp. 75–92.

precipitated by a specific event, against a background of distrust and frustration.[30]

Nevertheless, an analytic distinction needs to be maintained between spontaneous and planned violence. There have been armed attacks without immediate provocation being visible. We need systematic study of the conditions that lead to one or the other and to various mixtures. Probably many underlying conditions are the same. Planned insurrections and sniping develop, however, only when additional factors are present: prolonged frustration, unusually harsh harassment from the police, certain personality configurations, and a supporting ideology that violence is not only effective, but a positive good.

This last has been furnished by Frantz Fanon and others who see violence as psychologically liberating, as essential to an oppressed population striving to free itself, not only from domination by others, but from self-hatred. Violence ". . . is a cleansing force. It frees the native from his inferiority complex and from his despair and inaction. . . ."[31] Angela Davis expressed the same belief in a lecture at U.C.L.A., when she declared that ". . . the first condition of freedom is an open act of resistance—physical resistance, violent resistance."[32] This sentiment is caught up by Jean-Paul Sartre in the preface to Fanon's book: ". . . this irrepressible violence is neither sound nor fury, nor the resurrection of savage instincts, nor even the effect of resentment; it is man recreating himself."[33]

Persons who become involved in planned violence by participation in guerrilla activity, are decisively cut off from the dominant society, and thus their loyalty to the violent group is more nearly assured. They are also cut off from part of themselves—from that part that recognizes a shared humanity or shared values and goals with those being attacked. Violence may function to repress feelings of ambivalence.

The critical question concerns the total, long-run consequences of violence (a question we shall raise in the final chapter); but here we see it as one of the responses to serious disprivilege. We are inclined to agree with Bertrand Russell, in his attack on the approach of D. H. Lawrence, similar to that of the Sartre quote, that such "thinking with the blood . . . led straight to Auschwitz."[34] Nazism also appealed, as Oppenheimer has observed, to the unity of the folk and the recovery of self-confidence through violence. The critical question remains: At what cost?

3. Some counterassertion or aggression is more appropriately seen as against the whole status system than against specific individuals or situations. Efforts on the part of a member of a minority group to climb the economic ladder, and to demonstrate that climb by purchases appropriate to his new status, are usually interpreted as aggression by the dominant group. For a Negro of moderate income to drive a high-priced automobile is, in effect, to say: This is my mark of equality. He attacks the status pattern not only by economic advance but by exaggerating his economic advance. (This is, of course, a phenomenon found widely among majority-group members as well. As *The New Yorker* would have Mrs. Smith say to Mrs. Jones: "You mean to say that all the while we have been trying to keep up with you, you have been trying to keep up with us?")

Ostentation is not to be interpreted solely as a means of aggression against a confining definition of economic "place." In part it is a mode of self-expression that may become exaggerated under conditions which prevent other modes of self-expression from being used. Thus it is likely to be exaggerated among minority-group members who have made some advancement, particularly in income, but whose activities are blocked from many channels. It should also be noted that

[30] See Terry Ann Knopf, "Sniping—A New Pattern of Violence?," *Transaction*, July–Aug., 1969, pp. 22–29.

[31] Frantz Fanon, *The Wretched of the Earth*, Grove Press, 1963, p. 73. For biographies that give insight into Fanon's thought, see Peter Geismar, *Fanon*, Dial Press, 1971; and David Caute, *Frantz Fanon*, Viking, 1971.

[32] *The New York Times*, Aug. 23, 1970, p. 5.

[33] Jean-Paul Sartre in Fanon, *op. cit.*, p. 21.

[34] Quoted by Oppenheimer, *op. cit.*, p. 60.

the dominant group's interpretation of efforts to climb the economic and occupational ladder as aggression may be reason to hide and disguise, not display, any success in this regard, in order to avoid retaliation from the majority.

4. Members of a minority group can express their hostility by withdrawing trade from the businesses of the dominant group, or from those individuals in the group who show the most prejudice and discrimination. This is partly an avoidance device, as we have seen, but it is also a sign of aggression. Where there is legal protection, this way of expressing resentment may take the form of organized boycotts, of "don't buy where you can't work" movements.[35] The device is effective only where the minority group has substantial purchasing power and is important to the success of specific individuals in the dominant group. That this is not a new tactic is shown by the following statement:

In St. Louis, for example, when a white-owned chain store which did business almost exclusively with Negroes refused to employ Negro help, the local Urban League organized a boycott. Later, this campaign extended to the employment of Negroes in trucking companies and bakeries, and to motion-picture operators in houses that catered to Negroes. A Negro Housewives' League was formed by the Pittsburgh *Courier* to demonstrate the buying power of Negro customers to white advertisers. When one large dairy company, which served Negroes, refused to hire them, the Housewives' League launched a boycott that caused the company's sales to drop alarmingly.[36]

In some minority-majority situations, the modes of wage payment, of purchasing, and of finding housing are so much under the control of the dominant group that any expression of resentment by members of the minority at the kind of treatment they receive can be made only at the risk of loss of wages or of poorer shopping and housing conditions. This is true, for example, in plantation settings. With the development of an urban economy, however, with its regular wage payments and increased purchasing power, the situation changes. The boycott becomes a powerful weapon. We shall comment on its use in the desegregation process in Chapter 22.

5. A form of aggression often used by even the most powerless member of an oppressed group is to work slowly or to leave a job entirely if the treatment is too offensive. Inefficient, lazy—and therefore costly—work is a source of a great deal of complaint from members of the dominant group. They usually assume it to be a proof of inferiority, failing to see that, whether by conscious intent or by lack of motivation, it is an expression of hostility and primarily a result of a low ceiling on opportunities. Irresponsible or awkward work is a natural personality consequence of the situation. A Negro field hand or unskilled factory worker or janitor may not dare to stop work entirely, but he can be careless with the white man's time and goods. The situation is somewhat similar to the low efficiency and low motivation often characteristic of "buck privates" in the Army. They too are caught in a status that many of them resent; they feel hostility that cannot be expressed openly against those who give them orders; their response is to "soldier" on the job, to do only what they are told to do, and that only to the barest minimum.[37] The same principle applies, in fact, to any work situation in which lack of confidence in the employers and lack of hope for advancement lead to low morale.

[35] The opposite side of the coin says "support the businesses of fellow Blacks." For a variety of documents related to this issue, see John H. Bracey, Jr., August Meier, and Elliott Rudwick (eds.), *Black Nationalism in America*, pp. 235–245, 371–386, and 486–503.

[36] Roi Ottley, *New World A-Coming*, Houghton Mifflin, 1943, pp. 113–114.

[37] The authors of *The American Soldier* found that the Army situation produced among white soldiers many of the same protests that Negroes had long used in reference to their treatment. "When white soldiers wrote about authoritarian practices in the Army, 'They treat us like dogs,' or 'This is supposed to be a democracy,' or 'Why don't they treat us like men?' the phrases have a familiar ring to those acquainted with Negro protests." See Samuel Stouffer, Edward Suchman, Leland DeVinney, Shirley Star, and Robin Williams, Jr., *The American Soldier: Adjustment During Army Life*, Princeton, 1949, pp. 502–503.

High labor turnover can be a similar expression of resentment. It may not be an effective method of hostility, but it brings some satisfaction as a sign of independence. In many situations the unreliability of servants is a source of much complaint but is little understood as an expression of aggression against inferior status. The cook who leaves her job without warning must look upon her action as a form of aggression, and she therefore fears to reveal her intention in advance. By leaving an unpleasant situation she says, "I may be inferior and you may have many advantages over me, but at least you do not own my body."[38]

6. Aggression may be expressed under some circumstances by the withdrawal of the forms of deference and etiquette, by the loss of earlier feelings of affection, and the development of feelings of distrust and suspicion. In societies where status lines are sharply drawn, violation of prescribed patterns of etiquette are quickly interpreted as aggressive acts. In the South, until recently, variation from established forms of deference—recognized as attacks on the system—were often severely punished. Most Negroes disguised their feelings of distrust and resentment and overtly accepted the required forms.[39] Overt acceptance, however, may cover—or indeed fail to cover—resistance to the system. Many Negroes have learned the skillful use of etiquette, allaying any fears on the part of the white man that he doesn't accept the status patterns, to wring some small advantage from a difficult situation.

When stable patterns of dominance and submission break down, familiar deference forms quickly change, because they so obviously represent the old order. There may, indeed, be symbolic reversal: a civil word from adolescent to parent or Black to White may seem to smack too much of former inferiority. Johnson cites the case of an accomplished Negro woman lawyer in Chicago:

On one occasion she went to shop in a fashionable district. First, the elevator girl refused to take her upstairs, and then after she got upstairs nobody waited on her. When a man finally came to order her out, the lawyer attacked him verbally with great violence. She reported the story in part:

"I really shouted then. I was pointing my finger in his face and I said, 'If you touch me again (the man had touched her hand while she rang for the elevator), even my little finger, I'll have you arrested, and I've practiced in the courts long enough to have just enough influence to do it. Why,' I said, 'I kick your kind around every day in court. You've been used to Negroes who tuck their heads and run when you scowl. Well, let me tell you, this is a new kind of Negro and there are plenty more like me, so you'd better watch out. If I were a man I'd knock you down.' "[40]

Persons of different temperament, or in different areas, who have the same feelings of hostility that this woman had may feel the need to inhibit their direct expression. We shall seriously misunderstand them, however, if we fail to see that these feelings will strongly affect their behavior in other ways.

7. Aggressive feelings may be embodied in art. Whether art can and should be used for "political" purposes and remain art is, of course, a long-standing issue. We think it can be, provided something of the situation of common humanity, and not of one group alone, is involved, and provided the "politics" is indirect, latent, and secondary to the artistic statement. These rather stern criteria may leave open whether various forms of minority-group expression are art, but that makes them none the less important.[41]

Among the arts, literature is undoubtedly the most clearly involved in expressing the protest theme. Much more reading in of the presumed message is needed, for example, in music.[42] In many settings, literature has

---

[38] John Dollard, *Caste and Class in a Southern Town*, Yale, 1937, p. 301.

[39] *Ibid.*, pp. 301–307; and Bertram Doyle, *The Etiquette of Race Relations in the South*, Univ. of Chicago Press, 1937.

[40] Johnson, *op. cit.*, p. 311. It is instructive to note, at a time when we may exaggerate the recency of the Negro protest movement, that Johnson reported such incidents as this over 30 years ago.

[41] We will develop the theme of art and minority-majority relations more fully in Chapter 20.

[42] See Frank Kofsky, *Black Nationalism in Music*, Pathfinder Press, 1970.

been an articulate voice for the deep-seated but unexpressed hostilities of large numbers of people. This may take the form of folk tales and myths or of written literature. Among the American Indians, for example, many of the original myths have gradually taken on a content that helps them express their resentment against the white conquerors, giving support to Malinowski's remark: ". . . Myth . . . is not an idle rhapsody, not an aimless outpouring of vain imaginings, but a hard-working, extremely important cultural force."[43]

Written literature may contain a much more explicit aggressive theme in protest against prejudice and discrimination. Claude McKay wrote:

If we must die, let it not be like hogs
Hunted and penned in an inglorious spot
While round us bark the mad and hungry dogs,
Making their mock at our accursed lot.
If we must die, Oh let us nobly die,
So that our precious blood may not be shed

In vain; then even the monsters we defy
Shall be constrained to honor us though dead!

Oh, kinsmen! we must meet the common foe!
Though far outnumbered let us show us brave,
And for their thousand blows deal one
      death-blow!
What though before us lies the open grave?
Like men we'll face the murderous cowardly
      pack
Pressed to the wall, dying, but fighting back![44]

Autobiographies and books of personal essays are a rich source of guidance to the person seeking to understand minority experience from "the other side." They do not stand as representative, in any sampling sense, any more than autobiographies of majority-group members are representative. On the current scene, the authors are articulate, angry, and self-confident, doubtless beyond the usual range. Yet several autobiographies have become significant documents of the time, throwing experiences that have been widely shared onto a large screen, bringing a deep sense of personal recognition to minority-group readers, who see slices of their own lives made vivid. Majority-group readers may experience a jolt to the imagination that helps them to grasp something of the meaning of life to the minority, and also, if they are fortunate, gain insight into their own experience. We define these autobiographies too narrowly by noting them here as one expression of aggression against discrimination, but that is clearly one of their dimensions.[45]

8. An almost universal way of expressing aggression is humor. Members of a dominant group are sometimes surprised to learn that their stereotyped jokes about minority-group members are matched in number and barbed sharpness by the jokes which the "inferior" people tell about them.

That humor is found in most conflict situations gives point to Myrdal's remark that it is a mode of adjustment.[46] It may be used as a means of social control, to prevent individuals from following a disapproved course of action or to stop the action. It may, however, have no effect on the objective situation but serve rather to make one's own role in that situation seem more desirable, or to make the whole situation seem less important—and therefore one's own disadvantaged role of less consequence. Burma cites a number of authors who hold that the conflict element is essential to humor: "Jowett has said that every amusing story must of necessity be unkind, untrue, or immoral. Thomas Hobbes believed that humor arises from a conception of superiority in ourselves by comparison with the inferiority of others. Crothers has called it the 'frank enjoyment of the imperfect,' and more recently James L. Ford has said that humor 'is founded on the deathless principle of seeing someone

---

[43] Bronislaw Malinowski, *Myth in Primitive Psychology*, Norton, 1926, p. 12.

[44] Reprinted from *Selected Poems of Claude McKay* by Claude McKay through permission of Twayne Publishers, Inc., copyright 1953.

[45] See Richard Wright, *Black Boy*, Harper & Row, 1937, which has become a classic; Malcolm X, *The Autobiography of Malcolm X*, Grove Press, 1966, even more important as a document of the times; Claude Brown, *Manchild in the Promised Land*, New American Library, 1965; Eldridge Cleaver, *Soul on Ice*, Dell, 1968; Julius Lester, *Search for the New Land*, Dial Press, 1969.

[46] Gunnar Myrdal, *An American Dilemma*, Harper & Row, 1944, pp. 38–39.

get the worst of it.' "[47] Often, in fact, "humor and sorrow are allies," as Louis Lomax puts it. Out of many tragic situations comes "gallows humor" that may help to make a vastly difficult situation more bearable. Some unhappy East Germans, it is reported, have invented a new compass: "If you're lost in the woods without a compass on a dark and foggy night, just stretch out your left arm and slowly turn in a circle. When your wristwatch is snatched off your arm, that's East."[48]

Despite the numerous insightful interpretations, it is difficult to speak with confidence about the causes and the consequences of humor. Little is known about who invents humor, who communicates it to what audiences.[49] There is clearly an in-group dimension, involving morale and social control, but also expressing, and seeking to handle, self-hatred. More obviously there is an out-group dimension, involving both an effort at accommodation and conflict.[50]

In the late 1950s, Middleton and Moland found that Negro students told over four times as many anti-Negro as anti-White jokes—perhaps expressing social distance from lower-class Negroes and indicating student use of a white reference group. Were a similar study made today, the results might be quite different, for humor is a flexible instrument of adjustment that adapts quickly to the immediate situation.[51]

Humor used for internal social control is often designed to pull a member down to size, to remind him of his common plight:

A Jewish man who had been successful financially attempts to cement his status improvement by purchasing a yacht. In order to impress his parents with their son's success, he invited them aboard for a cruise one day. He meets them at the dock resplendent in his new gold-braided yachting cap, blue jacket with white pearl buttons and white duck trousers. His father carefully studies the son and asks, "Look, son, by your papa you're a captain, and by your mama you're a captain, but by the captains are you a captain?"[52]

When status patterns are under sharp attack, humor is part of the arsenal. Godfrey Cambridge, for example, tells how he handles a major problem for Blacks—getting a taxi in New York. One of his methods is the "try and look innocent method": "I stand there with a big broad smile on my face. I remove my sunglasses so no one thinks I'm a drug addict. I try to show them I'm a white Negro, carrying my attache case. I hail them with my attache case. They think I'm an executive."[53]

Or Dick Gregory says: "There's only one difference between the North and the South. In the South, they don't care how close I get, as long as I don't get too big. In the North, they don't care how big I get, as long as I don't get too close."[54]

Humor may be used to blur a line of distinction, to expose our friendly as well as our unfriendly rigidities: "High noon in New York, August: The crowded bus jogged to a stop at Fourteenth Street. All the passengers got off, except two women who had been sharing a seat—one Negro, the other white. Both were stout. *If I move to another seat,* the white woman thought, *this Negro will think I don't want to sit by her.* Two stops later the Negro looked at her seatmate and said: 'Honey, there's plenty room on this bus; why for then are you crowding me?'"[55]

Some jokes require simply the addition of color to the persons involved to express race conflict: ". . . When a *colored* boy could not do his geometry, his *white* teacher says he should be ashamed, for when George Washington was his age he was a surveyor.

[47] John H. Burma, "Humor as a Technique in Race Conflict," *ASR*, Dec., 1946, p. 710.

[48] Edward Shields, *Cleveland Press*, Aug. 1, 1963.

[49] See Milton L. Barron, "A Content Analysis of Intergroup Humor," *ASR*, Feb., 1950, pp. 88–94.

[50] See Irwin D. Rinder, "A Note on Humor as an Index of Minority Group Morale," *Phylon*, Summer, 1965, pp. 117–121.

[51] Russell Middleton and John Moland, "Humor in Negro and White Subcultures: A Study of Jokes among University Students," *ASR*, Feb., 1959, pp. 61–69.

[52] Rinder, *op. cit.*, p. 119.

[53] Quoted by Langston Hughes, *The Book of Negro Humor*, Dodd, Mead, 1965.

[54] See Nancy L. Arnez and Clara B. Anthony, "Contemporary Negro Humor as Social Satire," *Phylon*, Winter, 1968, p. 341.

[55] Louis Lomax, "The American Negro's New Comedy Act," *Harper's Magazine*, June, 1961, p. 41.

To which the Negro youth replies, 'Yes, and when he was your age he was President.' "[56] A joke may cut two ways, revealing both the Negro's plight and the white man's meanness or susceptibility to flattery: "A Negro drives through a red light in a Mississippi town. The sheriff yells, 'Hey, boy, where you think you going?' The Negro thinks fast and answers: 'Well, boss, when I see that green light come on an' all them white folks' cars goin' through, I says to myself, "That's the white folks' light!" So I don' move. Then when that ol' red light comes on, I jus' steps on the gas. I says, "That mus' be us niggers' light!"' The sheriff replies, 'You're a good boy, Sam, but next time you kin go on the white folks' light.' "[57] Negroes have jokes that help them to laugh at Jim Crow incidents or the commands of Whites. Two Negro maids are comparing notes: "At my place I have a terrible time; all day it's 'Yes, Ma'am,' 'Yes, Ma'am,' 'Yes, Ma'am.'" "Me, too," says the other, "but with me it's 'No, Sir,' 'No, Sir,' 'No, Sir.'"[58]

Most people have experienced the feelings of solidarity, the release of tension, and the tightening of social control that come from humor. We are beginning to get some experimental evidence to support personal insights and clinical observations. Freud's "catharsis" theory, for example, is given some support by an experimental study of the effects of hostile humor on tension. Negro respondents heard either a recording designed to mobilize aggressive impulses toward segregationists or a control recording of music. Then they heard Negro performers deliver hostile, antisegregationist humor, neutral humor, or a benign speech. For those subjects who were moderately aroused and involved by the stimulus, both the hostile and the neutral humor reduced aggression and tension, as measured by a mood check list. For those highly aroused, the hostile humor was particularly aggression reducing, and only the hostile humor reduced tension.[59]

Displaced Aggression

In Chapter 6 we discussed some of the attitudes that members of minority groups develop with regard to their fellow group members. We also noted that much of the aggression that might be expected to be directed against the dominant group is redirected, instead, against one's fellows or other substitute targets. These two ideas need now to be combined briefly in order to observe the hostility and tensions that characterize the interaction *within* a minority group. Two cautions are necessary at this point. Along with the forces making for conflict within these groups there are, as we have seen, a number of other forces that encourage cohesion and group solidarity, the balance varying with many factors. Secondly, it should not be supposed that all the aggression within a minority group is displaced from the dominant group, which is the real target and cause of the hostility. Some of it is simply a product of the normal interaction *within* the group, the prejudice of the majority being, at most, an indirect factor.

Despite these qualifications, it seems apparent that some of the violence and hostility that, for example, Negroes show toward other Negroes is to be explained by displaced aggression and is properly included in this discussion of the aggressive response to prejudice and discrimination. Not knowing the true source of one's difficulties, or being unable to attack what one believes is the true source, one turns upon an easily accessible and relatively powerless fellow group member. This person then receives not only the hostility that his own acts might have caused, but all the pent-up and blocked hostility that the accumulated experiences with the dominant group have caused. A higher level of conflict within a minority group is to be seen, then, not as a sign of a different nature, but as a product of prejudice.

Having discussed the many ways in which Blacks in the United States express direct

[56] Burma, *op. cit.*, p. 711.

[57] St. Clair Drake and Horace Cayton, *Black Metropolis*, Harcourt, Brace Jovanovich, 1945, p. 723.

[58] Burma, *op. cit.*, p. 712.

[59] See David L. Singer, "Aggression Arousal, Hostile Humor, Catharsis," *JPSP*, Monograph Supplement, Jan., 1968, pp. 1–14; and see the similar findings of Earl S. Dworkin and Jay S. Efran, "The Angered: Their Susceptibility to Varieties of Humor," *JPSP*, June, 1967, pp. 233–236.

aggression, we do not want to exaggerate the extent to which aggression is displaced. By many important indexes, however, it seems clear that most hostility is expressed toward substitute targets near at hand—and less able to retaliate—than against a member of the dominant group. It is critical to note that most of the victims of Negro murderers probably 90 percent or more) are Negroes (and that Whites kill Whites).[60]

The displacement may be not only toward one's immediate associates but also toward other minorities with whom one happens to be in contact. (Again, a feeling of solidarity *with* other minorities may also be a product of prejudice.) Negroes are sometimes susceptible, as we have seen, to anti-Semitism, beyond their hostility to other Whites. Mexicans in the United States often show a strong anti-Negro feeling, partly in an effort to dissociate themselves, in their own minds and in the minds of the dominant Whites, from identification with Negroes and partly as a form of displaced aggression. The hostility may be between subgroups of a minority— between Negroes from the West Indies and those born in the United States, between European and "Oriental" Jews.

Not all of the tendencies toward aggression —direct and displaced—of minority-group members are to be explained, of course, by prejudice and discrimination. Hostile feelings and impulses are part of the equipment of all human beings because of the gap between what they want and what they attain. Physical laws of the universe, social rules, competing desires all combine to frustrate, to some degree, even the best-satisfied individual. It is not necessarily true that a person of inferior status will have more aggressive tendencies than the one who is dominant over him, because there are so many sources of aggression, prejudice being only one. Moreover, a member of a minority group may make an avoidance or an acceptance adjustment in-

stead. On the other hand, the tendencies for aggression in the minority-group member may be stronger than can be explained by the prejudice he has experienced. Personal maladjustment or failures from other causes may be blamed on discrimination. A Negro, for example, may be sensitive not only to real racial barriers but to imagined ones, every act of a white person being interpreted in racial terms, every criticism being an expression of prejudice, any failure to advance a sign of a categorical barrier. If such a person were white, he would find some other reason than race prejudice to explain his failure.

Variables Affecting Types and Extent of Aggression

In the last several pages we have seen that minority-group members can express their hostility toward the dominant group in a number of ways. It is important not to mistake the absence of overt aggression for a lack of feelings of hostility or for a lack of effects. If these effects are covert or heavily disguised, if they are obscured by external gestures of acceptance of an inferior status, they are nevertheless exceedingly important in the analysis of the personality tendencies of minority-group members. The powerful underlying feelings may be revealed overtly only in unusual circumstances—when anger overcomes fear, or a mob situation reduces the usual inhibitions—but the feelings are there at all times.

There are important class, locality, and other group differences in expressing aggression, because of different personality tendencies, different traditional modes of expression of a particular minority group, different attitudes and culture patterns in the dominant group, different chances of success, and the chance factors of a specific situation.[61] "The weapons employed by lower-class Negroes in expressing hostility covertly may

[60] Pettigrew and Spier, *op. cit.*, p. 621. See also Earl Moses, "Differentials in Crime Rates between Negroes and Whites," in Marvin Wolfgang, Leonard Savitz, and Norman Johnston (eds.), *The Sociology of Crime and Delinquency*, Wiley, 1962, chap. 21; and Lee N. Robins, "Negro Homicide Victims—Who Will They Be?" *Trans-Action*, June, 1968, pp. 15–19.

[61] Howard Schuman and Barry Gruenberg have recently shown that various aspects of the city of residence shaped racial attitudes. See "The Impact of City of Racial Attitudes," *AJS*, Sept., 1970, pp. 213–261.

take the form of petty sabotage, unexplained quitting of jobs, gossip, pseudo-ignorant malingering. Middle-class Negroes are in a better position to use the economic weapon of controlled purchasing power. Upper-class Negroes may use this also, but in addition they find it effective to use the method of indirect attack on the offending institutions by arousing outside public opinion."[62]

Because opportunities for successful direct aggression are much more limited for low-status members of a minority group than for those of middle or upper status, they are more likely to employ displaced aggression to express their pent-up hostility against fellow group members. They less often see their problems as a result of a generalized prejudice and are therefore more likely to attack the persons immediately around them. Physical violence has a more important place in the culture of lower classes, so that both direct and displaced aggression will take this form for low-status persons more often. Their feelings of hostility may also be more intense. "Because of the large amount of family disorganization among lower-class Negroes, the child fails to enjoy the security, affectional as well as economic, which children in the middle and upper class enjoy. The child not only sees violence, but is also the object of the violent behavior of his parents."[63]

There are important regional differences in the types and extent of aggression, because of class differences, different chances of success, and different personality tendencies that result from varying processes of socialization. The regional contrast is less vivid than it used to be, for today a *national* movement for civil and human rights binds the regions together. Urbanization in the South and the extensive migration of Negroes to the North and West have reduced the differences among the regions; both the cooperation and the competition among civil rights groups have tended to give them national perspectives. Thirty years ago Frazier wrote: "The border Negro struggles with rage where the

southern Negro suffers from fear. The unconstructive wish fulfilling fantasies that are evoked by these states are respectively malevolent and escapist."[64] This insightful comparison may still be accurate to some degree; but it is also clear that fear and escapism have been much diminished in the South; and oppositely, escapism of many varieties is found wherever human beings with few resources are confronted by enormous obstacles.

Altogether, it is important to see the wide variety of ways aggressive feelings may be expressed and to keep carefully in mind the many influences which affect the extent and types of aggressive response to prejudice and discrimination.

ACCEPTANCE OF STATUS AS A FORM OF ADJUSTMENT

Contemporary sociology and cultural anthropology have shown that people can learn to adjust to, and even accept, extremely diverse circumstances that seem strange, painful, or evil to those who have received different training. Standards of value by which the desirability of a given status is judged, as well as the status itself, are a product of society. A whole group may accept what to others seems to be an inferior role, because it seems perfectly normal to them; it is taken for granted. Only contact with other standards, the acquisition of levels of aspiration that are blocked in the old status, may destroy acceptance of that status.

Types of Acceptance

1. Whole-hearted. Under some circumstances members of a minority may fairly whole-heartedly accept an inferior position. However, since unwillingness to accept one's status fully is one of the defining characteristics of a minority, as contrasted with a caste, "whole-hearted acceptance" is always qualified. This pattern of adjustment was fairly common, several decades ago, among

[62] Johnson, *op. cit.*, p. 302.

[63] E. Franklin Frazier, *Negro Youth at the Cross-ways*, ACE, p. 52.

[64] *Ibid.*, p. 232.

American Negroes but is now far less common.

2. Specific. Far more common than this acceptance of the whole status pattern is acceptance of some specific situation or some phase of a relationship that implies inferiority, either out of belief or out of desire to escape some unwanted aspect of the relationship. In the latter case, acceptance borders closely on avoidance.

3. Unconscious. There is also a measure of acceptance in the attitude toward oneself and one's group that we have discussed in the preceding chapter. Even those members of a minority group who have come in closest contact with the dominant society, and thus are least willing to accept a categorical position of inferiority, often acquire, by that very contact, attitudes toward themselves and their group that characterize the majority. Thus we find feelings of inferiority and even of self-hatred, often deeply unconscious or disguised by assertions to the contrary, in many members of minority groups who have come to see themselves from the point of view of the majority.

It is clearly necessary to distinguish carefully among these three varieties of acceptance, for they have very different consequences. Nearly complete acceptance is closely correlated with resignation and passivity. It becomes the dominant factor in the life of the individual who follows this pattern. Acceptance of some specific situation that requires an inferior role is far more likely to be a conscious or even a rational decision. It tells little about the total personality of the individual, for were he faced by a different situation he would make another mode of adjustment. Members of the dominant group may well misinterpret this kind of acceptance, mistaking it for passivity and a *general* acceptance. The unconscious adoption of feelings of inferiority and self-hatred produces ambivalence and tension in the individual that are important in his behavior. It may arouse an extraordinary amount of striving and even of aggressiveness, in order to overcome the feelings of inferiority. It may, however, be related to a disorganizing ambivalence, a tendency that is often found

among "marginal men." Stonequist refers to the dual self-consciousness and identification of the marginal man, the fluctuating and contradictory opinions, the irrational, moody, and "temperamental" behavior, the "inferiority complexes" accompanied, in overcompensation, by "superiority complexes."[65] Such personality tendencies may come from an unconscious acceptance of inferiority alongside contrary feelings and hopes of equality.

The whole-hearted acceptance of inferiority is characteristically a product of isolation—physical and/or social. There are few points of contact between the lower-class rural Negro and the white social world, for example, so that the segregation and discrimination involved are often not questioned.

Acceptance may be based on a role that, despite the inferiority implied, brings security and a reflected glory. A Negro servant may feel rewarded by the friendly atmosphere, by the economic and personal security his job brings him, and by a sense of pride when appreciation is shown for his work. He can, in addition, have a feeling of identification with his employers, thus sharing their prestige and position. Acceptance may be based on a genuine belief in the inferiority of one's own group—a result of accepting the standards of the dominant group.

The number of persons in the United States and, one may say with confidence, around the world who are willing to accept whole-heartedly an inferior status is declining sharply. The picture of the "folk Negro" is important, not so much because it is a common type as because it is an important part of the background out of which the other three types of acceptance are emerging. Belief in inferiority may be gone, but one may still accept his status to hold a job, to gain a favor, or simply to avoid trouble.

4. Qualified. At the beginning of the chapter we noted a reformist or conciliatory response to discrimination. This does not fit any of the three major types closely, for it

[65] Everett V. Stonequist, *The Marginal Man*, Scribner, 1937, pp. 144–156.

shares elements of each. Perhaps it is best understood, nevertheless, as a qualified form of acceptance—not acceptance of one's own status, but of the system as capable of reform. This shades off toward aggressive actions, but remains different because of the stronger hopes, the greater readiness to trust members of the dominant group, and feelings that life is satisfying. In February, 1965, Gallup asked a random sample of Whites and Nonwhites, "In general, when you look forward to the coming year, that is, the next twelve months, would you say you are very optimistic, fairly optimistic, or not so optimistic? Forty-seven percent of the Nonwhites answered "fairly optimistic," and 21 percent "very optimistic," compared with percentages of 47 and 27 for the Whites.[66]

In December, 1967, Negro respondents to a Roper poll divided equally, 40 percent saying "happier" and 40 percent saying "less happy" when asked to compare Americans with a generation ago. Twenty-three percent of white respondents said happier and 45 percent said less happy.[67]

Whatever the ratio of any given group that might be thus classified, we think it wise to have, as one analytic category, "qualified acceptance," to refer to those whose dominant response is one of relatively hopeful belief that the system they live in is capable of improvement.

VARIABLES AFFECTING TYPES AND EXTENT OF ACCEPTANCE

In acceptance, as in avoidance and aggression, one cannot speak of the reaction of "the" Negro, or "the" Mexican-American, or "the" Indian. In each instance there are variations among classes, age groups, regions, and many other types of groups. There are also individual variations that affect the nature of the response. We cannot discuss all the possible variables but for illustrative purposes will refer to the differences in amount of acceptance of status found among Negroes of different ages.

A generation ago, Powdermaker found that older Negroes were much more likely to express accommodative responses and even to accept the white man's ideas of their appropriate status. Middle-aged Negroes did not, typically, agree with these ideas, but often acted as though they did—to avoid trouble. And younger people neither agreed with the ideas nor acted out accommodative behavior.[68] This tendency for older persons to be more likely to accept their situation and for younger persons to oppose it is still found, although the whole curve has shifted to lower levels of acceptance.[69]

Two qualifications are necessary, however, to avoid misinterpreting this correlation. The studies cited refer largely to the more visible forms of acceptance, types one and two in our commentary above. Older and younger persons may not be so different in the tendencies toward unconscious acceptance—a product of self-feelings drilled into them by the power of the dominant community. Such acceptance does not result in a lack of protests. The ambivalence with which it is associated, however, affects the nature of the protests, making them more emotional and probably less effective.

It is necessary to qualify, secondly, by noting that the influence of age on types and levels of acceptance is highly complicated by other variables. House and Fischer found, for example, that when they specified the relationship of age and militancy by the level of authoritarian tendencies, younger persons of low authoritarianism were less militant than were older persons of low authoritarianism, perhaps because of the greater amount of integration of the young. Among those with medium and high authoritarian scores,

[66] Hazel Erskine, "The Polls: Negro Philosophies of Life," *POQ*, Spring, 1969, p. 150.

[67] *Ibid.*, p. 152. Various polls have also found that more Negroes believe people "more concerned" and "more considerate," compared with a generation ago, than Whites who believe these things.

[68] Hortense Powdermaker, *After Freedom: A Cultural Study in the Deep South*, Viking, 1939, pp. 325–333.

[69] See Brunswick, *op. cit.*; and Marx, *op. cit.*, pp. 53–54, 185–186.

on the other hand, younger persons were more militant.[70]

Thus age itself is probably not the important variable. It happens simply to be correlated with education, degree of urbanness, knowledge of "the American dream," and availability of contact with social movements and ideas that expose and oppose the old status patterns.

It is well to recall again that seldom will a response be purely of an acceptance, reformist, aggressive, or avoidance variety. In studying acceptance one must particularly avoid mistaking surface accommodation for a thoroughgoing willingness to stay in one's "place." As Elkins reminds us, accommodation is morally and psychologically a very complex phenomenon, involving a principle of interpersonal relations that operates in many settings. The admixture of types of response is shown in

. . . the principle of how the powerless can manipulate the powerful through aggressive stupidity, literal-mindedness, servile fawning, and irresponsibility. In this sense the immovably stupid 'Good Soldier Schweik' and the fawning Negro in Richard Wright's *Black Boy* who allowed the white man to kick him for a quarter partake of the same tradition. Each has a technique whereby he can in a real sense exploit his powerful superiors, feel contempt for them, and suffer in the process no great damage to his own pride. Jewish lore, as is well known, teems with this sort of thing. There was much of it also in the traditional relationships between peasants and nobles in central Europe.[71]

Thus overt acceptance may hide opposition. It is well to note, moreover, the opposite situation: Overt expressions of hostility and aggression may hide a deep-seated sense of inferiority and acceptance of inferior status. It is probably true that most southern Negroes have much stronger feelings of aggression than their accommodating behavior indicates; and northern Negroes have more unconscious feelings of acceptance ("self-hatred") than their avoidance or aggressive behavior indicates.

ORGANIZED PROTESTS AND SOCIAL MOVEMENTS AMONG MINORITY GROUPS

One of the consequences of prejudice and discrimination for minority groups is the development of a wide variety of social movements and organized group pressures to escape from, or to improve, their status. These range from highly emotional religious or nationalistic mass movements to the carefully planned use of legal, political, and economic weapons. They stem from the individual personality tendencies we have discussed above; but as these tendencies come to focus in organized groups and mass movements, they take on an analytically distinct new element—that of collective behavior. They cannot be understood simply by studying the needs and tendencies of isolated individuals because the *interactional* aspects of group phenomena require additional analysis.

We shall not at this point make a detailed study of such group effects, for they will be involved in a number of places in the analysis of social structure, and those that are especially concerned with social change will be discussed in Part III. Here, however, a brief statement of the general principles underlying such groups is necessary to relate them to the theme of this chapter.

Some of the social movements among minority groups are primarily attempts to escape or avoid the difficulties of their status; some are primarily aggressive protests against their lot; some, which on the surface may seem to be escape devices, are indirectly attacks upon the dominant group. Insofar as it becomes concentrated in protest organizations, the sense of group solidarity tends to lead to attacks on the distribution of power and prestige. All over the world in the twentieth century, minority groups have organized for more effective

---

[70] James S. House and Robert D. Fischer, "Authoritarianism, Age and Black Militancy," *Sociometry*, June, 1971, pp. 174–197.

[71] Stanley Elkins, *Slavery: A Problem in American Institutional and Intellectual Life*, Univ. of Chicago Press, 1959, pp. 132–133.

opposition to their status. The group factor has focused their individual feelings of frustration, has given them some measure of common objectives, has *intensified*, by the reciprocal exchange involved, their antagonism to specific situations. The Catholics in Northern Ireland angrily demand political and economic equality. Basques struggle to maintain their uniqueness in Spain. Bengalis in what was formerly East Pakistan vehemently protested against domination by Punjabis from West Pakistan. In the United States, Chicanos, Indians, Blacks, and other groups found new organizations and strengthen old ones, in a wide variety of protest and/or escape activities—religious, political, and economic.

In later chapters, we shall study a number of these organizations. One can understand them only by analyzing the personality tendencies of the individuals involved and by studying the emergent new forces that result from more or less formalized group structure. The resentment of inequality by individual Negroes is one thing; the same resentment focused through the organized legal activity of the NAACP or, in a different vein, the Black Panthers, is another; and both need analysis.

Studies of group patterns among Americans have almost universally agreed that participation increases with social status. Except for church and to some degree labor union membership, lower-class persons are much more likely to interact within a narrow circle of family, friends, and neighbors than in organized groups. It has generally been believed that Negroes share this pattern, except that semiorganized clubs and cliques to some degree take the place of kinship associations. Recent evidence, however, reveals a different pattern. Babchuk and Thompson found in one city that if the bowling clubs and birthday clubs and Saturday Nighters societies were included, Negroes had a high rate of participation in voluntary associations.[72] The groups represented are primarily recreational and ex-

pressive groups that furnish an opportunity for status recognition, leadership, and a release from the restrictions of the larger society.

Orum found that the relationship between social class and organizational membership was much less strong among Negroes than it was among Whites. Lower-class Negroes were more likely to belong to organizations than their white counterparts, while the relationship was reversed in the upper class. He also found that Negroes were more likely to participate actively.[73] This latter finding is reenforced by Olsen who found, when class and age were controlled, that Blacks were more active than Whites in every type of activity investigated. He postulates that the difference reflects an "ethnic community" influence among Negroes—a sense of sharing that encouraged participation. This interpretation is supported by his finding that those Blacks who identify with their group are more active than the nonidentifiers.[74]

Membership in the nationally prominent protest organizations is less common—probably fewer than one Negro in ten being formally affiliated. The local associations are important, however, because of the opportunity they furnish for leadership experience and because they are a link in the chain of public opinion on which the national organizations depend.

Minority-Group Leadership. The balance of forces leading toward avoidance, acceptance, conciliation, or aggression is clearly shown in the kinds of leaders who come to the fore. Beginning, perhaps, during World War II and becoming steadily more powerful, the United States has witnessed a movement that pushed aside the moderate, accommodating, class-oriented leader in favor of the assertive, impatient, mass-oriented leader. Following Thompson we can define the former as a person primarily interested in raising the cultural level of minority-group members and winning better conditions by

---

[72] Nicholas Babchuk and Ralph Thompson, "The Voluntary Associations of Negroes," *ASR*, Oct., 1962, pp. 647–655.

[73] Anthony Orum, "A Reappraisal of the Social and Political Participation of Negroes, *AJS*, July, 1966, pp. 32–46.

[74] Marvin Olsen, "Social and Political Participation of Blacks," *ASR*, Aug., 1970, pp. 682–697.

negotiation and persuasion. The mass-oriented leader works toward the removal of police brutality, unemployment, voting discriminations, and other disprivileges. He pursues these goals more by arousing mass support for demonstrations, boycotts, and picketing than by conversations on interracial committees.[75]

By the late 1960s, political activity was occupying a more important place in protest movements. Scores of Mexican-American and black city councilmen and state legislators had been elected. The mayors of several large cities were black. In 1970, the first Puerto Rican congressman was elected; and in that year, black representation in Washington was the largest in history, with 12 congressmen and one senator.[76]

New men have come to the fore because the context of race relations has changed. The development of an urban, literate constituency, the Supreme Court challenges to segregation, the appearance of independent African nations, and other forces have dramatically changed Negroes' perceptions of what is possible. ". . . compromise leaders held their positions primarily because they were acceptable to white leaders. They were also accepted by Negroes because accommodation was regarded as the most practical and effective mode of adjustment in the existing power situation."[77] In a context of hope and aspiration, however, new voices are demanded. A broad attack on the whole range of discriminatory patterns is demanded *now*. "You don't stop beating your wife with all deliberate speed, you stop right now."[78] Not to have been in jail or at the head of a picket line is to risk loss of influence. Thus the heads of the major protest organizations, including those who have worked in the past through negotiation and legal action, join the demonstration, lest those whom they lead get too far ahead of them (a situation that political leaders not uncommonly find themselves in).

This reference is primarily to leaders who are prominent nationally. On the community level, accommodating leadership is less uncommon, because of variation in local conditions and the greater vulnerability of local leaders to reprisals from the dominant group. Yet even on the community level, protest, not accommodation, has become the mode.[79] Those who believe that the demand for full equality now is unwise are either fairly quiet or are limited to assertions that demanding rights too aggressively and rapidly will lead to retaliation and failure.

Will a Separate Negro Culture Emerge? The tone of most Negro protest today is integrationist, not pluralistic. The goal is to win full and equal opportunity in the larger society. This point is difficult to document, because conflict-oriented and separationist activities are more visible. But the evidence is decisive. A Louis Harris poll for *Time* asked a nationwide cross section of Blacks whom they respected most. The sharpest contrast was between the NAACP and the Black Panthers, with 75 percent saying they had a "great deal" of respect for the NAACP, compared with 25 percent for the Black Panthers, while the negative response, "hardly at all," was given by 3 percent to the former and 37 percent to the latter.[80] When Campbell and Schuman measured racial attitudes in 15 American cities, they found that only a small minority of Negroes accepted separationist statements: "Negroes should have nothing to do with whites if they can help it" (from zero to 18 percent of the several age

---

[75] Daniel Thompson, *The Negro Leadership Class*, Prentice-Hall, 1963.

[76] For an articulate statement of the political style of the "new" black congress member, see Shirley Chisholm, *Unbought and Unbossed*, Houghton Mifflin, 1970.

[77] Lewis Killian and C. U. Smith, "Negro Protest Leaders," *SF*, Mar., 1960, p. 253. Harold Isaacs emphasizes the impact of world affairs, particularly the changes in Africa, on American Negroes. See *The New World of Negro Americans*, John Day, 1963, especially Part 3, "Negroes and Africa."

[78] *Newsweek*, quoting Philadelphia Councilman-at-Large Marshall L. Shepard, July 29, 1963, p. 31.

[79] A good description of local protest activity is found in the paper by Harold Nelson, "The Defenders: A Case Study of an Informal Police Organization," *SP*, Fall, 1967, pp. 127–147. Negroes in a southern city responded to the inadequate performance of the law enforcement agencies by forming a private organization to perform various police duties. Despite sharp conflict over the action, more satisfactory law enforcement resulted.

[80] *Time*, Apr. 6, 1970, p. 28.

and education categories); "Whites should be discouraged from taking part in Civil Rights organizations" (from five to 14 percent); "Should be a separate black nation here" (from zero to 10 percent).[81] It is important to note that the largest number of separationist answers, in each instance, were given by the less well educated, younger groups.

In the last several years, however, a new tone has been heard. Acceptance of inferior status has almost disappeared as a response, but avoidance responses—separation from the dominant group—continue to compete with the stronger efforts toward integration. We are thinking here not so much of the self-segregation in community and association that is found among many deprived ethnic and racial minorities, nor of the calls for separation made by the Black Muslims and other "nationalist" groups, important as these phenomena are. Our reference, rather, is to a more classic pluralism that is expressed by a few Negro intellectuals, artists, professional men, and musicians. Let us not, they say in effect, integrate ourselves out of existence. While joining fully in the economic and political life of the nation, let us maintain our distinctive identity.

What we are witnessing is a culture-building process. The extent of the contribution of the African background to North American Negroes is controversial. Some lingual patterns perhaps, some contribution to music and dance, to folk literature and religion have been incorporated. But on these beginnings, new forms have grown. Their African community and tribal identities were broken, but Negroes have become a community of suffering. Their widely different origins and contemporary conditions are, to an important degree, obscured by their shared fate. When they were powerless this "community of suffering," although it created some major cultural products, was too split and demoralized to weld these products into an ethnic subculture.[82] When they gained some

power—but not much—they sought to eliminate the special burdens they carried, to win equality in an integrated society. Now some few, seeing integration bearing down upon them, are beginning to wonder if its full accomplishment will not mean the fading of a valued culture, a loss of recognition of special Negro accomplishments, a reduced opportunity to wring from their vastly difficult experience a valuable and unique contribution to the total human endeavor, and a weakening of the sense of pride and identity that has been so painfully won.

Perhaps we will not be misunderstood if we say that a few Negroes are becoming "Jewish." There is something of the same community of feeling that comes from having been through enormously destructive experiences together—and come out of them with something creative and valuable. Jazz is a widely-heralded musical style that is predominantly Negro in origin; there has grown an insightful body of literature; drawing on their religious traditions, Negroes in their fight for equality, are contributing to the culture of social change, and in the process are helping to bring the country more fully in touch with the contemporary world; they have vitally influenced the civil rights activities of other minorities; Negro contributions to sports are not insignificant.

In the United States today, we may be witnessing the beginnings of what Bernard Siegal has called "defensive structuring," a form of adaptation ". . . that recurs with great regularity among groups that perceive themselves as exposed to environmental stress of long duration with which they cannot cope directly and aggressively."[83] His illustrations are drawn primarily from smaller and more homogeneous groups than America's Negro population (specific Indian tribes, for example, or religious sects), so we might expect to find tendencies toward de-

---

[81] Campbell and Schuman, *op. cit.*; cited by Brunswick, *op. cit.*, p. 365.

[82] Virginia H. Young has recently argued, in opposition to many interpretations of the Negro family,

that a distinctive, organizationally strong, and functional family system is one of the elements in "an indigenous American Negro culture." See her "Family and Childhood in a Southern Negro Community," *AA*, Apr., 1970, pp. 269–288.

[83] "Defensive Structuring and Environmental Stress," *AJS*, July, 1970, p. 11.

fensive structuring, rather than a full expression of it, in the black group. These would be tendencies to support "solidarity, harmony, and interdependency" by means of ". . . authoritarian control over members, exercised by a small specially knowledgeable elite; a high rate of endogamy; cultivation of cultural-identity symbols; and early socialization for impulse control."[84] These are characteristics of the Black Muslims and other Negro groups to some degree.

We have no desire to exaggerate the strength of the movement toward pluralism among American Negroes. It is doubtless in its early stages, as culture-building processes go, and may not develop far, if discrimination is rapidly reduced. It seems more likely, however, to grow in importance in the years ahead. Louis Lomax takes a somewhat different view:

It pains me, now, to remember those days, to recall just how close we Southern Negroes were to becoming a first-rate culture group. We had so many things going for us: a way of worship that, in time, would have produced a Negro God; a historical heritage that we passed on as if it were an Ark of the Covenant between the Almighty and us; although we shared the common language, we spoke a jargon of our own; and our social outlets satisfied the ambitions we then felt. But there was a fatal flaw in the foundation of our emerging way of life: We had come together as a tribe for negative, not positive, reasons; we were bound together by the animus of the white man, not by historical customs and traditions such as those that have fashioned the world's peoples into culture groups.[85]

The reign of terror and injustice, Lomax believes, so crushed Negro self-respect that he turned away from the task of building his own culture and embraced integration,

"thereby changing the social history of the nation."[86] Lomax may exaggerate both the negative forces at work (or perhaps overlooks the extent to which negative forces have been involved in the building of every culture) and the extent to which Negroes have embraced integration. Although few are pluralistic or openly separationist on the basis of a distinctive Negro culture, there may be many for whom this theme has some resonance, amid the more dominant sounds of integration. (And such as the Black Muslims, although too impoverished and poorly trained to be masters of the Negro contributions, nevertheless by their symbolic invention of a whole culture manifest the pull of the pluralistic idea.) We expect in the years ahead, in fact, to hear more voices—not simply from the impoverished, but from the talented and creative—calling for the preservation of a distinctive Negro culture and supporting associations. This movement is unlikely in the foreseeable future to be large, compared with the drive for desegregation. But short of an unexpectedly rapid integration of American society or the opposite, the renewal of massive segregation, we believe some of the most sensitive and creative of Negroes, as well as some of the angry, will continue to emphasize the possibility and desirability of a distinctive Negro subculture.[87]

---

[84] *Ibid.*, p. 11.

[85] Louis Lomax, *The Negro Revolt*, New American Library, 1963, pp. 63–64.

[86] *Ibid.*, chap. 5.

[87] Is this a happy possibility? Perhaps in view of the speculative quality of this section we should indicate our own value perspective. We tend to be integrationist; but we also believe that a dash of Negro pluralism in this large and complex society may be desirable. From our point of view, if this perspective is maintained by only a few, or becomes only a small part of the perspective of all, it may well add flexibility and enrichment to American society and help to maintain pride among Negroes. As a strong movement, however, promoted by a slow pace in the elimination of injustice, it could contribute to a vicious circle by strengthening tendencies toward prejudice and schism rather than a mutually respecting pluralism.

We have seen in the preceding two chapters that prejudice and discrimination have important consequences for the personality development of minority-group members and important influences on the nature of social movements among them. The consequences for the dominant group are no less significant. Again it is difficult to separate causes from effects. Once set in motion, many "consequences" become, in their turn, "causes" of further prejudice and discrimination. Feelings of guilt in the prejudiced person (effect) may be allayed by projection—by further prejudicial activity—and thus be the immediate "cause" of that activity. Or discrimination in the form of segregated schools (usually an effect of prejudice) may, because it proves to be an expensive luxury for a community, set in motion a host of other events which increase prejudice. The effect thus becomes a cause: Segregation will minimize the kind of equal-status contact that reduces prejudice; blinding stereotypes will be perpetuated.

Before indicating some of the consequences of prejudice for members of the dominant group, we must also point out that they are almost always discussed in terms of some value stand, implicit, or explicitly stated. One can speak, for example, of the gains and costs of prejudice. These may be gains and costs in terms of the values of the prejudiced person himself, or according to some scheme of "generally agreed-upon values," or in light of the premises of the person making the judgment. Often these three value schemes will coincide, but they may not. There are conflicts of value within a society and particularly there are differences in the ranking of values. "Freedom from contact with the members of a minority group" may in itself become a value, high in the ranking of some persons, of lower

importance for others, and completely lacking for others.

The present authors do not see how the indication of value stands can be avoided in this discussion; nor do they see any reason to avoid them. The only requisite of a scientific approach in this regard is that the premises be made explicit. As we discuss the gains and the costs of prejudice and discrimination, we shall try to make clear to whom the particular consequence is a gain or a cost. If the reader has a different value stand or a different order in his hierarchy of values, he will, of course, make a different judgment. Description and analysis of the effects themselves, however, will, if they are valid, be agreed upon by all.

We must distinguish the gains or losses to individuals from those to groups—the community, nation, or world. We must remember that what is a gain to one member of the dominant group (granted his value hierarchy) would be a loss to another member of the dominant group with different preferences. And we must discriminate carefully between short-run and long-run consequences, for they may be very different—if not, indeed, opposites.

THE GAINS FROM PREJUDICE AND DISCRIMINATION

It seems unlikely that man would show such an enormous capacity for prejudice and discrimination were it not for the gains he seems to acquire. To be sure, these may be primarily short-run individual gains, tied inextricably with serious long-run losses. Most of us, however, prefer a bird in the hand (the immediate gains from prejudice) to two in the bush (the gains to the whole society in the long run from abolishing prejudice), particularly if the concerted community action necessary for the long-run gain seems to be lacking. Moreover, the complicated interaction that makes prejudice costly in the long run is difficult to understand. The international consequences of my discriminatory treatment of Mexican migrant workers is far less apparent to me than the desirability of getting my crops picked as cheaply as possible. If this means gross underpayment, unsanitary living quarters, and great insecurity for the workers, a rationalizing prejudice will help me to justify the situation or see it as inevitable.

John Dollard described the three primary gains made by white people in the South in terms of economic, sexual, and prestige advantages, all closely related (and, it should be noted again, all tied to disadvantages). These have applicability to many minority-majority situations.[1]

1. Almost all efforts to calculate economic gains refer to individual gains, summed across the majority group. This is essential, because it locates the areas of vested interest in discrimination, where resistance to change is at a maximum. It should not lead us to forget, however, the possible— indeed probable—economic costs to the whole society, to which we shall refer later. The situation is analogous to private gain from the overcutting of forests, strip mining without environmental restoration, or dumping of wastes into public water ways— all likely to be profitable—set against the long-run public costs. We need a social budget, and not simply a series of individual budgets to understand the full range of economic effects of discrimination.

With that distinction in mind, we can note that white men clearly profited from slavery,[2] that employers who can keep Mexican workers at minimum-wage levels reap larger profits,[3] that dominant groups are able to reduce the necessity for their own employment in heavy manual, monotonous, and poorly paid jobs if they keep minorities relatively powerless.[4]

Thurow, in a careful appraisal of the American situation, estimates that white workers gain about $15 billion (plus or minus $5 billion, for a precise calculation is impossible) per year from discrimination against nonwhite workers. This gain comes from a combination of employment, wage, human capital, occupational, and labor monopoly discrimination.[5]

The apparent economic gains are often reduced by the inefficiency of workers with low morale and the "pseudo-ignorant malingering" that we discussed in the preceding chapter, as well as by the long-run social costs we shall discuss later; but there remains a residue of economic advantage for those able to command the labor of minority-group members or otherwise take advantage of their relative powerlessness. When one rents a house to a person of low status, he often is able to charge a rent considerably higher than he could get from a member of the dominant group, because of the limited opportunities for housing that the minority group person has. It may be an immediate gain to an individual to reduce his competition for jobs by branding minority groups "inferior," keeping them out of his union, his social clubs (where jobs are often found), his medical association (for this is not simply a practice of the lower classes),

[1] *Caste and Class in a Southern Town*, Yale, 1937.

[2] See the careful assessment by Kenneth Stampp, *The Peculiar Institution: Slavery in the Ante-Bellum South*, Knopf, 1956, chap. 9.

[3] See Leo Grebler, Joan W. Moore, and Ralph C. Guzman, *The Mexican-American People: The Nation's Second Largest Minority*, Free Press, 1970, chap. 10.

[4] See, for example, W. H. Hutt, *The Economics of the Colour Bar: A Study of the Economic Origins and Consequences of Racial Segregation in South Africa*, Deutsch, 1964. But it should be added that nowhere is it more clearly illustrated than in South Africa that such individual gains are achieved at great societal costs.

[5] See Lester C. Thurow, *Poverty and Discrimination*, The Brookings Institution, 1969, pp. 130–134. See also Norval D. Glenn, "White Gains from Negro Subordination," *SP*, Spring, 1966, pp. 159–178. We should emphasize that it is an intricate problem to separate the effects of discrimination from other forces affecting minority-group economic levels (including the surviving effects of past discrimination). O. D. Duncan has examined this question in a valuable way in "Discrimination against Negroes," *Annals*, May, 1967, pp. 85–103.

or limiting their chances for vocational and professional training. The short-run, individual economic gains that come from prejudice are the opposite side of the same coin that we discussed at length in Chapter 4.

2. Often, in the relationships between a dominant and an oppressed group, a pattern of sexual contact between the men of the majority and the women of the minority group develops that allows some of the men of the dominant group to gain an immediate sexual advantage. The total effects of this pattern are, of course, distinct from the immediate physical gratification. Sexual contacts between "superior" and "inferior" influence, in many important ways, the nature of the relationship between the dominant men and women, the family patterns of the majority and minority groups, the feelings and frustrations of the men of the oppressed group, the status position of the mixed offspring who may result, etc. Some of the costs of the sexual gain—the price paid—we shall discuss in the next section. This advantage will be seen as actually part of a vicious circle (vicious in terms of the total values of the dominant men themselves) and thus very costly.[6]

3. Most normal people enjoy the feeling that they are not just average members of society but are to some degree special and important. The enthusiastic way with which most of us identify with a winning baseball team or a glamorous movie star indicates our appetite for prestige, vicarious as well as real. If my school is best, my community most attractive, and my nation all-powerful and all-wise, I somehow have gained in significance. If a whole group of fellow human beings can be kept in an inferior position and especially if they can be made to give daily signs of deference and humility—and if I can persuade myself that they really are inferior—I can get a comfortable feeling of prestige that my own individual achievements might not command.

The prestige gain of belonging to a "superior" group is seldom unambiguous; there are often self-doubts and doubts over the whole-hearted acceptance of his status by the minority-group member. These lead to an almost compulsive need for reassurance in some instances, and thus to a rigid insistence that all the deference forms be followed to the letter.[7] The long-run total consequences, moreover, may add up to losses that far exceed the prestige gain, as we shall see. From the point of view of day-to-day adjustments, however, the feeling of mastery and importance may seem to be a real gain. It also assists in achieving the economic and sexual advantages. And, particularly for those of the dominant group who are most frustrated and least successful, it may have an adjustment value that prevents their lot from seeming unbearable. In a society where the "success pattern" is stressed but in which the technically open-class system imposes obstacles to success on a great many, egos are constantly being convicted of inferiority. The pseudo success of prejudice may allay the fear and sense of failure (even while it contributes to the likelihood of failure).

Therapists who fail to see this prestige gain, and the other gains as well, may attempt a head-on attack on prejudice instead of trying to create a situation in which prejudice is relatively useless. Where individuals are given some chance at economic security and advancement, where sexual contacts within the approved cultural framework are free of anxieties, rigidities, and internal contradictions, where members of the dominant group have genuine opportunities for achievement, however small, that will give them a feeling of self-confidence and worthiness—under these conditions prejudice will decline progressively and may come to be seen as a costly and inefficient way of achieving human values.

4. The nature of human society makes one gain of prejudice a peculiarly difficult one to reduce rapidly. Once established as a value, the sheer maintenance of a status system—even in the face of obvious costs—is considered desirable, an end in itself. The pattern of superiority-inferiority comes to be

---

[6] On this whole question, see Dollard, *op. cit.*, pp. 134–172.

[7] *Ibid.*, pp. 173–187, and Bertram Doyle, *The Etiquette of Race Relations in the South*, Univ. of Chicago Press, 1937.

looked upon as good and right. To violate it is bad, an attack on one's sense of selfhood and feelings of solidarity with the community. Evidence that prejudice and discrimination are costly in terms of a person's desires will not persuade him to abandon them, at least in a hurry, if he thinks they are essentially right. Few of us choose our course of action only after weighing the costs. Many a white South African, for example, might be shown that his discrimination against Negroes costs him money, produces a schizophrenic morality and religion, confuses the political life of the nation, and weakens its international position, but he would continue to insist, probably into the second and third generation after the demonstration, that segregation and discrimination are right, are good in themselves—in spite of the cost. Such beliefs may have been, in the first place, rationalizations to justify other gains, but after being built into the whole fabric of a society, they tend to take on an independent existence. This assertion does not mean that they cannot be changed (see Part III of this volume), but it does mean that there will be a lag between the reduction of the functions of prejudice and the reduction of prejudice itself. Many of us are capable of saying: That which is, is good—even if it's bad.

THE PERSONALITY COSTS OF PREJUDICE

Our discussion of the gains from prejudice and discrimination was continually qualified by the need for referring to the concomitant losses. Seldom are the gains achieved without cost to the individual and to the group. The evidence indicates, in fact, that in almost all instances the costs greatly outweigh the gains in terms of the values of prejudiced persons themselves. The great *interdependence* of all people within a society, and today of all the people in the world, makes it impossible for a dominant group to inflict penalties on minority groups without being penalized itself. In the eloquent words of John Donne,

"No man is an *Iland,* intire of it selfe; every man is a peece of the *Continent,* a part of the *maine;* if a *Clod* bee washed away by the *Sea,* Europe is the lesse, as well as if a *Promontorie* were, as well as if a *Mannor* of thy *friends* or of *thine owne* were; any man's *death* diminishes *me,* because I am involved in *Mankinde;* And therefore never send to know for whom the *bell* tolls; It tolls for thee."[8]

Booker T. Washington expressed something of the same idea when he said that the white man could not keep the colored man in the ditch without getting down there with him. Or we might put the notion of interdependence in the no less vivid terms of *The New Yorker* cartoon: Three mountain climbers are tied together as they climb a steep canyon wall. The woman at the top begins to slip and the man in the middle calls to the man below him, "There she goes!" "What do you mean," comes the reply, " 'There *she* goes'?" In a very real sense, the death of or the confining discrimination against any person "diminishes *me.*"

We cannot write with great confidence of the personality costs of prejudice, because of the lack of well-controlled studies and the difficulty of separating cause from effect. In such a situation, implicit value judgments are particularly likely to slip into the discussion and interfere with objective analysis. (With the present authors, these would take the form of tendencies to exaggerate the personality damage that results from prejudice.) Keeping this danger in mind, we think that the evidence, nevertheless, indicates that prejudice is an expensive luxury *in terms of the prejudiced person's own total interests and values.* The costs will differ, of course, from individual to individual and from situation to situation. It is necessary to distinguish, for example, between the consequences of a prejudice that is taught to a child as a normal part of his culture and of one that is seized upon by an insecure person as an attempted adjustment pattern. The former prejudice may create guilt, tension, and tendencies toward projection in a per-

[8] From *Devotions upon Emergent Occasions,* Cambridge, 1923, p. 98.

son who is simultaneously taught democratic ideas of nonprejudice; but it may not pervade the whole personality in such a way as to affect most aspects of his behavior. The latter prejudice, however, may result not only in guilt, tension, and projection, but in a rigidity of mind and a compulsiveness in adjustment that block a realistic appraisal of one's problems. We cannot in this brief discussion make a refined analysis in terms of types of individuals and types of situations involved. We shall speak in terms of some of the general consequences, only noting that the degree to which each consequence is applicable to a particular situation and the combination of consequences found there will vary widely.

The Cost of Ignorance

By definition, prejudice is a categorical prejudgment of an individual because he is classified as a member of a particular group. One of the inevitable effects, applying to a greater or less degree, is a loss of contact with reality. Rationality is highly valued by most people. It is contradicted by prejudice, which furnishes a greatly oversimplified or completely inaccurate "explanation" of one's difficulties, and often also a program of action that is supposed to solve them. Because it is blind to the real causes, this program of action is unable to effect a real cure. Keeping the Negro "in his place" will somehow reduce our tensions, improve our economic position, and boost our shaky feelings of self-esteem. But what if this protection of our place in the status system actually has very little to do with our tensions, our economic insecurity, or our lack of self-confidence; what if, in fact, it is one of the *causes* of our difficulties (as we shall see below)? Then our prejudice blocks us from a realistic appraisal of the problems we face. Its program of action is a modern form of magic that manipulates symbols and follows rituals but knows nothing of the true course of events. When a great many Germans came to believe the most of their difficulties were caused by Jews, when they adopted a program of action dominated by

anti-Semitism, they were blinded to the true causes of their problems. They were led then to accept leadership that was equally lacking (or uninterested) in understanding the basic forces at work, with the result that they soon faced the overwhelmingly greater problems of war. One pays a penalty for ignorance in interhuman relations as he does for ignorance of the physical world.

Myrdal speaks of "the convenience of ignorance." He refers to the almost studied lack of information and the misinformation with which the white American tries to protect the status system and make it seem reasonable and moral:

One need not be a trained student of the race problem to learn a lot in a couple of days about the Negroes in a community which is not known by even its otherwise enlightened white residents. To an extent this ignorance is not simply "natural" but is part of the opportunistic escape reaction.

It thus happens that not only the man in the street, but also the professional man, shows ignorance in his own field of work. One meets physicians who hold absurd ideas about the anatomical characteristics of the Negro people or about the frequency of disease among the Negroes in their own community; educators who have succeeded in keeping wholly unaware of the results of modern intelligence research; lawyers who believe that practically all the lynchings are caused by rape; ministers of the gospel who know practically nothing about Negro churches in their own town. In the North, particularly in such groups where contacts with Negroes are lacking or scarce, the knowledge might not be greater, but the number of erroneous conceptions seems much smaller. The important thing and the reason for suspecting this ignorance to be part of the escape apparatus is that knowledge is constantly twisted in one direction—toward classifying the Negro low and the White high.

The ignorance about the Negro is the more striking as the Southerner is himself convinced that he "knows the Negro," while the Yankee is supposedly ignorant on the subject. The insistence on the part of the Southern Whites that they have reliable and intimate knowledge about the Negro problem is one of the most pathetic stereotypes in the South. In fact, the average Southerner "knows" the Negro and the interracial problem as the patient "knows" the toothache—

in the sense that he feels a concern—not as the diagnosing dentist knows his own or his patient's trouble. He further "knows" the Negro in the sense that he is brought up to use a social technique in dealing with Negroes by which he is able to get them into submissive patterns of behavior.[9]

Myrdal might as aptly have entitled this observation "the *in*convenience of ignorance," for one must point out not only the lack of information and the functions of that lack in serving the dominant group, but also the serious problems that result from faulty knowledge and attempts to make magical cures. When energies are directed by misinformation into activities that cannot possibly produce the desired result, the prejudice which helps to create that misinformation becomes a heavy cost.

The Cost of Moral Ambivalence

Another personality consequence of prejudice is the development of seriously ambivalent, mutually contradictory views of life that cause one to be at odds with himself. What are the effects on the white child of being taught a democratic and Christian ideology and then also being taught the contrary ideology of intergroup prejudice? The prejudice encourages him to displace his hostilities onto members of the "inferior" groups, but his democratic and Christian training prevents him from being quite sure of himself. There is a burden of guilt that will not, for the most part, be consciously recognized (although some of it may be revealed in the nature of the religion which a person accepts) but will be projected onto the minority group, with further feelings of hostility, more aggression, and intensified feelings of guilt. This vicious circle wastes one's resources and diverts his energies into ineffective actions. Myrdal considers this moral ambivalence the most important factor in race relations in the United States.

Though our study includes economic, social, and political race relations, at bottom our problem is

the moral dilemma of the American—the conflict between his moral valuations on various levels of consciousness and generality. The "American Dilemma," referred to in the title of this book, is the ever-raging conflict between, on the one hand, the valuations preserved on the general plane which we shall call the "American Creed," where the American thinks, talks, and acts under the influence of high national and Christian precepts, and, on the other hand, the valuations on specific planes of individual and group living, where personal and local interests; economic, social, and sexual jealousies; considerations of community prestige and conformity; group prejudice against particular persons or types of people; and all sorts of miscellaneous wants, impulses, and habits dominate his outlook.[10]

There has perhaps been a tendency to accept Myrdal's thesis too quickly. He did not clearly demonstrate that most Americans do, in fact, feel guilty about racial discrimination nor indicate what the range of variation was. For some persons, segregation is morally good and they defend it with moral fervor.

Westie examined, among a random sample of Indianapolis households, the degree of agreement to a general value statement related to "the American creed" and then to a specific application of that value. For example: "Everyone in America should have equal opportunity to get ahead," and "I would be willing to have a Negro as my supervisor in my place of work."[11] Of 1030 item pairs, answers to 383 were inconsistent, with the general value being the one most frequently accepted. Westie notes that 81 percent of the American Creed items were accepted, but only 56 percent of the specific valuations. Only 12.6 percent of his respondents were entirely consistent, and thus had no "American dilemma," as measured. There were many ways for the others to handle the inconsistencies, for example by repression ("what conflict?"), by appealing to the relativity of the value ("there are different kinds of brotherhood"), by projection ("a Negro juror would be prejudiced"). It is also interesting to note, however, that some felt

---

[9] Reprinted from *An American Dilemma* by Gunnar Myrdal, pp. 40–41. Copyright 1944 by Harper & Row.

[10] *Ibid.*, p. xliii.
[11] Frank R. Westie, "The American Dilemma: An Empirical Test," *ASR*, Aug., 1965, p. 531.

obliged to explain their lack of prejudice, their unwillingness to discriminate. "Thus, people with no dilemma in Myrdal's sense seem to experience another type of dilemma: a conflict between their endorsement of democratic action and yet *another normative system,* which exists in the majority of American local communities: the system which says that one ought to be prejudiced and one ought to discriminate."[12]

In their study of ministers in Little Rock, Campbell and Pettigrew found little guilt among the sectarian leaders or even among the segregationist ministers of the established churches. Their total system of values gave them protection against any discomfort that the race issue by itself might have brought.[13] In a study of 279 students in the Deep South, Campbell found some evidences of guilt, but also of moral defense of segregation. He asked each student how he would feel if, when he was a junior in high school, it had just been announced that ten percent of the students next year would be Negroes, admitted for the first time. Then he asked for their feelings when, at the end of the senior year, it was clear that the Negroes had done well, or had done poorly. For comparison he asked how they believed they ought to feel about these things. One hundred twelve expressed little guilt (measured by one or no scale step differences between how they would feel and how they should feel, on a five-step scale). Those lacking feelings of guilt were more likely to come from small towns or rural areas in the South. The American Creed on race relations had not reached them; the segregated system had provided them with counternorms.[14]

This evidence qualifies the application of the thesis of "the American dilemma," and should make us cautious about the assumption of a homogeneous moral view regarding race relations at some basic level of the national conscience. There is little doubt, however, that many white persons, and probably most, sense a contradiction between their religious and political ideology and their race relations practices. The moral ambivalence produced by prejudice is illustrated in an important way by the tensions and the sustaining beliefs that are created by sexual activity between majority- and minority-group members. Lillian Smith, in *Killers of the Dream,* has given an insightful account of the costs to white men and women of the race-sex situation in the South. Although the pattern of relationship has changed a great deal in the last several decades, many of the beliefs and attitudes of earlier days survive to affect significantly the personality development of those who share them. The effects of contact between the races were sharply influenced by the religious and moral teachings that white children received: God was a God of love, and yet of wrath. "We were told that He loved us, and then we were told that He would burn us in everlasting flames of hell if we displeased Him."[15] They were taught that their bodies were things of shame and mystery, and yet that their white skin was a thing of glory, a source of strength and pride. They were taught that the black person was inferior and evil, yet many of their warmest relationships were with a colored nurse, and in adult life many white men found sexual pleasure with Negro women.

What a strange ugly trap the white race made for itself! Because these slaveholders were "Christian," they felt compelled to justify the holding of slaves by denying these slaves a soul, and denying them a place in the human family. Because they were puritan, they succeeded in developing a frigidity in their white women that precluded the possibility of mutual satisfaction. Lonely and baffled and frustrated by the state of affairs they had set up in their own homes and hearts, they could not resist the vigor and kindliness and gaiety of these slaves. And succumbing to desire, they mated with these dark women whom they had dehumanized in their minds, and fathered by them children who, according to their race philosophy, were "without souls"—a strange exotic new kind of creature, whom

[12] *Ibid.,* p. 538.
[13] Ernest Campbell and Thomas Pettigrew, *Christianity in Racial Crisis. A Study of Little Rock's Ministry,* Public Affairs Press, 1959.
[14] Ernest Campbell, "Moral Discomfort and Racial Segregation—An Examination of the Myrdal Hypothesis," *SF,* Mar., 1961, pp. 228–234.

[15] Lillian Smith, *Killers of the Dream,* Norton, 1949, p. 79.

they made slaves of and sometimes sold on the auction block. The white man's roles as slave-holder and Christian and puritan were exacting far more than the strength of his mind could sustain. Each time he found the back-yard temptation irresistible his conscience split more deeply from his acts and his mind from things as they are.

The race-sex-sin spiral had begun. The more trails the white man made to back-yard cabins, the higher he raised his white wife on her pedestal when he returned to the big house. The higher the pedestal, the less he enjoyed her whom he had put there, for statues after all are only nice things to look at. More and more numerous became the little trails of escape from the statuary and more and more intricately they began to weave in and out of southern life. Guilt, shame, fear, lust spiralled each other. Then a time came, though it was decades later, when man's suspicion of white woman began to pull the spiral higher and higher. It was of course inevitable for him to suspect her of the sins he had committed so pleasantly and often. *What if*, he whispered, and the words were never finished. *What if. . . .* Too often white woman could only smile bleakly in reply to the unasked question. But white man mistook this empty smile for one of cryptic satisfaction and in jealous panic began to project his own sins on to the Negro male.[16]

Thus the white man confronted himself with guilt and fears that required a great deal of emotional energy to try to dispel— the fear of "mongrelization" (which he projected onto the black man); guilt over the rejection of some of his own children; confusion in trying to free himself from a deep-seated childhood affection for a colored nurse, a second mother; fear "lest their sons, and especially their daughters should feel the same attraction they felt and should perhaps continue the blending of races to which they and their forefathers had made such lavish contributions. And because they feared this, knowing the strength of temptation, they blocked their children's way by erecting as many barriers as possible, extracting energy from their own guilt to build fortifications of law and custom against what they considered an 'irresistible sin.' "[17]

[16] *Ibid.*, pp. 116–117.
[17] *Ibid.*, pp. 121–122.

In this setting, a combination of circumstances set in motion a vicious circle. Religious training, particularly with regard to the sinfulness of sex; the teaching of race superiority; but along with these a warm and satisfying relationship to a black nurse— these had helped to shape an individual's personality when, in adult life, he sought for a satisfying physical relationship.

This total combination of circumstances was shared directly by only a small minority perhaps, but a minority important in affecting the nature of southern society and culture. Others shared many of the traditional attitudes that grew up in this situation and participated, by identification, in its support. Although the elements in this pattern have all been modified, they survive with sufficient strength to be a primary factor in the personality development of many Whites. The energy with which segregation has been defended, the feeling that one has asked the really profound question when he asks, "Would you want your daughter to marry a black man?" represent a deep separation in the personality of the white man.

Not only the white men, of course, but also the white women were strongly influenced by this whole pattern. There was a strong tendency for the cultural sex taboos to be referred primarily to white women; the repressed sex feelings were directed, whether in action or fantasy, toward Negroes. "Sacred" white womanhood came to symbolize not just a barrier to Negro males but part of the ambivalent attitude toward sex of white men as well. White women who were taught that sex was to be shunned, and at the same time often experienced the loss of their own men, came to feel that sex was indeed largely an evil that split their homes. Their sexual unresponsiveness then encouraged their men to direct more of their sexual interest and to project more of their ideas of sexual vitality onto black people, which further enhanced the dogma of sacred white womanhood, which in turn further frustrated the white women and blocked them from a normal warm relationship with their husbands.

This vicious circle was (and to a lesser degree is) costly to the white men and women involved. A few women fought against it by trying to adopt a masculine role. In recent years, more have fought against it by organizing to resist some elements in the whole pattern of relationship.

Such protests, however, were from a minority. The majority tried to fill the gaps that their social role left in their lives by piety, by mastery of an elaborate social etiquette, by loving care of a garden— "planting and transplanting little secret dreams, making them live in an azalea, a rose, a camellia, when they could not live in their own arid lives."[18]

Culturally stunted by a region that still pays nice rewards to simple-mindedness in females, they had no defenses against blandishment. They listened to the round words of men's tribute to Sacred Womanhood and believed, thinking no doubt that if they were not sacred then what under God's heaven *was* the matter with them! Once hoisted up by the old colonels' oratory, they stayed on lonely pedestals and rigidly played 'statue' while their men went about more important affairs elsewhere.[19]

The women thus affected did not escape feelings of resentment, some of which were expressed in the form of rigid and repressive control over their own families. Having been among the victims of a tradition that repressed them and tried to make of them "psychic children," they became the vigilant guardians of that tradition.

Many a man went into politics, or joined the KKK, had a nervous breakdown or forged checks, got drunk or built a great industry, because he could no longer bear the police-state set up in his own home. But this would have been a hard thing for these good mothers and wives to believe, and for the men also. . . . With a rigid training they armored their children against their fantasies and sex feelings, preparing them for human relations as if for a cruel medieval battle. Thus they segregated sex from love and tenderness and obligations, and did not see how inevitably it would slip into secret back-door union with hate and guilt.[20]

Our discussion of some of the personality consequences of prejudice has been only illustrative. It has shown that in a society where rationality is prized and where the values of democracy and sexual fidelity are widely held, prejudice is a costly item. Further consequences could be discussed. Most people believe that a realistic appraisal of one's own worth and a lack of arrogance are to be prized. These are blocked by prejudice. Dominant individuals in a society characterized by discrimination bear an often overwhelming burden of fear and insecurity. White South Africans sometimes show an almost obsessive fear of revolt and violence from the repressed black men. The small southern town in the United States is characterized by locked doors and incidental firearms to a greater extent than in an equivalent town in other parts of the country that lack a minority group. Today many New Yorkers have three or four locks on their doors and are afraid to walk the streets at certain hours and in certain neighborhoods. Thus a pattern of discrimination is supported only at the cost of much irrationality, moral confusion, arrogance, and fear.

THE ECONOMIC COSTS OF PREJUDICE

It is of course impossible to designate in precise dollar figures how much it "costs" to maintain a pattern of prejudice and discrimination, although there have been careful estimates by economists that the bill may be as high as $30 billion a year in the United States.[21] We can, however, indicate some of the ways in which specific groups among the dominant members of society are injured economically and in related ways by prejudice, and how society as a whole suffers.

Prejudice that takes the form of segregated areas in housing and severe limitations on the economic opportunities of minority-group members is an important factor in the development and continuation of slums. Beyond the loss of skills and the loss of pur-

[18] *Ibid.*, p. 138.
[19] *Ibid.*, p. 137.
[20] *Ibid.*, p. 147.

[21] See chapter 11.

chasing power that such a situation creates, there is the direct financial cost of large expenditures for public health, for fire protection, for police and courts, and for relief. These costs are much higher per capita in slum areas than in other parts of a community. The tax yield, moreover, is low. Discriminatory limitation on the supply of housing for minority groups means that owners of the houses that are obtainable have less incentive to maintain their property in decent condition—they can rent anyway. This deterioration lowers the value of the bordering property of white persons and injures the whole community through the total costs of slums.[22]

Sometimes the economic costs of discrimination are given symbolic emphasis: When a feed store that had traded with Koinonia Farm, an interracial community in Georgia, was bombed for violating a boycott, the windows of the Citizens Bank and the Sumter County Court House were also shattered.[23] We are tempted to say that the two bastions of community life—economic stability and orderly government—are thus shown to be vulnerable to the destructive power of discrimination.

An unmeasured but undoubtedly large amount of money has been spent since 1954 by state governments, and agencies which they support, in efforts to prevent desegregation of schools and other public facilities. Direct tuition payments to children attending private schools (often hastily created to avoid integration), maintenance of "sovereignty commissions," and the costs of opposition to desegregation in the courts illustrate these expenditures. By 1971, some 500,000 students in the 11 southern states were attending segregated private schools. Although direct public support for these schools has disappeared, they continue to enjoy tax-exempt status (despite challenges), and their presence makes it more difficult to pass school bond issues for the public

schools, whose support from the states also declines when their enrollments decline.[24]

Costs of the federal government's attempts to enforce laws and court orders are difficult to measure but may run into the hundreds of millions. In 1963, for example, expenses for federal marshals, national guard and regular army units used in the conflict over the desegregation of the University of Mississippi were several million dollars.[25]

Both the economic costs and the economic gains of prejudice are clearly apparent in other parts of the world. In South Africa, for example, the dominant white group is thoroughly dedicated to a policy that keeps the nonwhites in a subservient position. During the last 25 years, South Africa has experienced rapid economic development. The standard of living for the 20 percent of the population that is white is among the highest in the world; but the per capita income of the colored and Indian population is scarcely one-fifth as high, and for the two-thirds of the country who are of full African ancestry, less than ten percent as high.[26] The Whites feel threatened and have sought to preserve their advantages by "apartheid," a term that refers to a presumed long-run goal of separate, but related communities of Europeans and Africans. In practice, however, apartheid has meant massive oppression and restriction of Nonwhites within the white-dominated society.

So long as agriculture and mining were the foundation of the economy, such a policy was at least economically possible (and, in fact, is currently supported by a strong demand for uranium and gold). But South Africa is undertaking extensive industrialization. There is need for skilled workers, rationally organized into productive enterprises, and sufficiently well-paid to be able to

---

[22] See Elmo Roper, in R. M. MacIver (ed.), *Discrimination and National Welfare*, Institute for Religious and Social Studies (distributed by Harper & Row), 1949, pp. 23–35.

[23] *Civil Liberties*, Oct., 1957, p. 4.

[24] See *The Washington Post*, Feb. 7, 1971, p. A-12. On December 20, 1971, the U.S. Supreme Court ruled against the tax-exempt status of segregated private schools.

[25] It is clear that in all of this a person starting from different moral premises will say: these are not the costs of prejudice but the costs of defending one's self against federal interference or efforts to enforce an unconstitutional ruling.

[26] F. P. Spooner, *South African Predicament: The Economics of Apartheid*, Praeger, 1961, p. 173.

afford the products of their own making. The Whites of South Africa, therefore, face a dilemma: They can have apartheid or they can have an expanding, modern industrial society; they cannot have both. Having chosen the former, the government now faces serious obstacles to the achievement of the latter. Their goods are widely boycotted abroad, especially by the newer nations, and investment by foreigners has been made less attractive.[27]

South Africa faces, as do other segregated systems, the costs of duplicate facilities. There are substantial expenditures to maintain the agencies of control and repression. Enforcement of residential segregation, regardless of its costs, means reliance on migratory labor to a major degree. In addition to the direct costs of transport, this reduces efficient allocation of skills and lowers the morale of workers.

I. D. MacCrone notes the political-moral costs of a growing intolerance—demands for rigid conformity, isolation from the world, authoritarian patterns throughout the society.[28] On a strictly economic level, the cost of apartheid is shown in the difficulty of getting investment capital, despite help from American and British investors. Why? ". . . the country's manufacturing industry . . . does not distribute sufficient buying power to the majority of its workers—the non-Whites—to enable them to buy the products of industry."[29]

Contemporary studies of industry, moreover, have shown that failure to pay attention to the workers' need for being treated with respect leads to lower productivity, higher labor turnover and, in the last analysis, higher costs. Workers from minority groups are particularly likely to lack the sense of being treated with full respect; hence this factor in the loss of efficiency applies especially to them. In Chapter 7 we noted that a partially intentional, partially unconscious inefficiency on the job was one of the aggressive responses to prejudice. It can be seen in the present context as one of the costs of prejudice.

Prejudice prevents the training and use of manpower at the highest possible skill. This is expressed not only in the failure to employ fully the trained carpenter or pilot or teacher if he belongs to the "wrong groups," but more particularly in the failure to train many individuals in the first place. Ginzberg stresses the importance of discrimination and segregation in affecting the ways in which Negroes prepare themselves for work.[30] This influence stretches back into the family, where a child first sees the occupational world through the experience of his parents. A boy's attitudes toward work and his conception of appropriate and available jobs are strongly affected by his father. In many Negro families the father is not the responsible head of the house; he may well be oriented negatively toward his job, in which he feels trapped; he does not convey to his son the belief that hard work and careful preparation will lead to success. Most Negroes have access to poorer schools in which the occupational world is not opened to them nor standards of achievement held up to them.

Much of the potential of the Negro minority goes to waste because it fails to be developed. Many just coast through school; others drop out prematurely because they see no point in continuing. Still others, because of a lack of opportunity, never become

[27] Paradoxically, the major exceptions to this statement are Great Britain and the United States which, between them, purchase nearly half of South Africa's exports and are the main sources of foreign investment capital. In the face of repeated United Nations resolutions (28 by 1963) condemning apartheid and despite the resentment of other African nations, the American government and American businessmen help to sustain the South African government. To American businessmen investing there, apartheid is a matter of internal "politics." A State Department spokesman says: "We respect the right of Americans to invest where they want to invest"— a statement one would do well not to take too literally. See *The New York Times*, Aug. 18, 1963.

[28] Cited in Vernon McKay, "Apartheid in a Hostile World," *Africa Report*, Dec., 1960, p. 14.

[29] Spooner, *op. cit.*, pp. 210–211. On the costs of apartheid, see, in addition to McKay, *op. cit.*, pp. 3 ff.; and Spooner, *op. cit.*, especially pp. 157–236; Gwendolen Carter, *The Politics of Inequality: South Africa Since 1948*, Thames and Hudson, 1958; Leo

Kuper, "The Control of Social Change: A South African Experiment," *SF*, Oct., 1954, pp. 19–29; and Pierre L. Van Den Berghe, *South Africa: A Study in Conflict*, Wesleyan Univ. Press, 1965, pp. 183–216.

[30] Eli Ginzberg, "Segregation and Manpower Waste," *Phylon*, Winter, 1960, pp. 311–316.

aware that they possess special aptitudes.[31] The South is particularly hurt because of out-migration. As Ginzberg notes, if a southern Negro is trained in electronics in the armed forces, he almost certainly will relocate, after his discharge, in the North.

The economic costs of segregated schools and other facilities must be measured not only in terms of duplicated expenditures but also in terms of the long-run expense of inadequate education and less efficient services. It is a case of buying a poorer product with more money. And in a society where millions of persons live outside the regions of their birth, poor schools in one area affect the life of other areas. It is well to recognize, however, that despite the long-run economic costs of segregated schools, the immediate fact is that in some communities desegregation is costly. This is true in communities with a high proportion of Negro pupils, if, as is often true, the expenditure per Negro child has been much less than the expenditure per white child. Desegregated schools that tried to maintain the standards set for white children would be more costly. The standards for Negro children have of course, been very low in many areas and vastly need raising, and the long-run gains would be extensive; but it is unwise to forget the immediate fact that desegregation in some areas is expensive, for this is one of the sources of opposition.

It is sometimes supposed that, although the upper classes—the employers and professional people—pay an economic price for prejudice in the loss of consumers and less choice among workers, the working classes—those who would face the most immediate competition from the labor of minority-group members—profit from a system that protects their advantages in the job market. We have seen that this is sometimes true for certain individuals, if one disregards the costs they carry as members of the

general community. For many more, however, prejudice has proved to be a great economic burden. It has made it possible for some employers to pay them less—making up the difference in the currency of racial superiority. Racial, religious, and national prejudices have often stood in the way of union organization, whether through the conscious manipulation of the employer or the unintended effect of divided feeling. Recognition of this experience stands behind the vigorous attempts on the part of some labor unions to eliminate prejudice from their ranks.

A prejudice that has permitted a minority of the dominant whites in the South to exploit Negro labor is one of the key factors in the poverty of many of the *white* people of the region. Johnson noted that this situation goes back to the time of slavery:

The plantation system did not require whites in any large numbers, and the lack of industries limited the growth both of a middle class and of white-collar workers. The "tarheelers" and "sand hillers" of the Carolinas, the "crackers" of Georgia, the "red necks" of Alabama, the "wool-hats" of Mississippi, the "piney woods folks," the "swamp dwellers" of Louisiana, together with others of the lower middle and lower classes, felt the brunt of the slave system. While the planters lived in the rich river bottoms, the poorer whites lived in the hills, nursing their illusion of a common destiny by virtue of a common color. The two classes seldom came into contact where dangerous economic contrasts could be made. The interclass struggle, hatred, and antagonism of the poorer whites were mitigated both by this geographical segregation and by the consoling rationalization of a superiority to the black labor that was controlled by the planters.[32]

Large numbers of "poor whites" continue to suffer economically from a system that tries to get a large share of its labor from a suppressed group. The adverse effects for the whole nation are heightened in any economy based on specialization and the division of labor, where the functional interrelatedness makes each individual highly dependent on others.

[31] *Ibid.*, p. 315. Much of the recent work on this subject deals particularly with educational motivation. For a valuable summary, see Irwin Katz, "A Critique of Personality Approaches to Negro Performance, with Research Suggestions," *JSI*, Summer, 1969, pp. 13–27; consult also the other articles in that issue of *JSI*.

[32] Charles S. Johnson, *Patterns of Negro Segregation*, Harper & Row, 1943, p. 79.

PREJUDICE AND THE NATIONAL WELFARE: POLITICS

It is generally held in the United States that a nation unified by common purposes and a shared allegiance is greatly to be desired. Virtually everybody also defends a political system in which differences of interest are resolved in a process of free discussion and by democratically elected representatives. It is a truism to say that prejudice and discrimination attack these values; but some of the precise ways in which they injure the democratic process should be noted. Not everybody, of course, shares these values or gives them top priority. Some people have political power or hold office precisely because of prejudice and tend, therefore, to look upon the results that we mention below not as costs but as gains. A reader who takes this position will want to reverse the value orientation of the following discussion but will concur, if the analysis is accurate, on what the effects are.

In the South, one important political concomitant of prejudice has been the long series of devices, used since the days of Reconstruction for keeping the Negro disfranchised. These have largely been swept away, by judicial decision and legislative enactment, so that we are now witnessing more residual than direct consequences. We shall not at this point describe the role of minority groups in the political process (see Chapters 13 and 14), but simply note some of the costs of this situation for the majority. Not only has the Negro been prevented until recently from achieving the gains that he might make by using the political instrument, but the great majority of *white people* of all classes have been injured. The lower-class Whites have been made politically ineffective by the prevailing system; all the people of the southern region, even those who technically manage the governmental machinery, have been affected by the limitation on issues that come to the fore in a political situation geared to protecting a status system; and the nation as a whole is vitally influenced in a federal system in which the votes of representatives from each area determine policies that affect citizens in every area. Let us examine each of these situations briefly.

1. Some of the laws that were devised to disfranchise the Negro had a similar effect on many of the Whites. If the poll tax stood as an economic barrier to black citizens, it was scarcely less of one to an even larger number of Whites. (It is now outlawed.) The poorer Whites were also affected to a minor degree by educational and property requirements in some states. Actual disfranchisement, however, is far less significant than a general political ineffectiveness. For generations, a significantly lower percentage of eligible voters participated in elections in the South than in the North. This is still true, although the differential has been reduced. It reflects not only inability to vote but also a lack of interest in government. The lower classes have little power in party circles, except for the few who actively enter politics. (This is an important avenue of vertical social mobility for some, but seldom do they stand as representatives of the lower classes.)

A political system whose key function, at least on the surface, has been to keep the Negro from political power puts a sharp limitation on the kinds of issues that will be discussed. There is a tendency for all candidates to center their claims around their enthusiasm for, and their ability to enforce, the status system. "Personalities" thus tend to be the "issues" of the campaign. In a one-party system—the product of a desire not only to disfranchise the Negro but to control the average white citizen—significant local, national, and international issues are obscured even more than they are in the usual dual-party or multiparty campaign. When all candidates must try to prove that they are the "true" representatives of *the* party, they inevitably tie themselves to old slogans and traditions.

Not only do the masses of Whites in the South find themselves, because of their desire to keep the Negro down, faced by a political system that obscures the central political issues; they also put themselves more largely under the influence of demagogues. With one-party politics enforcing a kind of unnatural political unity on white men, they are reduced to a negative least common denominator of solidarity—white supremacy. The person seeking political power is encouraged to appeal to this common emotion. A candidate who tried to make a rational analysis of an issue would divide the electorate, but one manipulating the theme of white supremacy could count on a vigorous emotional agreement from the great majority. In recent campaigns in the South, it should be noted, racist appeals have been sharply reduced; and in those states with significant numbers of black voters, conciliatory campaigns are not uncommon.

2. It is usually assumed that even if the Negro and the poorer Whites suffer from an oligarchic political situation, at least the small group of dominant Whites profit by the one-party system, the small electorate, and their own controlling position in political activity. Even this assumption is not entirely correct. They too suffer from a political system that easily gives power to men who play upon hate, fear, and prejudice. They suffer from the support this gives to all the other costs discussed above. And although it is not eliminated, the power they might have in national political circles is reduced. It is not by accident that Lyndon Johnson was the first American president since the Civil War to be elected from the South. (Woodrow Wilson may be looked upon as a partial exception, since he was born in Virginia; but he was elected from New Jersey.) Until recently, the Democratic party has largely been able to count on the southern vote and thus has been able to give its major rewards to other sections. (We shall see shortly that some other factors increase the national power of southern political leaders.) Middle- and upper-class persons who are part of the rapidly expanding urban South are less effective politically whenever the race issue is the central problem of southern politics. Even more than in the rest of the country, rural areas have been overrepresented in southern legislatures. So long as the race theme dominates political discussion, urban leaders are in a poorer position to work for policies much more important to their interest than segregation. Recent "one man,

one vote" rulings of the Supreme Court, it should be added, have sharply reduced rural overrepresentation.

3. The political costs to the whole nation of a political system that rests in an important measure on race prejudice must also be noted. Each legislator in Congress, no matter how elected, represents every citizen in the country; he sets policies and votes on laws that affect everybody. A senator elected by a small percent of the adult population of Mississippi represents every citizen of Maine and South Dakota. Because of the one-party system and the small electorate, politicians in the South tend to have a longer tenure of office than those in the North. Thus, owing to the seniority system in Congress, southern representatives have a large number of committee chairmanships when the Democratic party is in power. They have the additional advantage of experience, which increases their power.

4. The political effects of prejudice in the North are somewhat different from those in the South but are also costly to people who start from a democratic value premise. There is little actual disfranchisement of Negroes or other minority-group members. By crowding them into slums, however, by limiting their economic opportunities and the educational incentives, the North helps to encourage bossism, political corruption, and apathy. And the whole community is affected by the political machine thus sustained. Democratic representation is also sometimes blocked in the North by gerrymandering—determining the boundaries of election districts in such a way that the vote of a minority group is cut into small segments, each too small to elect a candidate. Here, again, we should note that in the last few years, legal and judicial actions, the civil rights movement, and the further concentration of blacks in many cities has reduced these political effects. There are many more black politicians and they are much less dependent on white support and mass apathy.

5. A final political cost of prejudice to the majority has not yet loomed large in the United States but under some circum-

stances grows in importance. This is the appeal to minority groups of political movements and ideologies that the dominant community considers subversive and dangerous. Every imperialist nation in recent years has carried the burden of arms, and often of battle against nationalist uprisings, as a price for its discriminatory treatment of colonial peoples. Where discrimination has been strongest, the national protests have taken the form of a reflexive prejudice that has reduced the chances for peaceful and cooperative interchange. Thus the relations of the nations of the West with the emerging nations of Asia and Africa are complicated not simply by the desire for freedom, but by the suspicion and the prejudice that many of the people of these continents have for the nations of the West.

The situation in the United States is not entirely different, although it has not developed very far. Negroes, for example, have become Communists in insignificant numbers, despite intensive efforts by the Communist Party to win them. A big recruiting drive in 1930 persuaded several hundred to join, but many resigned after a few months. The total had not reached 3000 by 1940, a figure representing less than ten percent of the membership. There may have been a few years in the early 1940s when the Negro membership constituted a little more than ten percent of the total.[33] The Communist Party expelled anti-Negro members for "white chauvinism"—often fairly trivial signs of personal prejudice—and promoted many Negroes to responsible positions in an effort to recruit more Negroes, but with little success.[34]

Comparing the experience of American Negroes to those from other parts of the world whom he met in Paris at a Conference of Negro-African Writers and Artists, 1956, James Baldwin wrote: ". . . we had

been born in a society, which, in a way inconceivable for Africans, and no longer real for Europeans, was open, and, in a sense which has nothing to do with justice or injustice, was free. It was a society, in short, in which nothing was fixed and we had therefore been born to a greater number of possibilities, wretched as these possibilities seemed at the instant of our birth. Moreover, the land of our forefathers' exile had been made, by that travail, our home."[35]

However, it would be a mistake to conclude that American Negroes have no difficulty in giving unqualified allegiance to a nation that makes them second-class citizens. Baldwin's ambivalence is shown by his remark, a few sentences after the statement quoted above: "We had been dealing with, had been made and mangled by, another machinery altogether."[36] We have seen in Chapter 6 that the highly disprivileged are the least supportive of civil liberties, and the most likely to approve the use of violence. Negroes were far less willing in World War II than in World War I to postpone their demands for equal rights; and they are far less ready in the 1970s than ever before to wait for some natural process of evolution or the reform of white men to bring them equality. Civil disobedience —the explicit and open violation of hated laws—has become a major part of their civil rights campaign. So far this has been mainly a highly disciplined and restrained violation of laws of doubtful constitutionality. To their opponents it threatens anarchy; to their defenders it expresses another step in America's continuing revolution, with strong kinship to a movement that goes back at least to the Boston Tea Party. But to all it documents the depths of their opposition to a segregated and discriminatory society.

In the late 1960s, even as political participation by Blacks and election to office increased, a sharper attack on the legitimacy of the political system, paradoxically, also increased. The attack, expressing extreme

---

[33] Nathan Glazer, *The Social Basis of American Communism*, Harcourt Brace Jovanovich, 1961, pp. 174–175.

[34] *Ibid.*, chap. 5; Wilson Record, *The Negro and the Communist Party*, Univ. of North Carolina Press, 1951; Wilson Record, *Race and Radicalism: The NAACP and the Communist Party in Conflict*, Cornell Univ. Press, 1964; Harold Cruse, *The Crisis of the Negro Intellectual*, Morrow, 1967, pp. 147–170.

[35] James Baldwin, *Nobody Knows My Name*, Dell, 1961, p. 20.

[36] *Ibid.*, p. 21.

alienation, ranged from violent rhetoric to a few instances of open attack. Even the full range includes only a small minority of America's black population, but they represent the most severe expression of political alienation since the days of the Communist Party's campaign to attract black adherents.

At various points we have cited instances of this alienation, and will add only a few items here: 25 percent think Negroes should arm themselves.[37] The same proportion think "a great deal" of the Black Panthers, whose image is of militant pressure against the system.[38] For some, Castro, Mao, and Che are heroes; they see Blacks in America as a colony under white domination—with every right and obligation to break out. "The Black Panther Party is a revolutionary Nationalist group and we see a major contradiction between capitalism in this country and our own interests. . . . We have two evils to fight, capitalism and racism. We must destroy both racism and capitalism."[39]

If America has not yet faced the problem of a thoroughly restive political minority in her midst it is partly because of the inarticulateness of the masses of minority-group members, the compelling hope of the American dream, the progress toward equality that has been made in the last fifty years, and the lack, until recently, in the world outside, of a powerful and successful competing system. If these conditions change, as the first and last have already changed, one can look for sharper internal conflicts, with the costs they entail.

PREJUDICE AND THE NATIONAL WELFARE: INTERNATIONAL RELATIONS

Closely related are the effects of prejudice on the relationships among nations of different race or religion. In times of inter-

[37] *Newsweek,* June 30, 1969, p. 15.
[38] *Time,* Apr. 6, 1970, p. 28.
[39] "An Interview with Huey Newton" in August Meier, Elliott Rudwick, and Francis L. Broderick (eds.), *Black Protest Thought in the Twentieth Century,* Bobbs-Merrill, 2nd ed., 1971, p. 496.

national tension these become a particularly heavy cost and command the careful attention of policy makers. It has been widely noted that American treatment of minority groups receives world-wide attention. During World War II the forced relocation of Americans of Japanese ancestry and the discrimination against Negroes in the United States were exploited by Japan as propaganda among the colored peoples of the world. Even Germany, whose basic philosophy and practice were thoroughly discriminatory, played upon the theme of American hypocrisy. The propaganda was often exaggerated or distorted, but there were many instances of violence and injustice upon which to build, so that our enemies had only to cite our own papers to get evidence. A riot, a lynching, or a case of legal injustice in the United States was, and is, a subject of great interest in Peking, in Oslo, in Tokyo, in Moscow.

In the current tensions between the Soviet Union and the United States, Communist policy makers and propagandists are given a genuine advantage by past history and present incidents in American race relations. Both the imperialism and the color prejudice of many of the Western powers have been of great advantage to the Communists in winning the support of large numbers of Negroes in the East. Winning the war was complicated for the United States by the mistrust, and often hostility, of non-white allies who had heard of and experienced so much of the white man's prejudice. And now the even more important problem of finding a road to international cooperation under law is confused by the barriers of prejudice. Negroes have petitioned the United Nations for an investigation of their treatment in the United States—an indication of the fact that our prejudice is even less of a local issue than it used to be. In a world that has become so thoroughly interdependent white people dare not disregard the growing power and population of predominantly colored nations. If they wait until colored people have achieved great power before they "grant" them equality, they may well face a reciprocal prejudice which will not be content simply with equality. As Myrdal said, a generation ago, "Their race pride and race prejudice is still mostly a defensive mental device, a secondary reaction built up to meet the humiliations of white supremacy. . . . It should be apparent that the time to come to an understanding on the basis of equality is rapidly running out. When colored nations have once acquired power but still sense the scorn of white superiority and racial discrimination, they are likely to become indoctrinated by a race prejudice much more akin to that of the whites—a race prejudice that can be satisfied only by the whites' humiliation and subjugation."[40] If, on the other hand, Myrdal goes on to say, America now moves toward a fuller realization of her own creed, if she takes the lead in abolishing color prejudice, she will gain immensely in prestige and power around the world. "In this sense the Negro problem is not only America's greatest failure but also America's incomparably great opportunity for the future."[41]

It is almost a truism to note that world opinion of American race relations is highly negative, and has become more so in recent years.[42] That time for adjustment of America's racial policies has not yet run out is due, perhaps, both to the modification of those policies in significant ways and to the fact that few nonwhite nations have, as yet, achieved great power.

This does not mean that America's past and present racial policies cause her no difficulties. It requires perhaps an excessively vivid imagination to think of a world divided between the Whites and Nonwhites in hostile confrontation. Despite recent events, it does not require too much imagination to think of China trying to lead a coalition of Asiatic and African nations

held together in part by resentment of the past (and present) imperialisms and prejudices of the white man. During a conference of the Afro-Asian People's Solidarity Organization in Tanganyika, in February, 1963, the Chinese delegation sought to expel the Soviet group on the grounds that it was noncolored.[43] The first formal statement ever issued under the name of the Chinese Communist leader, Mao Tse-tung, August, 1963, was an appeal to the world's Nonwhites to unite.[44] We doubt that such appeals will succeed. Political, economic, and military interests do not coincide with race lines; and African and Asian nations will look with a wary eye at any new attempt to dominate them, no matter the slogans used. Nevertheless, lines of cleavage can be deepened by appeals to race, and failure on the part of the United States to improve her race relations weakens her international position. In this sense we agree with Lomax ". . . that to the degree that the Negro wins his battle for total involvement in the American mainstream, the world will move just that much farther away from a race war."[45] A well trained and motivated black population in the United States could be one of the world's greatest resources for peace.

Some of the precise ways in which prejudice and discrimination have been costly to the United States need to be indicated. The attitudes of the people of East Asia, one of the critical areas of the world today, have been greatly influenced by American action. Beginning with the Chinese Exclusion Act of 1882 and coming to a climax in the comprehensive immigration law of 1924, we proclaimed to the Asiatic people that they were unfit for citizenship, that they were racially unqualified to associate with us. From the very beginning, this attitude affected international relations. Carey McWilliams points out that in 1882 an active anti-Semitic movement was being organized in Germany and that it immedi-

[40] Myrdal, *op. cit.*, p. 1018.

[41] *Ibid.*, p. 1021.

[42] See Hazel Erskine, "The Polls: World Opinion of U.S. Racial Problems," *POQ*, Summer, 1968, pp. 299–312. These opinions, it should be noted, are not themselves without bias. It is not clear that America has some special capacity for making invidious distinctions, over and beyond the capacity so widely shared among the peoples of the world.

[43] *The New York Times*, Aug. 13, 1963.

[44] *Ibid.*, pp. 1, 21.

[45] Louis Lomax, *The Negro Revolt*, New American Library, 1963, p. 260.

ately used the anti-Oriental laws and activities in the United States as an example to prepare German opinion to favor exclusion of Jews.[46] In East Asia there were many reverberations of our "yellow peril" agitations; the Boxer Rebellion in China and the rise of militarism in Japan both drew power from American prejudice. Particularly after the passage of the Immigration Act of 1924 (which explicitly barred further Japanese immigration to the United States despite the fact that a "gentlemen's agreement" of almost two decades' standing had effectively achieved the same result with less resentment), nationalists in Japan began to exploit antiwhite sentiments. The act was very important in the defeat of Japanese liberals and in the rise of militarists to political power. Our prejudice was used ". . . as a means of inflaming Japanese public opinion against America; as the excuse for ever-increasing military and naval appropriations; as an excellent issue to exploit for domestic political purposes inside Japan; as a *quid pro quo* in dealings with the United States; and as a means of diverting widespread social discontent in Japan into chauvinistic channels."[47] We do not imply that American prejudice completely explained or justified Japanese activity; but it was an important factor, and a heavy cost, in America's international relations.[48]

Discrimination is also an expensive luxury for the United States in Central and South America. Our treatment of the five million people of Mexican descent is a continuing problem between the United States and a nation whose friendship is of great importance to both the security and the economic interests of Americans. Particularly in the Southwest, along the extensive boundary that divides the two countries,

people on both sides are continually asking favors that depend upon good will.

The Good Neighbor Policy, which has been such an important part of American policy in recent years, is vitally affected by prejudice and discrimination. Our protestations of friendship sound less than sincere to the nations of the south when they are followed by expressions of race prejudice, either against them, against the citizens of other nations, or against residents of the United States itself who have migrated from these lands. Most of the Central and South American countries are complicated mixtures of Indian-Negro-White stock. Race lines are relatively unimportant and race prejudice is looked upon as an affront not only to the individual but to the nation as well.

As a result of independence for many African nations in the last several years, the number of African diplomats in Washington has increased greatly. Much to the injury of American interests, they have had serious difficulty in finding adequate housing. Representatives from Asian countries also experience some difficulty. Even though this problem has been reduced, the difficulty is not solved, for ". . . these diplomats need only look about to see that they are being singled out for special and isolated treatment and that an American Negro otherwise just as qualified cannot move into the same building."[49]

SUMMARY

We have examined only a few of the costs of prejudice for members of the dominant group. Although there may be some gains, there are far more losses in the long run. One could scarcely expect otherwise among a people who proclaim a democratic ideology with great fervor and in a highly inter-

---

[46] Carey McWilliams, *A Mask for Privilege*, Little, Brown, 1948, p. 16.

[47] Carey McWilliams, *Prejudice, Japanese-Americans: Symbol of Racial Intolerance*, Little, Brown, 1944, p. 8.

[48] We noted in Chapter 4 that America's immigration law was modified in 1952 and significantly changed in 1965, sharply reducing the racial and ethnic biases it had contained.

[49] See United States Commission on Civil Rights, *Civil Rights U.S.A. Housing in Washington, D.C.*, 1962, p. 26. The statement was made by Angier Biddle Duke, who at the time was the State Department Chief of Protocol.

active world of many races and religions. For those who rank "race purity" and segregation as in themselves among the most desirable of values this assertion is, of course, not true. But for those who give such values a low ranking or even a negative position, the costs of prejudice are demonstrably great. The threat to a democratic society—and the opportunity—are well put in the poetic words of James Baldwin:

If we—and now I mean the relatively conscious whites and the relatively conscious blacks, who must, like lovers, insist on, or create, the consciousness of the others—do not falter in our duty now, we may be able, handful that we are, to end the racial nightmare, and achieve our country, and change the history of the world. If we do not now dare everything, the fulfillment of that prophecy, re-created from the Bible in song by a slave, is upon us: *God gave Noah the rainbow sign, No more water, the fire next time!*[50]

Many people agree with Robert MacIver that the greatest cost of discrimination is the loss of purpose and solidarity that are the strength of a people. His statement may well sum up the whole question:

Whatever is distinctive about this country, its spiritual heritage, comes from the recognition and the liberation of the universal in man, transcending division and harmonizing differences. It is this heritage, exalting the rights and the liberties of men, that more than anything else America must stand for if it stands for anything. It cannot stand on alien traditions but on this thing that is peculiar to its own being. Without that, we are spiritually impoverished, voiceless, and inarticulate before the world.[51]

[50] James Baldwin, *The Fire Next Time*, Dial Press, 1963, pp. 119–120.
[51] MacIver, *op. cit.*, p. 6.

Chapter 9 / ANTI-SEMITISM—A CASE STUDY IN PREJUDICE AND DISCRIMINATION: THE SOCIOLOGY OF ANTI-SEMITISM

In the preceding six chapters we examined the major factors involved in prejudice and the consequences of prejudice for both the dominator and the dominated. Our primary concern has been with general principles, not with prejudice as it refers to any particular group. Throughout the rest of the book we shall continue to approach the question topically, not by the study of particular minorities. In this chapter and the next, however, our aim is to use the principles already discussed to analyze the prejudice against a specific group. By a detailed study of one minority, the usefulness of the concepts we have employed may be tested and a more unified picture of the complex interactions involved may be observed.

Anti-Semitism is in many ways the "classic" prejudice. Through the course of centuries it has illustrated all of the intricately related forces at work. It has ranged all the way from "polite" social exclusion to vicious pogroms. Insecure persons have found the Jews a convenient scapegoat—available in almost every land, relatively powerless, distinguishable by religion and in some instances by culture, and approved by tradition as a target for hostility. In almost every major economic or political conflict in the Western world in the last several centuries one of the opposing forces, or both, has employed anti-Semitism as a weapon. Millions of people who have never known a Jew are equipped with a ready-made picture of his supposed physical appearance and personal characteristics.

Hasty observers—including many Americans—are likely to say "there must be something to it" if a prejudice has existed so long and expressed itself in so many different settings. They overlook the self-perpetuating nature of a deep-seated prejudice, once it has become thoroughly established. Nowhere is the cumulative force of

several factors more clearly shown than in the discriminations directed against Jews. A careful study of anti-Semitism is a magnifying glass of great value in the examination of prejudice. There are unique elements, of course, for no two cases of prejudice are exactly alike. But the uniqueness consists largely in the particular combination of forces in the history of anti-Semitism. Most of the forces involved are also found in other cases of prejudice, which will, therefore, be better understood by the analysis of anti-Semitism.

Anti-Semitism may be defined as any activity that tends to force into or to hold Jews in an inferior position and to limit their economic, political, and social rights. It is not simply opposition to Jews because they are different, although that has sometimes been the explanation. It is more often, at least in the modern world, opposition to Jews because they are not different, i.e., because they have become effective competitors for the values being pursued by the prejudiced person.

The term "anti-Semitism" calls attention to the Semitic origin of (many) Jews in order to identify them as a "race" and thus make use of feelings of race prejudice against them. In Chapter 2 we noted the errors involved in designating the Jews as a race; we need only repeat here that they are a very mixed group, by no means purely Semitic, that there are many Semites who are not Jews and many Jews who are not Semites, that Semites are simply a branch of the Caucasian race, and that even were the Jews a distinct race the fact would create no consequences of importance for human behavior.

THE ORIGINS OF ANTI-SEMITISM

Although the term "anti-Semitism" is comparatively new, having first been used by a German journalist, Wilhelm Marr, in 1873, opposition to Jews is very old. Its recent manifestations can be understood only by an account of the historical conditions out of which they emerged. Historical analysis cannot reveal the contemporary forces that sustain this attitude. It can, however, reveal the traditional source of the prejudice and help in understanding its functions and dysfunctions. Although the circumstances that led to modern anti-Semitism are probably impossible to discover, they are doubtless related to the conflicts between the Jewish people and their neighbors in the ancient world. Located at a strategically important point in the Near East, their land was under almost constant pressure from the succession of ancient empires (and pressure on that area continues down to the present). Out of these early conflicts the Jews developed a strongly unified religion-culture. Their unity was doubtless at first a reflection of the continuous threats and attacks that their geographical position encouraged. But, once established, that unity, with its ethnocentrism, reacted upon the situation, making them more vulnerable to attack. Their land was invaded and many were driven into other areas.

There were three major dispersals of Jews during antiquity: the Babylonian captivity of the sixth century B.C., the dispersals of the Hellenic period, especially under Alexander the Great in the late fourth century B.C., and the migrations caused by the Roman conquests, particularly in the first century A.D. This last dispersal saw Jews following the Romans into Italy, Spain, and France. Many crossed the Rhine into what is now Germany, and that was the home of a large proportion of European Jews during the Middle Ages. Not until the first Crusade (A.D. 1096) did this group begin to move east of the Rhine valley.[1]

Conflicts accompanied these migrations and contacts. There was no anti-Semitism as we know it today, for the conflicts were probably similar to other national and im-perial struggles of the time; but owing to the constantly repeated pressures on the Jews, and their reciprocal intense group cohesion, the opposition gradually became traditional. There was conflict between the ancient Greeks and the Jews because the national, economic, and religious interests of the two nations frequently collided. But this was scarcely anti-Semitism; there was also strong opposition between Greek and Persian, Greek and Roman, and finally Greek and Greek. While the Roman Empire dominated the land of the Jews, it was relatively tolerant of religious and cultural differences if they did not obstruct political allegiance. Not until Christianity became the dominant force in Europe did opposition to the Jews begin to develop into categorical anti-Semitism. This fact has led many people to suppose that religious conflict is the "ultimate" cause of anti-Semitism. It is more likely that several causes were involved from the beginning. Although religious symbols were often used to describe the conflict, this can be understood only against the earlier conflicts of empire and the dispersals.

One of the most puzzling problems is that the Jews survived at all as a distinct group, rather than disappearing into the ranks of the dominant society or changing too much to be recognizable. No other ancient cultural-national group has survived with such distinctness. It is tempting, in trying to explain this continued identity, to rely on some simple one-factor theory. Many authors believe that religion is the basic cause of their survival. Carl Mayer says:

I contend that the *prima causa* of their survival is *religion*. The term "religion" must be understood here not in any narrow theoretical or abstract way but in the meaning it has to the Jewish people, inextricably interwoven as it is with the whole social and political texture. . . . The pure idea of monotheism is the first powerful factor for the preservation of the Jews. The second reason for their survival is to be found in the Messianic idea with its accompanying idea of the kingdom of God on earth, for it has provided the Jews with the supreme certainty that the kingdom of God on earth will eventually be realized if only they remain faithful and true to

[1] R. H. Lowie, *The German People*, Holt, Rinehart & Winston, 1945, p. 87.

the one God. Another potent factor in the situation is the idea of the special mission that the Jews as the chosen people have to fulfill. This gave them a rare confidence in themselves which proved of tremendous survival value. Finally, there is the ritual whose importance in the survival of the Jews as a people can hardly be exaggerated.[2]

These four characteristics of Judaism have doubtless contributed. We would add only that these elements themselves have to be explained. Judaism was not carved in all its complexity on the tablets of Mount Sinai, but is itself one of the adjustments of a people to the circumstances of their history. If we replace the idea of religion as the *prima causa* with the concept that religion is one of a complex series of interacting causes, then an analysis of the elements in Judaism that give it survival power is valuable. Mayer himself describes some of the other elements that resulted in the continued identity of the Jews as a people (only, it must be added, he sees them as working in the opposite direction): "They persist despite all temptations and threats to merge which they have encountered in their history. They persist in the face of pressure, hardship, hatred, and persecution which have constantly been their lot. They persist despite their loss of statehood, despite dispersion and exile, and despite their precarious existence everywhere."[3] Threats, persecution, loss of statehood, dispersal, and a precarious existence, in the total setting within which they functioned, actually brought cohesion to the Jews. As Hertzler says:

This sentiment of solidarity, exclusiveness, and superiority was not created by the Jews themselves. Originally they were a conglomeration of tribes, distracted by internal dissensions between families, classes, tribes, and the major cleavage between Israel and Judah. Extraneous pressure and a common protective need forced them so closely together that there was no room for intranational fighting and they were forced to think in terms of unity and act in effective concert. The Jews, in brief, were crushed into the cohe-

sion of an invincible national cultural solidarity. In no other people is this common cultural consciousness so emphatic and so enduring.[4]

Keeping in mind the concept of interacting causes, we can profitably examine the role of religious differences in anti-Semitism. These differences alone would probably not have produced the observed results, but they intensified and sustained them. In A.D. 313 Christianity became the official religion of Rome. By the fifth century full citizenship rights became dependent upon religion—as contrasted with the relatively tolerant view of the early empire. Jews were forbidden to try to convert Christians; intermarriage became a crime, as did the acceptance of Judaism. These developments occurred, significantly, at a time when the Roman Empire was torn by conflict and dissension. Christians were no longer available as targets for hostility, a role they had filled in earlier conflicts not perhaps so much for their religious difference as for their lack of enthusiasm for the secular power of Rome. In his *Apology*, Father Tertullian described the earlier situation sharply: "If the Tiber rose to the walls of the city, if the inundations of the Nile failed to give the fields enough water, if the heavens did not send rain, if an earthquake occurred, if famine threatened, if pestilence raged, the cry resounded: 'Throw the Christians to the lions.'"

Now the Jews, easily distinguished as a religiously different group at a time when religious beliefs were of great importance, began to fill the same role.

There was especially sharp conflict between Christianity and Judaism because of the nature of their relationship. The Christian inevitably felt ambivalent toward the Jew. Both shared belief in the Old Testament but interpreted it differently. Jesus was a Jew, but he was accepted only as a prophet or rejected entirely by those who clung to the older religion. The strength of the antipathy toward Jews was in part a result of the very fact that Christianity was in such an important measure of Jewish

[2] In Isacque Graeber and S. H. Britt (eds.), *Jews in a Gentile World*, Macmillan, 1942, pp. 316–317.
[3] *Ibid.*, p. 315.

[4] J. O. Hertzler, in *ibid.*, p. 71.

origin. Christians got rid of their doubts and ambivalent feelings on this score by projecting exaggerated hostility onto the Jews. An "intolerant minority under an intolerant majority" produced a sharp line of cleavage. Once politically disfranchised and religiously condemned, the Jew was subjected to a long chain of pressures that made hostility toward him progressively easier. He was not to be an employer of labor, a physician, an artisan with a Christian apprentice—on the basis of the fact that he was not a believer, and was therefore a dangerous person.[5]

It would be a mistake to assume that these religious differences were not involved, just as it is a mistake to assume that they are the basic cause of anti-Semitism. They help to explain why the Jews were selected as a target for hostility but do not explain the need for that hostility. Judaism was the only non-Christian religion in Europe. Owing to the background we have discussed, it was an especially ethnocentric religion; the Jews' god was the only god, their customs were the divinely revealed and therefore true way of life. This attitude is characteristic of all people, but, perhaps as a compensation for the sufferings they had experienced, Jews gave it special emphasis. They turned suffering and persecution into a kind of religious victory; their pains "were actually a matter of congratulation, pride, and self-glorification, because they were to result eventually in historic vindication."[6] Their very emphasis on religion, in the midst of a dynamically expanding Christianity, made the Jews particularly vulnerable to attack. And they clung to their religion with a rigid conservatism—it seemed to be their one dependable source of security—that made it at many points out of place in a changing civilization.[7]

The idea that they were God's "chosen people" was doubtless an attempt to compensate for the fact that they had obviously not been "chosen" to lead a life of security and power on earth. To the medieval Christian, however, this arrogant belief was just a fact. His own life had not always been comfortable, and here were those who challenged his religion—one of the few things that brought, or at least promised, him comfort. So the Jews became the "Christ killers." It was believed that they sometimes got hold of sacred bread and tortured it until it bled. In 1243, scores of Jews at Beelitz near Berlin were burned at the stake on this charge, and in 1420 the whole Jewish community of Vienna was exterminated on the same allegation.[8] Such violence created an ever more intense need for anti-Semitism to justify it. It is very difficult not to hate someone whom you have harmed.[9]

One of the aspects of this cumulative and self-sustaining process was the segregation of Jews in ghettos. At first segregation was voluntary, if not actually a right demanded by the Jews for services rendered the rulers of a city. Within the ghetto they could more readily protect their way of life from the invasions of the surrounding culture and they could protect themselves more easily. This self-imposed segregation, however, encouraged the very differences by which anti-Semitism justified itself. There was a transition from voluntary to compulsory segregation. By the time of the Crusades, the church was restricting contact, for fear that the alien beliefs of the Jews would weaken the faith of Christians. "The Lateran Council of 1179 definitely forbade true believers to lodge among the infidels, lest they be contaminated by false beliefs. The Counter Reformation perfected this system

---

[5] For an examination of the influence of theology and church policy in the growth of anti-Semitism, see James Parkes, *The Conflict of Church and Synagogue*, Meridian Books, 1961.

[6] Hertzler, *op. cit.*, p. 70.

[7] *Ibid.*, pp. 67–70; see also Jacob Katz, *Exclusiveness and Tolerance: Studies in Jewish-Gentile Relations in Medieval and Modern Times*, Oxford, 1961.

[8] Louis Golding, *The Jewish Problem*, Penguin, 1938.

[9] It is a measure of the tensions in Jewish-Christian relations that this distortion of history was not officially repudiated by the Catholic Church until the Second Vatican Council acted, in 1965. Even after that, anti-Semitic passages were removed only slowly from various catechisms. See *The New York Times*, July 14, 1967. Efforts at reconciliation, however, should also be noted. See, for example, Katharine Hargrove (ed.), *The Star and the Cross*, Bruce, 1966.

and made it universal as far as Catholic Europe was concerned. Pope Paul IV in 1555 decreed that Jews were henceforth to be segregated strictly in their own quarter, which was to be surrounded by a high wall and provided with gates, closed at night."[10]

The religious terms in which opposition to Jews was phrased disguised even in earliest times, but more and more from the time of the Crusades, an equally fundamental economic conflict. Before the tenth century, Jews were the chief merchants of Europe; many of them were international traders, bringing together the mutually hostile Christians and Mohammedans. Probably only a fraction of the Jewish population of Europe were traders; some of the Jewish communities on the Rhine had the longest record of continuous European settlement to be found; there were many agriculturists and artisans. Nevertheless, their loss of citizenship after the fifth century and their isolation in the midst of a civic-religious society forced a relatively higher proportion of them into marginal economic activities.

Beginning about the tenth century, trading became less marginal. Cities grew; there was an increase in business and in prosperity. More and more Christians turned to trade and soon outnumbered the Jews. As citizens, the Christians had a great competitive advantage over their rivals.

They formed themselves into municipal corporations and trade guilds for competitive purposes. Using their commercial resources to increase their political power, and joining with the prelates in their agitations against the Jews, they presently had the Jews limited in their property-owning and industrial activities by various restrictions. Being unable to compete with their Jewish rivals, who were both more experienced and better connected with coreligionists in distant commercial cities, the Christian businessmen urged the actual exclusion of Jews from trading. In this they were soon successful.[11]

The growth of cities in Italy in the tenth century and in Germany in the eleventh brought with it a strong increase in the

[10] Hertzler, *op. cit.*, p. 72.
[11] *Ibid.*, p. 87.

practice of, and demand for, a money economy. The church prohibited the lending of money at interest, but the canon law allowed Jews to lend to non-Jews. Being gradually forced out of the large-scale trading ventures, many Jews turned to usury. This established a complicated series of relationships with the emerging commercial and industrial economy. The lending of money was an important contribution in the transition from a barter to a money economy; but while making the contribution, Jews made themselves targets for a many-sided attack—from merchants who wanted to borrow from them but at the same time to fight them as competitors, from the church which condemned their usury, from the nobility who used them as tax collectors and bankers but wanted, at the same time, to exploit them as much as possible, and a little later from Christian bankers and usurers who wanted to drive them out. It was not the fact that they were traders and bankers that made the Jews subject to attack in the new commercial world, for they had occupied those roles in the early medieval world with much less prejudice shown them. Anti-Semitism grew rapidly after the tenth century because Jews were traders and bankers in a setting that made these occupations increasingly profitable and therefore led to their being invaded by Christians in large numbers.

The church's condemnation of usury made sense in the relatively self-sufficient, largely barter economy in which a large proportion of the population lived, even down to the eighteenth century. Under those circumstances, a person borrows money only when he has suffered some unusual loss—long illness of the breadwinner, loss of crops, a destructive fire. To charge interest in such a situation is to kick a man when he is down. To the great majority of people, this continued to be the perspective on interest-taking: it was robbery; money was unproductive and yet one had to pay for its use. Since Jews were identified as the usurers, they were hated for this injustice. There was a great deal of stereotyping in this judgment, of course. Not all Jews (in fact, only a small minority of them) were usurers nor were all usurers Jews. "The statement that one constantly meets that 'all usurers were Jews, because the church forbad usury' is as true as that all adulterers were Mohammedans because the church forbad adultery."[12] But at first there were more Jewish money-lenders, especially of the pawnbroking variety with which the average man might have dealings; Christian moneylenders were likely to work in secret, for their activities were condemned. Thus the stereotypes held by the masses of medieval citizenry were reinforced.

Prejudice and discrimination against Jews by the Christian merchants themselves had a different motivation. "Those who speak of the 'Shylocks' in medieval ghettos seldom ask themselves: What were the rest of the townspeople doing? How could they have borrowed, had they not been earning enough to meet a high interest on loans?"[13] The tradition-minded peasantry may have opposed the Jewish merchant and moneylender because his activities were bad according to their standards, but the Christian townspeople attacked the Jew because his activities were good—i.e., profitable. Having found trading a profitable venture, many Christians, by the thirteenth century, had turned to banking. The church's condemnation of usury was not enforced or it was circumvented by accommodating formulas. Anti-Semitism, involving both projection (the Christian bankers were perhaps not without some guilt feelings) and economic conflict, was a natural product of this situation.

A third group was related to the Jews in an ambivalent way during this period. The Jew, lacking citizenship, was permitted to reside in a city only at the will of its prince. The prince exchanged protection for certain economic services. "The royal method of collecting a substantial proportion of their revenue was to license their Jewish serfs to lend money to their Christian subjects, and then collect the profits."[14] It was in the interests of many of these princes to keep their Jewish subjects as dependent as possible, and yet they found them of great assistance in financial undertakings such as the purchase of war supplies. Only when Christian bankers became so powerful that the Jews were no longer indispensable did the princes join in open opposition.

The medieval church was involved in the discrimination against Jews not only because it regarded the religious difference as dangerous but also because it was an enormous secular power, particularly in Italy and southern Germany. One of the important supports to the Reformation in northern Europe was the effort of the emerging industrial and merchant class to free itself from domination by Italian financial houses. This secular aspect of the church involved it in discrimination not only against Jews, who could be robbed under the pretext of their disbelief, but also against the whole heretical Protestant movement.[15]

Opposition to Jews was not the only significant conflict of the period. There is good evidence that much of the stereotype of the medieval Jewish "Shylock" is a result of the selective memory of modern historical accounts, and it tells as much about contemporary anti-Semitism as about the anti-Semitism of medieval Europe. Such works as Sombart's *The Jews and Modern Capitalism* try to show that the Jews were primarily responsible for the first stages of capitalist development. Extensive commercial activity was carried on by gentiles in Italian cities as early as the tenth century, however, and the inevitable strains connected with the emergence of a new society led to their condemnation as well as to dislike of Jews. Miriam Beard writes:

The medieval mind did not, in fact, regard the Jew as the financial master of Europe. On the contrary, it recognized the far more dangerous threat to feudal economy emanating from Gentile Italians, in particular the papal bankers of Florence. . . . The grasping extortioners who

---

[12] James W. Parkes, *An Enemy of the People: Antisemitism*, Penguin, 1946, p. 64. This book has been revised under the title *Antisemitism* (1963). Our citations are from the earlier version.

[13] Miriam Beard in Graeber and Britt (eds.), *op. cit.*, p. 379.

[14] Parkes, *op. cit.*, p. 65.

[15] Beard, *op. cit.*, pp. 382–383.

are seen writhing on the burning sands of Dante's Hell, expiating their usurious crimes, are all excellent Christians of the best Italian families. . . .

The myth of Shylock, then, has persisted largely because we lack two important histories: (1) we have no complete story of the *friendly* relations between Jews and Christians and (2) we have no history of the *popular animosity toward Gentile bankers and monopolists* through the Middle Ages and Renaissance.[16]

These observations should help us to keep the anti-Semitism of medieval Europe in perspective. They do not, however, eliminate the long story of discrimination, expulsion, and bloody violence that characterized European treatment of the Jews from the time of the Crusades on. ". . . In north European lands, Ashkenazim Jews were no sooner forced to make debtors of nobles and neighbors than they enlarged the risks of being discriminated against . . . Those who owed him money at a high rate of interest were only too easily tempted by the incitements of fanatics and demagogues."[17] The course of some of the Crusades could be traced by the trail of violence against Jews that they left. In 1290 the Jews were expelled from England, in 1306 from France, and during the fourteenth and fifteenth centuries from many of the cities in Germany and Austria. In 1298, 146 Jewish communities in Germany were utterly destroyed on a charge of ritual murder in one of them. During the middle of the fourteenth century, a quarter to a third of the population of Europe was wiped out by the Black Death. Greatly in need of an "explanation" to allay its fears and a scapegoat upon whom to thrust its hostilities, community after community turned on the Jews. Owing to religiously prescribed diet and cleanliness, Jews were struck down less often by the disease. They were in league with the devil; they had poisoned the wells. Driven by this myth, many towns did not wait for the plague to hit them but attacked the Jews as potential well-poisoners. "Within two years nearly

three hundred and fifty Jewish communities were exterminated."[18]

In 1492 the Jews were expelled from Spain.[19] The push to the northeast which began with the Crusades was given another impetus. In earlier centuries the Sephardic Jews of Spain and Portugal, who had not been forced into moneylending, had been an accepted part of the population. But by the late fourteenth century they were caught by the conflicts of the Inquisition and a century later were driven out of the Iberian Peninsula. Year by year, from the Crusades on, Western Europe forced its Jewish population back. When Russia threw up a barrier on the east by prohibiting Jewish migration into her lands, the waves of refugees settled in the ancient kingdom of Poland. Here, until the twentieth century, resided the largest Jewish population of the world. And here the vicious attacks on Jews that had characterized Western Europe were repeated. Hundreds of Jewish communities were exterminated in repeated pogroms from the sixteenth to eighteenth centuries. ". . . The outbreak of the Ukrainian Cossacks against Polish misrule in the seventeenth century was accompanied by a series of onslaughts on the Jews. The toll of Jewish lives between 1648 and 1658 may be reckoned at 100,000. A hundred years later, bands of 'Haidamack' rebels rose again in the Ukraine, perpetrating atrocities which at least rivalled these."[20]

ANTI-SEMITISM IN CZARIST RUSSIA

By the nineteenth century, Russia had become the center of anti-Semitic violence. Although she had excluded Jews, her own imperial expansion, both into Poland and into the Black Sea area, had brought millions

[16] *Ibid.*, pp. 380–384.
[17] Hertzler, *op. cit.*, pp. 87–88.

[18] *Ibid.*, p. 95.
[19] Although this edict was annulled by the Constitution of 1869, which proclaimed religious toleration, it was not until 1968 that the order expelling Jews from Spain was explicitly repealed. See *The New York Times*, Dec. 17, 1968, pp. 1 and 14.
[20] Louis Golding, *op. cit.*, quoted in Alain Locke and B. J. Stern (eds.), *When Peoples Meet*, Hinds, Hayden and Eldredge, 1946, p. 269.

of Jews under her domination. They were not to be absorbed, however. A series of decrees limited their rights, restricted their mobility, and severely discriminated against them. An edict of Nicholas I in 1827 regulated military service. Although Jews received none of the privileges of citizenship, they were forced to give a double share of military service, 25 years, often at great distance from their homes. During this period every effort was made to force them to accept Christianity—their food was confined to pork for long periods or they were compelled, under threat of severe military discipline, to perform some Christian rite.[21] Almost complete segregation of Jews was the rule in Russia.

Down to the end of Tsardom she remained determined to exclude this unwanted mass from penetration into the old provinces of Russia. A new kind of ghetto was created in the form of a series of provinces along the western frontier in which the Jews were compelled to live, and even within these provinces their rights of settlement and choice of occupation were severely restricted. Outside of these provinces selected categories of Jews might reside, visit certain fairs, and, provided they did not exceed a small proportion of the total enrollment, study at the universities. The area of settlement was known as the Pale, and it contained more than a half of the Jewish population of the world.[22]

Anti-Semitism was not simply an official Czarist policy. Time after time it took the form of a mass movement. The complete destruction of Jewish communities that had characterized the earlier anti-Semitism of Western Europe, was common. The government was indifferent to these attacks or, more probably, actively interested in funneling off hostility onto the Jews. Russia had been least affected by the economic and political changes of the nineteenth century. Her standard of living was very low, her government highly oligarchic and inefficient.

Alexander II, to be sure, was somewhat liberally inclined. During his rule educated and wealthy Jews gained a few rights—to live outside the prescribed area, for example —and the military inquisition was replaced by universal military service. More Jewish students attended Russian schools and universities. The great masses of Jewish people, however, remained culturally isolated and outside the protection of the law. And when, in 1881, Czar Alexander was murdered—a symbol of the great discontent in the land— renewed waves of anti-Semitism began. The government virtually invited the masses to riot on Easter to punish the Jews (no Jew had been among the murderers). There followed two weeks of pogroms that the government explained as the incitements of revolutionary parties. Further rioting occurred that summer and during the spring of 1882, followed by new decrees (the "Temporary Rules"—which lasted for 35 years) that even more sharply limited the freedom of Jews. (During these years millions of Jews fled from Russia and Poland, a majority of them to the United States.)

Anti-Semitism in Russia, particularly after 1881, was closely related to the rising revolutionary pressure against the czarist regime. It is not that Jews were the primary leaders in the revolutionary movement. The repressive measures, to be sure, made radicals of many Jewish youth. The protests, however, went far beyond them. The rulers sought, by attacking Jews, to make "the struggle for liberty appear detestable to the people by representing it to be the work of the Jews."[23] Alexander III showed some personal dismay at the pogroms; he wrote in the margins of the government reports on the pogroms such remarks as "extremely sad and perplexing." But it did not occur to him that his own anti-Semitism—he and his son Nicholas II had the traditional stereotyped views of the Jew as a parasite and extortioner—and the activities of his own officials were important causes of the violence.

Not all of the Russian ruling class looked

[21] James W. Parkes, *The Jewish Problem in the Modern World*, Thornton Butterworth, 1939, pp. 82–83.
[22] *Ibid.*, p. 80.

[23] Hugo Valentin, *Anti-Semitism Historically and Critically Examined* (trans. from the Swedish by A. G. Chater), Viking, 1936, p. 81.

with favor on anti-Semitism as a weapon against reform or revolutionary activity. In speaking against the severely repressive "Temporary Rules" that Count Ignatyev, Minister of Interior, was seeking to apply against the Jews, Count Reutern declared, "The governmental authorities remain inactive in the face of obvious Jew-baiting. . . . Today they hunt and rob Jews, tomorrow they will go after so-called kulaks, who morally are the same as Jews only of the Orthodox Christian faith, then merchants and landowners may be next. In a word, in the face of such inactivity on the part of the authorities, we may expect in a not distant future the development of the most horrible socialism. . . ."[24] Count Reutern was not demonstrating a personal lack of anti-Semitism or a liberal view but was pointing to the inefficiencies of hatred as a weapon.

Events seem to have proved him correct. Political anti-Semitism continued to grow (there were 100 openly anti-Semitic members in the second Duma and more in the third), and pogroms continued; but they did nothing to slow down the demands for drastic changes. The short-lived Kerensky republic brought complete emancipation to the Jews. The Bolshevik revolution, however, and the civil war that followed caught them between the opposing forces. The aristocracy identified Bolshevism with Jews, the Bolsheviks identified the Jews with wealth and power, whereas in fact the great majority of Jews had supported the liberal and social-democratic movements.

Thus the great final struggle between the Bolsheviks and their opponents in 1919–20 brought upon Russian Jewry a catastrophe of dimensions previously unknown. The desperate Bolshevist troops and robber bands, who looked on the Jews as hated bourgeois and, moreover, were themselves by no means free from anti-Jewish feelings, often started pogroms, which, however, were punished as far as possible by their leaders. But the White generals deliberately handed over the Jewish communities to the mercy of their soldiery. The orthodox Jewish masses of the Ukraine, to whom Bolshevism was a godless abomination, were put to the sword as—Bolsheviks.[25]

THE REVIVAL OF ANTI-SEMITISM IN MODERN EUROPE

The treatment of Jews in czarist Russia might be called the last expression of medieval anti-Semitism. Russia was still largely a feudal society, and the complex causes operating there were quite similar to those in western Europe centuries earlier. The fall of the czarist regime, however, by no means brought an end to anti-Semitism. That cycle was completed, but another was already under way. As early as the middle of the nineteenth century in Western Europe a new wave of anti-Semitism, based on the old antipathies that had been carried along as tradition, but with new factors added, began to rise. For a hundred years or more, economic improvement, the Enlightenment, and the growth of traditions of religious liberty and political democracy had brought more and more freedom to the Jews. Almost everywhere the rising middle classes, looking for support in all quarters, won the active support of Jews. Slogans of liberty and individualism, so appropriate to their battle against the feudal society, did not harmonize with the surviving restrictions on Jewish life. Jews, for their part, saw in the new society the possibilities of far greater freedom. In 1791 the National Assembly declared that all Jews in France were full-fledged citizens. The Edict of Toleration, issued by Emperor Joseph II in 1781, removed some of the restrictions in Austria. One by one the German states granted civic equality to Jews. By 1870 virtually all of the legal restrictions on their economic, political, and religious activities had been abolished in Western Europe.

This freedom had scarcely been accomplished, however, before a new revolutionary struggle began to shake the foundations of the European social structure. Unemploy-

[24] Quoted by Mark Vishniak from the diary of E. A. Peretz, in K. S. Pinson (ed.), *Essays on Antisemitism*, Conference on Jewish Relations, 1946, p. 134.

[25] Valentin, *op. cit.*, pp. 93–94.

ment and economic distress brought new frustrations to the masses. And the ruling groups found themselves faced with strong revolutionary pressures. It was soon apparent that the traditions of anti-Semitism were still strong and that many of the economic causes of antipathy toward Jews were still operative despite the legal changes of the nineteenth century. By 1870 anti-Semitism was surging up with renewed vigor as a manifestation of the tensions and conflicts of the time. There was a strong resurgence in Germany and Austria, where diverse groups found anti-Semitism a common rallying ground or, equally, an effective weapon with which to fight each other.[26] The last third of the century brought to Germany, more rapidly than to almost any other country, the social strains that everywhere accompanied the industrial revolution—threatened loss of power for the old landed aristocracy; insecurity for the lower middle class; the emergence of a large class of toolless proletariat, subject to the vicissitudes of the economic market; and a peasantry that found its accommodations continually upset by the new society. Granted a tradition of anti-Semitism, the Jews could be made to seem responsible for the troubles of these widely differing groups. To many of the peasants they were the symbol of urbanism,[27] to the middle class they were direct competitors and symbols of "big business;" to the old aristocracy they were leaders of the new radicalism; and to some of the proletariat they were powerful industrial and financial leaders. One of the key factors in Germany's tragic history since 1870 is that these groups, whose accommodation somehow had to be worked out, directed much of

their energy into attacking their opponents with the weapon of anti-Semitism while disregarding any real issues. Each group could, to be sure, find evidence to support its stereotype of the Jew. He was largely urban middle class. Having been forced into cities by earlier restrictions, he was in a favorable position to take part in the growth of urban industrial society. German Jews were not only "town-dwellers in the first century of an almost entirely urban civilization; but they were most numerous in just those groups which were rapidly rising through prominence to the control of political and national life."[28] They were merchants and financiers and, as the educational system was opened to them, lawyers, doctors, journalists. Jews not only were urban but had an international cosmopolitanism that was of great advantage as they joined in the expansion of trade throughout the world during the nineteenth century.

Besides being deeply involved, *although as a small minority*, in the development of the urban industrial society, Jews oppositely occupied an important place in economic and political movements that carried direct and indirect threats to the power of the ruling group of that very society.

The nineteenth century was the century of constitutional radicalism, of liberalism and individualism—all the movements in which Jews found themselves most at home. It was natural that they should play their part in these parties, for it was to the great ideas of the French Revolution and the idealism which preceded it that they owed their emancipation; it was to liberalism and "the Manchester School" that they owed the removal of the bars to their economic advancement; and in the new spirit of social reform, and the new demands of social justice, they found a field of practical activity for which the deepest principles of their rabbinic inheritance had admirably prepared them.[29]

Thus Jews had a part in almost every phase of the development of industrial society. There were Jews among the proletariat, among the lower and upper middle classes,

[26] See Peter G. J. Pulzer, *The Rise of Political Anti-Semitism in Germany and Austria*, Wiley, 1964.

[27] George Kren notes how their urbanism was interpreted as rootlessness and a lack of feeling for traditional virtues, contrasted with the simple German peasant, in a famous German anti-Semitic novel, Wilhelm von Polenz's *Der Büttnerbauer*, 1895. "In the novel the Jew lends the peasant money at usury and the latter, unable to repay it, loses the land to the Jew who, without regard for the true purpose of the soil, builds a factory on it. The peasant, unable to bear this sacrilege, hangs himself on an old tree on the land." See George Kren, "Race and Ideology," *Phylon*, Summer, 1962, pp. 171–172.

[28] Parkes, *The Jewish Problem in the Modern World*, p. 39.

[29] *Ibid.*, pp. 39–40.

and among the wealthy financiers. There were conservative Jews, stanch supporters of Bismarck, who defended nineteenth-century capitalism, and others who were important in the growth of social democracy and communism. Such a variety of roles cannot explain anti-Semitism, but it helps to describe the supports to the traditional prejudice which the various groups were able to find in the environment around them. Start with this tradition that reaches back for more than a thousand years, add intense economic and political conflict with all the personal insecurities and frustrations that accompanied it, and you have the background for the revival of anti-Semitism in Germany after it had receded for a century or more.

The tradition of anti-Semitism had survived most completely among the isolated peasantry and "among the more obstinate of those who stood to lose from the developments of the century—the old landowning aristocrats, and the clericals anxious to retain the privileged position of the churches. They hated the entry of the Jews into their 'Christian' society; they hated the democratic, urban, commercial and secular civilization in which the emancipated Jews found themselves at home."[30] This latter group soon discovered that the tradition of anti-Semitism was still widespread and could be used effectively to confuse political issues, to unite otherwise divergent groups—all those who, for widely different reasons, disliked the nineteenth century—and to fight the rising liberal and radical movements. They were not without support from members of the German élite. Some intellectuals, perhaps most importantly Heinrich von Treitschke, expressed anti-Semitic beliefs.[31] We showed in Chapter 4 how Bismarck, despite the important roles that several Jews had occupied in his government, used anti-Semitism to hold together the alliance upon which his power rested. Needing the support of the Catholic center parties, whom he had offended by his earlier Kulturkampf with its anti-Catholic and secular elements, he

could represent the Kulturkampf as a Jewish-led secular movement. Hoping to kill the attraction of radical socialism, the conservatives gave some support to the mild reform program of Adolf Stoecker, founder of the Christian Social Workers' party and leader of the Antisemitic League. By using or at least accepting anti-Semitism, Bismarck hoped to split this group sharply from any feeling of identity with left-wing socialism, which was continuously identified as a Jewish product.

Stoecker at first had also hoped, with his Christian Social Workers' party, to keep the workers from social-democratic leanings. During the early years anti-Semitism was unimportant in his pronouncements, and demands for social reform for the workingman were important in his program. Stoecker failed, however, to appeal to the workers. His group became more and more of lower-middle-class composition, and in 1881 it officially dropped the word "Workers'" from its name. Beginning in 1879, anti-Semitism occupied a much more important place. Stoecker became the leader of the "Berlin Movement"—a group of diverse forces united in opposition to liberalism and clearly anti-Semitic "in the fight for God, Kaiser and Reich."

The anti-Semitism of the conservative forces was to some degree limited by traditions of western civilization and by religious symbols. By 1890 there were signs that it would lose out to an anticonservative anti-Semitism appealing more thoroughly to mass frustration and confusion. "When in November, 1892, against all expectations, more than twice as many votes were cast for the anti-Conservative anti-Semite Ahlwardt as for the Conservative candidate, the *Kreuzzeitung* emphatically called the event to the party's attention: 'Anti-Semitism which once in the Berlin Movement was the bridge for crossing over from the Liberal to the Conservative Party,' could again serve Conservative interests if the party took the lead in the battle against Jewry."[32] It was

[30] Parkes, *An Enemy of the People: Antisemitism*, p. 4.

[31] See Pulzer, *op. cit.*, chap. 26.

[32] Paul W. Massing, *Rehearsal for Destruction. A Study of Political Anti-Semitism in Imperial Germany*, Harper & Row, 1949, p. 65.

becoming apparent that the use of anti-Semitism in the political battles of the time could not be limited to the relatively conscious manipulations of the conservatives. Equipped for anti-Semitism by tradition, made ready for scapegoatism by the frustrations growing from a deeply rifted society, encouraged to hate the Jews by a ruling group that wanted to control them, and aroused to passion by rabble rousers, a small proportion of lower- and middle-class Germans were intense anti-Semites. They supported political parties whose main platform was anti-Semitism. This group was never large before World War I; its political representation, at least on the national level, was tiny. But it foreshadowed the developments of later years when defeat in war, a ruinous inflation, an ever sharper class conflict were to combine to increase its numbers enormously.

This extreme anti-Semitism was in itself a complex phenomenon, drawing together individuals of widely differing tendencies. One branch was composed largely of small-town people and was justified, by a perverted interpretation of Christianity, by religious symbols. Some of its leaders were drawn from the clergy who had links with the political anti-Semitism of the upper class, but many of the followers were from the traditional-minded lower middle class. Another branch, which later was to prove to be the dominant type, was anti-Christian as well as anti-Jewish. It opposed the Junkers and the big industrialists and, on the surface at least, supported the radical political tendencies of the time. This was a very unstable support, however, for the movement was essentially negativistic, drawing far more from personal frustration than from organized economic interest. Its members came from the most unstable elements of the middle class, who mixed their anti-Semitism with other panaceas—"body-building, vegetarianism, soul-breathing, monetary reform."[33] In the last analysis it was not the peasantry or the landed aristocracy, but the urban lower middle class who formed the core of the anti-Semitic movement. Not clerical power but deep-seated antireligious sentiments furnished much of the motive force.

The Beginning of "Racial" Anti-Semitism

At the end of the nineteenth century an anti-Semitism based on a traditional economic-religious conflict and on a contemporary political-economic struggle was being complicated by the addition of the "racial purity" myth. Perhaps more than any other one factor, this myth permitted modern anti-Semitism to become the focal point for the most diverse hostilities and frustrations. The tying together of individuals with enormously varying needs and desires inevitably made anti-Semitism a thoroughly nihilistic movement. The one common denominator was made up of fear, frustration, and hostility. If the various segments of the movement had been guided by their differing economic, political, and religious interests they would have attacked each other or some part of the social structure. But the times were too confused and insecurity was too great for them to know where to strike. Here was the answer, supported by tradition, reinforced by the cumulative effects of the allegiance of differing groups, and now made utterly definitive by an absolute racial ideology. Until the end of World War I there were relatively few converts or at least few active supporters for this myth; but it was elaborated and perfected in heavy tomes and propagandistic pamphlets and was ready at hand as an all-embracing explanatory principle when the enormous frustrations of the postwar period descended upon Germany.

The earlier anti-Semitism of the nineteenth century was rarely based on the supposed racial difference and inferiority of Jews. The historian Treitschke, for example, based his opposition to Jews on cultural grounds: "If it were possible to get our Jewish fellow citizens to feel themselves solely as German citizens of Israelitic faith, many a one-sidedness in the German character might find its salutary complement in Judaism. But only a part of the German Jews have so com-

[33] Carey McWilliams, *A Mask for Privilege: Anti-Semitism in America*, Little, Brown, 1948, p. 98.

pletely fused with our culture. . . ."[34] Even Houston Stewart Chamberlain, a British-born German citizen who became the intellectual leader of the "Aryan cult," did not rationalize his prejudice against the Jews in biological-racial terms. He used the term "race" in a very ambiguous way. It was not something entirely innate: non-Aryans might acquire the Aryan "spirit," and an Aryan might lose it. Nevertheless, Chamberlain developed a sharp contrast between the supposed traits of the Semite and of the Aryan and made the conflict between the two a leading principle of history. If anything was good, it was Aryan; if it was bad, it was Semitic. This distinction led to complications, because followers of the Aryan-Semitic conflict myth often did not agree on what was good and what was bad. "Thus to Chamberlain himself Goethe was so perfect an example of the purest Aryan that he quoted him in his *Foundations* no less than 127 times (according to the index). But another writer of the same school, Lenz, calls Goethe a 'Teutonic-Western-Asiatic cross-breed,' and proves it by an examination of the poet's mentality; while yet a third, Otto Hauser, proves his mongrel nature by the fact that in *Faust* there are 'hundreds of quite pitifully bad verses.' "[35]

Other writers, however, anticipated the extreme racial anti-Semitism of Hitler by declaring that the supposed inferiority of Jews was entirely innate. In 1886 George von Schönerer, an Austrian politician, proposed an immigration ban on Jews (modeled after the American anti-Oriental legislation) and special laws for native-born Jews. Religious differences were unimportant, he declared; it was the racial characteristics of the Jews that mattered. We shall see how this became the central item in the Nazi world mythology.

The Dreyfus Affair

Having discussed in some detail the revival of anti-Semitism in late-nineteenth-century Germany, we cannot undertake an analysis of the use of the prejudice in other countries. A brief statement concerning the famous Dreyfus case, however, will indicate that the political and social conflicts in Germany were matched by similar (not identical) struggles elsewhere. Massing gives an interesting interpretation of the differences in social structure—and therefore differences in conflict patterns—in Germany, France, and England.

In Germany, the forces that bred and used anti-Semitism were stronger and resistance to them weaker than in England or France. Politically speaking, conservative-clerical France, the France of the anti-Dreyfusards, had been beaten in 1789 and ever since had been engaged in a difficult comeback fight. Its counterpart in Germany had never lost its paramount position in state and society. In England and France, a national ideology had been developed by the middle classes which regarded themselves as the backbone of the modern state. In Germany conservatism took the national ideology away from the middle classes, its erstwhile herald, infused it with conservative-clerical values, and monopolized it to the exclusion of all other groups. By the end of the century Germany had become a leading industrial nation but its astounding industrial transformation was grafted upon a pre-industrial political structure. Groups victimized by industrialization saw the villain in "liberalism," in those forces which made for the socio-economic transformation of the nation but did not have the power or will to account also for its political life. In Germany, anti-Semitism thus found allies it could not have found at all or not in such strength in nations where the industrial revolution was accompanied by one in politics. In France and England the same social groups suffered from the advance of capitalism which in Germany registered their protest through anti-Semitism and antiliberalism. But in these countries they found no semifeudal, semiabsolutistic forces in power with which to align themselves against the upper bourgeoisie. They had to fend for themselves but they also had the opportunity to participate in forming the political will of the nation.[36]

The French Revolution had indeed produced a different distribution of power from that in Germany, but it had not created a

---

[34] Quoted by Lowie, *op. cit.*, p. 96.
[35] Parkes, *An Enemy of the People: Antisemitism*, pp. 49–50.

[36] Massing, *op. cit.*, pp. 80–81.

liberal, democratic state.[37] After 1870 the chief political conflict concerned the desirability of a lay state, with lay education, as opposed to a state and educational system tied closely to the church. French Jews were among the anticlericals and were therefore opposed by the old aristocracy.[38]

The Dreyfus affair pointed up this conflict. In September, 1894, it became known to the French general staff that the German military attaché in Paris had received secret military information from a French officer. Captain Alfred Dreyfus, the only Jew on the general staff, was accused, tried in an atmosphere of national tension, and sentenced to life imprisonment. The French conservative press and aristocracy made full use of the conviction to attack the Third Republic as a corrupt "Jew Republic," and for a time the conservatives made political gains from the controversy.

Gradually, however, the facts came to light. In 1896 Major Picquart, new chief of the Intelligence Department, learned that the papers on the basis of which Dreyfus was convicted were the forgeries of a Major Esterhazy. Major Picquart was thereupon transferred to Tunis by the general staff— in the hope of silencing him. In 1898, however, further forgeries by a Colonel Henry were exposed (Henry had been among the leaders of those who had accused Dreyfus), strengthening the hand of those who, like Clemenceau and Zola, were demanding a new trial. Colonel Henry committed suicide, and shortly thereafter Esterhazy was convicted of embezzlement and dishonorably discharged. He fled to England where he confessed his part in the forgeries. But even this did not settle the affair. The opponents of the Republic were not willing to give up the powerful weapon of anti-Semitism with which they had made some gains. The affair was an important issue in election campaigns, and the forces backing the anti-Dreyfusards were so strong that in the new trial in 1899, despite the evidence, Dreyfus was not acquitted. His sentence was reduced to ten years for "treason in extenuating circumstances," and then he was pardoned. In 1903 he appealed for a retrial; but this was not granted until 1906, when Clemenceau had become prime minister. Dreyfus was then acquitted and reinstated in the army with the rank of major. The issue was formally closed.[39]

This case is a very interesting example of the way anti-Semitism has become involved in the political struggles of modern nations. By playing on the insecurities and patriotic sentiments of the masses, the conservative and clerical forces were able to win some support from them. That Dreyfus was a wealthy man whose family had fled from Alsace to Paris when the Germans had taken over the province, that he was a fervent French patriot and hater of the Germans, that he was among the Jews who had assimilated to the French upper class to the point, in some instances, of adopting anti-Semitism —these facts did not prevent the conservatives from manipulating the trial to their own advantage for a time. In the long run, the forgeries boomeranged, and the political use of anti-Semitism was largely stopped in France until the confusing days of the Vichy regime during World War II.

During the early years of the Dreyfus affair, even some of the socialists—vigorous opponents of the conservatives and clericals —were convinced of Dreyfus' guilt.[40] They could not believe that such a wealthy man would be given an unfair trial. They looked upon the struggle as nothing but a conflict between two bourgeois groups. Jaurès, the leader of the socialists, took this view at first and was only gradually persuaded by the

[37] The period of the Enlightenment and Revolution in France was not entirely free of anti-Semitism. Diderot and Voltaire, for example, expressed some anti-Semitic beliefs. More important, however, was the development of civil equality. See Arthur Hertzberg, *The French Enlightenment and the Jews*, Columbia Univ. Press, 1968.

[38] See Thomas Anderson, "Édouard Drumont and the Origins of Modern Anti-Semitism," *Catholic Historical Review*, Apr., 1967, pp. 28–42. See also Paul Catrice, "L'Antisemitisme Social Français au Miroir de la Littérature des XIXe et XXe Siecles," *Revue de Psychologie des Peuples*, Sept., 1967, pp. 248–281.

[39] See the analysis of the Dreyfus affair by Hannah Arendt, in Pinson (ed.), *op. cit.*, pp. 173–217.

[40] For a general account of anti-Semitism among European socialists, see George Lichtheim, "Socialism and the Jews," *Dissent*, July–August, 1968, pp. 314–342.

course of events—and by Clemenceau—that a victory for the anti-Dreyfusards would be a victory for a conservative-clerical state and against the Republic.

Thus the Dreyfus forgeries did not "work." They did not succeed in assuring aristocratic control of the army or in destroying the Republic. But they were sufficiently powerful to keep France in political turmoil for years and to obscure basic political issues. It remained for the same kind of claims, repeated a hundred times in a defeated and confused postwar Germany, to occur in an environment more favorable to their success—with what results we are all too well aware.

ANTI-SEMITISM IN GERMANY AFTER WORLD WAR I

We have sketched some of the background against which one can begin to understand the most extreme and violent expression of anti-Semitism in history. In the 1890s, when the use of anti-Semitism as a political device was common in Germany, and even more common in Austria, a young Austrian came to Vienna. There he saw a frankly anti-Semitic party win two-thirds of the seats on the city council and witnessed the political manipulations of anti-Semitism by Karl Lueger, who for fourteen years was burgomaster of the city. Lueger's anti-Semitism ". . . was an open anti-liberal platform device. His pupil really set out to destroy physically those whom his master so constantly taught him to regard as the most dangerous enemies of the German people."[41] We shall not undertake to analyze the personality basis for Hitler's anti-Semitism. Apparently he had an overpowering need for a prejudice that would allow him to thrust off his frustrations and would "explain" a complex conflict situation. His personal frustrations were matched by the frustrated nationalism of an Austrian-German. It may well be that a rigid, authoritarian upbringing had created in him a self-splitting need for the contradictory feelings of dependency and domination described by Eric Fromm in *Escape from Freedom*. The important thing about Nazi anti-Semitism is not the personality of Hitler but the millions of times these same personality needs were repeated, for whatever reasons, in other Germans (and in people of many other lands), and the tremendous impetus given to the growth of those needs by the utter disorganization of the postwar period.

Even widespread personality tendencies, however, cannot account for the Nazi movement. Why did they coalesce into a social movement? What aspects of German tradition, social structure, and societal conflict prepared the way for Nazism instead of some alternative form of expression of those tendencies?

The masses did not ask for anti-Semitism, they wanted hate. They did not ask for the racial doctrine, they wanted to feel superior. They did not ask for the legend of the "stab in the back," they desired to rid themselves of what they felt to be a national humiliation. They did not demand the leader principle, but they wanted once more to obey instead of taking their own decisions.[42]

Reichmann's statement perhaps minimizes the anti-Semitic potential in the Germany of the 1920s, but it helpfully suggests that the final result was not simply the consequence of individual prejudices. These were drawn upon as resources by a revolutionary movement. They must be seen against a tradition of anti-Semitism that reaches back hundreds of years. In his detailed account of the Nazi policy of extermination, Hilberg notes the precedents of discrimination, stereotypy, and violence—even if not of genocide—in medieval Canon law, in the writings of Martin Luther, and in later German history.[43] We have briefly described the use of anti-Semitism as a political-economic weapon in the generation just preceding the rise of Hitler. To this we must add, as background influences, military defeat, the loss of colonies and homeland territory, the Versailles Treaty with its "guilt clause," the political

[41] Parkes, *An Enemy of the People: Antisemitism*, p. 18.

[42] Eva Reichmann, *Hostages of Civilization: The Social Sources of National Socialist Anti-Semitism*, Beacon Press, 1951, p. 191.

[43] Raul Hilberg, *The Destruction of the European Jews*, Quadrangle Books, 1961, pp. 1–17.

conflict of the left and right (with the Weimar Republic, in between, being torn to pieces), and the utter confusion of the inflation. These so enlarged the group of the hopeless, cynical, and confused that the basis was laid for the development of a strong anti-Semitic movement.

The active core of the Nazi party was at first drawn largely from the demobilized soldiers. Intensely nationalistic, embittered by defeat, unable to find a stable place in a shattered economy, accustomed to violence, they turned to a party that promised once again to exalt their nation above all others, that gave them a sense of power to overcome the feelings of hopelessness and a political philosophy that explained all their problems in simple terms: The Jews are to blame.

There is no way of knowing how large a proportion of the German people were staunch Nazis, even during the time of the party's greatest success. During the 1920s any slight improvement in the political-economic situation, as during the Locarno period, brought a reduction in members. By 1930, however, the Nazis were a major force. At least five groups could be distinguished then, and later during the period of Nazi rule, according to their attitude toward the party: There was the fervent group of active members. There was a larger group who agreed with many of the things for which Nazism stood or were persuaded by its propaganda, though they may have disliked some aspects of the movement. They voted the National Socialist ticket and supported its growth while not taking an active role in the party or its related groups. Its nationalism, its anti-Semitism, anticommunism, antidemocracy took their generalized, vague fears and insecurities and focused them, thus seeming to bring them under control. It "explained" things. A third group supported Nazism for rather conscious political-economic reasons—it could be used to defeat communism. By 1930 a world-wide depression was compounding Germany's internal economic problems; both the Communist and the Nazi parties began to get more votes; the balance of power in the German cabinet shifted to the right. In 1932, however,

the Nazis lost a few votes while the Communists continued to gain. At that point Hitler was invited to become premier, a position he assumed in January, 1933. Fear of communism on the part of the military and industrial rulers of Germany was an important factor in this legal *coup*.

The fourth group of German citizens were opposed to the Nazi movement generally but were unwilling or unable to take an active stand against it. The enormous risks to themselves and their families, or the feelings of helplessness, prevented them from open resistance. Another factor which reduced their opposition, however, was their partial sharing of the beliefs of Nazism. We are describing here a continuum, not sharply separate groups, and to *some degree* a high proportion of Germans were appealed to by the anti-Semitism and ultranationalism of Hitler. These were not the dominant beliefs of this fourth group, but their feelings were sufficiently ambivalent to make them helpless and ineffective in the conflict. The party propaganda machine skillfully played on these underlying attitudes in order to keep this group confused and helpless. The fifth group was composed of active and convinced anti-Nazis. Some fled the country to escape the Nazi regime or to fight it from abroad (not all who fled were anti-Nazi). Others opposed it from within the country; and a large number of Germans, Christians as well as Jews, faced the firing squad or were sent to concentration camps, beginning as early as 1934.

Whatever the relative proportions of these various groups, it is clear that a large number of Germans, by about 1935, supported or tolerated the Nazi movement. And in its growth to power anti-Semitism was the central coordinating belief. It was a theory of history, a source for a scapegoat, and a weapon for fighting both communism and democracy all rolled into one. The Jews made up less than 1 percent of the population of Germany, so they could hardly strike back. Yet they were sufficiently prominent, owing to geographical and occupational concentration (itself in part a result of anti-Semitism) for adroit propaganda to show, to the person ready to believe, how they "dominated" certain occupations. Before 1933 the leaders of the Weimar Republic, thoroughly insecure and on the defensive, were unwilling to endanger their shaky position by defense of the Jews,[44] whereas large numbers of Germans were entirely ready to accept just such an "explanation" of their woes as the Nazi anti-Semitic doctrine. Perhaps the most skillful use of anti-Semitism by Hitler was the way he won the support—or at least held off the opposition—of some of the most powerful industrial and military figures of Germany by making communism seem to be a Jewish product. This idea also appealed to many of the middle class, who identified themselves with the old regime in opposition to the urban proletariat. A traditional prejudice can be played upon in such a way that judgment is thoroughly lost, when the will to believe is strong. Only one out of 89 Communist members of the 1932 Reichstag was a Jew; there were only 600,000 Jews in Germany, but the Communists received almost six million votes—yet Nazi propaganda was able to link the Jews with communism in many people's minds.

Thus Hitler used anti-Semitism to forge a superficial unity out of intrinsically contradictory appeals.[45] The basis had been laid in *Mein Kampf* where he developed a theory of history that solves, at one blow, all the complicated problems with which modern social science contends. Success and failure, the good and bad are all to be explained by race:

Everything that today we admire on this earth—science and art, technique and inventions—is only the creative product of a few peoples and perhaps originally of *one* race. On them now depends also the existence of this entire culture. If they perish, then the beauty of this earth sinks into the grave with them.

The blood-mixing . . . is the sole cause of the dying-off of old cultures.[46]

Starting from this premise that race is the most important thing in the world, Hitler developed his conception of the Jews and their

role in Germany's problems. He distinguished three types of races: the culture-founders, the culture-bearers, and the culture-destroyers. Only "Aryans" are culture-founders; some other "races" are culture-bearers, although their role is precarious, depending upon contact with the superior Aryans; but Jews, said Hitler, are culture-destroyers. He pictured them simultaneously as weak and cowardly yet enormously powerful and dangerous, giving his followers a sense of fear, but then a way to escape their fear—if they would follow him. He exploited the individual feelings of powerlessness and terror in the modern world of confusion by describing the supposed plots and strength of the Jews, then gave his followers a sense of collective strength by making the Jews out to be cringing weaklings and by encouraging attacks against them. The mutually contradictory qualities in these stereotypes are no obstacle for those ready to believe and needing a security-giving formula.

If the Jews were alone in this world, they would suffocate as much in dirt and filth, as they would carry on a detestable struggle to cheat and ruin each other, although the complete lack of the will to sacrifice, expressed in their cowardice, would also in this instance make the fight a comedy.

. . . The Jew is led by nothing but pure egoism on the part of the individual.

Slowly the fear of the Marxist weapon of Jewry sinks into the brains and souls of decent people like a nightmare.

One begins to tremble before the terrible enemy, and thus one has become his final victim.

If we let all the causes of the German collapse pass before our eyes, there remains as the ultimate and decisive cause the nonrecognition of the race problem and especially of the Jewish danger.[47]

Using that kind of doctrine as rationalization, the Nazis launched the most extensive campaign against the Jews that the world has ever seen. We cannot undertake to list here in any detail the legal and economic discriminations, the systematic expulsion from almost every phase of German life, and the violence that characterized it. A few items will illus-

---

[44] Parkes, *An Enemy of the People: Antisemitism*, pp. 46–47.

[45] Martin Needler, "Hitler's Anti-Semitism: A Political Appraisal," *POQ*, Winter, 1960, pp. 665–669.

[46] Adolf Hitler, *Mein Kampf*, Reynal and Hitchcock, 1940, pp. 396, 406.

[47] *Ibid.*, p. 416, 447, 451. See especially chap. 9, "Nation and Race."

trate the cumulative attack. In 1933 a new civil service law dismissed all "non-Aryan" officials, excepting ex-servicemen or those who had held their jobs before August 1, 1914. This affected teachers, university professors, judges, public prosecutors, as well as the staffs of government bureaus. Non-Aryan lawyers were debarred and non-Aryan doctors deprived of their panel practice, with the same exceptions. In 1934 the "Aryan clause" was adopted by the army. In 1935 the Nuremberg laws deprived all Jews of citizenship and therefore eliminated all exceptions to the employment of Jewish officials that previous decrees had allowed. In 1936 the expropriation of Jewish-owned firms without compensation began. On November 10, 1938, an anti-Jewish pogrom started simultaneously in all German towns; all Jewish stores were demolished and thousands of Jews arrested. Jews were then required to repair all the damage; they forfeited any insurance claims to the government and were fined, collectively, about $400 million (one billion marks). On February 25, 1939, the Jewish community of Berlin was given orders to produce daily the names of one hundred persons who were to receive two weeks' notice to leave the country.[48]

That is only a very partial list. Both before and after Hitler's rise to power, threats and violence were part of the plan. After the outbreak of World War II and the extension of German domination over most of Europe, any restraints that still protected the Jews of Europe were abandoned. The Nazis systematically overworked, starved, and murdered them in every land they occupied. The outside world could scarcely believe the reports of the slaughter until German records, brought into the Nuremberg trials after the war, gave conclusive evidence. By 1945 the Nazis had killed six million Jews. Before the war there were over three million Jews in Poland; today there are only 32,000. At the end of the war scarcely 10,000 of the Jewish population of Germany remained. To the personal violence of the Crusades and the

planned violence of the czarist regime the Nazis added a technological violence that virtually destroyed the Jewish population of Europe outside of Russia. Perhaps a million escaped (to Russia, Palestine, the United States, Latin America, and elsewhere); perhaps a million are yet alive in Europe (not including Great Britain and the Soviet Union); but six million were killed.[49]

The brutality of the campaign is almost beyond comprehension. Lest we assume, however, that this somehow sets the Germans apart as altogether depraved, we ought to note, with Everett Hughes, that the capacity for violence and torture—or indifference to these things in others—is, most tragically, widely shared.[50] The need is to isolate, as precisely as possible, the cultural, structural, and personality conditions under which this capacity is maximized and the conditions that can minimize it.

ANTI-SEMITISM IN EUROPE AFTER WORLD WAR II

The defeat of Nazism and the virtual destruction of European Jewry removed anti-Semitism as a major political force in Europe. It did not, however, mean the disappearance of anti-Semitism from Europe. In the summer of 1949 the voters of West Germany held their first free election since 1933. Parties that were rather frankly ultra-nationalistic, pro-Nazi, and anti-Semitic received a vote variously estimated at from three to six millions, out of a total of 25 million. Since then, political anti-Semitism has faded. In the national election, September, 1969, the National Democratic Party, the major ultranationalist, rightist party in Germany, received less than 5 percent of the

---

[48] For a more complete listing of decrees, see "Twentieth Century Ghetto" in *Living Age*, Apr., 1939, pp. 154–160.

[49] For a detailed account of the Nazi definition of "Jew," the expropriation of their property and exclusion from occupations, their geographical concentration, and their final near annihilation, see Hilberg, *op. cit.*

[50] See Everett Hughes, "Good People and Dirty Work," *SP*, Summer, 1962, pp. 3–11; and also the exchange between Hughes and Arnold Rose, "Comment on 'Good People and Dirty Work,'" and "Rejoinder to Rose," *SP*, Winter, 1963, pp. 285–286 and Spring, 1963, p. 391.

vote, and thus failed to qualify for the Bundestag. However, the party's percentage of the national vote did go up to 4.3 from the 1965 percentage of 2.0. In three state elections, June, 1970, and two in November, 1970, the NPD suffered heavy losses, failing to qualify for any of the state legislatures.[51] There remain scattered acts of violence, vandalism against synagogues, publication of anti-Semitic pamphlets, and the expression of some Nazi sentiments. These persist against the opposition of the federal government and even though the Jewish population of West Germany is only 5 percent (30,000) of its prewar number.[52]

Other countries of Western Europe exhibit similar tendencies. This is particularly true of France, where remnants of her wartime regime, deep-seated political conflicts, and the migration of over 100,000 Algerian Jews combine to maintain a potentially difficult anti-Semitic situation.[53] Although the nearly half-million Jews in France are quite diverse ethnically, they tend to be highly assimilated to French culture. This does not eliminate the possibilities of anti-Semitic attitudes. The French Public Opinion Institute has reported that 10 percent of a sample of French adults admitted to being confirmed anti-Semites. Another 10 percent admitted feelings of antipathy toward Jews.[54] That these sentiments are not merely of the "genteel" or "aristocratic" variety sometimes deemed most prominent in France[55] is shown by the fact that the highest rate of anti-Semitism was among members of the Communist Party (14 percent). When Charles de Gaulle, provoked at Jewish resentment of his shift of support from Israel to the Arab states, characterized the Jews as an "élite people, sure of itself and domineering," L'express found that a larger proportion of those polled agreed with the General (44 percent) than disagreed (35 percent). The remark, made in 1967, brought sentiments to the surface in France that had been largely dormant since World War II.[56]

In other parts of the world, those countries with strong European ties experience persistent, even if minor, anti-Semitic outbreaks. This is perhaps most true of Argentina, with its Jewish population of over 400,000.[57]

Anti-Semitism in the Soviet Union

In Eastern Europe and the Soviet Union anti-Semitism continues to be used on occasion as a weapon of government. After the purge of Rudolph Slansky in Czechoslovakia, Premier Antonin Zapotocky declared: "We shall not tolerate any foreign influence in our affairs whether from Washington, or London or Rome or Jerusalem." He added that this was not the first time that "Jewish and other capitalists" had tried to interfere in Czechoslovakia.[58] After Soviet repression of the liberalization tendencies, in 1968, over 4000 Jews left Czechoslovakia in a few weeks time. In 1969, several thousand Jews left Poland, at least partly in response to government actions. "For about two years the Polish Communist Party has been purging Jews from its ranks and from public offices and jobs."[59] To the Polish government, Jews were uniformly Zionists; but in fact most would have preferred to remain in Poland. The largest number have migrated to Scandanavia. Perhaps 10,000 Jews remained in the country by 1970.[60] The situation is somewhat

---

[51] See Die Zeit (Hamburg), Oct. 3, 1969, pp. 4 and 6; The Times (London), June 6, 1970, p. 4; The New York Times, Nov. 9, 1970, pp. 1, 5; The New York Times, Nov. 23, 1970, p. 11E.

[52] See H. G. Van Darn, "Antisemitismus ohne Juden," Politische Studien, Mar.–Apr., 1965, pp. 133–138.

[53] See The New York Times, Nov. 11, 1962.

[54] Reported in The New York Times, Dec. 5, 1966.

[55] See Pierre Aubery, Milieux Juifs de la France Contemporaine, Plon, 1962.

[56] See The New York Times, Dec. 12, 1967, p. 2.

[57] For data on contemporary anti-Semitism in Europe and elsewhere, see the journal Patterns of Prejudice, which was started in 1967 by Institute of Jewish Affairs, London.

[58] See The New York Times, Dec. 23, 1951; Claire Sterling, "Anti-Semitism in the Satellites: The Wave of Fear Advances," The Reporter, Apr. 14, 1953, pp. 17–20; Arnold Forster and Benjamin Epstein, Cross-Currents, Doubleday, 1956; Peter Meyer, Jews in the Soviet Satellites, Syracuse Univ. Press, 1953; and Morris Fine and Milton Himmelfarb (eds.), American Jewish Yearbook, Vol. 70, American Jewish Committee and Jewish Publication Society of America, 1969, pp. 395–418.

[59] The New York Times, Oct. 5, 1969, p. 27.

[60] See Margaret Reynolds, "Reluctant Emigrés," New Republic, March 21, 1970, pp. 17–19.

different in Rumania, the home of about 100,000 Jews, where they live in comparative freedom.

The situation is most critical in the Soviet Union, where nearly one-quarter of the world's 12 or 13 million Jews live (estimates range from 2.2 to 3.0 million).[61] Against the background of generations of violence in pre-Soviet days and an official policy of non-discrimination today, we see a pattern of prejudice and attacks on the equal rights of Jews that seems designed both to use them as scapegoats and to destroy them as a distinctive ethnic group. The situation has become particularly acute since the 1967 Arab-Israeli war and the increase of Soviet military involvement with the Arab states.

It is difficult but important to keep distinct, in the analysis of Soviet policy and actions, three separate although highly interactive aspects: (1) policies that apply to all religions and ethnic groups in the USSR—or at least to all minority religions and ethnic groups; (2) political-military policies related to Soviet interests in the Eastern Mediterranean—policies that influence their treatment of Israel, their attitudes toward Zionism, and their efforts to repress any sympathy toward Israel expressed by Jews in the USSR; (3) and anti-Semitism in the more precise sense of opposition toward Jews as Jews. There is some tendency on the part of Jews outside the country, who are deeply concerned over the treatment of coreligionists in the Soviet Union, to put all Soviet actions into category three. Official interpretations from the Soviet Union take an opposite stand: There is no anti-Semitism; Jews are subject to the same laws and policies as are other "national" groups; "Zionist disloyalty" is of course repressed, but that is not anti-Semitism.

It is easy to read into a complex and ambiguous situation the interpretation most congenial to one's values. In our judgment, the Soviet Union is characterized by a disturbing amount of anti-Semitism. It is expressed particularly by the obstacles placed in the way of maintenance of Jewish religious and secular culture, beyond the obstacles placed in the way of other groups. There are severe limitations on publications, on religious training, on contact with coreligionists abroad, on the study of Hebrew or Yiddish. This judgment should be qualified, however, for there has been some abatement, certainly on the official level, of anti-Semitism since the days of Stalin. "For our society, nationalist vestiges in any form—be they manifestations of nationalism, or of Great Power chauvinism, or racism or anti-Semitism—are thoroughly alien, are in contradiction to our world outlook."[62] This 1965 statement by Premier Kosygin may be considered merely a pious gesture, but nothing like it had been heard in the country since the days of Lenin.

The position of Jews in the Soviet Union is complicated by the fact that they are rather widely scattered throughout the country. The "nationalities" policy refers particularly to regions, or to enclaves within regions, where a given cultural nationality has a majority. More than that, the liberal aspects of the policy have always been severely constrained by continuing pressures toward Russification. Zvi Gitelman describes this ambivalent situation well:

Soviet nationality policy is dualistic: it seeks to promote the culture of backward nationalities and, at the same time, to push many national cultures toward a merger with the Great Russian. This Stalinist dialectic posits as its final synthesis the "drawing together" and even the "merging" of all the cultures into one supranational culture. Since the Jewish people are politically and culturally weak, and geographi-

---

[61] According to the 1970 USSR Census, 2.15 million listed themselves as Jews, a figure 5 percent lower than the 2.27 million in 1959. Demographers in the USSR claim that assimilation accounts for the drop. See *The New York Times*, Apr. 17, 1971, p. 13; and *The New York Times*, May 8, 1971, p. 11.

[62] Quoted by William Mandel, "Soviet Jewry Today," *Issues*, Summer, 1968, p. 8. This whole number of *Issues* is devoted to articles on "Soviet Jews: An Investigation." See also Moshe Decter, "The Status of the Jews in the Soviet Union," *Foreign Affairs*, Jan., 1963, pp. 420–430; Solomon Schwartz, *Jews in the Soviet Union*, Syracuse Univ. Press, 1951; Fine and Himmelfarb, *op. cit.*, pp. 385–394; Ronald Rubin (ed.), *The Unredeemed: Anti-Semitism in the Soviet Union*, Quadrangle, 1969; and Joel Cang, *The Silent Millions: A History of the Jews in the Soviet Union*, Taplinger, 1970.

cally dispersed, the repressive arm of nationality policy can be raised against them. They feel only one of the two contradictory thrusts of Soviet policy. Furthermore, individual members of the Soviet apparatus, especially at the lower and middle levels, are often anti-Semitically inclined, especially in regions where anti-Semitism has strong native roots.[63]

The combination of traditional anti-Semitism, of persistent Russian nationalism, of opposition to traditional religions, and of a foreign policy that sets the Soviet Union on the side of the Arabs against Israel has produced a difficult situation for Jews in the USSR. To be sure, they are significantly "overrepresented" in professional and technical occupations. They still attend universities at a rate perhaps four times as high as their proportion of the population would indicate; (this rate has been reduced by the increased representation in universities of previously underrepresented groups). There is little discrimination on the social level. Yet Jews are severely constrained as a cultural and religious group. And even quasi-official anti-Semitism persists.

In 1971, Jews in the Soviet Union and those attending the World Conference Of Jewish Communities On Soviet Jewry in Brussels made strong appeals for the right to practice religious and cultural freedom and the right to emigrate. Members of the Jewish Defense League in New York pursued these goals more militantly, by shouting obscenities and harassing Soviet officials, for example. Whether because of, or in spite of, these pressures, some 2500 Jews were permitted to emigrate from the Soviet Union to Israel during the first four months of 1971—more than in any full year since the founding of Israel.[64]

In sum, despite the defeat of Nazism and despite the revulsion against its ideology and policies throughout Europe, we may not have seen the end of anti-Semitism, even of the organized and political type, in Europe and

the Soviet Union. Individual frustration focused by a traditional prejudice and the presumed usefulness of a scapegoat in internal and international affairs keep it alive.

ANTI-SEMITISM IN THE UNITED STATES

Some Americans assume that anti-Semitism is a characteristically European phenomenon with no hold in the United States. Others, stirred to action by the rise of Nazism in Germany, have perhaps overestimated the strength of anti-Semitism in this country. Our task is to examine the evidence to discover, as nearly as possible, its actual strength.

Overt manifestations of anti-Semitism were rare in the early period of American history. From the establishing of the federal government, Jews had complete legal and political equality, and it has never been lost. This is an important part of the total interacting pattern, for we have seen how the picture of the Jew as a noncitizen helped to shape the attitudes and actions of Europeans. Most Americans were Europeans, of course, and they brought much of their culture—including their prejudices—with them. The liberalizing influence of the American Revolution, however, and the vast opportunities available in the new land did not encourage the growth of anti-Semitism. The relatively small number of Jewish colonists and early immigrants, largely from Spain, Germany, and other countries of western Europe, was absorbed without a great deal of discrimination. The number grew slowly during the first century of the nation's history, and by 1880 there were 230,000 Jews in the United States.

At about that time several forces converged to stimulate the growth of anti-Semitism in America. "The second American Revolution," as Charles Beard calls it, was being won by large-scale business and industrial enterprise. The earlier pattern of small competitive firms was being broken by the rise of dominance of large oligopolistic concerns; and that shift demanded a whole chain of other adjustments. "Once trium-

[63] Zwi Gitelman, "Soviet Jews vs. Other Minorities: Similarities and Differences in Treatment," *Issues*, Summer, 1968, p. 13.

[64] See *The New York Times*, Jan. 17, 1971, p. 1-E; Feb. 22, 1971, p. 2; Feb. 26, 1971, pp. 1–2; May 1, 1971, pp. 1, 8.

phant, the industrial tycoons discovered that they could not function within the framework of the social and political ideals of the early Republic."[65] An open-class structure with rapid social mobility and free competition (and not simply free "enterprise") would be a serious obstacle to their power. Most of the men in this group of industrialists and financiers were of north European ancestry. Perhaps the most important challenge to their dominance came from the German Jews who had climbed with great speed to positions of power in middle-western and western cities.

Competition was felt not only at the top of the status ladder but also among members of the urban middle class. Parsons distinguishes between the "snobbish" anti-Semitism of the elite and the "envious" variety perhaps most common in the lower middle class. The former is expressed primarily in exclusion from "select" residential districts, clubs, and resorts. "Essentially these people are expressing through the scapegoat mechanism, their own sense of guilt that no longer are they basing their claims to status on the achievements of the individual, in which they are tacitly forced to admit that the Jew is fully their equal, but rather on social class and its symbols. It is not a matter of what you do, but of who you are . . . 'envious' anti-Semitism . . . is a rationalization of failure or of fear of it. The keynote is always that the Jew wins because he fights unfairly."[66]

After the Civil War a new stereotype began to develop in the United States and was added to those inherited from Europe. ". . . the Jew became identified as the quintessential parvenu—glittering with conspicuous and vulgar jewelry, lacking table manners, attracting attention by clamorous behavior, and always forcing his way into society that is above him."[67] This picture was not without some accuracy, but it ". . . held up a distorted mirror to the immigrants' foreignness

and cultural limitations and above all to their strong competitive drive and remarkable social mobility."[68]

Both among the elite and in the middle class, discriminatory action accompanied the stereotype. Jews began to be barred from some hotels, resorts, and residential areas. After about 1875, social exclusion spread rapidly, justified on the grounds that a person has a right to pick his social companions but ignoring the important place that clubs and other "prestige organizations" have in economic power struggles. They ". . . help to maintain higher and lower ranking in the community; . . . they function as a mechanism for placing people in the class hierarchy; and . . . they serve to impede movement out of the middle class into the upper class. In short, they organize and regulate upward social mobility. . . . Institutions of this character are not based on the innate congeniality of like-minded persons, but rather on the strategical consideration of consolidating a power relationship. Social power is organized by exclusion."[69]

The existence of a political democracy and the important role that many Jews played in the civic life of many American cities prevented a direct attack on their economic and political rights. The American upper class adopted a different approach, much less characteristic even of fairly intense anti-Semitism in Europe, that of blocking Jewish entry into the "social" life of the upper class and thereby restricting Jewish ability to compete economically and to win full status credentials.

The growth of political anti-Semitism in Europe after 1870 also had effects, both direct and indirect, across the Atlantic. Cultures exchange their prejudices as well as other practices. In the 1880s an Austrian politician modeled his anti-Jewish legislation after the pattern of the anti-Chinese acts in the United States. Similarly, the rising tide of anti-Semitism abroad gave impetus to it in America.

[65] McWilliams, *op. cit.*, p. 9.

[66] Talcott Parsons, *Religious Perspectives of College Teaching in Sociology and Social Psychology*, Edward W. Hazen Foundation, no date, p. 41.

[67] John Higham, "Social Discrimination against Jews in America, 1830–1930," *Publication of the American Jewish Historical Society*, Sept., 1957, p. 9.

[68] *Ibid.*, p. 10.

[69] McWilliams, *op. cit.*, p. 116. See also W. Lloyd Warner and Paul S. Lunt, *The Social Life of a Modern Community*, Yale, 1941, pp. 112 ff.

One of the important effects of European anti-Semitism on the United States was the tremendous force it gave to immigration, especially after the Russian pogroms of 1881–1882. From 1881 to 1914 nearly two million Jews, mostly from Russia and Poland, fled from eastern Europe. This influx did not contribute immediately to an increase in anti-Semitism in the United States. The Jewish immigrants came in, for the most part, on the lowest levels of our economy. The economy was still expanding rapidly so that, except during years of depression, it absorbed the newcomers with relative ease. Most of the powerful groups in America still encouraged immigration as a source of unskilled, and cheap, labor; and the native workers had not yet come to identify immigration as a major cause of their troubles—most of them were too close to the immigrant role themselves. By the turn of the century, however, America began to feel the effects of the closing up of the frontier; her economy took on a rigidity, a "stickiness," that it had not known before. Workers from abroad were not so readily absorbed, and agitation for their exclusion, which had already begun with the Chinese, grew in strength.

Meanwhile, many of the new Jewish immigrants, a majority of them skilled laborers to begin with, exhibited some of the same ability to improve their status that their western European predecessors had shown. They climbed in class status just when the "native" middle class was feeling strongly the effects of the increasing rigidity of the economy. The middle class was hard hit by the recurring depressions. And those in small businesses were being progressively weakened by the growing power of the larger concerns. The hostilities of the middle class were readily directed against the Jews because they, more than any other recent immigrant group, were in open competition with it. Moreover, the Jewish immigrants continued to be a distinguishable group into the second and third generations. Cultural differences did not of themselves, of course, cause prejudice. They simply assisted the revival of a tradition of anti-Semitism. As middle-class groups felt more competition from the Jews, they found the prejudice ready at hand and a fairly distinct group against whom to direct it.

The cultural contrasts not only separated the Jewish immigrants from the "native" population but also divided the Jews from Germany and west Europe from those who fled from Russia and east Europe after 1881. This distinction had a number of consequences, reflected in the relationships between Jews. The recent immigrants had been affected very differently by the growing nationalism of the period. "The older members of the western Jewish communities had become citizens before nationalism has become a dominant disease. They, therefore, when they became nationalists, became patriotic Englishmen, Frenchmen, Germans, or others. But these new arrivals had become nationalists while they were still living as Jews in an environment which did not desire to assimilate them. Their nationalism, therefore, was Jewish; and this division led to a violent, and still enduring conflict within the Jewish community."[70] Some German Jews, in fact, supported the restrictive legislation that would sharply curtail further Jewish immigration from Eastern Europe.[71]

In the period immediately following World War I there were a number of overt anti-Semitic developments in the United States. The forgery of the *Protocols of the Elders of Zion* (purported to be the plot of "international Jewry" to overthrow governments and conquer the world) was circulated. Part of the "red scare" was in the form of claims that communism was a Jewish product. The Ku Klux Klan, with its violent anti-Semitism, took on renewed vigor. In May, 1920, Henry Ford began a series of anti-Semitic articles in the Dearborn *Independent,* a paper with a circulation of 700,000, and in four pamphlet reprints from the articles. Ford gave wide currency to the *Protocols* and other anti-Semitic ideas, continuing his compaign, with various interrup-

[70] Parkes, *An Enemy of the People: Antisemitism,* p. 74.

[71] See Bernard Weinryb, Marshall Sklare (eds.), *The Jews: Social Patterns of an American Group,* p. 17.

tions, until 1926. In 1927 he became convinced that the *Protocols* was a forgery and —after a threatened libel suit, it might be added—publicly apologized.

Some of the anti-immigrant agitation of the postwar years involved opposition to the further entry of Jews into the United States. The laws of 1921 and 1924 were so drawn as to reduce the Jewish immigration to a small fraction of what it had been.

Overt anti-Semitism receded after 1927, only to come to the fore with renewed force in 1933. A deep depression, a slight rise in revolutionary sentiment (tempting reactionary forces to use the rusty weapon of anti-Semitism), opposition to changes brought about by the New Deal, and the coming to power of Nazism in Germany were among the factors contributing to its growth.[72] Strong records the founding of five anti-Semitic organizations in the United States between 1915 and 1932, nine in 1933, and 105 between 1934 and 1939—a clear indication of the rapid increase in organized prejudice during the 1930s.

During this period political anti-Semitism made its first significant appearance here. At no time did it reach a position of important political influence or become the central rallying point of a political party; but it appeared often enough in political debate to show that the United States is not immune, under certain conditions, to organized anti-Semitism. An occasional congressman (e.g., Representative Louis T. McFadden, Senator Theodore Bilbo) attacked Jews. The most prominent and probably the most influential of the political anti-Semites from 1938 to 1942 was Father Charles Coughlin. Anti-Semitism did not occupy an important place in his speeches and writings until he had already won national prominence by exploiting the fears and frustrations from depression at home and the growth of communism abroad. It is not possible, therefore, to know how much his support rested upon agreement with his anti-Semitism; but other issues were doubtless more important. Yet

the fact that he reached millions of persons every week through his radio broadcasts, his newspaper, and his extensive correspondence makes it likely that ". . . in him we have the foremost exponent of political anti-Semitism the United States has yet seen."[73]

More important than such scattered political efforts were the activities of the 121 or more frankly anti-Semitic organizations. We cannot undertake here an analysis of these groups, but they occupy an important place in American anti-Semitic agitation in the 1930s. Since 1941 such organizations, although they were perhaps more numerous in the immediate postwar years than at any other time, have been insignificant in the United States.[74]

Throughout the administration of Franklin Roosevelt anti-Semites sought to attack his policies by identifying them with Jews. Though their ideas were recorded in dozens of pamphlets and periodicals, they won little hearing even during the sharp controversy

[72] See Donald S. Strong, *Organized Anti-Semitism in America*, American Council on Public Affairs, 1941, p. 15.

[73] Gary T. Marx, *The Social Basis of the Support of a Depression Era Extremist: Father Coughlin*, Survey Research Center, Univ. of California, 1962 (mimeographed), p. 119. For another careful study of the social groups from whom Coughlin derived his strongest support, see Seymour Lipset, "Three Decades of the Radical Right: Coughlinites, McCarthyites, and Birchers," in Daniel Bell (ed.), *The Radical Right*, Doubleday, 1963, pp. 313–377.

[74] See, in addition to the works of McWilliams and of Strong, Leo Lowenthal and Norbert Guterman, *Prophets of Deceit. A Study in the Techniques of the American Agitator*, Harper & Row, 1949; and John Roy Carlson, *Under Cover*, Dutton, 1943. Using a somewhat different listing from Strong (who, they say, included moribund as well as active hate groups for his prewar estimate), the Anti-Defamation League listed the following totals for anti-Semitic organizations in the United States: 1940, 60; 1941, 73; 1942, 69; 1943, 73; 1944, 91; 1945, 112; 1946, 130; 1947, 115; 1948, 78; 1949, 66. See Arnold Forster, *A Measure of Freedom* (an ADL report), Doubleday, 1950, p. 81. Such groups have been given some new support by the desegregation conflicts. The National States Rights Party, in its publication *Thunderbolt*, Ed Fields (ed.), the Ku Klux Klan, the American Nazi Party, led by the late George Lincoln Rockwell, *Common Sense*, published by Conde McGinley, and *The Cross and the Flag*, published by Gerald L. K. Smith, all mix anti-Semitism with the fight against desegregation. These were among the most prominent of the 40 or more hate groups active in the United States in the early 1960s. See Allyn Robinson, Milton Ellerin, Robert Koenig, and Herman Reissig in *SA*, (whole issue), Nov., 1960, on "Anti-Semitism."

over isolationism before World War II. The same type of attack was directed against President Eisenhower, as illustrated by the following statement:

. . . The election of Eisenhower means that Baruch and his gang of powerful international Jews have captured the White House again. . . . This vicious international Jew machine . . . is as powerful among Republicans as it is among Democrats. . . .

The first step of Baruch and his ruthless ilk of international manipulators . . . will be to complete conscription of all human beings from 17 to 70. Their second gesture of tyranny will be to repeal the McCarran Immigration Act so that 20 million Jews and colored will be dumped on American shores. They propose to see to it that never again will the great white Christian population of America be able to express majority power. . . .[75]

It is paradoxical that anti-Semitic beliefs in the United States had some resurgence during and just after World War II, despite the ideological aspects of the war against Nazi Germany. Anti-Semitic beliefs declined in the 1950s and 1960s, as we shall see, but they did not disappear. In the spring of 1963 when Senator Thomas Kuchel spoke in the Senate on the "fright peddlers," he indicated that he was receiving 60,000 letters a month, perhaps 10 percent of which implored him to help get the United States out of the United Nations, clean out the traitors, and get rid of the income tax. If he tried to answer these letters, he received more appeals and more leaflets. His speech elicited a great deal of mail, about 4 to 1 supporting his view that the radical right represented a danger to the country. Some of his correspondents, however, wrote such things as this: "Pray tell us why the Senate is allowing Kennedy to disarm America and leave us at the mercy of the Communist Jews in the Jewnited Nations." Some identified the Catholic Church as the great threat; others put Catholics and Jews together. Some expressed dismay at the thought of the "94

Jews" President Kennedy had placed in key government positions.[76]

A publicly more visible phenomenon is the series of small acts of anti-Semitic vandalism that, at times, reach "epidemic" proportions. Such was the case following a widely publicized desecration of a synagogue in Cologne, Germany on Christmas Day, 1959. Within a month incidents had been reported from 34 countries, including hundreds in the United States. By March 1, 1960, the Anti-Defamation League of B'nai B'rith had recorded anti-Semitic acts in 236 American cities. "Eighty-four per cent of these incidents involved the construction and display, through various means, of swastikas and/or anti-Jewish epithets and slogans; 11 per cent involved mail, telephone, and personal threats; and 5 per cent of the incidents consisted of physical damage (other than mere defacement) of personal and community property."[77] Most of the participants were adolescent boys from working-class backgrounds. For perhaps half of them, the attack had no particular ideological significance. It was a prank or an expression of random hostility focused on Jews partly because of the publicity given the "epidemic." For others, however, there was specific hostility toward Jews. These boys were drawn in large proportion from broken homes, or homes where the father was weak; they had made poor school adjustment; many were personally unstable, with strong feelings of inferiority and with sadistic tendencies.[78]

During the course of this "swastika epidemic" 24 neo-Nazi clubs were discovered by Anti-Defamation League researchers. They previously had information on 13 others. These clubs had almost no connection with adult hate groups, with their political interests, but were preoccupied with symbols

[75] From the newsletter of Gerald Smith, quoted by Forster and Epstein, *op. cit.*, pp. 61–62.

[76] Reported in the *Progressive*, July, 1963, pp. 7–8.
[77] Howard Ehrlich, "The Swastika Epidemic of 1959–1960: Anti-Semitism and Community Characteristics," *SP*, Winter, 1962, p. 265.
[78] Herman Stein and John Martin, " 'Swastika Offenders': Variations in Etiology, Behavior, and Psycho-Social Characteristics," *SP*, Summer, 1962, pp. 56–70; see also Ehrlich, *op. cit.*, pp. 264–272; and David Caplovitz and Candace Rogers, *Swastika 1960: The Epidemic of Anti-Semitic Vandalism in America*, ADL, 1961.

of Nazi militarism, "the uniforms, flag, insignia and slogans of the Third Reich."[79]

It would be a mistake to exaggerate the importance of such incidents, making them appear to be a major anti-Semitic movement. To some degree they represent random adolescent aggression given focus on Jews by reports of earlier such acts. The appearance of an "epidemic" is partly a function of greater public awareness and greater police vigilance after a few dramatic incidents have occurred. And, as Caplovitz and Rogers wisely observe, the effect is not necessarily a net increase in prejudice. Some with mild predispositions toward anti-Semitism may become less prejudiced when they see the vandalism toward which their attitudes lead and the public censure which follows. Even some who are drawn into the action may be shocked into an awareness of their own intolerance. "Just as the epidemic may have taught some to be anti-Semitic, it may have taught others not to be."[80]

It would equally be a mistake, however, to disregard acts of desecration and vandalism or to dismiss them as unimportant. They indicate the presence of a tendency among some persons to focus hostile feelings onto Jews when a strategic incident triggers aggressive actions. And the absence of a clearly stated public standard against which participants in such actions can judge their own behavior could seem to lend legitimacy to their behavior.

Acts of vandalism, participation in hate groups, and political movements with anti-Semitic doctrines have attracted only a small minority of the American people. "Politer" kinds of discrimination, however, have been more widespread. These reflect particularly the transition of many Jews from the insecurities of immigrant status to effective competition for middle-class positions. By the 1920s, barriers to their entrance into white-collar jobs, colleges and graduate schools, and many professions had been erected.[81] Twenty years later, however, these barriers were beginning to crumble under the combined effect of several forces: the war against

Nazism, with its important ideological aspects, state laws against discrimination in employment and education, high levels of talent and training among Jews that give them valuable skills, and the high average level of motivation for advancement have been among the significant influences. On the basis of evidence from over 250 communities, Dean concluded in the mid-1950s that Jews were excluded from relatively few economic activities. Chief exceptions were the locally owned industries and local legal, banking, and financial institutions.[82] These were not, of course, unimportant exceptions. Where extensive training is required, barriers to Jewish employment have receded notably; ". . . discrimination has declined sufficiently so that young Jews no longer regard independent self-employment as the only guarantee of security. The importance of specialized training for breaking into traditionally non-Jewish occupations is apparent in the fact that salaried Jews in business usually work for other Jews, but salaried professionals are just as likely (or more likely) to be working for non-Jewish firms —a relatively recent development in employment conditions."[83]

These statements indicate an important trend, but do not establish the absence of discrimination against Jews in employment. Particularly in banking, insurance, and heavy industry, barriers remain. On the margins between economic and social discrimination is the opposition to Jewish membership in various clubs. Epstein and Forster report, for example, that the Merchants Club of New York (with membership drawn from the textile industry) admits no Jews. It claims, on the one hand, to be a social club, but also claims, for income tax purposes, to be a business organization.[84]

A large number of more clearly private

---

[79] Caplovitz and Rogers, *op. cit.*, p. 37.

[80] *Ibid.*, p. 53.

[81] McWilliams, *op. cit.*, and chaps. 12, 19 below.

[82] John P. Dean, "Patterns of Socialization and Association between Jews and non-Jews," *Jewish Social Studies*, July, 1955, pp. 247–284.

[83] Judith Kramer and Seymour Leventman, *Children of the Gilded Ghetto*, Yale, 1961, pp. 136–137. See also N. C. Belth (ed.), *Barriers: Patterns of Discrimination Against Jews*, ADL, 1958, pp. 43–51.

[84] See Benjamin Epstein and Arnold Forster, *"Some of My Best Friends,"* Farrar, Straus & Giroux, 1962, pp. 34–39.

city and country clubs and of residential areas also exclude Jews. Claims that these are purely private associations—which are not entirely false—disregard or disguise the fact that overtly social clubs may have significant economic and political functions. They also exaggerate the degree of sociability. A country club or residential area of several hundred members is scarcely a friendship circle. Rules to determine eligible membership are clearly designed not to include those who feel close to one another but to exclude certain categories of people. A study conducted by the Anti-Defamation League documents the frequency of exclusion of Jews. Information on 1152 out of the 1288 civilian country and city clubs with professional managers indicates that 32 percent are religiously nondiscriminatory, 60 percent were "Christian" clubs that admitted no Jews or only a few, and eight percent were "Jewish" clubs that barred Christians or admitted only a few. In only ten percent of the clubs were the restrictions written into constitutions or by-laws; in most they were carried out by informal gentlemen's agreements.[85]

One scarcely speaks of discrimination if Jews are kept out of the Newman Club or Wesley Fellowship or if non-Jews are kept out of B'nai B'rith. Most of the clubs in the study just cited, however, are large and heterogeneous in membership, secular in purpose, and of significance in their communities beyond the realm of recreation. They draw not a religious but a status line, a line that is sharpened by the appearance of the numerous reciprocal clubs—equally exclusive—in the excluded group. As the Anti-Defamation League remarks: "When, as and if Jewish community relations agencies conclude that the problem of the 'Christian club' merits their attention, they will inevitably have to cope with the other side of the coin—the 'Jewish club.' "[86] For our purposes here, the interesting thing is the way in which organizations presumably designed for recreational and sociable purposes get involved in the strains of intergroup relations.

How Widespread Is Anti-Semitism in the United States?

It is easy to play up the activities of a few violent agitators, a handful of politicians, a tiny number of desecrators of synagogues. But it is also easy to overlook the receptivity that many Americans might show to anti-Semitism under conditions of prolonged economic hardship. The United States government almost without exception (the immigration laws of 1924 and 1952 may be an exception) has consistently opposed anti-Semitism.[87] Many individual citizens, however, have shown by word and action that they are not free from it. Most studies that seek to discover the amount of this prejudice measure willingness to accept certain anti-Semitic statements. This technique may yield very different results from attempts to measure participation in stated kinds of anti-Semitic activities (joining "hate groups," attacking Jews, discriminating against them in employment or education, etc.). Polls tell little about intensity of feeling or readiness to act. Often people who verbalize the traditional attitudes of prejudice will not take part, at least at the present time, in discriminatory acts. Knowledge of attitudes, however, may help to predict potential hostile acts if conditions change.[88]

There have been significant changes in responses to poll questions during the last several decades. Among samples of the American population, the percentage who "definitely would not marry a Jew" fell from 57 to 37 between 1950 and 1962.[89] A number of polls have asked: "Do you think the Jews have too much power in the United States." The percentage answering "yes" went up from 41 in 1938 to 58 in 1945; but by 1962 it had fallen to 17 and by 1964 to 11.[90] A more stringent question produced the same varia-

[85] *Rights*, Jan., 1962, pp. 83–86.
[86] *Ibid.*, p. 86. On discrimination in clubs, hotels, and resorts, see also Belth, *op. cit.*, pp. 10–39.

[87] See Cyrus Adler and Aaron M. Margolith, *With Firmness in the Right: American Diplomatic Action Affecting Jews, 1840–1945*, American Jewish Committee, 1945.
[88] For an examination of the validity of poll data, see Thomas Pettigrew in *Jews in the Mind of America*, by Charles H. Stember (ed.), Basic Books, 1966, pp. 380–381.
[89] Stember, *op. cit.*, p. 106.
[90] *Ibid.*, p. 121, and Gertrude Selznick and Stephen Steinberg, *The Tenacity of Prejudice*, Harper & Row, p. 16.

tion. Samples were asked, "In your opinion, what nationality, religious, or racial groups in this country are a menace [threat] to America." Between 1940 and 1946, the percentages citing Jews ranged from 17 to 22 (with a peak of 24 percent in 1944). But Jews were mentioned by only 5 percent in 1950, by 2 percent in 1953, and by 1 percent in various polls in 1954, 1955, and 1962.[91]

It is important to note that when respondents are asked to name the groups that they believe have various characteristics, the percentages are low. Most poll questions, however, "trip" latent or low-level prejudices by mentioning specific groups and asking for responses to them. There is also a persistent tendency for poll questions to be stated in the negative, thus inviting respondents who have random negative feelings to use the groups furnished them as targets for their hostilities. When only one group is mentioned, this tendency is maximized. A certain amount of prejudice and hostility is likely to be directed, in a poll, toward any group. Until we learn how to subtract this nonspecific or random prejudice, we must treat poll data with caution.

These methodological problems help to account for some of the contrast between the findings and interpretations of Stember and his associates in *Jews in the Mind of America* and Selznick and Steinberg in *The Tenacity of Prejudice*. In the former, poll data from a variety of sources and years (primarily 1938–1962) are used. In the latter, the interpretations rest primarily on data from a national poll taken in 1964. In general, Stember stresses the decline of anti-Semitism; Selznick and Steinberg stress its tenacity. To some degree this is a matter of one group saying a glass is half full, the other that it is half empty. There are more important differences, however. *The Tenacity of Prejudice* is primarily a discussion and multivariate interpretation of one index of anti-Semitism used with one sample at one point in time. (Hazards of interpretation are revealed by the fact that without measures

at more than one time, the authors cannot confidently speak of the "tenacity" that is used in the title. When other data are used to give a time dimension, they tend to show that better-educated and younger persons have lower levels of prejudice. Such facts might lead other authors to entitle a book "The Mutability of Prejudice.")

Selznick and Steinberg state that "We are confident that neither acquiescence nor a negative response set is a serious problem in this study."[92] We are inclined to be less confident. Variations in questions, samples, and time make it difficult to test the effects of wording, but such data as the following must at least give us pause: In 1956, 1959, and 1964, national samples were asked to respond to the statement: "Jewish businessmen are so shrewd and tricky that other people don't have a fair chance in competition." Percentages agreeing were 35, 30, and 35, for the three years. In 1952 and 1966 a more neutral question was asked: "Compared with most people of your religious beliefs, would you say most Jews are about the same, better or not as good in being fair in business?" The proportion saying "not as good" declined from 37 to 26 percent between the two years.[93] When a positively worded item was asked in 1964, 19 percent accepted the anti-Semitic stereotype by disagreeing somewhat (14 percent) or disagreeing strongly (5 percent) with the statement: "Jewish businessmen are about as honest as other businessmen."[94]

Methodological problems associated with a possible tendency on the part of some respondents to acquiesce to a series of negatively worded items cannot, in our judgment, be set aside by the belief that "discriminatory practices and political anti-Semitism typically depend on the acquiescence of the many and the actions of the few."[95] The implication here is that if acquiescence is being measured, it does not seriously distort the picture, since acquiescence may be part of the anti-Semitic syndrome anyway. The dif-

[91] Stember, *op. cit.*, p. 128; and Hazel G. Erskine, "The Polls: Religious Prejudice, Part 2: Anti-Semitism," *POQ*, Winter, 1965–1966, p. 655.

[92] *Op. cit.*, p. 12.
[93] *Ibid.*, p. 17.
[94] Erskine, *op. cit.*, p. 660.
[95] Selznick and Steinberg, *op. cit.*, p. xx.

ficulty is that the same thing can be said of liberal actions, hence acquiescence cannot be used as a distinctive element of anti-Semitism.

Keeping problems of interpretation in mind, we can profitably note some of the findings reported by Selznick and Steinberg. Their index was based on the following eleven questions (proportions of the sample who agreed with each item are noted):

1. Do you think Jews have too much power in the United States? (11%)
2. How about the business world—do you think Jews have too much power in the business world? (29%)
3. Jews are more willing than others to use shady practices to get what they want. (42%)
4. Jews are more loyal to Israel than to America. (30%)
5. Jews are [not] just as honest as other businessmen. (28%)
6. Jews have a lot of irritating faults. (40%)
7. International banking is pretty much controlled by Jews. (30%)
8. Jews don't care what happens to anyone but their own kind. (26%)
9. Jews always like to be at the head of things. (54%)
10. Jews stick together too much. (52%)
11. The trouble with Jewish businessmen is that they are so shrewd and tricky that other people don't have a fair chance in competition. (35%)[96]

Thirty-one percent of the sample agreed with none or one of these statements (the least anti-Semitic third), 32 percent agreed with two, three, or four of the statements (the middle anti-Semitic third), and 37 percent agreed with five or more (the most anti-Semitic third). Selznick and Steinberg wisely observe that there are a variety of themes in these statements, representing different kinds of attitudes. They note that three themes are of particular importance and that they fall into a rough scale. Theme one, represented by the tenth statement above, characterizes Jews as clannish; theme two, as given in the eleventh statement, emphasizes alleged business practices; and

theme three, expressed in the first statement, sees Jews as overly powerful. These form a scale in the sense that over 90 percent of the respondents who give judgments on all three of the statements fall into one of the four possible scale types:[97]

Stick Together Too Much	Shrewd and Tricky	Too Much Power in U.S.
Yes	Yes	Yes
Yes	Yes	No
Yes	No	No
No	No	No

Forty percent of the respondents accept none of these statements; 29 percent accept one—almost always the reference to clannishness; and 31 percent accept two or three. Since this division into thirds is roughly the same as that obtained by use of all 11 statements, and has the additional advantage of forming a scale, it can profitably be used as a short measure of anti-Semitism, insofar as the prejudice can be measured by a few, short, rather stereotyped, one-directional, noncomparative statements. (We repeat these qualifiers lest the numbers be given greater credence than they deserve. In particular, we emphasize again the distinction between accepting a few furnished verbal stereotypes and anti-Semitism as discrimination.)

The data we have cited are difficult to interpret because they classify together persons of very different intensities of feeling and with widely varying readiness to act. They do indicate, however, the extensive sharing of verbal stereotypes and point out, to some degree, the potential followers of an anti-Semitic movement if the level of anxiety and confusion is raised. Ten percent of the American people might, under highly disorganized conditions, be direct supporters of such a movement, and perhaps half of the remainder would be sufficiently vulnerable to its appeal to give it some support or fail to resist it. Americans who oppose prejudice and discrimination cannot afford to be indifferent to this possibility.

On the other hand, there are strong forces

---

[96] *Ibid.*, pp. 22 and 28.

[97] *Ibid.*, p. 30.

in America opposing such a possibility. There has been a significant reduction of discrimination against Jews in the last 25 years. It may be too easy, in the shadow of the catastrophe in Europe during the Hitlerian era, to fail to take national differences into account. Without exaggerating the point, we should note, with Halpern, that "America is Different."[98] The emancipation of Jews was on the agenda of most revolutionary movements in Europe; this issue became an important symbol of the schism between revolutionaries and traditionalists; and anti-Semitism has had ". . . a natural place in the programs of European counterrevolutionary parties."[99]

[98] See his chapter by that title in Sklare, *op. cit.*, pp. 23–39.

[99] Halpern, *op. cit.*, p. 26.

To be an anti-Semite in England or the United States, however, has only minimal association with desires to repeal their revolutions, in which freedom for Jews was never an issue. Reactionary movements in the United States cannot launch their programs from islands of traditionalism—a disinherited nobility, an established church, a semiautonomous army, or exclusive universities—which somehow "escaped the levelling influence of Revolution." Although there are shadows of such institutions in America, they are too strongly opposed by institutions of an open society to furnish a rallying point for organized anti-Semitism. So long as our institutions remain healthy, anti-Semitism as a movement will be found mainly only on "the lunatic fringe."

In the preceding chapter some aspects of the history of anti-Semitism were described. That analysis was largely concerned with the conflict and traditional factors that caused and renewed the prejudice. We turn now to an examination of some of the individual factors. What experiences, tendencies, and group memberships are most likely to predispose a person to accept and act upon antipathy toward Jews? This problem, as applied to prejudice in general, was the theme of Chapter 3; hence we may be brief in our examination of it here, needing only to refer it specifically to prejudice against Jews. In the next section we shall ask: What are the personality consequences of anti-Semitism for Jews?

WHAT TYPES OF PERSONS AND GROUPS ARE LIKELY TO BE ANTI-SEMITIC?

There have been many attempts to discover whether certain occupational groups, classes, regions, or character types are likely to be more anti-Semitic than others. References to this problem were made in Chapter 9, but we need now to direct our attention specifically to it, in terms of the interaction of all the basic factors in prejudice. Not all individuals or groups are equally susceptible to anti-Semitic beliefs or actions. Studies seeking to isolate the factors that predispose an individual to accept this prejudice are somewhat contradictory, but it is well to examine them to discover the degree of agreement and to make clear that any easy explanation is impossible. They point to the need for distinguishing carefully among the various kinds of anti-Semitism (from sharing the verbal stereotypes to active discrimination) and for continuing analysis of its many different roots.

Of the large number of variables that have been examined in connection with levels of anti-Semitism, we shall comment on four: education and class, character structure, religion, and race.

Education and Class

In studies of prejudice, no variable has proved to be of more consistent explanatory value than level of education. In 1958, the American Institute of Public Opinion asked a cross section of the American population this question: "If your party nominated a generally well-qualified man for president, and he happened to be a Jew, would you vote for him?" Those answering "yes," divided into four educational levels, were as follows:

Grade school	59%
Some high school	68%
Completed high school	69%
College	82%[1]

It is important to recognize the limitations and weakness of this kind of measurement. Anti-Semitism must be defined, in this context, as willingness to make the verbal responses that have been designated as anti-Semitic by the poll taker. And one cannot tell how much the influence of education is affected by other variables, or how much it qualifies their impact. Selznick and Steinberg, in their test of the effects of education, allow us to see that other differences in level of anti-Semitism—e.g., among classes or occupations —are, to a substantial degree, reflections of differences in education. There is a difference of 25 percent between blue collar workers and white-collar workers, when no control is made for education, with 56 percent of the former, but only 31 percent of the latter being recorded as anti-Semitic on their

[1] Charles Stember, *Education and Attitude Change*, Institute of Human Relations Press, 1961, p. 62.

	Grade School	High School	Some College	College Graduate	Total
Blue Collar	71% (249)	48% (348)	26% (31)	(too few) (2)	56% (630)
White Collar	58% (50)	35% (203)	31% (110)	17% (144)	31% (507)
Percentage difference	+13	+13	−5	(no comparison possible)	+25

Source: Adapted from Gertrude Selznick and Stephen Steinberg, *The Tenacity of Prejudice*, Harper & Row, 1969, p. 76.

scale. When education is controlled, however, the differences are sharply reduced, and in one instance reversed.[2]

These data lend support to Jean-Paul Sartre's view that anti-Semitism is "a poor man's snobbery." That is not the whole story, of course, but status envy and insecurity play an important part. Sartre is describing many more than Frenchmen, when he says of one who senses only insecurity in tests of individual merit: ". . . he finds the existence of the Jew absolutely necessary. Otherwise to whom would he be superior? Indeed, it is vis-à-vis the Jew and the Jew alone that the anti-Semite realizes that he has rights. If by some miracle all the Jews were exterminated as he wishes, he would find himself nothing but a concierge or a shopkeeper in a strongly hierarchical society in which the quality of 'true Frenchman' would be at a low evaluation, because everyone would possess it."[3] In this remark we see the importance of interaction between the nature of society and an individual's experience in it. In less hierarchical societies, the search for a sense of individual importance is not so likely to take the form of prejudice.

Social mobility experience, as well as education and class, may be related to anti-Semitism. An intensive study of 150 veterans in Chicago revealed a number of significant relationships between personal and group

characteristics and anti-Semitism in this largely lower-middle-class group. On the basis of exploratory interviews with a small group of veterans not included in the final sample, Bettleheim and Janowitz developed a classification of four types of veterans according to their attitudes toward Jews:

1. The *intensely anti-Semitic* veteran was spontaneously outspoken in expressing a preference for restrictive action against the Jews even before the subject was raised. . . .

2. The *outspokenly anti-Semitic* veteran revealed no spontaneous preference for restrictive action against the Jews. Instead, outspoken hostility toward the Jews emerged only toward the end of the interview when he was questioned directly. As in the case of the intensely anti-Semitic veteran, his thinking contained a wide range of unfavorable stereotypes.

3. The *stereotyped anti-Semitic* veteran expressed no preference for hostile, or restrictive action against the Jews, either spontaneously or when questioned directly. Instead, he merely expressed a variety of stereotyped notions about the Jews, including some which were not necessarily unfavorable from his point of view. . . .

4. The *tolerant* veteran revealed no elaborate stereotyped beliefs about the Jews although even the most tolerant veterans expressed isolated stereotypes from time to time. Moreover, neither spontaneously nor when questioned directly, did he advocate restrictive action against the Jews. In fact, on policy questions, the tolerant person either denied any just grounds for differentiating between Jews and non-Jews, or affirmed his lack of concern about such differences.[4]

[2] See table above; see also Hazel G. Erskine, "The Polls: Religious Prejudice, Part 2: Anti-Semitism," *POQ*, Winter, 1965–1966, pp. 649–664.

[3] Jean-Paul Sartre, *Anti-Semite and Jew*, Schocken Books, 1965, p. 28.

[4] Bruno Bettelheim and Morris Janowitz, *Dynamics of Prejudice. A Psychological and Sociological Study of Veterans*, Harper & Row, 1950, pp. 12–13.

When the 150 men in the study were classified on the basis of these types, the following distribution resulted:[5]

	Distribution of Anti-Semitism		Distribution of Anti-Negro Attitudes	
	No.	%	No.	%
Tolerant	61	41	12	8
Stereotyped	42	28	40	27
Outspoken	41	27	74	49
Intense	6	4	24	16
Total	150	100	150	100

For purposes of comparison, attitudes toward the Negro, based on the same classification, are also given. For the most part, as intolerance toward the Jew increased, even greater intolerance toward the Negro was exhibited. There was only one case in which tolerance toward the Negro was accompanied by outspoken anti-Semitism.

By what personal and group characteristics were the tolerant veterans distinguished from the intolerant? An answer to this question helps to reveal the causes of anti-Semitism. Bettelheim and Janowitz found a significantly greater number of aggressive attitudes among the downwardly mobile group than among those who had advanced in social status since the period of their last civilian employment. Those who had experienced no mobility were in between. It seems, from this study, that the level of status is not related to anti-Semitism but that the direction of change of status is important.[6]

These data cannot be taken without qualification. Twenty of the original 150 veterans could not be classified according to social mobility with the data in hand. Twelve of the twenty were in the tolerant group and five in the stereotyped. If a large proportion of these were in the downward mobility group, the hypothesis would not be substantiated. This situation is unlikely, but the possibility should not be overlooked; it is conceivable that lack of data is precisely a sign of downward mobility.

A more serious qualification demands that we not assume a causal relationship. This study does not prove that several of the veterans are outspokenly and intensely anti-Semitic *because* they are downwardly mobile. The causation may run another way. Persons who are frustrated, aggressive, rigid-minded (and therefore anti-Semitic) are unable to do the kind of work (or get along with the boss) that allows upward social mobility. Only carefully controlled observation can reveal which of these time sequences, or what other, most accurately explains the relationship. An interactional pattern may be involved. Bettleheim and Janowitz cite evidence from the German situation that points in the direction of a time sequence running from downward mobility to intense anti-Semitism:

The socially and economically downward-moving lower middle class groups (frequently referred to as the "squeezed-out group") were the followers of Hitler, while the "respectable," relatively secure, and static middle classes (those who had not yet experienced downward mobility) held apart from this extreme form of nationalism (and anti-Semitism). Before Hitler, they were the followers of Stahlhelm, of the conservative parties who embraced "stereotyped" anti-Semitism without being outspokenly intolerant. All this changed with the advent of Hitler. Then anti-Semitism became not only respectable, but the social norm. Moreover, these middle classes which had formerly enjoyed relative security now themselves became part of the squeezed-out group, squeezed first by the new ruling group of National Socialists and then by the war mobilization economy. At this point, most of them became intensely hostile to the Jews, both because they were again following the accepted and successful pattern and also because they needed more violent outlets for the hostility aroused by sudden and severe frustration.[7]

[5] *Ibid.*, pp. 16, 25.
[6] See table on page 286; from *ibid.*, p. 59.

[7] *Ibid.*, p. 60; see also Hans H. Gerth, "The Nazi Party: Its Leadership and Composition," *AJS*, Jan., 1940, pp. 517–541.

Anti-Semitism and Social Mobility

	Downward Mobility		No Mobility		Upward Mobility		Total	
	No.	%	No.	%	No.	%	No.	%
Tolerant	2	11	25	37	22	50	49	38
Stereotyped	3	17	26	38	8	18	37	28
Outspoken and intense	13	72	17	25	14	32	44	34
Total	18		68		44		130	

The relationship between prejudice and social mobility is a complicated one. Under some conditions it may be a climb in status, not a fall, that makes one sensitive to the appeals of anti-Semitism. Greenblum and Pearlin found in their sample from Elmira that the upwardly mobile had a somewhat larger proportion of persons ready to accept anti-Semitic statements than the downwardly mobile. The difference was small, however, and when the comparison is limited to gainfully employed men under 35 years of age (a group more comparable to the Bettelheim and Janowitz respondents), the downwardly mobile are somewhat more anti-Semitic. In each instance those whose status has remained stable are less prejudiced.[8]

Silberstein and Seeman refined the concept of mobility by relating it to the attitudes and expectations that their respondents had about status change. They reasoned that if a person were strongly motivated to improve his status, downward mobility or a stationary position would be more frustrating—and related to more prejudice—than if he were "achievement motivated"—interested in a job for its own sake. The results, in the measures of anti-Semitism, were as follows:[9]

Mobility History	Achievement-Oriented	Mobility-Oriented
Downwardly mobile	12.4	14.0
Stationary manual	12.5	12.6
Stationary nonmanual	11.6	12.9
Upwardly mobile	11.1	11.9

Note: Low score equals low prejudice.

In each instance, the mobility-oriented were the more prejudiced; and the downwardly mobile were more prejudiced than the upwardly mobile.

This approach is given support in a study by Kaufman. He designed a "Status Concern" scale to measure the extent to which persons were worried about maintaining or improving their status. Among 213 non-Jewish college undergraduates, he found that a high score on this scale was more closely related to anti-Semitism than high score on the F Scale designed for *The Authoritarian Personality*. The correlation of the latter to anti-Semitism dropped to .12 when the effects of Status Concern are partialled out, but the correlation of Status Concern with anti-Semitism drops only from .66 to .48 when the influence of the F Scale scores are partialled out.[10]

Comparing respondents from four small southern towns with those from four small northern towns, Pettigrew was able to introduce another variable. Controlling for age and education, he found that the down-

[8] See Joseph Greenblum and Leonard Pearlin, "Vertical Mobility and Prejudice: A Socio-Psychological Analysis," in Reinhard Bendix and Seymour Lipset (eds.), *Class, Status, and Power*, Free Press, 1953, pp. 480–491. The difference in definition of mobility should be noted: For Bettelheim and Janowitz mobility referred to an individual's own occupational climb or fall; for Greenblum and Pearlin mobility referred to changes in occupational status in comparison with one's father.

[9] Fred Silberstein and Melvin Seeman, "Social Mobility and Prejudice," *AJS*, Nov., 1959, p. 263.

[10] Walter Kaufman, "Status, Authoritarianism, and Anti-Semitism," *AJS*, Jan., 1957, pp. 379–382.

wardly-mobile tended to be more anti-Semitic in the North, but less anti-Semitic in the South. Although neither contrast was statistically significant, their importance may be increased by the fact that the same pattern was found in anti-Negro scores. The downwardly-mobile were significantly more anti-Negro in the North and less in the South. Pettigrew argues that those who have lost status in the North are alienated from norms of tolerance, while the downwardly-mobile in the South are alienated from norms of prejudice.[11]

Is There an Anti-Semitic Character Structure?

These brief references to variables that affect the meaning of social mobility lead to more general questions regarding the possible influence of character structure on anti-Semitism. In Chapter 3 we examined the evidence for the hypothesis that prejudice was not simply a specific attitude but, in many instances, part of a total character configuration. This hypothesis is based on the observation that prejudices tend to come in clusters and that, moreover, they are associated with other tendencies—rigidity of mind, high anxiety, ambivalence (outward submissiveness and conventionality but an unconscious hostility and desire to break free from social inhibitions). According to this conception, one understands prejudice by examining the needs of the prejudiced individual. If we avoid the danger of assuming that this is the only explanatory principle, that all prejudice is to be explained by the presence of unconscious hostility and ambivalence, the hypothesis can be of great help in understanding anti-Semitism. The evidence of many studies indicates that the most extreme opposition to Jews, at any rate, cannot be explained simply by analyzing economic competition and traditional factors. Anti-Semitism seems to be highly correlated with a character structure that contains the following tendencies:

a. *Conventionalism.* Rigid adherence to conventional, middle-class values.

b. *Authoritarian submission.* Submissive, uncritical attitude toward idealized moral authorities of the ingroup.

c. *Authoritarian aggression.* Tendency to be on the lookout for, and to condemn, reject, and punish people who violate conventional values.

d. *Anti-intraception.* Opposition to the subjective, the imaginative, the tender-minded.

e. *Superstition and stereotypy.* The belief in mystical determinants of the individual's fate; the disposition to think in rigid categories.

f. *Power and "toughness."* Preoccupation with the dominance-submission, strong-weak, leader-follower dimension; identification with power figures; overemphasis upon the conventionalized attributes of the ego; exaggerated assertion of strength and toughness.

g. *Destructiveness and cynicism.* Generalized hostility, vilification of the human.

h. *Projectivity.* The disposition to believe that wild and dangerous things go on in the world; the projection outwards of unconscious emotional impulses.

i. *Sex.* Exaggerated concern with sexual "goings-on."

These variables were thought of as going together to form a single syndrome, a more or less enduring structure in the person that renders him receptive to antidemocratic propaganda.[12]

Many persons object to the idea that one can think of anti-Semitism as an unidimensional tendency, ranging from the acceptance of verbal stereotypes to active participation in violence against Jews. Samuel contends, as we shall see, that the basic factor in intense anti-Semitism is hatred for Christianity—a hatred that cannot be openly acknowledged and is therefore projected onto Jews. When this factor enters, according to Samuel, an essentially unique phenomenon, not just another prejudice, is created. Similarly, Ackerman and Jahoda draw a distinction between dislike of Jews as a prejudice and anti-Semitism as an emotional disorder based on unconscious hostilities that are involved in the personality of the individual. The

---

[11] Thomas Pettigrew, "Regional Differences in Anti-Negro Prejudice," *JASP*, July, 1959, pp. 28–36.

[12] T. W. Adorno, Else Frenkel-Brunswik, D. J. Levinson, and R. N. Sanford, *The Authoritarian Personality*, Harper & Row, 1950, p. 228.

former is ". . . based on nothing but erroneous prejudgment or stereotyped thought process."[13] The latter is rooted in a fundamental personal insecurity. This kind of analysis is correct insofar as it emphasizes that when the deeply irrational and unconscious forces of self-conflict and ambivalence become involved in anti-Semitism, it takes on a rigidity, an intense motivational energy, and a complexity that give it a highly important place in the total personality of the individual and make explosive and vicious social movements more likely. Such an analysis is in error, however, in its tendency to draw a sharp distinction between the emotionally disturbed and the well. There is no sharp break between those who have an anti-Jewish prejudice and those who exhibit the more intensive anti-Semitism. The analysis is in error, also, in failing to describe the interaction among the many causes of anti-Semitism. Political, economic, and cultural factors are not ranged on one side, producing anti-Jewish sentiments, while personal confusion and hostility, on the other, create the more intense anti-Semitism. There are numerous ways in which a person could "adjust" to the frustrations of an authoritarian upbringing or to the confusions of modern life. That anti-Semitism is often chosen in some societies cannot be understood by even the most intensive analysis of the personality unless that analysis is accompanied by a study of the cultural and conflict factors in the environment of the person involved. Some persons make a different "adjustment;" and in some societies, where anti-Semitism is unknown, *all* unstable and confused persons make a different response.

In sum, there can, from our point of view, be anti-Semitism without serious personality disturbance, and there can be serious personality disturbance without anti-Semitism. This prejudice is most likely to occur among emotionally disturbed individuals in a society where a traditional anti-Jewish prejudice is available, and under circumstances in which political and economic conflicts encourage the attitude and give the disturbed individual "good" reasons for thinking his anxiety will be reduced by attacks against the Jews.

Religion and Anti-Semitism

As we noted in Chapter 9, there are some observers who believe that anti-Semitism is primarily a Christian phenomenon, the result of specific teachings about Jews, of specific Christian beliefs, and of the close but ambivalent relationship between Judaism and Christianity. It is peculiarly difficult to test this idea because the difficulties of measuring anti-Semitism are matched by those involved in measuring Christian belief. Moreover, there is little chance for comparative study of other religions, since most Jews have lived, for many hundreds of years, primarily in societies where the great majority of the populations were Christian. The largest exceptions to this statement, the societies of North Africa, vary so widely from the predominantly Christian societies in economic, political, educational, residential, and other patterns that specifically religious comparisons, unaffected by other influences, are nearly impossible.

We must speak on this question, therefore, with caution. Some issues, to be sure, can be stated with some confidence. It appears that in the United States, the levels of Catholic and Protestant anti-Semitism are about the same, or perhaps slightly lower for Catholics.[14] Each of the categories "Protestant" and "Catholic" is quite heterogeneous, however, so that averages tell us little. Ethnic group, denomination, class, and degree of religious involvement are among the variables that should be taken into account. Among white Protestants who go to church at least once a month, Selznick and Steinberg found that 43 percent scored high on their anti-Semitism scale, compared with 35 percent among the Catholics. (This ex-

[13] Nathan Ackerman and Marie Jahoda, *Anti-Semitism and Emotional Disorder*, Harper & Row, 1950, p. 6.

[14] See Erskine, *op. cit.*; Selznick and Steinberg, *op. cit.*, chap. 7; Charles Stember *et al.*, *Jews in the Mind of America*, Basic Books, 1966, pp. 228–229; Charles Glock and Rodney Stark, *Christian Beliefs and Anti-Semitism*, Harper & Row, 1966, p. 129.

cludes those who gave no opinion.) When they divided their Protestant sample along denominational lines, however, they found scores of 24 percent among the members of the "liberal" churches and 46 percent among the "conservatives."[15]

This denominational comparison doesn't tell us much without controls for class, educational level, and other secular variables. When the authors controlled for education, the contrast between liberal Protestant and Catholic is virtually eliminated. A large share of the apparent higher level of anti-Semitism among conservative Protestants is also shown to be a function of their lower levels of education. The difference of 22 points between the conservative and liberal Protestants seen as a whole is reduced to 13, 16, and 4 points on the three educational levels where comparisons are possible.[16] Even this reduction may underestimate the extent of educational influence on the total scores, since the educational categories are large. "Some college" may mean an average of one year for the conservatives and three years for the liberals.

Perhaps the most ambitious attempt to measure empirically the relationship between religious beliefs and anti-Semitism has been made by Charles Glock and Rodney Stark. Their book has been widely discussed[17] and deserves careful study. Their major conclusions can be summarized in these words:

The causal chain that links Christian belief and faith to secular anti-Semitism begins with orthodoxy—commitment to a literal interpretation of traditional Christian dogma. Orthodoxy, in turn, leads to particularism—a disposition to see Christian truth as the *only* religious truth. Particularism produces a two-fold response toward religious outsiders. On the one hand Christian particularism prompts missionary zeal: The faith is open to all mankind if only they will accept it. But when others reject the call to conversion

the hostility latent in particularism is activated.

The hostility is directed against all religious outsiders whether they are of another faith or none. Because of their historic link with Christianity, the Jews are singled out for special attention. The specifically religious hostility toward the Jews generated by particularism is not merely a result of blaming the historic Jews for the death of Jesus. Particularistic Christians are not alone in holding such a view; less orthodox and unparticularistic Christians are also likely to implicate the ancient Jews in the Crucifixion. The difference lies in the interpretation given this view of history. In the eyes of most particularists, the Jews *remain* guilty; the Jews provoked God's wrath by crucifying Jesus, and have suffered under divine judgment ever since. Their tribulations will not cease until they extirpate their guilt by accepting salvation through Christ. Less orthodox and less particularistic Christians are unlikely to draw this link between the ancient and the modern Jews.

This process—orthodoxy to particularism to religious hostility—culminates in secular anti-Semitism.[18]

Serious problems of methodology leave these conclusions in doubt. We shall not examine the numerous issues that inevitably arise in connection with complex survey designs (problems of sampling, of diversity of meaning in questions asked, of controlling for several test variables simultaneously, of the adequacy of indexes used, and the like). In our judgment the most critical question in connection with the work of Glock and Stark has to do with time sequence. Does orthodox and particularistic training lead naturally to anti-Semitism among Christians? Or are many of those individuals who continue to accept fundamentalist beliefs and to participate in orthodox churches precisely the individuals who also use anti-Semitism as *another* way to struggle with their anxieties? It is important to remember several things about the data presented in *Christian Beliefs and Antisemitism:* (1) A substantial proportion—perhaps half, depending upon the measure being used—even of the orthodox and particularistic have low scores on the anti-Semitism scale. (2) There is no infor-

---

[15] *Op. cit.*, pp. 108–109.

[16] *Ibid.*, p. 110.

[17] See, for example, reviews by Robin Williams, Andrew Greeley, and Daniel Levinson, *ASR*, Dec., 1967, pp. 1004–1013; Gordon Allport, *JSSR*, Spring, 1967, pp. 138–139; and James Dittes, *Review of Religious Research*, Spring, 1967, pp. 183–187.

[18] Glock and Stark, *op. cit.*, pp. 208–209.

mation on those who were taught the presumably anti-Semitic fundamentalist beliefs and who later left such churches (or all churches); nor is there information designating those who joined such churches as adults, presumably with their attitudes toward Jews already largely shaped. Without such sequential data, we cannot tell how much the "Christian Beliefs" shaped attitudes as contrasted with the influence of selective dropping out and selective joining. (3) The valuable controls used by Glock and Stark on education, income, age, political preference, and the like, need to be complemented by controls on various elements of character. This is particularly valuable in a situation where large proportions of even those groups high in anti-Semitism record low scores.

We think that survey designs are of great value in research, but they require extremely careful attention to the problem of establishing the time order of the variables observed. With apologies to Alexander Pope: A little control is a dangerous thing. Before we can speak with confidence about

the specific influence of Christian teachings on anti-Semitism, we shall need even more complex designs than that shown in the table below.

Comparisons of levels of anti-Semitism among these eight categories could help reveal the extent to which fundamentalist training *per se* was involved. Similar comparisons would be needed for other educational levels and with other controls introduced.

It is clear that some persons who are active participants in Christian churches have high anti-Semitism scores, as measured by the indexes designed by Glock and Stark. At the least, they do not find certain fundamental teachings of their religion incompatible with anti-Semitic ideas. These teachings, indeed, may support such ideas under particular constellations of other conditions. In our judgment, Christian belief is not only not a sufficient cause of anti-Semitism; it is not a necessary cause in the contemporary world. Nevertheless, some kinds of Christian teachings for some people in some contexts do give additional support to anti-Semitic beliefs that are sustained by other forces as well.

Level of Anti-Semitic Beliefs as a Function of Contemporary Church Membership, Past Membership, and Level of Need for Security, Education Controlled (High School Graduates Only)

Contemporary members of churches with high average anti-Semitism				Contemporary members of churches with low average anti-Semitism			
Raised in such churches		Joined such churches as adults		Raised in such churches		Joined such churches as adults	
1 High generalized need for security, low tolerance of ambiguity	*2* Low generalized need for security, high tolerance of ambiguity	*3* High generalized need for security, low tolerance of ambiguity	*4* Low generalized need for security, high tolerance of ambiguity	*5* High generalized need for security, low tolerance of ambiguity	*6* Low generalized need for security, high tolerance of ambiguity	*7* High generalized need for security, low tolerance of ambiguity	*8* Low generalized need for security, high tolerance of ambiguity

Anti-Semitism Score	1	2	3	4	5	6	7	8
High								
Low								

Anti-Semitism Among Negroes

In Chapter 6 we commented briefly on anti-Semitism among Negroes. That topic has been discussed extensively in recent years and requires some additional attention here, in connection with this examination of the causes and extent of anti-Semitism. There are some who believe that black opposition to Jews has reached "crisis level," particularly with reference to the school situation in New York City.[19] Schlomo Katz introduced a recent book on *Negro and Jew* with the statement:

It is now widely accepted as an incontrovertible fact that, 1) there exists a pronounced anti-Jewish sentiment among the Negro masses in this country, despite the active participation of many idealistic young Jews in the Negro struggle for equal rights, and the moral support given to the Civil Rights movement by organized Jewish groups, and, 2) that Jews are reacting to this sentiment with an emotional backlash. Though no exact studies of substantial reliable data about this situation are available, the prevalence of anti-Jewish myths among Negroes is undeniable.[20]

As Katz noted, exact studies are scarce. At least one national sample, however, taken in 1964, allows us rather close comparison of the level of anti-Semitism among Negroes with levels among the white samples studied by Glock and Stark and by Selznick and Steinberg. The results are reported by Gary Marx in *Protest and Prejudice*.[21] Since the Negro samples were taken from metropolitan areas and cities only, and the questions used were somewhat different from those asked of the white population, exact comparison is impossible. In particular it is important to note that three of the nine questions used by Marx to build his index of anti-

Semitism were stated positively—a yes answer showed friendliness toward Jews.[22] Remembering the imprecision involved, we can profitably compare the range of scores among Negroes with those recorded by the white population. In the western church member sample studied by Glock and Stark, 32 percent scored high (8–12) or medium high (5–7) on their 12-point scale. (About 2 percent of the sample was black. The scale was based on answers to six anti-Semitic statements, two points being assigned when a respondent said he agreed with a statement, one point when he agreed "somewhat.") Thirty-seven percent of the Selznick-Steinberg national sample had scores of five or above on their 11-point scale. (About 12 percent of this sample was Negro.) And 24 percent of Marx's Negro sample were designated as high or very high on anti-Semitism, with scores of five or above on his nine-point scale. If those who agreed with only four of the nine statements are added, thus cutting the scale at about the same point used in other studies, 35 percent of the Negro sample were "anti-Semitic."[23] On the basis of this evidence it appears that readiness to accept verbal anti-Semitism is about the same for Blacks and Whites in the United States.

Approaching the question from a different perspective, the Harris Poll asked a national sample of Negroes whether they believed certain groups were more helpful or more harmful in their efforts to achieve equality. Forty-four percent stated that they thought Jews were more helpful, 9 percent thought them more harmful, and 47 percent were not sure. These figures can be compared with 58, 5, and 37, which were the percentages falling in the three categories when they were asked about Catholic priests, and with 24, 24, and 52, which were the percentages with reference to white churches.[24]

---

[19] See *The New York Times,* Jan. 16, 1969, p. 48; Jan. 23, 1969, pp. 1 and 51; and Feb. 3, 1969, p. 25.

[20] Schlomo Katz (ed.), *Negro and Jew,* Macmillan, 1967, p. vii. See also the various views expressed by Earl Raab, "The Black Revolution and the Jewish Question," *Commentary,* Jan., 1969, pp. 23–33; Milton Himmelfarb, "Is American Jewry in Crisis?" *Commentary,* Mar., 1969, pp. 33–42; Nathan Glazer, "Blacks, Jews, and the Intellectuals," *Commentary,* Apr., 1969, pp. 33–39; and Harold Cruse, *The Crisis of the Negro Intellectual,* Morrow, 1967, pp. 476–497.

[21] Harper & Row, 1967, Chapter 6.

[22] See *ibid.,* pp. 128–129.

[23] Marx, *op. cit.,* p. 131.

[24] William Brink and Louis Harris, *The Negro Revolution in America,* Simon & Schuster, 1964, p. 133. See also Celia S. Heller and Alphonso Pinkney, "The Attitudes of Negroes Toward Jews," *SF,* Mar., 1965, pp. 364–369; and Eugene Bender, "Reflections on Negro-Jewish Relationships: The Historical Dimension," *Phylon,* Spring, 1969, pp. 56–65.

Data that tend to show general levels of verbal anti-Semitism to be about equal among contemporary American Blacks and Whites are not sufficient to answer the questions about the influence of race on the prejudice. We need to ask also: Are there variations within the belief system that differentiate the anti-Semitism of Blacks and Whites, even if they seem to come out about the same "on the average"? And what are the levels of anti-Semitic behavior? Selznick and Steinberg found that 54 percent of Negroes scored high on measures of anti-Semitism related to economic questions, compared with 32 percent of Whites; but on noneconomic questions, Negro scores were lower (26 percent compared with 29 percent).[25] The large differences on economic questions were not a function of educational level, for the scores were higher for Negroes than Whites in every educational category.[26] On the other hand, Negroes were more likely to reject various forms of discrimination against Jews than were Whites. They were less likely to believe that clubs had a right to discriminate against Jews, less likely to be opposed to their political party nominating a Jew for president, more likely to say that an employer should hire the best man without regard to his religion.

Opposition of some Negroes to Jews on the basis of economic questions rests to an important degree on two considerations: In metropolitan areas, Jews make up a high proportion of the landlords, merchants, and employers with whom Negroes have contact. That two-thirds of the 750 stores destroyed in the Watts section of Los Angeles in 1965 were owned by Jews is scarcely a measure of anti-Semitism. We need to note, with Harry Golden, that "Jewish stores were the only ones to burn"—an exaggeration that can help us understand the relationship of Negro to Jew if not taken literally. In many more instances around the country, of course, the landlord, merchant, or employer of Negroes is a gentile. It is perhaps some Negro writers, more than the average black man, who distinguish between Jew and whitey. They may help to create an inadequate picture of the actual range of beliefs. As Golden says: "I think of the thousands of Southern Protestants who have built vast fortunes on Negro slum housing. In every city and town the richest man, next to the mill-owner and the Coca Cola distributor, is the man with what are called 'nigger houses.' "[27]

In the years ahead, it may be job competition and the related question of control over school opportunities which will present the sharpest points of conflict between Jews and Negroes. And once again this is best seen as a particular expression of a more general conflict situation between Blacks and Whites. "What the Negro wants is what the White has, and he wants it now. The Whites who have what Negroes are going to want to take next are very often Jews. The stores in Harlem, the teaching and civil service appointments, are rungs on the ladder Negroes have to climb over the toes of Jews, just as they have to make Irish and Italians move over in the construction trades."[28]

In our judgment, when anti-Semitism is measured by discriminatory behavior, there are few signs of it being more common among Blacks than among Whites. It seems more accurate to say that discriminatory anti-Semitism has fallen among Whites while it has increased somewhat among Blacks, so that it is no longer clear that a more favorable situation obtains among Negroes. This shift is matched by some increased hostility among Jews to Negro demands. This hostility is sometimes described as a "backlash"—expressive of resentment against growing Negro anti-Semitism. Such an interpretation is inadequate in two ways: As we have tried to show, it is not at all clear that there has been a significant increase in anti-Semitism among Blacks. A few Negro extremists have sought to exploit anti-Semitism and some Jewish leaders have responded with expressions of deep concern. It is understandable that there should be distress at any sign of new or renewed anti-Semitism; but it is possible to over-read the signs, and it is possible to

[25] Op. cit., p. 120.
[26] Ibid., p. 121.

[27] Harry Golden in Katz, op. cit., p. 63.
[28] Ben Halpern in ibid., p. 68.

cover one's own sense of guilt at having backed off from the more serious demands of the civil rights movement. The Anti-Defamation League of B'nai B'rith has declared that "Raw, undisguised anti-Semitism is at a crisis level in New York City schools. . . ."[29] We think the same evidences could be read to mean, however, that there is a sharp and difficult conflict between Jews and Negroes over control of teaching and administrative positions in New York City schools, over curriculum, and over control of school policy generally. This has led some Negro leaders and would-be leaders to speak in harsh and uncompromising terms. A few have used and encouraged severe anti-Semitic statements. Opposition to those statements is on soundest ground when it is carried through in a context in which the realistic basis of conflict and the severe disadvantages of Negroes are recognized. Arthur Hertzberg puts the matter sharply:

The issues between Jews and Negroes are not misunderstandings between the two groups but hard questions about power and position. It is ridiculous to pretend that at this moment in American history, the texture of Jewish and Negro experiences are similar. The Jews are the most vulnerable of the haves, and the Negroes are the most unfortunate of the have-nots. They may have some rhetoric in common; they are together the heirs of moral imperatives; but the real question is what love and justice mean, concretely: how many Jewish school principals are commanded by the joint Negro-Jewish commitment to morality, and Jewish memories of persecution, to go sell shoes, so less well-trained Negroes can hold their jobs.[30]

In the last sentence, Hertzberg leaves his analytic position. Whether Negroes are "less well-trained" depends upon what one wants accomplished. Are they less well-trained to motivate Negro boys to stay in school, to be sensitive to the aspirations and perspectives of the black population, to introduce perspectives on American culture and history that express more fully the roles of

black men? Or, even granted that they are less well-trained now, is there any other way to achieve parity than to offer special opportunities for experience to overcome past disprivilege?

A second reason why "backlash" may be a poor way to describe Jewish concern over Negro-Jewish conflict is that Jewish behavior may have changed first or concomitantly: It is the Negro actions, according to this interpretation, that are backlash or, more neutrally, response. As Nathan Glazer has noted, Negroes are making demands for entry on an equal footing into institutions ". . . which are the true seats of Jewish exclusiveness—the Jewish business, for example, the Jewish union, or the Jewish (or largely Jewish) neighborhood and school. Thus Jews find their interests and those of formally less liberal neighbors becoming similar: they both have an interest in maintaining an area restricted to their own kind; an interest in managing the friendship and educational experiences of their children; an interest in passing an advantage in money and skills to them."[31]

We think "backlash" is a poor term to describe this complicated, difficult, and often poignant situation. The term implies a causal priority, and often a moral assessment of greater and lesser responsibility and guilt, which we find unfortunate. The contemporary situation puts some Jews and some Negroes into sharp confrontation. Various outcomes that we regard as unfortunate—stereotyping, mutual insensitivity, and discrimination—can develop out of such confrontation. Such outcomes can be minimized only when the full range of causes is objectively studied and their impact eliminated.

THE EFFECTS OF ANTI-SEMITISM ON JEWS

In Chapters 6 and 7 we discussed the influence that prejudice and discrimination have on the personalities of minority-group members. It is well now to raise this question

[29] *The New York Times*, Jan. 23, 1969, p. 1. See also Morris Fine and Milton Himmelfarb, *American Jewish Yearbook*, 1969, pp. 76–89.

[30] In Katz, *op. cit.*, p. 74.

[31] Nathan Glazer, "Negroes and Jews," *Commentary*, Dec., 1964, p. 34.

specifically with reference to Jews. Many people "justify" their anti-Semitism by pointing to the supposed characteristics of Jews. Is there any evidence that Jews have, on the average, a greater tendency for this or that characteristic than other groups with which they may be compared? If so, is there any way in which these differences may be looked upon as a "cause" of prejudice?

Evidence on this subject is highly inadequate. Assertions range all the way from the belief that Jews are fundamentally different (innately so, many anti-Semites would say) to the claim that there are no differences in group averages, that Jews have the same range and distribution of personality tendencies as other groups (a proposition resting upon a democratic ideology; but not always fully informed). Although our evidence is incomplete, based almost entirely on uncontrolled observation, not on controlled study, these statements seem to be in harmony with present knowledge of the nature of personality:

1. There are no inherited differences between Jew and non-Jew.

2. Differences in experience (including discrimination) have produced some differences in tendency between some Jews and members of the dominant group.

3. These differences are frequently exaggerated and misinterpreted by anti-Semites and others (sometimes including Jews). They are often assumed to apply universally, without regard to individual variation; the anti-Semite pays attention only to what he regards as unfavorable differences; his selective perception distorts the picture enormously; and he has an entirely inadequate idea of why there are differences.

Referring to the generations of anti-Semitism and of ghetto life, Friedmann describes a number of consequences for Jews:

(1) The exaggeration of certain physical features, a bio-social phenomenon observable in isolated communities characterized by inbreeding; . . . (2) the exaggeration of certain psychological features well described in the literature of the ghetto, including overdevelopment of the critical sense and of destructive analysis, escapism in dreams, an active imagination . . . , a cruel sense of humor, self-denigration and denigration of the community to which they belong; (3) an intensification of cultural autarky, in other words an attempt to find within the segregated community something with which to satisfy all needs, from the prescriptions of the dietary laws to food for the mind, the need for beauty, metaphysical truth, mystic communion with God.[32]

It would be surprising indeed if Jews, having experienced the kinds of discrimination that we have described in the preceding chapter, had not developed some tendencies different (in degree, not kind) from those of persons with very different experiences. Among the most important consequences of prejudice and discrimination, for example, are the attitudes toward oneself and one's group. Many Jews have had sufficiently stable early experiences to be able to adjust on a "reality" level to the discriminations they meet. Others, being unable, in a social context that defines them as inferior or obnoxious, to develop a satisfying sense of selfhood, react by overemphasizing their Jewishness or by trying to hide it. Neither of these extremes is likely to be an effective adjustment from the individual's own point of view. Overemphasis on one's status as a Jew (with consequent underemphasis of one's statuses in a given occupational role, educational level, community, nation, and other group associations) requires that one identify himself closely with a group that the majority treats with prejudice. Minimization of one's role in the Jewish group, on the other hand, or an attempt to break completely one's identification with Jews, requires the denial of a strong sense of community and often leads to a feeling of guilt that one has deserted his group. In either event, anxiety and feelings of unworthiness are likely to follow. When he came to the United States, Kurt Lewin observed that many Jewish students adjusted to the discriminatory aspects of college life by displaying well-adapted and balanced behavior. "There are, however, a large number

[32] Georges Friedmann, *The End of the Jewish People?* Doubleday, 1967, pp. 268–269.

of Jewish students who show decided lack of adjustment. To one who has come to America from pre-Hitler Germany it is quite impressive to find such typical signs of Jewish maladjustment as over-tension, loudness, over-aggressiveness, excessively hard work—sometimes to an even higher degree than over there."[33]

Sklare and Vosk asked a sample of the Jews in an industrial city of 130,000 whether they had experienced any anti-Semitism. Seventy-five percent of the adults and 86 percent of the adolescents said yes. Their experiences, doubtless ranging from imagined slights to serious discrimination, are part of the setting in which Jewish personality development takes place.[34]

Jewish Anti-Semitism

In Chapter 6 we referred to the phenomenon of self-hatred, particularly among Negroes. It is a tendency found also among Jews, among some second-generation immigrant groups, and among others who feel caught in a status that is defined as inferior by the dominant group. The self-hatred is seldom an open and uncomplicated reaction. It is more often indirect, even unconscious, and accompanied by ambivalent feelings of superiority and chauvinism. Self-hatred is the product of three interacting factors. Those of high status define one's group as inferior; one experiences discrimination because of group membership, yet the attitudes of the majority prevent one from leaving the group. Those who try to solve this problem by accepting the definitions of the dominant group are caught in a difficult situation so long as prejudice continues.

Under these circumstances one attacks himself (feelings of unworthiness and blame) or one's group ("negative chauvinism") or some part of one's group (an "inferior" part which endangers one's security

because the majority draws no distinctions)[35] or one's family (the cause of one's group location). Lipset sees this last source of Jewish anti-Semitism as an expression, in part, of a belief on the part of children that their parents are hypocritical. "Many Jewish parents live in lily-white suburbs, go to Miami Beach in the Winter, belong to expensive country clubs, arrange *Bar Mitzvahs* costing thousands of dollars—all the while espousing a left-liberal ideology. This is their hypocrisy, and it is indeed the contradiction which their children are rebelling against."[36] This Jewish anti-Semitism is a psychologically somewhat different phenomenon from the anti-Semitism of non-Jews.[37] Both expressions represent an attempt to achieve a satisfying sense of self by identifying with the dominant group. This is more difficult for the Jew, for he must deny more of himself. In the study of a group of emotionally disordered persons Ackerman and Jahoda found two differences between Jewish and gentile anti-Semitism.

First, in examining the content of the anti-Semitic projections of Jewish anti-Semites, the absence of "good" qualities is conspicuous. Here, there are no conscious claims that Jews are in-

[33] Kurt Lewin, *Resolving Social Conflicts*, Harper & Row, 1948, p. 170.

[34] Marshall Sklare and Marc Vosk, *The Riverton Study. How Jews Look at Themselves and Their Neighbors*, American Jewish Committee, 1957, p. 45.

[35] Benjamin Ringer found that long-time residents among "Lakeville's" Jews in a majority of cases saw Jewish newcomers ". . . as seriously lacking in propriety, as unduly concerned with material wealth and possessions, as capable of misusing power, and finally as standoffish and ethnocentric." See *The Edge of Friendliness: A Study of Jewish-Gentile Relations*, Basic Books, 1967, p. 78.

[36] Seymour Lipset, " 'The Socialism of Fools': The Left, The Jews, and Israel," Anti-Defamation League, 1969, p. 25. See also Joseph Adelson, "A Study of Minority Group Authoritarianism," in Marshall Sklare (ed.), *The Jews*, Free Press, 1958, pp. 475–492; and Moshe Anisfield, Stanley Munos, and Wallace Lambert, "The Structure and Dynamics of the Ethnic Attitudes of Jewish Adolescents," *JASP*, Jan., 1963, pp. 31–36. There is some danger that any desire or action to disaffiliate from Judaism or the Jewish group is labelled anti-Semitism or self-hatred by current observers. Is it possible to become a non-Jew? Hitler said no and, paradoxically, so also do some Jews. Can disaffiliation be a result of normal personality and social change—as some persons have been known to leave the Presbyterian and Methodist Churches? We think it a mistake to foreclose such a possibility.

[37] See Bernard Segal and Peter Thomasen, "Status Orientation and Ethnic Sentiment Among Undergraduates," *AJS*, July, 1965, pp. 60–67.

telligent, powerful, successful, sexually potent, or ethical. The reason for this probably lies in the precarious illusion of not belonging to the Jewish group, the even greater ambivalence stemming from a dread of discovery, and even more, "conversion" to their Jewishness. Their anti-Semitism seems better fortified by denying the "good" elements of the cultural stereotype. Knowing deep down that they are Jews—and failures, to boot—they cannot reconcile the culturally favorable aspects of the Jewish sterotypes with their own state of being.

Second, it appears that while most Gentiles in our case material hate not only Jews but also other groups as well, the Jewish need for hatred is more exclusively directed against Jews. None of the Jewish patients and clients mainfested significantly any other form of prejudice.[38]

Negative chauvinism and self-hatred seem particularly strange in view of the undoubted achievements of many Jews. They are well represented in numerous lines of endeavor that are held in high regard in modern society—in science and art, in business and the professions. In Germany, for example, 13 of the 38 who won Nobel prizes before 1933 were Jews. The cultural traditions of Judaism, the community solidarity (in important measure a result of discrimination), high individual desire for achievement (again in part a result of discrimination), the intellectual alertness which comes from the marginal position of membership in two cultures—these and other factors have encouraged high achievement.

We know of no way to demonstrate that anti-Semitism has been a driving force that helps to account for the achievements of Jews, because the positive pull of Jewish culture and the negative push of discrimination (leading to group solidarity and strong efforts to overcome discrimination) are indissolubly linked. The achievements, however, by generally accepted standards, are of a high order. We shall not try to list the many accomplishments of Jews, for they are a matter of public record. We simply note here the continuing encouragement to high attainment found in Jewish culture and

socialization practices,[39] and suggest that when a group with strong resources is caught in circumstances that they regard as unjust, they will respond with extraordinary effort and achievement.

In a context of prejudice, however, even notable contributions become a source of embarrassment, not of pride. What is a virtue in the dominant group becomes a vice in the minority group. Episcopalians or Texans or Americans of Swedish descent may boast of the number of their members who have become important businessmen, scientists, doctors, musicians. But some Jews and opponents of anti-Semitism spend a great deal of energy to prove that the Jews have *not* made extraordinary contributions, whereas anti-Semites document the "dominance" (contributions) of Jews to many lines of endeavor. Merton describes the situation well.

In a society where, as a recent survey by the National Opinion Research Center has shown, the profession of medicine ranks higher in social prestige than any other of ninety occupations (save that of United States Supreme Court Justice), we find Jewish spokesmen manoeuvred by the attacking ingroup into the fantastic position of announcing their "deep concern" over the number of Jews in medical practice, which is "disproportionate to the number of Jews in other occupations." In a nation suffering from a notorious undersupply of physicians, the Jewish doctor becomes a deplorable occasion for deep concern, rather than receiving applause for his hard-won acquisition of knowledge and skills and for his social utility. Only when the

[38] Ackerman and Jahoda, *op. cit.*, pp. 79–80.

[39] See, for example, Bernard Rosen, "Race, Ethnicity, and the Achievement Syndrome," *ASR*, Feb., 1959, pp. 47–60; and Fred Strodtbeck, "Family Interaction, Values, and Achievement," in Marshall Sklare (ed.), *The Jews*, Free Press, 1958, pp. 147–165. As Strodtbeck remarks, it is implicit in most studies that working hard and improving one's status is good. Persons who start from a different value premise will interpret the facts differently.

It is doubtless possible to exaggerate the influence of cultural forces and socialization. Slater argues that the rapid mobility of American Jews is primarily to be accounted for by socioeconomic factors, not by cultural support for intellectual activities. See Miriam Slater, "My Son the Doctor: Aspects of Mobility among American Jews," *ASR*, June, 1969, pp. 359–373.

New York Yankees publicly announce deep concern over their eleven [twenty, 1963!] World Series titles, so disproportionate to the number of triumphs achieved by other major league teams, will this self-abnegation seem part of the normal order of things.[40]

The opposite side of this self-abnegation is the claim by many anti-Semites that Jews are highly gifted, "of admirable endurance and resilience." This approach was formulated by Wilhelm Marr in his pamphlet, *Sieg des Judentums über das Germanentum,* 1873, in which he tried to prove that the Jews were not weak and inferior but talented and strong, "the first major power in the West."

It must not be assumed that Jewish efforts to minimize their own achievements are necessarily signs of self-hatred. They may be simply a strategy (very ineffective in the writers' judgement) to reduce hostility. But they shade off into doubt over the accomplishments of one's group and into feelings of antipathy.

Other Personality Effects of Prejudice

The effort to minimize achievements or to escape identification with the group and the tendency even to hate oneself or one's group are not the only personality consequences of anti-Semitism. To some degree, Jews exhibit compensatory feelings of superiority (illustrated by the orthodox religious conception of the "chosen people"), of individual aggressiveness, and of incomplete identification with the dominant society. When anti-Semitic allegations were introduced into a school board election in a New Jersey community, Jewish ethnocentrism and anomic feelings increased. The increase was not uniform, however. Jews with numerous contacts with gentiles were less likely to become more ethnocentric, but more likely to have a greater sense of anomie. Having invested trust in intergroup relations, they felt more threatened by the anti-Semitic episode,

less certain of their place in the community.[41]

It is important to emphasize the range of Jewish tendencies and to stress, with Sartre, the situational sources of those tendencies.[42]

During the centuries in which they were deprived of citizenship, limited in occupational and residential choice, and liable to physical attack, Jews inevitably developed modes of response that involved individual aggressiveness and group cohesiveness. Periods of tolerance have encouraged assimilation, but they have seldom lasted long enough to get rid of the fear and doubt that centuries of discrimination have encouraged. In Germany, for example, during the greater part of the nineteenth century and the first two decades of the twentieth, Jews were assimilated more and more into the dominant pattern. Intermarriage was quite common. There were periods of political anti-Semitism, as we have seen, but a mass following was not achieved. With the devastating conditions of the twenties and thirties, however, came virulent attacks on Jews. Their fears were confirmed; the liberal, democratic dream faded; and the conviction that only in their own community could they find strength and freedom from anxiety was encouraged. The effects were felt in America; a renewed interest in Judaism, a revived sense of Jewish community, an increased opposition to intermarriage resulted. Jews in the United States have one of the lowest rates of intermarriage of any "immigrant" group.

[41] Martin S. Weinberg and Colin J. Williams, "Disruption, Social Location and Interpretive Practices: The Case of Wayne, New Jersey," *ASR*, Apr., 1969, pp. 170–182.

[42] Sartre, *op. cit.*, chap. 3. Empirical studies of tendencies among Jews compared with others are scarce, although a number of writers offer valuable insights. See James Yaffe, *The American Jews*, Random House, 1968; Thomas Pettigrew, *A Profile of the Negro American*, Van Nostrand, 1964, pp. 80–82; A. P. Sperling, "A Comparison Between Jews and Non-Jews with Respect to Several Traits of Personality," *Journal of Applied Psychology*, Dec., 1942, pp. 828–840; Keith Sward and Meyer Friedman, "Jewish Temperament," *Journal of Applied Psychology*, Feb., 1935, pp. 70–84.

[40] Robert K. Merton, *Social Theory and Social Structure*, Free Press, rev. ed., 1957, pp. 432–433.

The pull toward assimilation and the internal splits within the Jewish group are still strongly operative in the United States, of course. But the period of Nazi anti-Semitism revived the feelings of biculturality. In a tiny minority it stimulated radical political views. We have noted that reactionary and counterrevolutionary movements have often employed anti-Semitism. The opposite side of that coin shows that Jews have strongly supported the liberal, democratic, socialist, and communist movements, which have promised them liberty and equality.[43] Many members of the American Communist Party, for example, have been immigrants from Russia and Eastern Europe, most of them Jews. This fact, however, must be studied carefully. Even at its peak the party had scarcely more than 50,000 members and by the late 1950s had fallen to a small proportion of that number. This means that at the most a small fraction of 1 percent of Jews were party members. Why did even this number join? The answer is complex: For generations reactionary movements in Europe had been anti-Semitic while the "left" had fought for their full citizenship. Most Jews supported the center parties or the democratic left, but wherever there was a tendency toward a polarization of far right *versus* far left, some Jews left the weakening center for the radical position. In the United States, Jews with high educational and professional training felt the sting of ethnic prejudice. They thus experienced the status discrepancy often associated with radical politics. American Communists were much more likely to be middle cass than working class; they were almost entirely urban; they felt alienated from the traditional ways of doing things; some were idealists who wanted to change the world in a hurry; and most were literate persons familiar with the currents of change around the world. Each of these factors tended to increase the proportion of Jews among those attracted to radical politics.[44]

A more important manifestation of the effects of insecure status and attacks on Jews is the complex of attitudes regarding the meaning of Jewishness. These problems are involved in the remark of Rabbi Stephen S. Wise: "I may have been an American for sixty-four years, but I have been a Jew for four thousand years." They lie behind the conception that Judaism is not simply a religion but a nation or the unifying center of a "people." They have been the sustaining force of the Zionist movement, whose founder developed his ideas in the context of the Dreyfus affair in France. "The dominant motive which goaded Theodor Herzl on in the last decade of the nineteenth century was not Judaism, with its attendant age-old allegiance to culture and 'race,' but persistent anti-Semitism with its intolerable contemporary realities."[45] The fervor with which the idea of Zionism has been embraced can be understood only against the background of Nazi persecution and mass exterminations. As Kurt Lewin says:

I remember how, as an adolescent, I was deeply disturbed by the idea that the accusation against Jews as being incapable of constructive work might be true. I know that many Jewish adolescents growing up in an atmosphere of prejudice felt similarly. Today, a Jewish youth who has watched Palestine grow is in an infinitely better situation. Whatever one's opinion about Zionism as a political program may be, no one who has observed closely the German Jews during the fateful first weeks after Hitler's rise to power will deny that thousands of German Jews were saved from suicide only by the famous article of the *Jüdische Rundschau*, with its headlines "Jasagen zum Judentum" ("Saying Yes to Being a Jew"). The ideas expressed there

---

[43] See Louis Ruchames, "Jewish Radicalism in the United States," and Daniel Aaron, "Some Reflections on Communism and the Jewish Writer," in Peter Rose (ed.), *The Ghetto and Beyond: Essays on Jewish Life in America*, Random House, 1969, pp. 228–252 and 253–269. See also Robert Michels, *Political Parties*, Collier Books, 1962, pp. 245–250; and Nathan Glazer, "The Jewish Role in Student Activism," *Fortune*, Jan., 1969, pp. 112–113, 126–129.

[44] For a careful review of the facts and a valuable commentary, see Nathan Glazer, *The Social Basis of American Communism*, Harcourt Brace Jovanovich, 1961, chap. 4. See also Gabriel Almond, *The Appeals of Communism*, Princeton, 1954; and Morris Ernst and David Loth, *Report on the American Communist*, Holt, Rinehart & Winston, 1952.

[45] J. O. Hertzler, in Isacque Graeber and S. H. Britt (eds.), *Jews in a Gentile World*, Macmillan, 1942, p. 85.

were the rallying point and the source of strength for Zionist and non-Zionist alike.[46]

Most American Jews support Zionism, of course, not for themselves, but for the remnants of Central and Eastern European Jewry who survived the Nazis. The great majority of the Jews of the world now live in the United States, Israel, and the Soviet Union. The degree and direction of their biculturality will be *primarily* determined by their experiences in the United States and the Soviet Union. Persecution anywhere in the world, however, will affect their identification with Judaism.

One might imagine a continuum along which can be ranged the various attitudes of American Jews toward Zionism, from the most strongly supportive to the opposed:

1. All Jews owe national allegiance to Israel, for they constitute a nation. Residence anywhere else in the world is a continuing diaspora.
2. Israel has added strength and pride to the Jewish people. It is almost a second home to me, although I have no wish to move there, and I try to help it any way I can.
3. Israel has been a great boon to European and "Oriental" Jews. I feel a strong interest in my coreligionists there and wish the nation well.
4. Israel interests me no more than other countries.
5. Jews are a religious group, not a nation. Zionist claims weaken their positions in their various native lands. I wish no harm to Israel, but I am anti-Zionist.

This is not, of course, a true scale, but it may suggest both the range of attitudes and the fact that there is wide disagreement. Without having any precise evidence, we would guess that only a small proportion of American Jews takes either position one or five, and not many would agree with statement four. Perhaps the majority would fall somewhere between position two and three. Such an attitude is not different in kind from the views toward their homelands held by many immigrants to the United States. Recency of migration, prejudice, and

international conflict are three variables that strongly affect these attitudes.

In their study of "Lakeville," Sklare and Greenblum used a scale not dissimilar to the one we have suggested, with the first position, however, not stated or blended into the second. Their respondents approved the following levels of support for Israel:

	percent
Raise money, influence U.S. policy, and additional action	33
Raise money, influence U.S. policy	32
Raise money only	28
None	7

Source: Adapted from Marshall Sklare and Joseph Greenblum, *Jewish Identity on the Suburban Frontier,* Basic Books, 1967, p. 226. See chap. 6.

Zionism as a political movement can be understood and evaluated only by reference to the problems and rights of the Arab masses in Palestine, the strategic conflicts of the major powers, the interests of the Arabian ruling groups, as well as the claims and rights of the Jews. But from the point of view of the social psychology of Jews, it is strongly affected by anti-Semitism, with the attendant encouragement to the sense of separate "nationality."[47] Other factors, of course, are involved. There is some tendency among those who identify with the "new left" in the United States—including some Jews—to be anti-Israel. Israel is seen as somehow part of the "establishment"; and Soviet support for the Arabs influences their beliefs. For other Jews, however, support for Israel has stronger salience than their sympathy for leftist views. They respond to the dilemma by adopting a more conservative perspective.[48]

[46] Lewin, *op. cit.,* p. 198.

[47] See Samuel Halperin, *The Political World of American Zionism,* Wayne State Univ. Press, 1961.
[48] See Melvin Tumin, "The Cult of Gratitude," in Rose, *op. cit.,* pp. 69–82. On opposition to Israel

Assimilation Versus Pluralism

Minority status has significance not only for individuals but for group structure and survival. It has often been the experience in the United States that persons of common national or ethnic origin have felt a strong bond of kinship here, have settled in particular areas of a city, have set up churches and other associations along traditional lines, have published newspapers in their original language, and have married within the ethnic circle. In many instances, however, these patterns begin to change more or less rapidly (depending upon the size, location, and ideology of the group, among other things) in the second generation. In school, the children learn English and absorb much of the culture of the surrounding society. The parental model is sometimes seen as a handicap to success and happiness in the new world. The rate of internationality and interethnic marriage goes up. Within three or four generations, any communal base for a national identity is almost lost, and the fact that one's ancestors came in a majority or plurality from Germany or England or Holland is a matter of minor interest. Assimilation has taken place.

One should not exaggerate the extent of this process or fail to note the differences among groups. It has proceeded farthest among those from North Europe, who have been in the United States longest. Racial or quasiracial differences greatly slow the process, as can be seen among the Americans of Mexican descent in the Southwest. Our interest here is in the Jews. How far has the process gone with them? Will they lose their separate identity? Most American Jews are now second and third generation in this country—time enough to be fully acculturated but not yet long enough to have felt the full assimilationist pull of the American setting. We must speak, therefore, with some caution; but we can explore the situation as it now appears.

Many early students of the question applied Robert E. Park's "natural history" approach to the Jewish population of the United States, and on the basis of their observations of the contrasts between first and second generation, concluded that assimilation would be the eventual outcome. Continuing immigration would retard the process; crises abroad and anti-Semitism at home would postpone full absorption; but in time, the open society so weakens the functions of ethnic groups that they would disappear.[49] One of the basic assumptions of the "Chicago school" was that community structure was related in a profound way to geographical concentration in "natural areas." Dispersion of an ethnic group would be a sign of the weakening of its associations and would undermine them further.

One is tempted to say, overly simply, that this thesis is pre-automobile, and presuburb. If it is correct, a distinctive Jewish group is rapidly disappearing in the United States, for perhaps two-thirds of them have moved to suburbs which, even if largely Jewish, are often too small to support the full range of ethnic associations; many suburbs, moreover, are religiously mixed, with Jews in a minority. Accompanying this trend is an increase in interethnic contacts in schools and in jobs, the growth of friendship patterns between Jews and Gentiles, a slight increase in the rate of intermarriage, and a shift away from Jewish Orthodoxy toward the Conservative and Reform congregations.

In the face of these trends, paradoxically, there are clear signs of continuing strong group identity and even of revival among Jews.[50] In the last 30 years an increasing

[49] For the best known statement of this thesis, see Louis Wirth, *The Ghetto*, Univ. of Chicago Press, 1928. For a valuable critique see Amitai Etzioni, "The Ghetto—a Re-evaluation," *SF*, Mar., 1959, pp. 255–262; and Erich Rosenthal, "Acculturation Without Assimilation? The Jewish Community in Chicago, Illinois," *AJS*, Nov., 1960, pp. 275–288.

[50] There is a rich literature describing the influence of suburbanization and other current trends on American Jews. See, for example, Sidney Goldstein and Calvin Goldscheider, *Jewish Americans: Three Generations in a Jewish Community*, Prentice Hall, 1968; Benjamin Ringer, *op. cit.*; Marshall Sklare and Joseph Greenblum, *op. cit.*; Stuart Rosenberg, *The Search for Jewish Identity in America*, Doubleday, 1965; James Yaffe, *Jewish Americans*, Random House, 1968; Rose, *op. cit.*; Albert Gordon, *Jews in*

among Jews, see *The New York Times*, Feb. 17, 1971, p. 37.

proportion of Jewish families have joined and participated in the programs of synagogues. Between 1900 and 1958, the number of Jewish children enrolled in schools for religious instruction increased from 45,000 (approximately 4 percent of the Jewish population) to over 550,000 (over 10 percent). Between 1950 and 1958 the number more than doubled.[51] In suburbs where Jews may be a small minority, they tend to come together not only around their institutions, but in informal friendship circles. There are many interreligious friendships, but best friends are usually Jewish, and evening leisure-time activities particularly are likely to be shared within the ethnic group. This is not necessarily the result of conscious choice but is the consequence of a search for a relaxed setting for the pursuit of shared interests.[52]

Thus in the United States today the forces of assimilation seem to be weaker among Jews than the forces of pluralism. Despite their rapid acculturation, drastic changes in their traditional ways, and highly successful involvement in most phases of American life, most Jews continue to think of themselves and to be thought of as a distinctive ethnic community. Or to put this in Milton Gordon's terms, there has been substantial cultural and civic assimilation, but relatively little structural, marital, or identificational assimilation.[53] What accounts for this? There are, we believe, a number of factors involved. The list given here is surely not exhaustive; nor are the items mutually exclusive and of equal importance for all

persons. But these influences seem important:

1. Continuing pride in a tradition of great strength and accomplishments promotes group identity.

2. Centuries of experience in survival surrounded by non-Jews has led to a group cohesiveness that prepared them for the assimilationist influences of the American environment. Other immigrant groups had no such experience in minority status. Related to this is a lack of dependence upon language as a unifying factor. Yiddish has certainly been an important influence among American Jews in the past, but there are several "native languages" among Jews, not one; and their unifying tradition does not rest upon a shared language.

3. Movement to the suburbs, out of all-Jewish ghettoes, leads children—and adults —to ask: Who am I? In what way am I different from those around me? Since, in a friendly environment, the answer to this question is not laden with difficulty, a traditional, ethnic-group response is often made. Closer association with the synagogue comes readily; and religious education for the children, to establish their identity becomes important. It may well be, as Herberg, Gans, and others have suggested, that this tendency is reenforced by a widespread *anomie* in American society. One fights normlessness, and the personal alienation that may accompany it, by identifying closely with the more cohesive subcommunity.

4. Religious and ethnic professionals— traditionally held in high regard by Jews —vigorously reaffirm the strength and viability of the group and its values. There is a rich and complex associational structure, covering the full range of attitudes, values, and degrees of acculturation. Almost any Jew can find one or more groups that view the world as he does, and each— though they vary widely—identifies with the total Jewish group. One can be pro-Zionist or anti-Zionist, Orthodox or Reform, even assimilationist or pluralistic and remain Jewish in orientation. This is not a unique development. The Catholic Church,

---

Suburbia, Beacon Press, 1959; Nathan Glazer, *American Judaism*, Univ. of Chicago Press, 1957; Judith Kramer and Seymour Leventman, *Children of the Gilded Ghetto: Conflict Resolutions of Three Generations of American Jews*, Yale, 1961; C. Bezalel Sherman, *The Jew Within American Society*, Wayne State Univ. Press, 1961.

[51] *Ibid.*, p. 210.

[52] See Herbert Gans, "The Origin and Growth of a Jewish Community in the Suburbs: A Study of the Jews of Park Forest," in Marshall Sklare (ed.), *The Jews*, Free Press, 1959, pp. 205–248.

[53] Milton Gordon, *Assimilation in American Life*, Oxford Univ. Press, 1964. See also Edward O. Laumann, "The Social Structure of Religious and Ethnoreligious Groups in a Metropolitan Community," *ASR*, Apr., 1969, pp. 182–197.

for example, has shown the same kind of heterogeneity in many settings. It represents successful adaptation to change in situation and variety among its constituency (successful in terms of the goal of group survival).

5. The horrors of Nazism undercut many of the assumptions of an assimilationist policy. For many years to come, even those who have experienced no anti-Semitism are likely to say: Do not be misled by the contemporary situation; yesterday is a better guide to our experience tomorrow than is the present. (There is a close parallel with this in international relations.) In Rosenberg's words,

. . . it is no small thing that the highly acculturated and the often de-Judaized Jew of the 1940's was stopped cold in his assimilating tracks, and what seemed like an inexorable, progressive process of submersion in the general culture was reversed." But the sentence preceeding this statement should also be noted: "How long into the future the recent drama of rebirth will be able to excite the Jewishness of American Jews remains, of course, a moot question.[54]

6. There is enough anti-Semitism in the United States, particularly barriers to some jobs, residential areas, and educational opportunities, to lend weight to the arguments of those Jews who hold that identity with the ethnic group is the only sure support.

7. Jews are still relative newcomers. Though most are native-born, and third-generation persons will soon be in a majority, only a small proportion are "old American" in the sense of fourth generation or more. Thus the assimilationist pull has not reached its strongest intensity.

8. The development of Israel has strengthened the group identity of many Jews. This is not to suggest that they are Zionist in the sense that they feel a national allegiance to Israel or a desire to migrate there, for it is clear that only a small minority of American Jews take this position. (In the years after the 1967 Arab-Israeli war, "a small minority" has meant several thousand migrants a year from the United States to Israel.) Much more widespread, however, is a sense of pride in the accom-

plishments of Israel, a belief that it has contributed greatly to the lives—and even survival—of their coreligionists in Europe, North Africa, and the Near East, and a feeling of attachment that derives from Israel's deep traditional significance for Jews.

These are powerful forces. Together they help to account for the vitality of the American Jewish community. It would be a mistake, however, to assume that all of them will remain strong and that assimilationist forces will not grow in strength. There is tremendous pressure on *all* traditions and group identities in a period of drastic social change and extensive social and physical mobility. More specifically with regard to Jews one should note that they have not yet felt the full power of assimilationist influences. These appear after one or two generations of persistent intergroup contact in schools, jobs, and neighborhoods. Those who support a continuing distinctive group, moreover, face a dilemma, for its preservation is aided by segregation and even anti-Semitism. As barriers to various jobs, clubs, and residential areas are torn down, barriers to interpersonal contact, friendship, and intermarriage are also lowered.

In the contemporary balance, pluralistic influences outweigh assimilationist ones, and seem likely to continue to do so in the decades ahead. The assimilationist forces, however, if we may hazard a prediction, are likely to grow stronger. The result will not be to eliminate a separate Jewish community in the United States. What seems more likely will be continuing identity with a group that becomes less and less distinctive. This is not to say that Jews will become "just another denomination," pulled in the direction of the majority, but rather that interaction will mutually modify the present separate religious groups and that all of them together will be vastly affected, for the most part in the same ways, by the dynamic forces at work in the world in the last decades of the twentieth century.[55]

---

[54] Stuart Rosenberg, *op. cit.*, p. 151.

[55] See Marshall Sklare, *Conservative Judaism: An American Religious Movement*, Free Press, 1955; Will Herberg, *Protestant-Catholic-Jew*, Doubleday,

*Are Jewish "Traits" the
Cause of Anti-Semitism?*

If the above discussion is correct, prejudice and discrimination against Jews (as against other groups) have created some differences in individual and group behavior. They have been among the factors causing a high level of individual achievement but have also caused self-doubt, frustration, and hostility. They have encouraged solidarity but also intragroup conflict and barriers to adjustment with the dominant groups. To the anti-Semite, these differences are the causes of his attitudes. Basically he is wrong. He exaggerates the differences enormously, he forgets differences favorable to the minority group, and he has a thoroughly inadequate idea of the cause of the differences. Selective and adroit use of the facts can, however, give a superficial support to his prejudices. In the study of anti-Semitism as in the study of other prejudices, failure to examine the whole process of the vicious circle that we discussed in Chapter 5 will lead to an incomplete understanding of the roots of prejudice and an underestimation of the tenacity with which it resists direct, rational attack. However one may explain the origin of tendencies of minority-group members, to the contemporary generation—few of whom can be counted on to be moral philosophers—these tendencies are simply there, as facts of his environment. Thus prejudice and discrimination can be sustained in part by their own consequences.[56]

THE INTERACTING CAUSES
OF ANTI-SEMITISM

To get a more unified picture of the complicated spiral of forces that have created and support anti-Semitism, it might be well

1955; H. J. Gans, "American Jewry: Present and Future," *Commentary*, May, 1956, pp. 422–430, and "The Future of American Jewry," *Commentary*, June, 1956, pp. 555–563; Nathan Glazer, "The Jewish Revival in America," *Commentary*, Dec., 1955, pp. 493–499, and Jan., 1956, pp. 17–24; and J. Milton Yinger, *The Scientific Study of Religion*, Macmillan, 1970, pp. 500–507.
[56] See William Catton and Sung Chick Hong, "The Relation of Apparent Minority Ethnocentrism to Majority Antipathy," *ASR*, Apr., 1962, pp. 178–191.

to draw together, in summary, the many factors we have traced above. Some of these factors have already been discussed, and so will only be listed here; others that have been disregarded until now will need fuller treatment. It is especially important to keep in mind that these forces are interactive, mutually reinforcing, and to an important degree self-perpetuating. Once a group has been set apart as a target for hostility, it is chosen more readily for that role the next time, because tradition suggests it, guilt feelings demand it, and perhaps the responses of the minority group, having differentiated the group more sharply, encourage it. These are among the interactive forces:

1. In the pre-Christian era, the Jewish people, living astride important trade routes and in a strategically vital area, were caught up in conflict with many nations. The conflicts were so continuous that traditions of antipathy were given root. They helped to develop a strong Jewish ethnocentrism which, at the same time, reinforced the antipathy.

2. With the domination of Europe by the Christian Church, Jews stood out as the only large minority religious group at a time when religious symbols were of enormous importance. The conflict between Christianity and Judaism was more than usually sharp because of the ambivalent relationships between the two—the Jews denied Christ, yet he was a Jew.

3. By the fifth century, Jews had been deprived of their citizenship. This action may have begun as religious intolerance, but it led to many social and economic consequences. Jews had no role in the gradual development of the nation-state system that was to predominate in Europe; they had no legal rights or powers until the end of the eighteenth century. Thus their differentiation from the rest of the "body politic" was increased.

4. Having no legal rights in the medieval world, Jews were permitted to reside in the cities only at the pleasure of the princes. The princes used them as revenue officers and "royal usurers." The royal treasuries seemed always to be empty, so Jews were

continually forced to demand payment from the unwilling citizenry. While being drawn into these "banking" activities, Jews were, oppositely, driven from many other occupations, forbidden to own land, and excluded from the artisan guilds. Thus their economic differentiation increased.

5. The rapid growth of cities and the development of commerce from the tenth century on encouraged more and more Christians to come into the formerly marginal occupations associated with trade. They used their advantages as citizens and members of the dominant religion to fight their Jewish competitors, even succeeding in driving them out of most of western Europe.

6. In eastern Europe, to which most of the Jews fled, they were still barred from citizenship, and the violent attacks that they had experienced at least since the days of the Crusades were repeated. This treatment kept in motion the forces of anti-Semitism.

7. Inevitably the lack of citizenship, economic discrimination, and personal violence to which the Jews were subjected intensified their cohesiveness. Their ethnocentrism was maintained. The Jewish community seemed to be their only protection against the hostilities they continuously experienced. They were bicultural and binational; they could scarcely give full allegiance to the nation or culture in which they resided because of the interaction between the discrimination against them and their own ethnocentrism. They were blocked from the full participation that would have led, in time, to assimilation, and then were accused of being different. They could see no advantage in deserting a rich cultural heritage for a precarious position in the dominant society. Just how precarious that position might be has been shown again by the destruction of German Jewry, one of the most "assimilated" groups in the world. Biculturality has been an important part of the vicious circle that has kept anti-Semitism alive. Being different, Jews were more easily selected for hostile treatment; they were forced back upon their own group and its traditions, thus maintaining its differences. In earlier days, this vicious circle revolved mainly

around religious symbols. Only with the decline of feudalism and the rise of nations, often with relatively distinct cultures, did the position of Jews as "foreigners" become vital. Having evolved painfully into unified nations, the European countries found the Jewish aliens (whom they themselves had kept alien) in their midst. It is doubtless significant that there is a high (but not perfect) correlation between the areas where independent statehood was achieved with great difficulty and the areas where anti-Semitism has been most prevalent. Compare England and France with Germany and Poland. There is also a social psychological aspect to the emphasis on nationalism. As Parsons says:

It is a striking fact that the extreme kind of nationalistic sentiment is often found in groups where frustration of the sort described above is likely to be most severe; as for instance, in the *lower middle class*. The pattern of sentiments seems to be somewhat as follows: "I may not be a successful person, able to live in luxury the way others do; but there is one thing you can't deny—I am just as much an American (or German or Englishman) as anybody." Part of the intensity of national sentiment may undoubtedly be interpreted as "compensation" for frustration elsewhere. National identification allows the individual to participate in the glory of the achievement of *his* nation and relieves him of the blame for lack of *personal* achievements. Patriotism is very much of a social and economic leveler, and a very appropriate way in which to appease one's own uneasy conscience (usually on an unconscious level) and to "run down" the superior achievements or good fortune of others. The fact that the Jews form a suitable symbol in both these contexts is important in understanding the concentration of aggression on them.[57]

In an era when nationalism has loomed large, Jews have been simultaneously more provincial (with staunch loyalty to the Jewish community) and more international (with a sense of identification with the Jewish culture in every part of the world and frequently with friends and relatives residing in many different lands).

[57] Talcott Parsons, in Graeber and Britt (eds.), *op. cit.*, p. 117.

8. With anti-Semitism established by the factors listed above, it became fixed in tradition and passed on to each new generation in the socialization process. Once used, a pattern of prejudice is more likely to be used again than is a new pattern, for the old has acquired reinforcements. It has the sanction of tradition; it has helped to create some of the very differences by which it was at first justified; and the minority group has absorbed some of the projections of the dominant group—to admit that the prejudice was not "justified" would then require of the dominant group that they re-examine the projected evils which they have thrust from themselves. Since this is too painful an experience for most individuals, they maintain the old prejudice. Many Germans today have strong unconscious guilt feelings about the anti-Semitism of the Nazi regime, whether they participated in it or simply failed to oppose it. Those very guilt feelings may well *increase* their anti-Semitism. And in some individuals at least, the stronger the guilt, the stronger must be the prejudice to try to allay the tensions. Here is another important factor in the vicious circle of anti-Semitism.

9. Part of the tradition of prejudice is the stream of stories, jokes, and stereotypes that carries the culturally established attitude on to the next generation. Millions of people who have scarcely ever seen a Jew "know" why a joke is funny when it shows a "typical" Jewish trait or has a Jew acting in a way completely unfitting to the stereotype. By laughing at the joke we share a bond of common "knowledge" with our associates, we get a feeling of superiority, and by acknowledging its humor we get a twisted kind of proof that our original attitude was correct. Literature contains a number of stereotyped and hostile pictures of Jews, beginning with the medieval miracle plays and the later morality plays—indicating their connection with the popular forms of medieval Christian teachings. Chaucer's "Prioress's Tale," Marlowe's *The Jew of Malta,* and Shakespeare's *The Merchant of Venice* have helped to reenforce attitudes toward the Jew. Of themselves, they would not create a prejudice; it is the reader, more than the writer, who makes them reinforce a belief already established. In a different context they would have a wholly different effect.

It mattered little in the ultimate anti-Semitic effects that Shakespeare's Shylock is presented with great imaginative penetration. The name became in time the popular designation for all Jews, and the subtler humanity of the great dramatist's character remained unknown to the vast majority who have since its creation used the name Shylock as synonymous with Jew. . . . Most would agree that it is invidious and incompetent criticism which stresses anti-Semitism as such in creative literature like Shakespeare's. As Dickens once said in reply to Jewish criticisms of his character Fagin in *Oliver Twist,* "All the rest of the wicked dramatis personae are Christians."[58]
Even great literature, however, read from the perspective of an already established prejudice, can be made into stereotypes.

10. Anti-Semitism has been sustained to some degree by the wide dispersion of Jews around the world. When a gentile moved from one nation to another, his pattern of prejudice was not broken, for in the new land he was likely to find Jews. International contacts did not challenge the traditional prejudice against the Jew. ". . . Because he is a continuous minority in all the communicating lands of the Western world, the apprehensions regarding him as a minority were transferable, interchangeable, and even cumulative to a degree."[59]

11. Some of the interactive forces that sustain anti-Semitism are particularly prominent in the modern world. They have given it a force and a tenacity unmatched even by medieval pogroms. Freud (and many others following him) contended that anti-Semitism is in part simply a way of attacking Christianity itself. The anti-Semitic person is protesting against Christ as a symbol of brotherhood, peace, and equalitarianism; he is protesting against the demands on his behavior that Christian teachings make. A

[58] Joseph W. Cohen, *ibid.*, pp. 354–355.
[59] Hertzler, *ibid.*, p. 82.

song of the Hitler Youth declared: "Pope and Rabbi shall be gone. We want to be pagans once again. No more creep to churches." And another said: "We are the joyous Hitler Youth. We do not need any Christian virtue. Our leader, Adolf Hitler is our Saviour."[60] "No more creep to churches"—an important phrase of self-revelation. Anti-Semitism thrives among those who feel Christianity as repression. They attack Jews not as Christ killers but as Christ givers. This hostility may break into the open, as in the case of the Hitler Youth, or it may be unconscious displacement, as with the more traditionally religious Americans.[61] The unconscious hostility that the latter feel toward Christian authority over their lives is displaced onto the Jews. Maurice Samuel insists that this is *the* cause of anti-Semitism. He draws a sharp line between anti-Jewish sentiment and anti-Semitic hallucination: "Anti-Jewish sentiment (a dislike of Jews based on contact, direct or indirect, with some Jews) is in fact the ordinary variety of racial, religious and economic bitterness, overflowing in ordinary human abuse. Anti-Semitic hallucination is a unique phenomenon (the word unique must be taken quite literally here) in modern group relations."[62]

That anti-Semitism, like all other prejudices, has some unique aspects, and that the desire to attack Christianity obliquely is one of them seem to be highly probable. (We do not need to share Samuel's enthusiasm for this as the only explanation, or assume, as he does, that those who disagree with him are obstinate, naïve, or themselves anti-Semitic.) This aspect of anti-Semitism has become increasingly important in recent years, particularly in Nazism, which was thoroughly antithetical to Christianity as

well as to Judaism, but also in many other movements and in many individuals.[63]

12. Having discussed the personality factors in prejudice at length above, we need only mention them here to bring them into the list of interacting forces. The loss of an integrating system of values, the "freedom" that is felt as loneliness and confusion, the alienation from satisfaction with one's work, the gap between achievement and one's desires—these and the other aspects of modern society that have contributed to insecurity have made a great many of us particularly susceptible to prejudice.

13. Akin to the theory that modern anti-Semitism rests in part on a reaction against Christianity is the theory that it is a disguised attack on liberal democracy as it has developed since the eighteenth century. This source of opposition to Jews is often a consciously chosen weapon in political-economic conflict. Anti-Semitism can obscure basic problems, can divert the hostility of the masses, can cloak an attack on democracy as "necessary" for protection against the dangerous Jews. "The history of anti-Semitism, in both its classical and modern form, shows that it is profoundly symptomatic of political, economic, and institutional change."[64] In periods of rapid change, with their attendant frustrations, a nation with a tradition of anti-Semitism can be led away from democracy and liberalism by the manipulation of hostility toward the Jews.

14. One of the forces involved in modern anti-Semitism implied above is explicit propaganda and the work of organized groups. Propaganda and "hate groups" are a "cause" of anti-Semitism only when there is already a favorable attitude toward their message. In such a situation they can increase and intensify the prejudice. Propaganda to whip up hatred of the Jews was carried on systematically by the Nazis and

[60] Quoted by Carl J. Friedrich, *ibid.*, p. 8.

[61] It is unfortunate that there were no questions regarding individual psychodynamics in the interview schedules of the important Glock and Stark and Selznick and Steinberg studies. Such questions would have allowed an elaboration of the research designs in a valuable direction.

[62] Maurice Samuel, *The Great Hatred*, Knopf, 1940, p. 10.

[63] See, in addition to Samuel, Jacques Maritain, *A Christian Looks at the Jewish Question*, Longmans, Green, 1939.

[64] Carey McWilliams, *A Mask for Privilege: Anti-Semitism in America*, Little, Brown, 1948, p. 108.

has been used extensively by "hate groups" in the United States.

15. Modern anti-Semitism has been sustained not only by the attacks on Christianity and democracy that characterize some aspects of our society, but also by the increasing importance of commerce and industry. The Jews, having been forced into the cities and into commercial occupations by the process that we have discussed, naturally took an important part (although one that is often exaggerated by anti-Semites) in the development of the modern economy. They became competitors of the increasingly powerful middle class, while at the same time representing to those who were suffering from the new order the essence of the society they opposed. This latter group included the old ruling class, who often identified Jews as the key factors in the new economy; and it included the masses of people in many situations. As trade developed in eastern Europe, Jews in high proportion took over the "marginal" job of buying and selling cattle. "Since a cattle dealer is never a popular figure in agricultural communities, the only living contact between the precapitalist peasant masses of central and eastern Europe and the market economy of modern industrial society was the Jew."[65]

16. Oppositely, Jews have been used as symbols of communism—sometimes, as in the case of Hitler, by the same person who identifies them as the epitome of capitalism. Jews have, of course, participated in the growth of communism and other left-wing developments in the last century. It scarcely matters, for a theory of anti-Semitism, whether they have furnished more or less than a proportionate number of left-wingers, for prejudice can create the necessary observation.

17. Jews have been important in the rise of the trade-union movement. Since trade unionism has been able to get increasing rewards for workers in all industrialized western nations, employers and others have often fought it vigorously. Those who already had a prejudice against Jews could easily convince themselves that unionism was a Jewish product.

Modern urban industrial society is thus not only prejudice-prone, but peculiarly prone to anti-Jewish prejudice. The Jews, who occupy places on almost every status level of society, are more apt scapegoats for more diverse groups than is a minority that is concentrated primarily in lower status levels. Jews are importantly involved in most of the sharply conflicting developments of modern life. The prejudices of various groups are thus mutually reinforced. The long history of violence against Jews has created such deep-going guilt feelings that many people dare not admit—their ego involvements being so intricately related to the question—that their hostility to Jews is a categorical prejudice. Thus economic conflict, personal insecurity, traditional stereotypes, cultural disorganization, and propagandistic distortion have come together to create and sustain the blinding prejudice of anti-Semitism.

THE FUTURE OF ANTI-SEMITISM

In Part III we shall examine the question of techniques in the reduction of prejudice and discrimination. That analysis will apply to anti-Semitism as well as to other kinds of categorical group judgments. At this point we wish simply to comment briefly on the kinds of conditions likely to increase and those likely to decrease anti-Semitism. Many writers take the position that there will be anti-Semitism so long as Jews continue as an identifiable religious or cultural group. J. F. Brown declares that the prejudice will be overcome only ". . . by immediate cultural and final racial assimilation." He thinks that Jewish leaders should encourage a wider distribution of Jews into all occupations.[66] (The pattern of occupational distribution is, to a large degree, the

[65] Friedrich, in Graeber and Britt (eds.), *op. cit.*, p. 5.

[66] *Ibid.*, pp. 143–146.

result of prejudice.) I. S. Wechsler takes the same position: "The only condition on which it can be eliminated, the Jew is neither willing nor able to meet. For anti-semitism to disappear the Jew must cease to be; but this is precisely what he cannot do and the price he is unwilling to pay."[67] J. O. Hertzler says, even more strongly, that

. . . to cease to be a cultural irritant the Jew must be completely assimilated. Any old sense of allegiance to his "chosen people" idea will have to disappear; he must consciously remove characteristics of behavior which are recognizably Jewish; he must deliberately mold himself and his life on Gentile patterns. . . . He will have to be completely absorbed ethnically. . . . He will have to give up all pride in his group and his people's history and denationalize himself as a Jew. Parodoxically he will have to individualize himself completely so far as a Jewish nation is concerned, and become a 100 percent conformist so far as the nation of his sojourn is concerned. . . . He will have to thrust himself into the background in his economic activities and never allow himself to be numerous or conspicuously successful as a competitor in any occupation, profession, or other economic pursuit. . . .[68]

It is not surprising that these authors take a pessimistic view of the chances of eliminating anti-Semitism. Strong in-group feelings among Jews, some feeling of identification with an international Jewish community, religious differentiation, and an occupation distribution that varies from that of most other groups are, to an important degree, the *result* of prejudice. To ask that these be changed *before* the prejudice can be reduced is to ask that an effect eliminate a cause. If the prejudice were not there, members of the majority would not be concerned with the cultural, religious, or occupational differences between themselves and Jews. Few Americans are disturbed over the fact that Episcopalians have had more than "their share" of occupants of the White House, or that Baptists insist upon immersion.

If Jews were to disappear completely as identifiable individuals, anti-Semitism, to be sure, would disappear. But that this is in no way useful as an approach to the reduction of anti-Semitism is indicated by two simple facts. So long as there is prejudice, the dominant group will not let them disappear (German Jews were among the most assimilated, but Hitler created the idea that one Jewish grandparent makes a Jew); and so long as there is prejudice, Jews will not want to disappear (they look upon their own community and religion as a source of strength and solace). Such a "solution" is certainly not in the American tradition. The complex pattern of national, religious, racial, and cultural groups in the United States rests upon the thesis that there can be unity in diversity.

We do not mean to suggest by these remarks that Jewish response to discrimination is uninvolved in the cycle of causes and therefore unimportant in programs seeking to reduce anti-Semitism; for we have noted the importance of the vicious circle. Nor do we imply that there will not be continuing change among Jews, as among non-Jews. It is not at all clear, however, that the nature of that change in the next several decades implies the disappearance of a distinctive Jewish subcommunity.

. . . despite the obvious and often less than obvious patterns of their accommodation to the revolutionary environment of the New World, certain fundamental vestiges remain embedded in the depths of the Jewish psyche. In America, as elsewhere in the long history of their Diaspora, psychologically, Jews are still in exile. And as one wit has said, it is often more difficult to get the Exile out of the Jews than to get the Jews out of Exile."[69]

Halpern suggests that we can see in Europe the unfolding of an Hegelian dialectic: The ghetto was the thesis, the emancipation movement the antithesis, and Zionism, seeking to transcend the failures of the emancipation while absorbing its successes in a new, now fully self-chosen ghetto, is the synthesis. In the United States,

[67] In K. S. Pinson (ed.), *Essays on Antisemitism*, Conference on Jewish Relations, 1946, p. 39.

[68] In Graeber and Britt, (eds.), *op. cit.*, pp. 98–99.

[69] Rosenberg, *op. cit.*, p. 268.

however, quite different processes are at work. Perhaps we have seen so far only a thesis: the continuing affirmation of a Jewish community in the face of "assimilation" (in the sense of rejection of the institutions of the immigrant ghetto).[70] What the antithesis (or the dominant one among several) may be it is not easy to guess, but perhaps it will be a religio-cultural movement now only partly foreshadowed in these late years of the thesis. And some future synthesis may develop along the lines suggested by Arnold Toynbee—who has not always been friendly to Judaism: a religion at home in every land, not tied, as virtually all religious expressions are, to the limited experience of tribe, nation, or civilization, and therefore at home in the emerging world society of the atomic age.[71]

One should not take the application of an Hegelian formula nor our speculations too seriously. What we want to suggest is the likelihood of continuous development of the Jewish tradition and continuation of Jewish identity. We do not believe that the elimination of anti-Semitism is dependent upon the self-liquidation of Jews as a distinct group. Virtual disappearance as a group may, after some centuries, be a result of the elimination of prejudice, but it can scarcely be the cause. Anti-Semitism will be reduced when and if the causes that we have discussed in several of the preceding chapters are reduced. The reduction of personal insecurity; the growth of an integrated set of values; an increase in economic security; encouragement of political processes based on free discussion, on acceptance of majority rule, and on conciliation of differences; education that reveals the cultural roots of prejudice, that exposes stereotypes, that reduces the learned and unlearned ignorances about other groups that most of us share—these and additional changes can attack the foundation of anti-Semitism and other prejudices and can simultaneously free man's energies for the solution of other problems.

[70] Ben Halpern, in Marshall Sklare (ed.), *The Jews*, pp. 34–39.
[71] *The New York Times*, Sept. 11, 1960.

Part II / MINORITIES IN
THE SOCIAL STRUCTURE:
THE INSTITUTIONAL PATTERNS
OF INTERGROUP RELATIONS

Chapter 11 / MINORITIES
IN THE ECONOMY
OF THE UNITED STATES

Among the most important indications of the status and power of a group is its place in the economic structure. Nowhere are prejudice and discrimination more clearly shown than in the barriers to economic improvement that are thrown in the way of minority-group members. Job opportunities are important not only in the narrow economic sense, but also in terms of their influence on the whole style of life of individuals and on the institutional structure of groups. The political influence of a group, its family patterns, religious beliefs, educational ambitions and achievements, even the possibilities of good health and survival cannot be understood until the place of that group in the total economy is studied. The relationship is, of course, reciprocal; political, familial, religious, and other institutional patterns also affect the economic situation.

This analysis deals with the roles of minority groups in the American economy. The degree to which similar forces are involved in other societies may be seen by referring to some of the general principles discussed in Chapter 4. Since Negroes not only represent the largest minority but are the group most affected by economic discrimination, we shall be largely concerned with their place in the economy.

POPULATION DISTRIBUTION

While the percentage of Negroes living in the South has been declining, it has been increasing in other parts of the country. In 1969, Negroes constituted nearly one-fifth of the population in the South, less than one-tenth in the North, and one-twentieth in the West.

The average annual out-migration from the South of nonwhite persons declined from

Negroes as a Percent of the Total Population in the United States and Each Region, 1940, 1950, 1960, and 1969

	1940*	1950*	1960	1969
United States	10	10	11	11
South	24	22	21	19
North	4	5	7	9
Northeast	4	5	7	9
North Central	4	5	7	8
West	1	3	4	5

*Data exclude Alaska and Hawaii
Source: U.S. Department of Commerce, Bureau of the Census, *The Social and Economic Status of Negroes in the United States*, 1969, p. 4.

159,700 in the 1940s to 145,700 in the 1950s, and to 88,300 from 1960 to 1969. Thus, nearly 4,000,000 nonwhite persons, mostly Negroes, left the South in 30 years.

The Negro population increased from 18,793,000 in 1960 to 22,331,000 in 1969, an average annual increase of 2.3 percent from 1950 to 1960 and 2 percent from 1960 to 1969. The white population increased from 158,051,000 in 1960 to 175,311,000 in 1969, an average annual increase of 1.6 percent for the 1950s and 1.2 percent from 1960 to 1969. Fifty-five percent of all Negroes now live in metropolitan areas. Approximately three-fourths of all whites live outside metropolitan areas and central cities, either in suburbs or small places.

AGRICULTURE

Although agricultural employment of nonwhite workers has been declining, both absolutely and relatively, for half a century, farm work continues to be an important part of their occupational pattern. Agricul-

Percent Distribution of Population by Location, Inside and Outside Metropolitan
Areas, 1950, 1960, and 1969

	Negro			White		
	1950	1960	1969	1950	1960	1969
United States	100	100	100	100	100	100
Metropolitan areas	56	65	70	60	63	64
Central cities	43	52	55	34	30	26
Suburbs	13	13	15	26	33	38
Outside metropolitan areas	44	35	30	40	37	36

Source: U.S. Department of Commerce, Bureau of the Census, The Social and Economic Status of
Negroes in the United States, 1969, p. 7.

ture is even more important for Americans
of Mexican descent.

Farms Operated by Nonwhites

In 1964, there were 199,952 nonwhite farm
operators in the United States. Negroes constituted 92 percent of this total, and 8 percent were classified as other nonwhite. Of
all nonwhite farm operators, approximately
92 percent were in the South, and 98 percent
of these were Negroes.

Two-thirds of the nonwhite operators,
other than Negroes, resided in the West,
mainly in California and Hawaii. Most of
the nonwhite farm operators in California
were Orientals; most of those in Hawaii
were Hawaiians and Orientals. Most of the
2500 nonwhite operators in North Carolina
and of the 1100 in Oklahoma were Indians.

From 1959 to 1964, the total number of
nonwhite farm operators decreased approximately 91,000, and about 87,000 of the
decrease was in the South. The number of
nonwhite operators in 1964 was only one-
third as large as it was in 1950. Almost
three-fifths of the change in the number of
nonwhite operators from 1959 to 1964 occurred on tenant farms. The table below
shows the totals for Negro and other nonwhite farm operators for 1900 to 1964.

In 1964, the average size of farm of nonwhite operators in the South was 56.6 acres
as compared to 282.6 acres for farms of
white operators, and approximately two-
thirds of all farms operated by nonwhite

Negro and Other Nonwhite Farm Operators,
1900–1964

Year	All Nonwhite Operators	Negroes[1]	Other Nonwhite[1]
1964	199,952	184,004	15,948
1959	290,831	272,541	18,290
1954[2]	483,650	467,656	15,994
1950	585,917	559,980	25,937
1945[2]	689,215	(NA)	(NA)
1940	723,504	681,790	41,714
1935[2]	855,555	(NA)	(NA)
1930	921,400	882,852	38,548
1925[2]	(3)	(NA)	(NA)
1920	954,284	925,710	28,574
1910[4]	924,450	893,377	31,073
1900	769,528	746,717	22,811

Notes:

NA—Not available

[1]. For Hawaii for 1959, 1950, and 1940, Negroes were
not separately identified; for these years "other non
white" includes "all other" races for Hawaii.

[2]. Coterminous United States only; Alaska and Hawaii
were not included in censuses of 1954, 1945, 1935,
and 1925.

[3]. Available for South only.

[4]. Forty-nine states; no classification by color for
Alaska for 1910.

Source: U.S. Bureau of Census, Census of Agriculture,
1964, Statistics by Subjects—Chapter 8, p. 760, Color,
Race, and Tenure of Farm Operator, Government
Printing Office, 1968.

operators in the South were less than 50
acres in size. The small-scale nature of nonwhite farming in the South is shown in the

report that approximately 70 percent of the nonwhite farms of less than 50 acres sold less than $2,500 worth of farm products in 1964.[1]

Negro Farmers

Despite the changes that have occurred since 1940, the poorest farm families in the United States are concentrated in the cotton region of the Old South. Everything about them testifies to their meager existence. The shacks that pass for houses, their unbalanced diet, their low incomes, their rudimentary farm equipment, their lack of medical care, their semiliteracy, and their political impotence mark them as a forlorn, low-status segment of the population. Many of these families are white, but the Negro families have a racial handicap in addition to the group's other disabilities.

The percentage of nonwhite workers in agriculture decreased from 21.1 in 1948 to 13.0 in 1959 (the percentage of white workers in agriculture in 1959 was 8),[2] to 11.2 in 1962 and 5.3 in 1967.[3] The actual drop in the number of Negro farm workers between 1962 and 1967 was more than 350,000, with Negroes leaving the farms at twice the white rate. Consequently, the proportion of all Negro workers employed as farm workers was halved by 1967, and agricultural work now accounts for about the same proportion of black as white employment. An important difference is found, however, in types of farm work performed by the two racial groups. Three-fifths of all white farm workers are farmers and farm managers, while Negro farm workers were primarily farm laborers and foremen.[4]

The tenure of Negro farm operators in the South is shown in the following table. Full owners operate only the land they own.

Part owners operate land they own as well as land rented from others. Managers operate land for others and are paid a wage or salary and/or a commission for their services. Tenants rent from others, or work on shares for others, all the land they operate, and are divided into five subclasses. Cash tenants pay cash rent, either on a per acre basis or for the farm as a whole. Share-cash tenants pay part of the rent in cash and part in a share of the crops and/or of the livestock and livestock products. Crop-share tenants pay a share of the crops but not of the livestock or livestock products. Livestock-share tenants pay a share of the livestock or livestock products. They may or may not also pay a share of the crops. Other and unspecified tenants include those who do not pay any cash rent or share rent; they may have the use of the land rent-free or in return for a fixed quantity of product, payment of taxes, maintenance of buildings, etc.[5]

The worst types of exploitation that formerly characterized tenancy, and especially the sharecropper status, have been eliminated or greatly reduced.[6] However, for Negro sharecroppers in the South considered as a group, Demerath's observation is too optimistic:

. . . In the social relations of the economy, the South has today a new kind of farmer and sharecropper, white and Negro. Instead of being con-

---

[1] U.S. Bureau of the Census, *Census of Agriculture, 1964, Statistics by Subjects*, chap. 8, p. 762.

[2] Conrad Taeuber, "Some Recent Population Changes in the United States," *JIR*, Spring, 1960, p. 113.

[3] Claire C. Hodge, "The Negro Job Situation: Has It Improved?", *Monthly Labor Review*, Jan., 1969, p. 22.

[4] *Ibid.*, p. 27.

[5] U.S. Bureau of the Census, *Census of Agriculture, 1964*, pp. 747–748.

[6] As Rubin points out, parts of the plantation area of the Old South are in transition from feudal agrarianism to an industrial mass society. If the traditional image of the society was based on the plantation owner's agrarian, paternalistic, white supremacy value systems, we now have a new image based on the merchant and industrialist with values centered in the town, rational economic qualifications for jobs, and money as a medium for the achievement of power and prestige. Economic crisis and scientific-education movements have forced the traditional plantation owner to convert to a rational operation that might be called a factory-in-the-field. The plantation house, domestic service, and other symbols of the old regime function for prestige and power only after the demands of rational economic institutions are met. Morton Rubin, "Social and Cultural Change in the Plantation Area, *JSI*, 1954, First Quarter, pp. 34–35.

Number of Farms, by Color and Tenure of Operator, for the South: 1900–1964 [Data for subclass of tenants for 1964 and all data for 1959 are based on reports for only a sample of farms.]

Color and tenure of operator	Number of farms					
	1964	1959	1945	1935	1920	1900
The South						
All farm operators	1,372,732	1,645,028	2,881,135	3,421,923	3,206,664	2,620,391
Full owners	808,500	946,613	1,509,056	1,339,946	1,405,762	1,237,114
Part owners	303,612	322,952	193,607	234,720	191,463	133,368
Managers	7,120	9,196	13,193	15,782	18,318	18,765
All tenants	253,500	366,267	1,165,279	1,831,475	1,591,121	1,231,144
Cash	47,322	49,231	232,234	(NA)	219,188	[1]458,790
Share-cash	17,393	18,025	20,829	(NA)	22,672 }	
Crop-share	133,284	233,895	801,813	(NA)	1,212,315 }	772,354
Livestock-share	13,349	14,144				
Other and unspecified	37,007	50,972	110,403	1,831,475	136,946 }	(NA)
White, total	1,188,154	1,379,407	2,215,722	2,606,176	2,283,750	1,879,721
Full owners	737,701	856,864	1,348,076	1,189,833	1,227,294	1,078,635
Part owners	272,349	285,418	165,355	198,768	152,432	105,171
Managers	6,975	8,906	12,751	15,401	16,548	17,172
All tenants	171,129	228,219	689,540	1,202,174	887,566	678,743
Cash	35,365	34,376	159,092	(NA)	118,913	[2]187,088
Share-cash	15,185	15,619	15,549	(NA)	14,465 }	
Crop-share	} 90,201	{ 128,794	437,689	(NA)	701,891 }	491,655
Livestock-share		13,198				
Other and unspecified	26,574	36,232	77,210	1,202,174	52,297	(NA)
Nonwhite, total	184,578	265,621	665,413	815,747	922,914	740,670
Full owners	70,799	89,749	160,980	150,113	178,558	158,479
Part owners	31,263	37,534	28,252	35,952	39,031	28,197
Managers	145	290	442	381	1,770	1,593
All tenants	82,371	138,048	475,739	629,301	703,555	552,401
Cash	11,957	14,855	73,142	(NA)	100,275	[2]271,702
Share-cash	2,208	2,406	5,280	(NA)	8,207 }	
Crop-share	} 56,432	{ 105,101	364,124	(NA)	510,424 }	280,699
Livestock-share		946				
Other and unspecified	10,433	14,740	33,193	629,301	84,649	(NA)

Notes:

NA – Not available

[1]Less than 0.05 percent.

[2]For 1920 standing renters were included with "Other tenants"; for 1910, standing renters were included with "Cash tenants"; for 1900, standing renters and unspecified tenants were included with "Cash tenants"; for 1890 and 1880, all tenenats were classified as either renting for fixed money rental or for share of products. In determining increase-decrease 1910–1920, the 27,072 white and 77,924 nonwhite standing renters reported for the South for 1920 were included with "Cash tenants."

Source: U.S. Bureau of the Census, Census of Agriculture, 1964 Statistics by Subjects—Chapter 8, p. 765, Color, Race, and Tenure of Farm Operator, Government Printing Office, 1968.

tinuously in debt to the credit merchant or the plantation store, he rents from the finance company a thirty-five hundred dollar automobile, a TV set, and a variety of kitchen and farm appliances his father never imagined. Out of cash, the county welfare will take him on or he can seek work in a nearby plant. He and his family are consumers in the new mass market in which newness is of the essence; and traditions, even in race, tend to go by the boards more rapidly than ever before, though not rapidly enough for those who feel their pince or drag.[7]

When Bogue says that "instead of the ragged sharecroppers, we are becoming used to the skilled operators of tractors and complicated agricultural machinery—men who draw good wages and have more security because they are indispensable,"[8] it is clear that he is not referring to the generality of tenant farmers, and especially not to the remaining Negro sharecroppers. The majority of Negro farmers have not benefited from the important developments in southern agriculture (improved methods, bigger investments in capital and fertilizer, larger farm units, a shift from cotton and tobacco to diversified farming and cattle raising). Negro farmers have not had the education, capital, and credit to take advantage of these developments themselves, and very few Negroes have well-paid employment on the large scientific commercial farms.[9]

INCREASING MECHANIZATION IN AGRICULTURAL PRODUCTION

The mechanization of cotton production has continued apace during the postwar period. The experimental models of earlier years were replaced with more than 18,000 mechanical cotton harvesters of the spindle type and 23,000 mechanical cotton strippers

were in use by 1957.[10] In 1955 nearly three-and-a-half million bales of cotton, constituting nearly one-fourth of the American crop, were harvested mechanically. Two-thirds of the California crop was harvested by machines. By 1959, 40 percent of the cotton crop was machine harvested.[11] Almost as significant in its long-run effects as mechanical pickers and strippers is the bringing of other stages of cotton production under mechanical control. Much has been accomplished along these lines in the western sections of the cotton region, and the feasibility of completely mechanizing the crop in important localities has been established.[12]

In a study of 15 Arkansas counties, Dillingham and Sly found that the number of mechanical cotton pickers increased from 482 in 1952, or an average of 28.3 per county, to 5061 in 1963, an average of 297.7.[13] The smaller-sized machine can harvest an acre of cotton in six man-hours compared to 74 man-hours of hand labor. In 1958, 27 percent of the Mississippi Delta cotton crop was harvested by mechanical pickers. Six years later the percentage had increased to 81. Such changes contributed greatly to the reduction of Negro tenancy.[14]

In Arizona, the all-time high for hand cotton pickers was reached in 1953 (48,500); machine-harvested cotton reduced the hand pickers to 5300 in 1963, nearly a 90 percent drop. Nevertheless, hand technologies in cotton persist. The number of seasonal workers required, especially in thinning and weeding (5469) exceeds the peak numbers needed in either lettuce or

[7] Nick J. Demerath, "Desegregation, Education, and the South's Future," *Phylon*, First Quarter, 1957, p. 44.

[8] Donald J. Bogue, "Population Distribution and Composition in the New South," in Jessie P. Guzman (ed.), *The New South and Higher Education*, Tuskegee Institute, 1954, p. 28.

[9] Eli Ginzberg, *The Negro Potential*, Columbia, 1956, pp. 16–17.

[10] James H. Street, *The New Revolution in the Cotton Economy*, Univ. of North Carolina Press, 1957, p. v.

[11] Fay Bennett, "The Condition of Farm Workers in 1962," Report to the Board of Directors of National Sharecroppers Fund, 1963, p. 2.

[12] Street, *op. cit.*, pp. v–vi. Modern cultivation of cotton includes mechanization in disposal of plant residue from the preceding crop, application of the fertilizer, planting, thinning, and weed control, insect control, defoliation, picking, and ginning.

[13] Harry C. Dillingham and David F. Sly, "The Mechanical Cotton-Picker, Negro Migration, and the Integration Movement," *Human Organization*, Winter, 1966, p. 346.

[14] *Ibid.*, pp. 346–347.

citrus. Padfield and Martin point out that where wages are relatively low, the percentage of cotton that is machine harvested is low. California's wage rate is highest, and it has the highest percent of machine harvest. With the lowest wage rate, South Carolina is fourth lowest in machine harvested cotton.[15]

The rapid spread in the use of the cotton picker is not the only major change in the production of cotton. In 1969, the 300,000 cotton farmers in the United States harvested approximately 11 million bales, compared with 18 million in 1955. In that year, the United States produced half the world's supply; by 1969, the proportion was down to one-fifth. Competition had increased from growers in Brazil, Mexico, Egypt, Pakistan, and Turkey. In 1968, the United States exported only 2.7 million bales of cotton, compared with 4.2 million in 1967. Also in 1968, synthetics outsold cotton 2 to 1.[16]

Padfield and Martin say that social evolution has accompanied technological change. In the lettuce industry, the shift from the shed pack to the field pack resulted in the displacement of the top occupational classes by the lower occupational classes, and the displaced groups were out permanently. In cotton, the top class, a new elite made up mainly of Anglos, began to displace the bottom class—the hand pickers. But in cotton, the groups that were gradually being displaced by machines—Indians, Negroes, and Mexican-Americans—began to move up in the occupational system and eventually acquired some of the machine operators' jobs. Of course, many thousands of seasonal workers were forced out of work in cotton, but it is not uncommon to find non-Anglo machine operators. In citrus, technological changes have been minor. Efficiency comes primarily from loading, transporting, warehouse labor and space-saving systems, and from more formal organization of picking crews.[17]

A report on the sugar cane industry during the past 25 years shows some interesting consequences of technical developments on racial groups in Louisiana. Mechanization was accelerated by the invention of a harvesting machine in 1938. Whereas the average hand laborer had been cutting two tons of cane daily, the first harvesters could cut approximately 25 tons per hour. Harvesters replaced 21,000 workers in Assumption Parish in 1944, and the use of the machine spread rapidly after World War II. Now hand cutting is limited almost entirely to damaged and stunted canes; almost 96 percent of the crop is now harvested mechanically. Supplementing the harvester are such inventions as: mechanical cane loaders; ditching, burning, and fertilizing machines; and machines for expediting and improving cultivation. A new machine combines the cutting, stripping, and loading of sugar cane into a single operation. New and improved herbicides and insecticides are widely used. In the county studied by Pellegrin and Parenton, all sizes of farms between 10 and 260 acres declined in number between 1950 and 1959. More importantly, the traditional pattern of Negro-white relationships underwent significant change, a shift from a paternalistic to a contractual relationship. The farmer has been freed from dependence on hand labor. Industrial plants that would absorb surplus labor are not likely to be established in rural Louisiana. Automation and other technical changes have created a labor surplus in the industrialized areas in the part of the state reported on in this study.[18]

In the past, the failure to diversify crops in the South was due to the fact that no crop could compare with cotton as a source of cash income. In recent years greater crop diversification has been stimulated in the cotton areas of the Old South by such factors as exhaustion of the land through continued use of the one-crop system; the ravages caused by the boll weevil; the programs of state and federal agricultural

[15] H. Padfield and W. Martin, *Farmers, Workers, and Machines,* Univ. of Arizona Press, 1965, pp. 90, 135.

[16] *Time,* Oct. 10, 1969, p. 94.

[17] Padfield and Martin, *op. cit.,* pp. 285–286.

[18] Roland J. Pellegrin and Vernon J. Parenton, "The Impact of Socio-Economic Change on Racial Groups in a Rural Setting," *Phylon,* Spring, 1962, pp. 56–60.

agencies; a growing interest in livestock, in the food and feed grains, and in other products which can be produced with less labor; the mechanization of cotton cultivation; and a decline in the share of the world's cotton supply that is produced in the United States. Even in the Delta, the alluvial plain in the northwestern corner of Mississippi, diversification has proceeded rapidly. More than twice as many acres in the Delta are planted in corn, wheat, soybeans, and rice as in cotton. In addition, the raising of cattle and hogs has increased greatly.

Recently the perfection of a mechanical tomato picker has had a drastic effect on jobs formerly performed by Mexican-American workers in the Southwest, an effect comparable to that produced by the mechanical cotton picker in the mid-1950s.[19]

MIGRATORY FARM LABORERS

Hired farm workers fall into three groups: regular workers (those employed for more than 150 days a year by one employer, more than half of whom work on farms of more than 1900 acres), seasonally employed workers, and foreign farmhands. The seasonal farm workers are employed less than 150 days a year, and they work for more than one employer. Hundreds of thousands of people—native white, Negroes, and Mexican-Americans—move each year from state to state harvesting fruit and vegetables. They follow three main "streams" (1) along the Pacific Coast from southern California to Washington and back, (2) from the south-central region of Texas, Louisiana, and Oklahoma northward through a wide area, terminating in Minnesota, Michigan, and Wisconsin, and (3) along the Atlantic seaboard, starting in Florida and moving up through Georgia, the Carolinas, Virginia, Delaware, New Jersey, and New York, with a few going on to New England, and a return to Florida.

Robert Coles, a psychiatrist who has car-ried on extensive research among migrant farmers, refers to the "subculture" of these workers and their families. They are on the move much of the time, usually they do not vote, and they are rarely eligible for local unemployment assistance. Their rights to adequate schooling for their children, to police protection, and to sanitary and fire inspection and regulation of their homes are, in many cases, limited. They are isolated from the life of the various communities where they work. The diet of most migrants is poor in vitamins and protein, and they receive inadequate medical care. Coles found that migrant children learn to respond to two worlds, that of their family and that of "others" (the comfortable, middle-class world of America). Migrant children move early and unceremoniously into adulthood when two elements are fulfilled, experience in working in the fields and the onset of puberty. Many of the younger migrants attempt to leave the migrant stream, and some succeed by finding jobs in the cities or at least by buying a car so that they can travel alone rather than in trucks and buses. Lack of education, unemployment, and fear of the city, however, work against them. One migrant (aged 17, two children) said: "I tried the city for a job, and I moved in with a cousin, and no go. . . . They was all on relief and I was supposed to get on when I could, after applying; but we got tired of waiting, and we just left one day. . . . I'd rather keep 'on the season' and feel right than sit all day as they do and do nothing."[20]

In an intensive study of ten migrant families, six black and four white, Dr. Coles found a striking number of children infected with diseases of the intestines, blood, mouth, eyes, and ears. At five or six, migrant children seem cheerful, spontaneous, affectionate to one another, and relaxed; later, physical health deteriorates and often a variety of "symptoms" develop. Heavy drinking before and after work, violence, apathy, gloom, and severe depressions are seen in many migrants. Growers and others

[19] E. Galarza, H. Gallegos, and J. Samora, *Mexican-Americans in the Southwest*, McNally-Loftin, 1969, p. 34.

[20] Robert Coles, *The Migrant Farmer*, Southern Regional Council, 1965, p. 20.

who work with migrants are likely to regard them as unreliable, unkempt, unthrifty, quarrelsome, heavy drinkers, destructive of property, sullen, and unresponsive. According to Coles, their way of life results in two distinct personality styles. With members of their own families they are often warm and open, but at work, with strangers, and often with one another, they are guarded, silent, sullen, bitter, or touchy. His psychiatric observations, however, do not support many of the claims made about the "laziness" of farmhands. Those he has studied "are *motivated* toward work, *want* to work, and *will* work."[21]

The largest group of domestic seasonal farm laborers is the Mexican-American. Although these people have worked in the Southwest for more than six decades, they have not, as a group, moved up on the economic ladder. As Samora points out, this lack of mobility is due in part to the fact that no new immigrant group has sought the unskilled and semiskilled jobs, and enough labor was available from Mexico to prevent a shortage that might have raised wages. Attempts to adopt a settled life pattern and to improve their economic and social status have been hindered by their lack of adequate education, lack of machine skills, and the interest in communities in holding them available for seasonal farm work. This last factor is reflected in the unwillingness of many employment offices to recommend them for other jobs. From 1945 to 1955, the main competition to Spanish-speaking farm labor came from the "wetbacks," persons who crossed the Rio Grande River illegally to work in the United States. During 1954, 1,035,282 deportations were listed, and, since many were deported more than once and others were never apprehended, from half a million to a million wetbacks entered illegally.[22] Public Law 78, passed in 1951 as a temporary program on the claim that there was a shortage of farm labor because of the Korean War, and renewed in 1954, 1956, 1958, and 1960, provided for the admission of seasonal farm workers from Mexico. Under this law, Mexican citizens were admitted as contract workers for temporary employment in United States agriculture in the numbers shown below during the years 1957 to 1967.

1957	436,049
1958	432,857
1959	437,643
1960	315,846
1961	291,420
1962	194,978
1963	186,865
1964	177,736
1965	20,284
1966	7,647
1967	6,125[23]

The law provided that no Mexican nationals (braceros) could be employed if domestic labor was available, but numerous ways were found to discourage domestic workers. The latter were believed to be less docile and to expect higher wages. In December, 1963, Congress renewed Public Law 78 for one year as the final extension. Samora says that the expected competition for labor began in early 1965 and that wages and working conditions began to improve. Predicted shortages of labor generally did not materialize.[24]

The Subcommittee on Migratory Labor of the United States Senate, headed by Walter F. Mondale, has held hearings on the problems of migrant workers for a decade, but Congress has specifically excluded migrants and other farm workers from workmen's compensation. (The migrants' accident rate is 300 percent higher than the national average.) Also, the migrants averaged only 78 days of work for pay of $891 in 1969, but they are specifically excluded from coverage by the unemployment law. The minimum wage law has been applied by Congress only

[21] *Ibid.*, pp. 21–29.

[22] Julian Samora, *La Raza: Forgotten Americans*, Univ. of Notre Dame Press, 1966, pp. 65–70.

[23] Galarza, Gallegos, and Samora, *op. cit.*, p. 89.

[24] Samora, *op. cit.*, pp. 70–71. Galarza, Gallegos, and Samora point out that "the question whether poor men shall go north or investment shall go south is never finally settled. Now that public opposition holds the bracero importation in check, the growing, packaging, and processing of fruits and vegetables may move south of the border on a larger scale than in the past." Galarza, Gallegos, and Samora, *op. cit.*, p. 13.

to the largest farms and the minimum for farm workers is 30 cents an hour below that for other workers. Employers of migrants who pay on a piecework basis avoid even this minimum. Migrants and other farm workers are excluded from coverage by the National Labor Relations Act, which protects the rights of other workers to organize to improve their situation. The child labor law does not prevent migrant families from taking their children into the fields to work. If no one is able to work, usually the family is unable to qualify for welfare assistance. The $15 million voted by Congress in 1969 for the Migrant Health Act is said to be used mainly in the local machinery of the Public Health Service.[25]

Coles concludes that if anything is to be done by middle-class citizens about the lot of migrant workers, they must be prepared for some tiresome work, for "the coordinated planning, in education, medicine, agriculture, housing, and a host of associated fields, required for the job."[26] With the success in 1970 of AFWOC (the Agricultural Farm Workers Organizing Committee) led by Cesar Chavez and Larry Itliong in carrying on a strike to organize Mexican-Americans, Filipinos, and other minorities in California, some anticipate the building of a strong union among minority farm workers. According to Leggett's assumptions, the strike and the union should also foster class consciousness, class politics, and status-group political action.[27]

Cooperatives. According to the executive director of the Federation of Southern Cooperatives, a central service organization for member cooperatives, the cooperative movement is "weak, small, in many ways inef-

fectual in the face of hunger, despair, and disease." Lack of investment capital hinders it from moving into such areas as health and life insurance, low-cost housing, specialized farms, community-owned recreational facilities, restaurants, civic educational programs, day-care centers, small industries, large-scale farming operations where each member owns a small plot but where grazing lands are cooperatively owned. Prejean says that efforts to begin small industries owned collectively by workers are being made throughout the South. These cooperatives include gasoline stations, bakeries, grocery stores, credit unions, and clothing suppliers. The Federation of Southern Cooperatives is owned by 45 different co-ops representing approximately 15,000 families. For poor people, the cooperatives offer economic advantages, and they provide a power base from which attempts can be made to obtain better schools, better public services, and open access to the public resources of the community.[28]

EMPLOYMENT AND UNEMPLOYMENT

During the latter part of the nineteenth century, and in fact until World War I, the Negro population in both northern and southern cities was small. The usual occupations followed by Negroes were those of servant, porter, janitor, and, to a smaller extent, common laborer. Gradually, as labor disputes occurred, Negroes were brought in to break strikes and weaken labor unions. It was through strikebreaking that Negro workers obtained their first jobs in northern steel plants and in the meat-packing industry.

At the time of World War I, Negroes were brought into the great industrial centers of the North to overcome the shortage of unskilled workers. It was no mere trickle of workers who came, but hundreds of thousands of migrants. These people went into heavy industries, into domestic service, and into construction work. Within a few years Negroes had demonstrated that they

[25] William Robbins, "Migrant Workers: A Life of Brutal Hardship," *The New York Times*, July 26, 1970.

[26] Coles, *op. cit.*, p. 31.

[27] John C. Leggett, *Class, Race, and Labor: Working Class Consciousness in Detroit*, Oxford Univ. Press, 1968, pp. 145–146. Leggett points out that the AFWOC was supported by Walter Reuther, the California AFL-CIO, the U.A.W. (United Auto Workers), the I.U.D. (Industrial Union Department of the AFL-CIO), and the I.L.W.U. (the International Longshoremen and Warehousemen's Union).

[28] Charles Prejean, "Rural Poverty—1968 Style," in Patricia Romero (ed.), *In Black America*, United Publishing Corporation, 1969, pp. 247–248.

Number of Employed and Unemployed Persons, 1960–1969 (In millions. Annual averagees for 1960 to 1968; January-November averages for 1969)

	Employed		Unemployed	
	Negro and other races	White	Negro and other races	White
1960	6.9	58.9	.8	3.1
1961	6.8	58.9	1.0	3.7
1962	7.0	59.7	.9	3.1
1963	7.1	60.6	.9	3.2
1964	7.4	61.9	.8	3.0
1965	7.6	63.4	.7	2.7
1966	7.9	65.0	.6	2.3
1967	8.0	66.4	.6	2.3
1968	8.2	67.8	.6	2.2
1969	8.4	69.5	.6	2.3
Change 1960–1969:				
Number	+1.5	+10.6	−.2	−.8
Percent	+21	+18	−27	−27

Note: The information on employment and unemployment is obtained from a monthly sample survey of households. All persons 16 years of age and over are classified as employed, unemployed, or not in the labor force for the calendar week containing the twelfth of the month.

The unemployed are persons who did not work or have a job during the survey week, and who who had looked for work within the past four weeks, and were currently available for work. Also included are those waiting to be called back to a job from which they had been laid off or waiting to report to a new job.

The sum of the employed, excluding military, and the unemployed constitutes the civilian labor force.

Source: U.S. Department of Commerce, Bureau of the Census, *The Social and Economic Status of Negroes in the United States,* 1969, p. 28.

were satisfactory workers in the urban environment.

When the industrial development of the South was accelerated in the years that followed World War I, Negro workers were already employed in the fertilizer, tobacco, turpentine, steel, and furniture manufacturing industries. The rapid expansion of industry, together with the increase in service industries and in hotel and restaurant operations, provided new job opportunities for the urban Negro. The bulk of the new jobs in domestic service also went to Negroes.

With the coming of the depression the northern Negro industrial worker lost much of the ground he had gained. He had very little seniority, he had not yet acquired much skilled status, and white workers were clamoring for such jobs as there were. Southern Negro workers experienced less unemploy-

ment and less occupational shifting, but the wage differentials based on race were continued. The trend whereby Negro artisans were displaced by Whites in the building and hand trades was heightened in depression years. According to R. C. Weaver, "Almost a half of the skilled Negro males in the nation were displaced from their usual types of employment during the period 1930 to 1936; a third of those outside their usual occupations were in unskilled work, and over 17 percent were unemployed."[29]

Minorities and Employment in Defense Industries

The economic position of the Negro at the time the defense program was inaugurated in

[29] R. C. Weaver, *Negro Labor,* Harcourt Brace Jovanovich, 1946, p. 9.

1940 was discouraging. The proportion of Negroes in manufacturing (5.1 percent) was lower than it had been in 1910 (6.2 percent), and, with the exception of domestic service, similar losses had occurred in other kinds of employment. Also, the Negro was greatly underrepresented in the industries that are important in war production. In aircraft and parts, 0.1 percent of the workers were Negro; in electrical machinery, 0.5 percent; other machinery, 1.0 percent; rubber products, 2.1 percent; apparel, 2.3 percent; nonferrous metals and their products, 2.4 percent; automobile equipment, 3.6 percent; iron and steel, 5.5 percent; ship and boat building, 6.4 percent. Negroes had not forgotten the dismissal, during the depression, of a high percentage of black workers brought into industry during boom years, and they campaigned for training, employment, and upgrading in all war industries.

During the war years a number of significant changes occurred in the Negro employment situation. The number of Negroes in skilled, single-skilled, and semi-skilled jobs doubled. The percentage of Negro women employed as domestic servants decreased sharply, and Negroes were employed in industries and plants where few had held jobs before the war. More industrial and occupational diversification for Negroes occurred in four years during World War II than in the whole post-Civil War period.

Negro and Other Nonwhite Races as a Percent of All Workers in Selected Occupations, 1960 and 1969 (Annual averages for 1960 and January-November averages for 1969)

	1960	1969
Total employed	11	11
Professional and technical	4	6
Medical and other health	4	8
Teachers, except college	7	10
Managers, officials, and proprietors	2	3
Clerical	5	8
Sales	3	4
Craftsmen and foremen	5	7
Construction craftsmen	6	8
Machinists, jobsetters, and other metal craftsmen	4	6
Foremen	2	4
Operatives	12	14
Durable goods	10	14
Nondurable goods	9	14
Nonfarm laborers	27	24
Private household workers	46	44
Other service workers	20	19
Protective services	5	8
Waiters, cooks and bartenders	15	14
Farmers and farm workers	16	11

Source: U.S. Department of Labor, Bureau of Labor Statistics, in U.S. Department of Commerce, Bureau of the Census, *The Social and Economic Status of Negroes in the United States*, 1969, p. 43.

Employment of Whites and Nonwhites

The number of employed and unemployed persons by race, is shown in the following table.

OCCUPATIONS OF NONWHITE WORKERS

Although there were significant changes in the occupational distribution of nonwhite workers between 1960 and 1969, a disproportionate share of the lower-paid, less-skilled jobs were still held by Negroes and persons of other races in 1969.

THE EXTENT OF UNEMPLOYMENT AMONG NONWHITES

In 1968 and 1969, the unemployment rate for nonwhites was the lowest it had been since 1953, but it was still about twice as high as that of the white rate. In those years, the unemployment rates for both groups had decreased to approximately half the rate in 1961, a recession year.

The following table shows the reasons given in official reports why men are not in the labor force.

It should be noted that unemployment, as defined by the Bureau of Labor Statistics, is based upon the number of persons in the labor force actively seeking work. Figures of

Unemployment Rates, 1949–1969 (Annual averages
for 1949 to 1968; January-November averages for 1969)

	Negro and other races	White	Ratio: Negro and other races to White
1949	8.9	5.6	1.6
1950	9.0	4.9	1.8
1951	5.3	3.1	1.7
1952	5.4	2.8	1.9
1953	4.5	2.7	1.7
1954	9.9	5.0	2.0
1955	8.7	3.9	2.2
1956	8.3	3.6	2.3
1957	7.9	3.8	2.1
1958	12.6	6.1	2.1
1959	10.7	4.8	2.2
1960	10.2	4.9	2.1
1961	12.4	6.0	2.1
1962	10.9	4.9	2.2
1963	10.8	5.0	2.2
1964	9.6	4.6	2.1
1965	8.1	4.1	2.0
1966	7.3	3.3	2.2
1967	7.4	3.4	2.2
1968	6.7	3.2	2.1
1969	6.5	3.2	2.0

Note: The unemployment rate is the percent unemployed in the civilian labor force.
Source: U.S. Department of Labor, Bureau of Labor Statistics, in U.S. Department of Commerce, Bureau of the Census, *The Social and Economic Status of Negroes in the United States,* 1969, p. 29.

the BLS do not include the unemployed persons who have left the labor force as a result of long-term joblessness and who are no longer seeking employment. Many thousands of older Negroes who have exhausted their unemployment insurance benefits, as well as a large number of young persons who have never entered the labor market, are not included in official unemployment statistics. Thus many labor economists regard these statistics as an understatement of actual employment conditions. "Hidden unemployment" is especially marked in Negro ghettos.[30] Also, current population surveys of the United States Government do not enumerate a part of the working-age population. The undercount for black workers is estimated to be from 13 to 15 percent, compared with 2 percent for whites. Considering the high unemployment rates and the estimated undercount, the true unemployment rate for Negro working-age males probably is significantly greater than reported in official publications.[31]

Unemployment rates for nonwhite teenagers are the highest in the labor force. In 1969, the rate for this group was twice that for the white teenage group.

Early in 1970, black unemployment rose from 7.1 percent to 8.7 percent; again it was twice that of whites. According to official figures, seasonally adjusted unemployment

[30] Herbert Hill, "Black Labor in the American Economy," in Patricia Romero (ed.), *op. cit.*, p. 179.

[31] *Ibid.*, p. 179.

Men Not in the Labor Force, by Age, 1969 (January-November averages)

	Total not in labor force (thousands)	Reason not in labor force (percent)			
		Total	Going to school	Unable to work[1]	Other[2]
16 to 19 years					
Negro and other races	461	100	80	1	19
White	2,566	100	82	1	17
20 to 24 years					
Negro and other races	120	100	62	6	32
White	959	100	77	3	20
25 to 54 years					
Negro and other races	261	100	11	35	54
White	1,026	100	16	35	49
55 to 64 years					
Negro and other races	169	100	1	38	62
White	1,236	100	–	28	72
65 years and over					
Negro and other races	495	100	–	19	81
White	5,314	100	2	9	89

Notes:

– Represents zero or rounds to zero.

[1]Includes only those who have serious, long-term physical or mental illness.

[2]Includes retired workers and unpaid family workers, those keeping house, and a large number preparing to enter or reenter the labor force or awaiting military service.

Source: U.S. Department of Labor, Bureau of Labor Statistics, in U.S. Department of Commerce, Bureau of the Census, *The Social and Economic Status of Negroes in the United States,* 1969, p. 35.

for nonwhite teenagers in poverty neighborhoods was 34.2 percent in July, 1970, compared with 24.7 percent a year earlier. The actual situation was more serious because official statistics do not include many school dropouts who have never begun to look for work, or those 16- to 18-year-olds who are officially registered at, but seldom attend, school. Nor do they include the angry early teenagers who are on the street all the time.[32]

Although many localities in the Southwest are rated normal in unemployment rates for the total labor force, from 7 to 10 percent of the male Mexican-American labor force may be unemployed at a given time. In Los Angeles, unemployment rates of 12 to 25 percent have been found in some Mexican-American neighborhoods. During the low point in agricultural production in the Lower Rio Grande, the Salt River valley, and the central valley of California, some communities have a male unemployment rate of one-third. Mechanization in canneries and other food processing plants has eliminated thousands of jobs. For decades, these cannery jobs were regarded as the next step up from farm labor. In the cities, mechanization in laundering, car washing, and other fields has eliminated jobs that have provided employment for many Mexican-Americans.[33]

[32] Jacob Cohen, "Jobs: Source of Much Black Unrest," *The New York Times*, July 19, 1970.

[33] Galarza, Gallegos, and Samora, *op. cit.*, pp. 32–34.

Unemployment Rates by Sex and Age, 1967–1969 (Annual averages for 1967 and 1968; January-November averages for 1969)

| | Negro and other races | | | White | | |
	1967	1968	1969	1967	1968	1969
Total	7.4	6.7	6.5	3.4	3.2	3.2
Adult men	4.3	3.9	3.7	2.1	2.0	1.9
Adult women	7.1	6.3	6.0	3.8	3.4	3.4
Teen-agers[1]	26.5	25.0	24.4	11.0	11.0	10.8

[1] "Teen-agers" includes persons 16 to 19 years old.

Source: U.S. Department of Labor, Bureau of Labor Statistics, in U.S. Department of Commerce, Bureau of the Census, *The Social and Economic Status of Negroes in the United States*, 1969, p. 30.

THE PRESENT ECONOMIC STATUS OF NEGROES

The Basic Causes of the Negro's Present Economic Disadvantages

Killingsworth holds that racial discrimination, as a present source of economic disadvantage, is probably less important than is often assumed. An understanding of this disadvantage requires an analysis of the changes in the Negro's rate of progress in the past three decades.[34] A study of the great progress made by Negroes from 1940 to 1953, as well as the slowing down of some aspects of that progress since then, is attributed to a complex set of labor market interactions. World War II created an acute labor shortage, due largely to a great increase in government spending and to a massive withdrawal of men from the civilian labor force. Industrial growth and an extensive system of government subsidies resulted in a redesigning of production techniques to utilize large numbers of low-skilled workers. Southern Negroes migrated in great numbers to centers of heavy industry in the North Central and the East Coast regions. These migrants settled in the "central cities" and were joined by new migrants from the South. Backlogs of demand for durable goods and the Korean War provided jobs and postponed the transition to usual peacetime conditions.

[34] This summary is based on Charles C. Killingsworth, *Jobs and Income for Negroes*, Institute of Labor and Industrial Relations, Univ. of Michigan Press, 1968, pp. 45–48. See later sections in this chapter: "Discrimination on Ethnic and Racial Grounds" and "Economic Losses from Discrimination."

Before the end of the Korean War, Negroes began to be affected adversely by the movement into the urban labor market of white farmers who had been displaced by technological developments in agriculture. At the same time, the demand for less-skilled workers in manufacturing began to decline. The industrial investment boom of the 1950s furthered the decentralization of manufacturing activity, and the central cities became less attractive as locations for new stores and offices, in part because whites were migrating to the suburbs in large numbers.

Killingsworth traces some of today's "gross unemployment" among Negroes to the response they made to the "distorted patterns of demand" in the labor market during World War II. When these patterns started to change in conformity to long-run trends in the economy, Negroes "were in the places and the occupations that had the greatest burdens of adjustment." Those burdens were increased by continuing migration and by a population explosion among big city Negroes. The latter phenomenon had been occasioned by the transference of a substantial part of the reproductive capacity of the entire Negro population to northern cities and to a falling death rate. The inundation of the public schools, together with *de facto* segregation, resulted in a failure of education to contribute substantially to social and economic mobility of Negroes as it had for earlier newcomers to the cities. The effects of the Negro population explosion began to be felt in the late 1950s and the early 1960s. Despite reduced participation rates (percentage of the population of working age that is in the labor force) among young Negroes, as well as a long economic boom, special employment and training programs, and the draft calls of a new war, the unemployment rate among young Negroes remained at alarming levels. Killingsworth concludes that economic trends indicate that " 'gross unemployment' among young Negroes will persist or even worsen as the very large numbers of Negro children now in the big cities reach working ages, and that this blight will spread as today's teen-age Negroes grow older." This conclusion is not intended to suggest that the problem of reducing economic inequalities for Negroes is irremediable, but it does warn against underestimating the difficulties and the enormity of the problem.[35]

Economic Growth. Some economists think that the major explanations for the South's low incomes and general economic backwardness are essentially the same as those propounded for many underdeveloped countries. They see the South as the most underdeveloped region of the United States because its socioeconomic structure has occasioned shortages of well-educated and skilled manpower, inadequate supplies of capital, a lack of modern techniques of production, and a scarcity of innovating entrepreneurs.[36]

Nationally, as well as for the South, economic growth is essential if there is to be an improvement in employment for workers. For the black population a continuing strong demand for workers is critical, for, as Hodge points out, it is often in the rapidly growing occupations that Negroes can make substantial gains. Growing occupations, and occupations with higher turnover, have greater hiring needs and upgrading is more prevalent than in declining fields. Negro gains of recent years could be lost if the economy does not grow. When workers are needed, discriminatory barriers are more quickly lowered.[37]

Changes in the Job Market. In 1930, about 56 percent of the work force produced goods;

by 1960, the proportion had dropped to 44 percent. Within the central cities of the country, the change in the job market was even more drastic. Moreover, this rapid shift came at a time when the immigration to urban centers was at a peak. New York City lost 84,000 jobs in manufacturing between 1959 and 1963. At the same time, the city gained 69,000 jobs in service fields, 45,000 in government, and 21,000 in finance, insurance, and real estate.[38]

Since 1945, a net total of approximately two million farm workers have left rural areas each decade to seek city work. Dentler and Warshauer say: "This cityward movement of less educated job seekers . . . intensified over [the] postwar years when unskilled jobs in urban as in rural areas were shrinking. Employment of professional and technical workers increased by 47 percent between 1950 and 1960. This was a growth rate more than three times greater than that for all occupational groups taken together. Most of this growth, and nearly all of the 34 percent increase in clerical workers over the same period, occurred solely in metropolitan areas."[39]

High school dropouts constitute a large and growing proportion of that part of the work force which is "static, shrinking, or expanding least rapidly." Educational attainment for the adult with no more than a grade school education have become more and more atypical, yet less and less employable.[40] In Chapter 18, we call attention to the higher dropout rates and the lesser educational attainments of Negroes, Mexican-Americans, Puerto Ricans, and American Indians. The economic consequences of these differentials is substantial in today's rapidly changing job market.

Discrimination on Ethnic and Racial Grounds. Duncan and Duncan say that the experience of non-Negro minorities in America, as shown by their educational and occupational achievements, argues against the existence of

[35] *Ibid.*, p. 48.

[36] James G. Maddox, E. E. Liebhafsky, V. Henderson, and H. M. Hamlin, *The Advancing South: Manpower Prospects and Problems*, The Twentieth Century Fund, 1967, p. 5.

[37] Hodge, *op. cit.*, p. 28.

[38] R. A. Dentler and M. E. Warshauer, *Big City Dropouts and Illiterates*, Praeger, 1969, p. 61.

[39] *Ibid.*, p. 61.

[40] *Ibid.*, pp. 61–62.

pervasive discrimination on purely ethnic grounds. According to these investigators, the notion of equal opportunity "irrespective of national origin is a near reality, challenged most severely by the cumulative over-achievement of Russian-Americans and the cumulative under-achievement of Latin-Americans." The experience of the Negro minority, however, leads them to a different conclusion. They say: "The current occupations of Latin-Americans are reflected in a mean socioeconomic status score which falls short of the mean score for all non-Negro, non-farm, native males by 15 points. The current occupations of Negro-Americans are reflected in a mean score which falls short of the same (non-Negro) mean by 24 points."[41] Adjusting for starting point in the social structure and formal educational qualifications, they find that Latin Americans have a handicap of one point on the socioeconomic status scale. Negroes have a handicap of twelve points on this scale. Such evidence of discrimination in the competition for jobs cannot be easily disregarded.

Are Racial Employment Practices Changing? A marked improvement in recent years in the number and kinds of jobs held by Negroes is seen by some economists. Hodge says that some of this occupational upgrading occurred between 1957 and 1962, but that substantial gains were made in the period 1962–1967. During those years, nearly 1.1 million black workers moved into jobs that offered higher pay and status. Despite these gains, the Negro continues to hold a disproportionate share of the lower-skilled, lower-paying jobs.[42] A 1970 special report of the Census Bureau shows that Negroes, who constitute 11 percent of the population, got 28 percent of the new crafts and operative openings that went to family men between 1960 and 1969. During the same period, the median income of married Negro blue collar workers rose by 44 percent, while the income for white married men in the same occupations rose

by 27 percent. Sar Levitan, of George Washington University's Center for Manpower Policy Studies, says that these figures represent real changes, not limited to any particular geographic area or to any specific industry. He predicted that these gains against racial barriers would continue if the national economy avoided a prolonged recession.[43]

Racial employment practices may improve in the South, in part because of equal employment opportunity programs included in Title VII of the Civil Rights Act of 1964. This part of the act went into effect in July, 1965, for employers of 100 or more workers; after 1968 it was extended to those who employed 25 or more. The act has several weaknesses: "the machinery for redress in employment discrimination is completely complaint-oriented, providing for investigations and hearings, conferences and conciliations, referrals to state and local agencies, and civil court actions; it includes various exemptions; and there are few real penalties for violations." Although he predicts that change will be slow and that resistance will create turmoil, Maddox concludes that Title VII represents substantial progress in national attitudes toward the basic right to a job, without discrimination because of race, color, religion, sex, or national origin.[44]

The Philadelphia Plan. The Philadelphia Plan, the Nixon Administration's plan to increase minority employment in construction trades, was put into effect September 23, 1969. Under this plan, the Labor Department's Office of Federal Contract Compliance requires contractors to make [good-faith] efforts to hire specified percentages of Blacks in federally-aided projects costing $500,000 or more. In each case the hiring goal to be applied to federal contractors is to be governed by the overall nonwhite percentage of the local labor market. The minimum level for most job categories is 11 percent, the nonwhite share of the national

[41] Beverly Duncan and Otis D. Duncan, "Minorities and the Process of Stratification," *ASR*, June, 1968, pp. 363–364.
[42] Hodge, *op. cit.*, p. 20.

[43] *The New York Times*, June 21, 1970, p. 28.
[44] Maddox, Liebhafsky, Henderson, and Hamlin, *op. cit.*, p. 152.

labor market. In some cities, Blacks constitute 25 to 30 percent of the total work force, and in such cases federal contractors are expected to use a standard of nonwhite hiring that more closely approximates the local labor market. In Philadelphia, where more than one-third of the population is black, the plan's ground rules call for contractors to pledge to try to hire Blacks at a rate of at least 4 percent of their new employees for projects undertaken in 1970, 9 percent in 1971, 14 percent in 1972, and a top range of 19 to 26 percent after that. The government has said that tests of "good faith efforts" would include whether a contractor relied solely on unions to assign workers to him, or, if necessary, participated in federally funded training programs and went to community organizations that had agreed to supply Blacks. In January, 1970, it was predicted that the Nixon Administration would move cautiously to extend some features of the Philadelphia Plan to virtually all work done under federal contract.

Objections to the Philadelphia Plan were advanced by the Controller General of the United States and by some members of Congress on the ground that it required racial quotas in violation of Title VII of the 1964 Civil Rights Act. In January, 1970, the Contractors Association of Eastern Pennsylvania sought an injunction against the plan, claiming that it was unconstitutional. On March 13, 1970, federal District Judge Charles R. Weiner upheld the constitutionality of the plan and ruled that it did not violate the Civil Rights Act of 1964. On the latter question, Judge Weiner pointed out that the plan does not require the contractor to hire a definite percentage of a minority group.

The Philadelphia Plan was slow in getting under way in Philadelphia, in part because of the dispute over its legality. Initial progress reports in May, 1970, indicated that the plan had fallen short of expected minority hiring goals. The head of the Office of Contract Compliance in Philadelphia said at that time that there was no doubt the contractors were behind in compliance. A committee was set up to monitor the projects already started. Mr. Benjamin Stalvey, of the OCC, said that "contractors should have no problem recruiting because we know the number of minority workers available and we can aid them with recruitment sources. One or two contractors have called us and we referred them to sources. But we haven't heard any contractors say that they couldn't find workers."[45] The federal agencies with projects under construction included the Departments of Housing and Urban Development, Transportation, and Health, Education, and Welfare. Agencies with projects can send out simple reminders to contractors or they can order compliance. Traditionally the Government has gone slow in contract compliance because it does not want to interfere with its procurement practices. Political pressures have built up on the application and extension of the Philadelphia Plan, with contractors, the AFL-CIO, and some congressmen opposing the plan, and the NAACP, the Urban League, other civil rights organizations, and some congressmen supporting it. It remains to be seen how successful the plan will be in increasing the representation of Negroes in federally aided construction projects.

Sullivan's Opportunities Industrialization Center. A highly successful black business enterprise, described in more detail in the following chapter, has provided training for more than 50,000 persons, with a job placement, in Philadelphia at least, of 90 percent. Founded and sponsored by Leon Sullivan, pastor of Zion Baptist Church in a slum area of Philadelphia, the Opportunities Industrialization Center was established in an idle jail building refurbished in part by seed money provided by Sullivan's 4000 parishioners. Eventually Sullivan interested Philadelphia businessmen, including executives of General Electric, Westinghouse, IBM, and Bell Telephone in his undertaking, and in fiscal 1969

[45] *The New York Times*, May 3, 1970, p. 50. See also Laurence Stern, "Nixon's 'Philadelphia Plan' To Be Enforced Nationwide," *The Plain Dealer*, Dec. 28, 1969; John Herbers, "Gains Are Made in Federal Drive for Negro Hiring," *The New York Times*, Jan. 25, 1970, p. 1; and Donald Janson, *ibid.*, March 15, p. 30.

OIC received $10 million in funds from the Departments of Labor and HEW (a cutback the following fiscal year reduced government involvement to $1.8-million). OIC has grown slowly to 70 loosely confederated branches in 70 cities.[46]

FUTURE EMPLOYMENT IN THE SOUTH

If the South succeeds in attracting an increasing proportion of capital-intensive manufacturing industries in the future, professional and technical occupations will rise in importance and put those workers who are inadequately trained and undereducated in an unfavorable competitive position. The employment outlook for the southern Negro is not a promising one so long as he is undereducated, lacks industrial experience, and is subjected to racial discrimination.[47] This is not intended to suggest that employment opportunities for Negroes will not expand at all in occupations other than professional and technical fields. A recent federal estimate is that 11.6 percent of the textile industry's workers are Negro, compared with 3.3 percent in 1960. Dr. Richard Rowan, of the University of Pennsylvania, estimates that the proportion is higher in the South, and nine-tenths of the textile industry is located in the South. His study of 46 companies in the latter half of 1968 showed that Negroes constituted 12.7 percent of the production workers in the industry and 13.4 percent in the South. Cleghorn says that the percentage has risen since then.[48]

The U.S. Bureau of Labor Statistics (BLS) has projected a 1975 U.S. labor force of approximately 93.6 million persons, part of which will be in the armed forces. The assumption is that approximately 90.5 million persons will be in the civilian labor force in the 48 continental states, an increase of 20.2 million over the 1960 labor force of about 70.3 million. The number of Negroes of working age is expected to increase from approximately 6.3 million in 1960 to 7.1 million in 1975, but Negro migration from the South is expected to result in a continued decrease in the proportion of Blacks in the South's working-age population, from 22 percent in 1950 to 20 percent in 1960 and to 17 percent in 1975. The changes that are expected in the occupational distribution of employment with the generally upward shift of workers into the service-type of occupations will not increase job opportunities for Negroes unless there are substantial changes in the educational achievements of Negroes and in hiring practices. On the latter point, it should be noted that many of the white-collar, clerical sales, and other service jobs involve face-to-face relations between fellow workers and between workers and their customers or clients. These are the kinds of jobs in which discrimination against Blacks has been most prevalent in the South.[49]

It is hardly to be expected that new laws, court decisions, and expanding employment opportunities will have revolutionary effects on Negro employment in the South in the 1970s. Two important projected changes in the occupational distribution of black employment in the South are in agriculture and government. In 1960 Negro agricultural employment in the South was 563,000; by 1975 it is expected to decline to 240,000. The employment of Negroes in government in the South—federal, state, and local—is expected to almost double between 1960 and 1975, from 73,000 to 140,000.[50] This increased employment will be largely in the lower echelons of public administration and will involve a small number of Blacks compared to the number that will leave agricultural employment. The projected gain in government employment is important, however, in establishing a new pattern of nondiscriminatory employment of Negroes. Total Negro

[46] Charlayne Hunter, "The New Black Businessmen," *Saturday Review*, Aug. 23, 1969, p. 59.

[47] Maddox, Liebhafsky, Henderson, and Hamlin, *op. cit.*, p. 79.

[48] Reese Cleghorn, "The Mill: A Giant Step for the Southern Negro," *The New York Times Magazine*, Nov. 9, 1969, p. 35.

[49] Maddox, Liebhafsky, Henderson, and Hamlin, *op. cit.*, pp. 159, 163–164, 188, 190.

[50] This projected increase will be due in considerable part to the enforcement of new laws and regulations, as well as pressures from civil rights groups. An example of this trend is seen in a federal court decision of July 28, 1970. In Montgomery, Alabama,

employment in the South is expected to increase from approximately 3.3 million workers in 1960 to 3.6 million in 1975. This is a projected increase of almost 400,000 employed Negro workers, compared with the decrease of more than 200,000 which occurred in the 1950s when unemployment among Negroes was high. Unemployment and underemployment among Negroes in the South, though slightly lower than in sections outside the South, may still be twice as high as for southern Whites in 1975. Negro employment is expected to rise much more rapidly outside of the South (86 percent) than within the South (12 percent), largely because "a relatively high proportion of southern Negro boys and girls who enter the labor force during the next decade, plus many Negro workers between 25 and 45 years of age who leave southern farms, will seek employment in the North and West."[51]

NEGROES, MEXICAN-AMERICANS, AND PUERTO RICANS AND LABOR UNIONS

The role of labor organizations in encouraging or discouraging Negro, Mexican-American, and Puerto Rican members is an important part of the industrial experience of these groups. In earlier years the techniques used by labor unions to retard the employment of persons in all these groups, but especially Negroes, included withholding membership by means of constitutional provisions, by means of ritual pledges, or as an unwritten policy of the international or local union; accepting black members but discriminating against them in referrals; hindering the upgrading of members of these minorities; and sponsoring the employment and upgrading of Negroes in plants in which the union had no bargaining agreements, while failing to try to correct discrimination in plants in which the union had an agreement.

For more than 40 years there have been differences between the racial and ethnic policies of trade or craft unions on the one hand and industrial unions on the other. Unions of the industrial type include all workers in a mass-production industry regardless of craft, skill, or lack of skill. In general, the industrial unions have been more favorable to the admission of racial and ethnic minorities than have the trade unions. Also, these unions have been much more likely to have members of these groups on executive boards, and as officers and job stewards, than have the craft organizations.

In recent years AFL-CIO affiliated unions have engaged in discriminatory practices in four main ways: (1) Exclusion of black workers from union membership; (2) Segregated locals; (3) Separate racial seniority and other discriminatory provisions in union contracts; (4) Discrimination in union controlled apprenticeship training programs.[52]

Although clauses limiting membership to Caucasians have been removed, Nonwhites are still excluded from certain craft unions by tacit agreement. State and federal court orders have forced several unions to admit a small number of Negroes, but this tokenism has not affected the basic pattern of discrimination. Federal court decisions have involved the International Brotherhood of Electrical

Judge Frank M. Johnson ordered seven government agencies of the state of Alabama to stop discriminating against Negroes in their hiring practices. Judge Johnson held that the state "engaged in, and continues to engage in, a systematic pattern and practice of discrimination against qualified Negro applicants . . . by preferring lower-ranking white applicants." The agencies involved handle about $110 million a year in federal grants. State agencies that do not receive substantial federal appropriations were not specifically included in the order. Johnson ordered that 62 Negro applicants be given immediate priority consideration for jobs previously held by Whites, and he called for a report within 30 days indicating what steps had been taken toward compliance with his order. Johnson said that Alabama was the only state which had refused, despite urging by federal officials, to adopt a regulation prohibiting racial discrimination and providing for a system of appeals in such cases. He said also that the evidence showed that virtually all state jobs at the clerical level and above were open only to Whites, while custodial, domestic, or laborer jobs were filled almost entirely by Negroes. *The Plain Dealer*, July 30, 1970.

[51] Maddox, Liebhafsky, Henderson, and Hamlin, *op. cit.*, p. 200. See also pp. 175, 193, 197–198.

[52] Hill, *op. cit.*, pp. 202–203.

Workers, the United Association of Plumbers and Pipe Fitters, and the Sheet Metal Workers Union.

The building industry is one of the most important industries where jobs are increasing, but it is also one where trade union practices have been the decisive factor in determining the status of Negro workers. Craft unions in the building and construction trades control access to employment by controlling the assignment of union members to jobs. Denial of membership denies black workers the opportunity to obtain employment. Hill says that Negro craftsmen, denied union membership, are excluded from work in white residential areas, in new commercial construction, and in public works projects. Many skilled black workers are, therefore, limited to maintenance and repair work within the Negro community.[53]

From its establishment in 1965 through 1968, the Equal Employment Commission processed almost 250 complaints against building trades unions. In a majority of these cases, the commission found "reasonable cause" to support the allegations of the complaint. By the end of 1968, lawsuits charging a pattern of discrimination had been filed by the Justice Department against 16 building trades unions and one building trades council of the AFL-CIO, and private suits had been brought in U.S. district courts in several cities.[54]

When the American Federation of Labor and the Congress of Industrial Organizations merged in 1955, policy resolutions were issued promising the rapid elimination of racial discrimination and segregation within unions. Thirteen years later, the civil rights record of the AFL-CIO could only be characterized as tokenism.[55]

In January, 1970, the EEOC completed its first comprehensive survey of minority members in referral unions, that is, those that have hiring halls or that supply quotas of workers for employers. The survey, based on reports from 3700 local unions, was for 1967,

but the commission said that the situation had changed little since then. In the building trades, Negro membership was 8.4 percent, but most of these workers were in the lower-paying categories, including laborer. In the mechanical trades, only 0.8 percent of the membership was black. In these trades, the percentages of Negroes ranged from 8.2 percent in New York City to zero in Houston, Birmingham, and Kansas City. Atlanta had 0.1 percent; Chicago and Cleveland, 0.4, and New Orleans, 9.3. In referral unions other than the building trades, mainly building, hotel, and restaurant employees, and teamsters, 12 percent of the membership was reported to be Negro. In these unions, however, as well as in the building trades, the high-paying categories included few black workers.[56]

Demonstrating black militants shut down construction projects in Chicago and Pittsburgh in 1969, demanding triple the number of building jobs to equal the proportion of Negroes in the U.S. population (approximately 12 percent). We refer earlier to the Philadelphia Plan for increasing minority employment in the construction trades. Negotiations for similar arrangements had been started in 1970 in Newark, Boston, Pittsburgh, St. Louis, Oakland and San Jose, California, Detroit, Atlanta, Seattle, and other cities. In Chicago, where the building trades had only 3 percent Negro membership, an agreement was reached in January, 1970, to provide 4000 new jobs a year for five years in private and public construction. The latter agreement was praised by the Secretary of Labor, even though it did not contain the guarantees the Labor Department thought were necessary to insure that a fair share of the jobs would be in the better-paying mechanical trades.

During 1968 segregated locals continued to exist in some manufacturing plants where all the white workers were included in AFL-CIO craft unions and all the black workers belonged to a separate industrial union. For

---

[53] *Ibid.*, pp. 195–196.
[54] *Ibid.*, p. 201.
[55] *Ibid.*, p. 201.

[56] John Herbers, "Gains Are Made in Federal Drive for Negro Hiring," *The New York Times*, Jan. 25, 1970, pp. 1, 71.

Negroes in Building Trades, 1967

Union	Member-ship	Negro	Per-cent Negro
Asbestos workers	6,104	61	0.9
Boilermakers	23,946	934	3.9
Bricklayers	34,069	3,300	9.6
Carpenters	315,538	5,284	1.6
Electrical workers	133,904	915	0.6
Elevator construc-tors	6,728	33	0.4
Operating engi-neers	103,677	4,200	4.0
Iron workers	70,273	1,197	1.7
Laborers	266,243	81,457	30.5
Lathers	4,660	177	3.7
Marble, slate, stone polishers	4,355	387	8.8
Painters	66,714	2,498	3.7
Plasterers	28,182	3,947	14.0
Plumbers	147,862	320	0.2
Roofers	10,807	1,461	13.5
Sheet metal workers	34,867	92	0.2
Totals	1,257,929	106,263	8.4

Source: The New York Times, Jan. 25, 1970, p. 71. ©1970 by the New York Times Company. Reprinted by permission.

Negroes in Referral Unions

	Building Trades		Non-building Trades
	All Con-struction Trades	Mechan-ical Trades	
Albuquerque	1.3%	0.0%	5.9%
Atlanta	22.8	0.1	.3
Birmingham	16.3	0.0	unavail.
Chicago	4.6	0.4	37.6
Cleveland	4.6	0.4	37.6
Houston	18.1	0.0	40.9
Kansas City	10.8	0.0	10.2
Los Angeles	8.2	0.5	9.4
Memphis	16.6	0.9	.7
New Orleans	21.7	0.3	18.7
New York	12.3	8.2	17.9
San Francisco	13.2	4.5	10.0
Washington	10.7	3.4	40.5
Detroit	14.7	0.5	4.3
United States	8.4	0.8	12.0

Source: The New York Times, Jan. 25, 1970, p. 71.

example, an auxiliary unit is part of all-white Local 60 of the International Garment Workers Union in New York City. The auxiliary (60-A) is made up mainly of Negro and Puerto Rican shipping clerks, "push-boys," and delivery men. The auxiliary (60-A) has twice as many members as Local 60, but it has never been chartered as a separate local and the manager of Local 60 also serves as the manager of 60-A.

Although there are hundreds of thousands of Spanish-speaking men and women in organized labor, there has never been an attempt to organize them in auxiliary unions. Galarza, Gallegos, and Samora say that Mexican-American workers are now too numerous in the Southwest to be taken casually. "In some industrial plants in Texas and California one-half or more of the membership is Spanish-speaking. One of the largest locals of a construction union, with 15,000 members, has a registered membership that is 60 percent Mexican. A garment workers' union with 8,000 members is 75 percent Spanish-speaking."[57] These authors add that these are industries in which unemployment is common and that trade-unionism must deal with the Mexican-American worker in and out of the union hall.

A serious type of discrimination on the part of many major unions affiliated with the AFL-CIO is the provision in their contracts for separate lines of seniority promotion. Such agreements limit Negro workers to unskilled or menial job classifications that deny them equal seniority rights and prevent them from developing skills which would make them eligible for more desirable classifications. Hill reports several important federal court decisions, involving the Tobacco Workers Union, the Papermakers and Paperworkers Union, the Asbestos Workers, and the Pulp, Sulphite, and Paper Mill Workers, in which separate racial seniority lines and

[57] Galarza, Gallegos, and Samora, *op. cit.*, p. 42.

other provisions in union contracts that result in job assignments on the basis of race are held to be violations of the law.[58]

Apprenticeship Training Programs. An equally serious type of discrimination occurs in apprenticeship training programs. Many labor unions control admission into apprenticeship programs, and the majority of these continue to exclude black applicants or severely limit their number. Well-known among these organizations are the printing industry, the skilled metal crafts, the building trades, and the railroad craft unions. Litigation has resulted in limited progress among some of the building trades and the metal crafts, but the basic pattern of discrimination remains. Despite acute manpower shortages, both the Amalgamated Clothing Workers and the ILGWU have prevented the use of federal funds for training purposes in the industries in which they operate. In Chicago,

. . . the taxpayers pay for the Washburne Trade School, but the unions decide what student can enter this public school as part of their apprenticeship training. For years, Negroes made up less than one percent of the student body because the unions denied them entry. Today after court contests, civil rights protests, newspaper exposés and Herculean efforts by the school board, there are 167 Negro students among the 2,958 pupils, but 37 were brought in under so-called open enrollment—they are not part of the union apprenticeship program and get a diploma instead of a union job.[59]

In Massachusetts, there were no Blacks among 137 structural iron worker apprentices at the end of 1968; of 661 electrician apprentices, eight were black; of 300 plumber apprentices, 11 were black; of 353 sheet metal worker apprentices, none was black; of 256 pipe fitters, one was black; and of 167 newspaper-compositor apprentices, one was black.[60]

In 1961, the U.S. Commission on Civil Rights found that the Bureau of Apprenticeship and Training of the Department of Labor had been "unsuccessful even in its limited efforts to promote equality of opportunity" and said that, under the authority it then had, the Bureau was unlikely to have any appreciable effect on the exclusion of Negroes from apprenticeship training programs. The Commission also said that even a more extensive educational program to reduce the indirect barriers that discourage Negro youth from seeking apprenticeship training probably would be unsuccessful unless an attack were made on the discriminatory practices of indenturing organizations.[61]

On June 27, 1963, Secretary Wirtz "issued strict new standards . . . designed to prevent racial discrimination in labor apprenticeship programs." A new regulation (Title 29, Part 30) authorized BAT to decertify all apprenticeship training programs shown to discriminate. According to Hill, the construction unions bitterly protested the new regulation as "unwarranted interference." In the five years following the new ruling no apprenticeship training program was deregistered. During those years the federal courts, the FEPC and other administrative civil rights agencies found many of these programs to be in violation of anti-discrimination statutes and executive orders.[62]

Some idea of the magnitude of the resistance of certain labor unions to equal employment opportunities for Negroes is shown in the number of complaints against these organizations. From July 2, 1965, the date that Title VII of the Civil Rights Act of 1964 went into effect, until the end of 1968, the EEOC received more than 4200 complaints about unions. According to Hill, the commission entered a finding of "reasonable cause" in almost 70 percent of the complaints investigated, but it has been unable to secure compliance through conciliation procedures in many of these cases. Consequently, in 1968 there were approximately 170 civil

[58] Hill, *op. cit.*, p. 202.

[59] Jack Starr, "A National Disgrace: What Unions Do to Blacks," *Look*, Nov. 12, 1968, pp. 33–37. Quoted in Hill, *ibid.*, p. 203.

[60] *Ibid.*, p. 203.

[61] 1961 *U.S. Commission on Civil Rights Report*, Book 3, "Employment," p. 110.

[62] Hill, *op. cit.*, p. 199.

rights cases pending in the federal courts against labor unions.[63]

Exceptions to the general patterns of discrimination among labor unions include the United Packinghouse Workers of America, the United Automobile Workers Union, and the American Federation of State, County and Municipal Employees. The latter union organized a number of Negro workers during 1968. Other exceptions are District 65 in the distributive trades and Local 1199 of the Hospital Workers Union, both of New York City, as well as certain local unions in several cities. While these unions have organized thousands of Negro and Puerto Rican workers on an equal basis, organized labor in general has resisted demands for changes in their traditional policies.[64]

After two years of efforts and the expenditure of nearly $4 million in federal funds to help train Negro and other minority group apprentices, in September, 1969, the construction unions included only about 4 percent Negroes—5280 out of a total of 132,000 apprentices. Adding American Indians, Spanish-Americans, and Orientals, the 12 skilled construction unions had, at that time, approximately 9500 persons. The 7.2 percent total minority group representation in the building trades was about the same or a little better than apprenticeship openings in the metal, manufacturing, public utilities, mining and transportation industries, and trade and service jobs.[65]

BLACK CAUCUSES AND INDEPENDENT BLACK UNIONS

From 1969 on, black caucuses have appeared in several major labor unions and the number of independent black labor organizations has increased. A nationwide black caucus of steelworkers emerged at the 1968 convention of the United Steelworkers of America, AFL-CIO. Hill says that this black caucus, known as the Ad Hoc Committee, "succeeded in making Negro exclusion from leadership positions within the union and the union's discriminatory collective bargaining agreements a major public issue for the first time." Among other statements the Ad Hoc Committee said that black workers no longer try to use the civil rights department of the AFL-CIO to seek redress of their grievances, but appeal directly to the courts or to various public agencies such as the National Labor Relations Board, FEPC commissions, and the EEOC. Going further, the committee said that the AFL-CIO civil rights department had often sought to maintain the status quo by intervening with state and federal agencies on behalf of affiliates charged with violating fair employment practice laws.[66]

The importance of black caucuses operating within labor unions is twofold—their attack on discriminatory practices, and their threat to established union bureaucracies. In addition to the United Steelworkers of America, active caucuses have been held in the American Federation of Teachers, the Amalgamated Transit Union, the United Automobile Workers, and the ILGWU. Negro drivers in Chicago struck against the Amalgamated Transit Union, AFL-CIO, and threatened to form their own independent union if they were not given equal representation in the union leadership. A black nationalist group at Chrysler's Hamtramck assembly plant carried out "wildcat strikes" against the company's failure to promote Negroes to supervisory jobs, but it also attacked the UAW for not exerting sufficient pressure on the company to eliminate discriminatory employment practices. Black members of the AFL-CIO have come into conflict in recent years with the union's leaders. Black caucuses have represented the black community within the teaching profession, and, in some cities, black teachers are considering a separate union. Black caucuses within the National Maritime Union

[63] Hill, *op. cit.*, pp. 203–204.

[64] *Ibid.*, p. 204. For additional information on labor unions and racial and ethnic discrimination, see H. Hill, "The Racial Practices of Organized Labor: The Contemporary Record," in Julius Jacobson (ed.), *The Negro and the American Labor Movement*, Doubleday, 1968, pp. 286–357.

[65] *Plain Dealer*, Sept. 22, 1969, p. 6A. Figures were compiled by the Associated Press from U.S. DOL reports.

[66] Hill, *op. cit.*, p. 206.

and the ILGWU have attacked the rules that required at least ten years of membership to become eligible for national office. In the case of the former union, federal Judge Constance Motley voided the election of officers. The union brought suit, but her decision was upheld by the U.S. Court of Appeals.[67]

Among the independent black unions that have been attempting to bring about fundamental changes in the racial policies and practices are The Independent Alliance of Skilled Crafts in Ohio, the Maryland Freedom Labor Union, the United Community Construction Workers of Boston, the United Construction and Trades Union in Detroit, the Allied Workers International Union in Gary, and similar organizations in Chicago, Seattle, Boston, Oakland, and elsewhere. These organizations have appealed especially to two groups of black workers: those in the building trades who have long been excluded from AFL-CIO craft unions, and those who work in ghetto areas where the AFL-CIO makes no organizational efforts. As a result of a 1967 court decision (Ethridge v. Rhodes), which held that contractors must show that they have an integrated labor force, black-controlled hiring halls are now being used by some contractors. Confrontations of importance have occurred in the construction field in Detroit and in Boston between independent black workers unions and AFL-CIO unions over opportunities to work on public construction.[68]

A summary on black labor in the American economy by a leading student in this area seems accurate.

[67] *Ibid.*, pp. 208–213.
[68] *Ibid.*, pp. 206–207. According to Hill:

The Detroit Community Relations Council found that the Iron Workers Union, the Riggers Union, the Glass Workers Union, the Asbestos Workers and Insulators Union, with a combined membership of 2,960 have no Negro journeymen. Only "trowel" trades show a significant number of Negro members. The Plasterers and Cement Masons locals are 50 percent Negro. In Laborers Local 334, some four thousand out of five thousand members are Negro. These workers do demolition and other rough, hazardous and back-breaking work. Excluding the "trowel" unions, there were 131 Negroes among the 14,166 journeymen—less than 1 percent. Among carpenters, bricklayers and painters there has been

There is now emerging a new Black working class, concentrated both in heavy industry and in the service occupations, especially in the public sector. Negroes constitute 85 percent of those teaching in Washington's public schools and 50 percent of those teaching in Philadelphia's public schools; there are Black majorities in the labor force employed at several major auto-manufacturing plants in and around Detroit; over 90 percent of the garbage collectors in Memphis are Negro; Black workers constitute 25 percent of the membership of Local 1014 of the United Steelworkers of America employed at the huge U.S. Steel plant in Gary, Indiana; and in District 8 of the Steelworkers Union in the Baltimore area, Negroes constitute approximately 40 percent of the membership. A number of the largest ILGWU locals in New York City now have a large majority of nonwhite members. The presence of Black majorities or near-majorities in major industrial plants and labor unions means that Negroes are now strategically concentrated, both geographically and occupationally, to exercise a new leverage within organized labor.[69]

INCOME

In 1967 the median income of primary families and individuals was $4,187 for Negroes and $7,409 for Whites. Almost 37 percent of the Negro households had incomes below $3,000, compared with 19 percent of the white households. In the higher income range, 12 percent of the black households had incomes over $10,000, while 31 percent of the Whites had such incomes. The following table shows that the greatest disparity between Negro and white family income is in the South, where the Negro median family income is about half that for Whites.[70]

some integration. The 1960 Census shows that 11.6 percent of Detroit building workers were Negro. They were in the Laborers, Carpenters, Plasterers and Cement Workers locals. Eight years later the percentage was about the same. *Ibid.*, p. 207.

[69] *Ibid.*, p. 213.
[70] Lester C. Thurow, *Poverty and Discrimination*, The Brookings Institute, 1969, p. 19.

Median Family Income in 1968, and Negro Family Income, 1965–1968, as a Percent of White, by Region

	Median family income, 1968		Negro income as a percent of white			
	Negro	White	1965	1966	1967	1968
United States	$5,359	$8,936	54	58	59	60
Northeast	6,460	9,318	64	68	66	69
North Central	6,910	9,259	74	74	78	75
South	4,278	7,963	49	50	54	54
West	7,506	9,462	69	72	74	80

Source: U.S. Department of Commerce, Bureau of the Census, *The Social and Economic Status of Negroes in the United States,* 1969, p. 15.

In the postwar period the median family income of Nonwhites has been relatively stable at 55 percent ($\pm$ 4 or 5 percent) of Whites, with a slight increase in 1966–1967.[71] Between 1947 and 1952 median nonwhite family incomes increased from 51 to 57 percent of median white family incomes, but by 1958 nonwhite incomes were again 51 percent. Improving employment opportunities in the mid-1960s caused nonwhite incomes to rise to 55 percent of white incomes, and by 1967 they had returned to a level slightly above that for 1952. In short, during every recession in the postwar period, the ratio of nonwhite to white incomes dropped sharply.[72] In absolute incomes, the average gap between white and Negro families widened from $2,300 to $3,100 (in 1967 dollars) between 1947 and 1967.[73]

Schooling is only one of the influences on income, and its effects vary from one racial group to another. Differences in years of education seem to explain less than a third of the difference in earnings among individuals after race, region, age, and sex have been taken into account. Negroes gain less from an additional year of schooling than do Whites, and the ratio of expected lifetime earnings of Whites with a given level of education to the expected lifetime earnings of Blacks with a similar level of training rises with increasing years of education. These

differences in the gains from education reflect, in part, differences in the quality of education received by different racial groups. Present evidence indicates, however, that the economic gains from additional education would be substantially different even if Negroes and Whites had the same achievement scores. The Coleman report shows that in the metropolitan Northeast a constant percentage of Whites score above the Negro mean achievement score on the verbal-achievement test at all grade levels. Nevertheless, the proportion of Whites earning more than the Negro mean by years of education increases from grade to grade.[74]

A Bureau of the Census report for 1968 shows that the median income of Negro men 25 to 54 years old who have completed four years of high school was lower than that for white men in this age group who have completed only eight years of schooling.

Thurow shows the effects on income when education and experience increase simultaneously. "If the effects," he says, "were no greater than the sum of the two separate effects, thirty-five years of experience and sixteen years of education would raise white incomes by $2,090 above what they would have been with no education and no experience. In fact, sixteen years of education and thirty-five years of experience are worth $8,155—or almost four times as much as the

---

[71] *Ibid.,* pp. 24.
[72] *Ibid.,* pp. 60–61.
[73] *Ibid.,* pp. 153–154.

[74] Samuel Bowles, "Towards Equality of Educational Opportunity?" *Harvard Educational Review,* Winter, 1968, pp. 96–97.

Median Income of Men 25 to 54 Years Old, by Educational Attainment, 1968

		Median income, 1968		Negro income as a percent of white
		Negro	White	
Elementary:	Total	$3,900	$5,844	67
	Less than 8 years	3,558	5,131	69
	8 years	4,499	6,452	70
High School:	Total	5,580	7,852	71
	1 to 3 years	5,255	7,229	73
	4 years	5,801	8,154	71
College:	1 or more years	7,481	10,149	74

Source: U.S. Department of Commerce, Bureau of the Census, The Social and Economic Status of Negroes in the United States, 1969, p. 21.

sum of the separate parts. Similar complementarities exist for Negroes, though the absolute income levels are lower: three and one-half times the sum of the separate parts. Similar complementarities exist in both the North and the South."[75]

Economic Losses from Discrimination. The total earnings of employed Negro males 18 to 64 years of age in 1959 were about $12 billion, but they would have been approximately $18.7 billion if the average income of Negroes had been the same as the earnings

of Whites with the same schooling. Thus Negro males lost about $6.7 billion in earnings because of discrimination in employment. Estimates for Negro females 18 to 64 years of age indicate a loss of approximately $1.3 billion as a result of discriminatory practices, a total loss of $8 billion resulting from the underutilization of Negro skills and abilities. This loss in earnings was equal to about 1.7 percent of GNP in 1959.[76] In 1966, a larger estimate of the economic loss resulting from discrimination was given by the Council of

[75] Thurow, op. cit., p. 83.

[76] Maddox, Liebhafsky, Henderson, and Hamlin, op. cit., p. 147.

Annual Increase in Income of Males Resulting from Education and Experience, by Color and Region, 1960 (in Dollars)

Color and region	Experience only[a]	Education only[b]	Experience and Education[c]
All white	1,409	681	8,155
All nonwhite	1,148	244	4,856
Northern white	1,658	616	8,385
Northern nonwhite	1,702	144	5,260
Southern white	1,257	719	7,293
Southern nonwhite	811	252	3,724

Notes:
[a.] Thirty-five years of experience, no education
[b.] Sixteen years of education, no experience
[c.] Thirty-five years of experience and sixteen years of education

Source: Lester C. Thurow, Poverty and Discrimination, The Brookings Institution, 1969, p. 83. Reprinted with permission. Basic data are from U.S. Bureau of the Census, U.S. Census of Population: 1960, Subject Reports, Educational Attainment, Final Report PC(2)-5B, 1963.

Economic Advisers. According to the annual report of the Council:

If economic and social policies could be specifically designed to lower Negro unemployment to the current unemployment level of whites, the resulting gain in GNP would be $15 billion. Part of this gain would be in wages of the new Negro employees, and part would result if all Negroes were able to obtain jobs which would better utilize their abilities and training.

National output can be further expanded by improving the average level of productivity of each individual. Education and training are two of the most important means to this end. If the average productivity of the Negro and white labor force were equalized at the white level, total production would expand to $22 billion. If both unemployment rates and productivity levels were equalized, the total output of the economy would rise about $27 billion—4 percent of GNP. This is a measure of the annual economic loss as a result of discrimination.[77]

Thurow estimates that $15 billion—plus or minus $5 billion—would be a good range for the annual white gains (or Negro losses) from discrimination in the United States. This is not regarded as the maximum gain that could be achieved by discrimination if the system were efficiently run.[78]

Strictly from an economic point of view, eliminating discrimination would be a profitable social investment. This does not mean that the elimination of discrimination would mean no losses for some Whites, or that Whites as a group might not have some losses economically. To many persons, including the authors of this book, the social benefits from eliminating discrimination, or drastically reducing it, would far outweigh any possible economic losses. One of the unresolved policy questions, however, concerns the failure of American society, and other changing societies, to distribute the costs of change. They tend to be borne overwhelmingly by those "majority-group" members who themselves live a somewhat marginal existence.

Poverty of Nonwhites. The poverty line is that level which is generally accepted in the United States as the minimum necessary to meet basic needs in modern society. The most frequently-used figure is $3000 (in 1962 prices) stipulated by the CEA. According to this definition, the incidence of poverty among nonwhite families decreased in the postwar years. In 1947, two-thirds of all nonwhite families were below the poverty line; by 1962, 44 percent lived in poverty. The total nonwhite families, however, increased so rapidly that the actual number of persons living in poverty in 1962 was only 3 percent below the number for 1947. According to Killingsworth, white families moved out of poverty at a more rapid rate, and their total increased at about half the rate of nonwhite families. By 1962, nonwhite families constituted a larger percentage (22 percent) of all poor families than in 1947.[79] More elaborate standards for the determination of poverty show that the number of Whites below the poverty level dropped by about 39 percent in the period 1959–1968, compared with a 23 percent drop in the number of Negroes in that category. In 1968, one-tenth of the white population and about one-third of the Negro population was below the poverty level.

In 1968, approximately 27 percent of all Negro families, but 43 percent of poor Negro families, resided outside metropolitan areas. The proportion of poor Negro families living in central cities was less than for Negro families in general, 45 percent compared with 59 percent. The percentage of Negro families below the poverty line was largest outside metropolitan areas. Within metropolitan areas, the proportion of Negro families below the poverty level was approximately the same for those living in central cities as for those living in suburbs.

Approximately 70 percent of the Negro and white men living in poverty neighborhoods of six large cities in the United States worked full time all year in fiscal 1969, compared with about 50 percent of the Negro and white women. Teenagers in these areas tended to be employed on a part-time or seasonal basis.

A report shows that income for families of

[77] *Ibid.*, pp. 149–150.
[78] Thurow, *op. cit.*, p. 134.

[79] Killingsworth, *op. cit.*, p. 14.

Persons Below the Poverty Level 1959–1968 (Numbers in millions)

	Negro and other races	Negro	White	Percent Negro and other races	Negro	White
1959	11.0	9.9	28.5	56	55	18
1960	11.5	(NA)	28.3	56	(NA)	18
1961	11.7	(NA)	27.9	56	(NA)	17
1962	12.0	(NA)	26.7	56	(NA)	16
1963	11.2	(NA)	25.2	51	(NA)	15
1964	11.1	(NA)	25.0	50	(NA)	15
1965	10.7	(NA)	22.5	47	(NA)	13
1966	9.7	(NA)	20.8	42	(NA)	12
Based on revised methodology[1]						
1966	9.2	8.9	19.3	40	42	11
1967[2]	8.8	8.5	19.0	37	39	11
1968	8.0	7.6	17.4	33	35	10

Notes:
NA—Not available.
[1]Reflects improvements in statistical procedures used in processing the income data.
[2]Due to a processing difference, data for 1967 are not strictly comparable with those shown for 1966 and 1968.

Source: U.S. Department of Commerce, Bureau of the Census, *The Social and Economic Status of Negroes in the United States,* 1969, p. 24.

Negro and other races living in poverty areas of six large cities was highest in Chicago and lowest in Atlanta and Houston.

Thurow estimates that if being nonwhite were the only factor leading to nonwhite poverty, Nonwhites would constitute only 4.7 percent of the total number of poor families. In 1960, Nonwhites made up 21.1 percent of the total. This poverty model recognizes that many other factors adversely affect Negroes:

Location of all Negro Families and of Negro Families Below the Poverty Level, 1968

	Percent distribution of Negro families Total	Below the poverty level	Negro families below the poverty level in each location Number (thousands)	Percent
United States	100	100	1,366	29
Inside metropolitan areas	73	57	779	23
Central cities	59	45	620	23
Suburbs	14	12	159	24
Outside metropolitan areas	27	43	589	47
Farm	3	7	94	61
Nonfarm	23	36	496	46

Source: U.S. Department of Commerce, Bureau of the Census, *The Social and Economic Status of Negroes in the United States,* 1969, p. 23.

Extent of Employment and Unemployment of Men, Women, and Teenagers in Poverty Neighborhoods of Six Large Cities Combined, July 1968–June 1969

	Adult men		Adult women		Teenagers	
	Negro	White	Negro	White	Negro	White
Total civilian labor force (thousands)	168.5	79.8	168.4	48.9	46.8	15.1
Percent of total[1]	100	100	100	100	100	100
Worked full time all year (50–52 weeks)	70	71	50	51	12	15
Worked full time part year (less than 50 weeks)	23	21	30	33	46	44
Worked part time	5	6	16	13	31	34
Unemployed at any time during the year[2]	20	18	17	16	49	38

Notes:

[1] Percents total more than 100 because of overlap between those who were unemployed at any time during the year and other categories.

[2] Employment and unemployment were not confined strictly to the time period July 1968–June 1969. Depending on the actual week of interview, "at any time during the year" could extend as far back as late 1967.

Note: Six large cities: Atlanta, Chicago, Detroit, Houston, Los Angeles, and New York City.

Source: U.S. Department of Labor, Bureau of Labor Statistics, in U.S. Department of Commerce, Bureau of the Census, *The Social and Economic Status of Negroes in the United States,* 1969, p. 93.

less education than Whites, greater likelihood of being outside the labor force, an unequal share of full-time jobs, and residence in areas with poorer industrial structures.[80] Thurow estimates, also, that being black accounts for 38 percent of the difference in the incidence of poverty for Whites and Negroes.[81]

WELFARE POLICIES

Among nonwhite poor persons, slightly less than half received welfare assistance in 1968.

[80] Thurow, *op. cit.,* p. 41.

[81] *Ibid.,* p. 111.

Median Family Income in Poverty Areas of Six Large Cities, July 1968–June 1969

	Atlanta	Chicago	Detroit	Houston	Los Angeles	New York City
Negro and other races	$4,700	$7,000	$6,200	$4,700	$5,800	$5,700
White	$6,200	(B)	$6,300	$6,000	$6,600	$5,300
Negro and other races as a percent of white	76	(NA)	98	78	88	108

Notes: B—Base of percentage too small to be significant.
NA—Not available.

Source: U.S. Department of Labor, Bureau of Labor Statistics, in U.S. Department of Commerce, Bureau of the Census, *The Social and Economic Status of Negroes in the United States,* 1969, p. 96.

Number and Percent of Persons Below the Poverty Level and of Persons Receiving Welfare, 1968 (In millions)

	Negro and other races	White
Total population	24.5	175.6
Below poverty level	8.0	17.4
Percent of total population	33	10
Receiving welfare	3.8	5.6
Percent of total population	16	3

Source: U.S. Department of Commerce, Bureau of the Census, U.S. Department of Health, Education, and Welfare, in *The Social and Economic Status of Negroes in the United States*, 1969, p. 26.

Among the white poor, about one third received welfare assistance.

Numerous criticisms have been made of the welfare system in effect in the 1960s and the early 1970s. The system covers only 8 or 9 million of the 25 to 30 million persons living below the poverty level, and it is demeaning and inefficient. Created during the depression years of the 1930s, welfare is a puzzling mixture of 50 separate programs with each state setting its own level of payments, deciding on its own regulations and eligibility standards, and determining whether or not to accept federal funds available for public assistance. (Twenty-two states do not accept all of the federal funds available for assistance purposes.) The great majority on relief are too young, too old, too sick, or too disabled to be self-supporting. Only about 60,000 are able-bodied men; the others include: 4,000,000 children whose parents cannot support them; 1,100,000 mothers of these children; approximately 100,000 physically or mentally incapacitated fathers of these children; 2,000,000 persons aged 65 or over; and 700,000 are totally blind or disabled.[82] A major criticism has been the low payment levels of contemporarary welfare, and the variation in grants from state to state. For example, in 1966

[82] Sylvia Porter, "Humiliation, Conflict in Welfare System," *The Plain Dealer*, May 29, 1969, p. 24.

payments in the Aid to Families with Dependent Children were less than $8 per person in Mississippi, while New York paid $48.[83]

Despite the criticisms of the current welfare program, the public welfare rolls have risen at unprecedented rates. An outstanding example is New York state, where the rolls rose at a rate of about 20,000 each month in 1967–1968 and reached a total of approximately 1,000,000 by 1969. Since Blacks constitute 11 percent of the total population of the United States, but approximately half of all AFDC recipients are black, some have attributed the rising AFDC rolls to the "deterioration" of the black family. Cloward and Piven reject this explanation, and give migration as the main cause of the increasing number on AFDC. Referring to the large redistribution of Negroes from rural to urban areas and from South to North, they say: "Had the economically obsolete black poor remained in the rural areas, the welfare rolls would not have shown nearly so dramatic a rise over the past two decades . . . as long as unemployment was also rising, both trends appeared to move together, and unemployment seemed to be determining AFDC levels; but even when unemployment turned downward, the impact of migration continued to push AFDC rates upward."[84] Mass migration has led to an increase in two ways: first, people have moved from a region where benefits are relatively difficult to obtain to places where becoming eligible for benefits is relatively easy; and second, the increasing political power of black people in cities has affected public policies, causing many more families to go on the rolls.

Regional variations in rules and attitudes governing eligibility for AFDC benefits are seen in this statement:

A woman with illegitimate children over the age of three who is alleged to maintain a relationship with a male could be disqualified in most Southern states under any one of several rules: either she maintains an 'unsuitable home,' or

[83] Richard Cloward and Frances F. Piven, "Migration, Politics, and Welfare," *Saturday Review*, Nov. 16, 1968, p. 32.

[84] *Ibid.*, pp. 31–32.

her children have a 'substitute parent,' or she is an 'employable mother.' But if she moves to a state outside the South, she is likely to qualify for benefits. In 1960, the Southern region granted assistance to 48 percent of those who applied. Elsewhere, the rates were appreciably higher: 57 percent in the Western and North Central regions; 63 percent in the Northeast. At the extremes, Texas admitted 34 percent, while Massachusetts admitted 80 percent.[85]

Most migrants do not go on the welfare rolls soon after their arrival in a new location. A Baltimore study concluded that welfare rolls have risen primarily because federally sponsored programs in the cities have encouraged families with long-standing eligibility to apply for public aid. Among the federal programs that have contributed directly or indirectly to the increase in applications for aid are urban renewal, the antipoverty program, and national health programs. As a result of urban renewal programs, thousands of families that have had to relocate have been referred by the Housing Agency in Baltimore to the Department of Welfare. By informing people of their entitlements, agencies of the antipoverty program (Office of Economic Opportunity) have produced increased applications for welfare in the cities. Also hospitals have referred poor patients to welfare agencies to establish their eligibility for assistance. The result has been the addition of thousands of eligible people to the welfare rolls.[86]

The National Welfare Rights Organization, an association of welfare recipients and other poor people, the majority of whose members are families receiving AFDC, lists three main demands for the "Poor Peoples Campaign." This organization calls for: first, the repeal of the welfare sections of the 1967 Social Security Amendments (Public Law 90–248) that accept existing state practices requiring mothers to accept work or be cut off welfare; second, a national guaranteed minimum income of $4000 (1968 figure; the 1970 minimum is given as $5500) for every family of four; and third, the allocation of federal funds for the immediate creation of at least

three million jobs for men "to permit them to assume normal roles as breadwinners and heads of families."[87]

REDUCING THE ECONOMIC INEQUALITY OF NONWHITES

Importance of Discrimination in Income

Equalizing the distribution of white and Negro incomes involves a number of factors, including increasing human capital (skills), improving labor mobility, and eliminating the handicap of discrimination. Negroes have less human capital, receive less remuneration for the human capital they do have, and suffer from a more adverse distribution of market imperfections. Racial discrimination is an important aspect of the greater market imperfections confronting Negroes. The poverty of Negroes cannot be eliminated nor can Negro and white income distributions be equalized without eliminating discrimination.[88]

Discrimination is important in its effects on income, but it also reduces the effectiveness of many of the instruments used in combatting poverty. If discrimination reduces Negro returns to education, and the evidence seems quite clear on this point, education is a less effective weapon for reducing Negro poverty than for reducing white poverty. The emphasis on training in preference to antidiscrimination measures that was characteristic of the Johnson administration has been continued during the Nixon Administration. For the fiscal year 1971–1972, $3.2 billion was budgeted for manpower training programs, an increase of 20 percent over the previous year. This policy led Charles B.

[85] *Ibid.*, p. 32.
[86] *Ibid.*, p. 34.

[87] *Now!* (National Welfare Leaders Newsletter), May 6, 1968, p. 13. According to the NWRO, the guaranteed minimum income should also provide annual cost-of-living adjustments, be administered by a simple affidavit, similar to the income tax, and include a work incentive allowing families to keep all earnings up to 25 percent of their guaranteed minimum income and some portion of additional earnings. NWRO advocates job programs that focus on building low-income housing and community facilities in the ghettos, contribute manpower to extend health care, education, and community organization, and give preference to contracts with organizations controlled by poor people.
[88] Thurow, *op. cit.*, p. 110.

Markham, former research director of the EEOC to say: "I am for education programs, too, but I do not think we should spend 99 percent of the resources on a third of the problem."[89] In a study of the Negro labor market done for the OEO, Lester C. Thurow concluded: "Discrimination lowers black incomes, but it is difficult to eliminate. Direct attacks on discrimination generate political protest and pressure. Therefore, we will attempt to circumvent the discrimination problem. We will first use other instruments, such as education and training, to equalize black and white incomes and after this has been accomplished we will worry about discrimination." He added: "Unfortunately, all of my research indicates that this strategy will not work."[90] Thurow, Markham, and other economists say that the major problem is not in initial entry to jobs but in the advancement of blacks once they are employed. Concern has been expressed both in and outside the government that some of the manpower training programs are more of a holding action to keep people out of the unemployed list than a device for getting them permanently into the work force. In some cases, men have gone from one training program to another.[91]

Role of Education in an Antipoverty Effort. A careful analysis of education and poverty shows that improved general education results in average private financial gains that are less than costs, implying, therefore, that education is a relatively expensive and inefficient means of bringing people out of poverty.[92] Perhaps the most convincing explanation of the empirical results of this study lies in education's numerous potential by-products of a social and nonpecuniary nature. Such by-products include equality of opportunity, improvement in citizenship, and the perpetuation of a cultural heritage. For these

reasons, educational efforts may be intensified even though these efforts may result in private financial gains that fall short of costs. Although Ribich's results are not conclusive, his study suggests that one cannot assume that any and all new educational expenditures will produce returns greatly in excess of costs. Even if one assumes that the improvement of general education, including increased per-pupil expenditures, compensatory and preschool education, is not the most efficient way to alleviate poverty, no clear-cut rule on policy emerges. Ribich lists six positions from which a policy maker might choose.

1. The intangible benefits of education are more important than the goal of generating income gains.
2. Large amounts of transfers (guaranteed annual income; negative income tax, etc.) are inadvisable, so an apparently less efficient approach to the alleviation of poverty is required.
3. Poverty is more than a matter of income. Transfers change income, but changes in attitude and motivation come only from education and other nontransfer programs.
4. Revolutionary changes in the school system are called for. Large amounts of new personnel and equipment should be brought into schools in poverty neighborhoods.[93]
5. A heavier emphasis should be placed on transfers and other forms of direct help.
6. A somewhat greater emphasis than now exists should be placed on direct-help programs, but such programs should be tied closely to education programs.[94]

In any case, no program to increase income through improving education will succeed

[89] John Herbers, "Discrimination Held Main Cause of Income Inequality," *The New York Times*, Feb. 24, 1970. Markham's statement was based on an analysis made by Orley Ashenfelter of a commission survey of 43,000 employers covering 26 million workers. The survey was based on 1966 figures.

[90] *Ibid.*

[91] *Ibid.*

[92] Thomas I. Ribich, *Education and Poverty*, The Brookings Institution, 1968, p. 125.

[93] On this point, Ribich says that analysis of Project Talent schools, which involved "reasonably large dollar differences in expenditures per student, did not establish that large changes are more efficient than small ones." He adds that perhaps the real need lies "in a revolution of attitudes, organization, and approach of public school systems" but that it is unclear what the efficacy or permanence of such a revolution would be. *Ibid.*, p. 128.

[94] In support of this position, it can be argued that additional marginal expenditures intended to improve directly the economic situation of poor families might do more for educational performance than marginal expenditures in the schools. Since socioeconomic class has a strong effect on educational outcomes, a relatively small improvement along this line might result in substantial improvements in educational performance. *Ibid.*, pp. 128–129.

unless other steps are also taken. Raising general education standards will have relatively little effect unless such improvement is combined with training opportunities and job opportunities. As Thurow says: "As long as there is discrimination, more education produces little payoff."[95] From our theoretical perspective, the income status of a group, as well as other aspects of its status, reflects interactions among three sets of variables: the structure of opportunities available to them, the system of values that supports or challenges that structure, and the training, motives, and aspirations of individual members of the group. These make up a "tough" system. Strategies that deal with only one of these factors cannot break through the mutually reenforcing lines that maintain the system (in our case, the system of discrimination).

Eliminating Government Discrimination. Since government is the strongest force in creating and enforcing many of the monopoly powers that are behind various types of discrimination, the elimination of discrimination at all levels of government may be one of the most effective means of reducing the effect of discrimination throughout the economy. Government is the major instrument for restricting investment in nonwhite education. Its housing codes prevent Whites from selling to Negroes in certain locations. It permits union-management agreements that facilitate discrimination. It encourages the export of Negro capital by refusing the governmental cooperation necessary to operate a Negro business.[96] Rationally, it is relatively easy to see the basic role that government plays in discrimination. It is not so easy to prescribe how discrimination by government can be eliminated or drastically reduced, but there is some value in recognizing that attacking human capital discrimination will not, by itself, raise nonwhite incomes.

STRATEGIES FOR REDUCING POVERTY

Coordinated programs for creating tight labor markets, improving the distribution of human capital, drastically reducing discrimination, increasing labor mobility, and providing for those outside the labor force are all essential in the attempt to eliminate poverty and discrimination. Theoretically, direct income transfers are an exception to this principle, but politically they have been unacceptable.[97] Recent action, however, makes it appear likely that this principle will be adopted on the federal level.

The difference between a tight labor market (3 percent unemployment) and a loose one (7 percent unemployment) produces a relative increase in nonwhite median family incomes from 50 to 60 percent of Whites. Such a change does not eliminate discrimination, but it represents a greater change than can be obtained through the application of any other policy designed to alter the income distribution.[98]

Creating tighter labor markets has certain advantages: aggregate economic policies are impersonal; they do not require state and local cooperation; they can be implemented without recruiting a bureaucracy of administrators, teachers, and social workers; they do not interfere with personal choice; they are cheaply implemented; and they can become effective in a short period of time. Unbalanced labor markets (markets in which labor demands exceed labor supply) are not however, without their costs. Such markets would bring some inflation, and price and wage controls might become necessary. On the other hand, balanced labor markets and price stability will result in only small relative gains in the income position of the poor.[99]

Efforts of Businessmen to Provide More Jobs for Nonwhites. In February 1968, former President Johnson announced that the National Alliance of Businessmen had agreed to join a private-public effort to find jobs for the hard-core unemployed in the slum areas of the United States. The names of 60 leading businessmen were listed for this job program, including Henry Ford 2d, chairman; J. Paul Martin, president of the Coca-

---

95 Thurow, *op. cit.*, p. 157.
96 *Ibid.*, pp. 27, 158.

97 *Ibid.*, pp. 159–160.
98 *Ibid.*, p. 61.
99 *Ibid.*, pp. 64–65.

Cola Company; James Cook, president, Illinois Bell Telephone Company; Orville Beal, president, Prudential Insurance Company of America; Harold S. Geneen, chairman of the board, International Telephone and Telegraph Corporation; and John H. Sengstacke, president, Robert S. Abbott Publishing Company. The aim of the program, called Job Opportunities in the Business Sector (JOBS), was to train and employ 100,000 hard-core unemployed persons in private industry by June, 1969, and 500,000 by the middle of 1971.[100] Nine months later NAB claimed that 145,000 of the hard-core had been hired and that 60 percent of them were still on the job. In March, 1969, Donald M. Kendall, president of Pepsi Cola and the new head of NAB, announced that the goal had been raised to 614,000 people in jobs in 1971.[101] By July, 1970, the NAB said that 23,520 cooperating business concerns had placed 360,140 of the hard-core unemployed in jobs. Because of the business decline, however, half of those hired by the Alliance had left their jobs by July, 1970, and "the companies that formed the alliance in 1968 seem to be showing less zeal in seeking and keeping these employees."[102]

In December, 1967, the Chase Manhattan Bank started a program for training unskilled high school dropouts; six months later the results with these "unemployables" had been so successful that the bank said it would train 1000 in a three-year period. In July, 1968, the First National City Bank opened a training center to provide remedial and technical skills for entry-level jobs for 700 young men and women from the hard-core unemployed. The 18-month instruction period was arranged under a contract between the bank and the United States Department of Labor. Also in July, 1968, the American Institute of Banking opened classes in basic education and banking terminology for ghetto residents who were employed by

34 commercial and savings banks in the New York area. It expected to train 700 minority group members in the course of a year.[103]

Guaranteed Jobs. Sheltered employment is one possibility for those who are outside the labor force because they are not acceptable to private employers or those whose handicaps cannot be overcome by training programs. Such employment is provided for the individual by the public rather than the private sector, and wages are set by the desired income distribution rather than the productivity of the worker. These jobs are in part an income transfer program and partially a work creation program. The government can become an employer of last resort or subsidies can be given to private employers to hire specific workers. The National Commission on Technology, Automation, and Economic Progress has suggested that the guaranteed jobs be provided in public services or private nonprofit organizations. Useful jobs with low skill requirements are not difficult to find in schools, hospitals, conservation, city sanitation, and elsewhere. Since needed services would be produced by such jobs, the real cost would be much lower than that of an income transfer. The major benefit, however, is seen in the increased self-respect that comes to the worker. Three main objections are given to guaranteed jobs: (1) employed workers may feel threatened by sheltered workers; (2) these jobs may create dead-end work that is unacceptable to the poor; and (3) public institutions require a stable work force to be efficient. Thurow thinks that the first two objections can be met, or at least reduced, but that the third objection cannot be avoided. On this point he says: "Society must simply decide if the benefits of guaranteed job programs exceed the costs of inefficiency that they may cause in public institutions."[104]

[100] Roy Reed, "Top Businessmen Join U.S. Effort to Find More Jobs," *The New York Times*, Feb. 25, 1968, p. 1.

[101] Nick Thimmesch, "NAB Gets New Effervescence," *The Plain Dealer*, March 28, 1969.

[102] Jacob Cohen, "Jobs: Source of Much Black Unrest," *The New York Times*, July 19, 1970.

[103] Leonard Sloane, "Banks and Dropouts, Now Getting Acquainted," *The New York Times*, July 14, 1968, p. F1.

[104] Thurow, *op. cit.*, pp. 144–146. In August, 1970, an amendment to the Nixon Administration's family assistance legislation, designed to create at least 30,000 jobs in the public service sector, was introduced in the Senate. *The New York Times*, Aug. 23, 1970, section 4, p. 3.

Direct Income Transfers. The unrest of the ghettos, the shortcomings of the welfare system, and the failure of job programs to reduce significantly the number of hard-core unemployed have given support to the concept of a guaranteed annual income. Proposals along this line take two forms: the "negative income tax" and the guaranteed annual income. The first proposal is based on the assumption that families who earn too little to file a tax return are deprived of the automatic exemptions ($600 for each member of the family) and the deductions (for medical bills, sales taxes, etc.) that amount to tax savings. It is suggested that a family reporting no income should be paid an allowance equal to half the sum of the standard tax exemptions and deductions ($1500 for a family of four). In this reverse income tax, a family that reported a nominal income would have this allowance reduced by 50 percent of each dollar earned. If a family of four earned $1,000, the allowance would be reduced by $500, leaving an allowance-income total of $2,000. This sum is small, but it is more than many states now provide in welfare payments.[105]

The proposal for a guaranteed annual income would award all families under the "poverty level" (variously defined, currently, as ranging from $3000 to $3500) an allowance of $400 to $500 each for the parents and the first four children, $150 for the fifth and sixth child. Family income from wages would reduce the subsidy by about 40 percent of each dollar earned. This plan would continue in effect until the combined allowance-earnings reached $5000, or some other point well beyond the designated "poverty level."

Both proposals offer some incentive to beneficiaries to improve their economic position. Milton Friedman, a strong advocate of the negative income tax says: "We already have a guaranteed income of sorts. The trouble is it is a mess . . . Our present welfare system keeps a group of people in a state of dependency and creates a two-class society . . . The negative income is a way in which you can meet your obligations to the disadvantaged and establish a gradual means of getting them off welfare."[106]

The question of the costs of direct income transfers has received considerable attention. Estimates of the cost to the federal budget of a "family allowance," "negative income tax," or "guaranteed annual income" program vary from $15 billion to $25 billion, depending on the nature of the program. In 1965 James Tobin, one of the principal advocates of a "family allowance," gave the former figure for a rather modest proposal.[107] Tobin pointed out that this cost would be offset partially by savings in public assistance, on which governments were then spending $5.6 billion a year ($3.2 billion of which came from federal funds), and from a number of other income maintenance programs, notably in agriculture. In 1969, Thurow estimated that a negative income tax program with a marginal tax rate of 50 percent would cost $25 billion to bring every household up to the poverty line. He says: "Approximately $12 billion would go to those who are technically below the poverty line and the rest would go to individuals above that line. If the positive incentive effects on those who are now on welfare were larger than the negative incentive effects on those who are now working, the costs would be less. If the reverse were true, the costs would be higher."[108]

In 1968, OEO sponsored an income maintenance project involving 1359 families, with the average family containing five or six members. The income guarantee that these families received was set at a percentage of the poverty-line income of $3300 per year. Annual income-guarantee payments averaged $1100 per family, and the study attempted to determine whether guaranteed payments had a deleterious effect on the work behavior of the recipients. The work earnings of 29 percent of the families declined after they began to benefit from the new welfare plan,

[105] *Newsweek,* July 1, 1968, p. 29.

[106] *Ibid.,* p. 29.
[107] James Tobin, "On Improving the Economic Status of the Negro," *Daedalus,* Fall, 1965, pp. 891–893.
[108] Thurow, *op. cit.,* pp. 150–151.

53 percent of the families increased their earnings during the experiment, and 18 percent earned the same. A control group that received the ordinary welfare support during the same period had the following earnings record: 31 percent earned less, 43 percent earned more, and 26 percent earned the same. The OEO study found that the administrative costs for a welfare system like the experimental one are $72 to $96 annually per family, compared to an estimated $200 to $300 for a family under the present welfare system.[109]

Many students think that poverty cannot be eliminated without direct income transfers. This does not mean that the disadvantages of such plans are not recognized nor that they are advocated as the single policy measure that will remedy all or most of the complex problem of economic inequality. For example, if work incentives are to be maintained, providing good job opportunities with training and advancement are essential.[110] Also, giving the poor money instead of more services perhaps puts too much faith in the doctrine that "the market" is the most responsive and accurate apparatus for providing the things that people really want and that the poor will be better off getting what they want through the market than in having it prescribed for them. As Killingsworth points out, this approach ignores the fact that some needs are not met or are met very inadequately by the market. The outstanding example is housing. The market has failed spectacularly to provide low-cost housing for the poor. Another example is the improbability that the market could effectively organize a system of remedial education for slum dwellers.[111] The present writers conclude that integrated poverty programs, with direct income transfers, combined with complementary productivity and guaranteed job programs, could provide about as satisfactory an approach to the elimination of poverty as could be devised. We agree with Thurow that general economic growth

and foreseeable changes in the private economy will not eliminate either discrimination or poverty. Special programs must be designed specifically to change the distribution of income.[112]

The Nixon Administration's Welfare Reform

President Nixon and spokesmen for his Administration say that it is clear that AFDC doesn't work and that mending it is out of the question. The Administration's Family Assistance Program which was approved by the House, provided for an income maintenance plan by which a family of four with no other income would receive an annual minimum of $2465—$1600 in cash payments and $865 in food stamps. Payments on a diminishing scale would be provided for the working poor. In addition to placing a uniform income floor under all the nation's impoverished, the FAP would offer them job training and would continue financial support after they had obtained work and until they passed the poverty line.[113] The estimated cost of the FAP is $4 billion annually. In September, 1970, the Senate approved the program on the condition that it not become effective until it is tested in at least three selected areas of the country. The amendment to the FAP bill postponed the nationwide start of the program.

CONCLUSION

Killingsworth makes an interesting comparison between the present economic status of Negroes with what it was a century ago, saying that the progress of Blacks has been impressive and undoubtedly greater than reasonable persons would have anticipated at the end of the Civil War. Then, most Negroes were totally illiterate, landless, and destitute, and they were concentrated in the rural South. Today the majority of Negro families have risen above the poverty level. Less than one-tenth of the Negro labor force is in agriculture, and more Negroes live in the

---

[109] *Science News*, Feb. 20, 1970, pp. 216–217.
[110] Thurow, *op. cit.*, p. 151; Killingsworth, *op. cit.*, p. 81.
[111] Killingsworth, *op. cit.*, pp. 80–81.

[112] Thurow, *op. cit.*, 154.
[113] *The Plain Dealer*, Aug. 30, 1970, p. 8AA.

North and West than in the South. But the progress of the past century does not console those who are still deprived for the inequities that remain. Here, as in other parts of the world, political and economic progress has furthered a "revolution of rising expectations."[114]

According to the official definition of poverty, the percentage of the population that is impoverished has slowly but steadily declined since World War II, but at a rate that would require at least 40 additional years to eliminate it.[115] The failure of federal contract compliance, the inability of fair employment commissions to change the patterns of employment discrimination, the inability of the private sector to solve the problems of the ghetto, and the inadequacy of the antipoverty program indicate that new programs are necessary.[116] The combination of an expanding economy together with the special measures mentioned earlier would provide the basis for further progress. Extensive economic planning will be required, as well as some reordering of national priorities.

In one sense the issue of poverty and discrimination becomes, as Willhelm and Powell say, "a question of human—not only civil—rights and involves White and Negro alike . . . As more of us become unnecessary—as human energy and thought themselves become increasingly unnecessary—the greater will be our social anxiety. Then perhaps we will become aware that racial strife today is not between Black and White, but is instead a search for human rights in a world of machines that makes so many human beings utterly dispensable."[117]

---

[114] Killingsworth, *op. cit.*, pp. 2–3.
[115] Thurow, *op. cit.*, p. 153.
[116] Hill, *op. cit.*, p. 214.

[117] Sidney M. Willhelm and Edwin H. Powell, "Who Needs the Negro?" *Transaction*, Sept.–Oct., 1964, p. 6.

MINORITY BUSINESS

In this chapter we shall be concerned with the extent of the participation of Negroes in professional and business life in the United States. Although we shall not examine the place of other minorities in the business and professional world, many of the principles and trends discussed here are applicable to other groups. The degree to which groups occupy higher status jobs is a sensitive index to the minority-majority situation in a society. Changes in the levels of participation in such jobs are of special importance as indicators of social trends.

NEGRO BUSINESS
AND BUSINESSMEN

Negro businesses in the United States have always been small businesses, and today there are only "a relative handful of Negroes who can seriously be classified as businessmen."[1] There are fewer Negro businesses of significant size now than there were four decades ago. During the 1950s business ownership in the United States increased, but Negro business ownership decreased by 20 percent. According to DeLorean, less than 3 percent of all industry in the United States, less than 2 percent of construction enterprises, less than 1 percent of manufacturing, are owned by minority persons, and 75 percent of the businesses that are owned by Negroes is located "in the profitless barrens of the ghettos, catering to a segregated clientele."[2] In the 1950s, the greatest decline

among Negro businessmen occurred in transportation, where small-scale operators were replaced by large truck and taxi firms.[3] The number of restaurants owned by blacks declined 33 percent between 1950 and 1967, and other retail businesses declined more than 33 percent. Funeral homes declined 6 percent and barber shops 16 percent. Samuels says that the ghetto businessman of today is affected as much as 25 times harder by crime than is his nonghetto counterpart.[4]

Specific cities reveal the Negro business situation. In Washington, D.C., the population is 65 percent black, the school population is 95 percent black, and the city is an important center of black affairs. The black businesses, however, constitute less than 8 percent of the total of 28,000 business enterprises, and fewer than 2000 of them are black-owned.[5] In Newark, New Jersey, more than 50 percent of the population is black, but only 10 percent of the approximately 12,200 licensed businesses are owned by Blacks. In New York City, one out of every 1,000 Blacks, compared with one out of every 40 Whites, owns a business of any kind.[6] In Philadelphia in 1964, about ten Negro-owned businesses—insurance, publishing, catering, cosmetic supplies, and contracting —were quite successful, but most of the 4242 Negro businesses of Philadelphia, comprising 9 percent of the total businesses, were "marginal in profit-making, stability,

---

[1] John Z. DeLorean, "The Problem," in William F. Haddad and G. Douglas Pugh (eds.), *Black Economic Development*, Prentice-Hall, 1969, p. 10.

[2] *Ibid.*, p. 10. Samuels points out that it is difficult to ascertain the actual number of Negro businesses. The agricultural business census enumerates race, but the general business census does not. He estimates that there are 50,000 to 150,000 nonwhite

businesses in a total business population of 5.2 million, or from 1 to 3 percent of the total. If Nonwhites were proportionally represented in business ownership, they would own 15 percent of the businesses, or 750,000. See Howard J. Samuels, "Compensatory Capitalism," in Haddad and Pugh (eds.), *op. cit.*, p. 63.

[3] Lawrence Johnson and Wendell Smith, "Black Managers," in Haddad and Pugh (eds.), *op. cit.*, p. 113.

[4] Samuels, *op. cit.*, p. 63.

[5] *Ibid.*

[6] DeLorean, *op. cit.*, p. 10.

and physical condition."[7] According to the Drexel Institute of Technology study cited by Foley, the type of business was of the pattern found in other American cities: "Nearly all were retail and service trades, and most were single proprietorships. Personal services were the most numerous, hairdressing and barbering comprising 24 percent and 11 percent, respectively, of the total number of Negroes in business. Luncheonettes and restaurants comprised 11.5 percent of the total. Many of the businesses would be submarginal if free family labor were not available."[8]

Typically, then, the Negro businessman has been a very small businessman, and, according to Foley, generally he has not been a very good businessman, nor a very significant factor in the Negro community. In fact, the Negro businessman was scarcely more advanced in the middle 1960s than he was in the 1820s.[9] Nonwhite persons in the professional and technical category have been increasing at the rate of 11 percent per year, compared with a white increase of 2.5 percent, but a "business exit" from the ghetto has hardly existed.[10]

The Myths Held by Negro Businessmen and by Negroes in General

In Philadelphia, Foley investigated three myths concerning Negro business that are widely held by Negro businessmen and by many Negroes. These myths are: lack of financing, competition from Jewish merchants, and the state of poverty of the Negro community. On the first point, Foley found that the Negro businessman has a difficult time getting credit, but that he has no more trouble getting credit than any other very small businessman.

Banks have branches in the Negro areas of Philadelphia, and they do make loans to Negroes. They make two types of loans: consumer loans and mortgage finance loans. They make them every day and have been for years. But they do not make business loans to Negroes for the same reason that they do not make them to the same type of white businessmen anywhere else in the city of Philadelphia: business loans are very risky loans. For instance, since World War II, one branch has been making on the average, fifty consumer loans a month to Negroes; but in its history it has made only two loans to Negro businessmen. I think it is very important to overcome the myth. It is true that Negro businessmen lack credit, but it is not because of a special prejudice peculiar to financial institutions. The banks are in the Negro area to make loans and therefore, to make money. Very small businessmen—Negro or white—cannot get loans simply because of the risks to the banks.[11]

In a consumer survey involving 84 housewives in a two- or three-block area in Philadelphia, Foley found that nine-tenths of the women shopped for groceries and for drugs exclusively at white stores. For cosmetics and for dry cleaning a slight majority

[7] Eugene P. Foley, "The Negro Businessman," *Daedalus*, Winter, 1966, p. 113.

[8] *Ibid.*, p. 113.

[9] *Ibid.*, pp. 115, 125.

[10] Samuels, *op. cit.*, p. 63.

[11] Foley, *op. cit.*, pp. 425–426. In the middle 1950s, Frazier wrote about "the social myth of Negro business," the belief that Negroes would own factories, banks, and stores in large numbers and that they would employ many Negroes. According to Frazier, the "black bourgeoisie" dreamed of gaining a monopoly of the Negro market, but it rejected identification with the masses. Identification with the white propertied classes was said to be impossible, so the black bourgeoisie—living in a world of make-believe—attempted to maintain the style of living of wealthy Whites. In this analysis, most of the members of the "black bourgeoisie" were said to fear competition with Whites "partly because such competition would mean that Whites were taking them seriously, and consequently they would have to assume a more serious and responsible attitude towards their work." This book by Frazier, based more on personal observations than detailed data, was a tract as well as a social scientific document. Frazier was attacking what he considered to be a failure on the part of too many professionals and intellectuals in the Negro group to live up to their potentialities. Because of the dual nature of the work, it exaggerated the situation under study. It was hailed and denounced by members of the Negro community. In any case, ten years later the situation was considerably different. The black nationalism movement had narrowed the social psychological gap between social classes within the Negro population. Black consciousness and black pride were significantly greater than they were in 1955. The "social myth of Negro business" as described by Frazier is much weaker today, if it exists at all. E. Franklin Frazier, *Black Bourgeoisie*, Free Press, 1957, pp. 166, 168, 216. See E. Holsendolph, "Middle-Class Blacks Are Moving Off the Middle," *Fortune*, Dec., 1969, p. 154.

shopped at Negro stores. A considerable majority bought gasoline at white stations. These housewives invariably said they shopped in white stores because they are "lower priced" and their reason for shopping in Negro stores was invariably because they are "more convenient." Foley found that the median prices in white stores were slightly higher than in Negro stores, contrary to the overwhelming impressions of the Negro housewives. The Jewish merchant is not, in his judgment, an unfair competitor.[12]

Concerning the third myth, the poverty of the Negro community, Foley found that although the area studied was a poor one, there were many white merchants who were making a very good profit.[13]

Why Have Negro Businessmen Not Been Successful?

The three major barriers to entry into business and for success in business for black entrepreneurs have been: (1) inability to raise capital, (2) the attitudes of buyers, black and white, and (3) the lack of management skills. We refer above to Foley's finding that Negro businessmen in Philadelphia have no more difficulty getting credit from banks than other small businessmen. Johnson and Smith emphasize the fact that Negro businessmen have lacked the assets needed by borrowers to protect business loans, and that the inability to find funds to build assets locks the small businessman into a vicious circle.[14] Efforts of the federal government to free some capital for the black community have not resulted in much risk-taking by nonwhite banks.[15] Church groups and some charitable organizations are now making limited amounts of risk capital available to black entrepreneurs through black banks, and, to some extent, competition from

these banks provides an inducement to white lending institutions to liberalize credit to the black community.

On the basis of service, value, or skin color, many Whites have been unwilling to patronize Negro businessmen, and not infrequently black customers have dealt with black businessmen only if circumstances have necessitated such buying. Such actions are attributed to a lack of confidence in the black businessman.[16] Related to the effect of attitudes of the Negro public toward the Negro businessman is the lack of business success symbols available to Negro businessmen themselves and to potential entrepreneurs. Foley says that "the culture has simultaneously unduly emphasized achievement in business as the primary symbol of success and has blindly developed or imposed an all-pervading racism that denied the Negro the necessary opportunities for achieving this success."[17] As a consequence of this stance, the Negro has been limited to "a modest, marginal retail or service operation." Recently the new mood of black awareness that has developed in the United States has done much to offset the attitudes formerly widely held in the black community. Skin color alone, however, will not be sufficient reason for expecting the patronage of black customers; black entrepreneurs will have to acquire the business skills essential to making their goods and services competitive.

The need for training and developing managerial skills requires different approaches for each aspect of the business situation: the small entrepreneur, the manager of a ghetto-based enterprise, and the manager operating within the framework of a major corporation. Attention is given later in this chapter to this problem, as well as to the other barriers to Negro business success.

One limiting factor in the future of Negro business may be the coinciding of the arrival of Negro Americans in the nation's cities and the decline of opportunities for establishing small businesses.[18] The arrival coincides also

---

[12] *Ibid.*, p. 426.

[13] *Ibid.*, p. 426.

[14] Johnson and Smith, *op. cit.*, p. 114.

[15] Johnson and Smith, *ibid.*, p. 114, explain that banks are held responsible by the government for checking the risk factor. While banks can recover in case of failure, they are cautious in their lending to avoid compiling a high failure record with the federal agency.

[16] *Ibid.*, p. 116.

[17] Foley, *op. cit.*, p. 124.

[18] Daniel P. Moynihan, "Employment, Income, and the Negro Family," *Daedalus*, Fall, 1965, p. 754.

with the decline in manufacturing jobs, a point which is made in Chapter 11, where the employment opportunities in the inner city were discussed.

A possibility for an increase in the number of Negro businesses is the replacement of a number of white (often Jewish) small businessmen in the urban ghettos by Negroes. Such a change may occur in part as a result of governmental, philanthropic, and educational help, furthered by black nationalism, linked, in some cases, with anti-Semitism. Jencks and Reisman say that "to the extent that the Black Muslims and similar organizations can create a patriarchal, prideful 'Protestant' methodical middle class, they may in time assist the development, now mainly confined to propaganda."[19]

Another possible change in the Negro business situation is the establishment of community-owned black retailing operations. White-owned chains now avoid the ghettos, and brand names tend to be unavailable because manufacturers refuse to allow them to be sold at higher than list prices. As a result, ghetto residents often buy shoddy, off-brand merchandise at inflated prices from small merchants. Theodore Cross argues that community-owned black stores would have a better chance than small merchants to get permission from brand-name manufacturers to charge what they had to, and that they would have a greater chance to obtain subsidies from government or from the manufacturers themselves to enable them to do business even while charging list prices.[20]

The Negro Market

The total value of the Negro consumer market has been estimated up to $30 billion annually. According to the highest estimates, black business serves only 10 to 15 percent of this market.[21] A study of consumer behavior in the inner core of Toledo, Ohio indicates that "differentiation in demand may be as great among black people as among whites."[22]

In addition to general advertising, most important national advertisers now prepare special campaigns for the Negro market. Among these companies are: Coca Cola International Corporation, Pet Milk Company, Carnation Company, Radio Corporation of America, Daggett and Ramsdell, Hamilton Watch Company, F. and M. Schaefer Brewing Company, Jacob Ruppert Brewing Company, American Oil Company, and Greyhound Bus Lines. These campaigns range from advertising in Negro newspapers and magazines, and on the 700 Negro-oriented radio stations, to the publication of a guide to conventions of Negro organizations and the distribution of a travel guide for Negroes listing service stations, restaurants, motels and parks at which they are welcome.[23]

In the middle 1960s, a nationwide campaign for "integrated advertising"— launched by the New York City Labor Department and supported by the Advertising Council and the American Association of Advertising Agencies—encouraged more than 120 leading United States corporations to run one or more integrated advertisements. These companies include: American Telephone, General Electric, International Business Machines, Manufacturers Hanover Trust Company, American Airlines, and Scott Paper Company. Nearly all the large national publications now run integrated advertisements regularly. Companies such as Lever Brothers use spot television commercials throughout the United States, including the Deep South, with identifiable Negroes demonstrating company products. Businessmen say that such advertising is "good" business. Consumer studies have shown that on a per capita basis, "the average Negro outspends his white counterpart in many product areas—including cosmetics, appli-

[19] Christopher Jencks and David Reisman, "The American Negro College," *Harvard Educational Review,* Winter, 1967, p. 14.

[20] See A. A. Altshuler, *Community Control,* Pegasus, 1970, pp. 212–213.

[21] Samuels, *op. cit.,* p. 63.

[22] *The Plain Dealer,* Nov. 23, 1969. Report on a study by G. Allen Brunner and Thomas A. Klein, "The Ghetto Consumer: Matching Problem."

[23] Ray Show, "The Negro Consumer," *Wall Street Journal,* June 30, 1961.

ances, stockings, soft drinks, hair preparations, phonograph records, and movies . . .
in many product areas, the Negro 'trades up'
to quality levels higher than his white counterpart."[24] From the standpoint of the Negro,
the integrated advertising campaign may help
him to get off the unemployment and welfare
rolls. New York City Labor Commissioner
James McFadden says: "Lack of skills and
education is not the whole story. Confronted
with an image of life in which only whites
are successful, minority groups lose the ambition to acquire the skills necessary for advancement." The New York City Labor Department found that the campaign had
spurred some Negroes to apply for better
jobs and to seek the additional education or
training the jobs require.[25]

Black Insurance Companies, Banks, Manu-facturers, Wholesalers, and Contractors

Until after the turn of the century, Nonwhites were unable to buy life insurance
from national companies; when they could
get coverage, often higher premiums had to
be paid. This situation stimulated the development of a number of black-controlled insurance companies. In 1962, there were
about 50 of these companies, but they played
a very limited role in the sale of insurance
even to black policyholders. The National
Insurance Association, composed of 46 Ne-
gro-managed insurance companies, had combined assets of $343 million in 1963, $1.9
billion in life insurance in force, and approximately 10,000 employees.[26] The largest
company had total assets of about $77
million, and the 20 leading companies had
combined assets of approximately $300 mil-
lion, a small part of the more than $30 bil-
lion total for the insurance industry.[27]

Banks have been owned and operated by
Negroes for decades, but they have generally
been marginal and weak. In 1921, there were
49 Negro-owned banks in 38 cities in the
United States. Thirty years later, there were
only 14 such banks, with total assets of $32
million and total deposits of $29 million.
In 1951, with the exception of one bank in
Philadelphia, another in Washington, D.C.,
and a third in Kansas City, all were located
in the South. At that time, these banks employed from 3 to 15 persons, each.[28] In 1963,
there were only 13 black banks in the country, but by 1969 the number was up to 20
operating in 19 cities. Freedom National
Bank, Harlem's first black-chartered and
black-operated commercial bank, was opened
in 1965. This bank has been growing fast,
but five huge banks still maintain branch
offices in the area.[29] According to Andrew
F. Brimmer, Negro member of the Federal
Reserve Board, "adverse loan experience"
caused Negro-owned banks as a group to
have "no after-tax profits" during the years
1965–1968.[30] Brimmer said that, in part, the
difficulty is "that the market for their services is circumscribed by the general conditions in the ghetto—high unemployment, low
incomes, a low rate of savings and the marginal character of local businesses. These
obstacles are reinforced by the severe shortage of trained management personnel."[31]

In Negro manufacturing and wholesaling,

[24] Sylvia Porter, "Integrated Ads Spur Negroes,
Products," *The Plain Dealer*, June 3, 1965.

[25] *Ibid.*

[26] *The New York Times*, Aug. 18, 1963, p. 52.

[27] Johnson and Smith, *op. cit.*, p. 113. For a detailed analysis of Negro-owned life insurance companies, see Andrew Brimmer, "The Negro in the National Economy," in John P. Davis (ed.), *The
American Negro Reference Book*, Prentice-Hall,
1966, pp. 309–322; on Negro-owned banks, see *ibid.*,
pp. 297–308.

[28] E. Franklin Frazier, *op. cit.*, p. 57.

[29] Johnson and Smith, *op. cit.*, p. 113.

[30] DeLorean, *op. cit.*, p. 16.

[31] *Ibid.*, p. 16. Theodore Cross argues that black
lending institutions can operate more effectively in
the ghettos than can white ones. To make a profit, or
even to break even in the ghettos, it is necessary to
charge higher interest rates than elsewhere. The reasons include: high rates for bad debts, small average
loans, necessity of providing intensive counseling
for customers, a small resource base of highly active
accounts, and the need to devote considerable effort
to community improvement activities. White banks
tend to stay out of the ghettos because charging
higher interest rates would lead to charges of racial
discrimination. Some large white financial institutions have channeled limited amounts of money for
ghetto lending through black banks. This procedure
makes bank-style credit available at rates only 1.5 or
2 percent higher than elsewhere instead of the 30,
50, or 1000 percent figures charged by loan sharks,
small loan companies, and individual merchants. See
Altshuler, *op. cit.*, pp. 212–213.

Philadelphia seems to be typical. In 1964, 13 manufacturing concerns, all small, owned by Negroes, were distributed as follows: eight beauty products, two clothing, one casket, one ironworks, and one meat products. In addition, Negroes owned fourteen wholesale distribution companies: eight beauty products, three food, one clothing, one casket, and one of candy, notions, and novelties.[32] Most of the two dozen ghetto plants established in the United States in 1967 and 1968 were modest in size, involving investments of $1 to $2 million, and were engaged in turning out relatively unsophisticated products. Approximately 8000 jobs were provided by these plants, but peak employment had not been reached.[33]

In September, 1968, the American Insurance Association told the Small Business Administration that—"As contractors, Negroes and other American minorities lack the necessary management and technical skills, experience and financial capacity. As a result they operate at a low level of efficiency, organization, and profitability."[34] In view of the experience of black contractors and aspiring contractors, the issuance of such a statement is not surprising. Exclusion from construction craft unions has made it almost impossible for black workers to acquire the skills to enter the construction business through the normal channel of going from skilled worker and foreman to small-scale contracting, and later into large-scale work. It has also made it impossible for them to have available the number of skilled workers necessary for large enterprises. In addition, the black contractor lacks access to financing. For these reasons, black contractors are almost completely unable to qualify for surety bonds needed for participation in most FHA insured projects and in public construction work. A study of seven major cities showed that 67 percent of all minority contractors have been unable to obtain a single surety bond. The construction industry is expected to grow from the 1960 level of $105 billion annually in new construction, maintenance, and repairs to $180 billion in the 1970s. In this expanding field, black contractors "find themselves in a kind of circular trap where their lack of experience in bonded work makes it virtually impossible to obtain surety bonds for construction work requiring such bonds and thereby gain experience on this type of work, even though they might otherwise have the ability to perform."[35]

BLACK CAPITALISM

Although the War on Poverty in the late 1960s developed a number of manpower employment programs, most of the jobs for Negroes continued to be menial and dead-ended, with little opportunity for advancement. In addition, government-sponsored manpower programs tended to "cream" the labor market, leaving almost untouched the hard-core of the chronically unemployed and underemployed.[36] The relative lack of success of these programs, together with the widespread unrest in the ghettos, has occasioned, along with other proposals, a new emphasis on "black capitalism" as a means of helping Negroes become more competitive in a capitalistic society. As described by DeLorean, this idea involves the development of black entrepreneurs on a large scale through the following approaches:

Branch operations of big industry in the inner city.

Indigenous inner-city industries assisted by partnership arrangements or by technical and managerial support from outside corporations.

Individually operated inner-city enterprises made possible through compensatory devices such as Small Business Administration loans, managerial and technical training programs, sheltered markets, etc.

[32] Foley, *op. cit.*, p. 113.
[33] Martin Skala, "Inner-City Enterprises: Current Experience," in Haddad and Pugh, *op. cit.*, pp. 151–152.
[34] DeLorean, *op. cit.*, pp. 14–15.

[35] G. Douglas Pugh, "Bonding Minority Contractors," in Haddad and Pugh, *op. cit.*, pp. 138–139. On the bonding problems of minority contractors, see Gilbert B. Friedman, "The Unbondables," *The New Republic*, July 6, 1968, pp. 27–29.
[36] DeLorean, *op. cit.*, pp. 10–11.

Community-owned corporations financing local enterprises and social services.[37]

Despite difference in the viewpoints of black and white business analysts, DeLorean thinks that agreement can be reached on an order of priorities for ghetto economic development. The imperatives are:

The location of capable black businessmen.
The liberalization of concepts and standards of lending, bonding, and insuring.
The provision of managerial training, technical assistance and support, and identification of stable markets.
The provision of easier access to markets for minority entrepreneurs and, if necessary, the provision of sheltered markets.[38]

Although the Reverend Sullivan, of Philadelphia, hopes to see by the year 2,000 at least 100,000 new black businesses making or selling things for the total American community, employing five million people and generating $50 billion in new wealth, the more modest hope of the Small Business Administration is that the number of minority-owned businesses can be doubled by 1975. An agency report says: "Our analysis recognizes that greatest opportunities will arise in the retail trade and service industries, but contemplates principal expansion in the more substantial segments of these industries (shopping centers, franchises, supermarkets, business, professional and technical services). It also proposes progressive growth of minority ownership in other industries, especially in contract construction, but also in wholesale trade and manufacturing."[39]

In the debates inside and outside the ghetto on the significance of black enterprise, two points of view stand out. One group emphasizes the cost aspect of the cost-benefit question, arguing that the ghettos offer the least fruitful areas for enterprise development because land, facility, and maintenance costs are extremely high, circulation is limited, housing facilities and transportation are inadequate, crime and ghetto hostility

prevent the employment of competent management and clerical staffs, and insurance costs are excessive. Many in government and business hold this viewpoint, with the result that the attempts to promote economic well-being in the ghetto have depended almost solely on employment programs supported by social services. A second group stresses the benefits, or social utility, side of the question. Those in this group hold that the economic system puts the ghetto at a competitive disadvantage because resource allocation policies (highway, housing, tax) have built up the infrastructure of the suburbs and small cities at the expense of urban communities. This school argues that our investment policies should be changed to aid ghetto areas, concentrating on the social utility of the program in the same way that we emphasize the benefits of the defense, space, and highway programs rather than their costs. According to Green and Faux, these two views are complicated by the current disagreements between the integrationists and the separatists. In general,

the 'cost effectives' hold the integrationist view that blacks can best assimilate into American life through opening up housing and jobs in suburban growth areas, and that the tools, legal and programmatic, are now at hand. . . . The 'social utilitarians' argue that recent data indicate a slight opening-up of the suburbs to blacks and that the trend will increase, but that such movement has affected only the black upper-middle class and has thus further reduced the leadership in the ghettos, leaving the great mass of blacks doomed to decades of existence in deteriorating neighborhoods.[40]

Along with all the discussions of black capitalism, three main developments have been taking place: business organized in the black community by major industry, businesses organized in the ghetto by black businessmen, and capital and technical assistance by government sources, foundations, and church groups. Business organized by major industry takes two forms, that of establishing a plant in the ghetto, maintaining control but

---

[37] *Ibid.*, pp. 11–12.
[38] *Ibid.*, p. 17.
[39] *Ibid.*, p. 17.

[40] Gerson Green and Geoffrey Faux, "The Social Utility of Black Enterprise," in Haddad and Pugh, *op. cit.*, pp. 21–22.

employing minority persons at as many levels as possible, considering their training and experience. In the other form, the company sponsors the business in cooperation with the black community with the intention of transferring control of the firm at some future date to investors from the black community, complete with management and other personnel. An example of the former plan is the electrical manufacturing plant built in 1968 by the IBM Corporation in Brooklyn's Bedford-Stuyvesant area. This plant, which employs 300 people, has a lower turnover rate than similar operations in which minorities do not predominate, and its productivity rate compares favorably with other plants. Another major industry that has established a plant in a ghetto is AVCO, a company that built a $2.3 million printing establishment in the Roxbury area in Boston. An example of the type of business development in which a major firm helps to organize, finance, and staff a business in cooperation with the black community is Fairmicco in Washington, D.C. Fairmicco is a conglomerate of community organizations in the Shaw urban renewal area and Fairchild Hiller Corporation, an aircraft and electronics manufacturing firm. Among other things, Fairchild Hiller agreed to provide interim management until a black successor could be recruited and trained.[41]

One of the most noteworthy developments of black-owned and controlled businesses was Reverend Leon Sullivan's organization in 1968 of the Progress Plaza Shopping Center in Philadelphia. This center consists of ten stores owned and operated by Negroes, and seven stores, including a supermarket, shoe store, and bank that are managed by Negroes. The center was financed by a pledge of $10 monthly for 36 months from the 650 members of the Zion Baptist Church, of which Sullivan is pastor, a $1.3 million bank loan, and a $400,000 Ford Foundation grant. In St. Louis, a Negro group is developing a seven-acre urban renewal site for a ten-store shopping center, and another shopping center is being organized in the Watts area in Los Angeles. The latter project involves a pledge by the Pacific Mutual Insurance Company to supply up to $1.5 million in funds and management skills. In Harlem, a $4.5 million motor hotel is to be built by Harlem investors and the Hotel Corporation of America.[42] Jim Brown's Negro Industrial and Economic Union is helping to finance black entrepreneurs in six cities.[43]

Among the government agencies that have affected significantly the development of black entrepreneurships are the Small Business Administration (SBA) and the Economic Development Administration (EDA). In the 1965 Housing and Urban Development Act, the Small Business Administration was given the authority to guarantee the leases of small businessmen (one who grosses less than $1 million annually) up to ten years. This action meant that private mortgage money of insurance companies and pension funds that had not been invested previously in slum areas could be protected against changed economic conditions of these areas or defaults in rental payments by small businessmen.[44] A SBA program, which has not been used extensively, is the Local Development Company Program. This program lends to a local, nonprofit economic development corporation 80 percent of the funds needed for land, buildings, and equipment for 25 years at 5.5 percent interest. The maximum allowed is $350,000 per small business aided, but if ten small businesses are assisted, the total can be $3,500,000. This program has given assistance to factories, shopping centers, industrial parks, parking garages, nursing homes, and other job-creating enterprises. This program can be coordinated with an urban renewal program to include total land use of a slum area and total community needs.[45] An important development in 1968 was the initiation of "Project Own" by Howard J. Samuels, then Administrator of SBA. The purpose of this program

---

[41] Edward D. Irons, "Black Capitalism—1968," in Patricia Romero (ed.), *In Black America*, United, 1969, pp. 218–220.

[42] *Ibid.*, p. 225.

[43] James J. Kilpatrick, "Black Capitalism, Sullivan Style," *The Plain Dealer*, November 22, 1968.

[44] Foley, *op. cit.*, p. 129.

[45] *Ibid.*, pp. 129–130.

was to facilitate the development of minority business and the entrance of minority entrepreneurs into the mainstream of American business. Project Own involves capital acquisition, managerial training, and technical assistance.[46]

The Economic Development Administration of the U.S Department of Commerce has made a number of "seed money" grants to selected trade associations representing the black business community, including the National Bankers Association, the National Insurance Association, and the National Business League. These are not new organizations, but the grants from EDA enabled them to launch the first substantial programs in their careers.[47]

A number of construction programs have been administered by the Department of Housing and Urban Affairs (HUA; HUD) to provide opportunities for Negro contractors and Negro employees, and for the economic development of ghettos. These include: (1) FHA's 3 percent insured loans for the construction or rehabilitation of housing projects for low- and moderate-income families; (2) the grant program for small public facilities (community centers, health centers, etc.) that are related to the community action programs of the OEO, and (3) the construction and leasing program of public housing units.[48]

Guaranteed Markets

One means of furthering minority economic development is through the provision of a guaranteed market for new businesses and industries. In suggesting that American governments launch set-aside programs for ghetto procurement, Eugene Foley, former Assistant Secretary of Commerce points out that the Department of Defense and many other federal procurement agencies have long followed this practice by reserving certain contracts for exclusive bidding by small business, and have required prime contrac-

tors to demonstrate attempts to subcontract to small business. Although it has been little used, a 1960 order, which is still in effect, requires the Department of Defense to give preference, where prices are equal, to firms that will do a substantial part of their work in labor surplus areas. (Since the federal government defines labor market areas in terms of one or more local political units, subareas within cities, such as Harlem, are ineligible for designation as labor surplus areas.)[49]

Under the GHEDIPLAN and similar proposals, a portion of a city's purchases and small contracts would be set aside for ghetto businesses. A set-aside of 10 percent in New York City would provide a market for an estimated $50 million worth of goods and services. If the example set by the public sector were followed in the private sector by foundations, trade associations, private industry, educational and religious institutions, and social organizations, as well as some federal and state governmental purchases, another $50 million might be provided. Thus a guaranteed market of approximately $100 million would exist in New York City.[50]

The rationale of a governmental set-aside program might rest on neighborhood poverty and unemployment, or on these together with race. The justification for including race as a factor would be the same as in public hiring—severe current underrepresentation. The preferential treatment would be regarded as transitional, with the targets designed to avoid the demand that all government contracts be awarded on a group quota basis.[51]

To avoid the delays usually associated with seeking new markets, some firms use ghetto plants as a source of supply for internal needs. An example is IBM's Bedford-

---

[46] Irons, *op. cit.*, pp. 220–221.

[47] *Ibid.*, p. 222. Brief accounts of these programs are given in *ibid.*, pp. 223–224.

[48] Foley, *op. cit.*, p. 130.

[49] Altshuler, *op. cit.*, pp. 174–175.

[50] Dunbar S. McLaurin and Cyril D. Tyson, "The GHEDIPLAN for Economic Development," in Haddad and Pugh, *op. cit.*, p. 133. The GHEDIPLAN (Ghetto Economic and Development and Industrialization Plan) was developed by Mr. McLaurin. See section on "Black Economic Development" later in this chapter.

[51] Altshuler, *op. cit.*, pp. 175–176.

Stuyvesant plant that makes computer cables, a product needed throughout IBM's manufacturing system.[52]

Preferential Treatment: Easing of Requirements in Lending

Another form of preferential treatment of minorities involves lending. An early experiment in more liberal lending policies for Negro business men was the "6 × 6" Pilot Loan and Management Program started in Philadelphia in 1964 by SBA. Under this program, loans up to $6000 for six years were made to very small businessmen, and management training and counseling were provided. In 1964, 219 loans were approved totaling $912,547; 98 of these loans for the amount of $379,657 were made to Negroes. Sixty-eight of the latter loans went to established Negro businesses for $272,757, and 30 went to new Negro businesses for $106,900. Traditional bank barriers were overcome by considering loan applicants principally on character, integrity, and ability to repay the loan from earnings, rather than on collateral. Subsequently this program was expanded to five other cities, and its provisions were included in Title IV in the Economic Opportunity Act of 1964 on an expanded basis with loans up to $25,000 for 15 years.[53]

Howard Samuels, who is also a former head of the SBA, says that loans to minorities must be made on a different basis than other business loans. The loss rate of regular bank loans is less than half of one percent. The SBA takes about a 3 percent loss ratio, but SBA experience with minority loans is approximately 12 percent. Banks cannot be expected to risk that type of loss, but SBA can guarantee loans up to 90 percent. Since a bank cannot lose more than 10 percent on a given loan, no bank takes an unreasonable risk, even with 12 percent loss on new minority businesses.[54]

A part of what Samuels calls "compensa-tory capitalism" is the new ethic being practiced by "the socially and economically aware banking and business communities." He refers specifically to his work at the Department of Commerce in coordinating the JOBS (Job Opportunities in the Business Sector) program with the National Alliance of Businessmen, and to the acceptance by some bankers of the principle of less stringent requirements for loans to minorities, with the same kind of risk guarantees that are provided when loans are made to underdeveloped countries.[55] An indispensable aid in raising outside financing for a new business is a long-term purchasing contract with a powerful corporate sponsor. A guaranteed market of this type is one of the best forms of collateral.[56]

The Training of Managers

The training of managers to operate ghetto enterprises is a matter of great importance. For managers other than small entrepreneurs, three techniques have been suggested. In the first place, formal training is a necessity and work beyond the undergraduate level may be required. In the case of plants that are set up as independent profit centers, it is necessary to train other people in such areas as accounting, marketing, and finance

---

[52] Skala, *op. cit.*, pp. 155–156.

[53] Foley, *op. cit.*, p. 127.

[54] Howard Samuels, "How to Even the Odds," *Saturday Review*, Aug. 23, 1969, p. 23.

[55] Samuels, "Compensatory Capitalism," pp. 66–67. An influential economist, Milton Friedman, asks what it means to say that the corporate executive has a "social responsibility" in his capacity as businessman. He says: "If this statement is not pure rhetoric, it must mean that he is to act in some way that is not in the best interest of his employers." One example he cites is that of hiring "hardcore" unemployed, at the expense of corporate profits, instead of better-qualified workmen to contribute to the social objective of reducing poverty. He argues: "Insofar as his actions . . . reduce returns to stockholders, he is spending their money. Insofar as his actions raise the price to customers, he is spending their money. Insofar as his actions lower the wages of some employees, he is spending their money." If he spends someone else's money in a different way than they would have spent it, Friedman says, the executive is exercising "social responsibility," but he is in effect imposing taxes and deciding how the tax proceeds shall be spent. Milton Friedman, "What Are the Social Responsibilities of American Business Executives?," *The Plain Dealer*, Oct. 16, 1970, p. 14A.

[56] Skala, *op. cit.*, p. 153.

to assist the manager. A second technique in managerial preparation places a black in training with a trained white from within the corporation to run the plant until the black learns the operating methods. Johnson and Smith say that learning under these circumstances is difficult at best and the results are usually unsatisfactory. The third technique is an accelerated program that measures the new manager's weaknesses in relation to the job he will have, and then designs a program that will enable him to acquire the skills that he needs. Many companies have established programs of this type, and some management experts think this may be the most efficient way rapidly to train a ghetto manager.[57]

To assist black entrepreneurs of small businesses, consulting services involving daily support have been started by some schools of business in major cities in the United States. In 1966, a group of Harvard MBA candidates started the Business Assistance Program. BAP was underwritten by a three-year grant from the Ford Foundation and was designed to introduce modern, rational methods into small-business operations.[58] At Columbia University a nonprofit corporation called MBA Management Consultants, Inc. was formed in 1968. The clients in the Harlem community "control" the organization, but a spirit of cooperation between the two groups has been maintained. In 1970, the organization had 55 clients; usually two consultants are assigned to each company. The MBAs have their advisers too in a group of volunteer professors at the Graduate School of Business and experts at Arthur D. Little, Inc., a management consulting company which supports the program. Another consulting service formed by students at New York University Graduate School of Business, called the Urban Business Assistance Corporation, has been providing assistance to black businessmen in such sections as Bedford-Stuyvesant in Brooklyn.[59]

The Interracial Council of Business Opportunity, founded in 1963, has assisted approximately 3000 minority-owned businesses to open, stay open, or improve. This organization's 1500 volunteers provide free management counseling, and 2500 people have attended the special management training courses sponsored by the group at colleges and universities. The ICBO Fund, Inc. partially guarantees bank loans which would not otherwise be made; over $9,000,000 worth of loans have been generated. Another aspect of the ICBO program is National New Enterprise, a plan to foster the formation of business ventures with a capitalization of no less than $100,000 and affording maximum opportunity for minority employment. Ten such businesses were started in 1969. The Major Industries Program encourages large corporations to assist in creating businesses of significant size to be owned and operated by minority entrepreneurs. In addition, ICBO has established a government procurement office in Washington, D.C. to assist government, as well as the private sector, in coordinating the flow of contracts to minority businesses.[60]

Among black colleges, Texas Southern is the only undergraduate school that is an accredited member of the American Association of Collegiate Schools of Business. Atlanta University is the only black university in the nation with a graduate school of business. A consortium of predominantly white universities (Indiana, Rochester, University of Southern California, Washington University, and Wisconsin) seeks young graduates from predominantly black colleges and offers them the opportunity to study for a master's degree in business at any one of the five campuses. This program is expected to produce about 100 graduates annually. Stanford University has instituted a similar program, and has plans for a summer preparatory course. The Graduate School of Business at Harvard has established approximately 100 scholarships for black students. The University of Massachusetts has created a pro-

[57] Johnson and Smith, *op. cit.*, pp. 121–122.
[58] *Ibid.*, p. 119.
[59] Leonard Sloane, "Management Aid for Harlem Business," *The New York Times*, May 3, 1970, pp. 1, 14.

[60] Brochure issued by the Interracial Council for Business Opportunity, 1970.

gram called ABLE (Accelerated Business Leadership Education) to train young men and women currently employed in industry who have been identified by their firms as having potential for upper management positions.[61]

According to Johnson and Smith, any closing of the gap where 100 jobs exist at the management level for every five trained black managers in existence must await the crop of present high-school graduates who might be encouraged to consider business as a career. In addition to the general disenchantment with business common among many college students, there are two additional reasons for lack of interest in black students in looking at the business option. Some black students doubt that business is really serious about hiring and utilizing black people in meaningful jobs, and the number of black people in such jobs who serve as models to young people is exceedingly small. Some business administration educators think that industry, government, and educational institutions will have to join forces in providing a clear message to young black Americans that industry is receptive and that upward mobility is possible.[62]

Franchising

One of the most promising opportunities for the black businessman is through the expanding field of franchising—automobile dealerships, ice cream stands, gas stations, shoe stores, restaurants, muffler repair shops, and other types of business. Franchising provides an ideal system of management aid, including helping the owner to select a site, apply for a loan, prepare advertising, and learn inventory. Such outlets need not be limited to the black community. Howard Johnson restaurants, A & W root beer stands, and Holiday Inn motels are examples of franchising outside the ghetto. Although blacks have been almost wholly excluded from franchises in the past, there have been small gains in the last several years. The Depart-

ment of Commerce and the SBA have started a program to facilitate franchising.[63]

DIFFICULTIES INVOLVED IN EXPANDING BLACK CAPITALISM

Black capitalism, defined by an eminent black economist now serving as a member of the Federal Reserve Board as small-scale, limited-employment, Negro-owned businesses located in the ghetto, offers a very limited potential for economic advancement for the majority of Negro Americans. Andrew Brimmer says that the low income, high levels of unemployment, and poor net financial position of urban Negro families provide a poor economic environment for business investment. Paradoxically, economic advances by urban Negro families do not necessarily improve the prospects for Negro-owned businesses. Greater affluence brings greater mobility, more diverse tastes, and an interest in consuming in the larger national economy. Another serious problem is the lack of human capital among ghetto residents. Black businessmen find it difficult to recruit employees with high levels of education and on-the-job work experience. The acquisition of human capital by ghetto residents will not necessarily increase the supply of qualified employees to black businessmen because many qualified black workers are interested in the higher expected returns and the greater job security in a company operating in the national economy.[64]

Other difficulties in expanding black entrepreneurship include the almost nonexistent supply at present of black managers, the skimpy information about potential markets for black businesses; and the difficulty of finding capital, especially in a tight money market. On the last point, the tradi-

---

[61] Johnson and Smith, *op. cit.*, pp. 121, 123.

[62] *Ibid.*, p. 124.

[63] See Foley, *op. cit.*, p. 128, and Samuels, "How to Even the Odds," p. 24.

[64] Andrew Brimmer, "Black Capitalism, *South Today*, Mar. 1970, p. 6. Excerpts from a paper by A. F. Brimmer and H. S. Terrell, "The Economic Potential of Black Capitalism," given at the meetings of the American Economic Association on December 29, 1969.

tional view is that equity investment in marginal businesses is an inadvisable use of capital, and "even by the high-risk, high-gain standards of venture capital, the ghetto is scarcely seen as a promising locale for investment."[65]

Brimmer has questioned the view that a large number of plants will be located in the ghetto, saying that ". . . the economics of scale and of plant location in most instances will seldom if ever tip the decision in favor of concentrating a substantial part of the output of any major firm in the ghetto—but removed from its principal markets in the country at large."[66] Brimmer's doubts are shared by others who emphasize the high-risk character of ghetto plants. Labor costs for upgrading the "hard-core" unemployed are high, even in cases where assistance is received from manpower training grants. The wage rate does not reflect the heavy overhead charges—indirect costs that come from absenteeism, high turnover, and extensive supervisory efforts. At Aerojet-General's Watts Manufacturing Company, a plant set up after the Watts riots, 10 to 15 percent of the work force was illiterate, 90 percent had never held a steady job, and the average man had at least three arrests and a felony conviction. In the first year, Watts hired 1000 people to maintain a staff of 500; four years later the turnover was still 45 percent annually.[67]

According to Skala, "the road to profitability will be a long and hard one." John Garrity of McKinsey and Company predicted that his company would lose money without government aid in the form of tax incentives, low-cost loans, or even operating subsidies. Fred J. Borch, chairman of General Electric Company, says that the "unknowns" and the "conflicting viewpoints among the experts" will cause most major corporations to be hesitant about inner-city manufacturing.[68] This may be too severe a statement; there is now a small, but not unimportant black capi-

talism. It seems unlikely, however, that major economic improvement for Blacks will come as a result of separate economic activities.

Opposition to the special help that has been extended to new black businesses has come from existing small companies, whether owned and managed by Blacks or Whites. If special assistance is to be continued, it may be necessary to work out some arrangement to balance the competitive situation between the less successful established enterprises and their new competitors.[69] Objections to the proposal to grant special tax privileges to businesses that locate in the ghetto have come from the AFL-CIO executive council. This group said that legislation introduced in Congress in 1969 would, if enacted, create tax "loopholes" that would encourage the location of sweatshops or some marginal plants of large companies in ghetto areas.[70] Also, basic differences in the viewpoints of some white businessmen and some black leaders, as well as mutual distrust, make the future of business partnership uncertain.[71]

Finally, many share Brimmer's concern that the pursuit of black capitalism may retard black economic development by discouraging many from participating in the national economy,[72] and Arthur Lewis' view that American economic life is inconceivable except on an integrated basis.[73]

BLACK ECONOMIC DEVELOPMENT

Some economists and some black leaders distinguish between job training, or even black capitalism, and what they call black economic development. According to this view, job training is seen as having only one objective —employment—while "economic development" has multiple objectives, one of which is employment. Under the Economic Oppor-

[65] Haddad and Pugh, *op. cit.*, pp. 2–3.

[66] Andrew F. Brimmer's commencement address at Clark University, Atlanta, Georgia, June 3, 1968. Reported in *The Plain Dealer*, June 4, 1968.

[67] Skala, *op. cit.*, pp. 153–154.

[68] *Ibid.*, pp. 158–159.

[69] A. W. Elliot, " 'Black Capitalism' and the Business Community," in Haddad and Pugh, *op. cit.*, p. 78.

[70] *The Plain Dealer*, Feb. 23, 1969.

[71] Haddad and Pugh, *op. cit.*, p. 5, and DeLorean, *op. cit.*, p. 12.

[72] Brimmer and Terrell, *op. cit.*, p. 6.

[73] W. Arthur Lewis, "Black Power and the American University," *University: A Princeton Quarterly*, Spring, 1969, p. 9.

tunity Act, approximately $2 billion annually are spent on the War on Poverty. More than $800,000,000 are devoted to OEO's Community Action Program in rural and urban areas. Under the Model Cities Program, urban areas may receive a significant increase in resources. These programs rely mainly on manpower training and social service programs rather than on the economic development of black ghettos. Critics of these programs say that job training and other employment programs do not create jobs. Unless there are, or will be, vacancies for which qualified personnel are not available, the training simply provides the trainees with the opportunity to become more competitive.[74]

Advocates of the position mentioned above say they are not talking about black capitalism. They speak about "the creation and acquisition of capital instruments by means of which we can maximize our economic interests. We do not particularly try to define styles of ownership; we say that we are willing to cooperate pragmatically and let the style of ownership fit the style of the area of its inhabitants."[75] In the final analysis, they say, the interest is not in jobs but in the instruments that create jobs. They are not interested in bringing white businesses into black communities, but in creating instruments that can hire blacks. Nor are they interested in substituting black ownership of small businesses for white ownership of such businesses. They want to acquire capital instruments on a major scale "to maximize the flow of money to the community and begin that geometric progression toward economic well-being."[76]

The black economic development view calls for a complete restructuring of the ghetto economy. Such restructuring would require a total plan for ghetto development and industrialization. In this viewpoint, the ghetto is regarded as an underdeveloped nation whose economic productivity and stability are to be increased. The goal would be "to redress the adverse balance of payments between the ghetto and the outer white world, and to attain capital and profits under local control and within the geographical area of the ghetto."[77] Instead of piecemeal approaches, the GHEDIPLAN envisions a program similar to those followed by the United States in helping an underdeveloped country. Included in such programs outside the country is the establishment of a central banking system, insurance networks, and other instruments of capital accumulation. Favorable tariff rates are set, and production machinery as well as consumer items are sold to the underdeveloped country. The goal is "to establish a balanced, diversified, and self-supporting economy that will generate capital and support a stable friendly society."[78] According to McLaurin and Tyson, the New York Urban Coalition has liberally borrowed ideas from the GHEDIPLAN and has set up a corporation to provide venture capital along the lines suggested in the plan and has established a GHEDIPLAN-type management assistance corporation.

Some black nationalists regard the control of economic instruments as a part of the total situation in the community that must be controlled by Blacks. Innis says: "We must control our schools if we are to upgrade education and pass on positive values to our children. We must control health facilities if we are to cut down our mortality rate. We must control the law enforcement in our areas if the police are to serve their proper function . . . In short, we must control every institution that takes our tax moneys and is supposed to distribute goods and services equitably for us."[79]

[74] Green and Faux, *op. cit.*, pp. 22–23, 26–27.
[75] Roy Innis, "Separatist Economics: A New Social Contract," in Haddad and Pugh, *op. cit.*, p. 53.
[76] Ibid., p. 58. Some black nationalists have suggested that organized black groups should seek to establish a "community rebate plan." Black people would not patronize merchants and contractors who did not agree to "reinvest" 40 to 50 percent of net profits in the black community. "This contribution could take many forms: providing additional jobs for black people, donating scholarship funds for students, supporting certain types of community organizations." Stokely Carmichael and Charles Hamilton, "The Search for New Forms," in Sethard Fisher (ed.), *Power and the Black Community*, Random House, 1971, p. 380.

[77] McLaurin and Tyson, *op. cit.*, p. 128.
[78] *Ibid.*, p. 131.
[79] Innis, *op. cit.*, p. 55.

The ultimate goal of those who advocate community-based economic development is the total renewal of the ghetto. Instead of the urban renewal programs of the past (programs which have often failed to achieve their intended goals due to the resistance of the ghetto), urban renewal of primarily residential ghettos, it is argued, could drastically alter the whole environment. Theoretically, such developments could create large-scale entrepreneurial opportunities for ghetto-controlled community corporations in the construction of housing, office buildings, and retail centers, and in the financing and management of such structures and businesses. Some say that this is the only approach available to the government that is acceptable to ghetto leadership, and they see in it a way of achieving both urban renewal and black economic development.[80]

Others say that clearly economic development, in the context of domestic urban problems, does not have the meaning it carries when applied to underdeveloped nations, that is, the problem of increasing the output and productivity of the population of a large, self-contained geographical unit, the solution to which involves capital accumulation. The analogy breaks down, they say, because of the difficulty of defining the ghetto in economic terms and in identifying and controlling such economic factors as imports and exports. In the inner cities, the problems they see are those of the redistribution of income, employment, and ownership among income classes, and, to a lesser degree the development of a business infrastructure within the ghetto.[81]

Those who question the analogy between the ghetto and an underdeveloped nation point out that unlike such nations, the ghetto has only one indigenous resource—its own manpower. This resource can be developed only if industry, materials, and capital are imported. Such importation would promote a new "colonialism" in which outside investors would take profits, exploit indigenous labor and skills, yet would create little capability in the community. Such persons insist, therefore, on guarantees of early divestiture by outside partners or complete internal control through community corporations.[82]

Regardless of how the ghetto is viewed, the federal programs discussed earlier in this chapter seem to be inadequate to bring about substantial economic change in the ghetto. We refer to Title IV of the Economic Opportunity Act, which provides loans and technical assistance to poverty area entrepreneurs; SBA, which may be having some effect upon improved access to capital and technical assistance by minority businessmen; the Economic Development Administration, which has had limited funds and program authority to provide for urban programs; and OEO, which has not regarded economic development as an area of major program interest.[83]

Green and Faux argue that black economic development, as they define it, will not encourage racial segregation and undo the progress toward integration that has been made during the past decade. In this view, integration is not simply interaction between Blacks and Whites, but a relationship on the basis of equality. Institutions that interact with the white community on this basis have been lacking in the ghetto. The creation of black-owned businesses, it is hoped, will help to build such institutions by developing black economic and political power within the ghetto. Green and Faux say that the establishment of a black business increases the amount of real integration in the nation by providing opportunities for both parties to bargain as equals.[84]

The question of community control is often a difficult issue. Companies tend to assume that they will be welcomed for the new job opportunities they provide, and often do not realize that the community desires a voice in management and a share in the ownership. Several companies, including

[80] Ibid., pp. 30–31.
[81] Green and Faux, op. cit., pp. 23–24.

[82] DeLorean, op. cit., pp. 12–13.
[83] Ibid., p. 24.
[84] Green and Faux, op. cit., pp. 28–29.

Aerojet-General, EG&G, and Warner-Swasey have shared ownership of new enterprises with the employees and the community. Others, including Xerox and General Electric, have given free managerial, marketing, and technical assistance to a community group that raised "seed money" and provided a management team.[85] The demands for early divestiture made by black militants are regarded by many corporate officials as unrealistic. The fear is that ghetto residents may end up with a poor investment or one that fails. Skala cites the case of Fairmicco, where the backers had intended to issue 100,000 shares at $1 each in the Shaw area. In this way Fairchild's ownership share would have been substantially reduced, but business losses made it necessary for the sponsoring company to put additional capital into the project and to discard its timetable for withdrawal.[86]

In 1968, a group of CORE leaders, law professors, businessmen, politicians, and graduate students of business prepared numerous drafts of an ambitious bill known as the Community Self-Determination Act. This proposal authorized the establishment of federally chartered development corporations in ghetto communities of up to 300,000 population. This bill to institutionalize black enterprise as a community-wide cooperative venture was not adopted.[87] Frederick Sturdivant, of the University of Texas Graduate School of Business, opposed the Community Self-Determination Act, saying that the bill

ignores the great challenge that confronts this nation, which is to find ways to surmount the racial barriers erected by the dominant society and create a truly pluralistic democracy. Any legislation that ignores this objective and enforces a concept of 'separate but equal' economic development moves the world toward apartheid

. . . If economic integration . . . is to be viewed as a step toward the goal of equal rights and opportunities for all citizens of this nation, then this approach of black capitalism is not the answer.[88]

A moderate position on black economic development is the partnership concept between black ghetto institutions and white business, with government playing an intermediary role by providing the ghetto institutions with the fiscal base to negotiate as equals. Without this intervention, Green and Faux say that "marriages" between ghettos and business will not be made in the foreseeable future.[89] Finally, in the attack on poverty and racism, community-based economic development should not supplant the current manpower and social service programs.

Minority Business Programs

Despite the many disputes within the Negro community and between Blacks and Whites concerning the merits or demerits of diverse programs and projects for bettering the economic situation of Negroes and other minorities in the United States, no single formula can be designated as the most promising means of attaining the desired goal. The following list of organizations, methods, and projects, a number of which have been mentioned earlier, seem to be among the most significant developments of recent years. The items given are not necessarily mutually exclusive. We reiterate that manpower training programs and social service programs should not be abandoned.

Community Development Organizations. The New York Urban Coalition, formed with the help of a committee of bankers, includes three subsidiary operations. The first program will utilize the Small Business Investment Company Act to finance businesses. The second operation will establish a Venture Capital Corporation to finance businesses that are potentially successful but involve a greater risk factor. The third subsidiary will

---

[85] Skala, *op. cit.*, p. 153.

[86] Elliot points out that communities expecting that community corporations will devote a certain percentage of gross net profits to "social or supportive services" for the community as a whole should be aware that not all corporations succeed and that in marginal years it may be impossible to provide any supportive services. A. W. Elliot, *op. cit.*, p. 77.

[87] DeLorean, *op. cit.*, pp. 18–19. See also, John McClaughry, "Black Ownership and National Politics," in Haddad and Pugh, *op. cit.*, pp. 40–49.

[88] DeLorean, *op. cit.*, p. 13.

[89] Green and Faux, *op. cit.*, pp. 34, 36.

provide management assistance in ghetto areas. It will assist in defining local business opportunities, locate potential managers and owners, initiate apprenticeship programs to train managers, and prepare the investment for consideration by traditional banking sources or the Venture Capital Corporation. The Board of Directors of this cooperative plan includes representation of both the white financial institutions and the black community leaders.[90]

The Harlem Commonwealth Council obtained a grant from the Demonstration Office of OEO to organize a nonprofit, tax-exempt corporation that would invest in profit-making businesses and use the accumulated income to reinvest in other businesses. Assistance has also been provided by The National Association of Manufacturers and McKinsey and Company.[91]

In 1968–1969, more than 40 minority group members in Rochester, New York started businesses, expanded their stores, or bought out existing white merchants. Most of these new ventures involved retail goods and services, but a few were in contracting, camera repair, and plastic molding. The leading role in the establishment of new independent businesses has been played by the Rochester Business Opportunities Corporation, a nonprofit organization supported by more than 60 Rochester corporations devoted to "giving the minority entrepreneurs a chance." RBOC provides a wide range of financing and counseling services to aspiring entrepreneurs. The organization's largest commitment is FIGHTON, inc., a $600,000 manufacturing company organized by FIGHT with the assistance of Xerox. FIGHTON makes vacuum cleaners, metal stampings, and transformers for Xerox's internal use. In addition to purchasing most of the output during the first two years, Xerox provides free technical and managerial services. RBOC has agreed to assist in finding customers other than Xerox to put the company on an independent basis. The FIGHTON project grew out of nearly four years of collaboration between FIGHT, a black self-help organization, and Xerox on job training programs for the disadvantaged.[92]

Private Organizations. A number of private organizations operated by Blacks are helping to start, finance, or staff black business enterprises. Among these are NEGRO, NIEU (Jim Brown's Negro Industrial and Economic Union), and Opportunity Industrialization Centers. The latter, developed by Reverend Leon Sullivan, is the largest of these undertakings. We referred earlier to the Progress Plaza Shopping Center in Philadelphia, built and operated by Negroes under the sponsorship of OIC. Reverend Sullivan has also created a nationwide chain of more than 75 job-training centers, the nation's largest self-help group for the disadvantaged. The OICs teach elementary job skills and seek to increase morale and motivation among the trainees. Philadelphia's centers alone have trained 7000 graduates, 90 percent of whom were placed on jobs. In addition to the shopping plaza and the OICs, Reverend Sullivan has established an aerospace firm and a garment factory.[93] In 1965, a group of Negroes organized the nonprofit Greater Philadelphia Enterprises Development Corporation to stimulate loans for small businessmen, foster employment opportunities, and provide counseling. In 1969, this organization helped six major industrial concerns expand employment opportunities in target areas through sponsorship of mortgage loans totaling more than $8 million.[94]

Private Business. In 1970, the American Bankers Association set a goal of lending $1 billion for minority businesses during a five-year period. Fifty-five cities were selected for "a concentrated effort to improve minority business."[95] We have referred to programs started by companies such as IBM, AVCO, Fairchild Hiller, Aerojet, EG&G, Warner-Swasey, Xerox, and General Electric,

[90] DeLorean, *op. cit.*, pp. 17–18.
[91] Innis, *op. cit.*, p. 55.

[92] Skala, *op. cit.*, pp. 166–168.
[93] DeLorean, *op. cit.*, p. 18; Skala, *op. cit.*, p. 163.
[94] *The New York Times*, Feb. 22, 1970.
[95] *The Plain Dealer*, May 1, 1970. For an account of bank-lending programs to minority small business enterprises in New York City, Detroit, Philadelphia, Seattle, Baltimore, Boston, and Washington, D.C., see *The New York Times*, Apr. 11, 1971, pp. 1, 8.

as well as by the National Alliance of Business and the Interracial Council for Business Opportunity. One business leader and former government official says that despite current and proposed changes, industry is "still falling far short of both its obligations and its potentialities."[96]

Government. In 1968–1969, the SBA had black entrepreneurship teams promoting black business in more than 40 cities throughout the country. The agency sought also to increase substantially SBA loans for ghetto businesses, under liberalized lending concepts.[97] We have mentioned SBA's Project OWN for the promotion of bank credit for minority entrepreneurs with a system of government guarantees. A proposal by the Federal Task Force on Urban Problems for the establishment of an urban development bank to finance ghetto business projects with low cost loans, as the World Bank does for underdeveloped countries, has not been accepted.[98] Programs sponsored by such government agencies as the EDA of the Department of Commerce, HUD, and OEO have been mentioned previously.

Methods and General Principles. Earlier discussions in this chapter have included such general principles and methods as: guaranteed markets, preferential treatment in lending, consultation through business assistance programs, the training of managers, and franchising.

A Special Report on Minority Businesses

To our discussion of minority businesses, we append excerpts from the deliberations of the participants in the Thirty-fifth American Assembly[99] on BLACK ECONOMIC DEVELOPMENT, at Harriman, New York, on April 24–27, 1969. According to the final report of the Thirty-fifth Assembly, "the statement represents general agreement; however no one was asked to sign it, and it should not be assumed that every participant subscribes to every recommendation."

Black economic development is not a panacea for the nation's racial ills. It is a vital thrust of the drive toward equality among the races—the logical culmination of a decade of disillusionment in which integration and employment programs by themselves were seen to have effected little improvement of the social order.

Having tested the programs for change and found them wanting, blacks now seek the opportunity to evolve their own options. It should be recognized that there can be no separate and autonomous black economy over the long run, for this would stifle the free commerce from which such an economy must draw its vitality, and it would thus be self-defeating. But blacks want effective control of the economic institutions in their own communities. This should not preclude general involvement elsewhere.

To do this most will initially need, in addition to their own talents, energies and efforts, the advice, assistance and support of the white business community. The exclusion of blacks from business opportunity in the past has left them with neither the capital nor a reserve of trained, experienced, and immediately available talent upon which to build business structures in the present.

. . .

Here and there in the nation are signs of nascent movement toward fairer and more creative lending and bonding policies. A number of large corporations have recently created urban affairs divisions and are beginning to investigate ways and means of promoting and assisting black enterprises. A few corporations are already supporting black manufacturing ventures. The emergence of dynamic new black enterprises and the performance of the few spin-off ventures thus far formed are perhaps more encouraging. Black communities have developed a sharpened focus on capital formation. Many diverse attempts are

[96] Howard J. Samuels, "Prejudice in the Marketplace," in C. Glock and E. Siegelman (eds.), *Prejudice, U.S.A.*, Praeger, 1969, p. 157.

[97] DeLorean, *op. cit.*, p. 18. For an interesting account of the SBA's attempts to establish "a meaningful program of black capitalism," see Howard J. Samuels, "How to Even the Odds," *The New York Times*, Dec. 21, 1969, pp. 22–26. In December, 1969, Mr. Samuels criticized the Nixon Administration for "abandonment" of the SBA. He said that the money spent in capital loans fell far short of the mark for a successful program.

[98] DeLorean, *op. cit.*, p. 18.

[99] The American Assembly, an affiliate of Columbia University, with offices in the Graduate School of Business holds meetings and publishes books on matters of public interest. Haddad and Pugh, *op. cit.*, Appendix.

being made within these communities to develop more job skills, more black managers, and new black enterprises.

But the commitment of the mass of the white business community still must be made. For example, even under the 90 percent guarantees of the Small Business Administration, white financial institutions remain generally reluctant to make funds available to black enterprises.

Only by recognizing its repressive role in the disparity of the economic order can business begin to make the fundamental change in operational behavior that is so urgently required. Given the willingness, the alert businessman working with the black community can find attractive opportunities and the promise of profit. Incentives such as tax allowances, write downs, and the like may stimulate his interest, yet he can enter into a relationship with black entrepreneurs in the sense of sharing a responsibility for change. The motives, pecuniary or compassionate, need not be mutually exclusive.

Black economic development is bound to no formula. It can proceed in a number of possible ways, including among others:

Community-owned corporations supporting local enterprise and social services;

Black-white partnership arrangements which may include provisions for gradual divestiture of interest by the white partner;

To insure and expedite parity within the system, The American Assembly makes the following recommendations:

1. It is urgent and critical that the national effort and emphasis designed to curtail poverty in our nation be intensified. Therefore the Assembly strongly urges the Administration and the Congress not to cut but to substantially expand current levels of federal participation in housing, community development, poverty, manpower, and educational programs.

. . .

2. The Assembly urgently calls upon the President, the Congress and the American people to reallocate budget funds in adequate volume to launch immediately a massive program of economic development, not unlike the Marshall Plan, to achieve rapidly emancipation for black and other minority Americans who have been denied the opportunity to participate equally in the rewards of the American economy.

. . .

3. The Assembly calls for the formation of a "National Development Corporation" and a variety of local development corporations, to carry out the mandate of the second recommendation.

This proposed Corporation, although chartered by the Congress, would be non-governmental, and operate as a quasi-public institution.

The Corporation would make effective use of available governmental resources, but not be dependent on yearly Congressional appropriations. It would have the authority to issue stocks and bonds for capitalization and expansion.

The Corporation would provide loan and equity capital for minority enterprises, provide technical assistance and managerial training, and conduct research and demonstration programs. It would participate in both secure and high risk ventures.

. . .

Autonomous inner-city industries assisted, if necessary, by compensatory devices such as sheltered markets, guaranteed loans, and technical and managerial help from outside agencies and corporations;

Location of branch operations of big business in the inner-city, especially where they are used to increase black involvement throughout the total enterprise.

Within the framework of a black-white alliance, inner-city entrepreneurs might also be able to evolve their own unique economic organizations such as cooperatives and profit-sharing ventures.

The long-range goal of black economic development is to generate the wealth to achieve social, political, and economic parity—in short, to enable the black community to build a more satisfying and self-sufficient life for its people and all Americans. The more immediate goal is to raise incomes.

. . .

These plans must provide for maximum encouragement of individual private enterprise, including cooperatives, while at the same time recognizing total community needs.

4. These plans must also take into account the needs of the community as *defined* by the community.

Therefore the Assembly also recommends the creation of autonomous local development corporations with wide powers to raise and use private and public resources, and calls upon municipal governments and private institutions to stimulate the rapid development of these local corporations by the use of local purchasing powers, and other such devices, to channel economic prowess to the local community corporations.

The Assembly calls upon an organization such as the Urban Coalition to take the next step and organize the effort to draft and implement the blueprint for a "National Development Corporation."

5. The Assembly recommends the establishment of a loan "discount" mechanism to accelerate the involvement of financial institutions in the rapid expansion of black economic development. This could be done through a new network of federally chartered and financed regional "discount banks" that could function through use of the existing physical facilities of the Federal Reserve banks. These so-called "discount banks" would be prepared to purchase on presentation at face value without interest and without recourse to the seller, loans made to the black and other minority communities in urban and rural centers. The creation of such a system would provide added incentive and protection to those who enter this field of lending, and would expand existing loan guarantee programs. It would also be helpful to liberalize the existing discount practices at the Federal Reserve banks.

6. The requirements of surety companies for securing bonds are experience and sufficient working capital to execute construction projects under consideration. This generally means a small contractor must be able to provide sufficient working capital to carry his job to 20 percent of completion before he is reimbursed. This lack of working capital is an insurmountable problem for small contractors and a constraint on their growth.

One device exists which will permit the smaller contractor to compete—the use of licensed builder's control companies. This service is currently available in the private sector at competitive prices with bonding companies. It provides support to the contractor and assures that the building project will be completed as planned.

Therefore we recommend a shift in private and governmental policy to a position which would permit the contractor the option of either obtaining a bond for a job or using the services of a local builder's control company. The Assembly recognizes this may require special regulations to protect the government's investment.

7. The Assembly recommends that a national effort be initiated to assist potential black entrepreneurs and to train and educate future executives. These programs can be initiated at the graduate business school level, and at the community level where, with the help of local in-

dustry, rapid business training programs can be developed. A continual flow of this trained talent will be needed to supply the demands of rapid economic growth.

8. The Assembly recommends that tax and other incentives be used, as they have been used and are now used, to interest traditional investors to participate in the rapid development of an underutilized national resource.

9. Black economic development* also requires the immediate ending of racial discrimination in labor unions. Certain unions have been among the organizations most reluctant to permit members of minority groups to participate in the important task of rebuilding our nation. This must stop. The Assembly calls upon federal, state and local governments, the unions themselves, and the industries which contract with them, to provide equal opportunity for training and employment to minority groups.

It would seem imperative that all private and governmental efforts be used to relieve the overt and covert economic, social and political restraints which have served as effective barriers to full participation.

These barriers have been clearly identified. What remains now is to organize the effort to remove them.[100]

NEGROES IN THE PROFESSIONS

We have described some of the obstacles and some of the accomplishments related to Negroes in business. Their participation in professional jobs is somewhat more extensive, and perhaps growing more rapidly, but there are major difficulties in this segment of the economy as well.

The Medical Field

In 1965, Negro physicians and surgeons comprised only 2 percent of the profession in the United States, compared with 10.7 percent in the field of social welfare, 7.8 percent of the teachers, and 3 percent of the college teachers.[101] In 1968, the proportion of Negro

* The phrase "black economic development" is an expedient. It should be understood to embrace not only blacks but all disadvantaged cultural groups in urban and rural America.

[100] 35th American Assembly, *Final Report*, pp. 4–9.

[101] H. M. Bond, "The Negro Scholar and Professional in America," in John P. Davis, (ed.), *The American Negro Reference Book*, Prentice-Hall, 1966, pp. 579–580.

physicians was still 2 percent; less than 2 percent of the dentists were black and fewer than 5 percent of the nurses. Of the more than 300,000 doctors in the United States in 1968, the number of black physicians was estimated to be between 5800 and 7000. An average of 6400 physicians in the black population of 22,000,000 represented a ratio of one black doctor to 3500 people, compared with one physician for 670 people for the United States. The number of black practitioners has decreased in some parts of the country, particularly in the Deep South. In Georgia, there was a decrease in the number of black physicians from 150 in 1958 to about 100 in 1968, with most of the decrease occurring in the rural areas. In Mississippi the number of black doctors has decreased to the point that they constitute less than 5 percent of all physicians in a state where 42 percent of the population is black. On the West Coast, however, there has been a marked increase in the number of Negro physicians. In Los Angeles, the number of black doctors rose from 50 in 1963 to 400 five years later, and in San Francisco from approximately 100 to between 150 and 200.[102]

Special efforts have been made in recent years to recruit black medical personnel. The talent recruitment program of the National Medical Association has been enlarged and has received support from the American Medical Association and the Association of American Medical Colleges. A survey conducted by the latter association in 1968 showed that 24 medical colleges had special recruiting programs for minority groups at four-year colleges and 20 at senior-high, junior-high, and grade schools. Scholarships and fellowships to offset much of the high cost of medical education have become plentiful. Morais says that in 1968 there were more financial grants available for tuition and other needs than there were black applicants applying for them.[103] A report prepared by the National Medical Association-American Medical Association Liaison Committee, published in the *Journal of the American Medical Association* in October, 1969, cited the increase in the percentage of Blacks enrolled in the class of 1972 and called for an adequately financed special recruitment program to end the shortage of Negro physicians. The report mentioned two obstacles in the present recruitment of Negro medical students—"the use of white, middle-class-oriented tests and too little flexibility to help the Negro student adjust to medical school standards." The report said also that recruitment of disadvantaged students requires a special form of financial assistance that goes beyond the usual tuition needs and provides for living expenses as well. According to the authors of this report, federal funds will be needed to meet this need.[104] In November, 1970, the Association of American Medical Colleges reported that minority student enrollment "has increased by almost 50 percent over that in last year's freshman class." According to this report, Negroes numbered 697, or 6.1 percent of the first-year class, an increase of 257 students from 1969 when that group constituted 4.3 percent of the medical student enrollment. The association said that "American Indians increased from 7 to 11; Americans with Spanish surnames from 44 to 73; Orientals from 140 to 190; Puerto Ricans increased from 96 to 113 and the number in medical schools other than the University of Puerto Rico showed a jump from 5 to 23."[105]

As a result of various efforts and pressures, about 300 Negro students entered the nation's medical schools in 1968, an increase over previous years. These students constituted 3.1 percent of the first-year class of 9653. Less than 2.5 percent of the medical students in 1967–1968 were black. During that year, only 51 students in the 27 medical schools in the South were nonwhite.[106] More than two-thirds of the approximately 200 Negro graduates of medical schools in the United States in 1968 came from Howard

[102] H. H. Morais, "Medicine and Health," in Romero, *op. cit.*, pp. 365, 374.

[103] *Ibid.*, p. 366.

[104] Lawrence K. Altman, "Funds Urged to Attract Negro Doctors," *The New York Times*, Oct. 5, 1969.

[105] *The New York Times*, Nov. 2, 1970.

[106] Morais, *op. cit.*, p. 368.

(88) and Meharry (49). Excluding these two medical schools, Negroes comprise only 1 percent of the students in American medical colleges. The Pacific region, with 11 medical schools ranks first in the percentage of Negro enrollment.[107]

Northwestern University's medical school has committed itself to an Urban Doctors Program that, beginning in 1972, will admit annually 25 selected inner-city high school graduates to a six-year program leading to the M.D. The plan calls for students to spend two years in an intensive premedical program at the Central Y.M.C.A. Community College, which is located near low-income areas of Chicago. This training will be followed by four years at the medical school. Throughout the six-year period, the student will commute from home and will be involved constantly in health and medical services in his own home area. A majority of the students will be black, but some will come from other disadvantaged minorities, including poor whites. Funding will be largely private, but some federal aid may be available. It is not expected that all, or perhaps even most, of these special students will remain in the ghettos after they become successful physicians. The sponsors of the program hope that the student who remains in close touch with his background will be more likely to respond to the needs he knows. Four other medical schools in the Chicago area have indicated that they may join the program at a later date.[108]

Because of the shortage of physicians, 137 medical school graduates in 1968 had no difficulty in obtaining internships at sixty-four hospitals. In contrast to earlier years, black doctors now have no problem in obtaining residencies. More posts are available than there are applicants for them.[109]

In the 1950s and 1960s, policies with respect to the admission of Negroes to county medical societies varied regionally. In typical cities of the Northeast, Midwest, and Pacific Coast—Philadelphia, New York, Boston, Chicago, Gary, Indianapolis, Detroit, and Los Angeles—there was no discrimination, although in some, e.g., Detroit, some Negro physicians complained that the associations had not done enough to bring about integration in the hospitals. Membership in a county medical society is a prerequisite to membership in the AMA, and it has often been charged that many state and county societies make it impossible for a Negro physician to join these groups. In the past, if an applicant alleged that discrimination in a local society kept him out of the AMA, the complaint was simply registered with the House of Delegates. New by-laws adopted by the House of Delegates in December, 1968, open the way for admission to the AMA of nearly 1000 black doctors hitherto barred by local branches in Alabama, Mississippi, Florida, Georgia, South Carolina, and Louisiana. Since 1969, a complaint concerning discrimination is referred to the AMA judicial council. If the council finds that the allegations are true, it is required to "admonish or censure" the local association. Repeated violations could lead to the expulsion of the local group from the AMA. Since physicians are required in most states to belong to the local medical society in order to practice at the leading hospitals, exclusion from the local association has meant a virtual ban on Negro physicians practicing in major metropolitan hospitals, particularly in the South.[110]

While the AMA was making changes at the national level, black physicians complained about slow progress at the local level. According to a survey in the fall of 1968, black practitioners in county medical societies were disappointed that their " 'views (were) not sought in policy making and

---

[107] Altman, *op. cit.* Eighty-four American medical schools have at least one black student enrolled. Most of those with no Negro enrollment are state-supported schools, some in states that have a small Negro population. In general, private schools have a larger Negro enrollment than state-supported schools and showed a slightly greater increase in this enrollment over the past few years. Of the predominantly white schools, the University of Illinois graduates the largest number of black physicians. *Ibid.*

[108] Fred Hechinger, "A Plan to Get M.D.'s Into the Ghettos," *The New York Times*, May 9, 1971, Section 4, p. 9.

[109] Morais, *op. cit.*, p. 368.

[110] Fraser Kent, "Negro Doctors May Get Full AMA Membership," *The Plain Dealer*, June 19, 1968, p. 39.

little effort (was) made to advance them to responsible posts.'" Negro doctors, especially in a number of southern local medical units, "felt that they were being accepted in a limited and formal sense and not as members of a team."[111]

Noteworthy developments in the medical field at the national level during 1968 included the election of Dr. Paul B. Cornely, head of the Department of Preventive Medicine at Howard University, as president of the American Public Health Association. During the annual meeting, the organization's black members formed a caucus to work for definite objectives within the national organization. Also, at the annual meeting of the American Hospital Association in 1968, a group of approximately 30 black hospital administrators formed a new unit within the national group. The purpose of this caucus is to "improve educational facilities for health workers of minority groups and to study the problems involved in supplying health care to impoverished communities."[112]

Racial discrimination is still prevalent in the important matter of gaining admission to hospital staffs. Dr. Howard A. Rusk commented in The New York Times of April 7, 1968, that "of the 23,000 physicians in New York City, 7,000 (had) no hospital affiliations and more than half of these (were) Negro physicians." Time reported on August 23, 1968, that "in Chicago and other major cities, it is still far more difficult for a Negro doctor to get into a good hospital than it is for a white." In 1968 the president of the National Medical Association said that "the number of Negro physicians admitted on hospital medical staffs, particularly in large cities, remains relatively small." Dr. James M. Whittico, Jr. and the delegates to the annual NMA convention welcomed an AMA offer to work closely with the AMA to investigate cases of alleged racial discrimination, including those involving hospital staffs. The NMA stands for a universal system of open staffs for all hospitals.[113]

Discrimination and segregation are still far from uncommon in the treatment of black hospital patients. Morais says: "Often black patients were consigned to basements, attics and deteriorating older wings of hospitals. In the South Negro patients were not infrequently relegated to segregated quarters, while in the North they were at times ingeniously placed in separate wards and semi-private rooms. And if they were poor —as many of them were—they were treated by an over-worked staff in cramped, dilapidated wards devoid of some of the most elementary sanitary safeguards." In 1968, medical civil rights leaders felt that there had been only token enforcement of Title VI of the Civil Rights Act of 1964. Under Title VI, government agencies were directed to withhold federal funds from hospitals practicing discrimination. From 1966 until early in 1968, HEW initiated enforcement proceedings against 35 hospitals. Only 12 of these lost federal financial assistance because of noncompliance with the law. Considerable concern has also been expressed because of the passage of the Talmadge Amendment to Title VI, which made it possible for non-complying hospitals to be paid by Medicare and Medicaid for "emergency" treatment of patients.[114]

Medicare and Medicaid now play an important part in providing badly needed health services to the poor. In 1968, nearly 20 million persons 65 or over were covered under the law. Approximately a third were impoverished, and Blacks comprised a disproportionate share of this group. Since 1968 OEO has increased its program of comprehensive health-care centers in poor neighborhoods. This program was instituted to provide services that would include medical

---

[111] Morais, op. cit., p. 369.
[112] Ibid., p. 369.
[113] Ibid., pp. 369, 371.

[114] Ibid., p. 371. Of the more than 21,000 emergency Medicare claims filed in the country in one fiscal year, 17,700 cases came from the South, and more than half of these were from Alabama and Mississippi. Two hospitals in Mississippi which did not meet the civil rights standards for Medicare submitted 2700 claims. In November, 1968, HEW tried to close the loophole by proposing a new regulation providing payment to a noncomplying hospital only if it was the nearest one to the patient involved or the nearest one equipped to meet the particular emergency. Ibid., p. 371.

and dental care, immunization, diagnostic tests, rehabilitation, and care of drug problems. Government financed, these health-care centers are administered by medical schools, county medical societies, health departments, hospitals, and community associations. Black physicians have taken an active part in the development of these centers and have been appointed to major administrative positions in a number of them. Among the best known of these centers are those in the Bedford-Stuyvesant area in Brooklyn, N.Y., and in Nashville, Tennessee.[115]

Some Negro physicians and dentists have been concerned as to whether their position is threatened by the growing provision of free clinical and hospital care for low-income people. The NMA, however, adopted a resolution favoring the Medicare program. The lack of confidence in Negro physicians shown by some Negroes, especially persons in the higher- and middle-income brackets, is a matter of concern to the Negro practitioner.[116] Some Negro doctors—in cities such as Atlanta—still object to the efforts on the part of other Negro physicians to bring about complete desegregation of medical facilities on the grounds that open facilities will lead eventually to the loss of patients to white physicians.[117]

The shortage of Negro dentists is even greater than is that of physicians. According to the dean of the Howard University College of Dentistry, the number of black dentists has decreased in the last 30 years to the point that in 1968 there was only one black dentist per 11,500 black people. In addition, fewer and fewer black students are enrolling in dentistry.[118]

The situation that prevails in dentistry with reference to the enrollment of students is found also in nursing. The American Nurses' Association abolished its racial restriction on membership in 1946, and by 1962, 1152 professional schools of nursing had no racial or religious restrictions on admission.[119] In May, 1968, the American Nurses' Association adopted a resolution calling for an intensification of efforts to eliminate discriminatory practices within and outside the health field.[120]

The Ministry

The ministerial profession was the first to be established among Negroes, and for many years ministers were the principal leaders of the Negro race. During the second quarter of the twentieth century, this leadership was shared, to a considerable extent, by lawyers, physicians, dentists, social workers, teachers, and journalists. Nevertheless, the ministry has continued to be an important profession in the Negro group, and clergymen are second in numbers only to teachers among Negro professional people. The clientele of Negro ministers, like that of Negro teachers and lawyers, is limited mainly to the Negro group.

On the whole, the religions of Negroes in the United States and elsewhere have tended to reinforce the social and political status quo, but nearly everywhere some religious leaders and groups have sought to change existing structures. This was true during the periods of slavery and Reconstruction and, in recent years, the role of priest-political leader has been played with considerable success by such men as Adam Clayton Powell, Martin Luther King, Jr., and Jesse Jackson. Since 1965, many ministers of black churches have emerged as leaders of the black rebellion. Clifton Brown says that black clergymen in white denominations have often had a second-class status, that is, they often earn less than their white colleagues, generally they are kept with black congregations, and they are relegated to lesser positions in the hierarchies, if they are included at all. There are, of course, exceptions to this—black bishops in the Methodist and Episcopal churches, for ex-

---

[115] *Ibid.*, pp. 374–375.
[116] Bond, *op. cit.*, pp. 579–580.
[117] E. Holsendolph, *op. cit.*, p. 154.
[118] Morais, *op. cit.*, p. 366.

[119] Mary E. Carnegie and Estelle M. Osborne, "Integration in Professional Nursing," *The Crisis*, Jan., 1962, pp. 5–9.
[120] Morais, *op. cit.*, p. 369.

ample, interracial ministerial staffs in a few churches, and vigorous support for civil rights on the part of many white clergymen. But judged against their own standards, churches have not made major progress in eliminating separation and discrimination. Partly because some black clergymen have felt stymied within the regular channels of these churches, and in part in response to an increasing sense of black identity, "black power" had begun to emerge in white churches by 1967.[121]

The significance of black awareness among black clergymen and of the caucuses that had been formed among these clergymen became obvious at a meeting of the Committee of Black Churchmen held in St. Louis in October, 1968. According to Brown, "many delegates expressed the opinion that there was no justification for black churchmen participating in predominantly white churches if those churches were not willing to involve themselves in the plight of black people."[122] Another event in 1968 was the formation of the Association of Black Seminarians. Black seminarian caucuses began at Princeton University but soon spread to other theological schools in the Northeast. At these consultations, the theology in the black church and the curricula of predominantly white seminaries were examined in relation to black institutions.[123]

Priests attending the Black Catholic Clergy Caucus in Detroit in April, 1968, denounced the Catholic Church in the United States as "primarily a racist institution." In its list of demands, the caucus asked for increased efforts to recruit Negroes for the priesthood and that a department be established to deal with "the Church's role in the black people's struggle for freedom." Even within the Roman Catholic religious orders, black consciousness has become evident. The first National Black Sisters' Conference, held in Pittsburgh in 1968, was attended by 150 black nuns from 76 religious communities.[124]

Brown's assessment of the "black power" movement among the clergy is incisive.

It was among the black membership (particularly the clergy) of mainly white churches that the most vocal element of black religion was found in 1968. The black caucuses were the agents of this. Yet these caucuses represented only two million of the twenty-two million black church members in the United States. Consequently the indictments, the challenges and the innovative schemes of the black caucuses lacked the broad power base by which they could have assumed a leadership role in black religion. Furthermore, the black caucuses, too, have often spoken in different voices, reflecting the sad fact that as in the traditional Negro churches, denominationalism has created barriers which prevent concerted action on common problems.[125]

Further attention is given to the black clergy and to the leadership of the Black Muslim movement in Chapter 17, "Minorities and Religion."

The Legal Profession

Thirty-five years ago the practice of Negro lawyers was limited largely to civil cases or divorce and to the affairs connected with Negro churches and fraternal orders. At that time a Negro attorney had little chance of winning a case in a southern court where "protection by a 'respectable' white person usually counts more . . . for a Negro client than would even the best representation on the part of a Negro lawyer." Johnson reported that by 1938 the courts had improved in many southern cities in the sense that Negro lawyers did not have to give as much thought to dealing with racial factors as they did with law.[126]

Edwards found that even in the border areas and in some parts of the North, skepticism concerning the Negro lawyer's ability to obtain justice in the courts was evident in the 1950s. Many Negroes in these places gave legal work to white attorneys, and some important Negro lawyers refused to

[121] Clifton F. Brown, "Black Religion—1968," in Romero, *op. cit.*, p. 349.

[122] *Ibid.*, p. 349.

[123] *Ibid.*, p. 350.

[124] *Ibid.*, pp. 350–351.

[125] *Ibid.*, p. 352. It should be noted that there are 22 million Blacks in the United States, not 22 million black church members.

[126] Charles S. Johnson, *The Negro College Graduate*, Univ. of North Carolina Press, 1938, p. 237.

take a case to court without having a white practitioner as an associate. The same research, however, showed that the Negro public's conception of the Negro lawyer was changing. Several reasons were given for this change. Negro lawyers no longer associated themselves with white counsel; an increasing number of Negroes believed that Negro lawyers were competent and that they would be able to obtain a fair hearing in court. Negro lawyers played a leading part in the drive to expand the civil rights of Negroes.[127] Negroes have been appointed to federal judgships and appointed or elected as judges in municipal courts. Opportunities for Negroes to be more active in politics, especially in the South, have helped to enhance the status of Negro lawyers.[128]

For 30 years the majority of civil rights cases in the United States have been handled by the NAACP Legal Defense and Educational Fund, Inc. (LDF). In 1968, LDF consisted of 25 full-time staff lawyers and several hundred cooperating attorneys on call for occasional work. The LDF budget increased from $295,000 in 1958 to $2.4 million in 1968.[129]

Negro lawyers and judges of both sexes were 1.02 percent of the total engaged in the legal profession in 1960. In 1970, only 3000 (1 percent) of the 325,000 lawyers in the United States were black. To reduce this imbalance the LDF is expanding its lawyer-training program and plans to award scholarships to 300 students each year over the next five years. This program will attempt to double the number of black lawyers throughout the United States during the next seven years.[130] In 1963, it was estimated that 75 of the nation's 8000 judges were Negro. According to this estimate, Negroes constituted about 1 percent of the judiciary, the same proportion they were of employed lawyers in the United States. In 1967 Thurgood Marshall, former director of the NAACP LDF was appointed associate justice of the U.S. Supreme Court.[131]

The Teaching Profession

In the Negro group, the number of persons engaged in teaching far exceeds that in other professions. The development of a competent group of Negro teachers has been greatly complicated in the past by the extremely low salaries offered, by racial wage discrimination, by racial differentials in teaching loads, by lack of professional training, and by the strong controls exerted on Negro teachers by the white community. Not all of these conditions have changed, particularly the degree of white control over Negro schools in the rural South, but, as we point out in Chapter 18, there has been considerable improvement in the overall Negro public school situation in the past 20 years.

Depending upon the nature of the school system and the school, the status and role of the Negro public school teacher changed to a greater or lesser degree in the 1960s. In Chapter 18 we discuss some of the consequences of: increasing or decreasing racial isolation and desegregation in the public schools, the reduction of differences in school environments, the growing emphasis on black awareness and pride among both teachers and students, greater decentralization and a larger degree of community control of schools in some northern cities, the strain and tension for black and white teachers and administrators alike in the integration of schools, the loss of thousands of jobs by black teachers and principals through nominal desegregation, and the

---

[127] Greenberg says: "The Howard [University] graduates have in recent years been joined by those from southern state law schools desegregated under the law. In Arkansas, Maryland, North Carolina, Texas, and elsewhere Negroes who have attended state schools now appear in civil rights cases. The Negro lawyer handles 99 percent of the southern antidiscrimination litigation, and most of it in the North. . . . The southern white attorney who will handle a desegregation case is almost unique. Yet many large Negro centers and even some important cities in the South still have no Negro lawyer or but a few. . . ." Jack Greenberg, *Race Relations and American Law*, Columbia, 1959, p. 22.

[128] G. Franklin Edwards, *The Negro Professional Class*, Free Press, 1949, pp. 135–138.

[129] James M. Nabrit, III, "The Law—1968," in Romero, *op. cit.*, p. 162.

[130] *The Christian Science Monitor*, May 25, 1969.

[131] Bond, *op. cit.*, p. 583.

quality of integration where it has occurred.

In recent years, several predominantly white educational organizations and institutions have selected black men and women as their leaders. Mrs. Elizabeth D. Koontz was elected president of the National Education Association in 1968. The Los Angeles board of education has chosen the Reverend James E. Jones as its president,[132] and, in the 1960s, the New York public school system appointed several black principals.

Earlier studies of Negroes engaged in college teaching revealed considerable dissatisfaction with the profession. The problems that Negro colleges and college teachers have faced in the past and those that are being confronted now are discussed in Chapter 19. In a study of the Negro professional class, Edwards found that 92 male college teachers (84 were members of the liberal arts faculty of Howard University) listed "interest in work" as the primary motivation and "best job opportunity at the time of beginning" as the next most important reason for entering the teaching profession. Further analysis, however, revealed that few of Edwards' respondents were interested in teaching and the academic way of life. In interviews, the teachers in the sample said they were interested in a particular field—philosophy, mathematics, language, etc.—and that the opportunity to teach was the only employment open to them upon the completion of their training. Teachers listed a larger number of alternate occupational choices than did those interviewed in other professions. One-fourth said that their primary interest had been in becoming physicians, and many of these persons said they had begun teaching with a view to saving money to enter medical school. Many of the teachers included in this study expressed dissatisfaction with their present employment, due, in considerable part, Edwards thinks, to two main factors: (1) the low pay received by teachers, and (2) the institutional controls to which teachers are subjected. No significant difference was found between teacher and physician respondents in intelligence as measured by high-school grades, and this is true also of the parental income of the two groups. There was a significant difference between the amount of financial support given by the parents for professional training.[133]

Among recent developments that have strongly influenced the position of Negro college and university teachers is the increasing number of black students seeking admission to and entering colleges, the distribution of students in publicly and privately supported institutions, the spread of the black power movement to higher education, the introduction of black studies programs, and the competition among both black and predominantly white institutions for black scholars and administrators. An increasing number of white universities have appointed black educators to serve black students. Andrew Billingsley served as assistant chancellor of academic affairs at the University of California, Berkeley. A former president of two Negro colleges, Samuel D. Proctor, has served as dean of special projects for the University of Wisconsin. Carl A. Fields was appointed dean at Princeton University in 1968, and Columbia University chose Franklin H. Williams as director of its Center of Urban and Minority Affairs. At least three white institutions have appointed a Negro as president. C. R. Wharton is president of Michigan State University, Arthur Banks is president of a junior college in Connecticut, and James Colston has been appointed president of Brooklyn Community College.[134] Wade Ellis, formerly of Oberlin College, is now serving as associate dean of the Graduate School at the University of Michigan, and there are many other Negro educators holding administrative posts in predominantly white institutions.

Engineering and Related Professions

Before 1950 few jobs in engineering were open to Negroes and few Negroes were be-

[132] Prince E. Wilson, "Education of Blacks, 1968," in Romero, *op. cit.*, p. 98.

[133] Edwards, *op. cit.*, pp. 138–141.
[134] Wilson, *op. cit.*, p. 98.

ing trained in this field. The strong demand for engineering and related technical personnel following the outbreak of hostilities in Korea brought increased job opportunities to Negroes.[135] Since then the enrollment of Negro students in engineering has increased, but the increase has not been large. In 1955, only 150 (.65 percent) of 23,000 graduating engineers were Negroes.[136] Among the 30,000 engineering graduates in the United States in 1970, only 200 (.67 percent) were Negroes. In 1970, efforts were being made to correct this imbalance. For example, the Cleveland Urban League started a pilot program to prepare inner-city high school students for careers in engineering and architecture.[137]

According to the U.S. Census taken in 1960, 3378 male Negro engineers constituted four-tenths of 1 percent of all employed engineers in the country. Bond points out that engineering is a relatively new profession among American Negroes. The School of Engineering of Howard University, the principal training school for this professional group, graduated its first class in 1910. During the next 55 years, the school granted 987 degrees in civil, electrical, and mechanical engineering as well as in architecture. In addition to these graduates, Negroes have studied at a number of predominantly white technological institutions in the United States, including, in recent years, such southern schools as Georgia Institute of Technology and Clemson University. Recently several predominantly Negro engineering schools have been inaugurated in the South —at South Carolina Agricultural and Technical College, Tennessee State Agricultural and Mechanical University, Tuskegee Institute, and Prairie View Agricultural and Mechanical College. According to Bond, none of the predominantly black institutions has the facilities to conduct engineering educa-

tion "over the broad scope presented by modern technology."[138]

Negroes in Government Service

The Civil Service Act of 1883 ended half a century of the spoils system. Negroes had not been the recipients of many jobs under the spoils regime, and at the time of the creation of the Civil Service Commission only 620 Negroes were employed by the government in Washington.[139] In the years 1885 to 1889 the number of Negro federal employees increased to 2393. As the total number of government employees grew, there was an increase in Negro employees, but the number of Negroes in responsible jobs declined. In 1912 Negroes held more than 19,000 jobs in the federal service, including a number of important positions as collectors of customs, collectors of ports, postmasters, paymasters, and diplomats which had carried over from previous years.

During the administration of Woodrow Wilson, "humanitarian and citizen of the world," Negroes were completely eliminated from responsible government positions. A Negro auditor of the Navy and other officials were asked to resign, and Negro postmasters were ousted. This was no mere party action; these men were not replaced by other Negroes.

Appointing officers during Wilson's administration used two personnel procedures to keep Negroes out of clerical and other desirable civil service jobs. The first method, the "rule of three," dated back to the early years of the civil service; it allowed the appointing officer to choose among the three highest eligibles. The second method was the requiring of a photograph. These two practices made it possible to avoid appointing most Negro applicants, and they were continued under Harding, Coolidge, and Hoover. The number of Negroes employed

[135] Eli Ginzberg, *The Negro Potential*, Columbia, 1956, pp. 12–13.

[136] L. T. Hawley, "The Negro's New Economic Life," *Fortune*, Sept., 1956, p. 254.

[137] Michael A. Hobbs, "Program Encourages Blacks to Be Engineers," *The Plain Dealer*, Aug. 31, 1970, p. 13A.

[138] Bond, *op. cit.*, pp. 586–587.

[139] For the experience of the Negro in government service prior to World War II, see John A. Davis and Cornelius L. Golightly, "Negro Employment in the Federal Government," *Phylon*, Fourth Quarter, 1945, pp. 337–340.

by the government steadily increased, but the jobs were mainly those of custodians.

During the depression the government had special problems of relief for Negroes. President Roosevelt and other white government officials attempted to get a fair share of employment for Negroes. However, most of the Negro appointees under Roosevelt in peacetime were not regular federal jobholders, but advisers dealing exclusively with Negro problems. The rank and file of Negro workers in the federal government continued to be mainly in custodial categories. Hayes found that Negroes constituted 8.4 percent of a total of 115,552 federal employees in Washington in 1938. This percentage was low in view of the fact that the 1940 census showed 28.2 percent of all persons in Washington to be Negroes. In 1938, 82,000 Negroes, or 9.9 percent of the total 861,914 government employees, were listed in the annual report of the Civil Service Commission. For the District of Columbia, 90 percent of the Negro government employees were in custodial service; 9.5 percent were in the clerical, administrative, fiscal, or clerical-mechanical classifications; and 0.5 percent were subprofessional.[140]

President Roosevelt issued Executive Order 8802 on June 25, 1941, and the Committee on Fair Employment Practice was appointed. The President asked all heads of departments and independent establishments to examine "their personnel policies and practices to the end that they may be able to assure me that in the Federal service the doors of employment are open to all loyal and qualified workers regardless of creed, race, or national origin." In March, 1942, Mr. Roosevelt authorized the FEPC to obtain employment data from all government agencies and departments.[141] By November 1942, the number of Negro government workers in the District of Columbia had increased to 17 percent of all employees. On July 31, 1943, Negroes constituted 12 percent of all federal workers as compared with 9.9 percent in 1938; they made up 18 percent of all persons

in departmental service (chiefly located in the District of Columbia).[142]

The war agencies in the federal government employed a large number of Negroes. According to Davis, 12 percent of their employees were Negroes, with black workers forming 11.8 percent of the army employees and 14.6 percent of the navy employees. Most of the army and navy workers were not in the classified service, although the war agencies as a group showed the best classification distribution of Negro employees. The highest utilization in terms of classifications and grades within these classifications came in the National War Labor Board, the Office of Price Administration, the War Manpower Commission, and the War Production Board.

During World War II the executive departments compared unfavorably with other agencies in the employment of Negroes. The Departments of Commerce, Interior, and Labor increased the numbers of Negroes employed and utilized them in more classifications during wartime. "The Treasury and the Post Office have usually hired large numbers of Negroes, but utilization has left much to be desired. On the whole, the records of Justice, State, and Agriculture have not been good, although some wartime improvement has been noted."[143]

The rule concerning the submission of photographs with applications was abolished in December, 1940; but an applicant's race can usually be ascertained. Ordinarily professional workers are interviewed by the official under whom they are to work. Formerly it was possible, when a newly appointed person proved to be a Negro, to find his work unsatisfactory and have him dismissed after a short time. It was also relatively easy to prevent Negroes from being upgraded. These procedures have been more difficult to invoke since the establishment of fair employment practices committees in the federal government beginning in 1948. These agencies are treated more fully in Chapter 14.

Negro employment at the Tennessee Valley

[140] *Ibid.*, p. 340.
[141] *Ibid.*, pp. 340–341.

[142] John A. Davis, Nondiscrimination in the Federal Services," *Annals*, Mar., 1946, p. 72.
[143] *Ibid.*, pp. 72–73.

Authority has varied from 8 to 12 percent in a region whose population is about 10 percent Negro. Most of the Negro TVA employees are found in trades and labor jobs rather than in white-collar positions, but Daves says that TVA has made as much, if not more, progress in the placement of Negroes in clerical, professional, and technical positions than any federal or private industry in the South.[144] This agency regularly conducts a campaign of recruitment and placement, including the seeking of qualified applicants in Negro schools and colleges.

The number of Negroes in federal service increased markedly during the 1960s, as did the proportion of Negroes holding positions of high rank and salary. In 1961, approximately 1000 Negroes (one-third of 1 percent) were employed in GS-12 to GS-18 categories, roughly the $10,000 to $25,000 salary range of 1966. In large part due to the urging of President Johnson and John Macy, chairman of the Civil Service Commission, executive agencies added 1411 Negroes to these categories between June, 1962, and early 1966, an increase of more than 100 percent. Of the "blue collar" federal employees in the "wage board" classification, the number of Negroes earning more than $8000 annually increased 582 percent between 1962 and the end of 1965. Of the 18,420 federal employees added in one year, June, 1964 to June, 1965, more than half were Negroes. During 1965 Johnson appointed 30 Negroes to positions paying from $25,000 to $35,000. In that year another 20 Negroes were appointed to positions paying from $19,000 to $25,000. In addition to the importance of these appointments to the recipients themselves, many of these appointees acquired the ability to influence the pattern of hiring, firing, and promotion in government, where full equality of opportunity does not yet exist.[145]

On February 24, 1966, the Civil Service Commission issued new regulations designed to open more federal jobs to Negroes and other minorities. These regulations included, for the first time, procedures for appealing grievances concerning racial discrimination to the commission from the agencies where they originate. Commission members said that a survey of minority employment in the federal government in July, 1965, showed that Negroes held 13.5 percent of federal jobs.[146]

In 1966, the postmasters of the nation's three largest post offices—New York, Chicago, and Los Angeles—were Negroes. A representative of the Post Office said that there was no design in this situation, but that it was the natural result of hiring large numbers of Negroes over a period of 40 years. In 1966 more than 100,000 of the department's 685,000 employees were Negroes. According to an official of the Post Office, while others were discriminating against Negroes, the department was hiring many competent Negroes and promoting them.[147]

By April, 1968, employees belonging to minority races held 497,725 (18.9 percent) of the 2,621,936 full-time federal government jobs—74,098 more than in June 1966. Most of the job gains during this period were made by Negroes, who held 14.9 percent of the federal jobs, compared with 13.9 percent in 1966. The chairman of the Civil Service Commission said that the gains registered by Negroes were in all grades and at all salary levels even though most were employed in the low and middle levels.[148]

Romero lists 70 Negroes appointed to major government positions during the Johnson administration. Among these appointments to positions carrying high levels of official responsibility were: Robert Weaver, Secretary of Housing and Urban Development; Thurgood Marshall, Associate Justice, U.S. Supreme Court; William H.

[144] J. H. Daves, "TVA and Negro Employment," *JNE*, Winter, 1955, pp. 87–90.

[145] Carl T. Rowan, "LBJ Opens Door for Negro," *The Plain Dealer*, Feb. 13, 1966.

[146] *The Plain Dealer*, Feb. 25, 1966.

[147] *The New York Times*, Nov. 13, 1966.

[148] *The Plain Dealer*, Apr. 25, 1968. The federal civilian work force dropped by nearly 8700 in the period November, 1969 to May, 1970, but minority group employees increased by approximately 1400. Minority groups (Negroes, Spanish-surnamed Americans, Oriental Americans, and American Indians) held 19.2 percent of federal jobs in May, 1970. *The New York Times*, Jan. 24, 1971, p. 48.

Hastie, Judge, U.S. Court of Appeals, Third Circuit; Constance Baker Motley, U.S. Judge, Southern District of New York; Andrew F. Brimmer, Member, Federal Reserve Board; Howard Jenkins, Jr., Member, National Labor Relations Board; Samuel Nabrit, Member, Atomic Energy Commission; Hobart Taylor, Jr., Member, Board of Directors, Export-Import Bank; Walter E. Washington, Mayor, Washington, D.C.; Samuel C. Adams, Jr., Overseas Director, Agency for International Development; Theodore M. Berry, Director, Community Action Program, OEO; Roy K. Davenport, Deputy Undersecretary, Department of the Army; and Harold Wood, Associate Director, United States Information Agency.[149]

The Armed Forces

On July 26, 1948, President Truman established, through Executive Order 9981, an advisory committee known as the President's Committee on Equality of Treatment and Opportunity in the Armed Services. This order declared it "to be the policy of the President that there shall be equality of treatment and opportunity for all persons in the armed services without regard to race, color, religion or national origin. This policy shall be put into effect as rapidly as possible, having due regard to the time required to effectuate any necessary changes without impairing efficiency or morale." While the scope of the committee's work included persons in the armed services of all racial, religious, and nationality groups, no evidence was presented to the committee indicating formally defined service policies denying equality of treatment and opportunity except in the case of Negroes. Inequality of treatment and opportunity for Negroes had official sanction and was incorporated in regulations. Although the committee sought a formula that would be applicable to all minorities, its report is limited throughout to recommendations affecting Negroes.[150]

The two basic questions that have faced military staffs in considering the question of Negro utilization are: (1) Do Negroes have the mental and technical qualifications to be used in the full range of military jobs?; and (2) Shall Negroes be utilized only in Negro units? The committee found that until quite recently the first question had been answered negatively and the second in the affirmative.

Negroes had served as enlisted men in the Navy's general service until the end of World War I, but Negro enlistments were stopped at that time. When enlistments were reopened in 1932, only the messman's branch recruited Negroes, and this situation continued until the middle of 1942. Several changes in policy were made in 1945; and on February 27, 1946, the Navy ordered that ". . . all restrictions governing types of assignments for which Negro naval personnel are eligible are hereby lifted. Henceforth, they shall be eligible for all types of assignments in all ratings in all activities and all ships of the naval service. . . . In the utilization of housing, messing, and other facilities, no special or unusual provisions will be made for the accommodation of Negroes." Within five years the Navy changed from a policy of complete exclusion of Negroes from general service to a policy of complete integration in general service.

The racial policy of the Air Force during World War II was that of the Army—a 10 percent quota on enlisted men, segregated units, and severely limited job opportunities. After the issuance of Executive Order 9981 in July, 1948, the Air Force began to develop a new policy. The new program provided that there be no strength quotas of minority groups on a troop basis; that qualified Negro personnel be assigned to any position vacancy; that all individuals, regardless of race, be given equal opportunity for appointment, advancement, professional improvement, promotion, and retention in all components of the Air Force. Among the conclusions of the President's committee on

---

[149] Romero, op. cit., pp. 469–472.
[150] President's Committee on Equality of Treatment and Opportunity in the Armed Services, Free-

dom to Serve, Government Printing Office, 1950, pp. 4–5. See also, Richard M. Dalfiume, Desegregation of the U.S. Armed Forces: Fighting on Two Fronts, 1939–1953, Univ. of Missouri Press, 1969.

the experience of the Navy and Air Force were these: The enlisted men were much more ready for integration than the officers had believed; segregation results in wastage and malassignment of manpower; integration, instead of presenting insurmountable difficulties, had brought a decrease in racial friction.[151]

The Army had had Negro units since the establishment of two infantry and two cavalry regiments in 1866. During World War I Negroes served in supply and supporting units, and also in two combat divisions. Despite the recommendations of several studies made by the Army War College between World War I and World War II that the Army never again form Negro units of divisional size, two Negro divisions were reactivated in World War II. According to the President's committee, the historical record proved that segregated units do not result in maximum efficient utilization. The Gillem Board, a special board of general officers appointed in October, 1945, concluded that segregation was necessary and recommended the retention of a Negro quota in proportion to the civilian population. This board made five specific recommendations, but two of these were not approved by the Army, and nothing was done about one of the recommendations that was approved. The committee found in 1949 that a large number of jobs in the field of Army occupations were still closed to Negroes. The same serious deprivation existed with respect to the opportunity to attend Army schools. The committee recommended to the Army in May, 1949, a four-point program for the achievement of the objective in Executive Order 9981:

1. Open up all Army jobs to qualified personnel without regard to race or color.
2. Open up all Army schools to qualified personnel without regard to race or color.
3. Rescind the policy restricting Negro assignments to racial units and overhead installations, and assign all Army personnel according to individual ability and Army need.
4. Abolish the racial quota.[152]

Between September, 1949, and March, 1950, the four recommendations were accepted by the Army.

The performance of Negro soldiers in segregated units both in World War I and in World War II was less effective than that of Whites. In World War II the quality of performance seemed to depend largely on the organization of the Negro troops. When they fought in platoons together with white soldiers, Negroes did well; most of those organized into larger units, such as companies, did less well.[153] The explanation of this difference is attributed to factors other than innate racial qualities. The great majority of the Negro soldiers were handicapped by inadequate schooling and by their home and community backgrounds. Their inferior status in American society had given them little understanding of the values for which the United States was fighting and little familiarity with the complex structure and technology of an organization such as the Army. Segregation in training and utilization had a depressing effect on morale, as did the shortage of competent officers, white and Negro. Many Whites who became officers had strong prejudices concerning Negroes and their abilities. Some who were unprejudiced became impatient at the slow learning ability of many Negroes. Color made the Negro soldier who did a poor job highly conspicuous.[154] There were numerous exceptions to the general performance referred to above. The 99th Fighter Squadron and the 332nd Fighter Group made outstanding records, the 2000 volunteer infantry replacements at Ardennes performed very well, and Negro troops gave strong support to combat units at Iwo Jima, Anzio, Okinawa, Salerno, and elsewhere.

---

[151] President's Committee on Equality of Treatment and Opportunity in the Armed Services, *op. cit.*, p. 44.

[152] *Ibid.*, p. 61.

[153] Eli Ginzberg, *The Negro Potential*, Columbia, 1956, p. 76. Ginzberg presents a thorough review of the status of the Negro soldier during and following World War II.

[154] *Ibid.*, pp. 76–86.

Integration in the Army, begun in Europe in 1951, went ahead swiftly in 1952.[155] By the summer of that year, segregation in that command had virtually disappeared.[156] The Marine Corps was the last of the services to admit Negroes at all, but its last two all-Negro units were integrated by the summer of 1952.[157] In visiting several military bases from coast to coast in 1953, Nichols found "that the wall of racial segregation was almost gone."[158]

Negroes in the Armed Forces, 1956–1970

At the time of the Truman order in 1948, Negroes constituted 8.8 percent of the Army personnel. In 1964, the proportion was 12.3 percent. Negroes serving in the Air Force increased from less than 5 percent in 1949 to 8.6 percent in 1964. The proportion of Negro personnel in the Navy has remained around 5 percent for the period 1944–1964. After integration was begun in the Marine Corps, the proportion of Negroes increased from 2 percent in 1949 to 8.2 percent in 1964.[159] The trend toward higher percentages of Negroes in the armed forces is shown in the following table.

[155] Lee Nichols, *Breakthrough on the Color Front,* Random House, 1954, pp. 129–230.
[156] Ginzberg, *op. cit.,* p. 87.
[157] Nichols, *op. cit.,* p. 203.
[158] *Ibid.,* p. 143.
[159] Charles C. Moskos, "Racial Integration in the Armed Forces," *AJS,* Sept. 1966, pp. 135–136.

According to a 1970 Bureau of the Census report, on March 31, 1969, Negroes constituted 9 percent of the armed forces, 11 percent of those serving in Southeast Asia, and 12 percent of those who died in Vietnam combat.[160]

[160] Harris attributes the higher ratios for Negroes serving and dying in Vietnam to several factors: (1) in some instances, low educational attainments disqualify Negroes for safer administrative duties; (2) a large number of black servicemen volunteer for overseas duty even if it means assignment to combat in Vietnam for several reasons—the hope that the people of other lands will be more accepting than those at home, the risks of combat increase the odds in favor of rapid promotion, the extra pay for hazardous duty is tempting or it is essential for the support of relatives, and the ego satisfaction of testing one's courage in a legally sanctioned altercation. Theodore D. Harris, "The Military and the Negro," in Romero, *op. cit.,* p. 363.

Negro Men in the Armed Forces, March 31, 1969 (In thousands)

	Total	Negro	Percent Negro
Total	3,439	323	9
Outside Southeast Asia	2,801	256	9
In Southeast Asia	638	67	11
Deaths in Southeast Asia	34	4	12

Source: U.S. Department of Defense, in U.S. Department of Commerce, Bureau of the Census, *The Social and Economic Status of Negroes in the United States,* 1969, p. 85.

Trend Toward Higher Percentages of Negroes (Enlisted Men/Officers) in Armed Forces over Selective Years, 1949–64

	Army		Navy		Marine Corps		Air Force		Total Percent in Defense Department
	Enlisted Men	Officers	Enlisted Men	Officers	Enlisted Men	Officers	Enlisted Men	Officers	
1949	12.4	1.8	4.7	0	2.1	0	5.1	.6	N.A.
1954	13.7	3.0	3.6	.1	6.6	.1	8.6	1.1	N.A.
1962	12.2	3.2	5.2	.2	7.6	.2	9.2	1.2	N.A.
1964	13.4	3.4	5.8	.3	8.7	.4	10.0	1.5	11.7

Source: Richard J. Stillman, II, *Integration of the Negro in the U.S. Armed Forces,* Praeger, 1968, p. 64. Based on unpublished data obtained from Civil Rights Office, Department of Defense.

The pattern of rank distribution within the defense organization is less favorable for Negroes than the overall proportion. In 1962, there were few Negro officers in the senior grades; the great majority were lieutenants and captains. The number and percentage of Negro personnel in each officer rank in 1962 are shown in the following table.

In 1964, the ratio of Negro to white officers was approximately 1 to 30 in the Army, 1 to 70 in the Air Force, 1 to 250 in the Marine Corps, and 1 to 300 in the Navy.[161] In July, 1968, the Defense Department announced the increase in Negro officers after 20 years of racial integration in the armed forces. The Army had more than quadrupled its number of black officers, from 1306 in 1948 to 5637 in 1968. Included in this group were one brigadier general and 27 full colonels, compared with one colonel in 1948. In 1948, the Navy had only four Negro officers, but a total of 330 in 1968, including three captains. The Air Force increased its black officers from 330 in 1948, with only one colonel, to 2417 in 1968. Many of these officers were combat pilots, and there was one lieutenant general and 19 full colonels. In 1948, there

[161] Moskos, *op. cit.,* pp. 136–137.

was only one Negro officer in the Marine Corps, compared with 180 in 1968, and an attempt was being made then to double that number.[162]

On March 31, 1969, Negroes made up 2 percent of all officers in the armed forces and 3 percent of the officers stationed in Southeast Asia. Approximately 3 percent of the Negroes in the armed services are officers as compared with 13 percent of the whites.

[162] Harris, *op. cit.,* pp. 360–361.

Negro Officers and Enlisted Men in the Armed Forces, March 31, 1969 (In thousands)

	Total	Negro	Percent Negro
Total	3,439	323	9
Officers	419	9	2
Outside Southeast Asia	354	7	2
In Southeast Asia	65	2	3
Enlisted men	3,020	314	10
Outside Southeast Asia	2,447	249	10
In Southeast Asia	573	65	11

Source: U.S. Department of Defense, in U.S. Department of Commerce, Bureau of the Census, *The Social and Economic Status of Negroes in the United States,* 1969, p. 86.

Number and Percentage of Negro Personnel in Each Officer Rank, 1962

Rank		Service			
Army, Air Force and Marine Corps	Navy	Army	Navy	Air Force	Marine Corps
Generals (all types)	Admirals (all types)	0(0%)	0(0%)	1(0.29%)	0(0%)
Colonels	Captains	6(0.11%)	0(0%)	6(0.14%)	0(0%)
Lt. Colonels	Commanders	117(0.95%)	3(0.03%)	67(2.54%)	0(0%)
Majors	Lt. Commanders	424(2.47%)	17(0.14%)	124(0.60%)	0(0%)
Captains	Lieutenants	1,532(5.21%)	88(0.35%)	615(1.74%)	7(0.17%)
1st Lieutenants	Lieutenants (j.g.)	650(4.33%)	57(0.39%)	317(1.56%)	16(0.44%)
2nd Lieutenants	Ensigns	421(2.26%)	29(0.22%)	170(1.45%)	9(0.28%)
Total Officers and Percentages		3,150(3.2%)	194(0.26%)	1,300(1.24%)	32(0.21%)

Note: 1962 Data for all Services. The Air Force figures include only officers assigned to duty in the 48 states of the continental United States. All other figures are complete and worldwide in scope.

Source: Gesell Committee (President's Committee on Equal Opportunity in the Armed Forces) Initial Report, June 13, 1963, p. 10. In Richard J. Stillman, II, *Integration of the Negro in the U.S. Armed Forces,* Praeger, 1968, p. 67.

In the lower noncommissioned officer ranks in all the armed forces, but especially in the Army, there is a concentration of Negroes. Among enlisted men, Negroes are underrepresented in the top three ranks in the Army and the top four ranks in the other three services. The data show that the Army, followed by the Air Force, has the largest proportion of Negroes in the total personnel, and, also, the most equitable distribution of Negroes throughout the ranks.[163]

Occupational Opportunities for Negroes in the Armed Forces. Negro enlisted men and officers have somewhat better occupational opportunities than do Negroes in civilian employment. Negroes constitute a higher proportion of the enlisted men than they do of the civilians in every clerical, technical, and skilled field for which a comparison is possible. These occupations include electronic, medical and dental, drafting, and other kinds of technicians, aircraft and automobile mechanics, electricians and communications linesmen, construction and related craftsmen, and printing craftsmen. Negroes make up 9 percent of those in the craftsmen and foremen categories, compared to 5 percent in civilian life. The occupational pattern is somewhat different among officers. Negroes constitute a smaller percentage of military than civilian personnel in law, medicine, dentistry, nursing, and the clergy. In a number of fields, however, Negroes comprise a larger proportion in the armed forces than in civilian life. Among these fields are engineering, the applied sciences, finance and accounting, aviation and navigation, and a variety of management fields. Marked differences are found in the armed services in the occupational distribution of their Negro personnel. In most of the clerical, technical, and skilled fields, the Army's proportion of Negroes is from two and one-half to four times higher than it is in comparable civilian jobs. The Army also has a higher percentage of Negroes in most professional, scientific, and management fields than does the civilian economy. In most occupational categories, Negroes are better represented in the Air Force than in civilian life. The Navy is the only branch of the armed forces where the Negro is less well represented than in the civilian economy in almost every occupational category, from the professional, scientific, and managerial to the technical, administrative, clerical, and craftsmen personnel.[164]

An important trend within the military establishment is that of ever greater technical complexity. A rough measure of this trend toward the "professionalization" of military roles is the decrease in the proportion of men assigned to combat arms. The proportion of men in combat arms dropped from 44.5 percent in 1945 to 26.0 percent in 1962. The proportion of white personnel in traditional military specialties approximates the total proportional decrease during this period. The likelihood of a Negro serving in a combat arm was, however, three times greater in 1962 than it was in 1945. Also, when comparisons are made between military specialties within the combat arms, the Negro percentage is higher in "line" than it is "staff" assignments. Integration of the military has led to great improvement, but racial egalitarianism within the armed forces cannot entirely eliminate the effects of the disadvantages that Negroes encounter earlier in American life.[165]

In 1965, the re-enlistment rate of Negroes for all four services was approximately twice that of white servicemen. At that time about half of all first-term Negro servicemen chose to stay for at least a second term. One expected effect of the high rate of re-enlistment of Negroes is an increase in their representation in the advanced NCO grades.[166] In 1967, 30 percent of all Negroes in the armed forces who were eligible re-enlisted after their first tour of duty, a substantial decline from the rates of 1964, 1965, and 1966. During the years 1964–1967, the re-enlistment rate for whites declined from 20

---

[163] Moskos, *op. cit.*, 137.

[164] Eli Ginzberg and Dale L. Hiestand, "Employment Patterns of Negro Men and Women, in John P. Davis, (ed.), *The American Negro Reference Book*, Prentice-Hall, 1966, pp. 229–231.
[165] Moskos, *op. cit.*, pp. 137–138.
[166] *Ibid.*, p. 139.

percent to 15 percent.[167] According to Harris, Negroes re-enlisted in the Army in 1968 at three times the rate of Whites, while the ratio was two-to-one in the Navy, Air Force, and Marines.[168]

In recent years, the armed services have emphasized the expanding career opportunities for black women as well as for black men. All the women's service branches seek to attract a larger number of young Negro women for both the enlisted and commissioned categories. In 1968, 12.4 percent of the women Marines were black, but in that year only 4 percent of the personnel of the Navy's WAVES were Negro.[169]

The Service Academies and the ROTC. An important means of increasing the number of professional Negro officers is the service academies. In 1966, there were only 52 black cadets among the 9800 students at West Point, Annapolis, and the Air Force Academy, or .5 percent of the total enrollment. Eleven Negroes graduated from these schools in June, 1965, one-eighth of all Negro graduates since 1887.[170] In 1968, the academies sought to broaden racial representation in their student bodies by active recruitment of potential Negro appointments from the nation's high schools, including schools in black neighborhoods. West Point had 32 black cadets in 1968 and expected to triple that number at an early date. Between 1964 and 1968, the number of black midshipmen at Annapolis increased from four to 31, and in the same period, the Air Force Academy increased its black enrollment from six to 55.[171]

The largest single source of Negro officers is the Reserve Officers Training Corps at predominantly Negro colleges. At 15 schools, from 1964–1965, the Army ROTC had 7622 cadets, an increase of 353 students over the 1963–1964 period, and the Air Force ROTC

had 3106, a gain of 406 over the previous year.[172] In 1968, all the services moved toward the establishment of additional ROTC units in predominantly Negro colleges, and, in addition, black students at predominantly white colleges were encouraged to enroll. The Navy established a NROTC unit at Prairie View A. M. College in Texas, the first Navy unit ever located at a black institution.[173]

The National Guard. In 1964, 5780 of the 442,410 Army and Air Guardmen, 1.5 percent of total Guard strength, were Negroes, compared with the 11 percent representation of Negroes in the national population. Unlike the regular military services, the National Guard has always had low Negro participation and few officers. In 1964, only 20 states reported having Negro officers. The Air Guard has had a smaller proportion of black men than the Army. The smallest number of Guard members is found in the southern states with the largest Negro populations and the highest percentages in northern cities.[174] In 1968, serious efforts were made to recruit more Negro personnel in both the enlisted and officer categories for the state National Guard units and the Organized Reserve components of all the services. These efforts were hindered to some extent by the hostility of some ghetto youths because of recent Guard participation in riot control actions, but the hostility was balanced by several practical considerations. National Guard or Reserve membership provides deferment from selective service. Another reason is the unlikelihood that Guard or Reserve units will be mobilized for duty in Vietnam, and a third factor is the supplemental income that participation provides to disadvantaged young men.[175]

Off-duty Facilities, Social Relations, and Racial Tensions. Color barriers at the formal level have disappeared from today's military establishment. The official policy is equal treatment regardless of race in such nonduty

---

[167] U.S. Department of Commerce, Bureau of the Census, *The Social and Economic Status of Negroes*, Government Printing Office, 1969, p. 87.

[168] Harris, *op. cit.*, p. 359.

[169] *Ibid.*, p. 359.

[170] Richard J. Stillman, *Integration of the Negro in the Armed Forces*, Praeger, 1968, p. 65.

[171] Harris, *op. cit.*, p. 360.

[172] Stillman, *op. cit.*, p. 70.

[173] Harris, *op. cit.*, pp. 359–360.

[174] Stillman, *op. cit.*, pp. 95, 98.

[175] Harris, *op. cit.*, pp. 358–359.

facilities as swimming pools, chapels, barber shops, post exchanges, movie theaters, snack bars, and dependents' housing, as well as in the living conditions of members of the armed services. The general pattern of integration during combat and garrison duty is not, however, carried over into social relations behind the front lines or during off-duty hours. Moskos found that, on the whole, "racial integration at informal as well as formal levels works best on-duty vis-à-vis off-duty, on-base vis-à-vis off-base, basic training and maneuvers vis-à-vis garrison, sea vis-à-vis shore duty, and combat vis-à-vis noncombat. In other words, the behavior of servicemen resembles the racial (and class) separation of the larger American society, the further they are removed from the military environment."[176] On a visit to Vietnam in 1967, Whitney M. Young, Jr. found that Whites and Negroes "usually split up during their off-duty hours," especially in the bars and clubs, which are self-segregated. (The exceptions to this rule are the places frequented by members of the Green Berets.)[177] In 1968, this trend seemed to be continuing among white and black soldiers in Vietnam, Germany, and Japan. Generally, these men sought entertainment and recreation in voluntarily segregated places rather than in the integrated military facilities. In that year, several interracial brawls, involving men from all branches of the military, occurred in rear areas in Vietnam. Harris attributed these troubles to ingrained prejudices on the part of individuals of both races that military regulations and the association of combat duty had not eliminated.[178]

In 1967, some racial conflicts occurred among U.S. troops in Germany. During the summer of 1968, and in October of that year, racial fights took place in Vietnam. In 1969, a number of racial assaults occurred at the Marine Corps base at Camp Lejeune, North Carolina. During the first half of 1970, racial troubles broke out among the U.S.

troops stationed in Germany. These racial tensions have been attributed to a number of factors. Major General Michael P. Ryan, commander of the Second Marine Division at Camp Lejeune has emphasized the difficulty of building morale during the period of rapid turnover that the division has had. He and his predecessor, Major General Edwin B. Wheeler, have also stressed the effect of local mores on the black marine. Many of the town's facilities—barbershops, bars, and amusement centers—are segregated. Many Negro marines attribute much of the friction to their feeling that black men are discriminated against in various ways. Their complaints range from epithets they say are used by some white officers and noncommissioned officers to the allegation that Blacks are punished more severely for minor offenses, that Whites are promoted more readily than Blacks, that housing facilities are unequal, and that Blacks are more likely to be sent to Vietnam than Whites. A survey of race relations at U.S. Army bases throughout the world reported that many young Negro soldiers said that they resented having their newly found racial pride interpreted as evidence that they are black militants or black racists.[179] Johnson says that many of the younger men come "with a strong sense of blackness and with a need for involvement with the racial struggles in the outside world."[180]

A number of suggestions have been made, and some steps have been taken, to reduce the racial tensions that have developed in the armed forces since 1967. In September, 1970, the Pentagon sent a team of military and civilian experts to West Germany to investigate the situation there and to make recommendations for its improvement. The Seventh Army headquarters at Heidelberg has estab-

[176] Moskos, op. cit., pp. 141–142.
[177] Whitney M. Young, Jr., "When the Negroes in Vietnam Come Home," Harper's Magazine, June, 1967, p. 69.
[178] Harris, op. cit., pp. 361–362.

[179] Ralph Blumental, "Racial Tension at Bases Is Increasing, Army Finds," The New York Times, Jan. 25, 1970, pp. 1, 2. See also, Carl T. Rowan, "Racial Woes for Pentagon," The Plain Dealer, Aug. 27, 1969; and E. W. Kenworthy, "Lejeune Commandant Worried Over Growing Racial Tension," The New York Times, Aug. 15, 1969.
[180] Thomas A. Johnson, "Newer Negro Marines Are Looking for Identity with Blackness," The New York Times, Dec. 21, 1969.

lished an Equal Opportunities Discussion Group to study the dissension and to suggest new procedures.[181] The director for civil rights of the Department of Defense has stressed the need for human rights councils within the military, better communications between the races, and courses in race relations and black history for many service personnel. Some black marines have expressed a desire to form their own committees for taking problems to superiors in the Corps. Other proposals include the establishment of human relations programs at the service academies, in schools for noncommissioned officers, and in basic training; and increasing the number of black high-ranking civilian and military officials in the Pentagon.

In referring to one report on race relations in the armed forces, Blumenthal said that while it is bleak, encouraging programs have been instituted at U.S. Military Academy and other colleges to increase the opportunities for Blacks who want to enter the military service. He quotes the report as saying that "aggressive command action, firm but impartial discipline and good leadership" could still prevent serious racial confrontations at United States bases.[182]

[181] *Time*, Sept. 21, 1970, p. 36.

[182] Blumenthal, *op. cit.*, p. 1.

Chapter 13 / MINORITIES AND THE AMERICAN POLITICAL AND LEGAL PROCESSES

As societies have become more complex, a larger and larger proportion of key decisions have been made through political processes, and law has come to occupy an increasingly influential place in our lives. Our study of the place of minority groups in the social structure, therefore, must give careful attention to the ways in which these groups influence and are influenced by political decisions and legal processes. Some of the political and legal aspects of American minority life are dealt with in other chapters and recent decisions of the United States Supreme Court on educational questions, as well as fair educational practice legislation, are examined in later chapters.

LEGAL STATUS OF THE NEGRO BEFORE 1900

In the matter of voting, even free Negroes were disfranchised throughout the South and in most of the North and the West as of 1860. New England, with the exception of Connecticut, permitted Negroes to vote. New York required Negroes who wished to vote to own a certain amount of property, a qualification that did not hold for Whites. Wisconsin granted the suffrage to Negroes in 1849. Other northern and border states disfranchised them as follows: Delaware in 1792, Kentucky in 1799, Maryland in 1809, Connecticut in 1818, New Jersey in 1820, Virginia in 1830, Tennessee in 1834, North Carolina in 1835, and Pennsylvania in 1838. Other states in the South and West did not permit Negroes to vote.[1]

After the adoption in 1865 of the Thirteenth Amendment abolishing slavery and involuntary servitude, except as a punish-ment for crime after due conviction, special restrictive legislation was enacted in the southern states. These laws, which became known as the Black Codes, virtually reintroduced the slave codes. They covered apprenticeship, labor contracts, migration, vagrancy, civil and legal rights.[2] The passage of the Black Codes brought about the adoption of the Fourteenth Amendment containing the famous statement: "No State shall make or enforce any law which shall abridge the privileges or immunities of citizens of the United States; nor shall any State deprive any person of life, liberty, or property, without due process of law; nor deny to any person within its jurisdiction the equal protection of the laws." The Fifteenth Amendment—"The right of the citizens of the United States to vote shall not be denied or abridged by the United States or by any State on account of race, color, or previous condition of servitude"—was also a reaction to the Black Codes, as was the federal Civil Rights Act of 1875. This act was declared unconstitutional in 1883, and soon thereafter the southern states began to enact segregative legislation.[3]

One of the controversial aspects of the early years of the Reconstruction period was the program carried on by the Bureau of Refugees, Freedmen, and Abandoned Lands. The Freedmen's Bureau in the War Department was created by a bill passed in 1865 and was in operation until 1872. It was criticized for the tactlessness, ineptitude, and corruptness of some of its officials. On the other hand, especially in recent years, this agency has been acclaimed for its positive accomplishments. At the time it was abolished, it had 2600 day and night schools in

---

[1] C. S. Mangum, Jr., *The Legal Status of the Negro*, Univ. of North Carolina Press, 1940, pp. 371–372.

[2] See E. Franklin Frazier, *The Negro in the United States*, Macmillan, rev. ed., 1957, pp. 126–127.

[3] Carey McWilliams, "Race Discrimination and the Law," *Science and Society*, Winter, 1945, p. 11.

operation, with 3300 teachers (most of them trained by the bureau). It established Howard, Fisk, Hampton, and St. Augustine Normal School. In many parts of the South it was responsible for setting up what later became tax-supported public schools. Institutions were founded to care for the aged, the crippled, and the mentally diseased. A medical-aid program for Negroes was organized, and hospitals were established. Orphans and the destitute were furnished aid, and some 30,000 displaced freedmen were returned to their former homes. The bureau was instructed by Congress to give every freedman 40 acres and a mule. Some abandoned and confiscated land was distributed, but the bureau never had more than 800,000 acres to dispose of (only 2/10 of 1 percent of the land of the seceding states was ever held by the bureau). Even if all these lands had been available, less than one acre could have been given to every freedman. As McWilliams indicates, most of the lands were quickly repossessed by the former owners as a result of wholesale amnesties, and Negroes who had acquired small tracts were dispossessed.[4]

Many interesting developments occurred during the Reconstruction years. In 1869 a Georgia court declared invalid a prewar statute preventing anyone with one-eighth or more Negro ancestry from holding public office. An article of the Louisiana constitution requiring racial separation in the schools was suspended in 1868, and the South Carolina public schools were opened to both races in the same year. It is reported that the University of South Carolina admitted Negro students in the first Reconstruction years, and that Richard T. Greener, a Negro graduate of Harvard, was librarian. Negroes were elected to Congress for the first time during the forty-first session (1870–1871). H. K. Revels, of Mississippi, came to fill the Senate seat of Jefferson Davis; Jefferson F. Long was a representative from Georgia. From 1870 to 1901, 20 Negroes were seated as representatives and two as senators. The largest number

elected for any one Congress during these 30 years was seven (1876–1877).[5]

There is no need for us to present a detailed account of the Reconstruction period. Most readers are more or less familiar with the martial law; the arbitrariness of some military officers and officials of the Freedmen's Bureau; the New England schoolteachers who came south; the collaboration of some Negroes, carpetbaggers, and scalawags; the waste and corruption; the positive achievements such as the new state constitutions, new laws on voting, new schools, etc.; and the disappointment and resentment of southern leaders at the loss of the war.

The famous "Bargain of 1876" restored "white supremacy" to the South. The Republicans agreed not to oppose the election of Democrats to state office in South Carolina, Louisiana, and Florida and to withdraw troops from these states; the Democrats agreed to hand Hayes the presidency that Tilden had won. The bargain carried with it the nullification of the Civil War amendments insofar as the Negro was concerned. From then on Negroes were to be "eliminated from politics."[6]

THE DISFRANCHISEMENT AND RE-ENFRANCHISEMENT OF NEGROES

To assure the permanent elimination of the Negro from political affairs in the South, various devices were invented. "Grandfather clauses" were included in a number of the

---

[4] Carey McWilliams, *Brothers Under the Skin*, Little, Brown, rev. ed., 1951, pp. 357–359.

[5] Charles S. Johnson, *Patterns of Negro Segregation*, Harper & Row, 1943, pp. 164, 342.

[6] McWilliams, *Brothers Under the Skin*, p. 265. According to Moon, Negroes "played a minor role in the corrupt practices of the post-war period in which there was nationwide relaxation of standards of political morality." More importantly Negroes did not dominate the state governments of the South. "The majority of state executive offices and the most important were always filled by white men. The congressional delegations were composed of the same class of individuals. The leading men in both branches of every state legislature were representatives of the dominant race. . . .'" Every attempt was made by white southerners to assure the failure of the Reconstruction governments; the participation of Negroes in the political process was unthinkable. See H. I. Moon, *Balance of Power: The Negro Vote*, Doubleday, 1948, pp. 62–64.

disfranchising constitutions adopted by southern states in the 1890s. The Louisiana constitution of 1898 provided that one might register permanently before September 1, 1898, if he was entitled to vote in any state January 1, 1867, or if he was the son or grandson of a person so entitled and 21 years of age or over in 1898. North Carolina included a "grandfather clause" in her revised statutes of 1905.[7] These clauses excluded Negroes from voting while permitting white persons of all kinds to vote. The United States Supreme Court held these clauses to be unconstitutional in 1915.

Between 1889 and 1908, ten southern states (Alabama, Arkansas, Florida, Louisiana, Mississippi, North Carolina, South Carolina, Tennessee, Texas, and Virginia), through constitutional provision or statutory law, adopted a poll tax requirement for voting. The effectiveness of the poll tax as a device to regulate voting was considerably enhanced in Alabama, Mississippi, Louisiana, and Virginia by the provision that there would be no proceedings to collect the tax until it was three years overdue. North Carolina eliminated the poll tax from her voting requirements in 1920 and later four other states eliminated this qualification. The tax existed in five states—Alabama, Mississippi, Arkansas, Texas, and Virginia until 1964, when the required 38 states had ratified an amendment to the Constitution that would prohibit such taxes as requirements for voting in a federal election. In a test case of the 24th Amendment, the Supreme Court unanimously struck down a Virginia law requiring voters in federal elections to pay a poll tax or file a certificate of residence.[8] On March 24, 1966, the Court ruled unconstitutional Virginia's poll tax law on state elections. Other states affected by this ruling were Alabama, Mississippi, and Texas.[9]

Another device for disfranchising Negroes was the "white primary." Since nomination in the Democratic primary usually was equivalent to election in the South, exclusion from the primary election meant the removal of

Negroes from participation in the democratic process. In 1923 Texas passed the first "white primary" law, in which it was stated that "in no event shall a Negro be eligible to participate in a Democratic party primary election held in the state of Texas." This law was based on the Supreme Court's declaration in Newberry v. United States (256 U.S. 232, 1921) that Congressional primaries were not "elections" within the meaning of the Constitution. This statute came to the Supreme Court in 1927 in Nixon v. Herndon (273 U.S. 536), and the Court ruled that it violated the equal-protection clause of the Fourteenth Amendment. Governor Dan Moody of Texas announced that Texas would not permit Negroes to vote regardless of what the Supreme Court said. He then called a special meeting of the Texas legislature, and a new statute was passed empowering every political party in the state through its executive committee "to prescribe the qualifications of its own members" and permitting it to determine "who shall be qualified to vote or otherwise participate in such political party." The state executive committee quickly adopted a resolution which read, "All white Democrats who are qualified under the Constitution and laws of Texas and none others are to be allowed to participate in the primary elections." By a vote of five to four the Court held the second Texas law unconstitutional (Nixon v. Condon, 286 U.S. 73, 1932). Three weeks later the state Democratic convention, instead of the state executive committee, voted to exclude all but whites from the primary. In 1935, in Grovey v. Townsend (295 U.S. 45) the Supreme Court held that a vote of the state convention of a political party to restrict participation in the primary of that party did not violate the Fourteenth and Fifteenth amendments, provided the expenses of such primaries were paid by the party and not by the state. The Court took the position that this rule was simply the action of a private group acting on its right to determine its own membership and policies.[10]

On April 3, 1944, the Supreme Court re-

---

[7] Johnson, *op. cit.*, p. 165.
[8] *The Plain Dealer*, Apr. 28, 1965.
[9] *The New York Times*, Mar. 27, 1966.

[10] See R. E. Cushman, "The Laws of the Land," *Survey Graphic*, Jan., 1947, pp. 14–15; and Walter White, *A Man Called White*, Viking, 1948, pp. 83–88.

versed its 1935 ruling on the white primary. The case involved Lonnie E. Smith, who contended that he was denied the right to vote in a 1940 primary by Houston, Texas, election judges because of his race. The majority opinion of the Court said that the Democratic party in Texas is required to follow state legislative procedure in selecting party nominees in primary elections and thus the party becomes a state agency. It held that when primaries become a part of the machinery for choosing state and national officials, the same tests for discrimination apply to a primary as to a general election.[11]

In 1898, the Supreme Court held that Mississippi's requirement that electors be able to read any section of the state constitution or to understand it when read did not, on its face, discriminate between the races, and did not violate the equal protection clause of the Fourteenth Amendment. However, state and federal courts placed limitations on the use of literacy tests as a qualification for voting. After 1949, registrars were no longer legally free to ask any questions they desired. In the case of Davis *v.* Schnell, a three-judge federal district court held unconstitutional the Alabama law requiring a prospective elector to be able to understand and explain any article of the Constitution of the United States to the reasonable satisfaction of the board of registrars. Summarizing this important decision, the *Race Relations Law Reporter* says:

The federal court, though holding that these provisions of the Alabama law were unconstitutional, recognized the right of states to prescribe a literacy test for electors. But as no uniform, objective or standardized test or examination was provided whereby an impartial board could determine whether the applicant had a reasonable understanding and could give a reasonable explanation of the articles of the Constitution, the provision of the Alabama Constitution was held to be unconstitutional.[12]

States that have some form of literacy qualification for voting, including 12 states outside the Deep South, are shown in the following table.

Individual State Voting Requirements for Literacy

Understand Constitution	Read and Write
Alabama	Alabama
Arizona	Arizona
California	California
Connecticut[a]	Connecticut
Delaware	Delaware
Georgia	Georgia[b]
Louisiana	Louisiana
Maine	Maine
Massachusetts	Massachusetts
Mississippi	Mississippi
New Hampshire	New Hampshire
	New York
North Carolina	North Carolina
Oklahoma	Oklahoma
	Oregon[c]
South Carolina	South Carolina
	Washington
Wyoming	Wyoming

Notes:
[a] And Statutes.
[b] Or pass test on citizenship.
[c] Read election law and write.
Source: *Race Relations Law Reporter*, Apr., 1958, pp. 390–391.

The Civil Rights Act of 1964 prohibited registrars from applying different standards to white and Negro voting applicants and from disqualifying applicants because of inconsequential errors on their forms. It required that literacy tests be in writing, and that any applicant desiring one be given a

---

[11] See Thurgood Marshall, "The Rise and Collapse of the 'White Democratic Primary,'" *JNE*, Summer, 1957, pp. 249–254.

[12] *RRLR*, Apr., 1958, p. 384. For a discussion of the Boswell Amendment, Alabama's response to the Supreme Court's decision in *Smith v. Allwright* (the white primary case), see Donald S. Strong, *Registra-tion of Voters in Alabama*, Bureau of Public Administration, Univ. of Alabama Press, 1956, pp. 22–25. The key passage of this amendment, proposed by the legislature in 1945 and ratified by the voters in Nov., 1946, required new applicants to "read and write, understand and explain any article of the Constitution of the United States."

copy of the questions and his answers.[13] (A summary of the 1964 Civil Rights Act is given at the end of Chapter 14.) To overcome the ineffectiveness of Title I (Voting) of the 1964 law, Congress enacted the Voting Rights Act of 1965. (A summary of this law is given at the end of this chapter.) A basic feature of the 1964 law is that it provides a statistical formula to define discrimination. This provision makes it unnecessary to bring a particular county official to trial and convince a judge of his misconduct. According to the law, a state or county is practicing discrimination if *both* of these conditions are present: (1) Less than 50 percent of the voting-age population was registered as of November, 1964 or voted in the presidential election of that year, and (2) any "test or device" is required of prospective voters.[14] The phrase "test or device" is defined to mean: ". . . any requirement that a person as a prerequisite for voting or registration for voting: (1) demonstrate the ability to read, understand, or interpret any matter; (2) demonstrate any educational achievement or his knowledge of any particular subject; (3) possess good moral character; or (4) prove his qualification by the voucher of registered voters or members of any other class."[15] Under this formula, a state (New York, for example) that has more than half its adult population registered can retain its literacy test. Although less than half of its adult population voted in November, 1964, Texas is unaffected because it employs no test or device. The 1965 law provided for a "freeze" on state voting requirements for five years. That law provides also for the appointment of federal examiners in those counties where local officials refuse to comply, or do not expand their facilities and working hours to accommodate the new Negro applicants. The Attorney General has virtually unlimited discretion in the assignment of registrars. Strong says that by June, 1967,

federal examiners had been sent to a total of 60 counties: 13 in Alabama, 4 in Georgia, 9 in Louisiana, 32 in Mississippi, and 2 in South Carolina.[16] In June 1970, the 1965 law was extended for five years.

The Negro Vote

Despite the use in some counties of techniques to circumvent the provisions of the Voting Rights Act of 1965, including gerrymandering, the merging of Negro districts into large units with white majorities, changing positions from an elected to an appointed status, the abolition of offices being sought by Negro candidates, withholding information about political affairs from potential Negro candidates, extending the terms of incumbent white officers, raising filing fees, adding qualification requirements for offices, and failing to certify nominating petitions for

[16] *Ibid.*, pp. 92–93.

Estimated Number and Percentages of Voting-Age Negroes Registered to Vote in Eleven Southern States, 1940–1966

Year	Estimated number	Percentage
1940	250,000	5
1947	595,000	12
1952	1,008,614	20
1956	1,238,038	25
1958	1,266,488	25
1960	1,414,052	28
1964	1,907,279	38
1966	2,306,434	46

Sources: Adapted from U.S. census data on nonwhite population and Negro registration estimates in Gunnar Myrdal, *An American Dilemma,* Harper & Row, 1944, p. 488; M. Price, *The Negro Voter in the South,* Southern Regional Council, 1957, p. 5; "The Negro Voter in the South—1958," *Special Report,* Southern Regional Council, 1958, p. 3; U.S. Commission on Civil Rights, *1959 Report,* Government Printing Office, 1959, and *Voting,* Government Printing Office, 1961; *The New York Times,* Aug. 8, 1965 (official U.S. Civil Rights Commission estimates for 1964); Southern Regional Council, *New South,* Winter, 1966, p. 88; Donald R. Matthews and James W. Prothro, *Negroes and the New Southern Politics,* Harcourt Brace Jovanovich, 1966, p. 18.

[13] "Summary of Main Provisions of Civil Rights Bill, *The Crisis,* Aug.–Sept., 1964, pp. 430–431.
[14] Donald Strong, *Negroes, Ballots, and Judges,* Univ. of Alabama Press, 1968, pp. 91–92.
[15] *Ibid.,* pp. 92–93.

Negro-White Voter Registration in the South, Spring-Summer, 1968

State	White Voting-age pop.	Negro Voting-age pop.	White reg.	Negro reg.	Percent White reg.	Percent Negro reg.
Alabama	1,353,058	481,320	1,117,000	273,000	82.5	56.7
Arkansas	850,643	192,626	640,000	130,000	75.2	67.5
Florida	2,617,438	470,261	2,195,000	292,000	83.8	62.1
Georgia	1,797,062	612,910	1,524,000	344,000	84.7	56.1
Louisiana	1,289,216	514,589	1,133,000	305,000	87.9	59.3
Mississippi	748,266	422,256	691,000	251,000	92.4	59.4
North Carolina	2,005,955	550,929	1,579,000	305,000	78.7	55.3
South Carolina	895,147	371,873	587,000	189,000	65.6	50.8
Tennessee	1,779,018	313,873	1,448,000	228,000	81.3	72.6
Texas	4,884,765	649,512	3,532,000	540,000	72.3	83.1
Virginia	1,876,167	436,720	1,256,000	255,000	67.0	58.4
Totals	20,096,735	5,016,100	15,702,000	3,112,000	78.1	62.0

Note: Voting-age population figures are from the 1960 census.
Source: Voter Registration Project, Southern Regional Council, *Voter Registration in the South*, 1968, p. 2.

Negroes,[17] the number of registered Negro voters in the South has increased substantially since 1965.

An estimate of the number of Negroes who voted in the South during the 1920s is 70,000.[18] The table on page 392 shows the estimated number of Negro adults who were registered to vote in the Old South from 1940–1966.

The table above shows the registration of Negro and white voters in the South, by states, in the spring-summer of 1968.

The effects of the Voting Rights Act of 1965 can be seen in some before-and-after figures. In Alabama as a whole, only 23.6 percent of the voting-age Negroes were registered before the law was passed. This figure more than doubled within seven months, and by April, 1966, nearly half of the black adults in the state were registered. In Mississippi, only 6.7 percent of the black adults were registered in August, 1965. Three years later the proportion was 59.4. In

the six states wholly covered by the Voting Rights Act (Alabama, Georgia, Louisiana, Mississippi, South Carolina, and Virginia), black registration has increased from 30.9 percent to 57 percent. (White registration for these states is 79.2 percent of those of voting age.)[19]

By February, 1970, black voter registration in eleven southern states had reached 3,248,000, or 64.8 percent of those eligible to vote.[20] Concerning this substantial increase in registration, a political observer says: "Black registration has swelled voter rolls in every state of the Old Confederacy and separate black party movements have challenged the established Democratic organizations. Realizing that without the Negro vote their preeminence is seriously jeopardized, many white political leaders have begun *counting* the Negro vote and consequently changing their tune."[21]

A tabulation of black elected officials in the southern states, made by the Southern

[17] U.S. Commission on Civil Rights, *Political Participation, 1968*, pp. 177–178.
[18] H. L. Moon, "The Southern Scene," *Phylon*, Fourth Quarter, 1955, pp. 357–358.

[19] Marvin Wall, "Black Votes," *South Today*, Aug., 1969, p. 6.
[20] *The New York Times*, Feb. 8, 1970, pp. 1, 50.
[21] *The New York Times*, Jan. 24, 1971, p. 10E.

Regional Council in 1971, showed a total of 735. The number of Negroes holding these posts had increased from a handful in 1960 to 78 in 1965, 528 in 1969, and 711 in 1970.[22] Perhaps the most dramatic change occurred in Greene County, Alabama, where Negroes outnumber Whites 10,000 to 3000. When the Voting Rights Act of 1965 went into effect, only 425 Blacks, less than 11 percent of the voting age population of 5001, were registered to vote. White names on the lists totaled 1736, 87 more than the white population of voting age. By March, 1966, black registration totaled 3781—nearly 2000 of whom had registered with federal examiners sent in under the Voting Rights Act.[23] In August, 1969, Blacks won control of Greene county by electing four members of the County Commission. Three white officials who still held office (sheriff, county attorney, and probate judge) said they would aid the new Negro officeholders. Three Negro candidates also won election to the five-member Greene County School Board.[24] A widely known example of a local government headed by Negroes is Fayette, Mississippi, a community of 1800 presided over by Mayor Charles Evers. With the help of black and white supporters throughout the United States, Mayor Evers has brought in new industries and a manpower training school that serves four counties.[25]

In recent years, black candidates have suffered political losses along with numerous gains. In the South in 1968, nearly 300 Blacks were defeated by white opponents.[26]

[22] *The New York Times*, Feb. 8, 1970, p. 50; May 2, 1971, Sec. 1, p. 17. According to Hosea Williams, vice president of the Southern Christian Leadership Conference, there are 70 counties in the South with black majorities. He says: "There could and should be at least 1695 black elected officials in these counties if we are to have representative government." In August, 1970, the SCLC had field workers in 23 of these 70 counties working with local people on voter registration and education in an operation called SCOPE. *Ibid.*, Aug. 30, 1970, p. 65.

[23] Wall, *op. cit.*, p. 6.

[24] Martin Waldron, "Negroes Confirmed as Winners and Control Alabama County," *The New York Times*, Aug. 2, 1969. *Ibid.*, Aug. 30, 1970, p. 65.

[25] *Ibid.*, Aug. 30, 1970, p. 65.

[26] Edward F. Sweat, "State and Local Politics in 1968," in Romero (ed.), *In Black America*, United, 1969, p. 142.

The Negro Vote in the North and West

In Chicago only a few prominent Negroes took an active part in politics before the Great Migration, and the Negro vote was not important until 1915. Although both the Republican and the Democratic machines sought control of the Negro vote, Chicago was strongly Republican throughout the twenties. Roosevelt received only an estimated 23 percent of the Negro vote in 1932. Hoover was not popular with Chicago Negroes, but they were doubtful about a candidate who had served in the Wilson administration and they did not want to take the chance that a man like Garner would succeed to the presidency in the event of Roosevelt's death. Opinion shifted in 1936 and 1940; 49 and 52 percent, respectively, of the Chicago Negro vote went to Roosevelt. After Roosevelt's personal appearance in Chicago in November, 1944, where he mentioned the poll tax, the FEPC, and equal opportunity for all men, the Democratic ticket polled 65 percent of the Negro vote. Some shift back to the Republicans with the beginning of World War II was a convincing demonstration that Negroes, voting as a bloc whenever they feel they have vital interests at stake, may sometimes hold the actual balance of power.[27]

A generation ago, Negro political behavior differed little from white political behavior in the North. Negroes voted in almost the same proportion as Whites, they were not tied to one party, and they went along with the machines rather than with third parties and reformers. However, Negroes carefully appraised the attitudes of candidates and parties toward their group. Professional politicians quickly realized the potentialities in the Negro vote and organized Negroes as they had formerly done with the Irish, the Germans, the Poles, and other newcomers to city life. In Chicago, Big Bill Thompson's rise to political power was coincident with the Great Migration. The Negro population in that city rose from 44,103 in 1910 to 109,458 in 1920 and 233,903 in 1940 and was concentrated in a few wards. Although

[27] St. Clair Drake and Horace Cayton, *Black Metropolis*, Harcourt Brace Jovanovich, 1945, pp. 109, 352–354, 359–360.

Black Elected Officials in the South, August, 1971

State	Total	U.S. Congress	State — Senators	State — Representatives	State — Others	County — Commissioners, Supervisors	County — Election Commissioners	County — Others	City — Mayors	City — Councilmen, Aldermen	City — Others	Law Enforcement — Judges, Magistrates	Law Enforcement — Constables, Marshals	Law Enforcement — Justices of Peace	Law Enforcement — Others	School Board
Alabama	96			2		6		13	4	38		1	6	15		11
Arkansas	97			1				2	6	27			4	6	12	39
Florida	41			2					2	30	3	1	1			2
Georgia	54		2	13		6		1		20	1	1				10
Louisiana	71			1					4	24	1		8	10	9	14
Mississippi	98			1		4	18	3	4	31			8	11		18
North Carolina	85			2		3			4	63		2				11
South Carolina	59			3		7			3	31		9				6
Tennessee	41		2	6		1				14		9		6	1	2
Texas	41		1	2					2	22						14
Virginia	52		1	2		4			30		2			12	1	
Totals	735		6	35		31	18	19	59	300	7	23	27	60	23	127

Source: Voter Education Project, Southern Regional Council, Black Elected Officials in the United States, 1971. Reprinted with permission.

Thompson was a corrupt politician, he treated Negroes more fairly than they had ever been treated before. With his blessing, Negroes developed their own ward machines and in return they demanded concessions for support.

Oscar DePriest quickly learned the ways of political machines and, during the first three decades of the century, built a powerful organization in Chicago. His precinct captains and ward committeemen "fixed" such matters as getting exceptions made to zoning ordinances, arranging for beds in the county hospital or the sanitarium, getting constituents "out of trouble" with the police, finding jobs, getting immediate relief, lending a hand to a church with mortgage problems, arranging for a club to use a public park for an outing, or straightening things out with the Bureau of Licenses. Payment for these services came in the form of votes or actual cash.[28] Similar developments occurred in Detroit, Philadelphia, Cleveland, New York, and St. Louis.

In the North and West, Negroes remained Democratic in the 1956 election, but with smaller margins. Although there was a definite trend away from the Democratic ticket, it was not strong enough to give President Eisenhower a majority in any major area of northern Negro registration. Harlem voted Democratic but by substantially reduced percentages; four assembly districts gave four-fifths of their votes to the Democrats in 1952 but only two-thirds in 1956. Only a slight shift was shown in the Chicago Negro vote. Mr. Stevenson's pluralities were a slightly smaller percentage than they were in 1952. In the Detroit area in Michigan, neither party claimed any shift of Negro votes, but there was a slight shift from the Democrats to the Republicans in California. In Philadelphia and several other cities, the falling off of the vote in a number of Negro districts was interpreted as an indication of dissatisfaction with the performance of both major parties.[29] As in the case of the much

greater shift in the South, the changes in Negro voting behavior in the North in the 1956 election may be attributed in part, but by no means entirely, to school segregation-desegregation and other civil rights issues.

From the beginning of the New Deal until 1952, 75 to 80 percent of the Negro voters cast their ballots for Democratic presidential candidates. Some change occurred in the elections of 1952, and in 1956 the Negro vote dropped to between 60 and 65 percent. In 1960, it is estimated that nearly 80 percent of the Negro voters voted for Mr. Kennedy. That vote played a crucial role in the election. In Texas, the statewide Kennedy margin was only 45,000, but he was estimated to have received more than 100,000 Negro votes. In South Carolina he won by less than 10,000 votes, but more than 40,000 Negroes voted for him. In North Carolina his majority was 58,000, but 70,000 Negroes voted for him. Mr. Kennedy carried Illinois by only 9000 votes, but 250,000 Negroes are estimated to have voted for him. Michigan went Democratic by 67,000 votes, with an estimated Negro vote of 250,000. Other northern states where his margins were exceeded by his votes from Negroes included New Jersey, Missouri, and Pennsylvania.

The Negro vote for the Democratic ticket in 1960 represented a 16 percent gain over 1956, as compared with an overall gain by Democrats of 8 percent. In 1964, almost all southern Negro precincts supported President Johnson.[30] Some heavily Negro precincts in New York, Pennsylvania, Maryland, and Ohio showed a better than 90 percent vote for President Johnson. Negroes were crucial in swinging Virginia, Tennessee, and Florida back to the Democrats after several years of Republican control.[31] Although the Nixon-Agnew ticket won the 1968 presidential elec-

---

[28] Ibid., pp. 342, 348, 351, 368–364.
[29] The New York Times, Nov. 11, 1956; The Crisis, Dec., 1956, pp. 614–615. A postelection poll made by the Survey Research Center of the University of

Michigan and published in March, 1957, showed that the Republicans received 35 percent of the Negro vote in 1948 and 36 percent in 1956. A Gallup Poll release in January, 1957, showed that the Republicans received 39 percent of the Negro vote in 1956. David Lawrence, " 'Rights' Minimized as a Vote Getter," Washington Post and Times-Herald, July 21, 1957.
[30] James Q. Wilson, "The Negro in Politics," Daedalus, Fall, 1965, p. 952.
[31] The New York Times, Nov. 4, 1964, p. 26.

tion, it received 10 percent, or less, of the black vote. Mr. Wallace and the various splinter and extremist groups secured such a small part of the Negro vote that it was hardly measurable. Miller says that it is apparent that Negroes, realizing that the three black presidential candidates, Charlene Mitchell, on Communist Party ticket; Eldridge Cleaver, on Peace and Freedom Party slate in Arizona, Iowa, Michigan, and Minnesota; and Dick Gregory, on Peace and Freedom ticket in New Jersey and Pennsylvania, and Freedom and Peace ticket in New York, Colorado, and Virginia, could not win, did not cast their votes for them merely on grounds of race.[32]

It is difficult to obtain complete information on the numbers of black elected officials outside the South. A list published in 1968 listed such officials for 22 other states; in each of these states at least one Negro was serving in either the state senate or the lower house. California, Illinois, Maryland, Michigan, Missouri, New York, and Pennsylvania had the largest black representations, and these were also the states in which substantial numbers of Blacks were serving in city councils.[33] According to a national survey of the Joint Center for Political Studies, three-fifths of the elected black officials are in eleven southern states. In 1971, more than 700 of the 1860 blacks who held elected offices resided outside the South.[34] In 1970, the black elected officials included more than 200 state legislators, compared with 36 in 1960. In 1970, 12 blacks were serving in, or had been elected to the U.S. House of Representatives, and one was in the U.S. Senate.[35]

Despite the marked increase in the number of black elected officials, the total still represents only three-tenths of 1 percent of all

officeholders. The principal interacting factors in the increased number of such officials seem to be: (1) the Voting Rights Act of 1965, (2) voter education and registration campaigns, (3) more black candidates seeking office, (4) perception by Negroes of enhanced chances for success in the election of black candidates, (5) the black nationalist and black power movements, and (6) the decisions of the U.S. Supreme Court in the reapportionment cases forcing state legislators to draw Congressional district lines so that Blacks will have a better opportunity to send representatives to many positions.[36]

Community Characteristics and Negro Voting in the South

A comprehensive study of political participation in the South found that community characteristics exert a strong influence on Negro political behavior.[37] In this analysis, comparisons are made of four counties: Piedmont (Peripheral South, Urban), Camelia (Peripheral South, Rural), Bright Leaf (Deep South, Urban), and Crayfish (Deep South, Rural). Matthews and Prothro found that the most important characteristic for Negro participation is the proportion of Negroes in the population. They found also that higher levels of Negro income and education were related to higher rates of political participation, and that Negroes in white-collar employment were not only more likely to participate politically but that their presence in an area seemed to lead other Negroes to participate. Correlated negatively with Negro political activity were levels of white education and rates of farm tenancy.[38] Daniel found that his correlations for Alabama for 1960 were very similar to those found by Matthews and Prothro. However, Daniel's correlations for 1966 differ considerably from those for 1960 and those reported by Matthews and Prothro. In Daniel's findings for 1966, nonwhite socioeconomic status and employment in manufacturing changed from a positive to a negative re-

[32] J. Erroll Miller, "The Negro in National Politics in 1968," in Romero, *op. cit.*, p. 36.

[33] Sweat, *op. cit.*, p. 139.

[34] *The New York Times*, May 2, 1971, Sec. 1, p. 17. The number of black officials rose 22 percent between February 1970 and February 1971. The total of 1860 for 1971 compares with 475 black officials elected in 1967.

[35] *The Plain Dealer*, Dec. 22, 1970, Sec. 1, p. 14. For a comprehensive list of elected Negro officials elected in 1968 or of those who held office in that year, see Romero, *op. cit.*, p. 448–468.

[36] Miller, *op. cit.*, p. 7.

[37] Matthews and Prothro, *op. cit.*, pp. 133–135.

[38] *Ibid.*

lationship with political mobilization. Also, "poverty, percent of farms operated by tenants, and percent Negro of the total population, changed from a negative to a positive relationship with Negro political mobilization, and there was an increase in the negative relationship between this variable and nonwhite urbanization."[39] Daniel says that changed conditions in Alabama between 1960 and 1966 affected the relationships between some of the political and socioeconomic components of the social system. For example, a positive correlation between a high Negro percentage of the total population and low political participation by Negroes was altered by the introduction of federal examiners and the voter registration drives. The exception to the patterns of change found by Daniel is the increase in the negative relationship between nonwhite urbanization and Negro political mobilization. His explanations of this relationship are (1) that an urban Negro tends to feel little identification with his community, (2) the perception by urban Negroes of a low probability of success in influencing elections, and, possibly, (3) that the measure of urbanization that was used, a county statistic, is too general.[40]

The Impact of Negro Voting on Social and Economic Status

Many political observers have assumed that the vote will automatically give southern Negroes influence over public policy commensurate with their numbers. They have argued that when Blacks vote in substantial numbers, southern state and local officials will respond to black demands or suffer at the polls. By means of political leverage, governments will be forced to eliminate many types of segregation. Claiming that this argument is too simple, Matthews and Prothro say:

. . . the translation of votes into power, and power into policy, is by no means automatic, and . . . public officials and political leaders

have far more freedom of maneuver in dealing with their constituents than had been initially realized. . . . The experience of northern Negroes—who have been voting in large numbers for many decades and yet are still distinctly 'second-class citizens'—is not very comforting to those who would place primary reliance on the vote as the 'solution' to the Negro problem in the South.[41]

Keech found that the Negro organizations in Durham, North Carolina and in Tuskegee, Alabama that have been so successful in mobilizing Negro voters and in obtaining important decisions in the courts are no longer leading the "Negro revolution." Having entered the mainstream of American life, the middle-class business and professional people who head these organizations are unable to articulate the problems of low-income Negroes.[42] In Keech's view, the steps essential for enabling rank-and-file Negroes to enter the American mainstream are, for the most part, programs that demand federal action. Local governments have too limited resources, financial and professional, to attack these problems. Local votes can help to elect national officials who will support programs that deal with local problems, and help elect local officials who will cooperate with the Federal programs. But Keech warns:

Lest there be undue optimism on this, at one point the U.S. Department of Labor ruled Durham schools ineligible for a Neighborhood Youth Corps project because the city school board had not yet complied with the Civil Rights Act. . . . the Durham school board chose not to participate in Project Headstart because of changes which were requested in its application. . . . On still a third occasion the board turned down a Neighborhood Youth Corps program. One of the board members' argument against it was that 'I don't think the school board should get into a welfare program.'[43]

A comparison of the effects of Negro voting in Durham and in Tuskegee may be significant in other situations. When Negro

[39] Johnnie Daniel, "Negro Political Behavior and Community Political and Socioeconomic Structural Factors," *Social Forces*, Mar., 1969, p. 278.

[40] *Ibid.*, pp. 279–280.

[41] Matthews and Prothro, *op. cit.*, pp. 477–478.

[42] William R. Keech, *The Impact of Negro Voting: The Role of the Vote in the Quest for Equality*, Rand McNally, 1968, p. 91.

[43] *Ibid.*, pp. 91–92.

voters in Tuskegee became a majority, their votes produced a marked change in the distribution of public services, including garbage collection, street paving, and recreational facilities. Also, Negroes were employed for the first time in municipal service positions and appointed to boards and commissions, and local public accommodations and fair employment ordinances were passed. According to Keech, Negro votes played a smaller role in eliminating discrimination in hospitals, and discrimination in schools and jury selection was handled through court suits started before Negro voting had reached sufficient proportions to deal with them. He concludes, though, that none of these things would have been impossible for Negro votes to obtain in contemporary Tuskegee if voting were used to secure them.[44] It is important, however, to point out that to say ". . . votes bring fair treatment of Negroes in Tuskegee is different only in degree from saying votes bring fair treatment of Jews in Tel Aviv. Negroes are a majority of the electorate in Tuskegee. More important than the fact that this majority secured the specified gains is the fact that having 25, 40 and 45 percent of the electorate was not enough! Saying that the vote is a protector of majorities in a democracy means little. Cohesive and intensive majorities do not as a rule need protection."[45]

Durham demonstrates that some gains can be made by Negroes when they constitute less than a majority of the electorate, as well as some of the limits on what voting can obtain in a situation more nearly typical than that which prevails in Tuskegee. In Durham, the Negro vote has influenced the outcome of elections, equal treatment by law enforcement agencies, equal distribution of parks and fire stations, employment of Negroes in municipal service, and reappointments to boards and commissions. The failures of Negro voting in Durham are as noteworthy as its successes. The vote has not helped pave streets in Negro sections, but Keech says that this lack is due at least partially to Durham's

requirement that residents pay for paving their own streets. On other failures of the Negro vote, he says:

The failure of the vote to be useful in integrating parks, schools and libraries is more significant, and more directly attributable to the limitations of the vote as a political resource for minorities. Fair employment and integration in the private sector of social life was even further removed from the influence of the vote in Durham. The general picture there seems to be that the vote is most useful for the least important gains. Surely the greatest strides made by Durham Negroes themselves have been the integration of schools and public accommodations, and the extension of fair employment. The things the vote has most clearly helped them secure are far less dramatic than these changes.[46]

Based in large part on studies and comparisons of Negro voting in Durham and Tuskegee, Keech's major conclusions are:

1. The effects of past discrimination are more resistant to Negro voting than is present discrimination. (His points here are: nobody, including Negro leaders, seems to know what to do about these effects; many Americans, including some Negro leaders seem not to have begun to think in terms of these effects; and programs that are designed to eradicate the effects of past discrimination may generate opposition because they appear to discriminate in favor of Negroes.)
2. In attacking present discrimination against Negroes, Negro votes are less able to secure fair and equal treatment in the private sector of social life than in the public sector. Negro votes are far less useful in leading governments to pass laws that integrate public accommodations, insure fair employment practices, and guarantee equal access to housing than they are in leading government to eliminate government discrimination itself. Tuskegee's public accommodations and fair employment practices ordinances were the last major payoffs of Negro voting there, and Durham's city council has never acted on requests that it pass such ordinances.
3. In attacking present discrimination in the private sector, votes will be more useful in eliminating such discrimination in public ac-

[44] *Ibid.*, p. 93.
[45] *Ibid.*, pp. 93–94.

[46] *Ibid.*, p. 94.

commodations and employment than in housing. While votes have brought public accommodations and fair employment ordinances in Tuskegee, the prohibition of discrimination in the sale and rental of housing has scarcely become a public issue. In Durham, fair housing only became a public issue in 1967, four years after the peak of demands for action in fair employment and public accommodations.

4. Within the public sector, votes more easily secure a fair and rapid distribution of public goods than their integration. In Durham the school board has resisted school integration. Negro votes have been more effective in obtaining a fair distribution of school facilities on a "separate but equal" basis than in integrating the schools. In public recreation, votes have not been as useful in achieving integration as in equalizing the distribution of facilities.

5. When public facilities are distributed as a result of bond issue elections, Negro votes have a better chance of insuring equal distribution than when facilities are distributed as a result of an independent decision by city officials. When a facility or service is the sole issue of an election, it is easier to achieve the desired results than when it is buried among other issues or when it cannot be tied to any single election.

6. Votes are less useful where elected officials do not have direct responsibility for policy than where they do. Although the city council in Durham appoints the school board, it disclaims any responsibility for school policy. The same is true of public housing policy.

7. Negro votes more easily secure an incremental adjustment in existing policies than a totally new program. Example: placing streetlights and traffic signs on all corners, compared with obtaining a new program of paving all streets at city expense when this has been, hitherto, a private responsibility.

8. The less salient a policy change is, and the less visible it is to the public eye, the more influence Negroes (or other groups) can have on it through voting. Example: the success of Negro votes in obtaining better parks and recreational facilities in Negro areas and the repeated failure of Negro votes to secure school integration.[47]

In short, in Durham and Tuskegee, fair and equitable administration of the laws has a relatively high legitimacy, and votes have been useful in achieving such ends. Programs that would contribute to the elimination of basic inequalities have less legitimacy in these cities. As Keech says, "the formal mechanisms of democracy do not assure much more than that elites will have incentives to meet demands that do not conflict with the values of the elites and of the majority of the voters."[48]

An interesting political development of recent years at the national level is the formation of the Black Caucus. The thirteen black congressmen feel that their constituencies include the majority of black Americans, a group that is underrepresented in Congress. In 1971, the Black Caucus planned to establish a staff comparable to the staffs of congressional committees, except that the caucus staff will not be paid with public funds. According to Representative Charles C. Diggs, Jr., some of the work of the caucus will lead to legislation, but not all of it. He said that the caucus will continue "to examine ways of convincing the executive branch that our approach to some problems may offer better solutions than theirs. In some cases we are talking about laws or executive orders that are already on the books but are not being enforced. We will be challenging interpretations of existing laws that we consider to be in error."[49]

Important gains may come to Negro minorities through resources other than votes. In Durham, litigation has brought about school integration; demonstrations and boycotts have brought changes in the private sector, including concessions in fair employment and the integration of numerous public accommodations. In these areas, the vote failed to produce changes. Now that most local practices have been brought into line with local and federal law, litigation is less useful than it was. According to Keech, the kinds of concessions that blacks need most now are changes in law, and these are no longer forthcoming from the courts.[50]

[48] *Ibid.*, p. 108.
[49] William Raspberry, "Black Caucus: Why and How," *The Plain Dealer*, June 25, 1971, p. 11.
[50] Keech, *op. cit.*, pp. 108–109.

[47] *Ibid.*, pp. 95–98.

Coalitions with White Voters

Negroes constitute a minority almost everywhere in the South. In order to win, southern Negroes usually have to enter into coalitions with at least some white politicians and voters. Matthews and Prothro point out that in situations where there is strong white agreement in favor of segregation, biracial coalitions are almost impossible. Thus, many Negroes in the South "may finally win the right to vote only to find themselves in a more or less permanent political minority." The vote for southern Negroes is a necessary but not a sufficient condition for change in the South. Also necessary are continued pressures from other regions and realistic views on the part of Negro and white Southerners.[51]

Wilson says that the Negro is a partner "in a set of tacit, though unorganized coalitions" and adds that they are probably the only viable ones, particularly in the South. In his view, the Negro needs

. . . many different and often conflicting alliances which take into account the different bases of support available for different kinds of issues. Nationally, organized labor may support civil rights and income-transfer measures but locally it is often likely to support (at least tacitly) segregated housing and economy in government. Religious groups are very effective when the issue is voting rights; they are much less effective in dealing with economic questions where simple morality is not at issue. Upper-class business men may support Negro voting claims in Southern cities and Negro oriented public works programs in Northern cities, but nationally they will oppose large-scale income redistribution. A grand Negro-liberal coalition, if achieved, may so rationalize these inconsistent positions as to deliver the leadership of would-be allies into the hands of those elements who are least in favor of (or least effective on behalf of) Negro causes.[52]

A similar view has been expressed by Bayard Rustin. In stressing the desirability of alliances, Rustin says that the civil rights struggle is no longer in the era of demonstration and ideological absolutes but is now

a matter of practical politics. Sweat adds: "The facet of broad strategy chosen by Negro elected officials will, in all likelihood, be determined by the exigencies of their own peculiar local conditions, as well as by their ability to manipulate the existing power structure. The most fruitful approach at the moment would seem to be a judicious mixture of alliances combined with confrontation—both securely anchored in a black voting power base."[53]

BLACK POWER

In the mid-1960s, a political concept known as "black power" began to develop. No single definition is adequate to describe this movement, but it is concerned "with organizing the rage of black people and with putting new, hard questions and demands to white America."[54] Hamilton says that black power must "(1) deal with the obviously growing alienation of black people and their distrust of the institutions of this society; (2) work to create new values and to build a new sense of community and of belonging; and (3) work to establish legitimate new institutions that make participants, not recipients, out of people traditionally excluded from the fundamentally racist processes of this country." The ghetto is looked at from the standpoint of "internal" and "external" problems. Internal problems range from "exploitative merchants who invade black communities, to absentee landlords, to inferior schools and arbitrary law enforcement, to black people unable to develop their own independent economic and political bases." External problems include: jobs, open occupancy, medical care, and higher education.[55]

Some advocates of black power take a "provincialistic" posture, attributing precedence to a quality—skin color—over actual performance of black Americans. They justify this position with the claim that racial

---

[51] Matthews and Prothro, *op. cit.*, pp. 478–479, 481.
[52] Wilson, *op. cit.*, pp. 960–961.

[53] Sweat, *op. cit.*, p. 143.
[54] Charles V. Hamilton, "An Advocate of Black Power Defines It," *The New York Times Magazine*, Apr. 14, 1968, p. 79.
[55] *Ibid.*, p. 79.

discrimination has so retarded Negro Americans that only a few Blacks can perform competitively with white Americans. Historic handicaps, it is said, can only be overcome by separation from Whites, at least temporarily, and by preferential treatment.[56]

In the rhetoric of race relations in the late 1960s, "black power cannot exist within white power. One or the other. There can only be one or the other. They might exist side by side as separate entities, but never in the same space. Never. They are mutually exclusive."[57] The white man is regarded as "irrelevant to blacks, except as an oppressive force. Blacks want to be in his place, yes, but not in order to terrorize and lynch and starve him. They want to be in his place because that is where a decent life can be had."[58]

Proponents of black power argue that without separation, "whites will dominate blacks, with the result that blacks will acquiesce to or rage against whites."[59] Leaders in the movement insist that black people must form independent political parties rather than waste their time trying to reform or convert "the racist parties." According to this view, the election of a few black people to local or national office does not solve the problem of political representation. For example, of the ten black people on Chicago's City Council of 50, only two or three are said to speak out forcefully. Carmichael and Hamilton say that if independent Blacks are continuously outvoted on official bodies to which they are elected, it will become necessary ". . . to devise wholly new forms of local political representation. There is nothing sacred about the system of electing candidates to serve as aldermen, councilmen, etc., by wards or districts. Geographical representation is not inherently right. Perhaps political interests have to be represented in some entirely different manner—such as community-parent control of schools, unions of tenants, unions of welfare recipients actually taking an official role in running welfare departments."[60]

Another assumption of the black-power advocates is that white decision makers will yield nothing without a struggle and a confrontation by organized power. Black people will make gains only through their ability to organize bases of economic and political power, that is, through boycotts, electoral activity, rent strikes, work stoppages, and pressure-group bargaining. It must be made clear that Whites "will have to bargain with Blacks or continue to fight them in the streets of the Detroits and the Newarks."[61]

We point out in Chapter 7 that black power, at least in its more extreme form, is the position of a small minority. Gerlach and Hine say that leadership and organized activity above a local group level in the black power movement is ephemeral; cohesion comes through "a range of integrating, cross-cutting links, bonds, and operations, including ties between members and group leaders, by the activities of 'traveling evangelists,' or spokesmen, large scale demonstrations and 'in-gatherings,' sharing of basic ideological themes and collective perception of, and action against, a common opposition." They see this "decentralized, segmented, and reticulate" movement as adaptive in bringing about social change.[62]

[56] Wayne C. Rohrer, *Black Profiles of White Americans*, F. A. Davis, 1970, pp. 133–134; Hamilton, *op. cit.*, p. 81.

[57] LeRoi Jones, "The Need for a Cultural Base to Civil Rites and Bpower Mooments," in Floyd B. Barbour (ed.), *The Black Power Revolt*, Porter Sargent, 1968, p. 120.

[58] Stokely Carmichael, "Power and Racism," in Barbour, *op. cit.*, p. 70.

[59] Rohrer, *op. cit.*, p. 134.

[60] Stokely Carmichael and Charles V. Hamilton, "The Search for New Forms," in Sethard Fisher (ed.), *Power and the Black Community*, Random House, 1970, pp. 380, 382.

[61] Hamilton, *op. cit.*, pp. 23, 79. The most extreme form of black power is found in the Black Republic of New Africa, a small group which advocates setting up an independent Negro republic in a tract of land to be taken out of Alabama, Georgia, Louisiana, Mississippi, and South Carolina. Robert Franklin Williams, president of the organization, has been living in exile for a decade in Cuba, Mainland China, and Tanzania. This state would be established peacefully if possible, with bloodshed, if necessary. *The Plain Dealer*, July 14, 1968.

[62] Luther P. Gerlach and Virginia H. Hine, "The Social Organization of a Movement of Revolutionary Change: Case Study, Black Power," in Norman E. Whitten, Jr., and John F. Szwed, *Afro-American Anthropology*, The Free Press, 1970, pp. 385–401. In their field work in a local community of 100,000 (three-quarters of this population are English-speak-

The Role of Whites in the Black Power Movement

Black power leaders do not want Whites in decision making or leadership positions in the institutions of the black community. New welfare and development agencies, public and private, have been criticized for ignoring existing Negro organizations and trying to do the job of delivering social services themselves. Often such agencies "have storefront locations and hire some 'indigenous' workers, but the class and racial gap is difficult to cross."[63] It is claimed that if black power is to be a motivating force to energize black communities, the ideal leadership is "the kind of black competence which affords pride and holds onto hope in uniquely saving ways."[63a] At present, such leadership is in short supply. The fact that many successful blacks no longer feel it necessary to maintain social distance from less advantaged blacks does not affect the situation materially. Comer says: "Because the functions of Negro organizations have been largely preempted by white agencies, however, no Negro institution is available through which such people can work to overcome a century of intraNegro class alienation."[64]

Black power advocates recognize the need for the help of Whites, mainly technical and financial. Eldridge Cleaver's widely quoted statement that Whites "could best help the black movement by donating machine guns"

is simply an extremist statement of the hope that sympathetic white people will provide resources other than manpower to black programs.[65] Also, such Whites are frequently asked to attack white racism (prejudice). Specific objectives outside the Negro community suggested for concerned Whites include bringing as much pressure as possible on local and national decision makers to adopt sound policies on an open housing market and an expanding job market.[66] Comer says that white people of good will with interest, skills, and funds are needed and "contrary to the provocative assertions of a few Negroes—are still welcome in the Negro community."[67] A related view holds: "It is not necessary that Blacks create parallel agencies—political or economic—in all fields and places. Richard Hatcher did so in Gary, but he first had to organize black voters to fight the Democratic party machine in the primary. The same is true of Mayor Carl Stokes in Cleveland. At some point it may be wise to work within the existing agencies, but this must be done only from a base of independent, not subordinated, power."[68]

Centralizing-Decentralizing Trends in Government and Black Power

Black power advocates say that as the federal government becomes more involved in the lives of people, the base of citizen participation must be broadened. The new forms, agencies, and structures, developed by the black power movement, are seen as linking these centralizing and decentralizing trends.[69] Wilson points out the effects of the greater and more direct involvement of the federal government in the affairs of cities and metropolitan areas. This increased participation, occurring "under circumstances which require that federal authorities not visibly deny the precept of equal justice for all means that Negroes, through injunctive procedures as well as political pressure, will be able to

---

ing; most of the other people are Spanish-speaking Latin Americans) within a metropolitan area, Valentine and Valentine found that the quality of the adaptation by poor people is distorted in many printed and electronic reports. Usually, these reports do not point out the positive strengths of the ghetto, including "the ability to deal with misfortune through humor, the capacity to respond to defeat with renewed effort, recourse to widely varied sacred and secular ideologies for psychological strength, and resourceful devices to manipulate existing structure for maximum individual or group benefit." Charles A. Valentine and Betty Lou Valentine, "Making the Scene, Digging the Action, and Telling It Like It Is: Anthropologists at Work in a Dark Ghetto," in *ibid.*, pp. 403–418.

[63] James P. Comer, "The Social Power of the Negro," in Barbour, *op. cit.*, p. 81.

[63a] Nathan Wright, Jr., "The Crisis Which Bred Black Power," in Barbour, *op. cit.*, pp. 115–116; Rohrer, *op. cit.*, p. 135.

[64] Comer, *op. cit.*, p. 82.

[65] Rohrer, *op. cit.*, pp. 135–136.

[66] Hamilton, *op. cit.*, p. 81.

[67] Comer, *op. cit.*, p. 83.

[68] Hamilton, *op. cit.*, p. 81.

[69] *Ibid.*, p. 83.

compel changes in the administration of local programs in schools, housing, and the like as a precondition to resolving the growing volume of federal aid."[70]

Effectiveness of Black Officials and Attitudes of Black Voters

Because of the recency of acquisition of office by most black local officials, it is too early to tell whether they can operate more effectively in areas of social blight than did their white predecessors. It is known that these officeholders are under strong pressure to achieve results quickly on problems of long standing such as housing and recreation.[71] Usually this is impossible, and the situation is compounded by the burden of political inexperience carried by black officials as a result of years of exclusion from the political process, especially in the South.

Expert help has been made available to new officeholders, particularly in the South. In addition to the work of the Southern Regional Council's Voter Education Project, that organization sponsored the Southwide Conference of Black Elected Officials in Atlanta, December 11–14, 1968. Earlier, SEDFRE (The Scholarship, Education, and Defense Fund for Racial Equality) gave limited assistance to inexperienced officeholders. Recently, this organization inaugurated a privately funded technical assistance program for newly elected public officials, with headquarters in New York City.[72]

Sweat predicts that the more active and more sophisticated black voters become the less inclined they will be to vote for a charismatic leader or for a particular political party. This means that some Blacks who are opposed by Whites will lose Negro votes unless they can persuade voters that their programs are pertinent to pressing problems.[73]

Community Control

When black leaders use the term "community control," they mean greater participation of

Blacks in the political and economic affairs of urban communities. Specifically, they include the following:

1. Devolution of as much authority as possible to neighborhood communities. (A neighborhood community usually is defined as an area of about 50,000 people. These communities are conceived of as units that would give Blacks something like parity with suburbs.)
2. Direct representation of such communities on the city council, the board of education, the police commission, and other significant policy bodies.
3. Black representation at all levels of the public service in far more than token members.
4. Similar representation on the labor forces of government contractors.
5. The vigorous application of public resources to facilitate the development of black-controlled businesses.[74]

In addition, an informal agenda involves getting federal, state, and local administrations to give top priority to the pursuit of racial equality. Black leaders insist, however, that they want such administrations to concentrate on assisting them to obtain power and wealth of their own, either as communities or as individuals.[75]

Some advocates of community control recognize that the great problems of cities— poverty, segregation, and air pollution—require regional solutions and metropolitan values rather than narrowly conceived remedies. Altshuler suggests the following program:

(1) elimination of all special districts, leaving a simple two- or three-tier system of general purpose governments within each urban region; (2) the top tier, regional in scale, to exercise responsibility for such functions as pollution control, general land use and transportation planning, the equalization of public services (via grants-in-aid), and securing integration opportunities for those who wish to exploit them; (3) the bottom tier to exercise the kinds of responsibility that suburbs now exercise; (4) each tier, or at least the top two, to be organized along strong mayoralty lines, with all agency

---

[70] Wilson, *op. cit.*, p. 966.
[71] Sweat, *op. cit.*, p. 136.
[72] *Ibid.*, p. 144.
[73] *Ibid.*, p. 143.

[74] Alan A. Altshuler, *Community Control: The Black Demand for Participation in Large American Cities*, Pegasus, 1970, p. 14.
[75] *Ibid.*, pp. 14–15.

heads serving at the pleasure of the mayor; and (5) civil service regulations to be made far more flexible, so as to enable chief executives to combat the three bureaucratic diseases of stagnation, unresponsiveness, and racial imbalance.

Where a middle tier—the central city—persisted, neighborhoods within it would continue to exercise less authority than suburbs. Thus, the neatest and most equitable arrangement would be two tiers, if it were feasible. A two-tier system . . . might be one in which the suburbs themselves had substantially less power, e.g., to exclude low-income housing, to maintain lily-white schools, than at present.[76]

Altshuler recognizes that sources of conflict exist between advocates of black community (neighborhood) control and white residents who now control a city. Where Blacks had hoped to gain a central city majority in the near future, now they would probably oppose the transfer of any of its functions to the metropolitan level. In such a case, Blacks would be likely to become less enthusiastic about community control itself, while white city residents in the process of losing control would be likely to acquire some interest in it.[77]

Despite the arguments against community control, Altshuler says that it is probably the most feasible major demand that Blacks are now making. In his view, "white resistance to massive desegregation and redistribution is overwhelming, and it comes from all segments of white society. The resistance to community control, by contrast, is centered in the big city public bureaucracies. Many other Whites are hostile—out of family, ethnic, or racial solidarity, but they really have no stake in who governs the ghettos."[78] The present authors do not share Altshuler's hope that community control "will help cement the American union by providing an adequate outlet for racial pluralism." We see no reason to believe that the idea of community control as presently set forth will prove acceptable in more than very limited ways in most American cities. A democratically successful pluralism requires significant crosscutting memberships.

[76] *Ibid.*, pp. 46, 50–51.
[77] *Ibid.*, pp. 51–52.
[78] *Ibid.*, p. 197.

PROTESTS, ALLIANCES, CONFRONTATIONS, VIOLENCE

Definitions and Prevalence of Protests. Protest activity is defined by Lipsky as "a mode of political action oriented toward objection to one or more policies or conditions, characterized by showmanship or display of an unconventional nature, and undertaken to obtain rewards from political or economic systems while working within the systems."[79] According to this view, protest is one of the few ways in which relatively powerless groups can achieve a bargaining position. Bargaining resources also can be created by increasing group solidarity. Typically, protest efforts are intended to activate reference publics in such a way that a target group or individual will respond along lines that are favorable to the protesters. If the protest consists of efforts to induce third parties to join the conflict, but where the value orientations of these parties are similar to those of the protesting group, it may be called "alliance formation." Where groups have sufficient resources to bargain on their own, as in the case of some economic boycotts and labor strikes, they may be said to engage in "direct confrontation."[80]

Some advocates of black power insist that the disorders of 1965–1967 were revolts rather than riots. Their argument is that many who participated in the disturbances deny the legitimacy of the sociopolitical system. They claim that the present value structure supports property rights over human rights and that an oppressive notion of "law and order" relegates black people to a subordinated status.[81]

Left-wing spokesmen say that the riots of the 1960s were incipient colonial uprisings, but Fogelson points out profound differences between these two types of events.

The recent American riots were spontaneous and unorganized, opposed by the Negro leadership, confined almost entirely to the ghettos, and quelled with vigor but not without restraint by

[79] Michael Lipsky, *Protest in City Politics*, Rand McNally, 1970, p. 2.
[80] *Ibid.*, p. 3.
[81] Charles V. Hamilton, "Riots, Revolts and Relevant Response," in Barbour, *op. cit.*, p. 174.

the authorities. The colonial uprisings, by contrast, developed out of nonviolent demonstrations against colonial exploitation; the African leaders led the demonstrations and then directed the uprisings. The rioters attacked government buildings and did other damage outside native districts; and the authorities, relying largely on the military, responded relentlessly and ruthlessly. Hence the American riots were more restrained than the colonial uprisings—which suggests that the stakes are higher and the frustrations deeper in Africa than in America.[82]

The disorders of the 1960s differed from the race riots that followed World War I and World War II in that they were not mass confrontations of Blacks and Whites. Typically, the riots of earlier periods involved a dispute between Whites and Blacks over rights of residence or the use of parts of urban territory (parks, playgrounds, beaches, etc.). Nearly all the disturbances of the 1960s involved only Blacks and law enforcement agents. According to Rossi: "Blacks did not attempt to move out of their neighborhoods and the few scattered attempts by Whites to enter black ghettos were turned back by the police and troops. The revolts of the 1960s were directed toward the police and toward property."[83] Reasons for the differences between the riots before and after 1960 include the following: (1) the great expansion of white suburbs and black ghettos has insulated the racial groups from one another; (2) the children of the first- and second-generation immigrants who rioted in 1917, 1919, and 1943 are middle-class citizens who, for the most part, do not need to resort to violence to maintain their socioeconomic status; (3) except in the deep South, governmental authorities are highly professional today, and no racial group can riot with impunity; and (4) except in the deep South, white leaders are committed to orderly change and cannot sanction rioting even

when they might be sympathetic with a cause espoused by persons inclined to riot.[84]

Masotti, Hadden, Seminatore, and Corsi have identified a series of patterns of violence in the history of the United States that consists of: suppression and insurrection; lynching; white-dominated, person-oriented rioting; racial warfare; person-oriented rioting; and Negro-dominated, property-oriented rioting. Admittedly, there is considerable overlap between the patterns. This study found that each pattern was, for a time, hardly noticeable, then became more important, and eventually became the dominant pattern. It concludes also that the dominance in violence of the Negro may not yet be complete. If the patterns operate in a full cycle, "the Negro would next orient his violence toward the white person, not the white's property—just as the whites initially oriented their violence toward the persons of their slaves. In any event, the Negro is dominant in this final pattern . . . virtually the only white participation is that of white police or other organized forces that attempt to suppress the riot."[85]

The table on page 407 shows the patterns of violence found in the Hasotti, Hadden, Seminatore, Corsi study in chronological order.

The revolts of the 1960s were ubiquitous. They occurred in cities where the proportions of Blacks were both large and small. Both liberal and conservative city administrations faced revolts. There were riots in Rochester, Omaha, and Lansing, as well as in New York, Chicago, Philadelphia, Cleveland, and Detroit. The South had fewer riots than the North, "not simply because Southern Negroes have lower expectations than Northern Negroes and Southern policemen fewer inhibitions than Northern policemen. The South . . . has far fewer ghettos. . . . It is only recently that as the racial status quo has been vigorously challenged in the South,

[82] Robert M. Fogelson, "Violence as Protest," in Robert H. Connery (ed.), Urban Riots: Violence and Social Change, Proceedings of the Academy of Political Science, Vol. 29, No. 1, 1968, p. 33.

[83] Peter H. Rossi, "Introduction," in Ghetto Revolts, Aldine, 1970, p. 6.

[84] Fogelson, op. cit., p. 31.

[85] Louis H. Masotti, Jeffrey K. Hadden, Kenneth F. Seminatore, and Jerome Corsi, A Time to Burn?: An Evaluation of the Present Crisis in Race Relations, Rand McNally, 1970, pp. 127–128.

Patterns of Violence

I	Slavery	White-dominated	Person-oriented
	Insurrections	Negro-dominated	Person-oriented
	Suppression	White-dominated	Person-oriented
II	Lynching	White-dominated	Person-oriented
	Rioting	White-dominated	Person-oriented
III	Warfare	White/Black-dominated	Person-oriented
IV	Rioting	Negro-dominated	Property-oriented
V	Rioting	Negro-dominated	Person-oriented
	or		
	Warfare	White/Black-dominated	Person-oriented
	or		
	Suppression	White-dominated	Person-oriented

Source: Louis H. Masotti, Jeffrey K. Hadden, Kenneth F. Seminatore, and Jerome Corsi, *A Time to Burn?* Rand McNally, 1970, p. 130. Reprinted with permission.

Southern whites . . . have retreated to segregated suburbs and left Negro ghettos behind. Where this happened, as in Atlanta, Southern Negroes, like Northern Negroes are more resentful of their grievances and less concerned about society's restraints, more conscious of their strength and less reluctant to test it through violence."[86]

Causes of the Civil Disorders of the 1960s

The statement in the *Report of the National Advisory Commission on Civil Disorders* that "white racism is essentially responsible for the explosive mixture which has been accumulating in our cities since the end of World War II"[87] fails as an explanation of the riots of the 1960s. Granted that white racism (prejudice) is an important feature of American society, it is, as Grimshaw points out, as much an effect as it is a cause. A sociological explanation of the disorders emphasizes the structural characteristics that support the subordination of certain groups. A sociological interpretation would regard discrimination and segregation, black migration and the white exodus, and the black ghetto as

sources rather than as results of prejudice.[88] An important corollary of the latter explanation of violence is the greater amenability of structural factors to planned social change. In the light of what is known about the difficulty of changing attitudes by direct attacks, the Commission's stress on white racism suggests that the problem of black-white relations is essentially insoluble. Apart from the greater publicity that it received and its wider distribution, the Kerner report added little to earlier reports. In testifying before the Commission, Kenneth B. Clark said: "I read that report . . . of the 1919 riot in Chicago, and it is as if I were reading the report of the investigating committee on the Harlem riot of '35, the report of the investigating committee on the Harlem riot of '43, the report of the McCone Commission on the Watts riot. . . ."[89]

Some black observers say that the rioting seemed not to be directed toward any particular civil rights goal, but was an unorganized, spontaneous "lashing out" at "the system." Lockard says: "The destruction of property and the attacks on police suggest a

[86] Fogelson, *op. cit.*, p. 40; Rossi, *op. cit.*, p. 9.
[87] *Report of the National Advisory Commission on Civil Disorders*, Bantom Books, 1968, p. 10.

[88] Allen D. Grimshaw, *Racial Violence in the United States*, Aldine, 1969, p. 5.
[89] *Report of the National Advisory Commission on Civil Disorders, op. cit.*, p. 29.

desire to destroy what ghetto residents cannot control. The burning, demolition, and looting of property is symbolic of the have-not frustration felt by ghetto dwellers, and the violence directed at the police expresses resentment at the symbols of control over their lives."[90]

Expressing a revolutionary view that is not held by most Blacks, Hare says that all black power advocates, "except the deceptive and dishonest few who occupy positions in all groups, appear to have lost faith in the old ways of righting the black man's wrongs. . . . They recognize the basic incompatibility of reform and revolutionary tactics."[91] To bring out a similar view, Silver contrasts a statement in the Kerner report with one made in the majority report of the Commission on Industrial Relations in 1915. The 1968 report said: "Those few who could destroy civil order and the role of law strike at the freedom of every citizen. They must know that the community cannot and will not tolerate coercion and mob action." The 1915 report said: "Through history where a people or group have been arbitrarily denied rights which they conceived to be theirs, reaction has been inevitable. Violence is a natural form of protest against injustice." Silver sees violence as "a matter of natural law, of elemental and self-evident justice. . . . collective violence as a response to injustice is rooted in the innate order of things."[92]

An analysis of the causes of civil disorders should distinguish between precipitating and underlying conditions. Precipitating incidents often involve emotionally charged offenses committed by one group against the other—attacks on women, police brutality, murder, and assault. Recently, violation of segregation taboos by Blacks have been precipitants. Lieberson and Silverman find that the functioning of local government is important in determining whether a dis-

turbance will follow a precipitating event. Inaction or actual encouragement on the part of police can increase the possibilities of a racial riot. Riot cities "not only employ fewer Negro policemen, but they are also communities whose electoral systems tend to be less sensitive to the demands of the electorate. Local government illustrates the possibility that riots occur when a community institution is malfunctioning, from the perspective of one or both racial segments." In riot cities, Negroes are less likely to be store owners, Negroes are closer to Whites in their proportion in "traditional" Negro occupations, and Negro-white income differences are smaller. These findings suggest that malfunctioning of local government and conflicts of interests in the economic world are among the leading underlying causes of racial riots.[93]

Purposes of the Riots of the 1960s

Some observers hold that the riots of the 1960s were meant to alert America; others say that their purpose was to contribute to overturning it.[94] Typical of the first view, Boskin sees the riots as an integral part of the protest of the 1960s, adding that the ultimate objective of the civil rights and other Negro movements is to introduce revolutionary change within the framework of the American social and political structure.[95] Representing the other view, Killian finds that the new black radicals reject the economic system, the American political system, the bourgeois values of America, and the nationalism of the late twentieth century. Also, they align themselves with the anti-Vietnam war movement and with the Third World.[96] An example of the current rhetoric of violence is taken from an essay by Hare: ". . . Voting is institutionalized and sacred, and it is virtually impossible to

[90] Duane Lockard, *Toward Equal Opportunity*, Macmillan, 1968, p. 141.

[91] Nathan Hare, "How White Power Whitewashes Black Power," in Barbour, *op. cit.*, p. 187.

[92] Allan A. Silver, "Official Interpretation of Racial Riots," in Connery (ed.), *op. cit.*, p. 152.

[93] Stanley Lieberson and Arnold R. Silverman, "The Precipitants and Underlying Conditions of Race Riots," *ASR*, Dec., 1965, pp. 896–897.

[94] Fogelson, *op. cit.*, p. 35.

[95] Joseph Boskin, *Urban Racial Violence in the Twentieth Century*, Glencoe, 1969, p. 148.

[96] Lewis R. Killian, *The Impossible Revolution*, Random House, 1968, p. 143.

vote in a revolution; most certainly it is inconceivable, given the present methods of choosing candidates. Besides I may be able, through superior fighting skills and stealth to kill a number of men, slitting the throat of one, choking another, dropping a hand grenade among the rest. But I can vote only once. If my numbers are too few to fight back in self-defense they are too few to vote out white supremacy. . . . Black men must bring an irresistible black power force to clash with the immovable object of white oppression with such velocity that America will either solve her problem or suffer the destruction she deserves."[97]

Some black power advocates maintain that the movement is consistent with democratic ideals, but admit that it does have a violent facet. Scott draws three conclusions from rhetoric of violence: (1) one hears what must be interpreted as the advocacy of violence; (2) the violent rhetoric is justified as a response to prior white violence and is considered as self-defense; (3) this rhetoric is intended to maximize "the slender hope that may exist for a relatively peaceful, constructive working out of the cry for Black Power."[98]

Rossi regards the revolts as expressions that challenge the legitimacy of existing institutions: "In defying the police and looting commercial establishments, ghetto blacks suddenly expressed attitudes which they had held all along, to the effect that local institutions were not of their making, were inimical to their interests and had a legitimacy only by virtue of definitions which they did not share."[99] In some respects the attitudes of black power advocates coincide with a mood that seems to be growing in American politics, that is, a greater tendency to work outside of established channels. Smith says that today there are "more demonstrations and fewer quiet remonstrances behind the scenes, a weakening of the tradi-

tional political parties as vehicles for managing conflict, direct action exalted and closed politics distrusted, a push for wider participation along with a vague feeling that government officials are aloof and no longer representative."[100]

Gains and Costs of Civil Disorders

Riots have been called short-lived "opportunity structures." There is no single "rioter," but rather persons who play many different roles—looter, sniper, police attacker, sympathetic bystander, ideological interpreter, and others. The riot "has an ideological meaning for the participants; it is not simply a diversion which allows for criminal activity." The greater the financial damage of the looting and burning, the more the looter's feelings about his world are emphasized. In addition, the riots become a kind of primitive attempt at an income redistribution.[101]

Turner concludes that interpreting public disorders as furthering reform requires that the protests "be capitalized quickly, while the conditions are favorable, through programs that can be implemented on a continuing basis by a more routinized and impersonal bargaining." He suggests also that reformers should not overestimate the efficacy of disorderly protest compared with other means for bringing about change.[102]

The theat of violence works both ways—it can make public officials more responsive to Negro demands, but it can also make them more resistant to Negro objectives. In some cases, violence may merely escalate the level of conflict and inflame the atmosphere without changing the political situation.[103] Rossi expects that an increase in the political strength of urban Blacks will be accompanied by an increased white backlash. Working-class Whites may interpret the political struggle for better conditions for Blacks as a con-

[97] Hare, *op. cit.*, pp. 186, 188.

[98] Robert L. Scott, "Justifying Violence: The Rhetoric of Militant Black Power," in R. L. Scott and Wayne Brockriede (eds.), *The Rhetoric of Black Power*, Harper & Row, 1969, p. 134.

[99] Rossi, *op. cit.*, p. 9.

[100] Bruce R. Smith, "The Politics of Protest: How Effective is Violence?" in Connery, *op. cit.*, p. 127.

[101] Lee Rainwater, "Open Letter on White Justice and the Riots," in Rossi, *op. cit.*, p. 71.

[102] Ralph H. Turner, "The Public Perception of Protest," *ASR*, Dec., 1969, p. 829.

[103] Keech, *op. cit.*, p. 109; Smith, *op. cit.*, pp. 127–218.

test in which black gains are made at their expense. At one extreme, this could mean that the civil disorders of the 1970s would be communal riots in which masses of Whites and Blacks would confront each other in street warfare. A less extreme development would mean the replacement of liberal mayors who have responded to black demands with "law and order" mayors committed to holding the line on the urban ghettos. The latter tactic might radicalize the political attitudes of Blacks still further.[104]

The Future Role of Civil Disorders

Hacker predicts that the number of attempts to sabotage the American government and society will increase; peaceful demonstrations such as marches and picketing will be augmented by less peaceful methods in the form of blocking traffic, interfering with business, and disrupting white America's usual routines. In time, he expects serious destruction: "dynamiting of bridges and water mains, firing of buildings, assassination of public officials and private luminaries."[105] On the other hand, Rossi says that as the ghetto becomes better organized (more political organizations claiming more and more allegiance of black people), the revolts will decrease in frequency. According to Rossi, a revolt is an inefficient political device compared with disciplined political action, and as black leaders "emerge and press their demands on local administrations and national officials, the political messages will become clearer and the accompanying manifestations of collective strength will become more coherent."[106]

Writing about the ability of relatively powerless groups, in general, to engage in successful protest, Lipsky says that the outcome is influenced not only by manifest, immediate behavior but by more remote, environmental factors. In part, the response of communications media, potential allies, and target groups to protest depends upon the reputations of the protest groups in the wider community, and the extent to which sympathy or hostility exists for the general group of which the protesters are considered a part. Also important in the success or failure of protest are the political and legal system prior to the protest; and the general social context within which the protest is viewed.[107]

Altshuler writes hopefully about the possibility of domesticating American racial conflict as we have done with labor-management conflict. He points out that labor makes new demands at every opportunity, but that it is far from being a revolutionary force. His argument is:

Blacks want many things. They want more and better jobs. They want massive redistributive public programs. They want integration. They want to own property. They want to be treated with respect by civil servants, employers, and merchants. They want to see their own kind in positions of power, prestige, and wealth. They want credit, insurance, and decent merchandise at prices comparable to those paid by whites. And, of course, many of them want community control. There is almost surely a good deal of substitutability among these wants. The trade-offs cannot be specified with . . . precision; but . . . higher relative incomes would probably alleviate the intensity of black anger as effectively as integration. More responsive substantive policies could do as well as participatory reform. And even within the participatory realm, jobs, contracts, and elaborate consultation could doubtless reduce . . . the pressure for transfers of authority to the neighborhood level.[108]

Whether civil disorders increase or decrease in the 1970s and 1980s will depend largely on how well American economic and social institutions provide the life chances that a substantial part of the population wants. Perhaps, as Rainwater says, the necessary condition for any permanent solution to riots is the provision of reasonable ap-

[104] Rossi, *op. cit.*, p. 12.

[105] Andrew Hacker, "The Violent Black Minority," *The New York Times Magazine*, June 2, 1970, p. 67.

[106] Rossi, *op. cit.*, pp. 11–12.

[107] Lipsky, *op. cit.*, pp. 188–189. See *ibid.*, pp. 189–191 for a discussion of the political and legal system in New York City, as well as the "mood" of the city during the period 1963–1965, that favored the success of the rent strikes.

[108] Altshuler, *op. cit.*, pp. 196–197.

proximation of the "average" standard of living for every family.[109] If political institutions fail to provide remedies, "the aspirations of the people begin to spill over into forms of activity that the dominant society regards either as unacceptable or illegitimate —crime, vandalism, noncooperation, and various forms of political protest."[110]

Conclusion on the Negro in Politics

In bringing the discussion of the Negro in politics to a close, we cannot do better than to summarize the conclusions of an astute political scientist. James Q. Wilson says that the best ways to understand the political position of Blacks in the United States today is to compare what some Negroes are asking of politics with what politics can provide. He refers to politics in the narrower sense— "the competitive struggle for elective office and deliberate attempts to influence the substance of government decisions—and not, in the broadest sense, as any activity by which conflict over goals is carried on. Although something is sacrificed by limiting the definition (rent strikes, boycotts, and sit-ins may have consequences for officeholders and legislators), the sacrifice is necessary if we are to understand what is meant by the statement that the civil rights movement, and Negro protest generally, ought to become a political movement."[111] Wilson them summarizes Rustin's argument "that the problems of the Negro cannot be solved by granting him even the fullest civil rights, for it is his legal privileges which must be changed. Such changes, in the magnitude necessary, require radical—indeed revolutionary—programs in education, housing, and income redistribution; these programs, in turn, will be attained only by an organized radical political coalition of Negroes, trade unions, church groups, and white liberals."[112]

Above all, perhaps, it is important to realize that the Negro demand for economic equality is no longer simply a demand for economic opportunity. Instead, it is a demand for economic results. Wilson points out that American politics has long been accustomed to dealing with ethnic demands for recognition, power, and opportunity, but it has not hitherto been confronted with a demand for equal economic shares. Hence the race issue throughout the country has become one between liberty and equality, an issue which, among other things, will distinguish the white liberal from the white radical.[113]

Political Activities by Americans of Mexican, Puerto Rican, Indian, and Oriental Descent

Voluntary associations among Mexican-Americans have a long history (La Alianza Hispano-Americana—1894; La Sociedad Mutualista Mexicana—1918; La Sociedad Union Cultural Mexicana—1924; and others), but politically oriented organizations were not formed until after World War II. In 1948, Strong wrote that there was no comparison between the degree of Negro political sophistication and that of Mexican-Americans.[114]

The views of the 250,000 or more Mexican-Americans who served in the armed forces during World War II were broadened. Industrial workers and a slowly increasing middle class have shown more interest in political action. In the 1950s, Mexican-Americans were elected to city councils or other offices in Texas cities and in Denver and Los Angeles, and to the state legislature in Arizona. Unity Leagues stressed voter education, and such organizations as the League of United Latin-American Citizens, the Latin-American Educational Foundation, and the Alianza Hispano-Americana worked to improve the status of Mexican-Ameri-

[109] Rainwater, *op. cit.*, p. 81.

[110] David Boesel, Richard Berk, W. Eugene Groves, Bettye Eidson, and P. H. Rossi, "White Institutions and Black Rage," in Rossi, *op. cit.*, pp. 44–45.

[111] Wilson, *op. cit.*, p. 949.

[112] *Ibid.*, p. 949. See Bayard Rustin, "From Protest to Politics: The Future of the Civil Rights Movement," *Commentary*, Feb., 1965, pp. 25–31.

[113] Wilson, *op. cit.*, pp. 964–965. On the Negro demand for economic equality, Wilson cites Nathan Glazer, "Negroes and Jews: The New Challenge to Pluralism," *Commentary*, Dec., 1964, p. 34.

[114] Donald S. Strong, "The Rise of Negro Voting in Texas," *American Political Science Review*, June, 1948, pp. 510–522.

cans.[115] In recent years there has been a substantial shift away from the mutual-aid and self-improvement approach to a more vigorous demand for equality and the elimination of discrimination. Meager financial resources, lack of staff and of organizational skills, and little help from outside the community have handicapped the efforts of these organizations.[116]

Grebler, Moore, and Guzman say that Texas, with a Spanish-surname population about as large as California's presents a far more favorable picture—"despite the fact that Texas ranks far lower than California on almost any yardstick of socioeconomic position for this group, despite the fact that its social system generally is more hostile to Mexican-Americans, and despite voting procedures that militate against its minority population."[117] For example, in 1967, ten members of the Texas legislature were Mexican-Americans and one of them was a senator. The great concentration of a Mexican-American population in the Rio Grande Valley explains most of this difference between Texas and California.[118] With nearly two million Mexican-Americans in California, only one congressman, Edward R. Roybal, of Los Angeles, is of Mexican descent. No Mexican-Americans sit in the California legislature, or on the city council or the elected board of education in Los Angeles.[119] The Democrats have taken Mexican-Americans for granted (traditionally 90 percent of the relatively small registration votes Democratic), and the Republicans have not concerned themselves much until recently. The Reagan organization made some successful efforts in the 1968 campaign, notably in the Los Angeles area, but the Democrats believe that for the state as a whole they received 75 percent of the Mexican-American vote. As a result of the losses in California, a Mexican-American was appointed to the Democratic National Committee.[120] Both Arizona and Colorado have had some ethnic representation in their legislatures. New Mexico is the only state that has proportional representation; in that state, almost 30 percent of all legislators are Mexican-American.[121]

Political alignment with Negroes was rejected by the respondents in the Grebner, Moore, and Guzman study both in Los Angeles and in San Antonio. Poorer residents in mixed neighborhoods were more likely to favor interminority coalition, but this was not true in city areas having concentrations of Mexican-American people. In such sections, ethnic identity seemed to be stronger than class solidarity with Negroes. Among the reasons given in the negative responses were: the distinctiveness of Mexican-Americans, prejudice against Negroes, the differences in the problems faced by the two groups, and, in Los Angeles, opposition to Negro militant strategy as "distasteful to the Mexican-American tradition of 'quiet fighting.'"[122]

Grebner, Moore, and Guzman found that one of the main problems of Mexican-American leadership is the need for dual validation by the ethnic clientele and the dominant group. At present, approval by one source of power often means rejection or mistrust by the other, a situation that has been a problem for other kinds of ethnic leaders. Another problem is the conflict between young and old, a conflict that is not limited to Mexican-Americans. The generational gap has been widened by the example of militant action set for Mexican-American youth by the black power movement. One militant youth group, the Brown Berets, has staged walk-outs, sit-ins, boycotts, and, occasionally, violent types of protest at colleges, high schools, and elsewhere. According to Grebner, Moore, and Guzman, the most

[115] J. Milton Yinger and George E. Simpson, "The Integration of Americans of Mexican, Puerto Rican, and Oriental Descent," *Annals*, Mar., 1956, pp. 126–127.

[116] Leo Grebner, Joan W. Moore, and Ralph C. Guzman, *The Mexican-American People: The Nation's Second Largest Minority*, Free Press, 1970, p. 554.

[117] *Ibid.*, p. 561.

[118] *Ibid.*, pp. 561, 564–565, 569–570.

[119] Helen Rowan, "A Minority Nobody Knows," in John H. Burma (ed.), *Mexican-Americans in the United States*, Schenkman, 1970, p. 300.

[120] *Ibid.*, p. 300.

[121] Grebner, Moore, and Guzman, p. 561.

[122] *Ibid.*, p. 569.

serious problem of Mexican-American leadership is its fragmentation and parochialism. Regional unity is still a distant goal,[123] but there have been some noteworthy developments. In 1970, at least 750,000 of the 4,000,000 registered voters in Texas were of Mexican-American descent. La Raza Unida had no official political organization, but it had demonstrated its potential as a third political party by electing candidates in Crystal City, Carrizo Springs, and Cotulla, all in southwest Texas. Established chicano groups in southeast Texas are joining forces with the United Party. Senator Ralph W. Yarborough, who was defeated in the spring of 1970 for the Democratic nomination, was the first victim of La Raza Unida. In the fall of 1970, candidates for both the Senate and the governorship sought Mexican-American votes. The victory of Cesar Chavez's United Farm Workers Organizing Committee in the California grape area has raised the morale of Texas Mexican-Americans. Current demands by Mexican-American political leaders in Texas include: an end to the importation of cheap Mexican labor for farms and factories, appointment of Mexican-Americans to state and federal jobs, equal employment opportunities, better housing, integration of schools, and the hiring of more Mexican-Americans as teachers.[124]

Somewhat over half of the approximately 1,500,000 mainland Puerto Ricans live in New York City. Prior to the middle 1960s, only a small proportion of those eligible to vote were registered and their vote was light. Nevertheless, Puerto Ricans have been important in a number of voting districts in New York City. The recognition of Spanish as a language of native-born Americans in the New York voter registration law of 1965 has contributed to greater political activity in recent years. Increased political awareness and cultural pride in the years since 1968 have stimulated the formation of scores of grass-roots organizations in New York City,

Chicago, Boston, and in other cities. Associations such as the Citizens Committee for Unity in New York City are concerned with neighborhood improvement and aiding residents. In the same city, the Citywide Puerto Rican Action Movement couples militancy with underground techniques, organizes demonstrations, and plans political strategy.[125] The Young Lords who pattern themselves after the Black Panthers, have less support than the militant reform groups of "advocacy planners." Boston's Emergency Tenants Council has been active in leading rent strikes, and it succeeded in getting the city to reject its planner's redevelopment scheme for part of the South End in favor of one submitted by ETC. In Chicago, La Comunidad Latin, a Puerto Rican citizens' group, asked the Board of Education for a new school.[126] Unquestionably voting and other forms of political participation will continue to increase in cities where there are large Puerto Rican populations.

American Indian voting has lagged because of a lack of knowledge of issues and candidates, experience in the mechanics of voting, and effective organization. Largely because of the development and growth of their own organizations, tribal and intertribal, and of the Congress of American Indians, marked increases have been recorded in registering and voting on many Indian reservations since 1956. Although the American Indian population is small, the Indian vote could be—and in some cases has been—a decisive factor in Montana, Idaho, Colorado, Washington, Oregon, North Dakota, Utah, Minnesota, Nebraska, and Alaska. In recent years, voting has been supplemented by protest activities (mainly demonstrations), on the part of new Red Power organizations against various types of discrimination.[127]

In Hawaii, the only state where non-Caucasians constitute a majority of the population, one United States Senator is of Chinese descent, the other is Japanese-American.

---

[123] *Ibid.*, pp. 554–555.
[124] Martin Waldron, "Chicanos in Texas Bid for Key Political Role," *The New York Times,* Aug. 2, 1970, pp. 1, 30.

[125] *The New York Times*, Apr. 23, 1968, pp. 49, 57.
[126] *Newsweek*, June 15, 1971, p. 97A.
[127] For an account of some of these organizations, see Chapter 22.

One of the two representatives in Congress is of Japanese origin.

In 1970, mainly in some of the state colleges and universities in California and in New York, third-world organizations were formed by Mexican-American, Puerto Rican, and Chinese students. These united-front groups demanded separate or joint minorities programs of study, took positions on the war in Vietnam and on various domestic economic and political issues pertaining to racial and cultural minorities.

A SUMMARY OF THE VOTING RIGHTS ACT OF 1965

Suspends literacy tests and other devices (found to be discriminatory) as qualification for voting in any Federal, State, local, general or primary election in the States of Alabama, Alaska, Georgia, Louisiana, Mississippi, South Carolina, Virginia and at least 26 counties in North Carolina.

Provides for the assignment of Federal examiners to conduct registration and observe voting in States and/or counties covered by the Act.

Directs the U.S. Attorney General to initiate suits immediately to test the constitutionality of poll taxes because the U.S. Congress found that the payment of such tax has been used in some areas to abridge the right to vote.

Extends civil and criminal protection to qualified persons seeking to vote and to those who urge or aid others to vote.

The Voting Rights Act of 1965 is the fourth bill to be enacted by the U.S. Congress since 1957 that attempts to safeguard the right of every citizen to vote, regardless of his race or color. The previous three legislative measures attempted to secure the right to vote through court cases initiated largely on a case-by-case, county-by-county basis. These cases, brought either by the U.S. Attorney General or an individual, did not adequately meet the dimensions of the problems of racial discrimination in voting.

The 1965 Act provides new tools to assure the right to vote and supplements the previous authority granted by the Civil Rights Acts of 1957, 1960 and 1964. It is intended primarily to enforce the Fifteenth Amendment to the Constitution of the United States which provides in Section 1:

The right of citizens of the United States to vote shall not be denied or abridged by the United States or by any State on account of race, color, or previous condition of servitude.

Source: The Voting Rights Act of 1965 by the United States Commission on Civil Rights (CCR Special Publication, Number 4, Government Printing Office, August 1965).

The law has two central features:

1. Provision for suspending a variety of tests and devices that have been used to deny citizens the right to vote because of their race or color.
2. Provision for the appointment of Federal examiners to list voters in those areas where tests and devices have been suspended.

In this Act, the term "voting" includes all action necessary—from the time of registration to the actual counting of the votes—to make a vote for public or party office effective.

VOTER REQUIREMENTS OUTLAWED BY THIS ACT

No State or political subdivision (counties, municipalities and parishes) covered by the Voting Rights Act may require the use of any test or device as a prerequisite for registration or voting.

Tests or devices included in this Act are those which require:

1. A demonstration of the ability to read, write, understand or interpret any given material.
2. A demonstration of any educational achievement or knowledge of any particular subject.
3. Proof of good moral character.
4. Proof of qualifications through a procedure in which another person (such as an individual already registered) must vouch for the prospective voter.

COVERAGE

The Voting Rights Act of 1965 states that no person shall be denied the right to vote in any Federal, State or local election (including primaries) for failure to pass a test if he lives in a State or political subdivision which:

1. Maintained a test or device as a prerequisite to registration or voting as of November 1, 1964, *and*
2. Had a total voting age population of which

less than 50 percent were registered or actually voted in the 1964 Presidential election.

If the above two factors are present, the State or political subdivision is automatically covered by the 1965 Act. If an entire State meets these qualifications, all of its counties come under the provisions of the Act. If only one county in a State meets them, the single county is subject to the requirements of the law.

States covered by the Act include Alabama, Alaska, Georgia, Louisiana, Mississippi, South Carolina, Virginia, and approximately 26 counties in North Carolina.

Cessation of Coverage

A State or political subdivision may be removed from coverage by filing a suit in a three-judge District Court for the District of Columbia. The State or political subdivision must convince the court that no test or device has been used for the purpose or with the effect of denying the right to vote because of race or color during the five years preceding the filing of the suit.

However, if there has been a previous court judgment against a State or political subdivision determining that tests or devices have been used to deny the right to vote, the State or political subdivision must wait five years before it can obtain an order from the District Court for the District of Columbia removing it from the coverage of the Act.

A judgment may be obtained more quickly if the Attorney General advises the court that he believes that the tests have not been used to discriminate on the basis of race or color during the five years preceding the filing of the action. He may also ask the court to reconsider its decision anytime within five years after judgment.

Changes in Voting Laws

When a State or political subdivision covered by the Act seeks to change its voting qualifications or procedures from those in effect on November 1, 1964, it must either obtain the approval of the U.S. Attorney General or initiate a Federal Court suit. If the Attorney General objects to these changes, or if they have not been submitted to him for his approval, the new laws may not be enforced until the District Court for the District of Columbia rules that the changes will not have the purpose or the effect of denying the right to vote because of the race or color of any person.

FEDERAL EXAMINERS

Once it is determined that a political subdivision is covered by the Act, the U.S. Attorney General may direct the U.S. Civil Service Commission to appoint Federal examiners to list voters if:

1. He has received twenty meritorious written complaints alleging voter discrimination, *or*
2. He believes that the appointment of examiners is necessary to enforce the guarantees of the Fifteenth Amendment.

The times, places and procedures for listing will be established by the Civil Service Commission.

Authority of the Examiners

The Federal examiners will list (that is, declare eligible and entitled to vote) those who satisfy state qualifications that have not been suspended by the Voting Rights Act. Examples of valid qualifications would be those of age and residence.

The examiners will prepare a list of qualified voters and send the list each month to State authorities who must register them—that is, place their names in the official voting records. This list must be available for public inspection. Each person on the examiner's list will be issued a certificate by the examiners as evidence of eligibility to vote in any Federal, State or local election.

No person listed by the examiner will be entitled to vote in any election unless his name has been sent to local election officials at least 45 days before that election thereby allowing the State election machinery to run without complication.

Enforcement of Action by Federal Examiners

At the request of the Attorney General the Civil Service Commission may appoint poll watchers in counties where Federal Examiners are already serving to observe whether all eligible persons are allowed to vote and whether all ballots are accurately tabulated.

If anyone who is properly listed or registered is not permitted to vote in any political subdivision where examiners are serving, a complaint may be made to the examiners of this denial within 48 hours after the polls close. If the examiner believes that the complaint has merit, he must inform the Attorney General immediately. The Attorney General may seek a district court order that provides for the casting of the ballot and suspends the election results until the vote is included in the final count.

Challenge of Listed Persons

A formal objection challenging the qualifications of a person listed by the Federal examiner may be filed (at a place to be designated by the Civil

Service Commission) within ten days after the list of qualified voters has been made public and must be supported by at least two affidavits. The validity of the challenge will be determined within fifteen days after filing by a hearing officer appointed by the Civil Service Commission. The U.S. Court of Appeals may review decisions of the hearing officer.

Until the final court review is completed, any person listed by the examiner is still eligible and must be permitted to vote. If a challenge is successful, the name of the registrant will be removed from the examiner's list.

Withdrawal of Federal Examiners

Examiners may be withdrawn from a political subdivision when the names of all persons listed by the examiners have been placed in the official records and when there is no reason to believe that persons in the subdivision will be prevented from voting.

The removal may be accomplished by action of:

1. The Civil Service Commission after it receives notification from the U.S. Attorney General, *or*
2. The District Court for the District of Columbia in a suit brought by a political subdivision after the Director of the Census has determined that more than 50 percent of the nonwhite voting age population in the subdivision is registered to vote.

A political subdivision may petition the U.S. Attorney General to end listing procedures and to request that the Director of the Census conduct a survey to determine whether more than 50 percent of the nonwhite voting age population is registered.

POLL TAXES

The Act contains a Congressional finding that the right to vote has been denied or abridged by the requirement of the payment of a poll tax as a condition to voting.

The U.S. Attorney General is directed to institute suits against Alabama, Mississippi, Texas and Virginia which require the payment of poll taxes in order to determine if such taxes violate the Constitution. While a suit is pending, or upon a finding that the poll tax is constitutional, persons registered or listed for the first time in areas covered by the Act need only pay the tax for the current year. The poll tax may be paid up to 45 days prior to an election regardless of the timeliness of the payment under State law.

VOTING SUITS

The Voting Rights Act of 1965 gives new enforcement powers to the courts in voting cases. When the court finds that there has been a denial of the right to vote in a suit brought by the U.S. Attorney General, the court must:

1. Authorize the appointment of examiners by the Civil Service Commission unless denials of the right to vote have been few in number, they have been corrected by State or local action, and there is no probability that they will reoccur.
2. Suspend the use of tests or devices in an area where it has been proved that at least one such requirement has been utilized to deny the right to vote because of race or color.

When examiners have been authorized by court order, they may be removed by an order of the authorizing court.

LANGUAGE LITERACY

If a person residing in a State where tests or devices have not been suspended has completed at least six grades in an "American-flag" school (a school in the United States or its territories), his inability to speak the English language shall not be the basis for denying him the right to vote. For example, a person who completed six grades of school in the Commonwealth of Puerto Rico but who now resides on the mainland of the United States would satisfy literacy requirements.

CRIMINAL AND CIVIL PENALTIES

Public officials or private individuals who deny persons the right to vote guaranteed by the Voting Rights Act of 1965 or anyone who attempts to or intimidates, threatens, or coerces a person from voting are subject to criminal penalties. It is also made a crime to attempt to or to intimidate, threaten or coerce anyone who urges or aids any person to vote. Criminal penalties are provided for applicants who give false information about their eligibility to vote or who accept payment to register or vote in a Federal election. The U.S. Attorney General is also authorized to bring action for injunctive relief to restrain violations of the Act.

THE CIVIL RIGHTS OF MINORITIES[1]

We have referred to the Supreme Court's decision declaring the Civil Rights Act of 1875 unconstitutional. This act, which provided that Negroes should have full equality in the use of theaters, hotels, and public conveyances, was part of the legislation designed to give the former slaves the status of free men. In 1896 the Court, in Plessy *v.* Ferguson (163 U.S. 537), confirmed a Louisiana law requiring racial segregation on common carriers. This ruling held that separate but equal accommodations did not violate the equal-protection clause of the Fourteenth Amendment. Later this principle was extended to cover schools, parks, playgrounds, hotels, places of amusement, restaurants, and all types of public transportation facilities.

The "separate but equal" doctrine held that the separation of Negroes and Whites in public places prevented conflicts, insured better race relations, and was therefore a proper exercise of the state's police power. The northern states used their police powers through civil rights laws to forbid the segregation that southern states required. In several decisions the Court's interpretation of the Fourteenth Amendment was that "mathe-

matical" equality of treatment in the treatment of segregated groups was not required, but only "substantial" equality. In some cases very little equality was considered to be "substantial." In Cumming *v.* Board of Education (175 U.S. 528, 1899), "the Court found that a Georgia county had not denied substantial equality in failing to provide a high school for 60 qualified colored children although it had a high school for white children. The Court seemed entirely satisfied by the county's argument that it could not afford to maintain two high schools." By 1914 the Court had begun to tighten its definition of equality in segregation cases. In McCabe *v.* Atchison, T. & S. F. Ry. Co. (235 U.S. 151), it decided that an Oklahoma law did not provide equal accommodations when railroads were allowed to offer sleeping, dining, and chair cars for Whites without furnishing them on demand for Negroes. In June, 1946, the Supreme Court ruled against segregation on interstate buses, and in September, 1946, a federal court of appeals for the District of Columbia held unconstitutional the segregation of interstate Negro passengers by a railroad company. In the same year a United States district court of southern California enjoined school authorities from establishing separate grade schools for "Mexicans."[2] Of importance in defining the meaning of equality under segregation is the ruling of the Circuit Court of Appeals in 1940 in Allston *v.* School Board of the City of Norfolk (112 Fed. 2d 992). Here it was held that Negro and white teachers must be paid the same salaries for the same work. By refusing to review the case the Supreme Court affirmed the decision of the lower court.

The courts have consistently ruled that the Fourteenth Amendment requires publicly

---

[1] Konvitz distinguishes political rights, such as the right to vote, from civil liberties (freedom of speech, freedom of the press, freedom of assembly, religious freedom, the right to bear arms, the right to security against unreasonable searches and seizures, security against double jeopardy and excessive bail, the right to trial by jury, security against self-incrimination, and other rights mentioned in the Bill of Rights) and civil rights. "In its more technical, limited sense, the term civil rights, as distinguished from political rights and civil liberties, refers to the rights of persons to employment, and to accommodations in hotels, restaurants, common carriers, and other places of public accommodation and resort. The term contemplates the rights enumerated in the federal Civil Rights Act of 1875 and the various acts against discrimination found on the statute books of eighteen states." Milton R. Konvitz, *The Constitution and Civil Rights*, Columbia, 1946, p. vi.

[2] R. M. MacIver, *The More Perfect Union*, Macmillan, 1948, p. 172.

owned and operated swimming pools to be operated without discrimination or segregation. Furthermore, the courts have not permitted alleged leases to dummy corporations to be used to evade the intent of the Fourteenth Amendment. The policy of the courts on publicly owned swimming pools was extended by the Pennsylvania courts to privately owned pools open to the public. Under the Pennsylvania Civil Rights Act, it was held in the case of Everett *v.* Harron that "a privately owned swimming pool soliciting patronage from the general public could not refuse admission to Negroes while admitting whites generally."[3] The court rejected a so-called "club" membership card as a device to exclude Negroes. In 1971, the Supreme Court held that Jackson, Mississippi could close its public swimming pools rather than integrate them.

On June 8, 1953, the Supreme Court upheld an 1873 law that required District of Columbia restaurants to serve persons of any race provided they are well behaved. The 1873 law, unenforced for many years, came to the Supreme Court after the U.S. Court of Appeals had ruled it and a similar law of 1872 invalid. The Justice Department, in joining the District of Columbia in urging the Supreme Court to overrule the Court of Appeals, called attention to statements by President Eisenhower that he would "use whatever authority exists in the office of the President to end segregation in the District of Columbia, including the Federal government."[4] During 1953 the three main theaters in downtown Washington began to admit Negroes, and two legitimate theaters soon opened on a nonsegregated basis. Later, neighborhood theaters began to admit Negroes.[5]

The public-school decision of the Supreme Court in 1954 opened the way for further legal attacks on segregated facilities. On March 14, 1955, the U.S. Fourth Circuit Court of Appeals in Richmond, Virginia, reversed a decision of the federal district court at Baltimore which had held that segregation in public recreational facilities was permissible if both races were given equal facilities. The Circuit Court said that the May 17, 1954, decision of the Supreme Court "swept away" as well any basis for separating the races in public parks or playgrounds.[6] By 1955, several southern cities had opened their public libraries and museums on a nonsegregated basis.[7] Also, since 1955 golf courses in Nashville, Fort Lauderdale, Florida, and other southern cities have been desegregated.

A continuing series of cases at the end of the 1950s indicated that some states and cities were resisting the desegregation of public facilities as much as possible. Additional delays were discouraged by a decision of the Supreme Court in 1963. In response to a suit by Negroes, Memphis had presented a plan in 1960 that called for full desegregation by 1971. Concerning this case, Berger says:

The Court, in Watson v. City of Memphis, found this rate too slow, pointing out that it was then eight years since it had first outlawed segregation in public recreational facilities. . . . The rights guaranteed by the Constitution, said Justice Goldberg for the unanimous Court, are 'present rights,' not promises. The city authorities, he went on, could not legally delay desegregation because it feared disturbances; its fears, moreover, were only vague and problematical, since previous desegregation had been peaceful.[8]

On July 14, 1955, the Circuit Court of Appeals in Richmond, Virginia, held in a Columbia, South Carolina, bus case that the Supreme Court decree outlawing public-school segregation "should be applied in cases involving transportation."[9] On June 5, 1956, a three-judge U.S. district court panel in Montgomery, Alabama, ruled segregation on Montgomery and Alabama public

---

[3] *Ibid.,* p. 260.

[4] Associated Press release, June 9, 1953.

[5] Carl Rowan, *Go South to Sorrow,* Random House, 1957, p. 228.

[6] *The Plain Dealer,* Mar. 15, 1957.

[7] C. Vann Woodward, *The Strange Career of Jim Crow,* Oxford, 1955, pp. 142–143. This was not true of Atlanta in 1955. In July of that year the Atlanta Public Library Board declined to open the main library to Negroes, *The Plain Dealer,* July 15, 1955.

[8] Monroe Berger, *Equality by Statute: The Revolution in Civil Rights,* Doubleday, 1967, pp. 130–131.

[9] *The Plain Dealer,* July 15, 1955, p. 6.

conveyances unconstitutional. The court traced the evolution of the law from the Plessy *v.* Ferguson doctrine of 1896 to the public-school decision in 1954, saying that the latter ruling had completely "destroyed" the "separate but equal" point of view. The court said: ". . . Statutes and ordinances requiring segregation of the white and colored races on . . . motor buses of a common carrier of passengers . . . violate the due process and equal protection of the law clauses of the . . . Constitution."[10] The U.S. Supreme Court upheld this ruling on November 13, 1956, and on December 17, 1956, it rejected pleas by Alabama and the city of Montgomery for reconsideration of this decision. Attorney General Brownell called a conference of district attorneys from 14 states to meet in Washington on December 10, 1956, for the purpose of outlining a campaign to end racial segregation in intrastate transportation.[11]

The theme of nonviolence introduced into the Montgomery, Alabama, campaign against bus segregation by Martin Luther King, Jr., of Montgomery, was a noteworthy development in southern race relations.[12] After several months Montgomery buses resumed operation on a nonsegregated basis. Integrated bus systems then became the rule in southern cities. Much of this desegregation occurred following protests of the Freedom Riders in the early 1960s.

Civil rights statutes covering racial and religious discrimination in places of public accommodation have been enacted by 38 states.[13] In some of these states, violation of these laws is a misdemeanor and is punishable by fine and imprisonment. Other states permit the aggrieved individual to sue for damages. One state provides for civil damages only, and in the others either civil damages or a criminal proceeding, but not both, is permitted. The minimum fines or minimum recoveries in civil suits are small, varying from $10 to $100.

During 1969 29 laws strengthening civil rights protection were adopted by various states. More than half of these new state laws dealt with discrimination in housing. One law barred discrimination in public accommodations; most of the others were prohibitions against discrimination in employment.[14] Specific references are made to some of these new laws in the sections of this chapter concerned with housing and employment practices.

On the whole, the laws pertaining to public accommodations have not been effective, although there are some notable exceptions. Some public prosecutors consider such offenses insignificant and are unwilling to prosecute unless provided with unquestionable cases. The injured individuals often prefer to ignore humiliation rather than spend the time and money necessary to carry through a lawsuit in view of the small minimum recovery allowed and the difficulty of demonstrating larger damages. Because jail sentences are seldom imposed and fines are small, many of those subject to the statutes regard the occasional fine as a business expense, try to avoid detection, and continue to discriminate. Leskes says that a statute guaranteeing equal rights in places of public accommodation, resort, or amusement should be deemed only the beginning of the struggle for equality of opportunity.[15]

President Truman's Committee on Civil Rights recognized the weaknesses of the existing civil rights machinery:

The civil suit for damages and the misdemeanor. penalty have proved to be inadequate sanctions to secure the observance of these laws. Additional means, such as the revocation of licenses, and the issuance of cease-and-desist orders by administrative agencies are needed to bring about wider compliance. We think that all of the states should enact such legislation, using

[10] *SSN*, Dec., 1956, p. 13.
[11] See Luther A. Huston, "Desegregation on Buses Presents Legal Problems," *The New York Times*, Nov. 25, 1956.
[12] For an excellent account of the Negro boycott of buses in Montgomery, see Rowan, *op. cit.*, chap. 6.
[13] Anti-Defamation League, *Law*, 1970, p. 1.

[14] *Ibid.*, pp. 1–3.
[15] Milton R. Konvitz and Theodore Leskes, *A Century of Civil Rights*, Columbia, 1961, p. 180. On legislation and court tests of state laws pertaining to public accommodations, see *ibid.*, chap. 6.

the broadest possible definition of public accommodation.[16]

The first two states to follow this recommendation were New Jersey and Connecticut. Each enacted laws in 1949 "giving administrative state agencies authority to handle charges of discrimination in places of public accommodation by persuasion and conciliation or, if such attempts at mediation fail, by cease-and-desist orders."[17] By 1955 New York, Rhode Island, and Massachusetts had passed similar laws.[18] By 1961, Pennsylvania and Ohio had strengthened their civil rights laws by giving state administrative agencies authority over charges of discrimination in places of public accommodation.

In addition to extending the administrative technique used in combating discrimination in employment to discrimination in places of public accommodation, Connecticut amended its definition of such places. The amendment deleted from the law the limited list of specific places that had been considered "places of public accommodation" and substituted this definition: "Any establishment . . . which caters or offers its services or facilities or goods to the general public. . . ." Another important part of the amendment was the specific statement, for the first time, that "segregation" and "separation" were discrimination within the meaning of the act and were therefore prohibited.[19]

Extralegal techniques sometimes used to circumvent state civil rights laws and discriminate against Negroes include finding that a "mistake" has been made in a hotel reservation; stating that all tables or all rooms are reserved; claiming that only "members" of an association or club are admitted to some recreational facility; quoting differential prices on the basis of race; ignoring minority customers or serving them after a long delay.

A national study of resort hotels and motels revealed that approximately one-fourth of the places on which data were obtained excluded Jews from their facilities. These were places of public accommodation, and, in many states, legally obligated to serve all patrons, regardless of race or religion.[20]

In 1969, Maine became the first state to enact a law dealing with the problem of discrimination by private clubs that hold state liquor licenses. The new law prohibits any person, firm, or corporation holding a state or local license for the dispensing of food, liquor, or any other service from withholding membership, facilities, or services to any person on account of race, religion, or national origin. Organizations that are "oriented to a particular religion, or which are ethnic in character" are exempted from the provisions of the law. License holders who violate this provision may have their license revoked. According to a B'nai B'rith Anti-Defamation League report, although this law was intended originally to be used against clubs with discriminatory admission practices, "the language of the law seems broad enough to cover every person who operates under a state license, including physicians, dentists and real estate agents."[21]

The situation in the area of religious liberty has changed. In June, 1962 the U.S. Supreme Court handed down a 6 to 1 decision declaring unconstitutional a requirement of the State of New York that each school class at the beginning of each school day recite a prayer expressing belief in God and asking His blessings on the children, their parents, their teachers, and their country. Children who wished could remain silent or be excused. The majority of the Court held that the formulation and use of a school prayer meant taking a position on a religious matter. In the Court's judgment, this law violated the intent of the First Amendment, which was in Justice Black's

---

[16] President's Committee on Civil Rights, *To Secure These Rights*, Simon & Schuster, 1947, p. 171.

[17] Arnold Forster, *A Measure of Freedom*, Doubleday, 1950, pp. 206–207.

[18] Elmer Carter, "Policies and Practices of Discrimination Commissions," *Annals*, Mar., 1956, p. 74.

[19] Sol Rabkin, "Racial Desegregation in Places of Public Accommodation," *JNE*, Summer, 1954, pp. 249–261.

[20] Benjamin R. Epstein and Arnold Forster, *Some of My Best Friends*, Farrar, Straus & Giroux, 1962, p. 58.

[21] ADL, *op. cit.*, p. 3.

words, "that each separate government in this country shall stay out of the business of writing or sanctioning official prayers." This decision threw into question the constitutionality of the programs in more than a third of the schools of the country involving the recital of the Lord's Prayer or Bible reading sessions, as well as the requirement of teaching about religion, usually without sectarian emphasis, in approximately one-fifth of the nation's public schools.[22] In the decade following this decision of the Supreme Court, the practices mentioned above gradually declined because of (1) the impact of the Court's decision, and (2) a continuing trend toward secularization that is independent of the decision. Significant differences geographically are apparent in the changes that have occurred since 1962. The two sections of the country where these practices had been most common were the Deep South and the Northeast, especially Pennsylvania, New York, and Massachusetts. The greatest decline in these programs has been in the Northeast, and the least decline has been in the South. Since practices of this type were barred from the beginning in state constitutions in the Middle West and the West, they have never been an issue in states in those sections of the country.[23] The use of school property for released-time religious practices in the public schools was banned in 1952.[24]

Earlier developments in the area of religious liberty included the protection of Jews denied unemployment compensation because they refused jobs requiring work on Satur-

day, the defense of Jewish shopkeepers arrested for violations of Sunday blue laws, prohibition of the distribution of the New Testament in the public schools, and legal representation in the courts for Jewish foster parents seeking to adopt non-Jewish children.[25]

The exclusion of Negroes from service on juries persists in a few states. Until recently, combating such exclusion rested entirely on private persons, usually defendants in criminal trials. It was thought that the federal government had available only criminal remedies, and it had successfully invoked a criminal statute only once, in the late 1870s. In 1961, the Commission on Civil Rights pointed out that civil actions instituted by the United States would provide a more effective way of preventing discriminatory exclusion from juries.[26] In 1968, Congress passed a Jury Selection Act providing that "all litigants in Federal courts entitled to trial by jury shall have the right to grand and petit juries selected at random from a fair cross section of the community in the district or division wherein the court convenes . . . No citizen shall be excluded from service as a grand or petit juror in the district courts of the United States on account of race, color, religion, national origin, or economic status."[27] Two decisions of interest were announced by the U.S. Supreme Court on January 19, 1970. In Carter v. Green County Jury Commission (on appeal from the U.S. District Court for the Northern District of Alabama), the Court held that the Fourteenth Amendment does not bar state's jury selection on the basis of reputation and "community esteem," in the absence of showing that a test was adopted or carried forward for the purpose of racial discrimination; absence of Negroes from a gubernatorially appointed jury selection commission in a predominantly Negro county does not constitute prima facie showing of discriminatory exclusion.[28] The other

---

[22] *The New York Times,* July 1, 1962.
[23] See Donald R. Reich, "The Impact of Judicial Decision Making: The School Prayer Cases," in David H. Everson (ed.), *The Supreme Court as Policy-Maker: Three Studies on the Impact of Judicial Decisions,* Public Affairs Research Bureau, Southern Illinois Univ., 1968, pp. 44–81. For an interesting study of the impact of the Court's 1962 and 1963 decisions on school prayers and Bible reading in Ohio compared with Wisconsin, see Donald R. Reich, "Schoolhouse Religion and the Supreme Court: A Report on Attitudes of Teachers and Principals on School Practices in Wisconsin and Ohio," *Journal of Legal Education,* 23, No. 1, 1971, pp. 123–143.
[24] For a discussion of Court decisions concerning released time for religious practices, see Stephen L. Wasby, *The Impact of the United States Supreme Court,* Dorsey, 1970, pp. 127–129.

[25] Will Maslow, "The Uses of Law in the Struggle for Equality," *Social Research,* Autumn, 1955, p. 307.
[26] *1961 Report of the U.S. Commission on Civil Rights,* Book 5, "Justice," pp. 111–112.
[27] *The United States Law Week,* The Bureau of National Affairs, Mar. 26, 1968, pp. 85–88.
[28] *Ibid.,* Jan. 20, 1970, Sec. 4, p. 4075.

decision handed down on January 19, 1970 (Turner v. Fouche, on appeal from the U.S. District Court for the Southern District of Georgia) made essentially the same point, but added that a prima facie case of jury discrimination is established by showing that a grand jury selection list for a county with a 60 percent Negro population was 37 percent Negro.[29]

In the past few years, the Civil Rights Section of the Justice Department has initiated such suits in a number of cases. Negroes have been added to juries in increasing numbers.[30]

FEDERAL CIVIL RIGHTS LEGISLATION

In July and August, 1957, the Republican administration, with the support of northern Democrats, sought passage of a civil rights bill with the following main provisions:

1. Establishment of a special Civil Rights Division within the Department of Justice.
2. Creation of a Federal Civil Rights Commission armed with subpoena powers to compel witnesses to testify and produce records.
3. Authority for the Department of Justice to intervene, in the name of the United States, in behalf of individuals in instances of actual or threatened violations of civil rights—such as the right to vote or to attend an integrated school.
4. Federal prosecutors could obtain injunctions from federal district judges against such real or threatened violations. Persons disobeying these injunctions could be fined or imprisoned for contempt by federal judges, without jury trial.[31]

This bill, passed by the House, was weakened by amendments in the Senate. The two

---

[29] *Ibid.*, p. 4075.

[30] Some legal critics have set forth a case for black juries. They say that the Supreme Court considers equal protection to be equal opportunity rather than equal results. In northern urban areas they propose that each black community constitute a jury district; the result would be all-black juries in these communities. In the Black Belt counties of the rural South, they propose that every jury be proportionately representative of the black population in the jury district. (In most cases, this would yield juries at least three-fourths black.) Note: "The Case for Black Juries," *The Yale Law School Journal*, Jan. 1970, pp. 531–550.

[31] *The New York Times*, July 21, 1957.

most important amendments limited Section 3 to cases involving the right to vote and provided for jury trials in all federal court criminal contempt cases. The final bill, the first civil rights legislation to come from Congress in 82 years, contained modifications of the jury trial proviso. The bill gives the federal government power to protect and enforce the right to vote with court orders. In cases of civil contempt (in which the judge is trying to compel obedience to his order) and in many cases of criminal contempt (in which the judge is punishing disobedience) the jury will be excluded. The bill provides that a judge may refuse to grant a jury trial, but that if he does so and subsequently assesses punishment above $300 in fines and 45 day's imprisonment the defendant can demand a jury to retry the action. The campaign for a new civil rights act had important political implications because of the increasing voting strength of Negroes. Striking evidence of the political power of Negroes was seen in the vote to make civil rights the business before the Senate. The border states—Maryland, West Virginia, Kentucky, Tennessee—and Texas, which have usually supported the South in previous struggles of this type, voted solidly with the North.

After extended litigation on the constitutionality of the Civil Rights Act of 1957, the federal government obtained injunctions against discrimination in registration in Terrell County, Georgia, and Macon County, Alabama. A court order was secured restoring 1377 Negroes to the registration rolls in Washington Parish, Louisiana. Also, the federal government tried suits in Bienville Parish, Louisiana, and in Bullock County, Alabama. Additional voting suits were filed in East Carroll and Ouachita Parishes, Louisiana; Dallas and Montgomery Counties, Alabama; and Forrest, Clarke, Walthall, and Jefferson Davis Counties, Mississippi. Also, under the provisions of this act, which prohibits threats, intimidation, and coercion of voters in federal elections, the government sued to end economic boycotts against Negro voters in Fayette and Haywood Counties, Tennessee, and in East Carroll Parish, Louisiana. Temporary injunctions were obtained in the Tennessee suits and an agreement was stipulated in the East Carroll case.[32] On May 6, 1963, the thirty-seventh voter registration case under the Civil Rights Act of 1957 was brought by the federal government. Eleven of the 37 suits were brought in Mississippi; the others were brought in Louisiana, Georgia, Alabama, and Tennessee.[33]

In 1960, Congress passed a second civil rights statute, strengthening and extending the 1957 Act. The *1961 Report of the U.S. Commission on Civil Rights* summarizes succinctly the main features of the Civil Rights Act of 1960 and some of the results of this act:

It provided that States, as well as the registrar, may be sued for discriminatory voting practices. Under Title III, the 1960 act required the preservation of voting records, and empowered the U.S. Attorney General to inspect them. Also, Title VI of this act introduced for the first time the possibility of Federal voting referees to see that persons who have been improperly disfranchised are in fact registered, where a court finds a "pattern or practice" of discrimination. In fact, only one court has found such a "pattern or practice," and in that case chose not to appoint referees. But ever since the enactment of the referee provision, the government has succeeded in obtaining broad and detailed decrees—decrees which, assuming continuing court surveillance over compliance, may well be as effective as the voting referees themselves. Under the records-inspection provision of the 1960 Act the Federal Government has made demands for the inspection and copying of registration records in 26 southern counties. Suits necessitated by refusals ended in favor of the Government, and since their disposition it has obtained voluntary compliance with demands for records in 18 of the 26 counties involved.[34]

It is of interest that the eight-week filibuster by 18 southern senators did not produce a single vote from the border senators or from Republican senators. Konvitz and Leskes find that although the 1960 act strengthened the 1957 act, it is not a strong statute.[35]

At the beginning of his administration, President Kennedy continued the Eisenhower policy of leaving to the judges the enforcement of law as defined by the courts. Later in 1961, and during the next two years, Mr. Kennedy committed the authority and prestige of his office to the cause of civil rights. Numerous executive decisions, speeches, and outspoken advocacy of new civil rights legislation gave new vitality to the civil rights movement. On June 20, 1963, Mr. Kennedy asked Congress to enact a new and much stronger civil rights law. A bill was passed by the House of Representatives in February, 1964, but discussions and maneuvering in the Senate delayed passage of a modified version of the original bill until June 19, 1964. Differences between the Senate and House versions of the bill were soon reconciled, and President Johnson signed the enactment. A summary of the main provisions of this law is given at the end of this chapter. Title I (Voting) of the 1964 Civil Rights Act proved to be ineffective and was succeeded by the much stronger Voting Rights Act of 1965.[36]

Some observers report "speedy compliance" with the public accommodations provisions of the Civil Rights Act of 1964 by thousands of southern hotel, motel, restaurant, and theater operators. According to this account, "many of them were pleased with the passage of the act, because it relieved them of the awkward and embarrassing responsibility of deciding whether or not to serve Negroes."[37]

FAIR EMPLOYMENT PRACTICES COMMITTEES

An important development with regard to the place of minorities in the American economy is the federal wartime Fair Employment Practices order and the numerous state and

[32] *1961 Report of the U.S. Commission on Civil Rights,* Book 1, "Voting," p. 134.

[33] *The Plain Dealer,* May 7, 1963.

[34] *1961 Report of the U.S. Commission on Civil Rights,* Book 1, "Voting," p. 134.

[35] Konvitz and Leskes, *op. cit.,* pp. 84–85.

[36] See the discussion of the effects of the Voting Rights Act of 1965 in Chapter 13. A summary of this law is given at the end of that chapter.

[37] James G. Maddox, E. E. Liebhafsky, V. Henderson, and H. M. Hamlin, *The Advancing South: Manpower Prospects and Problems,* Twentieth Century Fund, 1967, p. 33.

municipal employment laws that have been passed in the last few years.

The Federal FEPC During World War II

When Negroes continued to be greatly underrepresented in the defense industries in the months before Pearl Harbor, a march on Washington was organized by A. Philip Randolph, president of the Brotherhood of Sleeping Car Porters. Negotiations between the administration and Mr. Randolph resulted in the calling off of the march and the issuance by President Roosevelt on June 25, 1941, of Executive Order 8802. In part, this order stated:

I do hereby reaffirm the policy of the United States that there shall be no discrimination in the employment of workers in defense industries or government because of race, creed, color, or national origin, and I do hereby declare that it is the duty of employers and of labor organizations, in furtherance of said policy and of this order, to provide for the full and equitable participation of all workers in defense industries, without discrimination because of race, creed, color, or national origin.

All departments and agencies of the government of the United States concerned with vocational and training programs for defense production were instructed to take special measures to assure the administration of such programs without discrimination. All contracting agencies of the government were to include provisions obligating the contractor not to discriminate against any worker because of race, creed, color, or national origin. The order also established in the Office of Production Management a Committee on Fair Employment Practice, which consisted of a chairman and four other members to be appointed by the President. The committee was empowered to receive and investigate complaints of discrimination and to take "appropriate steps to redress grievances which it finds to be valid." The committee was also asked to "recommend to the several departments and agencies of the Government of the United States and to the President all measures which may be

deemed by it necessary or proper to effectuate the provisions of this order."

On May 27, 1943, Mr. Roosevelt issued Executive Order 9346, which amended Executive Order 8802 "by establishing a new committee on fair employment practice and defining its powers and duties." The revised order established a Committee on Fair Employment Practice in the Office for Emergency Management of the Executive Office of the President. This committee was to consist of a full-time chairman and not more than six members to be appointed by the President. The committee was now authorized to utilize the services and facilities of other federal departments and agencies, as well as such voluntary and uncompensated services as might be needed. Provision was also made for the acceptance of the services of state and local authorities and officials.

A total of 14,000 complaints of discrimination were handled during the five years that the federal FEPC was in existence. Eighty percent of the appeals for protection against discrimination were from Negroes. Discrimination on the basis of creed constituted 6 percent of the total, and most of these complaints came from Jews. The other 14 percent appealed because of national origin, and nearly all of these workers were Mexican-Americans. There were almost no charges of discrimination filed by American Poles, Czechoslovakians, Italians, Germans, Lithuanians, and other national groups.[38] Malcolm Ross is correct in saying that this record does not enable us to say that four-fifths of American prejudice is directed against Negroes, but it does give a rough indication of the exploitation that other Americans have found profitable.

In five years FEPC satisfactorily settled nearly 5000 cases by peaceful negotiation, including forty strikes caused by racial differences. FEPC held fifteen public hearings and docketed a total of 3485 cases, settling 1191 of them, during the last year of the war.

[38] For an excellent account of all aspects of the Federal FEPC, see Malcolm Ross, *All Manner of Men*, Reynal and Hitchcock, 1948.

These settlements were not publicized and generally escaped attention. The contrary impression, that FEPC normally met with unyielding opposition, was created by the comparatively few difficult cases which received emphasis through public hearings and public expressions of defiance by some recalcitrant employers and unions.[39]

On the question of whether the committee was successful in achieving its twin goals of creating greater economic opportunities for minority-group members and of fully utilizing our resources of manpower in the war effort, it may be pointed out that minority-group workers rose from less than 3 percent in 1942 to more than 8 percent in 1944; i.e., there was an addition of a million and a half Negroes and Mexican-Americans at work in vital war industries. However, it cannot be said that FEPC was the only factor in opening the plants to workers who had been previously excluded.

Such firms as the National Smelting Company of Cleveland and the Western Electric Company of Chicago accepted Negro workers in all capacities on their own initiative. So did many others. Moreover, the War Manpower Commission, the War and Navy Departments, the Maritime Commission, the War Shipping Administration, the Civil Service and other agencies had many staff members working on discrimination, and, on the whole, they did the bulk of the work under the wartime injunction to keep all gates open. FEPC was the specialist who took the cases which the other doctors along the row failed to analyze or cure. The healthy patients never entered its door.[40]

One might speculate, of course, on whether some of the "healthy" patients would have been so well if there had been no FEPC or no war.

Opposition to FEPC came from many sources and was not limited to the South.

Outside the South, the reaction to changes in racial patterns was less violent but often extremely critical. Many local chambers of commerce were alarmed by the new "militancy" of the Negro and the government's "encourage-ment" of it. The non-discrimination executive orders were blasted, usually in confidential letters or memoranda. The Negro press was severely scored, and Negro leadership was accused of being interested chiefly in self-aggrandizement and monetary gains. Some representatives of management dogmatically stated that Negroes and whites could not work together and that governmental efforts to force them to do so would result in widespread violence and serious loss of production.[41]

To the South "FEPC was an unpatriotic plot, contrived by rats and moral lepers, concealing under hypocritical guise a hope to cause disaster to the South."[42] A Mississippi Democrat in the debate in the House called on his party to kill FEPC, saying, " 'I come to you as an American asking you as another American for God's sake to help us.' "[43]

The assertion that FEPC was trying to impose social equality on the South echoed and re-echoed throughout the South. Righteous men proclaimed that only the South really understands Negroes and that the Negro race had made great progress under the guidance of wise southern leaders. As Ross says, FEPC was thought of as a radical movement, designed to eradicate the traditions of the South. It was, of course, bound to "subject white women to great danger." No one mentioned the personal economic advantage of the existing occupational arrangements that provided maids and yard men for upper- and middle-class white southerners.

In addition to being harassed constantly by powerful economic and political forces, the committee was badly handicapped by inadequate appropriations, insufficient staff, and excessive administrative controls. Also, FEPC was forced to produce immediate results. As a result, there was little opportunity for long-run planning and programming.

The committee had no authority to compel compliance with its directives. It had to rely on public censure. Some large and powerful corporations, such as Vultee Aircraft in

[39] Fair Employment Practice Committee, *Final Report*, Government Printing Office, 1947, p. viii.
[40] Ross, *op. cit.*, p. 48.

[41] R. C. Weaver, *Negro Labor*, Harcourt Brace Jovanovich, 1946, p. 239.
[42] Ross, *op. cit.*, p. 116.
[43] *Ibid.*, p. 115.

California, Buick Aircraft in Chicago, and Wright Aeronautical in Paterson, New Jersey, were cited and compliance was secured. The same is true of the exposure and pressure upon the International Association of Machinists at the Los Angeles hearings and the mechanical building-craft unions at the Chicago hearings. All of these efforts did help to increase the employment of minorities; Negroes did enter new occupations, plants, and industries; Negroes and whites did work together.[44]

It is important to note, however, that persuasion is not sufficient to end discrimination. From 1941 to 1946, employers needed war workers, their patriotism was aroused, and they disliked exposure. These were strong factors in reducing discrimination; but discriminatory policies "seldom disappeared spontaneously. The intervention of a third party, with authority to act if necessary, was required to start the process in motion." FEPC found that persuasion has its limits in a number of important cases that it was never able to settle. "Relatively few in number, these employers and unions which successfully defied the national policy of nondiscrimination proved that persuasion must be backed by final authority if conformity with the policy is to be realized."[45]

It was not until 1964 that a federal statute was enacted to cover fair employment practices. Later in this chapter, we point out that Title VII (Equal Employment Opportunity) of the Civil Rights Act of 1964 has been ineffective because it provides no enforcement powers.

Fair Employment Policies in the Federal Government After 1948

On July 26, 1948, two years after the refusal of Congress to enact permanent federal fair employment practice legislation, President Truman issued Executive Order 9980 to provide machinery for implementing fair employment policy and redressing the discrimination evident in the federal government.

[44] Weaver, *op. cit.*, pp. 137, 239.
[45] Fair Employment Practice Committee, *Final Report*, pp. viii–ix.

According to this Executive Order (1) the head of each department in the executive branch of the government was personally responsible for an effective program of fair employment policies within his department; (2) the head of each department was asked to designate an official thereof as Fair Employment Officer; and (3) the findings or action of the Fair Employment Officer were subject to direct appeal to the head of the department. The decision of the head of the department on such appeal was subject to the Fair Employment Board of the Civil Service Commission.

In January, 1955, President Eisenhower abolished the Fair Employment Board and established a five-man committee to carry out a nondiscrimination order. Instead of operating under the Civil Service Commission the new committee was asked to report directly to the President. This Executive Order stated that discrimination against any employee or applicant for employment in the federal government because of race, color, religión, or national origin was prohibited. The committee was empowered to conduct inquiries and advise the President concerning compliance with this policy.

In a study of the machinery established to provide equality of opportunity in federal civilian employment, the U.S. Commission on Civil Rights found that 1053 complaints of discrimination by federal agencies were filed between January, 1955 and December, 1960. One-fifth of these complaints were referred to President Eisenhower's Committee on Government Employment Policy for review and advisory opinion, the others were settled at the department or agency level. In 33 of the 225 referrals, the Committee disagreed with the findings of the departments or agencies concerned and recommended corrective action. The Committee, recognizing the limited role that complaints could play in the total program, instituted a program of information, education, and persuasion for top-level administrators, line supervisors, employment officers, personnel officers, and other management officials. Mainly this program consisted of conferences for officials and of training programs in nondiscrimination policy established by departments and agencies.[46]

On August 13, 1953, President Eisenhower abolished the Committee on Government Contract Compliance that had been established in December, 1951, and formed the Committee on Government Contracts. The new committee was charged with obtaining compliance for equal employment opportunity from contractors or subcontractors doing business with or for the federal government.

From 1957 through 1959, President Eisenhower's Committee on Government Contracts conducted 821 compliance surveys, and in 1960, 1022 surveys were undertaken. While they showed an increase in the number of plants employing Negroes in higher-skilled, professional and technical, clerical, and supervisory positions and a decrease in the number of plants having no Negro employees, there was no indication that any contracting agency denied a contract to a company because of its employment policies. No company was ever placed on an "ineligible" list provided for in the Committee's instruction procedures. Although no contract was terminated because of failure to comply with the nondiscrimination clause, the Committee itself, as well as some contracting agencies, used the threat of termination to induce some changes in contractors' employment practices. To "sell" its policy of merit employment to industry and labor, as well as to the compliance officers of the federal contracting agencies, the Committee distributed leaflets, posters, films, manuals, and other materials and conducted conferences with representatives of labor, industry, state anti-discrimination agencies, and private agencies. Also, the Committee planned a long-range educational program designed to motivate minority youth to train for nontraditional jobs. Despite these activities the investigations of the U.S. Commission on Civil Rights in Detroit, Baltimore, and Atlanta showed that in most of the industries studied, federal contractors conformed to local industrial

employment practices in the hiring of Negroes. The Commission's 1961 Report says: "The Committee lacked authority, it had only a vague charter, and its program was replete with weaknesses and loopholes." A common criticism was that many applicants for employment were unable to ascertain whether companies discriminating against them were government contractors. Often applicants apply not at a plant but to a local employment agency, and such agencies were often unable to determine which companies were current government contractors. The Commission found the major weakness of the program to be the limited jurisdiction that Executive Order 10479 gave the Committee. It attempted "to negotiate increased opportunities for minority group workers in training and recruitment services," but "its attempts were largely ineffective."[47]

On March 6, 1961, Executive Order 10925 established President Kennedy's Committee on Equal Employment Opportunity. For the first time responsibility for employment practices of the federal government, government contractors, and labor organizations was placed under a single committee.

A new post was created in the Civil Service Commission—Special Assistant for Minority Group Matters, and one of the duties of this officer was to promote recruitment of minority-group members for federal employment. Several federal agencies appointed full-time employment policy officers. Periodic employment surveys attempted to overcome, at least in part, lack of knowledge of discriminatory practices in the absence of specific complaints. The new Committee was authorized "to scrutinize and study employment practices," and it was given broad authority to enforce and implement its program. The Committee had some jurisdiction over labor unions in connection with employment under Government contracts, and theoretically, substantial indirect, as well as certain direct, pressures could be brought against discriminatory unions.[48]

[46] *1961 Report of the U.S. Commission on Civil Rights*, Book 3, "Employment," pp. 21–25.

[47] *Ibid.*, pp. 62–70.
[48] *Ibid.*, pp. 41–44, 71–72, 148–149. Also, as the U.S. Commission on Civil Rights points out, federal law imposes "a duty of fair representation upon

Although this arrangement was a significant change, the U.S. Commission on Civil Rights said that this executive order did not seem to affect training and recruitment services provided by federal funds. Also, it did not apply explicitly to all federally financed employment. Employment created through the grant of federal funds to state and local governments, to public institutions, and to private, nonprofit institutions for specific programs or activities was not covered in Executive Order 10925. The same thing was true of employment created by grant-in-aid programs. The Commission says: "Despite the clear authority of the Federal Government to attach nondiscriminatory conditions to the use of their funds—approximately $7.5 billion in fiscal 1961—such action has been taken only on a piecemeal basis."[49]

In the summer of 1961, representatives of nine large corporations, each holding defense contracts, pledged voluntary support for equal employment opportunities. The first "Plans for Progress" embodied a program designed to implement President Kennedy's Executive Order 10925, issued in March, 1961. In this order, the President's Committee on Equal Employment Opportunity was given power to require government contractors to eliminate discrimination in hiring and promotions. The "voluntary" and "affirmative" aspects of the Plans were to be important parts of the program. Lockheed Aircraft Corporation joined the program first, and by January, 1963 a total of 105 firms had signed up. Among the 52 original signers, 24 had plants, offices, or regional headquarters in the Atlanta area. A survey of these plants by the Southern Regional Council showed:

1. All had had at least one year in which to implement their plans, to take affirmative and voluntary action toward job elimination. Yet the results of the survey clearly indicate that, except for a handful of the companies, the Plans for Progress were, for the regional office in Atlanta, largely meaningless.
2. Only seven of the firms interviewed produced evidence of affirmative compliance with their pledges. Of the seven, three—Lockheed, Western Electric, and Goodyear—demonstrated what appeared to be a vigorous desire to create job opportunities.
3. The remaining 17 firms have paid varying degrees of attention to Plans for Progress, ranging from ignorance to indifference.[50]

Over periods ranging from six months to two years, 103 Plans for Progress companies increased the percentage of Negroes among their total work forces from 5.1 percent to 5.7 percent. During a 12-month period, 4600 establishments reported an increase in the representation of Negroes among their white-collar workers from 1.2 percent to 1.3 percent. While these increases seem insubstantial, the less than one percentage point rise among Plans for Progress signers meant that Negroes filled 40,938 of the companies' 341,734 vacancies, or 12 percent of them. That proportion was more than double the representation of Negroes among those hired before Plans for Progress. One-tenth of a percentage point rise in the representation of Negroes among white-collar workers represents a net gain of 1830 white-collar jobs, an increase of 17.4 percent in Negro white-collar employment at a time when total white-collar employment among the companies studied increased only 1.9 percent. Sovern says that it cannot be proved that these gains are attributable to the Committee's efforts, but that it is likely that some of them are.[51]

Executive Order 10925 remained in effect until October 24, 1965. Its successor, President Johnson's Executive Order 11246, repeated many of its provisions. The Johnson order abolished the President's Committee on Equal Employment Opportunity and as-

unions and presently proscribes discrimination in initial employment based on membership of nonmembership in a union. The NLRB, however, the federal agency authorized to administer these provisions has not effectively enforced the duty of fair representation nor has it had a significant impact on the hiring and referral practices in the building and construction trades." *Ibid.*, p. 161.
[49] *Ibid.*, pp. 5–17. For a discussion of the government's grants-in-aid programs see *ibid.*, pp. 81–95.

[50] SRC, *Plans for Progress: Atlanta Survey*, Jan., 1963.
[51] Michael Sovern, *Legal Restraints on Racial Discrimination in Employment*, Twentieth Century Fund, 1966, pp. 140–41.

signed its jurisdiction over government contractors to the Labor Department. The duties of contractors, found in section 202 of the Johnson order, remained essentially unchanged. Contractors were to undertake to refrain from discrimination, but in addition they were to promise to "take affirmative action to ensure that applicants were employed, and that employees were treated during employment, without regard to their race, creed, color, or national origin." They were required also to announce their policy in posters and in all "solicitations or advertisements for employees placed by or on behalf of the contractor" and in notices to all unions with which they had an agreement. They were required to comply not only with the executive order, but also with "rules, regulations, and orders of the Secretary of Labor." In addition, they were obliged to submit to compliance investigations, and to file reports giving information asked for by the Secretary of Labor.[52]

The Civil Rights Act of 1964

Title VII of the Civil Rights Act of 1964 establishes a federal right to equal opportunity in employment, and it created an Equal Employment Opportunity Commission to assist in implementing this right. Employers, labor unions, and employment agencies are required to treat all persons without regard to their race, color, religion, sex, or national origin. This treatment must be given in all phases of employment, including hiring, promotion, firing, apprenticeship and other training programs, and job assignments. Employers are subject to its provisions if they have 25 or more regular employees in an industry that affects interstate commerce. Generally speaking, labor unions are subject to the Act if they either operate a hiring hall for covered employers, or if they have 25 or more members who are employed by a covered employer. Employment agencies are also covered if they regularly undertake to supply employees for a covered employer.[53] The Equal Employment Opportunity Commission was established in July, 1965.

Title VII of the Civil Rights Act of 1964 produced optimism because it provided for a periodic survey by an agency of the federal government of all covered employers to check the racial composition and occupational distribution of their work forces. Thus far, the results have been disappointing. In 1969, Cousens concluded that the creation of the Equal Employment Opportunity Commission "did not fulfill either the promise or performance of a federal commission. Instead, it manifests many of the same weaknesses which have long characterized contract compliance programs in other federal departments."[54] Specifically, the main weakness of the EEOC is its lack of enforcement powers.

Title VII is not the only title in the Civil Rights Act of 1964 affecting employment discrimination. Title VI declares that "No person in the United States shall on the ground of race, color, or national origin, be excluded from participation in, be denied the benefits of, or be subjected to discrimination under any program or activity receiving Federal financial assistance." The precise number of programs and activities receiving federal financial assistance is uncertain, but they exceed 100. Included are such undertakings as: road, hospital, school, and airport construction; urban renewal; school lunch programs; and loans to small businessmen. Two limitations, however, are important on the power to cut off federal aid: (1) a "pinpoint" proviso in section 602 prevents the stopping of aid to any except the particular program and entity involved —discriminating in federally aided hospitals will not prevent a state from keeping its federal highway allocations; and (2) section 604 limits the use of the termination-of-aid sanction against employment discrimination. This section says: "Nothing contained in this title shall be construed to authorize

---

[52] *Ibid.*, p. 104.

[53] U.S. Commission on Civil Rights, *Civil Rights Digest* (Special Bulletin, August, 1964).

[54] Frances R. Cousens, *Public Civil Rights Agencies and Fair Employment*, Praeger, 1969, pp. 12, 114.

action with respect to any employment practice of any employer, employment agency,
or labor organizations except where a primary objective of the Federal financial assistance is to provide employment." Most
programs fail to pass the "primary objective" test and are not, therefore, subject to
Title VI.[55]

Conclusion on Federal Fair Employment Practices Programs

Title VII (Employment) of the Civil Rights
Act of 1964 is a poor instrument in that it
provides for conciliation but not the power
to compel. Title VI (Federal Aid) of the
same Act has added little to the FEP cause
because most programs or activities receiving
federal financial assistance fail to pass the
"primary objective" test of providing employment. Most of the state FEP laws are
strong, but the actions of the state commissions tend to be weak. The federal contractor
program is powerful but it cannot reach an
employer who does not have a federal contract or federally assisted construction contract. Sovern points out that Title VII of
the Civil Rights Act of 1964, the state FEP
commissions, and the federal contractor program, are complemented by other instruments whose responsibilities include equal
employment opportunity problems.

While Title VII withholds enforcement powers
from the Equal Employment Opportunity Commission, it grants them to the Attorney General
of the United States. His counterparts in a number of states can initiate enforcement proceedings under their anti-discrimination laws. The
National Labor Relations Board can help wipe
out remaining union resistance, a task in which
the Department of Labor can also lend a hand.
Although the NLRB's enlarged view of its powers mean a lesser role for the courts in the elaboration of the National Labor Relations and Rail-
way Labor Acts' restraints on discrimination,
the federal courts are taking on the new responsibility of deciding cases under Title VII, and
both state and federal courts continue to be
open to constitutional claims. State employment
services, civil service commissions, municipal

civil rights agencies, boards of education, and
licensing commissions are among the other government instrumentalities with power to inhibit
employment discrimination.[56]

If a federal employment commission with
enforcement powers were to be established,
it would need an enormous appropriation
from Congress, and its members and staff
would have to exhibit "energy, resourceful-
ness, and wisdom on a scale never yet
manifested by an anti-discrimination agency,
or, perhaps, by anyone else."[57] In short,
Sovern believes that "the reality of politics
and the limits of human capabilities require
a multifront assault on employment discrimination."

State and Local Fair Employment Practice Laws

Thirty-seven states have laws against discrimination in employment.[58] These laws
have been enacted because (1) of the lack
of a federal FEPC and (2) the state FEPC
has certain areas of operation that cannot
be covered by a national law. As Weaver
points out, a shift is under way to employment in the service industries and the distributive trades. Also, the number of persons
employed in public and semipublic utilities
is substantial. These branches of industry
are not reached by a federal employment
agency, which is limited to firms engaged in
interstate commerce.[59]

In the procedure followed by a FEP commission, the investigation of a complaint is
followed by an attempt to persuade the of-
fender to discontinue the discriminatory
practice. If that fails, a formal hearing may
be held. Following the hearing, a cease-and-
desist order may be issued, and this order
may be enforced, if necessary, by the courts.
In most cases, a formal hearing has not been
necessary, and only a very small fraction
of the cases in any state or city have gone
to the courts. In addition to handling complaints, and, in some states, initiating in-

[55] Sovern, *op. cit.*, pp. 99–101.

[56] Sovern, *op. cit.*, pp. 205–206.
[57] *Ibid.*, p. 207.
[58] ADL, *op. cit.*, p. 1.
[59] Weaver, *op. cit.*, p. 312.

vestigations on their own, some state and local FEP bodies have carried on extensive educational programs.

More than 50 cities enacted fair employment practices laws between 1948 and 1970. In California, Michigan, Minnesota, Ohio, and Pennsylvania one or more municipalities passed local FEP ordinances before such legislation was enacted at the state level.[60]

During the past decade, there has been a growing tendency to charge the state commission handling fair employment practices with the enforcement of laws against discrimination in housing (public and publicly assisted housing, FHA and VA-aided housing, and privately owned housing), places of public accommodation, and, in some cases, education. In New York, employment cases comprised 69 percent of the complaints brought to the State Commission for Human Rights (formerly the State Commission Against Discrimination) in 1958, but they declined to 62 percent in 1960, and to 46 percent in 1964. In that state, there have been three main types of complaints given in employment complaints: refusal to hire, 42 percent; dismissed from employment, 24 percent; and discriminatory conditions of employment, 14 percent. Berger lists five modes of settlement in the cases handled by the SCHR: (1) a complaint may be sustained (discrimination found and then eliminated by conciliation, except in the few cases that have gone to the stage of a public hearing) ; (2) a complaint may be dismissed for lack of evidence but the investigation reveals evidence of other discrimination, which is then eliminated by conciliation; (3) a complaint may be dismissed for lack of evidence, and the investigation may disclose no discrimination at all; (4) a complaint may be dismissed because the Commission lacks authority to deal with the question it raises; (5) the complainant may withdraw his complaint before it is settled. In a 20-year period, the last two dispositions ac-counted for only 7 percent of all the cases closed. In the same period, the Commission sustained approximately 19 percent of the complaints brought to it. (In the early years, a higher proportion of complaints was sustained—about 25 percent, but in 1964 the proportion fell to 10 percent.) The second category of complaints comprised about 20 percent of the total. The highest proportion of complaints in this category came in the late 1950s, but fell to 5 percent in 1964. Over two decades, more than half of all complaints fell in the third category, but unlike the first two categories, the proportion of these cases was lowest in the late 1950s and reached a high point of 76 percent in 1964. Concerning possible explanations for the small and declining proportion of complaints sustained, Berger says: "The complaints may be increasingly weak ones, or the commission's standard of proof of discrimination may be increasingly rigorous, or discrimination in employment may be declining or becoming so subtle that it has become harder to detect. Whatever the reason, or whatever the explanation one would like to test, the Commission does not make public the information needed to assess this trend."[61]

The findings of a study of hiring practices and beliefs of officials of 623 companies in 11 states is not encouraging with respect to the effectiveness of state fair employment commissions.[62] According to this study, there has been little improvement since 1945. Cousens says:

Employers are somewhat more receptive to the highly qualified Negro applicant, partly because of government contracts containing nondiscrimi-

---

[60] Among the cities prohibiting discrimination in public and private employment are: Chicago, Philadelphia, Minneapolis, Cleveland, San Francisco, Pittsburgh, Milwaukee, and Des Moines. Konvitz and Leskes, *op. cit.*, p. 220.

[61] Berger, *op. cit.*, p. 179; see also pp. 176–178.

[62] Cousens, *op. cit.*, p. 114. This study involved interviews with 800 executives in these companies, which had a work force of 450,000, and 82 additional companies in Michigan's construction industry, and 39 additional interviews in California investigating personnel testing. The industries included: financial institutions, public transportation, trucking, service establishments, utilities, and retail stores; interviewers attempted to interview executives at the highest levels. The "Project on the Effectiveness of Public Antidiscrimination Agencies," was sponsored by the Institute of Labor and Industrial Relations, Wayne State University.

nation clauses, partly because of greater awareness of existing inequities, but mostly because
of a tight labor market [the study was made in
1967–1968]. Nevertheless, we discovered not
only continuing widespread discrimination in
the industries and areas studied, but a rationale
largely unchanged since the era preceding FEP
legislation, i.e., the belief that Negroes are unsuitable for some occupations and hiring them
would create problems with employees and/or
customers. In brief, the same constellation of
stereotyped preconceptions and oppositions to
change which has deterred and delayed original
efforts for equal employment opportunity still
prevail.[63]

In the cases of discrimination by trade
unions, New York's SCHR has had more
success through investigations and one complaint brought by the Attorney General than
through individual complaints. In 613 complaints against unions, 30 percent were
upheld, a higher proportion than that for
employers but lower than that for private
employment agencies. In 50 "informal investigations," three-fifths were sustained, a
proportion lower than that for the employment agencies or the employers.[64] Compliance cases are particularly difficult to handle
in the construction industry. The closed shop
is illegal under the Taft-Hartley Act, but
labor unions informally control access
through apprenticeship programs to many
jobs over which contractors have only
nominal control. In a few cases, FEP agencies have taken the initiative and compelled
the admission of Nonwhites into unions. According to Lockard, the Human Relations
Commission in New York City used the
contract compliance method to force opportunities for Negro and Puerto Rican plumbers on a construction job which involved a
city contract. The New York SCHR forced
the cancellation of an all-white panel of
apprentice applicants of Local 28 of the
Sheet Metal Workers and the opening of
apprenticeships to qualified workers.[65]

In the face of continuing discrimination
in employment, critics ask what the state

and municipal agencies have been doing
since they were created. The answer seems
to be that they have been processing complaints. In terms of expanding opportunities
for minorities, the effects of this processing
have been minimal. More than half of all
the executives interviewed in the Wayne
State study did not know of the existence
of the civil rights agency in their state. Depending upon the industry, 40 to 45 percent
did not believe that FEP legislation was of
significance to their company, and more than
90 percent were not planning any change in
their policies or practices, because they did
not regard their employment patterns as
being discriminatory. On the other hand,
this study found that Negroes and other minorities regard such programs as largely
irrelevant in meeting their needs for jobs.
Cousens says: "If they are sufficiently motivated to file a complaint, the process takes
exceedingly long and then the odds are about
ten to one against actually getting the job
originally denied them."[66]

In assessing the New York state law,
Berger says that undoubtedly it has expanded
employment opportunities for minorities.
His reasons for this conclusion are that the
commission has: (1) settled thousands of
complaints brought by individuals, (2)
opened further opportunities in thousands
of additional cases affecting not only a single
worker but the entire labor forces of many
employers large and small, (3) made agreements with several industries concerning the
whole pattern of employment, (4) reduced
discrimination by commercial employment
agencies and trade unions, and (5) changed
the general conditions of the labor market
through the elimination of discriminatory
advertisements and through other devices intended to make individual qualification more
important to employment than the traditional
definitions of the marketplace that excluded
certain industries, firms, and kinds of jobs.
Berger does not argue whether something
has been achieved in the state of New York,
but rather how much has been achieved in
relation to the need. From this point of

---

[63] *Ibid.*, p. 114.
[64] Berger, *op. cit.*, p. 187.
[65] Duane Lockard, *Toward Equal Opportunity*,
Macmillan, 1968, p. 101.

[66] Cousens, *op. cit.*, p. 116. See also pp. 114–115.

view, the SCHR has serious weaknesses in the light of (1) the strong law under which it operates, (2) its nine commissioners, 200 staff members, and an annual budget of $2 million, (3) the urgency of its task, and (4) the more than two decades of its existence.[67] Lockard makes somewhat the same point about state antidiscrimination commissions in general in saying that the experience with FEP has been a failure to meet its potential. Specifically he says: "The predominant concern with individual cases, the failure to pursue contract compliance procedures, the bureaucratic slowness of many agencies, the failure to establish real contact with the Negro slum dweller and other shortcomings support the conclusion that FEP can in the future contribute more than it has in the past if the agencies get the internal leadership and external support to make possible an expanded and more effective program."[68]

Recommendations for strengthening state FEP programs include changes in the laws, less caution on the part of commissions, greater political support, and greater pressure by civil rights organizations for enforcement of the law. Ideally, a statute should include legal authorization for the agency to initiate investigations and it should contain specific authorization for investigation of the employment practices of contractors who are paid with public funds for construction, supplies, or services. A few commissions, most notably, perhaps, the New York state and city ones, have this authority and have taken actions along these lines. In addition to contract compliance, the SCHR has made agreements with more than 2000 firms over a period of 20 years through the use of informal pattern-of-employment investigations and follow-up checks on individual complaints. Most agencies have not used these devices because of lack of authority, manpower, or courage to make a frontal attack on the problem.[69] A second way of strengthening some of the state statutes would be to

include all employers regardless of the number of employees. Usually, the minimum varies from 4 to 50 employees, but the most common number is 6 or 8. A third provision that weakens the law in a number of states is a blanket exception for social, fraternal, educational and religious organizations not seeking a profit. Lockard says that the only variation that seems to have a compelling reason behind it is Ohio Civil Rights Commission's exemption of charitable and educational organizations where affiliation with a particular faith or creed is a bona fide qualification for employment.[70] A fourth recommendation is an explicit provision authorizing suits on conciliation agreements that a commission has concluded with offenders. Another change that emphasizes enforcement is the type of amendment enacted by the New York legislature permitting the investigating commissioner to omit the conciliation step.[71] Since nearly all of every commission's budget is required to handle the complaint load, a fifth recommendation calls for doubling present allocations to permit the spot checking necessary to uncover the large volume of discrimination that is uncomplained of at present. A related need is for full-time rather than part-time commissioners who have heavy commitments elsewhere.[72]

Most FEP commissions have not made use of all the tools given them by legislatures. Berger says that much has been made of the legislature's grant to New York's SCHR, in 1965, of the power to initiate complaints and to move from a finding of discrimination directly to a public hearing. He points out, however, that the Commission could always ask the Attorney General or the Industrial Commissioner to file a complaint. Also, "from the very outset, too, Section 297 of the law empowered a commissioner to skip the conciliation stage if he felt that a case warranted going directly to a public hearing."[73] A few commissions have gone beyond processing complaints by establish-

[67] Berger, *op. cit.*, pp. 200–201.
[68] Lockard, *op. cit.*, p. 101.
[69] *Ibid.*, p. 79.

[70] *Ibid.*, p. 82.
[71] Sovern, *op. cit.*, pp. 56–58.
[72] *Ibid.*, pp. 58–59.
[73] Berger, *op. cit.*, p. 204.

ing liaison with school systems, police departments, churches, and other institutions and by allocating staff resources to work with minority groups to encourage enrollment in manpower development and skill training. Cousens reports that each of the agencies in 11 states participating in the Wayne State "Project on the Effectiveness of Public Antidiscrimination Agencies" has legislative authority to conduct such action programs, but none of them had done so.[74]

Some evaluators see the lack of strong political support in both executive and legislative branches as the main obstacle to more effective FEP action. In New York, Pennsylvania, and some other states, the support of governors has been important in the enactment of the original laws and key amendments, as well as in increasing agency budgets and staffs, and governors and mayors have frequently complied with commission requests to inform other administrators that compliance with FEP was mandatory in government hiring and promotion. But the record is uneven. In some states, effective administrators have been removed because governors or legislators have resented their "trouble making." Some governors have become frightened at the possible political repercussions of too explicit commitment of support for FEP. Perhaps the most serious lack of support has come from state employment agencies. Lockard found that many of these agencies continue to refer job applicants on a discriminatory basis, and FEP administrators have been unable to gain the political strength needed to stop the practice.[75]

Finally, in the view of some appraisers, FEP programs have not realized their potential in part because civil rights groups have not been effective enough since the passage of antidiscrimination laws. Concerning these groups in New York, Berger says: "They have criticized the administration of it [the law] but have been only sporadic and not unified in pressing for stronger enforcement, have not stimulated enough complaints by individuals, and have not filed enough complaints themselves."[76]

HOUSING

Housing is both an essential commodity and one that provides numerous emotional satisfactions or dissatisfactions. Housing deprivations consist of physical shortcomings in dwelling units and of the inability to enter a neighborhood of one's choice.[77] Housing opportunities, together with educational and employment opportunities, are central areas of concern to racial and ethnic minorities in the United States.[78] The importance of housing is seen clearly in the school segregation-desegregation situation. Despite such measures as free choice of schools, pupil transfer plans, the placement of new school buildings, and the transportation of some pupils from crowded to uncrowded schools within a city school system, desegregation of the public schools proceeds slowly or actually declines, in part because of the concentration of racial and ethnic minorities within metropolitan areas. Residential segregation is also the *de facto* segregation underlying segregation in stores, places of employment, and other institutions. Taeuber points out, however, that each of these other types of segregation has additional support from general racial prejudice in the society and from specific social patterns.[79]

[76] Berger, *op. cit.*, p. 202.
[77] See David McEntire, *Residence and Race*, Univ. of California Press, 1960, p. 99.
[78] On this point McEntire says:

The middle class, including the minority middle class, seeks not just housing but neighborhoods. For families at this level, good housing means, in addition to an adequate dwelling unit, those qualities of quiet, order, cleanliness, good facilities, and social prestige, usually associated with a desirable neighborhood. Hence, for a middle-class family to be refused entry to a neighborhood of its choice is a serious deprivation not compensated for by the availability of housing elsewhere . . . at higher levels of income and cost, housing requirements become increasingly individualized . . . , *Ibid.*

[79] Karl E. Taeuber, "Negro Population and Housing: Demographic Aspects of a Social Accounting Scheme," in Irwin Katz and Patricia Gurin (eds.), *Race and the Social Sciences*, Basic Books, 1969, p. 186.

[74] Cousens, *op. cit.*, p. 117.
[75] Lockard, *op. cit.*, pp. 83–84.

According to one estimate, one-sixth of the population of continental United States is directly affected by housing discrimination. Earlier such discrimination included Irish, Italians, and other European immigrants, but today those most affected are Blacks, Puerto Ricans, Mexican-Americans, and American Indians, and, to a lesser extent, Orientals and Jews.[80] Housing discrimination does not apply with equal severity to all minority groups. In most cases, Jews can obtain housing that is equivalent in quality to that available to other Whites, but in many cities a number of good neighborhoods remain closed or are available only with difficulty. Today Jews do not suffer physical deprivation from residential discrimination, but exclusion from a neighborhood or community because of religious background represents a serious departure from democratic standards. The growth of Jewish enclaves in suburban areas, sometimes called "gilded ghettoes," constitutes a divisiveness in American society. This is true despite the fact that some have preferred to seek residence in these areas.[81]

Negroes face exclusion in every city, except in a relatively small number of neighborhoods. In addition, the housing available to Negroes is inferior to that of Whites. Both the housing and the neighborhoods in which Negroes live are more deteriorated; amenities are fewer; mortgages are harder to obtain; private investment in new buildings is rare; overcrowding is greater; schools, hospitals, and recreation facilities are inferior; and Negroes often get less housing value for their money than Whites.[82]

A careful study of the relationship between socioeconomic status and racial segregation in Chicago showed that the white-nonwhite residential segregation index expected on the basis of income in 1950 was 11, compared to the actual segregation index of 79. In that year, therefore, income differentials ac-

counted for 11/79—or 14 percent—of the observed racial segregation. In 1960, the expected segregation index was 10 and the actual index was 83—income differentials in that year accounted for only 12 percent of the observed racial segregation.[83] Taeuber estimates that 13 to 33 percent of the segregation in 15 cities analyzed is attributable to poverty and the rest to discrimination. Subsidized public housing or rent subsidies alleviate the problem of housing for Negroes somewhat, but if publicly aided housing is available to them only in the ghetto the low incomes that make them eligible also confine them to the ghetto. Nonwhites occupy half of all low-rent public housing, but a high proportion of this is segregated housing built in ghetto areas where Whites are unwilling to live.[84]

An improved economic status of Negroes cannot be used, except under exceptional circumstances, to secure unsegregated housing in Chicago and in most other cities in the United States. All the elements of compulsion—social, political, and economic—keep Blacks in place when they are willing and able to live outside the ghetto. These elements are present particularly on the outskirts of cities, where 80 percent of new houses are built. There exists, then, a separate housing market for Negroes. Unlike members of immigrant groups, including Puerto Ricans, Negroes have been unable to achieve much residential dispersion.[85]

In Chapter 3 we discuss the mutually reinforcing relationships between prejudice and discrimination. It is not sufficient to say that prejudice causes discrimination, but it

---

[80] Eunice and George Grier, *Discrimination in Housing*, ADL, 1960, p. 8.

[81] *Report of the U.S. Commission on Civil Rights*, 1959, p. 150.

[82] Charles Abrams, *The City Is the Frontier*, Harper & Row, 1965, p. 59.

[83] Karl E. and Alma F. Taeuber, "Is the Negro an Immigrant Group?" *Integrated Education*, June, 1963, pp. 25–28. Reprinted in August Meier and Elliott Rudwick, *The Making of Black America*, Atheneum, vol. 2, pp. 503–507.

[84] Lockard, *op. cit.* p. 108.

[85] K. E. and A. F. Taeuber, *op. cit.*, p. 506; Abrams, *The City Is the Frontier*, p. 64; John B. Lansing, Charles Wade, and James M. Morgan, *New Homes and Poor People: A Study of Chains of Moves*, Institute of Social Research, Univ. of Michigan, 1969, p. 68. See also, Reynolds Farley, "The Changing Distribution of Negroes Within Metropolitan Areas: The Emergence of Black Suburbs," *AJS*, Jan., 1970, pp. 512–529.

is important to recognize that misinformation, stereotypes, and myths serve to justify existing practices and to slow down or prevent changes. In the field of housing, many racial myths circulate widely and affect adversely the efforts of those who are concerned about the provision of more adequate housing for low-income families and open housing. One fiction is that the primary aspect of the Negro's housing problem is the slum, that is, insanitary or structurally deficient housing. Abrams pointed out that many Negroes do live in slums but that some do not. (About half the nonwhite renters in California and two-fifths of the nonwhite home owners live in substandard houses compared with one-fifth of the white renters and one-tenth of white homeowners.) The physical condition of homes in the black ghetto, however, is only one aspect of the housing situation there, and perhaps, not the most important aspect. Abrams said: "The neighborhoods are run-down; officialdom is less concerned with their maintenance, and their general atmosphere is demoralizing; the schools are segregated and inferior, and so are the recreational, hospital, and social facilities; there are also fewer new buildings erected in Negro areas, even for those who can afford them."[86] Overcrowding within the buildings Negroes occupy, and the high proportion of income paid for rent (36 percent of the black families in a 1965 U.S. Census survey in the renewal areas of 132 cities paid 35 percent or more of their incomes for their shelter), are other very important aspects of housing in black areas.[87]

A second fiction, especially characteristic of official policy in the mid-1960s, is that the best way to solve the Negro's housing problems is to tear down the slums.[88] As we point out later in this chapter, for years this policy usually resulted in clearing off blighted sections and replacing them with housing units priced beyond the means of the former residents. This policy often meant that displaced racial minorities crowded into already overcrowded segregated areas.[89]

A third fiction is that Negroes and Whites do not mix and that Negroes will destroy the social status of any neighborhood. Usually this fiction "is supplemented by claims that, once the Negro establishes a beachhead, more Negroes will follow—which is often the case—causing real estate values to topple —which may or may not be the case."[90] Laurenti found that prices rose in 44 percent of those areas that Negroes entered, were unchanged in another 41 percent, and declined in only 15 percent.[91] (Taeuber appropriately suggests, however, that the evidence produced by Laurenti's work does not support sweeping generalizations concerning the presence of Negroes in a neighborhood and property values.)[92]

A fourth fiction is that the federal government is, and always has been, the main advocate of equal rights in housing. In refuting this myth, Abrams pointed out that until 1948 the Supreme Court supported the use of the racial restrictive covenant as a private right, and that during the New Deal period the federal government required discrimination against Negroes as a condition of federal assistance.[93]

A fifth fiction is that the state and local antidiscrimination laws in housing provide the means for ending discrimination. More will be said later about this belief; the fact is that these laws have not solved the Negro's housing troubles. Of great importance is the inability of the city anti-bias laws to affect the suburbs, where most of the exclusionary practices exist. Concerning the state laws, Abrams said that it is "all but impossible to buck the concerted power of

[86] Charles Abrams, "The Housing Problem and the Negro," *Daedalus*, Winter, 1966, pp. 64–65.

[87] *Ibid.*, pp. 65–66.

[88] *Ibid.*, p. 66.

[89] Eunice and George Grier, "Equality and Beyond: Housing Segregation in the Great Society," in *Daedalus*, Winter, 1966, p. 84.

[90] Abrams, "The Housing Problem and the Negro," p. 67.

[91] L. Laurenti, *Property Values and Race,* Univ. of California Press, 1960. Cited by Grier and Grier, *op. cit.,* p. 82.

[92] Taeuber, *op. cit.,* p. 182.

[93] Abrams, "The Housing Problem and the Negro," p. 69.

the suburbs to which the political balance has shifted."[94]

A complementary set of myths concerning the causes and consequences of residential segregation that contributes to retarding efforts to create open housing is given by Taeuber. These fictions include: (1) Negroes prefer to live together; (2) prejudice and discrimination have nothing to do with the housing market; Negroes are free to live anywhere and do so to the full extent of their financial ability and preferences; (3) maintenance of the ghetto, at least in the short run, is beneficial to the Negro cause; and (4) the problem is a Negro one.[95]

The Role of Government in Housing Segregation and Desegregation

Residential segregation laws were declared illegal by the Supreme Court in 1917 when a Louisville, Kentucky, racial zoning ordinance was held to violate the Fourteenth Amendment. In 1925 the Court dismissed a New Orleans ordinance that sought to evade the prohibition on racial segregation by providing for written consent of the majority race inhabiting a block as a condition upon residence there by a member of the other race, by referring to its decision in the Louisville case. Racial discrimination in housing has taken many forms, and many techniques have been devised to effectuate it since 1917. A common device has been the racial restrictive covenant. This is an agreement between parties to the sale of real property whereby the purchaser agrees not to rent or sell his property to members of specified races, nationalities, or religions.

Prior to 1948, racial restrictive covenants could be enforced in state courts. When a party to a restrictive covenant brought suit against a violator, the court could order the proscribed purchaser or tenant to give up

possession of the property. In 1948 the Supreme Court held that restrictive covenants deny equal protection of the laws guaranteed by the Fourteenth Amendment. The Court held that restrictive covenants standing alone do not violate the rights guaranteed by the Fourteenth Amendment. If the agreements are carried out by voluntary adherence to their terms, in the Court's view, there is no action by the state and hence no violation of the Amendment.[96] It may be noted that the Department of Justice issued a statement saying that in its opinion the ruling of the Supreme Court in the racial restrictive covenant cases is "applicable with equal force to similar agreements based on creed."

Today many people disregard the covenants that appear in deeds not to sell to members of minority groups, but it has been shown that in some cities they are still used effectively. It is not clear why they continue to be effective despite the fact that they are no longer enforceable in the courts, but one possibility is that some homeowners are not aware of the 1948 Supreme Court decision. Also, it has been suggested that those who have entered into these agreements feel under moral pressure to keep them.[97] The U.S. Commission on Civil Rights thinks that the best explanation for the effectiveness of these covenants in the District of Columbia and environs is that simple exclusion is used to enforce the policy they declare.

The Commission was told that one of these builders, the W. C. and A. N. Miller Development Co. . . . uses the following clauses together with its exclusionary covenant:

Fourth. No lot or property . . . shall be occupied, leased, rented, conveyed, or otherwise alienated . . . without the written consent of

---

[94] *Ibid.*, pp. 69–70.

[95] Karl E. Taeuber, "The Problem of Residential Segregation," in Robert H. Connery (ed.), "Urban Riots: Violence and Social Change," *Proceedings of the Academy of Political Science*, 29, No. 1, 1968, pp. 103–112. Refutation of these myths is given in Taeuber's paper.

[96] Loren Miller, "Supreme Court Covenant Decision—An Analysis," *The Crisis*, Sept., 1948, p. 265.

[97] U.S. Commission on Civil Rights, *Civil Rights U.S.A.: Housing in Washington, D.C.*, 1962, pp. 10–11. The covenant usually used reads: "No part of the land hereby conveyed shall ever be used, or occupied by . . . Negroes, or any person . . . of Negro blood or extraction, or . . . any person of the Semitic race, blood, or origin, which racial description shall be deemed to include Armenians, Jews, Hebrews, Persians, and Syrians. . . ." *Ibid.*

the W. C. and A. N. Miller Development Co. [unless a majority of neighbors consent].

Fourteenth. . . . in order to facilitate operation of the covenant number "Fourth" . . . the grantee covenants . . . that in the event, at any time he . . . shall desire to lease, rent, or sell to another . . . he . . . will appoint the said W. C. & A. N. Miller Development Co. agent for such purpose.

The Commission's report adds that the effect of these clauses is to give the Miller Development Co. control "over the race and religion of all subsequent owners and tenants. This control the Millers have used to exclude Nonwhites and Jews from some areas."[98]

According to the U.S. Commission on Civil Rights, the most effective and widely used method of exclusion is the simple refusal to sell.

Despite the idealistic and liberal tone of New Deal legislation, it is interesting that Negro housing became increasingly segregated from 1934 to 1948. From the beginning of the FHA until the Supreme Court ruled against racial covenants, FHA policies emphasized racial unity as a condition for the highest evaluations of neighborhoods and insisted that racial homogeneity was essential to a neighborhood's financial stability.[99]

As a result of pressure from civil rights groups and the Attorney General, the FHA eventually ruled that it would no longer insure mortgages on properties having covenants that had been placed on them after February, 1950. It continued to insure properties on which covenants existed before that date.[100] This policy affected FHA financing guarantees for housing projects and one-unit dwellings, GI loans for veterans' housing, and slum clearance projects and land transactions by public agencies.

In 1949 a comprehensive housing bill passed by Congress provided for an urban redevelopment program. Title I included a writedown subsidy on land costs in slum or blighted areas, with two-thirds of the subsidy to be paid by the federal government and one-third by the municipality. The program was designed primarily for private developers, but public housing authorities could benefit from the subsidy.[101] The Housing Act of 1954 amended existing housing laws, putting major emphasis upon urban renewal.[102]

Urban Renewal Programs. The FHA's 221 program of assisting private industry in building rental projects for lower- to middle-income families has been almost entirely a central city program. Considering the high degree of residential segregation in urban areas, these projects often reinforce existing concentrations. Of two sites selected for FHA 221 projects in Chicago, for example, one was in a virtually all-white area; the other in an all-Negro area. When occupied, the projects had occupancies 99 percent white and 100 percent Negro. The elementary schools serving the projects are 98.5 percent white and 99.6 percent Negro. In Boston, three urban renewal projects have nonwhite occupancy of 87 percent, and the schools range from 91 to 100 percent nonwhite.[103]

The FHA says that it "examines carefully the site on every multifamily housing project which it insures, and particularly with respect to 221 (d) (3) projects." The U.S. Commission on Civil Rights points out, however, that FHA's concern is limited to economic feasibility. The Commission found that:

. . . . the main impact of urban renewal on residential patterns and racial composition of the public schools is through the relocation of families it displaces. More than 60 percent of the families displaced since 1949 whose color is known are nonwhite. The Department of Housing and Urban Development, which administers the program, sets certain standards of safety, sanitation, and costs to assure that the new homes of families and individuals who will be displaced will be adequate and within their

[98] *Ibid.*

[99] L. T. Hawley, "The Negro's New Economic Life," *Fortune,* Sept. 1956, p. 258; and Charles Abrams, *Forbidden Neighbors,* Harper & Row, 1955, pp. 161–162, 223, 231, 235.

[100] Abrams, *Forbidden Neighbors,* p. 24.

[101] *Ibid.,* pp. 244–245.

[102] B. T. McGraw, "The Housing Act of 1954 and Implications for Minorities," *Phylon,* Second Quarter, 1955, p. 171.

[103] Report of the U.S. Commission on Civil Rights, *Racial Isolation in the Public Schools,* vol. 1, 1967, pp. 34–35.

means. But the Department does not look into each relocation plan to determine the impact of relocation in intensifying or reducing racial concentration. Neither does it determine the impact of relocation on the composition of schools."[104]

According to Abrams, Congress has been unwilling to face the real issues, and despite the changes that have been made since the inauguration of the urban renewal program, the following defects remain:

1. It overemphasizes slum clearance and lacks an adequate housing program for those it evicts and for those who live in the slums it proposes tearing down. It makes no provision for rehousing these people except in the cities.
2. It relies almost exclusively on the speculative profit motive for the clearance of these slums and the rebuilding of slum neighborhoods. Some of the projects cannot show a profit and should be developed for other purposes—more parks, playgrounds, etc.
3. It deals primarily with only one aspect of the city's predicament, i.e., housing and slums, while it ignores the others—poverty, social unrest, school problems, racial frictions, physical obsolescence, spatial restrictions, decline of its economic base, and the lack of financial resources to cope with major difficulties. The poverty program is only a feeble start toward grappling with a few of these problems.[105]

It was Abrams' view that if cities could be made more attractive through having better schools, recreation, and environments, the demand for city living and housing would increase in many areas. Under these circumstances, he held that private builders and merchants would seek the profit opportunities available and urban renewal "could then become a more constructive tool for assembling land, replanning obsolete layouts, and providing recreation, schools, housing, and other amenities to new, well-planned neighborhoods."[106]

Despite the increased demand by low-income Negro families for public housing, some Negro leaders have been cool to attempts to expand such housing. The Mid-South Chicago Council, an organization formed to deal with blight and conservation problems, lasted only two or three years. One reason for its failure was the realization by businessmen, real estate brokers, and property owners that building code enforcement would result in a decrease in population density and thus a reduction of their market. In addition, neighborhood rehabilitation might mean the introduction of competition from new white businesses. In the Hyde Park–Kenwood neighborhood of Chicago, few Negro leaders were willing to take a public stand on public housing. A few advocates of extensive public housing, mainly leaders of labor unions with large Negro memberships, took a strong stand. A number of Negro civic leaders who occupied offices in voluntary organizations such as the NAACP spoke in favor of public housing to house Negroes being displaced from their homes. Their support of public housing was not enthusiastic. A number of Negro residents who owned desirable homes in the area opposed any public housing at all in that neighborhood. One of these men said:

When you get people living together whose actions and culture are far apart, then you are bound to have dissatisfactions arise, race notwithstanding. . . . You get some people who want to raise chickens or goats in their backyard. . . . Other people shouldn't have to suffer for that. It is better to have in one neighborhood people of like thinking and tastes.[107]

Negro politicians are reluctant to support proposals for open-occupancy ordinances. Wilson remarks that doing away with Negro wards by legislation is not an imminent possibility, but that it was widely believed in Chicago that the opposition of Negro politicians on this issue "stemmed from a realization that open occupancy would mean the end of the Negro wards which elect them." One Negro alderman explained his indifference to open occupancy in this way:

What it comes down to is this: It won't happen in my life time. This condition [Negro concentration] will be with us for a very long time, no matter what I do. . . . Negroes won't be

---

[104] *Ibid.*, p. 35.
[105] Abrams, *The City Is the Frontier*, p. 179.
[106] *Ibid.*, pp. 179–180.

[107] James Q. Wilson, *Negro Politics*, Free Press, 1960, pp. 202–203.

living just anywhere, and no whites are going to move in here. You couldn't pay a white family enough to move into this ward. I know.[108]

President Kennedy's executive order against discrimination went into effect on November 21, 1962. This order

. . . directs departments and agencies of the federal government to take all necessary action to prevent discrimination because of race, color, creed or national origin in the sale or leasing of housing owned or operated by the federal government, built in whole or in part with federal loans or grants, built with federally-insured loans, or constructed on real property handled under public agencies receiving federal assistance. Discriminatory practices in federally-insured lending are also prohibited. Provision is made for enforcement of the order, including legal action and cancellation of loans, grants, etc. A President's Committee on Equal Opportunity in Housing is created, and charged with the responsibility of coordinating departmental activities to implement the program.[109]

The Administration did not go as far in this order as the U.S. Commission on Civil Rights and a number of unofficial organizations had recommended. This order affected only a small part of the housing market. It covered only 23 percent of all new housing construction and only 13 percent of the housing not already covered by state or local laws. Also, it explicitly excluded the federally regulated and federally assisted savings and loan associations that are the main mortgage lenders in the United States.[110]

The 1965 Housing Act authorized $200 million in rent supplements. This program is designed to aid persons of limited incomes by making up the difference between one-fourth of their incomes and the rents charged by private, nonprofit, limited dividend, or co-operative sponsors. Families or individuals are eligible if displaced by government action, and also the elderly, physically handicapped, occupants of substandard housing, or victims of a natural disaster. The income must be within the limit established for low-rent public housing. Under this law, initiation of the housing operation depends on an interest on the part of private entrepreneurs or nonprofit corporations in going into suburbia. Shortly after this law was passed, Abrams said: ". . . it will be a miracle if the program produces more than a token number of suburban dwelling units for Negro families. The best of intentions can always be forestalled by devious zoning ordinances or obstreperous building codes. Much will still depend on how much pressure can be brought to bear on the federal housing agencies so that they will be forced to challenge suburban bias."[111] Abrams may have been somewhat too pessimistic, since the number of Negro suburbanites increased rather rapidly after 1965, albeit mainly in partially segregated suburbs.

In 1966 Congress passed the Demonstration Cities and Metropolitan Development Act. Title I (Model Neighborhoods in Demonstration Cities)

provides for a new program designed to demonstrate how the living environment and the general welfare of people living in slum and blighted neighborhoods can be substantially improved in cities of all sizes and in all parts of the country. It calls for a comprehensive attack on racial, economic, and physical problems in selected slum and blighted areas through the most effective and economical concentration and coordination of Federal, State, and local public and private efforts. The statute provides financial and technical assistance to enable cities to plan, develop and carry out comprehensive local programs containing new and imaginative proposals to develop 'model' neighborhoods.[112]

In large part, the neighborhoods selected for rehabilitation overlap the 'target' areas of the OEO. Unlike the OEO programs, the residents of the areas of focus in the Demonstration Cities program have no legislative right to official participation in the program.[113]

---

[108] *Ibid.*, pp. 205–206.

[109] *Race Relations Law Reporter*, Winter, 1962, p. 1019.

[110] Abrams, "The Housing Problem and the Negro," p. 69.

[111] *Ibid.*, p. 74; Robert Weaver, "Housing for Minority Families;" *Crisis*, Oct. 1966, pp. 425–426.

[112] Sethard Fisher, "New Techniques of Retardation," in S. Fisher, *Power and the Black Community*, Random House, 1970, pp. 430–431.

[113] *Ibid.*, pp. 431, 432.

The Federal Civil Rights Act of 1968. Title VIII of the Civil Rights Act of 1968 prohibits discrimination based on race, color, religion, or national origin in the sale, rental, financing, or advertising of dwelling units. In addition, it makes "blockbusting" illegal and opens membership on real estate boards and multiple-listing services to Nonwhites. On June 17, 1968, the Supreme Court reaffirmed the legality of the 1968 Civil Rights law, which provided that: "All citizens of the United States shall have the same right, in every state and territory, as is enjoyed by white citizens thereof to inherit, purchase, lease, sell, hold and convey real and personal property." Until the law of 1968 was enacted and the Court reinstated the law of 1866, federal law had been applicable only to certain dwellings constructed or sold with federal financial assistance. This decision and Title VIII provide the means for eliminating housing discrimination and segregation through three avenues of redress: complaints to HUD and state agencies, suits in the federal courts, and requests to the U.S. Attorney General to file suit on behalf of the aggrieved. At the end of 1968, Congress failed to appropriate sufficient funds to implement housing and civil rights laws. Funds to carry out the fair housing title of the Civil Rights Act were cut from $11 to $2 million.[114] By the end of 1970, 24 states are reported to have enacted open-housing laws "substantially equivalent" to the federal act, thus enabling them to receive complaints that otherwise must be sent to Washington. None of the southern states is among these 24. Some 373 towns and cities in the United States now have local open-housing ordinances; only 12 of these are in the South. Concerning Title VIII and the Nixon administration, Barker says:

Title VIII authorizes all departments and agencies of the federal government to administer their programs relating to housing and urban development in a manner which will promote open housing. Various federal government agencies dispense millions of dollars annually to local governments in the form of grants for programs such as sewer construction, highways, and metropolitan planning. Minimum standards to promote equal opportunity in housing should be part of the criteria for determining which local communities shall receive these grants. But the government regulations to establish these standards have not been issued.[115]

A modification in the Nixon administration's policy is seen in the case of Blackjack, Missouri. A nonprofit development corporation sponsored by religious organizations purchased approximately 12 acres of land in the area and planned to build a federally subsidized housing project for low- and moderate-income families of all races. After HUD had approved the application for federal subsidy, Blackjack residents incorporated themselves as a city and zoned out multifamily dwellings, including the proposed Park Valley project. Blackjack does not want federal aid, but other communities do. Difficult policy questions arise concerning what they must do, or not do, to qualify for financial assistance. In April, 1971, the federal government filed suit against Blackjack for excluding a racially integrated housing project and announced that communities rejecting federally subsidized housing for the poor would be denied other federal aid for community development. Secretary Romney announced that HUD would use its financial aid to encourage construction of federally subsidized housing in suburbs.[116] This development will bear watching. It should be noted, however, that a few weeks later President Nixon indicated refusal to use federal power to compel housing integration of different economic classes. Many thought this statement contradicted the Blackjack ruling, since freedom to exclude the poor mainly means freedom to exclude blacks.

---

[114] Paget L. Alves, Jr., "The Urban Scene: Housing and Poverty," in Patricia Romero (ed.), *In Black America*, United, 1969, pp. 235–237.

[115] Horace Barker, "Open Housing: No Southern State Has Moved to Enforce This Law of the Land," *South Today*, Mar. 1971, p. 4.

[116] Monroe W. Karmin, *The Wall Street Journal*, Jan. 19, 1971. Reprinted in *South Today*, Mar. 1971, p. 9. See also, *The Plain Dealer*, June 16, 1971, p. 9.

State Laws on Fair Housing. In the history of legislation against discrimination in housing, the approach of the legislatures was much more tentative than their approach in dealing with other forms of discrimination. The first laws in the field of housing were limited to public and publicly assisted housing and the first extension of such laws to private housing was to large multiple dwellings and whole housing developments. These laws have been extended slowly to cover most of the housing market.[117]

Prior to the enactment of Title VIII of the 1968 Civil Rights Act, state laws fell into five categories according to their coverage. The Alaska and Michigan laws covered all housing without stating exceptions. In the second category were the laws that included all sales, but which made exceptions for the rental of rooms within a residence (the so-called Mrs. Murphy rule) or exempted the rental of an apartment in an owner-occupied building. Such laws were in effect in Colorado, Connecticut, Indiana, Massachusetts, New Jersey, and New York. A third category excluded owner-occupied houses with regard either to sales or rental even if they were single-unit residences: California, Minnesota, Ohio, Pennsylvania, and Rhode Island. The fourth group excluded owner-occupied houses in a somewhat different way: Oregon's law applied to persons engaged in "a business enterprise" of selling or renting real property. Finally, New Hampshire and Maine prohibited discrimination only in the rentals of housing. Nearly all states included real estate agents (or the state commission had ruled that they were included as places of public accommodation or under the general terms of the housing law), as well as lending institutions. Most states excluded housing operated by religious, educational, or charitable groups from the effects of the law. The most outstanding deficiency in the state statutes was the widespread exemption for owner-occupied, one-family dwellings.[118]

The enactment of Title VIII of the 1968 Civil Rights Act stimulated state legislation against discrimination in housing. Because that law, like the provision against discrimination in employment in the 1964 federal Civil Rights Act, gives precedence to state laws that meet the standards established by the federal law, a number of states have adopted such laws, or have modified previously existing laws. Thus they obtain local control of their administration instead of federal control. In 1969, for example, five states enacted new fair housing laws, and eight states strengthened earlier laws. In 1970, 26 states had laws against discrimination in housing.[119]

For several reasons—scarcity of Negro complaints, a high proportion of no-probable-cause findings, procedural difficulties, and resultant delays in processing complaints—reliance on the case-complaint method alone is ineffective. The alternative to the complaint process is authorization for the state agencies to initiate investigations on their own. These pattern-centered approaches are similar to pattern-centered programs in employment. One pattern-centered approach used by the New York State Commission is called the Market Area Agreement. Under this arrangement, a group of housing developers agrees to admit occupants into rental units without regard to race, thereby eliminating the fear that one who admits Nonwhites will have difficulties in renting while competitors who discriminate take advantage of the situation.

Although militants dismiss the educational approach as useless, some evaluators find that it is necessary to counter the view held by many builders, rental agents, real estate brokers, and home owners that the presence of a Negro in a neighborhood means property value disaster.[120]

Lockard concludes that the fair housing law has considerable potential.

Granted that alone such laws can accomplish little, taken with other social change they could have an impact on the housing market especially because they provide a means to break the re-

---

[117] ADL, *Law*, 1970, p. 1.
[118] Lockard, *op. cit.*, p. 119.

[119] ADL, *Law*, pp. 1–8.
[120] Lockard, *op. cit.*, p. 125.

sistance of the hard core objector. Evasion of the law will undoubtedly be common, as the subjective factors in the renting and sale of housing leave many loopholes for the evader, but the blatant discriminator can be reached by imaginative, resourceful, adequately staffed and supported enforcement agencies.[121]

Additional Techniques and Programs Intended to Increase Open Housing. One approach to equality of housing opportunities is the private interracial housing development. By 1966 housing developments that had served a racially mixed market from their inception numbered several hundred—and possibly more than a thousand. The Griers say: "A few have been opened to Negroes only as a result of litigation or by direct threat of legal action. But in the majority, compliance has been voluntary once the developer has been faced with qualified Negro applicants."[122] The most serious limitation of these developments is that they are built by profit-oriented builders and most Negro families cannot afford to purchase or rent from them.

Another approach to equalizing housing opportunity is that of "benign quotas." In this plan attempts are made to maintain a certain ratio of Nonwhites to Whites (usually a white majority is maintained in the buildings) in order to prevent a project or a neighborhood from becoming totally segregated. The most successful of these plans have been developed by Morris Milgram, president of Planned Communities. This investment trust owns apartment buildings and housing projects in Pennsylvania, New Jersey, Virginia, New York, and Illinois. Despite defeats in Deerfield, Illinois and in Connecticut, the other projects organized by Mr. Milgrim have been successful financially and from the standpoint of integration.[123]

Fair-housing listing services perform valuable assistance by scattering the Negro families they place throughout the suburban areas of a city. The Griers say that the listing services open so many neighborhood in such quick succession that the chances of rapid racial turnover in any particular section become remote. Such services offer only a limited means to reduce residential segregation, and their activities are confined mainly to the more affluent segment of the Negro market.[124]

Voluntary neighborhood stabilization campaigns have tended to slow down racial transition and keep the change orderly rather than to stop it completely. According to the Griers: "As the change continues—and it is inevitable without the same kinds of tight restrictive controls which helped make the Negro ghettos what they are today—a segregated neighborhood is again likely to appear. . . . They are holding actions until other more fundamental efforts are made to lessen discriminatory practices throughout the whole metropolitan area."[125]

A number of "deghettoization" and integration projects of somewhat limited scope have been launched in recent years. A desegregation project in Washington, D.C. seeks to help the relocation of Negro families earning more than $7000 a year who work in the suburbs but have not been able to secure housing there. Designed by the Washington Center for Metropolitan Studies and the Housing Opportunities Council of Metropolitan Washington, the project received one grant of $300,000 and has sought additional funding from HUD.[126] In Westchester County (White Plains, New York), a nonprofit corporation called Westchester Residential Opportunities has operated since 1969. The purpose of the organization is to assist black families to move into predominantly white Westchester. The corporation sells its own notes to raise money for second-mortgage loans, which are used when a family is financially able to meet regular mortgage payments but does

[121] *Ibid.*, pp. 132–133.
[122] Grier and Grier, *Equality and Beyond*, Quadrangle, 1966, pp. 71–72.
[123] William Robbins, "Investment Trust Widens Assault on the Color Line in Housing," *The New York Times*, Feb. 11, 1968.

[124] Grier and Grier, *Equality and Beyond*, Quadrangle, 1966, pp. 79–80.
[125] *Ibid.*, pp. 74–75.
[126] National Committee Against Discrimination in Housing, *Trends in Housing*, May, 1969, p. 3.

not have enough cash for a down payment. A three-year foundation grant covers operating expenses. Cooperation of brokers increased after the Westchester group brought about a dozen complaints before the New York State Committee on Human Rights.[127]

Finally, one approach of private citizens interested in attempting to reduce residential segregation consists of exerting political pressure in favor of antidiscrimination housing legislation and comparable governmental action. The National Committee Against Housing Discrimination is a federation of several dozen religious, civil rights, labor, and civic organizations concerned with the problems of race on a national level. Today the NCDH's programs "are designed not only to provide professional service to its affiliate agencies and to the more than 1,000 local voluntary citizen groups across the nation . . . but also to assist local, state, and federal government agencies and private entrepreneurs whose operations affect patterns of residence and the availability of housing to families of different races."[128]

The Real Estate Industry and Open Housing

According to one study of the real estate industry the National Association of Real Estate Boards' Code of Ethics grows out of the experiences of people in this field. The primary emphasis is said to be on "the property owner's satisfaction and the protection of his property and neighborhood . . . although the tenant's satisfaction is also included." Helper says that NAREB and the lending agencies hold that "as long as white people think and feel the way they do about Negroes, real estate men must respect their wishes and serve them loyally, protecting equity, property value, and neighborhood by not selling to Negroes in the white area or block."[129] Her own conclusion

is that it is not the broker but the property owner or tenant and his conception of Negroes that is the basic problem in housing discrimination. This conception is said to be the result of conditioning by parents and others and by constant observation of the way of life of the poor, culturally impoverished portion of the Negro population. She says that the data of her study show that real estate men exercise influence over property owners, but that neither "the Board nor the 'legitimate' real estate broker urges white people to move when Negroes enter their area." It is the panic peddlers and the blockbusters who frighten people into moving, whereas most of her respondents insist that, when asked, they advise their clients to stay.[130] Finally, in her somewhat contradictory conclusions, Helper says that "right now real estate men are convinced of white people's opposition to Negro neighbors and of the adverse effects on property conditions and values when Negroes enter, and they tend in their business relations to reinforce white people's prejudice against Negroes."[131] In reviewing this study, Johnson calls attention to the evidence of the socializing impact that The National Association of Real Estate Boards, the Chicago Real Estate Board, and the real estate agencies themselves have on the new broker. Johnson says that the exclusion shown in Helper's data is the result of the ideology

which gives supremacy to the attitudes and feelings of the property owner. Brokers have tended to believe that white property owners demanded the exclusion of blacks, and moving-out rates tend to support the brokers' conception. . . . Unfortunately, Helper does not check the validity of the belief . . . a sample of whites might have been interviewed to determine the extent to which they wanted blacks excluded and a sample of blacks interviewed to determine the extent to which they wished to reside in white neighborhoods.[132]

[127] Linda Greenhouse, "Suburban Housing for Blacks Eases," *The New York Times*, Jan. 24, 1971, p. 55.

[128] Grier and Grier, *Equality and Beyond*, Quadrangle, 1966, pp. 80–81.

[129] Rose Helper, *Racial Policies and Practices of Real Estate Brokers*, Univ. of Minn. Press, 1969, p. 294.

[130] *Ibid.*, p. 295.

[131] *Ibid.*, p. 296.

[132] Norman J. Johnson, "A review of 'Racial Politics and Practices of Real Estate Brokers' by Rose Helper," *ASR*, Feb., 1971, p. 142.

An example of opposition by a real estate organization to open occupancy appeared in California after the Rumford Act was passed in 1963. That Act forbade discrimination on the basis of race, color, religion, national origin, or ancestry in the sale or rental of 70 percent of California's housing, including 25 to 30 percent of the single-family residences. The California Real Estate Association campaigned to nullify the law, and was the main force in getting Proposition 14 on the ballot in November, 1964. By a 2 to 1 vote, Proposition 14 became an amendment to the state constitution, and gave a property owner "absolute discretion" in the sale and rental of his property. It negated the Rumford Act and other laws in the civil rights field and prevented such legislation from being passed in the future. In June, 1966, the Supreme Court of California held that article of the state constitution void, and in May, 1967 the U.S. Supreme Court affirmed the judgment of the California Supreme Court.[133]

The first survey of real estate practices in the Tri-State New York Metropolitan Region since the passage of the 1968 federal open-housing law concluded that the law, in conjunction with state and local open-housing laws, had brought about "a considerable though slow and often reluctant" change in racial policies, attitudes, and practices of real estate brokers. But the survey concluded also that discrimination is "growing more subtle." The dilemma facing brokers in the region is the threat of losing their license or of losing listings because of refusal to accept restricted offerings. "Few brokers expressed concern about adverse findings of human rights commissions or about fines or court orders." The survey found that the most prevalent discriminatory practice is showing blacks a more limited selection. Other practices include: providing false information—no houses meeting buyer's specifications; stating that a specific house has been sold, or that the owner is out, or that it cannot be shown; offering black buyers only houses in black, fringe, or changing neighborhoods; failing to notify a black customer when a house suiting his needs becomes available; advising black buyers to make unusually large down payments; failing to assist black buyers in obtaining financing.[134]

Saying that public attitudes toward racially mixed neighborhoods are mediated largely by the real estate industry, Taeuber calls for more research directed to an analysis of the housing market as a social institution. He rejects the assumption that the agent represents simply the wishes of his clients, but says that careful study is needed to determine the powers he uses to perpetuate the industry view and the powers he might use to change traditional practice.[135]

Statements submitted to the U.S. Commission on Civil Rights by mortgage bankers in the Washington, D.C. area reflect the attitudes of many institutions engaged in financing housing. A spokesman for the Mortgage Bankers Association of Metropolitan Washington wrote: "Applications from minority groups are not generally considered in areas that are not recognized as being racially mixed, on the premise that such an investment would not be attractive to institutional lenders." The vice-president of Riggs National Bank testified that his bank had "loans in fringe areas or all-white areas on the verge of conversion. Where our survey would reveal that the conversion is just a matter of time anyway, we would make the loan."[136] Lockard found that despite some improvements in lending practices during the early and middle 1960s, banks were still an obstacle to the Negro family trying to borrow for housing outside the ghetto.[137]

The 1968 federal Civil Rights Act prohibits banks, mortgage houses, savings and loan

[133] Helper, *op. cit.,* pp. 280–281.

[134] National Committee Against Discrimination in Housing, *Trends in Housing,* Vol. 14, No. 4, Special Report 1, 1970, pp. 5–6. Practices used by rental agents to discriminate against black applicants are listed on p. 6.

[135] Taeuber, in Katz and Gurin, *op. cit.,* p. 184.

[136] U.S. Commission on Civil Rights, *Civil Rights U.S.A.: Housing in Washington, D.C.,* 1962, pp. 13–14.

[137] Lockard, *op. cit.,* pp. 115–116.

institutions, and other businesses making commercial real estate loans from refusing loans, or from discriminating on terms, because of a loan applicant's race, color, religion, or national origin. The actual fact is, however, that it is extremely difficult to prove that the refusal of a loan has been due solely or mainly to race or nationality.

Open Housing: Central Cities Versus Suburbs
Very little publicly subsidized low-rent housing was produced from the end of World War II to 1960. During the 1950s, the increase amounted to only 300,000 dwelling units in a total increase of 12,000,-000 homes. Most of these units—2½ percent of the total—were built within the central cities. According to the Griers, by "a general if implicit consensus among members of the real estate and home-building industries, federal and local governments, and, in most cases, those people already in residence, low-income families, regardless of race or origin, were kept out of the new suburbs."[138] Most Negroes who had the resources to buy homes in the suburbs were also prevented from doing so by builders, financing firms, and the federal and local governments. Racial antipathy was not the only factor in the phenomenal growth of the suburbs between 1950 and 1970. Of equal importance was the better housing sought by an increasingly prosperous white population. The movement of Whites to the suburbs, and the consequent increased growth of segregated residential patterns, has attained a powerful momentum. Most of the young white families have moved outside the city limits. The central cities continue to be the place of residence of most Negroes, including the young people who provide the potential for future population growth. Unless these patterns change, the color division between cities and suburbs will become even sharper.

We refer earlier in this chapter to President Kennedy's executive order of 1962 outlawing discrimination in federally aided housing. A year and a half later it was estimated that between 12 and 20 percent of all new residential construction was covered by this directive. The segregation that had grown with the construction of previous years, however, remained, and more importantly, that executive order did little to break down discrimination in the suburbs, where there were either no antidiscrimination laws or no enforcement of the law.[139] Bias is practiced in many suburbs by devices that are legal on their face; in particular, rigid zoning laws and building codes are relaxed for white developments but adhered to strictly for others. In some instances, condemnation for a park, school, or street is voted for in an area into which Negroes have come, and some inspectors, school officials, or police are skilled in employing subtle harassments to make life unpleasant for unwanted families.[140]

Reports of the 1970 Census show that very little racial integration of American suburbs occurred in the 1960s. About 15 percent of the Negro population lives in metropolitan areas outside the central cities, compared with 40 percent of all Whites. Approximately 5 percent of the nation's suburban population is black, the same proportion as in 1960.[141]

It is significant that some plans for the future presented by regional planning agencies do not take into consideration the effects of race. In metropolitan Washington, D.C., for example, regional planners prepared a "Plan for the Year 2000," describing the principles necessary for meeting the needs of a population expected to be twice its present size. The plan proposed that future growth be channeled along six radial "corridors" extending outward from the central city. No special consideration was given to the question of race. Concerning this plan the Griers say:

If the movement of the city's population continues in its present direction, three corridors

[138] Grier and Grier, *Equality and Beyond*, Quadrangle, 1966, pp. 20–21.

[139] Abrams, *The City Is the Frontier*, p. 63; Grier and Grier, *ibid.*, p. 61.
[140] Abrams, *The City Is the Frontier*, p. 65.
[141] *The Plain Dealer*, Mar. 14, 1971, p. 11.

will be heavily Negro. They will have their central origins in neighborhoods which currently are Negro and which already are expanding outward in the directions proposed by the plan. The other three corridors will be primarily white, and in similar fashion will originate in the only white residential areas that remain within the city of Washington. Thus segregation will be extended for an indefinite period into the new suburbs, and in a way that almost certainly will help to perpetuate the current relative status of whites and Negroes.[142]

If restrictive real estate practices should cut off Negro population expansion along the three corridors that this expansion is most likely to take, Negroes would be forced back into the city and would soon overwhelm remaining white or interracial areas. In this event, the District's population would become virtually all Negro within a short time.

"The Comprehensive Plan of the City of Chicago" takes race into account inadequately. An analysis of the recommendations and policies in this plan that bear on race, shows that the implicit priorities are: (1) restricting further loss of white population and maintenance of Chicago's proportion of its younger middle class, (2) increased desegregation rate for Negro middle-class families, and (3) residential accommodation of the Negro lower-income population. This order of priorities for a city where the number of Negroes in poverty areas could reach 900,000 by 1980 is likely to be impossible of realization. A Chicago Urban League critique of the Comprehensive Plan calls the priorities order "self-defeating," saying that "the achievement of the number one racial priority of restricting future losses of the white population is, and will be, limited by the racial conflicts created as Negroes seek more and better housing."[143]

Unless current trends are countered, the concentration of the poor, Blacks, and Puerto Ricans in older cities may grow until the financial strain causes such cities

to become wards of the state, or angry residents of ghettos create disorders that seriously affect the cities' transportation and commerce. Few counterforces seem capable of offsetting present trends. Legislatures could vote to open suburban sites for low- and moderate-income families, and corporations could make fair housing a requirement for locating in a community, but such steps do not appear to be imminent. HUD could withhold funds for some projects until suburban communities created more opportunities for low-income housing (see reference earlier in this chapter to Blackjack, Missouri). Another possibility is that the course toward "two societies, one black, one white—separate and unequal" may be slowed down by a labor shortage in suburban areas. Nassau County, New York is a case in point. A recent study says:

Unless the Long Island Railroad cuts down travel time appreciably, it is unlikely that many Nassau commuters will move willingly to Suffolk County. Meanwhile, the need for manufacturing, retailing, service and government employees in Suffolk continues to increase. Not much housing will "filter-down" in that rapidly developing county. Negro and Puerto Rican immigrants would require an available supply of new housing if they are to locate near new jobs.[144]

Because population growth occurs in the suburbs, these are the places where employment opportunities exist and will increase. If minority persons are not able to live in the suburbs, their representation in population-based employment will be minimal. The NCDH report points out that Westchester is so solidly upper-middle class and upper class that the shortage of help for the trade of the local population has become serious.[145]

Further evidence is given in the NCDH report concerning the relationship between lack of access to housing in the suburbs and the cutting off of employment opportunities

[142] Grier and Grier, footnote 138, p. 13.
[143] Edwin C. Berry and Walter W. Stafford, *The Racial Aspect of Urban Planning*, in Harold Baron (ed.), Chicago Urban League Research Report, 1968, pp. 17–21.

[144] Ernest Erber, *Jobs and Housing: A Study of Employment and Housing Opportunities in Suburban Areas of the New York Metropolitan Region*, National Committee Against Discrimination in Housing, 1970, p. 167.
[145] *Ibid.*, p. 170.

for Blacks and Puerto Ricans in a major and rapidly expanding segment of the New York metropolitan region's job market—the wholesale and retail industries. Nearly one-fifth of the jobs in the region are in these industries, and jobs in the retail and wholesale fields are increasing much more rapidly than are jobs in manufacturing. The projection for 1985 is that jobs in wholesale/retail will almost equal manufacturing jobs. Growth in the retail and wholesale industries occur overwhelmingly in suburban areas. Both industries have characteristics that are particularly suited to the needs of the minority work force: they include a wide range of skills and have openings for workers with minimal experience or job preparation. Since retailing is heavily dependent upon a part-time and seasonal work force, it is particularly appropriate for second wage earners (women who must work to supplement lower earnings by heads of households). Although every suburban shopping center visited showed evidence of a labor shortage, black and Puerto Rican representation in the work force was minimal, and the situation in wholesaling was similar. The study concludes: "Suburban governments and their taxpayers must realize that the limitations on access to local housing for low-income families also limits local chances to attract commercial and industrial ratables. Unless housing is available locally for lower-paid help and more efficient forms of public transit are devised, middle- and upper-income suburban residents will experience a deterioration in the quality and quantity of essential services."[146]

What Is Necessary to Increase Open Housing?
One group of policies intended to influence the supply of housing, and to contribute to an increase in open housing is in the field of financing. One approach is to offer long-term loans at below market interest rates. Interest rates are important, but for many low-income people, and especially Negroes, the major obstacle to becoming home owners is the down payment. Another group of financial policies is intended to influence demand. Two methods are suggested: programs to provide money that is to be used for housing, including rental allowances, or the negative income tax and family income supplements. A University of Michigan research study shows that for Negroes these policies in themselves will not be adequate.[147] Taeuber's analysis of trend data also demonstrates that no feasible indirect attack on residential segregation, including maintenance of a high aggregate rate of housing supply, is likely to have a marked effect on the degree of segregation.[148] Blacks have substantial disadvantages in the housing market in addition to that which results from low income.

Charles Abrams, a leading authority in the field of housing, concluded that neither antidiscrimination laws nor Supreme Court decisions would be sufficient to relieve the plight of the central city or give its black population better housing and a better environment. Opening the suburbs to Negroes would mean little because most black people could not afford housing there. In his view, a realistic program would involve federally subsidized housing in suburbs as well as in central cities. Abrams said: "Such a program must include access to ownership as well as rental. If private builders or the state and local governments refuse to build the housing, then the federal government must do so."[149]

The NCDH's study of housing and employment in the New York metropolitan region concluded that the movement of minority families to nonghetto areas in sufficient number to stop the expansion of the ghetto and provide free choice of residence to all minority families would require massive efforts involving government at all levels and private industry. NCDH estimates that providing nonghetto housing for a sufficient number of minority families to

[146] National Committee Against Discrimination in Housing, *Trends in Housing*, Special Report 1, 1970, pp. 5–6.

[147] Lansing, Wade and Morgan, *op. cit.*, p. 69.
[148] Taeuber, *op. cit.*, p. 183.
[149] Abrams, *The City Is the Frontier*, p. 67.

offset expansion of the urban ghetto's population would require housing in nonghetto areas for some 700,000 Nonwhites (about 200,000 households) annually on a national level. NCDH assumes that "there would be a large-scale response to new employment and housing opportunities in nonghetto areas, especially if the massive effort to provide these opportunities included affirmative action to bring them to the attention of minorities and to facilitate their relocation."[150]

The NCDH argues that it is not beyond the resources of the United States to make such a massive effort. Such effort would require stronger open housing laws, more efficient enforcement of such laws, a supply of housing at costs geared to the earnings of minority workers in nearby industries throughout an area such as the New York Metropolitan Region, fair employment practices and training programs designed to tap the full potential of the minority labor force, and a national commitment to an effort comparable to the commitment to production for military purposes in World War II.[151]

THE EFFECTIVENESS OF LEGISLATION, ADMINISTRATIVE ACTION, AND JUDICIAL DECISION IN THE FIELD OF CIVIL AND HUMAN RIGHTS

At the federal level, we believe that the laws pertaining to employment, housing, voting, and public accommodations through the 1964 Civil Rights Act, the 1965 Voting Rights Act, and the 1968 Civil Rights Act (with their amendments) are reasonably adequate instruments for the ends they are intended to attain. Further legislation is especially needed in such important areas as income supplements, education, welfare, and the composition of juries. In the categories mentioned first, the main legislative problem is the appropriation by Congress of

sufficient funds to implement the existing laws in more than a token way.

At the state level, the trend has been toward strengthening the earlier laws, as well as the enactment of antidiscrimination laws by additional states (in 1970, 37 states had laws against discrimination in public accommodations, 36 against discrimination in employment, 26 against discrimination in housing). Some of these laws are now quite strong, but the great lacks at the state level are overcautiousness on the part of state commissioners, insufficient funds and staff, lack of support from some state administrations, and the absence of such legislation in the southern states. Lockard concludes that public accommodations laws have been more successful than those on employment and housing. This judgment is based in part on his finding that only a third of the public accommodation cases in states for which detailed information is available resulted in dismissals, compared with two-thirds of the employment cases and half of the housing cases.[152]

Mayhew found that the enforcement activities of the Massachusetts Committee Against Discrimination were more vigorous and successful in housing than in employment.[153]

Some appraisers are relatively pessimistic about the contributions that state antidiscrimination laws can make to equalizing life conditions between the races. For example, Lockard says: ". . . my pessimism does not lead me to the conclusion that the marginal assistance that antidiscrimination laws can offer should be rejected as unimportant or perhaps productive of false expectations that will heighten the frustration. They are contributors to diminishing discrimination now, and their potential is higher than their achievements thus far."[154] Mayhew asks if the Massachusetts law is obsolete and replies that "even if the recognition of de facto problems of segregation

---

[150] Erber, *op. cit.*, pp. 174–175.

[151] *Ibid.*, p. 175. See also Eunice and George Grier, "Equality and Beyond: Housing Segregation in the Great Society," *Daedalus*, Winter, 1966, pp. 98–102.

[152] Lockard, *op. cit.*, pp. 137–138.

[153] Leon H. Mayhew, *Law and Equal Opportunity: A Study of the Massachusetts Commission Against Discrimination*, Harvard, 1968, p. 278.

[154] Lockard, *op. cit.*, p. 143.

and discrimination grows, the older civil rights agencies may continue to operate primarily at the level of intentional discrimination. New agencies and new institutions may come to embody and implement the new interpretations and compromises that will mediate race relations in the future."[155]

In the civil rights cases that were brought to the Supreme Court in the latter part of the nineteenth century, the first Justice Harlan pointed out that the purpose of the Civil War Amendments was to prevent racial discrimination. In the Plessy v. Ferguson case in 1896 involving racial segregation on common carriers, the Supreme Court said: "Legislation is powerless to eradicate racial instincts or to abolish distinctions based upon physical differences, and the attempt to do so can only result in accentuating the difficulties of the present situation. . . . If one race is inferior to the other socially, the Constitution of the United States cannot put them upon the same plane." In his dissent, Justice Harlan maintained that the Court had erred in basing the case on the issue that law cannot control social prejudice and then treating racial segregative attitudes as unchanging racial "instincts" that are beyond the power of law.

Earlier American sociologists tended to minimize the influence of the legal pattern and to emphasize the importance of the mores in race relations.[156] Increasingly, sociologists and legal scholars have concluded that legislation can be effective in reducing discrimination. This view does not hold that law, particularly in a nonauthoritarian society, is all-powerful. Concerning law and race relations, Greenberg writes: "But law alone, like other social forces, and like laws affecting other institutions, may not be able to alter these relations beyond a certain point, and in some situations it cannot make

much difference."[157] Burma makes the point that laws, of themselves, do not automatically eliminate the abuses they are intended to correct, but laws do establish criteria for judging actions. "Passage of civil rights legislation does establish the fact that certain behavior has been judged to be inimical to the public welfare and contrary to public policy, and such legislation does establish a frame of reference within which other necessary processes can be systematized and accelerated."[158] Roscoe Pound went further saying that laws may not only set standards but may also help to create habits of conformity to them.[159]

Court decisions reflect the climate of opinion, and from 1868 until 1936 the rulings of the Supreme Court functioned to support the prevailing racial system. The narrow and legalistic interpretations of the Court during these years had the effect of reducing to a minimum some of the liberties guaranteed by the Constitution. During this period the Court played an important part in "keeping the Negro in his place." Supreme Court decisions, however, modify as well as reflect opinion, and the decisions from 1937 to 1970 greatly influenced public opinion and prepared the way for legislative and executive action.

Important decisions have been handed down in the fields of education, housing, voting, and public accommodations by the U.S. Supreme Court, the lower federal courts, and many of the state courts. Berger emphasizes the point that the Supreme Court has had to assume the task of revealing the unfairness of some American institutions because other branches and levels of government "either would or could not speak with authority and justice on these issues."[160] The "Warren Court" of the 1960s is often called an "activist" court because of its in-

---

[155] Mayhew, *op. cit.*, pp. 287, 293–294.

[156] For a reconsideration of William Graham Sumner's views on law and social change, see Harry V. Ball, George E. Simpson, and Kiyoshi Ikeda, "Law and Social Change: Sumner Reconsidered," *AJS*, Mar., 1962, pp. 532–540.

[157] Jack Greenberg, *Race Relations and American Law*, Columbia, 1959, pp. 2–3. See all of chap. 1 of this work, "The Capacity of Law to Affect Race Relations." See also Konvitz and Leskes, *op. cit.*, chap. 10.

[158] John H. Burma, "Race Relations and Antidiscriminatory Legislation," *AJS*, Mar., 1951, p. 423.

[159] Greenberg, *op. cit.*, p. 2.

[160] Berger, *op. cit.*, p. 157.

clination toward social change. The "Burger Court" of the 1970s may come to be known as a "strict constructionist" court. (In July, 1971, Chief Justice Burger said that the courts should not be regarded as instruments for bringing about social change.) Despite legal ideologies and trends, it is clear that the Supreme Court's decisions may have considerable impact on national life, for example, the effects of the 1954 school cases in the rearrangement of many American cities.

Beginning with President Roosevelt's Executive Order 8802 in 1941 dealing with the employment of workers in defense industries, significant presidential orders have been issued concerning a number of civil rights, particularly employment and housing. The enforcement efforts of federal administrative agencies have not, on the whole, been impressive. A 1970 report of the U.S. Commission on Civil Rights found that "a few departments and agencies were doing a modest job in the area of protecting equal rights, but most were doing nothing. Advances have been made to some degree, in education, public accommodations, voting, and hospital services, but pervasive discrimination persists in housing, employment and other fields where the federal government has the power, but apparently not the will, to enforce the law."[161] Some members of the Commission see the solution as going beyond a revision of civil rights machinery and the replacement of "diffident bureaucrats who have been impelled to define narrowly their role and reduce the power of the federal government in some areas to a center for processing individual complaints." They call for "courageous moral leadership" by the President to inspire the American people to remove all the barriers to true equality.[162]

In Chapter 11 we showed that for many black people the emphasis has shifted from equality of opportunity to equality of results. An important question is whether the mood of most white Americans matches the change of concern on the part of Blacks.

CRIMINAL JUSTICE AND MINORITIES

Crime Rates. The Uniform Crime Reports show that generally and proportionately black Americans are arrested between three and four times more frequently than whites. In 1967, Blacks constituted 11 percent of the population, but they comprised almost one-third of persons arrested for all offenses. The following table indicates the arrest rates of Blacks and Whites for a variety of offenses in 1967. Wolfgang and Cohen point out that the rates for Blacks are consistently higher than those for Whites, ranging from twice as high, in the case of embezzlement, to 24 times as high, in the case of gambling.

In addition to being arrested proportionately more often than Whites, Negroes have much higher rates of conviction and imprisonment. Satisfactory national judicial statistics are lacking, but individual studies show that the Negro conviction rate is three to four times higher than their proportion in the population. Although Blacks constitute approximately 10 percent of the total population, they comprise about one-third of all prisoners.[163] Statistics on conviction and imprisonment, as well as the administration of justice itself, are affected by the operation of the bail system. The jailed defendant has much less chance of being acquitted than the defendant on bail. City jails are overcrowded with the poor and Nonwhites, often because these persons are unable to provide the amount of bail—in some cases as little as $25.[164] A related factor that affects minority crime is the greater difficulty, for financial reasons, of obtaining efficient legal counsel. Another influencing factor is the longer average prison sentence that Blacks, compared with Whites, receive for most criminal offenses. For ex-

[161] Jon Nordheimer, "A Highly Critical View of Progress on Rights," *The New York Times*, Oct. 18, 1970, p. E3.
[162] *Ibid.*, p. E3.

[163] Marvin E. Wolfgang and Bernard Cohen, *Crime and Race*, Inst. of Human Relations Press, 1970, p. 34.
[164] Haywood Burns, "Can a Black Man Get a Fair Trial in This Country?" *The New York Times Magazine*, July 12, 1970, p. 46.

Arrest Rates of Whites and Negroes (U.S., 1967)

Type of offense	Arrest rate (per 100,000 total population)		Ratio of Negroes' arrest rates to Whites'
	Whites	Negroes	
Gambling	20.84	507.26	24.34
Prostitution, commercialized vice	14.19	214.32	15.10
Robbery	22.42	325.00	14.50
Murder, non-negligent manslaughter	3.69	50.43	13.67
Weapons—carrying, possessing, etc.	36.83	359.31	9.76
Aggravated assault	49.05	438.53	8.94
Forcible rape	6.61	55.70	8.43
Other assaults	157.41	861.21	5.47
Disorderly conduct	383.67	1,860.82	4.85
Burglary—breaking or entering	169.90	755.62	4.45
Auto theft	84.55	351.91	4.16
Larceny—theft	332.25	1,345.69	4.05
Narcotics violations (except traffic)	65.83	236.50	3.59
Arson	6.27	19.14	3.05
Sex offenses (except forcible rape and prostitution)	42.18	126.50	3.00
Vagrancy	84.86	252.90	2.98
Drunkenness	1,234.11	3,375.94	2.74
Forgery and counterfeiting	26.50	70.33	2.65
Manslaughter by negligence	2.54	6.51	2.56
Vandalism	94.23	201.70	2.14
Fraud	52.02	109.35	2.10
Driving under influence of alcohol	252.40	499.52	1.98
Embezzlement	4.96	9.79	1.97

Sources: Arrest data from *Uniform Crime Reports*, 1967, Table *31*, p. 126 (4,508 agencies; 1967 estimated population 135,203,000). Arrest rates are based on 100,000 adult population. Populations 14 years of age or older were obtained for Negroes and Whites from *Current Population Reports, Population Characteristics, Negro Population, Mar. 1967*, Series P-20, No. 175, Oct. 23, 1968. Then the proportion of Negroes and Whites among reported population (135,203,000) was obtained. Next the number of Blacks 14 years and over (N=9,611,066) and Whites 14 years and over (N=86,803,571) was obtained by estimating proportion of Whites and Blacks 14 years and older among the reported population. Marvin E. Wolfgang and Bernard Cohen, *Crime and Race*, Institute of Human Relations Press, 1970, p. 32.

ample, a study of persons convicted of burglary and auto theft in Los Angeles County, most of them first offenders and unskilled laborers, showed that 45 percent of the Whites and 27 percent of the Blacks were given sentences for these crimes of four months' imprisonment or less, or probation; 42 percent of the Whites and 47 percent of the Blacks received four to nine months; and 13 percent of the Whites and

27 percent of the Blacks got 10 to 20 months.[165]

Wolfgang and Cohen point out that little research has been done on Mexican-American crime in Los Angeles or Puerto Rican crime in New York City. A study by Lemert and Rosberg showed that, for convictions, the felony rates per 100,000

[165] *Ibid.*, p. 38.

Mexican-Americans (356) in Los Angeles were somewhat higher than they were for the white rate (248), but lower than the Negro rate (835). When corrections were made for age and sex, the Mexican-American rate was lowered so that it approximated the white rate. Indians (2540) had a rate three times that of Negroes when computed per 100,000 male population; Japanese-Americans had the lowest rate of all ethnic groups included in this study.[166] Clarence O. Senior reports that 8 percent of the population in New York City is Puerto Rican, and that their share of the crime rate is only slightly more than 8 percent.[167] Puerto Rican juveniles constitute 25 percent of the New York City juvenile population, and comprise 27 percent of juvenile crime. Moreover, Puerto Rican delinquency was described as "of a milder type," such as ungovernability or truancy, while burglary and gang activities involving felonious assault and homicide were much less frequent than among non-Puerto Ricans.[168]

In a study of 300 institutionalized delinquents—179 Negro, 121 white—Axelrad found that the courts commit on a differential basis. The Negro children had been committed younger, for less serious offenses, with fewer previous court appearances, and with less prior institutionalization. Also, there were differences in family patterns. The white delinquents tended to have lived longer with their biological parents, the Negro delinquents with mother and stepfather, with mother only, with other relatives, or in unrelated families. The mother was the only person employed in 5 percent of the white families, as compared with 26 percent of the Negro families.[169]

A Buffalo, New York study showed that Negroes comprised 11 percent of the population between 7 and 20, but that they constituted 28 percent of the delinquents in this age group. Of those in this age category brought before the courts, the Negro rate was 42 per 1000 as compared with a white rate of 13 per 1000. In a larger northern urban area, 23 percent of the population from 7 to 17 were Negroes, but 59 percent of the delinquent children were Negro.[170]

In any discussion of criminal statistics, it is necessary to recognize their limitations and deficiencies. As Wolfgang and Cohen say:

We do not know with certainty the actual amount of crime among whites, Negroes, Puerto Ricans, or any other group. We do know that persons of all groups commit many offenses that are unrecorded. We cannot be sure of the degrees of seriousness of even the recorded crime without further study. . . . Among offenses for which non-whites as well as whites are arrested, crimes of homicide, rape, and other assaultive acts represent a small proportion compared to drunkenness, gambling, disorderly conduct and other relatively minor offenses against the public order. Interracial assaults are rare and no more threatening to whites than to non-whites.[171]

Such differences as are shown in the crime rates of ethnic groups cannot be attributed to innate racial characteristics. The figures demonstrate only that the average black citizen is more likely than the average white citizen to be exposed to a set of conditions that lead to arrest, conviction, and imprisonment. Nine-tenths of the Negro population in the North and West live in cities, and nine-tenths of these live in, or adjacent to, disorganized slum areas. Poverty, overcrowding, vice, crime, and social disorder characterize these areas. In addition to the socioeconomic factors that produce criminal patterns among Negroes, another set of factors involves the type of discrimination inflicted upon Negroes. Discriminatory barriers may encourage illegal behavior. Thus, crime may be utilized "as a means of escape, ego-enhancement, expression of ag-

---

[166] Wolfgang and Cohen, *op. cit.*, pp. 34–35.
[167] *Ibid.*, p. 35.
[168] *Ibid.*, p. 35.
[169] Sidney Axelrad, "Negro and White Male Institutionalized Delinquents," *AJS*, May, 1952, pp. 573–574.

[170] Orville R. Gursslin, *Delinquency and Youth Crime*, Buffalo Youth Board, 1958. Cited in Kenneth B. Clark, "Color, Class, Personality and Juvenile Delinquency," *JNE*, Summer, 1959, p. 241.
[171] Wolfgang and Cohen, *op. cit.*, p. 100.

gression, or upward mobility."[172] Finally, the higher rate of involvement with law enforcement "must be attributed to distortions introduced into the statistics by differential legal and penal treatment of whites and Negroes."[173]

Class position within the Negro group, as within the white population, affects the treatment of offenders by the police and by the courts. Lower-class Negroes in the Deep South are arrested more frequently for lower-court offenses than are upper-class Negroes; the latter, however, are not immune to the same extent that upper-class Whites are. The proceedings of the lower courts, especially the justice-of-the-peace courts, are similar in rural and urban areas. However, differences between Negro-white relations in the two types of areas influence the cases that come to court. In some of the Deep South rural areas the planter still exercises the kinds of controls over his Negro tenants that the police and courts exercise in urban communities.

Negro offenses against Negroes are treated, generally, in the South with undue leniency. A high percentage of Negro crime occurs within the Negro community, and most of it is found among lower-class Negroes, who bear the brunt of the racial stigma. Their personalities and motives are related to their subordinate roles in the community. Frustration leads to displaced aggression against other Negroes. The white viewpoint on Negro immorality and lack of restraint combines with the low social value placed upon Negro life to reduce the punishment of Negroes as long as they control their relations with Whites.

The Police

Recruitment. In the past, Negroes were not encouraged to apply for positions on the police force. To a considerable extent, these jobs were reserved for first and second generation immigrants who were on their way up socioeconomically. According to Alex, the opening up of a new set of jobs on a universalistic basis was due to (1) a shortage of white recruits, (2) the increase in Negroes' sense of social identity, and (3) the sharp increase in the proportion of Negroes living in the central city.[174]

The National Advisory Commission on Civil Disorders found that Blacks were underrepresented in every police department for which statistics were available. Of 80,621 personnel in 28 major cities, only 7046 were Nonwhite. The table on page 455 shows racial population ratios and the proportions of higher police officers to police officers according to race.

Since the publication of this report in 1968, the proportion of black policemen has increased significantly in several cities: in Washington, from 21 percent to 30 percent; in Detroit, from 5 percent to 9 percent; and in St. Louis, from 10 to 15 percent. Black policemen comprised 5 percent of the police force in New York City for many years, but recently the proportion has risen to 7.[175]

Increasing the number of Negroes on the police force accomplished at least two desirable objectives for white political leaders. Some relatively high-paying jobs were provided in the Negro community where unemployment rates were higher. Also, it was thought that Negro policemen might be more effective in dealing with ghetto populations.[176]

Most of the policemen interviewed in Alex's study had joined the department because civil service jobs provided them the best opportunities for upward economic mobility and relative security. Some explained their choice of job, in part at least, by saying that they can help Negroes, especially Negro youth, more than a white policeman can.[177] Recently, many of the

[172] Thomas F. Pettigrew, *A Profile of the Negro American*, Van Nostrand, 1964, p. 194.

[173] Richard R. Korn and Lloyd W. McCorkle, *Criminology and Penology*, Holt, Rinehart & Winston, 1959, p. 243. Quoted in Wolfgang and Cohen, *op. cit.*, p. 100.

[174] Nicholas Alex, *Black in Blue: A Study of the Negro Policeman*, Meredith, 1969, p. 200.

[175] John Darnton, "Color Line a Key Police Problem," *The New York Times*, Sept. 28, 1969, pp. 1, 69.

[176] Alex, *op. cit.*, pp. 200–201.

[177] *Ibid.*, pp. 201–202.

Racial Composition of 80,621 Sworn Personnel in Police Departments of 28 Major Cities, 1968

Name of Dept.	% Non-White pop.	% Non-White Police Officers	Ratio: Serg. to Officers N.W.	W.	Ratio: Lieut. to Officers N.W.	W.	Ratio: Capt. to Officers N.W.	W.	Ratio: Above Capt. to Officers N.W.	W.
Atlanta, Ga.	38*	10	1:49	1:73	1:33	1:16	0:98	1:58	0:98	1:145
Baltimore, Md.	41*	7	1:30	1:7	1:69	1:27	1:208	1:167	1:208	1:135
Boston, Mass.	11*	2	1:49	1:11	0:49	1:31	0:49	1:123	0:49	1:205
Buffalo, N.Y.	18*	3	1:37	1:22	1:37	1:14	0:37	1:56	0:37	1:42
Chicago, Ill.	27*	17	1:21	1:9	1:921	1:35	1:1842	1:127	1:307	1:140
Cincinnati, Ohio	28*	6	1:27	1:12	1:27	1:25	0:54	1:64	0:54	1:120
Cleveland, Ohio	34*	7	1:28	1:13	1:165	1:26	0:165	1:79	0:165	1:121
Dayton, Ohio	26*	4	1:16	1:7	1:16	1:30	0:16	1:67	0:16	1:100
Detroit, Mich.	39*	5	1:25	1:12	1:114	1:26	No such rank		1:227	1:66
Hartford, Conn.	20**	11	0:38	1:10	1:38	1:20	0:38	1:34	0:38	1:152
Kansas City, Mo.	20*	6	1:7	1:6	0:51	1:24	0:51	1:80	1:51	1:63
Louisville, Ky.	21*	6	1:35	1:13	1:35	1:18	0:35	1:53	1:35	1:75
Memphis, Tenn.	38*	5	No such rank		1:12	1:4	0:46	1:18	0:46	1:19
Mich. St. Pol.	9***	a[1]	0:1	1:11	0:1	1:63	0:1	1:79	0:1	1:500
New Haven, Conn.	19**	7	0:31	1:21	0:31	1:26	0:31	1:35	0:31	1:69
New Orleans, La.	41*	4	1:8	1:12	1:54	1:25	0:54	1:46	0:54	1:125
New York, N.Y.	16*	5	1:23	1:15	1:74	1:28	1:743	1:96	1:495	1:166
New Jersey St. Pol.	9***	a[1]	0:5	1:7	0:5	1:28	0:5	1:72	0:5	1:305
Newark, N.J.	40*	10	1:37	1:17	1:61	1:18	1:184	1:77	None listed	
Oakland, Calif.	31*	4	1:27	1:7	0:27	1:25	1:27	1:63	0:27	1:210
Oklahoma City, Okla.	15*	4	0:16	1:13	1:16	1:22	0:16	1:38	0:16	1:70
Philadelphia, Pa.	29*	20	1:53	1:18	1:172	1:40	1:459	1:120	0:1377	1:240
Phoenix, Ariz.	8*	1	0:7	1:8	1:7	1:32	0:7	1:70	0:7	1:175
Pittsburgh, Pa.	19*	7	1:36	1:11	1:36	1:31	0:109	1:362	1:109	1:242
St. Louis, Mo.	37*	11	1:11	1:9	1:75	1:40	1:56	1:107	0:224	1:165
San Francisco, Calif.	14*	6	0:102	1:8	0:102	1:25	0:102	1:110	0:102	1:165
Tampa, Fla.	17*	3	0:17	1:10	1:17	1:41	0:17	1:38	0:17	1:62
Washington, D.C.	63*	21	1:29	1:10	1:186	1:20	1:186	1:58	0:559	1:70

Notes:
a[1] Less than ½ of 1%.
* % Negro population figures, 1965 estimates by the Center for Research in Marketing, Cong. Quarterly, Weekly Report, No. 36, Sept. 8, 1967.
** % Negro population figures, 1966 estimates, Office of Economic Opportunity.
*** % Negro population figures for states of Michigan and New Jersey, 1960 Census Figures.

Source: Report of the National Advisory Commission on Civil Disorders, Bantam Books, 1968, p. 322.

new black recruits have been veterans who have come in through two Defense Department programs that permit servicemen to be released from duty in the United States three months earlier for police training. One of these recruits said, "Where else can a young black without a college education find a job that pays $11,000 a year?"[178]

Problems of the Negro Policeman. Along with the advantages, Negro policemen find that there are some drawbacks to being a member of the force. In the black community, they are regarded by some as agents of an outside, repressive, discriminatory, or even an anti-Negro, white society. Often, the black policeman finds himself in a position where he must make arrests for acts that are not regarded as particularly criminal by the community from which he has come, that is, the lower-class segments of Negro society. In this situation, he may become a legalist who makes arrests compulsively, or he may try to avoid situations, including policy operations, street gambling, and drunkenness, where he would be compelled to arrest for actions considered noncriminal by many in the Negro community. In civil rights demonstrations, his choice is very difficult. If he makes arrests, he may be condemned by the community; if he does not make arrests according to police standards, he is aware of rejecting part of his professional role. Because of the belief of department administrators that black policemen can be useful in ghetto areas, their assignments are likely to be primarily with a Negro clientele. For some black policemen, such placements result in greater or lesser isolation from friends and neighbors and to a desire on the part of the policeman to isolate himself.[179]

When a Negro policeman is assigned to a white neighborhood, he faces other problems. White citizens may prefer to deal with his white partners. They may abuse him, and he may be subject to unusual provocations if they are offenders. If he

overreacts, he may be subject to complaints and charges. In addition, he may have personal doubts about the way in which he is responding to the situation. If he advances to the position of plainclothesman, white civilians are likely to treat him as an intruder rather than as an officer. If he is unable to identify himself immediately, he may be subject to arrest and harsh treatment by white policemen coming from precincts other than his own. If the black plainclothesman needs to make an arrest, or even conduct an investigation in a white neighborhood, he may need to have a white policeman with him to confirm his official status.[180]

On the job, policy often requires that Negro and white policemen be paired. In some cases, this policy is not one of integration or equality. Often the Negro policeman is there, as Alex says, "to protect his white colleague and the department from charges of real or imagined brutality."[181]

To a degree, the personal tensions felt by black policemen are mitigated by the racial etiquette that tends to characterize the relationships between black and white policemen. Occupational ideology contributes to recognition of each other as professionals. Occupational solidarity is furthered by the campaign against their common enemy, the criminal, and by their separation from "the public." Also, the advantages that come to white policemen and to the department from having black officers help to reduce some racial tensions. At present, even in the best situations, the social equality of police personnel is limited to the work environment and official occasions; it does not include social life elsewhere.[182]

In summarizing the black policeman's lot, Alex says that he "is placed in a special category by the department, his white colleagues, white civilians, and the lower-class Negro community. He has received some of the rewards of his mobility but he has

[178] Darnton, *op. cit.*, p. 69.
[179] Alex, *op. cit.*, pp. 202–204.

[180] *Ibid.*, p. 207.
[181] *Ibid.*, p. 206.
[182] *Ibid.*, pp. 205–206.

paid for them with this double marginality."[183]

Police-Community Relations. According to the President's Crime Commission, the two basic reasons for minority-group resentment of the police are permissive law enforcement and police brutality. In the Bedford-Stuyvesant community of New York City, the Commission found eight factors mentioned in the antagonism between local residents and the police: the abrasive relationship between the police and black juveniles, police toleration of narcotics traffic in the ghetto, the small number of black patrolmen stationed in the black neighborhoods, inefficient handling of emergencies by local precincts, lack of respect toward black citizens, low police morale, not enough foot patrolmen, and inadequate patrol of black neighborhoods. Recent studies show greater dissatisfaction on the part of Blacks than Whites with the effectiveness of police law enforcement.[184]

A Crime Commission Survey found that the majority of white officers hold anti-Negro attitudes. One-tenth of the Negro officers in predominantly Negro districts also held extremely anti-Negro attitudes. While many policemen are anti-Negro in attitude, it does not necessarily follow that they behave in a discriminatory manner in contacts with Negroes. Studies by the Crime Commission indicate that "in the vast majority of encounters officers handle themselves with courage and restraint."[185] This finding does not mean that police brutality does not exist. The studies conducted by the Crime Commission reveal such behavior in northern as well as southern cities. Accompanying police on field patrol, Commission observers witnessed 20 instances of excessive force in 5399 police-citizen encounters during 850 eight-hour patrols.[186] In a study of four police departments in small and medium-sized cities in the Midwest during 1969, Walsh found that highly professional police officers (those who "view themselves as professionals, highly trained to provide service in meeting and solving problems the community itself cannot handle") appeared much more empathetic toward minority groups.[187]

In many cities the gulf between black police officers and white policemen and the white community has been widened as Blacks have withdrawn from established police organizations to form their own. The Society of Afro-American Policemen, founded in 1965, has chapters in Newark, Philadelphia, Chicago, Detroit, and New York. One member of this association said: "We don't meet as policemen. We meet as members of the black community." Darnton reports: "Unlike previous ethnic organizations in police departments, the blacks are bound by strong complaints, which they tend to take outside regular channels in an attempt to gain support and establish rapport with the black community." For example, in 1969 the Afro-American Patrolmen's League in Chicago announced that its members would not be used as "strikebreakers" against black pickets at construction sites. The following week, the Coalition for United Community Action reciprocated by holding a rally in support of the league, which had said that it was "under harassment" from the department. In San Francisco, the pledge of the Officers for Justice says: "We will no longer permit ourselves to be relegated to the role of brutal pawns in a chess game affecting the communities in which we serve. We are husbands, fathers, brothers, neighbors and members of the black community. Donning the blue uniform has not changed this."[188]

The Courts. In discussing crime rates, we pointed out that Blacks usually receive longer prison sentences than Whites for most

[183] *Ibid.*, p. 210.

[184] The President's Commission on Law Enforcement and Administration of Justice, *Field Surveys V, A National Survey of Police and Community Relations*, Government Printing Office, Jan., 1967, p. 14. Quoted in Wolfgang and Cohen, *op. cit.*, p. 67.

[185] Wolfgang and Cohen, *op. cit.*, p. 69.

[186] *Ibid.*, p. 70.

[187] James L. Walsh, "Professionalism and the Police," *American Behavioral Scientist*, Apr.–Aug., 1970, pp. 706, 708, 713.

[188] Darnton, *op. cit.*, p. 69.

criminal offenses. Another type of differential treatment on the basis of race is seen in jury service. The systematic exclusion of Blacks from grand and petit juries has been unconstitutional since 1880. Jury selection procedures, however, are such that it is difficult for Blacks to obtain juries on which black persons are fairly represented. For example, Finkelstein's analysis of venire records of persons selected for grand juries in Manhattan, the Bronx, and Westchester showed that Harlem districts contributed less than 1 percent of the Manhattan veniremen, although they comprised 11 percent of the voting population. Also, prosecutors are not required to give reasons when using their peremptory strikes from the jury panel. In cases involving black defendants, prosecutors frequently use their peremptory strikes to insure, if possible, the formation of a white jury.[189]

In the giving of testimony, it is generally the case in all parts of the country that judges and juries do not accord the same weight to Blacks as to Whites. Burns says: "When the issue is one of credibility, one white witness on one side of a lawsuit cancels out several nonwhite witnesses on the other."[190]

In concluding his examination of whether a black man can get a fair trial in the United States, Burns says: "The likelihood of the legal process being entirely uncontaminated by bias in any given case is small. Individual blacks can and do win civil suits and individual blacks can [be] and are acquitted of criminal charges, but in an institutional sense in almost all instances the law functions in a discriminatory and unfair manner when blacks (and poor people) are involved."[191]

Other minorities also experience discrimination from the police and the courts. For example, the U.S. Commission on Civil Rights has concluded that, in many localities, especially those near large reservations,

both reservation and nonreservation Indians are treated unfairly by the police and the courts. In some cases, Indian neighborhoods are not given adequate police protection by local authorities.[192]

Prisons. Earlier in this section we referred to the fact that Blacks comprise one-ninth of the population of the United States, but that they constitute one-third of the prison population. To an appreciable extent, jails and prisons are breeding places for crime. This is especially true in the South, where segregation invites discrimination in treatment. In many places there is a lack of special institutions for women and for juvenile offenders. Negroes are assigned the least desirable work, and "accidents" happen almost exclusively to Negro prisoners. Negro prisoners come out, in a relatively high proportion of cases, brutalized and embittered. Relatively more Negroes than Whites get the treatment of the jail, chain gang, and prison because of their greater inability to pay fines.

Approximately 10 to 14 percent more Whites than Blacks are annually granted some form of parole.[193] Data on executions show that, regardless of the offense, Blacks are executed more often than Whites. In the period 1930–1966, 3857 persons were executed in the United States—of these 53.5 percent were black, 45.4 percent were white, and 1.1 percent were members of other minority groups.[194]

Recommendations for Changes in the Administration of Criminal Justice

An Indigenous Police Force. Despairing of traditional views and practices in police-ghetto relations, and having no confidence in the recommendations that have been made by federal and state commissions that have investigated ghetto disorders and day-to-day interaction between the police

[189] Burns, *op. cit.,* p. 45. See discussion, earlier in this chapter, on the racial aspects of jury selection and jury service.

[190] *Ibid.,* p. 44.

[191] *Ibid.,* p. 46.

[192] *1961 Report of the U.S. Commission on Civil Rights,* Book 5, "Justice," p. 159.

[193] Wolfgang and Cohen, *op. cit.,* p. 84.

[194] "Executions 1930–1966," *National Prisoner Statistics Bulletin,* Bureau of Prisons, 1967. Quoted in Wolfgang and Cohen, *op. cit.,* p. 85.

and Blacks and other minorities, some critics have suggested a restructured police-ghetto relationship. Mast is particularly emphatic in his claim that police professionalization, that is, increased education and pay, better training, and more modern technology, will not lead to solutions of police-ghetto problems. He says: "to raise the rewards and self-esteem of policemen may assist somewhat, but the major thrust of modern police systems is toward centralization, mobility, and technology. Such a thrust may make criminal apprehension more efficient . . . , but it has little to do with causes of ghetto crime—minority status, low efficacy, and inadequate resources, and it unfortunately takes the policeman even further away from his constituency."[195] Altshuler says that some ghetto residents regard the police as an army of occupation, and adds that community control advocates say that the central issue in the ghettos today is legitimacy, not efficiency.[196] The indigenous police proposal rests on the following assumptions: "Ghetto self-determination efforts are proper and are to be encouraged; black ghetto dwellers form a natural community; decentralization and citizen participation are proper responses to bureaucratic centralization; local black norms are set by and belong to black people and should be in their control; the authority to regulate ghetto behavior rests more with indigenous people than with external sources."[197]

In the proposed restructuring, a gradual transfer of the present municipal police role—that of community manager—would be made to that of "community crime consultant." In the new role, the trained policeman would become a teacher and consultant on the techniques and objectives of professional police work, concentrating mainly on felonies or more serious crimes. Such crimes as theft, rape, murder, arson, and kidnapping would call for a close consulta-

tive relationship between municipal and indigenous police. Mast says that in criminal felonies it is likely that indigenous police would request assistance in the apprehension of criminals.[198] For misdemeanors, however, the police-ghetto relationship would be quite different. Such offenses are seen as being much more culture-bound and as varying from community to community. Problems such as assault and battery, drunkenness, domestic trouble, non-violent sexual conduct, and loitering would be looked at from the standpoint of local community standards under the authority of local people through their leaders. Thus, Mast says: "The indigenous police would have total control in the apprehension of individuals in the area of misdemeanors."[199] Municipal police would discontinue their patrolling of ghetto areas, and police stations would be taken over by the indigenous police force. Direct communications would be maintained between the municipal and indigenous police headquarters, but the relationship, it is said, would be based on technical cooperation rather than conflicts of interest. This technical cooperation is likened to the mutual assistance that has characterized police departments in large urban areas for some time.

The sponsors of the indigenous police proposal see the possible benefits as including a reduction of violence, a sense of efficacy on the part of Blacks as a result of determining the direction of their own communities, and strong efforts to create a successful self-policing program. As a result of taking on the role of teacher-consultant, they think that the municipal policeman would benefit through acquiring a higher status and greater prestige. They also say that the redefinition of roles might have a positive influence on the attitudes of both parties.[200]

Critics of the communal model say that letting each neighborhood, defined along the lines of race and class, determine its

[195] Robert Mast, "Police-Ghetto Relations: Some Findings and a Proposal for Structural Change," *Race*, Apr., 1970, pp. 453–454.

[196] Alan A. Altshuler, *Community Control: The Black Demand for Participation in Large American Cities*, Pegasus, 1970, pp. 37, 40–41.

[197] *Ibid.*, p. 456.

[198] *Ibid.*, pp. 457–458.

[199] *Ibid.*, p. 458.

[200] *Ibid.*, p. 459.

own style of law enforcement is no answer to crime and police problems of the central city. For one thing, as Wilson points out, the central city cannot be fully suburbanized because many people from all over the metropolitan area use it for work, governing, and recreation. The result of these varied uses is the frequent contact of different life styles and competing sets of community norms. Wilson says: "Necessarily, this generates political pressures to maintain order at the highest level expected by groups who use the city."[201] Also, many of the deepest social cleavages are found within the central city rather than between the city and its suburbs. Wilson's comment on this point is cogent:

Giving central city neighborhoods, many bitterly apprehensive and hostile toward adjoining neighborhoods, control over their own neighborhood police would be to risk making the police power an instrument for inter-neighborhood conflict. Proposals for communal police are often based on the tacit assumption that, somehow, only Negroes, and poor Negroes at that, would get control of the police. . . .Legislation that would give the police to Negroes would. . . give it to others as well. The exclusion of Negro residents, school children, and even passers-by that is now accomplished, to a degree, by informal controls and threats of violence could then be accomplished by police harassment, the subtle withdrawal of police protection, or both.[202]

The locally-minded police forces of small towns and homogeneous suburbs work reasonably well because they are not usually called upon to handle profound social conflicts. The central city is a different and much more complex kind of social situation.

The notion that different neighborhoods should be permitted to have different levels of public order has not worked well in the South. Dollard's remarks of some years ago on the southern double standard of justice are pertinent here: "The formal machinery of the law takes care of the Negroes' grievances much less adequately than that of the whites, and to a much

higher degree the Negro is compelled to make and enforce his own law with other Negroes. . . . The result is that the individual Negro is, to a considerable degree, outside the protection of the white law, and must shift for himself. This leads to the frontier psychology."[203]

It should be noted that critics of the communal model like Wilson question only those plans that would disperse the authority that governs the police. Decentralizing the functions of the police is another matter. Decentralization means giving component units within an administrative system greater freedom "within well-defined general policies, to handle local situations in a manner appropriate to local conditions. . . . Precinct commanders in a decentralized department would have greater freedom of action and more control over their patrolmen; precinct commanders in a dispersed department would surrender that control to whatever constellation of political forces the neighborhood might produce."[204]

Proposals for Change: The Police. Many recommendations have been made for the improvement of police operations short of the communal model discussed above. Among these suggested changes are the following: dramatic increases in both salaries and training of policemen, including more training in human relations; sharp increases in the recruitment of Black, Puerto Rican, Mexican-American and other minority-group police, as well as their promotion to leadership positions on the force; the creation of citizen advisory committees to work with local police precincts; better procedures for evaluating citizen complaints against the police; the development of policy guidelines for the exercise of discretion by police officers; stress on sensitivity and ability to deal with people as requisites for promotion; increased use of local civilians, male and female, for parking-meter patrol, school crossing guard duty and similar tasks; expanded

---

[201] James Q. Wilson, *Varieties of Police Behavior*, Harvard, 1968, p. 288.
[202] *Ibid.*, p. 289.

[203] John Dollard, *Caste and Class in a Southern Town*, Yale, 1937. Quoted in Wilson, *op. cit.*, p. 298.
[204] Wilson, *Varieties of Police Behavior*, p. 290.

early-warning systems for reporting accidents, disorders, and community tensions; the saturation of high-crime areas with police, and assigning priority in law enforcement to crimes of violence and to breaking up the syndicates behind the narcotics trade, numbers rackets, and other crimes that victimize the poor.[205] The recommendations of the National Advisory Commission on Civil Disorders include the establishment of a "Community Service Officer" program to attract ghetto youths between the ages of 17 and 21 to police work. "These junior officers would perform duties in ghetto neighborhoods, but would not have full police authority." The report suggests that the federal government should provide funds equal to 90 percent of the costs of employing CSOs on the basis of one for every ten regular officers.[206]

Undoubtedly, some of the suggestions that have been made by sociologists, lawyers, criminologists, police officials, community leaders, and others for the improvement of police operations have merit. Some of these recommendations have been or will be put into effect. Wilson's warning, however, that we should not expect too much from the redirection of police efforts should be carefully noted: "Order maintenance means managing conflict, and conflict implies disagreement over what should be done, how, and to whom. Conflict is found in all social strata and thus in all strata there will be resentment, often justified, against particular interventions (or the absence), but in lower-class areas conflict and disorder will be especially common and thus such resentment will be especially keen."[207] Wilson argues that race is not the decisive factor, that the urban poor have always distrusted the police and vice versa, and that this situation will not change until the poor become middle-class (or at least working class), or until "society decides to abandon its effort to maintain a common legal code and a level of public order acceptable to middle-class persons."[208]

In short, Wilson concludes that the police can cope with their problems but they cannot solve them. The attempt "to manage the unmanageable leads both sides to define the conflict as one between competing rights, moralities, and tests of manhood."[209]

Proposals for Change: Judicial Reform. Proposed changes in judicial reform include: the appointment of many more qualified judges from the membership of minority-groups, as well as the recruitment of minority-group lawyers, probation officers, and others concerned with the administration of justice; making juries more representative of the whole population; increasing free legal services; reducing the delays in the nation's courts; and utilizing more effective ways of handling minor forms of youthful offenders, before and after they are arrested.[210]

In view of the disorders experienced by numerous cities in the United States during the summers of 1965–1967, the National Advisory Commission on Civil Disorders has suggested plans for the administration of justice under emergency conditions. These measures, intended to supplement the criminal justice system during civil disorders, include: additional judges, bail, probation officers, and clerical staff; arrangements for volunteer lawyers to help prosecutors and to represent riot defendants; policies to ensure proper and individual bail, arraignment, pretrial, trial, and sentencing proceedings; procedures for processing arrested persons that permit separation of minor offenders from those dangerous to the community, in order that serious offenders may be detained and prosecuted effec-

---

[205] Wolfgang and Cohen, *op. cit.*, pp. 107–109.

[206] *Report of the National Advisory Commission on Civil Disorders*, p. 17.

[207] Wilson, *Varieties of Police Behavior*, pp. 296–297.

[208] *Ibid.*, p. 297.

[209] *Ibid.*, p. 299.

[210] Wolfgang and Cohen, *op. cit.*, pp. 109–114. See pp. 110–112 for specific suggestions for coping with delays in the courts, including ways of cutting down on the number of people who appear before the courts (alcoholics, homosexuals, drug addicts, petty criminals, and so forth). Suggestions for handling minor forms of juvenile delinquency are given on pp. 112–113.

tively; and adequate emergency processing and detention facilities.[211]

Proposals for Change: Corrections. Among the recommendations for changes in the correctional system are: wider use of bail, probation, and parole; raising standards for recruitment, selection, and training of correctional personnel; expansion of psychological and educational testing of inmates, and provision of a wider variety of educational and vocational opportunities; provision of in-service human-relations training for all correctional personnel; establishing machinery for receiving prisoner complaints; the use of better means of screening out insensitive, sadistic, and racially biased correction workers; making salaries of correctional personnel competitive with other civil-service jobs; and developing pre-release centers, halfway houses, and night-time or weekend prisons for selected prisoners with full-time employment.[212]

In addition to the many recommendations that have been made for changes in police operations, the judicial process, and corrections, numerous measures have been proposed for community action programs, ranging from volunteer neighborhood street patrols and drives for better street lighting to businessmen's committees to find job and training opportunities for high-school dropouts and young people returning to their neighborhoods from military service, juvenile detention, or prison terms.[213]

Proposals for Change: Improving the Quality of Life for the Urban Poor. Concerned and experienced social scientists, lawyers, members of government commissions, and others expect no significant reduction in crime unless drastic steps are taken to combat the underlying causes of criminal behavior by eliminating slum housing, upgrading education, increasing educational opportunities—including job training, expanding job opportunities, and reducing the social and psychological isolation of Blacks and other racial and cultural minorities from the society as a whole. The proposals for crime reduction through immediate reforms will have little effect unless serious attempts are made continuously to bring about more basic, long-run changes in the social system of the United States.[214]

[211] *Report of the National Advisory Commission on Civil Disorders,* p. 19.
[212] Wolfgang and Cohen, *op. cit.,* pp. 114–115.

[213] *Ibid.,* pp. 115–116.
[214] *Ibid.,* pp. 105–106. Comprehensive recommendations for national action outside the administration of criminal justice itself—recommendations in the fields of employment, education, the welfare system, and housing are given in the *Report of the National Advisory Commission on Civil Disorders,* pp. 23–29.

SUMMARY OF THE MAIN PROVISIONS OF THE CIVIL RIGHTS ACT OF 1964

Title I—Voting
Prohibits registrars from applying different standards to white and Negro voting applicants and from disqualifying applicants because of inconsequential errors on their forms. Requires that literacy tests be in writing, except under special arrangements for blind persons, and that any applicant desiring one be given a copy of the questions and his answers. Makes a sixth-grade education a rebuttable presumption of literacy. Allows the Attorney General or defendant state officials in any voting suit to request trial by a three-judge Federal Court.

Title II—Public Accommodations
Prohibits discrimination or refusal of service on account of race in hotels, motels, restaurants, gasoline stations, and places of amusement if their operations affect interstate commerce or if their discrimination "is supported by state action." Permits the Attorney General to enforce the title by suit in the Federal courts if he believes that any person or group is engaging in a "pattern or practice of resistance" to the rights declared by the title. The latter language was added in the Senate, which also authorized three-judge courts for suits under this title.

Title III—Public Facilities
Requires that Negroes have equal access to, and treatment in, publicly owned or operated facilities such as parks, stadiums and swimming pools. Authorizes the Attorney General to sue for en-

forcement of these rights if private citizens are unable to sue effectively.

Title IV—Public Schools

Empowers the Attorney General to bring school desegregation suits under the same conditions as in Title III. Authorizes technical and financial aid to school districts to assist in desegregation. The Senate strengthened a provision in the House bill saying that the title does not cover busing of pupils or other steps to end "racial imbalance."

Title V—Civil Rights Commission

Extends the life of the Civil Rights Commission until Jan. 31, 1968.

Title VI—Federal Aid

Provides that no person shall be subjected to racial discrimination in any program receiving federal aid. Directs federal agencies to take steps against discrimination, including—as a last resort, and after hearings—withholding of federal funds from state or local agencies that discriminate.

Title VII—Employment

Bans discrimination by employers or unions with 100 or more employes or members the first year the act is effective, reducing, over four years to 25 or more. Establishes a commission to investigate alleged discrimination and use persuasion to end it. Authorizes the Attorney General to sue if he believes any person or group is engaged in a "pattern or practice" of resistance to the title, and to ask for trial by a three-judge court. The Senate added to "pattern-or-practice" condi-

tion and shifted the power to sue from the commission to the Attorney General.

Title VIII—Statistics

Directs the Census Bureau to compile statistics of registration and voting by race in areas of the country designated by the Civil Rights Commission. This might be used to enforce the long-forgotten provision of the 14th Amendment that states that discriminate in voting shall lose seats in the House of Representatives.

Title IX—Courts

Permits appellate review of decisions by Federal District judges to send back to the state courts criminal defendants who have attempted to remove their cases on the ground that their civil rights would be denied in state trials. Permits the Attorney General to intervene in suits filed by private persons complaining that they have been denied the equal protection of the laws.

Title X—Conciliation

Establishes a Community Relations Service in the Commerce Department to help conciliate racial disputes. The Senate removed a House ceiling of seven employes.

Title XI—Miscellaneous

Guarantees jury trials for criminal contempt under any part of the act by Title I—a provision added in the Senate. Provides that the statute shall not invalidate state laws with consistent purposes, and that it shall not impair any existing powers of Federal officials.

"Summary of Main Provisions of Civil Rights Bill," *The Crisis*, 71 (Aug.–Sept., 1964), pp. 430–431.

Sociologists and anthropologists have long stressed the importance of familial and kinship institutions in the life of a given tribal or national group. These institutions govern the biological reproduction of the society, and through them many of man's economic and emotional needs are met. It would be inappropriate here to present a generalized picture of the place of the family in American social life,[1] and full accounts of the family life of all racial and ethnic groups in the United States cannot be given. Much of the interaction in minority families parallels that in other American families. We are primarily concerned in this chapter with the ways in which minority status affects family life. As examples of minority family life we shall consider the Negro family, the Italian family, the Mexican family, the Jewish family, the Chinese family, the Japanese family, and the Puerto Rican family. To these discussions we shall add, in Chapter 16, an analysis of intermarriage—interracial, interfaith, and interethnic.

THE NEGRO FAMILY:
1930–1964 STUDIES

During slavery the sexual impulses of American Negroes were no longer subject to control by African customs. In this situation, the range in types of mating was from purely physical contacts to permanent family associations based on strong affection between spouses and between parents and children.[2] There were cases, too, in which masters bred slaves as they bred their stock.

Differences in physical appearance, abilities, and work assignments on the plantations brought about differential assimilation into the world of the master race. Although some slaves closely approached the organization of family life characteristic of Whites, it was always possible for the economic interests of the master group to disrupt familial bonds. As Frazier pointed out, the Negro mother was the most stable and important figure in the family.

Within this world the slave mother held a strategic position and played a dominant role in the family groupings. The tie between the mother and her younger children had to be respected not only because of the dependence of the child upon her for survival but often because of her fierce attachment to her brood. Some of the mothers undoubtedly were cold and indifferent to their offspring, but this appears to have been due to the attitude that the mother developed toward the unborn child during pregnancy as well as the burden of child care.[3]

It should be remembered that, in addition to the children they bore to their spouses, some slave women bore children for the men of the master race, and that slave mothers were sometimes called upon to act as foster mothers to their masters' children.

It should be said that there were slave fathers who became deeply attached to their spouses and children. Some were able to buy their wives and children before emancipation. Approximately a half-million Negroes were free before the Civil War, and it was within this group that the family was first established on a firm basis. As time passed, these free families formed the nuclei of the

[1] For sociological analyses of the family, see Robert R. Bell, *Marriage and Family Interaction*, Dorsey Press; rev. ed., 1967; Robert O. Blood, *Marriage*, Free Press, 2nd ed., 1969; Ruth Shonle Cavan, *The American Family*, Thomas Y. Crowell, 1969; William F. Kenkel, *The Family in Perspective*, Appleton-Century-Crofts, 2nd ed., 1966; and Atlee Stroup, *Marriage and Family: A Developmental Approach*, Appleton-Century-Crofts, 1966.

[2] The authoritative work on the Negro family is E. Franklin Frazier, *The Negro Family in the United States*, Citadel, 1948.
[3] *Ibid.*, p. 361.

higher classes in both the North and the South.

Since World War I more than two million Negroes have migrated from the rural South to the urban South, and three times that number to the urban North and West. The migrants have included solitary, disorganized men and women, as well as illiterate or semiliterate impoverished families. Their children have contributed more than their share of juvenile delinquency in the urban slums. Illegitimacy, which was a relatively harmless matter in the country, has become an economic and social problem of some magnitude in the city.

In the past, lower-class Negro children were taught by their parents to conform to the prevailing mores with respect to Negro-white relations. They learned "to do as we were told, be as courteous as possible to white people, don't talk back to them, and do your work as well as possible. They said 'niggers' that are liked by white people are those who don't give any trouble and don't ask for much." Some of these children were taught that " 'if you can act big enough monkey, you can get almost what you want.' " There was a tendency among these children to rebel against such instructions and to display considerable hostility toward white people, but, despite their revolt, many lower-class children adopted the prevailing unfavorable stereotypes of the Negro and the techniques of "getting by" in the larger world. One mother said that she had never told her children anything about racial etiquette because she saw no reason for such advice. Frazier commented that apparently some members of the lower class regarded existing race relations as so natural and inevitable that everyone will know how to act.[4]

The indoctrination that the lower-class Negro child received in the home was supplemented in important ways by the neighborhood environment. As a result of studying lower-class children, Negro and white, in Chicago, Allison W. Davis concluded that

gang life in the slum taught the lower-class child to fear ". . . being 'taken in' by the teacher, . . . being a 'softie' with her. To study 'homework' seriously is literally a disgrace. Instead of boasting of good marks in school, one conceals them, if one ever receives any. The lower-class adolescent fears not to be thought a street-fighter; it is a suspicious and dangerous social trait. He fears not to curse. If he cannot claim early sex relations, his virility is seriously questioned."[5]

Some changes have occurred in the family life of lower-class urban Negroes. An increasing number of urban Negro workers are doing skilled and semiskilled work. The new body of black industrial workers has acquired an outlook on life based neither on an emulation of the behavior of the white group nor upon the ideals and standards of the brown middle class. According to Frazier, ". . . As the Negro worker becomes an industrial worker, he assumes responsibility for the support of his family and acquires a new authority in family relations. Moreover, as the isolation of the black worker is gradually broken down, his ideals and patterns of family life approximate those of the great body of industrial workers."[6] The emphasis on family stability among the Black Muslins also supports this trend.

The middle class in the Negro group as defined by Frazier included the families whose incomes are derived from skilled and semi-skilled occupations.[7] Children here are members of permanent family groups, and the father plays a much more important role both as breadwinner and as disciplinarian than does the lower-class father. School attendance and school records are carefully watched, and the child is sent to Sunday school and church. Play is closely supervised and playmates and clique mates are directly or indirectly selected. Parents exert influence upon their children to avoid aggression at

[4] E. Franklin Frazier, *Negro Youth at the Crossways, ACE*, 1940, pp. 42–44, 68.

[5] Allison W. Davis, *Child Rearing in the Class Structure of American Society*, Community Service Society of New York, Jan. 30, 1948, p. 8.

[6] Frazier, *The Negro Family in the United States*, p. 355.

[7] Frazier, *Negro Youth at the Crossways*, p. 55.

school, to inhibit sexual impulses, and to avoid poolrooms, gambling parlors, and cabarets. One of the most important pressures on the middle-class Negro child is that of staying away from the lower-class children and also abstaining from behavior that might identify him with the lower class.

While the majority of middle-class Negro families in Frazier's study seemed to be accommodated to their status, they were not as reconciled to their station in life as lower-class parents and their children. The middle-class families are less likely, as we noted in Chapter 7, to encourage their children to act in a subservient manner toward white people. Middle-class Negro children have been characterized by a greater awareness and sophistication about their racial status, and by more social and racial consciousness, than lower-class Negro children. They have had a more critical attitude toward the lacks in Negro life and a stronger resentment against the discrimination of the white group,[8] but in the current protest movement, both lower-class and middle-class youth have played important roles.

Upper-class Negro parents have never inculcated servile attitudes toward white persons in their children. They may tell children to ignore disparaging epithets on the ground that only "white trash" use such terms, and they make it clear to their offspring that fighting is not becoming to persons of their status. In the upper-class Negro family the man assumes the major economic responsibility and exercises the major authority. The family is usually smaller, although it may not be limited to parents and children. Supervision by parents is even more strict than in the middle-class family, and the child's friends are still more carefully chosen.

In their study of a number of New Orleans Negro subjects included 20 years earlier by Davis and Dollard in *Children of Bondage,* Rohrer and Edmonson divided the 20 individuals they scrutinized most closely into five major groups. Four of these "cultures" have a distinctive pattern of family life and socialization: the middle class, the matriarchy, the gang, and the [isolated] family. The fifth group is a residual group of the culturally marginal. Erikson's "ego identity" was adopted in analyzing the individual's mode of psychodynamic functioning —"the personal residue of the individual's experience in interaction with his society." Their middle-class subjects, all college graduates, identified with a variety of social roles, but all held a certain group of values: achievement, respectability, politeness, industry, and egalitarianism. All expressed antagonism toward the lower class and "its unprincipled way of life," as well as to the "snobbery" of the upper class. All of their middle-class subjects had been put in the position of choosing between their middle-class self-conceptions and their loyalties to family.[9]

In another group, Rohrer and Edmonson found a pattern of identification with the matriarchal family in dramatic contrast to class orientation. These lower-class women did not hold a class view, but saw sex as the basic social category and aligned themselves psychologically with their mothers "in a solidarity phalanx against men." These women viewed their mothers as the center of their lives and as the primary source of security. This is not "a solidarity of one kin group against another in the manner of the matrilineal clan, but rather of one sex against another . . . a mother-daughter solidarity against the world."[10]

The gang is the male "culture" corresponding to the matriarchy. According to Rohrer and Edmonson:

. . . the little boys who are recruited into gangs come out of matriarchal families. . . . It does not appear that they get markedly different maternal treatment from that accorded to little girls, but it seems clear that vesting all parental authority in a woman would have rather different consequences for boys and girls, and the spirit of rebellion against authority so promi-

---

[8] Frazier, *Negro Youth at the Crossways,* p. 55.

[9] John H. Rohrer and Munro S. Edmonson (eds.), *The Eighth Generation: Culture and Personalities of New Orleans Negroes,* Harper & Row, 1960, pp. 86, 92.

[10] *Ibid.,* pp. 126–127.

nent in the gang is mainly derived from this source. The matriarchs make no bones about their preference for little girls. . . . Boys cannot learn to be men in a manless family, and we may assert . . . that this learning is institutionalized in the gang for most Negro boys of the lower class. . . . Psychodynamically, gang members are characterized by deep-seated feelings of dependency and inadequacy. . . . While the gang furnishes male role models, it is neither stable enough nor emotionally secure enough to be a satisfying substitute for a family.[11]

Six of the subjects in the New Orleans restudy involved the "culture" of what Rohrer and Edmonson call the [isolated] family.[12] These persons were engaged in upper-lower or lower-middle-class occupations: postmen, maintenance workers, service station operators, janitors, and mail clerks.

All of them had been stably married for many years, and though they express a rather wide diversity of other social attitudes they are emphatic in the value they place on family life. . . . Such an emphasis places a special stress on the responsibility of parenthood, reliable and steady employment, and family support. . . . Most of them have no involvement whatsoever in outside social groups of any kind.[13]

Rohrer and Edmonson "guess that the gang, the matriarchy, and the isolated family . . . are the dominant social forms in the lives of a substantial majority of New Orleans Negroes," and they would expect "the patterns of role identification associated with them to be correspondingly prominent in any large sample of this population."[14]

THE NEGRO FAMILY:
1965–1971 STUDIES

Since 1965, many of the studies of the Negro family have concentrated on lower-class

life. A publication that has attracted considerable attention is the so-called Moynihan Report.[15] Although this report has been strongly criticized, Rainwater and Yancey claim that the purpose of the authors was "to present a sharply focused argument leading to the conclusion that the government's economic and social welfare programs, existing and prospective ones, should be systematically designed to encourage the stability of the Negro family." To this end, they sought to show

. . . first, that the Negro family was highly unstable (female-headed households produced by marital breakup and illegitimacy). This instability resulted from the systematic weakening of the position of the Negro male. Slavery, reconstruction, urbanization, and unemployment had produced a problem as old as America and as new as the April unemployment rate. This problem of unstable families in turn was a central feature of the tangle of pathology of the urban ghetto, involving problems of delinquency, crime, school dropouts, unemployment, and poverty. Finally, Moynihan wanted the Administration to understand that some evidence supported the conclusion that these problems fed on themselves and that matters were rapidly getting worse.[16]

Other scholars, however, took a different view of the Moynihan Report. Yinger points out that all necessary controls for class, education, recency of move to the city, and other relevant variables must be made before the facts are seen as signifying a peculiarly Negro pathology.[17] Because "the

---

[11] *Ibid.*, pp. 159–160.

[12] A concept similar to individuals and families who are called "routine-seekers" (versus "action-seekers") in Herbert Gans, *The Urban Villagers: Group and Class in the Life of Italian-Americans,* Free Press, 1962, pp. 28–31.

[13] Rohrer and Edmonson, *op. cit.*, pp. 186–187.

[14] *Ibid.*, p. 299.

[15] Office of Policy Planning and Research, U.S. Department of Labor, *The Negro Family: The Case for National Action,* Mar., 1965.

[16] Lee Rainwater and W. L. Yancey, *The Moynihan Report and the Politics of Controversy,* M.I.T. Press, 1967, pp. 27–28.

[17] J. M. Yinger, "Recent Developments in Minority and Race Relations," *Annals,* July, 1968, p. 140. Udry's analysis of 1960 census data shows the relationship between status and marital disruption to be inverse for both sexes and for both whites and non-whites, when status is measured by educational level. When measured by occupational status, the relationship of status to marital disruption is still inverse and clear for men. The far greater instability of non-white marriages is shown not to be attributable solely to the general low educational and occupational status of this group, but a characteristic of non-white groups of all educational and

vast majority of Negro families are stable, conforming, and achieving, and cause no problems to anybody, the tendency to view them in negative terms" is, according to Billingsley, a distortion of the actual situation.[18] This critic sees a further distortion in the singling out of instability in the Negro family as the causal factor for the difficulties Negroes face in the white society instead of the other way round. Billingsley criticizes Moynihan, and others as well, for comparing Negroes with Whites on standardized objective measures, implying incidentally that the Negro group is deviant, without taking into consideration two important facets of the Negro experience: social class and social caste.[19] Rainwater and Yancey point out that at two places in the report, Moynihan indicates that "the Negro community contained two broad groupings—an increasingly successful middle class, and an increasingly disorganized lower class." They attribute a part of the controversy over the

report to the circumstance that it was not written for a learned journal nor as an ordinary position paper prepared by a political executive. As a hybrid that sought to present certain social science findings and at the same time to argue a policy position, it reflects, they say, the intellectual difficulties of such an approach. The authors felt that the general direction of solutions to the problems they had considered—employment, income maintenance, better housing, and family planning were clear, but they did not formulate specific program proposals. Instead, they hoped that the Administration would develop such programs.[20]

As Billingsley shows in the table on page 469, there is a wide variety of Negro family structures. Regardless of race, it is an oversimplification to refer to middle-class and lower-class families, or to male-headed families and female-headed families. Billingsley distinguishes three general categories of family structure with twelve subtypes.[21] We shall return to this point later, but it should be said now that Billingsley asserts that the range and variety of Negro family structures does not suggest, as some have claimed, that the Negro family is falling apart, but rather "that these families are fully capable of sur-

---

occupational levels. By occupational status there is practically no overlap in rates between whites and non-whites of any status level, and the overlap between the two groups on disruption rates by education is slight. Of course, occupational and educational differences within the non-white group are relative to marital instability in the same way as among whites. The analysis here does not explain white-non-white differences but simply delineates them more clearly. Socioeconomic status differences not tapped by education and occupation may still explain much of the difference. For example, non-whites and whites matched on occupation or education are still grossly unequal in income, which may be related to divorce rates independently of occupational status. Perhaps the 'caste' position of Negroes has a relationship to marital instability. Perhaps a historical-cultural explanation, tracing the Negro family pattern to roots in the slavery system, is made more tenable in the light of the above data. Census data cannot lead to definitive choice among the possible explanations.

J. Richard Udry, "Marital Instability by Race, Sex, Education, Occupation and Income," in Charles V. Willie (ed.), *The Family Life of Black People*, Charles E. Merrill, 1970, p. 153 (reprinted from *AJS*, Sept. 1966, pp. 203–209 and May, 1967, pp. 673–674).

[18] Andrew Billingsley, *Black Families in White America*, Prentice-Hall, 1968, p. 199.

[19] *Ibid.*, p. 200. For other criticisms of the Moynihan Report, see William Ryan, "The New Genteel Racism," *The Crisis*, Dec., 1965, pp. 623–631, 644; *Institute of Race Relations Newsletter*, Oct., 1966, pp. 26–27.

[20] Rainwater and Yancey, *op. cit.*, pp. 7, 17, 29.

[21] In 1965, there were more than two and one-half million attenuated nuclear families in the United States, of which 733,000 were Negro families (approximately 6 percent of all Negro families). Females headed 689,000 of these families; males who were not married and not living with other relatives headed 44,000. This subtype can be divided into ten subsubtypes depending on whether the single parent is male or female and whether he or she is (a) single, (b) married with an absent spouse, (c) legally separated, (d) divorced, or (e) widowed. Concerning extended families in 1965, nearly 15 percent of all Negro families had one or more minor relatives living with them who was not their own child, and more than 25 percent of all Negro families had a relative living with them who was 18 or over. The number of augmented families is unknown but considered substantial. In 1965 there were almost half a million persons living in families with whom they were not related by marriage, ancestry, or adoption. Most of these persons were adults; 80 percent of the 326,000 men and 70 percent of the 173,000 women were 18 or over, and nearly one-third were 55 or over. Billingsley, *op. cit.*, pp. 18–21. Statistical data derived from U.S. Bureau of the Census, *U.S. Census of Population*, 1960; *The Negro Population*, Government Printing Office, 1965.

Negro Family Structure

Types of Family	Household Head		Other Household Members		
	Husband & Wife	Single Parent	Children	Other Relatives	Non-relatives
Nuclear Families					
I. Incipient Nuclear Family	X				
II: Simple Nuclear Family	X		X		
III: Attenuated Nuclear Family		X	X		
Extended Families					
IV: Incipient Extended Family	X			X	
V: Simple Extended Family	X		X	X	
VI: Attenuated Extended Family		X	X	X	
Augmented Families					
VII: Incipient Augmented Family	X				X
VIII: Incipient Extended Augmented Family	X			X	X
IX: Nuclear Augmented Family	X		X		X
X: Nuclear Extended Augmented Family	X		X	X	X
XI: Attenuated Augmented Family		X	X		X
XII: Attenuated Extended Augmented Family		X	X	X	X

Source: Andrew Billingsley, *Black Families in White America*, ©1968, p. 17. By permission of Prentice-Hall, Inc., Englewood Cliffs, N.J.

viving by adapting to the historical and contemporary social and economic conditions facing the Negro people."[22]

Having referred to some of the earlier studies of Negro families, and having presented general considerations in some of the recent thinking concerning these families, we turn now to a more detailed review of contemporary analyses. Rural versus urban residence has important consequences in both the structure and the functions of today's Negro families. In 1966, about one-half of all Negro families lived in the urban North, one-fourth in the urban South, and one-quarter in the rural South. According to Rainwater, in the 100 years since emancipation Negroes in rural areas have maintained full nuclear families almost as well as rural Whites.[23] Social class boundaries are difficult to specify in the Negro group. Billingsley's estimates of half of all Negro families in the lower class, 40 percent in the middle class and 10 percent in the upper

[22] On the basis of life styles, Hannerz categorizes the people in the "Winston Street" neighborhood of Washington, D.C., as: mainstreamers, swingers, street families, and streetcorner men. Ulf Hannerz, *Soulside: Inquiries into Ghetto Culture and Community*, Columbia, 1969, pp. 37–58. For an interesting statement on the limitations of relying solely on one of the dominant schools of interpretation (Africanist, slavery, macrostructural) of black family forms, see *ibid.*, pp. 71–78. For a valuable critique of the concepts of "the culture of poverty" and cultural deprivation, as well as Hannerz's analysis of the adaptation of the poor, see *ibid.*, pp. 178–188. See also Hylan Lewis, *Child Rearing among Low Income Families*, Washington Center for Metropolitan Studies, 1961, pp. 10–11; Charles V. Willie, ed., *op. cit.*, pp. 322–324; C. V. Willie and Janet Weinandy, "The Structure and Composition of 'Problem' and 'Stable' Families in a Low-Income Population," *ibid.*, pp. 193–194; and John H. Scanzoni, *The Black Family in Modern Society*, Allyn & Bacon, 1971.

[23] Lee Rainwater, "Crucible of Identity: The Negro Lower-Class Family," in Talcott Parsons and Kenneth B. Clark (eds.), *The Negro American*, Houghton Mifflin, 1966, p. 167.

class may underestimate the proportion of Negro families in the lower class and over-estimate the size of the Negro upper class, at least if social-class terms are to have the same meaning that they usually have with reference to the general population.[24] Despite the im-precision of class lines within the Negro group, the concept of social class looms as an important aspect in the study of Negro family life.

Although three-fifths of all Negro house-holds are headed by two parents,[25] it seems likely that as many as two-thirds of Negro urban poor children will not live in families headed by a man and a woman throughout the first 18 years of their lives.[26] Approxi-mately half of the nonwhite families with their own children of any age have no other members. Many of the multigenerational families live under crowded conditions: nearly one-third of all nonwhite members of households in 1960 lived in dwelling units with 1.5 or more persons per room. Crowd-ing is common among slum families in gen-eral, but it is more likely to occur and to be more severe among Negroes.[27] Under crowded living conditions in the slums, order —social as well as physical—in the child's social world is lacking. In addition to hous-ing accommodations themselves, type of neighborhood affects family life. Stable fam-ilies forced to live in the ghetto find it difficult to bring up children when they are surrounded by people whose patterns and standards are quite different.[28] One of the ironies of the civil rights movement is the acceleration of the moving of the more stable Negro families into black middle-class neighborhoods, or into integrated areas, or into the suburbs, leaving a higher ratio of

"problem families" to struggle, with scarce resources, with the difficulties of ghetto life.

Another pertinent factor influencing lower-class Negro family life is high fertility. Negro slum families have more children than do either white slum families or stable working- and middle-class Negro families. Because of family size and the greater likeli-hood that the father is absent, the mother in a family of this type has a more demanding task with fewer resources at her disposal.[29] Davies concludes that the evidence strongly indicates that high fertility is a major ele-ment in the etiology of poverty, adding that one policy measure aimed at improving the economic status of Negroes might take the form of a population control program among rural Negroes of the South.[30] This would check the very high fertility of this group, but it would operate also to reduce migration to urban areas in the future.

The extent to which lower-class Negroes aspire to establish a general middle-class style of life is somewhat in dispute. Rain-water says that Negroes of the lower class know what "the normal American family" is supposed to be like and that "they con-sider a stable family-centered way of life superior to the conjugal and familial situa-tions in which they often find themselves." In his view, many of them find it impossible, for economic or other reasons, to realize the ideals that they hold.[31] At this point in the history of race relations in the United States, however, others are not so sure that lower-class Negroes aspire to be middle-class Ne-groes in the usual middle-class white sense. For example, Billingsley says it is not true that middle-class Negro families have more in common with middle-class white families than they do with lower-class Negro families. His point of view is based on the concept of ethclass, that is, of a sense of participa-tional identification (behavioral similarities within a class plus a sense of peoplehood).[32]

[24] See Billingsley, op. cit., p. 7. Billingsley says: "If we consider family income as an index of social class, it may be observed that in 1966, 56 percent of Negro families earned less than $7,000, 32 percent earned between $7,000 and $10,000 and 12 percent earned over $10,000. There is a high, though by no means perfect, correlation among income, education, and occupation of family head."

[25] Jessie Bernard, Marriage and Family Among Negroes, Prentice-Hall, 1966, p. 118.

[26] Rainwater, op. cit., pp. 180–181.

[27] Bernard, op. cit., p. 130.

[28] Ibid., p. 133.

[29] Rainwater, op. cit., p. 182.

[30] Vernon Davies, "Fertility Versus Welfare: The Negro American Dilemma," Phylon, 1966, pp. 231–232.

[31] Rainwater, op. cit., pp. 182–183.

[32] Billingsley, op. cit., pp. 9–10.

It is difficult to determine the accuracy of this claim, that is, whether this viewpoint is widespread or is largely wish fulfillment and a mild form of nationalistic propaganda.

Keil observes that to accept Ralph W. Ellison's claim that Negro kinship is Western, one must overlook either the most striking aspect of Negro social structure—the battle of the sexes—or the core concept of middle-class kinship in the United States—marital companionship and the primacy of the nuclear family. According to Keil:

For the vast majority of Negroes, the battle of the sexes is no mere figure of speech. In the ghetto, men and women are considered to be separate and antagonistic species, and this division 'overrides the minor distinctions of creed, class and color.' Men are 'by nature' primarily interested in sexual satisfaction and independence (money will get you both); they are 'strong' sexually, and will take favors from anyone who will grant them. Women are said to be primarily interested in emotional support and their families (money is needed to keep the household intact); they are 'weak' sexually, and tend to become attached to one or two men at a time. Men call women self-righteous, money-grabbing, treacherous, and domineering. Women simply say that all men are no good. . . . The female forces on one side of the battle line consist of units like mother and daughter, sister and sister, niece and aunt, wife and mother-in-law, a matriarch with her daughters and grandchildren. Facing this formidable opposition is the independent Negro male who seeks allies where he can—in the gang, pool hall, blues bar, and barber shop. . . . However we characterize the anomalous position of the Negro male, he doesn't seem to fit gracefully into a conventional American or Western kinship system. Nor, for that matter, do the basic features of lower-class Negro kinship patterns match well with any non-Western kinship system that anthropologists have encountered. The battle of the sexes can . . . be found raging in many slums around the world . . . but in most of these 'cultures of poverty' the battle tends to be resolved in terms of male authoritarianism rather than 'mother-centeredness.'[33]

In the research that has been done on the American family, much has been said about

[33] Charles Keil, *Urban Blues*, Univ. of Chicago Press, 1966, pp. 9–10.

"broken homes" or "broken families." As Jessie Bernard observes, only in recent years has it been realized that for a sizable part of the population, white or Negro, the female-headed family is a standard phenomenon, acceptable even if it is not prescribed or preferred.[34] In 1960, half of all nonwhite families with incomes under $2000 in central cities were headed by women. Over a longer period, a larger proportion of women would find themselves, at some time or other, the heads of families. For the most part, these families are poor because they are headed by women, and they probably have women as heads because they are poor.[35]

In the "house of mothers," children learn early in life to fend for themselves. In many cases, Negro lower-class mothers try to keep their young children from the street, but as they grow up they inevitably become involved in "poor-group activities." Studies of the effects on personality development of being socialized in fatherless families indicate that children reared in one-parent homes find it more difficult to delay gratification. According to Pettigrew, they are less socially responsible, less achievement-oriented, more susceptible to delinquency. A study of Negro boys and girls from five to 14 showed that those without fathers had greater difficulty than others in differentiating the roles of the sexes.[36] Although the

[34] Billingsley points out that in 1966 there were approximately four million white single-parent families and about one million Negro single-parent families in the United States. Billingsley, *op. cit.*, p. 15. U.S. Census survey data reveal that about 27 percent of black families were headed by women in 1970, compared with 22 percent in 1960 and 17 percent in 1950. Throughout this period the white figure has been about 9 percent. *The Plain Dealer*, Feb. 27, 1971, p. 1.

[35] Bernard, *op. cit.*, p. 41.

[36] Thomas F. Pettigrew, *Profile of the American Negro*, Van Nostrand, 1964, pp. 17–24 (summarized in Bernard, *op. cit.*, p. 124). See also Elliot Liebow, "Fathers Without Children," chap. 3, *Tally's Corner: A Study of Negro Streetcorner Men*, Little, Brown, 1967. Keil takes exception to the view that lower-class Negro life style and its characteristic rituals and expressive roles are the products of compensation for masculine self-doubt. According to Keil, it is possible that "'the Oedipal problem of managing and diverting aggression against the father' may be easily resolved, mitigated, or avoided altogether in families in which the father is weak or absent and

evidence indicates that fatherless families are handicapped in the socialization of children, especially of sons, this point should not be overemphasized.[37] Bernard stresses that only a minority of Negro children are socialized in such families, and that not all of them suffer damage.[38] Also, some of the consequences associated with fatherlessness undoubtedly stem from deprivation, both of income and of maternal care as the mother tries to perform both parental roles.

Among slum Negroes, premarital sexual behavior and attitudes toward premarital pregnancy have a bearing on family life. In a study of families living in public housing projects in St. Louis it was found that

---

where a number of mothering women (grandmothers, aunts) are in or near the household. Even a large set of siblings and a string of visiting 'uncles' do not compete for a mother's attention as a potent and omnipresent father might. The 'uncles' and other males in the vicinity certainly offer some identity models to a young man growing up, but his sexual development is relatively unimpeded by them." Keil, op. cit., 1966, p. 23.

[37] Citing three existing national surveys that included questions on decision making in families and parental influence during childhood, Hyman and Reed point out that the differences between white and Negro responses are small and inconsistent. They say that a "black matriarchy" is seen to be an illusion when the findings on white respondents are considered. H. H. Hyman and J. S. Reed, " 'Black Matriarchy' Reconsidered: Evidence from Secondary Analysis of Sample Surveys," POQ, Fall, 1969, pp. 347–352. The samples taken in a recent study showed that among blacks, the authority of mothers tends to be stronger in intact than it is in broken families. Also, maternal household authority and identification with a female role model do not seem to have the negative effect on educational aspirations and school performance that have been attributed to them. Denise Kandel, "Race, Maternal Authority, and Adolescent Aspiration," AJS, May, 1971, p. 999.

[38] Bernard, op. cit., p. 126. Farley and Hermalin say the evidence suggests that family instability is associated with somewhat lower levels of such life chance variables as educational and occupational level, but that in nearly all studies the differentials are modest. Often other factors examined are more important, and by itself the family instability variable does not go far in accounting for differences between the races. One implication of this finding is that "programs designed to strengthen black family structure in the hope of thereby improving the socioeconomic status of blacks may be less effective than alternate strategies." Reynolds Farley and Albert J. Hermalin, "Family Stability: A Comparison of Trends Between Blacks and Whites," ASR, Feb., 1971, p. 16.

---

the informal social relations of slum Negroes begin to be highly sexualized in adolescence. Parents seldom feel that they can do much to prevent their children's sexual involvement. According to Rainwater, when a girl becomes pregnant "the question of marriage certainly arises and is considered, but the girl often decides that she would rather not marry the man either because she does not want to settle down yet or because she does not think he would make a good husband."[39] It was found that, in general, when a girl becomes pregnant while still living at home it is assumed that she will remain there and that her parents will take a major responsibility for rearing the children.

A study by Reiss shows the influence of factors other than slum dwelling on premarital sexual attitudes. His data show that Negroes and Whites differ considerably in the ways in which premarital sexual attitudes are produced and maintained. For his subjects, Reiss found that

within traditionally less permissive groups— women and whites—individual permissiveness is more likely to be affected by such social factors as church attendance, belief in romantic love, and falling in love. In the highly permissive groups—men and Negroes—individuals find support and justification for liberal sexual attitudes: their permissiveness is therefore less subject to alteration by social factors. Highly permissive individuals in less permissive social categories are permissive not because they have long-standing traditions to support it but because they are located in the social structure in such a way as to avoid inhibitory forces (e.g., church attendance and the idealistic version of romantic love) and to maximize experiences that promote permissiveness (e.g., falling in love). The highly permissive white college students are low on church attendance, tend not to believe in romantic love, and report falling in love relatively often. The equally permissive Negro students lack these characteristics; their permissiveness seems to be a consequence of a long-standing supporting tradition. This interpretation of the distinctiveness between more and less permissive subcultures is further supported by the contrast between the two extreme groups—Negro men and white women. White women's permissive-

[39] Rainwater, op. cit., p. 187.

ness is affected by *all* the variables investigated; that of Negro men is affected by *none* of them.[40]

In lower-class families, Negro and white, where husband and wife are both present, a high degree of conjugal role segregation tends to make the family group matrifocal in comparison to middle-class families. According to Rainwater, they are matrifocal "in the sense that the wife makes most of the decisions that keep the family going and has the greatest sense of responsibility to the family. In white as well as in Negro lower-class families women tend to look to their female relatives for support and counsel, and to treat their husbands as essentially uninterested in the day-to-day problems of family living."[41] These tendencies are all considerably exaggerated in the Negro lower-class family.

In learning their sex roles in the Negro slum community, boys and girls are not simply influenced by the fact that fathers are often absent but by male role models around boys that emphasize expressive, affectional techniques for getting along in the world. Rainwater reports that the female role models available to girls stress an exaggerated self-sufficiency (from a middle-class point of view) and the danger of becoming dependent upon men for anything that is important. Eventually the woman learns that "she is most secure when she herself manages the family affairs and when she dominates her men" and the man learns that "he exposes himself to the least risk of failure when he does not assume a husband's and father's responsibilities but instead counts on his ability to court women and to ingratiate himself with them."[42] Summarizing the experiences of Negro slum children during the socialization process, Rain-

water suggests that they learn that they are weak and can expect only partial gratification of their needs, and that even this level of gratification can be obtained only by less than straightforward means.[43]

The present authors disagree with the point of view that a large part of the difficulties faced by Negroes in the United States today, especially lower-class Negroes, is due to characteristics, racial or traditional, that are peculiar to Negro families. Instead, we agree with Rainwater, Billingsley, and the critics of Moynihan (and with what we understand to be Moynihan's actual basic beliefs) that the impact of the racial system of victimization is transmitted through the family.[44] Looking at the Negro family as a subsystem of the larger society, we agree with Billingsley that it is a highly adaptive mechanism for the survival of black people in a white world.

THE ITALIAN FAMILY

The study of family patterns among ethnic groups is a valuable approach to the analysis of the processes of acculturation and assimilation—and of the barriers thereto. Earlier writers called attention to the closely knit family of southern Italian background dominated by the father, a domination more benevolent than tyrannical. Authority over a child was held to be absolute until the latter's marriage, and included such important decisions as choice of occupation and selection of a marriage partner. Even after marriage the control often was maintained to a high degree.[45]

A report by Gans of a no-longer-existing inner-city Boston neighborhood called the West End, particularly of the native-born Americans of Italian descent who lived there prior to 1960, provides much material of interest on the Italian-American family. In

[40] Ira L. Reiss, "Premarital Sexual Permissiveness Among Negroes and Whites," *ASR*, Oct., 1964, pp. 697–698. This study is based on a high school and college probability sample of 903 students ages 16–22 and an adult sample of 1515 individuals aged 21 and older drawn randomly from across the nation.

[41] Rainwater, *op. cit.*, pp. 190–191. On the attitudes of lower-class Negro men and women toward getting married, as well as the causes of marital breakup, see *ibid.*, pp. 187–189, 192–194, and Bernard, *op. cit.*, pp. 70, 76–77.

[42] Rainwater, *op. cit.*, p. 199.

[43] *Ibid.*, pp. 205–206.

[44] Billingsley, *op. cit.*, pp. 32, 156–157; Rainwater, *op. cit.*, p. 200.

[45] For a review of studies of first-generation, second-generation, and third-generation Italian families in the United States, see Joseph Lopreato, *Italian Americans*, Random House, 1970, pp. 57–87.

this analysis, the life of the West Ender took place within three interrelated groups: the primary group (a combination of family and peer relationships that Gans calls the *peer group society*); the secondary group (the small array of Italian institutions, voluntary organizations, and other social groups that supported the peer group society, called by Gans the *community*); and the outgroup, called in this study the *outside world*, a variety of non-Italian institutions in the West End, in Boston, and in the United States that affected the West Ender's life. The peer group involves persons of the same sex, age, and life-cycle status, and it includes friendships, cliques, informal clubs, and gangs, as well as family life. During adulthood West Enders spent almost as much time with siblings, in-laws, and cousins as with their spouses and more time than with parents, aunts, and uncles. The *family circle* is the basis of the adult peer group society, but the informal rules of selection rest less on closeness of kinship ties than on compatibility. An important aspect of the relationship between marriage and the peer group society was the tendency of husbands and wives to take their troubles less to each other than to brothers, sisters, other relatives, or friends. Thus, "men talk things over with brothers, women with sisters and mothers; each . . . remains on his side of the sexual barrier." Although marriage partners at the end of the 1950s were much less "close" than those in the middle class, Gans discovered some signs of the eventual disappearance of the segregated conjugal pattern.[46]

Between the first and second generation, the major change has been that of bringing the men into the house for their evening activities. While Italians have never been frequenters of neighborhood taverns, the immigrant generation did set up club houses for card playing and male sociability that kept some men away from the house after work. These have disappeared, however, and . . . second-generation men now segregate themselves from the women inside the home, and spend only one or two evenings a week in activities 'with the boys.' The women

also have begun to conceive of their husbands as helping them in the home, although they are not yet ready to insist or even ask for their aid. The move to the suburbs is probably one indication of the ascendancy of the wife to greater equality, for in these areas, where the joint conjugal pattern is dominant, it is somewhat harder for the man to maintain the old pattern.[47]

The West End family was an adult-centered one, that is, a household where adult wishes were satisfied first. Early in life children were expected to behave in ways pleasing to adults, except that, in their own peer group, they could act their own age as long as they did not get into trouble. Gans found that parent-child relationships were almost as segregated as male-female ones. Parents brought up their children more or less impulsively, without the "self-conscious, purposive child-rearing" found in the middle class, and their concern about the possibility of downward mobility was stronger than a desire for upward mobility.[48]

Gans makes a distinction between his subjects in the West End as "working-class" people and persons of lower-class status. The working-class subculture is characterized by the dominant role of the family circle, and everything outside this group is viewed either as contributing to its maintenance or to its destruction. From his point of view, the lower-class subculture is characterized by the mother-centered family and the marginal male. If a family circle exists, it includes only female relatives. The middle-class subculture is based on the nuclear family and its desire for upward mobility. Where the family circle exists, it plays only a secondary role. The middle-class family is a child-centered family. Both in the lower-middle-class and in the upper-middle-class, people tend to participate in a larger number of peer groups, often based on specific interests, in contrast to working-class people who remain largely in one peer group. The professional upper-middle-class, organized around the nuclear family, emphasizes individual development and self-expression.[49]

46 Gans, *op. cit.*, p. 53.

47 *Ibid.*, p. 53.
48 *Ibid.*, pp. 36–60.
49 *Ibid.*, pp. 41, 244–248.

THE MEXICAN-AMERICAN FAMILY

Acculturation has been occurring at a slower rate and to a lesser degree among Mexican-Americans than in other ethnic groups in the United States. In material culture, Mexicans differ little from Anglo-Americans, and changes have been made in medical practices and in the customs regarding godparenthood. They have acquired English in varying degrees, and their Spanish has become somewhat Anglicized. Some changes have occurred in family organization, and significant changes have been taking place in child training and in courtship practices. Nevertheless, as Simmons remarks, "it is the exceedingly rare Mexican-American, no matter how acculturated he may be to the dominant society, who does not in some degree retain the more subtle characteristics of his Mexican heritage, particularly in his conception of time and in other fundamental value orientations, as well as in his modes of participation in interpersonal relations."[50] In Simmons' view, mutual stereotyping, the exclusionary practices of Anglo-Americans, and the isolation practices of Mexican-Americans maintain the separateness of the two groups. Mexican-American culture represents the most effective means Mexican-Americans have been able to develop for coping with their changed environment. Old ways will be exchanged for new ways only if these seem to be more rewarding and if the individuals have full opportunity to acquire and use the new ways.[51]

Bogue concluded that the Mexican-Americans constitute "the only ethnic group for which a comparison of the characteristics of the first and second generation fails to show a substantial intergenerational rise in socio-economic status."[52] The considerable variations in the background and social positions of the Mexican-American population are reflected in the three levels of acculturation given in Madsen's study of Hidalgo County in southeastern Texas: (a) traditional folk culture, (b) individuals caught in value conflicts between two cultures, and (c) those who have achieved status in the English-speaking world.

Heller's study of high school seniors suggests that an important factor in the slow upward mobility of Mexican-Americans is their high birth rate. She found that the avenues of mobility of Mexican-American students differed significantly with size of family but not much with parental occupation, education, or country of birth.[53] A study of 1950 Census data concerning the marital status by age and sex of second-generation Americans according to 13 countries of parental origin showed that in each of six age-sex classes the proportion of second-generation Americans who had never married was higher than that of the total white population of comparable age and sex. Considerable variation was found, however, among the ethnic groups, with Americans of Mexican descent least likely to marry late or never and Americans of Irish descent most likely to do so. Heer concludes that there is considerable support for the hypothesis that "the percentage never married among young adults in each ethnic group is a function both of the aspiration for high socioeconomic status in that group and of its attitude toward birth control."[54] There is a positive correlation between late marriage and membership in an ethnic group that exhibits high socioeconomic aspiration; and there is an inverse relationship between late marriage and ethnic-group opposition toward birth control.

Regardless of social class, the main social identification of Mexican-Americans continues to be with the family.[55] In a world that often seems to be hostile, it is a sanctuary. Today a conflict exists between the Anglo-

[50] Ozzie G. Simmons, "The Mutual Images and Expectations of Anglo-Americans and Mexican-Americans," *Daedalus*, Spring, 1961, pp. 286–299.

[51] *Ibid.*

[52] Donald J. Bogue, *The Population of the United States*, Free Press, 1959, p. 372 (quoted in Celia S. Heller, *Mexican American Youth: Forgotten Youth at the Crossroads*, Random House, 1966, p. 5).

[53] Heller, *op. cit.*, pp. 32–33.

[54] David M. Heer, "The Marital Status of Second-Generation Americans," *ASR*, Apr., 1961, pp. 233–239.

[55] William Madsen, *Mexican-Americans of South Texas*, Holt, Rinehart & Winston, 1964, p. 44; Arthur J. Rubel, *Across the Tracks: Mexican Americans in a Texas City*, Univ. of Texas Press, 1966, pp. 99, 100.

American value of individualism and the Mexican-American stress on family solidarity. In the upbringing of Latin children generally, the emphasis given to such values as family ties, honor, masculinity, and living in the present do not contribute to future advancement. Values that are conducive to the development of mobility aspirations—independence, achievement, and deferred gratification—are not stressed. Heller says that love for children is not conditional on level of performance, as it is often reported to be among middle-class Anglo-American parents, nor is the mechanism of shame, common among Jews and Japanese, used to spur achievement in Mexican-American families.[56] Heller found that few Mexican-American homes stress higher education or intellectual effort.

The nucleus of the Mexican-American family consists of parents and their children, but grandparents, especially paternal grandparents, and parents' brothers and sisters, particularly mother's sisters, are respected and obeyed. First cousins are almost as close as brothers and sisters; the relationship between female first cousins is unusually strong. In addition to the ties within the extended family, the *compadres* (coparents who are not genetic relatives) are bound to provide advice and help.[57]

Male dominance has been one of the noteworthy characteristics of the Mexican-American family. Also respect for one's family elders has been a major organizing principle. One young wife in a South Texas city said: "In *la raza,* the old order the younger, and the men the women." According to traditional norms, the father is the unquestioned head of the family and the mother is the affectional figure. The father is entitled to the respect, obedience, and services of his wife and children. Extraordinary respect is shown the mother and father by their children. In their study of Mexican-Americans in the village of Atrisco, Kluckhohn and Strodbeck found that no record of accomplishment was ever regarded as a substitute for a son's or daughter's obedient attitude to parents. They say: "A daughter might make a good marriage, a son might become more successful financially than others at his age; but should either fail to adhere to the standards of filial respect, he or she was a *mal hijo* or *mal hija* (bad son or bad daughter)."[58] Although respect for one's elders in general is largely a thing of the past, visitors are expected to acknowledge the supremacy of the male head within his own home.

Ideally, the wife and mother is submissive, unworldly, and concerned about the welfare of her husband and children. In a study of Americans of Mexican descent in a Spanish-speaking enclave on the edge of San Jose, California, Margaret Clark found that some change toward a more equal relationship between spouses—"not always apparent to Anglo observers"—is occurring. Actually, Heller says, the wife exercises a considerable amount of control within the home because the husband does not concern himself with the details of the household. In the absence of the father, family authority is vested in the oldest male wage earner. Even when the father is present, the oldest son, especially after adolescence, may have considerable authority. Clark cites a case of a brother siding with his sister in her dispute with their mother concerning American dating patterns. When the father agreed with the son, the mother said nothing more because, as the boy himself said: "even a mother won't dispute her oldest son."[59]

With the exception of children in lower-lower-class families, where boys and girls may be assigned exacting household tasks while their parents work in the fields, the relationship between parents and children is relatively permissive. In the parent-child relationship, the authoritative role of the

[56] Heller, *op. cit.,* pp. 34–35, 39; Madsen, *op. cit.,* p. 46.

[57] Madsen, *op. cit.,* pp. 46–47; Rubel, *op. cit.,* pp. 55–56; Heller, *op. cit.,* p. 34.

[58] Florence R. Kluckhohn and F. L. Strodbeck, *Variations in Value Orientations,* Harper & Row, 1961, p. 196.

[59] Margaret Clark, *Health in the Mexican-American Culture,* Univ. of California Press, 1959, pp. 133–157; Madsen, *op. cit.,* p. 54; Heller, *op. cit.,* p. 35.

father begins with the onset of puberty and "reason." Male children are indulged and are given much more freedom than are their sisters. Only in anglicized families are restraints on the behavior of teen-age girls relaxed.

Traditionally, the place of a woman in the Mexican-American family has been in the home. Rubel says: "Her friends and confidants are restricted to her mother, her sisters, and her close female relatives. . . . The striking dependence of a Mexican-American woman on a minimal unit of female relatives is intensified by the enjoined aloofness between the woman and her close male relatives. Given the little world of familiars upon whom an adult woman is forced to depend, each of the others in that group is of critical importance to her. . . . The marriage of a daughter threatens to fracture a group already overstrained by interdependency."[60] Heller attributes the changes in the norms of feminine behavior now occurring to the adolescent girl's revolt against female confinement at home rather than to changes in early home socialization.[61] Similarly, Clark found that the most effective control of teenagers comes from their peers.

According to traditional belief, the husband can hardly be expected to remain faithful to his wife, but she is expected to maintain absolute sexual fidelity and to regard his behavior with tolerance. Marital conflict may result from the male desire to prove his prowess outside the home. As Madsen points out, however, the Mexican-American community maintains a system of checks to prevent the male from threatening his domestic life with extramarital adventures, primarily through its expectation that no activity of a husband will interfere with his obligations to his wife and children. In New Lots, a city across the border from Mexico in southeastern Texas, where Mexican-Americans constitute 75 percent of the population, Madsen found that marital problems caused by sex are insignificant compared to the conflict in roles occasioned by

Anglo influences. He writes: "The husband's authority and the wife's submissiveness are both changing in response to the Anglo example. In general, the role conflict is weak in the lower-lower class and begins to emerge in the upper-lower class. It is primarily a middle-class phenomenon. Both the elite and the liberal upper class have worked out more clearly defined roles than have the partially-anglicized Latins in the middle segment of society."[62] Clark mentions that sometimes wives openly defy male authority despite the fact that theoretically they are subservient to their husbands. Madsen found that the conservative Latin wife is a skilled manipulator of her husband, using as her weapons in disguised form his own self-esteem, his *machismo* (manliness), and his role as provider and protector. Among Mexican-Americans the divorce rate is low. The involvement of two entire families strengthens the bonds of marriage, as do the sacred vows taken in the church.

Marriage patterns are influenced by, and influence, the extent to which wives work outside the home. This varies as Nye and Hoffman point out, by ethnic background. They note that in certain areas Japanese-American women are the most highly represented in the work force, followed by Negro women, Puerto Rican, "white" women, Chinese, Indian, and Mexican, respectively. They add that this order does not follow the economic position of these groups nor does it reflect directly such factors as family size. They say: "The Puerto Rican group has a relatively high female employment rate and the Mexican group, a low one, although both are predominantly Catholic, Spanish-speaking, and economically underprivileged." As they indicate, data on single women, married women without children, and married women with children would show whether attitudes toward gainful employment apply to women in general in these groups or to mothers only.[63]

In the city the Mexican peasant family

---

[60] Rubel, *op. cit.*, p. 78.
[61] Heller, *op. cit.*, p. 36.

[62] Madsen, *op. cit.*, pp. 49–50.
[63] F. Ivan Nye and Lois W. Hoffman, *The Employed Mother in America*, Rand McNally, 1963, pp. 21–22.

undergoes considerable change. Low incomes necessitate the keeping of roomers, and the resulting overcrowding has a deteriorating effect on family life. The father's exercise of moral protection over the wife and children decreases as the structure of the family is modified. In the urban environment the children speak English, attend church to please their parents but go irregularly, do not belong to any Mexican clubs, become competitive, give up holiday celebrations after marriage, and settle down as American working-class and white-collar people.

THE PUERTO RICAN FAMILY

One million of the three and one-half million Puerto Ricans live in the United States, more than 600,000 of them in New York City. The Puerto Rican way of life has persisted, especially among the low-income group, due in part to the maintenance of close ties with Puerto Rico. Puerto Rican migration to the States is a two-way rather than a one-way movement. In 1960 the net migration to the United States was 20,000, but Puerto Ricans made almost a million trips back and forth. In Lewis's sample of Puerto Rican migrants living in New York City, the majority had made a three-step migration—from a rural birthplace in Puerto Rico, to a San Juan slum, to New York.[64] A typical migration pattern involves the father migrating alone, staying with relatives and friends, finding a job and housing, and then bringing over the rest of the family. Thus, many families are divided for some time, and if they are ever united, show considerable differences in knowledge of English, assimilation, and in other respects. A second pattern is that of a woman with children who leaves because her husband has deserted her or who has decided to leave home and go to New York "where jobs are plentiful, where the government is reputed to be 'for the women and the children,' and where relief is plentiful."[65]

In the Lewis study, the average household size in New York was four per dwelling unit, smaller than in the Puerto Rican sample. Although Puerto Ricans in New York subscribe to no concept of family planning, the desired number of children seems to be two or three. In 1958, Padilla found that sterilization of women was the preferred means of birth control among those born in Puerto Rico. Among adults reared in New York, sterilization was regarded less favorably.[66]

Among Puerto Ricans in New York City two types of marriage are recognized: the legal and the consensual. A legal marriage is more desirable, but in everyday life there may be little difference between the two. In New York the nuclear family is more clearly distinguished from the extended ("united") family and it is of greater importance than it is in Puerto Rico.[67] In terms of patterns of household organization and living, the two main types of families are the nuclear family and the joint family. The nuclear family has several forms: (1) stable couple with no children; (2) stable couple and their children (their own, theirs "by rearing," and those who are "staying" with them); (3) stable couple and their children, plus children of prior relationships; (4) one parent and his or her children; and (5) one parent, his or her children, and a temporary spouse. Joint families consist of two nuclear families living as a single family unit under the same roof on a common budget.

Among adults who have grown up in New York, the desired residence is away from the parents' household, and, preferably, in their own household. With their greater emphasis on obligations toward kin, migrants are more inclined to modify household arrangements.

In the joint family, the members of three generations share the same household under the authority of a grandparent, usually a grandmother who is better off financially than her children. Her married children who have had difficulties maintaining their own

---

[64] Oscar Lewis, *La Vida*, Random House, 1965, pp. xi, xii, xxxviii.

[65] Nathan Glazer and Daniel P. Moynihan, *Beyond the Melting Pot*, M.I.T. Press and Harvard, 1963, pp. 122–123.

[66] Elena Padilla, *Up from Puerto Rico*, Columbia, 1958, pp. 111–112.

[67] *Ibid., passim.*

independent households, as well as her un-married grown children, find economic and social security there. Despite its advantages, the joint family has certain weaknesses. Padilla says: "The conflicts of the young with the old, of the individual who has grown up in New York with his Puerto Rican-oriented parents, and the conflicts which are generated by the constellation of authority versus roles of subordination may be exacerbated for those who live within such a unit."[68]

Lewis found that the proportion of couples living in free union increased in New York compared with Puerto Rican slums, as did the number of women who were divorced, separated, or abandoned. In the New York sample,[69] half of the marriages were con-sensual and one quarter of the households were headed by a woman who had separated from her husband. Forty percent of the wives in New York were gainfully employed, mostly in factories.[70] Incomes of the New York families were from three to four times larger than those of families in the San Juan sample. Forty-four percent of the New York group had family incomes of $4,000 or over, compared with 4 percent of all families in the La Esmeralda slum. Only 2 percent of the New York families had incomes below $1,000, compared to 44 percent for the San Juan groups.[71] The educational level of the New York sample was higher than the Puerto Rican average—6.5 years of school-ing compared to 3.6 in Puerto Rico. Among the migrants, school dropouts were high and only 4 percent of the New York families had children in school beyond the tenth grade.[72]

Despite recent social changes in Puerto Rico, boys are still left to a great extent to raise themselves. Girls, however, are care-fully watched and escape relatively early into marriage and motherhood. In New York, taking the perspective of the Puerto Rican parent, these traditional patterns raise serious problems. Glazer and Moynihan say:

If the boys are left to themselves they find bad friends, may take to drugs, will learn to be dis-respectful and disobedient. And even if a boy survives the streets morally, how is he to survive them physically, with cars and trucks whizzing by, and tough Negro and Italian boys ready to beat him up under slight provocation? If the girls are guarded, are raised in the house as proper girls should be, they become resentful at a treatment that their classmates and friends are not subjected to. In addition, guarding in Puerto Rico means to keep an eye on one's daughters in a community where everyone was known and you knew everyone. Here, since the streets are dangerous it means keeping the girl literally in the house.[73]

Puerto Rican migrants in New York place greater emphasis on close relationships with relatives on the mother's side than with paternal relatives. The mother is regarded as the dependable and loving person to whom children may turn for help, and she in turn may look to her own mother, brother, or sister for help. Her husband is supposed to be self-reliant and to protect his own family and kin. Although help may be denied be-cause "things have changed" or because one "cannot afford it," kinship ties through the mother's line remain strong, especially in those families where the mother brought up the children without much contact with the father or his family.

Special friends may be brought into the family group through coparenthood. Co-parents are selected from favorite relatives, immediate family members, and special friends, and, when an individual becomes a coparent to another, "he knows that from that moment on he is expected to give and can also expect to receive much greater loyalty, affection, respect, cooperation, and services from the person who has become his coparent."[74]

Children are regarded as essential to

---

[68] *Ibid.*, p. 142.

[69] Fifty families of migrants who were related to families in the Puerto Rican sample were located and studied. Lewis, *op. cit.*, pp. xxxvii–xxxviii.

[70] Employment opportunities open to Puerto Ricans in this New York sample were limited but greater than in Puerto Rico. All but a few of the adults' oc-cupations were jobs which required few formal skills or education. Two-thirds of the employed adults were operatives. In this survey, 80 percent of all working adults were unionized, but few were more than dues-paying members.

[71] Lewis, pp. xxxix–xl.

[72] Lewis, p. xl.

[73] Glazer and Moynihan, *op. cit.*, pp. 123–124.

[74] Padilla, *op. cit.*, p. 121.

married life, but whether the children are legitimate or not does not influence greatly the attitudes and feelings of the parents toward their offspring. According to Padilla, "essentially, all the children are treated alike, except that the real parent is expected to show greater favor and kindness to his own children."

Children become more of a strain for the Puerto Rican mother in New York. Instead of having someone around to relieve her in the care of her children—a mother, a sister, an aunt, a *comadre*—she may have no one next door or in the same housing project on whom she can rely. One social scientist who has observed these families feels that the more traditional Puerto Rican family in New York does a better job of bringing up children than the nuclear family. In the latter family the mother is likely to resent her lack of help in child care.[75] For Puerto Ricans, another aspect of child rearing in New York is that neighborhoods are no longer exclusive to one ethnic group. In the low-rent housing under its management the city insists that the groups be mixed as much as possible (one-fifth of the city's low-cost housing is now occupied by Puerto Ricans and one-seventh of the Puerto Rican population lives in these developments). The result is that the models of new conduct in rearing one's children include Negro, Jewish, and Italian styles of child rearing and child discipline, as well as the models advocated by welfare workers and the settlement houses. As Glazer and Moynihan point out, the Puerto Rican mother is at a loss in deciding the right course in rearing her children.[76]

Lewis attributes much of the high level of marital conflict among Puerto Rican families in New York to the employment of women outside the home. Such employment is seen as making the women more demanding of their husbands and as giving them a new sense of independence. Also, the male's position has been weakened by the stricter laws against wife-and-child beating and by larger family relief and child-aid programs. These factors are said to account largely for the increase in the number of abandonments, separations, consensual unions, and matrifocal families.[77]

Puerto Ricans in New York distinguish between "ancient" (*a la antigua*) families, authoritarian families ruled by the father or mother, and "modern" families, the "families of today." Younger parents, whether they grew up in New York or came recently from Puerto Rico, believe that fewer restrictions should be placed on children. A central authority, usually the father, still exists, but the difference is that the authority "is more flexible, less restrictive, and less formidable." Wives reared in New York express interest in an equalitarian type of family life, and, as a rule, husbands reared in New York do not object to their wives being employed, nor to helping in the household, nor to going out with their wives. Men who have migrated are likely to believe that a wife's place is "in the home." Wives in this group define a good husband as one who provides for his family's needs, exercises authority over the children, and shows his considerateness by helping in the house when his wife is sick.[78]

THE JEWISH FAMILY

Throughout their history Jews have placed a high value upon the family. Together with the synagogue and the school, it has constituted the basis of Jewish life. The founding of a family has been regarded not merely as a social ideal but as a religious duty. "The Rabbis declared that the first affirmative precept in the Bible was the injunction 'Be fruitful and multiply,' and they invested marriage with the highest communal significance. They despised the bachelor and pitied the spinster. Only he

[75] Joan Mencher, "Child Rearing and Family Organization Among Puerto Ricans in Eastville," unpublished doctoral dissertation, Columbia University, 1958. Quoted in Glazer and Moynihan, *op. cit.*, pp. 125–126.

[76] Glazer and Moynihan, *op. cit.*, pp. 126.

[77] Lewis, *op. cit.*, p. xlii.

[78] Padilla, *op. cit.*, pp. 150–152, 106, 160.

who had founded a house in Israel was worthy to be considered a full-fledged member of the community; only she who had become a mother in Israel had realized her destiny."[79] Jewish tradition stressed chastity of both the man and the woman before marriage, matrimonial fidelity on both sides, desire for large families, respect of children for their parents, and unlimited love and devotion of parents for their children. Women were not to enter public life but to devote themselves to domestic duties or assist their husbands in their work. Daughters remained at home until marriage, usually before the age of twenty. The husband's authority over his wife and children rested upon tradition rather than force.[80] Goldstein points out that in the time when the woman occupied a lower status in law and in the ritual of religion than the man, she was highly esteemed and the equal of man in the Jewish home.[81]

Today Jewish families have an overall pattern of stability. Comparative studies show that a smaller proportion of Jews than of the total population are divorced or have married more than once. Goldstein and Goldscheider observe that slight increases have occurred for more recent generations in the proportion of divorced or separated, in the extent of remarriage, and in the proportion living in nuclear households. These investigators found also that females were more concentrated in widowed and divorced categories than were men, due mainly to the greater longevity of women, the slightly higher rates of intermarriage among males, and the older ages at which males marry. A third finding concerning the stability of the Jewish family is that the social categories within the three generations that were more acculturated—suburbanites, the more educated, and Reform Jews—in general had higher divorce rates, a larger proportion of individuals who had married

more than once, and a higher proportion who were living in nuclear households. These differences were small, however, and the patterns were not distinct. The trend in age at marriage is downward among Jews, but Jews, continue to marry at later ages than do non-Jews.[82]

In the area of fertility and fertility planning, among religious groups, Jews (1) have the lowest current rate of reproduction, (2) expect and want the smallest families, (3) approve of contraception most strongly and are most likely to have used it, (4) are most likely to plan the number and spacing of their children, and (5) are most likely to use effective methods of contraception. In all of these matters, Catholics differ most from the Jews, with Protestants taking an intermediate position. Protestant-Jewish differences in the variables of the fertility complex appear to be a function of differences in a few strategic social and economic variables, and, when these background differences are controlled, the differences "are greatly diminished, disappear, or are even reversed." The differences between Catholics and non-Catholics increase rather than decrease when the effect of specific social and economic characteristics is controlled, indicating that "the persistent differences are unlikely to disappear simply as a result of movement to higher socioeconomic status among the Catholic population."[83] Goldstein and Goldscheider attribute the long history of low Jewish fertility in many countries to the social characteristics of Jews (long urban experience, high educational and economic status), cultural values (the aspirations of Jews for social mobility), and the insecurity of their minority status and desire for full acceptance in the non-Jewish world.[84]

An American Jewish social scientist who was born in Europe writes of the "degeneration in the American Jewish family" as the

[79] Israel Cohen, *Jewish Life in Modern Times*, Dodd, Mead, 1914, p. 40.

[80] Arthur Ruppin, *The Jews in the Modern World*, Macmillan, 1934, p. 277.

[81] S. E. Goldstein, *Meaning of Marriage and Foundations of the Family: A Jewish Interpretation*, Bloch, 1942, pp. 136–137.

[82] Sidney Goldstein and Calvin Goldscheider, *Jewish Americans*, Prentice-Hall, 1968, pp. 113–114.

[83] R. Freedman, P. K. Whelpton, and J. W. Smit, "Socio-Economic Factors in Religious Differentials in Fertility," *ASR*, Aug., 1961, pp. 608–614.

[84] Goldstein and Goldscheider, *op. cit.*, pp. 133–135.

"result of forces in the wider cultural scene: conflicting role expectations in marriage, discontinuity in the training process of children, emphasis on romantic irresponsibility in the courtship techniques, decline in useful functions performed by children in the home or out, lack of religious activities in the home, emphasis upon youth, speed, and material success, and the stress on enjoyment and consumption as against work and study." In addition, Kaplan says, there has been "an estrangement from traditional values of Jewish life, a stifling of the Jewish self-consciousness, and the general lack of identification with the broader aspects of Judaism."[85] He sees the typical Jewish child of today in rebellion against members of the older generation and the familial system they support.

Other students of the Jewish family do not share the point of view just stated. In a study concerned primarily with adolescence and religion, Rosen found that Jewish parents do not have as much influence as a religious referent as they do in the role of general significant other. In religion, parents compete with the rabbi and the religious teacher, persons who do not count as significant others in the everyday life of the adolescent. In Yorktown, the importance of the peer group in the development of religious attitudes proved to be quite strong. Informally organized cliques exerted greater power over teenagers than the formal youth groups. Peer group pressures resulted in a high degree of similarity of religious convictions, conduct, and self-evaluation among clique members. When the adolescent was caught between the cross-pressures of conflicting family and peer group expectation in religious matters such as the use of Jewish food, he tended to conform to the peer group's norms.[86]

In Lakeville, a midwestern suburban community of 25,000 with a Jewish population of 8000, Sklare and Greenblum found that the many Jewish residents who hold to a pattern of minimal ritualism rely primarily, and in some cases almost exclusively, on the religious school for the Jewish socialization of their children. Lakeville parents feel that their goal of transmitting a Jewish identity to their children is compatible with the modern views they hold on child rearing. Regardless of whether they are among the minority who feel that their homes should be more Jewish but find it difficult to change or among the majority who are satisfied with the level of Jewishness in their homes, the majority of Lakeville Jews are optimistic about the possibility of transmitting Jewish identity to their children. In this respect, they see one problem—the threat of intermarriage.[87]

It is estimated that two-thirds of American Jews live in suburban counties of metropolitan areas.[88] The consequences of this shift for Jewish family and community life, either for those who move or for those who remain in the city, are not entirely clear. Family life is affected to some extent by the change in organizational patterns in the suburbs. According to Fishman: "Whereas the earlier city organizational patterns frequently brought Jews together with non-Jews, or brought Jews themselves together for cultural-intellectual-ideological purposes, the newer suburban organizational patterns tend more frequently to involve only Jews, and . . . to bring Jews together for basically social-recreational purposes."[89] The movement of younger Jewish families out of the city has left "a numerically weakened and older Jewish population to cope with the problems of contributing to both Jewish and general facets of city life. The knowledge that they are a vanishing breed—that the Jewish future seems to be in another direction—may make the remaining Jewish city-dwellers even more sensitive to and resentful of the increas-

[85] Benjamin Kaplan, *The Jew and His Family*, Louisiana State Univ. Press, 1967, p. 171.

[86] Bernard C. Rosen, *Adolescence and Religion*, Schenkman, 1965, pp. 70, 199–200.

[87] Marshall Sklare and Joseph Greenblum, *Jewish Identity on the Suburban Frontier*, Basic Books, 1967, pp. 298, 306.

[88] Joshua A. Fishman, "Moving to the Suburbs: Its Possible Impact on the Role of the Jewish Minority in American Community Life," *Phylon*, Summer, 1963, p. 150.

[89] *Ibid.*, p. 151.

ing power of Negroes and other minorities that have nevertheless not risen as high as Jews in social status."[90]

Gordon says that the Jewish husband's position within the family has changed markedly because the demands of his business leave him little time for his family— at least this is what the businessman believes. The husband tends to regard, as his primary responsibility, providing economically for his family, and increasingly he may leave the rearing of the children to his wife. With the wife setting the standards, according to Gordon, a new "matriarchate" is developing.[91] Despite this observation, Gordon believes that the suburb has strengthened Jewish family life. He writes: ". . . the home remains the central institution in Jewish life, and the children are the center of attention and concern for their parents. Whatever the present weakness and defects of suburban life, it is my belief that they may be more than counterbalanced by a more closely-knit Jewish family life in the suburban home."[92] Many students of Jewish family life would not accept this sweeping generalization. Jewish family life is changing, but the changes depend in part on such factors as: type of city, region, proportion of Jews in the total population of the city, social class, generations in this country, religious subcategory, and so forth.

Goldstein and Goldscheider, in their study of Providence, Rhode Island, conclude that, in nearly all respects, Jews have become integrated into the majority community within three generations. While further social and cultural changes among Jews, as well as in the general population, will result in greater behavioral similarities among the members of the two groups, they predict that the Jewish community will remain structurally separate and that the Jewish identity will be continued. In their view, "through Jewish education, as well as through the expectations imposed on Jews by their Jewish and non-Jewish neighbors,

a new type of Jew is developing in the United States, one who feels equally comfortable being both a Jew and an American."[93]

Although its distinctiveness is decreasing, Jewish family life is still a strong unifying force. It is possible that Jewish family solidarity tends to be strengthened by existing prejudice, whereas the effect of prejudice and discrimination on more economically disadvantaged groups without traditions of family solidarity is to weaken the family.

THE CHINESE FAMILY

Family life among Americans of Chinese descent, as among other groups, is undergoing change. Lee reports that the practice of parental arrangement of marriages is less popular today, but that it has not been entirely abandoned. A study of 100 American-Chinese youths showed that 20 percent of their parents adhered to this custom and expected their children to comply. According to Lee, the arrival of foreign-born immigrant females since World War II has revived the custom despite the fact that these women grew up in China during a period when "blind marriage" had been denounced and laws against it had been enacted and enforced for more than twenty years.[94]

The selection of mates for the second generation is narrowed when clan and family exogamy must be observed strictly. ". . . The children whose parents belonged to either a four-clan association or a family association are considered 'cousins,' although no actual blood relationship is involved. . . . To solve the problem, Chinese-Americans have been forced to follow one of three courses: (1) remain single and stay in the city of their birth; (2) find mates in other Chinatowns; or (3) permit parents to arrange a suitable marriage."[95] According to

[90] *Ibid.*, p. 152.
[91] Albert I. Gordon, *Jews in Suburbia*, Beacon Press, 1959, p. 60.
[92] *Ibid.*, p. 84.

[93] Goldstein and Goldscheider, *op. cit.*, p. 243.
[94] Rose Hum Lee, *The Chinese in the United States of America*, Hong Kong Univ. Press, 1960, p. 194.
[95] Rose Hum Lee, "The Decline of Chinatowns in the United States," *AJS*, Mar., 1949, p. 430.

Lee, the second course is followed more extensively than the other two, with the result that the Chinese population has been undergoing redistribution to larger western and eastern Chinatowns where many clans reside.

Lee distinguishes four major family types: (1) early immigrant, (2) recent immigrant—the "separated" and the war brides, (3) the stranded, and (4) the established.[96]

The war wives were 10 years or more younger than the "separated" wives—most were between 20 and 22 years of age when they arrived, but the range was from 17 to 25. The great majority were from rural villages, had had a few years of education in the village schools, and were more "modern" than the "separated" wives. In the United States there was a tendency for husbands and wives to reverse roles. Husbands did some shopping and performed some housework, an unthinkable practice in China. Mutual affection, when it developed, tended to be based on the common goals of Chinese family life—children and the perpetuation of the family line. Where such feeling did not eventually appear, "antipathies and hostilities permeated every phase of family living."

Most of the stranded families are first-generation immigrants. As the result of two generations emigrating and settling here together, there are some second- and third-generation families in this group. Lee says:

The second generation of these families were the older China-born children of wealthier families whose parents brought them over during World War II so they might continue their studies in a more peaceful atmosphere. In other instances, the children came first and the parents joined them later. After the members of this generation finished their education they married, and their children constituted the third generation. However, it is this [third] generation that will experience more marginality while it is the second [generation] in the established families. The overwhelming majority of the

stranded families are young adults who married here after 1950, and their children are young.[97]

The established families include all the units that came before World War II and their second-, third-, fourth- and fifth-generation descendants, approximately 55 percent of the American Chinese population in 1950.

The 1965 immigration law allows a potential of 20,000 Chinese immigrants per year. For the years 1966–1968, Chinese immigrants from Asia (Taiwan) numbered: 1966, 13,736: 1967, 19,741; 1968, 12,738.[98] If continued, increments of this size will have a significant impact, on a relatively small group, by increasing the ratio of foreign-born. On the other hand, there is the rapid economic rise of Chinese in Hawaii and on the West Coast particularly.

Lee cites a study of 80 families, approximately half of the established families in Chicago in 1950, that showed how extensively the traditional Chinese rural family had been changed in the United States. The degree of acculturation varied greatly in these families with respect to food habits, language spoken in the home, recreation, the celebration of Chinese festivals, reading materials, music, clothing, ancestor worship, etc. Attempts to gain conformity on the part of children to the Chinese way of life had proved unsuccessful, and "the overwhelming majority of the parents compromised with their offspring to avoid conflicts."

In earlier years racial-cultural barriers cut many Chinese-American young people off from full membership in American society and threw them back upon their own group. During those years these barriers served to revive and stimulate pride in Chinese culture.[99] In the past few decades a number of influences have affected Chinese-American life in important ways. Wars and depressions have weakened the economic and social structures of Chinatowns and have helped

---

[96] Rose Hum Lee, *The Chinese in the United States of America*, p. 186. Unless otherwise indicated, the data in this section are based on chaps. 10 and 11 of this work.

[97] *Ibid.*, p. 232.
[98] U.S. Department of Justice, *Annual Report of Immigration and Naturalization Service*, 1968.
[99] Norman S. Hayner and Charles N. Reynolds, "Chinese Family Life in America," *ASR*, Oct., 1937, p. 637.

to bring about a redistribution of their populations.[100] With increasing acculturation the Chinese have tended to disperse outward from the ghetto. Prejudice and discrimination against the Chinese have decreased, making it unnecessary for them to practice voluntary segregation. In the metropolitan area of New York, only 8000 of the 33,000 Chinese live in and around Chinatown. The purpose of living in Chinatown has shifted from defense to business.[101]

The entrance of Hawaii as a state increased the Chinese population of the United States by one-sixth and added a group of relatively high occupational status. As the process of acculturation has continued, the Chinese have attained higher status through education, professional training, and entrance into American business and industry. Lee points out that as persons of Chinese ancestry lose all but their physical characteristics and as the larger society becomes more tolerant of white-Mongoloid marriages, intermarriage will increase. Thus the future of Chinese-Americans would seem to lie along the lines followed by other small minority groups which have become integral parts of American society.[102]

THE JAPANESE FAMILY

Prior to World War II, there were social, occupational, and economic barriers that restricted the Japanese in their relations with white persons and which caused them to associate largely with other Japanese.[103] The Japanese-American population was rather sharply divided into a young group and an old group, with virtually no middle-aged representatives. The average age of the Nisei, the native-born American generation, was 19 in 1939; of Issei, the original immigrant stock, 58; and the average period of residence was 30 years. To these two groups a third should be added: the Kibei (the Nisei who had spent much or all of their lives in Japan and who had returned to the United States).[104]

Bradford Smith points out that "the real trouble was that the Nisei, having rejected the land and culture of their parents, had been rejected by their own land. Though far more American that Japanese, they were not entirely at home in either culture. As a result of numerous rejections they developed a marginal culture of their own. They were socially at ease only among themselves, lacking the etiquette for Japanese company and fearing always the intrusion of prejudice in an American setting. . . ."[105]

About 112,000 Japanese, or 88.5 percent of the total Japanese population in the United States, lived in the Pacific Coast states at the time of Pearl Harbor. Between March and November, 1942, approximately 100,000 Japanese, two-thirds of whom were citizens, were moved from their homes, first into temporary assembly centers and then into the relocation centers in western and southwestern states.[106] They were faced with wholly new conditions of life. There was little family privacy, and the disciplining of children became difficult in the presence of many people. The centers stimulated the Nisei's emancipation from the family by granting economic independence and by strengthening peer groups against family groups.[107] Later, many families were split when older sons and daughters left the centers while the first-generation parents and younger children remained behind. Within two years after the relocation centers were closed Japanese-Americans "with great determination made substantial progress to-

[100] Lee, "The Decline of Chinatowns in the United States," pp. 430–431.

[101] D. Y. Yuan, "Voluntary Segregation: A Study of New York Chinatown," *Phylon*, Fall, 1963, pp. 255–265.

[102] Lee, *The Chinese in the United States of America*, p. 251.

[103] Bureau of Sociological Research, Colorado River War Relocation Center, "The Japanese Family in America," *Annals*, Sept., 1943, p. 153.

[104] F. J. Brown and J. S. Roucek (eds.), *One America*, Prentice-Hall, 1945, p. 329.

[105] Bradford Smith, *Americans from Japan*, Lippincott, 1948, p. 252.

[106] Carey McWilliams, *Brothers Under the Skin*, Little, Brown, 1943, p. 173; and Bureau of Sociological Research, Colorado River War Relocation Center, *op. cit.*, p. 150.

[107] Leonard Broom and John I. Kitsuse, *The Managed Casualty: The Japanese-American Family in World War II*, Univ. of California Press, 1956, p. 40.

ward again making a stable place for themselves in the metropolitan area [of Los Angeles county]."[108]

A study of Japanese-Americans in Chicago after World War II found that their quick adaptation to the American setting arises in considerable part from "the Japanese system of values and personality structure."[109] The values referred to here, and the adaptive mechanisms of the Japanese Americans, were found to be highly compatible with those of the American middle class. Because of this situation, Caudill concluded:

[the Nisei] tend to be favorably evaluated by the American middle class, not as isolated individuals, but as a group. Hence, in Chicago where they are removed from the high level of discrimination to be found on the Pacific Coast, the Nisei can be thought of as an entire group which is mobile toward the American middle class. They are tremendously helped in this process by the praise both of their parents and of the white middle class; conversely, they are thrown into conflict over their inability to participate as fully as they would like in the middle class way of life, and at the same time fulfill their Japanese obligations to their parents.[110]

Two decades later, Kitano confirmed this finding. He writes: "All in all, Japanese reverence for hard work, achievement, self-control, dependability, manners, thrift, and diligence were entirely congruent with American middle-class perceptions. . . . the most important single intervening variable in explaining the rapid upward mobility of the Japanese was its use of the educational opportunities provided it by the larger society."[111]

Even today, the model for the Japanese-American family is more vertically structured and male-dominated than comparable majority families. In the Japanese-American social system, strong emphasis is still placed on the intact family, prescribed roles, and a high degree of family and community reinforcement. The stress on duty, obligation, and responsibility, as well as on feelings of guilt and shame, has resulted in a high degree of conformity and little social deviance. Although the current generation is more likely to consult experts, inside or outside the ethnic group, the pattern of in-group dependence in solving problems is changing only slowly. Because of the influence of such factors as acculturation, generational differences, and social class, changes in Japanese family behavior are occurring. According to Kitano, among the Issei "considerations of security prevailed over considerations of advancement, and, as is typical of lower-class life, chance rather than plan played an important part in their view of life." Although considerable change is seen in the behavior of the Japanese-American especially among the Sansei (third generation), Kitano concludes that change in Japan has been more dramatic in terms of moving away from the old, traditional Japanese culture.[112]

CONCLUSION

A number of minority families have been briefly examined. All of them, as well as some that have not been considered here, have much in common with other families in the United States. Although each minority family has certain features peculiar to it, several qualities seem to characterize nearly all of them.

1. Each minority group includes a range of family types. One cannot speak of "the" Negro family, for example.

2. In the case of immigrant families, e.g., Chinese and Puerto Rican "separated" families, the nature of the husband-wife relationship in the United States depends, to a considerable extent, on the quality of the relationship achieved before the wife's arrival here.

3. A minority subculture represents the most effective means that the group has developed to adapt to its environment.

[108] Leonard Bloom and the Ruth Riemer, *Removal and Return: The Socio-Economic Effects of the War on Japanese Americans*, Univ. of California Press, 1949, pp. 4, 67.
[109] William Caudill, "Japanese-American Personality and Acculturation," *Genetic Psychology Monographs*, Feb., 1952, p. 29.
[110] *Ibid.*, p. 94.
[111] Harry H. L. Kitano, *Japanese Americans*, Prentice-Hall, 1969, p. 76.
[112] *Ibid.*, *passim*, especially pp. 66–78.

Family practices constitute an important part of that subculture.

4. There is often serious misunderstanding and conflict between parents and children in a minority group above and beyond that found generally in majority group families.

5. As they reach adulthood there is a strong tendency for minority children to establish more or less typical working-class, business-class, or professional-class American families.

The extent to which these new families approximate American family life in general would seem to depend upon several interrelated factors: amount of exposure to majority family patterns, urban, suburban, or rural residence, region of the country, degree of alienation between the elders and the young married people, and social class (with related variables such as occupation, income, education, neighborhood, etc.).

Chapter 16 / INTERMARRIAGE: INTERRACIAL, INTERFAITH, AND INTERETHNIC

Intermarriage here will include interracial, interfaith, and interethnic unions. The extensive sexual association of majority and minority men and women outside of marriage will also be considered.

RACE MIXTURE DURING THE SLAVERY PERIOD[1]

Sexual association between Whites and Negroes began with the introduction of Negroes into the colonies. Intercourse between the two races was not limited to white males and Negro females, and a considerable number of bastard children by Negro men were born to indentured white women. Marriages of Negroes and Whites occurred frequently enough to cause laws against such unions to be enacted. Later in the colonial period, censure and penalties were imposed almost exclusively on the association of Negro men and white women.

The evolution of slavery as a social institution did not decrease the sexual association of Negroes and Whites. The sale of mulatto women for prostitution became part of the slave trade in southern cities, and there were many casual relationships between white men and free Negro women. Where the associations became more or less permanent, as they did in Charleston, Mobile, and New Orleans, a system of concubinage developed. Intermixture of the races also occurred under various types of associations between the men of the master class and slave women on the plantations. At one end of the scale was physical compulsion and rape, with the

Negro woman becoming separated from her mulatto child at an early date. At the other extreme was the slaveholding aristocrat who took a mulatto woman as concubine and lived with her and their children affectionately and permanently. Between these two extremes were all degrees of attachment and involvement. Some men of the master class sold their own mulatto children. Others quickly abandoned their mistresses. The prestige of the white race was a factor in bringing about compliance of black and mulatto women. In many cases certain advantages came to the Negro woman, including freedom from field labor, better food and clothing, special privileges for her half-white child, and perhaps his eventual freedom.

NEGRO-WHITE EXTRAMARITAL SEXUAL RELATIONS IN RECENT YEARS

Emancipation brought profound social and personal disorganization to the former slaves. Promiscuity was common, and interracial sexual relations in the decades immediately following the Civil War were at least as frequent as they were during slavery. It is more difficult to ascertain early twentieth-century and present trends.[2] Most of the sociological investigations have brought the conclusion that interracial sexual relations have decreased.[3] In 1943 Charles Johnson found that the practice of sex relations, including the "keeping" of Negro "second wives," had been continued, particularly in the rural areas of the South.[4]

[1] This section is based largely on E. Franklin Frazier, *The Negro Family in the United States*, Citadel, rev. ed., 1948, chaps. 3–4. See also Otto Klineberg (ed.), *Characteristics of the American Negro*, Harper & Row, 1944, pp. 263–268; and Gunnar Myrdal, *An American Dilemma*, Harper & Row, 1944, pp. 123–127.

[2] Myrdal, *op. cit.*, pp. 127–128; also Klineberg (ed.), *op. cit.*, pp. 276–300.
[3] Charles S. Johnson, *Patterns of Negro Segregation*, Harper & Row, 1943, pp. 147, 292; Myrdal, *op. cit.*, p. 128.
[4] Johnson, *op. cit.*, p. 148.

The taboo on interracial sex relations seemed to be as strong in the border areas as in the South, although the penalties were not always so severe.[5] The taboo continues in the North, although it is often violated. Some interracial marriages occur and common-law alliances are more frequent. According to Johnson, ". . . The associations, while much limited and frowned upon in practice, are not as dangerously unnatural as in the South or in border areas; and this applies especially to the Negro residence districts in northern cities."[6]

INCIDENCE OF INTERMARRIAGE IN THE UNITED STATES

Racial intermarriage does not occur frequently in the United States. Religious intermarriage is somewhat more common, and ethnic intermarriage occurs most often.

Interreligious Marriages

A number of studies reveal the incidence of different types of religious intermarriage. A New Haven study was designed to discover whether general intermarriage or stratified intermarriage is taking place, that is, whether there is a single melting pot in the United States or one "with two or more separate compartments, each producing a special blend of its own." The main conclusions of this investigation follow:

The increasing intermarriage in New Haven is not general and indiscriminate but is channeled by religious barriers; and groups with the same religions tend to intermarry. Thus, Irish, Italians, and Poles intermarry mostly among themselves, and British-Americans, Germans, and Scandinavians do likewise, while Jews seldom marry Gentiles.

When marriage crosses religious barriers, as it often does, religion still plays a dominant role, especially among Catholics. The high frequency of Catholic nuptials sanctioning the outmarriages of Irish, Italians, and Poles implies

that their choice of spouses is determined largely by the willingness of their non-Catholic mates to be brought over to the church. Indeed, Catholic nuptials are increasing in marriages of Catholics with non-Catholics.

. . . Our main conclusion is . . . that assortative mating rather than random intermarriage has been occurring in New Haven since 1870 and that assimilation in this city is of a stratified character. The "melting-pot general-mixture" idea popularized by Zangwill and supported by others has failed to materialize in this particular community. Religious differences function as the chief basis of stratification.[7]

Hollingshead's study of five factors (race, age, ethnic origin, religion, and class) in the selection of marriage mates agrees with Kennedy's conclusions on the importance of religious barriers in New Haven intermarriages. Hollingshead, investigating all marriages in that city in 1948, found that religion divided the white race into three pools. "Persons in the Jewish pool in 97.1 percent of the cases married within their own group; the percentage was 93.8 for Catholics and 74.4 for Protestants."[8]

A comprehensive study of the rate of intermarriage between Catholics and non-Catholics by John L. Thomas indicates that New Haven is not representative, even of Connecticut, in its intermarriage patterns. According to Kennedy, the percentages of Italians, Irish, and Poles intermarrying with British-Americans, Scandinavians, Germans, and Jews were: 1870, 4.65 percent; 1900, 14.22 percent; 1930, 17.95 percent; and 1940, 16.29 percent. As we have noted, Hollingshead found that only 6.2 percent of the New Haven Catholics married outside their religious group. Thomas points out that the figures in the Kennedy and the

---

[5] *Ibid.*, p. 291.

[6] *Ibid.*, p. 150. For an interpretation of the attitudes of white persons toward alleged Negro sexuality, see chaps. 3 and 8 of this book.

[7] Ruby Jo Reeves Kennedy, "Single or Triple Melting-Pot? Intermarriage Trends in New Haven, 1870–1940," *AJS*, Jan., 1944, p. 339. A later report on intermarriage in New Haven resulted in approximately the same conclusions as the earlier study. In 1950, Italians and Poles were the only two large groups showing an increasing tendency toward intermarriage. Ruby Jo Reeves Kennedy, "Single or Triple Melting-Pot? Intermarriage in New Haven, 1870–1950," *AJS*, July, 1952, pp. 56–59.

[8] A. B. Hollingshead, "Cultural Factors in the Selection of Marriage Mates," *ASR*, Oct., 1950, p. 627.

Hollingshead studies refer to all intermarriages and not simply to those sanctioned by Catholic nuptials. In his study of interfaith marriages in Connecticut, Thomas discovered that "the rate for just the mixed marriages sanctioned by Catholic nuptials was 40.2 percent of all Catholic marriages in 1949." If the mixed marriages not sanctioned by Catholic nuptials were added, Thomas believes that the most conservative estimate would bring the total rate to more than 50 percent.[9] Thomas concludes that three

principal factors influence the intermarriage rates of Catholics: first, the relative percentage of Catholics in the total population (scarcity of prospective mates within the Catholic group occasions a high rate of intermarriage—provided that ethnic or other differences do not prevent contacts between Catholics and non-Catholics); second, the presence of cohesive ethnic groups within the community (loyalty to the group, social standing of the ethnic group, language, nationality prejudices, and religion combine to put a check on intermarriage); and third, the socioeconomic class of the Catholic population (in Thomas' study of the intermarriage patterns of 51,671 families distributed in thirty parishes of a large urban center the following percentages of mixed marriages in all Catholic marriages were found: lower rental area, 8.5; mixed lower and middle, 9.1; middle rental area, 12.0; mixed middle and upper, 16.3; upper rental area, 17.9; and suburban, 19.3).

The Kennedy and Hollingshead studies, as well as the special United States Census study of religion in 1957 (21.6 percent of Catholics were married to non-Catholics; 8.6 percent of Protestants were married to non-Protestants; and 7.2 percent of Jews were married to non-Jews) and the Thomas finding that approximately 30 percent of the marriages of Catholics are mixed, probably underestimate the extent of interfaith marriage. "Even if religion played no part whatsoever in marriage choice, approximately 70 percent of Protestant, 25 percent of Catholic, and 4 percent of Jewish marriages would be *intra*faith. For the country

[9] According to Thomas, there are no adequate data on the number of mixed marriages not sanctioned by Catholic nuptials. His study, which included all of the mixed marriages to be found in 132 parishes distributed throughout the East and Midwest, showed that 11,710 in 29,581 mixed marriages (39.6 percent) were not sanctioned by Catholic nuptials. He feels that this rate is fairly representative for the part of the country covered, but he does not predicate the same rate for other sections of the United States since his investigations show considerable sectional differences. Thus he finds that mixed marriages sanctioned by Catholic nuptials constituted 70 percent of the Catholic marriages in the dioceses of Raleigh, Charleston, and Savannah-Atlanta, but that they were only 10 percent for the dioceses of El Paso, Corpus Christi, and Santa Fe. "During the decade 1940–1950, mixed marriages sanctioned by Catholic nuptials approximated 30 percent of all Catholic marriages in the United States. The rate . . . for 1950 is 26.2." About 30 percent of the 912,851 Catholic marriages in the United States during the 1930s were mixed. John L. Thomas, "The Factor of Religion in the Selection of Marriage Mates," *ASR*, Aug., 1951, pp. 488, 489, 491. Loren E. Chancellor and Thomas P. Monahan, "Religious Preference and Interreligious Mixtures in Marriages and Divorces in Iowa," *AJS*, Nov., 1955, p. 237 report that state records in Iowa show that 42 percent of all marriages involving a Catholic in 1953 were mixed marriages. For "first" marriages the percentage was 35. If all civil marriages are eliminated, the percentages were 33 for the total and 29 for "first" marriages. (The *Catholic Directory* listed 30 percent of the marriages in Iowa in 1953 sanctioned by the Catholic Church as mixed.) For the years 1945 and 1955, Locke, Sabagh, and Thomas found high negative correlations between the interfaith marriage rates—at least for Catholics—and the percentage of Catholics in the population of the 48 states. Data on Catholics and Anglicans in Canada also support the hypothesis that the rate of interfaith marriage of a given religious group increases as the proportion of that group decreases in the population. Two additional hypotheses are stated: (1) that social distance may be one variable affecting the low intermarriage rates in some states in the United States (Catholics in Texas and New Mexico are predominantly Mexican-Americans, whereas a high percentage of Connecticut's Catholics are of Irish, Polish, or Italian origin), and (2) that the higher economic

status of a religious group, the higher the intermarriage rate (supporting data are cited from Arizona, where both income level and intermarriage rates of Catholics are higher than in Texas, and from two parishes in New Orleans). Harvey J. Locke, Georges Sabagh, and Mary Margaret Thomas, "Interfaith Marriages," *SP*, Apr., 1957, pp. 329–333. In 1962, 26.5 percent of all marriages involving Catholics were valid mixed marriages. According to the *Official Catholic Directory*, in the 26 Archdioceses in the United States, 24 percent were (valid) mixed marriages. In the Dioceses (covering smaller areas than the Archdioceses) 29 percent of the marriages were (valid) mixed marriages. Albert I. Gordon, *Intermarriage*, Beacon Press, 1964, p. 150.

as a whole, this means that about 55 percent of all marriages would be intrafaith and 45 percent interfaith if the religious beliefs of partners were a matter of pure chance. The 1957 census sample found that approximately 12 percent of the marriages were . . . across religious lines at the time of the census. In other words, over a quarter of the 'possible' interfaith marriages occurred."[10] Another reason for believing that these data underestimate the intermarriage rate is the failure in some studies to distinguish between interfaith couples prior to and after marriage. Because the conversion of one spouse after marriage is not uncommon, figures concerning interfaith marriage at the time of marriage are minimal figures.[11] Also, the census figures referred to are national data that do not take regional, class, educational, and racial differences into consideration. If white Protestants and Negro Protestants were tabulated separately, the inter-faith marriage rate of white Protestants would be found to be significantly higher than the total Protestant rate. Citing Heiss's midtown Manhattan finding that 21.4 percent of the Catholics, 33.9 percent of the Protestants, and 18.4 percent of the Jews in that area were intermarried, Yinger points out that a 25 percent intermarriage rate here means that 42 percent of the interfaith marriages that might have occurred did occur. While cautioning against generalizing from these data, he remarks that "they may indicate what takes place when the three religious groups live in quite close proximity."[12]

Rosenthal says that private communal surveys taken in the 1930s revealed that approximately 6 percent of Jewish families were intermarried. As mentioned earlier, the United States government survey of religious composition in 1957 showed that 7.2 percent of all Jewish families had a non-Jewish marriage partner. A survey of the Jewish population in Washington, D.C., indicated that the intermarriage rate is 12.2; in Montgomery County, 20.8 percent; in Prince George County, 20.8 percent; in Virginia, 34.2 percent. Marriage licenses in Iowa for 1953 showed that 31 percent of the marriages were mixed. In San Francisco, the proportion of mixed marriages was 17.2 percent, 20 percent on the Peninsula, and 37 percent in Marin County.[13] Cahnman says that it appears that high-status suburban counties have a high intermarriage rate, but that those for which data are available are not densely settled Jewish neighborhoods. Data from Forest Hills and West Rogers Park, as well as from New York and Chicago suburbs that are largely Jewish, might differ from those cited. Cahnman remarks that since "a high percentage of the younger generations in the newer areas receive a college education and . . . the intermarriage rate tends to be higher among college graduates . . . [the] chances are that the high-status neighborhoods, whether they harbor a considerable percentage of Jews or not, will be a jumping-off ground for accelerated social mobility and a large amount of out-marriage."[14]

Sklare points out a crucial element that has been generally overlooked in evaluating the 7.2 figure for Jewish intermarriage: that

---

[10] J. Milton Yinger, *Sociology Looks at Religion*, Macmillan, 1963, p. 83.

[11] In the Detroit area sample, Lenski found that 32 percent of the white Protestants and Catholics had outmarried, but at the time they were interviewed only 15 percent indicated that their marriage partner was of a different faith. See Gerhard Lenski, *The Religious Factor*, Doubleday, 1961. See also J. M. Yinger, "A Research Note on Interfaith Marriage Statistics," *Journal for the Scientific Study of Religion*, Spring, 1968, pp. 97–103; and P. H. Besanceney, "On Reporting Rates of Intermarriage," *AJS*, May, 1965, pp. 717–721.

[12] Yinger, *Sociology Looks at Religion*, p. 84.

[13] Erich Rosenthal, "Acculturation Without Assimilation? The Jewish Community of Chicago, Illinois," *AJS*, Nov., 1960, p. 288. Cahnman points out that available data on the intermarriage of Jews and non-Jews in the United States are insufficient because they do not include the cases where the spouse was converted to the religion of the other prior to marriage. The figures given in the government census, as well as the private studies in Washington, D.C., and San Francisco mentioned above, ascertain only those cases of intermarriage where the different religion of spouses is openly declared. In his opinion, as well as that of the Bureau of the Census, the recorded percentages of mixed couples are minimal figures. Werner J. Cahnman, "Introduction," in W. J. Cahnman (ed.), *Intermarriage and Jewish Life*, The Herzl Press, 1963, pp. 13–14, 179–181.

[14] Cahnman, *op. cit.*, p. 180.

figure constitutes the *ratio* of intermarried to inmarried couples and not the current rate of intermarriage among Jews. The statistic included persons who were married in Czarist Russia, members of the immigrant generation who were married in the United States, and people of the fourth generation. According to Sklare, the current rate may be at least double the 7.2 cumulative ratio. Even the cumulative ratio will increase greatly as first- and second-generation Jews constitute a smaller and smaller proportion of the total Jewish population.[15] Rosenthal says that the data on Washington, D.C. indicate that the intermarriage rate for Jews rises from about 1 percent among the first generation—the foreign-born immigrants—to 10.2 percent for the native-born of foreign parentage and to 17.9 percent of the native-born of native parentage (third and subsequent generations).[16] Analyzing 785 marriage records, the total number of all marriages involving Jews in Indiana in a four-year period (1960–1963), the same author found that the usual residence of groom and bride is a significant factor in the formation of Jewish intermarriages. His ecological analysis showed:

1. Couples who had eloped from contiguous states to Indiana had the highest level of intermarriage (67.4 percent). A detailed analysis of these extrastate marriages pointed to a causal relationship between elopement and intermarriage.
2. Couples with one partner usually residing in Indiana and the other outside the state had the lowest intermarriage rate (29.9 percent). It is assumed that these interstate marriages are arranged marriages or the result of a conscious effort to find a Jewish marriage partner.
3. Couples with both spouses residing within the state produce an intermediate level of intermarriage (49.0 percent). This means that a Jewish young man or woman who relies on finding a spouse close to home has a 50-50 chance of inmarriage.[17]

In a three-generational study of Jewish-Americans in Providence, Rhode Island, Goldstein and Goldscheider found that despite the relatively low rate of intermarriage, the rate is increasing among the young, the native-born American, and the suburbanites. They expect the overall rate of intermarriage to rise, but they point out that among the third generation of Jews and the suburbanites a higher proportion of intermarriages results in the conversion of the non-Jewish spouse to Judaism. Also, a large proportion of the children in such marriages are being raised as Jews. In Providence, the fertility patterns of the young intermarried couples more closely resemble those of the inmarried couples than was the case of the older age groups.[18]

A recent study of Jewish students in a

[15] Marshall Sklare, "Intermarriage and the Jewish Future," *Commentary*, Apr., 1964, pp. 46–52. Quoted in M. L. Barron, *Minorities in a Changing World*, Knopf, 1967, pp. 422–423.

[16] Erich Rosenthal, *Studies of Jewish Intermarriage in the United States*, The American Jewish Committee, 1963, pp. 52–53. The intermarriage rate here is computed by determining the ratio of intermarried families to the total number of families in which one or both partners to the marriage are Jewish, the procedure used by the U.S. Bureau of the Census. In Canada, the rate is the ratio of the intermarried to all Jews who marry. Rosenthal says: "We now know that a survey of the extent of Jewish intermarriage must be so designed as to cast a net over the whole Jewish as well as non-Jewish population rather than simply those identified as members in or contributors to a Jewish organization. The survey in Washington found a rate of intermarriage of 13.1 percent, more than twice the rate that would have been found if it had been based on a communal listing of Jewish families." Rosenthal thinks the Washington data provide support for the inference that other communities of this size (50,000 to 100,-000) have a similar level of intermarriage. *Ibid.*, p. 31.

[17] Erich Rosenthal, "Jewish Intermarriage in Indiana," *American Jewish Yearbook*, Vol. 68, 1967, p. 263. In this study a couple was considered to be intermarried if one spouse professed a religion different from that of the other. Those who changed their religion before marriage were considered to be inmarried. The intermarriage rate for Jews was computed by determining the ratio of intermarried couples to the total number of marriages (Jewish marriages) in which one or both partners were Jewish. This analysis deals with the formation of intermarriages during the period studied. It does not report on the percentages of all Jewish families in Indiana that are intermarried. *Ibid.*, p. 244.

[18] Sidney Goldstein and Calvin Goldscheider, *Jewish Americans: Three Generations in a Jewish Community*, Prentice-Hall, 1968, pp. 169–170. In discussing factors facilitating intermarriage later in this chapter, the special character of the Providence Jewish community is pointed out.

large midwestern state university, supplemented by a questionnaire from Jewish students in selected courses in a nearby private urban university, found that Reform Jews were more willing to make interfaith marriages than were Conservative Jews, students of both branches were more reluctant to marry Catholics than Protestants, and both were more willing to marry persons of no faith than either Catholics or Protestants. In intra-Jewish marriages, Reform Jews preferred Conservative to Orthodox Jews, and Conservative Jews were more willing to marry Orthodox than Reform Jews.[19]

In a nationwide survey of the United Lutheran Church of America, Bossard found that 58 percent of the members married outside their church.[20] Of all the Lutherans who married outside their faith, one-fifth married Roman Catholics; 18.8 percent married nonchurch members; and 23.7 percent married other Protestants. Cahnman comments that this study, as well as Thomas' study of the religious intermarriage of Catholics in the United States, indicates little concerning the ultimate gains and losses of these churches.[21]

By way of summary, we cite the interreligious marriage rate shown in the special U.S. Census of religion of 1957. Andrew M. Greeley points out that most research done on religious intermarriage lumps all Protestant denominations together. These studies indicate that Jews are the least likely to marry persons of other faiths, Catholics most likely, and Protestants fall in between. Using the tabulations of the 1957 Current Population Survey of Religion, Greeley shows that approximately four-fifths of the members of each of four Protestant denominations (Baptist, Lutheran, Methodist, Presbyterian) are married to people whose present religious affiliation is the same as their own. Greeley cites also NORC data collected on original and present religious denominations of both the respondent and

Husband	Wife	Marriage Rate (Percent)
Protestant	Protestant	91.4
	Catholic	8.4
	Jewish	0.2
Catholic	Catholic	78.5
	Protestant	21.2
	Jewish	0.4
Jewish	Jewish	92.8
	Protestant	4.2
	Catholic	3.0

Note: These figures are based on the religious affiliations of the spouses *after* marriage. Because a sizeable number of persons convert to the religion of their spouses after marriage, figures on the religious backgrounds of marriage partners prior to marriage would show a considerably higher rate of interfaith marriage.

Source: U.S. Bureau of the Census, *Current Population Reports*, Ser. P-20, no. 79, "Religion Reported by the Civilian Population of the United States: March, 1957," Feb. 2, 1958, p. 8.

spouse as given in its study of June, 1961 college graduates. The comparative data are given in the table on the following page. Greeley concludes that "one may say that America is still very much a denominational society to the extent that denominational homogeneity in marriage exists for at least three-quarters of the major religious denominations."[22]

A drastic redefinition of interfaith marriage suggested by Yinger would modify greatly present views of intermarriage. In his proposal, intermarriage would be regarded as a variable rather than an attribute. Two scales would be used to measure it. One would measure the degree to which the couple is intramarried, considering similarity on many possible religious factors. The second scale would measure the extent to which a married couple is related to an integrating or separating network of other persons and groups. In this approach, "if all the persons with whom they interact and all of their significant others are of the same

[19] Ruth Shonle Cavan, "Jewish Student Attitudes Toward Interreligious and Intra-Jewish Marriage," *AJS*, May, 1971, p. 1064.

[20] J. H. S. Bossard and E. S. Boll, *One Marriage, Two Faiths*, Ronald, 1957, p. 56.

[21] W. J. Cahnman, "Intermarriage and American Democracy," in Cahnman, *op. cit.*, p. 181.

[22] Andrew M. Greeley, "Religious Intermarriage in a Denominational Society," *AJS*, May, 1970, pp. 949–952.

Denominational Intermarriage (%)

Denominational Intermarriage	Catholic	Baptist	Lutheran	Meth- odist	Presby- terian	Jew
Proportion of U.S. population married to member of same denomination in 1957.	88	83	81	81	81	94
Proportion of 1961 alumni married to member of same denomination in 1968	86 (1130)	84 (355)	83 (354)	86 (712)	78 (402)	97 (353)
Proportion of alumni in which marriage took place between two people whose original denomination was the same and who currently belong to that denomination	75	35	34	30	15	94
Proportion of alumni whose original denomination has remained unchanged and whose spouse has converted to that denomination	11	14	22	16	15	2

Source: A. M. Greeley, "Religious Intermarriage in a Denominational Society," *AJS*, May, 1970, p. 950. Reprinted with the permission of the University of Chicago Press, publisher.

faith, then they are strongly intramarried on this group dimension. If they interact with many other persons of a different faith, if some of their relatives are intermarried, then they are partially intermarried, even if they are members of the same church and hold the same beliefs."[23] Intermarriage is seen as a phenomenon of a social structure as well as of a pair, and the second type of scale would take not only the memberships of significant others into account, but also their rankings on the several dimensions of religion used in the first scale. A multivariable definition (the product of the degree of religious heterogeneity in the marriage pair and in their social networks) in future research would make it possible to ascertain, much more accurately than is now possible, the consequences of religious intermarriage.

Interethnic Marriages

Nationality groups do not long remain endogamous in the United States. For example, in examining the rates—for sample years 1930–1960—at which residents of Buffalo, New York, with Polish or Italian names married persons of similar backgrounds, Bugelski found that ingroup marriages among Italians fell from 71 percent in 1930 to 27 percent in 1960, and among Poles from 79 percent to 33 percent. The parallelism of the trends for the two groups is striking, but the following differences are noted: (1) Polish males have always been

[23] J. Milton Yinger, "On the Definition of Interfaith Marriage," *Journal for the Scientific Study of Religion*, Spring, 1968, p. 105.

slower to outmarry, but by 1960 they reached a 50 percent point and were not far behind other categories; (2) Italian women started out more slowly, but by 1950 they passed Polish women, and in 1960 they had a slight lead; and (3) Italian men were the most rapid assimilators from the beginning of the period under study. On the basis of present data on Buffalo, Bugelski (unlike Kennedy in New Haven), does not draw the conclusion that assimilation along ethnic lines is proceeding so rapidly that national origins will soon become matters of indifference and that the groups studied were selecting marriage partners along lines of religious affiliation (Catholics, Protestants, and Jews). He does conclude (1) that the likelihood of Pole marrying Pole or Italian marrying Italian is diminishing at a faster and faster rate; (2) that intermarriage will result in even greater intermarriage on the part of children of such marriages; and (3) that before 1975, the "Polish Wedding" and the "Italian Wedding" will be a thing of the past.[24]

An analysis of 7492 marriage licenses issued in Los Angeles County during 1963 includes all marriages in which one or both spouses carried a Spanish surname. By the definition adopted, a total of 9368 Mexican-American individuals were identified.[25] Of these, 2246 (24 percent) were first-generation (born in Mexico); 3537 (38.2 percent) were second-generation, with one or both parents born in Mexico; and 3585 (38.2 percent) were third-generation, defined as Spanish-surname individuals whose parents were born in one of the five southwestern states where Mexican-Americans are concentrated. The overall rate of exogamy in these marriages was considerably higher than expected. Forty percent of the 7492 marriages involving Mexican-Americans were exogamous, and 25 percent of the Mexican-American individuals outmarried. Exogamy is much higher for Mexican-Americans in Los Angeles than it was in the past or in other urban areas. According to Mittlebach and Moore, the Mexican-American exogamy rate in Los Angeles approximates that of the Italian and Polish ethnic populations in Buffalo, New York a generation ago. Their data indicate that both men and women of the second and third generations are more likely to marry Anglos than to marry immigrants from Mexico. Among third-generation persons, the chances are higher that they will marry Anglos than either first- or second-generation Mexicans. Mexican-American men and women with both parents born in Mexico are more likely than those with mixed parentage to marry first- and second-generation spouses and less likely to marry third-generation spouses. Thus, the social distance between some categories of Mexicans is greater than between some categories of Mexicans and Anglos. In general, this study found that the higher the socio-economic status of the groom, the greater the rate of exogamy. For Mexican-American women, slightly more than half of those marrying high-status grooms married exogamously.[26]

In a study of every marriage in the city of New York of a first- or second-generation Puerto Rican in the years 1949 and 1959 (22,118 Puerto Ricans), Fitzpatrick found a significant percentage increase in outmarriage among second-generation Puerto Ricans. Nearly one-third of the second-generation brides and grooms married outside the Puerto Rican group. The increase was as great for grooms and greater for brides than the increase in outmarriage among second-generation immigrants in New York City in the period 1908–1912.[27] In these marriages, the correlation between higher occupational

[24] B. R. Bugelski, "Assimilation Through Intermarriage," *SF*, Dec., 1961, pp. 148–153.

[25] Frank G. Mittlebach and Joan W. Moore, "Ethnic Endogamy—The Case of Mexican Americans," *AJS*, July, 1968, pp. 50–62. Not all persons of Mexican-American descent who were parties to applications for marriage licenses in Los Angeles in 1963 are included. Specifically, persons of Mexican-American descent who did not carry Spanish surnames and second- and third-generation Mexican-Americans with Spanish surnames whose parents were not born in one of the five southwestern states where Mexican-Americans are concentrated were excluded.

[26] *Ibid.*, p. 55.

[27] Joseph P. Fitzpatrick, "The Intermarriage of Puerto Ricans in New York City," *AJS*, Jan., 1966, pp. 395–406. It should be noted that the number of second-generation marriages is still small relative to first generation, but the difference is evident in both years studied and indicates a consistent trend.

status and outgroup marriage is not consistent. Generation rather than occupational level is the significant variable among grooms, but among brides outmarriage increases as the occupational level of their husbands rises. Data on color were obtained from the marriage records, but Fitzpatrick says that it is difficult to make any reliable judgment about color in the case of Puerto Ricans. The designation of color on the marriage record is as it was given by the person who declared it, and the overwhelming majority of Puerto Ricans declared themselves white. It may or may not be significant that 90 percent of the marriages in the 1949 series were listed as "white-white," compared with 85 percent in 1959.[28]

A. I. Gordon found that ethnic considerations play a minor or passive role, if any at all, in the lives of people in the major religious groups as well as those who are unaffiliated. He says that among American Jews today, little thought is given to national origins. The division between Jews of Eastern and Western European descent are no longer significant. Marriages between the two groups occur regularly.[29] Reference is made above to studies by Kennedy, Hollingshead, and Bugelski indicating that in Catholic marriages ethnicity is receding as a factor to be given serious consideration. Interethnic marriages among the American people are becoming more common, but such marriages do not take place indiscriminately.

Interracial Marriages

From 1900 until the end of World War II, the Negro-white intermarriage rates in New York City, New York State, Boston, and Los Angeles were from 1 to 5 percent of all marriages in which Negroes participated.

Perhaps the fullest data on Negro-white

intermarriages in the United States are for Boston. Stone found that there were 143 such intermarriages for the period 1900–1904, or an average of 28.6 per year. The rate per 100 Negro marriages was 13.6.

The considerable decrease in Negro-white intermarriage in Boston cannot be explained by the hypothesis that the smaller the proportion of a minority race in the total population the higher will be the rate of intermarriage. The percentage of the Negro population in Boston was practically constant from 1900 to 1920 (1900, 2.1; 1910, 2.0; 1915, 2.1; 1920, 2.2). It was not markedly higher in 1930 (2.6). The Boston rate of Negro-white marriages in all Negro marriages in the period 1914–1938 was 3.9 as compared with 3.4 for New York urban areas exclusive of New York City in 1919–1937. The Boston rate changed little after 1919, whereas the New York rate, except during the period 1922–1924, dropped steadily. Whereas the former high rate of intermarriage in Boston was unique, the later Boston rate does not seem to be atypical.[30]

In his study of the four states with recent data, Heer shows that Hawaii has the highest reported incidence of Negro-white intermarriage. In this respect the other states, in descending order, are California, Michigan, and Nebraska. For Whites of both sexes the rates were: Hawaii, 0.38 percent; California, 0.21 percent; Michigan, 0.15 percent; and Nebraska, 0.02 percent. For Negroes of both sexes the interracial marriage rates were: Hawaii, 16.16 percent; California, 2.58 percent; Michigan, 1.56 percent; and Nebraska, 0.67 percent. The Negro-white intermarriage rate for Negroes in Hawaii during 1964 was higher than in any part of the United States at any period. The proportion of Negro men marrying white women in Boston in the period 1900–1904 was 13.7 percent as compared with 20.3 percent in Hawaii in 1964, and the proportion of Negro brides marrying white grooms was 1.1 percent in Boston during 1900–1904 as compared with 8.6 percent in Hawaii in 1964. Heer concludes

[28] The other percentages are:

	1949	1959
White/brown	.35	1.99
White/colored (Negro)	1.66	3.17
Brown/brown	2.37	4.14
Brown/colored	.11	2.64
Colored/colored	3.06	2.21
Other	2.20	1.12

Ibid., p. 396.

[29] A. I. Gordon, *op. cit.*, pp. 296–301.

[30] Louis Wirth and Herbert Goldhamer, "The Hybrid and the Problem of Miscegenation," in Klineberg, *op. cit.*, p. 280.

Intermarriage in Hawaii, 1957–1959

	Grooms					Brides				
	Total	Out	Percent Out	Group Intermarried Most and Number		Total	Out	Percent Out	Group Intermarried Most and Number	
Caucasian	5,204	2,058	39	P.H.	921	3,889	743	19	P.H.	366
Part-Hawaiian	2,312	894	39	Cauc.	366	3,244	1,781	55	Cauc.	921
Chinese	641	313	49	Ja.	150	659	331	50	Cauc.	126
Filipino	1,736	842	49	P.H.	382	1,539	645	42	Cauc.	317
Puerto Rican	328	188	57	P.H.	83	380	240	63	Cauc.	129
Korean	142	105	74	Ja.	56	159	122	77	Cauc.	49
Negro	145	90	62	P.H.	48	62	7	11	Cauc.	3
Hawaiian	227	62	27	Cauc.	38	269	149	55	Cauc.	60
Others	219					215				
Japanese	3,628	408	11	P.H.	185	4,166	826	20	Cauc.	398
Total	14,582	4,960	34			14,582	4,844	33		

Note: P.H. = part Hawaiian; Cauc. = Caucasian; Ja = Japanese. Out = Married out of group.
Source: Data courtesy of Professor Douglas Yamamura.

that racial intermarriage in the United States appears to be increasing, but that it is unlikely that Negro-white marriage rates will increase rapidly in the next 100 years. He argues that trends such as reductions in residential and school segregation may operate directly to decrease Negro-white status differences and indirectly to increase Negro-white intermarriage.[31] On the other hand, the recent increase in black awareness, and the emphasis on "black is beautiful," will tend to have the opposite effect.

According to Barron, the "other colored" races in the United States, especially the Filipinos and American Indians, have had considerably higher intermarriage rates than the Negro. Also, there has been a greater variation in rate among the Chinese, Japanese, Indians, and Filipinos than among Negroes. In some places where these minority races have had very small numbers, intermarriage has exceeded inmarriage.[32]

Between 1945 and 1954, 28.4 percent of those entering marriage in Hawaii married outside their group (Caucasian, Part-Hawaiian, Chinese, Filipino, Puerto Rican, Korean, Negro, Hawaiian, Japanese).[33] During the years 1957–1959, 34 percent of the grooms and 33 percent of the brides in Hawaii outmarried (see table above).

Burma's study of interracial marriages in Los Angeles County, 1948–1959, covered 3150 mixed marriages in over 375,000 total marriages. Mixed marriages here refers to taking out a marriage license in a county where about 5 percent of licenses applied for are not used within the time span of their validity. "Interethnic intermarriages" were

[31] David M. Heer, "Negro-White Marriage in the United States," *Journal of Marriage and the Family*, Aug., 1966, pp. 265, 266, 273.
[32] Milton L. Barron, *People Who Intermarry*, Syracuse Univ. Press, p. 189. On the basis of a small sample (28 couples) of Spokane reservation Indians, Roy estimates that between 80 and 90 percent of the individuals on the reservation manifest some form of amalgamation. Prodipto Roy, "The Measurement of Assimilation: The Spokane Indian, *AJS*, Mar., 1962, pp. 548–551. In a recent study, Berry reports on tens of thousands of "quasi-Indians" (people of mixed descent) who are not "official" Indians. Berry located 200 communities, and there may be others, comprised of people determined not to be Negroes. Brewton Berry, *Almost White*, Macmillan, 1963.
[33] C. K. Cheng and Douglas S. Yamamura, "Interracial Marriage and Divorce in Hawaii," *SF*, Oct., 1957, pp. 77–84.

Interracial Marriages in Los Angeles County, 1948–1959

Year	Total Marriages	Interracial Marriages	Interracial Marriages per 1000 Marriages
1948 (2 mo.)	5,376	28	5.2
1949	31,779	187	5.8
1950	31,915	168	5.3
1951	29,459	187	6.4
1952	30,178	171	5.7
1953	31,980	197	6.2
1954	32,095	238	7.4
1955	33,996	264	7.8
1956	36,365	268	7.4
1957	38,333	346	9.1
1958	37,700	465	12.3
1959	39,300	631*	16.1*
		3,150	

*In the 8 and one-half months of 1959 in which race could be recorded, there were 447 intermarriages, which were prorated to 631 for 12 months and 16.1 per 1000 per year. The 12-year total also includes this proration.

Source: J. H. Burma, "Interethnic Marriage in Los Angeles, 1948–1959," Social Forces, Dec., 1963, p. 157. Reprinted by permission of the University of North Carolina Press, publisher.

defined as cases in which an Anglo or Mexican married either a Negro, Filipino, Japanese, Chinese, Indian, or member of another non-European racial-ethnic group.[34] The above table shows that the number of interracial marriages that took place immediately after the old law was declared unconstitutional in October, 1948 was small, and it indicates that there was no great increase of interracial marriages during the next several years. By the mid-1950s an increase became apparent and it had become impressive by 1958 and 1959. Burma remarks that "even at its highest the rate is small but since some seven percent of Los Angeles County population is non-white, the rate conceivably could be eight to ten times as great as it actually is. On the other hand, this is a high rate compared to most of the remainder of the nation where the rate is

practically zero."[35] The total number of marriages increased by approximately 22 percent from 1953 to 1959, but the number of intermarriages during the period increased by approximately 220 percent. Since the 1959 law forbids asking race on licenses, there is no way of determining whether this rapid rate of increase has continued. It appears that the intermarriage rate per 1000 marriages in Los Angeles County is now about three times as high as it was in the late 1940s and early 1950s. Since this report does not include marriages between American Indians and any group except whites, marriages between two ethnic groups neither of which is white (for example, Chinese-Filipino), or the Mexican-Anglo or Anglo-Mexican marriages, this is a minimal rate. The following two tables from Burma's study provide additional data on interracial marriages in Los Angeles County, 1949–1959.

[34] John H. Burma, "Interethnic Marriage in Los Angeles, 1948–1959," SF, Dec., 1963, pp. 156–165.

[35] Ibid., p. 158.

Percentage of Males and Females in the Total Population, 1960, and Percentage of Total Intermarriages, for Selected Groups, Los Angeles County, 1948–1959

	Male			Female		
Group	Percent in Total Pop.	Percent in Intermarriage	Index	Percent in Total Pop.	Percent in Intermarriage	Index
White	90.2	42.0	.47	90.4	58.0	.64
Negro	7.6	21.5	2.83	7.7	6.5	.84
Japanese	1.3	7.4	5.70	1.2	12.6	10.50
Chinese	.4	4.2	10.50	.3	4.4	14.66
Filipino	.3	13.7	45.67	.1	8.1	81.00
Indian	.1	3.8	38.00	.1	4.0	40.00
Other	.1	7.4	74.00	.1	6.4	64.00

Note: The percentage of intermarriages divided by the percentage of population gives the index of probability of intermarriage by a person within that group.
Source: J. H. Burma, "Interethnic Marriage in Los Angeles, 1948–1959," *Social Forces*, Dec., 1963, p. 160. Reprinted by permission of the University of North Carolina Press, publisher.

Intermarriage by Ethnic Classification and Sex; 1958–1959

Classification	Total Number	Percent of Total
Negro-white	256	21.5
Filipino-white	163	13.7
White-Japanese	150	12.6
White-Filipino	96	8.1
Japanese-white	88	7.4
White-Negro	77	6.5
Hawaiian-white	63	5.3
White-Chinese	52	4.4
Chinese-white	50	4.2
White-Indian	48	4.0
White-Hawaiian	47	4.0
Indian-white	45	3.8
White-Korean	11	1.0
Korean-white	7	.6
Other	36	3.0
Total	1,189	100.1
Anglo-Mexican	1,433	
Mexican-Anglo	1,226	

Note: Male listed first in all cases.
Source: J. H. Burma, "Interethnic Marriages in Los Angeles, 1948–1959," *Social Forces*, Dec., 1963, p. 162. Reprinted by permission of the University of North Carolina Press, publisher.

Summarizing, Burma says: "This study indicates that in Los Angeles intermarriages are increasing significantly; the largest number of marriages include Whites and Negroes, but proportionately the smaller groups intermarry tremendously more than the larger groups; some evidence of intermarriage by cultural homogamy exists; intermarried couples are on the average somewhat older than are persons intramarrying, except if they themselves are the products of intermarriage; and, except for Whites, in most cases there was a greater likelihood that one party had been divorced than in comparable intramarriages."[36]

Except for the 25,000 Japanese war brides, Kitano reports that marital assimilation for the Japanese has been limited. One sample showed that Nisei parents overwhelmingly preferred that their children marry only other Japanese, but intermarriage brings little opprobrium. Among the Sansei (third generation), intermarriage is increasing. According to Kitano, undoubtedly the general direction of assimilation will include biological as well as social integration.[37]

[36] *Ibid.*, p. 165.
[37] Harry H. L. Kitano, *Japanese Americans*, Prentice-Hall, 1969, pp. 137–143. Concerning the Japa-

The "black is beautiful" theme in the current black nationalist movement, as well as in the continuing Black Muslim group, discourages association with Whites and, in those circles, may serve to reduce both extramarital Negro-white sexual relations and intermarriage.[38]

GREATER TENDENCY FOR MINORITY MEN TO OUTMARRY

There is a general tendency for the men of a racial, religious, or ethnic minority to outmarry to a greater extent than the women. Although the sexes in the Jewish group in Canada are almost equally divided, the number of Jewish men who marry non-Jews is regularly larger than the number of Jewish women who marry non-Jewish men.[39] Likewise, Jewish women in Europe have been more conservative than Jewish men in intermarrying.[40] In Koenig's Stamford, Connecticut study, the overwhelming majority of the Jewish partners in Jewish-gentile marriages (40 out of 59) were male.[41] In Minneapolis,

Gordon found that in nearly all cases of intermarriage, "it is the Jewish youth who marries the non-Jewish girl . . . in most instances the Jewish youth is financially better off than the girl he marries."[42] Sklare says that at least seven out of every 10 Jews who intermarry are men.[43] The majority of intermarriages in which the "other colored" races in the United States participate are between nonwhite males and white females.[44]

Barron reports that the most common type of Negro-white intermarriage is that of Negro men and white women,[45] and Heer found this to be the case in Hawaii, California, Michigan, and Nebraska. For example, for California in 1959 the intermarriage rate of white grooms was 0.09 percent and that of white brides 0.33 percent. Similarly, the interracial rate for Negro grooms was 3.96 percent and of Negro brides 1.16 percent.[46]

After California's antimiscegenation law was nullified by a state court in 1948, the intermarriage rate was not high. During a 30-month period (November, 1948, to April 30, 1951), 78,266 licenses were issued in Los Angeles County, of which 445 were between persons of the white and some other race (Mexicans are considered white). This rate of 56 per 10,000 marriages is slightly more than one-half of 1 percent of all marriages. Of the marriages between Whites and other races, 41 percent involved Filipino men; 20.5 percent, Negro men; 20.4 percent, Anglo men (because Mexicans are legally "white," the term "Anglo" is used to denote whites of non-Mexican descent); 7.6 percent, Chinese men; 5.3 percent, Mexican men, and 4.5 percent, Japanese men. For the women, 44.4 percent involved Anglo women; 29.2 percent, Mexican women; 7.4 percent, Negro women; 7.4 percent, Japanese women; 5.9 percent, Filipino women; and 3.9 percent, Chinese women. The rates of intermarriage according to race or nationality are shown in the following table.

---

nese war brides, Kitano says: "Their sociological position is marginal; the ethnic community has generally not accepted them, and their primary ties are to the husband's social group." *Ibid.,* p. 132.

[38] For an account of actual experiences with Negro-white intermarriage, including child-rearing, see Clotye M. Larsson, *Marriage Across the Color Line,* Johnson, 1965.

[39] One report says:

The intermarriage rate among Jews in Canada was more than twice as high among Jewish men than among Jewish women in each of the quinquennial periods since 1926, except in the periods 1931–35 and 1941–46, while the intermarriage rate among Protestants was from 12 to 30 percent higher among men than among women in the period from 1926 to 1930, and only 4 percent higher in the period from 1956 to 1960. Among Catholics, the intermarriage rate was higher among women than among men in each of the quinquennial periods, although the percentage by which the intermarriage rate among Catholic women exceeded that among Catholic men has decreased in each quinquennial period from 1926–30 to 1956–60.

Louis Rosenberg, "Intermarriage in Canada," in Cahnman (ed.), *op. cit.,* pp. 62–63.

[40] Barron, "The Incidence of Jewish Intermarriage in Europe and America," *ASR,* Feb., 1946, p. 9.

[41] *Ibid.,* p. 12.

[42] Albert I. Gordon, *Jews in Transition,* Univ. of Minnesota Press, 1950, pp. 206–207.

[43] Sklare, *op. cit.,* p. 422.

[44] Barron, *People Who Intermarry,* p. 189.

[45] *Ibid.,* pp. 189–190.

[46] Heer, *op. cit.,* pp. 265–266.

Rates per 1000 Marriage Licenses Issued to Mixed Couples of White and Nonwhite Races in Los Angeles County, November 1, 1948, to April 30, 1951, by Race or Nationality

Filipino-Anglo	217
Filipino-Mexican	193
Negro-Anglo	146
Anglo-Japanese	67
Anglo-Negro	58
Negro-Mexican	59
Chinese-Anglo	54
Anglo-Chinese	34
Anglo-Filipino	34
Japanese-Anglo	27
Mexican-Filipino	25
Chinese-Mexican	22
Japanese-Mexican	18
Mexican-Negro	16
Anglo-Korean	11
Mexican-Japanese	7
Mexican-Chinese	5
Other mixtures	7
Total	1000

Note: Male listed first in all cases.

The study did not record separately interracial marriages not including Whites, but the estimate of the total rate of intermarriage if these are included is 65 per 10,000 marriages. The sample seems to indicate that in the marriages of Whites to Whites about 3.5 percent, are between Anglos and Mexican-Americans, with marriages of Anglo males to Mexican-American females constituting about four-fifths of this total. The sample of 1000 marriages indicates that of the marriage licenses issued in Los Angeles County, about 75 percent are Anglo-Anglo, approximately 11 percent are Mexican-Mexican, almost 10 percent are Negro-Negro, and the other 4 percent are intraracial marriages involving other racial groups or interracial marriages. Since Los Angeles has a relatively large number of minority groups and of intermarriages, it should not be concluded that it is a typical city in the matter of intermarriage.[47]

[47] John H. Burma, "Research Note on the Measurement of Interracial Marriage," *AJS*, May, 1952, p. 587.

Exceptions to the greater tendency for minority men to outmarry are found in several studies previously cited. The atypical instances include: Mexican and Japanese women in Burma's 1948–1951 study in Los Angeles County; Yamamura's 1957–1959 report on Part Hawaiian, Puerto Rican, Hawaiian, and Japanese women in Hawaii; and Japanese and Chinese women in Burma's Los Angeles County study, 1948–1959.

Lewis F. Carter questions whether the preponderance of racial caste hypogamy in the United States is a sociological myth. A 1939 national sample reported 559 cases of hypogamy and 583 of hypergamy. A 5 percent sample, taken by the Census Bureau in 1960, showed 25,496 Negro males married to white females and 25,913 white males married to Negro females. Carter says that the major empirical studies of intermarriage in the United States have involved data from large urban areas and that these urban areas have been drawn exclusively from the northern and western sections of the country. It is his hypothesis that racial caste hypergamy, that is, white males marrying Negro females is more frequent in nonurban areas than is hypogamy, and, further, that these nonurban interracial marriages may be more numerous than urban ones.[48]

The factors responsible for the tendency of the men in a minority racial, religious, or ethnic group to out-marry more than the women do may be summarized as follows:

1. The women in these groups have fewer opportunities for meeting the men in other groups than the minority men have for meeting outside women.

2. Religious and other institutional controls may exert a stronger influence on minority women than on minority men.

3. Men take the initiative in dating and courtship.

4. Marrying a woman in the majority group, or a woman in the minority group whose appearance and manners closely approximate those of majority-group women, is a symbol of success, of prestige, of being ac-

[48] Lewis F. Carter, "Racial-Caste Hypogamy: A Sociological Myth?" *Phylon*, Winter, 1968, pp. 347–350.

cepted in the larger community. In the case of the Negro in the United States, it may also mean the realization of a wish, perhaps an unconscious wish, to have children who will be nearer to the ideal physical type of this country. Majority women who inter-marry typically are of lower socioeconomic status than the minority men they marry. They exchange majority prestige for higher socioeconomic standing. The woman in the minority group who is least visible from the standpoint of minority status has many com-petitors for marriage among majority women. Within the minority group she has marked advantages maritally.

In summary, we may say that people in the United States and elsewhere have been pre-dominantly endogamous with respect to race, religion, and ethnic group. Of these three types of intermarriage, racial intermarriage has usually been the least common and ethnic intermarriage the most frequent. Time, place, and conditions have affected the incidence of each type of intermarriage. There is no single pattern in the trend of intermarriage incidence.

THE LEGAL ASPECTS OF INTERMARRIAGE

The legal history of intermarriage in the United States is fascinating.[49] For example, until recently Mississippi had a criminal statute providing for the punishment of any-one who published, printed, or circulated any literature in favor of or urging interracial marriage or social equality, and the Texas court upheld an ordinance enacted by Fort Worth that it was unlawful for Whites and Negroes to have sexual intercourse with one another within the city limits.[50]

There has been so much intermixture in Louisiana that it was said that a marriage license would be refused only in cases where mixture was obvious from the appearance of the person making the application. Ordinarily the marriages of white persons to individuals with a small amount of Negro ancestry were questioned only by those interested in prop-erty succession, and the courts have dealt leniently with children of mixed ancestry.

California's antimiscegenation law was de-clared unconstitutional by a state court in 1948. Two Catholics, one Negro and one White, declared that their religious freedom was hampered by the law; the sacrament of marriage was being unconstitutionally denied them by the law.[51]

In 1964, the U.S. Supreme Court unani-mously struck down a Florida law that made it a crime for persons of different races to cohabit.[52]

Laws barring intermarriage were on and off the statute books of at least six southern states during the nineteenth century. Louisi-ana seems to have been the first state to enact such a law (1810), North Carolina followed

---

[49] See C. S. Mangum, Jr., *The Legal Status of the Negro*, Univ. of North Carolina Press, 1940, chap. 10; Klineberg (ed.), *op. cit.*, pp. 358–364; Johnson, *op. cit.*, pp. 162, 163, 169; and Barron, *People Who Intermarry*, pp. 50–58; Harriet F. Pilpel and Theo-dora Zavin, *Your Marriage and the Law*, Holt, Rine-hart & Winston, 1952, pp. 26–29; Richard V. Mackay, *Law of Marriage and Divorce Simplified*, Oceana Publications, 1961.

[50] ". . . The legislatures of quite a number of southern and western states have found it expedient to enact statutes expressly punishing members of dif-ferent races and sexes for living in a state of concu-binage or for indulging in acts of sexual intercourse with one another, whether it be fornication or adul-tery. Illicit interracial sexual relationships are also punishable under ordinary statutes prohibiting un-lawful cohabitation generally. Louisiana has even gone to the extent of enacting a statute that specifi-cally penalizes cohabitation between a Negro and an Indian. Texas punishes the continuance of a cohabi-tation between a white person and a Negro after a marriage either in or out of the state, but the mar-riage is an essential element of the offense and must be averred and proved." Mangum, *op. cit.*, pp. 256–257.

The evidence that was admissible in trying to es-tablish the race of anyone accused of miscegenation or of his or her accomplice is extremely interesting. Certain types of testimony were held to be accept-able, including bringing either the defendant or his or her paramour into court for the jury to view and to ascertain whether or not this individual is a Ne-gro. The same could be done with respect to "the immediate direct or collateral kindred of the person involved." It was even considered as proof, with or without photographs, of Negro ancestry if "one of the party's none-too-distant ancestors had kinky hair and other racial characteristics of the Negro." *Ibid.*, pp. 262–263.

[51] Burma, "Research Note on the Measurement of Interracial Marriage," p. 587.

[52] *The New York Times*, Mar. 13, 1966, p. 12E.

in 1830, Arkansas in 1838, and Mississippi and South Carolina in 1865. These laws were repealed for longer or shorter periods of time during Reconstruction, but all had reappeared by 1894.

At one time or another, 41 states had miscegenation laws. In the 1940s, 30 states prohibited, through constitutional provision or statutory law or both, the marriage of white persons and those who were defined in varying ways as "Negro." By 1963, through the repeal of statutes prohibiting interracial marriages or their nullification by state court decisions, the number was reduced to 21.[53] In the 1940s, 15 states possessed laws that expressly or impliedly prohibited the marriage of Caucasians and Mongolians, 10 states did likewise for Whites and Malays, and five forbade the marriage of Whites and Indians. Louisiana and Oklahoma prohibited unions of Indians and Negroes, and North Carolina banned the marriage of Cherokee Indians of Robeson County with persons of Negro ancestry to the third generation inclusive. Maryland forbade the marriage of Malays and Negroes.

States differed with respect to the amount of Negro ancestry that would prevent a person from entering a valid marriage with a white person. Mulattoes were specifically mentioned in the statutes of Arkansas, Delaware, Idaho, Kentucky, Mississippi, South Carolina, Tennessee, and Wyoming, but in most cases there was no reference to the amount of Negro ancestry that was considered to come within the law. Two states (North Carolina and Tennessee) prohibited the marriage of Whites to persons of Negro "blood" to the third generation inclusive. This was equivalent to making it illegal for a white person to marry an individual whose ancestry is one-eighth Negro. Five states (Indiana, Mississippi, Missouri, Nebraska, and South Carolina) had the same provision, but the language of the statutes was in terms of the marriage of Whites with persons of

one-eighth or more Negro "blood." Florida had contradictory rules, the constitution prohibiting marriage to the fourth generation inclusive (one-sixteenth Negro ancestry), whereas the definition of Negro in the statutory law prohibiting intermarriage was a person of one-eighth or more "Negro blood." Five states, (Alabama, Georgia, Oklahoma, Texas, and Virginia) prohibited marriages of Whites with persons who had any Negro ancestry. In Utah and West Virginia the statutes did not indicate what amount of Negro ancestry would make a person ineligible to marry a white person.

When the U.S. Supreme Court ruled against state laws prohibiting interracial marriage, 17 states still had such laws. The final decision of the Court against the state laws came in the case of the Lovings versus the Commonwealth of Virginia. Richard Terry Loving and his part Negro, part Indian wife, Mildred Jeter Loving, were married in Washington, D.C., in 1958, because they could not get a license in Virginia. They returned to their home state, were indicted for violation of the antimiscegenation law, and pleaded guilty. They were sentenced to one year in jail, but the prison term was suspended for a period of 25 years upon the condition that they leave the state and not return together for 25 years. In announcing the suspension of the sentence, the trial judge stated: "Almighty God created the races white, black, yellow, malay, and red, and he placed them on separate continents. And but for the interference with his arrangement there would be no cause for such marriages. The fact that he separated the races shows that he did not intend for the races to mix."[54] They left for a time, but in 1963 returned to challenge the conviction. In March, 1966, the Supreme Court of Appeals of Virginia held that nothing in the federal courts decisions of the previous 15 years had infringed upon the "overriding state interest in the institution of marriage." To upset the law in the courts would be "judicial legislation in the rawest sense of that term," the court said. It suggested that any change would have to come

[53] The states prohibiting Negro-white marriages were: Alabama, Arkansas, Delaware, Florida, Georgia, Idaho, Indiana, Kentucky, Louisiana, Mississippi, Missouri, Nebraska, North Carolina, Oklahoma, South Carolina, Tennessee, Texas, Utah, Virginia, West Virginia, and Wyoming.

[54] *The United States Law Week*, June 13, 1967, pp. 4679–4682.

from the legislature. The decision left the conviction of the Lovings in effect, but said that they could return to Virginia at the same time, as long as they did not cohabit.[55]

In June, 1967, the U.S. Supreme Court held that the Virginia law to prevent marriages between persons solely on the basis of racial classification violated the Equal Protection and Due Process Clauses of the Fourteenth Amendment.

Barron—among others—has pointed out the inconsistency in the conservative attitudes toward intermarriage held by many Americans and their activities in creating social and cultural conditions favoring intermarriage. The reference here is to public-school attendance, children being sent to colleges away from home, the campaigns against discrimination in employment and housing, and participation in interfaith activities. Inevitably an increase in intergroup contacts will lead to some intermarriages.[56]

RATIONALIZATIONS OF THE OPPOSITION TO INTERMARRIAGE

The taboo against intermarriage varies from section to section in its complexity and in the sanctions that enforce it. To many persons in the South such unions are unthinkable, and southern sentiments, attitudes, myths, dogmas, and customs work to prevent them. As Charles Johnson pointed out, "In this culture area the proscription involves not merely a 'climate of opinion' but a total ideology incorporating moral perspectives."[57]

The widespread opposition to Negro-white intermarriage finds expression, especially in the South, in the slogan of "no social equality." The term is vague; at times it covers and justifies all types of segregation and discrimination, whereas at other times it seems to be limited to intimate personal and social relations and intermarriage. Any

questioning about the doctrine will bring a stout insistence on preventing amalgamation and "preserving the purity of the white race." The ban on intermarriage is concentrated on white women, and it covers both formal marriage and illicit sexual relations. When the possibility of intermarriage is used to defend the whole caste system, "it is assumed both that Negro men have a strong desire for 'intermarriage,' and that white women would be open to proposals from Negro men, *if* they are not guarded from even meeting them on an equal plane. . . . The conclusion follows that the whole system of segregation and discrimination is justified. Every single measure is defended as necessary to block 'social equality' which in its turn is defended as necessary to prevent 'intermarriage.' "[58]

Myrdal concluded that the doctrine of "no social equality" is a rationalization of social segregation and discrimination that enables white people to avoid making "an open demand for difference in social status between the two groups for its own sake." In other words, *"what white people really want is to keep Negroes in a lower status."*[59]

Gross exaggeration of the likelihood of intermarriage has been utilized as a device for keeping the Negro "in his place." It has been utilized as the justification for not hiring Negro men in certain jobs, or as an excuse for separation in places of public accommodation, separate schools, or residential segregation. As Drake and Cayton say, "The ultimate appeal for the maintenance of the color-line is always the simple, though usually irrelevant question, 'Would you want your daughter to marry a Negro?' To many white persons this is the core of the entire race problem."[60]

Sklare and Greenblum found that relatively few of their respondents justify their feelings of being unhappy or somewhat unhappy in the event of an intermarriage on the basis of a concern with Jewish identity, Jewish survival, or the Jewish religion. Only 14 percent of those who opposed intermar-

---

[55] Fred P. Graham, "Miscegenation Nears Test in High Court," *The New York Times*, Mar. 13, 1966, p. 12E.

[56] Barron, "Research on Intermarriage: A Survey of Accomplishments and Prospects," *AJS*, Nov., 1951, p. 255.

[57] Johnson, *op. cit.*, p. 222.

[58] Myrdal, *op. cit.*, p. 587.

[59] *Ibid.*, p. 591.

[60] St. Clair Drake and Horace Cayton, *Black Metropolis*, Harcourt Brace Jovanovich, 1945, p. 129.

riage explicitly based their reaction on such grounds. Most Jews in Lakeville, a midwestern suburb of 25,000 with a Jewish population of 8000, explain their opposition in terms of the discord they say is inevitable in an interfaith marriage. These persons maintain that a Jewish-Gentile marriage is inherently an unstable union, emphasizing disturbed relations between husband and wife, or difficulties created for the offspring of an interfaith marriage, or the problematic relationship of the married couple to relatives, friends, and society at large. Concerning these respondents, Sklare and Greenblum say that they are far from being unbiased students of marital problems and that their opposition "seems to be a safe way of expressing the desire to continue the chain of tradition while at the same time avoiding the appearance of ethnocentrism."[61]

"SOCIAL TYPES" WHO INTERMARRY

For a sample of 1167 persons between the ages of 20 and 59, obtained in the Midtown Mental Health Project of Manhattan, five hypotheses were tested:

In general, the intermarried as compared with the intramarried are characterized by: (1) nonreligious parents, (2) greater dissatisfaction with parents when young, (3) greater early family strife, (4) less early family integration, and (5) greater emancipation from parents at time of marriage. The Catholic data supported all of these hypotheses. In the Protestant group, only two received substantial support—relatively weak ties to religion and to family. Most of the general hypotheses do not seem to apply to Jews. Heiss says: "The data suggest that intermarried Jews differ from intramarried Jews only in the strength of their family ties—while young and at the time of marriage.[62]

In Honolulu, Schmitt and Souza found that interracial households occupy a somewhat lower socioeconomic position. The members of such households hold, on the average, poorer jobs, have lower incomes, and live in less desirable housing than do those in unmixed households. They think it likely that the traditional Hawaiian tolerance toward intermarriage is more common among lower-income families, adding that "many Island parents still discourage intermarriage, a practice that may be more frequent (or effective) in the wealthier groups."[63]

PROBLEMS OF THE INTERMARRIED

The intermarried, especially the racially intermarried, in the United States face certain trials not faced by the homogamous. First, there is the matter of keeping a job. It may be necessary for both partners to keep their marriage a secret. Those who seem least vulnerable to economic reprisals are civil service employees, independent business people, Negro physicians, and labor leaders. Second, it is often difficult to find a place to live. The editors and correspondents of *Ebony* found that residential patterns for interracial families vary considerably from city to city. In Los Angeles mixed couples live in nearly every part of the city. In Chicago they spearheaded the drive that brought Negroes into Hyde Park for the first time. In Washington they settled in Negro areas. In Detroit they live in mixed communities. In New York they reside in Harlem and St. Albans, L.I., but many live in "white" sections of the metropolitan area.[64] According to Larsson, generally the sex of the white partner determines where an interracial couple lives. When the husband is white, the couple will ordinarily live in a white neighborhood; when he is Negro the reverse is usually true. Third, the intermarried couple will at times face ostracism from both the white and the black communities, including, in some cases, relatives and friends. Blood says that the main question for the white partner is whether he or she is prepared to

[61] Marshall Sklare and Joseph Greenblum, *Jewish Identity on the Suburban Frontier*, Basic Books, 1967, pp. 309, 311, 313.

[62] Jerold Heiss, "Premarital Characteristics of the Religiously Intermarried in an Urban Area," *ASR*, Feb., 1960, pp. 48–54.

[63] Robert C. Schmitt and Robert A. Souza, "Social and Economic Characteristics of Interracial Households in Honolulu," *SP*, Winter, 1963, p. 267.

[64] Larsson, *op. cit.*, pp. 44–45.

join the Negro race.[65] It may be difficult for each partner to maintain friendships with persons of his race. For some of the inter-married, outside pressures have had at least occasional inside repercussions. One study found that "after marriage the Negro partner tended to be touchy about seeming racial slurs and to insist on the white partner's need to learn to 'understand' Negroes."[66] Fourth, children of an intermarriage may create problems.

One of these [problems] is the attitude of the parents and relatives of the white partner. To them, the Negro spouse is a difficult enough problem to adjust to, but still is not a blood relative. The child of the intermarriage, how-ever, is a blood relative, and must be either accepted or rejected. This can be a real emo-tional crisis. Some couples reported that they had not informed white relatives of the exist-ence of children for this reason.[67]

Some interracial couples have refrained from having children because of possible difficulties or embarrassments, but they seem to have been the exceptions. Most of the Negro-white couples in Chicago have chil-dren, but they are Negro children. According to Drake and Cayton, good adjustment for the children of interracial marriages is diffi-cult but not impossible. Such persons are usually not accepted by the white community unless they pass, but, in Chicago at least, the stigma of having a white parent is not very strong and the community may forget the interracial background completely. If the child of an interracial marriage wishes to pass but cannot do so, he may become seri-ously maladjusted. In Chicago such "in-betweens" constitute a small percentage of the children of mixed parentage. Most make a successful adjustment to life in the Negro community; a few pass completely over into the white group.[68]

Rosenthal says that intermarriage usually means the end of belonging to the Jewish group, citing the fact that in at least 70 per-cent of the mixed families in Greater Washington the children were not identified with the Jewish group. He writes: "This finding, which repeats earlier European ex-periences, takes on special significance if viewed against the fact that the fertility of the Jewish population in the United States is barely sufficient to maintain its present size."[69]

Bossard and Boll say that the lower birth-rate and higher rate of childlessness among those who enter interfaith marriage suggest that these persons expect that children will cause problems or will have problems. These authors found that differences between re-ligions in such matters as attitudes toward sexual relations, rearing of children, friend-ships outside the faith, "private life," proper reading material, tithing, food taboos, fast-ing before religious services, religious holi-days, and the Sabbath day affect marital and familial relationships.[70]

According to Bossard and Boll, six type patterns of adjustment have been found ac-ceptable to persons who have intermarried religiously.

1. One marriage partner accepts the religious culture of the other.
2. The intermarried couple withdraws from most social contacts.
3. Each spouse goes his own way religiously, with the sons being brought up in the father's faith and the daughters in the mother's reli-gion.
4. The couple agrees not to have children.
5. Both persons may be indifferent to religion, regardless of their religious backgrounds.
6. Compromise between spouses who both give and take on the issues involved in a mixed marriage.[71]

A recent review of Catholic-Protestant mar-riages and Jewish-Gentile marriages con-cludes that children tend to follow their mother's footsteps. According to Blood; "Child-rearing is primarily the mother's re-

[65] Robert O. Blood, *Marriage*, Collier-Macmillan, 2nd ed., 1969, p. 96.
[66] *Ibid.*, p. 96.
[67] Drake and Cayton, *op. cit.*, p. 155.
[68] *Ibid.*, pp. 154, 158.

[69] Rosenthal, *Studies of Jewish Intermarriage in the United States*, p. 53.
[70] Bossard and Boll, *op. cit.*, chap. 6.
[71] *Ibid.*, pp. 155–168.

sponsibility and religious and cultural training are her special province; as a result, her values are transmitted to the children more often than her husband's."[72]

PASSING

One of the results of marital and extra-marital race mixture is the appearance of a number of persons who cannot be distinguished physically from members of the majority group. Such individuals may or may not "pass" for Whites. This question was discussed in Chapter 7 in connection with the avoidance type of adjustment of minority-group members.

There are no accurate figures on the extent of passing that occurs in the United States. Estimates of those who leave the Negro group permanently and are absorbed by white society vary from a few thousand to tens of thousands annually.[73] It is impossible to estimate the number of Negroes who pass only temporarily or occasionally. Probably most of those who "cross to the other side" remain in the white group, but thousands have returned after a trial period has shown that life for them in the Negro community is more enjoyable and more comfortable.

FACTORS THAT FACILITATE INTERMARRIAGE

A number of factors seem to facilitate intermarriage. One is the attitudes of individuals toward intermarriage. The nature and the effectiveness of these attitudes are determined by the marriage mores and the other influencing factors to be mentioned shortly. In his study of intermarriage in Derby, Connecticut, Barron found that attitudes alone are not responsible for intermarriage patterns.[74] There were general similarities between intermarriage attitudes and practices, but the attitudes were more liberal than the practices.

The second group of factors are demographic, and include the sex ratio and the numerical size of minority groups. A marked disparity in the distribution of the sexes, as is the case with the Filipinos in the United States, favors intermarriage. Generally speaking, intermarriage varies indirectly and breadth of selection varies directly with the relative size of the minority group. This tendency is seen clearly among the Jews of Iowa. They live in relatively small Jewish communities and, during a seven-year period, the intermarriage rate fluctuated between 36.3 and 53.6 percent. While the average rate was 42.2 percent, in cities of 10,000 or more, the intermarriage rate was 34.2 percent; it was almost twice as high in towns and rural areas.[75] For the Jewish community of about 80,000 persons in Greater Washington, the intermarriage rate was found to be 13.1 percent. However, the intermarriage rate of in-migrants from larger communities, particularly from the New York metropolitan area, was significantly lower.[76] Although the Jewish population of 20,000 in Providence, Rhode Island is relatively large, the intermarriage rate in that city is relatively low. According to Goldstein and Goldscheider:

---

[72] Blood, *op. cit.*, p. 88.

[73] In an interesting paper on "The African Ancestry of the White American Population," Stuckert finds that approximately 23 percent of the persons classified as white in 1960 have "an African element in their inherited biological background." He estimates that 77.4 percent of the Negro population of the United States had some degree of non-African ancestry in 1960. His estimates on the number of persons passing from the Negro group into the white group are: 1861–1890, 90,900; 1891–1910, 101,300; 1911–1930, 183,200; 1931–1940, 42,700; 1941–1950, 155,500; 1951–1960, 96,900. The annual mean average for these periods ranged from 3030 for 1861–1890 to 15,550 for 1941–1950. For 1951–1960 it was 9690. The lowest annual rate of passing (rate per 1000 Negro population per year) was 0.36 percent for 1931–1940, the highest was found for 1941–1950 (1.21 percent). The annual rate of passing for 1951–1960 was 0.64 percent. Robert S. Stuckert, "The African Ancestry of the White American Population," *Ohio Journal of Science*, May, 1958, pp. 155–160. A revised version of this article appears in Peter B. Hammond, (ed.), *Physical Anthropology and Archaeology*, Macmillan, 1964, pp. 192–197.

[74] Barron, *People Who Intermarry*, p. 326. Our treatment of the factors that facilitate intermarriage is based in part on Barron's analysis of why people intermarry.

[75] Rosenthal, *Studies of Jewish Intermarriage in the United States*, p. 51.

[76] *Ibid.*, p. 53.

The Providence Jewish community is an old one and has strong roots and strong organizational structure, and therefore it provides the framework for a close identification with the community, and . . . compared to such other communities as Washington and Los Angeles . . . Providence has a much more stable population and one that contains a higher proportion of first and second-generation Americans. But even among third-generation Jews in Providence the intermarriage rate was lower than that for the comparable group in Washington, D.C.[77]

In the case of the Jews, not only does the small size of the group facilitate intermarriage, but the low birth rate of native-born Jews, at a time when the general population of the United States is growing, probably will mean further attrition by randomization.[78]

In the Chinese population in metropolitan New York there is a general excess of males. For example, when men aged 25–29 are compared with women aged 20–24, there is an excess of 54 men in the sex ratio of the Chinatown population and of 20 in the non-Chinatown population. In general, the non-Chinatown population has a better income, education, and occupational status than the Chinatown population; hence the former group is more likely to be accepted by the majority population. Yuan says that some Puerto Rican girls in New York and some Mexican girls in Los Angeles marry Chinese men in order to support their families, adding that this practice is perhaps more acceptable to the lower-class Chinese and to the lower-class Puerto Ricans and Mexicans due to economic necessity.[79]

A demographic factor of some importance in facilitating intermarriage is the high spatial mobility of the American people. More than one-fifth of the native-born population live in states other than those in which they were born. Thirty million persons changed their residence during World War II. In the age group 7 to 13 years, more than a third live in places other than where they were born. Changes in recreational habits, including increased travel, as well as the increased emphasis on higher education, new employment opportunities, and the requirements of military service, expose younger people to contacts with different backgrounds, and, also, weaken the hold of old group controls.[80]

The third set of factors that affect intermarriage rates are the propinquous factors. They include place of residence, place of work, place of recreation, place of education, etc. Segregated minority groups tend to in-marry, whereas dispersed minorities tend to intermarry. (One should not infer a causal connection here. It may be that dispersed minorities intermarry more for the same reason that they are dispersed, namely, a lower prejudice against them.)

The fourth category of factors influencing the incidence of intermarriage consists of cultural similarities. Included here are similarity of cultural background, length of residence in the United States, occupational and economic class, amount and type of education, church affiliation or lack of it, and linguistic similarity. The Washington data show that the most important social factor influencing Jewish intermarriage is distance from immigration. Among the third and subsequent generations, the intermarriage rate was 18 percent.[81] In Providence, the reaction of the third-generation Jews of East European origin differed little from the second and the first: about one-fifth in each generation would be indifferent to an intermarriage in their own family and none would be happy with it. Among those of German or mixed descent, more than half of the fourth generation feel indifferent or even happy about their child's intermarriage, compared with much smaller proportions among the less advanced generations.[82] To a greater extent than formerly, Jews are now working with Gentiles as colleagues occupa-

[77] Goldstein and Goldscheider, *Jewish Americans: Three Generations in a Jewish Community*, p. 169.

[78] Sklare, "Intermarriage and the Jewish Future," pp. 422, 433.

[79] D. Y. Yuan, "Chinatown and Beyond: The Chinese Population in Metropolitan New York," *Phylon*, Fourth Quarter, pp. 321–332

[80] Bossard and Boll, *op. cit.*, pp. 6, 60.

[81] Rosenthal, *Studies of Jewish Intermarriage in the United States*, p. 31.

[82] Sklare and Greenblum, *Jewish Identity on the Suburban Frontier*, p. 309.

tionally instead of serving them as merchants or free professionals.[83]

To these rather specific factors might be added the general social conditions of "political emancipation, intermingling of culture, and the spread of tolerance and growth of fellowship" in modern times.[84] Thomas' investigations lead him to believe that there will be a gradual but steady increase in the number of marriages between Catholics and non-Catholics. His reasons are as follows: First, the decline in immigration, the horizontal and vertical mobility of our population, and the increased cultural contacts due to modern means of communication will reduce the influence of ethnic groups over individuals' choices of marriage partners; second, mixed marriages have a cumulative effect because the children of mixed marriages tend to marry outside their religious group more often than do the children of in-group marriages; third, the attitude of young people, both Catholic and Protestant, appears to be increasingly tolerant; and fourth, both the family and the church have less control over youth than they did in former years. Although Burma's data on interethnic marriage in Los Angeles give no causal inferences, it is the author's opinion that assimilation, decreasing social distance, improved social status of minorities, and decreasing intolerance are likely to be found among the causal factors for all intermarrying groups.[85]

Despite sharp segregation from both Anglo whites and Negroes in Los Angeles, including the existence of three high schools that are predominantly Mexican-American, Mittlebach and Moore concluded that prejudice against the Mexican-American population is comparatively low and opportunities for status advancement quite high in comparison with other parts of the Southwest. They say: "Los Angeles is an environment which facilitates interaction with the larger system."[86]

One of the factors that prevents some Jewish parents from upholding traditional norms is their desire to be consistent with a liberal orientation to intergroup relations.[87] A study of the Jewish population of Champaign-Urbana, numbering about 250 families almost equally divided between town and gown, showed that the intermarriage rate for faculty members was 20 percent compared with a 6.5 ratio for townspeople. Considering the backgrounds of the two groups, this finding was unexpected. Most of the Jewish faculty members have arrived in Champaign-Urbana in recent years, are descended mainly from East European immigrants, had parents who were affiliated with either Orthodox or Conservative synagogues, and grew up in predominantly Jewish neighborhoods. The townspeople, chiefly manufacturers, wholesalers, retailers, and professionals, include a group descended from German-Jewish families of longer residence in the community and whose predominant background is Reform. Cohen concluded: "Once the memories of Jewish culture become vague, the town Jew can find reasons to remain within the fold: he retains a latent supernatural faith, and the larger community expects him to be Jewish. By contrast, once the faculty Jew ceases to find meaning in the ethnic fellowship or the folkways, he has neither traditional belief nor strong social pressure to help him maintain his commitment."[88] A new factor in relation to Jewish-Gentile intermarriage is a change in the position of the Gentile. Richard Rubenstein, a Hillel rabbi at the University of Pittsburgh, observes that "in the course of 'emancipating' themselves, many of the bright middle-class Gentile girls who attend the better colleges are attracted by the political liberalism characteristic of Jewish students or by their equally characteristic avant-gardism in intellectual and esthetic matters."[89]

Rosenthal says that our understanding of

[83] Sklare, "Intermarriage and the Jewish Future," pp. 430–431.
[84] S. E. Goldstein, *The Meaning of Marriage and the Foundations of the Family*, Bloch, 1942, p. 161.
[85] Burma, "Interethnic Marriage in Los Angeles, 1948–1959," p. 160.
[86] Mittlebach and Moore, "Ethnic Endogamy: The Case of Mexican Americans," p. 52.
[87] Sklare and Greenblum, *Jewish Identity on the Suburban Frontier*, p. 317.
[88] Sklare, "Intermarriage and the Jewish Future," p. 428.
[89] Quoted in *ibid.*, p. 430.

the marriage market in Iowa communities was enhanced by studying the combined effects of residence and remarriage on intermarriage. In the rural areas, the chances of intermarriage were as high in a first marriage as in a remarriage. In cities of more than 10,000, the marriage market for first marriages for Jews was relatively well organized, and the interfaith marriage rate for Jews was 28.4 percent. In remarriages the intermarriage rate was 47.5 percent.[90] In Indiana the same author found a sharp contrast between individuals who had been previously widowed and those who had been previously divorced. The former had a high inmarriage rate, higher than those who had never been married before; the latter had a high rate of intermarriage, higher than the one found for the previously-never-married.[91]

In the light of recent studies, Sklare discusses three "dated notions" about the psychological and social conditions under which Jewish-Gentile intermarriage takes place, and, to some extent, his summary applies to other types of intermarriage. The explanations that he questions are: social climbing, escape from the harassments of prejudice, and hostility toward—or revolt from the mores and aspirations of—parents. Citing Rosenthal's Iowa data, Sklare says that it seems clear that if social climbing were a leading cause of intermarriage, Jewish men in that state would ignore many of the girls they choose to marry. The second interpretation is increasingly beside the ·point, he says, at a time when the penalties and risks of being Jewish are obviously on the wane. If the hostility-revolt theory were true, Sklare says that one would expect to find Jewish-Gentile marriages most prevalent in the second generation, where generational conflict is greatest. Instead, it is highest in the third generation.[92] He refers to the analysis of the data in Jerold Heiss' Midtown Manhattan Study where the assumption was that those whose early family life showed marked signs of disruption or had otherwise been unsatisfactory would be more likely to intermarry than those with relatively stable childhoods. Instead, it was found that the family backgrounds of the exogamous Jews in the study were not exceptional in terms of conflict, and actually showed fewer cases of parental divorce, separation, and desertion than did the backgrounds of the endogamous Jews.[93]

Gordon's assessment of intermarriage seems judicious. He sees it as the product of urbanization, mobility, propinquity, and related factors that play such an important role in present-day American society. As the generations succeed each other, he predicts that intermarriage will become more frequent because people "by some fortuitous circumstance, happen to meet, fall in love, and—as the result of the general weakening of contemporary family and religious ties as well as the possession of similar educational, economic, and social backgrounds—decide to marry."[94]

FACTORS THAT RETARD INTERMARRIAGE

Many of the parents of persons considering intermarriage use their influence to prevent it. There are no laws in the United States forbidding interfaith or interethnic marriages, and in June, 1967 the U.S. Supreme Court struck down the laws in 18 states that forbade Negro-white or other interracial marriages. With the exception of certain subcultures in the United States, the mores contain a strong taboo against interracial marriages and, to a lesser degree, against interfaith marriages. Some religious faiths, through teaching and the personal influence of clergymen, have always tried to discourage intermarriage.[95]

---

[90] Rosenthal, Studies of *Jewish Intermarriage in the United States*, pp. 51–52.

[91] Rosenthal, "Jewish Intermarriage in Indiana," p. 263. For a more detailed analysis of the data in the Iowa and Indiana studies, see Erich Rosenthal, *Journal of Marriage and the Family*, Aug., 1970, pp. 435–440.

[92] Sklare, *op. cit.*, pp. 424–426.

[93] *Ibid.*, p. 426.

[94] Gordon, *Intermarriage*, pp. 54, 60.

[95] For a detailed report on the positions that have been taken by various Protestant denominations on interfaith marriages, see A. I. Gordon, *Intermarriage*, chap. 5; on the Catholic point of view, see chap. 6;

In 1966, the Catholic Church relaxed some of its regulations concerning marriages between Catholics and other Christians. The non-Catholic partner was no longer required to sign a statement that he would allow his children to be reared Catholic, but he was still asked to make the promise orally. The written promise is still required for the Catholic partner. In May, 1970, Pope Paul VI announced that, beginning on October 1 of that year, the non-Catholic partner is relieved of the obligation to make the oral promise as a condition for the granting of a dispensation to his spouse.[96] Formerly, the Nuptial Mass was restricted to unmixed Catholic couples, but mixed couples may now use any Catholic rite they wish. Also, if the local bishop approves, Catholics may marry non-Catholics in places other than Catholic churches without a priest being present.[97] The new bilateralism includes encouragement of mixed couples to receive instruction in both partners' faith before marriage and to attend both churches every Sunday. The requirement that the Catholic partner wholeheartedly practice his own faith places a moral obligation on the couple to practice Catholic teaching about birth control and to attempt to raise the children in the Catholic faith.[98] Blood says that invalid mixed marriages are contracted by American Catholics almost as often as valid ones. Many are entered into by nominal Catholics to whom religious affiliation is

relatively meaningless. In other instances, the non-Catholic partner is unwilling to accept the Catholic conditions or one party is divorced and therefore ineligible to contract a valid Catholic marriage.

Gordon says that the great majority of the 250 varieties of organized Protestantism in the United States have expressed through church documents their disapproval of interfaith marriages involving non-Protestants. Some denominations oppose marriage between members of their group and members of certain other Protestant churches. Fundamentalists and literalists often oppose marriage with liberals and vice versa.[99]

Many Jews have opposed intermarriage on two grounds: first, because of the importance that the home has in religious life, and second, because there is no other way to preserve the Jewish community.

Twenty years ago Gordon noted that there had been considerable change in the attitudes of Jews in Minneapolis toward intermarriage. He pointed out that traditionally intermarriage had been considered calamitous and that the early Jewish residents in Minneapolis felt sick when they heard about it. "When it occurred among the children of Orthodox Jews, parents 'sat Shiva'—they observed the traditional seven-day period of mourning as if the child had died. Parents were distraught and ashamed to face their friends."[100] Later, despite disapproval, the outmarriage of Jews took place in ever increasing numbers. According to Gordon, nearly all those who intermarried remained in the Jewish group. "They join synagogues and temples, the golf club, and other organizations. They usually go to the Reform or Conservative synagogues, feeling, correctly, that their wives will be more readily accepted than at Orthodox ones. Even when the wife has not been formally converted to Judaism, she is permitted to join the women's organization of several of the synagogues and occasionally even plays a role of some prominence in its affairs."[101]

As a three-part device designed by Jews

---

and for Jewish views, see chap. 7. See also, Barron, *People Who Intermarry*, pp. 22–47, and Bossard and Boll, *op. cit.*, chap. 5. J. F. Doherty states the position of the Catholic Church on interracial marriage as follows:

1. The Roman Catholic Church in no way forbids interracial marriage as such. 2. The natural right to marry includes also the natural right to marry the person of one's own choice, to marry this person regardless of race. 3. The exercise of this right involves great benefits to the individual and to society regardless of the undesirable concomitants in many sections of this country. The parties to an interracial marriage may justifiably enter such a marriage to secure these benefits despite the undesirable consequences they may suffer. 4. The entrance upon an interracial marriage is in itself, a morally good act.

J. F. Doherty, *Moral Problems of Interracial Marriage*, Catholic Univ. of America Press, 1949, p. 154.
[96] *The New York Times*, May 3, 1970, p. E9.
[97] *The Plain Dealer*, Dec. 5, 1970, p. 6B.
[98] Blood, *op. cit.*, p. 84.

[99] Gordon, *Intermarriage*, p. 121.
[100] Gordon, *Jews in Transition*, pp. 205–206.
[101] *Ibid.*, pp. 206, 207.

in Chicago to forestall "large-scale assimilation," Rosenthal lists (1) a modicum of Jewish education, (2) voluntary segregation, and (3) residence in a high-status area. In explanation of the latter point, he says: "Settlement there removes the stigma that is usually attributed to a separate ethnic community which, according to the scheme of the race-relations cycle, is reserved for unacculturated immigrants. Residence in a high-status area indicates the voluntary nature of the settlement of Jews as well as non-Jews and lifts the burden of alienation from the younger generation in particular."[102]

The finding in an Indiana study that interstate marriages have the lowest level of intermarriage led to the inference that they are arranged marriages. Rosenthal remarks that the data "therefore underline the wisdom of or necessity for the old Jewish tradition of arranged marriages to secure Jewish group survival."[103] This inference was strengthened by the finding that elopements had an intermarriage level of from 67 to 77 percent, and that local marriage market marriages showed a 50–50 chance for intermarriage. A rabbi who is a student of intermarriage advises parents who are opposed to intermarriage to "try, lovingly and persuasively, to dissuade the young people from intermarrying," adding that "to do more—to coerce, to threaten, or to use force—only hastens the likelihood of intermarriage." He says further that by the latter approach parents may drive their children away forever.[104]

Intermarriage is opposed by some Jews even when the non-Jew joins the Jewish group because "an alien element is introduced."[105] Other viewpoints, however, are expressed in a symposium on intermarriage and Jewish life. Cohen, viewing the "threat of intermarriage" as the necessary "leaven in the dough," says: "The price of freedom is the tension caused by our desire to survive in the face of inevitable competition. In the long run, then, the answer to intermarriage is the quality of Jewish life, for the enhancement of which Jewish education is the main instrument."[106] Pointing out that Americans are "certain to look with disfavor upon any culture which seeks to maintain itself by decrying the intermarriage of its adherents with those of another culture," Cahnman advocates acceptance of "a policy which does not decry marriages of Jews with Gentiles, provided the homes they establish are Jewish and their children are given a Jewish upbringing." Such an attitude, he says, would eliminate the charge of "exclusiveness and tribalism" and "racial pride;" what is valuable is the "Jewish social heritage, or civilization, and not physical descent."[107] In the Lakeville study, it was found that many Jewish parents are not capable of reacting in the traditional manner with respect to intermarriage. Only 1 percent would reject their child, and 93 percent were prepared to accept the intermarriage, retain their connections with their child, and also attempt to build a meaningful relationship with his Gentile spouse.[108] Some parents hope that their friendly stance to the non-Jewish partner will be interpreted as an invitation to join the Jewish group.

---

[102] Erich Rosenthal, "Acculturation Without Assimilation? The Jewish Community of Chicago," p. 287. Rosenthal remarks that if the national intermarriage rate, for Jews, of 7.2 percent found in the 1957 survey by the U.S. Bureau of the Census is accepted, and it is assumed that the statistics for Iowa and the San Francisco area are simply regional variations of the over-all rate, "we can probably be justified in defending the current survival formula as adequate for the preservation of the Jewish group. If we assume, however, that the findings for Iowa and San Francisco are the first indications of the future over-all rate of intermarriage, then the efficacy of the survival formula must be seriously doubted . . . the likelihood of intermarriage increases with increased acculturation." *Ibid.*, p. 288.

[103] Rosenthal, "Jewish Intermarriage in Indiana," pp. 263–264.

[104] Gordon, *Intermarriage*, p. 372. In his survey of the attitudes of college youth to intermarriage, Gor-

don found that 69 percent of his respondents believed that their parents are not opposed to interdating with a person of another religion. He thinks that this is important because the belief (not the fact) that parents are permissive on this point may play a significant role in the ultimate response of young people. He points out that whereas parents may have no serious objections to interdating, they may oppose intermarriage. *Ibid.*, p. 14.

[105] Goldstein, *op. cit.*, pp. 161–162.

[106] Jack J. Cohen, "Intermarriage and Jewish Education," in Cahnman, *op. cit.*, p. 208.

[107] W. J. Cahnman, "Intermarriage and American Democracy," in Cahnman, *op. cit.*, p. 189.

[108] Sklare and Greenblum, *Jewish Identity on the Suburban Frontier*, pp. 315, 317.

As far as Negro-white marriage is concerned, many white people will continue

. . . to exploit the fear of intermarriage as a means of retaining economic dominance, and as a devastating question to be raised in connection with any concessions, no matter how small, which the Negro community requests. A few intermarriages will no doubt continue to take place, as well as clandestine "affairs," but "crossing the line" is not uppermost in the minds of the Negroes. Relaxation of the taboos against intermarriage is something white people are most reluctant to grant. It is also the "concession" which Negroes, as a group, are least likely to request. That it looms so large in the white mind is the irony of race relations in Midwest Metropolis [Chicago].[109]

Contrary to a widespread belief among white persons that Negroes are strongly interested in intermarriage, a Chicago study showed that very few parents would encourage their children to marry whites (1.1 percent of a Negro slum sample and 2.5 percent of a Negro middle- and upper-class sample). About half of the respondents said they would tolerate intermarriage, stating that "it made no difference," and the other half opposed it. "Eighty percent or more of Negro parents would permit their child to marry a white person if the romance had already developed without their knowledge but there is no evidence of a desire for miscegenation or even interest in promoting it, except among a very tiny minority."[110]

Where integration increases, it is likely to be accompanied by an increase in Negro-white marriage. The recent growth of black consciousness and racial pride will tend to discourage intermarriage. In the near future, the rate of increase probably will be slow.

THE SUCCESS OR FAILURE OF INTERMARRIAGE

Evidence concerning the success or failure of intermarriage is not extensive. Intermarriage

—like inmarriage—does not always turn out well. In the event of marital difficulty, it may be difficult to discover whether the racial factor is directly or indirectly involved. Few studies control for class, education, residence, or other variables that influence the stability of marriages. Hence it is difficult to measure the possible impact of the factor of intermarriage.

Duvall and Hill report that from the first contact interfaith relationships are more subject to dissolution. Fewer interfaith couples who are "going steady" become engaged, and the proportion of broken engagements among them is high.[111] Burgess and Wallin found that 27 percent of the couples in their study who belonged to the same church broke their engagements compared with 41 percent of their interfaith couples.[112] A study in Iowa showed that interfaith couples are more likely to obtain divorces and that they divorce three years earlier than couples of the same faith.[113]

In a follow-up study of several hundred couples who attended the University of Minnesota, Dyer and Luckey found that interfaith combinations of Lutherans, Catholics, Protestants, and Jews are likely to be as happy as intrafaith marriages.[114] Duvall and Hill mention that none of the marital happiness studies list similarity of religious affiliation as an important predictive factor in marital adjustment.[115] They conclude that "if we define success in marriage as invulnerability to divorce, the interfaith marriage is more hazardous than the homogamous marriage. However, if we define success in marriage as happiness or adjustment in marriage and wait to take our measures of success until

[109] Drake and Cayton, *op. cit.*, p. 173.

[110] Donald J. Bogue and Jan E. Dizard, *Race, Ethnic Prejudice, and Discrimination as Viewed by Subordinate and Superordinate Groups*, Community and Family Study Center, Univ. of Chicago, 1964, p. 7. Mimeo.

[111] Duval and Hill, *Being Married*, Heath, 1960, p. 81.

[112] E. W. Burgess and Paul Wallin, *Engagement and Marriage*, Lippincott, 1953, p. 289.

[113] Thomas P. Monahan and Loren E. Chancellor, "Statistical Aspects of Marriage and Divorce by Religious Denomination in Iowa," *Eugenics Quarterly*, Sept., 1955, p. 170. Quoted in E. M. Duvall and R. Hill, *op. cit.*

[114] Dorothy T. Dyer and Eleanor Luckey, "Religious Affiliation and Selected Personality Scores as They Relate to Marital Happiness of a Minnesota College Sample," unpublished manuscript cited by Duvall and Hill, *op. cit.*, p. 2.

[115] Duvall and Hill, *op. cit.*, p. 82.

Desertions and Divorces of Jewish Men in Communally Mixed and Unmixed Marriages

| City | Percentages of Desertions and Divorces by Communal Homogamy | | |
	Communally Unmixed	Communally Mixed	Ratio
New Orleans	33.4%	57.4%	1.7X
Omaha	12.6%	62.2%	4.9X
St. Louis	8.6%	44.4%	5.2X
Boston	4.7%	25.4%	5.4X
Denver	8.4%	48.3%	5.8X

Source: Robert O. Blood, *Marriage*, Macmillan, 2nd ed., 1969, p. 87. Adapted from Carle C. Zimmerman and Lucius F. Cervantes, *Successful American Families*, Pageant, 1960, pp. 76, 153–154. Based on data for high school seniors and of friends of their families. In the five cities combined the total number of case studies was 1420 intracommunal marriages and 450 intercommunal marriages. Reprinted with permission.

after a few years have elapsed, interfaith marriages stand up very well."[116]

Zimmerman and Cervantes found a 70 percent higher rate of failure for Jewish-Gentile than for "communally unmixed" marriages (see table above).

When the data given above are compared with the data concerning Protestant husbands and Catholic husbands, St. Louis is the median city in the ratio of divorce-and-desertion failures in mixed compared with unmixed marriages. For Protestant husbands in that city the failure rate doubled, for Catholics it tripled, and for Jews, as indicated above, it is five times the homogamous rate. Blood remarks that this pattern suggests that Jewish-Gentile marriages are more hazardous than Catholic-Protestant marriages.[117] Although the divorce rates in a study of religiously homogamous and interreligious marriages in Iowa are relatively low because they are limited to high status couples in the early years of marriage, there is a marked difference between unmixed and mixed marriages. For both Catholic and Protestant women, the divorce rate in interfaith marriages was several times the rate for intrafaith marriages. In the Iowa study, the

denominational affiliation made little difference when one Protestant married another. Interdenominational Protestant marriages had about the same divorce rate as intradenominational marriages. When Catholics married Protestants, the more alike the two churches, the lower the divorce. When Catholics married members of "high" churches (Lutherans and Presbyterians) the divorce rate was two-and-a-half times the Catholic norm. When they married members of "low" churches (Methodists and Baptists), it was four-and-a-half times as high. The highest rate occurred in marriages of "unspecified Protestants' belonging to no church (almost 20 times the normal Catholic divorce rate). Evidently, it is easier for a person who holds religious values to get along with someone with a different religious orientation than with someone who rejects that whole orientation.[118]

A study in Hawaii of 324 war brides and husbands of European and Japanese ancestry found that the Japanese wives of non-Japanese were the happiest group, followed by the European wives of Japanese husbands. As a group, European wives of non-Japa-

[116] *Ibid.*, p. 81.
[117] Blood, *Marriage*, p. 84.

[118] *Ibid.*, pp. 85–86. The study referred to here is L. G. Burchinal and L. E. Chancelor, "Survival Rates Among Religiously Homogamous and Interreligious Marriages," *SF*, May, 1963, pp. 353–362.

nese husbands were third in marital adjustment, and Japanese wives of Japanese were fourth.[119] An exploratory study of 20 American-Japanese couples did not confirm the belief that such marriages would have a high rate of failure because they were hasty and involved sharp cultural conflict. "The serviceman's stay in Japan averaged over four years, and courtships averaged about two years. Severe cultural conflict was not found in in-group and out-group relationships; husbands identified themselves with their wives' circles; there were no regrets and no serious in-law problems. Cooperation and adaptation were common, wives were learning English, and there were no religious conflicts. A study of age at marriage, educational attainment, residence separate from in-laws, first marriage, and average number of children all indicated stability rather than conflict."[120] In a study in Chicago, Strauss found more harmony than strain in the American-Japanese war bride marriages he investigated. However, he says: "This is not to . . . claim that homogamy between husband and wife is of no importance in marital selection. . . . However, the easy assumptions that interracial marriages are doomed to destruction or that the couples must have something extra-special to make a go of the marriage are much over-simplified notions."[121] He recommends a reappraisal of this type of intermarriage in the light of the special conditions of contact, selection, and living conditions that make mixed marriages more vulnerable to difficulty.

Banton says a minority of the white wives who have married colored men in Britain could equally well have married white men but happened to have fallen in love with a colored man and married him despite opposition. He sees as the outstanding characteristics of most of the white women who associate with colored men: "firstly, an inferior economic position and low earning power; secondly, emotional insecurity, and a background of personal rejection."[122] Egginton says that "many mixed marriages are successful in Britain.[123] Collins shows that white women in Britain who marry colored men from British West Africa and the West Indies play an important role as intermediary between the wife's family and the white community, seeking to gain concessions from the privileged group.[124] Little points out that disapproval and ostracism of white friends and acquaintances lead the white wife to identify with the colored group, but when the child leaves school he may find it difficult to develop friendships with white persons at work without giving up the colored friends of his earlier years.[125]

Rosenthal points out that there are few scientific studies of religious intermarriage that deal with the widely held view that such marriages involve irreconcilable religio-cultural differences that lead to desertion and divorce. Even if it is assumed that religious intermarriages produce a higher divorce rate than do inmarriages, one must take into consideration the fact that a considerable number of intermarriages are remarriages. He adds: "We also know from an early study of marriage and divorce records in Iowa and Missouri 'that remarriages are not as enduring as first marriages

[119] Yukiko Kimura, "War Brides in Hawaii and Their In-Laws," *AJS*, July, 1957, pp. 70–71.

[120] G. J. Schnepp and A. M. Yui, "Cultural and Marital Adjustment of Japanese War Brides," *AJS*, July, 1955, p. 48–50. According to Schnepp and Yui, the International Institute estimated that there were from 40 to 50 Japanese war brides in the St. Louis area, and the Chicago Resettlers Committee estimates that between 2000 and 2500 resided in the Chicago area. Of the 15,500 marriages that went through the American consulates in Japan between 1945 and 1954, at least two-thirds were estimated to have been American-Japanese war marriages. *Ibid.*, p. 48. Between 1955 and 1960, at least 20,000 additional Japanese brides came into the United States, with the very likely probability that a similar number would come in before the law permitting this immigration expired.

[121] Anselm Strauss, "Strain and Harmony in American-Japanese War Bride Marriages," *MFL*, May, 1954, pp. 99–106. Cited in Duvall and Hill, *op. cit.*, p. 86.

[122] Michael Banton, *The Coloured Quarter*, Jonathan Cape, 1955, p. 152. See also, by the same author, *White and Coloured*, Jonathan Cape, 1959, pp. 126–131.

[123] Joyce Egginton, *They Seek a Living*, Hutchinson, 1957, p. 114.

[124] Sydney F. Collins, "The Social Position of White and 'Half-Caste' Women in Colored Groupings in Britain," *ASR*, Dec., 1951, pp. 796–802.

[125] Kenneth Little, "The Position of Colored People in Britain," *Phylon*, First Quarter, 1954, p. 62.

and that the probability of divorce rises with each successive marriage.' These findings clearly suggest 'divorce-proneness among divorced persons who remarry.' "[126]

Blood lists the same prerequisites for mixed marriages as for other marriages: compatibility, skill, effort, commitment, and support.[127]

CONCLUSION

Our conclusion on intermarriage may be stated briefly as follows:

1. From a statistical standpoint, the chances for success in marriage seem to be somewhat less for intermarriage than for inmarriage in the United States at the present time. Without the control of other variables, however, it is not clear how much the intermarriage factor itself produces this result.

2. The legality of intermarriage is an important aspect of equal civil rights. During the past two decades state laws against miscegenation have been repealed and/or declared unconstitutional by state courts in nine states, and in 1967, the U.S. Supreme Court struck down the laws forbidding interracial marriages in the 17 states that still had such legislation.

3. Race mixture is not biologically inadvisable.

4. Opposition by fervent church members to religious intermarriage has not decreased; otherwise, resistance to all types of intermarriage, except Negro-white, has declined significantly during the past three decades.

5. Religious intermarriage and ethnic intermarriage are increasing rapidly and, with continued acculturation, will continue to increase in the United States. Racial intermarriage is also increasing, with Negro-white marriages increasing more slowly than other kinds of racial intermarriage.

6. Intermarriage on a large scale would produce a relatively homogeneous population, physically and culturally. The elimination of intergroup conflicts based on race and culture would have societal advantages, although some would lament the passing of cultural pluralism.

---

[126] Rosenthal, "Jewish Intermarriage in Indiana," p. 262.

[127] Blood, *op. cit.*, p. 97.

Chapter 17 / MINORITIES AND RELIGION

Religious patterns are a sensitive index of the majority-minority situation in a society. Religious beliefs and institutional structures of a group show not only intrinsic religious aspects, but secular positions and secular problems as well. We shall be concerned primarily with some of the ways in which religious practices—of both dominant and minority groups—reflect and affect intergroup relations.

NEGRO CHURCHES

One does not speak accurately of "the" Negro church, for there are many varieties, indicating the wide differences among Negroes in all the forces that affect religious life—occupation, residence, education, secular group membership, and the like. Precise information on religious preferences is lacking, but we can note the broad outlines of identification. A NORC national poll, taken in 1964, revealed that 87 percent of the Negro respondents listed a Protestant preference, 9 percent a Catholic, and 5 percent had no preference.[1] Of the numerous Protestant denominations, most nonwhites belong to two: Baptist, 60.6 percent, and Methodist, 17.3 percent.[2] All these data refer to religious preference, not to membership. Al-

[1] Hazel Erskine, "The Polls: Negro Philosophies of Life," *POQ*, Spring, 1969, pp. 154–155. This is close to the estimate obtained by the sample census (30,000) taken in 1957: Of nonwhites over 14 years of age, 87.5 percent reported themselves as Protestant; 6.5 percent as Catholic. The latter figure, however, includes a higher ratio of Orientals and Indians than of Negroes. Thus somewhat fewer than 6.5 percent of Catholic respondents were Negro, indicating that there may have been an increase in Negro Catholics from 1957–1964. See U.S. Bureau of the Census, "Religion Reported by the Civilian Population of the United States: March, 1957." *Current Population Reports*, ser. P-20, no. 79, 1958.

[2] *Ibid.*

though exact figures are not available, at least two-thirds of Negroes, who belong to religious groups in somewhat higher proportion than do Whites, are members of the various churches.

Rural Negro Churches

Religious gatherings were the first forms of association permitted under the slave system, and the first leaders of Negroes were religious teachers. The other-worldliness doctrine provided an emotional escape from slavery and, later, from economic poverty and cultural isolation. After emancipation, churches were the first independent Negro institutions. And the rural church is still regarded as the outstanding social institution in the community, the only one that provides an effective organization of the Negro group. There is variation in style of worship and doctrine, depending to an important degree on the extent of isolation. Charles Johnson distinguished the plantation church from the church outside the plantation area. The plantation church is small and neglected, with a congregation consisting of 75 or 100 tenants and a few owners and their children. The average preacher is skilled in histrionic devices and "acts out" the journey to heaven and other favorite themes. His sermons are long and repetitious, and the congregation responds frequently with shouts of approval. Usually several persons experience hysterical seizures during which they testify to being saved or bemoan a hard life or some unjust treatment.

The rural church in the nonplantation areas has been more strongly influenced by the towns and cities. It provides a better-educated ministry and a type of Sunday school that is more subject to innovations and is characterized by greater participation by young people. The emphasis, nevertheless, is still on the "old time religion."[3]

Urban Negro Churches

Urbanization of a majority of Negroes in the United States has influenced their religious life in many ways; and their religious beliefs and practices have affected the nature of their responses to life in the city. These are among the consequences: (1) Some have become "unchurched." The city has shattered their older beliefs, they feel alienated from the existing churches—that some look upon as just another "racket." (2) For a majority, however, the church remains an important force. It is the association to which they are most likely to belong and in which they actively participate. (3) The urban world furnishes a wide variety of forms of belief and worship: small sects and cults like those in rural areas, denominations that are similar to the established churches of the white population, and dramatically new religious movements that depart widely—although not completely—from the Christian tradition. (4) In the city one finds the beginnings of a racially integrated church, in which lines of class, education, and residence determine membership more than does race.

The urban scene is illustrated by a study of Chicago, where Negroes have established hundreds of churches in more than 30 denominations. The details of this study, published in 1945, would have to be modified today; but the total picture has not changed substantially. The two Negro National Baptist Conventions included almost half of the churches and more than two-thirds of the members. Neither the Negro Baptist congregations nor the ministers had extensive contacts with white Baptists. Other denominations included Holiness, Spiritualist, and Community churches, and three varieties

of Methodists. In addition, there were a number of local denominations and "such all-Negro 'cults' as the African Orthodox Church, the Christian Catholics, the Temple of Moorish Science, and numerous fly-by-night groups organized around enterprising and untrained preachers."[4]

In Chicago, 10 percent of the Negro churches, but less than 10 percent of the church members, were affiliated with "white" denominations—Methodist Episcopal, Episcopal, Presbyterian, Congregational, Roman Catholic, Lutheran, Christian Scientist, Seventh-Day Adventist, and Disciples of Christ. Negroes were not welcomed in some of the white congregations of these churches, nor did they have much influence in the national organizations of these denominations. A number of "white" churches had educational or welfare projects *for* Negroes throughout the country. This picture has changed somewhat on the national scene, as we shall note below. It is still true, however, that the great majority of Negro churchgoers attend all-black congregations.

Sectarian Movements Among Negroes

A purely descriptive approach to the religion of minority-group members may cause us to overlook the ways in which religion is involved in the pursuit of life's values. If, on one occasion, it is a tranquilizer, on another it is a stimulant. There are some among the oppressed who use religion as a shield against the misfortunes of life; but others are armed with righteous anger. The student of majority-minority relations must attempt to discover the conditions under which these various patterns occur.

In briefest terms, those whose deprivation is so severe that even hopes and dreams for improvement of their earthly lot are denied them will be drawn to a religion that promises them a shield, and rewards in another life. Such persons are characterized by a particularly intense form of "status crystallization." Not only are they consistently low on measures of income, power, and prestige;

---

[3] Charles S. Johnson, *Growing Up in the Black Belt*, ACE, 1941. See also the same author's *Shadow of the Plantation*, Univ. of Chicago Press, 1934, chap. 5. Interesting accounts of revival meetings in rural Negro churches are given in Hortense Powdermaker, *After Freedom*, Viking, 1939, pp. 253–256; and in John Dollard, *Caste and Class in a Southern Town;* Yale, 1937, pp. 226–230, 231–232.

[4] St. Clair Drake and Horace Cayton, *Black Metropolis*, Harcourt Brace Jovanovich, 1945, p. 413.

but they have also been denied hope that their situation can be improved. In situations where income, power, and prestige are beginning to improve, however, hope will soar. Status becomes decrystallized for those who can hope; and religious values are among the clearest indicators of their inconsistencies of status.

Expressed in terms of a general sociology of religion, the former situation tends to promote withdrawal or avoidance sects, the latter to stimulate the development of aggressive sects that challenge not only the established religious structures, but the secular order as well.[5] Seldom is a situation so uniform that sects of only one type appear among a minority group. Hope can break through in the most discriminatory of circumstances, due to accidents of personal biography or some variation in the structure that "decrystallizes" the lives of some members of a minority. Although avoidance and withdrawal themes were predominant in the religious lives of American Negro slaves, for example, there were also tones of protest, of a nascent aggressive sect. "Certainly we must be struck by the appearance of one or another kind of messianic preacher in almost every slave revolt on record."[6]

The most widely held view has been, in the words of Benjamin Mays, that the Negroes' idea of God "kept them submissive, humble, and obedient."[7] This may be an accurate description of the most common view. It is subject to serious misinterpretation, however, if it is not put alongside the evidences of radical religious protest. These evidences are found not only in the lives of Denmark Vesey, Nat Turner, Frederick Douglass, Harriet Tubman, John Brown, and others who became well known; but also in the lives of the rank and file who came to believe in a gospel of freedom. This is well documented by Vincent Harding in his careful review of the theme of "religion and resistance." He notes, for example, that in 1800 ". . . South Carolina's legislature indicated a keen awareness of the possible connections between black rebellion and black religion, an awareness that was apparently the property of many southern white persons. In that year the legislature passed one of the first of those countless 19th century laws restricting black religious services. This one forbade Negroes 'even in company with white persons to meet together and assemble for the purpose of . . . religious worship, either before the rising of the sun or after the going down of the same.' "[8]

Protest themes have become more common in black religion, but the change should not be exaggerated. There are still strong tendencies toward avoidance. Most movements, however, are a mixture, as we shall see in our examination of a few twentieth century sects and cults.

Religion and Black Power

Perhaps the most interesting of current religious trends among Negroes are those associated with the black power movement, broadly defined. There are many aspects to the religious phase of this movement, of which we shall refer to four: the formation of new religions; heightened pressures from black ministers and laymen against the "white" church; the development of a "black theology;" and religious leadership in the civil rights movement generally.

The Black Muslims. New religions, or the transfer of loyalty to a new religion, are likely to occur under conditions of prolonged suffering, where the dominant religion appears implicated in the suffering, and where hope has been aroused.

[5] See J. Milton Yinger, *The Scientific Study of Religion,* Macmillan, 1970, chaps. 14 and 15 for development of this theme.

[6] Eugene Genovese, "American Slaves and Their History," *The New York Review of Books,* Dec. 3, 1970, p. 35.

[7] See Benjamin Mays, *The Negro's God as Reflected in His Literature,* Chapman and Grimes, 1938; E. Franklin Frazier, *The Negro Church in America,* Schocken, 1964.

[8] Vincent Harding, "Religion and Resistance among Antebellum Negroes, 1800–1860," in August Meier and Elliott Rudwick (eds.), *The Making of Black America,* Atheneum, Vol. 1, 1969, p. 182. For other indications of resistance in religious terms among nineteenth century Negroes, see John H. Bracey, Jr., August Meier, and Elliott Rudwick (eds.), *Black Nationalism in America,* Bobbs-Merrill, 1970, pp. 3–17, 123–155.

These conditions fit the situation of many American Negroes who have, as a result, participated in quite large numbers in a variety of new religious movements and cults. The Black Muslims are one of the largest and most important. We shall give a brief description of their doctrines and history by way of illustration of the "revitalization process" in religious movements.[9]

In their strongly puritanical code of behavior, their opposition to racial discrimination, and their search for security and dignity, the Black Muslims are similar to such groups as the cult of the late Father Divine. There are, however, important differences. They are more ascetic, more energetic in their pursuit of educational and economic improvement, more hostile to whites.[10] The Black Muslims attack integrationist Negroes as lackeys of the white man. They call, as did Marcus Garvey, for a separate Negro nation, but unlike Garvey they prefer to establish it in the United States, in a region set aside for that purpose or in Muslim sections of cities and states, where they can run their own farms and businesses.

Muslims in New York and Chicago and elsewhere now own and operate hundreds of businesses. Although most of these are small, they represent a substantial increase in the number of black-owned businesses in the central cities. The Muslims also are giving increasing attention to education. Curricula and methods in their schools tend to be traditional and stern, and the school year is 50 weeks long. Minister Louis Farrakhan, head of the Harlem Mosque commented on this: "We are 400 years behind, 100 years up from slavery. We have a lot of catching up to do."[11]

There is also a more psychological, "revitalization" quality to the Black Muslim movement. It fits quite closely Wallace's definition of such a movement as a deliberate and organized effort "to construct a more satisfying culture."[12] In their effort to cast aside all the punishing meaning of their identities as Negroes, they declare: We are the lost nation of Islam; salvation will come from a rediscovery of that tradition. All science stems from the work of 24 original black scientists, thousands of years ago. It is the black man, not the white man, who is good, and right, and powerful—or he can be, if he abides by the tenets of the faith, follows the stern requirements of self-denial and hard work, and breaks away from the evil ways of the white man.

There is a harshness about the way the Black Muslims speak, build up a quasi-military arm (called "The Fruit of Islam"), and ridicule nonviolent integrationist efforts that shocks most white men. It is startling to hear a Muslim minister proclaim as a goal: "To get the white man's foot off my neck, his hand out of my pocket and his carcass off my back. To sleep in my own bed without fear, and to look straight into his cold blue eyes and call him a liar every time he parts his lips."[13] When he is not startled by the vigor of the verbal attacks, the white man is likely to be amazed at the extravagant interpretation of history by which the Black Muslims justify their claims and sustain their self-respect.

How can we account for what appears to be a rather sudden rise of the Muslims, with their tens of thousands of members (estimates range from 10,000 to 200,000) and dozens of temples in over half the states? We should note, first, that the movement has had many predecessors. Garvey's Universal Negro Improvement Association, in the early 1920s, won a great deal of support among American Negroes by its appeal for a separate economy and separate nation.[14] Shortly before World War I a cult was founded by Timothy Drew (later known as Noble Drew Ali) which developed the theme

[9] See Anthony F. C. Wallace, "Revitalization Movements," AA, Apr., 1956, pp. 264–281.

[10] On their asceticism, see Lawrence L. Tyler, "The Protestant Ethic Among the Black Muslims," Phylon, Spring, 1966, pp. 5–14.

[11] The New York Times, Aug. 25, 1970, p. L-39.

[12] James Laue has applied "revitalization" to the Muslims. See "A Contemporary Revitalization Movement in American Race Relations: The 'Black Muslims,'" SF, Mar., 1964, pp. 305–323.

[13] Quoted by Eric Lincoln, The Black Muslims in America, Beacon Press, 1961, p. 27.

[14] See E. D. Cronon, Black Moses, Univ. of Wisconsin Press, 1955; also Lincoln, op. cit., pp. 56–66.

of the "Moorish" origin of Negroes. Symbols and worship in the "Moorish Holy Temple of Science" were strongly Muslim.[15] This cult may have influenced W. D. Fard, who became influential in Detroit in the early 1930s. He claimed to have come from Mecca to teach American Negroes that, they were the lost tribe of Shebazz, stolen by traders from Mecca many centuries ago. He came to restore their true names, language, nation, and religion.[16] About 1933 Fard disappeared. The cult was torn by schism, but gradually an officer of the cult, who had taken the name of Elijah Muhammad, the son of a Southern Baptist minister, won control.

For 25 years, Muhammad's Black Muslim movement grew only slowly; but in the last several years it has gained membership and strengthened its program. Growing contact with "the American dream" (and growing frustration because it is being realized so slowly for them), disillusionment with Christian churches, the inadequacy of alternatives to religious response (political action or individual effort, for example), the rise to independence of the African states, and doubtless the publicity—some of it quite fearful—given to the cult by the mass media have been among the influences promoting its growth. As James Baldwin has remarked, Negroes had been hearing the message of the Muslims for a generation, but few had listened. Now the time is ripe; the message gets through.[17] Even those Negroes—probably a large majority—who oppose its message and its strategy recognize the appeal of the movement and are likely to say that there is a little "Muslim" in most Negroes today.

But who are the dedicated followers? For the most part, the message of Muhammad has attracted the same kinds of persons who were drawn to Garvey, Fard, and Noble Drew Ali—the recent migrants to large cities. Their ambitions have been raised by the promises of an affluent society, their sense of power increased, their old accommodative way of life destroyed; yet their hopes are frustrated. Those who join are mostly young men, lower-class, often functionally illiterate. Some have been converted in prison. These are the persons who are ill-equipped to struggle for status in the urban world. They are poorly trained; they face discrimination; they are uncertain of their own manhood. They may seek to escape the trap by use of drugs, alcohol, and mental illness, as some do. They may attack the frustrating society by random aggression or criminality, as some do. They may, by happy chance, get a good start in family and school, seize the rare opportunity, and win success by the dominant group's own criteria, as a few do. But for some, the former responses are unacceptable and the latter unattainable. They join such movements as the Muslims. We should not be misled by their anti-white tone. Far more importantly, the Black Muslim movement is a radical attack on the inferiority complex and sense of powerlessness of Negroes.

It is impossible to speak with confidence about the extent of Muslim appeal. At most, 1 percent of the black population belongs to the sect. In 1964, five metropolitan and city samples of Negroes gave it a low rating in chosing among the NAACP, CORE, and the Muslims as having "done most" for Negroes. In the five samples, from 70 to 92 percent selected the NAACP, from 2 to 12 percent selected CORE, and from 0 to 8 percent selected the Muslims. On the basis of leadership, Malcolm X, who was then the most prominent of the Muslims (although he had been suspended from leadership), was selected as the person who had done most by 0 to 5 percent of the samples, compared with Martin Luther King's 85 to 95 percent.[18] Later polls, however, may indicate a more favorable attitude toward the Muslims. The martyred Malcolm X has become a hero to diverse groups, and 27 percent of a national sample rated him favorably (40 percent of

[15] A. H. Fauset, *Black Gods of the Metropolis*, Univ. of Pennsylvania Press, 1944, pp. 41–51.

[16] See E. D. Benyon, "The Voodoo Cult Among Negro Migrants to Detroit," *AJS*, May, 1938, pp. 894–907.

[17] See James Baldwin, *The Fire Next Time*, Dial Press, 1963, pp. 61–65.

[18] See Gary Marx, *Protest and Prejudice*, Harper & Row, 1969, pp. 25–28.

those under 30). In another poll, 23 percent of a national sample of Negroes indicated that they respected Elijah Muhammad "a great deal," and another 23 percent replied that they respected him "some."[19] The figures for Muhammad Ali—though scarcely based on his religious leadership—were 33 and 24.[20]

Variation in time, samples, and questions make it difficult to be certain, but support for the Muslims—during a period when they had become less violent in their rhetoric, more oriented to improved education and economic advancement for Blacks—seems clearly to have increased.

The appearance and growth of the Black Muslims are testimony to the impatience of American Negroes. If their aspirations continue to be seriously frustrated, the potential for violence that the movement carries may grow. If, on the other hand, the United States rapidly removes the special burdens imposed on Negroes, the Black Muslims may prove to be an effective instrument for the development of discipline, thrift, responsibility, and stable family patterns. Norms of behavior that are unlikely to be adopted when they are seen as the coercive demands of white men become deep commitments when they are seen as commandments of a specifically black man's religion. The divisiveness of the sect's approach to Whites may also decline. Minister Farrakhan claims that Muslim attitudes toward Whites have been misunderstood. Charges of anti-white racism are unfounded, he declares; the group is pro-Black.[21] This, in any event, has been the recent trend. Thus the latent functions of the Black Muslims may be quite different, for its members and for society, than quick observation of its manifest symbolism and beliefs would lead one to expect.[22]

The Black Muslims, like many other sects, have a tendency to schism. Malcolm X, who was suspended as the New York leader in December, 1963, at first talked of organizing a "black nationalist party," presumably to promote a sharper attack on discrimination, with implications of mounting violence. After a trip to Mecca, however, and other parts of the Islamic world, he proclaimed himself an orthodox Muslim, denounced black racism, and broke sharply with Elijah Muhammad. In a letter to a friend, Malcolm X wrote:

Nothing will stop them [racial explosions] but real meaningful actions, sincerely motivated by a deep sense of humanism and moral responsibility to remove . . . the very basic causes that produce the 'materials' for these explosive conditions. We must forget politics and propaganda and approach this as a Human Problem which all of us as human beings are obligated to correct. The well meaning whites must become less vocal and more active against racism of their fellow whites . . . and Negro leaders must make their own people see that with equal rights also go equal responsibilities.[23]

His murder a few months later leaves unresolved the question of how he might have developed these ideas organizationally. He has become a hero to quite contrasting kinds of people, because in his lifetime he stood for sharply contrasting kinds of goals and means. But above all, he stood for unmitigated attack on racial discrimination; he challenged "whitey." And by the strength of that challenge he has become a saint to many of the most militant participants in the black power movement.

Black Power Activities Within Predominantly White Churches. Today there are more black participants in predominantly white churches than ever before, more black leaders in those churches, more cooperation and integration between formerly separate denominations. And there is also a sharper challenge to the continuing evidences of prejudice in the churches than ever before. This is not an uncommon situation: A few changes, won at what seems the cost of great effort, open up the vision of much more extensive change. Against this vision, the

[19] *Newsweek*, June 30, 1969, p. 13.
[20] Harris poll in *Time*, Apr. 6, 1970, p. 28.
[21] *The New York Times*, Jan. 13, 1969, p. 26.
[22] For valuable studies of the Muslims, see E. U. Essien-Udom, *Black Nationalism: A Search for Identity in America*, Univ. of Chicago Press, 1962; and Lincoln, *op. cit.*

[23] *The New York Times*, Oct. 4, 1964, p. 59.

new, slightly improved situation is even less acceptable than the old.

Breaking into public view in 1967, black challenges to the churches began to crystallize into "black caucuses" of clergymen and laymen. These vary widely in size and degree of support, but the "Black Methodists for Church Renewal," "Union of Black Clergymen and Laymen of the Episcopal Church," "Black Affairs Council" of the Unitarians, and various other caucuses and organizations among Lutherans, Roman Catholics, and others express a decisive new aspect of the American "Social Gospel" movement. There are various demands and goals, but perhaps they center on the following: More positions of responsibility for black clergymen; greater support from the churches for the economic, educational, and housing needs of Negroes; incorporation of elements of "black Christianity" into worship, church-school, and music programs; control of inner-city activities by Blacks, to replace what are seen as well-meaning but ineffectual white efforts. As these themes are developed in conferences and pronouncements, two basic sectarian styles emerge: There is an element of aggressive prophecy, seeking to bring the church to justice, to make it an instrument of radical change. "We must stop worshipping a cute white baby and recognize the adult, black revolutionary that Christ was."[24] There is also a withdrawal theme, indicating another sectarian approach rooted deep in Christian history. Some caucus members are seeking to achieve a purely black fellowship, a situation in which a "black religious experience" can be achieved without bending to white styles and dominance. It is not surprising that "soul" should be sought in the churches, as elsewhere.

Although protest and avoidance themes are mixed in most activities of black churchmen, some express one or the other predominantly. The prophetic-aggressive approach has been most vividly expressed in the demands for $500 million in "reparations" from white churches and synagogues.

With a little change of wording, James Forman's "Black Manifesto" could be attributed to Gerrard Winstanley, that uncompromising seventeenth-century English radical, for whom Christ "is the true and faithful leveller."[25]

The Manifesto was presented to a meeting of the Black Economic Development Conference in Detroit, April, 1969. It achieved a great deal of national publicity in May, 1969, when Forman repeated the demands at Riverside Church, New York, from a pulpit that had been vacated by the church's ministers; (although the Rev. Ernest Campbell returned later and spoke favorably of the idea of "restitution"). Some of Forman's supporters attracted further attention, and opposition, when they occupied national offices of the Presbyterian church in an effort to attain some of the goals of the Manifesto.[26] Forman's accusations and demands shocked most white churchmen. He called for "total control" of their own lives by black people, and declared that their hearts went out to the Vietnamese, who like themselves suffered under the domination of a racist America. The accusations, the radicalism, the economic costs, the very idea of reparations were not likely to win support from major church bodies. The Roman Catholic Archdiocese of New York, for example, rejected the Manifesto completely. The Council of Bishops of the United Methodist Church, in a "message on reconcilliation," stated that "The violent Marxism of the black manifesto is utterly unacceptable to United Methodists."[27] The National Council of Churches discussed the issue carefully, but without the aid of experts who might have examined its economic implications. Two years after the Manifesto was issued, less than $4 million had been raised by American churches in response to its demands,

---

[24] Speaker at a black caucus, quoted by *The New York Times*, Nov. 9, 1970, p. 30.

[25] Comparative study can enrich our understanding and help us escape the feeling that the current situation is unique. One can learn a great deal about contemporary America by study of the Civil War period in England, for example. For an effort along this line, see Yinger, *op. cit.*, pp. 293–298.
[26] For the Manifesto and a series of valuable comments on it, see Robert S. Lecky and H. Elliott Wright, *Black Manifesto: Religion, Racism and Reparations*, Sheed & Ward, 1970.
[27] *The Plain Dealer*, Nov. 14, 1969.

and the document had largely been forgotten.[28]

There was some support, it should be noted, for the idea of reparations.[29] The Manifesto appealed to the prophetic-sectarian elements that are not unimportant in the contemporary American church. But the church as a whole is not likely, suddenly, to begin to act like a sect. The effects of the Manifesto on the church are likely to be indirect; it may influence programs, the allocation of funds, and policies in ways congruent with its message, but it is unlikely to win substantial direct support.

Black Theology. Crises that drastically disorganize or reorganize the lives of a group of people are usually accompanied by a body of thought that seeks to bring the new experience into a framework of systematic religious interpretation. Among minority-group members, theology often interprets disprivilege as a peculiar sign of God's grace, of the special mission of the group, of its unique insight based on its unique experiences. The theology cuts two ways: As the "suffering servant," the persecuted group has been chosen to bring a message to all mankind; but as a group treated unjustly, the minority is told by some of its theologians that they are destined to prevail in a holy war. Thus they hear, "If God is for you, must you not also be for yourself" (C. Eric Lincoln) but also, when Jesus said walk a second mile, "he meant only with your brother" (Albert B. Cleage Jr.). These messages mingle in the work of most contemporary black theologians, with the latter perhaps dominant over the former.[30]

Black theology is being given some attention in predominantly white Protestant seminaries; it is the focus of an Institute for Black Ministries, established in Philadelphia in 1970; and it has been developed in a large number of books and articles. We shall not try to examine the wide range of materials, but a few quotations may indicate some of its dimensions.[31]

What is Black Theology? . . . It is black people reflecting religiously on the black experience, attempting to redefine the relevance of the Christian Gospel for their lives. . . . To study theology from the perspective of Black Theology means casting one's mental and emotional faculties with the lot of the oppressed so that they may learn the cause and the cure of their humiliation. . . . Black Theology is revolutionary in its perspective . . . Relating this concept to our contemporary situation in America, Black Theology affirms that the church of the Oppressed One must be a black church.[32]

Theological work everywhere is filled with effort to state the integral, true, authentic expression of a religious tradition. Thus "Christianity cannot be alien to Black power; it *is* Black Power."[33] "It is the Cross which reveals war and revolution as the life-giving means to counteract the misuse of freedom by men with absolute power who tend to use it irresponsibly to abridge freedom of the powerless."[34] These revolu-

---

[28] See *The Christian Century*, Apr. 14, 1971, pp. 451–453.

[29] See, for example, the chapters by William Stringfellow, James Lawson, and Harvey Cox in Lecky and Wright, *op. cit.*

[30] Theology is not immune from the pressures toward polarization during a time of crisis, when the "he who is not for us is against us" mentality prevails. Even the more universalistically inclined are pushed toward one pole. Note the shift, for example, in the thought of Martin Luther King, Jr., toward more support for disruptive resistance. Compare *Stride Toward Freedom*, Harper & Row, 1958, with *Why We Can't Wait*, Harper & Row, 1963, and *The Trumpet of Conscience*, Harper & Row, 1968. Vincent Harding raises a critical question with regard to

the polarization: "An interim goal is now to make white men 'invisible' while black men are brought into the light. Can it be brought off by blacks with any less poisoning of the spirit than occurred in whites who invented 'tuning out'?" "The Religion of Black Power," in Donald R. Cutler (ed.), *The Religious Situation*, Beacon Press, 1968, p. 7.

[31] For a variety of views, see Albert B. Cleage Jr., *The Black Messiah*, Sheed and Ward, 1968; James H. Cone, *Black Theology and Black Power*, Seabury Press, 1969; Joseph R. Washington Jr., *Black and White Power Subreption*, Beacon Press, 1969, chap. 5; Joseph R. Washington Jr., *The Politics of God*, Beacon Press, 1967. For a useful, brief statement, see James H. Cone, "Black Consciousness and the Black Church: A Historical-Theological Interpretation," *Annals*, Jan., 1970, pp. 49–55.

[32] Cone, "Black Consciousness and the Black Church," *op. cit.*, p. 53.

[33] James H. Cone, in C. Eric Lincoln (ed.), *Is Anybody Listening to Black America?* Seabury Press, 1968, p. 8.

[34] Washington, Jr., *Black and White Power Subreption*, p. 125.

tionaries, these Marxists, as some have called them, have somehow failed to get the message that "religion is the opiate of the people."

Black Religion and the Protest Movement. Preceeding sections have indicated many ways in which religion is involved in the civil rights movement; but it may be useful to conclude this discussion of religion and black power with a few more general observations. Although the message of solace is still the predominant one in many Negro churches, it would be a mistake to overlook two important qualifications: Many leading churches and clergymen occupy major roles in the movement to end discrimination; and even the most otherworldly of approaches has implications for a system of repression.

Almost all the largest urban Negro churches have become "race churches;" they are involved in the civil rights movement, they support Negro businessmen, and they exert pressure against discriminatory white businesses. In no other institution can so many Negroes be reached and mobilized to action so quickly. This is not to suggest that economic activity is a dominant part of the work of urban churches—for it surely is not —but only to indicate the continuing influence of religious leaders, on both local and national levels, and their growing interest in economic affairs. The importance of Negro ministers rests not so much in ideology as on certain historical and structural facts. The ministry was the first profession to gain recognition, and Negro preachers became the principal race leaders. Ministers have a great deal of freedom of action. They answer to no one except their congregations and they are expected to be real "race men." This is not a new phenomenon. Drake and Cayton described the situation among Negro clergy in Chicago nearly 30 years ago: "They can say what they please about current affairs and race relations; there are no church superiors to discipline them and no white people to take economic reprisals. . . . Preachers are subjected to continuous community criticism, and to retain the allegiance of their followers they are forced to

concern themselves with a wide range of secular activities—political action, protest against discrimination, advice on securing jobs and legal aid, and the encouragement of Negro business enterprises."[35]

Negro ministers no longer hold the great preponderance of leadership positions, because civil rights workers, lawyers, physicians, teachers, journalists, social workers, businessmen, and politicians have come increasingly to the fore. Experts in these secular fields, often with more academic training than the ministers, are rendering many services formerly performed only by preachers. A "call to preach" no longer guarantees respect and influence. There has been an absolute as well as a relative decline in the number of Negro clergymen since 1930.[36] Nevertheless, clergymen remain among the most important Negro leaders. Probably only a minority of them are militant, but the ratio is much higher among the younger and better educated clergy.[37]

It should also be noted that the theme of aggression that underlies much of the "otherworldly" emphasis in the religion of lower strata can break out into the open when hope rises and movements appear to create rallying points. Religion serves, as Baldwin says ". . . as a complete and exquisite fantasy revenge: white people own the earth and commit all manner of abomination and injustice on it; the bad will be punished and the good rewarded, for God is not sleeping, the judgment is not far off. It does not require a spectacular degree of perception to realize that bitterness is here neither dead nor sleeping, and that the white man, believing what he wishes to believe, has misread the symbols."[38]

[35] Drake and Cayton, *op. cit.*, pp. 427–428.
[36] See E. Wilbur Bock, "The Decline of the Negro Clergy: Changes in Formal Religious Leadership in the United States in the Twentieth Century," *Phylon*, Spring, 1968, pp. 48–64.
[37] Ronald L. Johnstone classified 20 percent of his Detroit sample as militant. See his "Negro Preachers Take Sides," *Review of Religious Research*, Fall, 1969, pp. 81–89. On the whole, he does not see Negro ministers as a strong leadership resource for the civil rights movement.
[38] James Baldwin, *Notes of a Native Son*, Beacon Press, 1955, p. 66.

What are the conditions under which this potential for religious militancy develops? What have been the trends in the United States? A generation ago, observers of the plantation South emphasized the reinforcement that the belief system and the church structure furnished for segregation.[39] By furnishing extramundane satisfactions, religion draws attention away from injustices on earth. This tendency was supported by many planters, who welcomed churches and revival meetings for "their Negroes," but were unenthusiastic about schools. When opportunities improve, however, when hope rises, aggression begins to be focused on segregation and discrimination. James Baldwin describes the remark of Dr. Marcus James, a priest of the Anglican church, to a Conference of Negro-African Writers and Artists in Paris. Dr. James quoted the old saying that when Christians arrived in Africa they had the Bible and the Africans had the land; but after a while, Africans had the Bible and Christians had the land. Sharing this sentiment, the group responded with laughter; but James went on to say ". . . that the African not only has the Bible but has found in it a potential weapon for the recovery of his land."[40] So it is in the United States: under some conditions, Negro churches have been bulwarks of segregation; under others they have been the focal points of opposition to segregation.

One of the problems in dealing with this question empirically is that "religion" has been seen as a uniform thing. Using a national sample of Negroes and various single measures of religion, Gary Marx found that the more "religious" a person was, the less likely it was that he would be militant in civil rights; or, the more subjective importance he assigned to religion, the less likely he was to support militant activities. When he specified the variable "religiosity," however, by distinguishing between those who interpreted religion in otherworldly terms and those who believed it involved interest in the "here and now," a sharp difference appeared. Among those who rated high on the "otherworldly" religious scale, only 15 percent were militant; of those who rated high on the "temporal" religious scale, 39 percent were militant.[41]

In our judgment, the distinction developed by Marx needs to be carried further. Most studies have said little more than that persons who hold *traditional, fundamentalist* religious views are likely to hold traditionalist views about race relations. It is clear that those who are developing a very nontraditional black theology do not hold traditional views about race relations. It is critical that one know the measures by which religiosity has been determined. Statements about "religion in general" and its presumed relationship to civil rights activism are of little value.

PREJUDICE, SEGREGATION, AND THE DOMINANT CHURCHES

The religious life of the dominant group, as well as of minorities, reflects and affects intergroup relations. We need to ask, therefore, how religious belief and practice affect individual prejudices and how dominant churches respond to minority-group members. On the basis of the principles of the sociology of religion we would expect to find the intergroup patterns of churches and the religious attitudes of individuals deeply imbedded in secular structures and attitudes.

ARE RELIGIOUS PEOPLE MORE PREJUDICED?

Judging solely on ideological grounds, one might suppose that highly religious people would be less prejudiced against minority groups than would nonreligious people. On this, as on so many social scientific questions, it is mainly Christians and American Jews who have been studied, hence generaliza-

[39] See, for example, Allison Davis, B. B. Gardner, and M. R. Gardner, *Deep South*, Univ. of Chicago Press, 1941, and Dollard, *op. cit.*

[40] James Baldwin, *Nobody Knows My Name*, Dell, 1961, pp. 38–39.

[41] Gary Marx, "Religion: Opiate or Inspiration of Civil Rights Militancy Among Negroes," *ASR*, Feb., 1967, pp. 64–72.

tions are rather severely limited. From a distance one may assume that the Muslim, because his tradition opposes race prejudice, is immune from majority-minority problems. Yet in many Muslim societies, women are clearly a minority and religious prejudice is severe. Hinduism draws no sharp race lines and is religiously tolerant but it is integrally associated with a caste system in most interpretations. Although Buddhism is highly tolerant, devout Buddhists have often withdrawn from the societies in which they live and shown little concern for rigid class systems. These lines are not written to prove that every religion and everybody is equally likely to be prejudiced; but to emphasize the need for careful, comparative study.

On studies of Christians, to which our observations will be limited, it is easy to document the fact that religious motives play an important part in current integration efforts (see below). On the other hand, churches have often been strongholds of bigotry and religious people among the most intolerant—not simply of those who disagree with them religiously but of minority groups as well. In a study of over 1000 students from 13 eastern and southern colleges, Putney and Middleton found that there were significantly more high authoritarian scores among those who took a conservative Christian position than among those who were skeptics.[42] In a random sample of 800 from the Detroit area, however, Angell found no relationship between religiosity and prejudiced responses to questions about integrated schools and nonwhite playmates for children. There were interesting differences *within* the church groups, showing the need for controls. Middle-class Protestants, for example, showed less prejudice than lower-class, because the latter contained a fairly large proportion of rural southerners. Middle-class Catholics, however, were slightly more prejudiced than lower-class.[43]

Studies of the relationship between individual religiosity and prejudice are extremely sensitive to the questions asked, the sample, and the measures of religiosity. In virtually every instance, verbal, not behavioral measures of the dependent variable are used. It remains problematic whether there is a close link between attitudes and behavior in this area. Behavioral measures for the independent variable (church attendance, for example) are more commonly employed. Samples are often fairly small, moreover, so that controls for critical variables—particularly age and education—are often impossible.[44]

Keeping these methodological problems in mind, we can profitably examine some of the continuing research on religion and prejudice. Working with a national sample of 1400 adult Americans, Rokeach measured the relationship between various indicators of religiosity and a range of values. Of most interest to us are the findings relating to compassion as a value.

. . . those who place a high value on *salvation* are conservative, are anxious to maintain the status quo, and are generally more indifferent and unsympathetic with the plight of the black and the poor. They had reacted in a more fearful and calloused way to the assassination of Dr. Martin Luther King, were more unsympathetic with the student protest movement, and were more opposed to the church's involvement in everyday affairs. The data also suggested that they suffered more from feelings of anomie. Value for *forgiving* (the second most distinctively Christian value) was also found to be negatively related to social compassion but to a generally lesser extent than was the case for salvation.[45]

A number of studies have found a curvilinear relationship between religiosity and prejudice. Twenty-eight percent of the college students interviewed by Allport indicated a

[42] Snell Putney and Russell Middleton, "Rebellion, Conformity, and Parental Religious Ideologies," *Sociometry*, June, 1961, pp. 125–136.

[43] Robert Angell, "Preference for Moral Norms in Three Problem Areas," *AJS*, May, 1962, pp. 650–660.

[44] For a careful statement of the need for a highly differentiated study of the relationship between religion and prejudice, see Frederick Whitam, "Subdimensions of Religiosity and Race Prejudice," *Review of Religious Research*, Spring, 1962, pp. 166–174.

[45] Milton Rokeach, "I. Value Systems in Religion. II. Religious Values and Social Compassion," *Review of Religious Research*, Fall, 1969, p. 24.

marked influence of religious training, 41 percent reported a moderate influence; and this 69 percent was more prejudiced than the 31 percent who reported little or no religious influence. The difference was significant at the 1 percent level. Sixty-two percent of the Protestants, 71 percent of the Catholics, but only 22 percent of the Jews and 27 percent of those with no religious affiliation were in the "more anti-Negro" half.[46] Frenkel-Brunswik and Sanford also found that the more anti-Semitic girls were more conventionally religious. Both studies discovered, however, that many of the persons who were least prejudiced also reported a strong religious interest—an interest, to be sure, that was less often tied to traditional forms. Bettelheim and Janowitz, in a study of 150 veterans, asked their interviewees, among other questions dealing with army experiences: "How did the fellows feel about religion?" In the discussion that followed, it was revealed that veterans who stressed ". . . the acceptance and importance of religion in the army were significantly more tolerant than the rest of the sample. . . . Intolerance, however, was concentrated in the group whose answers indicated their indifference to religion by statements to the effect that 'most soldiers followed their own habits' or 'everybody has his own opinions.' "[47]

How can we interpret these diverse findings? Is the variation best accounted for by differences in the measuring instruments or contrasts among the groups being studied? Or do we have here a "real" difference indicating the complexity of the relationship between religion and prejudice? We believe the latter is more nearly correct. It is impossible to speak of the effects of "religion" —as if it were a wholly homogeneous phenomenon—on prejudice. The first need, of course, is for careful controls that eliminate the influence of other variables. Religion may have nothing at all to do with the relationship. Middle-class people seem to be more anti-Semitic in our society than lower-class people; they are better educated; they are more likely to attend church and to be "religious"; but they are also in more direct economic competition with Jews. To say that middle-class people are more anti-Semitic because they have received more education or because they go to church more often, when other variables have not been controlled, is clearly unwarranted. Nor can we assume that this might not be true. To make the issue absurdly clear—or perhaps just absurd —middle-class people are fatter than lower-class people, and also more anti-Semitic; therefore, corpulence leads to prejudice. Descriptive studies can be of use in science only when they are related to a general theory that prevents one-sided surface "explanations."

After the application of controls we may find that the relationship between religion and prejudice is still complex. We need further, therefore, an analysis of the kind of religious training a person has received, a study of why and how he is religious.

Maranell found significant correlations between anti-Semitic and anti-Negro attitudes and eight dimensions of religion in two samples of university undergraduates in the South, but not in two samples of northern undergraduates.[48] This casts doubt on any intrapsychic causal link, and suggests instead an explanation in terms of regional subcultures.

One persistent finding that throws doubt on the religiosity-prejudice relationship is that the clergy, at least in this period in American history, are less prejudiced, on the average, and more likely both to support and to participate actively in civil rights efforts than are laymen.[49] Several thousand par-

---

[46] Gordon Allport and B. M. Kramer, "Some Roots of Prejudice," *JP*, July, 1946, pp. 25–27; see also Charles T. O'Reilly and Edward J. O'Reilly, "Religious Beliefs of Catholic College Students and Their Attitudes Toward Minorities," *JASP*, July, 1954, pp. 378–380.

[47] Bruno Bettelheim and Morris Janowitz, *Dynamics of Prejudice. A Psychological and Sociological Study of Veterans*, Harper & Row, 1950, pp. 51–52; see also Robert Friedrichs, "Christians and Residential Exclusion: An Empirical Study of a Northern Dilemma," *JSI*, 1959, Fourth Quarter, pp. 14–23. It should be added, however, that Rokeach, *op. cit.*, found no curvilinear relationship.

[48] Gary M. Maranell, "An Examination of Some Religious and Political Attitude Correlates of Bigotry," *SF*, Mar., 1967, pp. 356–363.

[49] See Jeffrey K. Hadden, *The Gathering Storm in the Churches*, Doubleday, 1969; Lawrence L. Kersten, *The Lutheran Ethic: The Impact of Religion on Laymen and Clergy*, Wayne State Univ. Press, 1970, chap. 4.

ticipated in the Selma march, 1965, for example, and perhaps 25,000 in the 1963 March on Washington. Clergy make up a high proportion of those who have organized conferences to protest racial injustice; in opinion polls dealing with race relations, ministers take more liberal views than laymen almost without exception. In Hadden's view: "Conflict between clergy and laity in recent years over the civil rights issue is deeply rooted in fundamentally different views about civil rights and the role that the church and clergy should be playing in this struggle. What is perhaps surprising is that the overt conflict has not been even more serious."[50]

It is not enough, of course, simply to assume that a stronger religious interest accounts for the clergy's attitudes and actions. Various structural and role factors are also involved. When 48 Protestant clergymen attending an urban training program were asked to participate in a civil rights demonstration, most joined in, and 25 chose to be arrested. Those arrested ". . . tended to be younger, occupied positions that were not directly responsible to all-white congregations, came from denominations that had taken a strong stand in favor of integration, and tended to have roommates who also chose arrest."[51] A structural variable was shown by James Wood to influence significantly the chances that church leaders would adopt a controversial policy on racial integration. In a study of 28 major religious bodies, he found that leaders working with a church polity that gave them significant formal authority were more likely to adopt strong civil rights positions. The structural influence was shown most decisively by the fact that a hierarchical, as contrasted with a congregational, polity had its strongest influence under conditions that might have made policy makers most vulnerable, namely, the small, fundamentalist, southern church.[52]

Related to comparisons of clergy and laymen are various comparisons of type of religiosity. Gordon Allport drew a distinction between extrinsic beliefs that are used simply as instruments of self-interest by insecure persons, and intrinsic beliefs that are the results of normal socialization and security. Children with various personal needs, taught the same religious-prejudice syndrome, may have quite different outcomes. A child who has deep feelings of insecurity and distrust may tie his religion to prejudice: I am of the elect (which implies that many others are not); God is partial to me. Such beliefs in the insecure lead easily to categorical condemnation of out-group members in an effort to bolster a shaky security. A secure person, on the other hand ". . . does not need to look on people as threats to his well-being,"[53] he does not need to use religious revelation or the doctrine of election to downgrade others in order to bolster himself. Indeed his capacity for reciprocity of perception—seeing the world from another's point of view—encourages the use of religion for brotherhood rather than self-defense.[54] Wilson devised an "extrinsic religious values" scale to measure motives for affiliating with religious groups. He found a significant positive correlation between the scores on this scale and an anti-Semitism scale among 10 small, rather diverse groups.[55]

The extrinsic-intrinsic idea is useful. Unfortunately, efforts to employ it in research have yielded contradictory results. From a total sample of 497 college students, Allen and Spilka selected the 210 who were "most religious," on the basis of their rated importance of religion, frequency of church attendance, religious identity, and attitudes

---

[50] *Ibid.*, p. 159.

[51] Jeffrey K. Hadden and Raymond C. Rymph, "Social Structure and Civil Rights Involvement: A Case Study of Protestant Ministers," *SF*, Sept., 1966, pp. 51–61.

[52] James R. Wood, "Authority and Controversial Policy: The Churches and Civil Rights," *ASR*, Dec., 1970, pp. 1057–1069.

[53] Gordon Allport, *Personality and Social Encounter*, Beacon Press, 1960, p. 264. He suggests that extrinsic religion and prejudice are simply correlated, each an effort to achieve security. We wonder if there is not a functional connection between them.

[54] Allport noted that the extrinsic-intrinsic distinction is best seen as a continuum, not a dichotomy. For his full discussion, see *ibid.*, pp. 257–267; see also Gordon W. Allport and J. M. Ross, "Personal Religious Orientation and Prejudice," *JPSP*, Jan., 1967, pp. 432–443.

[55] Cody Wilson, "Extrinsic Religious Values and Prejudice," *JASP*, Mar., 1960, pp. 286–291.

toward the church. These were then given a 16-item prejudice scale, on the basis of which those highest in prejudice ($n = 29$) and those lowest in prejudice ($n = 32$) were selected for further study. This further study consisted of extensive tape-recorded interviews, in which the aim was to determine the extent to which their religious views were "committed" or "consensual" (a distinction related to intrinsic-extrinsic). Neither interviewers or those who rated the subjects from the tapes knew the prejudice or religious scores of the respondents. The results, in brief, were that a strong correspondence was found between committed religion and low prejudice, and between consensual religion and high prejudice.[56] Allen and Spilka did not find, however, that the Extrinsic Religious Values scale used by Wilson successfully distinguished between their subjects holding a committed or consensual orientation. The measurement processes and instruments used by Allen and Spilka are, in our judgment, somewhat richer and more likely to be valid than Wilson's; but in this line of research, each scale must be used with caution until more extensive validation has been undertaken.

Photiadis and Biggar, in another study employing the extrinsic-intrinsic distinction, discovered that extrinsic beliefs were not significantly related to attitudes of social distance when the effects of a number of other variables were controlled. There was a significant simple correlation, due particularly to the effects of status concern, conservatism, and authoritarianism. When their influence was removed, extrinsic religious belief and social distance were no longer significantly correlated.[57] Church participation was related negatively, although not at a significant level, to expressions of social distance.

These negative results do not prove that the quality of individuals' religious orientations is unrelated to prejudice. We are a long way from the use of validated instruments on standardized populations, hence all generalizations in this area are subject to doubt. At this time we believe that two statements are justified: the nature of one's religious belief as a personality tendency (intrinsic-extrinsic or some other measure) is largely a dependent variable, reflecting most directly, perhaps, the degree of inner security. Secondly, the extrinsic or intrinsic quality of one's religious beliefs is partly a cultural phenomenon, as is the linkage or lack of linkage between prejudice and religion. These things may simply be taught to one as part of his cultural training: God ordained that races shall be separate, or God ordained brotherhood. On this level, it is cultural analysis, not personality analysis that is most fruitful.

One source of evidence for cultural analysis is the printed material used by churches in their religious education programs. These vary widely in the frequency with which they refer to intergroup relations and in the content of their messages, so that within a society there is a wide range of teaching regarding other religions and races. In a careful content analysis of the publications of four Protestant groups, for example, Olson noted the way in which the authors treated other religious, ethnic, and racial groups.[58] Scores from $+100$ to -100 were determined by classifying the material in 14 categories as favorable or unfavorable. A large share of the publications contained intergroup references, the range in the four

[56] Russell O. Allen and Bernard Spilka, "Committed and Consensual Religion: A Specification of Religion-Prejudice Relationships," Journal for the Scientific Study of Religion, Fall, 1967, pp. 191–206.

[57] John Photiadis and Jeanne Biggar, "Religiosity, Education, and Ethnic Distance," AJS, May, 1962, pp. 666–672. The study was made in a town of 8000 in South Dakota, using as respondents 300 persons attending Presbyterian, Baptist, and Episcopal churches. See also John Photiadis and Arthur Johnson, "Orthodoxy, Church Participation, and Authoritarianism," AJS, Nov., 1963, pp. 244–48.

[58] Bernard E. Olson, Faith and Prejudice, Yale, 1963. The four series of publications were from the Beacon Press curriculum for the Council of Liberal Churches—liberal; the Christian Faith and Life and other curricular materials of the Presbyterian Church, U.S.A. (now United Presbyterian)—neo-orthodox; the Lutheran Church, Missouri Synod—conservative; and the Scripture Press, serving mainly fundamentalist churches. See also Bernard Weinryb, Trafford Maher, and Bernard Olson, "Intergroup Relations in Religious Textbooks," Religious Education, Mar.–Apr., 1960, pp. 109–138.

Ratings Given to Publications

Group referred to	Liberal	Neoorthodox	Conservative	Fundamentalist
Non-Christian	80.0	37.4	−58.1	−33.5
Jewish	48.6	44.3	−15.4	7.9
Catholic	36.6	23.4	−66.9	−52.8
Other-Christian	45.9	79.3	−38.2	−2.1
International	73.6	77.3	35.2	8.0
Other Ethnic	61.5	87.8	72.0	23.7
Negro	85.7	93.8	33.3	56.7

Source: Bernard Olson, *Faith and Prejudice*, Yale, 1963, p. 386.

series being from 67 to 88 percent, with interreligious relations occupying the most important place. The publications varied widely in their handling of these themes, as can be seen from the above table.

It is clear that these Protestant writers drew their least favorable pictures of Catholics. Although there was condemnation of prejudice, the fundamentalist and conservative materials would frequently have to be "classed as anti-Catholic." Treatment of the Negro, on the other hand, was positive in all four curricula and was aimed generally at the reduction of prejudice.

SEGREGATION AND THE CHURCHES

When we shift our attention from individual attitudes to institutional practices, we find the same mixed picture. American churches are predominantly segregated by race. This fact requires careful study, however, for there is wide variation among churches and growing pressures toward change. There is a trend toward integrated churches, which we think will continue at an accelerated pace. And there is also some pressure toward separation or resegregation, as one manifestation of the "black power" movement broadly defined. We must keep these various trends in mind as we study the contemporary situation in America.

Shortly after World War II Loescher found that perhaps 6 percent of Negro Protestants belonged to predominantly white denominations; and of these not more than 8000 attended integrated local churches.[59] No "white" church in his study of 18,000 churches in six denominations had an "open" or mixed membership in an area undergoing transition. Only when Negroes were in the majority was membership open in transition areas. The usual pattern in Protestantism, then and now, is initial resistance to the coming of Negroes; but when the transition has occurred, the church property is sold to a Negro group.

To what degree has this situation changed since Loescher wrote? Speaking generally, one can say "only a little";[60] but this requires some examination. A list of some of the changes on the national and local levels may give an indication of the trend, although we can scarcely speak in precise quantitative terms. In 1952, the Presbyterian Church in the U.S. (southern) "voted to abolish its Negro synod and absorb the Negro congregations into the regional synods."[61] In 1952 the Methodist Church began the abolition of its segregated Central Jurisdiction for Negro churches. Several

[59] F. S. Loescher, *The Protestant Church and the Negro*, Association Press, 1948, pp. 76–77.

[60] See David Reimes, *White Protestantism and the Negro*, Oxford, 1965; Robert W. Spike, *The Freedom Revolution and the Churches*, Association Press, 1965; Joseph C. Hough, Jr., *Black Power and White Protestants: A Christian Response to the New Negro Pluralism*, Oxford, 1968.

[61] W. A. Visser 'T Hooft, *The Ecumenical Movement and the Racial Problem*, United Nations Educational, Scientific, and Cultural Organization (UNESCO), 1954, p. 28.

general conferences, which meet every four years, have re-emphasized this policy; but have also spoken of "reasonable speed" and emphasized voluntary procedures.[62] These reflect, to an important degree, the large southern membership of the Methodist Church. After 20 years, the Central Jurisdiction has been, by voluntary action of the Annual Conferences, officially disbanded. There continues to be opposition to the national policy of integration, however, on the local and state levels, in the form of reduced support for race relations work, reduced use of Methodist literature, formation of a Methodist Layman's Union to resist integration, and the like.[63]

In 1956, the United Presbyterian Church of North America voted for "complete integration of all churches, agencies, and institutions,"[64] and in 1964 elected a Negro moderator (the membership is 95 percent white). The Protestant Episcopal Church and the Methodist Church have Negro bishops serving mainly white constituencies.

Although such changes are modifying the segregation structure it is doubtless still true that more than 90 percent of Negro Protestants are in separate denominational organizations. There are equivalent changes at the local congregational level. Although only a small minority of Protestant churches in the United States are racially integrated, the pace of desegregation has increased in the last few years. The following items may indicate that segregation is no longer the virtually universal rule: In a study of 13,597 churches (United Lutheran, Congregational-Christian, and Presbyterian Church in the U.S.A.) Kramer found that 1331, or nearly 10 percent, reported racially integrated congregations. Most of the integrated churches had only a few nonwhites (83 percent reported fewer than five).[65]

In a survey of four of the city's boroughs, the Protestant Council of the City of New York found that about half of the city's Protestant churches have at least some interracial aspects. Questionnaires filled out by 315 of the 1500 Protestant churches showed that 51 percent were segregated (that is, had membership all of one race, or only a tiny minority from another race), 25 percent were nonsegregated ("a reasonable percentage of persons from minority groups in membership, in church attendance, and/or in the church school and other organizations"), and 24 percent were integrated (persons from minority groups were serving as officers, on boards and committees "to a degree that indicates minority groups are participating in the leadership and activities of the church").[66] Most of the segregated churches were in segregated neighborhoods. The majority indicated that they would welcome members from other races. The degree to which the 315 churches are representative of the city's Protestant churches is not known. In 1956, the Disciples of Christ reported that out of 7000 congregations studied, 464 local groups in 40 states were racially mixed to some degree.[67]

Interviews with ministers and church officials from 1054 of the 1500 Congregational-Christian Churches in Standard Metropolitan Areas revealed, for 1958, the following racial patterns in the congregations:

Pattern	Percent
All White	69.6
All Negro	2.9
All Oriental	0.7
All "Spanish"	0.2
White-mixed, no Negro members	12.1
White-mixed, with Negro members	12.1
Negro-mixed	2.1
Oriental-mixed	0.3

A 1946 survey had found 17 percent, compared with the 26.6 percent racially mixed

---

[62] See *Doctrines and Disciplines of the Methodist Church*, Methodist Publishing House, 1964.

[63] See James R. Wood and Mayer N. Zald, "Aspects of Racial Integration in the Methodist Church: Sources of Resistance to Organizational Policy," *SF*, Dec., 1966, pp. 255–265.

[64] B. E. Mays, *Seeking to Be Christian in Race Relations*, Friendship Press, 1957, pp. 51–52.

[65] Alfred S. Kramer, "Patterns of Racial Inclusion Among the Churches of Three Protestant Denominations," *Phylon*, Third Quarter, 1955, pp. 283–294.

[66] *The New York Times*, Feb. 10, 1957.

[67] J. Oscar Lee, "The Churches and Race Relations—A Survey," *Christianity and Crisis*, Feb. 4, 1957, p. 4.

reported here; but that study had included rural churches, thus the net gain is smaller than it appears to be.[68]

Loth and Fleming, in a survey of church desegregation, received reports of 130 churches which, in the two years, May, 1954, to May, 1956, had included Negroes for the first time as members, worshipers, or program participants.[69] A survey by the Cleveland Church Federation revealed that 52.5 percent of the churches affiliated with the Federation had more than one racial group in active membership. This was a recent development; 40 percent of the churches indicated a change of attitude regarding interracial membership within the preceeding five years. It should be noted that the number of persons from minority races was not large: only 1385 Negroes, for example, were active in the affairs of predominantly white churches in the Cleveland area.[70]

It is difficult to speak with precision on this matter, but it can be estimated reasonably that 10 to 15 percent of northern and western Protestant churches are interracial to some degree (with a denominational range of perhaps 5 to 20 percent). The number of individuals involved is small. Probably no more than one or two percent of Negroes are in interracial churches. Interracial ministerial staffs or appointment of Negro ministers to predominantly white churches is a rare phenomenon.[71]

Continuation of racially homogeneous churches is not simply a sign of prejudice in the churches. To some degree it reflects housing segregation (often defended, of course, by church people). It also signifies denominational loyalty and a desire for separate churches on the part of some non-whites. In the last several years there have been strenuous efforts by national church leaders and conferences to break down racial barriers, both in the churches and in other institutions. In 1963, Catholic, Jewish, and Protestant leaders joined in a National Conference on Religion and Race in an effort ". . . to increase the leadership of religion in ending racial discrimination in the United States."[72] For many spokesmen in the churches, "Racism is our most serious domestic evil," ". . . the number-one scandal of the church."[73] Such declarations have been made before, though perhaps not with such frequency and urgency. Churches, deeply involved as they are in the institutional structure of society, are seldom leaders in social reform; yet they are often important in carrying a movement along and conditioning the process by which change is accomplished. Some 25 years after segregation and discrimination became vital public issues in the United States, the churches may be ready to take an active part in the process of change. (This is written without cynicism; our aim is simply to describe the situation as accurately as possible.) We expect churches to be more actively involved in desegregation in the decade ahead. Even in the South, where church segregation remains a massive fact, except for a few temporary incidents of integration as a result of protest marches, the sharpness of the line of separation seems likely to be reduced.

Segregation and Integration in Catholic Churches

Many of the forces that affect Protestant responses to segregation also affect Catholics. There are, however, some differences. In Catholic countries generally, the race line has been drawn less sharply than in Protestant countries. During slavery, the Catholic

[68] See Herman Long, *Fellowship for Whom? A Study of Racial Inclusiveness in Congregational-Christian Churches*, Department of Race Relations, Board of Home Missions, 1958.

[69] See David Loth and Harold Fleming, *Integration North and South*, The Fund for the Republic, 1956, pp. 37–44, 91–96.

[70] *Cleveland Press*, Jan. 17, 1958.

[71] Rare, but not completely lacking, even in the South. See John Collins, "Student Interracial Ministry: A Venture in Reconciliation," *Interracial News Service*, Sept.–Oct., 1962, pp. 1–4.

[72] See Mathew Ahmann (ed.), *Race: Challenge to Religion*, Regnery, 1963; see also Emory S. Bucke (ed.), "Race Relations and the American Church," *Religion in Life*, Summer, 1957, pp. 322–387; Kyle Haselden, *The Racial Problem in Christian Perspective*, Harper & Row, 1959; Liston Pope, *The Kingdom Beyond Caste*, Friendship Press, 1957; *Thomas B. Maston, Segregation and Desegregation, A Christian Approach*, Macmillan, 1959.

[73] Ahmann, *op. cit.*, p. 171; and *Christian Century*, Oct. 10, 1962, pp. 1215–1216.

Church insisted upon baptism and religious instruction for slaves, in contrast with the "property" emphasis in Protestant areas. Some of this contrast of attitude survives today. The emphasis on liturgy and worship in Catholicism, compared with the more informal "social" patterns found in many Protestant churches, has supported an interracial perspective. And the hierarchical, rather than local, control removes some decisions from the influences of local prejudices. On the other hand, Catholic churches are affected by the values and prejudices of their constituents and by the traditions and practices of the communities of which they are a part. Catholics exhibit about the same range of prejudices as Protestants,[74] and local traditions and pressures affect decisions concerning the time and place to integrate.

Although most American Negroes are Protestants, there are, as we noted above, more than 800,000 Negro Catholics. One-quarter of these live in Louisiana and 40 percent in six cities (Washington, New York, Chicago, Philadelphia, Galveston-Houston, and Los Angeles). The Catholic Church has participated in and been influenced by the civil rights movement; but whether in the depth demanded by the critical issues involved is a matter for dispute. One does not need to follow the news for many months before he sees such contrasting headlines as: "Gain by Catholics on Race Bias Seen," and "Negro Catholics Say Church Fails."[75] The first story indicated that the Southern Regional Council believed that the reputation of the Roman Catholic Church in the South, in matters of race, had begun to improve. It cited the opening up of Catholic hospitals and schools to Negroes. The other story reported a letter written by the National Convention of Black Lay Catholics that stated ". . . that the Roman Catholic Church was dying in the black community 'because of the tragic and total failures of those who have so long exercised the "missionary" role among us to be sensi-

tive to us as a people with a particular culture, heritage and history.' "

We know of no way to measure the rate of change confidently or to state precisely how strongly the Roman Catholic Church has participated in the movement to reduce racial discrimination in the United States; but our strong impression is that the Roman Catholic Church, like the other churches, has not played an important part. On the one hand we should note the establishment, in 1961, of the National Catholic Conference for Interracial Justice, an outgrowth of the Catholic Interracial Council movement begun by Father John LaFarge in New York in 1934. Under the leadership of its director, Mathew Ahmann, the Conference played a critical role in creation of the Conference on Religion and Race, along with the National Council of Churches and the Synagogue Council of America.[76] One can cite numerous statements by priests and bishops denouncing race prejudice, for example the pastoral statement by the National Conference of Catholic Bishops calling on all men of goodwill to combat discrimination and to support open housing.[77]

It is also important to note that in the early days of school desegregation, Roman Catholic schools often took the lead, especially in southern and border states. In 1925, Xavier University in New Orleans was opened to Negroes, with an integrated faculty; Catholic University, in Washington, D.C., admitted Negro sisters in 1933 and other Negro students to the undergraduate and graduate programs in 1936. In 1944 St. Louis University began the first integration on the college level in Missouri; and in 1947 the archdiocese of St. Louis began school desegregation. Seven high schools and 32 elementary schools in Virginia were desegregated in 1958, at that time the only integrated schools below the college level in the state. By 1959, Catholic schools in most southern states had been desegregated.[78]

74 Angell, *op. cit.*, p. 659.
75 *The New York Times*, Oct. 4, 1970, p. 46, and Aug. 24, 1970, p. 21.

76 See Ahmann, *op. cit.*
77 *The New York Times*, Nov. 20, 1966, pp. 1 and 85.
78 Foy, *op. cit.*, pp. 105–107. It should be noted that the Negro Catholic population in most of these

At the same time, the number of Negro priests has increased slowly, from 26 in 1949, to 120 in 1961, to 167 in 1968.[79] There are seven Negro priests in the Chicago archdiocese, which contains about 80,000 Negro communicants—or less than one per 10,000.[80] (The ratio of priests to white communicants is about one per 1000.) Although there are over 100,000 Negro Catholics in New York, it was not until 1968 that the first Negro priest was appointed to head a parish in the New York archdiocese.

A special source of tension between Negroes and Catholics arises because of housing patterns. Catholics are slightly more tied to the city than Protestants because they more frequently identify with an ethnic community and, until the recent past, had lower incomes. They are more likely, therefore, to be in the path of expanding Negro communities, and more likely to be involved in efforts—some of them violent—to resist that expansion. It should be noted both that such resistance has little to do with their religion as such, and that Church appeals to tone down the resistance have had little effect.[81]

Churches in the South

The classic "dilemma of the churches"[82] is nowhere more clearly shown than in the activities of southern churches during this period of dramatic racial change. It may be well, therefore, to comment on the religion-segregation picture in this region separately.

Southern religious history broke with that of the rest of the nation over the slavery issue in the 1830s, and has continued, since then, to be somewhat distinctive.[83] In the Methodist Church, despite a national bureaucratic structure, regional and local forces are very strong. Interregional migration, instead of reducing contrasts, tends to increase them, as the more liberal clergy leave the South and, to a lesser degree, more conservative clergy from the North move in.[84] We do not disagree substantially with Frady's judgment of the largest Protestant church: "The South, the most thoroughly churched corner of our country, is a humid gospel region largely under the cultivation of the Southern Baptist Convention. . . . Here in the South the moral challenge of the post-1954 civil rights movement was mounted—and here it was for the most part ignored, sidestepped, and in some cases opposed by the churches of the Southern Baptist Convention."[85]

It is perhaps too easy, however, to caricature the southern church, or simply to moralize about its activities rather than seeking to understand their causes. A few years after the Supreme Court school desegregation decision, Waldo Beach noted that some persons were using religion to defend racism; others had joined the struggle against racism on religious grounds; but, as Beach said: "By far the great majority of the churches are in the middle, maintaining a troubled, uncertain silence."[86]

Since that time the situation has not changed greatly, but we must note several facts and try to interpret them carefully. Many Negro ministers, of course, have taken the lead in the civil rights movement; but we should also note that white ministers have not been absent completely from the

---

states, except for Louisiana and Texas, is small, ranging from 1000 to 7000 in 10 southern states in 1960.

[79] *Newsweek*, Mar. 4, 1968; and Foy, *op. cit.*, p. 74. In addition, there are 200 Negro brothers, serving as teachers, hospital attendants, and office or manual workers. There are 986 Negro Catholic nuns, three-fourths of them in three orders founded specifically for Negro women and one-fourth scattered among 109 communities of nuns. See *Crisis*, Oct., 1962, p. 473.

[80] *The New York Times*, Feb. 18, 1968, p. 84.

[81] See Margaret E. Traxler, "American Catholics and Negroes," *Phylon*, Winter, 1969, pp. 355–366.

[82] Yinger, *op. cit.*, pp. 234–239.

[83] See Samuel S. Hill, Jr., *Southern Churches in Crisis*, Holt, Rinehart & Winston, 1967; Marshall Frady, "God and Man in the South," *Atlantic Monthly*, Jan., 1967, pp. 37–42; Kenneth K. Bailey, *Southern White Protestantism in the Twentieth Century*, Harper & Row, 1964; Raymond C. Rymph and Jeffrey K. Hadden, "The Persistence of Regionalism in Racial Attitudes of the Methodist Clergy," *SF*, Sept., 1970, pp. 41–50.

[84] See Rymph and Hadden, *op. cit.*

[85] Frady, *op. cit.*, p. 37.

[86] Waldo Beach, "Storm Warnings from the South," *Christianity and Crisis*, Mar. 19, 1956, p. 30.

scene. In 1957, 74 Protestant clergymen in Atlanta issued ". . . a statement on race relations calling for obedience to law, preservation of public schools, protection of free speech, and maintenance of communication between white and Negro leaders."[87] This both reflected and helped to set the tone for changes beginning in Atlanta. When desegregation began in New Orleans schools, white students at first boycotted the integrated schools. At William Frantz School ten white children joined one Negro child during the second week. Seven of those ten were children of clergymen. Ministerial associations in several cities have supported school board plans for school desegregation. In 1963, 28 young Methodist ministers in Mississippi issued a manifesto proclaiming their belief in "freedom of the pulpit" and "opposing racial discrimination in the state of their birth." All were subjected to boycotts by their congregations or other forms of harassment.[88]

But these are fairly isolated incidents. The troubled, uncertain silence of which Beach wrote or outright opposition to desegregation is still the norm among southern churchmen. During the period of crisis in the desegregation of schools in Little Rock, ministers of all faiths cooperated in arranging for special church services to pray for a calming of the fever of racial passing—in segregated services! Eight of a group of clergymen who had been among those in January, 1963, to sign "An Appeal for Law and Order and Common Sense" in dealing with racial problems in Alabama, wrote Martin Luther King, Jr., in May urging him to call off demonstrations in Birmingham. ". . . we are now confronted by a series of demonstrations by some of our Negro citizens, directed and led in part by outsiders. . . . We do not believe that these days of new hope are days when extreme measures are justified in Birmingham. We commend the community as a whole, and the local news media and law enforcement officials in particular, on the calm manner in which these demonstra-

tions have been handled."[89] This last statement struck King, who was then in jail, as somewhat ironic, since order had been kept in part by the use of dogs, who had bitten six demonstrators, by vigorous use of firehoses, and by the jailing of hundreds of persons.

The most systematic study of the dilemma of southern churchmen and their ambivalent behavior has been made in Little Rock by Campbell and Pettigrew. On the basis of interviews, they classified 25 Protestant ministers (representing largely the more prominent churches) and two rabbis into three groups: five segregationists, 16 inactive integrationists, and 8 active integrationists. On the first day of desegregation of Central High School, four white and several Negro clergymen escorted Negro children to school. Two of the white ministers were from the city—the only two from among the many who were asked to help. When Governor Faubus surrounded the school with troops in an effort to block integration, 15 prominent ministers objected strongly. Campbell and Pettigrew note that different "reference systems" pulled the men in varying directions. Typically the self-reference system—personal values and training—pulled them toward integration. The professional-reference system—the regional and national church—rewarded a minister for keeping up membership and attendance. "Promotions for him are determined far less by the number of times he defends unpopular causes, however virtuous their merit, than by the state of the physical plant and the state of the coffer."[90] Finally, the membership-reference system, his own congregation, encouraged segregation or inaction. Pulled by these diverse forces, most of the clergymen took the ambivalent position of inactive integrationism. They felt little guilt, for their sense of worth was based largely on success in managing their churches; they readily assumed that a slow process of education was what was needed,

---

[87] *The New York Times*, Nov. 3, 1957, p. 84.
[88] *The New York Times*, June 30, 1963, p. E 8.

[89] Quoted in *Liberation*, June, 1963, p. 9.
[90] Ernest Campbell and Thomas Pettigrew, "Racial and Moral Crisis: The Role of Little Rock Ministers," *AJS*, Mar., 1959, p. 514.

and "you can't teach those you can't reach;" they avoided commitment by reference to "deeper issues"—humility, brotherly love; and they felt rather courageous in the little bit they did toward integration because stanch segregationists attacked the clergy for being race-mixers.[91] Among those who attacked them were the ministers of the fundamentalist sects, all of whom were vigorous segregationists.[92]

Faced with strong cross-pressures, the southern ministry today is relatively ineffective in supporting the desegregation process. Nevertheless there is good evidence that many of them, particularly the younger men in the established denominations, support racial integration. If the southern scene continues to change, as we believe it will, the dilemma will become less sharp, and churchmen who did not make the first moves may be involved significantly in the less dramatic task of consolidating and extending the gains. In this sense, we agree with Campbell and Pettigrew when they say: "We are convinced that the Protestant ministry is potentially the most effective agent of social change in the South in the decade ahead."[93]

All of this is to say that for the most part the church acts like a church, not like a sect. This may cause discomfort from various moral perspectives—it does from ours—but should not occasion surprise. Why, then, do we suggest that the years ahead may bring some increase in integration activity in southern churches? It is because the social context of their work is rapidly changing. If the "church" as a sociological type is accommodated to its social setting—not without some sectarian deviants in its midst—it should be emphasized that the social setting is being rapidly urbanized and industrialized. Slow as school integration is, the percentage of Negro children attending schools with white children in the South has increased from 0 to about 35,

1954–1971. It is in this context that one begins to read that 300 Baptists leave their local church in Birmingham, which had denied membership to two Negroes, to set up a church with the Negroes as members; that after having twice been turned away, Negroes attend service at St. Paul's Episcopal Church, Selma; that, by 1963, at least 234 Southern Baptist congregations in Texas had adopted policies to admit Negroes into full membership.[94]

To the student of the sociology of religion, the ambivalence and the range of attitudes on race relations among churchmen, whether ministers or laymen, is not surprising. Church members are also bankers, Legionnaires, householders, status seekers, etc. Their interracial behavior may occur in spite of their religious perspectives, not because of them. Moreover, the religious life of man is not something aloof from the rest of his experience; it is intimately tied to the whole of life, with its tensions and errors as well as its sublime moments. Churches will move toward desegregation as the rest of society moves, affecting and being affected by all the other forces at work.

The Churches' Interest in the Desegregation of Other Institutions

When we examine the evidence concerning the role of the churches in promoting an integrated society, we find the same mixed picture that we found in the church situation itself; support of segregation or indifference on the one hand, and the beginnings of vigorous efforts to promote integration on the other.

Although the churches stress the dignity and worth of the individual and the brotherhood of man, the racial behavior patterns of most church members have not been substantially affected by these principles. With the exception of the financial support that white churches contributed to Negro secondary schools and colleges, they have given, until recently, very little attention to

[91] *Ibid.*, pp. 509–516.
[92] Ernest Campbell and Thomas Pettigrew, *Christianity in Racial Crisis: A Study of Little Rock's Ministry*, Public Affairs Press, 1959, chap. 3.
[93] *Ibid.*, p. viii.

[94] *The New York Times*, Dec. 20, 1970, p. 34; *The Plain Dealer*, Mar. 29, 1965, p. 1; Bailey, *op. cit.*, p. 153.

the American racial situation. They have issued pronouncements, passed resolutions, conducted "interracial Sunday" once a year, held occasional conferences, sponsored summer camps and work camps with an interracial aspect, published a number of pamphlets, and used racial or interracial themes in study groups.

In the 20-year period before the Depression, the Protestant churches were almost completely silent on the subject of race relations. The number of resolutions increased during the 1930s, but these pronouncements were quite general and dealt mainly with the gross aspects of the disabilities and injustices that Negroes experience. "The majority of the statements focus on the most obvious evil—lynching—and scarcely a word is uttered on the more controversial and more basic issue of economic discrimination. Indeed, discrimination is rarely mentioned. And there is only a single use of the word segregation."[95] During the first half of the 1940s a flood of pronouncements on race relations materialized. In March, 1946, the Federal Council of Churches of Christ in America declared that it renounced ". . . the pattern of segregation in race relations as unnecessary and undesirable and a violation of the Gospel of love and human brotherhood. Having taken this action, the Federal Council requests its constituent communions to do likewise. As proof of their sincerity in this renunciation they will work for a non-segregated Church and a non-segregated society." Subsequently, four denominations adopted the statement as their own, and three other denominations, without adopting the council statement, have recommended that their churches welcome Negroes.[96]

These pronouncements have certain limitations. They are verbal acts, and in many cases they represent minority opinions. There is little evidence that the rank-and-file membership of Protestant denominations is greatly influenced by these official actions.

To what degree have churches been drawn into the current activity and debate over desegregation and the reduction of discrimination? At the top organizational level there was almost unanimous approval of the Supreme Court decision calling for desegregation of the schools. "Every major Protestant denomination in the South has made public pronouncements commending the decision."[97] Catholic leaders and the National Council of Churches have repeatedly declared that discrimination and segregation are evil. In 1963, The World Council of Churches issued its strongest statement condemning racism. Reaffirming a 1954 declaration that ". . . any form of segregation based on race, color or ethnic origin is contrary to the Gospel and is incompatible with the Christian doctrine of man, and with the nature of the Church of Christ," they added that "wherever and whenever any of us Christians deny this, by action or inaction, we betray Christ and the fellowship which bears his name."[98] Protestant churches, which have left the inner-city by the hundreds when neighborhoods have shifted from white to nonwhite, have established new programs in several cities. These inner-city parishes are deeply involved in the full range of community life, not simply in religion. Their role in a period of emphasis on local community control, however, has become problematic.

Thousands of Catholic, Jewish, and Protestant ministers have taken part in recent freedom rides, sit-ins, and protest marches and dozens have been sent to jail for their efforts. Various "social action" groups of northern Protestant denominations are beginning to direct their attention toward desegregation in housing, an activity that Quakers and other sects have engaged in for several years. For example, the American Baptist Convention,

[95] Loescher, *op. cit.*, p. 31.
[96] *Ibid.*, p. 42.

[97] John Hope, II, "Trends in Patterns of Race Relations in the South Since May 17, 1954," *Phylon*, Second Quarter, 1956, p. 107.
[98] *The New York Times*, Sept. 1, 1963, p. 40. In response to the interracial crises of 1963, the National Council of Churches established a Commission on Religion and Race to mobilize the resources of its members on race relations matters. Staffed at the beginning by an "emergency committee of six," the Commission is to be on a permanent basis and financed by the constituent members of the National Council.

Disciples of Christ, Methodist Church, Presbyterian Church, U.S.A., and United Church of Christ are seeking in a combined effort to supply professional leadership in study-action programs concerned with housing.

These are small beginnings. But if these illustrations prove to be beginnings, and not simply slightly more dramatic gestures than previous religious involvement in race relations, the churches of the United States may yet significantly influence the integration process.

As these items indicate, there has been a shift from pronouncement, to protest, to activity, paralleling shifts that have occurred elsewhere in society. Where words once seemed to be sincere participation, they now can be taken, if not accompanied by action, as hypocrisy. Thus it is more meaningful when 17 church groups pledge themselves to buy only from bias-free companies—a decision affecting the expenditure of hundreds of millions of dollars a year.[99] The United Presbyterian Church has recently undertaken to raise $70 million to support a Fund for the Self-Development of People.[100] And, in an interesting internationalization of the issue of racial justice, tieing it to the question of peace, clergymen of all the major world religions have set up a lobbying group beside the United Nations in New York. The group is designed to focus the opposition of religious leaders throughout the world to racial discrimination and war.[101]

THE RELIGIONS OF
SPANISH-SPEAKING AMERICANS

We cannot undertake a full description of religious patterns among other minorities in the United States, for each deserves much longer treatment than we can give. Brief reference to a few situations, however, may further suggest the importance of the study of religion in the analysis of minority-majority relations.

The majority of Spanish-speaking persons in the United States belong to the Catholic faith, but the number of Protestants among them is growing. In many instances, adherence to Catholicism seems to be nominal, while many of the Protestants have the fervor of new converts. In New York City, about 14,000 Spanish-speaking people, mainly Puerto Ricans, belong to major Protestant denominations, perhaps 10,000 of them in their own all-Spanish churches.[102] In addition there are, according to a 1960 estimate of the Protestant Council of New York, 25,000 in Pentecostal-type churches. Among them, enthusiasm and participation are at a high level. "The tight Pentecostal congregation is one of the most important expressions of community that exists among Puerto Ricans in New York."[103]

There are also some Protestants among Americans of Mexican descent, perhaps 5 percent, although it is difficult to state an accurate figure.[104] They tend to interact closely among themselves, cut off by their group programs and to some degree by values from Catholic Mexicans, and also isolated from the dominant Protestant churches. This latter separation was first justified by the language difference but tends to be perpetuated on purely ethnic grounds.[105]

About 95 percent of Spanish-speaking Americans, according to the *Catholic Almanac*, are baptized Catholics, but a large proportion are inactive; ". . . about 10 percent of the Spanish-speaking coming to

[99] *The New York Times,* July 3, 1968, pp. 1 and 21.
[100] *The New York Times,* June 7, 1970, p. 66.
[101] *The New York Times,* Jan. 31, 1971, p. 3.

[102] Nathan Glazer, "The Puerto Ricans," *Commentary,* July, 1963, pp. 1–9.
[103] *Ibid.,* p. 5. The figure of 39,000 Protestant Puerto Ricans in New York may well be an underestimation. A Columbia University study found 83 percent Catholic, 9 percent Protestant in the established churches, 5 percent in sects and "storefront" groups, 2 percent "spiritualist." Protestants attended church more regularly than Catholics. See Clarence Senior, *Strangers—Then Neighbors,* ADL, 1961, pp. 72–73.
[104] See Leo Grebler, Joan W. Moore, and Ralph C. Guzman, *The Mexican-American People: The Nation's Second Largest Minority,* Free Press, 1970, pp. 486–488.
[105] See Margaret Sumner, "Mexican-American Minority Churches, U.S.A.," *Practical Anthropology,* May–June, 1963, p. 121.

this country since World War II are, by U.S. standards, practical Catholics."[106] As among the Protestants, most Spanish-speaking Catholics attend separate churches, although integration is the ultimate aim of the Church. "It is a matter of practical necessity, now and for many years to come, to provide the Spanish-speaking with services in their own language and in a manner corresponding to their native culture."[107] It remains a question whether or not separation started out as practical necessity reenforces that necessity and is later sustained by class, ethnic, and racial lines after the lingual difference is gone.

Because of the relative lack of Spanish-speaking priests and the European orientation of much American Catholicism, the indoctrination of Mexican-American children in Catholic dogma involves problems that are not encountered in training Catholic children of immigrant European families. The latter have Catholic doctrines presented to them in a way they can understand, and they are fairly well prepared in the teachings of the church by confirmation time. Few Mexican-American children go to parochial schools because of the tuition fees. What they learn of the church doctrines is acquired in catechism classes before first communion and later on at confirmation. At the same time that instruction in the catechism is being received in English from Catholic officials, their mothers tell them folk tales in Spanish and provide interpretations of religious occurrences.

Teenage Spanish-speaking Americans tend to judge the Catholic Church in their community by the priest. His interest in the needs of young people is more important to them than the number of persons attending Mass or the number of confessions he hears. " 'What we need,' say the boys and girls in the Mexican communities, 'are priests who want to help us—you know, how to get jobs and better houses, real men in Los Angeles . . . not just priests hidden in the

church. There's a world around us and he should be in it like we are, if he's going to really help us.' "[108]

Although the Catholic Church has been quite traditional in dealing with its members of Spanish-speaking descent, one should not disregard the exceptions to that statement. Long before governmental and educational institutions began to think about their special problems, the churches (both Catholic and Protestant) had tried, even if not very successfully, to design programs for their Spanish-speaking members. There was little experience to go on, resources were limited, but perhaps most importantly, there were, and are, disagreements over methods and goals which limited the success of these programs. Grebler, Moore, and Guzman describe the situation well in their examination of the continuum from conservative to liberal in church policy, from pastoral to social action among Catholics, from evangelical to social gospel among Protestants. They see this continuum in terms of its general significance:

The conservative tradition requires that the "client" should become totally immersed in the values of the institution; the liberal position maintains that the institution is there to serve the "client". Of course, neither position is mutually exclusive, and the difference between the conservative and liberal is a matter of emphasis. . . . Adherence to values at either end of the continuum will be shown to imply special stances toward Mexican Americans—from paternalism through self-determination, from priority on conformity to the institution's norms of conduct through priority on the institution's assistance to the client in his non-institutional roles. The value continuum suggests a fundamental difference: the institution as an end versus the institution as a means.[109]

The institutional emphasis has been predominant, but not exclusively so. In 1945, the American Board of Catholic Missions began support for a "Bishops' Committee

[106] Foy, *op. cit.*, p. 495.
[107] *Ibid.*

[108] Beatrice Griffith, *American Me*, Houghton Mifflin, 1948, pp. 184, 186.
[109] Grebler, Moore, and Guzman, *op. cit.*, p. 447.

for the Spanish-Speaking," which has gradually shifted from strictly pastoral to more social action programs. It supported termination of the *bracero* program and, somewhat belatedly, the union organization of Mexican farm workers.[110] A few priests have worked in nonchurch programs, in the factories and fields. Some support and are members of the Cursillo Movement, brought from Spain in the late 1950s as a program to intensify and renew religious dedication by three-day sessions of discussions, lectures, and devotion. Social action concerns are not inherent in the Cursillo Movement, but many of the participants are inclined in that direction.

The Protestant social action ministry among Americans of Spanish-speaking descent goes back more than half a century. The National Council of Churches (then the Federal Council) established its Council on Spanish-American Work in 1912. A "migrant ministry" program, started in 1920, was a response to the extremely difficult conditions of farm workers of Mexican descent. Its budget in 1966 was greater than $1 million; many of its members were direct participants in the unionization campaign of Cesar Chavez.[111] Most Spanish-speaking Protestants, however, are members of fundamentalist sects oriented more toward individual salvation and achievement than social action. Only in recent years have they begun to get involved in the civil rights movement.

THE JEWISH RELIGION

The Jewish religion in its traditional form, more than language, tradition, or secular culture, distinguished European Jews from their Christian neighbors through the Middle Ages and into the nineteenth century. Through these centuries, and until the present time, Judaism has provided the basis for group solidarity among the Jews. As the religion of a specific people, however, Judaism is strongly mixed with other cultural elements. "Much of its religious culture, custom, and tradition is interwoven with the national history of Jews. Judaism is thus not a church with a body of doctrine and a system of theology: it is, in effect, the national, religious civilization of the Jewish people."[112]

From the period of heavy Jewish immigration, 1880–1915, until the mid-1930s, Judaism was changed rapidly by the new American setting. Religion continued to be an extremely important part of life for most Jewish Americans, but practices and beliefs that were functionally connected with life in different societies, in Eastern Europe for example, seemed awkward or irrelevant in the United States. Ritual in particular has been significantly revised. Sklare and Greenblum note how this revision represents the pull of the contemporary Christian and secularist environment, on one hand, and the desire to express Jewish identity and continuity on the other. A home ritual, for example, is most likely to be retained when it ". . . (1) is capable of effective redefinition in modern terms, (2) does not demand social isolation or the adoption of a unique life style, (3) accords with the religious culture of the larger community and provides a 'Jewish' alternative when such is felt to be needed, (4) is centered on the child, and (5) is performed annually or infrequently."[113] Individuals will vary in their judgments on whether these criteria indicate successful adaptation or only the preservation of a nominal Jewish connection.

Until the 1930s most observers emphasized the assimilationist pull of the American environment. It was difficult for Judaism to withstand the influences toward assimilation that prevailed in small communities, and the result was that the intermarried abandoned the Jewish faith in appreciable numbers. Also, the concentration of Jews in

[110] Ibid., p. 462.
[111] On all of this, see *Ibid.*, pp. 443–512.

[112] Stuart E. Rosenberg, *The Search for Jewish Identity in America*, Doubleday, 1965, p. 40.
[113] Marshall Sklare and Joseph Greenblum, *Jewish Identity on the Suburban Frontier*, Basic Books, 1967, p. 57.

urban centers made it easy for those who wished to avoid the synagogue to do so.

In the large American cities some Jews have come to admire liberal Christian preachers and have joined Unitarian or other liberal churches. A few have become members of the Christian Science Church. Still others are "nonreligious" or "antireligious." Their Jewish identity is ethnic and cultural, not religious.

Despite these trends, the predominant fact is the continuing strength of the sense of identity with Judaism. Indeed, since about 1933 the pressures toward assimilation have been countered to an important degree by forces that have renewed the Jewish community in the United States. What we observe today, therefore, is the paradox of the continuing "Americanization" of Judaism at the same time that the feeling of a distinctive identity with Judaism persists and perhaps even grows among its members. Having discussed this development in Chapter 10, we need here only to suggest some of the factors involved. In part, it shares in the general emphasis on ethnicity and religious community that characterizes the contemporary scene. The religions with which Protestants, Catholics, and Jews identify in substantial numbers seem to many observers to be glossy, secularized attempts to establish "confident living." They are efforts to overcome the sense of anomie, to escape the loneliness of the crowd, by close identity with a religious group. Jews can now do this as Jews more readily than they could a generation ago, for they are less insecure, less "foreign." The American pattern of freedom of religion and the separation of church and state allows religion to be the carrier of this attempt to find a place. The continuing identity with Judaism was also reinforced by the rise of Nazism. If such vicious anti-Semitism could appear in Germany, where Jews were as fully assimilated as anywhere in the world, the whole idea of assimilation must be thought through again. Biculturalism of an Eastern European model was certainly unattractive to most American Jews; but a more vigorous empha-sis on cultural pluralism—attention to their religious and, to some degree, their cultural distinctiveness as well as to their ties to American society—became common.[114]

In any religious group whose members differ widely in background, level of education, occupation, and social class, denominations with different types of belief and practice tend to appear. Although there has been a blurring of the lines of distinction in recent years, one can readily distinguish the Orthodox, the Conservative, and the Reform branches of Judaism in America. Reform Judaism bears somewhat the same relationship to Orthodoxy that Protestantism does to Catholicism. The Reform group is less mystical, its ceremonies are less elaborate, and it makes fewer demands on its members. It represents the influence of modern urban life, the improvement of status, the sharp reduction of disprivilege, the increased secularization that many Jews experienced, first in western Europe and then in the United States. A sociologist's comment on the Reform group in an American industrial city is of interest:

As to doctrine, the Reformed group, of course, has made the most complete compromises. Protestants who visit the Temple say they recognize little difference between its services and those which they attend in their own churches. Only the brief recitations in Hebrew, the letters on the windows, are there to remind them that the very pew in which they sit bridges a cultural gap. Here no hats are worn, the men and women sit together, there is an organ loft and a choir, and the ghetto seems very far away. The mild Sunday-morning exhortation of Rabbi Golder is equivalent to that of the Methodist minister across the way. Indeed, Rabbi Golder calls himself "ambassador to the Christians." They understand him well, for he is cut out of the same cloth as their clergy. He visits in their pulpits and is a leader in the social work of the city. His congregation is proud that its leader is so

[114] See Marshall Sklare, *Conservative Judaism*, Free Press, 1955; Marshall Sklare and Marc Vosk, *The Riverton Study, How Jews Look at Themselves and Their Neighbors*, American Jewish Committee, 1957; Will Herberg, *Protest-Catholic-Jew*, Doubleday, 1955; C. Bezalel Sherman, *The Jew Within American Society*, Wayne State Univ. Press, 1961.

universally a respected and an important factor in the larger community. In his hands Judaism is no vital, compulsive force, but a mannerly social practice in the best Gentile taste. The Orthodox part of the community frankly distrusts him.[115]

Conservative Judaism is traditional in its outlook, although in some respects it is closer to Reform Judaism than to Orthodoxy. In contrast to Reform Judaism, Orthodox and Conservative Jews have avoided the formulation of a general Jewish creed. The two latter groups try to arrange public services on weekdays as well as on the Sabbaths and holidays. Also, in both, the men pray with covered heads. Many Conservative congregations have these characteristics in common with Reform Jews: abolition of the separation of the sexes in the synagogue, admission of women to the choir, the synagogues being spoken of as temples, and the expectation that the Messianic age will come about through the efforts of many thinkers and teachers.[116] Conservative Judaism is essentially an American denomination. Its programs and doctrines can be seen as an effort to preserve what is believed to be essential in Judaism while at the same time encouraging practices and beliefs harmonious with the American environment. Sklare describes its development in functional terms:

The greatest contribution of the German Reform movement may be said to be its function as the provider of a cushion for the disintegrative effects of emancipation. It helped to indicate a *modus vivendi* between assimilation and a no-longer acceptable Orthodoxy. In the same tradition, American Conservatism has cushioned the effects of the dissolution of Judaism as an integrated and highly traditional sacred system. It too has offered a *modus vivendi* for the alienated. . . . The signal contribution of Conservatism would seem to be that of offering an acceptable pattern of adjustment to the American

environment for many East-European-derived Jews.[117]

For many years Orthodox Judaism reflected Eastern European life. It was maintained largely by a fairly steady stream of European immigrants. The virtual cutting off of European immigration does not necessarily mean that Orthodoxy will die out in the United States. According to Rabbi Pool, Orthodox Judaism has shown that it is adapting itself to the American environment, and he cites such innovations as the late Friday evening service, the removal of the women's gallery, the confirmation of girls, and the community *seder* (celebration on Passover eve). The goal of some Orthodox Jews is to harmonize unquestioning faith with modern living.[118] The unprecedented persecution of Jews in Europe during the Nazi regime increased the strength of Orthodoxy by intensifying the consciousness of the Jewish heritage.

There are distinctive currents within Orthodoxy, so that no one description is accurate. In recent years, the accommodative trend has been slowed, classical Orthodoxy reemphasized, and some young people drawn back into the denomination. Liebman overstates the case, but calls our attention to an interesting fact when he observes that

the only remaining vestige of Jewish passion in America resides in the Orthodox community. . . . the old antagonisms to the world of Orthodoxy are gone from many intellectuals furthest removed from Orthodox life. . . . there is a recognition and admiration for Orthodoxy as the only group which today contains within it a strength and will to live that may yet nourish all the Jewish world.[119]

The many elements of Judaism have resisted the organization of a denominational group, and it seems unlikely that this in-

---

[115] Leonard Bloom, "The Jews of Buna," in Isacque Graeber and S. H. Britt (eds.), *Jews in a Gentile World*, Macmillan, 1942, p. 186.

[116] Louis Finkelstein (ed.), *The Jews, Their History, Culture, and Religion*, Harper & Row, vol. 2, 1949, chap. 35.

[117] Sklare, *op. cit.*, p. 249.

[118] David de Sola Pool, "Judaism and the Synagogue," in O. I. Janowsky (ed.), *The American Jew*, Harper & Row, 1942, pp. 53–54.

[119] Charles S. Liebman, "Orthodoxy in American Jewish Life," in Morris Fine and Milton Himmelfarb (eds.), *American Jewish Yearbook*, The American Jewish Committee and the Jewish Publication Society of America, 1965, p. 92.

dependence will give way in the foreseeable future. In spite of the differences between the Orthodox and the Reform groups, however, each regards the other as a part of Judaism.

It is possible for them to do so, because of the principle that even an unobservant or a heretical Jew does not cease to be a member of the covenant made between God and Israel at the time of the Revelation. Only actual rejection of Judaism, by affiliation with another faith, is recognized as separating one from the Jewish community. So long as a follower of the Jewish faith has not by overt act or word and of his own free will declared himself a member of another religion, other Jews are bound to regard him as one of their own faith, and to seek his return to its practice and beliefs.[120]

In the absence of any central organization or authority, the only bond that unites the Jewish people is a "consciousness of a *Kenesset Yisrael* (the congregation of Israel) which Solomon Schechter translated into 'Catholic Israel.' "[121]

There is no exact knowledge of the numbers of Jews who belong to the three denominations. In 1958 the Reform group was composed of 548 synagogues with about 1 million members, the Conservatives had 650 synagogues (plus 200 related but nonmember synagogues) with 1.2 million members.[122] The Orthodox group does not list its members, but claimed 2500 synagogues in the United States and Canada in 1960.[123] It is well to remember that one generation's reform may be a later generation's orthodoxy. There seems to be a tendency for the Conservative movement to emerge as the dominant one among American Jews, but even as it does so, it continues to change. Kramer

[120] Finkelstein (ed.), *op. cit.*, pp. 1333, 1352.
[121] *Ibid.*, pp. 1352–1353.
[122] Sherman, *op. cit.*, p. 209.
[123] Morris Fine and Milton Himmelfarb (eds.), *American Jewish Yearbook*, The American Jewish Committee and the Jewish Publication Society of America, 1962, p. 210. Liebman gives a figure of 1607 Orthodox synagogues for the United States alone, with 204,815 male worshippers. This latter figure is affected by, perhaps, 5 percent of dual memberships. See Liebman, *op. cit.*, pp. 24–25. Altogether, about 60 percent of America's 5.5 million Jews belong to one of the three denominations.

and Leventman report the following pattern in a midwestern city:

	Fathers		Sons	
	Number	Percent	Number	Percent
Orthodox	17	20.2	1	1.2
Conservative	44	52.4	49	58.3
Reform	16	19.1	14	16.7
None	7	8.3	20[a]	23.8
	84	100.0	84	100.0

Note:
[a]Eleven of the sons will join within the next few years.
Source: Judith Kramer and Seymour Leventman, *Children of the Gilded Ghetto*, Yale, 1961, p. 155.

Something of the same pattern appears in "Riverton," studied by Sklare and Vosk:

	Grandparents	Parents	Children
Orthodox	81%	16%	9%
Conservative	11	43	42
Reform	5	30	31
Nonreligious	2	4	8
Don't know, it depends, or no answer	1	7	10
	100%	100%	100%

Source: Marshall Sklare and Mark Vosk, *The Riverton Study: How Jews Look at Themselves and Their Neighbors*, American Jewish Committee, 1957, p. 16.

Only 23 percent of the children in Orthodox families intend to remain Orthodox; half of them plan to turn Conservative.

Despite their differences, the three Jewish denominations share in common a need to respond to the American environment. Not only is the society around them different from Europe, but their members have acquired new perspectives, hopes, and values. One response is to elaborate the programs of the synagogues. The "institutional synagogue" is regarded by some religious Jews as "one of the most promising features in American Jewish life."

The synagogue center has come to stay, despite fears that Judaism might be diluted by the secular attractions of the gymnasium, the swimming pool and similar extension activities. The house of worship, whether orthodox, conservative or reform, is gradually being transformed into a center of social life in the Jewish community. The week-end synagogue is again assuming the character of the *beth hakneseth* of older times, the seven days a week rallying center of Jewish life. The synagogue center attempts to embrace the totality of Judaism—worship first and foremost, but, along with it, forums and institutes for the study of the Hebrew language, Jewish history and literature, a Jewish library, family celebrations such as *bar mitzvah* or confirmation and weddings within the synagogue. The synagogue is tending to become once more a focus for Jewish needs and causes. In this lies a strong hope of a Jewish life once more reintegrated in and around the synagogue.[124]

The recency and the severity of anti-Jewish policies in Nazi Germany have made many Jews in the United States dubious about complete assimilation.[125] We have also suggested that the desire to find personal identity in a complicated society has supported allegiance to one's traditional religious community. But whether or not the current revival of Judaism is a long-run trend, or a short-run reversal of a dominant trend toward assimilation, is not entirely clear. It is our guess that we shall see a paradoxical result: continuing identity with Judaism for most Jews, but at the same time a reduction

[124] de Sola Pool, *op. cit.*, p. 54.
[125] See, for example, Marshall Sklare, "Assimilation and the Sociologists," *Commentary*, May, 1965, pp. 63–67.

in the elements that differentiate it from other religions in the American environment. This does not mean that only Judaism will change. It means that all alike, as they struggle with religious problems in the fundamentally new content of a mobile industrial society, will revise many aspects of religious traditions that developed in vastly different settings.

CONCLUSION

We know little about the consequences of religious traditionalism and religious change for minority status, but there is some evidence that it is the persons more strongly motivated toward status improvement among minority groups who leave traditional religion. Their shift is probably both symbol and cause of their more rapid acculturation. It also establishes cross-cutting memberships that influence majority-group opinion and behavior.

It is perhaps not so much the *direction* as the *fact* of religious change that is important. Thus many persons of Chinese descent in Hawaii have become Catholics (although more are Protestants) and have moved rapidly up the status ladder. Japanese in Hawaii, who have become Protestants in larger proportion, have climbed more rapidly than those who have remained Buddhists. Among Spanish-speaking Americans, the shift is from Catholicism to Protestantism. And among Jews, from Orthodox to Conservatism and Reform. Because religion is embedded in the whole social system within which people interact and in terms of which they respond to one another, status change often requires a break with earlier religious identities.

Chapter 18 / THE EDUCATION OF RACIAL AND CULTURAL MINORITIES IN THE UNITED STATES

THE EDUCATION OF MINORITIES AND THE SOCIAL ORDER

The education of minorities cannot be treated exhaustively in a work that attempts to cover many aspects of majority-minority relations. Instead of examining the educational status of all minority peoples, we shall concentrate mainly on educational policies for Negroes as the most severely handicapped group. Some attention is given to Mexican-American, Puerto Rican, and American Indian children because of the linguistic, economic, and residential factors which affect their education. In analyzing this phase of intergroup relations, it is well to keep in mind the importance of education in a free society.

Public-school systems are responsive to the dominant social influences of the communities of which they are parts; their operations cannot be understood unless this point is grasped.[1] State commissions of education, as well as county, city, and town boards of education, exercise control over educational policies. All are subject to political forces, and inevitably they vary in competence and in social attitudes. The policies of principals and teachers are limited by the authority of superintendents and assistant superintendents, and often the latter are not well qualified in the field of intergroup relations.

During Reconstruction years both conservatives and radicals in the South seemed to feel that proposals for Negro education were based on the assumption that the Negro population was to acquire the same general social standing and stratification as the white population. The development of the sharecropping type of tenancy nullified much of the earlier discussion of Negro education.

Bond points out that under such an exploitative system an educated labor force would be a liability rather than an asset. There was no reason for "spoiling a good plowhand" or letting the Negro "get ahead of himself." In the Alabama constitutional convention of 1910 a planter "said that there was no fear of the illiterate Negro, but of 'the upper branches of Negro society, the educated, the man who after ascertaining his political rights forced the way to assert them.'"[2]

For several decades after Reconstruction a debate raged over "industrial education" for Negroes. This term had varying meanings for different white people. Some believed that such education was "practical" and the only kind of public education worth stressing. Others thought that advocacy of "industrial" training was the only politically feasible way of improving Negro education. A good many advocated the formula as a means of rationalizing discrimination and keeping appropriations low for Negro schools.[3]

The ineffective educational programs for Negroes fitted in well with the developing industrialization of certain parts of the South. It helped to keep Negro labor cheap and presumably it would provide insurance against labor troubles.[4]

The earlier attitudes and policies of southern industry were modified somewhat in the early 1900s by the coming of new concentrations of capital. In Alabama the larger industrial concerns, especially those in coal and iron, decided to elevate Negroes slightly in the socioeconomic scale. Bond shows the educational implications of this

---

[1] For pre-World War I references, see H. M. Bond, *The Education of the Negro in the American Social Order*, Prentice-Hall, 1934; also E. Franklin Frazier, *The Negro in the United States*, Macmillan, 2nd ed., 1957, chaps. 17–18.

[2] H. M. Bond, *Negro Education in Alabama, A Study in Cotton and Steel*, The Associated Publishers, 1939, pp. 141–142.

[3] Gunnar Myrdal, *An American Dilemma*, Harper & Row, 1944, pp. 897–899; also S. J. Wright, "Hampton-Tuskegee Pattern," *Phylon*, 1949, Fourth Quarter, pp. 340–342.

[4] Bond, *Negro Education in Alabama*, pp. 145–147.

change in the self-conscious planning of the Tennessee Coal and Iron Company.

The Tennessee Company began at once to build up complete industrial and housing units, fitted with hospitals, welfare centers, and schools, by which means it was frankly hoped to regularize the uncertain Negro labor. It was officially stated that this was not a philanthropic movement: "The Steel Corporation is not an eleemosynary institution," and its first object was "to make money for its stockholders."[5]

It is apparent that during the development of industrial centers like Birmingham, Negro education was adjusted to the needs of the dominant members of the white group.

A close relationship has existed also between rural Negro schools and the agricultural system of the Old South. The dates for the opening and closing of school in the cotton belt were not set in advance but were determined by the landlords watching the crop. "In the spring and fall the internal school program is changed to accommodate the farming system. Chapel exercises, lunch hours, and recreational periods are either shortened or eliminated entirely in order that school may close at an earlier hour, to let children get away to the farms."[6]

The net result of the financial, political, and social forces playing upon education for Negroes, until very recent years, is well pointed up in a report of the U.S. Commission on Civil Rights. In 1959, 23.5 percent of Nonwhites 25 years of age or over were deemed functionally illiterate (completed less than five years of school), compared to 6.4 percent of Whites. The median number of school years completed by Nonwhites 25 years old and over was 8.1, compared to 11.4 for Whites. Only 20 percent of Nonwhites compared to 45.3 percent of Whites had high school or better education; 49.5 percent of Nonwhites compared to 80.8 percent of Whites had elementary school or better.[7]

Several relationships may be discerned be-

tween the social order of the South and Negro schools. First, the lower classes have not exerted much influence on public-school legislation and educational policies. Many Negroes have been disfranchised since Reconstruction days, and, for the most part, the white working population has been politically impotent. Second, Negro public education has been keyed to the interests of those in the white group who have been in control of legislation and finance at a given time. Third, better provision for Negro education appears to have been made in (1) urbanized industrialized communities than in rural areas and in (2) counties with a small Negro population than where a large population would require a greater expenditure.[8] In connection with these points, Myrdal's observation concerning Negro education at the time of World War II is pertinent:

. . . *The Southern whites have never had the nerve to make of Negro education an accomplished instrument to keep the Negroes in their caste status.* . . . The Southern whites' caste policy has been halfhearted all through. . . . The interest of educating the Negroes to become faithful helots has been obvious, but the Southern whites have not even attempted to make it effective in practice. Instead, they have merely kept Negro education poor and bad.[9]

THE SUPREME COURT'S DECISIONS OF MAY 17, 1954, AND MAY 31, 1955

What we have described has been rather significantly modified in the last several years.

The decisions of the U.S. Supreme Court in the public-school cases in 1954 and 1955 were not sudden legal developments. These decisions were preceded by the Murray case of 1936, the Gaines case of 1938, and the Sweatt and McLaurin decisions of 1950 (see Chapter 19). Notable decisions in other areas included the ruling on the white primary in 1944, the racial restrictive covenants decision of 1948, and the banning of segregated interstate travel in 1946.

[5] *Ibid.*, p. 240.
[6] Charles S. Johnson, *Patterns of Negro Segregation*, Harper & Row, 1943, p. 21.
[7] *1961 Report of the U.S. Commission on Civil Rights*, "Voting," Book 1, p. 9.

[8] Bond, *Negro Education in Alabama*, pp. 290–291.
[9] Myrdal, *op. cit.*, p. 896.

On May 17, 1954, the Supreme Court, consolidating cases arising in Delaware, Kansas, South Carolina, and Virginia, ruled unanimously that the separate-but-equal doctrine (Plessy *v.* Ferguson), which had been used to exclude Negro children from public schools maintained for white chlidren, was unconstitutional. The Court held that the plaintiffs, by being required on the basis of race to attend separate schools, were deprived of the equal protection of the laws assured by the Fourteenth Amendment. In a related case, the Supreme Court ruled on the same day that the separate-but-equal doctrine, when applied to exclude Negro children from admission to the public schools of the District of Columbia, violates the due-process clause of the Fifth Amendment.[10]

The Court pointed out that the Plessy case, long used to justify separate schools, was concerned with transportation rather than education. In none of the previous education cases had the Court actually decided that the Plessy doctrine applied to education. Since separate but equal facilities existed in the South Carolina and Virginia cases, the 1954 decisions could be based only on this ground. The Court found that education today is not merely "social" as in 1896 but "is perhaps the most important function of state and local governments" and "is a principal instrument in awakening the child to cultural values, in preparing him for later professional training, and in helping him to adjust normally to his environment." The Court concluded that racially separate schools have "a tendency to retard the educational and mental development of Negro children and to deprive them of some of the benefits they would receive in a racially integrated school system." Whereas the Plessy opinion held that segregation does not necessarily imply a badge of inferiority, the 1954 decision said that to separate grade- and high-school children from others solely because of race "generates a feeling of inferiority as to their status in the community that may affect their hearts and minds in a way unlikely ever to be undone."

In the District of Columbia case, the Court held that "segregation in public education is not reasonably related to any proper governmental objective. . . ." Pointing out that the Fourteenth Amendment contains a due-process clause in the same language as the Fifth Amendment, Hill and Greenberg conclude that "from now on all segregation by state as well as federal governments will have to pass the apparently unpassable test of 'reasonable relationship.' "[11]

Recognizing the complexity of implementing its far-reaching decrees of May 17, 1954, the Supreme Court postponed arguments on how the ruling should be carried out. The attorneys general of the separate-school states were invited to submit proposals in the fall of 1954 for accommodating their school systems to the new legal principle. The Court's second unanimous decision, handed down on May 31, 1955, stated: "All provisions of federal, state or local law requiring or permitting such discrimination must yield to this [the May 17, 1954] principle." Trial courts (federal district courts) that had originally heard the cases were instructed to order a "prompt and reasonable" start toward desegregation with a view to "good faith compliance at the earliest practicable date." No deadline was set for the desegregation of the public schools, but the Court said that it should be carried out "with all deliberate speed."

The Supreme Court did not require immediate compliance with its two decisions because it recognized that local conditions vary and that time must be allowed for administrative changes. Legitimate grounds for delay included "problems related to administration, arising from the physical condition of the school plant, the school transportation system, personnel, revision of school districts

[10] *RRLR*, Feb., 1956, pp. 5, 9. Because of the volume of court decisions, new legislation, and policy changes by school boards, any discussion of the desegregation process is soon outdated. In this section we attempt to summarize developments at the local, state, and national levels in the three years following the May 17, 1954, decision. Students will find the following publications indispensable in keeping abreast of current changes: *Southern Education Report, Race Relations Law Survey,* and *Journal of Negro Education* (quarterly).

[11] Herbert Hill and Jack Greenberg, *Citizen's Guide to Desegregation,* Beacon Press, 1955, p. 120.

and attendance areas into compact units to achieve a system of determining admission to the public schools on a non-racial basis, and revision of local laws and regulations which may be necessary in solving the foregoing problems."

What Do the 1954 Decisions Mean?

In the simplest terms, the historical decisions of 1954 mean that the rigid and arbitrary separation of the races in the public schools solely on the basis of race is no longer legal. An explanation of the Court's decisions was given in Judge Bryan's memorandum in the Arlington school cases.

It must be remembered that the decisions of the Supreme Court of the United States in Brown *v.* Board of Education, 1954 and 1955, 347 United States 483 and 349 United States 294, do not compel the mixing of the different races in the public schools. No general reshuffling of the pupils in any school system has been commanded. The order of that court is simply that no child shall be denied admission to a school on the basis of race or color. Indeed, just so a child is not through any means of compulsion or pressure required to stay in a certain school, because of his race or color, the school heads may allow the pupil, whether white or Negro, to go to the same school as he would have attended in the absence of the ruling of the Supreme Court.[12]

In Houston, Texas, in May, 1957, U.S. District Judge Ben Connally made the same point in distinguishing between racial desegregation and "forced integration."[13]

Acceptance of and Resistance to the Decisions of the Supreme Court

The public-school decisions were welcomed enthusiastically by supporters of civil liberties, liberal political leaders in both major parties, and spokesmen for minority-group organizations. Within four months of the decisions, public-school desegregation had been started in four large cities (Baltimore, St. Louis, Washington, and Wilmington) and

in more than 40 smaller cities and towns. By the end of 1954, 25 of West Virginia's 55 counties had begun or completed desegregation. Separate schools in Arizona were practically eliminated by the Court's decisions. Within less than a year, nine of the 12 cities in Kansas that were authorized by local option to have segregated schools had started to integrate. In Missouri, Negro children were admitted to previously all-white schools in 110 school districts.[14] Kansas and Missouri did not argue questions of implementation in the Court in May, 1955, and other states asked only for recognition of their plans for desegregation and for time for their completion.

Pro-segregationists criticized the decisions and the justices of the Supreme Court. Senator Russell remarked that the Court had substituted psychology for law, and Senator Eastland said that the South "will not abide by or obey this legislative decision by a political court." M. D. Collins, Georgia's State Superintendent of Schools, said he was "not certain" the ruling applied to Georgia. Senator Byrd called the decisions "the most serious blow that has yet been struck against the rights of the states in a matter affecting their authority and welfare," and Representative Thomas B. Abernathy of Mississippi stated: "The white and Negro children of my state are not going to school together despite the Constitution." In the spring of 1956, 19 senators and 82 representatives from 11 states signed a manifesto denouncing the Supreme Court's decisions on school segregation. In addition, this statement commended "the motives of those states which have declared the intention to resist forced integration by any lawful means."[15] Segregationist public officials continued to comment on court decisions. When Judge J. Skelly Wright ordered the desegregation of the first six grades of New Orleans public schools beginning in September, 1962, Senator Allen J. Ellender said: "I am very surprised and disappointed by Judge Wright's ruling. It seems to me he is working for a place on the Supreme Court." John Deer, director of the

---

[12] *SSN*, Sept., 1956, p. 8.
[13] *Ibid.*, June, 1957, p. 2.

[14] Hill and Greenberg, *op. cit.*, pp. 130–131.
[15] *SSN*, Apr., 1956, p. 1.

State Sovereignty Commission of Louisiana remarked: "It's most unfortunate for Judge Wright . . . to strike the people of New Orleans with a blow which will shatter public morale." Representative Hale Boggs of New Orleans said that the only solution to school integration is an amendment to the Constitution which he is sponsoring which would return to the states "complete jurisdiction over school problems."[16] In his inaugural address January 14, 1963, Governor George C. Wallace reaffirmed his determination to defy any efforts to desegregate schools in Alabama. He referred to desegregation as "communistic amalgamation" and claimed the South had been "footballed about to the favor of the Afro-Asian bloc." Governor Wallace also said: "In the name of the greatest people that have ever trod this earth, I draw the line in the dust and toss the gauntlet before the feet of tyranny and I say segregation now, segregation tomorrow, segregation forever. . . . What I have said about segregation goes double this day and what I have said to or about some federal judges goes triple this day."[17]

On the official political level, opposition to the school segregation decisions took many forms: legislative acts and resolutions, amendments to state constitutions, and decisions by state supreme courts.[18] By November, 1962, legislatures of 16 states had adopted 379 new laws and resolutions to prevent, restrict, or control school desegregation. According to Southern Education Reporting Service: ". . . Alabama, Arkansas, Georgia, Louisiana, North Carolina and Virginia have adopted tuition grant laws. Legislatures in Alabama, Arkansas, Florida, Louisiana, Mississippi, North Carolina, South Carolina, Tennessee, Texas, and Virginia set up pupil placement plans. Alabama, Arkansas, Florida, Georgia, Louisiana, Mississippi, South Carolina and Virginia legislators have approved interposition resolutions.[19] Local-option provisions for closing schools were on the law books in Alabama, Florida, Georgia, Mississippi, North Carolina, and Texas. Compulsory school attendance laws were amended or repealed in Alabama, Arkansas, Florida, Georgia, Louisiana, Mississippi, North Carolina, South Carolina, Tennessee and Virginia had laws to encourage or facilitate private schools."[20]

In 1961, Pollitt listed the following techniques for preventing or slowing down school desegregation:

1. Nonlegal resistance, including riotous demonstrations and manipulating the location of school buildings.
2. Interposition resolutions
3. Restrict-the-Court Actions
   Resolution of Georgia legislature calling upon the state's Congressmen to introduce impeachment proceedings against the justices of the Supreme Court.
   Amendment to United States constitution proposed by Florida whereby all Supreme Court decisions would be reviewable by the U.S. Senate.
   Senator Eastland's bill to deprive Supreme Court of jurisdiction to hear school desegregation cases (defeated by a 41–40 vote). Arkansas, Georgia, Louisiana, Texas, and Virginia authorized the governor to operate the school system with the hope that suits against the governor would be suits against the state and thus beyond the jurisdiction of the federal courts under the 11th Amendment. [As Pollitt points out, none of these efforts to restrict the Supreme Court have achieved their purpose.]
4. Barratry Statutes
   Six states have enacted laws prohibiting the NAACP from providing legal aid.

---

[16] *Ibid.*, May, 1962, p. 2.
[17] *Ibid.*, Feb., 1963, p. 10.
[18] *Ibid.*, May, 1957, p. 1.
[19] According to Professor Wylie H. Davis, of the law school of the University of Texas, "'Interposition' is a label for the doctrine that any one of the American states has the legal right to 'interpose' its sovereignty against an exercise of national governmental power deemed by that state to violate the federal Constitution, and specifically deemed to violate it by usurping powers not delegated to the national government but reserved to the states or to the people. The idea is that the state's sovereign, protective right of resistance is 'placed between' the national government's act and the state's citizens." Davis calls "interposition" a euphemism for nullification; and in his opinion, "as anything more than a formal and official protest against federal action, the doctrine is a legal absurdity." *Ibid.*, Mar., 1956, pp. 1–2.
[20] SERS, *Statistical Summary of School Segregation-Desegregation in the Southern and Border States*, Nov., 1962, p. 4.

5. Crippling the NAACP

Statutes requiring discharge from state employment of all those who belong to or contribute to NAACP.

Tenure laws repealed and all teachers and state employees required to list annually organizations to which they belonged or to which they contributed.

Identification statutes. Arkansas requires all organizations promoting school desegregation to submit lists of members and contributors. Similar statutes found in Tennessee, Texas, and Virginia.

Legislative investigative committees. Appointment of State Sovereignty Committee, Un-American Activities Committee, etc. with authority to subpoena witnesses and investigate "racial activity." Arkansas, Florida, Georgia, Louisiana, Mississippi, Virginia.

6. Close the Schools

Series of statutes ending compulsory education.

Statutes permitting school closing on a local option basis.

Statutes requiring closing of any integrated schools and, also, Negro schools if white schools are closed because of integration.

School closing laws usually accompanied by supplementary laws that preserve teacher benefits and which provide tuition grants, tax benefits, etc. so that "private" education will be more likely.

7. Pupil Assignment Laws

Most effective technique yet devised (but see comment later in this chapter concerning recent court decisions on the use of such laws). Virginia and Louisiana laws were declared unconstitutional because race was mentioned. The North Carolina criterion is "orderly and efficient administration of public schools" and the "effective instruction, health, safety, and general welfare of the pupils." [Pollitt says: "The assignment laws make provision for appeal from the original assignment, generally by way of a request for a transfer, and an appeal procedure from denial of the transfer request is generally available. The practical consequence of the pupil-assignment laws is that, with minute exceptions, each Negro child is originally assigned to a Negro school, and each white child to a white school. The Negro child who is dissatisfied with his segregated status then applies for transfer or reassignment."] Parents are usually required to be present at the hearing conducted by the School Board and are asked to explain why the Negro school is not adequate. If the transfer is denied, the school child either appeals to the State Superintendent of Schools, or, in some states, goes to court.[21]

In many parts of the South, White Citizens' Councils were organized to intimidate Negroes who supported desegregation. Negroes who signed petitions to admit their children to nonsegregated schools often lost their jobs and had little or no opportunity for other employment. In addition to other types of economic pressure such as the stopping of credit, loans, and supplies, some of the councils discouraged Negroes from voting and from belonging to the NAACP. Although the membership and leadership of the councils vary considerably, many of the leaders have been persons of some standing in their community and state.[22] The original leaders, six citizens of Sunflower County, Mississippi, agreed that violence should not be a part of the movement. Apparently actual threats of physical violence usually come from unofficial sources, but the Clinton, Tennessee, incidents and the attack on Nat King Cole indicated the steps that some councils were prepared to take.[23] One speaker at an organizing meeting in Dallas County, Alabama, explained the principle of economic coercion in this way: "The white population in this county controls the money, and this is an advantage that the council will use in a fight to legally maintain complete segregation of the races. We intend to make it difficult, if not impossible, for any Negro who advocates desegregation to find and hold a job, get credit or renew a mortgage."[24] After the condemnation that this widely publicized statement received in the South and elsewhere, some Citizens' Council leaders mini-

[21] Daniel H. Pollitt, "Equal Protection in Public Education: 1954–1961," *AAUP Bulletin*, Autumn, 1961, pp. 201–202. See also *RRLR*, Fall, 1961, pp. 905–922; and J. Kenneth Morland, *Token Desegregation and Beyond*, SRC and ADL, 1963, pp. 15–19.

[22] F. B. Routh and P. Anthony, "Southern Resistance Forces," *Phylon*, First Quarter, 1957, pp. 50–52. See also J. M. Nabrit, Jr., "Desegregation and Reason," *Phylon*, Third Quarter, 1956, pp. 287 ff.

[23] Routh and Anthony, *op. cit.*, pp. 51–52.

[24] Montgomery *Advertiser*, Dec. 1, 1954.

mized or disclaimed organizational responsibility for economic sanctions. Harold C. Fleming points out that regardless of the degree of direct responsibility attributed to the councils, both economic and social reprisals have been used extensively against those who favor desegregation.[25] It should be added that white citizens who advocate compliance have been subject to economic and social pressures, and that the councils have threatened to screen all candidates for local, state, and national offices for pro-Negro sentiments.[26]

In September, 1961, the U.S. Commission on Civil Rights declared that "the nation's progress in removing the stultifying effects of segregation in the public elementary and secondary schools—North, South, East and West—is slow indeed," and it made 12 recommendations to speed up the process. The most far-reaching of these recommendations asked Congress to require every local school board operating segregated schools to file a desegregation plan with the federal government within six months providing for an immediate first step toward compliance with the 1954 decision and envisaging complete desegregation as soon as practicable.[27]

For the first time since it issued the "all deliberate speed" order in 1955, the Supreme Court on May 27, 1963, commented on the pace of desegregation. In a decision that public parks in Memphis, Tennessee, must be desegregated at once, not with "deliberate speed," Justice Goldberg said: "The basic guarantees of our Constitution are warrants for the here and now and, unless there is an overwhelmingly compelling reason, they are to be promptly fulfilled." Commenting on school integration in the same opinion, he said that the Court "never contemplated that 'deliberate speed' would countenance indefinite delay in elimination of racial barriers in schools. . . ."[28]

THE EXTENT OF SEGREGATION IN PUBLIC SCHOOLS, 1965–1970

In 1965, 80 percent of all white children in the United States were attending schools that were from 90 to 100 percent white. About 65 percent of all Negro students attended schools in which 90 percent of the students were Negro.[29] Segregation was the norm wherever the proportion of Negroes was large. The Office of Education survey found that Mexican-Americans, American Indians, Puerto Ricans, and Oriental Americans are also segregated, but to a lesser extent than Whites. A report of the U.S. Commission on Civil Rights points out that such national or regional averages do not show the full extent of school segregation. The Commission's investigation indicated that in metropolitan areas, where two-thirds of both the Negro and white populations now live, school segregation is more severe than the national averages suggest. In 15 large metropolitan areas in 1960, 79 percent of the nonwhite public school enrollment was in central city schools; 68 percent of the white students attended suburban schools. In Cleveland, 98 percent of the nonwhite metropolitan public school children were enrolled in central city schools in 1960, while 69 percent of the white children were in suburban public schools. In Philadelphia, 77 percent of the nonwhite metropolitan public school children were in the city schools in 1960, and 73 percent of the white children attended suburban schools. Such racial concentration is typical of major metropolitan areas.[30]

Racial concentration, especially in elementary schools, also is severe within central cities. The next table indicates the extent of such segregation in 75 cities. In these cities, three-fourths of the Negro students are in elementary schools with enrollments that are nearly all-Negro (90 percent or more Negro), and 83 percent of the white students

[25] Harold C. Fleming, "Resistance Movements and Racial Desegregation," *Annals*, Mar., 1956, p. 49.

[26] Hodding Carter, "A Wave of Terror Threatens the South," *Look*, Mar. 22, 1955, p. 34.

[27] "Education," *1961 U.S. Commission on Civil Rights Report*, vol. 2, pp. 181–185.

[28] *SSN*, June, 1963, p. 5.

[29] James S. Coleman, Ernest Q. Campbell, Carol J. Hobson, James McPartland, Alexander M. Mood, Frederick D. Weinfield, and Robert L. York, *Equality of Educational Opportunity*, U.S. Office of Education, 1966, p. 3.

[30] U.S. Commission on Civil Rights, *Racial Isolation in the Public Schools*, Vol. 1, 1967, p. 3.

were in all-white schools. Approximately nine-tenths of the Negro elementary school students attend majority-Negro schools.

Racial isolation does not differ greatly from the North to the South. The table on page 556 indicates the extent of Negro elementary school segregation in 20 Southern and Northern cities in 1965–1966.

Not only is racial isolation in the public schools intense, it has been increasing. In the early and middle 1960s, Negro elementary school enrollments in northern city school systems increased, as did the number and proportion of Negro elementary students in majority-Negro and nearly all-Negro schools. The evidence suggests that a school that has become half- or majority-Negro tends rapidly to become nearly all-Negro.[31] In southern and border states the proportion of Negroes in all-Negro schools has decreased since the 1954 decision of the U.S. Supreme Court, but an increasing enrollment of Negroes, together with only slight desegregation through 1965–1966 had resulted in a substantial increase in the number of Negroes attending nearly all-Negro schools.

The metropolitan area populations of the United States are growing and have become increasingly separate racially. From 1940 to 1960, Negro population increases in metropolitan areas occurred mainly in the central cities; white increases occurred mainly in the suburbs. These trends continued during the 1960s and they are reflected in school attendance. Thus, central city and suburban school districts, like the cities and suburbs themselves, include separate racial and social groups.[32]

Racial and social separation between city and suburb is attributed, in large part, by the U.S. Commission on Civil Rights both to the practices of private industry and government at all levels.[33] Specifically, the main causal elements in this situation are past and present housing policies (or the lack thereof), and the antimetropolitan nature of school district organization. Concerning the latter point, most of the recent consolidation of districts in the 27,000 school districts of the United States has been limited to the rural areas. In the Boston metropolitan area, there are more than 75 districts, and there are 96 in the Detroit metropolitan area.[34] Increasing enrollments in private and parochial schools also is an important factor in the rising concentration of Negroes in central city school systems. In 1960, approximately one-sixth of the nation's school enrollment (Grades 1 to 12) was in private schools. In metropolitan areas, about one-third more elementary school children attend nonpublic schools than in the suburbs, and nearly all these students are white. In the larger metropolitan areas, and particularly in the central cities, the trend is even stronger. The report of the U.S. Commission on Civil Rights says that the absorption by nonpublic schools of a disproportionately large segment of white students poses serious problems for city school systems. In 1965, 40 percent of the total white elementary school population in St. Louis attended nonpublic schools; in Philadelphia, more than 60 percent; and in Boston, 41 percent.[35]

In discussing the number of black students in desegregated public schools, some have expressed disappointment that 15 years after Brown v. Board of Education only 30 percent of the Negro students in the South were in

[31] *Ibid.*, p. 199. In 1968, Massachusetts was the only state that had a racial imbalance law (adopted in 1965), but it reported that racial imbalance had spread to more schools that year than ever before. In the same year, Detroit reported the failure of its large-scale efforts to maintain racial balance in three selected neighborhoods as Whites continued to leave the center city. P. E. Wilson, "Some Aspects of the Education of Black Americans," in Patricia Romero (ed.), *In Black America*, United Publishing Corporation, 1969, pp. 99–100.

[32] U.S. Commission on Civil Rights, *Racial Isolation in the Public Schools*, Vol. 1, p. 200.

[33] *Ibid.*, pp. 200–201. See the section on housing in Chapter 14 of this book. According to recent reports, Negro suburban population has been growing more rapidly than had been thought. This increase, however, often means that Negroes live in segregated suburbs or segregated sections of suburbs.

[34] T. F. Pettigrew, "A Social Psychological View of the Predominantly Negro College," *JNE*, Summer 1967, pp. 279–280.

[35] U.S. Commission on Civil Rights, *Racial Isolation in the Public Schools*, pp. 38–39.

Extent of Elementary School Segregation in 75 School Systems

City	Percentage of Negroes in 90 to 100 percent Negro schools	Percentage of Negroes in majority-Negro schools	Percentage of Whites in 90 to 100 percent white schools
Mobile, Ala.	99.9	99.9	100.0
Tuscaloosa, Ala.	99.6	99.6	100.0
Little Rock, Ark.	95.6	95.6	97.1
Pine Bluff, Ark.	98.2	98.2	100.0
Los Angeles, Calif.	39.5	87.5	94.7
Oakland, Calif.	48.7	83.2	50.2
Pasadena, Calif.	None	71.4	82.1
Richmond, Calif.	39.2	82.9	90.2
San Diego, Calif.	13.9	73.3	88.7
San Francisco, Calif.	21.1	72.3	65.1
Denver, Colo.	29.4	75.2	95.5
Hartford, Conn.	9.4	73.8	66.2
New Haven, Conn.	36.8	73.4	47.1
Wilmington, Del.	49.7	92.5	27.3
Miami, Fla.	91.4	94.4	95.3
Tallahassee, Fla.	99.7	99.7	100.0
Americus, Ga.	99.3	99.3	100.0
Atlanta, Ga.	97.4	98.8	95.4
Augusta, Ga.	99.2	99.2	100.0
Marietta, Ga.	94.2	94.2	100.0
Chicago, Ill.	89.2	96.9	88.8
East St. Louis, Ill.	80.4	92.4	68.6
Peoria, Ill.	21.0	86.9	89.6
Fort Wayne, Ind.	60.8	82.9	87.7
Gary, Ind.	89.9	94.8	75.9
Indianapolis, Ind.	70.5	84.2	80.7
Wichita, Kans.	63.5	89.1	94.8
Louisville, Ky.	69.5	84.5	61.8
New Orleans, La.	95.9	96.7	83.8
Baltimore, Md.	84.2	92.3	67.0
Boston, Mass.	35.4	79.5	76.5
Springfield, Mass.	15.4	71.9	82.8
Detroit, Mich.	72.3	91.5	65.0
Flint, Mich.	67.9	85.9	80.0
Minneapolis, Minn.	None	39.2	84.9
Hattiesburg, Miss.	98.7	98.7	100.0
Vicksburg, Miss.	97.1	97.1	100.0
Kansas City, Mo.	69.1	85.5	65.2
St. Joseph, Mo.	39.3	39.3	91.3
St. Louis, Mo.	90.9	93.7	66.0
Omaha, Nebr.	47.7	81.1	89.0
Newark, N.J.	51.3	90.3	37.1
Camden, N.J.	37.0	90.4	62.4

City	Percentage of Negroes in 90 to 100 percent Negro schools	Percentage of Negroes in majority-Negro schools	Percentage of whites in 90 to 100 percent white schools
Albany, N.Y.	None	74.0	66.5
Buffalo, N.Y.	77.0	88.7	81.1
New York City, N.Y.*	20.7	55.5	56.8
Charlotte, N.C.	95.7	95.7	94.7
Raleigh, N.C.	98.5	98.5	100.0
Winston-Salem, N.C.	88.7	95.1	95.6
Cincinnati, Ohio	49.4	88.0	63.3
Cleveland, Ohio	82.3	94.6	80.2
Columbus, Ohio	34.3	80.8	77.0
Oklahoma City, Okla.	90.5	96.8	96.1
Tulsa, Okla.	90.7	98.7	98.8
Portland, Oreg.	46.5	59.2	92.0
Chester, Pa.	77.9	89.1	37.9
Harrisburg, Pa.	54.0	81.3	56.2
Philadelphia, Pa.	72.0	90.2	57.7
Pittsburgh, Pa.	49.5	82.8	62.3
Providence, R.I.	14.6	55.5	63.3
Columbia, S.C.	99.1	99.1	100.0
Florence, S.C.	99.1	99.1	100.0
Sumter, S.C.	99.0	99.0	100.0
Knoxville, Tenn.	79.3	79.3	94.9
Memphis, Tenn.	95.1	98.8	93.6
Nashville, Tenn.	82.2	86.4	90.7
Amarillo, Tex.	89.6	89.6	98.3
Austin, Tex.	86.1	86.1	93.1
Dallas, Tex.	82.6	90.3	90.1
Houston, Tex.	93.0	97.6	97.3
San Antonio, Tex.	65.9	77.2	89.4
Richmond, Va.	98.5	98.5	95.3
Seattle, Wash.	9.9	60.4	89.8
Milwaukee, Wis.	72.4	86.8	86.3
Washington, D.C.	90.4	99.3	34.3

Notes:

*"These percentages make no reference to the large Puerto Rican enrollment in New York City elementary schools. The data provided to the Commission by the New York City public school system are based on classroom count by teachers. According to Mr. Leonard Moriber, research associate, New York City Board of Education, students with Spanish surnames are counted as Puerto Rican regardless of their race. Thus it is likely that the actual number and proportion of Negro elementary school students is somewhat higher than the data show. According to the school system's data, of the total of 592,000 elementary school students in the New York City school system, 183,000 are Negroes and 130,000 are Puerto Ricans. Of the total of 313,000 Negro and Puerto Rican students, 177,000 (56 percent) are in schools whose student bodies are 90–100 percent Negro and Puerto Rican. 267,000 (85 percent) are in schools whose student bodies are majority-Negro and Puerto Rican." *Ibid.*, p. 5.

Percentages shown in this table are for 1965–66 school year, except for Seattle, Wash. (1964–65), Los Angeles, Calif. (1963–64), and Cleveland, Ohio (1962–63).

Source: U.S. Commission on Civil Rights, *Racial Isolation in the Public Schools*, 1967, vol. 1, pp. 4–5.

Extent of Elementary School Segregation in 20 Selected Northern and Southern Cities—Based on Proportion of Negro Students in 90–100 Percent Negro and Majority-Negro Elementary Schools

Southern cities	Percent in 90–100% Negro schools	Percent in majority-Negro schools	Northern cities	Percent in 90–100% Negro schools	Percent in majority-Negro schools
Richmond, Va.	99	99	Gary, Ind.	90	95
Atlanta, Ga.	97	99	Chicago, Ill.	89	97
Little Rock, Ark.	96	96	Cleveland, Ohio	82	95
Memphis, Tenn.	95	99	Chester, Pa.	78	89
Marietta, Ga.	94	94	Buffalo, N.Y.	77	89
Houston, Tex.	93	98	Detroit, Mich.	72	92
Miami, Fla.	91	94	Milwaukee, Wis.	72	87
Winston-Salem, N.C.	89	95	Indianapolis, Ind.	71	84
Dallas, Tex.	83	90	Flint, Mich.	68	86
Nashville, Tenn.	82	86	Newark, N.J.	51	90

Source: U.S. Commission on Civil Rights, *Racial Isolation in the Public Schools,* 1967, vol. 1, p. 7.

schools having substantial numbers of Whites. Others find this figure encouraging, saying that the proportion in June, 1970 was 40 percent and that perhaps it had reached 50 percent by September, 1970.[36]

Equal Educational Opportunities. In reviewing the findings of the Coleman report, Sewell points out that, on the average, no very large differences were found between the schools attended by various racial and ethnic groups on such objective indicators of school quality as buildings, equipment, special-purpose rooms, class size, teachers' qualifications, textbooks, library, free lunch, school psychologists and nurses, art and music instruction, curriculums offered, programs for exceptional children and for pupil evaluation and placement, and extracurricular programs. The one school environment factor where the minority student is consistently at a disadvantage is in the economic, social, and psychological characteristics of his fellow students. Sewell summarizes the report's findings on this point: "On the average, he attends a school in which he is exposed primarily to other minority children; most of the students in his school come from homes

of relatively low educational and economic level; fewer of his classmates are enrolled in the college preparatory curriculums; a smaller proportion of his fellow students will actually go to college; fewer will finish high school; and fewer will be optimistic about their life chances."[37] Although the black student was, therefore, associated primarily with students whose academic conduct and achievements were less likely to assist or stimulate him to his best academic performance, the differences in the school environments, on the average, were not massive according to the indicators used in this survey.

Despite the overall conclusion of the Office of Education survey, significant inequalities in educational opportunities still exist. Smaller school systems must choose between college preparatory or vocational curricula, and generally they select the former even though few of the Negro students will attend college. In larger high schools relatively more Negroes than Whites are enrolled in vocational curricula, but little preparation is offered for occupations in which employment opportunities are expand-

[36] John Herbers, "School Integration Entering Critical Stage," *The New York Times,* June 21, 1970, p. 6E; *Time,* Sept. 14, 1970, p. 39.

[37] William H. Sewell, "Review Symposium," *ASR,* June 1967, p. 476. For an interesting discussion of the Coleman report, see *ASR,* Apr., 1970, pp. 228–252.

ing most rapidly. Frequently, the vocational curricula are of poor quality and are symbols of debasement. Also, relatively little progress has been made in providing Negro youth with equal educational opportunity after they have left school. Educational extension is an important factor in improving economic status in farming areas, but the almost exclusively Negro staff assigned to Negro residents in the South has had such a high caseload that adequate service has been almost impossible.[38] In another aspect of educational equality, faculty desegregation lags behind pupil desegregation in southern states. West points out that the loss of contact with Negro teachers may mean that there are fewer adequate role models for the desegregated Negro students.[39]

Educational Attainments of Whites and Negroes. The gap between the educational attainments of Whites and Negroes is rapidly being reduced. In 1962, the median educational attainment for the 25–29 age group was 11.2 for Negroes and 12.4 for whites. In 1966, the median in the same age range for Negroes was 12.0 and 12.5 for Whites. In the middle 1960s, 99 percent of the children of both races in the 6–15 age range were in school. The enrollment gaps in the age groups above and below this age range have been considerably reduced. In 1960, 51 percent of the Negro five-year olds and 66 percent of the Whites were enrolled, while in 1966, 66 percent of the Negro children and 74 percent of the Whites were enrolled. Among 16- to 17-year-old youth, 77 percent of Negroes and 85 percent of Whites were enrolled in 1960, compared with 83 percent of Negroes and 89 percent of Whites in 1966.[40]

DIFFERENCES OF PERFORMANCE IN RACIAL AND ETHNIC GROUPS ON STANDARD ACHIEVEMENT TESTS

According to the Office of Education survey, the results on the various tests (verbal ability, nonverbal ability, reading comprehension, mathematics achievement, and general information in other subject matter areas) at twelfth grade showed considerable differences among racial and ethnic groups and regional differences for Whites and Negroes. In general, the same results were found for the lower-grade levels.

The white students obtained the highest average scores followed by Oriental Americans, American Indians, Mexican-Americans, Puerto Ricans, and Negroes. Negro average scores were about one standard deviation below those of whites. This means that about 85 percent of the Negro scores were below the white average. The lowest scores were consistently for those in the nonmetropolitan South. The highest scores were for students in the metropolitan North. Both whites and Negroes do better in the North and West than in the South and Southwest, but regional variation is much greater for Negroes than for whites. Metropolitan students on the average score significantly higher than nonmetropolitan students, whatever the region.[41]

Figure 8 (page 558), showing average grade level performances, illustrates the relationship between the racial composition of schools, the social class level of individual Negro students and their schools, and student performance for twelfth-grade Negro students in the metropolitan Northeast. The first four bars indicate that when relatively disadvantaged Negro students are in class with a majority of similarly disadvantaged white students, their performance is higher than when they are in a class with a majority of equally disadvantaged Negroes. The situation is similar when more advantaged Negroes, in school with similarly advantaged Negroes, are compared with those in school with similarly advantaged Whites. Disadvantaged Negro students in school with more advantaged Negroes also show an improvement in performance. Since only a small proportion of Negroes is in the middle class, disadvantaged Negroes generally must attend school with Whites if they are to be enrolled with a majority of more advantaged students. As the U.S. Commission on Civil Rights report says: "The combined effects of

[38] E. H. West, "Progress Toward Equality of Opportunity in Elementary and Secondary Education," *JNE*, Summer 1968, pp. 215–216.

[39] West, *op. cit.*, p. 218.

[40] *Ibid.*, pp. 212–213.

[41] Sewell, *op. cit.*, p. 476.

*Figure 8 / Average Grade Level Performance of Twelfth Grade
Negro Students by Individual Social Class Origin, Social Class
Level of School and Proportion White Classmates Last Year;
Metropolitan Northeast*

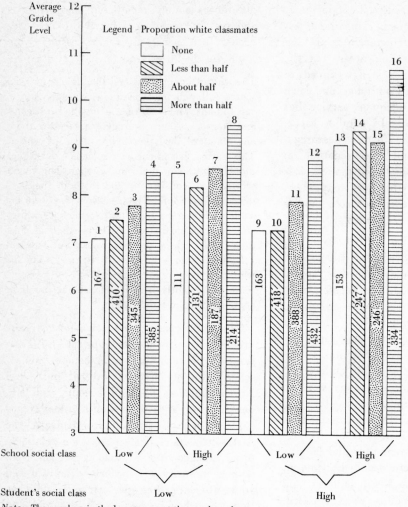

Note: The numbers in the bars represent the number of cases.
Source: USCCR analysis of *OE Survey* data.

social class integration and racial desegregation are substantial. When disadvantaged Negro students are in class with similarly
situated whites, their average performance is
improved by more than a full grade level.
When they are in class with more advantaged
white students, their performance is improved by more than two grade levels."[42] According to this report, these comparisons
suggest a relationship between the per-

formance of Negro students and the racial
composition of classrooms, but they do not
explain it. Among the possible explanations
are: (1) differences in the quality of education provided in majority-Negro and
majority-white schools; (2) a process of selection, with only initially more capable Negro students attending majority-white schools;
and (3) student environment factors associated with racial composition that affect the
attitudes and performance of Negro students.
It may be said further that predominantly
Negro schools are widely considered by the

[42] U.S. Commission on Civil Rights, *Racial Isolation in the Public Schools*, Vol. 1, p. 91.

community as inferior institutions, and that black students in such schools often come to share this view. Teachers and administrative staff may also hold this view and communicate it to students. Presumably, this stigma influences the scholastic achievements and attitudes of Negro students.[43]

DESEGREGATION VERSUS INTEGRATION

Much has been said about racial "imbalance," but it is difficult to define a "balanced" school. Fischer says that no "balance," however logical it may be statistically, is likely to be workable if it includes either a majority of Negroes or so few that they are individually conspicuous. In practice this means a Negro component ranging from a minimum of 15 to 20 percent to a maximum of 40 to 45 percent.[44] It is important to make a distinction between school desegregation and integration. Desegregation involves only a certain mix of students, preferably more than half white. Merely desegregated schools may be effective or ineffective. A U.S. Commission on Civil Rights reanalysis of the data on this point in the Coleman report suggests that the crucial variable is interracial acceptance. In the integrated schools, most teachers report no racial tensions, and Negro students show higher verbal achievement, more definite college plans, and more positive racial attitudes than in merely desegregated schools.[45] The Office of Education report found also that those Negro pupils who first entered integrated schools in the early grades made consistently higher scores than the other groups, but the differences were small.[46]

A further analysis of the Coleman report data by McPartland concluded that the increased achievement of Negro students enrolled in desegregated schools is not a func-

tion of the proportion of Whites within the total school, but of classroom composition. Although substantial progress has been made in the South toward school desegregation, McPartland shows that school tracking, which results in largely Negro classes within a desegregated school, may have a slightly negative effect on achievement.[47]

The Coleman data show that the scholastic achievements of students of various racial and ethnic groups is enhanced as the proportion of white students is increased. Thus, the results cited in the case of Negro students are found also for Puerto Rican, Orientals, Mexican-Americans, and American Indians. Other studies corroborate these general findings, and the reason given is the addition of a large proportion of middle- and upper-class students.[48] The Coleman survey showed that white pupils do not suffer academically when mixed with Negroes in predominantly white schools. While a priori, as Thompson says, such a mix should bring better race relations, there is no convincing evidence of the advantage of this situation for white pupils.[49] Concerning substantial changes in school procedures, Fischer says:

Few persons of either race are willing to accept inconvenience or to make new adjustments in family routines if the only discernible result is to improve the opportunities of other people's children. A still smaller minority will actually forego advantages to which their children have become accustomed merely to benefit other children. Most parents, liberal or conservative, hesitate to accept any substantial change in school procedures unless they are convinced that their own children will have a better than even chance of profiting from them.[50]

In view of the fears on the part of middle- and upper-class Whites that mixing their children with ghetto pupils, nearly all of whom are lower class, would be detrimental for the education of their offspring academically and otherwise, the choice of schools

---

[43] *Ibid.*, pp. 90–91, 204.

[44] John H. Fischer, "School Parks for Equal Opportunities," *JNE*, Summer 1968, p. 303.

[45] Pettigrew, *op. cit.*, p. 281.

[46] Coleman, James S., et. al., *Equality of Educational Opportunity*, U.S. Office of Education, p. 29.

[47] West, *op. cit.*, p. 218.

[48] Charles H. Thompson, "Equality of Educational Opportunity," *JNE*, Summer 1968, pp. 196–197.

[49] *Ibid.*, p. 202. We comment later on the tendency of a school that has become more than 40 percent Negro to become majority-Negro.

[50] Fischer, *op. cit.*, p. 302.

enrolling a majority of Negroes will be relatively uncommon if any alternative is available.[51] Borderline sites or school pairing on the periphery of a ghetto seldom bring together children of different social classes. Antagonisms between lower-class Whites and Negro children increase the problems of the school and lessen the benefits of intercultural contact.[52] Some survey data show that those who had biracial schooling in the early grades associate integration with more positive attitudes toward Negroes and biracial situations. These data show further that white Americans who had had as children interracial schooling are more likely as adults to live and associate with Negroes now and are more likely to send their children to interracial schools.[53] Such findings, however, are unlikely to carry much weight at present with a majority of white parents.

THE INFLUENCE OF FAMILY AND SCHOOL INFLUENCES ON THE ACHIEVEMENT SCORES OF RACIAL AND ETHNIC GROUPS

The Office of Education survey shows that in the South and the Southwest, where the educational disadvantage is greatest to begin with and continues to increase, school effects appear to be negligible. The report argues that if differences between schools in test scores were due to the differential influence between schools, the difference should become proportionally larger at each higher grade level due to the fact that the students would have been exposed longer to the effects of the school. Between-school variance, however, increased only slightly, if at all, from grade to grade, suggesting that school effects are probably small. Other analyses

showed that family background is important to achievement, and that this relationship does not decrease over time.[54]

There are differences among ethnic groups in school-to-school variation in scholastic achievement. Variations in achievement for Negroes are larger than they are for Whites, and are especially high in the South. Also, for Negroes and the other minority groups, but not for Whites, the school-to-school component of variance increases from grade 1 to grade 3. According to this survey, the indirect evidence suggests that "it is those children who come least prepared to school, and whose achievement in school is generally low, for whom the characteristics of a school make the most difference." The investigators say that these children seem to differ in sensitivity to variations in school quality, and that, in general, those children from groups where achievement is lowest at the beginning of school are the most sensitive. A rough order of the sensitivity to school effects is as follows: Puerto Rican, American-Indian, Mexican-American, Negro (South), Negro (North), Oriental American, white (South), white (North).[55]

On the school-to-school effects of elementary and secondary education, the Coleman report concludes:

Taking all these results together, one implication stands out above all: That schools bring little influence to bear on a child's achievement that is independent of his background and general social context; and that this very lack of an independent effect means that the inequalities imposed on children by their home, neighborhood, and peer environment are carried along to become the inequalities with which they confront adult life at the end of school. For equality of educational opportunity through the schools must imply a strong effect of schools that is independent of the child's immediate social environment, and that strong independent effect is not present in American schools.[56]

Some of the phrases in the above statement, especially "a child's achievement that

---

[51] The U.S. Commission on Civil Rights report on racial isolation in the public schools lists three underlying fears that motivate opponents of desegregation: (1) Fear of loss of the neighborhood school, (2) fear of lowering of standards in erstwhile Caucasian schools, and (3) fear that contact with Negro children will be harmful to Caucasian children. Also given in this report are arguments against these fears in a world that is now interracial. U.S. Commission on Civil Rights, *Racial Isolation in the Public Schools*, Vol. 2 (Appendices), 1967, p. 293.

[52] Fischer, *op. cit.*, p. 302.

[53] Pettigrew, *op. cit.*, p. 281.

[54] Coleman, et. al., *op. cit.*, pp. 290 ff; Sewell, *op. cit.*, p. 477.

[55] *Ibid.*, p. 297.

[56] *Ibid.*, p. 325.

is independent of his background and general social context" and "the inequalities imposed on children by their home, neighborhood, and peer environment" merit further attention. Although it is difficult to specify precisely the ways in which the student environment affects performance and attitudes, two elements stand out. The U.S. Commission on Civil Rights suggests:

First, different backgrounds influence what students see as attainable goals. A disadvantaged student in school mostly with other disadvantaged students is exposed primarily to youngsters for whom immediate work and earnings are the most concrete need. While it may be easy for a given student to express his desire for a college education, there is little around him which suggests that his own friends and social equals regard such a thing to be possible. Since, as they move through the grades, students increasingly measure their behavior by the standards accepted by their friends and associates, such a student is unlikely to follow through on his aspiration for college.

Second, a similar process is probably involved in academic achievement. Students from poor backgrounds do not perform as well in school— even in the early grades—as more advantaged students. . . . This performance gap increases as students move to higher grades. Students in schools where early and continuing academic difficulty are typical are likely to suffer from the cumulative disadvantage of their classmates. The students provide each other with academic standards with varying degrees of academic interchange. Where the majority of students have low achievement, others will be likely to follow suit.[57]

Community attitudes that label schools as inferior affect the attitudes and performance of many teachers in majority-Negro schools. At a Commission on Civil Rights hearing in Rochester, the superintendent of schools in Syracuse, N.Y. said that in such schools teachers often "average down" their expectations of students. In Harlem, a study of low teacher expectations found that: "The atmosphere stemming from such expectation cannot be conducive to good teaching, and is manifest in friction between teachers, abdic-

tation of teaching responsibilities . . . (and) a concern with discipline rather than learning . . ."[58] The Commission report points out that this conclusion is consistent with the data from the *Equality of Educational Opportunity* survey that Negro students were more likely to have teachers who did not want to remain in their present school. Also, their teachers were more likely to think that other teachers considered their school as a poor one.[59] Conversely, the children in a desegregated school tend to assume that they will succeed in school and in their future careers. Although Negro children may have problems of racial identification in desegregated schools, the high aspirations that they hold are more likely to be supported by the similar aspirations of their schoolmates.

Change in the Concept of Equality of Educational Opportunity

Coleman has stated clearly the change that has occurred in the concept of equality of educational opportunity, a change that will have important consequences in future educational planning. Earlier, the role of the community and the educational institutions was relatively passive; it was their duty to provide a set of free public resources. The use of those resources was the responsibility of the child and his family. Now, according to Coleman, the responsibility to create achievement lies with

---

[57] U.S. Commission on Civil Rights, *Racial Isolation in the Public Schools*, Vol. 1, pp. 88–89.

[58] *Ibid.*, p. 105. Although the research by Robert Rosenthal and Lenore Jacobson is subject to various criticisms, their basic point is sound: The attitudes and expectations of others toward a child in the classroom strongly influences that child's academic performance. See their *Pygmalion in the Classroom*, Holt, Rinehart & Winston, 1968. For a careful summary of methodological problems in the study, see William Gephart and Daniel Antonoplos, "The Effects of Expectancy and Other Research-Biasing Factors," *Phi Delta Kappan*, June, 1969, pp. 579–583. See also Kenneth B. Clark's comments on the self-fulfilling prophecy aspect of much of the teaching in ghetto schools. He says that ghetto children, ". . . by and large, do not learn because they are not being taught effectively and they are not being taught because those who are charged with the responsibility of teaching them do not believe that they can learn, do not expect that they can learn, and do not act toward them in ways which help them to learn." Kenneth B. Clark, *Dark Ghetto: Dilemmas of Social Power*, Harper & Row, 1965, pp. 127, 131 ff.

[59] *Ibid.*, p. 105.

the educational institution rather than with the child. The emphasis now is on the effects of schooling, and, if there is a difference in achievement between the average child in one racial group and the average child in another racial or ethnic group, the reduction of that inequality is a responsibility of the school. Under this concept, the school's obligation has shifted from increasing and distributing equally its "quality" to increasing the quality of its students' achievements.[60]

ATTEMPTS TO IMPROVE THE SCHOOLING OF MINORITY CHILDREN BY BUSING

Despite the fact that bus transportation has been used for many years, and on a large scale, for a number of purposes other than mixing the races, it has become a controversial means of desegregating public schools. With the South's large number of rural schools and its mixture of housing patterns, busing was often essential to the preservation of segregated schools. In the West, long bus trips for school children are common, and school buses are used in all sections of the country to transport children to private and parochial schools, to relieve overcrowding in classrooms, or for other purposes. Approximately 40 percent of the public-school students in the United States are transported at public expense. In 1968–1969, the number of school systems known to be using busing as part of a desegregation program, on the other hand, was small, and the percentage of the students transported for this reason was quite small.

Desegregation plans that most frequently use pupil busing are: school pairing, central schools, school closing, magnet schools, education complexes, education parks, and free-choice open enrollment. Under open enrollment programs, the school district may be able to utilize public-transit systems instead of providing buses. After arrival at their school, the transported students may be kept

intact as a unit, even to the point of being kept separate from the other children during recess and lunch periods. In other cases, the bused students are distributed throughout the receiving school or are distributed under quotas for each grade or class.[61]

Leeson provides summaries on four of the country's important busing programs. New York City's busing program, operated on a voluntary basis since 1960, involves 40,000 children and is the largest in the nation. Thus far, suburban districts have been unwilling to accept even small numbers of pupils from New York's poor sections. When the bused children were matched with ghetto students of similar ability and background, the achievement scores of the bused children were not significantly different.

In Berkeley, California, a city of 120,000 with a Negro population of approximately 30,000, students from every grade level are bused where necessary to achieve racial balance. This is one of the few busing programs that uses cross-busing—the transporting of Whites as well as Negroes. In 1968–1969, about 2000 white pupils in an elementary-school enrollment of 9000 were bused from their neighborhoods to formerly predominantly black schools, and approximately the same number of black students were bused to formerly predominantly white schools. According to Leeson, these changes gave each of the 14 elementary schools a Negro enrollment of 36 to 45 percent (Negro pupils constitute 41 percent of the total elementary enrollment). Teachers and white residents did not flee from the city, and the added cost of the integration program was less than 3 percent of the total annual budget.

In Connecticut, Project Concern included Hartford, New Haven, and Waterbury in 1968–1969 and involved two dozen suburban communities that received 800 Negro and Puerto Rican children into their predominantly white schools. The estimated cost of busing one pupil and paying the tuition to the suburban community is $1500 annually,

[60] James S. Coleman, "The Concept of Equality of Educational Opportunity," HER, Winter 1968, p. 22.

[61] Jim Leeson, "Busing and Desegregation," Southern Education Report, Nov. 1968, p. 18.

with state and federal programs reimbursing the city for about half of this cost. This program has not operated without opposition; ten school boards rejected the invitation to participate in the program in 1968–1969 and there were angry debates at public meetings in several towns. Within the city of Hartford, an internal busing project transported 182 children in grades kindergarten to sixth from eight inner-city schools to six predominantly white schools in other parts of the city. Roman Catholic parochial schools have started a program that transports more than 100 elementary school children in Hartford to church schools in the city and in three suburbs.

In Massachusetts, a racial imbalance law prohibits school systems from maintaining schools that are more than 50 percent non-white. The penalty is loss of state aid. The law also forbids forced busing, thus virtually eliminating the possibility of busing white students into predominantly black schools. About one-fourth of Boston's students are black, but half of the city's schools in 1968–1969 were defined as racially imbalanced. Under the city's open enrollment plan, the responsibility for providing transportation lies with the parents. Boston has two separate busing programs, one a voluntary project transporting central city children to suburban schools and the other privately organized to enroll Negro ghetto children in less-crowded city schools. In 1965, Operation Exodus began the intracity busing program. During 1967–1968, this program bused 930 students to 32 schools within the city at a weekly cost of $6400. Beginning in 1965–1966, four Boston suburbs formed the Metropolitan Council for Educational Opportunity to transport ghetto children in kindergarten through high school. Three other suburbs later joined the project, and 200 inner-city students, including some Whites, were enrolled in the seven communities. In 1968–1969, this project sent more than 850 Boston students to twenty communities. Some of the suburban systems have reduced tuition fees so that they can enroll more Metco students. State and federal funds support the program in the approximate ratio of $400,000 from Title III of the Elementary and Secondary Education Act to $100,000 from the state.[62]

Dissatisfaction with inner-city schools and a desire to obtain a better education for their children have been the main reasons for the interest of Negro parents in busing programs. With the growth of black nationalism, opposition to busing proposals on the part of Negroes has increased. Some black parents ask: "Why are our children bused out and white children not sent in?" Black militants say that busing out takes the better students out of the black community and makes Negro students think "white" instead of "black."[63] School officials trying to bring about some degree of desegregation find that they lack enough Whites to go around. Some educators fear that continued or increased busing in the face of resistance from parents would cause even more middle-class Whites to leave the cities and thus make the situation worse in the long run.[64]

A survey of ten "segregation academies" by the Southern Regional Council concluded that white parents in the South "do not move their children from public to private schools because of threats of increased busing." This study of schools in eight states chosen at random as being representative of their type showed that public schools in these states are busing an average of 49.5 percent of their pupils and the academies are busing an average of 62 percent. Also, the figures indicated that bused students in public schools travel an average of 10.1 miles a day each way, compared with 17.7 miles each way for the students in the segregation academies.[65]

From the evidence available in 1970 and 1971, it appeared that in most large cities, only intercity busing (central city-suburbs) would provide a significant amount of racial balance. On January 10, 1972, a U.S. District Court in Richmond, Virginia ordered the consolidation of the two-thirds-black city

[62] Jim Leeson, "Busing and Desegregation—II," *Southern Education Report*, Dec. 1968, pp. 14–17.
[63] Jim Leeson, "Busing and Desegregation," *ibid.*, Nov. 1968, pp. 18–19.
[64] Eunice and George Grier, "Equality and Beyond," *Daedalus*, Winter 1966, p. 92.
[65] *The New York Times*, May 3, 1970. Quoted from *South Today*, Apr., 1970.

school system of Richmond with the 91 percent white schools of suburban Chesterfield and Henrico counties. If this decision is not reversed by the U.S. Supreme Court, many cities and their suburbs will be required to combine their separate school systems into a single, integrated, metropolitan-wide school district.[66]

FACTORS IN SUCCESSFUL SCHOOL DESEGREGATION

In its analysis of racial isolation in the public schools, the U.S. Commission on Civil Rights concluded that whether school desegregation is effective depends on a number of factors, including the leadership provided by state and local officials; the involvement of all schools in the community; the steps taken to minimize the possibility of racial friction in the newly desegregated schools; the maintenance of educational standards; the avoidance of racial isolation within the desegregated school; and the availability of supportive services for individual students who lag in achievement. Instances of the importance of each of these factors in specific school situations are given in the Commission's report. For example, to meet the community's apprehension about the possible

lowering of educational standards in school desegregation, Xenia, Ohio closed an all-Negro elementary school in 1964 and converted it into a demonstration school. With the support of a grant, new educational techniques have been introduced and a cross-section of the children in the community attend.[67]

Because environmental deprivation and school retardation are disproportionately the lot of Negro students, academic segregation in racially integrated schools tends to become also racial segregation. Such segregation denies many black children the advantages of integrated schools.[68] Among others, John Goodlad has addressed himself to the question of preventing and remedying segregation in the integrated school. According to this point of view, there is no need to segregate slow learners in a nonpromoted or "homogeneous" class because they are unable to do the work of the grade. It is argued that the traditional practices of nonpromotion and interclass grouping in the graded school system do not remedy the learning problems of pupils who are so segregated, and that certain side effects of these policies aggravate the conditions that education for disadvantaged children is supposed to remedy. Instead, it is proposed that:

The norms of expectancy simply are spread out to reach them; there are no grades. It is not necessary to overlook the limited accomplishments of a child simply to keep him with his age group. By spreading out the ages in the total group, it is possible both to adapt academic work to individual needs and to provide appropriate peer associations. There is no shifting of slow learners,

[66] *The Plain Dealer*, Jan. 13, 1972, p. 7F; Jan. 16, 1972, p. 1A. President Nixon's antibusing bill, sent to Congress on March 24, 1972, proposed a moratorium on all new court orders requiring busing until July 1, 1973, or until Congress passes legislation establishing desegregation guidelines. Controversy over this bill—as well as over a second presidential proposal providing for the concentration of federal funds in poor, segregated schools to improve the educational level and the establishment of desegregation guidelines that would include a ban on further busing for children through the sixth grade—produced a deadlock between the administration and Congress. Civil rights groups campaigned against the antibusing bill, asserting that busing is not so much of a burden as the President has claimed it is. Supporting this view are figures from the Department of Transportation cited by the U.S. Commission on Civil Rights showing that of the increased cost for school busing in 1971, less than 1 percent was used to carry out desegregation. Approximately 95 percent of the increase was due to population growth. John Herbers, "Roadblocks for the Nixon Proposals," *The New York Times*, April 23, 1972, Section 4, p. 2E.

[67] U.S. Commission on Civil Rights, *Racial Isolation in the Public Schools*, Vol. 1, pp. 154–163.

[68] Analyzing data on 5075 ninth-grade Negro students from a sample of schools selected from the metropolitan areas of the New England and Middle Atlantic states, McPartland found that only the Negro students in mostly white classes demonstrate any added achievement growth due to attendance at mostly white schools. He reports, however, that classroom desegregation "has an apparent beneficial effect on Negro student verbal achievement no matter what the racial enrollment of the school." James McPartland, "The Relative Influence of School and of Classroom Desegregation on the Academic Achievement of Ninth Grade Negro Students," *JSI*, Summer, 1969, pp. 101–102.

usually those who are environmentally disadvantaged, to academically and often racially segregated classes because youngsters of all academic levels are provided for within the nongraded, team-taught cluster.[69]

STRATEGIES USED TO ACHIEVE GREATER RACIAL BALANCE

Various communities have been trying to achieve greater racial balance while retaining the neighborhood school. The strategies used have included busing, pairing, redistricting, consolidating, and many other ways. According to the Office of Education report, many have failed; some have had at least partial success. In New Haven, pairing (attendance areas of two or more schools are merged and grades are regrouped so that each school serves different grade levels for the new area) was tried at the junior-high level. In contrast to this compulsory integration, a voluntary transfer plan was implemented at the elementary level. The reason given for the transfer plan was the relief of overcrowding, but greater racial balance was achieved. The provision for new school buildings in New Haven, however, means that the indirect stimulus to desegregation will not exist.[70]

Although greater problems are ecountered in large cities, some plans to broaden school attendance in these areas have been developed. It is hoped that these proposals will also enhance the quality of education. They are of three general types: supplementary centers and magnet schools, education complexes, and education parks. Plans for supplementary centers and magnet schools would provide specialized school programs in existing schools or in new facilities. Students from all or from many sections of the city would attend, mainly on a part-time basis. The advocates of supplementary centers hope they will help to reduce the exodus of white families to suburbs and they expect to operate these centers desegregated by race and social class. Magnet schools offer unusual curricula meeting special needs. For example, a Philadelphia program financed, in part, with federal funds, provides for an area of specialization in each of three high schools: commerce and business, space and aeronautical science, and government and human service.

In the educational complex, attendance areas would be broadened by grouping existing schools and consolidating their attendance zones. Presumably the clusters would draw on a more racially and socially heterogeneous student group, and specialized teachers and facilities could be available to more students.[71]

Proposals for education parks are similar to the plans for educational complexes, but they embody two differences: the parks would be new facilities consolidating a range of grade levels on a single site, and, in some cases, they would draw students from other school districts. In Syracuse, N.Y., for example, it is planned to close 31 elementary schools and to have all students attend one of four educational parks. Most of the proposals thus far advanced include a grouping of several racially desegregated schools serving a student body of 5000 to 30,000. Proposals vary concerning size, grade organization, population to be served, and whether there should be one or several parks to serve a city or a metropolitan area.

Some educators are concerned about the impact of size upon the education of children in huge educational facilities; others think that the parks may facilitate new approaches to teaching and learning that would offer greater individual attention to each child's needs.[72] Some educators maintain that the graded school system, with its practices of nonpromotion, interclass, and homogeneous grouping leads both to segregation in the integrated school and to loss of interest in school. It is said that children who are not promoted, "when compared with promoted children of equal past performance and

[69] John I. Goodlad, "Desegregating the Integrated School," U.S. Commission on Civil Rights, *Racial Isolation in the Public Schools*, Vol. 2, p. 268.

[70] Coleman, et al., *op. cit.*, pp. 32–33.

[71] U.S. Commission on Civil Rights, *Racial Isolation in the Public Schools*, Vol. 1, pp. 163–167.

[72] *Ibid.*, p. 167 ff.

measured intelligence, perform at a somewhat lower academic level, decline in their social relations with other children and in their self-image, and lose interest in school." To offset these tendencies, they recommend the nongraded school and team teaching.[73]

While favoring the education park idea, some educators point out the problems involved in the establishment of such enterprises. Lortie discusses the possibilities of resistance from teachers, saying that most teachers now support the neighborhood school even where it contributes to racial segregation.[74] Fisher says that a metropolitan school park would have to be approached from the outset as a problem in metropolitan planning. He mentions the importance of quantitative projections of population and housing data, but also the relation of a park to the character of housing and occupancy policies, and to ethnic considerations. According to Fisher: "To build a park only to have it engulfed in a few years by an enlarged ghetto would be a sorry waste of both money and opportunity. No good purpose, educational or social, would be served by creating what might become a segregated school enclave. . . ."[75] Estimates of the cost of building classrooms in education parks range from an amount approximately equal to the cost of regular classrooms to twice that amount. Other questions concerning feasibility include the use of existing facilities. Among suggested uses are the expansion of nursery school programs and adult education in in-city structures.

COMPENSATORY EDUCATIONAL PROGRAMS IN RACIALLY ISOLATED SCHOOLS

Compensatory education refers to attempts made to improve the quality of education for disadvantaged children. Of the several approaches employed, remedial instruction gives intensive assistance to students in academic difficulty. Techniques include a low student-teacher ratio, tutors to help students during and after school, counseling, and the use of special teaching materials to increase basic skills. The cultural enrichment approach offers activities that go beyond those traditionally provided to students. Such programs try to broaden the horizons of poor children by giving them access to museums, concerts, the theater, other schools, and college campuses. A third type of compensatory education program attempts to overcome attitudes that inhibit learning. Here efforts are made to increase self-esteem through black studies or similar programs, and to instill confidence through academic success and recognition. A fourth approach is preschool education. This approach makes use of some of the elements in the other approaches as it tries to increase the verbal skills of the disadvantaged child and to provide cultural enrichment activities for him before he enters primary school.[76] As the Commission report points out, one element common to most compensatory education is an effort to involve parents in the school program. It is believed that the motivation of children for academic work can be increased if parents are assured that the schools are concerned about their problems and if they are given suggestions concerning ways in which they may contribute to their children's success. In some cases, adult education is offered in an attempt to correct inadequacies in the home environment.[77]

It is important to emphasize that compensatory education programs in predominantly Negro schools are established on the assumption that the major cause of academic disadvantage is the poverty of the average child and the environment in which he lives. It is claimed that children from poverty families enter school poorly motivated and lacking in verbal skills. The Commission report says that the children's disadvantage increases as they go through school, and that

[73] *Ibid.*, pp. 171–172, and John I. Goodlad, "Desegregating the Integrated School" in U.S. Commission on Civil Rights, *Racial Isolation in the Public Schools*, Vol. 2, pp. 260–268.

[74] Dan C. Lortie, "Towards Educational Equality: The Teacher and the Educational Park," *ibid.*, pp. 273–285.

[75] John H. Fisher, "School Parks for Equal Opportunities," *JNE*, Summer, 1968, pp. 301–309.

[76] U.S. Commission on Civil Rights, *Racial Isolation in the Public Schools*, Vol. 1, p. 116.

[77] *Ibid.*, pp. 116–117.

this is attributed to failure of the schools to provide necessary services.[78]

Among the federal educational programs launched in recent years to improve the skills and motivation of children in a number of minority groups are Head Start, Talent Search, and Upward Bound. The results of studies, mainly of summer Head Start children, show that Head Start "is making a promising first step toward raising the achievement level of deprived children." Most of the studies report an increase in the test scores of children after the Head Start experience.[79] Thus far, the long-term effects of the Head Start program have been disappointing. Gordon says that a review of almost 100 studies of Head Start shows that the persistence of gains in intellectual function in three- and four-year-old children is not consistent. Changes in social-emotional maturation and in readiness to benefit from primary school experience are more generally reported and are seen by teachers as being more persistent. Gordon concludes that "the long term impact of Head Start as an antidote to the destructive influence of poverty and inferior status on educational and social development is yet to be established."[80]

Follow Through, an extension of Head Start, was started in 1967 to provide continued services to former Head Start pupils through the primary grades. Funding restrictions caused Follow Through to be changed from a nationwide program, as first planned, to a research program devoted to seeking alternatives to present educational systems. Another program funded by Head Start, but jointly sponsored by OEO, HEW, HUD, and the Department of Labor, is the Parent and Child Care Center (PCC). Since OEO had found that very poor children in Head Start had developed serious handicaps by age three, this project was designed as a preventive measure to provide comprehensive services to all members of a family in the program.

Talent Search, a program with a very limited budget, attempts to find disadvantaged high-school students with potential for higher education and to assist these students in gaining admission to college. In 1969, 72 Talent Search projects were reported by the Office of Education, but no information was available on the number of students who had entered college as a result of the program.[81]

Upward Bound, a more comprehensive federal program than Talent Search, provides supplementary training to assist in preparing "medium risk" high school students for college.

In 1965, the National Teachers Corps was started to assist in recruiting and training the future teachers of disadvantaged children. The program emphasizes sensitizing these teachers to the cultural differences of poor families, and often includes actually living in low-income communities.[82]

On the basis of raising the academic achievement of disadvantaged children, as a group, compensatory education in majority-Negro schools has not shown evidence of much success within the periods that have been evaluated thus far. Various reasons are given for this finding. Glickstein attributes the questionable impact of federal involvement in the education of minority students to "poor program management, a piece-meal legislative response, a splintered and uncoordinated approach and . . . insufficient funding."[83] Sewell suggests that the Coleman report shows the need for preschool programs of greater scope than any yet started and for new experimental and innovative programs, especially in the early grades, to improve the educational capacities of the disadvantaged child and to stimulate and maintain his motivation for educational achievement.[84] Some advocates of compensatory education say that such programs as Higher Horizons and More Effective Schools in New

[78] *Ibid.*, p. 117.

[79] Howard A. Glickstein, "Federal Programs and Minority Groups," *JNE*, Summer, 1969, pp. 308–309.

[80] Edmund W. Gordon, "Compensatory Education in the Equalization of Educational Opportunity," *JNE*, Summer, 1968, p. 270. For a review of Upward Bound, see David Hunt and Robert Hardt, "The Effects of Upward Bound Programs on the Attitudes, Motivations, and Academic Achievement of Negro Students," *JSI*, Summer, 1969, pp. 117–129.

[81] Glickstein, *op. cit.*, pp. 312–313.

[82] *Ibid.*, p. 311.

[83] *Ibid.*, p. 314.

[84] Sewell, *op. cit.*, p. 479.

York City have not had sufficient time to succeed, and they claim also that thus far the compensatory projects have not differed enough from traditional practice.[85] The U.S. Commission on Civil Rights suggests that one possible explanation, and a more basic one, is that compensatory programs do not wholly compensate for the depressing effect of racial and social class isolation upon the aspirations and self-esteem of black students.[86] The present comments do not suggest that compensatory education is incapable of reducing the effects of poverty on the academic achievement of individual children. Probably cultural enrichment, better teaching, and supplementary educational services can be helpful to disadvantaged children.

It is difficult to speak with confidence about the effects, or lack of effects, of educational enrichment programs, because there are few carefully controlled studies. Ex post facto research, using survey designs—even those, such as the Coleman report, carried through in a highly sophisticated way—are subject to almost endless debate, as critics cite one or another additional control that might have been added. Field research, on the other hand, may suffer from lack of scope, but it can introduce comparisons of experimental and control groups, thus achieving greater validity.

Such research has been undertaken at Oberlin College, where, for a number of summers, about 65 pupils who had just finished the seventh grade were brought to the campus for an intensive academic program, enriched with trips, plays, concerts, and recreation. There has also been a follow-up program, through their junior-high and senior-high years, consisting of counseling, reunions, support for additional summer activities, newsletters, contacts with the families, and the like. For the summers of 1964 through 1966, these pupils (from Cleveland, St. Louis, Lorain, Elyria, and Oberlin) were prematched with another panel, and randomly assigned to either experimental or control groups. Their academic records, aspirations, and achievements were followed through the spring of 1970. The impact of the program has not been spectacular; but it has been significant—statistically and otherwise. Only the first group—the 56 1964 participants and their "controls"—have reached college age. Of these, 35 of the experimental group entered college, compared with 19 of the control group. Equally significantly, those in the experimental group have entered four-year colleges in greater proportion. These data are somewhat soft, for two reasons: it is not yet clear what the staying power of the college entrants will be; and complete information is lacking on 17 of the 112 in the 1964 panel. Full information may qualify, but it cannot upset the major finding: Carefully planned programs of educational intervention can alter aspiration and performance. These programs must avoid a "hit-and-run" approach; for each step along the road brings new problems and unexpected requirements to students who come from educationally deprived backgrounds. It is clearly not true, however, that kindergarten is "already too late," as some believe. Failure to start educational enrichment early is costly; but a "middle start" is possible for a significant number when adequate resources are provided. In our judgment, many programs have proved to be ineffective because they have concentrated either on the students, in an effort to raise their skills, motives, and aspirations, or on the whole structure of opportunities, in order to expand the options of disadvantaged persons. It is the *product* of these two factors, however, that determines the outcome. Changing one factor only is of little value. With apologies to Kant: aspirations without opportunities are blind; opportunities without aspirations are empty.[87]

[85] Editors of *Harvard Educational Review*, *HER*, "Policy Issues," Winter, 1968.

[86] U.S. Commission on Civil Rights, *Racial Isolation in the Public Schools*, Vol. 1, pp. 138–139.

[87] See J. Milton Yinger, Kiyoshi Ikeda, and Frank Laycock, *Middle Start: Supportive Interventions for Higher Education Among Students of Disadvantaged Backgrounds*, U.S. Office of Education, Bureau of Research, Final Report for Project No. 5–0703, Nov., 1970; and J. Milton Yinger, Kiyoshi Ikeda, and Frank Laycock, "Treating Matching as a Variable in a Sociological Experiment," *ASR*, Oct., 1967, pp. 801–812.

Recommendations of the U.S. Commission on Civil Rights on the Establishment of Equal Educational Opportunity

As an important means of providing equal educational opportunity of high quality for all children, the U.S. Commission on Civil Rights recommended that the President and Congress give serious consideration to new legislation embodying the following principles:

1. Congress should establish a uniform standard providing for the elimination of racial isolation in the schools.
2. Congress should vest in each of the 50 states responsibility for meeting the standard it establishes and should allow the states maximum flexibility in devising appropriate remedies. It also should provide financial and technical assistance to the states in planning such remedies.
3. The legislation should include programs of substantial financial assistance to provide for construction of new facilities and improvement in the quality of education in all schools.
4. Congress should provide for adequate time in which to accomplish the objectives of the legislation.
5. Prohibit discrimination in the sale or rental of housing.
6. Expand programs of federal assistance designed to increase the supply of housing throughout metropolitan areas within the means of low- and moderate-income families.

In addition, the Commission recommends that HUD:

7. Require as a condition for approval of applications for low- and moderate-income housing projects that the sites will be selected and the projects planned in a nondiscriminatory manner that will contribute to reducing residential racial concentrations and eliminating racial isolation in the schools.
8. Require as a condition for approval of urban renewal projects that relocation will be planned in a nondiscriminatory manner that will contribute to reducing residential and racial concentrations and eliminating racial isolation in the schools.[88]

To this discussion of compensatory education, two postscripts may be added. Some educators do not believe that the evidence supports the hypothesis that school resources are ineffective in raising achievement levels. Bowles says that the evidence of the Equality of Educational Opportunity Survey itself suggests that student achievement is related to the level of resources devoted to the school. Preliminary analysis of the Survey data showed that the achievement levels of Negro students were particularly sensitive to the quality of teaching staffs assigned to them.[89] On this point, a finding of the Office of Education survey is of interest—

The preferences of Negro future teachers are more compatible with the distribution of needs in the market than are those of the majority; too few of the latter, relative to the clientele requiring service, prefer blue-collar or low ability children or prefer to teach in racially heterogeneous schools, or in special curriculum, vocational, or commercial schools. These data indicate that under the present organization of schools, relatively few of the best prepared future teachers will find their way into classrooms where they can offset some of the environmental disadvantage suffered by minority children."[90]

Finally, one solution assumes that Negro achievement is "basically a result of irredeemably bad inner-city public schools paralyzed by rigid bureaucracies." It has been suggested, therefore, that every child from a family earning under the poverty criterion be eligible for a $1200 educational allowance. The child's parents could then purchase the best available education—from a suburban public school, a private or parochial school, or a school operated by a university as a business (Job Corps type of training). A variation of this proposal is to permit the public schools to subcontract out particular tasks to any public or private group that offers a new program. According to this point of view, the public school would have to improve or close for lack of students. It is argued that the ability to decide what school

---

[88] U.S. Commission on Civil Rights, *Racial Isolation in the Public Schools*, Vol. 1, pp. 209–212. Comments on each of these recommendations are given in the Commission's report.

[89] Samuel Bowles, "Towards Equality of Educational Opportunity," *HER*, Winter, 1968, pp. 91–94.
[90] Coleman, et al., *op. cit.*, p. 27.

a child attends would improve parent morale.[91]

Cooperation of Suburbs and Parochial School Systems

In discussing busing we pointed out that only intercity busing (central city-suburbs) would provide a significant amount of racial balance in the large metropolitan areas. Most educators have concluded that comprehensive desegregation cannot occur without organizing units that cut across present local lines, enlarging attendance areas, and eliminating the neighborhood school. Such restructuring cannot be accomplished without the collaboration of suburbs surrounding the largest cities and/or parochial school systems.

Educational Equality and the Job Market

Equality of educational opportunity has little meaning unless equality of employment opportunity also exists. Attempts to improve academic achievement are closely related to the problem of reducing racial discrimination in the job market. Some social critics go further, saying that preoccupation with reorganization of the schools is too narrow a view and that educational change is simply a part of broader social change. They advocate changing the country's social class structure rather than establishing programs to compensate for social inequalities. At present, plans for such a sweeping change are not available.

SCHOOL ENROLLMENT AND DROPOUTS

Studies based on Census data and a nationwide survey using a sample of 35,000 households show that 17 percent of Negro adolescents (ages 16 and 17) have dropped out of school; for white adolescents the figure is 9 percent. Most of this difference comes from differences outside the South. The dropout rate varies, however, with socioeconomic level. The nonenrollment rate is 3 percent for adolescents from white-collar families,

but it was 13 percent for families where the head was in a blue-collar or farm occupation, unemployed, or not in the labor force at all. The difference in dropout rates by parental occupation existed for both male and female Negro and white adolescents.[92] Thus, racial differences in the dropout rate are sharply reduced when socioeconomic factors are considered.

In a study of 131 of the largest central cities in the United States, Dentler and Warshauer found that variations in high school dropout rates, as well as variations in levels of adult illiteracy, are due, to a significant extent, to differences among the cities in levels of poverty, occupational mix, economic opportunity, and social mobility. A static city is defined as one that is growing much more slowly—or is declining at a faster rate—than comparable communities. While better educated, more mobile adults and their children tend to migrate to new centers of opportunity, less well educated adults accumulate in static centers. According to this study, as the context of social and economic opportunities declines, the level of graduation from high school among adolescents is depressed. Thus, for example, cities such as Nashville, St. Louis, Louisville, Cincinnati, and Jacksonville offer fewer work opportunities and carry relatively larger numbers of impoverished families than do such cities as Dearborn, Portland, Berkeley, and Pasadena. They found also that a large community in decline tends to sustain a larger per capita burden of welfare and related municipal services. As the process continues, the proportion of educationally less advantaged adults increases, the better educated migrate to growing areas, and an increase in school failure or withdrawal occurs in the declining city.[93]

Dentler and Warshauer explored the relationship between educational and welfare programs designed to remedy or cope with the problems of high school withdrawal, adult illiteracy, and welfare dependency.

[91] Kenneth B. Clark, "Alternative Public School Systems," *HER*, Winter, 1968, pp. 100–113.

[92] Coleman et al., *op. cit.*, p. 28.
[93] Robert A. Dentler and Mary Ellen Warshauer, *Big City Dropouts and Illiterates*, Praeger, 1968, pp. 54–62.

They predicted that cities with far fewer dropouts than expected would support preventive or rehabilitative programs that differed in extent and quality from programs maintained by cities having high dropout rates. They found that cities having higher proportions of dropouts and illiterates than expected tended to have higher than average educational, health, and public welfare expenditures, but they did not find a relationship between high dropout and illiteracy rates and the qualitative side of school and welfare programs. They suggest that the public sectors of American municipal economies "do not equalize, and usually fail to do so much as compensate slightly for gross differences in life prospects, let alone remedy insecurities or strengthen individual opportunities."[94]

According to these investigators, welfare and social security programming should come from a national plan for protecting citizens from changing contingencies. In their view, programs to prevent or reduce dropouts and to teach adults to read are nowhere so pertinent as unemployment insurance, disability insurance, and other forms of social insurance that transcend local variations. They do not, however, regard community action programs, innovations in welfare and educational services, training and retraining programs as useless or irrelevant. The attempts they make may lead to other means of dealing with insecurity, and the educational efforts in welfare may contribute to the vitality of welfare agencies. They say: "Programs that in some respects do not work must be maintained, and changed periodically, or the very formal organizational machinery for doing anything will grow inflexible or will disappear."[95]

BLACK AWARENESS, BLACK PRIDE, BLACK NATIONALISM, AND BLACK EDUCATION

Because integration had not been attained to any great extent 14 years after the U.S.

Supreme Court's Brown decision of 1954, some Negroes had concluded, by 1968, that integration was unrealistic. Militant blacks began to emphasize black awareness and pride and to advocate the withdrawal of Negroes in order to develop skills, strength, and dignity before agreeing to negotiate the terms of integration. Some of the ultramilitant blacks rejected even this approach and turned toward Africa or the "Third World" for inspiration and future identification.[96]

Other observers of—and activists in—racial affairs criticized black nationalists who claimed that "white teachers are ruining Negro children and that only black teachers can be trusted to teach black children." Morsell says that such arguments are beguiling until one remembers how long scorn was poured on the illogic of white segregationists that birds of a feather flock together.[97]

Poussaint, a black psychiatrist, says that the growth of black consciousness and pride has had salutary effects on the black's self-image. His evidence suggests that the consequences of self-image as a motivator for behavior is like a self-fulfilling prophecy: "Negroes were told and believed that they were inferior and would fail and therefore they failed . . . for the black child to be motivated to achieve in school, the school must negate everything that the society affirms; it must tell the child that he can succeed—and then he will succeed."[98] Poussaint and Atkinson cite the evidence in the Coleman survey to indicate, moreover, that the motive to self-assertion and aggression is even stronger than self-concept in its influence on behavior. For this reason, they suggest that structural changes in societal institutions in the direction of providing blacks with greater opportunity to be more self-assertive and aggressive would be improvements. The decentralization of New York

---

[94] *Ibid.*, pp. 63–65.

[95] *Ibid.*, pp. 67–68.

[96] P. E. Wilson, "Some Aspects of the Education of Black Americans," in Pat Romero (ed.), *In Black America*, United, 1969, pp. 89–100.

[97] J. A. Morsell, "Racial Desegregation and Integration in Public Education," *JNE*, Summer, 1969, p. 283.

[98] Alvin F. Poussaint and Carolyn O. Atkinson, "Negro Youth and Psychological Motivation," *JNE*, Summer, 1968, p. 250.

City schools, the development of black business, and the organization and channeling of black political power are seen as significant steps in such change. Since Negro youth and their parents generally have high educational and occupational aspirations that are not reflected in achievement levels, these authors ask if there is not some way in which these aspirations could be associated with their interests and proficiencies—and rewarded consistently.[99] It remains a moot question whether educational and economic decentralization do, in fact, serve this purpose.

Negro Teachers, Desegregation, and Jobs

Many Negro teachers and principals in the South have lost their jobs in the process of school desegregation. Often the closing of all-Negro schools has meant sending the pupils to schools staffed largely by white teachers. In 1965, at least 350 teaching positions formerly held by black teachers in southern states were eliminated because of school desegregation. In May, 1968, the Georgia Teachers and Education Association, a Negro organization, complained of the "unethical and unfair practice in Georgia relating to the dismissal, transfer and demotion of Negro personnel." Similar protests have been made in Georgia and in other states since 1968. National education officials estimate that 5000 black principals, teachers, and school employees have been dismissed or demoted regardless of qualifications as nominal desegregation has occurred.[100]

Recent graduates in the field of education do not seem to be having difficulty in finding teaching jobs. A study of graduates of the class of 1968 in predominantly Negro teacher-training institutions in the southern and border states showed that only 15 among 1211 graduates who were certified to teach and who wanted to teach had not found teaching jobs. The seven deans and placement directors who provided information said that school systems had made a greater effort to recruit Negro education graduates in 1968 than in previous years. They also said that their graduates were more likely to begin teaching in an integrated faculty than those who graduated three years earlier. Two colleges in the Deep South reported that recruiters from the West and the Midwest had been especially active on their campuses in 1968. Southern University said that 40 percent of their 1968 graduates left Louisiana for teaching positions elsewhere. An official of Texas Southern University commented that the guidelines on faculty desegregation issued by HEW for the federal compliance program under the Civil Rights Act of 1964 were a major factor in opening job opportunities in desegregated schools.[101]

COMMUNITY CONTROL

A widely discussed proposal for improving education for black children is community control of the schools. This plan is closely related to the larger issue, considered in Chapter 13, of community control of ghetto affairs.

Advocates of community control say that the idea is not as revolutionary as it sounds. They point out that white communities take for granted their control of local school boards and budgets, and they propose that in large city systems a set of powers and financial resources be assigned to the local community. In this way, it is argued, the community could develop an educational structure and process that would be responsible to the needs of the local community and accountable to it for its success.[102]

It should be indicated at the outset that "neighborhood" or "community" in discussions of community control refers to an area in the range of 50,000 to 75,000 people in a city of up to two million people. Only three

[99] *Ibid.*, pp. 250–251.

[100] Jack Rosenthal, "Integration: South Finds New Ways to Say 'Never'," *The New York Times*, June 28, 1970.

[101] Robert F. Campbell and Frank Richardson, "How Are New Negro Teachers Faring?" *Southern Education Review*, Dec., 1968, pp. 25–27.

[102] Whitney M. Young, Jr., "Minorities and Community Control of the Schools," *JNE*, Summer, 1969, p. 286.

American cities had populations significantly larger than two million in 1960. Altshuler suggests that "districts" in Chicago and Los Angeles might be thought of in the 100,000 range. With a population of eight million, New York might have either larger districts or a greater number of units.[103] The idea is to give blacks something like parity with suburbs.

In the case of education, participation would provide an involvement with the system which, it is hoped, would diminish alienation and also serve to stimulate educational change. The "community" in community control proposals includes not only parents of school children but also other segments of the public that have had no role in public education. It is a type of "participatory democracy" intended to remedy the alleged failure of public school systems, particularly those in large cities that have sizeable minority populations.[104] It is seen as a social policy that could help to remove an obstacle to change in the educational system—the trained incapacity of educational administrators, curriculum specialists, principals, and teachers to change the school systems to deal adequately with the members of minority groups.[105] In black insistence upon "meaningful involvement" as it relates to curriculum offerings, administration, instruction, and other aspects of the academic enterprise, Lincoln says that the basic intention is the destruction of the "racial caste structure" and that it cannot be seen in isolation from that interest.[106]

According to its proponents, community control of the schools involves local control over key policy decisions in four areas: personnel, budget, curriculum, and public policy. Local governing bodies would be locally selected, and mechanisms would be developed to encourage broader community participation.[107]

The most extensive general proposal in community control advanced thus far is the Bundy Plan presented to the mayor of New York City in the fall of 1967. This plan called for citywide decentralization by dividing the systems into subsystems—between 30 and 60—and for wide community control. It recommended a citywide educational structure for special schools, the establishment of minimum standards, control of capital construction, and provisions for voluntary services when requested by local districts. It provided for local selection of a majority of the members of the local school boards, and community control of personnel, the expense budget, student policy, and curriculum.[108]

Soon after the appearance of the Bundy Plan, Mayor Lindsay offered a modified school desegregation plan designed to have greater appeal to the state legislators. The latter ignored the Mayor's plan, and the New York State Board of Regents presented another plan. In May, 1968, James Allen, then the Commissioner of Education of the state of New York, succeeded in getting the several plans coordinated and presented to the state legislature as the Regents Plan. This plan failed to pass, but the legislature enacted a bill empowering the Mayor to appoint four additional members to the New York Board of Education. It ordered the Board to recommend a decentralization plan the next year. The Board submitted a plan in December, 1968, providing for some community control, but it retained existing personnel procedures. The defeat of both the Bundy Plan and the Regents Plan ended the first phase of the political decentralization struggle.

Part of the struggle over decentralization came as a result of the creation in 1967 by the New York Board of Education of "ex-

---

[103] Alan A. Altshuler, *Community Control: The Black Demand for Participation in Large American Cities*, Pegasus, 1970, pp. 130–131.

[104] Marilyn Gittell, "Community Control of Education," in Robert H. Connery (ed.), *Urban Riots: Violence and Social Change*, Academy of Political Science, 1968, p. 62.

[105] P. H. Rossi, "The Education of Failure or the Failure of Education," *JNE*, Summer, 1969, p. 332.

[106] C. Eric Lincoln, "The Relevance of Education for Black Americans," *JNE*, Summer, 1969, p. 222.

[107] Gittell, *op. cit.*, p. 63.

[108] *Ibid.*, p. 65. For an account of the main features of the Bundy Plan, see Marilyn Gittell and Alan G. Hevesi, *The Politics of Urban Education*, Praeger, 1969, pp. 261–274.

perimental" decentralized school districts in Harlem, Ocean Hill-Brownsville, and lower Manhattan. In these districts, conflicts arose over the powers to be given to the elected governing boards and the administrators of the districts. According to Gittell and Hevesi, the community groups felt that they had been given structural changes but no actual power. The Board contended that it could not, under state law, delegate power to the districts.[109] Escalation of the Ocean Hill-Brownsville district controversy constituted the second phase of the conflict over decentralization.[110]

The third phase of the conflict consisted of further debate in the state legislature, with the United Federation of Teachers and the Council of Supervisory Associations opposing legislation and ghetto groups and civic committees of various kinds supporting it.[111]

Legislation for independent districts and for community control has been introduced, since 1967, in California, Massachusetts, Michigan, and Kentucky. Discussion of community control plans has occurred in several cities, including Boston, Detroit, Chicago, Los Angeles, Minneapolis, Philadelphia, and Washington, D.C. The arguments against community control emphasize two themes: parochialism and the lack of qualifications on the part of community people to deal with the technical problems in education. Claims that black racism and extremism could be met by safeguards in the form of state legislation and administrative regulations, as well as in the provision of funds from the city, state, and federal governments, are not convincing to the opponents of community control. The same may be said concerning the proponents' claim that community representatives who make decisions would have to rely, to some extent, on professional educators for help in policy making. Members of

the UFT and the Council of Supervisory Associations contend that parent and community control would result in a return to corruption, patronage, and chaos.[112]

In all the discussions of the Bundy Report and similar proposals for community control, a basic question remains unanswered. The question is whether local autonomy would result in children learning more than they learn under the control of a single, mainly white board. Epstein says that discussions of pedagogical tactics, for example, different methods of teaching reading, as well as of different methods of administering the schools, do not explain whether a common language can be taught at all "once the children sense the hostility to their style of life and their color of an alien and overpowering environment."[113] Epstein finds somewhat disingenuous, however, the suggestion that the ghettos now run their own schools in the hope that children can learn from the specialized culture of the black community. It is unclear how the decentralization proposals, in themselves, would generate faith in ghetto children that their academic efforts will lead to chances to participate as responsible citizens in their city and country.[114]

Jencks notes that the main reason that employers hesitate to hire dropouts is not that they can't read, but that "dropouts don't get to work on time, can't be counted on to do a careful job, don't get along with others in the plant or office, can't be trusted to keep their hands out of the till, and so on." Altshuler agrees with Jencks's interpretation of this and other evidence that there is often little relationship between skills and variations in earnings, saying that black poverty and unemployment are more the prod-

---

[109] Gittell and Hevesi, *op. cit.*, p. 13. The editors point out that the Harlem chapter of CORE introduced legislation into the New York State Legislature at this time to create an independent school district for the Harlem community. This legislation failed to pass in 1967, and again in 1968.

[110] For accounts of both sides of this controversy, see *ibid.*, pp. 338–350 and 352–362.

[111] *Ibid.*, pp. 371–372.

[112] For a statement by an active proponent of community control of the public schools, see Gittell, *op. cit.*, pp. 60–71 (revised and expanded version in Gittell and Hevesi, *op. cit.*, pp. 363–377). A criticism of community control of education, particularly as proposed in the Bundy Plan, is given in Council of Supervisory Associations, "Interim Report No. 2, January, 1968: The Bundy Plan," in Gittell and Hevesi, *op. cit.*, pp. 277–287.

[113] Jason Epstein, "The Politics of School Decentralization," in Gittell and Hevesei, *op. cit.*, pp. 296–297.

[114] *Ibid.*, pp. 297–298.

ucts of poor socialization than of poor reading and arithmetic skills. In his view, black-controlled educational systems might fail to do better, but he thinks that they could hardly do worse.[115]

The interests of professionals, black and white, is a part of the controversy over community control. Integration involves strain and tension for black and white administrators and teachers alike. Community control offers jobs and promotion to administrative and supervisory positions for Blacks without the discomfort of going into "foreign" schools and neighborhoods, and it does so under the ideology of helping one's own community. The development of the black professional class is an important element in the struggle in New York City, where there are 6500 Negroes on the public school staff of 60,000. Only a small fraction of the school administrators is black.[116]

The controversy over community control of the public schools is not likely to subside soon. Apart from the self-interests of professionals, the question of the bearing of these proposals on integration is of great importance. Opponents of community control are concerned about the "balkanization" of a city system under what they regard as such rigid conditions that integration would become more, rather than less, difficult. They urge those working for the improvement of the schools by decentralization to see to it that the chances for integration are maximized rather than reduced by whatever district lines are drawn.[117] Altshuler says that to endorse the demand of Blacks that they sometimes, at the lowest tier of American government, be permitted the experience of majority status is not to suggest that opportunities for integration should be curtailed, or that neighborhood boundaries should be drawn on racial lines. His position is that the effort to extend integration opportunities to those who want them must be increased, but he admits that an incidental effect of community control might be to increase the present, almost total degree of segregation.[118]

PROSPECTS FOR SCHOOL DESEGREGATION

To estimate the prospects for school desegregation during the 1970s, it is necessary to review some of the main legal and political developments in education since 1965. In April, 1965, the Office of Education announced that public schools in the United States must integrate at least some grades by September of that year if they expected to qualify for federal aid. At the same time, it was said that the aid might be cut off unless steps were taken to integrate the faculty, transportation, and other facilities. The basic requirements for the beginning of school in the fall of 1965 were integrated classes in at least four grades—the first grade, the lowest grade of junior high, and the first and last high-school grades. Some exceptions to these guidelines were to be made because of special circumstances in some of the nation's 27,000 school districts. To qualify for federal funds, it was necessary for a school district to submit a plan demonstrating "substantial good faith" to desegregate. Title VI of the 1964 Civil Rights Act provides that all recipients of federal aid must operate in a nondiscriminatory manner, and that state and local agencies must provide a pledge of compliance, a court order providing for integration, or a voluntary plan of desegregation. By March, 1965, documents had been received from 22,400 school districts, and approximately 19,000 were found acceptable.

[115] Altshuler, *op. cit.*, pp. 213–214.

[116] See *ibid.*, p. 201, and Epstein, *op. cit.*, p. 290.

[117] J. A. Morsell, "Racial Desegregation and Integration in Public Education," *JNE*, Summer, 1969, p. 283.

[118] Altshuler, *op. cit.*, pp. 203–204. It is of interest that the Puerto Rican community does not oppose the idea of decentralization, but that it is concerned about the way community control would work out. Vazquez says: "Since Puerto Ricans are dispersed throughout the city and must share community leadership with the more powerful Negro groups in some areas, or with the mainland whites in others, these doubts are not entirely unfounded. In the resolution of this problem may lie the future development of the Puerto Rican community in New York because . . . the struggle for decentralization is essentially a struggle for political power as well as educational reform." Hector C. Vazquez, "Puerto Rican Americans," *JNE*, Summer, 1969, p. 255.

The Commissioner of Education had said that an acceptable plan must include assignment of pupils by neighborhood zones or give a pupil and his parents free choice of a school.[119]

Freedom of choice did not result in much desegregation in the Deep South. By the spring of 1967, less than 3 percent of Negro students in Mississippi were in classes with whites. Reluctance on the part of many Negro parents to send their children to predominantly white schools was attributed to fears concerning their jobs or personal safety, or to fears that their children would be lonely or mistreated in such schools. In some districts where Negroes did apply in large numbers, the white school officials turned away many of these pupils. Often in the latter cases, the school superintendent said that there wasn't enough room in the white schools for all the Negroes who applied. Since freedom of choice seemed to be achieving considerable integration in such states as Texas and Virginia, the Office of Education did not want to ban this procedure outright. In the spring of 1966, guidelines were issued for use in determining whether freedom of choice was achieving enough in desegregating public schools. Under these guidelines, school districts with 8 or 9 percent of their Negro students in classes with Whites were expected to double that proportion within a year. Districts with less than that proportion were asked to make "substantial" efforts to catch up. The South took this issue into the federal courts, and in April, 1967 the Supreme Court refused to delay the enforcement of a ruling by the United States Court of Appeals, Fifth Circuit, which had said that if freedom of choice was not putting substantial numbers of Negroes in formerly all-white schools, the school officials had the responsibility to try other procedures.[120] The governors of Louisiana, Mississippi, and Alabama met immediately to develop strategy to oppose the court order.

In March, 1969, four federal judges ordered 22 South Carolina school districts to work with federal experts to develop "acceptable" desegregation plans within 30 days. The districts were asked to conform to a Supreme Court decision of May, 1968 that held freedom-of-choice plans unacceptable if "there are available other ways, such as zoning, promising speedier and more effective conversion to a unitary school system." All 22 districts affected by this order had used freedom-of-choice plans, but none had reached even the 15 percent school desegregation achieved by the district involved in the Supreme Court case of May, 1968—New Kent County in Virginia.[121]

On April 7, 1969, a cutoff of federal funds for three school districts in the South, two in Georgia and one in Mississippi, as well as three hospitals in Mississippi, was announced by HEW. Termination in these instances was approved because of failure to comply with the nondiscrimination provisions of the 1964 Civil Rights Act.[122] In October, 1969, the Supreme Court issued a new order, saying: " 'All deliberate speed' for desegregation is no longer permissible . . . The obligation of every school district is to terminate dual school systems at once."[123] The government's figures in this case showed that only 262 of the 1129 school districts in nine southern states were operating unitary desegregated systems at the beginning of the 1969–1970 school year. It was estimated that 202 more had abolished the dual system since the opening of the fall term. In August, 1970, either on their own volition or by order of the federal courts, 543 school districts in eleven southern states had plans to convert to unitary school systems that would no longer discriminate on the basis of race.[124]

By the spring of 1970, the national movement in support of public school integration had lost some of its momentum. John Herbers points out that for the first time since 1954, southern Whites and some northern liberals

[119] Associated Press, The Plain Dealer, Apr. 30, 1965, p. 2.
[120] The New York Times, Apr. 23, 1967.

[121] Ibid., Apr. 1, 1969.
[122] Associated Press, The Plain Dealer, Apr. 8, 1969.
[123] Anthony Lewis, "School Segregation," The New York Times, Nov. 2, 1969.
[124] The New York Times, Aug. 30, 1970, p. 1.

had joined forces to maintain segregation. The following developments are cited as indicators of a lessened drive for integration: (1) A number of liberal and Negro journalists have questioned the accomplishments of forced integration and have argued for improving the quality of schools, whatever their racial composition, (2) many educators question the value of integration and are not in favor of extensive reshuffling of students, (3) groups that support school integration were having trouble raising funds, and (4) most northern Congressional liberals found little support on the part of their constituents in early 1970 for opposing the several southern amendments designed to weaken enforcement of desegregation under the 1964 Civil Rights Act. Some observers held that the extent of the erosion of the integration movement had been exaggerated, pointing out that the great majority of Negro citizens favor integration, citing both the Coleman study finding that integration is the most consistent mechanism for improving the quality of education for the disadvantaged and the fact that integration has been successful in a number of communities in the United States.[125]

On March 14, 1970, President Nixon issued a long statement listing the "basic principles and policies" that his Administration would follow on school desegregation. He said: "Racial imbalance in a school system may be partly de jure [by law or official policy] in origin and partly de facto [by neighborhood racial patterns]. In such a case it is appropriate to insist on remedy for the de jure portion, which is unlawful, without insisting on a remedy for the lawful de facto portion. De facto racial separation, resulting genuinely from housing patterns, exists in the South as well as in the North; in neither area should this condition by itself be cause for federal enforcement actions." In effect, Mr. Nixon indicated that the relationship that had existed between the Supreme Court and the Executive branch in working to achieve desegregation of the public schools has ended.

Especially during the Johnson administration, the Court had issued a series of rulings expanding and strengthening its 1954 decision that a dual system is unconstitutional, and the Executive branch had backed up the Court with its guidelines and actions enforcing the school fund cutoff provisions of the 1964 Civil Rights Act. The meaning of the President's statement seems to be that his Administration will not assist in the breaking of new ground as far as civil rights enforcement is concerned. Among other things, the President said that "transportation beyond normal geographic school zones for the purpose of achieving a racial balance will not be required." In devising school desegregation plans, he said that "primary weight should be given to the considered judgment of local school boards—provided they act in good faith, and within constitutional limits," and that "the neighborhood school will be deemed the most appropriate base for such a district." The Supreme Court has not yet ruled on de facto segregation, but some observers think the President has served notice that if it declares de jure and de facto segregation to be the same thing, it will do so at its peril.[126] Perhaps the most telling criticism of the politically conservative presidential statement came from the U.S. Civil Rights Commission. This independent governmental agency said that the President had placed too much emphasis on the "neighborhood school" concept, that he had overemphasized busing as an issue, and that experience had shown that "good faith" promises by school boards to desegregate cannot be relied upon.[127] Pointing out that while 20 percent of the black pupils in the South were in integrated classes in September 1968, and 30 percent attended them in September, 1969, and almost 40 percent of southern Negro students were attending formerly all-white schools in April, 1970, the NAACP Legal Defense and Educational Fund decried President Nixon's statement limiting the applicability of constitutional principles.

Not all of the steps taken by the Nixon

[125] John Herbers, "National Push for School Integration Losing Momentum," *The New York Times*, Mar. 22, 1970.

[126] John Herbers, "President Draws the Line on Integration," *The New York Times*, Mar. 29, 1970.
[127] *The Plain Dealer*, Apr. 12, 1970, p. 1.

administration in 1970, however, were in the same direction. In June, it prevented Mississippi from destroying the Head Start program in that state. HEW and OEO officials eliminated the previous federal rule requiring Head Start to comply with state laws setting certification standards for teachers. A new law in Mississippi, effective July 1, sharply increased educational requirements for Head Start employees, most of whom are black. According to one estimate, 512 of 537 teachers would have lost their jobs. Earlier, Governor Bell had vetoed grants to five of the 28 Head Start operations in the state, but HEW Secretary Finch overrode that veto. Head Start, with a budget of $39,000,000, is the third largest industry in Mississippi, and it is the only important institution in the state controlled by blacks.[128] On July 9 and 10, 1970, after months of negotiations and threats of lawsuits, the Department of Justice sued 52 southern school districts that had refused to eliminate dual school systems. At the same time, an earlier Administration position was reversed when the Internal Revenue Service said that it would hereafter deny tax benefits to private schools that exclude black students. This ruling affected hundreds of "segregation academies" that had been started in the South for 400,000 or more white children from newly desegregated public schools. These schools had relied heavily on the previously held tax advantages.[129]

In the light of various developments in 1970, many observers thought that school integration was entering a critical stage. Extensive desegregation in the towns and rural areas of the Deep South occurred in September, 1970. Desegregation came to hundreds of school districts that had been in the process of integrating or that did so all at once. It was estimated that the number of Negro students in the South in schools with substantial numbers of Whites would increase to 60 percent or more. In the larger cities, the Supreme Court must decide whether integration is complete or partial. In either case, desegregation will be substantial, and additional integration was expected on a voluntary basis in both North and South through the expenditure of $1.5 billion in a special program the President proposed to facilitate desegregation.

On April 20, 1971, the U.S. Supreme Court decided unanimously that the cities of the South must bus children to schools beyond their neighborhoods, if necessary, to comply with the Court's 1954 ruling against segregation by law. The Court added that its decision would not apply to Northern-type segregation based on neighborhood patterns. This decision differed from the Nixon Administration's desegregation policy that desegregation should not override children's rights to attend neighborhood schools, and that the law of school integration should be the same in North and South. (After the decision was announced, the White House press secretary said: "The Supreme Court has acted . . . and it is up to the people to obey that law.") The Court's decision upheld a federal district judge in Charlotte, N.C. who had ordered massive busing in an effort to approximate the same racial ratio in every elementary school in the county. The Supreme Court said that the Constitution did not require these busing programs to eliminate all-black schools or to create the same racial balance in all schools, but that a judge who established such a guideline for a recalcitrant community would be upheld by the Court.[130]

In 1970, the crucial question was what the quality of the integration would be. Senator Walter Mondale of Michigan said that many schools in the South are "desegregated only in the most strained and token way" and that this would continue to be the situation. He and others have cited schools such as those in Kemper, Mississippi where white and black children attend classes in the same building, but Blacks have black teachers in separate all-black classes and even have a

[128] Jack Rosenthal, "U.S. Says It Kept Mississippi From 'Destroying' Head Start," *The New York Times*, June 14, 1970.
[129] Jack Rosenthal, "Schools: Some Gains But Still Large Problems," *The New York Times*, July 12, 1970.

[130] Fred P. Graham, "Supreme Court, 9–0, Backs Busing to Combat South's Dual Schools, Rejecting Administration Stand," *The New York Times*, Apr. 25, 1971, p. E-2; *The New York Times*, Apr. 21, 1971.

segregated school bell. In some schools, white administrators were said to be planning to bar Blacks from a number of school events. The Senate Select Committee on Equal Educational Opportunity was told of a new technique to perpetuate discrimination, "resource transfer." In some Louisiana school districts, desks, sports equipment, microscopes, and school buildings have been declared surplus and transferred to new private schools. Louisiana adopted a program of state financial aid for all private schools. Julian Bond, the Georgia legislator, told the Senate Select committee that because of discriminatory practices in the white schools, the massive desegregation would be "a fraud perpetrated under the guise of paper compliance." Elliot Richardson, the new Secretary of HEW, promised, however, that the government would prosecute any discrimination against black students or teachers in otherwise desegregated schools.[131]

A political development of some importance occurred in Michigan in July, 1970, when the state Legislature enacted a law that (a) overturned a plan to shift 3000 students in the Detroit school system in order to change the school racial composition (the school board plan had changed the feeder pattern into high schools on the city's fringes to move more Negro students into white high schools and shift Whites into racially mixed schools), (b) provides for eight school districts with a 13-member central board of education, but also stipulates that the majority of the central board members will come from the eight local boards, and (c) made the Detroit school system "open," allowing white pupils to transfer from racially mixed schools. The Detroit school board was surprised at the legislative coalition that defeated the Detroit plan—liberal Whites, conservative Whites, and Negro legislators. The Negro legislators traded the integration plan for more community control, the conservative Whites opposed forced integration,

and the liberal Whites, fearful of a racial confrontation, did not fight for integration.[132]

MEXICAN-AMERICAN, PUERTO RICAN, AND AMERICAN INDIAN CHILDREN IN THE PUBLIC SCHOOLS

The education of Mexican-American children has been notable for the low rate of school attendance. There are numerous reasons. The parents of many of them are migratory laborers whose swing through the cotton-growing areas continues until December or January. Half a year's schooling is lost in this way. Although many of these children enroll for the second semester, they are placed, year after year, in the same grades because of the time they have lost. Some areas have crop schools, but these schools have not been successful. The economic need for each grown member of the family to be self-supporting or to help support the family constitutes a strong pressure in many families during the adolescent's last two years in high school. Another reason for the nonattendance of many Mexican-American children is the attitude of the Anglo-American children or teachers. An additional factor is the attitude of parents toward education. Many Mexican-American parents have not regarded education for their children as important. Finally, the compulsory school attendance laws have not always been enforced.

In 1959, the U.S. Commission on Civil Rights found it impossible to evaluate from available sources the extent of segregation of Spanish-American children in New Mexico. It concluded that the patterns of segregation and discrimination "had long been diminishing" and added "one is led to believe that there is now no compulsion in whatever segregation may still exist." The Commission found that Spanish-American pupils had often been segregated in Arizona, but that this practice had been dying out when in 1951 a federal district court held that deficiencies in English language did not "justify the general and continuous segregation in

---

[131] John Herbers, "School Integration Entering Critical Stage," *The New York Times*, June 21, 1970; Jack Rosenthal, "Integration: South Finds New Ways to Say 'Never'," *The New York Times*, July 28, 1970.

[132] Jerry M. Flint, "Shift in Schools in Detroit Beaten," *The New York Times*, July 5, 1970, p. 17.

separate schools of children of Mexican ancestry from the rest of the elementary school population." According to the Commission, the compulsory type of school segregation has been eliminated in New Mexico and Arizona.[133]

There are more than 1,750,000 Spanish-speaking children in the five-state area of Arizona, California, Colorado, New Mexico, and Texas. This is one-sixth of the school enrollment of the area; the great majority of this group is Mexican-Americans.[134] Educational opportunity has been restricted to the extent that Mexican-Americans lag, by three to four years or more, behind the attainments of the country as a whole.[135] A study of average achievement of Mexican-American and Anglo school children in Los Angeles does not answer the important question of language introduction and transition.[136]

One-fourth of the children in the public schools of New York City are Puerto Rican. According to Vazquez, these children have the lowest record of achievement of any group within the New York City public school system. New programs introduced to improve the situation have produced no significant change in performance.

Puerto Rican families live in the oldest housing structures in New York City: 40 percent in deteriorating and dilapidated housing, compared with 33 percent for Nonwhites and 11 percent for Whites. Puerto Rican living space is more crowded than it is for Nonwhites and Whites. Average incomes for white families and for nonwhite families are considerably higher than they are for Puerto Rican families. Comparisons with other groups on education and training are unfavorable, and unemployment rates are more than twice as high as they are for all races combined. The average Puerto Rican child comes from a family that carries heavy burdens, and he is faced with cultural and linguistic differences. In his report on Puerto Rican children in the public schools, Margolis concluded that these children "tend to learn less, lose heart more and drop out sooner."

With the passage of a voter registration law in New York in 1965 recognizing Spanish as the language of some native-born Americans, and the enactment of the Bilingual Education Act in 1968 specifying the right of Puerto Ricans to have their children educated bilingually, Vazquez sees a new trend toward cultural pluralism.[137]

Separate federal schools for Indians were established primarily as a result of the treaties entered into by Indian tribes and the federal government. In the early 1880s the government gave subsidies to schools established by missionaries, and these responsibilities were expanded in accordance with provisions in treaties made up to 1880 and, in some cases, when treaties made no provision for education. Following church-state separation discussions around 1870, the government gradually withdrew its support of mission schools and began to increase the number of federal schools. When citizenship was given to all Indians residing in the country in 1924, education became a state responsibility. Laws enacted by Congress since 1936 have provided financial aid to states and local districts and have increased the public-school enrollment of Indian children.[138] Many public schools that Indian children attend are all-Indian.

In 1960, approximately 60 percent of the 125,000 Indians of school age were in public schools, 27 percent were in federal schools, and 9 percent were in mission schools. The majority of the Indian pupils in public schools have been accepted on a nondiscriminatory basis, although not always without

[133] *Report of the U.S. Commission on Civil Rights,* 1959, p. 280.

[134] A. Clift, "Higher Education of Minority Groups in the United States," *JNE,* Summer, 1969, p. 293.

[135] Ernesto Galarza, Herman Gallegos, and Julian Samora, *Mexican-Americans in the Southwest,* McNally & Loftin, 1969, p. 76.

[136] Leo Grebner, Joan W. Moore, and Ralph C. Guzman, *The Mexican-American People,* Free Press, 1970, p. 171.

[137] Vazquez, *op. cit.,* pp. 247–254.

[138] See E. P. Dozier, George E. Simpson, and J. Milton Yinger, "The Integration of Americans of Indian Descent," *Annals,* May, 1957, p. 163. For an excellent review of past policies on the education of American Indians, see Hildegard Thompson, "Education Among American Indians: Institutional Aspects," *Annals,* May, 1957, pp. 95–105.

special financial inducement by the federal government. Difficulties have arisen in Louisiana, Mississippi, and North Carolina in securing admission of Indian children to public schools on a nondiscriminatory basis, but some Choctaw children in Mississippi and some Cherokee children in North Carolina attend such schools with white students.[139]

In 1968, the Bureau of Indian Affairs spent $96 million of its $241 million budget on the education of Indian children, and "there was little to show for it." Approximately 60 percent of these students attended BIA boarding schools. Since there is only one federal high school in Alaska, two-thirds of the Alaskan Indians are sent to a boarding school in Oregon and 267 attend school in Chilocco, Oklahoma. The Navajo constitute a third of the children for whom the BIA is responsible educationally. Nine-tenths of these children are in boarding schools, and these schools have a 60 percent dropout rate, compared with the national average of 23 percent.[140]

CONCLUSION

It seems to the present writers that the fourth stage of the process of public school desegregation has begun. In the first stage, the least resistant communities were desegregated rather quickly. In the second stage, roughly 1957–1962, resistance to desegregation reached a peak and numerous tactics were devised to prevent or delay desegregation. By 1963–1964 opposition to desegregation had by no means disappeared, but many segregationists were resigned to at least token desegregation. Resistance to *de facto* as well as intentional segregation had increased and demands for faster school desegregation were included in the platforms submitted by various civil rights groups in the demonstrations and campaigns that began in 1961. Those federal courts that continued to regard pupil placement acts as proper desegregation measures appeared to be dissatisfied with their administration.[141] The Supreme Court declared in May, 1963, that it would not countenance indefinite delay in the elimination of racial barriers in the schools, and at the same time former President Lyndon Johnson took strong and forthright stands on the necessity for action by the Executive branch, the Congress, and private organizations against discrimination in employment, housing, and related matters. State governments, as in California, and some local school boards had begun to explore new plans for achieving more desegregation. In the fourth stage, 1969 to the present, it is apparent that desegregation is stymied in northern cities by the massive migration of whites to the suburbs. If the resegregation trend in these states is to be reversed, it will be necessary for central cities and their suburbs to collaborate in one way or another. In the South, school desegregation increased substantially in the fall of 1970, but, in many places, the crucial question was the quality of the integration.

Developments in the school situation are part of the vast changes that have taken place in almost every aspect of American society in the past quarter of a century. Urbanization, political realignments, a shift toward more skilled jobs, and international developments are among the factors in the situation within which school desegregation is proceeding.

[139] *1961 U.S. Commission on Civil Rights Report*, Book 5, "Justice," pp. 156–157. In 1959, the Commission reported that one-third of the Indian Children attending school in Arizona are enrolled in regular public schools. Most of the other two-thirds attended federal schools on Indian reservations, but approximately 2500 were in sectarian mission schools. Of about 35,000 Indian school children in the Gallup Administrative Area of the Bureau of Indian Affairs (New Mexico and part of Arizona; New Mexico has majority of Indians in this area), 11,000 were in public schools. *Report of the U.S. Commission on Civil Rights 1959*, pp. 252–253.

[140] Clift, *op. cit.*, p. 292.

[141] In *Bush v. Orleans Parish School Board*, Aug. 6, 1962, the Court of Appeals for the Fifth Circuit said: "This court . . . condems the Pupil Placement Act when, with a fanfare of trumpets, it is hailed as the instrument for carrying out a desegregation plan while all the time the entire public knows that in fact it is being used to maintain segregation by allowing a little token integration." U.S. Commission on Civil Rights U.S.A., *Public Schools Southern States 1962*, p. 11.

MINORITIES IN HIGHER EDUCATION

*Undergraduate Instruction
for Minority Peoples*

Estimates vary concerning the number of Negro students enrolled in college in the United States. According to a Bureau of the Census report, 434,000 black college students were enrolled in the fall of 1968, an increase of 85 percent over the 234,000 in college in 1964. These students constituted 6 percent of the total college enrollment of 6,801,000 in 1968.[1] Based on a survey of 50,-000 households, the U.S. Census Bureau estimated 492,000 blacks were in college in 1969.[2] In 1966–1967, Negro college students constituted about 15 percent of the Negroes of college age; the figure for the white college age group is 45 percent.[3]

Clift's estimate of 55,000 "other non-white" students in American colleges in the fall of 1969 must include American Indians, Orientals (Japanese, Chinese, Filipino), all other races (Asian Indians, Koreans, Polynesians, Indonesians, Hawaiians, Aleuts, Eskimos, and other races), and it may include some Mexican-Americans (Mexican-Americans and Spanish-Americans are classified as white in the U.S. Census) and some Puerto Ricans (the majority of Puerto Ricans are classified in the Census as white, a minority as Negro). Later statistical data are available in the 1970 Census.[4]

In the 1960s, Negroes lagged behind Whites in moving up to college. In 1960,

among 18- to 19-year-old persons, 35 percent of Negroes and 40 percent of Whites were enrolled in higher education; by 1966, the proportions were 39 percent for Negroes and 48 percent for Whites. In the 20- to 24-year-old group in 1960, 8 percent of Negroes and 10 percent of Whites were enrolled in school, but by 1966, 14 percent of Negroes and 21 percent of Whites were enrolled.[5]

In the mid-1960s, over 100,000, slightly more than half of all American Negro college students, attended the one hundred-plus primarily Negro colleges located mainly in the South. By the fall of 1968, 36 percent of the Negro college students were enrolled in predominantly black colleges.[6] It is esti-

---

[1] U.S. Department of Commerce, Bureau of the Census, *Current Population Reports*, Series P-23, No. 29, "The Social and Economic Status of Negroes in the United States, 1969," p. 53.

[2] *The New York Times*, Oct. 11, 1971, p. 80.

[3] Charles H. Thompson, "The Higher Education of Negro Americans, Prospects and Problems," *JNE*, Summer, 1967, p. 201.

[4] Virgil A. Clift, "Higher Education of Minority Groups in the United States," *JNE*, Summer, 1969, p. 291.

[5] E. H. West, "Progress Toward Equality in Education," *JNE*, Summer, 1968, pp. 213–214.

[6] U.S. Bureau of the Census, *op. cit.*, p. 53. Reported enrollments in the fall of 1968, in 28 predominantly white state universities and land-grant colleges in 17 southern and border states, showed 6004 Negro students (1.76 percent) in a total undergraduate enrollment of 398,249, and 1552 Negro students (1.69 percent) among the total of 91,732 graduate and professional students. In this group of colleges and universities, the University of Virginia had the smallest number of Negro undergraduates (30) and Louisiana State had the largest number (828). The range for the graduate and professional schools was from the University of Delaware and Texas Technological College (five each) to the University of North Carolina (264).

For 1968–1969, reported enrollments in 11 state universities and land-grant colleges in nine eastern states included 3106 Negro students (1.84 percent) in 169,070 undergraduates, and 456 (1.69 percent) black students in the total graduate and professional school enrollment of 32,835. Vermont had the smallest number of Negro undergraduates (seven) and the State University of New York the largest number (1439). In the graduate and professional schools, Maine and Vermont (one each) had the smallest enrollments, and Rutgers, the State University of New Jersey, had the largest (175).

In 1968–1969, reported enrollments in 15 state universities and land-grant colleges in seven midwestern states included 10,418 Negro students (2.98 percent) in a total undergraduate enrollment of 348,978, and 3164 Negro students (2.85 percent) among the total of 110,981 graduate and professional students. The

mated that in 1950, 60 percent of the Negro college students were enrolled in Negro colleges. The decrease in the proportion of all Negro college youth attending predominantly Negro colleges is attributed by West mainly to three factors: the large volume of out-migration from the South, the recent increase in public two-year, integrated colleges in a number of southern states, and the increasing attendance of Negroes in primarily white colleges in the South.[7] Nevertheless, the total number of Negroes attending these colleges has increased in recent years due to increasing population and numbers of high school graduates.[8] By 1975, the number of southern Negro high school graduates is expected to be 700,000 as compared with 300,000 in 1960. Despite differences from state to state and expected increases in the enrollment of Negro students in predominantly white colleges and universities, much of the growth in Negro college enrollments in the next five years or so is likely to be in the primarily Negro colleges in the South.[9]

College enrollment figures for Puerto Ricans are the lowest for any ethnic group in New York City. The 1967 Ethnic Census of the City University of New York showed that 81.8 percent of the university enrollment is "white," 10.2 percent Negro and 2.9 percent Puerto Rican. Of the 1932 Puerto Rican students, 1562 were in the nonmatriculate category.[10] Most Puerto Rican youths attend vocational high schools or take a general course of studies in an academic high school. In 1963, only 331 (1.6 percent) of the academic diplomas granted in New York City went to Puerto Ricans. In 1969, fewer than 2 percent of the Puerto Ricans attending high schools graduated with academic diplomas, and fewer than half of those graduates were expected to go to college.[11]

Clift estimates that approximately 1 percent of the eligible Spanish-speaking Americans of the Southwest are in colleges and universities. High dropout rates and low levels of achievement in the lower grades leave few who are eligible for college admission.[12]

The Predominantly Black Colleges and Universities

With the exception of four institutions, in 1968 all of the approximately 120 institutions of higher learning referred to as "Negro," "predominantly Negro," or "black" were located in the South. As Wilson points out, these institutions range from the small unaccredited junior college to the full-fledged university such as Howard or the "consortium" known as Atlanta University. With the exception of Cheyney State College and Lincoln University in Pennsylvania, all these colleges and universities

---

range for the undergraduate enrollments was from 69 at Iowa State to 1688 at Southern Illinois, and for graduate and professional schools from five for Miami University of Ohio to 1000 at Wayne State.

In the same year, reported enrollments in 26 state universities and land-grant colleges in 16 western states included 4102 Negro students (1.34 percent) in a total undergraduate enrollment of 306,085, and 977 Negro students (1.13 percent) among 86,521 graduate and professional students. For undergraduates, one university (South Dakota State) had no Negro students and the University of California had 1500; in graduate and professional schools, there were no Negro students at Montana State and 500 at the University of California. John Egerton, "Almost All-White," *Southern Education Report*, May, 1969, pp. 2–17.

[7] For an account of desegregation in predominantly white colleges and universities in the decade following the U.S. Supreme Court's decision in the public school cases in 1954, see G. E. Simpson and J. M. Yinger, *Racial and Cultural Minorities*, Harper & Row, 3rd. ed., 1965, pp. 451–453. Special attention is given to the states (Mississippi and Alabama) where the greatest resistance to desegregation at the college level occurred.

[8] A. J. Jaffe, Walter Adams, and Sandra G. Meyers, *Negro Higher Education in the 1960s*, Praeger, 1968, pp. 3–4.

[9] *Ibid.*, p. 123. The Coleman report estimates that in 1965 there were 148 colleges where more than 5 and less than 50 percent of the students were Negroes. The weighted average size of these institutions

was about 10,000 students, but some were quite small. They included institutions in every part of the United States and were evenly divided among public and private colleges and universities. Cited in Christopher Jencks and David Riesman, "The American Negro College," *HER*, Winter, 1967, p. 39.

[10] H. I. Vazquez, "Puerto Rican Americans," *JNE*, Summer, 1969, p. 251.

[11] Clift, *op. cit.*, pp. 294–295.

[12] *Ibid.*, p. 294.

were founded after 1864. For two decades after the Civil War, private colleges were founded by northerners and were church related. During the second period of development, 1885–1916, Negro churches took the lead in establishing these colleges, but some of the southern states began to support college education for Blacks. In 1890, support for the so-called "land-grant" colleges for the Negro came from the passage of the second Morrill Act.[13]

Most of the students who attend the predominantly Negro four-year colleges are of southern origin and come from the state in which their college is located. Relative to all southern Negro youth, they come from high socioeconomic backgrounds, but this is a low-income level in relation to southern white youth. More girls than boys enroll in the primarily Negro colleges. Most of the black students have attended separate primary and secondary schools and stand high in their classes. Their performance on achievement tests, however, is poor relative to that of the generality of students in this country.[14] Not more than 10 or 15 percent of the students at most Negro colleges rank above the national average on verbal or mathematical tests.[15]

Among other findings concerning degree-seeking Negro college students in the United States, the Coleman survey found that— "(1) In every region Negro students are more likely to enter the State college system than the State university system, and further they are a smaller

proportion of the student body of universities than any other category of public institutions of higher education, (2) Negro students are more frequently found in institutions which have a high dropout rate, (3) they attend mainly institutions with low tuition cost, (4) they tend to major in engineering, agriculture, education, social work, social science, and nursing."[16]

According to two Negro educators, one of the major pitfalls in discussing the higher education of Negroes stems from the effort by black colleges to offset the effects of the prior educational experience of a large number of these students. They say that a large proportion of the students applying for admission to these colleges are so handicapped that they cannot respond to remediation and then continue with a sound program of higher education. In their view, in the long run, the correction for this situation lies in compelling the communities from which these students come to provide the quality of lower education they should receive. Colleges cannot completely "remake" individuals harmed by inadequate local school systems. They advocate, however, that there should be some Negro colleges whose primary purpose is to provide higher quality education for students with very high potential. Because of the competition these colleges will have, as more "white" colleges seek to recruit such students, these educators are doubtful whether more than four or five black colleges could concentrate on this highest level type of program. Such concentration would require special funding to provide staff and facilities, and, in their opinion, a college devoted to a program of that quality would have to offer a minimum of remedial work. They question "whether a really high-quality program of higher education can be achieved when any substantial proportion of the entering students have woefully inadequate backgrounds."[17]

Later data are not available, but in 1953–1955, two-thirds of the black students who

---

[13] P. E. Wilson, "Some Aspects of the Education of Black Americans," in Pat Romero (ed.), In Black America, United, 1969, p. 116.

[14] Jaffe, Adams, and Meyers, op. cit., p. 124.

[15] Jencks and Riesman, op. cit., pp. 24–25. For data on student-faculty ratio, percent of faculty with earned doctorate, average faculty salaries, per student expenditure, number of library books per student, library expenditure per student and per faculty member, tuition charges, and other pertinent information concerning higher education by percentage of degree-seeking Negro students attending public and private colleges, and according to region, see James S. Coleman, Ernest Q. Campbell, Carol J. Hobson, James McPartland, Alexander M. Mood, Frederic D. Weinfield, Robert L. York, Equality of Educational Opportunity, U.S. Department of Health, Education, and Welfare, 1966, pp. 23–27, 386–446.

[16] Coleman et al., op. cit., p. 25.

[17] J. Bayton and H. Lewis, "Reflections and Suggestions," JNE, Summer, 1967, p. 288.

ranked in the top tenth of their graduating classes in segregated southern high schools preferred a Negro college. Presumably, the proportion has always been lower in the North, and is lower in the South today.[18] At least one-third of the more able southern black entrants enter substandard colleges, and, in addition, approximately half of the more able students do not enter college at all.[19] Slightly more than half of the students who attend primarily Negro colleges are enrolled in public, four-year institutions, and a little less than half are in private, four-year schools. Today there are very few, if any, primarily Negro public junior colleges.[20] Jaffe, Adams, and Meyers say that the most important single finding in their study of Negro higher education in the 1960s is that the "poor" colleges seem to have had the greatest increases in enrollments in recent years. This finding applies especially to colleges in the "Deep South" where the less selective, less expensive colleges seem to be attracting an increasing proportion of southern black high-school graduates seeking to enter college.[21] An important factor in this trend is the availability now of federal student loan and work-study funds. Many students from low-income homes apply to the less selective schools. Continuation of this trend will depend on future federal policies.[22]

While social and legal barriers will continue to be lowered, the poor primary and secondary schooling of southern black students is not likely to improve markedly in the near future. Consequently, poorly prepared Negro high-school graduates in the South are likely to continue to seek admission to the Negro college. For the country as a whole, the hard fact of the situation is that the black colleges offer the only opportunity that a very large segment of Negro youth has for higher education. Unquestionably, the predominantly black colleges will continue, including those that lack accreditation.[23]

On the basis of personal characteristics of the Negro students examined in a recent study, it has been questioned whether they are able to enter on an equal basis with their white age-mates into the educational or vocational life of the country. The test scores of the southern Negro male subjects indicate qualities associated with lack of achievement motive. Likewise, the scores of the female students reflect the world from which they came, a world in which heavy responsibilities encourage women to be practical and efficient.[24]

In their assessment of Negro colleges in the United States, Jencks and Riesman list Fisk, Morehouse, Spelman, Hampton, Howard, Tuskegee, and Dillard as the leading private institutions, adding that the number of strong public ones such as Texas Southern and Morgan State is quite small. In their view, these institutions fall near the middle of the institutions of higher learning in the United States. They say that these colleges "attract a few brilliant students, employ a few brilliant professors, and run a few very lively programs. . . . their faculties are comparable to those of small and not very distinguished sectarian colleges or fairly typical state colleges. Both intellectually and economically, the students approximate the latter somewhat more closely than the former."[25] The other 50 relatively large public colleges and approximately 60 small private ones are characterized by these authors as "academic disaster areas." Faculty members in these latter colleges are said to be insecure, marginal, and pedantic. Comparing student bodies, they say that Negro colleges are almost never academically se-

[18] Jencks and Riesman, *op. cit.*, p. 47.
[19] Jaffe, Adams, and Meyers, *op. cit.*, p. 133.
[20] *Ibid.*, p. 126.
[21] *Ibid.*, p. 127.
[22] Jaffe, Adams, and Meyers recommend the allocation of "considerable moneys and effort to the problem of the more able southern Negro high-school seniors who currently enter inferior colleges." *Ibid.*, p. 132.

[23] According to Jencks and Riesman, 12 of the 49 private Negro four-year colleges and 17 of the 21 private Negro junior colleges lacked accreditation in 1964. Jencks and Riesman, *op. cit.*, pp. 50–51.
[24] E. McClain, "Personality Characteristics of Negro College Students in the South," *JNE*, Summer, 1967, p. 324.
[25] Jencks and Riesman, *op. cit.*, p. 25.

lective by white standards.[26] At the same time, Jencks and Riesman found pockets of vitality, that is, a few zealous and imaginative faculty members and students when they visited these institutions; the same thing is true, they added, in equivalent white institutions.[27]

Somewhat similar findings are given in a study of Negro colleges and the students they enroll that was undertaken by Jaffee, Adams, and Meyers. Their two main conclusions are: (1) "Most of these colleges are either academically 'poor' or very questionable in quality, and they enroll students who are predominantly ill-prepared for college-level work. The value of an education at these colleges for such students appears slight. In turn, it seems highly unlikely that the college experience would particularly enhance the student's later contribution to his community." And (2) "These conditions will continue to be the case—and probably will hold true for considerably larger numbers of students—in the foreseeable future, unless concerted contravening measures are brought to bear on the problem."[28]

Several presidents of predominantly Negro colleges have responded to such criticisms of their institutions, especially to those of Jencks and Riesman. These replies include Wright's assertion that the article is replete with unsupported generalizations, speculations, and errors; Mays' comment that in 1965 there were 401 predominantly white colleges in the United States whose academic performance was such that no regional accrediting agencies would rate them; and Gloster's prediction that, by steadily raising their academic standards, Negro colleges will be able to compete effectively with other institutions for Negro as well as white students.[29] According to Gloster, if Negro colleges could get adequate

financial support, they could design academic programs that would successfully develop talent among the masses of Negro students.[30]

Black Public Colleges

A recent commentary that the black public colleges are less free, more provincial, and less imaginative than private institutions does not deal sufficiently with the handicaps faced by these colleges.[31] For decades the increased demand by Negroes for college and professional education has been met predominantly through existing institutions. As a result of this practice, "new curriculums have been added to the state institutions whenever an emergency arose. The typical land-grant college is now a mosaic of every kind of curriculum demanded by Negroes; and it has become everything but what its name signifies, for it serves simultaneously as an agricultural and mechanical college, a liberal arts college, and teacher's college, a professional school, a graduate school, or more generally as the Negro state university."[32] According to Reddick, the Negro land-grant college, with a few exceptions, has been a makeshift that enabled the white college to get federal

---

[26] *Ibid.*, pp. 24–25.

[27] *Ibid.*, p. 28.

[28] Jaffe, Adams, and Meyers, *op. cit.*, p. 122.

[29] Stephen J. Wright, *HER*, Summer, 1967, p. 452; Benjamin E. Mays, *ibid.*, p. 456; Hugh M. Gloster, *ibid.*, pp. 459–460. For an excellent series of papers on the black college, see *Daedalus*, Summer, 1971, whole issue.

[30] Although the increase in federal funds for higher education has brought a new source of support for Negro colleges, Henderson points out that these colleges received only 3 percent of the $4 billion that went into higher education in 1969. The most significant support came under Title III of the Higher Education Act of 1965, the "Developing Institutions" provision. Vivian W. Henderson, "Negro Colleges Face the Future," *Daedalus*, Summer, 1971, pp. 637–638. In 1971, the federal government agreed to waive the required matching funds for student loan money for those colleges that enroll 50 percent or more of their students from families whose incomes are below $7500. Nabrit says that if this principle could be extended to include loans for academic facilities and dormitories, it would greatly assist the poorer colleges. He adds: "Almost all of the black colleges would fall into this category." S. M. Nabrit, "Reflections on the Future of Negro Colleges," *ibid.*, p. 675. See Andrew F. Brimmer, "The Economic Outlook and the Future of the Negro College," *ibid.*, p. 570, for a relatively optimistic view of the future of Negro colleges.

[31] Jencks and Reisman, *op. cit.*, pp. 55–58.

[32] G. N. Redd, "Present Status of Negro Higher and Professional Education," *JNE*, 1948, vol. 17, p. 400.

funds. State officials have refused to allocate to Negro institutions a fair share of the funds that come to the states from Washington for experiment stations and research.[33] Although this situation has changed somewhat during the past decade, many of the Negro public colleges have been largely institutions for training teachers. Massive support will be required to keep Negro colleges supported by public funds from remaining far behind other institutions in nearly every respect.[34]

Nine of the southern states have been directed to eliminate their dual systems in higher education, and these states will have to present acceptable plans to achieve this end. On the surface, North Carolina has brought all its colleges into a common system by making each college responsible for higher education in its geographic area. Nabrit points out that "the difficulty arises in that some areas will have only colleges while others will have graduate schools. Another complication arises when a Negro school and a branch of the university exist in the same geographic area."[35] Among the consequences of furthering racially unified systems of higher education will be the dropping of specialized programs such as engineering, agriculture, law, and pharmacy in the black public colleges. The loss of these highly specialized programs may militate against developing leadership in these areas among blacks.[36] Drake sees the future role of publicly supported black colleges as quite different from that of private colleges. The basic task of the former institutions probably will be "training for careers in the public white-collar sector—teachers, state civil servants, agriculturalists, home economists, and personnel for business and industry. Through their interchange arrangements with predominantly white institutions in a unitary system they will have the opportunity to continuously feed students into the state schools of law, medicine, dentistry, library science, and social work where they do not offer such work themselves."[37]

The Faculties of Predominantly Black Colleges

Predominantly Negro colleges continue to have serious staffing problems. Most predominantly black colleges are in small towns or rural areas where the setting is quite different in nature and either actively or potentially hostile. Typically there is limited access to the meager resources of the community for intellectual or leisure-time activities. The tendency to confine activity to the campus has created morale problems that affect human relations in the college community as well as in the educational process. Earlier studies showed that learning and working in the separate college often came to be regarded as a tour of duty during which one looks forward to the periodic "return to civilization" in a metropolitan center. Newer teachers felt the greatest pressure because their high expectations of recognition and congenial association could rarely be satisfied in the isolated Negro college. Faculty-administration clashes have been common. The lack of productivity and of enthusiasm in teaching have been widespread and have been rationalized as the individual made an uneasy peace with a "tough" situation.[38] Twenty

[33] L. D. Reddick, "Critical Review: The Politics of Desegregation," *JNE*, Summer, 1962, p. 417.

[34] Hurley H. Doddy, "The Status of the Negro Public College: A Statistical Summary," *JNE*, Summer, 1962, p. 379.

[35] Nabrit, *op. cit.*, p. 668.

[36] *Ibid.*, p. 670.

[37] St. Clair Drake, "The Black University in the American Social Order," *Daedalus*, Summer, 1971, p. 891.

[38] Hylan Lewis, " 'Tough' Aspects of Higher Education," *Phylon*, 1949, pp. 359–361. In a recent study, Tobe Johnson found that the internal system of most black schools produces a discrepancy between the activities black faculty would like to engage in and the survival needs of the colleges. The desire to teach in one's area of specialization is offset by the schools' need for faculty members to offer instruction across their subject fields and sometimes outside that field, and, in some cases, to provide remedial teaching. The desire to do research, to write, and to engage in other scholarly pursuits tends to be countered by heavy teaching loads. Funds to attend professional meetings are not always available. Tobe Johnson, "The Black College as System," *Daedalus*, Summer, 1971, p. 809–810.

years ago Myers was impressed with the lack of confidence in the students on the part of the faculty, the harsh and repressive regulations, and the absence of cordial faculty-students relationships. This observer added that these comments did not apply to all Negro colleges, and he pointed out that the same things are found—although in his opinion in less pronounced form—in white colleges.[39]

Franklin Frazier's critical evaluation in the mid-1950s held that many Negro teachers refused to identify with the black masses and regarded teaching mainly as a source of income. Frazier said: "In many cases they have nothing but contempt for their Negro pupils. Moreover, they have no real interest in education and genuine culture and spend their leisure in frivolities and in activities designed to win a place in Negro 'society.' " He said also that that generation of black college students thought of education mainly in terms of the money it would enable them to earn as professional and business men.[40]

Of the "elite" black colleges listed by Jencks and Riesman (Atlanta, Clark, Morehouse, Morris Brown, Spelman, Dillard, Fisk, Hampton, Howard, and Tuskegee), only Tuskegee is not located in a relatively large city. According to Jencks and Riesman:

These colleges generally offer prospective faculty more academic freedom, higher salaries, and better schools for their children than do most of their Negro rivals. They are not . . . all intellectually exciting or innovative . . . when young Negro Ph.D.s from leading universities decide which of many tempting offers to accept, the only Negro colleges they are likely to consider seriously on a long term basis are the wealthy private ones. Similarly, although some young white faculty members will, for idealistic reasons, want to spend a term at impoverished commuter colleges, like Miles, or try their wings at Tougaloo or Virginia Union, more will be attracted, at least if they have school-age children, into the Fisk or Morehouse league.[41]

These authors question whether certain types of white faculty will be assets in the years ahead. Their point is that idealistic persons often become disillusioned when they discover that Negro students "have no higher motives and fewer academic interests or aptitudes than the whites they rejected."[42] Kuritz reports that in these colleges such faculty members find "a cloistered atmosphere, a coolness and a diffidence, and aloofness which confuses and confounds them."[43]

One of the problems besetting administrators in predominantly Negro colleges is the struggle to retain black scholars. The recruiting effort is mainly northern-based, "selective in nature and lethal in effect." Stephen J. Wright, former president of Bluefield State College and of Fisk University and now president of the United Negro College Fund, which represents 36 private institutions, all of them accredited, says: "The thing that makes it serious is that in order to maintain accreditation you have to have a certain percentage of persons on your staff who have a doctorate degree. If you go below, say, 25 per cent, you're in trouble." None of the UCF colleges can afford to match the salaries being offered by predominantly white institutions. In 1969, Martin Jenkins, president of Morgan State, claimed that "every one of our Negro scholars" has received offers from white institutions. Benjamin Quarles, professor of history at Morgan State, said: "If a young

---

[39] Alonzo F. Myers, "The Colleges for Negroes," *The Survey*, May, 1950, pp. 234–236.

[40] E. Franklin Frazier, *Black Bourgeoisie*, Free Press, 1957, pp. 235–236.

[41] Jencks and Riesman, *op. cit.*, p. 45. Tobe Johnson says that the quality of nonblack teachers varies among the different black schools. "On many campuses, these teachers are all too often political refugees who neither understand the culture nor speak the language intelligently; retired professors whose energy level does not always measure up to their awesome responsibilities and wives of professors who are comfortably employed at neighboring white schools. On the other hand, some of the nationally better-known black schools, like Morehouse College . . . have been quite fortunate in the quality of white teachers they have attracted in recent years." Tobe Johnson, *op. cit.*, p. 806.

[42] Jencks and Riesman, *op. cit.*, pp. 45–46.

[43] Hyman Kuritz, "Integration on Negro College Campuses," *Phylon*, 1967, pp. 125–126.

man has nothing published at all and he's a Ph.D., normally he becomes an instructor. But we know of young men who haven't published a line and they have been offered professorships at one or two of the very best colleges. They make exceptions because the pressure is on from both students and alumni to produce black teachers."[44]

Another factor that complicates the up-grading of Negro colleges is the trend in the nation's predominantly white colleges, especially the high-prestige colleges, to at-tract the best prepared of black youth by offering strong scholarship support.

The dimensions of the financial side of the problems of providing higher education for black Americans are well summarized by P. E. Wilson. Despite increased attention to the situation, the total for the estimated annual budgets of 120 Negro colleges seeking to educate half of the 300,000 black students is $150,000,000. This means that approximately $1000 was available for feeding, housing, entertaining, and edu-cating each student on the black campuses. Estimates of the sources of income for the black private colleges were: 50 percent from student tuition; 25 percent from en-dowment earnings, earnings of auxiliary enterprises, and federal grants; and 25 per-cent from private gifts and grants, mainly from churches.[45]

Integration in Predominantly Black Colleges

On the question of integration in Negro col-leges other than the dozen top private in-stitutions, Jencks and Riesman say the chances are slight. In their view, the 60 "obscure" private colleges "typically have no endowment whatsoever, no alumni ca-pable of supporting them at more than a token level, little time or imagination to develop programs that would get federal or foundation support, few contacts with the men who distribute such funds, and no

obvious appeal to white philanthropy, fac-ulty, or students." Most of these schools enroll fewer than 500 students, and, ac-cording to these authors, operate with a small faculty, including badly exploited faculty wives, on a budget of half a million dollars. Jencks and Riesman refer also to the strong personal control exercised in many of these colleges by their presidents and to the difficulty of recruiting competent faculty.[46]

Only three public Negro colleges, all lo-cated in border states, have attracted sub-stantial numbers of white students. Most of the Whites coming to Lincoln University in Jefferson City, Missouri, Bluefield College in West Virginia, and West Virginia State College, are commuters who have no convenient alternative. (See table, page 590.)

In the 33 predominantly black private colleges in the South and the border states that were members of the United Negro College Fund in 1966, the average white en-rollment was about 1 percent. Jencks and Riesman expect that only a few of the col-leges founded for Negroes will attract sub-stantial white enrollments in the foresee-able future, adding that this in itself need not be disastrous.[47]

---

[44] Richard M. Cohen, "Black Colleges Face Brain Drain," *The Washington Post*, Mar. 23, 1969, p. F1.

[45] P. E. Wilson, "Some Aspects of the Education of Black Americans," in Romero (ed.), *op. cit.*, p. 95.

[46] Jencks and Riesman, *op. cit.*, pp. 48–49.

[47] *Ibid.*, p. 44. Looking ahead, these authors pre-dict that the southern situation will approximate that in Pennsylvania and Ohio. In these relatively industrialized states, Negroes have had the vote for some time and both have had a public Negro college for many years. There has been no strong demand to close these colleges, and neither has attracted many white students. Neither college is known for academic distinction, yet 40 to 50 percent of the Ohio Blacks who go to college choose Central State, and 25 to 30 percent of the Pennsylvania Negroes who go to college attend Cheyney State. *Ibid.*, p. 58. In 1969 the director of the Federal Department of HEW's Office for Civil Rights pressed Pennsylvania, under threat of losing millions of dollars in federal aid, to end a pattern of enrolling most white stu-dents at 13 of the colleges in the system and most Negroes at the fourteenth. Other states with state college systems maintaining racially identifiable schools that were queried about desegregation plans in 1969 included Arkansas, Louisiana, Mississippi, and Maryland, and the federal agency planned to ask other southern and border states to submit de-segregation plans. *The New York Times*, Aug. 25, 1969.

Reported Enrollments, Fall 1968, in 17 Originally All-Negro State Universities and Land-Grant Colleges in 16 Southern and Border States

Name of Institution	Full-time Undergraduate Students		All Graduate and Professional School Students	
	Total	Nonblack	Total	Nonblack
(11 Southern States)				
Alabama A&M College	1,930	6	146	30
Arkansas AM&N College	3,445	13	0	0
Florida A&M University	3,367	7	615	8
Fort Valley (Ga.) State College	1,963	1	139	0
Southern (La.) University	6,814	5	670	6
Alcorn (Miss.) A&M College	2,322	4	0	0
North Carolina A&T College	3,390	2	190	6
South Carolina State College	1,602	0	336	22
Tennessee A&I State University	4,372	6	164	0
Prairie View (Tex.) A&M College	3,576	30	482	29
Texas Southern University	3,330	12	470	30
Virginia State College	2,104	50	314	75
Totals	38,215	136 (0.3%)	3,526	206 (5.8%)
(5 Border States)				
Delaware State College	906	206	0	0
Kentucky State College	1,610	559	0	0
Maryland State College	717	83	0	0
Lincoln (Mo.) University	2,019	968	50	30
Langston (Okla.) University	1,336	41	0	0
Totals	6,588	1,857 (28.2%)	50	30 (60.0%)
Grand Totals, Southern and Border States	44,803	1,993 (4.4%)	3,576	236 (6.6%)

Source: Southern Education Report, May, 1969, p. 7.

Proposals Concerning the Predominantly Black Colleges

Views concerning the future of the predominantly black colleges, as well as proposals for strengthening them, differ widely. McGrath recommends that most existing institutions be maintained and strengthened. He contends that none of these colleges should be allowed to die until their present and prospective students can be assured of better educational opportunities elsewhere. According to McGrath, the most pressing curricular need is the strengthening of the liberal arts fields that prepare students for advanced training in related graduate departments or in professional schools such as law, medicine, dentistry, or social work. The most serious deficiencies are found in the sciences, but inadequacies exist in other subjects.[48] Some observers think that there should be no

[48] Earl J. McGrath, *The Predominantly Negro Colleges and Universities in Transition*, Columbia, 1965, pp. 159–160, 164.

escalation of funds or efforts expended on improving the "poor" or most of the "fair" black colleges because they doubt that these schools can be improved at a reasonable cost in a reasonable time.[49]

Bayton and Lewis question whether the black school's immediate task of combatting inadequate secondary preparation requires as many special programs as have been sponsored recently by foundation and government grants. In their opinion, the real key to the educational problems of predominantly Negro colleges and universities is money; money in amounts at the disposal of the "great" colleges and universities. Such funds, they say, are needed to provide freshmen "tutorials," small classes, fewer lecture courses, and other instructional changes.[50]

The federal government offers three programs of financial aid to disadvantaged students: College Work Study, National Defense Student Loans, and Educational Opportunity Grants. In 1968–1969, the total appropriations for these programs amounted to $473.9 million, and the estimated number of students benefited was 710,000. Often the individual student grants or loans are too small to meet the disadvantaged student's need, and recently the number of students to be served by these federal programs has been reduced by a cut in EOG funding.[51]

Criticism by the National Association for Equal Opportunity in Higher Education of the Nixon administration's alleged insensitivity to Negro education resulted in an increase of 30 percent in federal aid to predominantly black colleges in October 1970. The new commitment increased aid from HEW from $95 million a year to $125 million. These funds are used for construction loans, work-study programs, and for strengthening teaching, administrative, and student-service programs.[52] Later, a report of the Carnegie Commission on Higher Education said that financial pressures threaten the future of black colleges, and recommended that federal aid be tripled to $360 million.[53]

White land-grant colleges in Alabama, Louisiana, Florida, and Tennessee had six times as many students as their black counterparts in 1970–1971, but they received 140 times as much money in federal grants. Public Negro colleges in several southern states have found it almost impossible to expand or to integrate as federal funds are now allocated among black and predominantly white institutions. Also opponents of the dual system of higher education have failed in court actions to stop the building of predominantly white campuses in Nashville and Montgomery. Other black public colleges that face major competition from new or expanding white colleges include Alabama A. and M. (and the University of Alabama-Huntsville), Alabama State (and Auburn University), Florida A. and M. (and Florida State University), and Southern University (and Louisiana State University in New Orleans, Baton Rouge, and Shreveport).[54]

In 1970, the Ford Foundation's funding of university study programs, mostly for undergraduates, in black studies was discontinued. The Foundation had made seven grants totalling $883,533 during 1968–1969 for these programs, as well as $796,800 in grants to a number of organizations and institutions for activities related to black studies: preparation of materials, library acquisitions and cataloguing, and summer faculty institutes. During 1969–1970, university study grants were increased to $1,046,350 and an additional $475,400 was awarded in supportive service grants. According to Foundation officials, the grants were designed to get black studies programs under way and were given only to those institutions that agreed to support the new programs at the same or higher levels after the Ford funds had been spent.[55]

[49] Jaffe, Adams, and Meyers, *op. cit.*, p. 129.
[50] Bayton and Lewis, *op. cit.*, p. 291.
[51] H. A. Glickstein, "Federal Educational Programs for Minority Groups," *JNE*, Summer, 1969, pp. 303–314.
[52] *The Plain Dealer*, Oct. 2, 1970, p. 3B.

[53] *Ibid.*, Feb. 18, 1971, p. 5C.
[54] *The New York Times*, Apr. 18, 1971, p. 54.
[55] *Race Relations Reporter*, Apr. 6, 1971, p. 8.

It has been suggested that one or two of the 70 private Negro colleges might establish a distinctively black curriculum. Such a program would go further than do the black studies courses now offered at many institutions. Jencks and Riesman say that present courses in black history, African history, or the legal problems of integration do not give these subjects the importance and legitimacy that Catholic colleges give to "Catholic" subjects. Such curricula would provide options and experimentation for students with a strong interest in black culture. The argument for this type of education is that a substantial number of young Negroes cannot be reached in any other way. These students "are often violently anti-white, and they are not likely to become less so in the foreseeable future. They tend to shun both public Negro colleges which are overtly repressive and responsive to white legislators, and private Negro colleges which accept white standards of excellence and concentrate their energy on getting students into white graduate schools. Seeing no other academic opportunities, they often reject education entirely, as another white conspiracy . . ."[56] Thus far no black college has gone very far in the direction of providing a curriculum that is almost entirely black-oriented.[57]

Another possible development for some black colleges would be for them to become thoroughgoing community colleges, providing services not just for the young Negro high-school graduate, but for local Blacks of all ages and with many kinds of nonacademic needs. Private Negro colleges might play an important role in channeling outside money and ideas into the local community and in organizing local black efforts at self help. It is not likely,

however, that many black educators would favor this proposal.[58]

In view of the wide variety of needs and in the absence of solid information on the consequences of education in predominantly black universities and colleges, we think a range of institutions is called for through the next several years.

The Federal City College

The new Federal City College is publicly supported and predominantly black, but it has unique aspects to justify giving it special attention. Washington, D.C.'s population is nearly 70 percent black, but FCC's student body is more than 90 percent black and its staff is about 50 percent black. The college has an open-door policy. In 1968–1969, students were chosen by lottery; in 1969–1970, those who applied first were accepted first. For 1968–1969, there were 6000 applications for 1300 available places, but the college expanded to 2000 students. By 1975, enrollment is expected to reach 20,000, and services will be extended to an additional 80,000 through extension and other "outreach" programs. Whether FCC's open door has attracted a true cross-section of D.C. residents, and particularly whether it has enrolled students from the bottom rung of society, are unsettled questions. Officials have been surprised by the low demand for financial aid. This may reflect a lack of poverty-level students, or it may reflect the working status of most FCC students.

FCC's tuition of $75 a year is among the lowest at four-year colleges in the nation. The location of the school, together with many night classes, facilitates work-study schedules, and the college helps students to obtain jobs, loans, and grants. It is developing child-care facilities for students with young children.

Between 15 and 20 percent of the college's first class did not return for the second quarter. More than half of the "dropouts" said they hoped to return to FCC within a year, and after two months about 10 per-

---

[56] Jencks and Riesman, *op. cit.*, p. 54.

[57] Eric Lincoln has suggested that the private Negro colleges be transformed into black national universities, with certain of these schools emphasizing research on such major interests as Third World studies, black slavery and its consequences, regional history, the art and culture of African and Afro-American peoples, and so forth. Eric Lincoln, "The Negro Colleges and Cultural Change," *Daedalus*, Summer, 1971, pp. 625–626.

[58] *Ibid.*, pp. 52–53.

cent had applied to, or were attending, other colleges. A Skills Center provides help in reading, writing, and other study skills, and other special facilities offer tutoring and both credit and noncredit courses, without the "remedial orientation" often associated with such programs.

Students are career-oriented and identity-oriented. One administrator compares them with second-generation immigrant groups and says that they "are not here for a liberal education, but for a passport to a better job." In addition, many students say they want training that will enable them to help others in the black community later. A four-year black studies course has been developed; its goal is to produce skilled technicians who will use their skills to meet the needs of the local and the world-wide black communities. Several hundred students have enrolled in the program, and hundreds of others have expressed an interest in taking black studies electives.

Efforts to introduce "participatory decision-making" involving faculty, students, and administrators have met with mixed results. Among FCC's problems, perhaps the most prominent is race, that is, "working out harmonious, trusting relations among faculty, staff members and students." Faculty chairman Joseph Brent, who is white, says: "While there is no racist problem, there is a deep element of cultural shock. Whites generally are profoundly unaware of the existence of a different and often unsettling culture among Blacks. On the other hand, it is often difficult for Blacks to work in a situation which approaches racial equality because they have been so deeply indoctrinated by a society which requires their servile behavior. In such a situation, any thoughtful person would expect a time of confusion and mistaken judgments."[59]

Alternatives to Education in Predominantly Negro Colleges

In addition to steadily increasing opportunities to enter predominantly white colleges or universities of the traditional type as an alternative to enrolling in a black college, many black students may find public junior colleges and public community colleges attractive. Public junior colleges are of especial interest to socioeconomically less fortunate and academically less well-prepared students, including many of the students who now enter the poorer Negro colleges. Such colleges are integrated and have the advantage of being more cosmopolitan than the less well-established black schools. Jaffe, Adams, and Meyers advocate that the moneys and efforts available for improving the "poor" or the great majority of the "fair" black colleges be used instead to expand rapidly a network of integrated public two-year colleges throughout the South. They contend that attendance at integrated colleges, where the resources are greater, offers more to students than attendance at small segregated institutions "with a long history of academic deficiencies."[60]

Advocates of the large, pluralistic public four-year community college point out that it does not suffer under the stigma of segregation, yet it does not make the psychological demands of an integrated residential college. It offers the promise

that Negroes with its B.A. will be able to leave the ghetto and enter the white world if he wants, but it does not demand that he make the break today. A Negro can come to such a college, attend classes, take his exams, collect his grades, credits, and diplomas and go home every night to his family and friends around the corner. A commuter college of this kind may be less demanding socially, despite the fact that it is predominantly white, than a residential Negro college would be. The commuter college does not ask its Negro students to acquire the habits and values of the old Negro middle class, much less of white society."[61]

[59] Laura G. Horowitz, "A New College With a City View," *Southern Education Report*, May 1969, pp. 18–23.

[60] Jaffe, Adams, and Meyers, *op. cit.*, pp. 129–132. For an account of the unconventional program promulgated at Malcolm X College (formerly called Crane Junior College) by President Charles G. Hurst, Jr., see *Time*, Aug. 16, 1971, pp. 50–51. Malcolm X is one of seven two-year community colleges maintained by the city of Chicago. Its student body is predominantly black.

[61] Jencks and Riesman, *op. cit.*, p. 41. The "open door" policy in the City University of New York City is discussed later in this chapter.

Some educators predict that the number of expense-free or inexpensive commuter colleges having extremely liberal admissions policies will increase significantly in the South during the 1970s and that increasing numbers of Negro students will enroll in them.[62]

Court Decisions Affecting Negro Higher Education Before 1954

Although the beginning of desegregation of American education is most decisively marked by the 1954 U.S. Supreme Court decision, there had been significant steps taken, particularly in higher education, through nearly two decades previous to that. A first step was taken in the Donald Murray case of 1936. Murray, an Amherst College graduate, was refused admission to the law school of the University of Maryland because he was a Negro. He applied to the court for a writ of mandamus to force the Board of Regents to admit him to the law school on the ground that exclusion on the basis of race was unconstitutional. The court issued a writ ordering the university to admit Murray. The Regents appealed to the court of appeals, which held that the state must provide equal educational facilities if it separated the races, and said that a scholarship to another state would not only mean additional expense for Murray but would deprive him of the opportunity of specializing in Maryland law.[63]

A landmark in the history of Negro education in the United States is the case of Lloyd L. Gaines v. University of Missouri. Gaines, who had an A.B. degree from Lincoln University, contended that he was denied admission to the law school of the University of Missouri solely because he was a Negro. The University of Missouri said that the admission of a Negro would be contrary to the constitution, laws, and public policy of the state. The university stated that the Missouri legislature had pro-

vided that Lincoln University, until it developed a law school for Negroes, should pay the tuition at the university of any adjacent state for Missouri Negroes wishing to study law. Gaines sought a writ of mandamus to compel the curators of the University of Missouri to admit him. The circuit court denied his petition and was upheld by the state supreme court. In 1938, the case was then taken to the Supreme Court of the United States on a writ of *certiorari*, which denied the university the right to exclude Gaines, saying that what would otherwise be an unconstitutional discrimination within the state could not be justified by providing opportunities elsewhere through scholarship aid. "The Court held further that, although the curators of Lincoln University had a discretionary obligation to reorganize that institution so that it would afford Negroes of the state an opportunity for training equal in standards to that of the University of Missouri, such an obligation was not sufficiently mandatory to relieve the state of the charges of illegal discrimination in the opportunities provided for the legal education of Negroes."[64]

From 1938 to 1954, in addition to offering out-of-state scholarships to Negroes who would accept them in spite of the ruling in the Gaines case, some of the southern states used other expedients in trying to comply with the Supreme Court's decision. Graduate work was added in existing Negro state colleges, separate professional and graduate schools for Negroes were established, and white state university faculty members were used on a part-time basis.[65]

Ranking in importance with the Gaines case are the Hemon Sweatt and the G. W. McLaurin cases ruled on by the U.S. Supreme Court on June 5, 1950. Mr. Sweatt began action on May 15, 1946, after being denied admission to the University of Texas Law School. The District Court of Travis County, Texas, granted the writ of mandamus against the Board of Regents. Issuance of the writ was stayed for six months to

---

[62] Jaffe, Adams, and Meyers, *op. cit.*, p. 124.

[63] Charles S. Johnson, *Patterns of Negro Segregation*, Harper & Row, 1943, p. 182.

[64] *Ibid.*, pp. 181–182.

[65] *Ibid.*, p. 19.

enable Texas to establish a "separate law school for Negroes substantially equal to the one at the University of Texas." When no other law school of any kind had been established six months later, another petition for mandamus was filed. A "law school" was then set up in the basement of a building in Houston, but Sweatt refused to enroll in it. The petition for mandamus was dismissed and an appeal was taken to the Texas Court of Civic Appeals. The lower court was ordered on March 5, 1947, to rehear the case. The case was reheard and was then reargued in the Court of Civil Appeals early in 1948. The higher court again affirmed the trial court's refusal to order the Regents to admit Sweatt to the law school. In the June 5, 1950, unanimous decision of the U.S. Supreme Court, Chief Justice Vinson said that the court could not agree with Texas that the 54-year-old precedent of "separate but equal" facilities for Negroes did not violate the equal protection clause of the Fourteenth Amendment and should, therefore, be affirmed.[66] He noted the reluctance of the Supreme Court to deal with constitutional issues except "in the particular case before it" and added that the Court did not "need" to rule on Mr. Sweatt's contention that the old ruling should be reexamined and abandoned. Mr. Vinson compared the faculties and the libraries of the school at Austin and the new Houston school. The law faculty at Austin had nineteen members and a library of 65,000 volumes. The plans for the Houston school

called for no independent faculty or library. The teaching was to be carried on by four professors from the University of Texas Law School, and few of the 10,000 volumes scheduled for Houston had actually arrived. He pointed out too that since the trial of this case had begun, a law school had been added at the Texas State University for Negroes and is "apparently on the road to accreditation" with five teachers and a library of 16,500 books. The Chief Justice wrote, "Whether the University of Texas Law School is compared with the original or the new law school for Negroes, we cannot find substantial equality in the educational opportunities offered white and Negro law students in the state." He said further that the University of Texas Law School "possesses to a far greater degree those qualities which are incapable of objective measurement but which make for greatness in a law school." Included here are "reputation of the faculty, experience of the administration, position and influence of the alumni, standing in the community, tradition and prestige." To these remarks a new point in cases of this type was added: the fact that the Negro law school "excludes" 85 percent of the population of Texas, and most of the lawyers, witnesses, jurors, judges, and others with whom Mr. Sweatt would deal when he became a member of the Texas bar. "With such a substantial and significant segment of society excluded," the decision said, "we cannot conclude that the education offered is substantially equal to that which he would receive if admitted to the University of Texas Law School." In his final conclusion Mr. Vinson held that legal education equivalent to that offered by the state to students of other races was not available to Mr. Sweatt in a separate law school as offered by the state, and that the equal-protection clause of the Fourteenth Amendment required that he be admitted to the University of Texas Law School.[67]

G. W. McLaurin, a retired Negro teacher

[66] The "separate but equal" dictum has a long and interesting Supreme Court history.

"In 1868 a Negro woman, Catherine Brown, tried to board a 'white' railroad car from Alexandria, Va., to Washington. When she was ejected, she brought suit. The Supreme Court ruled in 1873 that separate accommodations, even if identical, were not equal under the Constitution, and that the railroad had violated the law. However, in 1896 the court took a different view of segregation in Plessy versus Ferguson. The issue was whether a Louisiana provision for separate railroad accommodations denied equal protection. The court held that the segregation did not stamp Negroes 'with a badge of inferiority' and that segregation was justified under the 'separate but equal' ruling."

Benjamin Fine, "Education in Review," *The New York Times*, Apr. 9, 1950.

[67] Lewis Wood, "Supreme Court Rulings Bar Segregation in Two Colleges," *The New York Times*, June 6, 1950, pp. 1, 18.

in his early fifties and holder of a master's degree, applied for admission to the University of Oklahoma in 1948 to seek the degree of Doctor of Education. Originally he was denied admission because of race, but the Oklahoma legislature amended the state laws to allow admission on a segregated basis. This decision, also unanimous and written by Chief Justice Vinson, said that Mr. McLaurin was required first to sit in an anteroom to a classroom, at a special desk on the mezzanine floor of the library, and to eat at a different time from other students in the cafeteria. Later the arrangements were modified, and he was seated in a place railed off, and with a sign "Reserved for colored." After other changes he was, at the time of the trial, assigned to a classroom set apart for Negroes, assigned to a table on the main library floor, and allowed to use the cafeteria at the same time as other students, though at a designated table. Mr. Vinson held that such restrictions "set McLaurin apart" from other students and handicapped him in pursuing his graduate instruction effectively. "Such restrictions impair and inhibit his ability to study, to engage in discussions and exchange views with other students, and in general, to learn his profession." The ruling went on to say that it could be argued that Mr. McLaurin, even with restrictions removed, might still be set apart by his fellow students. This argument is irrelevant, according to the Court, because of the vast difference—a constitutional difference—between restrictions imposed by the state that prohibit the commingling of students and the refusal of individuals to associate where the state raises no such bar. Finally, the opinion said, the restrictions deprive Mr. McLaurin of his right to equal protection of the laws. "We hold under these circumstances, the Fourteenth Amendment precludes differences in treatment by the state based upon race. [He] having been admitted to a state supported Graduate School, must receive the same treatment at the hands of the state as students of other races."[68]

[68] *Ibid.*, p. 18.

Graduate and Professional Training for Negroes

The President's Commission on Higher Education reported that in 1940 no Ph.D.s were given by Negro colleges. By 1958 only two institutions of higher learning for Negroes, Howard University and North Carolina College at Durham, offered work leading to the Ph.D., and the doctoral program at the latter college was limited to the field of education. Only a very small percentage of the degrees awarded by Negro colleges are master's.

Before 1937 only five Negro institutions in the country offered instruction on the graduate level. After the U.S. Supreme Court declared, in the Gaines case in 1938, that a state must offer equal educational opportunities to Negroes, several southern states forced poorly equipped public Negro colleges to establish graduate work.[69] Ten years later, however, there were seven southern states where no graduate instruction whatever was offered in Negro institutions —Arkansas, Delaware, Kentucky, Maryland, Mississippi, Oklahoma, and Louisiana. A variety of professional and graduate work was available to white citizens in all of the southern states, and the opportunities for such work were provided for more than two-thirds of the students in these fields through public funds. Master's work could be taken by Whites in each of the 17 southern states, and there was at least one graduate school in each of 13 states that offered work leading to the doctorate. In professional training the southern states in 1948 provided, for Whites: 15 medical schools, 16 law schools, 17 schools of engineering, 14 schools of pharmacy, 11 schools of library science, 4 schools of dentistry, and 9 schools of social work.[70]

Much of the graduate work established after the Gaines case consisted of makeshift courses. The rapid development of much of this instruction was accompanied by low salaries, heavy teaching loads, a shortage

[69] Myrdal, *op. cit.*, p. 951.
[70] Redd, *op. cit.*, pp. 404, 407; C. H. Thompson, "Negro Higher and Professional Education in the United States," *JNE*, 1948, vol. 17, pp. 222–223.

of qualified instructors, a lack of funds and facilities for research, and a certain amount of cynicism due to frustration and professional isolation.[71] In 1960, the Dean of the School of Education at Howard University said that the programs of most of the schools and colleges of that university (probably the strongest Negro university in the United States) are ". . . only a little more than at a minimum point of adequacy, if we think of them in terms of a first-class university. Many more resources (intellectual, financial and personnel) will have to be put into these programs to raise them to a level necessary to achieve their goals."[72]

With the exception of training for the teaching profession, most professional education for Negroes in the South was carried on, prior to 1950, in private institutions. Education in law was provided at Howard University, in medicine and dentistry at Howard and Meharry, in pharmacy at Howard and Xavier, in social work at Howard and Atlanta, in theology at Johnson C. Smith and Atlanta, in nursing at Meharry, and in library science at Atlanta. During the first decade after the Gaines decision state law schools were established in Missouri, North Carolina, South Carolina, Texas, Oklahoma, and Louisiana.[73] In these years one school of journalism and one school of library science for Negroes were opened. By 1958, Howard University was training 42 percent of the students enrolled in professional work in the Negro institutions of higher education. Howard, Meharry Medical College, and Tuskegee Institute accounted for more than 70 percent of the professional training.

Predominantly Negro colleges and universities have continued to be mainly undergraduate schools, and graduate enrollment is not large at the 24 institutions which offer graduate work. In 1964, 18 of these schools enrolled a total of 1100 graduate students, and only two had more than 50 graduate

students (Howard, 523, and Atlanta, 273). At that time, between 40 and 50 graduate students attended Fisk, Alabama State, and Tennessee A. and I. State University. During that year, 12 institutions awarded 408 master's degrees: South Carolina State, 83; Howard, 71; Fisk, 38; Prairie View and Florida A. and M., 39 each; Virginia State and Tuskegee, 34 each; Texas Southern, 31; and Hampton, 30. Seven doctoral degrees were given that year, five in the physical sciences and one in education.[74]

Until recently, educational opportunities for Negroes have been greatly restricted in medicine. At the end of World War II, 20 of the nation's 77 medical schools were located in the South and did not admit Negroes. Only one-third of the 55 presumably nonsegregated schools actually admitted Negro students. In 1938 only 372 Negroes were enrolled in all medical schools; 40 of these in 17 of the 55 nonsegregated schools. In 1946, 507 of the 592 Negro medical students were enrolled in Meharry Medical College and Howard University; 85 were enrolled in 20 nonsegregated schools. The two Negro medical schools can train only a fraction of those who desire and are qualified for careers in medicine. The freshman class at Howard University Medical School was limited to 60 students in prewar years. By overtaxing its facilities the number was increased in 1947 to 75. At that time the principal limiting factor in the training of Negro physicians was the barring of Negro students from clinical facilities, even in tax-supported hospitals. Internship, an essential part of medical training, was another discriminatory area. With very few exceptions, Negro students

[71] L. H. Evans, "The Magnificent Purpose," *Phylon*, Fourth Quarter, 1949, pp. 319–320.

[72] Charles H. Thompson, "Editorial Comment," *JNE*, Summer, 1960, pp. 410–411.

[73] *Ibid.*, p. 407.

[74] Preston Valien, "Improving Programs in Graduate Education for Negroes," *JNE*, Summer, 1967, pp. 242–245. In July, 1971, the Ford Foundation announced grants of $1,750,000 each to Howard University and Atlanta University "to sustain their efforts to become graduate centers of excellence in the social sciences." At Howard, the new funds will be used to improve doctoral programs in history and political science; the grant to Atlanta will assist in inaugurating a doctoral program in political science. Both Howard and Atlanta universities are integrated. *Ford Foundation Letter*, July 15, 1971, p. 1.

trained only in Negro hospitals, and only 14 of the 112 Negro hospitals were approved for the training of interns.[75]

Dietrich C. Reitzes points out that the problems of Negro medical students have changed dramatically. Now the major problems are not associated with discriminatory admissions policies and the limited physical facilities of the Negro medical schools to train an adequate number of Negro students. According to Reitzes, the problems are

. . . the preparation of young Negroes for medical school, the motivation of qualified Negroes to select medicine as a career, and the provision of financial aid to pay for the required extended medical education. . . . In 1947–48 there were 93 Negroes in 20 predominantly white medical schools, while in 1955–56 there were 236 Negro students in 48 of these schools. Furthermore, there were many medical schools which had no Negro students in 1955–56 but which would have accepted qualified applicants. Also, there is evidence that those medical schools having Negro students would have accepted more, had more qualified Negroes applied.[76]

The number of Negro medical students remains inadequate because the proportion of Negro medical students to white medical students has not increased materially since 1947–1948 and does not approach the percentage of Negroes in the total population. From 1947–1948 to 1955–1956 Negro students increased from 588 to 761 (29.4 percent), but the total number of medical students increased from 22,739 to 28,639 (25.9 percent). The proportion of Negro medical students to all medical students in 1958 (2.6 percent) was only slightly greater than the percentage of Negro physicians to all physicians (2.2 percent). The problem of finding qualified Negro applicants for medical schools is complicated by the continued reduction of racial barriers in other professional fields. An increase in the number of Negro professionals in general may not provide more Negro physicians. Reitzes says that there are now open to young

Negroes professional careers not dependent on a Negro clientele, e.g., engineering, chemistry, and architecture.[77]

Dentistry has been more restricted for Negroes than medicine. Most of the responsibility for training Negro dentists has been placed on Howard University and Meharry Medical College.[78]

In the training of nurses, the President's Commission on Higher Education reported in 1947 that 1214 schools in the United States were for Whites only; 38 admitted Negroes and Whites, and 28 admitted Negroes only.[79] By 1962, 1152 professional schools of nursing had no racial or religious restrictions on admission.

In the professional fields, the underrepresentation of Blacks is striking. There are almost six times as many white physicians as Negro in proportion to their respective populations; nearly seven times as many white dentists; 40 times as many white engineers, 45 times as many white pharmacists; 57 times as many white architects; and 97 times as many white lawyers, as their black counterparts. In most of these fields, the majority of Blacks who are receiving training currently are enrolled in a predominantly Negro institution.[80] In the late 1960s and the early 1970s, many predominantly white universities, both in the South and in the North, were actively seeking additional funds to provide financial aid to black students wishing to attend professional schools. In addition to such efforts, a number of special programs have been started. Several major universities with private foundation support have established programs to encourage Negro students to consider, or to undertake, careers in law. Harvard Law School's Special Summer Program with Rockefeller Foundation support is one example. Emory University School

[75] President's Commission on Higher Education, *op. cit.*, pp. 33–34.

[76] Dietrich C. Reitzes, *Negroes and Medicine*, Harvard, 1958, pp. xxi–xxii.

[77] *Ibid.*, p. xxii. For a statement on new programs designed to increase the number of black medical students, see the section on "The Medical Field" in Chapter 12. ,

[78] President's Commission on Higher Education, *op. cit.*, p. 34.

[79] *Ibid.*

[80] Charles H. Thompson, "Equality of Educational Opportunity," *JNE*, Summer, 1968, p. 201.

of Law's Summer "Pre-Start" program with Field Foundation support is another. A Ford Foundation grant to the University of Mississippi is to be used in part to recruit black students for the Law School.

Indiana University, Washington University, and the University of Wisconsin have instituted graduate programs in business administration to prepare Negroes for careers in business with the assistance of a $300,000 Ford Foundation grant, which is to be matched by contributions from industry. At the University of Pittsburgh School of Public and International Affairs, the Jessie Smith Negro Foundation has established a fellowship program to train Negroes to serve in administrative positions dealing with urban problems. Similar programs in this field have been started at other graduate schools.[81]

College and University Admissions Policies
Underrepresentation of the poor and of Blacks and other minorities (6 percent of those admitted to college in 1968 were black, but Negroes constitute 12 percent of the college-age population; 7 percent of all students, regardless of race, come from the lowest quarter of family income), has led to a searching re-examination of admissions policies. A seven-year study of 2100 Brown University students concluded that colleges and universities can lower as well as raise customary admissions credentials without seriously affecting their standards if they consider other factors. It was found that the "risk" students do as well in graduate school as other students, although they are admitted less frequently, and the chances of their achieving success after graduation are equally good. Seemingly, the main factors of success are: graduation, an advanced degree, general reputation for success, occupational level, and income. The report proposes the use of an improved "admissions index" to determine whether high-school graduates are likely to be "good risks" as college students. The investigators

conclude that a summation of counselor ratings of motivation and student promise is as good as—or better—a variable than those used "from the cognitive domain." The reference here is to secondary school records or the scores that are obtained from national tests of scholastic aptitude achievement.[82]

An effort to provide the advantages of college training to disadvantaged youths was proposed by Leslie Berger at City College in September, 1965, and approved by the New York State Legislature in 1966. In 1969–1970, SEEK (Search for Education, Elevation, and Knowledge), financed by the state and the city, enabled 4000 students who would not otherwise have been accepted to attend the seven senior colleges of City University. The only criteria for admission are: age under 30, no previous attendance at college, a high-school diploma of some sort, and residence in a deprived area. Some courses are given in special sections intended to meet the needs of these students. If necessary, they are given special instruction in reading, writing, and other basic skills. Some tutoring may be required. SEEK pays all fees, supplies free books, and can pay the student a stipend of up to $50 a week, depending upon need. The program has had more success in some colleges than in others. Queens College was closed for a time in January, 1969, after violent demonstrations by SEEK students. More than 55 percent of the entrants at City College complete three years, and 30 to 40 percent are expected to graduate.[83]

"Open-door" proposals have generated considerable controversy. Perhaps the fullest discussion of such policies has occurred in New York City. The members of a special commission of the New York Board of Higher Education have disagreed on admissions to City University. All members of the commission favored open admission for all high-school graduates to some form of

[81] Valien, *op. cit.*, p. 245.

[82] M. A. Farber, *The New York Times*, Apr. 19, 1970, p. 72.
[83] Linda W. Scheffler, "What 70 SEEK Kids Taught Their Counselor," *The New York Times Magazine*, Nov. 16, 1969, p. 54.

higher education, but the more conservative wing advocated a sorting system that, in addition to the two-year colleges and the highly selective senior colleges, would include newly created comprehensive colleges where both two- and four-year courses would be available. The latter colleges would constitute an intermediate range similar to California's state colleges. In addition, this wing would continue the special programs that select underprepared students with high potential and give them special instruction after admission. The egalitarian wing of the commission insisted on a combination of procedures that would include the right on the part of every student to pick his college, with the college having the responsibility of finding ways of helping the student to succeed, and assignment by lottery to prevent lower level institutions from becoming predominantly black. Hechinger commented that "the road to nonselective egalitarianism would lead to a drastic change in the face and the mission of higher education. It would reduce intellectual discipline and quality controls, putting stress on emotional and social gains rather than intellectual accomplishment."[84]

By the spring of 1971, it was possible to make a tentative evaluation of open admissions at the City University of New York. During the preceding fall semester, 8500 Blacks and Puerto Ricans registered as freshmen at CUNY, in a total enrollment of 155,000. CUNY's new policy had guaranteed a place in the City University to every high-school graduate in New York City, regardless of his grades or the type of diploma he had. Since less than 5 percent of the black high-school graduates in New York City earn academic diplomas, this fact alone can have a marked effect on the number of Blacks eligible for college. Open admissions also affected the ethnic composition of the 34,500 members of the 1970–1971 freshman class through the inclusion of a large number of white Catholic stu-

dents from working-class families who would not otherwise have been eligible. Previously, the great majority of students were Jews.

Although every student is assured acceptance into one of the branches of CUNY, the school he attends depends on his high-school record. The choice of school and the particular program the student enrolls in is made as far as possible, but not entirely, by the student himself. His choice is limited by two criteria: his high-school average and his rank in his graduating class. Each student is placed in the highest category for which either his grade average or percentile ranking—whichever is higher —entitles him. Under these guidelines of the Board of Higher Education, the student enters one of the nine four-year senior colleges, which concentrate on the liberal arts, or one of the seven two-year community colleges, which have less stringent entrance requirements and concentrate on preparing technicians, hygienists, and so forth.

Faculty members and students are divided in their opinions concerning the effects of the new policy. Some complain about the lowering of standards. Some faculty members, including some who favor the policy, feel that their education and experience have not prepared them to teach open-admissions students. Others are enthusiastic about the "challenges" of the policy and the favorable results they hope will come from it. Since one of the central assumptions of open admissions is that there will be a lowering of standards for admissions only, the offering of supportive services is a crucial issue. The Board of Education requires that such services be provided, including financial aid, counseling, and remedial work, but the fact is that the amount and kind of help provided thus far varies greatly from school to school.[85]

Experience in some colleges and universities indicates that simply adopting a nondiscriminatory policy in admissions is

[84] Fred M. Hechinger, "A Growing Conflict Over the Effect of Open Admissions," *The New York Times*, Oct. 12, 1969, p. 11E.

[85] Solomon Resnik and Barbara Kaplan, "Report Card on Open Admissions: Remedial Work Recommended," *The New York Times Magazine*, May 9, 1971, pp. 26–28, 32, 34, 39, 42, 44, 46.

not only insufficient—it may actually be disastrous for many less-advantaged students. The lesser preparation for college work may result in low grades, feelings of inferiority, disenchantment with further education, probation, and dropping out. Colleges and universities that have given special attention to the question of how to maximize the chances of these "new" students for doing successful college work have found that singling out these students for special treatment is resisted and resented. What these students want is tutoring and counseling that will enable them to work out their destinies alongside students who have had better preparation for college training. Provision for teacher-counselors and advisers for these "new" students is expensive but essential if broadening the base of admissions is to accomplish more than going through the motions of higher education and certifying that a student has completed the formal requirements for a degree.

Some critics of present admissions policies say that until changes are made in the educational system, particularly of private colleges, it will be necessary to be selective. They advocate, however, a selective process based on criteria that will maximize the chances of minority students to survive in a "hostile" system. In a small experiment at Oberlin College, such characteristics as clear thinking, social adeptness, the ability to communicate, and self-reliance are being used to select students by interviews from a random sample of black applicants. At the end of the first semester of this procedure, there was no appreciable difference of grade point averages among three groups of black students: those selected by the regular procedure but not the new, those selected by the new procedure but rejected by the regular, and those selected by both.[86]

Since 1968, the proportion of Negro students admitted to northern private colleges has increased appreciably, but the increases have been on a small base. As one example, Ivy League universities (Brown, Columbia, Cornell, Dartmouth, Harvard, Pennsylvania, Princeton, and Yale) and the Seven Sisters (Barnard, Bryn Mawr, Mount Holyoke, Radcliffe, Smith, Vassar, and Wellesley) have admitted increased numbers of black students, in part as a result of recruiting efforts by the campuses' own Afro-American student groups.[87] Publicly supported institutions of higher education throughout the country have also sought to bring larger numbers of black students on their campuses.

Demands of Militant Black Students

Some black students on both black and white campuses who had been active in the civil rights movement of the early 1960s, and their successors, turned away from that movement in the late 1960s. Militant Negro college and high-school students utilized abrasive demands and sometimes violence in attempting to achieve their objectives. Black student alliances were organized under such names as: Afro-American Student Association, Black Students Union, and Black Pride, and, according to rumor, an underground national unification was achieved in late 1968. Some of these groups published magazines, pamphlets, and newsletters. In some cases, militant white students supported these black organizations.[88]

The demands made by black students of Northwestern University in April, 1968, are fairly typical of those that have been made on many predominantly white campuses in recent years, but in many instances the list of demands included an increase in the number of black faculty members.

1. That the Administration will accept and issue a policy statement [on racism in the United States and at Northwestern University] as outlined in this paper.

---

[86] William G. Davis and Gordon A. Welty, "The Old System and the New College Students." A paper presented in Panel No. 39, Admission and Orientation for the Educationally Disadvantaged, Apr., 1970, Conference, American College Personnel Association, St. Louis, Missouri.

[87] F. M. Hechinger, "More Negroes Accepted by Ivy League Colleges," *The New York Times,* April 14, 1968, p. 1.

[88] P. E. Wilson, *op. cit.,* p. 92.

2. That the Administration restructure the University Discipline Committee or create a new judiciary to adequately and justly cope with racial problems and incidents.

3. That the Administration effect a new judiciary standard (as outlined) and apply this standard retroactively to the UDC decision of April 15.

4. That the Administration allow the black community to (a) approve all appointments to the Human Relations Committee and (b) determine at least 50 percent of those appointments.

5. That each forthcoming freshman class consist of 10–12 percent black students, half of whom are from the inner city school systems.

6. That the Administration will institute a committee selected by the black community to aid the Admissions Offices, especially in recruitment, and which will have shared power with the Office of Admissions and Financial Aid in making decisions relevant to us.

7. That the members constituting this committee be in a salaried position.

8. That F.M.O. will be supplied with (a) a list of all black students presently enrolled at Northwestern, (b) a list including names, addresses, etc., of all accepted and incoming black freshmen, and (c) a similar list of each forthcoming freshman class.

9. That the process of evaluating financial need and administering financial aid be restructured in conjunction with our Admissions and Financial Aid Committee.

10. That our scholarships be increased to cover what is now included in our "required jobs" and that funds be allocated for those who want or need to attend summer session.

11. That the University provide us with a black living unit or commit themselves to immediately getting rid of the present fraternity and sorority housing arrangements.

12. That any hiring of personnel in the position of counseling the black community of NU be approved by that black community.

13. That a committee of black students selected by us work with the Administration in meeting our needs for a Black Student Union.

14. That we have access to the committee studying open occupancy and discrimination with review rights to the matters which they are discussing.[89]

Lists of demands such as those made by black students at Northwestern met with varying responses on the campuses where they were made, but the net effect of the demands, negotiations, and decision making was an increase in student power in college government and the establishment of a significant influence of the black community in these and other institutions.

Activism developed rapidly on Negro campuses in 1968. Protests occurred at Howard University, Tuskegee Institute, Fisk University, Virginia State College, Delaware State College, Bowie State College (Maryland), Atlanta University Center, and elsewhere. Student demands in these institutions included: the establishment of a black studies curriculum, changes in disciplinary authority, experimental courses and projects, liberalization of dormitory hours, membership of students on committees dealing with student affairs, and removal of student press censorship. According to Wilson, the development of black awareness in black colleges in 1968 produced gains in student power in many of these institutions.[90] Drake points out that the conventional black private institutions cannot radicalize themselves enough "to be acceptable to the most militant youth and there is no reason why they should try. They should state frankly what their distinctive contribution to the black liberation movement is—intellectual tasks, not 'street' tasks—and then develop a modus vivendi with the new experimental institutions that the angry young para-intellectuals . . . are setting up such as Malcolm X Liberation University in North Carolina." Such arrangements might include providing occasional lectures for the militant experimental institutions, making audiovisual aids available to them, extending them library privileges, and inviting their students to symposia and conferences for the enrichment of their own institutions.[91]

---

[89] "Revised Demands of the Black Students," in "Black and White at Northwestern University: Documents," *Integrated Education*, May–June, 1968, pp. 36–41. Reprinted in J. H. Bracey, Jr., August Meier, and Elliott Rudwick (eds.), *Black Nationalism in America*, Bobbs-Merrill, 1970, pp. 483–485.

[90] Wilson, *op. cit.*, pp. 117–119.

[91] Drake, *op. cit.*, p. 891.

Black Studies Programs

Interest in and demands for black studies programs have grown rapidly in recent years, many of them conceived as both an academic and a social environment. As the latter they offer the black student a greater opportunity for self-expression within his own group than has hitherto been possible at predominantly white institutions.[92] Often included in such programs are courses in black world history, Afro-American economics, Afro-American art and culture, Swahili, and African history and cultures.

Major reasons for the advocacy of black studies programs are to teach the black student about "his own culture,"[93] to improve his self-image, to strengthen his identification with the black group, and to analyze current problems from a new perspective.[94]

Many black scholars hold that Blacks have lacked substantial opportunities to obtain training and to do research in African and Afro-American studies. Some of these scholars see the possibility that Blacks will be put in charge of research projects in various fields of interest. They regard the participation of black scholars in studies dealing with black America as valuable in complementing what has been done in the past, and they think it may bring more comprehensive knowledge and a clearer perspective. The problem, of course, "is whether conscious advocacy will supplant the goal of research objectivity."[95]

Among more militant black scholars, an important reason for advocating new programs in black studies is the belief that white teachers cannot adequately interpret African and American black studies. On this basis, a group of dissident black scholars established in 1969 the African Heritage Studies Association. John Henrik Clarke, the leader of this group, said that his organization was prepared to begin major African and black studies "with or without the African Studies Association." At the November, 1969 meeting of the ASA and at the Conference on African and African-American Studies held a month later, a number of black scholars insisted that "they, not white educators or white institutions would be the interpreters, pace-setters and final authorities on black studies. They hoped to do this with a minimum of white participation."[96] An attempt to work out a compromise between the AHSA and the ASA failed and formal discussions between representatives of the two organizations came to an end in May, 1970.[97] Pettigrew advocates cross-campus cooperation in facilities, faculty, students, and programs, saying that the emergence of black studies programs "makes genuine partnership between primarily black and white institutions possible now in contrast to the often patronizing arrangements of the past." His view emphasizes four areas in which Whites

---

[92] Anne-Marie Henshel and Richard L. Henshel, "Black Studies Programs: Promise and Pitfalls," *JNE*, Fall, 1969, p. 424.

[93] In some cases, Blacks would like Whites to gain an understanding of these things, and in some colleges Whites form a large proportion of the Black Studies enrollment. At the University of Texas, where there are few black students, the enrollment is 85 percent white. In a few places, black hostility is so obvious that few Whites enter the program. At Cornell, the director of the African Study and Research Center said: "We have neither the time nor the resources to operate a race relations project wherein well-meaning but inexperienced and dysfunctional white students would occupy positions that might better be filled by blacks." Steven Roberts, "Black Studies Off to a Shaky Start," *The New York Times*, Nov. 23, 1969, pp. 1, 85.

[94] The extent to which blacks in America have a separate culture, rather than sharing a culture to which they have contributed, is, of course, a moot point. Belief in a distinctive culture, however, is very real for some Negroes. And that belief can be part of a self-fulfilling prophecy, adding cultural elements to those already shared by Negroes. See Chapter 20, "Minorities and Art," for discussions of "black culture," "soul," Negritude, and ideology and art. Henry A. Bullock advocates and follows a pedagogical procedure that he calls "cultural context teaching." He says that this method "introduces students to conventional disciplines through a black focus that is in fact black culture." This mechanism is said to produce "bicultural students—students who are sophisticated in handling the barrier of American racism." Henry A. Bullock, "The Black College and the New Black Awareness," *Daedalus*, Summer, 1971, p. 597.

[95] Henshel and Henshel, *op. cit.*, p. 427.

[96] Thomas A. Johnson, "Colleges Scored on Black Studies," *The New York Times*, Dec. 7, 1969.

[97] *African Studies Newsletter*, May–June, 1970, p. 1.

can play useful roles for black colleges of the future: financial support, cross-campus cooperation, increasing the supply of black Ph.D.s, and participating as teachers and students at the institutions themselves.[98]

Increased opportunities for black students to obtain training in all types of black studies programs, as well as increased participation and collaboration in research projects and in professional organizations and publications, is widely regarded as imperative. Most white and some black Africanists and Afro-Americanists, however, hold that social scientific scholarship does not depend on racial background. Also, the presence of black scholars does not insure the success of a black studies program. Roberts reports that "men who have long believed in the ultimate goal of integration often find it difficult to communicate with separatist-minded students." Dr. Sethard Fisher, chairman of the Black Studies Department at Santa Barbara, was forced to resign recently when students charged he was not "relevant to the black experience." Some black scholars are reluctant to teach in black studies programs because they think that the future of such studies is uncertain, or they do not want to "be harassed or dictated to by black students and they don't want to compromise their academic or professional integrity."[99]

Another major aim of black studies is to make education "relevant" to the problems of minority communities and to prepare students to deal with them. Cornell's plans call for a junior year in the ghetto; Dartmouth offers a quarter's work in Fourah Bay in Sierre Leone, the Roxbury ghetto of Boston, or the Institute of the Black World in Atlanta. In addition to their studies of the needs of black communities, it is hoped that the students enrolled in these courses could also contribute to the actual fulfillment of these needs. Henshel and

Henshel suggest that they could serve "as tutors or play monitors for the community children, even serve as living examples of a certain tangible success reached through motivation and scholarship." Also, it is thought likely that such programs will help to promote and expand Afro-American arts: music, dance, drama, poetry, painting, sculpture, and literature in general.[100]

While favoring the increase in interest and in courses in black studies, some scholars and administrators, black and white, express reservations concerning these programs. Apart from financial considerations, one of the major problems, at least initially, is the academic competence of the faculty members associated with the new courses. In the late 1960s and early 1970s, the demand for teachers, especially black teachers, far exceeds the supply. Henshel and Henshel say: "Low staff competence, reflected in lack of knowledge of the subject to be taught, lack of academic background in general, and lack of intellectual perspective, replaced in many cases by racial emotionalism, would result in low quality curricula."[101] According to Martin Kilson, ". . . a sad feature of the black studies movement is the absence of perspective in regard to those special habits and norms that govern scholarly activity."[102] Some black scholars, however, are not particularly concerned about the scarcity of teachers with the usual higher degrees, saying that they are trying to get away from the kind of course "the establishment" would offer. Troy Duster, a Berkeley sociologist, has pointed out that confusion in

---

[98] Thomas F. Pettigrew, "The Role of Whites in the Black College of the Future," *Daedalus*, Summer, 1971, pp. 827, 829.

[99] Roberts, *op. cit.*, p. 85.

[100] Henshel and Henshel, *op. cit.*, pp. 425–427. Since 1968, the creation of Black Studies programs has greatly stimulated the publication of books about the experience of blacks in America. Lester says: "In their eagerness to meet the heightened demand, however, some publishers are in danger of glutting the market. Over 4000 paperback books on blacks are now available, with every major publisher and numerous small independent publishing companies represented." Julius Lester, *The New York Times Book Review*, Feb. 15, 1970, p. 2.

[101] Henshel and Henshel, *op. cit.*, p. 428.

[102] Martin Kilson, "Anatomy of the Black Studies Movement," *Massachusetts Review*, Autumn, 1969, p. 719.

black studies programs at this stage is to be expected as new procedures and new criteria for courses and faculty are instituted.[103]

In addition to financial and academic problems, many schools have been confronted with political questions of ultimate control over black studies programs. In some cases, black students and faculty members have demanded control over the kinds of courses to be offered and the selection of teachers. At the outset of the black studies movement, the reason frequently given for these demands was that the courses were ideological, not sociological. Some said that only Blacks are capable of making decisions concerning Blacks. Most university officials disagreed with this view but favored giving black students important advisory roles.

A trend that has caused some concern in setting up black studies programs is the stress some students have placed on group discussion of black problems. According to the Henshels, overemphasis on discussion "has degenerated the curriculum in some cases to the level of the 'bull session,' in which verbal skills are sharpened at the expense of comprehension of competing ideas that it is a function of the university to provide."[104] Another possible drawback to black studies programs is that they may inadvertently become "a major agent of voluntary (and involuntary) segregation on both the social and the academic level." If such segregation occurs, and is accompanied by incompetence on the part of the staff and a meager scholastic background on the part of the student, there is a danger "of perpetuating indefinitely the relative academic impoverishment and isolation that is now the lot of the majority of black students."[105] Also, where a major in black studies is offered, there is the possibility that pressure might be brought on black students to enroll for this major as a way of showing black pride. Such pressure could result in considerable discomfort for black students who have a strong interest in another field.[106]

A related question is the effects of black studies programs on race relations. Henshel and Henshel point out that while fostering black identity and black pride, these programs may also encourage black racism. As examples of a trend that approaches racism they cite instances where white students were excluded from classes while certain topics were discussed by black students, requests in virtually all of the proposals for a totally black faculty, and the content of certain courses. According to these authors, ill will between the races in America may be stimulated at least for a while, by certain circumstances surrounding the black studies program. The segregation of Blacks behind the walls of their centers, ignoring the "white" world except to criticize it, may promote the estrangement of liberal Whites from the black cause. Among other Whites, who are not favorably disposed to the black situation, some of these programs may stimulate backlash, particularly if they should become instruments of political anarchy. Under these conditions, "racial tensions would be further exacerbated and elements of white reaction would be the ultimate beneficiaries."[107]

An important question concerning the rapid inncrease in black studies programs is the situation of graduates of such programs as they attempt to enter graduate schools or to find employment. Only a limited number of jobs are available to those who have taken some type of black studies major. On this point Sir Arthur Lewis, an internationally known economist who formerly taught at Princeton, is quite emphatic. Both from the standpoint of the career interests of most black students and in terms of the influence of the Negro community on the life of the nation, Lewis thinks it is

---

[103] Roberts, *op. cit.*, pp. 1, 85.
[104] Henshel and Henshel, *op. cit.*, p. 428.
[105] *Ibid.*, p. 424.

[106] For a statement concerning the experiences of a black student who opposed the all black dormitory and black studies institute at Antioch College, see *Civil Liberties*, Apr., 1971, p. 5.
[107] Henshel and Henshel, *op. cit.*, p. 426.

of great importance that the number of specialists in Afro-American studies be rather small in comparison with black scientists, engineers, accountants, and doctors.[108] Oppositely, the advocates of black studies hope that these programs will provide a favorable environment for the emergence of able black leaders. In 1970, many black students said that they intended to return to the ghettos and they felt that they needed skills tailored to black ghetto society.[109]

Other Ethnic Studies Programs

In addition to black studies programs, several western universities, including the University of Texas, have instituted ethnic studies programs. Others have begun Mexican-American programs, and the University of California, Berkeley, now has Asian and Native American (American Indian) programs. During 1969–1970, the Ford Foundation gave a grant of $149,428 to the University of California at San Diego for a "new college focusing on the experiences of blacks, Mexican-Americans, and American Indians."[110] Some Eastern schools, such as the City College of New York, have started Puerto Rican programs.[111]

In 1971, representing eight different tribes and pueblos, Indian students from

12 universities and colleges agreed to form a national association for the establishment and development of Indian Studies programs in higher-education institutions in the Southwest. Temporary headquarters of the group were established on the campus of the University of New Mexico, where four Indian Studies courses were said to have been successful during the fall of 1970.[112] Also in 1971, a board of 32 Indians and Chicanos established Deganawidah-Quetzalcoatl University. The school offered its first courses during the summer of 1971 and expected to have a full schedule for approximately 100 students in the fall of that year. As a result of scarcity of money, most or all of the teachers were expected to be volunteers at first. In addition to descriptive courses in Indian and Chicano history, the curriculum will include applied courses, including tribal business procedures, economic development, art, and dancing. The university expects to train teachers and design materials for Chicano and Native American studies programs. DQU is meant to complement existing institutions rather than to replace them, and officials hope to arrange exchange programs with other schools. Instead of being concerned about "segregation," the leaders see a positive value in separatism. The basic assumptions of the new school are that students will be involved in something of which they are proud, and that they will be doing something for themselves.[113]

Motivation and Aspiration

In a report on motivation and aspiration in the Negro college, Gurin and Katz distinguish between value-motive constructs and expectancy constructs. Expectancy factors— how people judge their chances for success —are considered relatively less generalized and less stable than motives and values, which are assumed to develop in early childhood and to persist as relatively stable characteristics of the individual. Because of his position in the social structure, these

---

[108] W. Arthur Lewis, "Black Power and the American University," *University: A Princeton Quarterly*, Spring, 1969, pp. 8–12. Reprinted in *The New York Times Magazine*, May 11, 1969, pp. 34–35, 39.

[109] Henshel and Henshel, *op. cit.*, p. 425.

[110] *Race Relations Reporter, op. cit.*, p. 8.

[111] S. Roberts, *op. cit.*, p. 85. In 1969, the Third World Liberation Front demanded the establishment of a Third World College at Berkeley to include an Asian Studies Department, a Department of Black Studies, a Department of Chicano (Mexican-American) Studies, a Department of Native American Studies, and other third-world studies programs as they developed. They demanded also third-world financial counselors, third-world persons as counselors in the Placement Office, third-world deans in the Arts and Letters and Science Departments, and third-world chancellors in the university system. They asked also for third-world control over third-world programs. Chinese students and members of other ethnic groups at San Francisco State College made similar demands. *East-West*, Jan. 15, 1969, pp. 1, 5. At neither institution were the demands, as stated by the students, granted.

[112] *The New York Times*, Mar. 7, 1971, p. 71.

[113] *The New York Times*, May 9, 1971, p. 45.

authors argue that the role of expectancy factors on his chances for success is accentuated for the Negro youth as compared with his white counterpart. How black students assess their chances for success appears to be important in accounting for all kinds of occupational aspirations, particularly the choice of a nontraditional job, in differentiating realistic from unrealistic aspirants among the high ability students, and in accounting for differences between students from different class backgrounds.[114]

Fichter found the aspirations of graduates of predominantly Negro colleges in the class of 1964 to be fairly high. A large proportion of them said that they wanted to go to graduate school, but a much smaller proportion expected to begin graduate work immediately after college. Even the black students who could not go on immediately said that they expected eventually to work for a graduate or professional degree.[115] Fichter attributes the reason for the high aspirations of the Negro college senior in part to his tendency to compare himself with the great majority of American Negroes who have not made it.[116] The role of financial disability in decreasing the number of Negroes who go to graduate school and in depriving some of them of attending the graduate school of their preference is seen in the seven-tenths of the male Negroes and more than one-half of the female Negroes who would have liked to study medicine but could not do so for financial reasons. Also, a significant number of male graduates could not apply for training in law and engineering, and a substantial minority of female graduates could not begin training in social work and for several health fields (nursing, physical therapy, and medical technology) because of financial problems.[117]

According to the Jaffe, Adams, and Meyers study, virtually all the Negro college students would prefer white-collar jobs, and the great majority wish to enter upper white-collar professions. This study found that "few aspire to become clerical and sales workers, or managers, officials, and proprietors . . . The majority hope to teach, chiefly at the primary and secondary levels . . . There is considerable evidence that career aspirations center about occupations for which the students feel . . . the least disadvantage relative to white competitors with equivalent preparation."[118] The authors say that these plans appear relatively realistic "if, and only if, they complete the full four years of college." Historically only half of Negro college entrants have done so. Of the graduates, approximately half continue in graduate or professional school. Between 80 and 90 percent of the graduates obtain professional employment. Most of those who drop out of college do not obtain upper white-collar jobs.[119] In terms of both academic performance and upper socioeconomic backgrounds, a small number of elite students who attend "good" colleges aspire to lives that are markedly different from those anticipated by all other Negro college students. Few plan to teach; the majority expect to enter occupations that most of the other students seem to regard as unrealistic goals. These elite students demonstrated the positive relationships that existed in the mid-1960s between favorable socioeconomic position, better academic performance, and more ambitious plans for the future.[120]

Educational Aspirations of Negro Women

According to Gurin and Katz, if one were to argue from the literature about the prominence of the black woman, one would expect to find the opposite of what one finds. They say: "Instead of having higher aspirations than the males, these Negro girls have lower aspirations. They are choosing

---

[114] Patricia Gurin and Daniel Katz, *Motivation and Aspiration in the Negro College*, Survey Research Center, Institute for Social Research, University of Michigan, 1966, pp. 296–302.

[115] Joseph H. Fichter, *Graduates of Predominantly Negro Colleges Class of 1964*, The National Institutes of Health, 1967, pp. 4–5.

[116] *Ibid.*, pp. 5–6.

[117] *Ibid.*, pp. 68–69.

[118] Jaffe, Adams, and Meyers, *op. cit.*, pp. 124–125.

[119] *Ibid.*, p. 125.

[120] *Ibid.*, p. 126.

jobs that are less prestigeful, demanding of less ability, and more traditional for Negroes. Instead of defining desirable jobs in terms of high ability demands as do the males, they consider the easier jobs as the most desirable or attractive to them."[121] Except for the fact that Negro girls in this study expect to work as long as the black men, these girls seem to have the orientation to work that is held by women generally. They attach less importance than men do to a career after college, and they have less interest in advancement in the occupations they have chosen.[122]

Educational Opportunities and the Job Opportunity Structure

Careful consideration needs to be given to the relationship between increased educational opportunities for blacks and the job opportunity structure. Geschwender cites Glenn's demonstration that Negroes do not make their greatest gains at the relative expense of whites. If blacks move into middle- and upper-status jobs only when whites move up to still higher occupations, racial inequality is not reduced. While suggesting that Negro youth get as much education as possible, Geschwender says that stronger equal opportunity legislation is also essential.[123]

Regional Compacts

In February, 1948, 14 southern states entered into a "regional compact" for the announced objective of arranging to pool their educational facilities so as to insure that students receive the best possible education. In June, 1949, 11 state legislatures created an organization known as the Board of Control for Southern Regional Education to investigate the possibilities of regional edu-

cation. The governor and three citizens of each state, appointed by the governor, constitute the board. The board's duties are, first, to administer service programs already approved by the state legislatures and, second, to conduct continuous long-range studies of regional educational needs and to develop cooperative arrangements among institutions and states to meet these needs.[124]

The first method of regional education was the "contract for services." In the first round of contracts, 14 institutions arranged to provide instruction in three fields: veterinary medicine, medicine, and dentistry. In veterinary medicine four schools (Alabama Polytechnic Institute, Tuskegee Institute, the University of Georgia, and Oklahoma A. and M. College) agreed to accept a total of 101 first-year students, and they were to receive $1000 for each student. Seven institutions (Duke, Emory, Louisiana State, Meharry Medical College, Tennessee, Tulane, and Vanderbilt) were to receive 173 students in medicine at $1500 per student. Dental training was arranged at six institutions (Emory, Loyola of Louisiana, Maryland, Medical College of Virginia, Meharry, and Tennessee) for 114 students at a cost of $1500 per student. All of these contracts provided for state quotas and for the selection of students according to the admission policies of each school. Students are certified as eligible for admission on the basis of any criteria the states wish to establish. These arrangements were scheduled to provide for 207 white students and 181 Negro students during 1949–1950 at a cost of approximately $1,500,000.[125]

The Board of Control for Southern Regional Education studied such additional fields as graduate studies, social work, architecture, forestry, phases of engineering, agriculture, and professional education. Also, it investigated methods of regional cooperation besides the contractual arrangements to exchange students and funds among the states. Other methods considered include joint use of research facilities, the movement

---

[121] Gurin and Katz, *op. cit.*, p. 275.

[122] *Ibid.*, pp. 275–276.

[123] James A. Geschwender, "Negro Education: The False Faith," *Phylon*, Winter, 1968, pp. 371–379. Norval D. Glenn's study is "The Relative Size of the Negro Population and Negro Occupational Status," *SF*, Oct. 1964, pp. 42–49. See also Gurin and Katz, *op. cit.*, p. 295.

[124] John E. Ivey, Jr., "Regional Education," *Phylon*, Fourth Quarter, 1949, pp. 381–384.

[125] *Ibid.*, pp. 385–386.

of students from one institution to another for training purposes, the exchange of faculty members, joint research projects, and voluntary specialization in curricular offerings.[126]

In August, 1967 the Southern Regional Education Board's Commission on Higher Educational Opportunity submitted a critical report on Negro higher education in the South. The aim of the report was "a total commitment of the region" to "provide equal opportunity for Negroes in the South," including the overall improvement of Negro colleges and universities. Perhaps the most important of the three broad goals designated by the Commission was the development of long-range plans to eliminate "the South's dual system of higher education and create a single system serving all students."

In 1968, South Carolina Governor Robert McNair, then SREB chairman, appointed a 12-member policy commission for a Regional Institute for Higher Educational Opportunities. By 1969 the Institute had five staff members and was receiving financial support of $10,000 annually from nine of the 15 member states of SREB. Funds from other states were expected. The commission specified eight areas in which the Institute should work to reach the goals of its report: statewide planning, providing mass opportunities for Negro students, facilitating student progress, improving instruction, improving curricula, promoting interinstitutional cooperation, improving administration of Negro institutions, and increasing financial support.[127]

Fair Educational Practices Legislation

Along with important court decisions regarding education for minorities, several state laws have been passed aimed at eliminating discrimination.[128] The first fair educational practices law (Quinn-Olliffe Law) was passed in New York State in April, 1948. Schools above the secondary level were prohibited from excluding or limiting or otherwise discriminating against applicants for admission because of race, religion, creed, color, or national origin. The law permits religious and denominational schools to select students exclusively or primarily from members of their religious faith, but a denominational school may not exclude a student because of his race.[129] In 1958, the antidiscrimination law was amended to prohibit discrimination in the use of the facilities of any educational association or corporation that classifies itself as tax-exempt and nonsectarian. This change in the law under which the New York antidiscrimination agency operates gave the agency overlapping jurisdiction with the Department of Education.[130]

New Jersey and Massachusetts adopted fair educational practices acts in 1949. The New Jersey law is an amendment to the fair employment law of that state, and a dual enforcement agency has been created. The Division Against Discrimination of the Department of Education is charged primarily with the power to prevent and eliminate discrimination in employment. The other body, the State Civil Rights Commission, was organized to supervise and implement the activities of the first group.[131] In 1956, enforcement of the Massachusetts law was transferred from the state Board of Education to the Massachusetts Commission

---

[126] *Ibid.*, pp. 386–387.

[127] Thomas W. Greene, "After the Explosion, Two Years of Fallout," *Southern Education Report*, May, 1969, pp. 32–37.

[128] On state legislation pertaining to fair educational practices see M. R. Konvitz and T. Leskes, *A Century of Civil Rights*, Columbia, 1961, chap. 8.

[129] As of June, 1949, 29 of these institutions filed certificates as Roman Catholic institutions, ten as Protestant, one as Russian Orthodox, and two as Jewish. In addition, two Roman Catholic and three Protestant junior colleges asked to be considered as religious or denominational institutions. The enrollment of these 47 institutions constitutes about 15 percent of the total enrollment in colleges and universities in the state. The University of the State of New York, The State Education Department, Education Practices Administration, *Annual Report, Aug. 16, 1948—June 30, 1949.*

[130] Commission on Law and Social Action of the American Jewish Congress, *Report on Twenty Anti-Discrimination Agencies and the Laws They Administer*, Dec., 1961, p. 6.

[131] *Report of the United States Commission on Civil Rights, 1959*, p. 263.

Against Discrimination. This Commission has the power to conduct conciliatory investigations and hearings upon complaints of possible violations and to issue cease-and-desist orders and dismissals of complaints. Judicial review of these decisions is provided.[132]

Certain differences appear in these three laws. Originally, the New York law covered only schools above the secondary level, but vocational and trade schools were added by legislative amendment in 1951. The *Report of the United States Commission on Civil Rights, 1959*, points out that while there is apparent restriction in the coverage of New York's education law, the legislature has given its Civil Rights Law almost universal application. Equal access is assured to: "kindergartens, primary and secondary schools, high schools, academies, colleges and universities, extension courses under the supervision of the New York Board of Regents," and in a general category, "any publicly supported school." Legislation in the other two states includes kindergartens, elementary and high schools, trade schools, undergraduate and graduate colleges, and professional schools. New Jersey and Massachusetts exempt from their coverage schools that are "distinctly private" in character.[133]

The term "distinctly private" is not clearcut, and determination of what is meant by it at times proves difficult. "The fact that an educational institution is not a public school in the sense of a school maintained and controlled by public authorities does not make it a school 'in its nature distinctly private.' To fall within the description 'distinctly private' such institutions must limit themselves to a very narrow group of persons. An ultra-exclusive private finishing school for girls would be an example. A private institution that accepts applications from the public generally certainly would remain outside the definition, as would an institution appealing to the public for funds."[134]

The New York law contains no stipulation concerning "distinctly private" schools, but it is limited to institutions "subject to visitation, examination or inspection" by the Regents or the commissioner of education. The University of the State of New York is a holding corporation that is in general charge of education in the state, both public and private. Even the so-called private colleges and universities in New York are incorporated as subsidiary corporations within the framework of the University of the State of New York. The State University of New York consists of the collection of institutions under public support. This latter organization has its own board of trustees and is subject to the supervision of the Board of Regents. The provisions of the fair educational practices act are applicable both to public and to private institutions.

Massachusetts follows the New York law in the matter of religious and denominational schools, but the New Jersey law exempts such schools altogether. In the latter state a denominational school may not be held for discriminating against applicants because of race or national origin. The Massachusetts law is limited in its scope to citizens of the United States and thus fails to make any provision for aliens.

Another difference in these laws is the provision in New Jersey against discrimination in the use of recreational, social, and other campus facilities after students have been admitted to educational institutions. The New York and Massachusetts laws are limited to prohibiting discrimination in admission. A final difference in these laws is the provision in Massachusetts that it is unlawful, except for religious inquiries in the case of denominational schools, "to cause to be made any written or oral inquiry concerning the race, religion, color or national origin of a person seeking admission." The New York law does not forbid questions pertaining to race, religion, or national origin on the application forms, but the Education Practices Administration conducted a survey during 1949–1950 of the controversial questions on the application blanks of all post-secondary institutions in the state for the purpose of securing the elimination

[132] *Ibid.*, p. 261.
[133] Forster, *op. cit.*, pp. 138–141. A model bill on fair educational practices is given in *ibid.*, p. 217.
[134] *Ibid.*, pp. 139–140.

of these items. By the end of that year "direct questions on race, color, religion and national origin had almost completely disappeared from the application blanks on file from 123 denominational and nondenominational colleges, universities and junior colleges, only one nondenominational unit had an optional question on religion, one unit a question on nationality and one unit a question on race. A total of 673 controversial questions had been eliminated to date."[135] By September, 1951, 952 of these questions had been eliminated.

In the State of Washington, the Civil Rights Law is sufficiently broad in its language to show an intent to provide protection to prospective students. It specifies that the right to full enjoyment of any public accommodation or facility will be preserved, and "public accommodation" is defined to include public educational institutions and nursery schools. Though exempting distinctly private or sectarian institutions, the law includes them "where public use is permitted therein."[136]

In 1957, Oregon gave its antidiscrimination agency jurisdiction over its existing law prohibiting discrimination in trade, vocational, and professional schools. The meaning of the Oregon statute is broadened by a reference to the type of institution in which "any form of State approval is required in order for it to operate."[137]

In 1961, Pennsylvania gave its antidiscrimination commission jurisdiction over colleges, universities and a limited number of other types of schools.[138]

Disagreement exists concerning the effectiveness of fair educational practices laws. Those who favor the legislation believe that the statutes have called attention to the problem of discrimination and that the educational work carried on by the commissioners is valuable. There have been fewer formal complaints than anticipated, but the commissioners have used their conciliatory powers to encourage a review of institutional policies on admission. A study of the New York Department of Education showed that 45 percent of three different classes in the nine medical schools in the state were Jews. The percentage of Jews in Cornell's medical school was 28, and in Columbia's 40. Jewish enrollment in these schools is estimated to have doubled during the first six years of the law's operation.[139]

Legislation probably can play a part in reducing discrimination in college admissions, but the question cannot be solved through legislation alone. Morroe Berger observes: "As a means of combating educational discrimination, legislation becomes increasingly unnecessary as the colleges grow more mindful of their democratic responsibility to all the people."[140]

[135] The University of the State of New York, *op. cit.*, July 1, 1949–June 30, 1950, p. 1.

[136] *Report of the United States Commission on Civil Rights, 1959*, pp. 263–264.

[137] *Ibid.*, p. 264.

[138] Commission on Law and Social Action of AJC, *op. cit.*, p. 6.

[139] Will Maslow, "The Uses of Law in the Struggle for Equality," *Social Research*, Autumn, 1955, pp. 303–304. For data on the restriction on admission of Jews to professional schools in the period 1925–1960, see G. E. Simpson and J. M. Yinger, *op. cit.*, pp. 454–457.

[140] Morroe Berger, "Fair Educational Practices Legislation," *Annals*, May, 1951, pp. 45–46.

Chapter 20 / MINORITIES AND ART

Art produced by and about minority-group members constitutes an important part of art as art, and, in reflecting the life of the social classes in given periods, it provides insights concerning majority-minority relations. Our discussion centers primarily on Negro materials as illustrative of the influences at work on this art.

Negro Folk Art

The folk songs, dances, and stories of the American Negro have had important effects upon life in the United States. Among popular dances that appear to have a Negro background are the Lindy Hop, the Big Apple, the Cakewalk tradition (". . . the urbanization of the plantation folk-dances incorporating in the whole such separate figures as the Black Annie, the Pas Mala, the Strut, the Palmer House, and later, Walkin' the Dog, Ballin' the Jack, and other individual expressions"), and the Charleston.[1]

Among American Negro folk tales are animal stories, tales of magic, human tales, moralizing stories, and some tales "that verge on the heroic or epic." Courlander comments on a large proportion of these tales:

. . . [they] stem from European oral tradition, some are from the Bible and many derive from daily life in slavery and postslavery days; but . . . an overwhelming number of the stories have prototypes in West and Central Africa. The African affinity is seen most readily in the animal tales first popularized in the white segment of the population by Joel Chandler Harris in his Uncle Remus series, but it is also apparent in stories of other kinds. Such tales have been found in which a king or another notable person replaces West African sky deities or culture he-

roes. Anansi, the Ashanti trickster here (originally a spider) as well as his son Intikuma, is called by name in a large cycle of tales told in the United States and in other New World Negro settings.[2]

As in all folk music, the authors of Negro folk songs are unknown. The songs have grown out of the Negro's experience as an American peasant. This art of untutored slaves came from cotton and tobacco plantations, the slave marts and slave quarters, camp meetings, factories, and forests. The titles of the spirituals are poetic—"Swing Low, Sweet Chariot;" "Sometimes I Feel Like a Motherless Child;" "Steal Away;" "Death's Goin' to Lay His Cold, Icy Hand on Me;" "We Shall Walk Through the Valley in Peace;" "Ride on King Jesus;" "He Never Said a Mumbaling Word;" "Go Down, Moses;" "Singing with a Sword in My Hand;" "No More Auction Block;" "Deep River;" "I Been Rebuked and I Been Scorned." These songs, molded by the hardships and suffering of folk Negroes, brought release from trouble and pain. But, as Zora Neale Hurston insists, they were not just "Sorrow Songs." There was, and there still is, much vitality and zest in the singing of these songs by folk singers. More recently, groups closer to the people than college choirs have carried modified spirituals throughout the country. Trios, quartets, and choruses, together with soloists like the late Mahalia Jackson, sing the spirituals in churches and concert halls, and on records. Tambourines, cymbals, trumpets, trombones, and bass fiddles are used in some churches as the spirituals are given a more pronounced rhythm and a jazz quality. The Gospel songs put an even greater emphasis on jazz and blues effects and are crowding out the spirit-

[1] Katherine Dunham, "The Negro Dance," in Sterling A. Brown, Arthur P. Davis, and Ulysses Lee (eds.), *The Negro Caravan*, Holt, Rinehart & Winston, 1941, pp. 997–999.

[2] Harold Courlander, *Negro Folk Music U.S.A.*, Columbia, 1963, p. 7.

uals. Evaluating these new songs, Sterling Brown says: "Many lovers of the older spirituals disdain the Gospel songs as cheap and obvious. But this new urban religious folk music should not be dismissed too lightly. It is vigorously alive with its own musical values. . . . To hear some fervent congregations sing 'Just a Closer Walk with Thee,' 'He Knows How Much You Can Bear,' and 'We Sure Do Need Him Now' can be unforgettable musical experiences. In sincerity, musical manner, and spirit, they are probably not so remote from the old prayer songs in the brush arbors."[3]

Among the secular songs of folk Negroes in the pre-World War II period, the blues were the most popular. Subject matter of the earlier blues included a woman's longing for her "man;" bewailing tornadoes, high water, hard times in farming; and the need for traveling, for leaving this cold-hearted town.[4] Although the blues are not the only Negro songs that express dissatisfaction, remorse, regret, accusation, hopelessness, weariness, and ridicule, "the blues is the everyday medium through which feelings of this kind are aired."[5]

Less well-known seculars are the work songs, social songs, ballads, and satires, but they too have had an important place in Negro life. In the rural South, better roads and more motor vehicles, radio, and television, the phonograph and juke box, movies, churches, schools, and the Negro press combine in reducing isolation. Although Negro folk culture is breaking up, it has by no means disappeared.[6]

In the large and somewhat controversial literature concerning the origin and nature of Negro folk music, Courlander's point of view is one of the most judicious. He writes:

We must not forget that this body of music is the result of an irrational blending process. Certain melodic lines may be indisputably European.

Certain rhythmic patterns may be almost identical to rhythms found in the West Indies or West Africa. Certain images may coincide precisely with those found in songs of English or Irish derivation, and certain themes may correspond with similar themes known in the non-Negro mountain communities, or recall songs typical of the western ranch country. But, with all the permutations and combinations, there remains the reality that, taken as a whole, the Negro folk music idiom is an integral and somewhat separate phenomenon and has a character completely its own. This will be modified in time, and it is being modified now, to the extent that Negro music accents more and more elements from other idioms, and to the extent that Negro music is drawn upon by jazz, popular music composers, and contemporary classical composers.[7]

When a musicologist, Dr. M. Kolinski, analyzed the songs appearing in several volumes of spirituals,

thirty-six were found to have the same scales (tonal structures) as specific songs in the West African collection, while identical correspondences in melodic line were even found in a few instances. Thirty-four spirituals had the same rhythmic structure as some of the West African melodies, while the formal structure of fifty spirituals—their phrasing and time—were found to have African counterparts.[8]

Motion pictures of some of the ceremonial dances taken by Herskovits in West Africa show a remarkable resemblance to the Charleston of the 1920s. Katherine Dunham writes concerning the Charleston:

. . . In Haiti, I found the Charleston in the dance La Martinique; and in terms of the retention of choreographic forms through transition periods, I would say that such a dance must have been known during the North American folk period. I have certainly seen possessed devotees in 'store-front' churches propelling themselves up and down the aisles with a practically pure Charleston step. It is not so surprising, then, that at one point the Charleston should have become such a popular and general expression of American culture.[9]

---

[3] Sterling A. Brown, "Negro Folk Expression," *Phylon*, First Quarter, 1953, p. 50.

[4] For an excellent statement on the blues, see Sterling A. Brown, "The Blues," *Phylon*, First Quarter, 1952, pp. 286–292. See also LeRoi Jones, *Blues People*, Morrow, 1963.

[5] Courlander, *op. cit.*, p. 128.

[6] Brown, "Negro Folk Expression," *op. cit.*, p. 60.

[7] Courlander, *op. cit.*, pp. 14–15.

[8] M. J. Herskovits, *The Myth of the Negro Past*, Beacon, 1958, p. 268. See Herskovits' remarks on the intangibles of singing techniques and motor habit accompanying song (pp. 265–267).

[9] Dunham, *op. cit.*, pp. 999–1000.

Artistic Achievements of Negroes, 1920–1960[10]

In 1932, Donald Young wrote concerning the "extravagant praise of ordinary accomplishments" in art produced by Negroes. Specifically mentioned was the poetry of Paul Lawrence Dunbar, James Weldon Johnson, Countee Cullen, Claude McKay, Jean Toomer, and Langston Hughes; the fiction of Jessie Fauset, Charles W. Chesnutt, Walter White, Nella Larsen, and W. E. B. DuBois. He spoke of "prejudiced overpraise" and "racial treason" in connection with the appraisal of the works of authors he considered average or above average, but not distinguished. This lack of outstanding literary work on the part of Negroes in the United States was attributed not to racial incapacity but to the limitations imposed by prejudice and socioeconomic conditions.

Criticism of Negro authors in the early and middle 1950s dwelt upon the small volume, in absolute or comparative terms, of writing done by Negroes and upon the need for a mastery of craftsmanship.[11] In the drama there had never been notable achievement by Negroes, and the situation changed little during that period. The most significant of the plays by Negroes through 1950 were the stage version of *Native Son*, Langston Hughes' adaptation of *Mulatto* (*The Barrier*), Owen Dodson's *Divine Comedy* and *Bayou Legend*[12] and Louis Peterson's *Take a Giant Step*.

Competently written short stories were produced by Langston Hughes, Chester Himes, and Richard Wright in the 1930s. Prior to World War II, Negroes had published more books of poetry than any other type of writing. In 1941, the editors of *The Negro Caravan* observed that "writing poetry is still popular among Negroes, but it is largely occasional verse, derivative, and escapist."[13] In 1960, Lash lamented the dearth of publications of poetry by Negroes in recent years. The situation, he said, is not merely critical, but alarming.

The *Phylon* reviews have not included much in the way of poetry that is worthy of the name since Gwendolyn Brooks' *Bronzeville Boys and Girls* of several years back, and even that was an isolated volume. Granting that the vocation of poetry may have fallen on evil days, so that poets generally are not as active as of yore, still it seems that Negro poets, and particularly talented new poets, could and would imbibe something of the new orientation which is apparent in the drama and in fiction . . . only Langston Hughes still versifies. And the new poets are so far naive and imitative and sophomoric in their efforts to scan and formalize what must first be known—perhaps intellectually or intuitively or emotionally or all of these and none of them.[14]

In the introduction to his 1963 collection of 171 poems by 55 Negro poets covering a period of 70 years, Arna Bontemps writes of the feeling of injustice felt by a number of poets during the Harlem Renaissance of the 1920s in the critics' tendency to call them *Negro* poets instead of poets. Bontemps says this attitude was especially displeasing to Countee Cullen, but that a few of his associates were not sure that it was bad. Today in view of the isolation of many contemporary poets, including some Negroes, and their private language, they are still wondering. "But," Bontemps says, "it can be fairly said that most Negro poets in the United States remain near enough to their folk origins to prefer a certain simplicity of expression."[15]

---

[10] For an interesting account of Negro writers in the United States, see Arna Bontemps, "The Negro Contribution to American Letters," in John P. Davis (ed.), *American Negro Reference Book*, Prentice-Hall, 1966, ch. 25. See also three papers delivered by Arthur P. Davis, Saunders Redding, and Langston Hughes at the First Conference of Negro writers in March, 1959, reprinted in Abraham Chapman (ed.), *Black Voices*, St. Martin's Press, 1968, pp. 605–622.

[11] Blyden Jackson, "An Essay in Criticism," *Phylon*, Fourth Quarter, 1950, p. 338; Thomas D. Jarrett, "Towards Unfettered Creativity: A Note on the Negro Novelist's Coming of Age," *ibid.*, p. 315: Nick A. Ford, "A Blueprint for Negro Authors," *ibid.*, p. 374; Blyden Jackson, "The Continuing Strain: Resume of Negro Literature in 1955," *Phylon*, First Quarter, 1956, p. 35; John Lash, "A Long, Hard Look at the Ghetto," *Phylon*, First Quarter, 1957, p. 8.

[12] Charles H. Nichols, Jr., "The Forties: A Decade of Growth," *Phylon*, Fourth Quarter, 1950, p. 379; Nick A. Ford, *op. cit.*, p. 374.

[13] Brown, Davis, and Lee, *op. cit.*, p. 282.

[14] John S. Lash, "Expostulation and Reply," *Phylon*, Summer, 1960, pp. 121–122. As noted later in this chapter, Gwendolyn Brooks published a volume of poetry (*The Bean Eaters*) in 1960.

[15] Arna Bontemps (ed.), *American Negro Poetry*, Hill and Wang, 1963, p. xiv.

Many interesting novels were written by Negroes in the early decades of the twentieth century, but none of first-rate distinction before the middle or late 1930s. In the 1940s critics praised such novelists as Richard Wright, J. Saunders Redding, Willard Motley, Ann Petry, Chester Himes, and Ralph Ellison, and they found that the best work of Gwendolyn Brooks, Margaret Walker, Owen Dodson, M. Carl Holman, and M. B. Tolson showed extraordinary mastery of craftsmanship and gave them a high place among contemporary poets.[16]

In 1952, Ralph Ellison won the National Book Award for *The Invisible Man.* Calling Ellison "a writer of the first magnitude," Bone says that *The Invisible Man* is "by far the best novel yet written by an American Negro" and "quite possibly the best American novel since World War II.[17] For many, Richard Wright's later work failed to carry conviction, but his earlier writings continue to be highly rated. Redding's appraisal seems fair and sound:

In going to live abroad Richard Wright had cut the roots that once sustained him; the tight-wound emotional core came unwound; the creative center dissolved; his memory of what Negro life in America *was* lost its relevance to what Negro life in America is—and is becoming. The people and the events in his latest books are not true. While Wright remained honest, he was honest only to the memory of things past, to passions spent, to moods gone vapid, and too often these moods found expression in vaporous language. . . .[18]

Using folk material in relation to the life of southern Negroes who have migrated to the big cities of the North, Langston Hughes for forty years was "prodigiously creative and worked with virtually every literary form, including novels, short stories, essays, opera librettos, popular ballads and blues, musical comedies, gospel plays, historical pageants, and children's verse and stories."[19] James Baldwin has been called "one of the most talented novelists alive today,"[20] and his fame is not limited to the United States.

LeRoi Jones says that only in music has any significant contribution been made by Negroes to a *formal* American culture. "For the most part, most of the other contributions made by black Americans in the areas of painting, drama, and literature have been essentially undistinguished." Jones attributes this "tragic void" to the fact that the only Negroes who have been able to pursue some art, especially the art of literature, have been middle-class Negroes.[21]

THE USE OF RACIAL THEMES IN ART PRODUCED BY NEGROES

In the ante-bellum period most of the literary expression of Negroes was along anti-slavery lines. This was true of speeches, many letters, pamphlets, poems, and a few items of fiction. Writing was thought of as a part of the struggle for freedom. After emancipation, Negroes wrote to advance the struggle for the rights and responsibilities of citizenship; and in the twentieth century, creative and social literature continued to be used as instruments of protest against racial discrimination.[22] Propaganda, racial defense, and racial advertisement, then, were characteristic, at least until the 1920s, of most of the art produced by Negroes in the United States.[23]

A subject of some importance in considering racial themes in the writings of Negroes is the use of dialect. The first Negro poet to use dialect consistently was James Edwin Campbell, who wrote at the end of the nineteenth century. Campbell's dialect more closely reproduced plantation Negro speech

---

[16] Ford, *op. cit.,* p. 374; Nichols, *op. cit.,* p. 378; Arthur P. Davis, "Integration and Race Literature," *Phylon,* Second Quarter, 1956, pp. 144–145; and Brown, Davis, and Lee (eds.), *op. cit.,* p. 144.

[17] Robert A. Bone, *The Negro Novel in America,* Yale, 1958, pp. 196–197, 212.

[18] Saunders Redding, "The Alien Land of Richard Wright," in Herbert Hill (ed.), *Soon, One Morning,* Knopf, 1963, p. 59.

[19] Herbert Hill, "Introduction," in Hill (ed.), *op. cit.,* p. 16.

[20] Nick Aaron Ford, "Walls Do a Prison Make: A Critical Survey of Significant Belles-Lettres By and About Negroes Published in 1962," *Phylon,* Summer, 1963, p. 123.

[21] LeRoi Jones, *op. cit.,* pp. 130–131.

[22] Brown, Davis, and Lee, *op. cit.,* p. 6.

[23] Hugh M. Gloster, *Negro Voices in American Fiction,* Univ. of North Carolina Press, 1948, p. 252.

than that of any other writer. Writing at about the same time, Paul Lawrence Dunbar, the best known of the Negro dialect poets, fashioned a synthetic dialect which was "modeled closer upon James Whitcomb Riley's colloquial language than upon the speech it was supposed to represent."[24] Dunbar's synthetic dialect could be read easily and with pleasure by northern whites "to whom dialect meant only an amusing burlesque of Yankee English," but it is impossible, as Redding remarks, "to speak the whole heart of a people . . . through such a bastard medium." Dunbar's dialect form limited him to the humorous and the pathetic.[25] Dunbar himself wished to achieve recognition as a writer of pure English, and he devoted himself assiduously to such writing. However, the minstrel tradition was so strong that his dialect poetry received far more attention than did his poetry, novels, and short stories, written in the pure tongue.[26]

Some of the Negro writers who followed Dunbar, especially Sterling Brown, have made effective use of dialect, but of a very different form of dialect. Commenting on Brown's work, James Weldon Johnson said ". . . He has made more than mere transcriptions of folk poetry, and he has done more than bring to it mere artistry; he has deepened its meaning and multiplied its implications. He has actually absorbed the spirit of his material, made it his own; and without diluting its primitive frankness and raciness, truly re-expressed it with artistry and magnified power. In a word, he has taken this raw material and worked it into original and authentic poetry."[27] In 1963 Bontemps said that Negro poets have abandoned the use of dialect because they believe its effective use is limited to humor and pathos.[28]

A new approach to the Negro character in fiction was introduced by Charles W. Chesnutt at the turn of the century. Chesnutt wrote objectively, utilizing southern folk material, the situation of near-whites in Cleveland, and the results of miscegenation (*The Conjure Woman, The Wife of His Youth, The House Behind the Cedars*). In his later novels (*The Marrow of Tradition* and *The Colonel's Dream*), Chesnutt became propagandistic, but Negro creative literature has been advanced by his exposure of the Negro to critical analysis in the early part of his career.[29]

In the years of confusion following World War I, much of the writing produced by Negroes, like that of white authors, was literature of escape. Spokesmen for the New Negro made extensive use of the racial theme, but they wrote mainly for a white audience and most of their critics were white. Rich Whites underwrote Negro poets; and Negro poetry, regarded as "the prattle of a gifted child," became a fad. This period was called the "Negro renaissance," but the viewpoint of Negro writers during the 1920s was limited by their isolation from the literary life of Whites and by the general pattern of racial segregation.[30] In spite of that, the devotion to racial defense and praise so characteristic of the prewar years was replaced to some extent by

. . . a wider range of creative activity, a greater diversity of techniques and ideologies, and a keener appreciation for universal values. Realistic portraiture was done of Southern folk life, the Mid-Western small town, Harlem, and West Indian peasant experience. Analysis was made of the problems of color and caste among the bourgeoisie of the metropolitan North. Agitation for racial justice was conducted on an international as well as a national or sectional basis. Attention was directed to the primitivistic and exotic aspects of Negro life in Harlem. Rollicking satire was employed to attack the American race problem.[31]

This is the period of Langston Hughes' *The Weary Blues*, Claude McKay's *Harlem Shad-*

---

[24] J. Saunders Redding, *To Make a Poet Black*, Univ. of North Carolina Press, 1939, pp. 51–52.
[25] *Ibid.*, p. 63.
[26] *Ibid.*, pp. 56–64.
[27] J. W. Johnson, Introduction to Sterling A. Brown, *Southern Road*, Harcourt Brace Jovanovich, 1932, pp. xiv–xv.
[28] Bontemps, *op. cit.*, p. xv.

[29] Redding, *op. cit.*, pp. 68–76.
[30] Margaret Walker, "New Poets," *Phylon*, Fourth Quarter, 1950, pp. 345–346.
[31] Gloster, *op. cit.*, pp. 253–254.

ows, Countee Cullen's *Color* and *Copper Sun*, Jean Toomer's *Cane*, Jessie Fauset's *There Is Confusion*, Wallace Thurman's *The Blacker the Berry*, James Weldon Johnson's *God's Trombones*, and George Schuyler's *Black No More*.

With the passing of time, Negro writers have developed greater skills in handling racial themes. In Langston Hughes' *The Ways of White Folks*:

> . . . The realities of Negro life swim into the consciousness of the reader, making him realize that there is a greater depth in Negro-white relationships of the most casual sort than other writers have suggested. Without truculence, Hughes counterpoises realized Negro characters and white types, disclosing to view several gradations of white attitudes. The result is a revelation of the breadth of unexplored areas available to Negro writers. Even when dealing with the tradition-bound problems of "passing" and miscegenation, Hughes is able to emphasize a phase of the subject that has generally escaped notice. This is because he accepts the fact of the situation as one which, readily understandable in itself, needs no explanation. It is the effect of the fact that interests him.[32]

The same critics regard all the stories in Richard Wright's *Uncle Tom's Children* (1938) as "worthy of study as a clinical case illustrating the extremes to which the unhealthy race relations of the plantation South can lead men, black and white alike."[33]

Additional insights on race have been provided by Hughes through a comic figure, Mr. Jesse B. Semple—or just Simple—in *Simple Speaks His Mind* (1950) and *Simple Takes a Wife* (1953). According to Davis, the Negro reader finds in Simple "all of the slightly mixed-up racial thinking, all of the 'twofold loyalties,' and all of the laughable inconsistencies which the segregation pattern produces in us. The pressure of jim crow living is so uniform that even though Simple is an uneducated worker his responses to this pressure ring true for all classes."[34]

Until recently, the prominence of the racial theme did not result in a distinctive artistic pattern. Adopting literary traditions that were useful for their purposes, Negro writers were influenced "by Puritan didacticism, sentimental humanitarianism, local color, regionalism, realism, naturalism, and experimentalism."[35] According to Bone, Baldwin succeeded in transposing the entire discussion of American race relations to the interior plane. He finds his first novel, *Go Tell It on the Mountain*, impressive, a work that "cuts through the walls of the storefront church to the essence of Negro experience in America."[36]

No serious student of literature or of race relations regards Negro material as the only "natural" province of the Negro writer. Bone points out that authors usually select source material on the basis of familiarity, but that this general principle does not exclude the right to use less familiar material whenever the writer can use it to advantage. This critic concludes: ". . . a high protest content is not likely to produce good fiction; a studious avoidance of Negro life is scarcely more promising; the treatment of race material though not necessarily race conflict, is by all odds the likeliest alternative."[37]

Social Protest Themes in Art Produced by Negroes

The protest against unemployment, poverty, slum living, and prejudice caused the Depression decade to be called the socially conscious 1930s Negro writers, especially the poets, joined their white confreres in producing "socially significant" books. Sterling Brown's poem "Old Lem" exemplifies the mood of these years.

I talked to old Lem
And old Lem said:
  "They weigh the cotton
  They store the corn
    We only good enough
    To work the rows;

[32] Brown, Davis, and Lee (eds.), *op. cit.*, p. 16.
[33] *Ibid.*
[34] Arthur P. Davis, "Jesse B. Semple: Negro American," *Phylon*, First Quarter, 1954, pp. 21–28.

[35] Brown, Davis, and Lee (eds.), *op. cit.*, p. 6.
[36] R. Bone, "The Novels of James Baldwin," in Seymour L. Gross and John E. Hardy (eds.), *Images of the Negro in American Literature*, Univ. of Chicago Press, 1966, pp. 265–266, 268.
[37] Bone, *The Negro Novel in America*, p. 225.

They run the commissary
They keep the books
   We gotta be grateful
   For being cheated;
Whippersnapper clerks
Call us out of our name
   We got to say mister
   To spindling boys
They make our figgers
Turn somersets
We buck in the middle
   Say, 'Thankyuh, sah.'
     They don't come by ones
     They don't come by twos
     But they come by tens"[38]

The coming of World War II did not immediately affect the mood of the 1930s, and Negroes continued to publish books of poetry in the social protest vein until the middle 1940s. The contrast between the poetry of the New Negro period (roughly 1920–1935) and that of the early 1940s is striking. An example of the latter is seen in Robert Hayden's poem, "Speech."

Hear me, white brothers
Black Brothers, hear me:
I have seen the hand
Holding the blowtorch
To the dark, anguish-twisted body;
I have seen the hand
Giving the high-sign
To fire on the white pickets;
And it was the same hand,
Brothers, listen to me,
It was the same hand.[39]

The same point of view is shown also in Margaret Walker's poem, "For My People."

For my people standing staring, trying to fashion a better way from confusion, from hypocrisy and misunderstanding, trying to fashion a world that will hold all the people, all the Adams and Eves and their countless generations;
   Let a new earth arise. Let another world be born. Let a bloody peace be written in the sky. Let a second generation full of courage issue forth; let a people loving freedom come to grow. Let a beauty full of healing and a

strength of final clenching be the pulsing in our spirits and our blood. Let the martial songs be written, let the dirges disappear. Let a race of men now rise and take control.[40]

Melvin Tolson's poem "Dark Symphony" is another illustration of this temper.

Out of abysses of Illiteracy
Through labyrinths of Lies
Across wastelands of Disease . . .
We advance!
Out of dead-ends of Poverty,
Through wildernesses of Superstition,
Across barricades of Jim Crowism . . .
We advance!
With the peoples of the World . . .
We advance![41]

After World War II, some lowering of racial barriers and the possibility of considerable integration in the foreseeable future tended to reduce the protest element in Negro writing. According to Davis, the Negro writer in the early and middle 1950s retained Negro characters and backgrounds but shifted his emphasis from protests against racial discrimination to problems and conflicts within the Negro group. In 1943, Chester Himes wrote *If He Hollers*; his *Third Generation* (1953) dealt with school life in the Deep South and the conflicts that color differences caused within a Negro family. Owen Dodson's *Boy at the Window* and Gwendolyn Brooks' *Maud Martha* portray Negro middle-class life. William Demby's *Beetlecreek* reversed the protest theme by showing the cruelty of a Negro to a white man. The main character in Richard Wright's *The Outsider* is a Negro, but this philosophical novel is concerned with the problems of living rather than with racial protest. Although the characters in Langston Hughes' *Sweet Flypaper of Life* are Negroes, there is no trace of protest based on race in this novel. William Gardner Smith's *Anger at Innocence*, Ann Petry's *Country Place*, Richard Wright's *Savage*

---

[38] Reprinted by permission of Sterling Brown. Copyright 1939 by Sterling Brown.
[39] Robert E. Hayden, *Heart-Shape in the Dust*, Falcon Press, 1940.

[40] Reprinted from *For My People* by Margaret Walker, by permission of Yale University Press. Copyright 1942 by Yale University Press.
[41] Reprinted by permission of Dodd, Mead & Company from *Rendezvous with America* by Marvin Tolson. Copyright 1944 by Dodd, Mead & Company, Inc.

Holiday, and Willard Motley's *Knock on Any Door* have either no Negro characters or no main Negro characters. With the exception of Motley's novel, all the others are second novels and followed successful first works that stressed racial protest. Davis cites the work of M. B. Tolson (*Rendezvous with America* as compared with his later *Libretto for the Republic of Liberia*), of Gwendolyn Brooks (*A Street in Bronzeville* and *Annie Allen*), and of others to illustrate the same tendency among Negro poets.[42] (An exception to the trend away from protest themes in the 1950s is found in Ralph Ellison's *The Invisible Man,* a novel showing why a normal life is almost impossible for Negroes in the United States.)[43] In Negro writings in 1954 and 1955, Jackson noted a trend away from the bitter and broken hero, or the hero who is just picturesque, to heroic heroes of a modest kind.[44]

Bone remarks that by the time Richard Wright's disciples mastered his technique, the social conditions that had produced it had changed. Negro writers turned their attention from the anguish and despair of slum life to wartime experience.

. . . members of the postwar generation came to maturity during a period of double catastrophe. Their depression experience tended to attract them to the party; their wartime experience decisively reversed the trend. This development can be illustrated by what might be called the Wright-Himes-Ellison configuration. During the Depression these three novelists were brought into the party fold primarily through their quest for racial justice. But when the party adopted a 'soft line' on the Negro question during the war, the very militancy which originally attracted them to the party now caused them to break away. This break, as recorded in their subse-

quent fiction, was in each instance a traumatic experience. And in each case the 'plunge outside of history,' as Ralph Ellison calls it, was followed by a reaction against racial protest as such.[45]

Ford says that despite the fact that James Baldwin would deny that *Another Country* is a protest novel, it is "a bitter recital of mistreatment, humiliation, and rejection of the Negro by white America." Before committing suicide, one of Baldwin's characters says to a white friend:

How I hate them—all those white sons of bitches out there. They got the world on a string . . . and they tying that string around my neck, they killing me. . . . Sometimes I lie here and listen, listen for a bomb, man, to fall on this city and make all that noise stop. I listen to hear them moan. I want them to bleed and choke, I want to hear them *crying,* man, for somebody to come and help them. . . . I think wouldn't it be nice to get on a boat and go someplace . . . where a man could be treated like a man. . . . You got to fight with the landlord because the landlord's *white.* . . . You got to fight with the elevator boy because [he's] . . . white. Any bum on the bowery can [lord it] all over you because maybe he can't hear, can't see, can't walk . . .—but he's white.[46]

Although he praises his talent and virtues, Ford concludes that Baldwin narrowly misses greatness because (1) his view is negative; (2) he fails in some cases to "satisfy a reasonable curiosity about the final actions of some of his major characters"; and (3) he follows the contemporary tendency to substitute too often obscenities, sexual stereotypes, and profanity for meaningful language. Another novel of 1962 of the protest type, John Oliver Killens' *And Then We Heard the Thunder,* deals with the humiliation suffered by Negro soldiers at the hands of white soldiers. According to Ford, it has the faults of *Another Country,* is just as bitter, more compassionate, but less comprehensive and profound. The racial overtones of a third protest novel of

---

[42] Arthur P. Davis, "Integration and Race Literature," *Phylon,* Second Quarter, 1956, pp. 141–146. More than half of the 36 poems in Gwendolyn Brooks' *The Bean Eaters* (1960) "deal with experiences that are characteristically Negro and most of the remainder are concerned with the poor and the underprivileged of the urban community." N. A. Ford, "Battle of the Books," *Phylon,* Summer, 1961, p. 128.

[43] Nick A. Ford, "Four Popular Negro Novelists," *Phylon,* First Quarter, 1954, p. 34.

[44] Blyden Jackson, "The Blythe Newcomers: A Resumé of Negro Literature in 1954," *Phylon,* First Quarter, 1955, pp. 9–10.

[45] Bone, *The Negro Novel in America,* p. 164.

[46] Quoted in N. A. Ford, "Walls Do a Prison Make: A Critical Survey of Significant Belles-Lettres By and About Negroes Published in 1962," *Phylon,* Summer, 1963, p. 124.

1962, William Melvin Kelley's *A Different Drummer,* are more subdued than those in *Another Country.*[47]

Social protest themes continued to appear in verses written by "new Negro poets" in the 1960s. Protests against racial exploitation and poverty, together with expressions of hope or hopelessness, are seen in the following three poems.

FEEDING THE LIONS

Norman Jordan

They come into
our neighborhood
with the sun
an army of
social workers
carrying briefcases
filled with lies
and stupid grins
Passing out relief
checks
and food stamps
hustling from one
apartment to another
so they can fill
their quota
and get back
before dark.[48]

FACES OF POVERTY

Lucy Smith

No one can communicate to you
The substance of poverty—
Can tell you either the shape,
  or the depth,
    or the breadth
Of poverty—
Until you have lived with her intimately.

No one can guide your fingers
Over the rims of her eye sockets,
Over her hollow cheeks—
Until perhaps one day
In your wife's once pretty face
You see the lines of poverty;

Until you feel
In her now skinny body,
The protruding bones,
The barely covered ribs,
The shrunken breasts of poverty.

Poverty can be a stranger
In a far-off land:
An alien face
Briefly glimpsed in a newsreel,
An empty rice bowl
In a skinny brown hand,
Until one bleak day
You look out the window—
And poverty is the squatter
In your own backyard.

Poverty wails in the night for milk,
Not knowing the price of a quart[49]

. . .

POEM BY J. OVERTON ROGERS

See the running of the roaches
Hear the gnawing of the rats.
See the dripping of the faucet
Hear the whining of the cats.

See the broken, falling ceiling,
Hear the wind blow through the sash.
See the unsafe stairs and railing,
And the lack of cans for trash.

No, I won't be bitter
'Cause weak laws favor you.
But I will complain,
'Cause that's all that I can do.

Take your goddamn' high-rent money
Let a curse be on your soul,
A curse from this black fellow
Living in your hell hole.[50]

---

[49] From *New Negro Poets U.S.A.* Edited by Langston Hughes. Copyright © 1964 by Langston Hughes. Reprinted by permission of Indiana University Press.

[50] J. Overton Rogers, *Blues and Ballads of a Black Yankee,* Exposition Press, 1965, p. 30. In his "Foreword" to this volume, Whitney M. Young says: "If he doesn't always write verse according to classic form, if, on occasion, his lines sound more like an outraged social commentary on injustice, Mr. Rogers in clear and succinct terms has written on a problem that must be faced by us all, both Negro and white, not from the standpoint of benefit to one or the other, but for the salvation of this nation." *Ibid.,* p. 6. From *Blues and Ballads of a Black Yankee,* by J. Overton Rogers. Copyright © by J. Overton Rogers. All rights reserved. Reprinted by permission of the publisher, Exposition Press, Inc., 50 Jericho Turnpike, Jericho, New York 11753.

[47] *Ibid.,* pp. 125–129.

[48] Clarence Major (ed.), *The New Black Poetry,* International Publishers, 1969, pp. 78–79. Reprinted by permission of International Publishers Co., Inc. Copyright © 1969.

Universal Appeal in Art Produced by Minorities

The general trend in the writings by Negroes passed from the exoticism and racial exhibitionism of the 1920s, through the social protest period of the 1930s and early 1940s, to the universal point of view from the late 1940s to the early 1960s, and, in recent years, to black nationalistic themes.

In *Native Son* (1940) Richard Wright makes it clear that Bigger Thomas is a Negro, but he makes it equally as clear that he could be "white." His experiences might well have been those of a white youth in the ghettoes of Chicago. The struggle of Lutie Johnson for a better way of life for herself and her son in Ann Petry's *The Street* (1946), despite what would seem to be occasional excessive sermonizing on the plight of Negroes, has undeniable universal appeal. In *Knock on Any Door* (1947), a work in which Willard Motley evinces a superb handling of sustained and meaningful imagery, Nick Romano, a victim of the ulcerous maladies of the city and the slums, might well have been a Negro, although for Motley's purposes is Italian.[51]

The career of Frank Yerby is of interest in considering the trend toward writing with universal appeal. His first work, *Health Card* (1944), was entirely devoted to a racial theme, but such later works as *The Foxes of Harrow* (1946) and *The Vixens* (1947) completely abandoned racial material. A racial symbol, the symbol of rejection, is substituted in all his nonracial novels.

He finds in the social rebels of the white race, in men and women who because of birth, or manner of livelihood, or disregard of social and moral proprieties have become pariahs among their own people, an archetype of racial rejection. But these white rejectees fight back. They build industrial empires, or pile up huge mountains of illicit wealth, or become swashbuckling pirates who defy the laws of the smug and the respectable. Thus, symbolically the white rejectees get their revenge on a proud and haughty society,

and through them the rejected Negro can feel a sense of vicarious triumph.[52]

Three books of poetry that appeared during the 1940s reveal a decided shift from social protest to the universal viewpoint. These are *From the Shaken Tower* (1944) by Bruce McWright, *The Lion and the Archer* (1948) by Robert Hayden and Myron O'Higgins, and *Annie Allen* (1949) by Gwendolyn Brooks. According to Margaret Walker: "Each one of these books is less preoccupied with the theme of race as such. Race is rather used as a point of departure toward a global point of view than as the central theme of one obsessed by race. . . . *Annie Allen* is a fine delineation of the character of a young Negro woman from childhood through adolescence to complete maturity, but with slight racial exceptions, it could apply to any female of a certain class and society."

We have referred earlier to Ralph Ellison's *The Invisible Man* (1952) as a novel that used race symbolically. In evoking a world "which perhaps only an American Negro can fully apprehend, a lunatic, febrile world where love and hate, pity and cruelty, are brutally intermingled," Hill says that Ellison's work "utterly transcends the traditional preoccupations of the Negro writer; ultimately he is concerned not with race but with man."[53] Williard Motley's *Let No Man Write My Epitaph* (1958) is not limited to race in its examination of drug addiction in Chicago's slums.[54] In 1959, Lorraine Hansberry's *A Raisin in the Sun* "wrote the

[51] Jarrett, *op. cit.*, pp. 315–316. In a later paper ("Recent Fiction by Negroes," *College English*, Nov., 1954, p. 87), Jarrett says that it is ". . . the general tendency of Negro fictionists today not only to move away from the racial problem *per se*, but also to treat more complex themes, and to strive for universality in the handling of them."

[52] Nick A. Ford, "A Blueprint for Negro Authors," p. 377. Later Yerby is quoted as saying that the novelist "hasn't any right to inflict on the public his private ideas on politics, religion, or race. If he wants to preach he should go to the pulpit." Nick A. Ford, "Four Popular Negro Novelists," p. 38. Blyden Jackson's point of view is that Yerby has race consciousness but kept it under control until he built up a large following. Jackson says: "In *Benton's Row* . . . he makes . . . the most heretical and blood-curdling comments about southern religion, southern womanhood, the Old Southern Mansion, planter culture . . . , the southern defense of lynching, and even southern cooking. . . . " Blyden Jackson, "The Continuing Strain: Resume of Negro Literature in 1955," pp. 38–39.

[53] Hill, *op. cit.*, p. 8.

[54] John Lash, "Dimension in Racial Experience," *Phylon*, Summer, 1959, p. 124.

human drama in the rich and colorful and transforming empathy of a Negro family's orientations: her play treats dreamers and schemers who are Negroes more than it treats Negroes who are dreamers and schemers."[55] Although James Baldwin is a powerful protest writer, a substantial part of his writing is universalistic. His *Nobody Knows My Name* consists of 13 essays on topics ranging from literary criticism to desegregation. Ford says that the "thread that binds the whole is the recurrent theme of Baldwin's and all other Americans' search for identity."[56] (To the angry black man, universal themes in the work of a black writer can be read as treachery or antagonism to one's own race. In 1968 Eldridge Cleaver, a prominent black nationalist, said: "There is in James Baldwin's work the most grueling, agonizing, total hatred of the blacks, particularly of himself, and the most shameful, fanatical, fawning, sycophantic love of the whites that one can find in the writings of any black American writer of note in our time. . . . A rereading of *Nobody Knows My Name* cannot but convince the most avid of Baldwin's admirers of the hatred for blacks permeating his writings. In the essay "Princes and Powers," Baldwin's antipathy toward the black race is shocking.")[57]

Ester Jackson has discussed the relationship of the American Negro to "the shape of human suffering" in the modern world as found in the works of Dostoevsky, Gide, Malraux, Mann, Camus, and Sartre. The realization that a large segment of mankind " 'seems to share the kind of existence which has been the lot of the Negro'—alienation from the larger community, isolation within abstract walls, loss of freedom, a legacy of despair—has led to a literary view of the Negro as the 'prototype' of the contemporary sense of existential dislocation."[58] A similar view is taken by De Mott when he asks about Jewish novelists: "Is it not probable that the extraordinary influence of works of serious Jewish novelists signifies only that the voice of powerlessness speaking in situations of humiliation, nakedness, and weakness is the voice that speaks most directly to the *common* conviction about the nature of present experience?"[59]

The Black Nationalist Theme. As the 1960s ended and the 1970s began, integration into present-day American society was no longer a concern of many black writers, especially the poets. Instead, Don Lee and others speak of launching a literary revolution intended to persuade Negro Americans to take pride in a distinct and separate cultural heritage. Today most of the younger black poets insist that they are writing for the black community. They say that only black people can judge their work; whites are believed to be unable to evaluate the black experience, and, "consequently, any work of art derived from it or addressed to those who live it."[60] Mari Evans, a black poet, takes a somewhat different position in saying:

[55] John S. Lash, "Expostulation and Reply: A Critical Summary of Literature By and About Negroes in 1959," p. 112.

[56] N. A. Ford, "Search for Identity: A Critical Survey of Significant Belles-Lettres by and About Negroes Published in 1961," *Phylon*, Summer, 1962, p. 128.

[57] Eldridge Cleaver, *Soul on Ice*, McGraw-Hill, 1968, p. 99.

[58] Seymour L. Gross, "Introduction: Stereotype to Archetype, The Negro in American Literary Criticism," in Gross and Hardy (eds.), *op. cit.*, pp. 25–26. Ester M. Jackson's paper is: "The American Negro and the Image of the Absurd," *Phylon*, Winter, 1962, pp. 359–371. Norman Mailer develops a similar theme in his essay "The White Negro" in *Advertisements for Myself*, Putnam, 1959. The Negro is viewed as "everyman," or perhaps as the prototype of what all men face.

[59] Benjamin De Mott, "Jewish Writers in America," *Commentary*, Feb., 1961, p. 133. Leo W. Schwartz, writer and anthologist, asserts that until World War II, books on Jewish themes "were considered parochial, non-commercial and alien," but that a reversal has occurred during the past two decades. He says: "The search for a definition of self, which once was characteristic of minorities has now become characteristic of the entire American people. We have come to seek the answer of what and who we are, and why. The Jew is more used to this question. He has been asking it of himself for a long time and it is this that accounts for the abundance of Jewish best-sellers—books by Jewish authors and on Jewish themes." *The Plain Dealer*, June 2, 1963.

[60] Stephen E. Henderson, " 'Survival Motion': A Study of the Black Writer and the Black Revolution in America," in Mercer Cook and S. E. Henderson (eds.), *The Militant Black Writer*, Univ. of Wisconsin Press, 1969, pp. 78–79.

"Some things should be said at home and some in the marketplace. Black writers should decide whether what they have to say *needs* to be said to white or black folks and attempt to market their work accordingly. There are some things whitey needs to be told—and some things the brother needs to hear."[61]

Militant black literary critics hope that black poets will help to save Negroes from entering the "mainstream" and from the "intellectual and spiritual arrogance which masquerades as integration." According to Henderson: "Our poets are now our prophets. They have come to baptize us in blackness, to inform us with Soul."[62] The themes of the militants are: praise for black people, pride in blackness, destruction of an oppressive society, and the creation of a new way of life. Addison Gayle, Jr., sees black poetry moving farther along "the path of the black esthetic, as black poets turn increasingly away from the preoccupation with 'titillating white folks' and toward the serious task of creating 'the values by which their race is to live or die.' "[63]

A NEW DANCE

S. E. Anderson

And there they were: with fire everywhere
brothers instantly bonded for life
for life
and there was fire everywhere;
in their hearts, in their eyes, in their shackhomes

But burn they must
and burn we must

Black is the spiralfire through corridors
of white halls enflaming

The white one must be cremated to be saved
and we must cremate to be saved

It will not be burning black streets
It will not be our burning homes
It will be the downtowns of ofayclowns
honking their pallid tunes across
this stolen land

and we dance the Blackflame dance
in tune to the rhythm of our times

We rebegin where our brothers began:
cleansing-fire spreads from city to city
to country to country
to world

and we dance the Blackflame dance
in tune to the rhythm of our times
to be alive for the world to be alive
we dance the Blackflame dance
we will
we are—
watch us . . . .   . . join us.[64]

KA 'BA

LeRoi Jones

A closed window looks down
on a dirty courtyard, and black people
call across or scream across or walk across
defying physics in the stream of their will

Our world is full of sound
Our world is more lovely than anyone's
tho we suffer, and kill each other
and sometimes fail to walk the air

We are beautiful people
with african imaginations
full of masks and dances and swelling chants
with african eyes, and noses, and arms,
though we sprawl in grey chains in a place
full of winters, when what we want is sun.

We have been captured,
brothers. And we labor
to make our getaway, into
the ancient image, into a new
correspondence with ourselves
and our black family. We need magic
now we need the spells, to raise up·
return, destroy, and create. What will be

the sacred words?[65]

A POEM SOME PEOPLE WILL HAVE TO UNDERSTAND

LeRoi Jones

Dull unwashed windows of eyes
and buildings of industry. What

[61] *Ibid.*, p. 79.
[62] *Ibid.*, p. 72.
[63] Addison Gayle, Jr., "Integrating Negroes with Black People," *The New York Times Book Review*, Sept. 27, 1970.

[64] Major, *op. cit.*, pp. 23–24. Reprinted by permission of International Publishers Co., Inc. Copyright © 1969.
[65] From *Black Magic Poetry, 1961–1967*, copyright © 1969 by LeRoi Jones, reprinted by permission of the publisher, The Bobbs-Merrill Company, Inc.

industry do I practice? A slick
colored boy, 12 miles from his
home. I practice no industry.
I am no longer a credit
to my race. I read a little,
scratch against silence slow spring
afternoons.

      I had thought, before, some years ago
that I'd come to the end of my life.
          Watercolor ego. Without the precise-
            ness
a violent man could propose.
          But the wheel, and the wheels,
won't let us alone. All the fantasy
          and justice, and dry charcoal winters
All the pitifully intelligent citizens
          I've forced myself to love.

          We have awaited the coming of a natu-
            ral
          phenomenon. Mystics and romantics,
            knowledgeable
          workers
          of the land.

          But none has come.
          (Repeat)
            but none has come.
Will the machinegunners please step forward?[66]

ART AND IDEOLOGY: BLACK NATIONALIST WRITERS

In introducing a symposium on Negro literature in the United States, Herbert Hill states that the debate about the conflict between art and ideology is a futile exercise.[67] In his view, a commitment to racial justice and social action requires intense devotion to literary technique and artistic discipline. In reply, it may be said that some writers attain this commendable goal, but that others do not. Undisciplined emotionalism and feelings of urgency often contribute to the production of shoddy work. Perhaps James Baldwin is a case in point. According to Bone, after Baldwin's return from Paris in

1957 he was unable to grow as an artist and fell back upon a tradition of protest writing that he had formerly denounced. In *Another Country*, *The Fire Next Time*, and *Blues For Mister Charlie*, Bone says that Baldwin "assumes the role of Old Testament prophet calling down the wrath of history on the heads of the white oppressor."[68] Saying that Eldridge Cleaver (*Soul on Ice*) has "a powerful facility with the written word," J. O. Killens, a novelist and fellow black nationalist, hopes that he will soon realize that "his forte is creative writing, that he has a true gift to give to the world and to the Black Revolt . . . and that that gift is his great pen, which is mightier than his sword."[69] LeRoi Jones, poet, playwright, novelist, essayist, and polemicist, has shifted from being an avant-garde writer to playing the role of an active black nationalist. Concerning five or six essays in *Home: Social Essays* (1966), Robert Bone says: "Ostensibly they announce the author's conversion to black nationalism; in reality they signal an esthetic breakdown, a fatal loss of artistic control. The prose disintegrates, the tone becomes hysterical, and all pretense of logical argument is abandoned. The style, shall we say, is severely disturbed."[70] According to J. O. Killens, some poets "are writing hurriedly these days, as are some novelists and playwrights, as if they fear that the great Black is Beautiful fad might not last long, that the Black Thing might swiftly go out of style . . . and that they'd better get on board the little Black train before it runs out of steam, or diesel, or Great White Tolerance."[71]

Earlier we pointed out that during the 1950s, the reaction against the protest motif or oppression aspect of race relations led to a concern with conflicts and tensions within the Negro group itself. Blyden Jack-

[66] From *Black Magic Poetry, 1961–1967*, copyright © 1969 by LeRoi Jones, reprinted by permission of the publisher, The Bobbs-Merrill Company, Inc.

[67] Herbert Hill, "Introduction," in Herbert Hill (ed.), *Anger, and Beyond*, Harper & Row, 1966, p. xiv.

[68] Robert Bone, "The Novels of James Baldwin," in Seymour L. Gross and John E. Hardy (eds.), *op. cit.*, p. 267.

[69] John O. Killens, "The Writer and Black Liberation," in Pat Romero (ed.), *In Black America*, United, 1969, p. 269.

[70] Robert Bone, "Action and Reaction," *The New York Times Book Review*, May 8, 1966, p. 3.

[71] Killens, *op. cit.*, p. 270.

son has said that the finest Negro novelists (Petry, Killens, Ellison, Smith) "demonstrated how a middle-class Negro organically develops from the Negro masses, which itself is becoming more and more middle class."[72] Jackson concluded that it was the duty of the contemporary Negro novelist to trace the growing incorporation of the Negro into the American middle class. As the black nationalist movement gained momentum in the middle and late 1960s, this position came increasingly under attack. LeRoi Jones maintains that until recently the work of Negro writers was an imitation of white middle-class literature. In his view, the Negro writer can only survive "by refusing to become a white man." He urges the development of a literature dealing with the culture of the black man, "the man who remains separated from the mainstream."[73]

In the separatist philosophy espoused by the more militant black nationalists, desegregation and integration for ghetto Negroes are regarded as impossibilities in the foreseeable future. (Many black nationalists say publicly or privately that their long-run goal is integration, but for the short run they hold that only through separatism can the black community develop self-confidence and techniques to the point where it can meet the white community on an equal basis. See discussion in Chapter 13). Some go further, saying that they do not want to be assimilated into what they regard as the hypocrisy, corruption, and meaninglessness of white middle-class America. These persons urge blacks to reject the values of "the establishment" and to accept what they consider to be the more satisfying values of the black world. Support for black culture in the United States bears some resemblance to the Negritude (Negroness) movement in West Africa. Difficult to define briefly, Negritude is both a reaffirmation of pride in the cultures of Africa and a reaction to white domination. It is an attempt both to find a gratifying identity in the modern world and to formulate a rallying cry for use in national and international power struggles. The concept of "soul," an important part of the idea of black culture, may or may not be associated with the political concept of black power. And black power may or may not include black separatism. In any case, black artists are being told by the black nationalists that they should "do their thing" and not be limited or ruined by the alien values of white art.

Another theme that stands out in the viewpoint of the nationalistic black writers of today is the relationship, as they see it, of black artists to "the problem" and the "challenge" of the twentieth century. One of the leading black writers says:

I take the position that, since man is a social animal, his literature should and does have social relevance. And further, that, since the Black Revolt . . . is part and parcel of the worldwide revolution of people of color against colonialism and white racism, literature by Black men and women will generally have a social relevance to this worldwide revolution and especially to the Black Revolt presently unfolding in these United States of America. Moreover, any literature worth the designation is social, has social significance, is engaged on one side or the other, for humanity or against. Put another way: all art is propaganda, notwithstanding all propaganda is not art.[74]

Among the writers named by Killens as shifting from social protest to "Human Affirmation in the Land of Revolution" are Paule Marshall, Julian Mayfield, Ossie Davis, John Clarke, Irving Burgie, John Williams, Loften Mitchell, LeRoi Jones, Ronald Milner, Rosa Guy, Alice Childress, Lerone Bennett, Charles Hamilton, and Lonne Elder. In Killens' words, the art of

[72] Quoted in Seymour L. Gross, "Introduction: Stereotype to Archetype, The Negro in American Literary Criticism," in S. L. Gross and J. E. Hardy (eds.), *op. cit.*, pp. 22–23.

[73] LeRoi Jones, "Philistinism and the Negro Writer," in H. Hill (ed.), *Anger and Beyond*, pp. 54–56. Julius Lester, a black literary critic, says that "the present emphasis on blackness and the corresponding denial of Americanness is as false as Cullen's denial of blackness. The black writer must realize that his blackness has been acted upon and has reacted to forces that are peculiarly American." Julius Lester, "Journey Through Black Literature," *The New York Times Book Review*, Nov. 30, 1969.

[74] J. O. Killens, *op. cit.*, pp. 265–266.

today's black writer is "a hand grenade blasting away at American complacency." The black writer has "the sense of urgency that the tide of change for Black people throughout the earth is here and now and that this tide is in the flood, and that we are now afloat on a full sea and so must take the current, or lose our ventures for another hundred years."[75] As examples of important novels published in 1968 and 1969, Killens cites John Williams' *The Man Who Cried I Am,* one of the few novels by a black writer that encompasses the international scene, and Sara Elizabeth Wright's *This Child's Gonna Live,* a book about black people in a fishing village on the eastern shore of Maryland.

Since literature reflects, to some extent, the social climate of the times, an important segment of Negro writings now deals with black culture, black revolt, and "social relevance."

The Increased Demand for Books by Negro Writers. In recent years, there has been a boom in books by and about blacks. In 1969, the Negro Book Club's pamphlet, "The Guide to African-American Books," listed more than 5000 available titles. Such books as *Black Rage* by William H. Grier and Price M. Cobbs, *Black Power* by Charles Hamilton and Stokely Carmichael, *Soul On Ice* by Eldridge Cleaver, and *Rivers of Blood,* and *Years of Darkness* by Robert Conot have had large sales. Richard Wright, Ralph Ellison, and James Baldwin have been the most influential and best-selling novelists, but Countee Cullen, Langston Hughes, Claude McKay, and Chester Himes have been rediscovered. Other novelists "with substantial reputations if not wide readership" include Charles Wright (*The Messenger* and *The Wig*), Carlene Hatcher Polite (*The People One Knows* and *Curling*), William Melvin Kelly (*A Different Drummer* and *Dem*), John Oliver Killens (*Youngblood* and *'Sippi'*), Ernest Gaines (*Of Love and Dust*), Ishmael Reed *The Free-Lance Pallbearers* and *Yellow Back Radio Broke-Down*). The educational divisions of the

major publishing houses have taken the lead in providing books about the black experience. Nearly 75 percent of the books listed in the Negro Book Club's brochure are intended for use in schools and colleges. Many of the other titles, including *The Autobiography of Malcolm X,* Claude Brown's *Manchild in the Promised Land,* LeRoi Jones's plays, and James Baldwin's novels and essays, were originally trade editions intended for a general audience, but have been taken up by educational institutions.[76]

Small, black-oriented publishing houses have been started in a number of cities, among them Broadside Press, in Detroit, and Drum Publications, in New York. The placement of Blacks in important managerial and editorial positions in established firms has lagged behind the publication of volumes by Negroes. Ronald Hobbs, a black literary agent, feels that "though the increase in publication of books on black culture and history is socially beneficial, greedy literary agents and uninformed publishers are saturating the field. There is a deluge of inferior books."[77]

Some literary critics think that the future of the "black revolution" depends largely on the relationship between black writers and the established publishing houses. Watkins says: "If black writers, expressing themselves freely, are accepted by the publishing world, they will contribute to the advancement of Afro-Americans and, in the process, more than likely broaden significantly the world of literature. If they are not, the gap between the races—in literature and in the streets—can only widen."[78]

JEWISH WRITERS: THE JEWISH THEME AND THE "MODERN MOVEMENT"

In the early part of the twentieth century, Jewish consciousness in art produced by Jews is seen most intensely in the novel.

[75] *Ibid.,* p. 268.

[76] Mel Watkins, "The Black Revolution in Books," *The New York Times Book Review,* Sept. 10, 1969, p. 8.

[77] *Ibid.,* 14.

[78] *Ibid.,* p. 14.

Mary Antin's *The Promised Land* (1912) proclaimed the delight of the persecuted immigrant from Central Europe in being in America and expressed a desire to renounce her European past. New York's Lower East Side furnished material for novels by Abe Cahan (*The Rise of David Levinsky*, 1917), Anzia Yezierska, and Fannie Hurst (*Humoresque*). Edna Ferber's *So Big* and *Cimarron* are "purely American in subject matter," but *Fanny Herself* (1917) traces the development of the native-born American Jew, including the leading character's consciousness of prejudice. In the 1930s there was an increasing awareness—implicit or explicit—of a Jewish problem in the United States. This awareness was expressed in, for example, the negative writings of Jerome Weidman (*I Can Get It for You Wholesale*, 1937, and *What's in It for Me?*, 1938), in the character studies of Budd Schulberg (*What Makes Sammy Run?*), and in the novels of the "proletarian" writers: Henry Roth (*Call It Sleep*, 1934), Albert Halper *Union Square* and *The Foundry*), and Michael Gold (*Jews Without Money*, 1930). The uncritical "melting pot" and "promised land" viewpoints and the denial of the past were discarded. The outstanding Jewish author of the latter school, Ludwig Lewisohn (*Upstream* and *The Island Within*), told and retold the story of the failure of assimilation.[79]

At the beginning of the 1960s, De Mott said that during "the present period of assimilation" it is not certain that a survey of specifically Jewish qualities in contemporary writing is justifiable. He questioned whether the difference between Jewish and Gentile experience in America for young people is as significant as that between American and European Jews during the previous 30 years, and also, whether there is a Jewish literature in the United States.[80]

According to Kazin, what saved Jewish writing in America "from its innate pro-

vincialism . . . was the coming of the 'intellectuals'—writers like Delmore Schwartz, Saul Bellow, Lionel Trilling, Karl Shapiro, Harold Rosenberg, Issac Rosenfeld, Lionel Abel, Clement Greenberg, Bernard Malamud, Irving Howe, Philip Rahv, Leslie Fiedler, Robert Warshow, Paul Goodman, Norman Mailer, Philip Roth, William Phillips." Many of the earlier writers had only their "hard story" to tell, but the Jewish "intellectuals" of the 1940s and later became a part of the worldwide "modern movement." According to Kazin:

. . . if the Jew has put his distinct mark on modern American writing, it is surely because, in a time when the old bourgeois certainties and humainst illusions have crumbled, the Jew is practiced in what James called 'the imagination of disaster,' and 'does indeed see life as ferocious and sinister.' The contemporary literary temper is saturnine, panicky, black in its humor but adroit in shifting the joke onto the shoulders of society. And the Jewish writer, with his natural interest in the social fact, has been particularly quick to show the lunacy and hollowness of so many present symbols of authority. Anxiety hangs like dry electricity in the atmosphere of modern American life and the stimulus of this anxiety, with all its comic overtones, is the realized subject in the novels of Bruce Jay Friedman, Joseph Heller, Richard Stern, Jeremy Larner, the plays of Jack Gelber and Arthur Kopit. There is real madness to modern governments, modern war, modern moneymaking, advertising, science, and entertainment; this madness has been translated by many Jewish writers into the country they live in, the time that offers them everything but hope. In a time of intoxicating prosperity, it has been natural for the Jewish writer to see how superficial society can be, how pretentious, atrocious, unstable—and comic. This, in a secular age when so many people believe in nothing but society's values, is the significance to literature of the Jewish writer's being a Jew."[81]

The approach to literature found in the writings of the Jewish "intellectuals" has not been unopposed within the Jewish com-

[79] Marie Syrkin, "The Cultural Scene: Literary Expression," in Oscar Janowsky (ed.), *The American Jew*, Harper & Row, 1942, pp. 99–100, 104–106.
[80] Benjamin De Mott, *op. cit.*, p. 133.

[81] Alfred Kazin, "The Jew as Modern Writer," in Peter I. Rose (ed.), *The Ghetto and Beyond*, Random House, 1969, pp. 428, 429, 431–432. Reprinted from *The Commentary Reader*, Atheneum, 1966.

munity. According to Guttmann: "Within the literary world, the campaign to win converts for Judaism has been three-fold—first, the attack on those who defect from or denigrate the Jewish community; second, continued emphasis on the dangers of anti-semitism; third, an affirmation of the positive aspects of Judaism and of the Jewish community." In 1937, Meyer Levin was asked by the secretary of the Anti-Defamation League why young Jewish writers felt impelled to "describe your people in this disgusting manner." Later, Guttmann says, Edward Adler, Jerome Charyn, Babette Deutsch, Leslie Fiedler, Norman Fruchter, Herbert Gold, Irving Howe, Alfred Kazin, Philip Roth, Muriel Rukeyser, L. S. Simckes, and Louis Untermeyer were denounced as anti-Semitic or criticized for their aloofness from the Jewish community. Among others, Roth has been advised to be more positive. This writer has been identified as one whose " 'criticisms, exaggerated by the self-hate of their alienation, cannot serve as an adequate guide to the true condition of the American Jewish community today.' " Roth's reply was: "The question really is—who is going to address men and women like men and women, and who like children? If there are Jews who have begun to find the stories the novelists tell more provocative and pertinent than the sermons of some of the rabbis, perhaps it is because there are regions of feeling and consciousness in them which cannot be reached by the oratory of self-congratulation and self-pity."[82]

The position of Roth and of other writers in the "modern movement" is that fiction is not written to affirm the principles and beliefs that are widely held, nor to guarantee readers of the appropriateness of their feelings. Rather, the world of fiction allows both the writer and the reader to respond to experience in ways that are not always possible in daily life. This expansion of moral consciousness is seen as valuable to an individual and to society.[83]

In contrast with the preoccupation of the current black nationalist writers with black culture, colonialism, and racism, the Jewish "intellectuals" are identified with the "modern movement" and write about the anxiety, the superficiality, and the pretentiousness of modern life. If secularization and assimilation continue, Guttmann says, "Negroes are more likely than Jews disproportionately to fill the ranks of dissent and to imagine in novel and in poem another country better than the one we live in now."[84]

BLUES AND BLUES PEOPLE

The music of American Negroes is an integral part of black culture and should be considered in that context. Charles Keil, musician and social scientist, points out that Negro culture is only partly dependent on the basic institutions in the black community, including religion and the family, that differ from white American specifications. On another level, he says, "the shared sensibilities and common understandings of the Negro ghetto, its modes of perception and expression, its channels of communication, are predominantly auditory and tactile rather than visual and literate . . . the prominence of aural perception, oral expression, and kinesic codes or body movement in Negro life—its sound and feel—sharply demarcate the culture from the irrational white world outside the ghetto."[85] Keil refers to "entertainment" from the white point of view and ritual, drama, or dialectical catharsis from the Negro viewpoint, as "that special domain of Negro culture wherein black men have proved and preserved their humanity." The important point is that Negro performances, called "entertaining" both by Negroes and by whites, have a special, usually unconscious, ritual significance for Negroes. The best of these entertainers of the "soul" tradition are identity experts—experts in "chang-

[82] Allen Guttmann, "The Conversions of the Jews," in Rose (ed.), *op. cit.*, pp. 439–440.

[83] Philip Roth, "Writing About Jews," in Rose (ed.), *op. cit.*, pp. 450–451.

[84] Allen Guttmann, *op. cit.*, p. 447.

[85] Charles Keil, *Urban Blues*, Univ. of Chicago Press, 1966, p. 16–17.

ing the joke and slipping the yoke."[86] Entertainers, including some preachers, and hustlers, then, must be seen as culture heroes rather than as deviants.[87]

Although Negro music in the United States is distinctive, it is inseparable from the total life of the United States. Albert Murray speaks quite clearly to this point:

. . . what American black musicians express represents far more than the fact that American black folks been 'buked and been scorned and nobody know de trouble dey seen . . . as an art form it is a direct product of the U.S. Negro sensibility, but it is the end-product . . . of all the cultural elements which brought that sensibility into being in the first place. . . . The spirituals . . . always expressed more than a proletarian reaction to poor pay and bad working conditions. . . . they were also a profound and universally moving expression of Protestant Christianity . . . the spirituals contained New England elements, frontier elements and American aspirations in general . . . , including an active physical existence and a rich, robust, and highly imaginative conception of life itself. . . . The blues affirm not only U.S. Negro life in all of its arbitrary complexities and not only life in contemporary America in all of its infinite confusions, they affirm humanity in the very process of confronting failures and existentialistic absurdities . . .[88]

[86] *Ibid.*, p. 15. In connection with a discussion of black culture, the concept of "soul" must be included. "Soul" is an elusive concept, an ineffable quality, but paraphrasing Keil's discussion of various soul components we can distinguish some of its features: spirituality given bodily manifestation; staying power, will to survive and surmount sufferings; food, sex, and song as energies that can substitute metaphorically for each other; sheer effort—trying is more important than success or failure; sharing feelings, emotions, experiences, and understandings with others; the language of the ghetto—reshaping current slang; gestures and exaggerated body movement correlated with a particular style of music; a sense of timing that runs through walking, talking, singing, dancing, preaching, and joking; the call and response pattern that is common in African and Afro-American ritual and singing, as well as in "signifying" ("playing the dozens" or "sounding"); a refusal to acknowledge the domination of machine over man—the tradition that is nonmachine, not antimachine; truth and sincerity; the trials of members of ethnic minorities; and negritude or racial identity—belonging. See *ibid.*, pp. 167–181.

[87] *Ibid.*, p. 20.

[88] Albert Murray, "Something Different, Something More," in Hill (ed.), *Anger and Beyond*, pp. 116–117.

Blues, jazz, and soul are key terms in the development of Negro music and the music produced by Whites in the United States that is related to Negro music.[89] The shouts, chants, and hollers, as well as the work songs and the spirituals, preceded the "primitive" blues. Although these blues had a component of social protest and social reform, they were, according to Jones, primarily a verse form and secondarily a way of producing music. The "primitive" blues was a vocal music, but as Negroes made more and more use of "European" instruments (brass and reeds), blues began to change and jazz was ushered in. Jazz developed out of the blues, but it is an original music and not simply a successor to the blues. Coming later, "classic blues" showed the Negro singer's inclusion of many aspects of popular American music, especially the music of vaudeville. The instrumental music associated with classic blues showed the same development. Ragtime, the most instrumental or nonvocal music inspired by Negro experience, appeared at approximately the same time as the classic blues. Whereas early blues singing had a notably personal quality, classic blues had a professional element—it could be used to entertain others formally. By the 1930s, jazz had made great headway in the Negro middle class and, also, white "swing" bands had appeared. Swing music, the music of arranged big-band jazz, developed a style that had little to do with most Negroes. Nevertheless, by the 1940s, swing dominated American dance music. "Real" blues returned to the Negro community; "rhythm & blues" was performed almost exclusively for black audiences. Then the "moderns" or "bebop-pers" appeared and restored jazz to its original separateness. Jones points out that bebop re-established blues as the most important Afro-American form in Negro music. Bebop was a reaction to swing, and progressive, Dixieland, and cool were white reactions to bebop. In turn, funky and soul are Negro reactions to progressive and cool. "*Cool* meant non-participation; *soul* means a 'new'

[89] This summary is based on LeRoi Jones, *Blues People*, pp. 50–223 (50, 59, 62, 70, 71, 81, 82, 163, 165, 166, 169, 172, 181, 194, 218, 219, and 223).

establishment. . . . rock 'n' roll is usually a flagrant commercialization of rhythm & blues (the 'vulgar' urban blues of the forties).". 'Soul' music (the hard-bop style) is often said to be a conscious re-evaluation "of the roots."[90]

Jones contributes to our understanding of the evolution of soul music (blues-jazz-gospel synthesis) by distinguishing between the Western emphasis on the artifact and the African or Afro-American stress on expression. According to Jones—

The Western concept of the cultivation of the voice is foreign to African or Afro-American music. In the West, only the artifact can be beautiful, mere expression cannot be thought to be. It is only in the twentieth century that Western art has moved away from this concept and toward the non-Western modes of art-making, but the principle of the beautiful thing as opposed to the natural thing still makes itself felt. The tendency of white jazz musicians to play 'softer' or with 'cleaner, rounder tones' than their Negro counterparts is, I think, an insistence on the same Western artifact. Thus an alto saxophonist like Paul Desmond, who is white, produces a sound on his instrument that can almost be called legitimate, or classical, and the finest Negro alto saxophonist, Charlie Parker, produced a sound on the same instrument that was called by some 'raucous and uncultivated.' But Parker's sound was *meant* to be both those adjectives. Again, reference determines value. Parker also would literally imitate the human voice with his cries, swoops, squawks, and slurs, while Desmond always insists he is playing an instrument, that it is an artifact separate from himself. Parker did not admit that there was any separation between himself and the agent he had chosen as his means of self-expression.[91]

The record is clear. Negro music (song and dance) has been borrowed by white America through the white-controlled music business (record companies, music publishers, radio stations). Among other examples, Keil points out that Benny Goodman's fame rests on Fletcher Henderson's arrangements, Elvis Presley's on the style of the Negro rhythm-and-blues performers of the late 1940s, and Peggy Lee's on many of Ray Charles' most

popular songs, adding that there are many notorious plagiarists in England. Appropriations by white musicians are resented to greater or lesser degrees by the Negro innovators in blues and jazz, and each appropriation leads to stylistic revitalization on the part of these innovators. According to Keil: "It is simply incontestable that year by year, American popular music has come to sound more and more like African popular music. The rhythmic complexity and subtlety, the emphasis on percussive sound qualities, the call-and-response pattern, the characteristic vocal elements (shout, growl, falsetto, and so on), blues chromaticism, blues and gospel chord progressions, Negro vocabulary, Afro-American dance steps—all have become increasingly prominent in American music."[92] The reasons for the appropriation of Negro-like music (swing, rock and roll, and so forth) on the part of Whites are less clear. Keil says that the needs of young white Americans "to reject and rebel, to dance and blow off steam, have often been cited in connection with various musical fads and crazes, the Beatles (and other British groups) being the latest case in point."[93]

Tynan has provided a vivid picture of the effectiveness with which a popular black musician communicates with an audience and conducts his ritual.

Observing the crowd was an unforgettable experience. From Charles' first opening wail, the mass of jam-packed humanity howled its joy. In groups they sang, chanting along with him. They stood on tables and waved hands above their heads in utter abandon. Even the sides of the bandstand were packed with admirers who wanted to get as close to Charles as they possibly could. On a raised platform to the right of the stand, normally used for a relief trio at dances, a young white couple began dancing until stopped by a ballroom guard. When the

[90] *Ibid.*, pp. 218–219, 223.
[91] *Ibid.*, pp. 30–31.

[92] Charles Keil, *Urban Blues*, Univ. of Chicago Press, pp. 44–46. Reprinted by permission of the publisher. Keil's annotated outline of blues styles consists of four main categories: Country Blues, City Blues, Urban Blues, and Soul Music, plus another division called Parallel and/or Derived Styles. The main headings and subheadings are arranged in chronological order, and regional variations are indicated. See *ibid.*, pp. 217–220.
[93] *Ibid.*, pp. 48–49.

singer launched into "Let the Good Times Roll" a deep-throated roar of recognition went up. All over the ballroom floor hands and arms, groping like lost souls striving for heaven reached up from the mass. Hysteria born of almost holy fervor gripped the crowd.[94]

According to Haralambos, the blues as a musical form is declining in popularity among Blacks, at least in northern cities. On the average, blues singers and audiences are in their forties. Younger Blacks are said to see the blues as relating to the past, "to a time of hardship and sadness which many don't want to be reminded of." In a study of popular radio stations, Haralambos found that black audiences prefer "soul music." He doubts that a satisfactory definition of this music will ever be produced, adding that disc jockeys "emphasized that aspects of gospel and blues are present in the harmonies, rhythms, diction, and subject matter of present-day soul songs."[95]

COMPOSERS

Most composers, including black composers, teach, have few opportunities for commissions and performances, and are relatively unknown. Dominique-René De Lerma, Director of the Black Music Center at the School of Music at Indiana University, has compiled a catalog listing some 850 black composers of serious music. The published work will be called: *Black Music: A Preliminary Register of the Composers and Their Works.* Another book, *The Legacy of Black Music*, will be published by Kent State University Press. The latter publisher has already published *Black Music in Our Culture.* Two new record albums were issued by Desto in 1971: *The Black Composer in America* and *Natalie Hinderas Plays Music by Black Composers.* Howard Klein, music critic of *The New York Times*, says that the works presented in these

records "could stand beside the best music written over the past twenty years and stand well."[96]

THE NEGRO IN THE PERFORMING ARTS

The Theater

During 1968, black performers were more visible to the American public than at any time since the 1920s, but in the total theatrical picture they occupied only a small place.[97] Many actors and actresses wondered whether they should work to develop a black theater or to try to succeed on Broadway. In 1968 the New York State Commission for Human Rights conducted hearings on discrimination in the theater. A report showed that of a total of 523 performers on Broadway in the 1967–1968 season, only 57 were black, and that number included the 45 cast members of the all-black company of *Hello Dolly!*[98] Barbara Ann Teer, actress and director of the off-Broadway musical play *The Believers* finds that the situation for the Negro in the theater and other mass media

[94] John Tynan, "Funk, Groove, Soul," *Down Beat*, Nov. 24, 1960, p. 19.

[95] Michael Haralambos, "Soul Music and Blues: Their Meaning and Relevance in Northern United States Black Ghettos," in Norman E. Whitten and John F. Szwed (eds.), *Afro-American Anthropology*, Free Press, 1970, pp. 367–383.

[96] Howard Klein, "Overdoing 'Benign Neglect'?" *The New York Times*, March 7, 1971. Section 13, p. 1.

[97] For a summary of the experience of Negro playwrights on Broadway and off-Broadway during the period 1930–1965, see Langston Hughes, "The Negro and American Entertainment," in John P. Davis (ed.), *op. cit.*, pp. 834–848. In 35 years, only ten Negro plays were produced on Broadway. During this period, Hughes says, the most hospitable theater in New York to the Negro playwright was the Greenwich Mews, an off-Broadway theater. According to Hughes, only the Karamu Theater in Cleveland was more active in presenting plays by or about Negroes than the Greenwich Mews. In a brief survey of the Negro theater up to 1964, Loften Mitchell said: ". . . it seems amazing that Negro theater workers have managed such a considerable output. It should be remembered that many of the ventures . . . were written, directed, and produced under harrowing circumstances. The artists generally worked full time at other jobs. They had no well-to-do relatives who could maintain them. They performed at night clubs, working or struggling during the day to pay their rents. And, too, these plays were supported by people whose incomes were at most, uncertain." Loften Mitchell, "The Negro Theatre and the Harlem Community," in John H. Clarke (ed.), *Harlem: A Community in Transition*, Citadel Press, 1964, pp. 155–156.

[98] Lindsay Patterson, "The Negro in the Performing Arts," in Pat Romero (ed.), *op. cit.*, p. 310.

"remains frighteningly depressing."[99] Another actress, Ellen Holly, wrote about the issue of color in the theater, citing the position taken by *The New York Times* Drama Section in favor of hiring only those Negro actors whose skins are black and whose features are 100 percent African. Miss Holly argues that black is not a color of the skin but a state of mind, adding that "if African criteria are to be the yardstick by which American blacks are hired few Americans will qualify, and we must consider importing actors from Uganda."[100]

Another question troubling black actors is that of the kind of roles they can and should play in an integrated theater. They are concerned about the relevance of a role to the black experience. After his success in *The Great White Hope*, James Earl Jones said that he didn't believe in integrated casting "unless the parts can be played psychologically and physically by Negroes. . . . Integrated casting is fine as long as it doesn't distort the scope of the play, but I'm not out to prove anything and I don't want to be used to further causes because I'm black."[101] Other actors hold that color is not important if the performer is sufficiently proficient.

Although the American Negro Theater had an excellent record of achievement during the early 1940s, it disappeared during the last half of that decade.[102] The Black Arts Repertory Theater and School, started in Harlem in 1965 by LeRoi Jones, was discontinued after seven months.[103] The year 1968 was a notable one for the black theater. The Negro Ensemble Group had a successful season; all of its plays were by black writers. Critics commented favorably on Ray McIver's *God Is (Guess What?)*, Lonne Elder's *Ceremonies in Dark Old Men*, and Errol Hill's *Man Better Man*. The New Lafayette Theater, founded by Robert Macbeth, produced Ed Bullins' *In the Wine Time*, "a stunning play about ghetto dwellers."[104] In addition to the production of plays by American Negro playrights, African writers were represented in the American theater of 1968 with plays by Wole Soyinka (*The Trials of Brother Jero, The Strong Breed*, and *Kongi's Harvest*).

Two plays by LeRoi Jones, *Dutchman* and *The Slave*, have been produced a number of times off-Broadway and elsewhere. Both plays have been praised by critics, and *Dutchman* received the ninth Obie Award for the best American play done off-Broadway. *Dutchman* is a violent one-act play set in a New York subway. The play consists of a dialogue between a Negro man and a white woman that ends in argument and a fatal stabbing of the man. *The Slave* is a violent, two-act play involving the leader of an uprising, his whie ex-wife and her husband, a liberal professor.[105]

Debates concerning the purposes and the quality of the black theater paralleled the controversies over the black graphic and plastic arts in the early 1970s. The points of view of Martin Gottfried and Clayton Riley exemplify these arguments. According to Gottfried, the theater, driven by a desire to be involved in contemporary problems and intimidated by black militancy in general (especially by the idea that only Blacks can write about Blacks), has surrendered to artistic racism. In his view, "professional and artistic standards are being compromised for the sake of black plays, playwrights and actors; standards of writing, production, performance and judgment are being lowered for blacks, and it is prejudice all over again, inverse this time."[106] If it weren't for the American racial situation, Gottfried says, the Negro Ensemble Company wouldn't exist. This critic's judgment is that the NEC "has suffered from overpraise and from the assumption that its blackness gives it a special reason to exist, whether or not the work is good. The company is admirably earnest in

[99] *Ibid.*, p. 305.
[100] *Ibid.*, p. 306.
[101] *Ibid.*, p. 306.
[102] Harold Cruse, *The Crisis of the Negro Intellectual*, Morrow, 1967, p. 209.
[103] *Ibid.*, p. 539.
[104] Patterson, *op. cit.*, p. 307.

[105] Miles M. Jackson, "Significant Belles-Lettres By and About Negroes Published in 1964," *Phylon*, Third Quarter, 1965, p. 225.
[106] Martin Gottfried, "Is All Black Theater Beautiful? No," *The New York Times*, June 7, 1970, pp. D1, 3.

its purpose but its qualities are social rather than artistic. . . ." Gottfried adds that this most famous of the country's black theaters does not get the best of the black scripts, the scripts of such writers as LeRoi Jones and Ed Bullins. Gottfried says that the American Place Theater, a white theater, presents at least one black play a season because the director has decided that there are times "when social needs come first; that a theater to be vital, must respond to the world in which it exists; that the energy of black playwrights' commitment and the relevance of their plays make them 'voices worth hearing.'" According to this critic, black writers feel compelled to write about black people and the racial situation, and this feeling "encourages propaganda and inevitably leads to agit-prop plays."

Most of the plays are situation melodramas, redefined as reflecting the *contemporary black experience*. . . . Ironically, Bullins—like so many black militants—is convinced that intellectual and cultural refinement (which it took to write 'The Pig Pen') is white and that a black man who sounds educated is trying to be white. Through such thinking, black playwrights write purposely coarse dramas, stereotyped in a way not very different from television's 'Amos 'n Andy' (a victim of rote liberalism that would surely be produced by the NEC and acclaimed as beautifully black were it written today by a black playwright.)

There are also new versions of the *coon show* —black folks singin' and dancin'. Not since 'Carmen Jones' . . . had anyone dared produce an all-black show for Broadway consumption. The all-black 'Hello, Dolly!' was appalling, all the more so for its success. What does 'Dolly' have to do with black people? Nothing, of course. Why were the characters—*all* of them—black? It was a 'Dolly' in blackface with no concern for the style or sense of the show.

'Dolly' wasn't the only recent coon show. There have been more each season ('Purlie' and 'Billy Noname' most recently), flecked here and there with reference to black beauty, sit-ins and militancy, but existing essentially to merchandise black bodies—have them on stage as a color motif, a racial motif.

Gottfried regards Charles Gordone's play, *No Place to Be Somebody* as "a disorganized

mixture of gangster movie melodrama, poetry, set pieces and surrealism. Parts of it were very impressive and Gordone is an extremely talented playwright, but his play is also long, clumsy and confused." Its overpraise, Gottfried argues, was unfortunate, for the reason that any playwright has the need and right to be judged as a professional and by professional standards.[107] Double artistic standards are racist, and racism destroys art.

In his vigorous reply, Clayton Riley, a black critic, said that Mr. Gottfried and his friends pray for the return of the nineteenth century. Riley agrees that Blacks in the theater are not functioning on the same standards of quality that are acceptable to most white people, but he says the standards that Gottfried praises are comprised "primarily of musical fantasies, inane, stupefying comedies and what tries to pass for profound dramatic commentary on our times."[108] Riley says that he too has criticized the work of black artists in the theater, but he questions whether

in a city where there is not a truly impressive white company at work in the performing arts . . . , the Negro Ensemble Company needs to justify its existence in terms of some vague, indeed nonexistent framework of excellence that Gottfried has dreamed up and applied to Black theater without mentioning anyone operating in whiteface in the same general area. If the NEC is a mediocre outfit, that mediocrity is basically attributable to an attempt by its director to run his shop as a dictator, and his further attempt to live up to the artistic requirements of white people (and some Blacks, as well) who have been dieting for years on such constipating fare as "Forty Carats" and "Last of the Red Hot Lovers."

Concerning Gottfried's comment ·that black playwrights feel compelled to write about black people and the racial situation, Riley says that virtually every white playwright feels a compelling desire to write about white people and nonracial situations. According to this critic, Blacks have "a rich legacy to call upon when we choose—onstage

107 *Ibid.*, p. 3.
108 Clayton Riley, "We Will Not Be 'A New Form of White Art in Blackface,'" *The New York Times*, June 14, 1970, pp. D1, 3.

or anywhere else—to tell one another about ourselves. Those who willingly chose to ignore what we were about until recently are hardly the ones to tell us what forms our craft and our artistic concerns should take, particularly since their silence and indifference were fundamental contributors to the exclusion of Blacks from America's cultural marketplace for so long."[109] In what Riley calls the "reality of dual activity by America's Black actors and playwrights," there is, first, a theater of Negro participation in which Blacks work "essentially as guests subject to the whims (sometimes known as 'standards')" of Whites who control the invitations and the output, and second, there is the Black Theater going back to the early 1960s. Riley wonders if Gottfried and his colleagues see only those black plays that are presented outside the black community. Among the productions commended by Riley are those at Ernie McClintock's Afro-American Speech and Drama Studio, 15 West 126th Street, where "the style and level of theater speak clearly of a concern for creating and maintaining a body of Black Theater classics." Riley says that the National Black Theater, another Harlem group, is examining "the use of dance and music structured to detail both the African and African-American tradition of the shared experience." He mentions also that Roger Furman's New Heritage Theater offers "solid, informative and entertaining productions of well-written, imaginatively produced original dramas and comedies." Riley concludes that—

None of the companies I have mentioned are beyond criticism; some of their works (and the works of similar community-based theaters) are better than others, and some of their playwrights, actors and directors are better equipped than others. This must all be measured by yardsticks of performance realistic to the artists and the community involved. But there is magic in what they do. Black magic for those who know the forms or are willing to sit and feel the effect without reaching to the shores and caves of Europe for guidance.[110]

Charles Gordone, a black playwright, takes a position different from both Riley and Gottfried. He doubts that there has ever been "such a thing as 'black theater.' What is called black theater has, as it should, come out of the civil rights movement." In Gordone's view, what is called the black experience in the United States is historically and existentially black American, and he asks whether any black writer can write anything and leave out the word "white." One of the reasons why Gordone believes that the idea of a black theater is dead is that after LeRoi Jones, "you can't write any more about how badly the black man is treated and how angry he is. LeRoi Jones has said it." Gordone suggests that "if you are a writer and you are going to talk about black people, include the humanity of all people, the love of all people, the humor of all people, the will to survive and the will to live —of all people—and the strength of people against fantastic odds. The black experience in this country has a hell of a lot to do with all that."[111]

Ossie Davis, a prominent black actor-author, says that he can understand the bitterness of young black writers and their rejection of the society in which they live. However, although he admires the honesty and sharpness of their work, he says that he cannot follow the same course. Davis sees a "sort of spiritual adolescence" in the work of these writers and looks "with confidence to the day when these young folks will no longer find it necessary to be as harsh, abrasive, bitter and jangling. . . ."[112]

The indications are that the controversies concerning the role of black playwrights and black actors in American life will continue for some time.

Dancers, Concert Artists, and Conductors

In the field of the dance, Katherine Dunham and Pearl Primus were leaders for many years. Both attained a high level of artistic achievement in the adaptation of folk dances of the Caribbean, the United States, and Africa, and in the modern dance field. More

[109] *Ibid.*, p. D3.
[110] *Ibid.*, p. D3.

[111] Charles Gordone, "Yes, I Am a Black Playwright, But . . . ," *The New York Times*, Jan. 25, 1970, p. D11.
[112] William Glover, "He Laughs at Racism," *The Plain Dealer*, Sept. 6, 1970, p. D13.

recently, other Negro women dancers whose work in modern dance has been noteworthy include Janet Collins, Mary Hinkson, Matt Turney, and Carmen de Lavallade. Outstanding among black male dancers in modern dance are Arthur Mitchell, Alvin Ailey, Donald McKayle, Geoffrey Holder, Al Minns, and Leon James. Arthur Mitchell, a star of New York City Ballet, has established the Dance Theater of Harlem to teach modern and ethnic dance, as well as classical ballet. In addition to the school, Mitchell has founded a new, young company, the Dance Theater of Harlem. His faculty includes Karel Shook, former ballet-master of the Netherlands National Ballet, Mary Hinkson, James Truitte, Thelma Hill, Pearl Reynolds, Mireille Briane, and Tanaquil LeClerq. The company has the services of a number of professional dancers, including John Jones and Walter Raines.[113] The Alvin Ailey American Dance Theater is widely praised by dance critics. Barnes points out that Ailey is an equal-opportunity employer in a field and at a time when integration is not too fashionable. In his company, ethnic variety has been eminently successful.[114] More than other performers, dancers seem to be involved with ghetto youth. For years, Arthur Mitchell, Alvin Ailey, Pearl Primus, Eleo Pomare, and others have conducted classes for children in their own studios or in community centers.[115]

Outstanding concert artists in the United States have included Marian Anderson, Dorothy Maynor, Roland Hayes, Paul Robeson, Todd Duncan, and Carol Brice. More recently Negro concert singers of distinction include: Leontyne Price, William Warfield, Mattiwilda Dobbs, Adele Addison, McHenry Boatwright, Laurence Winters, George Shirley, William Ray, and Reri Grist. Dean Dixon is an outstanding contemporary conductor. After ten years of conducting that included appearances with the New York Philharmonic and the NBC Symphony, Dixon moved to Europe because he could not get a steady job in the United States. During the past 21 years he has served as music director of the Sydney, Australia Symphony and held the same position with two European symphonies: the Goteborg Symphony in Sweden, and, since 1960, the Frankfurt Radio Symphony. In 1970, he returned to the United States to conduct the first week of the Philharmonic's summer season of concerts in New York City parks, to lead the Pittsburgh Symphony at Temple University's Ambler Festival in Pennsylvania, and to appear with the St. Louis Symphony in its summer season at Edwardsville, Illinois.[116] A number of aspiring and talented young black conductors are now beginning their careers. Henry Lewis is the first Negro to head a major symphony orchestra (the New Jersey Symphony) in the United States. After two years as associate conductor of the Dallas Symphony, Paul Freeman was appointed in 1970 to fill the newly created post of "conductor in residence" with the Detroit Symphony. One of his responsibilities will be to conduct a new youth orchestra sponsored by the Symphony. Everett Lee is music director of the Norrköpings Orkesterförening in Sweden. George Byrd, a black American now living in Munich, has conducted major orchestras in London, Paris, and Berlin. James DePreist was an assistant conductor of the New York Philharmonic for a year, and has since had guest engagements with leading orchestras in Europe and the United States. Other young black conductors include Karl Hampton Porter, Isaiah Jackson, Harold Wheeler, Coleridge Taylor Perkinson, and James Frazier.[117]

Graphic and Plastic Arts

In the first three decades of this century, there were few American Negroes of outstanding merit in the pictorial and plastic arts (Henry O. Tanner, Richmond Barthe, Aaron Douglas, and Augusta Savage).[118]

[113] Clive Barnes, "Shaping a Black Classic Ballet," *The New York Times,* Oct. 12, 1969.
[114] Clive Barnes, "A Great Lesson in Race Relations," *The New York Times,* Apr. 26, 1970.
[115] Patterson, *op. cit.,* pp. 314–315.

[116] Beatrice Berg, "Dixon: Maestro Abroad, Stranger at Home," *The New York Times,* July 19, 1970, p. D11.
[117] Allen Hughes, "For Black Conductors, A Future? Or Frustration?" *The New York Times,* Mar. 15, 1970, pp. D19, 32.
[118] Gunnar Myrdal, *An American Dilemma,* Harper & Row, 1944, p. 989.

Horace Pippin, a major discovery of the 1930s, became one of the leading American "primitives." This self-taught artist has been praised for his "vision, sensitiveness, social consciousness, precision, dramatic power and exuberant use of color."[119] Alain Locke pointed out that Afro-Americans were cut off from the African art traditions and skills by slavery, and that "stripped of all else, the Negro's own body became his prime and only artistic instrument so that dance, pantomime and song became the only gateways for his creative expression." In this way the American Negro was "forced away from the craft arts and the old ancestral skills to the emotional arts of song and dance. . . . No comment on the Negro in the plastic and pictorial arts would be sound without this historical perspective."[120]

A sampling of the work of Negro painters in 1961 mentioned the realism of John Biggers, John Wilson, and James Reuben Reed, as well as the semiabstractions and abstractions of Eugene Grigsby, Mildred Thompson, and Roosevelt Woods.[121] With the exception of Aaron Douglas' symbolic

geometrical work, most of the Negro muralists have been influenced by Rivera's style. According to Dover, this manner "was so suitable [for dramatizing the struggles and achievements of Negroes] that it confined originality, while the themes were sometimes too complex and intrinsically dramatic for pictorial narration without great gifts for selectiveness and design. . . . some transcended limitation and mere recording. . . . Among them Hale Woodruff is the pioneer and still the leader, though his brilliantly executed murals leave the uncomfortable impression that they only represent carefully chosen subjects."[122] Among the black painters who received favorable acclaim in the late 1960s were: Lois Mailou Jones, Samuel Gilliam, David Driskell, Al Hollingsworth, Jacob Lawrence, Richard Mayhew, Raymond Saunders, Hartwell Yeargans, Romare Bearden, and Hughie Lee-Smith. Fax says that of the dozens of living black artists, not more than two have really "made it"—and that, only in a relative sense.[123] Since representation in the established white galleries is extremely limited—or nonexistent—for black artists, Negroes increasingly are forming their own galleries.

In 1970, a controversy of some magnitude developed over the question of the meaning of "black art." Perhaps the argument is seen best in articles written by Hilton Kramer, an art critic of *The New York Times*, Benny Andrews, artist, and Edmund B. Gaither, curator of the Museum of the National Center of Afro-American Artists in Boston. The debate was caused by an exhibition called "Afro-American Artists: New York and Boston," that was organized for the Museum of Fine Arts in Boston by Gaither and Barnet Rubenstein. Kramer began the discussion by asking whether there is " 'a black esthetic' discernible in the visual expression of black American artists that distinguishes it from the work of their white contemporaries." If there is such an art, he asked

[119] Cedric Dover, *American Negro Art*, New York Graphic Society, 1961, p. 72.

[120] Alain Locke, *The Negro in Art: A Pictorial Record of the Negro Artist and of the Negro Theme in Art*, Associates in Negro Folk Education, 1940, p. 8. Locke states that there is

. . . a prevalent impression that the fine arts, with their more formalized techniques, are a less characteristic and less congenial mode of expression for the Negro's admitted artistic genius than the more spontaneous arts of music, dance, drama, or poetry. Such views ignore the fact that, although the interpretive, emotional arts have been the Negro's special forte in America, his dominant arts in the African homeland were the decorative and craft arts. These—sculpture in wood, bone, and ivory, metalworking, weaving, pottery—combined with skillful surface decoration in line and color, involve every skill in the category of the European fine arts, even if not in specific terms of the European traditions of easel painting, marble sculpture, engraving and etching. The Western world knows today, belatedly, that the Negro was a master artist in the idioms of his original culture, and that the characteristic African virtuosity was in decoration and design."

Ibid., p. 8.

[121] Dover, *op. cit.*, p. 51. Dover mentions also the work of four "youngish" painters: Humbert Howard of Philadelphia, Walter Sanford and Stan Williamson of Chicago, and Alvin Hollingsworth of New York. *Ibid.*, pp. 51–52.

[122] *Ibid.*, p. 92.

[123] Elton C. Fax, "The American Negro Artist," in Romero (ed.), *op. cit.*, pp. 283, 290. The same generally applies to white artists, Fax says, but the odds favor them.

what its characteristics are. If not, he asked if there are compelling social reasons now for encouraging segregated exhibitions of art by black artists. A distinction between a "black show" and "black art" is quoted from Mr. Gaither's Introduction to the catalogue of the show. According to Gaither:

At its simplest, a 'black show' is an exhibition of work produced by artists whose skins are black. The term seldom connotes the presence of properties or qualities intrinsic in the work and therefore it does not act as an art historical definition. A 'black show' does not belong to the same order as a 'cubist show.' The 'black show' is a yoking together of a variety of works which are, for social and political reasons, presented under the labels 'black' or 'Afro-American.' Such a show is thus a response to pressures growing out of racial stresses in America. At the same time, 'black shows' attempt to introduce a body of material to a race-conscious public in order to force that public to recognize its existence and its quality. And like socially motivated devices, the 'black show' has its strengths and weaknesses.

Kramer found this definition candid and precise but regards Gaither's definition of "black art" as less successful. Here Gaither referred to "artists who knowingly and intentionally base their art on peculiarly black experiences, on the history of blacks and on a view of Africa." Gaither added that their work "must be considered within legitimate art historical groupings which may be characterized by specific and observable traits." Kramer said that the "traits," if he understood Gaither's account correctly, are political rather than esthetic or stylistic. According to Gaither, "Black art is a didactic art form arising from a strong nationalistic base and characterized by its commitment to: a) use the past and its heroes to inspire heroic and revolutionary ideals; b) use recent political and social events to teach recognition, control and extermination of the 'enemy' and c) to project the future which the nation can anticipate after the struggle is won." In short, according to Gaither, "black art" is a "social art and it must be communicative." Apparently, Kramer said, it is art that is to be judged only in terms of political

ideology. In his view, esthetic quality suffered as a result of the use of criteria that are "patently ideological" in selecting "black art" for the show.[124]

In a second article on the Boston exhibition, Kramer pointed out that the show was not entirely devoted to "black art." Much of the work on exhibit belonged to "mainstream American art," and he mentioned especially the work of painters Norman Lewis, Alvin D. Loving Jr., Bill Rivers, Alma Thomas, and Felrath Hines, all abstractionists, and the sculptor Jack White. Others who were represented by works of "notable 'mainstream' quality" were Marvin Brown, Thomas Sills, Frank Bowling, Ellen Banks, Ronald Boutte, and the late Bob Thompson. Kramer said also that two of the best-known New York artists in the show—Romare Bearden and Benny Andrews—"work in styles which seem to derive their energy and expressiveness from a double commitment. On the one hand, they very consciously seek to utilize a 'black' subject matter. In theory, an art that draws its inspiration from this double commitment would seem to constitute an ideal synthesis. Yet in practice such an art seems to be extremely difficult to realize . . . the work of these two artists defines, if only in principle, a possible direction for a 'black art' that refuses to surrender itself entirely to the well-worn clichés of social realism." In concluding his critique of the Boston show, Kramer expressed doubt that any museum can handle the complex problems of a "black show" differently so long as "the imposition of rigorous artistic standards is regarded as one more form of white racism." He sees "no point in pretending that an exhibition such as the present one in Boston is anything but what it actually is: an art exhibition mounted under the pressures of political expediency that fails, by and large, to justify itself in terms of artistic accomplishment."[125]

[124] Hilton Kramer, "Trying to Define 'Black Art': Must We Go Back to Social Realism?" *The New York Times*, May 31, 1970, p. D17.
[125] Hilton Kramer, " 'Black Art' and Expedient Politics," *The New York Times*, June 7, 1970.

The replies to the Kramer articles by Andrews and by Gaither were spirited. Andrews called Kramer's review in *The New York Times* on May 22, 1970, "putrid and inappropriate." He said that Kramer was unable "to mentally penetrate the main essence of an exhibition of this kind." Andrews asks: ". . . why in hell is it so damn confusing to see the Black artist expressing his feeling about his people, his environment and life as something unfathomable, if artists like Goya, Picasso . . . and Durer, George Grosz, Ben Shahn, etc., can be dealt with critically?" Among the works that especially impressed Andrews were those by Dana Chandler, Romare Bearden, Barbara Chase Riboud, Edward Clark, Lovett Thompson, Lynn Bowers, Jack White, Russ Thompson, Gary Rickson, Reginald Gammon, Norman Lewis and James Denmark. In Andrews' view, ". . . just because the bulk of the art does not fit into a tidy outline of art criticism does not mean that there are not people capable of getting to what there is to say and explain about this body of work that makes it valid and artistic." Concerning Kramer's two-part article called "Trying to Define 'Black Art.' Must We Go Back to Social Realism?" Andrews said that his answer to the question: "Are artistic standards simply a form of white racism?" could very well be in the affirmative "if the white mainstream art oriented critic persists in the following":

1. Not being able to see a black figure done by a black artist without automatically assuming that the work is propagandistic, or politicizing.
2. Being unable to look at an all-black art exhibition with the same impartiality that he brings to an all-white exhibition.
3. Not criticizing curators or museums for putting on all-white exhibitions.
4. Giving the impression that art exhibitions are dropped down from heaven.
5. Not re-examining his attitudes about black people in general, and black artists in particular, before assuming so much knowledge about what blacks think or do not think.
6. Forgetting how easily he has lived with past discrimination against black artists.
7. Last, but not least, not asking himself, 'How many great all-white art exhibitions have I seen lately? . . .'[126]

According to Gaither:

Implicit in the critical notes of Kramer is a preference for art for art's sake ('objects having a purely esthetic end'), as well as a suspicion that, programmatically, social and/or political art cannot advance valuable formal or esthetic statements. Such a critical concept results in an unfortunate rigidity and inflexibility which then makes it improbable that its advocate could sympathetically and justly criticize the body of socially motivated art. A blindness results in which the critic misreads the art and incorrectly labels it. Moreover, esthetic values in such works are obscured by their radical or 'objectionable' content.[127]

Gaither says that the black artist "is not, as Kramer implies, 'exempt from the application . . . of critical discrimination based on purely artistic values.' Within his work, there are successes and failures reflecting his degree of mastery over the problem of synthesizing form and content. The visual test of his work is whether the art demands the viewer's attention and whether, after having seen it, the viewer continues to regard it as an exciting and significant experience. The test is concerned primarily with the visual power of the forms presented; however, it is not unaware of the consummation of a marriage between form and content. The critic of black art judges it for both these elements." Gaither then called attention to the stylistic differences of a number of black artists represented in the Boston show, and said that it is misleading to group them "simply as social realists." Finally, Gaither said that the exhibition presented all important tendencies in the current work of Afro-American artists and that its organizers made esthetic judgments in all sections of the show.[128]

It seems likely that the productivity of black artists will continue to increase, as

[126] Benny Andrews, "On Understanding Black Art," *The New York Times*, June 21, 1970, p. D21. © 1970 by the New York Times Company. Reprinted by permission.
[127] Edmund B. Gaither, "A New Criticism is Needed," *The New York Times*, June 21, 1970.
[128] *Ibid.*

will the controversies concerning artistic values of black art.

A different type of controversy arose in 1971 over the Whitney Museum's decision not to engage the services of a black adviser in mounting its April, 1971 show, "Black Artists in America." A demonstration against the exhibit was organized by the Black Emergency Cultural Coalition, the group of black artists that had persuaded the museum during six months of "consultations" in 1969 to present the attraction. The BECC had picketed the January, 1969 show at the Metropolitan Museum, "Harlem on My Mind," for its exclusion of works by black painters and sculptors. A few months later it brought pressure on the Whitney for better black representation. In September, 1969, the museum announced two steps for "the support and encouragement of black artists throughout the United States." Step 1 was the decision to hold "a major exhibition of work by black artists from all parts of the country." Step 2 was the establishment of a special fund for the acquisition of work by younger and lesser-known black artists. By January, 1971, the museum had purchased works by seven black contemporaries, increasing to 17 the number of Blacks in its permanent collection. It had also staged three small lobby shows of works by younger Blacks, and a fourth show had been scheduled for spring. The heart of the 1971 controversy seems to have been the extent of consultation of Blacks by the director of the show and the unwillingness of the museum to appoint a black codirector. Black artists were divided in their attitudes toward the boycott called for by the BECC. Some supported it; others questioned the idea of a "black" show but said they were pleased to have a chance to make a museum appearance.[129]

MINORITY THEMES IN THE ART OF MAJORITY GROUP MEMBERS

Racial themes are important not only in the work of minority artists but also among some members of the dominant group. They are often handled in a stereotyped, unimaginative way by persons of majority status.

Racial and Cultural Stereotypes and Counter-Stereotypes in Art

The first song-and-dance act impersonating a Negro was given about 1830, and the first minstrel show was staged in 1843. These shows reached their peak between 1850 and 1870; in 1880 there were 30 companies, but in 1919 only three first-class organizations were still playing.[130] According to Adams, the standard minstrel portrait of the plantation Negro "emphasized traits suggested by the adjectives lazy, shiftless, improvident, superstitious, stupid, ignorant, and slow, and those reflected in a fondness for watermelons, chickens, gin, crap games, razors, and big words."

Immigrants have been a poor second to Negroes in the amount of comical material they have provided for the American stage. Germans, Jews, the Irish, and many others have been presented, along with numerous other "character" types, in comedies, farces, and revues; even more frequently they have been caricatured in burlesque, variety, and vaudeville sketches.

The stereotyping of Negro character has occurred, and still occurs, in the works of both well-intentioned and prejudiced white writers. Although this had been the rule, there have been exceptions to the numerous literary interpretations which justify the exploitation of the Negro, and these exceptions have become more common. The most incisive analyses of the white stereotyping of the Negro have been done by Sterling Brown.[131]

In the ante-bellum period the Negro was

---

[129] Grace Glueck, "Black Show Under Fire at the Whitney," *The New York Times*, Jan. 31, 1971, p. D25.

[130] On stage caricaturing of minorities, see Harold E. Adams, "Minority Caricatures on the American Stage," in G. P. Murdock (ed.), *Studies in the Science of Society*, Yale, 1937, pp. 1–26.

[131] Sterling A. Brown, "Negro Character as Seen by White Authors," *JNE*, Jan., 1933, pp. 180–201. See also Brown, Davis, and Lee (eds.), *op. cit.*, pp. 2–5. Our discussion is based mainly on Brown's work. The stereotyping of Negro character, with specific reference to prejudice, is discussed in chap. 5.

often represented as a natural slave. In J. P. Kennedy's *Swallow Barn* (1832) Negro children are shown "basking on the sunny sides of cabins [like] terrapins luxuriating on the logs of a mill-pond." The complement of the *contented slave* was the *comic Negro* of the minstrel shows. Later variations of the latter type were found in Octavus Roy Cohen's pseudo-Negro dialect stories and in the "Amos 'n' Andy" radio and television programs. The *wretched freedman* stereotype is illustrated in Mrs. M. J. McIntosh's *The Lofty and the Lowly*, or *Good in All and None All-Good* (1854). Daddy Cato is given his freedom, of which he is not proud, late in life. After following his family to Boston, he is insulted when approached by abolitionists. "Make me free! how can I free any more? Dem da nonsense people, and what dem want take me from Miss Alice for? . . . I wonder if I been sick and couldn't do any'ting, ef dem would nuss me and take care o' me liken Miss Alice . . . I tink dem crazy 'bout free. Free bery good ting, but free ent all; when you sick, free won't make you well, free won't gib you clo's, no hom'ny, let 'lone meat." The rebellious, the ironic, the abused Negro failed to appear in the plantation tradition books. Miscegenation is absent from these stories, although it was commonplace; slavery was presented as a charitable institution.

The *brute Negro* stereotype was a specialty of Thomas Nelson Page in *Ole Virginia* (1887), *The Negro: The Southerner's Problem* (1904), *Red Rock* (1898), and *Pastime Stories* (1894). This stereotype was further developed by the Reverend Thomas Dixon in *The Leopard's Spots* (1902) and *The Clansmen* (1905). In *The Leopard's Spots*, "Dick, an imbecile, crushes with a rock the head of a white child and then attacks her. The assaulted child and the burning of the Negro are described with gusto. Drunk Negro soldiers drag white brides from their homes; criminal Negroes rove the countryside, forcing whites to take to the cities."[132]

The *tragic mulatto* was the principal stereotype produced by the writers of antislavery fiction; others were "the victim," "the noble savage," and "the perfect Christian." Antislavery novels concentrated on the abuses of slavery: whippings, the slave market, domestic slave breeding, slave hunts, persecuted freedmen, etc. The tragic mulatto appeared in Harriet Beecher Stowe's *Uncle Tom's Cabin* (1851) and *Dred, A Tale of the Dismal Swamp*, (1856). In Richard Hildreth's *Archy Moore, or The White Slave*, and in Boucicault's *The Octoroon*, Negroes of mixed ancestry play leading roles. George Washington Cable, a Confederate officer who later went to Massachusetts to live, made use of the tragic mulatto in *Old Creole Days* (1879) and in *The Grandissimes* (1880). However, Cable did not overidealize the Negro, and unlike Page and Harris he did not use his material to support old traditions. The tragic mulatto was often portrayed by prejudiced writers as a human being of divided inheritance, divided loyalties, and conflicting impulses. This theme persisted through the years in such works as *A Black Drop, Madame Margot, White Girl, The No-Nation Girl, A Study in Bronze, Gulf Stream*, and *Dark Lustre*. The woes of these mixed-ancestry characters, mostly female and the majority octoroons, are many.

One of the favorite stereotypes of the 1920s was that of the *exotic primitive*. In the reaction against Puritanism and Babbitry after World War I, the stereotyped primitivity of the Negro was very appealing. Those who were once shackled in slavery became the symbol of escape from a drab industrial civilization. White authors rushed to Harlem cabarets and the river fronts to see the unmoral, flamboyant, carefree children of nature. Their books portrayed what they regarded as the Negro's savage inheritance: hot jungle nights, tom-toms, esoteric rites, violence, and frankness. This is the formula of Carl Van Vechten's *Nigger Heaven* (1925), T. Bowyer Campbell's *Black Sadie* (1928), Sherwood Anderson's

---

[132] Sterling A. Brown, *The Negro in American Fiction*, Associates in Negro Folk Education, 1937, p. 94. In *The Negro Caravan* the editors say, "In

Reconstruction the wretched freedman became the brute, swaggering about, insulting, and assaulting, and it must be added, wanting to vote" (pp. 3–4).

Dark Laughter (1925), and many others.

As we have indicated earlier, not all white authors have stereotyped the Negro. Herman Melville (*Mardi*, 1849), George Washington Cable (*Old Creole Days*, 1879) and *The Grandissimes*, 1880), Mark Twain (*Huckleberry Finn*, 1884), Albion Tourgée (*One of the Fools*, 1879, and *Bricks Without Straw*, 1880), Upton Sinclair (*The Jungle*, 1905), Gertrude Stein ("Melanctha" in *Three Lives*, 1909), T. S. Stribling (*Birthright*, 1922, *The Forge*, 1931, *The Store*, 1933, *Unfinished Cathedral*, 1934), DuBose Heyward (*Porgy*, 1925, and *Mamba's Daughters*, 1925), E. C. L. Adams (*Congaree Sketches*, 1927, and *Nigger to Nigger*), Lyle Saxon (*Children of Strangers*, 1937), Paul Green (*In Abraham's Bosom*, 1924, *The House of Connelly*, 1932, and a number of short stories), Hamilton Basso (*Relics and Angels*, 1929, *Cinnamon Seed*, 1934, *Courthouse Square*, 1936), Erskine Caldwell (*We Are the Living*, 1933, *Kneel to the Rising Sun*, 1935, *Trouble in July*, 1940), Evelyn Scott (*Migrations*, 1927, *The Wave*, 1929, *A Calendar of Sin*, 1931), William March (*Come In at the Door*, 1934), Carson McCullers (*The Heart Is a Lonely Hunter*, 1940), Lillian Smith (*Strange Fruit*, 1944), and Bucklin Moon (*Without Magnolias*, 1949) are among the writers who have portrayed Negroes as many-sided persons rather than as caricatures of human beings. But for the most part, from 1830 to 1950, Negro life and character in American literature were presented in ways that gave support to prevailing social policies toward the Negro.

Of the four novels by white writers about American Negroes published in 1960, two made extensive use of stereotyped Negroes and two presented convincing Negro characters. In *Seed in the Wind*, Leon Odell Griffith stresses that the Negro's drive for equality means only one thing, an equal chance to have a white sexual partner. William Hoffman's *A Place to Lay My Head* portrays Negro integrationist leaders as dishonest opportunists and members of (white) citizens' councils as judicious leaders in the campaign to prevent desegregation. Exact opposites of these books are found in Harper Lee's *To Kill a Mockingbird* and Keith Wheeler's *Peaceable Lane*. The former novel relates the efforts of a white Alabama lawyer to bring up his young son and daughter without prejudice, his defense of a young Negro falsely accused of raping a white girl, and the attitudes of the white community toward him and his children. *Peaceable Lane* deals with the coming of a Negro family to a white suburb in Westchester County, New York, and "the slow conversion of the white community from hate and ostracism for those who show signs of admitting the Negro's constitutional rights, to tolerance and understanding."[133] In Ford's opinion, Erskine Caldwell's *Close to Home* (1962) is written with less understanding and conviction than some of his previous works, especially *Place Called Estherville* and *Kneel to the Rising Sun*.[134]

On literary grounds, William Styron's *The Confessions of Nat Turner* was favorably reviewed by some white critics and strongly criticized by others. Ten black critics angrily denounced the book as a deliberate subversion of history (John Henrik Clarke, ed., *William Styron's Nat Turner: Ten Black Writers Respond*). To the latter criticism, Styron replied (*The Nation*, Apr. 22, 1968) "by citing the lack of authentication for many of the 'facts' on Nat Turner (all sources are suspect), denying that his portrait was derogatory (Turner's fantasies were made up, but so was Turner's strategy for the rebellion, i.e., the evidence of leadership) and asserting, with supportive quotes from the Marxist critic, Georg Lukacs, the novelist's right and necessity to use imaginatively the tenuous material of history in the creation of 'larger truth.' "[135] The ten black writers have not only rejected "the larger truth" as untruthful and racially insulting, but have implied "that certain subjects, Nat Turner among them, are or should

[133] N. A. Ford, "Battle of the Books: A Critical Survey of Significant Books by and About Negroes Published in 1960," pp. 120–123.

[134] N. A. Ford, "Walls Do a Prison Make: A Critical Survey of Significant Belles-Lettres by and About Negroes Published in 1962," p. 131.

[135] Eliot Fremont-Smith, "Nat Turner I: The Controversy," *The New York Times*, Aug. 1, 1968, p. 32.

be, for esthetic and political reasons, the exclusive domain of Negro writers and ideologues."[136] Gilman points out that the prestige of literature can be used to make up for the lacks of history. In this way the historical Nat Turner can be used by Whites in a way that is comforting to Whites. Likewise, Negroes can repudiate Styron's myth and substitute another: "that of Nat Turner's nobility, grandeur, his representative existence as spearhead of Negro consciousness, as exemplar of clear, clean, undeviating urgency towards liberation."[137] The controversy over Styron's book illustrates again the role that ideology may play in art that embodies racial themes.

With the exception of the considerable use of the exotic primitive during the "roaring twenties" and the occasional appearance of the tragic mulatto, the favorite stereotypes of white authors do not appear frequently in the writings of Negroes. More often the Negro writer has produced counterstereotypes; that is, he has attributed ideal characteristics to his Negro characters. The Negro fictionists of the nineteenth century and of the first two decades of the twentieth felt called upon to meet propaganda with counterpropaganda, and in doing so they employed stereotyped situations and characters just as one-sided as those of the Negrophobe writers. Their stock in trade was the virtuous Negro and the vicious white man.[138] Gloster lists 25 of these writers in the years between 1853 (William Wells Brown's *Clotel, or the President's Daughter: A Narrative of Slave Life in the United States*) and 1918 (Sarah Fleming's *Hope's Highway*).[139]

One critic says that the characters of Negro novelists "usually become walking, talking propaganda, rather than completely rounded individuals. The Negro writer has hesitated, perhaps unconsciously, to temper the goodness of his Negro characters with the dialectical 'evil.' Fearful of reenforcing stereotypes in the white reader's mind, he has often gone to the other extreme, idealizing his characters, making them flat rather than many-sided." Or, according to this critic, in his desire to show that he is not idealizing his Negro characters the Negro writer may go to the other extreme and portray the American Negro "as an exaggerated Bigger Thomas, with all the stereotyped characteristics emphasized three times over."[140] In any event, Negro authors have given a picture of Negro life that has differed considerably from the simplified version so often presented in American literature.

Agencies of Mass Communication and Minorities in the United States

The agencies of mass communication—the motion picture, the radio, the newspaper, television, and the magazine—provide most of the "educational" stimuli that the great majority of the people in the United States receive after the completion of their formal schooling. Presumably these art and quasi-art mediums exert some influence on racial and religious attitudes.

Motion Pictures. Until World War II years no consistent effort was made by American motion-picture companies to dispel group prejudice through films. Minority-group characters were, in fact, generally treated in a stereotyped way. The industry's Production Code of Ethics, the only set of rules for Hollywood film-making, refers to "race" only once—in forbidding the depiction of "miscegenation (sex relationship between the white and black races)." The code forbids the portrayal of ministers as "comic characters or as villains" and the ridicule of any religious faith. Concerning "national feelings" the rules require that "the history, institutions, prominent people and citizenry of other nations shall be represented fairly." Apparently these sections of the code were

---

[136] *Ibid.*, p. 33.
[137] Richard Gilman, "Nat Turner Revisited," *The New Republic*, Apr. 27, 1968, p. 24.
[138] Gloster, *Negro Voices in American Fiction*, pp. 253–254.
[139] *Ibid.*, pp. 25–98.

[140] William G. Smith, "The Negro Writer: Pitfalls and Compensations," *Phylon*, Fourth Quarter, 1950, p. 298.

drawn up and have been interpreted in terms of safeguarding the industry from the wrath of influential groups rather than in the interests of "spiritual and moral progress . . . and correct thinking," as stated in the preamble.[141]

From 1942 to 1945 Hollywood made a conscious effort to promote better understanding among the racial, religious, and national groups in the United States and among the nations and races allied with us in the war. A number of films dramatizing and condemning Nazi anti-Semitism were produced, including *The Mortal Storm, Escape, Address Unknown, This Land Is Mine, The Hitler Gang, None Shall Escape*, and *Tomorrow the World*. Other films, such as *Pride of the Marines, Air Force, Winged Victory, Objective Burma*, and *The Purple Heart* portrayed Jewish characters as comrades in arms. During these years film audiences were introduced to many new Negro actors, musicians, and dancers; among them were Hazel Scott, Lena Horne, Duke Ellington, the late Fats Waller, Katherine Dunham, Teddy Wilson, and Kenneth Spencer. Nearly all these artists were presented either in an all-Negro film or in a segregated sequence. The film *In This Our Life* had one scene showing a young Negro law student in association with a white family. This scene, booed when the film was shown in the southern states, eventually disappeared from most versions. Memphis and other southern cities banned the showing of *Brewster's Millions* because Eddie ("Rochester") Anderson's role in the film placed him in charge of the office staff during the boss's absence.

Films that portrayed Negroes in a favorable light in the war years were *Bataan, Sahara,* and *The Curse of the Cat People*. The outstanding attempt to combat prejudice through the motion picture was the Army's *The Negro Soldier,* shown both in commercial theaters and by those using nontheatrical film libraries. The motion-picture industry did far less during World War II in trying to assist in the elimination of anti-Negro prejudice and in advocating the integration of the Negro in the nation's life, than it did in attempting to combat anti-Semitism. The explanation of this difference, given by competent critics, is that Hollywood seldom crusades, and the films dealing with anti-Semitism were merely in step with, and not in advance of, national sentiment and custom.[142] Two years after the war, however, the motion-picture executive who was responsible for *Crossfire*, a film attacking anti-Semitism, wrote, "It [*Crossfire*] says something. It says in no uncertain terms that bigotry and hatred and evil must be rooted out if our world is to know and enjoy peace. . . . It is time that our subjects became significant of our times and honestly reflect our changing society. . . ."[143]

Following his outstanding success as a Hollywood actor, Harry Belafonte said that *Island in the Sun* is a "stinking" picture and that he was "through with problem pictures about interracial relations." But, according to Landry, in producing *Island in the Sun*, Darryl F. Zanuck not only dared to portray the races romantically but he risked and lost a large part of the southern market, 20 percent of the total American film audience. Zanuck did this partly because Negro patronage is now important and in part because foreign peoples have great curiosity about the American Negro.[144] Turning down roles in *Porgy and Bess* and *The Emperor Jones*, Belafonte said of the first: "The music is great, but I wouldn't want to do it as the Dubose Heyward script is written. All that crap shooting and razors and lust and cocaine is the old conception of the Negro." The second, he said, "is an even worse conception of the Negro. I wouldn't consider it."[145]

---

[141] J. T. McManus and Louis Kronenberger, "Motion Pictures, the Theater, and Race Relations," *Annals*, Mar., 1946, p. 152.

[142] *Ibid.*, pp. 152–155.

[143] Dore Schary, "The Screen and Society," *National Jewish Monthly*, Oct., 1947, p. 60.

[144] R. J. Landry, "The Movies: Better Than Ever?" in Nathan C. Belth and Morton Puner (eds.), *Prejudice and the Lively Arts*, ADL, 1963, p. 11.

[145] Bob Thomas, "Power Is Difference to Richer Belafonte," *The Plain Dealer*, Aug. 11, 1957, p. 10. Belafonte's view of *Porgy and Bess* was not shared by Brooks Atkinson, dramatic critic of *The*

There is evidence that the use of the usual Negro stereotypes fell off sharply in films produced after the middle 1940s. Some "shockers" appeared later, but much of the standard stereotyping of former years disappeared. The movie version of William Faulkner's *Intruder in the Dust* was widely acclaimed, as were the films adapted from Broadway plays: *Home of the Brave, Lost Boundaries, Pinky,* and *The Quiet One.* Concerning these films Alain Locke said: "That they simultaneously register new seriousness and dignity in Negro characterization and new moral dimensions in theme makes for unprecedented progress. . . ."[146] Landry says that films such as *Gentlemen's Agreement,* concerning anti-Semitism, and *Pinky,* dealing with anti-Negro bias, did well at first, but that later films of this type were not successful critically or financially.[147]

Other developments of interest here include the rather considerable number of films concerning GI affairs and marriages with Japanese girls, as well as the "slow fade-out" (except in old movies on TV) of Indian, Mexican, and Oriental villains.[148] Landry says the Negro may have a complaint now and then against current movies, but he does not believe that the Jew has much complaint against present-day films.

One film critic's summary of the story of Negroes in American films since 1945 has three parts: up to 1954, Negroes as a social problem; through the 1950s, Negroes as emerging characters but showing the vestiges of Rastus; and the varied themes of the

1960s, the beginnings of the fully articulated character. This is not to say that there are no movies today that deal in the old sensationalism and the old stereotypes. Some recent films have gone to the other extreme and presented Negro characters as paragons of virtue. The absence of adult sexual behavior in many of Sidney Poitier's films has been commented on frequently.[149] Jim Brown, a former football star with the Cleveland Browns, and Raymond St. Jacques have joined Poitier as box-office attractions, and Hollywood has announced that it will produce the autobiographies of Ethel Waters and Malcolm X.[150]

According to one film critic, the race films of the 1970s suggest that Hollywood is searching for a formula that will be in line with contemporary race relations without offending. An example is Jim Brown's *tick . . . tick . . . tick,* a portrayal of a returned black war veteran who runs for sheriff in a Mississippi town and wins. The topic of this film "is timely; the treatment is cautious and illustrative, but not involving. . . . His (Brown's) devotion to law and order as a new sheriff should quiet the fears of the most uncertain white Southern viewer."[151] *The Liberation of L. B. Jones,* a film that attempts to depict subtle southern racial conflict, is only partially successful. This picture involves a comparatively well-

---

New York Times. When criticisms arose over the State Department's sponsorship of a *Porgy and Bess* company in Vienna and Berlin, Atkinson wrote that Europeans "do not have to be convinced that the decisive factor in any genuine work of art is less the material than the spirit of the authors and composers." Brooks Atkinson, "Negro Folk Drama," *The New York Times,* Sept. 9, 1952. Watts says that the "Porgy and Bess" tour which ended successfully in the Soviet Union turned out to be the opposite of "bad 'propaganda' "; Richard Watts Jr., "The Theater: Triumph Over Prejudice," in Belth and Puner (eds.), *op. cit.,* p. 13.

[146] Alain Locke, "Wisdom de Profundis: The Literature of the Negro, 1949," *Phylon,* First Quarter, 1950, pp. 10–11.

[147] Landry, "The Movies: Better Than Ever?," p. 11.

[148] *Ibid.*

[149] Thomas R. Cripps, "The Death of Rastus: Negroes in American Films Since 1945," *Phylon,* Third Quarter, 1967, pp. 271, 275. In 1968, Stanley Kramer, producer-director, traveled to nine campuses, showing his film *Guess Who's Coming to Dinner.* Many student filmmakers criticized the film claiming that falling in love with a person of a different race is no problem for them. Kramer points out that the students failed to recognize "the fact that they live in a world in which their own fathers and mothers and relatives and friends and neighborhoods do constitute for them a problem." Another objection was that Sidney Poitier was made such an ideal character that it was clear that the girl would marry him. Kramer's reply is that "the film is an adventure into the ludicrous—the characters so perfect that the only conceivable objection to this marriage could be ludicrously enough, the pigmentation of the man's skin." Stanley Kramer, "Guess Who Didn't Dig 'Dinner'," *The New York Times,* May 26, 1968, p. D21.

[150] Patterson, *op. cit.,* pp. 311–313.

[151] James M. Wall, "The Movies: The 1970s Intensify Hollywood's Struggle of Profits vs. Reality," *South Today,* May, 1970, pp. 4–5.

to-do black undertaker, a prominent white lawyer and his liberal nephew, white policemen, and a returned Black. The black ghetto school is the subject of *Blackboard Jungle*, *Up the Down Staircase* (Puerto Rican ghetto children), and *Halls of Anger*. Wall calls *Halls of Anger* "a genuine breakthrough in depicting young black anger" and says that it has audience-involving style.[152] An independently produced black-oriented film, *Nothing but a Man*, presents the struggle of a black couple to overcome their own differences in background as well as the oppressiveness of the southern Whites who appear peripherally in the picture. Although this film has been popular with film societies, it has had no commercial success.[153]

In 1968, Gordon Parks became the first Negro to direct a Hollywood film, a screen version of his novel, *The Learning Tree*. Another black director, Melvin Van Peebles, directed the film, *The Story of the Three-Day Pass* in France in 1968.[154] In 1970, Van Peebles directed *Watermelon Man* for Columbia Pictures. On this film, Van Peebles insisted on an apprentice program, with disadvantaged youths, "traditionally frozen out of the unions," given a chance to work and to learn the film-making process.[155] Because of the demands of some black actors and white directors, black technicians in something more than token numbers are being employed.

Television. While there were some protests by white southerners during the 1950s concerning the appearance of Negro actors on television programs (for example, Negro entertainers on the Ed Sullivan show, and the use of an allegedly interracial couple in the principal parts of a TV Playhouse presentation in which Sidney Poitier, a Negro actor, and Hilda Simms, a Negro actress, were starred),[156] there has been no substantial disapproval by southern audiences or viewers of programs in which Negroes were cast in roles other than stereotyped, submissive ones.[157]

In radio and television, especially in the latter, the potential for affecting intergroup relations positively or negatively may be greater than in any other medium at the present time. The director of the New York code office of the National Association of Broadcasters has said that the "presence in a television broadcast of a cruel stereotype is so immediate in one's living room, so pervasive, so irretrievable, so *shared* coast-to-coast, border-to-border as to be of enormous significance."[158] Constructive views of racial and ethnic differences are also thought to be of considerable significance. The code of the National Association of Broadcasters forbids: ". . . words (especially slang) derisive of any race, color, creed, nationality or national derivation, except wherein such usage would be for the specific purpose of effective dramatizations such as combating prejudice." The NBC network's rules state that "all program material presents with dignity and objectivity the varying aspects of race, creed, color and national origin. The history, institutions and citizens of all nations are fairly represented." Editors vary, of course, in the ways they interpret such policies. Ranson thinks that minority groups have no better friends today than the heads of the network continuity acceptance departments.[159]

One indication of television's sophistication in handling racial matters is its reversal of the fashion followed in old-time movies of representing American Indians as cowardly, blood-thirsty, or ignorant. Epstein says that today television westerns "are sociologically pure; in some cases, the principal character, without gun or badge, will act like a social or psychological case worker, trying to help the mixed-up villain

---

[152] *Ibid.*, p. 5.

[153] *Ibid.*, p. 5.

[154] Patterson, *op. cit.*, p. 312.

[155] Norman Goldstein, "Behind the Cameras, Blacks Now Start to Appear Too," *The Plain Dealer*, Apr. 12, 1970.

[156] Carl T. Rowan, *Go South to Sorrow*, Random House, 1957, pp. 193–196.

[157] Elmer Carter, "Policies and Practices of Discrimination Commissions," *Annals*, Mar., 1956, p. 71.

[158] Stockton Helffrich, "Editing the Airwaves," in Belth and Puner (eds.), *op. cit.*, p. 14.

[159] Jo Ranson, "On Key with Tin Pan Alley," in *ibid.*, p. 18.

gain better understanding of himself."[160] It should be pointed out, however, that television's extensive reuse of old movies has led to some problems. About 3500 old movies were purchased in Hollywood and approximately the same number were acquired in Britain and elsewhere. Syndicators rushed these products to market, and, in most cases, passed the "editing" problem to the local station. Landry reports that

. . . prohibition drama came replete with Italian gangsters, to the embarrassment of many homes. Dimly remembered Negro domestics cast for 'comic relief' in houseparty murder mysteries did not please the Negro trade. There were even echoes of the red-flanneled Irish, all pretty unfunny Mr. Dooleys. Viewers caught a hint or two of the venerable Yellow Peril. Jewish dialecticians returned—but hardly came back— in some 'vaulties.' Once, the acme of cinematic slapstick was a Jew and an Irishman on the town together. The remainder of such fictional partnership in vulgarity was partly quaint, partly nauseating.[161]

Marked changes in the policies of the mass media toward blackness occurred in 1968. Blacks were seen in soap operas, newscasts, television commercials, special features, and prime time productions.[162] Every major network concerned itself with the Negro's history in the United States.

CBS started the year off with a seven-part series called 'Of Black America,' which included programs on Black history, the Black soldier and slavery. The Westinghouse Broadcasting Company's Group W presented 'One Nation, Indivisible,' a three-and-a-half hour examination of America's racial crisis. 'Color Us Black,' a one-hour documentary on the student uprising at Howard University, was produced by the National Educational Television network. One of the most stunning documentaries was 'Still a Brother: Inside the Negro Middle Class.' A series on racism in America was presented by ABC. Its first program was 'Bias in the Mass Media.'[163]

In April, 1968, television covered the entire funeral of Dr. Martin Luther King, Jr. Also, more black actors appeared in continuing series: e.g., Robert Hooks in NYPD, Peter DeAnda and Ellen Holly in One Life to Live, Don Marshall in Land of the Giants, Nichelle Nichols in Star Trek, Darlene Cotton in Love of Life, Otis Young in The Outcasts, Clarence Williams, III, in Mod Squad, Greg Morris in Mission Impossible, and Hari Rhodes in Daktari. Black comedians, including Flip Wilson, Pigmeat Markham, and Sammy Davis, Jr., were seen often.[164]

Sesame Street, educational television's hour-long program, was designed to teach lingual, numerical, and reasoning skills to children between the ages of three and five. The program is concerned also with the hypothesis that poor children, as such, are deprived children. The thesis is that they are deprived because they go to school lacking the varied stimulation and the educational background and skills of middle-class children of the same age. Sesame Street attempts to reach these children in urban ghettos, on Indian reservations, in Appalachia, and elsewhere. The indications are that Sesame Street is reaching the middle-class child and that it has a large audience in urban ghettos. In 1970 audiences in rural poverty areas had not yet been tested; some station managers in the South expected to increase promotion of the program in such areas.

The effectiveness of Sesame Street in helping poor children to do better in school is controversial. Some critics say that the program does not recognize that many children fail because they are tired, hungry, or frightened. Others fear that the federal government, which has shared the costs of the program with the Ford Foundation, will conclude that Sesame Street is a money-saving substitute for Headstart. The latter persons say that Headstart provides a personal and individual approach to the problems of poor children, one that cannot be supplanted by the impersonal approach of educational television. Some see the showing of Blacks and Whites living together in harmony as one of the most important contributions of Sesame Street. (The setting of the show is a street in a rundown urban area.) In addition,

[160] Benjamin R. Epstein, " 'Art' vs. People: A Summing Up," in ibid., pp. 21–22.

[161] Landry, "The Movies: Better Than Ever?" p. 10.

[162] Pat Romero, "Introduction," in Romero (ed.), op. cit., p. xiv.

[163] Patterson, op. cit., p. 313.

[164] Ibid., p. 313.

Matt Robinson, the star of the show, projects a strong male image for black children. The program has been popular throughout the South. In 1970, 53 educational television stations in that region used *Sesame Street*. In addition, two commercial stations carried the program, giving up an hour of commercial time and profits daily.[165]

In November, 1970, the U.S. Office of Education allocated $2 million to enable the Children's Television Workshop to develop a second season of *Sesame Street*. This brought to $7 million the total funds received from the Office of Education for this program. The goal of the new program, broadcast over 250 stations, was to reach major ethnic groups through new programming techniques. In the 145-hour-long series, material reflecting black cultural life was again used, and an effort was made to develop an English vocabulary among Spanish-speaking children. Part of the new grant was used to provide viewing centers in major cities where many poor children did not have access to a television set.[166]

Room 222, an ABC television program of the 1969 season featured Lloyd Haynes as Pete Dixon, the American history teacher and his home-room class. His co-star, Denise Nicholas, was a guidance counselor at the integrated Walt Whitman High School.[167] The two principal actors in *Room 222* are black. Lou Gossett, a black actor, was one of the stars in *The Young Rebels*, a noteworthy ABC television series in 1970. Gossett portrayed the character Isak Poole, ex-slave, blacksmith, and guerrilla fighter in the American Revolution. In this show, Poole was a member of the fictitious Yankee Doodle Society, operating behind enemy lines with his white coconspirators. In the character of Poole, Gossett saw "an opportunity to portray a great deal of strength, mental and physical. He's not a superman. He has fallacies but he has an image that is not derogatory to black people—which I'm concerned about. . . ."[168]

The changes that occurred during the years 1968–1970 did not end discrimination in television programming. A number of black actors testified in hearings sponsored by The Commission on Human Rights in 1968, and William Booth, chairman of the commission, opened the sessions with this comment: "They [Negroes and other minority group members] are still not reflected in the everyday content of general programming and commercials. This is harmful because the public then sees the Negro and Puerto Rican solely as a rioter, a social problem, and not as a human being. For the most part Negroes are still limited to the stereotyped supporting and servant roles. The few programs which feature Negro performers treat them in such a nervous and unnatural manner as to make them seem hardly credible as human beings."[169]

Two years later, Jean Fairfax said that the broadcasting industry contributes to black rage by making black Americans invisible or by being unwilling to present them as serious and complex human beings. She summarized black anger about the broadcasting industry as follows:

1. The black experience is presented primarily in its socially pathological manifestations and without the kind of analysis that makes sense to black people.
2. Blacks feel that the industry is afraid to present black life in its strengths, its resiliency, and its qualities of endurance from the black point of view because this is too threatening and not what whites want to see.
3. The industry is more interested in presenting blacks as whites with dark skins than in discovering what the attitudes and life-styles of black people really are.
4. Blacks are not regarded as serious, intelligent citizens with broad civic concerns; it does not occur to program directors that there are knowledgeable blacks who can make contributions on issues other than race.[170]

A survey in 1968 showed that the percentage of blacks employed in 311 stations reporting was 2.7. A 1970 study of educational radio

---

165 Kitty Griffith and Todd Holland, "Sesame Street, South," *South Today*, Sept. 1970, p. 3.
166 *The Plain Dealer*, Nov. 22, 1970, p. 8A.
167 *The New York Times*, Oct. 5, 1969, p. D21.
168 *Ibid.*, Aug. 30, 1970, p. D13.

169 L. Patterson, *op. cit.*, p. 314.
170 Jean Fairfax, "Contributing to Black Rage," *The New York Times*, July 26, 1970, p. D15. © 1970 by the New York Times Company. Reprinted by permission.

and television stations revealed employment of minority group members at approximately 9 percent, most of whom were in clerical, talent, and production positions. No chief executive positions were held by minority group members, and they held only 3 percent of 451 major department head positions. Even at "soul" stations, blacks rarely hold executive positions. According to Miss Fairfax, if wise decisions are to be made in the broadcasting industry in the future, Blacks will have to be brought into top management positions.

Faith Berry has argued that the undercover agent role played by Bill Cosby in *I Spy*, along with similar roles played by black actors on such shows as *Mission Impossible, Mod Squad, NYPD*, and *Ironside*, has created "a new black stereotype of overwhelming dishonesty: the black man with no real personal life who is in the plot as a useful tool, the cooperative, all-too-often flunky accomplice made to look heroic in a scenario reminiscent of the old Lone Ranger–Tonto put-on." She characterizes the NBC *Bill Cosby Show* of 1969–1970 where Cosby plays Chet Kincaid, a physical education teacher in a high school, as "this barrel-of-fun-playing-it-dumb offering." Granting that the presentation of Blacks as human beings was a plus factor on this show, Miss Berry criticizes the program because it did not deal at all with the black experience.[171] A. S. Doc Young, a black reviewer, replied to Miss Berry's criticism of the Cosby show. According to Young, Cosby is "a comic, wit, humorist and storyteller." He asks what is wrong with laughter and why Cosby should alter his personality and repress his talent in an effort to become someone other than himself. "Bill Cosby is not Malcolm X or Dr. Martin Luther King, Eldridge Cleaver or Stokely Carmichael . . . as Bill Cosby . . . he is making an important contribution to Afro-Americans, to Americans as a whole." Young sees Cosby as the creator of a hit show, and as one who has opened the doors of opportunity for black professionals, artisans, and apprentices who previously were denied entrance to major network television and to Hollywood studios. From this viewpoint, the Cosby show is not an event for lament, but a source of black pride.[172]

An interesting exchange of views took place in 1970 on a black television show and the ability of a white critic to appraise such a program. Jack Gould, a *New York Times* reviewer, commented that *Black Journal* did not have "peripheral value . . . which is letting whites know the who, what, where and why of the black perspective." Tony Brown, the executive producer of the show, replied that the commitment of *Black Journal* was not to that concern, but "it is to a perspective which deals in Black on Black." Brown says that it is ludicrous "for a white reviewer for *The Times* to think that he can evaluate the assertion of manhood, womanhood and self-respect among my people." Asserting that black people are "bound together by spiritual and emotional ties which transcend any type of communication known to those who have not shared our experiences," Brown says that "our ability to communicate with one another is indigenous only to us." In his view, television continuously emphasizes white pride and teaches black people and white people to love white culture. It is necessary, therefore, for any program oriented to black people to combat the teaching of self-hate, and to include "as much emotionalism as possible, which can be used as a bridge to establish black culture in dignified perspective."[173] In replying, Gould said that Brown takes too much for granted with respect to the black audience for which he speaks. Citing Brown's contention that Blacks know all there is need to know about repression, Gould remarked that one would have thought that they, in particular, would be concerned with remedial proposals. But, he says, *Black Journal* gave "both blacks and whites emotion, not information." Acknowledging that "too much of television requires black people to embrace white culture,"

[171] Faith Berry, "Can 'Just for Laughs' Be Real for Blacks," *The New York Times*, Dec. 7, 1969.

[172] A. S. Doc Young, "Bill Cosby Is Not Malcolm X, He's Bill Cosby," *The New York Times*, Dec. 21, 1969.
[173] A "Letter to the Editor," printed in Jack Gould, "A Black Critic for a Black Show?" *The New York Times*, Oct. 11, 1970, p. D17.

Gould asks if gifted black people "should set an example against divisiveness by copying what they disapprove." He asked also what informative purpose the program served if the Blacks already know everything in *Black Journal?*[174]

Radio. Fifteen years ago the eventual death of radio was predicted, but in the late 1960s there were more radios in the United States than people—and more Americans listened to radio during the average week than watched television. A noteworthy development in radio is the limited-appeal program, and, increasingly, the elimination of short shows and a trend toward a single, 24-hour program addressed to a fraction of the population. In New York City, 63 different AM and FM stations compete for attention, including stations featuring "standard" rock-and-roll music introduced by disc jockeys with special accents, country-Western music, folk rock, all-talk or telephone-participation formats, middle-of-the-road music, "adult" music, music and news, all news, and ethnic broadcasting or "ghetto radio." New York City has three Negro stations. New York's WEVD, the formerly all-Yiddish station, now broadcasts in 13 different languages, including Japanese and Norwegian. Honan says: "So firm is the grip of the ethnic stations on their audiences that a recent Pulse survey shows the Spanish-speaking population, for example, listening to radio for an average of four hours a day, which is almost twice as much time as other Americans devote to the medium. This audience, according to surveys, is profoundly influenced by what it hears, whether commercials, news or comment."[175]

Spokesmen for the mass media predict that television will follow the fractionalization experienced earlier by newspapers and now by radio. Although these media may become a strong force promoting cultural diversity, the quality of that diversity remains to be seen. At present, the intellectual content of some of the ghetto and ethnic stations approaches zero, and little that might be considered public service is offered. Some ethnic stations are charged with exploiting commercially the linguistic handicap of their listeners and thus helping to perpetuate that handicap. To meet that charge it has been suggested that such stations might provide special counterbalancing educational services.[176]

In 1960, the black disc jockey was expected to follow a strictly commercial format while promoting records that dealt with noncontroversial subjects. In 1968, James Brown's hit record, *Say It Loud—I'm Black and I'm Proud,* appeared. In 1970, black activists—moderate and militant—accelerated their demands and broadcast reform became an important goal. Garnett says that the black critic of radio "is concerned about the image of him that is being portrayed to whites over the general market (or mainly white-oriented) media as well as how 'soul' radio affects the black man's image of himself."[177] Black critics note that fewer than 10 radio stations (and no TV channels) in the more than 7000 American radio and television outlets are black-owned and -operated. They point out that all seven Federal Communications Commission (FCC) commissioners are white. There is no nationwide black-oriented news network. Blacks still constitute a tiny minority in key executive positions at "soul" stations. Entertainment programs are based almost entirely on "rhythm-blues" or "rock" music, and little or no attention is paid to black performances in jazz, "pop," folk, or other music modes. Black radio critics wonder if white management's public affairs programs are intended to enlighten and serve the masses or merely to satisfy minimum FCC requirements. Black disc jockeys who do little more than play records and talk "jive" are said to be perpetuating old stereotypes. Black critics claim that the average white radio station manager seeks only to reap enormous profits at Black's ex-

---

[174] *Ibid.*
[175] William H. Honan, "The New Sound of Radio," *The New York Times Magazine,* Dec. 3, 1967, p. 70.

[176] *Ibid.,* pp. 72, 76.
[177] Bernard E. Garnett, "Are 'Soul' Stations Fair to Blacks?" *The New York Times,* May 3, 1970, p. D17.

pense. In challenging the renewal of WMAL's television license in Washington, D.C., William Wright said: "If we're going to talk about freedom and self-determination, we need to hear our black heroes performing in other art forms. We need to talk about drug addiction, about slum landlords, about jobs, about education. . . ." The reformers say that "soul" is popular, but they insist that broadcasters could offer information and public service without disturbing their profits.[178]

As is the case with estimates of the role and value of "black art," the ways in which Blacks participate in television and radio will continue to evoke varying responses among black people and among Whites. The inclusion of Blacks in television and radio programs increased during the 1960s, but Blacks are still greatly underrepresented in programming, in positions behind the scenes, and in management.

Popular Songs. In the past, Tin Pan Alley's songwriters frequently produced lyrics that were highly offensive to Jews, Negroes, Italians, Chinese, Japanese, and others. In recent years, according to Ranson, a vigorous reaction to the use of such slurs in popular songs has occurred. This change is seen as a result of general enlightenment and of the knowledge of the potential harm in racial and religious stereotypes.[179]

Comic Strips and Comic Books. The nature of the comic strip forces the artist to resort to caricature and oversimplification. A limit of three or four panels per day, with not more than 20 words per panel, allows little chance for qualifications and naunces. Frisbie remarks:

When the continuity requires the appearance of a Chinese laundryman, there is a strong temptation to draw him with buck teeth, pigtail and kimono under a balloon of "atlocious" dialogue. A Negro comes out jet black with fullness of lips and crinkly hair. A Mexican wears an enormous sombrero and may be crisscrossed with bullet-filled bandoleers. Indians have blankets,

feathers and big noses. The cartoonist's problem is that unless some such features are emphasized, his character can't be readily identified by comic readers as a Chinese, a Negro, a Mexican or an Indian, and such recognition may be essential to comprehension of the story line.[180]

The official creed of the National Cartoonists Society, to which many leading cartoonists belong, states:

. . . we should preserve our present high standard of artistic achievement and good taste in our relationship with the public and with those agencies that distribute cartoons for professional use . . . our work should comply with the established standards of morality and decency; and we should condemn any violations of such standards.[181]

The code of the Comic Magazines Association of America, which has been used to clean up the comic book industry, specifically states that "ridicule or attack on any religious or racial group is never permitted."

Despite the great popularity of television, comic books are still widely read. Nearly all English-language newspapers, with a total circulation of 57 million daily, contain comic strips. Frisbie says that the fact that this form of entertainment, which "offers so little support to racial and religious prejudice—and indeed, sometimes fights it—should encourage all concerned with better intergroup relationships."[182]

Newspapers and News Magazines. Newspapers and news magazines like the other mass media, can be impartial in how they report and yet highly biased in what they *select* to report. Objectivity in reporting crimes in which black Americans are involved may, for example, be coupled with a systematic avoidance of positive human-interest stories concerning the black community. Ordinary selection procedures usually result in an overall negative picture of minority groups. In

---

178 *Ibid.*, p. 17.
179 Ranson, *op. cit.*, p. 17.

180 Richard P. Frisbie, "The Comics: No More Funny Business in Prejudice," in Ranson, *op. cit.*, p. 20.
181 *Ibid.*
182 *Ibid.*

addition to the selection process, bias may enter news presentation in the way in which a story is featured. Different effects may result from front-page or back-page treatment, the content of the opening paragraphs, whether or not the story carries a byline, and whether pictures are used.

The Kerner Commission reported that the news media achieved reasonable balance in their reporting of the disturbances in the summer of 1967. When the commission studied the more qualitative findings, however, it found that the media "printed scare headlines unsupported by the mild stories that followed," "reported rumors that had no basis in fact," "staged 'riot' events for the cameras," "reported inaccurate information about the extent of the damage," and "tended to define the events as black-white confrontations," even though "almost all of the deaths, injuries, and property damage occurred in all-Negro neighborhoods." Very little is known about the effects on readers of such reporting.

Schary says that the media tend to present the black man in a light which reveals only white men's values, and questions whether this reverse stereotyping contributes to the reduction of prejudice. He asks whether the breakdown of prejudice requires that the white man come to recognize what it means to be black in a white society. In his view, the media may be accommodating unknowingly to today's prejudices by being silent on Mexican-Americans, Puerto Ricans, and American Indians. The indirect result of this unintended silence is the sustaining of prejudice.

It has been common practice for the news media to assign stories concerning minorities to reporters untrained in intergroup relations and recruited from the majority group. The Kerner Commission pointed out that the media have become more sensitive about these matters in recent years and have taken some steps to reverse old practices. Special fellowships for minority students interested in media careers are being provided, on-the-job training programs and collaborative efforts with journalism schools to broaden educational opportunities have been estab-

lished, and searches for black talent have been conducted.[183]

THE SOCIAL FUNCTIONS OF ART

In the main, the members of a public select artistic and quasiartistic products that present points of view along the lines of their own sentiments. When some prejudiced persons read all or part of *Native Son*, their anti-Negro feelings were intensified. Many nonprejudiced readers felt the book gave them much insight into lower-class life in general and lower-class urban Negro life in particular. In other words, art does not speak for itself. What one gets from a book or other artistic product, if one gets to it at all, depends to a considerable extent on what one takes to it.

The relationship between art and society is interactive, but art and quasiart doubtless reflect, more than they affect, their times. On a continuum of influence, presumably abstract music and abstract painting would stand at one extreme (least influence), and the motion picture and other mass agencies of communication at the other (greatest influence).

The social functions of art may be looked at from the standpoints of the minority artist, the members of a minority group, and majority-group members. For the minority artist, the creative process provides emotional release, social recognition, and perhaps some financial return. For minority persons, art by or about the members of the group provides entertainment and may inspire feelings of identity, pride, and confidence. For those in the majority group, such art affords amusement and tends to strengthen existing attitudes, whatever they may be, toward persons of minority status.

[183] This section on newspapers and news magazines is based on Dore Schary, "The Mass Media and Prejudice," in Charles Y. Glock and Ellen Siegelman (eds.), *Prejudice U.S.A.*, Praeger, 1969, ch. 4. For a report on the replies of 388 organizations—magazines, newspapers, radio-television—in 50 states concerning the number and percentage of Negro employees, coverage and understanding of the Negro, see Woody Klein, "New Media and Race Relations: A Self Portrait," *Columbia Journalism Review*, Fall, 1968, pp. 2, 11, 16.

Part III / PREJUDICE,
DISCRIMINATION,
AND DEMOCRATIC VALUES

Chapter 21 / THE REDUCTION
OF PREJUDICE AND DISCRIMINATION:
CHANGING THE PREJUDICED PERSON

In the first two parts of this volume we have followed the tangled patterns of relationship that develop between dominant groups and minority groups. We have examined the causes of prejudice and discrimination and described their results, for the individuals involved and for the social structure. We have seen that to some degree the institutional patterns of the minority groups can be understood only by reference to their statuses. Throughout this analysis, we have attempted to maintain an objective approach. Our own value stand has not been disguised, but we have tried to prevent it from distorting the picture.

In turning to the analysis of strategies that are effective in reducing prejudice and discrimination, our value stand becomes more explicit. We believe that the categorical judgment and treatment of human beings not only is evil in itself but brings with it a host of other evils. Having stated that premise, we shall attempt to analyze strategies on a thoroughly objective basis. The surgeon cannot afford to be sentimental.

Even in this section our concern is not simply with social-action programs—although we shall hope to contribute to them. One of the most effective ways of learning about the nature of intergroup hostility is to study the techniques that are effective, and those that are ineffective, in reducing it; for such a study to be valid it must be concerned with the causes and functions of that hostility.

In recent years, as we have seen, there have been important changes in many aspects of majority-minority relations. Vicious genocide and new waves of imperialism have arisen; but significant gains have also been made. Since 1940 there has been significant improvement in the status of the Negro in the United States, although many barriers to his full participation in society still stand.

These gains, however, have been so slow, compared with his soaring hopes, that the sense of relative deprivation has increased enormously. Anti-Semitism is at a low ebb, and the problems associated with the integration of many immigrant groups into America are being reduced; but the lot of those of Mexican and Puerto Rican descent, migrants and native-born alike, is still difficult. Americans of Japanese ancestry were treated with great injustice during World War II; but, perhaps as a reaction to that injustice, discrimination against Japanese is now minimal. The United States is once again discovering the Indians in her midst, and is finding them seriously disprivileged. In light of the conflicts of the day and the gap between her aspirations and the realities, it is clear that only a major, national effort can significantly reduce the costly burdens of discrimination.

VARIABLES TO CONSIDER IN THE DEVELOPMENT OF STRATEGIES

Effective strategy is based on a precise knowledge of the goals one wants to achieve and on a thorough understanding of the obstacles in the way. We need to consider (1) types of goals for which different groups are striving; (2) types of persons to be affected, in terms of their relation to prejudice and discrimination; (3) types of situations, in time and place, to which strategy must adjust.

The strategies of a given period reflect assumptions about these issues, but the assumptions are often unexamined. The result is less effective action. We want again to emphasize strongly, as we have throughout our discussion, the *system* quality to prejudice and discrimination. They express cultural norms; they are embedded in institutional and interpersonal structures; they are related to the motives, needs, and anxieties of majority and minority-group members. Strategies, unhappily, often focus on one element of the system. Perhaps we can illustrate this by a partially imaginary historical sequence, in which we will note major shifts in strategy.

The first stage in the break-up of patterns of dominance-submission is a slowly increasing readiness of dominants to admit some among the minority into relative equality of status if. . . . If, that is, they "improve themselves," take on "proper" attitudes and styles of behavior, and the like. The underlying theory is: disprivilege is caused by the inadequacies of minorities. Hence sound strategy requires the removal of those inadequacies. There is often generous and well-meaning help from the dominants, in the form of educational support for example. Considering the feedback mechanisms in complex social systems, this "cause" should not be set aside; but it is a third-level cause, and becomes meaningful only when preceeding "causes" are recognized and acted upon.

The next stage of strategic effort, with its underlying theory, shifts major concern to the majority-group member: Minority-majority relations are conflictful because of the prejudices of those on top. A major campaign of education and persuasion must be mounted to help them see, and to set aside, their own prejudices and the culture on which they rest. This approach is also valuable; but insofar as it fails to see how prejudices are tied into the social system—in particular, into the system of discriminations which the dominant-group members participate in regularly—it cannot be very effective.

It is exactly this system of discriminations that is the focus of attention in the next stage. The institutions of a "racist" society must be transformed, whether by organized legal and political action or by violent protest (the contrast, of course, is significant). According to those who take this approach, dominant-group prejudices are unimportant; at most they are reflections of the basic causes of injustice. And attention to the behavior of the minority-group members is a travesty, for it seems to blame him for being victimized. It

is essential, of course, to deal with the structure of discrimination. If the reenforcements to that structure which come from culture and character are overlooked, however, gains that are won by costly effort may fade out as the homeostatic forces in the total system bring it back to "normal."

In all this, there is room for strategic specialists who prefer to work on one part of the total system. There are times and places when one part of the system of discrimination is more vulnerable, suggesting that scarce resources should be expended there. There are no conditions, however, in which the several forces we have been dealing with are not operative, a fact that a general theory adequate to strategic requirements must emphasize. And in the long run, structure, culture, and character must all change.

Strategic disagreements sometimes rest on inadequate examination of conflicting goals, of variation among individuals in their readiness for change, and of differing situations. Hence we must comment on the dilemmas and problems that these circumstances present.

Types of Goals

Those who are seeking to reduce prejudice and discrimination do not all agree on the immediate or long-run objectives. Some believe that peaceful coexistence is most desirable. Others are willing to accept and work for economic and political equality and integration but are opposed to "social" equality (there is a vague and shifting line separating economic and political from social). Still others are working for complete integration, for a situation where each individual will be judged and treated as an individual and not in any way as a member of a *supposed* or functionless group. Functional group membership will continue to be important—it would be foolish to treat physicians as if they were engineers. Prejudice and discrimination, however, are characterized precisely by the fact that they disregard function; they treat the Negro physician and engineer and farm laborer and machine operator and teacher and unskilled worker as if they were all alike, although they share nothing in common *as Negroes* but a few physical traits—and these have a wide range of variation. That is why we call them a functionless group, just as "white" people are.

The present authors believe in the third goal mentioned above—complete equality and integration. This goal is harmonious with peaceful coexistence or pluralism, provided that the pluralism is chosen by individuals of the minority group as a matter of right and not enforced on them by the majority as a categorical requirement. Plural rights are limited, of course, by the legitimate needs for security and integration of the whole society. One of the great problems of modern society is the determination of differences that are allowable and are harmonious with the principle of the greatest good to the greater number. We believe these differences can be very broad—broader than most societies, in this day of crisis, are permitting. Differences in language, in religion, in belief in the best methods for achieving life's values—these are not only permissible but necessary for a society that is eager to find better ways to solve its problems. *Active allegiance* to a system of law that opposes the democratic method for settling disputes is doubtless beyond the range of differences that an integrated society may permit. Advocacy of such a system is less dangerous to democracy than its suppression; but active programs may well represent "a clear and present danger." Unfortunately, in the difficult and important task of separating advocacy from active programs, a legitimate and necessary pluralism has been weakened. Opposition to those who are working for an undemocratic state has been extended, by some, to opposition to those who have different ideas, believe different religious doctrines, have different conceptions of the proper extent of governmental activity, and trace descent from different ancestors. Thus reaction and prejudice frequently have been joined in our society. We believe that America can prosper only by encouraging the integration of all groups while permitting a wide and diversified pluralism.

In day-by-day moral decisions, one often has to decide between two values. Is it better

to make the maximum number of public housing units available to disprivileged black families, or to promote housing integration even at the cost of turning away some of the families in greatest need. This raises the difficult question of quotas. Can they be "benign," as Dodson, Cohen, and others have asked? This is, can they be designed to guarantee, in housing for example, that a neighborhood that has become integrated racially will not rather quickly be resegregated?[1] The word "quota" has powerful connotations of injustice to many people; and attaching the adjective "benign" to it may not eliminate those connotations, even if the goal is approved. The word quota is being attached at the present time to another process, with equally praiseworthy goals, and communication is blocked by the connotations of "quota." Many colleges, for example, are being urged to increase the proportion of minority-group students, to set goals considerably above their present enrollment, to set a floor under which their level of participation will not be allowed to fall. Now the word quota has traditionally meant a ceiling, not a floor; it has meant a barrier to fuller participation by a given group, rather than an active program to encourage participation. So long as a word can be attached to two such different sets of activities, clarity of goals will be impossible.

In the early days of the desegregation movement in the United States, there was not a great deal of disagreement over goals, or over priorities, because there was so much to do that any step seemed right. After a few gains, however, value priorities begin to emerge, and serious dilemmas, within and between persons, are revealed. Is it better to promote justice, even at the cost of conflict; or to promote peace, even at the risk of some injustice? In political campaigns, should minority-group members emphasize welfare goals or status goals? The former are more immediately important to the least privileged, the latter to the middle-class minority-group members for whom bread-and-butter issues

[1] See Dan Dodson, "Can Intergroup Quotas be Benign?," *JIR*, Autumn, 1960, pp. 12–17; and Oscar Cohen, "The Case for Benign Quotas in Housing," *Phylon*, Spring, 1960, pp. 20–29.

are less important, but prestige issues vital. As James Wilson has pointed out, the kinds of leaders and political arrangements needed to attain one of these goals are quite different from those required for the other; and if both are sought simultaneously, neither may be attained.[2]

Is liberty the primary goal—making certain that everybody has a fair start, that each has a choice among reasonable alternatives and the right to participate in decisions affecting his welfare, or, in a definition closer to John Stuart Mill, that everyman is free from tyranny of leaders and from constraints by the majority when those constraints are unnecessary for the larger good? Liberty has perhaps been the first goal of liberal societies during the last two centuries. For others, however, the first goal is equality. They believe, with R. H. Tawney, that liberty is impossible without equality, that the democratic society, therefore, must strive to achieve a relative equality in the distribution of scarce goods. Some would say that this is so important that equality should be sought even at the sacrifice of some liberty. Still others emphasize fraternity as the fundamental goal. In Max Weber's terms, this might be defined as relative similarity in the distribution of social honor, creating a situation in which men are not separated by rank. Each is therefore the brother—or perhaps more precisely, a potential brother-in-law—of every other.

It would take a long philosophical treatise to discuss the relationships among these goals. The French, and to an important degree the American, revolution assumed that they were not incompatible, but indeed mutually supportive. Many persons, however, would argue that they are mutually limiting; that efforts to attain one will reduce the chances of attaining the others, not because of their incompatibility, but because of the selective use of time and resources. Still others see them as mutually exclusive. In the United States, for example, there has always been an underlying tension between the goals of liberty and of equality, with the former

[2] See James Q. Wilson, *Negro Politics: The Search for Leadership*, Free Press, 1960.

being more strongly supported, and fear being expressed that too much equality means the end of liberty. Today, the pluralism-integration question raises the issue of fraternity in a crucial way. The goal of subgroup fraternity is receiving new emphasis, as for example in some phases of the Black Power movement.

We will not undertake the philosophical treatise required; but perhaps we may be permitted a moral aside. Is it possible that each of the three values can be carried to self-defeating limits? Ought the goal to be to maximize not any one of the values but the *product* value of the three? Ought we not to ask, in moral discourse about these goals, whether or not gain in any one of them contributes also to gain in the others? If not, perhaps the first gain has been pushed too far.

However one answers these questions, *some* answer is essential before meaningful strategic action is possible.

Types of Persons

Those who declare that *the* way to eliminate prejudice is "education" or "law" or "more contact between peoples," or those who, oppositely, declare that prejudice cannot be eliminated because *the* prejudiced person is torn by a deep-seated anxiety that is basic to his ego, both make the mistake of failing to distinguish among the many different types of persons who show intergroup hostility. The reduction of prejudice and discrimination demands that we make such distinctions, for a different strategy will be effective for each of the different types of persons.

Robert Merton has devised a useful classification of four types of persons for each of whom a different group of strategies is appropriate.

1. The unprejudiced nondiscriminator, or all-weather liberal; the person who accepts the "American creed" in both belief and action. Such a person must be the spearhead of any effective campaign to reduce prejudice and discrimination; but his force is reduced by several errors. There is the "fallacy of group soliloquies." "Ethnic

liberals are busily engaged in talking to themselves. Repeatedly, the same groups of like-minded liberals seek each other out, hold periodic meetings in which they engage in mutual exhortation, and thus lend social and psychological support to one another."[3] This activity does not appreciably spread the creed for which they are working. The fallacy of group soliloquies produces the illusion that there is consensus on the issue in the community at large and thus leads to the "fallacy of unanimity." The all-weather liberal mistakes discussion in like-minded groups for effective action and overestimates the support for his position. His isolation from other points of view also produces the "fallacy of privatized solutions."

The ethnic liberal, precisely because he is at one with the American creed, may rest content with his own individual behavior and thus see no need to do anything about the problem at large. Since his own spiritual house is in order, he is not motivated by guilt or shame to work on a collective problem. The very freedom of the liberal from guilt thus prompts him to secede from any *collective* effort to set the national house in order. He essays a *private* solution to a *social* problem. He assumes that numerous individual adjustments will serve in place of a collective adjustment. His outlook, compounded of good moral philosophy but poor sociology, holds that each individual must put his own house in order and fails to recognize that privatized solutions cannot be effected for problems which are essentially social in nature. For clearly, if each person *were* motivated to abide by the American creed, the problem would not be likely to arise in the first place.[4]

These fallacies lead to the paradox of the passive liberal's contributing, to some degree, to the persistence of prejudice and discrimination by his very inaction. They may be overcome by having the liberal enter groups that are not composed solely of fellow liberals (giving up the gratifications of consistent group support); by realization that discrimination brings rewards—or seems to

—and that exhortation, therefore, is not enough if the social environment is not changed at the same time; and by action on the part of the militant liberal to show the passive liberal how he contributes to prejudice and discrimination by his inaction.[5]

2. The unprejudiced discriminator, or fair-weather liberal. This is the person who, despite his own lack of prejudice, supports discrimination if it is easier or profitable. He may show the expediency of silence or timidity, or discriminate to seize an advantage. He may refuse to hire Negroes because it "might hurt business." The fair-weather liberal suffers from some degree of guilt and is therefore a strategic person for the all-weather liberal to work on. The need is to bring him into groups of all-weather liberals, where he will find rewards for abiding by his own beliefs.

3. The prejudiced nondiscriminator, or fair-weather illiberal. This is the reluctant conformist, the employer who discriminates until a fair employment practices law puts the fear of punishment and loss into him, the trade-union official who, though prejudiced himself, abolishes Jim Crow because the rank and file of his membership demands it, the bigoted businessman who profits from the trade of minority-group members. Like the fair-weather liberal, he is a person of expediency, but this disguises a basic difference. "Whereas the timid bigot is under strain when he conforms to the creed, the timid liberal is under strain when he deviates."[6] Adequate strategy must recognize this difference. The fair-weather illiberal can be kept from discrimination only by an environment that makes discrimination costly and painful, not by appeal to his value creed. Legal controls, strictly administered, may at first increase his prejudice—or at least his verbalization of it—but they will reduce his discrimination.

4. The prejudiced discriminator, or all-weather illiberal. He is consistent in belief

[3] Robert K. Merton, in R. M. MacIver (ed.), *Discrimination and National Welfare*, Institute for Religious and Social Studies (distributed by Harper & Row), 1949, p. 104.

[4] *Ibid.*, p. 105.

[5] For a somewhat impressionistic but useful attempt to study the all-weather liberal, see Alphonso Pinkney, *The Committed: White Activists in the Civil Rights Movement*, College and Universities Press, 1968.

[6] Merton, *op. cit.*, p. 108.

and practice. He believes that differential treatment of minority groups is not discrimination, but discriminating. Strategy in dealing with such persons must vary from region to region. In some subcultures of the United States the all-weather illiberal is a conformist, supported by the group norms; if he were to change, he would be alienated from the people important to him. In other subcultures he is isolated, and a change in his attitudes and behavior would help to bring integration with people significant to him. He can be moved toward type three. Change of the illiberal who is supported by group norms requires legal and administrative controls and large-scale changes in the economic supports to prejudice.

It is important to understand the distribution of these various types and to realize the kinds of strategies that are effective with each. To try to appeal to all of them in the same way, or to assume that a given proportion of each type is found, when they are in fact very differently distributed, is to make serious strategic errors.[7] We need to note that such a classification has little reference to the intensity dimension; two all-weather illiberals, for example, may have very different patterns of behavior because prejudice and discrimination occupy an important place in the personality organization of one and an unimportant place for the other. One cannot assume, moreover, that the same distribution would be true for each minority. In a given community one might find discrimination against both an Indian and a Negro group, but most of the white population may be fair-weather liberals toward the Indians and all-weather illiberals toward the Negroes.

These types are probably found everywhere, although certainly not in the same proportions. Campbell describes four types of white southerners that correspond to a large degree with Merton's list: those sensitive to discrimination and active in its reduction; the sensitive but quiet;[8] the indifferent; and the insensitive, who have been able,

because of their "psychic, group, and community jamming stations," to shut out awareness of much of the world around them.[9] In critical times, when judgments tend to be polarized, effective strategy requires that we be alert to such variation.

Levinson draws a valuable distinction between the openly antidemocratic individual and the pseudodemocratic individual. The former is nearly the equivalent of Merton's all-weather illiberal, except that Levinson emphasizes the deep-seated irrational sources (a specialized causal explanation that Merton might not share entirely). The pseudodemocratic person is somewhat similar to the fair-weather liberal; but Levinson places a useful emphasis on the ambivalence of such a person's feelings: he discriminates but has some sense of guilt about it; he is prejudiced but also believes in democratic values. This is probably a widespread type of individual in the United States; hence development of an adequate strategy in reducing his prejudice and discrimination is an important task. Levinson says:

An idea may be considered openly antidemocratic when it refers to active hatred, or to violence which has the direct aim of wiping out a minority group or of putting it in a permanently subordinate position. A pseudodemocratic idea, on the other hand, is one in which hostility toward a group is somewhat tempered and disguised by means of a compromise with democratic ideals. Pseudodemocratic statements about Jews are often introduced by qualifying phrases which deny hostility or which attempt to demonstrate the democratic attitude of the speaker, e.g., "It's not that I'm prejudiced, but . . ."; "Jews have their rights, but. . . ."[10]

The author notes the strategic importance of recognizing the ambivalence of the pseudodemocratic person. Such an individual is relatively unaffected by current literature that attacks prejudice as "un-American" or "un-Christian," for he has disguised his prejudice from himself by a group of rationali-

---

[7] For this whole discussion, see *ibid.*, pp. 99–126.
[8] For an interesting letter from one such in Mississippi, see John Ciardi, "Some Good Men There Are," *Saturday Review*, June 29, 1963, p. 17.

[9] Ernest Campbell, in a review of books by Harry Golden, James M. Dabbs, and Martin Luther King, Jr., *SF*, Oct., 1959, pp. 74–75.
[10] T. W. Adorno *et al.*, *The Authoritarian Personality*, Harper & Row, 1950, p. 60.

zations that seem to square his behavior with his value creed. Strategy must find a way not simply of exposing his rationalizations (for the problem is not essentially a rational one with the individual), but of lowering the need for prejudice while strengthening the belief in democratic values.

Many of us are pseudodemocratic. Our actions may seem to others to be discriminatory, but if they tell us so, it is easy to say, "Who, me? Why I believe in democracy, an equal chance for everyone. But why should I pay those Mexicans higher wages to buy more liquor with? They're just as happy the way they are. Why should I put in a bathtub for my Negro tenants? They'd just fill it with coal."

The human mind has an enormous capacity for holding mutually contradictory ideas without any feeling of discomfort. The pseudodemocratic individual will not become thoroughly democratic until the personal and group functions and the traditional supports of prejudice and discrimination are reduced sharply.

The strategic problem of distinguishing types of persons is also indirectly involved in Isidor Chein's discussion of "dimensions of prejudice." A person in whom one dimension is largest will respond to a different approach than the person in whom another dimension is largest. There is the "informational" dimension—for example, the holding of stereotyped beliefs—for which education is an important strategy. The "conformity" dimension represents a need on the part of the prejudiced person to conform to the prevailing pattern. Legal measures proscribing discrimination will affect him. The "status" dimension is the desire for ego satisfaction, for a position of superiority. Reduction of this factor in prejudice requires the equalization of opportunities and rights —giving ego motives less to thrive on. The "emotional" dimension involves attitudes of actual hatred and hostility toward minorities. The need here is for the minimization of frustration.[11]

A definitive classification of the types of persons involved in prejudice and discrimination would have to be far more complicated than those we have discussed. When so many variables are involved, a few types cannot cover the range of empirical combinations. Nevertheless, the distinctions drawn by Merton, Campbell, Levinson, and Chein can be of great value in strategic considerations.

Types of Situations

When one has distinguished the types of goals and types of persons involved, he has a great deal of information about a situation in which prejudice and discrimination are found. But other factors must also be considered if his strategy is to be effective. What is the legal pattern? Does it support discrimination or condemn it? Does the law condemn it ideologically but fail to provide enforcement techniques? To try the same strategy in a situation where one can count on legal support as he tries in a situation where the law is weak or actually supports discrimination is to be ineffective.

Is the situation one that requires immediate action, or is there time for more deliberate analysis? What is called for in one would be foolish in the other. Schermerhorn distinguishes between emergency problems and tractable problems.

Emergency problems are those in which a crisis arises, where a tangle of circumstances forces an immediate decision on responsible administrators. At this stage it is too late to alter the conditions that gave rise to the emergency. In a lynching, a riot, gang warfare, or violence of any kind between groups, it is useless at the moment to ask what preventive measures would have checked the trouble at the source. . . .

Tractable problems are those in which the need for immediate action is less urgent. Haste gives way to deliberation, and coercion to more strategic considerations. Time permits research, the marshaling of evidence, and comparison of alternative methods.[12]

[11] Isidor Chein, "Some Considerations in Combatting Intergroup Prejudice," *Journal of Educational Sociology*, Mar., 1946, pp. 412–419; see also

Daniel Katz, Irving Sarnoff, and Charles McClintock, "Ego Defense and Attitude Change," *HR*, Feb., 1956, pp. 27–45.
[12] R. A. Schermerhorn, *These Our People*, Heath, 1949, p. 519.

Strategic errors have been made in both directions. In a time of critical hostility a community may "appoint a committee" when what is most needed is training for their police in how to disperse a mob with the least violence. Or, oppositely, a group may "call in the cops," may throw down the gauntlet to discriminators when what is most needed is the careful analysis of causes, the skillful rallying of allies, and the creation of a more favorable environment for change. No easy formula can separate emergency problems from tractable problems, but to neglect to take account of their differences is to invite failure.

Is the discrimination supported mainly by lower-class members of the "dominant" group, themselves insecure and hoping to climb a little higher on the backs of minority-group members? Or is the pattern primarily set by powerful groups who are exploiting prejudice to maintain their authority? Or, more accurately, how are these two supports interrelated? Associated with this is the question of power in a community. Who makes the key decisions; whose support is vital? Much strategic counsel is based on the assumption that major support for change must come from "the conservative power elite." McKee argues, however, that this leads to failure to create ". . . support for new policies by building a constituency in the community who have a genuine stake, personal or ideological, in effecting changes in the community's policies."[13] In some contexts, a coalition can be built up among organized Negro groups, an active liberal middle-class group, the Jewish community, some church groups and women's organizations. In many instances, when such a coalition is mobilized, such "power elite" as there is may then find participation more desirable. Under other conditions, of course, this procedure may mobilize opposition. The need is for flexibility of judgment.

Is the strategy to be aimed at a large group of people or only a few? What will work for a small neighborhood, with an intimacy factor involved, will be ineffective in a large city, a state, or a nation, either because the principles involved may be different or simply because what is feasible for a few may be impossible for many.[14] Are the cultural differences between the majority and minority large or small? Migrants from peasant Mexican background, for example, with significantly different cultural values from those of an urban, industrial society,[15] require different kinds of strategy to improve their situation than do those from highly literate, urban situations (e.g., many Japanese and Jews).

Many aspects of the society under study are important situational influences. What is the level of unemployment, the degree of tension and frustration, the extent of status dissatisfaction? What subtle cues are people receiving on issues wholly unrelated to intergroup relations that influence their readiness for various kinds of intergroup behavior? In the United States, for example, the vast majority of motion pictures, television shows, and advertisements show no Negroes or use them only in stereotyped roles. In the last few years, however, Negroes have appeared as parts of casual crowds, juries, or as professional men; a small but increasing proportion of advertisements are "integrated." Were this trend to develop, what Americans come to look upon as "normal" may be slightly affected.[16]

Basic institutional structure is a vital part of the situation within which strategy must be worked out. Elkins observes that the abolition movement in England could build upon a *national* church, university system, press, and legal ethos; while in the United States, regional differences and isolation were im-

---

[13] James McKee, "Community Power and Strategies in Race Relations, *SP*, Winter, 1958–1959, p. 198.

[14] David Krech and Richard Crutchfield, *Theory and Problems of Social Psychology*, McGraw-Hill, 1948, pp. 500–501.

[15] Florence Kluckhohn, "Dominant and Variant Value Orientation," in Clyde Kluckhohn, Henry Murray, and David Schneider (eds.), *Personality in Nature, Society, and Culture*, Knopf, 2nd ed., 1953, pp. 342–357.

[16] See, for example, Royal Colle, "Color on TV," *The Reporter*, Nov. 30, 1967, pp. 23–25; *Newsweek*, July 15, 1968, pp. 74–75; *The New York Times*, Dec. 10, 1967, p. D25, and Jan. 18, 1968, p. 28.

portant facts.[17] Abolitionists in America were individualists, with little sense of the limits of history or the ways in which slavery was built into institutional structures. Some of these same influences are at work today: it is easy for Americans to view segregation as an individual, moral question (which it is, of course) and to disregard its institutional aspects. There continues to be regional isolation (northern liberal and Mississippi farmer live in significantly different cultural worlds). We have the beginnings of a national press, religious consensus, and university system; but compared with France or England, these are weak. This is an important situational fact for the strategist.

MAPPING OUT A PROGRAM

Having defined his goals and analyzed the kinds of persons and situational factors to be dealt with, the strategist is in a position to plan his antihostility program. Unfortunately, planning and testing are not common. Williams says:

It is clear that organized attempts to improve intergroup relations are numerous and significant. Considering the seriousness of the problems, the possibly dangerous results of inappropriate action, and the very great amount of time and money involved, it might be anticipated that these agencies of social engineering would systematically check the effectiveness of their efforts by appropriate research. With only a few exceptions, however, this has not been done until very recently. . . . . The administrator, student, or interested citizen who wishes to gauge the comparative effectiveness of given programs or techniques can find little scientific evidence to guide him.[18]

Well-intentioned but unguided programs can be useless or even harmful. When they fail, many people may conclude, as Williams points out, that intergroup hostility is inevitable. Others may decide that such hostility is so deeply embedded in our society that only revolutionary change can produce results. Assumptions of these kinds can be tested only by action that is guided by research. The effects of such action "should be to develop realistic confidence and to stabilize expectations in such a way as to reduce the dangers of unchecked utopianism on the one hand and fatalistic disillusionment on the other."[19]

One of the functions of research is to discover the points at which prejudice and discrimination can be attacked most successfully. Myrdal refers to the white man's "rank order of discriminations" toward the Negro, with particular reference to the South. He believes the white man is most willing (although not necessarily very willing) to grant economic and political gains to Negroes and is least willing to grant what he calls "social" equality. The Negro, on the other hand, is primarily concerned with just the "concessions" the white man will make most readily. This seems to carry the obvious strategic implication that action programs should center upon economic and political discriminations. MacIver also states that the "economic front" is a weak point in the defenses of the discriminator. Advances in this area, it is argued, do not encounter the emotional block that guards questions of segregation in social contact.

Evidence on this question is not decisive, for there is variation in time and place. Behavior may be different from the answer to interview questions (few Americans, for example, will verbally deny the right to freedom of economic activity, but their actions often speak louder); and rankings depend on what the actual situation is (if the right to vote has been won by Negroes, Whites may not state high opposition to it even though they had earlier strongly supported the disfranchising situation.)[20] It is also important

---

[17] Stanley Elkins, *Slavery*, Univ. of Chicago Press, 1959, pp. 202–214.

[18] Robin Williams, Jr., *The Reduction of Intergroup Tensions*, SSRC, 1947, p. 8.

[19] *Ibid.*, p. 10.

[20] On this question, see Gunnar Myrdal, *An American Dilemma*, Harper & Row, 1944, pp. 60–67; Edwin Edmunds. "The Myrdalian Thesis: Rank Order of Discrimination," *Phylon*, Third Quarter, 1954, pp. 297–303; and Lewis Killian and Charles Grigg, "Rank Orders of Discrimination of Negroes and Whites in a Southern City," *SF*, Mar., 1961, pp. 235–239.

to note, with Killian and Grigg, that the rank order tells you nothing about the absolute level of discriminatory tendency—which may be the more significant fact.

Empirical studies of the rank ordering hypothesis are not common. Williams and Wienir found, in a study of student attitudes at three universities, that there was a consistent ordering, but that it varied somewhat from the pattern described by Myrdal. Myrdal hypothesized (on the basis, as he noted, of observation, and not controlled study) the following order, with the relationships on which the white man was least willing to yield given first: Intermarriage, personal relations, public facilities (schools, churches, means of transportation), politics, legal and judicial activities, and economics. For the three student groups, the order was: Intermarriage, personal relations, economics, public facilities, politics, and legal and judicial activities.[21] The placement of economic privilege is undoubtedly crucial in understanding any given minority-majority situation.

Matthew and Prothro also throw doubt on the Myrdal thesis when it is observed from the Negro point of view. Recall that Myrdal's quite optimistic interpretation rested on the belief that the Negro rank order was just the reverse of the white. But Matthews and Prothro found that Negro political demands in the 11 southern states were sharply in opposition to what Whites were willing to grant. They also added a time dimension, and found that Negroes were expecting extremely rapid progress, while Whites were just beginning to get comfortable with the thought of glacial speed in changes of race relations.[22] We should observe, however, that their study, done a decade ago, would not have served as a good basis for prediction of the actual speed at which change in southern politics actually occurred in the 1960s. National political factors, of course, were critical in effecting this change.

Despite these qualifications knowledge of

the strong and weak points of opposition is essential to sound strategy. This does not mean that weak points should always be attacked first, for greatest opposition may be found on issues of greatest importance, which therefore must be confronted in spite of the difficulty. Only by knowledge of which issues are most difficult, however, can a rational decision on this question be made.

In addition to knowing the relative importance of various issues to the interacting individuals and groups, one needs to know, in mapping out a program, how a given type of strategy will be viewed by all those involved. Do they regard it as a legitimate way to express a grievance or as deviation from the accepted standards? Or, as is commonly the case in societies under serious stress, is a given strategy accepted by some— whatever their views of the goals being sought—and rejected by others? In America today, various forms of public protest are applauded by some as necessary and right, while others see them as acts of rebellion against legitimate authority. Marvin Olsen has designed a scale to measure the extent to which respondents grant legitimacy to various acts and has tested it with a largely upper-middle-class, urban, white group. The questions form a Guttman scale (coefficient of reproducibility = 96.6 percent):

If a group of people in this country strongly feels that the government is treating them unfairly, what kinds of actions do you think they have a right to take in order to try to change the situation? . . . Which of these actions do you think groups have a right to take in our country?

1. Hold public meetings and rallies. (92%)
2. March quietly and peacefully through town. (70%)
3. Take indirect actions such as economic boycotts or picketing. (60%)
4. Take direct actions such as strikes or sit-ins. (46%)
5. Stage mass protest demonstrations. (41%)[23]

That 59 percent of this highly educated group of respondents should oppose mass protest demonstrations is perhaps not so striking as the fact that 30 percent oppose the right to "march quietly and peacefully

[21] J. Allen Williams, Jr. and Paul L. Wienir, "A Reexamination of Myrdal's Rank Order of Discriminations." *SP*, Spring, 1967, pp. 443–454.

[22] See Donald R. Matthews and J. W. Prothro, *Negroes and the New Southern Politics*, Harcourt Brace Jovanovich, 1966.

[23] Marvin E. Olsen, "Perceived Legitimacy of Social Protest Actions," *SP*, Winter, 1968, p. 299.

through town." In any event, for those seeking change, it is necessary to know probable responses to various strategies.

Ralph Turner has extended our knowledge on this question by asking: Under what conditions will acts of disruption and violence be viewed as forms of legitimate protest and when will they be considered crime and rebellion?[24] He defines protest as an action with the following elements: it expresses a grievance, wrong, or injustice; protesters are unable to correct the condition directly by their own efforts; they seek to call attention to the grievance, to provoke ameliorative steps by some target groups; and some combination of sympathy and fear is invoked. The same act can be defined in many different ways; and the subsequent course of events is strongly affected by the definition that emerges. Those who define a disorder as a protest, in Turner's use of the term, see it as a form of communication. If they define it as deviation, they see it as an individual criminal act. When it is called rebellion or revolution, the disorder is seen, not as an effort to communicate with others or to change the system, but to destroy it.

What conditions support these various definitions; in particular, when will a more-or-less legitimate protest definition emerge? Turner notes the following conditions: Protesters must be seen as a major part of a group whose grievances are well known, who seem powerless to correct those grievances, and who seem deserving of support because they are customarily law-abiding and restrained in their methods. The appeal message must command attention; a combination of threat and appeal is required. "When the threat component falls below the optimal range, the most likely interpretation is deviance; above the optimal range, preoccupation with threat makes rebellion the probable interpretation."[25] The conflict expressed by the disorder must elicit some expression of conciliation if it is to lead to a protest definition. This leads to the further question: When will those who are the targets of protest be inclined to prefer conciliation, in an

effort to reduce the conflict potential? Turner suggests that this is likely to occur when there is risk of injury, to protesters and their targets, in a context in which norms against doing injury to others are strong; when the groups are interdependent in various ways; and when a conflict definition, rather than a protest one, seems likely to entail greater commitment of activity and resources. The points of view of third parties are also important. If they are affected by the disorder, but likely to be injured in some way by taking a partisan position, they may think of it as protest. Finally, official actions are significant parts of the process of definition. As Turner notes: "Official protest interpretations can serve as an effective hedge only in societies and communities where humanitarian values are strong relative to toughness values, so that failure of official action in the service of humanitarianism is excusable. But since this is true in many parts of American society, and because of the volatility of protest groups and the undependability of community support, official acknowledgment that disturbances are a form of protest has become progressively more common during the span of the last five years."[26]

Knowledge of the conditions under which conflictful or potentially conflictful action can win a protest definition—and thus presumably win attention while activating less resistance—is still rudimentary. What is clear is that acts formerly defined as deviant are now carried out under claims of legitimacy. Or, in the terms used by Robert Merton, what might earlier have been seen, by actor and outsider alike, as aberrant behavior, is now proclaimed as nonconformist, and is openly carried on under the presumed legitimacy of some higher authority.[27] This is well described by Horowitz and Liebowitz

[24] Ralph H. Turner, "The Public Perception of Protest," *ASR*, Dec., 1969, pp. 815–831.

[25] *Ibid.*, p. 821.

[26] *Ibid.*, p. 828. On this whole question, see also Robert M. Fogelson, "Violence as Protest," in Robert Connery (ed.), *Urban Riots: Violence and Social Change*, Academy of Political Science, 1968, pp. 25–41; Michael Lipsky, "Protest as a Political Resource," *American Political Science Review*, Dec., 1968, pp. 1144–1158.

[27] See Robert K. Merton in Robert K. Merton and Robert A. Nisbet (eds.), *Contemporary Social Problems*, Harcourt Brace Jovanovich, 2nd ed., 1966, pp. 808–811.

as a process of bringing various social problems out of the welfare arena and into the political arena. In the former, various forms of deviation are defined as public problems to be handled by social agencies according to various norms of administrative policy. In the latter, deviation (in matters of our interest, let us say Negro welfare parents demanding, by disruptive means, a voice in policy) is defined as a political problem to be fought out among the contending parties in an open and public process. "Deviance has been studied by employing a consensus welfare model rather than a conflict model because, for the most part, decision-making concerning deviance has been one-sided. The superordinate parties who regulate deviance have developed measures of control, while the subordinate parties, the deviants themselves, have not entered the political arena. The conflict, though existent, has remained hidden."[28] Thus, to cite an extreme contrast, if welfare mothers organize to demand an increase in welfare payments, saying they cannot feed their children on what they receive, they are defined as deviant, outside the legitimate process for reviewing and ameliorating such problems. If cotton farmers organize to demand payment for not growing cotton (five of them received over $1 million each in 1970 from the government), this is not deviant activity seeking welfare, since their efforts are carried out through political channels. Perhaps this issue can be stated in its most general terms in the following way:

When the distinction between deviation and political competition is easily drawn, we have:

1. Illegitimate deviation according to the powerful majority, and therefore Control by administrative means

2. Legitimate dissent accepted as such by majority and minority, and therefore Decision by political competition

But when decisive power of the majority or consensus break down:

1. Powerful minorities may rise to say: "Our view is legitimate," and try to push it into the political arena. E.g., Negro parents seeking control over welfare policies.

2. Powerful groups arise to say, of formerly accepted political dissent: "Your views are illegitimate," and try to push it out of the political arena into the deviation category. E.g., McCarthyism.

It is difficult to develop an objective statement of this situation, since long-run consequences are more difficult to see than the immediate actions of those with whom one feels much or little sympathy. Perhaps the more common error today among intellectuals is the belief that everything ought to be politicized, that there is little consensus to build on, and that therefore all issues should be made matters of public controversy. We think Merton's words, written in a somewhat different connection, are wise:

These future investigations into nonconformity will need to take care that they do not move from an unthinking orthodoxy to an equally unthinking heterodoxy by valuing nonconformity for its own sake. For what is nonconformity to the norms of one group is often conformity to the norms of another group. There is no joy or merit in escaping the error of taking heterodoxy to be inevitably false or ugly or sinister only to be caught up in the opposite error of thinking heterodoxy to be inevitably true or beautiful or altogether excellent. Put in so many words, this is a commonplace wrapped in banality. Yet people alienated from the world about them often do take heterodoxy as a good in itself, whatever its character. And others, perhaps in recoil against being tagged as hopeless Philistines or in reaction to the cases, familiar in every age, of true merit being neglected or punished because it was unorthodox, are quick to see value, all apart from its substance, in heterodoxy. . . .[29]

Whatever one's views on the value questions involved in this issue, it is clear that effective strategy requires an assessment of the various "definitions of the situation" made by those who will be affected by one's

[28] Irving L. Horowitz and Martin Liebowitz, "Social Deviance and Political Marginality: Toward a Redefinition of the Relation Between Sociology and Politics," *SP*, Winter, 1968, p. 281.

[29] Merton, *op. cit.*, p. 811.

actions. Since individuals are often ambivalent, more favorable rather than less favorable responses can be drawn out by actions appropriate to the tendency one wishes to encourage. And since this is a time of rapid change of views regarding the legitimacy of both means and goals, continuous appraisal is required.

STRATEGIES WITH MAJOR EMPHASIS ON CHANGING THE PERSONALITY

It has been noted frequently that attempts to reduce intergroup hostility can focus either on the prejudiced individual or on those aspects of the situation that allow and encourage discrimination. The former strategies try to change the values, the attitudes, the needs of individuals. They are sometimes based on the oversimplified theory that majority-minority conflict is "fundamentally" based on personality factors. But they are sometimes consciously chosen specialties that are used in full awareness of the value and necessity of other approaches. As Chein notes, "Many a program has been roundly condemned as inadequate or useless, the critics thinking in terms of one dimension of prejudice and failing to apprehend the suitability of the program for other dimensions. Many a program has been hailed as a panacea, its proponents failing to realize that it may be effective for only one dimension. Prejudice is multidimensional and the war against it must be carried on multidimensionally."[30]

We shall describe and evaluate five kinds of approaches that emphasize the need for changing the persons who show prejudice and discrimination: exhortation, propaganda, contact, education, and personal therapy. These are not analytically precise and mutually exclusive categories, but one can draw useful distinctions among them. It is particularly difficult to distinguish clearly among the first four, because of differences in the use of terms. Many people contend that any discussion about values or in controversial areas is "propaganda," or, since they usually

disparage such activities, "only propaganda." Other writers believe that any symbolic activity to change people's attitudes is "educational." This kind of conceptual poverty blocks understanding. Symbolic communication is of many varieties and we would do well to have that fact reflected in our vocabularies.

Propaganda is the manipulation of symbols on a controversial topic when the controversial element is disguised, emotional appeals are used, some or all of the relevant facts are left out or distorted, and the motives of the propagandist and/or the sources of the propaganda are hidden. Education is the transmission of noncontroversial information (it may or may not be true, but it is generally regarded as true in the society involved); or it is the handling of controversial topics by recognizing them as controversial, using an objective approach, bringing all relevant facts to bear, and noting clearly the sources and motives of the educator. *No empirical act will be simply propaganda or education.* We are describing "pure types" that may never be found. Each event can be placed along the continuum on the basis of the criteria used.

Exhortation seems ordinarily to be at about the midpoint between propaganda and education. It often minimizes the controversial nature of the topics with which it deals and uses emotional appeals; but it frequently marshals a great many facts and makes no effort to disguise its motives or its sources. Efforts to encourage contact between minority- and majority-group members are also near the midpoint, although perhaps somewhat more educational than propagandistic, as we have defined those terms. They are partially propagandistic because they frequently distort the facts in the guise of studying facts, for the contacts are selected on the basis of their ability to change attitudes, not according to their typicality.

Exhortation

Exhortation is perhaps the most frequently used method in trying to reduce intergroup hostility. Appeal to men's better selves;

[30] Chein, *op. cit.*, p. 419.

revivify belief in their value creed; change their hearts and they will change their ways. Despite the frequency with which this approach is used, its value has not been tested in any way that permits one to speak with confidence about the degree of its effectiveness. Myrdal's famous work has brought a strong emphasis on the importance of the "American creed" as an ideological weakness of the prejudiced person. There is a moral struggle going on *within* most Americans, says Myrdal, that prevents race relations from being worse than they are and makes an ideological approach to their improvement feasible. "The American Negro problem is a problem in the heart of the American." Because he believes in democracy, in the rights of the common man, in the rightness of free enterprise (no barriers to freedom of economic activity), the American cannot believe, without some mental gymnastics, that prejudice and discrimination are justified. The strategy of exhortation tries to bring this contradiction to the forefront of our attention, to revitalize the creed.

Although exhortation sounds quite old-fashioned, it is essentially the strategy of many current activities, from demonstrations and rallies to "guerilla theater." In this last, the players attempt, by a surprise dramatic event, to call vivid attention to an issue and to persuade those who see (or experience) the "play" that a given moral view is right. The theater group may stage a severe interracial argument on a bus; then speak words of reconciliation.[31]

Participants in these contemporary forms of exhortation doubtless feel quite secular in most instances. In many ways, however, such events are modernized versions of sermons, not lacking in surrogates for hell-fire and brimstone, followed by descriptions of the true road to salvation. As with all sermons, the central questions remain: are the sinners in the pews; are they listening?

In the context of other changes, exhortation may help to reduce prejudice—particularly by increasing the enthusiasm of those who are already convinced. It may also inhibit the discriminations, although it may not affect the prejudices, of many fair-weather illiberals who do not want to violate the community standards openly. It is easy, however, to exaggerate the influence of exhortation. As MacIver pointed out, the charge of inconsistency doesn't reach most men; they can easily get along on compromises. "It is well to expose their rationalizations but nevertheless they have great capacity for finding new ones. They may have some uneasiness on this score, but often it is not potent enough to make them change their ways."[32] This uneasiness, in fact, may lead to stronger intolerance, for it may raise one's guilt feelings, which are then allayed by a blinder defensiveness, by new discriminations that actually furnish new justificatons for the prejudices.

The American creed, moreover, is not of equal importance among all individuals or in all times and places. And persons who deviate from the creed can justify their actions by declaring that they are conforming with the spirit of the creed, not with the "sterile letter." Beyond that, one must recognize a contrary creed—a moral code that justifies prejudice and discrimination.

Effective strategy seems to indicate that exhortation can play only a modest role in the total efforts to reduce prejudice and discrimination. The moral premises on which it rests are not universally shared and are alloyed with countervalues; most of us are skilled at compartmentalizing our professions of belief and our other actions, overlooking any contradictions; and those who are most likely to show hostility to minority-group members are probably those who are least often reached by exhortation.

Propaganda

The "propaganda menace" and the "hidden persuader" have received so much attention

---

[31] For a brief account of some "guerrilla theater" events, see *Honolulu Advertiser*, Oct. 13, 1968, p. 32. For a critical appraisal of the theatrical approach to social change, see Robert Brustein, *Revolution As Theatre: Notes on the New Radical Style*, Liveright, 1971.

[32] R. M. MacIver, *The More Perfect Union*, Macmillan, 1948, pp. 88–89.

in recent years that many people have come to regard them as almost all-powerful. The success of the mass campaigns of persuasion by modern nations and the skill with which commercial propaganda (advertising) has converted cigarettes and chewing gum into necessities make us believe that a tremendously powerful instrument for controlling human behavior has been created. Why not turn this instrument to the purpose of reducing intergroup hostility?

Before examining attempts to use propaganda to control intergroup behavior, it may be wise to state briefly the contemporary answer to the question, How effective is propaganda? As we have learned more and more about the problem, we have seen that there is no *general* answer. The question must be more complicated: How effective is a specific propaganda campaign with a stated group of people in a particular situation? Gradually it has become apparent that far more limits are imposed on the power of propaganda than was generally believed to be true a few years ago.

Modern societies, to be sure, are more susceptible to propaganda than stable "sacred" societies. The entrance of more and more questions into the area of controversy, because of the breakup of traditional answers, concomitant personal insecurities that make many people eager for some simple answer to life's problems, the spread of mass media of communication, capable of bringing simultaneous stimuli to millions of people, and even the rise of the sciences of man—these and other factors have made propaganda more likely and more powerful than before.

Propaganda is limited, however, even under such favorable conditions. It is limited by knowledge of the facts on the part of propagandees; it is limited by a counterpropaganda; and above all, it is limited by the already existing values, needs, and hopes of the persons to whom it attempts to appeal. To put this point oppositely: Propaganda is most effective when it is dealing with a poorly informed public, when it has a monopoly in the field of communication (censorship), and when it either is working in an area in which the values and needs of the public are diffuse and poorly structured or ties its appeals closely to well-structured needs and values.

Propaganda may have wholly unexpected and unintended effects, for ultimately it is interpreted by specific individuals whose own values and needs are brought to bear. Unintended or "boomerang" effects of propaganda are particularly likely to occur when one tries to influence a heterogeneous group. A morale program, broadcast shortly after Pearl Harbor, had two dominant themes: the power and potentialities of the United Nations, to combat defeatism, and the strength of the enemy, to combat complacency. But what if the complacent heard only theme number one, and the defeatist heard only theme number two, the opposite arguments being disregarded? "To judge from interview materials, this is evidently what happened." The propaganda had the opposite effect from what was intended.[33]

Propaganda to Reduce Intergroup Hostility. On the basis of this brief discussion of some contemporary concepts employed by students of propaganda, we can perhaps evaluate more accurately the usefulness of propaganda as a strategy in the reduction of prejudice and discrimination. Literally millions of leaflets, pamphlets, cartoons, comic books, articles, and movies have been issued in the struggle against intergroup hostility. How effective are they? Flowerman suggests that this question can be answered only when we have the following information: To what degree do pro-tolerance groups control the media of communication? What is the level of saturation—the proportion of a population that is reached by the appeals? What is the attention level? (Mass media, with their aim of something for everybody, have developed a "deafness," a casualness toward the flow of stimuli. The intensity of attention varies with the specificity of the audience, the cruciality of the situation, and other factors.) How do the propagandees reinterpret the message?

[33] Robert K. Merton, *Social Theory and Social Structure*, Free Press, rev. ed., 1957, pp. 273–274, 517–522.

Does the propaganda conform to group standards? (If it does not, it can have little effect. And those standards may include prejudice.) What is the sponsorship? Is it held in high esteem?[34]

The evidence seems to suggest that on many of these counts antiprejudice propaganda has not been very effective. For the most part it reaches those who already agree with it. Radio programs of "intercultural education" that describe the culture and history of the Italians, Yugoslavians, and Greeks are listened to, respectively, by Italians, Yugoslavians, and Greeks. Each group may be made to feel better, more secure, more important, but they are scarcely informed about the others.

In some instances individuals have been confronted with antiprejudice propaganda involuntarily. Some fight it, openly or covertly; a few may accept it; but many evade it by managing to misunderstand its message. A number of studies have been made of the effects of a "Mr. Biggott" series of cartoons, designed to show an absurd man exhibiting ridiculous prejudices. "In each of them, Mr. Biggott, the central character, is shown as a cantankerous and unattractive man of middle age and moderate income. In each of them he displays the antiminority attitudes from which he earns his name."[35] Three cartoons are used in the study by Kendall and Wolf. One shows Mr. Biggott glowering at an "honor roll" billboard on which the community war heroes are listed. He says, "Berkowitz, Fabrizio, Ginsberg, Kelly—disgraceful!" In another cartoon, Mr. Biggott, lying sick in bed, says to a somewhat startled doctor, "In case I should need a transfusion, doctor, I want to make certain I don't get anything but blue, sixth-generation American blood!" In an "Indian" cartoon Mr. Biggott says to a humble American Indian, "I'm sorry, Mr. Eaglefeather, but our company's policy is to employ 100 percent Americans only."

The assumption behind the cartoons was that the picturing of an absurd man exhibiting absurd ideas would lead to reject his own prejudices. Cooper and Jahoda found, however, that prejudiced persons created many mechanisms of evasion. Understanding may be "derailed" by avoiding identification with Mr. Biggott (despite the sharing of prejudice). Mr. X, on seeing the "blood transfusion" cartoon, looked upon Mr. Biggott as an inferior *parvenu:* "I'm eighth generation myself. . . . He may not be the best blood either." Then Mr. X leads off into other subjects. Having understood the cartoon at first ("He don't want anything but sixth-generation American blood! Ha! That's pretty good."), he then felt it necessary to disidentify.[36]

Because of the difficulties of reaching the audience for whom the propaganda would be most useful and because of the ease with which its points can be evaded, we cannot rely heavily on propaganda as a strategy. To be sure, a cartoon series is a brief stimulus. We do not know what the effects of an intensive, long-run propaganda campaign would be. A movie is a stronger stimulus, on which we have some information. There have been many studies to test the effects of movies on attitudes; and, partly on the basis of the results obtained, several movies (some propagandistically and others educationally inclined) have aimed at the reduction of prejudice. Our knowledge of the total long-run effects of movies, however, is still far from adequate because of several methodological weaknesses. Sampling problems have not been given much attention (school populations are so readily available to the researcher); the distortions in evidence produced by the "before-after" type of experiment (the kind that has been most often used) have not been explored adequately;

[34] See S. H. Flowerman, "Mass Propaganda in the War Against Bigotry," *JASP*, Oct., 1947, pp. 429–433.

[35] Patricia Kendall and Katherine Wolf, in Paul Lazarsfeld and Frank Stanton (eds.), *Communications Research, 1948–49*, Harper & Row, 1949, p. 158.

[36] See Eunice Cooper and Marie Jahoda, "The Evasion of Propaganda: How Prejudiced People Respond to Anti-Prejudice Propaganda," *JP* Jan., 1947, p. 17. Many observers believe that the currently popular TV show "All in the Family" is subject to the same multiple interpretations. A liberal viewer regards it as an exposé of foolish prejudices; but others may identify with Archie Bunker and in so doing are given an opportunity to "rehearse" a variety of prejudices.

and the relation between pencil-and-paper responses and other kinds of behavior usually has not been studied.

Despite these weaknesses it seems fair to say that many movies do have a measurable effect on attitudes as recorded in verbal tests. L. L. Thurstone and his associates made the first extensive studies in this field. For example, *The Birth of a Nation,* which pictured Negroes in a very unfavorable light, was shown to 434 students, grades 6 to 12, in a small Illinois town containing no Negroes. The students were tested for their attitudes toward Negroes both before and after seeing the film. In the latter test they were, on the average, 1.48 scale points (on an eleven-point scale) more unfavorable to the Negro. After five months they were retested, and it was found that 62 percent of the change that had been attributed to the film remained.[37] We do not know if the nonverbal behavior of the children was affected, whether the new attitudes actually reshaped later experiences, whether giving them a test before the picture "sensitized" them to prejudice so that the movie was a different experience from what it would have been had they not been pretested. We do not know if the test five months after the movie was a stimulus that renewed memory associations with the movie and the earlier test—and so was inevitably highly correlated with that test. Tentatively, however, we may say that movies do seem to influence prejudices.

Can motion pictures also reduce prejudice? 329 students at a southern state university were shown *Gentleman's Agreement,* a successful Hollywood picture that took a strong stand against anti-Semitism. They had first recorded their attitudes on a ten-item anti-Semitism and ten-item anti-Negro scale. After seeing the film they were again asked to record their attitudes and were compared with 116 students who had not seen the film. The results were as follows:

	Saw the film	*Did not see the film*
Lower anti-Semitism score	228 (69.3%)	49 (42.2%)
No change or higher anti-Semitism score	101 (30.7%)	67 (57.8%)

This difference is significant at the .001 level. Interestingly, anti-Negro scores also fell among those who saw the film (p. = .05). Largest absolute gains were made by those whose anti-Semitism scores were highest at the beginning (they had more room in which to change); but those whose original scores were low showed the largest change when it is calculated as a percentage of possible change. Those persons low in status concern also had significantly greater reductions in their scores.[38]

Within the limits set by the present evidence it seems unwise to say either that antiprejudice propaganda is powerless or that it can, by itself, effect extensive changes. Flowerman points out these minimum requirements if it is to have any influence: The propaganda must be received under favorable conditions, so that it will be looked at or heard; it must attract and hold the attention of the propagandee; it must be enjoyed, not bring pain; it must be understood, not evaded by misunderstanding.[39] None of these is easy to accomplish. Propaganda usually is seen only by the already converted; if prejudiced persons happen to see it, they usually turn away; if they don't turn away, they often find it painful (because of guilt feelings or a sense of hostility); and if they don't find it painful, they frequently misunderstand its point. It is with the mildly

---

[37] See Ruth C. Peterson and L. L. Thurstone, *Motion Pictures and the Social Attitudes of Children,* Macmillan, 1933, pp. 35–38. Merton has made a pointed criticism of the weaknesses of this kind of measurement in "Fact and Factitiousness in Ethnic Opinionnaires," *ASR,* Feb., 1940, pp. 13–28.

[38] Russell Middleton, "Ethnic Prejudice and Susceptibility to Persuasion," *ASR,* Oct., 1960, pp. 679–686; see also Louis Raths and Frank Trager, "Public Opinion and Crossfire," *Journal of Educational Sociology,* Feb., 1948, pp. 345–368; and Alice Riddleberger and Annabelle Motz, "Prejudice and Perception," *AJS,* Mar. 1957, pp. 498–503.

[39] Flowerman, *op. cit.,* pp. 434–435.

prejudiced and the neutral, particularly with children, that these disadvantages are at a minimum.

Williams summarizes a number of principles that help one to understand the effectiveness of antiprejudice propaganda:

In intergroup relations, as in many others, word-of-mouth propaganda, especially that which appears spontaneous and informal, is more effective than visual or formal propaganda in influencing attitudes and behavior. . . .

In intergroup relations, as in many others, propaganda which makes an "emotional" (value-oriented) appeal is likely to be more effective than that which is restricted to factual appeal.

But this plausible assertion may be countered with the view that such appeals arouse relatively uncontrolled emotions which are not likely to lead to tolerant or humane behavior. It certainly appears that there are sufficient dangers in strongly emotional propaganda to warrant careful testing with different types of audiences. . . .

In intergroup relations, as in many others, the "propaganda of the deed" is especially likely to have effects upon attitudes and behavior. . . .

Propaganda which appeals to minority rights on the basis of the group's achievements tends beyond a certain point to arouse insecurity-hostility in the dominant group by stressing group differences and competitive success.

This hypothesis implies that appeals which suggest a status-threat to prejudiced groups are to be avoided. . . .

It is dangerous technique to employ mass propaganda emphasizing "rising tides of prejudice" as a means intended to mobilize defenders of minority rights and good intergroup relations. Such propaganda is likely to have a boomerang effect upon slightly prejudiced or wavering elements: it creates the presumption of group support for hostile actions.[40]

How Should Prejudiced Propaganda Be Handled? Wise strategy needs to understand not only the possible uses of propaganda but also the techniques that are most effective in counteracting prejudiced propaganda. In recent years there has been a vigorous debate, and sharp differences in action, between those who believed that "hatemongers" should be exposed, ridiculed, and made to stand in the glare of public attention and

those who contended that they should be disregarded and offset by positive action. Experience with the problem of counteracting rumors during World War II added strength to the arguments of those who held that hate propaganda should often be ignored, so far as a direct response is concerned. By "ignored" we do not mean "overlooked." One must pay careful attention to destructive rumors or propaganda against minorities; but they should usually be opposed indirectly, by positive action, not directly, by exposing them and pointing out their errors. If one tries to prove a rumor wrong by repeating it and then describing the truth, many of his listeners may hear only the rumor, if that is all they want to hear. Thus one accomplishes the opposite of what he intends. If one ignores the rumor but supplies truthful information, those who have not heard the rumor may to some degree be "vaccinated" against it. When the British movie production of *Oliver Twist* was brought to the United States, several groups opposed its release because *one* of the "villains" of the story is a Jew. They thought seeing the movie might increase anti-Semitism. Their opposition made it more likely that the movie would be widely attended and that those with mild or latent anti-Semitism would be sensitized to the unfavorable Jewish character. Such people would not, however, have read or understood the arguments of those who opposed the characterization. Violent anti-Semites, moreover, were given the rare opportunity of parading as defenders of civil liberties—upholding free speech and opposing censorship.

There is a danger that proponents of the "silent" treatment of hate propaganda will drift into a position of no treatment. If one ignores not only the hatemonger but the problem he represents, the silent strategy will fail completely.

Those who oppose giving publicity to the hatemonger and those who support it both give illustrations to demonstrate the effectiveness of their approach. The need is to see that there are very different ways of bringing public attention to an issue. Many professional haters are sensationalists who thrive best on exposure if it brings them into a conflict situation where they can pose as martyrs and heroes to their followers and potential followers. Publicity for them is clearly unwise antiprejudice strategy. Negative opposition that emphasizes a conflict situation and arouses emotions probably strengthens their appeal. Exposure of the hatemonger, however, need not be of this awkward variety. A competing program that emphasizes positive goals deprives him of many of his arguments. McWilliams describes a Los Angeles rally called in opposition to a demonstration led by Gerald L. K. Smith, well-known anti-Semite and racist. Smith's rally drew a small crowd and little attention, because the competing meeting did not interfere with him directly and did not make him the center of attention. It publicized the problem but not the man; it did not confuse the issue by opposing his right to speak.[41] In this question of strategy, as in all others, a flexible policy is necessary. These rules may help to guide one's decisions:

1. Do not overlook the importance of hate propaganda.
2. Where possible, deal with it indirectly, by furnishing true information, by developing people immune to prejudice, not by direct attack.
3. Do not exaggerate the extent of the rabble-rouser's following or the strength of his influence.
4. Stress the injury his actions bring to the whole society, not to some "poor, oppressed minority."

Contact

In recent years, in developing strategies for changing prejudiced persons, no factor has received more attention than the effects of contact between members of different groups. It is often said, "If there were only more contact, if people only knew each other better, there would be less prejudice." Yet it is also known that prejudice frequently seems most intense in areas where there is most

contact. How effective is contact with members of a minority group in changing attitudes and behavior toward that group? This question requires careful study, for there are many factors that affect the results. It is related to broader questions of international relations, where it is also frequently assumed that contact *per se* will improve understanding.

In interviews with 19 Indian and other Asian students in the United States, Lambert and Bressler discovered that contact—even when it was courteous and helpful—did not automatically create favorable attitudes. The effects depended not so much on the personalities of the individuals involved as on the total structure of the situation, especially the status conceptions of the two countries. Whenever the Indian students encountered certain "sensitive areas" that involved implications of low status for their country— even if the Americans involved were disagreeing with the implications—they tended to respond negatively. Ideas that Indians are basically inferior, that India is an undesirable place to live, that India's social structure is undemocratic, inhumane, unenlightened, and the like, created negative responses when they were discussed.[42]

Contact does not necessarily lead to improved understanding. The task is to discover the conditions under which attitude change does take place. Converging evidence from the sociology of knowledge and the psychology of perception shows that experience is situational; what we see or hear, what we believe, how we think are all dependent upon the total situation in which these actions occur and upon our total mental context. We never see an isolated unit of human behavior; we see behavior in a larger situation through the perspectives we have acquired. Most of us can look a "fact" squarely in the face and, if we already have a frame of reference that involves it, turn it completely around. In a study of the rumor process, Allport and Postman described to various per-

[41] Carey McWilliams, *A Mask for Privilege: Anti-Semitism in America*, Little, Brown, 1948, p. 258.

[42] Richard D. Lambert and Marvin Bressler, "The Sensitive-Area Complex: A Contribution to the Theory of Guided Culture Contact," *AJS*, May, 1955, p. 584.

sons a picture containing a Negro and a white man with a razor in his hand. After the description, each person was asked to tell all he could about the picture to a third person, the third to a fourth, and the fourth to a fifth. In over half of the experiments, the razor was reported to be in the Negro's hand; and in several the Negro was threatening the white man with it.[43]

The ambiguity of many aspects of human behavior makes it possible to perceive such behavior in a way that harmonizes with an already established belief. When a person greets you warmly, it is possible that he is a true friend, but it is also possible that he is busily engaged in opposing you behind your back and wants to prevent you from suspecting it. If you already "know" which is true, you will interpret his behavior in that light.

A strong prejudice can have an almost paralyzing effect on observation and rational judgment. Whatever the behavior involved, it can be "explained" by the prejudice. Even opposite kinds of behavior are used as "proof" of a supposed trait, as is well illustrated in the statement of General J. L. DeWitt concerning the evacuation of the Japanese from the West Coast in 1942:

In the war in which we are now engaged racial affinities are not severed by migration. The Japanese race is an enemy race and while many second and third generation Japanese born on United States soil, possessed of United States citizenship, have become "Americanized," the racial strains are undiluted. . . . That Japan is allied with Germany and Italy in this struggle is no ground for assuming that any Japanese, barred from assimilation by convention as he is, though born and raised in the United States, will not turn against this nation when the final test of loyalty comes. It, therefore, follows that along the vital Pacific Coast over 112,000 potential enemies of Japanese extraction are at large today. There are indications that these are organized and ready for concerted action at a favorable opportunity. The very fact that no sabotage has taken place to date is a disturbing and confirming indication that such action will be taken.[44]

The conclusion, the attitude, is found in the first part of this statement. The last sentence shows how *any* fact, even one that to the naïve observer must seem to be an exact refutation of the conclusion, can be made to seem to support it. Contact with the members of a minority group can scarcely weaken a prejudice that is so impervious to experience. Behavior that does not harmonize with the prejudice may not be seen at all; our perceptions are made selective and partial by the prejudice itself, which thus becomes self-confirmatory. Or if the behavior is seen, it is treated as an "exception": "Some of my best friends are Jews," but—they're not typical. Marrow and French showed that factory experience with "old" (over 30!) women workers who showed high production records and low rates of absenteeism did not change the stereotypes of management and foreladies that the "old" workers were liabilities.[45] Human beings have an enormous ability to resist the meaning of facts that contradict their already established beliefs.

Contact with the members of a minority group may, of course, be of an unpleasant variety. This is sometimes held to be a cause of prejudice—the attitude is simply a generalization from a few unfortunate experiences. Unpleasant experience with individual members of a minority group, however, can scarcely be the cause of prejudice, because that experience would not be generalized to the whole minority group unless the prejudice were already there. Moreover, we cannot be certain that persons who report more unpleasant memories of contact with members of minority groups have actually had more such contacts. Memory is selec-

[43] See Theodore M. Newcomb, Eleanor Maccoby, and E. L. Hartley (eds.), *Readings in Social Psychology*, Holt, Rinehart & Winston, 3rd ed., 1958, pp. 54–65.

[44] From United States Army Western Defense Command and Fourth Army, *Japanese in the United States, Final Report: Japanese Evacuation from the West Coast*, Government Printing Office, 1943, pp. 33–34.

[45] See A. J. Marrow and J. R. P. French, "Changing a Stereotype in Industry," *JSI*, Dec., 1945, pp. 33–37.

tive; they may remember (or invent) such contacts *because* they already have a stronger than average prejudice.

Thus we find that prejudice is sometimes explained as a result of the *lack* of contact with members of a minority group and sometimes explained as the result of the *presence* of such contact. Both theories explain only surface relationships.

Such observations do not mean, however, that one's experiences with individual members of a minority group have no effect on his attitudes toward that group. Prejudice does not entirely precede and coerce the interpretation of experience. Unpleasant contacts probably increase the strength of prejudice. Oppositely, *certain kinds of contact* are effective in reducing the strength of a tradition of prejudice. We are learning to examine contact against a background of knowledge of the total personality of the individuals involved, the leadership, the power structure, the place of one attitude in a total value system.[46]

Allport has prepared a valuable outline of the variables that we must have in mind in any analysis of the effects of contact between members of different groups.

Quantitative aspects of contact:
  a. Frequency
  b. Duration
  c. Number of persons involved
  d. Variety

Status aspects of contact:
  a. Minority member has inferior status.
  b. Minority member has equal status.
  c. Minority member has superior status.
  d. Not only may the individuals encountered vary thus in status; but the group as a whole may have relatively high status (e.g., Jews) or relatively low status (e.g., Negroes).

Role aspects of contact:
  a. Is the relationship one of competitive or cooperative activity?
  b. Is there a superordinate or subordinate role relation involved; e.g., master-servant, employer-employee, teacher-pupil?

Social atmosphere surrounding the contact:
  a. Is segregation prevalent, or is egalitarianism expected?
  b. Is the contact voluntary or involuntary?
  c. Is the contact "real" or "artificial"?
  d. Is the contact perceived in terms of intergroup relations or not perceived as such?
  e. Is the contact regarded as "typical" or as "exceptional"?
  f. Is the contact regarded as important and intimate, or as trivial and transient?

Personality of the individual experiencing the contact:
  a. Is his initial prejudice level high, low, medium?
  b. Is his prejudice of a surface, conforming type, or is it deeply rooted in his character structure?
  c. Has he basic security in his own life, or is he fearful and suspicious?
  d. What is his previous experience with the group in question, and what is the strength of his present stereotypes?
  e. What are his age and general education level?
  f. Many other personality factors may influence the effect of contact.

Areas of contact:
  a. Casual
  b. Residential
  c. Occupational
  d. Recreational
  e. Religious
  f. Civil and fraternal
  g. Political
  h. Goodwill intergroup activities

Even this list of variables that enter into the problem of contact is not exhaustive. It does, however, indicate the complexity of the problem we face.[47] Because of the large number of variables affecting the influence of contact on interracial attitudes and behavior, research conclusions are quite tentative. Yet certain principles are substantially supported. After one of the most intensive reviews of the effects of contact, Williams concludes that ". . . *in all the surveys in all communities and for all groups, majority*

[46] See Ronald Lippitt and Marian Radke, "New Trends in the Investigation of Prejudice," *Annals*, Mar., 1946, pp. 167–176.

[47] Gordon Allport, *The Nature of Prejudice*, Addison-Wesley, 1954, pp. 262–263. For another useful general statement, see Yehuda Amir, "Contact Hypothesis in Ethnic Relations," *Psychological Bulletin*, May, 1969, pp. 319–342.

White Contact with Blacks

	Great deal	Some contact	Almost none	Not sure
		(percentage)		
Coworkers on the job	10	22	67	1
Someone who works for you	5	10	83	2
A friend you see socially	3	17	79	1
Supervises you at work	2	4	92	2
Neighbor	1	9	88	2
Shop where you shop	7	36	56	1

Source: *The Plain Dealer*, July 6, 1970, p. 13-A. Reprinted by permission of the Louis Harris Political Data Center, University of North Carolina.

and minorities, the greater the frequency of interaction, the lower the prevalence of ethnic prejudice. (Note that the same correlation can be stated: the less the frequency of ethnic prejudice, the more frequent is the interaction.)"[48] Williams does not stop with this statement of a simple correlation. By the introduction of several test variables, he is able to strengthen a causal inference. "*If* contacts can be established"—an interesting and important qualification—even quite marked prejudices cannot nullify the prejudice-reducing influence of interaction.

Brief contacts, however, may not have a measurable impact. Trubowitz divided a group of grade school children into four categories, to participate in interracial contact through a three-day period. The categories were: joint trips and joint discussions; joint trips and separate discussions; separate trips and joint discussions; and separate trips and separate discussions. He hypothesized that planned interracial activity, particularly when heightened by discussion and trips, would produce positive attitude changes. He found, however, that little change occurred.[49]

Nor is pleasurable association by itself adequate to reduce prejudice. What Sherif calls "hedonistic associationism"—people like what is associated with their pleasures —overlooks the human skill in taking the pleasure and maintaining old attitudes. Sherif emphasized the impact of "superordinate goals." When individuals or groups are brought together within a situation that requires their active cooperation to achieve a mutually desired goal, stereotypy and prejudice fade.[50]

Selltiz and Cook, in their study of foreign students in the United States, emphasized the importance of opportunities for intergroup contact, the "acquaintance potential" of a situation. Those in smaller colleges, as compared with matched counterparts in intermediate and larger schools, had more personal contacts with Americans, contacts that were more than formal or official.[51] Availability of contacts is not simply a matter of propinquity. Interracial contact in the United States continues to be infrequent, despite the spread of the black population throughout the country. In his careful study of one American community, Molotch found that interracial contacts were infrequent in almost every activity, even in shopping, although there were some exceptions. It has often been remarked that "eleven o'clock Sunday morning is the most

[48] Robin M. Williams, Jr., *Strangers Next Door*, Prentice-Hall, 1964, pp. 167–168. See Chap. 7 of this work for a full discussion of contact.

[49] Julius Trubowitz, *Changing the Racial Attitudes of Children: The Effects of an Activity Group Program in New York City Schools*, Praeger, 1969.

[50] Muzafer Sherif, *In Common Predicament: Social Psychology of Intergroup Conflict and Cooperation*, Houghton Mifflin, 1966.

[51] Claire Selltiz and S. W. Cook, "Factors Influencing Attitudes of Foreign Students Toward Their Host Countries," *JSI*, First Quarter, 1962, pp. 7–23.

Contact and Fear

	High contact	Medium contact	Little contact
		(percentage)	
Feel uneasy about violence	34	43	55
Don't feel uneasy	66	56	44
Not sure	—	1	1

Source: The Plain Dealer, July 6, 1970, p. 13-A. Reprinted by permission of the Louis Harris Political Data Center, University of North Carolina.

segregated time of the week," but he found that eleven o'clock Saturday evening was even more segregated. In those few situations where interracial activity was quite common, as for example a city commission for civic activities, there were status contrasts and, within the commission, contrasts in power (for the blacks were chosen as "representatives," not because of their personal expertise or influence). Such contacts are as likely to confirm stereotypes as they are to create greater sensitivity to members of another race.[52]

The extent of black-white contact in the United States was recently recorded in a Harris survey. A representative cross-section of white people were asked: "Would you say you have a great deal of contact with blacks, some contact, or almost no contact with blacks in the following areas?" The Harris survey cross tabulated these results by the expressed fear of violence. Those with least contact are more worried about racial trouble. (See two preceding tables.)

The relationship between high contact and less fear of violence does not, of course, show the causal connections. It is perhaps significant, however, that those under 30 were more likely to say they were friendly with Blacks and less likely to express fears of racial violence. More intensive community studies, moreover, allow us to speak somewhat more confidently of a causal connection. Warren has shown that suburban Whites are not only individually isolated from Negroes, a situation which encourages

race tension, but also share a community atmosphere that reenforces that isolation and tends to furnish a community response to the conflict situation. Primary lack of contact generates a secondary, community sustained lack of contact.[53] In another community study, Jeffries and Ransford applied controls for the effects of proximity to the Watts riot and prejudice. They found that contact with Negroes prior to the riot was an important determiner of white attitudes toward the disorder, to some degree independent of the control variables. "Those lacking contact are more fearful of Negroes, cite more outside agitator explanations, evidence more feelings of increased social distance, and voice more punitive responses than those having contact."[54]

Effects of Equal-Status Contact. The influence that has been most carefully explored in recent research is the degree of status equality or status difference among the participants in intergroup relations. In exploring this issue we must remember how resistant stereotypes are to evidence. Moreover, equal-status contacts are perhaps more likely to involve competition. In his study of an interracial adolescent group, Irwin Katz found that, despite its liberal and friendly atmosphere, there was the danger that competition for leadership and the other inevitable group tensions—having nothing to

[52] Harvey Molotch, "Racial Integration in a Transition Community," *ASR,* Dec., 1969, pp. 878–893.

[53] Donald I. Warren, "Suburban Isolation and Race Tension: The Detroit Case," *SP,* Winter, 1970, pp. 324–339.

[54] Vincent Jeffries and H. Edward Ransford, "Interracial Social Contact and Middle-Class White Reactions to the Watts Riot," *SP,* Winter, 1969, p. 312.

do with race—would be seen as racial in origin and meaning.[55] This is especially likely when the surrounding environment in which the equal-status contact occurs does not support the implications of equality.

Nevertheless, there is good evidence that what might be called "stereotype-breaking contacts" reduce prejudice. MacKenzie found that among university students, when several variables that might influence the results were controlled, knowing professional Negroes and having a variety of contacts with Negroes produced statistically significantly more favorable attitudes.[56] In a study that is in better control of the time dimension, Mann assigned 78 graduate students at Teachers College, New York City, to six-person discussion groups. The groups, containing men and women, black and white, southerners and northerners, held four meetings a week for three weeks. At the beginning and at the end they were given sociometric tests and part of the Berkeley E-Scale for measuring prejudice. Contact in the group significantly reduced both the E scores and the use of race as a friendship criterion.[57]

A somewhat unusual kind of stereotype-breaking contact was experienced by many soldiers of the U.S. Army in Europe during the winter and spring of 1945. In March and April, 1945, several Negro rifle platoons were attached to white companies. Two months later, the Information and Education Division of the Army Service Forces conducted a survey to discover the response of white officers and men to this change. Five trained interviewers asked all available white company grade officers and a representative sample of platoon sergeants in 24 companies that contained Negro platoons, "Has your feeling changed since having served in the same unit with colored soldiers?" The responses were as follows:

	White Officers (Percent)	White Noncoms (Percent)
No, my feeling is the same	16	21
Yes, have become more favorable	77	77
No answer	7	2

Eighty-four percent of the white officers and 81 percent of the white noncoms answered "Very well" (the most favorable answer on a four-point scale) to the question, "How well did the colored soldiers in this company perform in combat?"[58]

Alongside these findings, however, it should be noted that in the last several years, contact in the American armed forces has been associated with extensive interracial conflict, indicating again the complexity of the issue with which we are dealing. Lacking formal study of the contemporary situation, we can only note the following variables as among those involved: (1) Conflict is brought quickly to public attention, friendly contact is not; hence we do not know how sharply the present situation contrasts with the earlier one. (2) The Black Power separatist mood affects current contacts. (3) There is a high ratio of black noncommissioned officers now, thus the contact is not always equal status (and there are elements of status inconsistency for members of both races). (4) The current war situation (1971) creates more general frustration than did World War II, because of motivational factors. (5) The ratio of black to white is much higher than it was in the period studied.

In many "contact" studies, there are methodological problems of self-selection and limitation to verbal behavior. Deutsch and Collins report the interesting results of

[55] Irwin Katz, *Conflict and Harmony in an Adolescent Interracial Group*, New York Univ. Press, 1955.

[56] Barbara K. MacKenzie, "The Importance of Contact in Determining Attitudes Toward Negroes," *JASP*, Oct., 1948, pp. 417–441.

[57] John Mann, "The Effects of Inter-Racial Contact on Sociometric Choices and Perceptions," *JSP*, Aug., 1959, pp. 143–152.

[58] Information and Education Division, U.S. War Department, "Opinions About Negro Infantry Platoons in White Companies of Seven Divisions," reprinted in Newcomb and Hartley (eds.), *op. cit.*, pp. 542–546.

Nature of Housewives' Relations with Negro People in Housing Projects

	Integrated		Segregated	
	Koaltown (%)	Sacktown (%)	Bakerville (%)	Frankville (%)
Friendly relations	60	69	6	4
Accommodative relations	24	14	5	1
Mixed relations	7	11	2	3
No relations	5	0	87	88
Bad relations	4	6	0	4
Total cases	102	90	100	101

Source: Morton Deutsch and Mary E. Collins, *Interracial Housing,* University of Minnesota Press, 1951, p. 79.

different patterns of interracial housing in which these problems are minimal. In two housing projects Negro and white families were assigned to apartment buildings regardless of race (the integrated pattern); in two other projects different buildings or different parts of the project were used for Negroes and Whites (the segregated biracial pattern). Interviews with the housewives in these situations revealed that the integrated pattern reduced prejudice much more sharply. (See above table.)

In the integrated projects only one-third as many women spontaneously expressed prejudice in the interviews as in the segregated projects (13 percent and 10 percent compared with 35 percent and 31 percent). About two housewives want to be friendly for one who wants to avoid contact with Negroes in the integrated arrangement; but in the segregated situation there are ten who want to avoid contact for one who wishes to be friendly. It is particularly interesting to know that 67 percent and 71 percent of the women in the integrated projects have positive attitudes toward the interracial aspects of their communities, many having come to like it more; but in the segregated projects most of the women liked the interracial aspects less than they did before they moved into the community.[59]

The effects of such types of contact would

[59] Morton Deutsch and Mary E. Collins, *Interracial Housing,* Univ. of Minnesota Press, 1951, chap. 11.

not be the same, of course, on persons whose prejudices were so strong that they would not join an interracial community; but among families who did accept housing on a biracial basis persons assigned (without regard to their original attitudes, for the type of arrangement was an administrative decision, not an individual choice) to integrated patterns discovered that their prejudices were very inadequate modes of adjustment. Those in the segregated projects had no such opportunity to revise their attitudes.

In a follow-up study of the effects of interracial housing, Wilner, Walkley, and Cook derived evidence that supports many of the findings of Deutsch and Collins, but also introduces some qualifications. In interracial neighborhoods, "the assumption that segregation is right and inevitable is challenged" by the authority of the community project; and the white resident is confronted with the problem of reconciling the evidence concerning the behavior of actual minority-group members with his stereotypes. Thus contact weakens the supports of prejudice. There are, however, a number of complicating factors:

the relation between *proximity and contact,* and the relation of each to attitude change; the influence of initial attitude on the outcome of the contact experience; the influence of social pressures—or social climate regarding intergroup association—on the outcome of the contact experience, and the ways in which the social climate is established and manifested; the effect that different proportions of minority group members has on the experience associated with proximity or contact; and the diminsions of attitude which undergo change.[60]

The four housing projects studied by Wilner, Walkley, and Cook had a small proportion of Negro residents; none had more than 10 percent. In all four projects, the extent of contact with Negroes was closely tied to proximity. The contacts that occurred were not simply unplanned conversation, but neighborly activities of various kinds—borrowing and lending, helping during sickness, visiting. The white women who lived near Negroes perceived, more often than those living farther away, that the opinions of other white women in the project were favorable to interracial contact. They also held Negroes in higher esteem and were more likely to believe that the races were equal in such things as cleanliness, manners, intelligence, and ambition. Although the attitudes toward Negroes that the white women had when they entered the project affected their responses, they were less important than proximity in the project.

Whether we consider the initially more favorable or initially less favorable respondents, those who live near Negroes in a project are more likely than those living farther away to report neighborly contact, to anticipate that white friends in the project will approve of such contact, to have high esteem for the Negroes in the project, to approve of the biracial aspect of the project, and to have a favorable attitude toward Negroes in general.[61]

Without discussing various refinements in the two studies of interracial housing, we show their major findings in the following table.

One uncontrolled aspect of these, and most studies of contact is the lack of any measures of selectivity of Negro participants. Are they more "contact prone"? Would the same results occur if a different pattern of selectivity prevailed? A study undertaken in Los Angeles may throw some light on these questions (although there are risks

Percentage Sharing at Least One Kind of Neighborly Activity

	%
Two integrated projects of the Deutsch and Collins study (192)	54
Integrated projects of the Wilner, Walkley, and Cook study (91)	50
Two segregated projects of the Deutsch and Collins study (201)	3
Segregated areas of the Wilner, Walkley, and Cook study (234)	5

Source: D. M. Wilner, R. P. Walkley, and S. W. Cook, *Human Relations in International Housing*, University of Minnesota Press, p. 143.

in making inferences through time and space back to the housing studies we have examined). Bonnie Bullough wondered why there had been a comparatively weak response to the growing opportunities for integrated housing among Negroes. Comparing two samples of Negroes in integrated neighborhoods (n = 224) with one in a solidly Negro area (n = 106), she found that the latter were significantly higher in feelings of powerlessness and anomia.[62] Without panel data, we cannot tell whether these feelings reflect or cause the housing patterns. From our interest here, however, they indicate the need to take account of Negro as well as white attitudes in studies of the effects of contact.

Studies of the effects of contact among children are of great theoretical and strategic importance. It is often possible more nearly to approximate experimental conditions in working with children than with adults and the effects of intergroup contact on children compete with fewer other stimuli. In a valuable study of intergroup relations in a boys' camp, Muzafer Sherif and his associates reveal the tension-building and stereotype-creating processes; and then

[60] D. M. Wilner, R. P. Walkley, and S. W. Cook, *Human Relations in Interracial Housing*, Univ. of Minnesota Press, 1955, p. 6.

[61] *Ibid.*, p. 95.

[62] Bonnie Bullough, *Social-Psychological Barriers to Housing Desegregation*, Univ. of Cal., Housing, Real Estate, and Urban Land Studies Program and the Center for Real Estate and Urban Economics, Special Report No. 2, 1969.

indicate how harmony may be established or reestablished.[63] Although this research has no direct interest in majority-minority relations, it skillfully reveals more general principles of intergroup relations that are of wide applicability. The subjects were 22 eleven-year-old middle-class boys. There were no problem children among them; each had a good school record; and all were strangers to one another at the start. So far as possible they were matched into pairs on weight, height, skills, and previous camping experience and then assigned randomly into two groups. For a week the two groups lived separately at an isolated camping site. They were then brought into frequent competitive and often frustrating interaction. At the end of this second stage, there were strong reciprocal prejudices and stereotypes; members of the two groups did not want to associate; there was name-calling and conflict.

How could these expressions of tension and disharmony be reduced? One might make appeals to a common "enemy," break up the groups by individual reward and rivalry, or shift attention to intergroup leaders. Sherif rejected these, however, in favor of an effort to reduce friction by introducing "superordinate goals"—a series of tasks that required, for a mutually esteemed outcome, intergroup cooperation. These tasks were preceded by seven unstructured contact situations. By themselves, these contacts did little to break down the group lines, reduce stereotypy, or end the conflict. When the two groups had to work together, however, to raise enough money to bring a movie to camp or to get water flowing again (after the staff had devilishly disrupted the supply), group lines blurred, antipathies receded, and the differential rating of in-group and out-group disappeared. "Patterns and procedures for intergroup cooperation were laid down at first on a small scale in specific activities. Only during interaction in a series of situations involving superordinate goals did intergroup friction begin to disappear and the procedures for intergroup reciprocity developed in specific situations extend spontaneously to widening areas of activity.[64]

Here is group-building and attitude-forming before our eyes. Undoubtedly new variables are introduced when one deals with group identities that have lasted for years, not weeks. It is valuable, therefore, to follow Sherif's study with one that deals with an interracial camp. Marian Yarrow and her colleagues describe the interpersonal relationships that develop between Negro and white children during the "equal status contact" of a two-week camping session.[65] Two camps for low-income children had been run on a segregated basis. During the summer of this study, three sessions, the first six weeks, remained segregated, but the last two sessions were integrated. The staff was integrated in all sessions. Six to ten children, chosen to get age homogeneity and to avoid prior friendships, were assigned to a cabin. Out of 32 cabins, eight were studied intensively during each of the two integrated sessions.

At the beginning of each period, a racial status structure was apparent, with white children definitely holding the top positions —as determined by interviews with the campers—in nine cabins and a more mixed picture in the other seven. By the end of the two-week sessions, this status differential had lessened but not disappeared. In the segregated camps, 45 percent of the children had formed themselves into mutual pairs— each choosing the other as best friend—by the time of the first interview. This had dropped to 35 percent by the end of the period. Almost the same pattern was found in the desegregated groups (44 and 33 percent), and 44 percent of these pairs were interracial, despite the status differential. "At the end of camp, in the eyes of the white children their Negro peers were significantly more desirable as friends than

[63] See Muzafer Sherif, *Intergroup Conflict and Cooperation: The Robbers Cave Experiment*, Univ. of Oklahoma Book Exchange, 1961; see also Muzafer Sherif and Carolyn Sherif, *Groups in Harmony and Tension*, Harper & Row, 1953.

[64] Muzafer Sherif, *op. cit.*, p. 210.

[65] See Marian Radke Yarrow (issue ed.), "Interpersonal Dynamics in a Desegregation Process," *JSI*, 1958, vol. 14, no. 1, pp. 1–63

they had been earlier in the session. Indeed, at the end of camp, white and Negro campers were about equally desired as friends by the white children."[66] There was also a significant growth in self-esteem among the Negro children and a reduction in the great sensitivity they showed at first to unfavorable behavior on the part of other Negro children.

In the light of the fact that the situation for Negro girls is often noted to be more favorable than that for Negro boys, it is significant to observe that in a camping setting—and doubtless elsewhere—desegregation held greater initial hazards for Negro girls: they were more likely to internalize their feelings than were the boys; and important camp values—strength and athletic skill for the boys, physical beauty for the girls—put them, but not the Negro boys, at a disadvantage. Nevertheless, there were gains:

For the girls this experience of equal-status contact results in a consistent change toward decreased self-rejection and a relaxation of tight control over their own behavior. . . . At the end of the camp the change is not complete (white girls, for example, still tend to stand as favored ideals for their Negro cabin mates, and the Negro girls still channel most of their aggression toward members of their own race), yet necessary beginnings of change have occurred, particularly changes reflecting an enhancement of the Negro girls' self concept.[67]

Equal-status contact in a two-week camp cannot, of course, offset the influence of years of segregation. A far more important "experiment" is taking place in recently desegregated schools, where hundreds of thousands of white and Negro children are seeing each other for the first time as fellow students. The results are exceedingly complex, varying with the attitudes of school and government officials, the responses of parents, the talents and tensions of the Negro and white children, the grade level, and many other factors. The transition from a segregated to an integrated school, as Robert Coles has reported, is undoubtedly somewhat easier, from a personality standpoint, for first graders than for high-school students.[68] Nevertheless, significant changes of attitude occurred even among many of the more segregationist-minded adolescents. Perhaps most important ". . . is the slow development of discretion and selection in the white child, the breakdown of quick and total vision and the beginning of particular vision based on daily experience."[69] Negro children also begin to see Whites as individuals, with their varying characteristics. In the learning process, the pull of opposite forces is strong. The ambivalences are nicely shown in the words of one of the white senior boys in Atlanta:

I've really changed a lot of my ideas. You can't help having respect for them, the way they've gone through the year so well. They're nice kids, that's what you find out after a while. They speak well, and are more intelligent than a lot of my friends. You have to understand how we've grown up. They were slaves to us, I mean even after the Civil War. . . . I was taught to expect them to do anything I wanted at home . . . they belonged in the kitchen, or fixing your socks . . . that's the way you grow up and that's what most of us expect . . . and then we're told that they're supposed to go to school with us . . . my daddy nearly died. . . . Mom told him he'd get a stroke if he didn't stop it . . . I sneered a few times the first few weeks, but I just couldn't keep it up, and I felt kind of bad and sorry for them. I used to get nervous when I'd see them eating alone. I wondered how I'd have felt if I were in their shoes . . . next thing I knew I was quiet when some of my friends were calling them all the old names. . . . I felt that I never again would look at them the way I did last September and before. . . .[70]

From the results of such studies as we have reported we cannot conclude that a

[66] Marian Yarrow, John Campbell, and Leon Yarrow, "Acquisition of New Norms: A Study of Racial Desegregation," *ibid.*, p. 27.

[67] John Campbell and Marian Yarrow, "Personal and Situational Variables in Adaptation to Change," *ibid.*, p. 36.

[68] Robert Coles, *The Desegregation of Southern Schools: A Psychiatric Study*, ADL and SRC, 1963. This is an intensive comparative study, by a child psychiatrist, concerned primarily with six- and seven-year-olds in New Orleans and 16- and 17-year-olds in Atlanta.

[69] *Ibid.*, p. 10.

[70] *Ibid.*, pp. 13–14.

decrease in prejudice is the inevitable result of equal-status contact. Ernest Campbell and Ray Schrader studied the attitudes of junior and senior high-school students of Oak Ridge, Tennessee, before school integration and then again a year after desegregation. On four scales measuring anti-minority attitudes they found a significant shift in a negative direction. Prejudices had increased.[71]

In the face of contradictory findings we must realize the need for a great deal of research to explore the effects of specific conditions. For example, when are there too few members of the minority to break stereotypes (a few can be regarded as "exceptions"), and when are there so many that a sense of threat to status develops? What is the impact of personal insecurity in response to equal-status contact? In a study of 106 white boys from New York, most of them from the lower class, who attended a four-week interracial camp, Mussen found that 28 boys became significantly less prejudiced against Negroes, but 27 boys became significantly more prejudiced. Those whose prejudice increased were those who had more aggressive feelings and needs and greater need to defy authority, felt themselves victims of aggression, felt that others were not kind and helpful, were more dissatisfied with the camp.[72] This might not have been the result had there been a different proportion of Negro campers (they made up about half the group), had the camp lasted longer, or had various other conditions prevailed. The study points up clearly, however, the need for careful attention to the complexity of the results of equal-status contact.

One can perhaps sum up the present knowledge about the effects of contact on prejudice in these four related propositions:

1. Incidental, involuntary, tension-laden contact is likely to increase prejudice.

2. Pleasant, equal-status contact that makes it unnecessary for the individuals to cross barriers of class, occupational, and educational differences as well as differences in symbolic (nonfunctional) group membership represented by such symbols as "race" is likely to reduce prejudice.

3. Stereotype-breaking contacts that show minority group members in roles not usually associated with them reduce prejudice. It must be added, however, that many people have little capacity for experiencing the members of minority groups as individuals; their stereotypes easily persist in the face of contrary evidence.

4. Contacts that bring people of minority and majority groups together in functionally important activities reduce prejudice. This is particularly true when those activities involve goals that cannot be achieved without the active cooperation of members of all the groups.

Do We Want Contact, Equal Status or Otherwise? In recent years there has been some increase in separationist sentiments in the United States, some of it in the name of pluralism—both Negro and white—but much of it renewing established prejudices. This takes us back to a topic we dealt with in Chapter One and elsewhere, but our interest in it here is in connection with the study of contact. In a valuable paper, Thomas Pettigrew summarizes the reasons often given by Whites today to support racial separation: (1) Each race feels awkward and uncomfortable in the presence of the other and benefits from separation; (2) since Whites are superior, they will lose by integration (in schools, for example); (3) contact increases conflict. Black separationists have somewhat matching assumptions: (1) Yes, each race does feel awkward and uncomfortable in the presence of the other; we're more comfortable by ourselves; (2) most Whites *think* they are superior, so white liberals should spend their time working on white racists, not worrying over integration; (3) yes, contact does mean conflict, and it will continue to until after a period of autonomy, when Blacks can enter

[71] Ernest Campbell, "On Desegregation and Matters Sociological," *Phylon*, Summer, 1961, pp. 140–142.

[72] Paul H. Mussen, "Some Personality and Social Factors Related to Changes in Children's Attitudes Toward Negroes," *JASP*, July, 1950, pp. 423–441.

*Figure 9 / Schematic Diagram of Autonomy and
Contact-Separation*

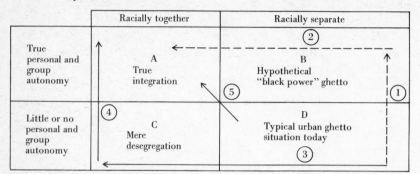

Source: Thomas Pettigrew, "Racially Separate or Together," *JSI*, Jan., 1969, p. 58. Dotted
lines denote hypothetical paths, solid lines actual paths.

into interaction on a fully equal basis.[73]

We shall refer only briefly to Pettigrew's comments on each of these points. It is true, he notes, that some interracial contacts are awkward, that intraracial contacts may seem more comfortable. But, he asks, at what cost do we gain this comfort? Isolation leads to mutual misinformation and, more importantly, it promotes differences. There has been a sharp reduction in racist beliefs in the United States during the last generation; wise policy should not be based on assumptions of its prevalence or increase. Contact does, under some conditions, increase conflict; but lack of conflict is no sign of progress. "One of the quietest periods in American racial history, 1895–1915, for example, witnessed the construction of the massive system of institutional racism as it is known today. . . ."[74]

Many people argue, Pettigrew notes, that "in the long run" full integration may be desirable, but that for the immediate and foreseeable future, separation is necessary and wise. The "white desegregationist," using some mixture of the three reasons given above, supports some public desegregation, but not extensive integration. This is basically a moderate version of the older segregationist view. Perhaps more interesting is the argument of some black leaders that autonomy must come first, then integration may be possible. The various positions are charted by Pettigrew, as shown in Figure 9 above.

Pettigrew marshalls substantial evidence to support "route 5." With reference to the "3–1–2 route," for example, he writes:

The black separatist route has a surprising appeal for an untested theory; besides those whites who welcome any alternative to integration, it seems to appeal to cultural pluralists, white and black, to militant black leaders searching for a new direction to vent the ghetto's rage and despair, and to Negroes who just wish to withdraw as far away from whites as possible. Yet on reflection the argument involves the perverse notion that the way to bring two groups together is to separate them further. One is reminded of the detrimental consequences of isolation in economics, through "closed markets," and in "genetic drift." In social psychology, isolation between two contiguous groups generally leads to: (a) diverse value development, (b) reduced intergroup communication, (d) uncorrected perceptual distortions of each other, and (d) the growth of vested interests within both groups for continued separation. American race relations already suffer from each of these conditions; and the proposal for further separation even if a gilded ghetto were possible, aims to exacerbate them further.[75]

Pettigrew may exaggerate the favorable outcomes of contact and overlook some of the costs.[76] But, in our judgment, he weighs the balance correctly.

[73] Thomas Pettigrew, "Racially Separate or Together," *Journal of Social Issues*, Jan., 1969, pp. 43–69.

[74] *Ibid.*, p. 57.

[75] *Ibid.*, pp. 58–59.

[76] See Russell Eisenman, "Comment on 'Racially Separate or Together?'" and Thomas Pettigrew, "Rejoinder," *JSI*, Autumn, 1969, pp. 199–206.

Education

Most Americans have a good deal of faith in the power of education (often accompanied by an anti-intellectualism that exalts the "practical" man, the man of "action," and disdains the expert and intellectual). It is frequently declared that education (empirically shading off into programs of contact, exhortation, and propaganda) could reduce prejudice sharply. Discussion of the value of education frequently fails to distinguish two levels of argument. One proposition might state: *If we were able to have a scientifically adequate and nation-wide program of education in majority-minority relations, prejudice would be reduced.* But the more frequent declaration is simply: Education can reduce prejudice.

The latter statement pays no attention to the obstacles in the way of getting an adequate program of education in intergroup relations. There is no likelihood that schools, communities, adult education programs, and the like will suddenly develop adequate and widespread studies of prejudice, for they are part of the total society, largely reflecting its traditions and power structure—and its prejudices.

Effective strategy requires that we distinguish these two problems in developing a program of education to reduce a prejudice and discrimination:

What are the barriers to setting up such a program? Who will oppose it, and how may their opposition be reduced? Who will finance it?

After one has set up the program, what techniques are most effective in changing the attitudes of different groups of people?

We perhaps know more about the second problem than about the first. One is justified in a modest optimism that when a program has been set in motion, particularly with children, it can be fairly effective in preventing or reducing prejudices. But under what circumstances will an educational program be set in motion? In March, 1971, the United States Department of Defense announced the creation of an Institute to train, within a year, 1400 instructors to staff a program in race relations. Classes will be required of every person who enters the service, with six-hour refresher courses each year thereafter. This ambitious program to prevent racial conflict and unrest reflects deep concern over the serious racial tensions in the armed forces during the last few years.[77]

It remains to be seen how effective the armed forces program will be, although smaller-scale efforts on some army bases have reduced conflicts. It is clear, however, that few institutions can match the armed forces in creating an extensive program by a decision from the top. Yet the school system is also an area where some action is possible. Despite the close connection between formal education and the rest of society, there is a measure of autonomy in the school system. This autonomy is easy to exaggerate, but it is a strategic error to dismiss it too lightly. Those professionally connected with education, because of their functional role in society, are somewhat more concerned with the pursuit of truth, a little less likely to be provincial. In our society they are also inclined to be somewhat more liberal than the average, although some are timid and others are emotionally identified with the upper classes. Coles observed, even among teachers who were unhappy with desegregation, "a kind of adherence in the end to professional responsibilities and obligations . . . a deep sense of professional integrity, of identity as teachers which transcended their private feelings about race."[78] Those who control the school systems, moreover (the school boards and trustees), are not inclined to determine every action of the teacher, because they are to some degree dependent on him as the conserver and pursuer of knowledge, as the expert and trainer of experts, who, despite the disdain in which he is held by the "practical" man, is indispensable to our society. An ideology of freedom for the teacher is also involved. The result is that the teacher has some autonomy, some power to attack prejudice if he wants to—and some teachers want to.

This modest resource has been used only slightly, although efforts to increase inter-

[77] *The New York Times,* Mar. 6, 1971, pp. 1, 14.
[78] Coles, *op. cit.,* p. 17.

group education have been expanded greatly in recent years. Educational institutions themselves still contain a great deal of discrimination. Few teachers are trained specifically in the analysis of majority-minority relations; seldom is a teacher chosen from a minority group (although the number of black teachers has recently increased); and few courses treat their material in a way designed to reduce prejudice.

In the last several years some labor unions have proved to be organizations in which the barriers to educational programs concerned with reducing prejudice have not been too high. The efforts of such unions as the United Automobile Workers and the National Maritime Union show that progressive leadership can take advantage of the functional unity of the members of various minorities and the majority to reduce prejudice.

What Kind of Education? The first job of strategy, in making use of education, is to determine the areas—such as schools and unions—where programs are most likely to be adopted. But that is only half the job. Having cleared the ground, one must decide how to proceed. Is it a matter simply of transferring information, for knowledge leads to action? Or are the ways in which the knowledge is acquired, the total situation of learning, as crucial as the facts themselves? More and more we see that the latter is the case. How one learns an idea is important to his mastery of it, to his acceptance of the idea as valid, and to the likelihood of his acting upon it. The total personality is involved in the learning process. One type of situation may stimulate a personality "set" that makes a person unable to acquire new knowledge. Or knowledge may be "learned" on a symbolic level but be so compartmentalized that it does not affect other ideas or overt behavior.

Education and re-education must be guided by the fact that prejudice is frequently "used" by the person; it is functional (not necessarily effective, be it noted). It will be "unlearned" only when the entanglements with the total personality are loosened by the nature of the learning situation, by the reduction of tension and the elimination of any threats to one's ego. At the very least, when one gives up a prejudice he admits an error—and most of us are reluctant to do this. Fineberg illustrates the way in which sensitivity to the feelings of the prejudiced person contributes to re-education:

Mrs. Tenney, a brilliant young woman active in community relations work, had remained silent at a dinner party when a woman whom she and her husband were meeting for the first time spoke of members of another race as mentally inferior to white people. It was an incidental remark. The conversation quickly drifted to something else.

Driving home, Mr. Tenney said to his wife, "I was watching you when Mrs. Hammond put in that nasty crack about colored people. Why didn't you speak up?"

"And spoil the chance of ever changing her mind?" asked Mrs. Tenney. "Had I spoken up, Mrs. Hammond would have defended her opinion. If I had won the argument, it would have been to my satisfaction but not to hers. She would have disliked me for embarrassing her among her new acquaintances. She looks like a sincere, capable person. I think we can change her views on several things. When she made that quip about racial inferiority, I put it down in my little mental notebook. And what do you think I did while we were getting our wraps?"

Mr. Tenney smiled. "Knowing you as I do, I'd say you made a date with Mrs. Hammond."

"Right! When we know each other better, I'll introduce Mrs. Hammond to Dr. Sanford and to Mrs. Taylor, who are as intelligent as any white person she ever met. One of these days Mrs. Hammond will be working for our Interracial Commission. That's not a promise, John, but I'll try hard."

In less than two months Mrs. Hammond had abandoned the notion of racial inferiority without having been forced to recant, apologize, or even to recall the invidious remark. Her mentor, Mrs. Tenney, is one of the few—there are altogether too few—who is concerned enough about racial and religious prejudice and astute enough to undertake the *reeducation* of mildly prejudiced individuals.[79]

[79] S. A. Fineberg, *Punishment Without Crime*, Doubleday, 1949, pp. 183–184.

Kurt Lewin was undoubtedly the leader in "action research"—the analysis of the conditions under which change in human relations takes place and the study of the processes by which it occurs. Out of his studies has come the emphasis on the involvement of the total personality in the educative process. This has led to the development of several principles: Create an informal situation; see education as a group process, not simply an individual process; maximize the individual's sense of participation in getting new ideas.[80]

We are not expounding a general theory of education. We are concerned with the learning process in an area where emotional attitudes and stereotypes affect observation and the acceptance of evidence. The degree to which different principles are involved in different learning situations is a problem that cannot be examined here.

Intergroup Education in the Schools. With the great increase in public awareness of intergroup relations and tensions in the last two decades, schools at every level began to pay more attention to interracial, intercultural, interfaith, and international questions. Specific courses have been introduced in a number of cities, and teacher training programs, literature designed for specific age levels, and some attention to intergroup relations in the total life of schools have increased.[81]

Several obstacles and weaknesses have become apparent in the short history of deliberately planned intergroup education. One fault on the part of many administrators is

[80] Kurt Lewin, *Resolving Social Conflicts*, Harper & Row, 1948.
[81] For studies of the extent of—and some of the problems faced in intergroup relations teaching, see *Teacher Education for Human Relations in the Classroom*, 1962, and *Human Relations in the Classroom*, 1963, prepared by the Subcommittee on Human Relations in the Classroom, Committee on Teacher Education, of the North Central Association of Colleges and Secondary Schools. For helpful guides to intergroup teaching see Gertrude Noar, *Teaching and Learning the Democratic Way*, ADL, 1963; and William Briggs and Dean Hummel, *Counseling Minority Group Youth: Developing the Experience of Equality Through Education*, Ohio Civil Rights Commission, 1962.

the segregation of teachers on racial or ethnic lines. Intergroup instruction is distorted if minority groups are not represented on the teaching staff. There have, however, been some notable changes in recent years. Thousands of Negro teachers are now assigned to interracial classes, in the North and in the South. Several hundred Negroes are members of formerly all-white faculties, and with the demand exceeding the supply, colleges and universities are now competing with one another in the effort to add black staff members. (Most of these teachers, of course, on all levels of education, teach subjects other than intergroup relations. Their influence on that topic is indirect and informal.)

A second type of difficulty in this new field lies in the attitudes of teachers. Intergroup education has no possibility of being effective unless those who are charged with carrying it out are competent and sympathetic. Routine performance of an assigned program accomplishes little or nothing. Subtle or obviously prejudiced remarks or acts on the part of the teacher outside the program itself may more than offset that which is included in formal instruction. Many pupils come from homes where prejudice is strong. If the teacher also harbors prejudice, the results of intergroup education are likely to be negligible. Some school systems now include interest and skill in intergroup relations among the criteria used in the selection of new teachers.

Closely related to teachers attitudes are school policies with regard to pupil assignment. In the matter of "ability level," schools are confronted with a dilemma: In some ways it is more effective to teach relatively homogeneous groups, because methods and materials can be adapted to their particular needs. On the other hand grouping and tracking tend to create self-fulfilling prophecies, to create expectations in the minds of students and teachers alike about levels of performance. The result is that those in "slow tracks" remain slow, those in "fast tracks" are given further support and encouragement. Most of this is without any intent on the part of those making the assignments. Although there are problems of interpretation in their study, Rosenthal and Jacobson have demonstrated their major point that teacher expectations affect, not simply the grading of pupils, but their actual performances. In a controlled study, they showed that teachers, without realizing it, sent cues to presumed slow learners and fast learners that tended to reenforce their original tendencies.[82] No amount of formal attention to intergroup relations will reduce the effects of such subtle and unintended discrimination. The policy of "ability grouping" is now the subject of a great deal of controversy, in educational circles and among parents. The sharpness of the dilemma it presents will encourage pendulum swings, as one or another force becomes stronger, until creative educational programs are designed that serve both the well-prepared and the less-well-prepared student.

Recent studies indicate that the imparting of specific information about minority groups does not materially alter attitudes toward those groups. This is not to say that transmitting such information has no value, but simply that its usefulness in producing more favorable attitudes toward "out-groups" is less great than many professional educators have believed. About all that can be claimed for purely factual instruction is that "it tends to mitigate some of the more extreme expressions of prejudice and that, where there is any readiness to receive it, it provides some protection against the mob-raising appeals to which ignorance is exposed. . . . Greater knowledge may not seriously change our evaluations, since the latter are so dependent on our prior indoctrinations. . . ."[83]

In short, knowledge may be helpful but its acquisition does not automatically produce understanding and appreciation. For effective action the main attack must be made on basic and often emotionally held attitudes rather than on opinions.

The way in which minority groups are described—or entirely overlooked—in textbooks and other school materials significantly affects intergroup relations in school and the formation of attitudes. In 1949 the American Council on Education surveyed 315 published sources used in schools and found relatively little support for a democratic perspective. Neglect of minority groups on the one hand and stereotypy, of a relatively moderate sort, on the other characterized many of the textbooks and other writings.[84] Twelve years later, Lloyd Marcus found important changes in his analysis of 48 leading junior and senior high-school textbooks in the area of social studies, but a still inadequate coverage and treatment.[85]

In a review of "readers" used in elementary grades, Otto Klineberg finds an even less adequate picture.

The American people are almost exclusively white or Caucasian. The only exception discovered in the fifteen readers refers to a visit to a Western ranch, near which lived an American Indian family, who spent most of their time "making beautiful things . . . to sell to the white people who came to the Indian country. . . ." The Americans in these readers are almost exclusively North European in origin and appearance . . . the exceptions . . . are themselves significant. An organ grinder is given an appearance which is stereotypically Italian or Greek . . . Americans in these readers are predominantly, almost exclusively, blondes. . . . There are occasional references to dark skin, but these usually relate to people far away. . . . Pandas, for example, are found in a distant land (India?) with dark-skinned people . . . and of course the illustrations for the stories about China, India, North Africa, etc., do show dark people. Not in the United States, however, apart from the exceptions noted above. Negroes are nonexistent.[86]

This was written in 1963. Since that time the situation has changed quite rapidly, particularly with reference to materials and courses dealing with Negro Americans, but

[82] Robert Rosenthal and Lenore Jacobson, *Pygmalion in the Classroom*, Holt, Rinehart & Winston, 1968; for a series of articles on "Institutionalization of Expectancy," see *The Urban Review*, Sept., 1968.

[83] MacIver, *op. cit.*, pp. 222, 223; chap. 5 of this work, "The Educational Front," is excellent.

[84] *Intergroup Relations in Teaching Materials*, ACE, 1949.

[85] Lloyd Marcus, *The Treatment of Minorities in Secondary School Textbooks*, ADL, 1961.

[86] Otto Klineberg, "Life Is Fun in a Smiling, Fair-Skinned World," *Saturday Review*, Feb. 16, 1963, pp. 75–76.

in connection with other minorities as well.[87]

Some of the problems in intergroup education found on the primary and secondary levels also characterize college work. Many general college programs are concerned with studying the democratic tradition and strengthening belief in the democratic heritage, but few have the specific aim of reducing prejudice, nor have they used techniques appropriate to that end. There are, of course, hundreds of courses in departments of sociology, anthropology, history, and social psychology concerned with minorities and prejudice. These are usually elective courses, dealing with self-selected students; and they therefore face different problems in reducing prejudice. The changing of attitudes, if it is recognized at all, is only one aim, although that hope probably lies behind most of the courses. Since the reducing of prejudices is not explicitly sought—and methods appropriate to that aim are not adopted—one does not judge the effectiveness of a course by measuring changes in attitude. Nevertheless, many such measurements have been made, and they reveal that one of the results—perhaps a by-product—of the study of minorities and prejudice may be an increase in tolerance. The results, however, are far from definite. About a third of the studies have found that the course of study produced no change of attitude.[88] The studies vary widely, moreover, in the degree to which they have controlled variables and eliminated the effects of self-selection that so often distort the analysis of human behavior. But their total weight gives some

support to the hypothesis that knowledge may reduce prejudice. It can undermine the rationalizations of prejudiced persons and make their attitudes seem less respectable. But the ambiguity of the results prevents any easy optimism. Courses that are not concerned with the functions of prejudice to the individual and are not designed to deal with them are unlikely to be very effective. Although facts may be stubborn things to the scientist, to most people they are extremely pliable compared with the stubborn quality of their stereotypes.

There is great need for research that will specify how different methods of teaching used with persons of different attitudes and tendencies will influence prejudice. Although they deal with only a brief "educational" situation, Mittnick and McGinnies illustrate the value of such specification. Having classified students from two high schools into low, middle, and high on a modified version of the California Ethnocentrism Scale, they randomly assigned persons of each category into six groups of nine members each. One month after this measurement, two groups from each category (six in all) saw a film "High Wall" and then engaged in a half-hour, nondirected discussion. The film treated group prejudice as a disease, tracing its origins to family experience and community influence. Six additional groups saw the film but did not discuss it. Six groups served as controls. After seeing the film, the 12 experimental groups were given a 33-item information test and all 18 were again given the E-Scale test. One month later, both tests were readministered. Significant reductions in ethnocentrism occurred among both the film and the film-discussion groups. Among those whose initial scores were high in prejudice, however, the opportunity for discussion significantly reduced the gain, counteracting some of the effects of the film, while for the middle and low groups, discussion increased the gain. The measurement after one month showed that those who discussed the film significantly retained the lower ethnocentrism scores, while the film-alone groups regressed toward their original attitudes. Those with low scores and those who actively participated

---

[87] The following bibliographies will give an indication of the range of materials available: Miles M. Jackson (ed.), *A Bibliography of Negro History and Culture for Young Children,* Univ. of Pittsburgh Press, 1968; Minnie W. Koblitz, *The Negro in Schoolroom Literature,* Center for Urban Education, 1966; NAACP, *Integrated School Books: A Descriptive Bibliography of 399 Pre-School and Elementary School Texts and Story Books,* 1967; Doris White, *Multi-Ethnic Books for Head Start Children, Part I: Black and Integrated Literature; Part II: Other Minority Group Literature,* National Laboratory on Early Childhood Education, Urbana, Illinois, 1969.

[88] A summary of the results of many of these studies is found in Arnold M. Rose and Caroline Rose, *America Divided: Minority Group Relations in the United States,* Knopf, 1948, p. 282.

in the discussions learned more from the films.[89]

Whether or not these findings on the differential effects of discussion are of general applicability, this study suggests the need for multi-variable research in attempts to understand the effects of education.

Not all the educational needs vis-à-vis majority-minority relations are found among members of the majority. A significant recent development, as we have noted in an earlier chapter, is the appearance of a black studies program in many schools. This is being followed by demands for, and to some degree action on, Puerto Rican, Mexican, Indian, and other programs. Jewish studies have long been a part of traditional curricula, but are now being developed in some places somewhat more along the "ethnic group" line of the newer programs.

The implications of these developments for the topic of this chapter are not clear. Black students, for example, make up the vast majority of students in black studies programs. They are presented with materials and educational philosophies ranging from scholarly emphasis on Negro history, literature, music, art (graphic and plastic), and experience to action programs designed to speed the destruction of "imperialistic societies." With such contrasts in basic premises, inevitably there are sharp disputes among those who design and work in these programs. Some see them as a necessary and appropriate way to emphasize black contributions to American culture and society; and others work to make the programs agents of black separation.

We do not know of any systematic studies that evaluate the influence of black studies programs on prejudice and discrimination, the topic with which we are concerned here. Effects will undoubtedly vary widely, depending upon the approach of the courses

and the materials used, and on the students who participate. General theory leads us to two opposite predictions: Courses that promote the growth of pride and the strengthening of self-identity may reduce prejudice. On the other hand, some of the materials and approaches seem likely to reduce the sense of common humanity, to promote stereotypes, and to create a world picture as inaccurately imaginary as the one white students have long suffered under. The balance, we suspect, will be determined, not only by struggles among the staffs and the schools where they work, but also by the total national setting. Slow progress in reducing discrimination and granting full rights to all citizens will support the chauvinistic elements in "ethnic studies." Rapid progress will support their broader humanistic potential, and thus help to break the vicious circle of majority-minority relations.[90]

Related to the question of the efficacy of intergroup education as such is the question of the general influence of education on anti-minority attitudes and behavior. In a careful review of the poll data over a number of years, Stember concludes that education has important, but limited effects:

Yet, as we go up the educational ladder, old images of minorities are replaced by new ones, often no less harmful. Covert discrimination continues to be acceptable and most important perhaps, the desire to keep minorities at some social distance remains.

It would thus appear that the impact of education is limited. Its chief effect is to reduce traditional provincialism—to counteract the notion that members of minorities are strange creatures with exotic ways, and to diminish fear of casual personal contact. But the limits of acceptance are sharply drawn; while legal equality is supported, full social participation is not.[91]

---

[89] Leonard Mittnick and Elliott McGinnies, "Influencing Ethnocentrism in Small Discussion Groups Through a Film Communication," *JASP*, Jan., 1958, pp. 82–90. For a study of the effects of attitude homogeneity among the members of an educational group, see Adrian Solomon, "Authoritarian Attitude Changes and Group Homogeneity," *JSP*, Feb., 1963, pp. 129–135.

[90] There has been a flood of materials on Black Studies. See, for example, Armstead L. Robinson, Craig C. Foster, and Donald H. Ogilvie (eds.), *Black Studies in the University*, Yale, 1968; Henry Rosovsky, *Report of the Faculty Committee on African and Afro-American Studies*, Harvard, 1969; "Black Mood on Campus," *Newsweek*, Feb. 10, 1968, pp. 53–60.

[91] Charles H. Stember, *Education and Attitude Change: The Effect of Schooling on Prejudice Against Minority Groups*, Institute of Human Relations Press, 1961, p. 171.

Not all prejudices, Stember notes, are affected in the same way by schooling. The more deeply rooted prejudices are affected only by a high level of training. Anti-Negro sentiments do not decline appreciably until one gets to the college level. As we have previously noted, one must be wary of poll data; they may only poorly indicate what individuals will do under various conditions. They are valuable if seen as one item of information among several that might help us understand prejudice and discrimination.

Personal Therapy

If prejudice and discrimination are frequently manifestations of personal insecurities or of a basic personality instability, then an effective program of strategy must be concerned with the reduction of emotional disturbances. The prevention and treatment of personality disorganization is a very large area that we can only touch upon; but we need to examine some of the general principles involved, as they refer to our problem. We need to avoid, as some specialists fail to do, exaggerating the effectiveness of personal therapy as a strategy. The authors of *The Authoritarian Personality* write, "The major emphasis should be placed, it seems, not upon discrimination against particular groups, but upon such phenomena as stereotypy, emotional coldness, identification with power, and general destructiveness."[92] Such a statement is the result of an inadequate theory of the causes of prejudice and discrimination. We need to remember Robert Coles' word of caution, with reference to the world-saving value of therapy: "If only more people could be analyzed! . . . The same logic and reason that finally had glimpsed the workings of the unconscious mind would take control of the body politic; the same insight that at last had characterized and defined the shadowy, unmentionable forces at work in the family would now set straight man's racial, religious, and national tensions."[93] But there are far too many feel-

ings of rancor, prejudice, and snobbery among the analyzed—and even those who analyze—Coles notes, to allow any longer such an easy interpretation. There are some situations, in the view of the present authors, in which personality factors are relatively unimportant, others in which they loom large; but more often the several factors are closely interlocked, and none should be chosen for "major emphasis."

Personal therapy is frequently most effective when the reduction of prejudice is simply a by-product of the larger goal of a stable personality. In this field, as in so many others, prevention is far more effective than cure. The creation of a society and interpersonal situation that make possible the maximum satisfactions of needs will reduce the likelihood of intergroup hostility. There is the danger in this strategy, as in education, of our adopting a "bootstrap" kind of thinking—asking unstable persons living in a prejudice-prone society to devise situations in which personal stability and tolerance prevail more widely. We have here no cure-all, but simply one approach, among many, that may contribute to the reduction of hostility. With this limitation in mind, we may say that anyone who contributes to the development of a strong economy, to a political situation that gives each individual some sense of control over his government, to a satisfying recreational program, to the growth of less restrictive and frustrating personal relations, particularly between parents and children—such a person is assisting, directly or indirectly, in the reduction of prejudice.

Even an extensive program of prevention, however, would be inadequate. For a long time to come we need to be equally concerned with a program of cure—of treatment for insecure persons who use prejudice and discrimination as modes of adjustment to their insecurities. Therapy may concentrate primarily on the tendencies of the individual or on the situations that are activating those tendencies. The latter approach is too often disregarded by psychiatrists and others concerned with personality reorganization; yet to treat "society as the patient" is frequently a more effective approach than the intensive

[92] Adorno *et al.*, *op. cit.*, p. 973.
[93] Robert Coles, *Children of Crisis*, Dell, 1967, p. 353.

analysis of each individual (who, in any case, can be understood only by examining the situational factors as well as individual tendencies).[94]

In the treatment of "problem children" particularly—children who may exhibit prejudice among other manifestations of insecurity—a change in the situation around them is often far more effective than direct attention to their problems. Often, in fact, the child can be disregarded completely. James Plant reports the case of a rebellious, truculent boy, the second son in a professional family of insistent ambition. The boy had much less native ability than his brother, was having a difficult time in school, and seemed badly "maladjusted"—the kind of person who could develop vigorous prejudices. At home, the parents frequently made invidious comparisons of the younger boy with the older. When the problem was brought to the school clinic, the doctor might have made complete psychiatric examinations of both the parents and the children. Actually, he scarcely saw them; he examined the situation. The younger brother, and four other boys who were having academic difficulties, were given special school work. They did their geography by reporting about ships that had docked, their civics by visiting city hall. The boy's rebellion disappeared; he was now the one who had the interesting stories to tell at meals and became the subject of his father's anecdotes. A whole constellation of family problems disappeared as a result of an interesting outlet for the boy in school. "One is tempted to compare this sort of therapy where the psychiatrist did not see the boy until he was gaily moving along both at home and in school a year later, with the approach which would have crystallized all his defeat and resentments in order that he and the psychiatrist might laboriously, but finally in triumph, erode away the last vestige of the difficulty."[95]

When personal insecurities are more deeply set, the situational approach is less likely to be effective. The responses of the individual may take on a rigidity that coerces the interpretation of every situation into the same mold. Alongside the therapeutic approaches that seek to modify the tension-laden situations, therefore, we need the direct treatment of unstable persons. This treatment can range from friendly counseling (simply listening, frequently) to intensive psychoanalysis.[96] Techniques that help an individual to face the causes of his hostility help to reduce its sharpness.

Public attention has been directed mainly to problems of therapy for dominant-group members. There is some tendency, in fact, to regard their prejudices and hostilities as pathological, while those of minority-group members are normal responses to abuse. This may be good strategy at certain points in history, or a relatively harmless error in dealing with a thoroughly oppressed group. When a pattern of discrimination is breaking down, however, the anxieties and hatreds of the oppressed are being released from repression, we need a more tough-minded analysis of the therapeutic problems and possibilities among them. Perhaps in the years to come America will discover that black anxieties and hatreds are also inimical to social welfare. This is probably already true in the most important sense, namely in the efforts to reduce their causes. But it is not yet true in the therapeutic sense that is our present focus of attention.

We are not referring, of course, to more or less rationally chosen opposition to discrimination, but to the unconscious problems that express themselves in ways unlikely to affect social practices, except negatively. Perhaps most important of these are the various paranoid symptoms. As Grier and Cobbs note: "For a black man survival in America depends in large measure on the development

[94] See L. K. Frank, *Society as the Patient*, Rutgers, 1948.

[95] James Plant, *Personality and the Culture Pattern*, The Commonwealth Fund, 1937, pp. 37–38.

[96] There is a vast literature on problems of therapy. See, for example, Fritz Redl and David Wineman, *Children Who Hate*, Free Press, 1951; and Bruno Bettelheim, *Truants from Life*, Free Press, 1955; Elliot Aronson, "Threat and Obedience," *Trans*-action, Mar.–Apr., 1969, pp. 25–27. It is unlikely that there are special principles that apply only to therapy dealing with prejudice. Processes that reduce hostility are likely also to reduce prejudice.

of a 'healthy' cultural paranoia. He must maintain a high degree of suspicion toward the motives of every white man and at the same time never allow this suspicion to impair his grasp of reality. It is a demanding requirement and not everyone can manage it with grace. . . . Of all the varieties of functional psychosis, those that include paranoid symptoms is significantly greater among mentally ill blacks than it is among mentally ill whites."[97]

Since the anxieties of black men, in the psychiatric sense, have not yet been defined by most observers as one of the critical factors in the cycle of causes that sustain racial animosities, they have not been studied much. In our judgment, however, direct and indirect methods of therapy to reduce those anxieties are a necessary part of a total strategic plan.[98]

Group Therapy

Individual therapy is certainly a strategy that any complete program must use, particularly in the treatment of persons having deep-seated prejudices. It suffers, however, from two disadvantages. It is costly in time and energy; and it is inadequate to cut the supports of prejudice that derive from groups.

Group therapy tries to overcome these disadvantages. It is an attempt to produce changes in the personality by using the knowledge of the effects of groups on attitudes and behavior. The activities of therapeutic groups may range all the way from doing simple rhythmic actions together—a major step for some isolated schizophrenics —to enacting a plot that contains the anxiety-laden problem, to discussions in which fellow "patients" get insight into their own problems by studying those of another. Group therapy has a long implicit history in religion, in drama, in other group practices; but as an explicit method of treatment for

disorganized persons it is quite new, and as a strategy in the reduction of prejudice it is even newer.

The underlying theory is that the feeling of belongingness of group members breaks down their feelings of isolation, facilitates interaction among them, encourages role-taking and self-knowledge. The sharing of symptoms and problems with others bring a sense of security and a lowering of guilt tensions —"I'm not the only one who faces this difficulty." The therapist attempts to create a situation that is thoroughly permissive and informal. Individuals are allowed to express their feelings of hostility freely, for self-discovery can scarcely occur in situations that require inhibition and concealment. Thus group therapy is closely related to the approach to education that we have discussed above. It is based on the same conception of change as a group process.[99]

Ronald Lippitt and his associates, in a series of studies, compared the effects of democratic and autocratic leadership on the behavior of ten- and eleven-year-old children. In the autocratic group, the children were told what to do, they were given no overall perspective of what they were doing (making masks), and the praise and criticism of the leader were given arbitrarily, with no objective reasons. In the democratic group all policies were determined by the members, the whole process was explained and technical help offered, alternatives were suggested, members chose freely what to do and with whom to work, praise and criticism were objective. These differences in group atmosphere had very different effects on the interaction of the children and on their relations with the adult leader. There was far more hostile domination of one child over another in the autocratic group, more demands for attention, more hostile criticism. On the

---

[97] William H. Grier and Price M. Cobbs, *Black Rage*, Basic Books, 1968, p. 161.

[98] For discussion of one critical issue, applicable to minority and majority alike, see Irwin M. Rubin, "Increased Self Acceptance: A Means of Reducing Prejudice," *JPSP*, Feb., 1967, pp. 233–238.

[99] Studies of group processes in the treatment of other problems are also of value to the student of prejudice. See, for example, Leon Yablonsky, *The Tunnel Back: Synanon*, Macmillan, 1965; Lamar Empey and Jerome Rabow, "The Provo Experiment in Delinquency Rehabilitation," *ASR*, Oct., 1961, pp. 679–695; and Rita Volkman and Donald Cressey, "Differential Association and the Rehabilitation of Drug Addicts," *AJS*, Sept., 1963, pp. 129–142.

other hand, the children were more submissive toward the leader in the autocratic group. Since there was no chance of becoming a leader, they expressed far less individuality. A scapegoat situation developed, in which the children, unable to resist the demands of the adult, attacked one of the other children.[100]

Illness, of course, as well as therapy, has a group dimension. Treatment is ineffective if this is not understood. One aspect of the group dimension of illness is that societies and smaller groups have culturally defined "sick roles," indicating how a person should (and may) behave when he is ill, and how he should be treated. The process of assignment of a person to the sick role, referring specifically now to mental illness, may begin when his behavior deviations are minor. The assignment is part of the adjustment process of others who interact closely with him; it expresses efforts to handle their own anxieties and guilts, for example. The result may be to solidify the minor symptoms of the first person. In this sense, it is not the individual who is ill and needs treatment, but the group process, although individual differences in vulnerability are also involved of course.[101] In the same way, prejudice is anchored in group processes and can be cured only by attention to group as well as individual factors.

The kind of principle of group process represented by such studies is basic to the attempts to reduce intergroup hostility by group therapy. Morris and Natalie Haimowitz report the effects of about 35 hours of group therapy in small groups with 24 persons. The individuals involved were from 25 to 60 years of age; they had masters' degrees or their equivalent in psychology and three years of experience. Before and after the six-week period they were given the Bogardus social-distance test, the group being divided into "friendly" and "hostile" in their attitudes toward 19 minorities on the basis of their willingness or unwillingness to admit members of the minorities to their clubs and neighborhoods (steps two and three on the scale), even if not to marriage (step one). The scores after the group therapy were significantly (at the 1 percent level) different from the scores before the therapy:

	Before	After
Friendly	7	13
Hostile	17	11

It is interesting to note that it was the mildly hostile, not the strongly hostile, who were most likely to change. Six of them moved into the friendly group, but only one strongly hostile person (out of nine) became mildly hostile. Four strongly hostile persons (and one mildly hostile) actually increased in prejudice during the sessions, apparently having been made more defensive about their attitudes by the experience.

The study gives tentative support, at least for the kind of people involved in the therapy, to the conclusion of the authors that

. . . with improved adjustment, hostility to minority groups declines. As the individual feels less threatened, he is less hostile in his reactions to the world. He becomes more able to cope with the sources of his frustrations directly and effectively. There is less hostility to be canalized, and less displacement in the expression of whatever tensions do arise. . . . The experience of releasing feelings about their own personal problems, and developing ways of constructively dealing with the problems of life, resulted in a decrease in the amount of ethnic hostility with which they came to the therapy experience.[102]

One may wonder whether a social-distance scale is a valid measure of "ethnic hostility"

[100] See Ralph White and Ronald Lippitt, *Autocracy and Democracy*, Harper & Row, 1960.

[101] See Thomas J. Scheff, *Being Mentally Ill: A Sociological Theory*, Aldine, 1966; but see also Walter R. Gove, "Societal Reaction as an Explanation of Mental Illness: An Evaluation," *ASR*, Oct., 1970, pp. 873–884. Gove's commentary is a valuable, but perhaps excessive, qualification of Scheff's thesis.

[102] Morris Haimowitz and Natalie Haimowitz, "Reducing Ethnic Hostility Through Psychotherapy," *JSP*, May, 1950, pp. 235, 238.

and whether the changes in attitude persisted, but the study suggests an approach that a complete strategic plan will contain.

In sum, as we examine the strategies that seek to reduce prejudice and discrimination primarily by changing attitudes, we find an increasingly effective approach which, in conjunction with other strategies, can help to reduce intergroup hostility.[103]

[103] See Gordon Allport, "Catharsis and the Reduction of Prejudice," *JSI*, Dec., 1945, pp. 3–10; S. R. Slavson, *An Introduction to Group Therapy*, The Commonwealth Fund, 1943; Virginia M. Axline, "Play Therapy and Race Conflict in Young Children," *JASP*, July, 1948, pp. 300–310; Dorothy F. Beck, "The Dynamics of Group Psychotherapy as Seen by a Sociologist," *Sociometry*, June, 1958, pp. 98–128, and Sept., 1958, pp. 180–197; and Max Rosenbaum and Milton Berger, *Group Psychotherapy and Group Function*, Basic Books, 1963.

Patterns of discrimination and segregation that lasted, in the United States, for three-quarters of a century after the abolition of slavery, began to break up in the 1940s. These patterns have become the target of a powerful movement, involving a larger share of Negroes than were ever before participants in active protests, a substantial number of Whites, and more recently Chicanos, Puerto Ricans, Indians, and others. The movement has evolved through several stages, with different strategies, different participants, and different kinds of conflict. Although there has been overlap and accumulation of strategies, rather than sharply divided periods, we might call 1944–1954 the "constitutional stage," marked at the beginning by the Supreme Court ruling against white primaries and at the end by the Court ruling against *de jure* school segregation.[1]

The next stage has two related but distinct parts. It is the period of nonviolent, but active protest against discrimination by private individuals and groups, but also of extensive statutory changes that register the same protest. Perhaps the beginning of the private campaign can be marked by the Montgomery bus boycott, 1955–1956, and its conclusion by the March on Washington, 1963, when 210,000 persons, Negro and white, joined Martin Luther King, Jr., to proclaim "I have a dream" of a society without discrimination and prejudice. Both frequency and intensity of protests had been mounting since 1955, and by 1963 there were, within a few months, over 1000 demonstrations, marches, sit-ins, and protest meetings that demanded equality of treatment. These actions registered themselves politically in a series of unprecedented legal actions by U.S. Congress (state legislative action had begun as early as 1945). In a series of civil rights bills, 1957–1965, the Congress removed any doubt that might have been left by the Supreme Court decisions that racial or religious discrimination that in any way involved public actions, officials, or monies was illegal.

The third stage to which we shall refer also has various elements. We might call it the "black power period," but with the involvement of numerous minorities it has become polychrome. It burst onto the scene, not without some preliminary noise elsewhere, in the form of the 1965 Los Angeles Watts riot and in a succession of other riots in Chicago, Cleveland, Detroit, Newark, and elsewhere, leaving scores dead, thousands wounded, and hundreds of millions of dollars of damage. Out of the ashes black power emerged as a rallying cry and to some degree as a strategy. Legal and political efforts were downgraded; cooperation with Whites was sharply reduced; Negroes were seen by some as a colony within the nation, unlikely to get out of their colonial status without militancy.

We shall examine some aspects of this third stage below. In the light of past experience, it seems likely that it will not last more than a few years into the 1970s, and by the late 1970s it may seem as outmoded as the "pre-Montgomery" pattern of mild constitutional reform appears today. What will follow depends upon national action. If seeds of constructive change that have already been planted are nourished and brought to fruition, the late 1960s may prove to have been the peak of conflict, to be followed by more constructive modes of change. Perhaps a congressional black caucus will be the more typical form of protest for the 1970s. However, if lack of imagination, inertia, unwill-

---

[1] This should not be read to mean that protests suddenly began in the 1940s. For comments on the immediately preceding period see Richard M. Dalfiume, "Stirrings of Revolt," in Allen Weinstein and Frank O. Gatell (eds.), *The Segregation Era: 1863–1954*, Oxford, 1970, pp. 235–247.

ingness to pay a large price for an even larger gain, distraction by other problems, and prejudice prevent effective action with reference to America's minorities, the nation may be faced with mounting tragedy.

These three stages have in common a shift from primary interest in prejudice to major concern over discrimination. Some scholars, as well as action leaders, have taken the position that prejudice has little to do with intergroup relations, that these vary with the social structure, not with changes in individual attitudes.[2] We support this emphasis on sociological factors as a strategic matter, and would only caution against swinging the pendulum too far in that direction. There are some situations in which attention to individual attitudes may be the most strategic approach. In general, these would be situations where the effort to improve the status of disprivileged persons has little community backing, where law, tradition, and the stratification patterns firmly support discrimination. Even under more favorable circumstances, it is a mistake to disregard individual prejudices entirely. Major attention should often be given to discrimination, but to overlook hostile attitudes is to be blind to a possible stumbling block.

Nevertheless, the recent shift in emphasis is based on sound observation and theory. Many studies show that individual behavior can be modified by changes in the situation, independently of personality structure. Or, to put this in terms that we believe theoretically more adequate, a high proportion of persons have tendencies toward nondiscrimination that may be called out by strategic situational changes even though such tendencies normally are dormant. There are, in Merton's terms, many fair-weather liberals and illiberals. Group supports, legal sanctions, economic pressures, firm action on the part of leaders can create the kind of climate in which their nondiscriminatory tendencies bloom.[3]

COMPROMISE VERSUS CONTENTION

Does this emphasis on discrimination mean that the extent of opposition is unimportant in strategic considerations? In our judgment it does not. It is an emphasis appropriate to the contemporary American scene, but not necessarily to all other situations. In facing problems of discrimination against members of minority groups, the wise strategist will try to decide to what degree the practices should be opposed directly and immediately, and to what degree they should be attacked indirectly by eroding away their supports. Enthusiastic supporters sometimes defend a particular approach as *the* strategy, as if a willingness to compromise or a flat refusal to compromise with discriminatory practices were wise in every situation. A skilled general knows when to retreat, when to consolidate, and when to advance. In intergroup relations, the problem is to determine when a vigorous program is likely to be successful *despite* the opposition it will arouse in some people, and when compromise is required *despite* the short-run sacrifice of some aspects of one's ultimate goal. It is scarcely necessary to note that the latter is more necessary when one has few allies, when prejudices are widespread, when the discriminatory practices are deeply embedded in the social structure.

The strategist must decide not only the degree of contention and the degree of compromise that he will use, but also the way in which his program will be carried on. There can be compromise that represents almost complete capitulation. ("We mustn't raise that issue, for it will arouse too much hostil-

[2] See, for example, Herbert Blumer, "Race Prejudice as a Sense of Group Position," *Pacific Sociological Review*, Spring, 1958, pp. 3–7; see also Arnold M. Rose, "Intergroup Relations vs. Prejudice," *SP*, Oct., 1956, pp. 173–176; Warren Breed, "Group Structure and Resistance to Desegregation in the Deep South," *SP*, Summer, 1962, pp. 84–94; Muzafer Sherif and Robert Faris in Muzafer Sherif (ed.), *Intergroup Relations and Leadership*, Wiley, 1962, pp. 3–45; Dietrich Reitzes, "Institutional Structure and Race Relations," *Phylon*, Spring, 1959, pp. 48–66; and Edwin H. Rhyne, "Racial Prejudice and Personality Scales: An Alternative Approach," *SF*, Oct., 1962, pp. 44–53.

[3] For a development of this point in general theoretical terms, see J. Milton Yinger, *Toward a Field Theory of Behavior*, McGraw-Hill, 1965, chap. 11.

ity; we need a program of education") ; and there can be compromise that keeps long-run goals clearly in mind while making necessary day-by-day adjustments. There can be contention that effectively prevents the very thing it is trying to do, by arousing hostile opposition; and there can be contention that destroys a discriminatory pattern. Ineffective contention is often the kind that attacks individuals, that blames them for their discriminations, rather than trying to understand them. It is usually necessary to secure the cooperation of the discriminator in changing an unhappy situation. This is not likely to be accomplished by exposing him to ridicule, attacking him as a person, and generally threatening his security. Opposition to discriminators is very different from opposition to discrimination.

The Place of Law and Administration

In recent years there have been substantial efforts to reduce discrimination through the use of law and administrative decisions. These efforts, many of which we have described in previous chapters, are indications that many people—including most social scientists—now challenge an earlier belief that law was impotent to enforce interracial justice. In this challenge, there has sometimes been a failure to seek out the conditions under which law is most likely to be effective. Some observers, looking at the problem from the perspective of the United States today, a setting in which the legal approach is relatively effective, have simply reversed the earlier dogma to affirm that law is the crucial weapon in the flight to improve intergroup relations. The scientific task, however, is not to assert one position or the other, but is to analyze factors involved in the variation in the effectiveness of an approach through law. In our judgment it can best be described as a "middle strategy." It is unnecessary to wait until everybody in a society is ready for a change before it can be incorporated into law, as the extensive emphasis on the situational approach that we have given throughout this volume makes clear. On the other hand, to pass a law that has little support

in other institutional patterns is a relatively ineffective move, although it may not be entirely meaningless. The fate of efforts in the United Nations to protect minorities shows that it is too early to hope to reduce discrimination substantially by international legal action. This does not mean that the efforts are not worth while; but it means that far more preparation by way of economic strength for minorities, shared values, the reduction of stereotypes and traditional prejudices, the relaxation of fear of war, and the like, is necessary before international legal action to protect minorities can be particularly helpful.[4]

Within the United States and many other societies, however, the necessary preparation for improving intergroup relations through the organized political community has been accomplished. Indeed, the analyses of social scientists concerning the nature and consequences of segregation are among the preparations. The Supreme Court and other judicial bodies and, more obscurely, the legislative branches of government have relied on the knowledge of social science for some aspects of their decisions.

With respect to the general strategic problem of compromise versus contention, in sum, we do not take an *a priori* position in favor of immediate legal and other forms of direct action or one that supports more indirect and long-run methods. What will be effective in one setting may fail in another; and in virtually every case a variety of approaches is required. An effort that might fail by itself can be a valuable element in a larger strategy. Education and conciliation, for example, may leave the tough institutional structure of discrimination undisturbed; but in a situation where vigorous direct action is also undertaken they may smooth the process of change. Legal action by itself may run into massive resistance or reluctant compliance that returns at once to the old patterns when surveillance is removed; but in a situation where educational and conciliatory processes

[4] For several valuable papers dealing with law and conflict, see David J. Danelski (issue ed.), "Law and Conflict Resolution," *Journal of Conflict Resolution* (whole issue), Mar., 1967.

have also been at work, gains won by legal coercion may gradually get the support of personal conviction and institutional practice.[5]

Underlying this statement on strategy is our belief that on the level of theory we also need a blend of separate, even superficially contradictory, views—a theory of conflict resolution, but also a theory of conflict. Neither is highly developed. Yet we are beginning to get the attention, building on often highly valuable earlier work, that both require. In 1957 the *Journal of Conflict Resolution* was founded; it is a focal point and symbol of growing scientific interest in this vital field.[6] We are also witnessing some revival of interest in the theory of conflict, building on the pioneering work of Georg Simmel.[7] In our view, the aim of policy should not be the elimination of conflict, but its redirection into constructive channels. The relatively open and public conflict of a strike may be preferable to the covert "sabotage" and demoralization of workers who have no way of expressing their grievances. A massive assault on segregation barriers by freedom marchers and crowds may be preferable to the self-destructive bitterness and the lack of motivation of the dispossessed. What we need, therefore, is a complex theory both of conflict resolution and of the consequences of various forms of conflict.

ORGANIZATIONS OPPOSING DISCRIMINATION

One of the most significant developments in recent years has been the growth of the pro-fession of intergroup relations and the increase in the number of organizations whose programs, wholly or in part, are dedicated to the reduction of prejudice and discrimination. Two forces are involved in this development. Minority-group members have established a vast variety of organizations whose aim is the elimination of their own disprivileges and those of other minorities; and out of the total community have come other groups, public and private, concerned with the full realization of democratic values. These two sources are, of course, not distinct.

Protest organizations and movements have a long history in the United States. Negro opposition to slavery, the abolition movement, immigrant protective associations were important in the nineteenth century. Requisites for effective organization, however, were often lacking. Literacy, trained leadership, some economic power in the hands of the minorities, and a growing awareness of the costs of discrimination in the dominant group create a situation in which opposition to disprivilege can be much more effective. By the twentieth century these influences had grown; and by 1940, in particular, an environment favorable to a massive attack on discrimination had been created.

This situation is reflected in the rapid growth in the number and power of organizations concerned with intergroup relations and in the concomitant increase in specialized personnel. There are several hundred intergroup relations agencies, local, state, or national, with paid professional staffs. Doubtless there are at least as large a number working on a continuous basis with volunteer personnel, in addition to scores of temporary commissions and committees that have been formed in recent years.

As more and more people have been drawn into the field of intergroup relations as a full-time occupation, it has gone through the process of "professionalization." A body of principles has developed to guide their work, a program of training for staff members, coordinating organizations for the exchange of experience, and professional publications for research and information. This process is by no means complete. It will doubtless be

[5] For an interesting study of the effects of law in another area of interest, see John Colombotos, "Physicians and Medicare: A Before-After Study of the Effects of Legislation on Attitudes," *ASR*, June, 1969, pp. 318–334.

[6] See, for example, the Mar., 1959 issue for a number of articles on a general theory of conflict reduction and nonviolence as a strategy.

[7] See Georg Simmel, *Conflict*, trans. by Kurt Wolff, Free Press, 1955; Lewis Coser, *The Functions of Social Conflict*, Free Press, 1956; Lewis Coser, *Continuities in* the Study of Social Conflict, Free Press, 1967; Clinton F. Fink, "Some Conceptual Difficulties in the Theory of Social Conflict," *Journal of Conflict Resolution*, Dec., 1968, pp. 412–460.

some time before we have graduate schools of "intergroup relations" to match our medical schools (or more probably, departments of intergroup relations in professional schools of "social engineering"). But steps in this direction have been taken at several universities and it seems highly probable that further development along this line will take place.

A focal point of this professionalization is the National Association of Intergroup Relations Officials (NAIRO), an organization founded in 1947, with a membership (1970) of 1600 professional workers. NAIRO describes itself as follows:

. . . an organization of individuals concerned with advancing intergroup relations knowledge and skills, improving the standards of professional intergroup relations practice, and furthering acceptance of the goals and principles of intergroup relations work.

NAIRO seeks to further these purposes through: Exchange of experience and knowledge among professional workers and others concerned with racial, religious, and ethnic relationships.

Study, analysis, and research on problems and developments affecting intergroup relations.

Collection, compilation, and dissemination of information and ideas regarding programs, methods, and techniques.[8]

Alongside public and private nonprofit agencies, there has developed a new kind of business firm, specializing in race relations consulting, recruitment of personnel from minority groups, and helping to design government programs. There are now perhaps 250 such firms, most of them owned and operated by Negroes. Their primary aim is not to reduce discrimination; they are businesses, not unlike white-operated agencies that specialize in consulting and employment services. Nevertheless, their work is partly motivated by the desire to change patterns of discrimination; and, whatever the intent, such work affects those patterns. Faced with legal and public pressure to add black employees, particularly on skilled and management levels, many companies have turned to these race-relations consultants for help. Won-

[8] *JIR*, Autumn, 1961, p. 291.

dering why their sales are low among Negroes, or hoping to expand their markets, firms have sought guidance from Negro market specialists—often discovering in the process how poorly tuned they were to the sensitivities, styles, and tastes of black Americans. This new occupation adds one more dimension to the intergroup relations profession.[9]

Public and Quasi-Public Agencies in Intergroup Relations

We cannot begin even to list the numerous agencies and departments of various organizations now concerned with intergroup relations. Among public agencies there are the staffs of fair employment and fair educational practices commissions,[10] administrators of public housing, school officers, and advisers in various branches of the federal government and in the armed services. We discussed some aspects of their work in earlier chapters. Although they often have legal powers to enforce their decisions, their emphasis is much more strongly on conciliation and education. In only a small proportion of cases are the coercions of law employed.

Perhaps the most general of the agencies is the U.S. Civil Rights Commission. Its mandate is extremely broad, with its emphases changing from year to year as the national situation changes.

The U.S. Commission on Civil Rights is a temporary, independent, bipartisan agency established by Congress in 1957 and directed to:

Investigate complaints alleging that citizens are being deprived of their right to vote by reason of their race, color, religion, or national origin, or by reason of fraudulent practices;

Study and collect information concerning legal developments constituting a denial of equal protection of the laws under the Constitution;

[9] See Saul Friedman, "Race Relations Is Their Business," *The New York Times Magazine*, Oct. 25, 1970, pp. 44–69.

[10] For a careful study of one state agency, see Leon H. Mayhew, *Law and Equal Opportunity: A Study of the Massachusetts Commission Against Discrimination*, Harvard, 1968.

Appraise Federal laws and policies with respect to equal protection of the laws;

Serve as a national clearinghouse for information in respect to denial of equal protection of the laws; and

Submit reports, findings, and recommendations to the President and the Congress.[11]

On the local level there has been an extensive development of "community relations boards" or "mayor's committees," as they are frequently named. Some of these may be called quasi-public, for they are primarily advisory and have no official status. But many have been established by community ordinance and have professional staffs (with membership from one to over 30) financed out of public funds.[12]

The municipal agencies have handicaps as forces in the movement to reduce discrimination, but they also have some significant strengths and accomplishments. Most of them work on small budgets; but financial support is increasing, and by 1962 the largest municipal commission, that of New York City, had a budget of nearly half a million dollars. They are often affected by the local political situation. This can be an advantage insofar as minority groups are in a balance-of-power position. More often, however, it is a disadvantage, because those seeking to hold or gain political power will give only token support to the agency if powerful interests in the community oppose the agency's recommendations on housing, recreation, or job opportunities. This is not to criticize the skill of the various mayor's committees, but only to suggest that they work within the framework of an often difficult political structure. Matching difficulties are found on the national level, of course, as any student of Congress will attest.

Partly because of policy and partly because of budget limitations, mayor's committees usually work closely with the schools, with private agencies, with other municipal organizations. Again, this is a source of both strength and weakness. The agency gains in strength if it can get the support and employ the facilities of other groups. Wide community sponsorship may thus be secured for a project that could not be sustained by the community relations board itself. But the need to rely on other groups for implementation can also be a source of weakness. As every professional staff person knows, the best of plans may be seriously weakened as they are passed from group to group, from community relations board to coordinating committee to city council.

Despite the obstacles faced by local civic unity groups, they have made important contributions to intergroup relations in many cities. They have countered violence and the threat of violence with firmness, with facts and open discussion. They have helped to reduce discrimination in city employment, particularly by increasing the employment of Negroes in police departments, schools, and public transportation. They have worked closely with city administrations, school officials, and fair employment practices commissions (which in some instances—Cleveland, Gary, Youngstown, Philadelphia—are part of the same agency). A few community relations boards have been assigned responsibilities in connection with public housing, and most of the boards are concerned with housing problems. There is little doubt that these agencies occupy a strategically important place in the efforts to reduce discrimination in American cities.

Private Organizations in the Field of Racial and Cultural Relations

Complementing the official agencies concerned with intergroup relations are many private associations dedicated wholly or in part to the reduction of prejudice and discrimination and the enlargement of opportunities for minorities. They range from temporary local groups formed to try to solve a particular problem to permanent national groups with large professional staffs and an-

[11] U.S. Commission on Civil Rights, *For All the People . . . By All the People*, Government Printing Office, 1969, p. ii.

[12] For a discussion of the comparative effectiveness of private councils and public commissions, see Richard Robbins, "Local Strategy in Race Relations: The Illinois Experience with Community Human Relations Commissions and Councils," *JIR*, Autumn, 1961, pp. 311–324.

nual budgets over a million dollars.[13] Some are concerned with civil rights generally, others with the special problems of particular racial or ethnic groups. Some emphasize education, others are involved in action programs. We cannot describe fully even a small number, but will mention a few here in order to note the range and importance of their programs.

National Association for the Advancement of Colored People. The NAACP, founded in 1909, works for the elimination of segregation and discrimination against Negroes and other Americans. For the most part, it seeks its objectives through court and legislative action, although it has participated to some degree in the demonstrations and protest marches of the civil rights movement and has given legal and financial support to others in this movement. Campaigns for equality have been waged in the fields of housing, employment, education, recreation, law, travel, the armed forces, voting, and officeholding. Efforts have also been made to ban residential segregation, to secure passage of antilynching laws, and to bring about cooperation between religious organizations and the NAACP. The Research Department has compiled a large quantity of material on race relations and civil rights, and the national office has published a monthly journal, *The Crisis,* since 1910.

The NAACP is a militant organization but one that operates within the framework of the democratic ideology and the democratic society. Before the "Negro revolt" of the 1960s, it was regarded by many Whites, especially in the South, and by some upper-class Negroes, as a radical organization; actually it had adopted at an early date various measures to exclude Communists from its membership. And in the spectrum of current organizations in the civil rights field, the NAACP seems quite conservative.[14]

At the local level the NAACP serves as a legal-aid society; but in fighting for the Negro's rights at the national level it selects cases for their strategic importance, and insofar as possible, enters the courts only where there is good chance of success. Lawyers of national reputation, who may or may not be members of the organization's legal staff, cooperate with local attorneys in arguing a case of key importance. Frequently it is expected that the decision will be adverse in the lower courts, but cases are prepared with extreme care so that they will stand up in the higher courts. In Chapter 14 we discussed some of the outstanding cases that the NAACP has taken to the U.S. Supreme Court. Among these are the white primary, residential segregation by municipal ordinance, private residential restrictive covenants, and the admission of Negroes to schools, colleges, and graduate training supported by public funds. The NAACP has won most of the several dozen cases it has argued before the Supreme Court.

The NAACP is an interracial organization, but its membership is preponderantly Negro. As its strength has grown and as the number of trained Negroes has increased, the influence of white members and officers has declined at the national level. It is doubtless more effective on the national than on the local level, but local activity has increased in recent years. There are about 1750 branches, youth councils, and college chapters, with a total membership of 462,000. The professional staff, headed by Roy Wilkins, totals about 150 persons; income in

[13] Figures for budgets, membership, and staff change from year to year. Those that we cite, for illustrative purposes, are mostly for the late 1960s or 1970. Those interested in the data for the current year may consult standard reference works and the official publications of the agencies themselves. In the material that follows we have drawn on the *Encyclopedia of Associations, National Organizations of the U.S.,* Gale Research Co., vol. 1, 6th ed., 1970; National Association of Intergroup Relations Officials, *Directory* of Intergroup Relations Agencies with Paid Professional Personnel, 1959; Morris Fine and Milton Himmelfarb (eds.), *American Jewish Yearbook,* Vol. 71, American Jewish Committee and Jewish Publication Society of America, 1970; *The New York Times,* July 5, 1970 and June 28, 1970; and various official publications.

[14] Not, however, to the Army. In a 1968 directive to its intelligence agents, released in 1971, the Army sought information on "Aims and activities of groups attempting to create, prolong, or aggravate racial tensions." NAACP, SCLC, CORE, and SNCC were among the groups listed. *The Plain Dealer,* Feb. 28, 1971, p. 1.

1969 was nearly $4 million.[15] In addition, there is the associated, but legally separate, NAACP Legal Defense and Education Fund, with a staff of 25 lawyers, of which Jack Greenberg is the chief counsel, and a $3 million annual budget. It serves as the legal arm of the civil rights movement generally.

The NAACP has been the subject of rather continuous criticism, either for being too militant (as segregationists believe, of course, but as some "moderates"—e.g., William Faulkner and Chet Huntley—also declare) or for being too conservative (as some participants in the current "Negro revolt" believe). In our judgment, however, the NAACP has been, and continues to be, an unusually effective organization in the fields of civil rights and civil liberties. Because it has specialized in legal and court action, it has not been the major force in the direct protests of recent years. Before turning to a brief statement concerning some of the organizations that have been more thoroughly involved in those protests, we should like to comment on their relationship to the NAACP and to such other "older" organizations as the National Urban League. Our judgment is as follows: (1) There is a need for several types of organization; too closely unified a movement would be weaker than present diversity. (2) There was a "lag" after the surge of the Negro revolt was apparent, before the NAACP and the Urban League recognized their power and their importance; they were dominated by a middle-class perspective that did not at once alert them to the strength of the demands for "freedom now." Faced by the challenges of new organizations, however, they joined the revolt in their own ways and have supported it effectively; as organiza-

tions they have proved to be highly adaptable. (3) There is some conflict among the groups, and perhaps some undesirable rivalry akin to "jurisdictional disputes" among labor unions. Strategy—particularly the question of the degree of militancy—sometimes has been influenced by leadership competition rather than an analysis of the problems at hand. There are more important structural sources of these disputes, however, as we shall note below.[16] The result is that the NAACP, while it has expanded its National Board, to bring in a wider range of Negro views, has reduced the proportion of white Board members (from 22 percent, 1963, to 12 percent, 1969), has endorsed—and to some degree participated in—nonviolent action projects, and has severely criticized President Nixon's Administration for its racial policies, nevertheless maintains its essentially integrationist approach. For example, Roy Wilkins has criticized Negro students for separatist policies, their willingness to withdraw into campus ghettos. In return, Roy Innis, national director of CORE, declared that Wilkins consistently opposed "the legitimate aspirations of black people. . . . We are against the policy of integration and assimilation being offered by Mr. Wilkins."[17] Judging by most evidences, however, the majority of black people interpret their aspirations differently from Mr. Innis. As of the early 1970s, the policies and goals of the NAACP continue to be most frequently approved by black Americans.

Southern Christian Leadership Conference. In 1955–1956 the Montgomery Improvement Association, in Alabama, successfully carried through a long and difficult boycott of city buses. The well-disciplined, nonviolent technique of the Negro group attracted national attention and brought its leader, the Reverend Martin Luther King, Jr., into the front ranks of the civil rights movement. To extend the use of nonviolent but direct resist-

[15] See Langston Hughes, *Fight for Freedom. The Story of the NAACP*, Norton, 1962; Wilson Record, "Negro Intellectual Leadership in the NAACP," *Phylon*, Fourth Quarter, 1956, pp. 375–388; Walter White, *A Man Called White*, Viking, 1948; Anthony Lewis, *Portrait of a Decade: The Second American Revolution*, Random House, 1964; Loren Miller, *The Petitioners: The Story of the Supreme Court of the United States and the Negro*, Pantheon, 1966; Clement E. Vose, *Caucasians Only: The Supreme Court, the NAACP, and the Restrictive Covenant Cases*, Univ. of California Press, 1959.

[16] See Elliott Rudwick and August Meier, "Organizational Structure and Goal Succession: A Comparative Analysis of the NAACP and CORE, 1964–1968," *Social Science Quarterly*, June, 1970, pp. 9–24.

[17] See *The New York Times*, Jan. 15, 1969, p. 42-M and Jan. 22, 1969, p. 25.

ance to segregation and discrimination, King and others formed the Southern Christian Leadership Conference. For two or three years SCLC was active in several local campaigns but was not a major influence in the desegregation process. Then beginning with the sit-ins of 1960, the freedom-rides of 1961, and the crescendo of protests in 1963, SCLC leaped to prominence. By 1963 it had a paid staff of 43, with the Reverend Wyatt T. Walker as executive director, and a budget of nearly half a million dollars. King had become, by almost any reckoning, the most influential Negro of the day, not as the administrator of an organization, but as a charismatic leader and the most articulate voice of Negro aspirations.

Something of the approach of the SCLC to race relations is expressed in the following statement:

The Southern Christian Leadership Conference has the basic aim of achieving full citizenship rights, equality, and the integration of the Negro in all aspects of American life. . .

The basic tenets of Hebraic-Christian tradition coupled with the Gandhian concept of *satyagraha*—truth force—is at the heart of SCLC's philosophy. Christian nonviolence actively resists evil in any form. It never seeks to humiliate the opponent, only to win him. Suffering is accepted without retaliation. Internal violence of the spirit is as much to be rejected as external physical violence. At the center of nonviolence is redemptive love. Creatively used, the philosophy of nonviolence can restore the broken community in America. . . .

SCLC sees civil disobedience as a natural consequence of nonviolence when the resister is confronted by unjust and immoral laws. This does not imply that SCLC advocates either anarchy or lawlessness. The Conference firmly believes that all people have a moral responsibility to obey laws that are just. It recognizes, however, that there also are unjust laws. From a purely moral point of view, an unjust law is one that is out of harmony with the moral law of the universe, or, as the religionist would say, out of harmony with the Law of God. More concretely, an unjust law is one in which the minority is compelled to observe a code which is not binding on the majority. . . . In the face of such obvious inequality, where difference is

made legal, the nonviolent resister has no alternative but to disobey the unjust law. In disobeying such a law, he does so peacefully, openly and nonviolently. Most important, he *willingly* accepts the penalty for breaking the law.[18]

Although King preached nonviolence throughout his career, which ended with his murder in 1968, he did adopt a more militant stance in the last two years. He spoke of civil disobedience to disrupt American society; urged black control and ownership of the ghettos; and used a rhetoric that was close to that of Black Power advocates. He continued to call for cooperation with Whites, however, and for the attainment of an integrated society. In an article written shortly before he was killed, he opposed those who were suggesting that rioting was a necessary and valuable strategy. ". . . I am convinced that if rioting continues, it will strengthen the right wing of the country, and we'll end up with a kind of right-wing take-over in the cities and a Fascist development, which will be terribly injurious to the whole nation."[19]

Some observers, particularly those who take a radically militant point of view, believe that King's approach reached its peak in 1963 and was replaced by a nonintegrationist black power strategy in the mid-1960s. The evidence does not support this belief. The new-breed radicals appeal to a minority of the American black population; their calls for drastic change and the elimination of discrimination, of course, are joined by the vast majority; but full equality within society, achieved by forceful but nonviolent methods, are the policies receiving most support. When the Harris poll, in 1970, asked a national sample of Negroes which leaders they thought "very effective," the percentages were as follows:

[18] From a leaflet, "This Is SCLC," quoted in August Meier, Elliott Rudwick, and Frances L. Broderick (eds.), *Black Protest Thought in the Twentieth Century*, Bobbs-Merrill, 2nd ed., 1971, pp. 303–305. For various statements of SCLC perspective, see pp. 291–306, 346–351, and 584–595 of this work. See also Martin Luther King, Jr.'s books, *Stride Toward Freedom*, Harper & Row, 1958; *Why We Can't Wait*, Harper & Row, 1963; and *The Trumpet of Conscience*, Harper & Row, 1968.

[19] Meier, Rudwick, and Broderick, *op. cit.*, p. 592.

Elected black officials	71%
Civil rights leaders, such as the NAACP	67%
Black ministers and religious leaders	56%
Leaders of black militant groups	29%[20]

A *Newsweek* poll taken one year earlier showed that King remained a dominant figure. ". . . King, in death, remains by far the most revered Negro leader—and . . . no one alive is even close. King's standing today has passed from hero-worship to beatification: he is rated favorably by 95 percent of the sample, excellent by 83 percent. The martial young loved King as much as the walk-soft old, the North as well as the South."[21]

It is difficult to interpret these data. Perhaps King is revered, but his difficult strategy not followed; perhaps those who oppose the philosophy of the SCLC are more active and influential than those who support it— clearly they are more visible and articulate. His full impact can certainly not be assessed until the survival value of his approach is tested through two or three further stages in the race relations process.[22]

It is not clear what the influence and direction of SCLC will be, whatever the continuing importance of militant, nonviolent integrationism may be. After three years, the Reverend Ralph D. Abernathy has been more successful in holding the group together than many thought possible, considering the overriding symbolic importance of King. There are disagreements over strategy within the group, however, and some competition for leadership, with the Reverend Jesse Jackson, a younger, more charismatic, and more aggressive leader, challenging Abernathy for authority. As with the other major organizations, the national setting, more than the individuals involved, will influence the

[20] *Time*, Apr. 6, 1970, p. 29.
[21] *Newsweek*, June 30, 1969, pp. 14–15.
[22] Two useful books about King seemed rather heavily influenced by the critical mood of the late 1960s. We think they underestimate his long-run significance. See C. Eric Lincoln (ed.), *Martin Luther King, Jr.*, Hill and Wang, 1970; and David L. Lewis, *King: A Critical Biography*, Praeger, 1970.

direction of development of SCLC. It will fade out or change drastically if racial discrimination is not reduced rapidly. In a more favorable environment, it will evolve in ways consonant with the life and view of Martin Luther King.

Student Nonviolent Coordinating Committee. Following the dramatic and successful desegregation of lunch counters in Greensboro, North Carolina, in February, 1960, student groups throughout the South adopted the nonviolent method of seeking equal treatment in parks, restaurants, theaters, swimming pools, and other facilities. In April, Martin Luther King called together leaders of various student groups, meeting at Shaw University, Raleigh, North Carolina, and out of their conversations came the Student Nonviolent Coordinating Committee. Although intended, perhaps, as an arm of SCLC, SNCC soon broke away. There was some rivalry over leadership, some disagreements over the timing and coordination of protests between the student leaders and King. After a few months SNCC was more formally organized, established a central office in Atlanta, and became separate not only from SCLC but also from the informal student groups on college campuses. By 1963 it had a staff of about 70 persons, headed by John Lewis, many of them drawing only subsistence pay, and a budget of $160,000. It was particularly effective in voter registration, often in the "hard-core" areas least influenced by the integration movement.

Disagreements over strategy and goals became more severe within SNCC during the mid-1960s. It was caught up in the Black Power movement, Stokely Carmichael became its chairman in 1966, and the nonviolent philosophy was set aside. H. Rap Brown, Carmichael's successor as chairman, was even more vehement in his verbal attacks. The organization continued to support voter registration effectively, but began to organize all-Negro parties, as in Lowndes County, Alabama, under the Black Panther emblem.[23]

[23] See Stokely Carmichael and Charles V. Hamilton, *Black Power*, Random House, 1967, chap. 5.

In 1970, the name of the organization was changed to the Student National Coordination Committee; but by that time it had faded out as a major national organization, its new militant approach being taken up by CORE, and in a more extreme way by the Black Panthers.[24]

National Urban League. One of the oldest Negro organizations, the National Urban League, founded in 1910, has operated primarily as a social work agency. A large part of its work is devoted to the extension of economic opportunities to Negroes in industry, business, and the professions and to the improvement of housing. This objective is sought through discussions and conferences with business executives, industrialists, and labor union officials. Many Urban Leagues now provide clients with expert testing and counseling services in the professional, technical, clerical, skilled, and semiskilled job categories. Other activities include providing information about Negroes, serving as adviser to governmental agencies and industry on health, welfare, and employment matters affecting Negroes, developing programs to provide for the adjustment and social needs of in-migrant Negro workers, and assisting in the interracial planning of social services and community projects.

The Urban League maintains 98 branches in cities throughout the country. Its professional staff of 1200 persons is the largest of the predominantly Negro civil rights groups. Although the League has taken little direct part in the protest demonstrations of the last several years, preferring to specialize in job training and placement and various social welfare programs, it has recently taken a more militant stand. The late Whitney Young, Jr., executive director for 10 years, proposed programs for Negroes similar to

veterans' benefits to compensate for the years of disprivilege, or a domestic "Marshall plan" to bring Negroes rapidly into the mainstream of American society. The plan would guarantee a job for everyone willing and able to work and called for the building of one million low- and medium-income housing units a year to eliminate slums.

Young was fairly optimistic, for he could see changes, particularly in the job situation. He estimated, for example, that through the work of the National Urban League, 40,000 jobs were opened to Negroes in 1966, compared with 2000 in 1961.[25] He was among the most caustic and vigorous in his descriptions and condemnation of discrimination and injustice; but he preferred to try to persuade people to change rather than to attack them.[26] He did not accept the label "moderate." "No one is for gradualism; no one counsels patience; no one thinks in terms of compromise. So the famous 'moderate versus militant' is imaginary. What exists is militancy versus extremism, and that is really a question of responsibility against irresponsibility; sanity against insanity; building versus burning."[27]

Young died in March, 1971. Beginning in 1972, Vernon Jordan, a lawyer who is director of the United Negro College Fund became executive director of the National Urban League. For several years, Jordan was involved in the Voter Education Project; and he may complement the previous interest of the Urban League in jobs and housing with more interest in political participation by Blacks.

Southern Regional Council. Successor to the Commission on Interracial Cooperation, which was founded in 1919, the Southern Regional Council is a research and action agency primarily devoted to keeping open and extending the channels of communication be-

[24] On the first several years of SNCC, see Howard Zinn, *SNCC: The New Abolitionists*, Beacon Press, 1966. For documents showing the changes in strategy, See Meier, Rudwick, and Broderick, *op. cit.*, pp. 307–315, 352–360, 484–490. A book expressing the highly militant view of SNCC after 1966 is Julius Lester, *Look Out Whitey, Black Power's Gon' Get Your Mama*, Dial, 1968. There are many references to SNCC in Harry Edwards, *Black Students*, Free Press, 1970.

[25] *The New York Times*, Jan. 8, 1967, p. 54.
[26] Two books are essential reading for the student of Young's approach and the National Urban League: Whitney M. Young, Jr., *To Be Equal*, McGraw-Hill, 1964; and Whitney M. Young, Jr., *Beyond Racism: Building an Open Society*, McGraw-Hill, 1969.
[27] Whitney M. Young, Jr., quoted in *The Plain Dealer*, Aug. 21, 1967, p. 11.

tween Negroes and Whites in the South. The 100 persons who make up the interracial council are drawn primarily from religious and educational organizations. There is a staff of 23. It is one of the few interracial groups in the South to have worked steadily through many years to reduce the tension and conflict that rest upon lack of information and lack of communication. Closely associated with the Council is a panel of social scientists and human relations workers and a number of affiliated agencies and councils throughout the South.

Congress of Racial Equality. Founded in 1942, CORE had quietly applied the techniques of nonviolence and the sit-in, largely in the North, for many years before it was brought to prominent attention by the Negro revolt of the 1960s. CORE was established first as a committee of the pacifist Fellowship of Reconciliation in an effort to apply Gandhian techniques of vigorous, nonviolent resistance to American race relations. It has pioneered in the training of interracial groups for peaceful picketing, sit-ins, and negotiation. In recent years it has greatly expanded its activities and now has 70,000 members and a staff of 70 plus a number of "subsistence workers."

The first president was James Farmer, one of the original organizers, a conscientious objector during World War II, and a disciple of Gandhi. During its first 15 years, CORE was primarily a middle-class organization; but with the success of the Montgomery bus boycott in 1956, under King's leadership, Negro organizations throughout the country began to see possibilities in mass action. CORE began to move quite rapidly in that direction with the sharp increase in sit-in protests and freedom rides in 1961. Thus King, who had been influenced by CORE and its nonviolent programs, in turn brought CORE, somewhat paradoxically, into a more militant phase of the civil-rights movement. The transformation from an integrationist, nonviolent, yet very active and uncompromising organization, into a separatist, angry, and highly militant if not violent organization, took place over a period of just a few years.

Farmer himself marks the transformation by a dramatic event: "For CORE, nonviolence—never a way of life, but only a strategy—ended on a balmy night, September 1, 1963, in a sleepy town on the Mississippi, when a uniformed mob screamed for my blood. The casketless hearse in which I escaped became for CORE a symbol of the burial of peace."[28]

Whatever the timing, by 1964 CORE was a black nationalist, not an integrationist organization. Its membership, which had been predominantly white, was by that time mainly black. Some Whites remain, however, on the advisory committee. Floyd McKissick became the national director in 1966 and Roy Innis in 1969, both more separatist than Farmer, although the latter had moved significantly in that direction and remains as chairman of the advisory committee.[29] It is somewhat ironic to read that CORE, a pioneer in breaking down walls of segregation, in 1970 proposed separate schools for Blacks and Whites, with each race controlling its own. Innis said that CORE had talked with the governors of Georgia, Alabama, Mississippi, and Louisiana, and "all conceded that the plane could fly, that their side could live with it."[30] Thus, for some, has the civil rights movement come full circle.

There has not been extensive sociological study of private, voluntary race relations organizations that would help us to explain why one remains "on course," while another changes its direction sharply or disappears.[31]

[28] James Farmer in the Foreword to Inge P. Bell, *Core and the Strategy of Nonviolence*, Random House, 1968. The shift also unfolds, somewhat ambivalently, in James Farmer, *Freedom—When?*, Random House, 1966. On the history and development of CORE, in addition to these two works, see Meier, Rudwick, and Broderick, *op. cit.*, pp. 233–249, 567–583; Rudwick and Meier, *op. cit.*; and August Meier and Elliott Rudwick, "How CORE Began," *Social Science Quarterly*, Mar., 1969, pp. 789–799.

[29] Farmer's less ideological or perhaps his more ambivalent approach to black nationalism is shown by his service for two years as President Nixon's Assistant Secretary of Health, Education, and Welfare, a position he left at the end of 1970.

[30] *The Plain Dealer*, Mar. 6, 1970, p. 2-A.

[31] The literature on bureaucracy is a valuable source of theory on this question; studies of trade unions and churches are useful, and we shall apply some theory derived from the latter below. Probably

Rudwick and Meier have raised that problem in a very helpful way by comparing the ways in which the NAACP and CORE responded to the sharply increased militancy of the black protest movement in the 1960s. It is tempting to explain the difference by individual, leadership factors, and these doubtless play some part. Rudwick and Meier wisely stress the structural differences between the two organizations. Following Sills, they note that the NAACP fits the "corporate type" of formal organization quite closely. The national headquarters is strong and dominant, with legal control over the local branches, although in practice the local groups exercise considerable autonomy. CORE is a "federated type" of organization. It did not have a salaried national secretariat until 1957, 15 years after it was founded; local groups were highly autonomous. Related to this is the continuity of leadership, illustrated by the fact that the NAACP has had three chief executive officers in 50 years, and CORE has had three in ten years. These differences partly reflect historical origins, with NAACP chartered under the laws of the state of New York, with a legally designated, self-perpetuating Board of Directors. CORE was founded by a more alienated group of pacifists, many of them theological students.

As a result of these and other differences, when the severe protests of the 1960s began to be felt by the major civil rights organizations, NAACP responded as corporately organized groups do: They took some of the opposition onto the board, encouraged college and youth chapters in their direct-action programs, reduced even further the proportion of Whites, and took a more critical stance with regard to the major issues of discrimination. But they did not drastically change their policies and goals. Between 1966 and 1968 there was substantial pressure on the NAACP from the more black nationalist members, on the Board and in the chapters; but their criticism was assimilated into the ongoing program rather than being substi-

tuted for it. CORE, on the other hand, with its strong local autonomy, its longer history of direct action programs, its rapid change of leadership, was much more strongly influenced by the changing mood of the 1960s.[32]

The Black Panthers. The left wing of the black protest movement has been occupied during the last five years by the Black Panthers. The organization was founded in Oakland, California, in 1966, in some ways a product of the split in strategy of SNCC, or at least illustrative of the radicalizing of one segment of the black nationalist movement in the mid-1960s. Although it has never been a large group, having reached a peak of about 5000 members in 1968, and dropping to perhaps 1000 by 1971,[33] it has been the object of a great deal of attention and controversy. The aims of the Black Panthers are similar to those of other black nationalist groups, except perhaps for the violence of the verbal attack on the government, accompanied by affirmation of the sentiments of the Declaration of Independence, and demands that the government furnish jobs and decent income for all.

What we want now!:

1. We want freedom. We want power to determine the destiny of our black community.
2. We want full employment for our people.
3. We want an end to the robbery by the white man of our black community.
4. We want decent housing fit for shelter of human beings.
5. We want education for our people that exposes the true nature of this decadent American society. We want education that teaches us our true history and our role in the present day society.
6. We want all black men to be exempt from military service.
7. We want an immediate end to *police brutality* and *murder* of black people.
8. We want freedom for all black men and women held in federal, state, county, and city prisons and jails.
9. We want all black people when brought to trial, to be tried in court by a jury of their peer group or people from their black com-

---

the most valuable direct study of a voluntary organization is that of David Sills, *The Volunteers: Means and Ends in a National Organization,* Free Press, 1957.

[32] On all of this, See Rudwick and Meier, *op. cit.*
[33] *The New York Times,* Mar. 1, 1971, pp. 1, 14.

munities, as defined by the Constitution of the United States.

10. We want land, bread, housing, education, clothing, justice and peace.[34]

From the beginning there were differences over strategy and aims among the Black Panthers, as there are in any "sectarian" group. These differences have become sharper, in the context of intense public opposition to the severity of Panther rhetoric and their violent stance. Huey Newton, the present chairman, says that their aims have shifted from black nationalism, to revolutionary nationalism (there were some tentative approaches to white radicals of the "new left" in 1969), to international radicalism (concern for black men everywhere), to "revolutionary intercommunalism."[35] This last is not defined, but probably represents major attention to black community control and development, a position close to that of CORE in the early 1970s. Whether this will be the line of development remains problematic, since serious disagreements continue. In his most recent remarks, Newton calls for avoidance of confrontations with the police, increased church attendance, and greater effort to win support from the black community. From their self-imposed "exile" locations in Algeria, however, Eldridge Cleaver and Mr. and Mrs. Michael Tabor call for intensified guerrilla attack on the United States. Stokely Carmichael broke with the Black Panthers in 1969, presumably in opposition to their policy of direct confrontation with the police. By 1971 he believed they were "practically finished," and called on black Americans to shift their attention to building "mother Africa."[36]

[34] Meier, Rudwick, and Broderick, *op. cit.*, pp. 492–493.
[35] *The New York Times*, Feb. 5, 1971, p. 56.
[36] *The New York Times*, Feb. 6, 1971, p. 11; and Mar. 21, 1971, p. 61. To get something of the underlying feelings and range of view of Black Panthers, as well as a picture of their organization and history, see Eldridge Cleaver, *Soul on Ice*, Dell, 1968; Bobby Seale, *Seize the Time: The Story of the Black Panther Party*, Random House, 1970; Earl Anthony, *Picking Up the Gun: A Report on the Black Panthers*, Dial, 1970 (a somewhat bitter attack by an ex-officer, indicating the sharp differences in view); Meier, Rudwick, and Broderick, *op. cit.*, pp. 491–515; "The Panthers: Personal Freedom vs. Public Order," *Social Action* (whole issue), Nov., 1970.

About one-quarter of America's black population, in the early 1970s, look with favor on the Black Panthers as a source of pride and for their efforts in favor of black control of their own communities. Their violence is written off as defense against police brutality. About another quarter are "not sure" about Panther activities (it is difficult to separate the uncertain in this category from those who don't know about the Panthers; together they make up 34 percent). Whites, on the other hand, are strongly in opposition. In April, 1970, the Harris poll asked respondents in a cross-section of American households: "In general, do you feel the Black Panthers are a serious menace to this country, annoying but not very serious, or a force for good in the country?"[37]

Attitudes Toward the Black Panthers

	Whites	Blacks
	(percentage)	
A serious menace	66	21
Annoying but not serious	24	19
Force for good	3	26
Not sure	7	34

Source: *The Plain Dealer*, May 11, 1971, p. 3-B.

National samples by the Gallup poll produce similar results. (These are not broken down by race, and presumably are mainly white respondents):

Attitudes Toward the Black Panthers

	Highly favorable	Highly unfavorable
	(percentage)	
College students (1971)	8	42
General public (1970)	2	75

Source: *The New York Times*, Feb. 7, 1971, p. 54.

In assessing the place of the Black Panthers in efforts to reduce discrimination, one

[37] *The Plain Dealer*, May 11, 1971, p. 3-B.

of the most difficult questions has to do with the rhetoric and reality of their violent guerrilla activity, particularly in dealing with the police, and the degree to which the police tried to crush them. It is impossible to describe the Black Panther–police interaction "in general." The details of each encounter require examination. Perhaps this much, however, can be said to indicate our judgment about the context. In a day of sharp interracial conflicts, stereotypes have hardened on both sides. Police, seeing the Black Panthers through the prism of violent rhetoric and riots, have often acted first, and looked for specific law violations second or not at all. Members of the Black Panthers, seeing the world through years of discrimination, excessive use of police repression, and frustrated hopes, have talked hatred, gathered weapons, and in some instances, employed violence. They have also fed some hungry children. In the face of several court decisions in the spring of 1971, finding Black Panthers innocent of charges or finding insufficient evidence even for an indictment,[38] it seems clear that police actions during the preceding several years were much more repressive against the Panthers than was warranted or than the law allowed. The courts, on the other hand, in a somewhat calmer period, have recognized the right of Panthers to scream with pain and to demand change. They may also find, in some instances, that the rights of others, including police, have been violated. The basic question remains: Have the Black Panthers helped to jolt the United States into action, or frightened it into retrenchment? The importance of this one organization should not be exaggerated; its approach and activity is more symbolic than causal. It is our judgment, however, that the 1968–1969 confrontation period caused retrenchment rather than change, that it helped to elect reactionary politicians, slowed implementation of laws designed to achieve equality, and broke up essential alliances. It remains to be seen whether "revolutionary intercommunalism"

—self-selected segregation and community control—will have different results.

Black Power. Black power, of course, is not an organization but a movement, or perhaps a style. Some see it as the successor to the civil rights movement; or it can be thought of as one of the forms that the rights movement took, beginning about 1964. Although as a movement it overlaps with the Black Panthers, CORE, and other organizations, it may be useful to comment briefly on it as a general approach to contemporary minority-majority relations. Black power has a wide variety of meanings. "The larger and more diverse a political movement's constituency, the more vague and imprecise its unifying symbols and rallying cries are likely to be. A slogan like black power has no sharply defined meaning; it may excite many different emotions and may motivate individuals to express their loyalty or take action for almost contradictory reasons."[39] Despite this range, we can identify black power as a movement that emphasizes confrontation strategies and "nationalistic" (separatist) goals more strongly than did most previous movements. "We must fill ourselves with hate for all white things." Such white things include the American political and economic system to some advocates of black power. "We must destroy both racism and capitalism" (Huey Newton).

Since black power is an outlook, a point of view, more than a program, we shall not examine the range of views further in this discussion of strategy. Indeed, it is not clear from such writings as Carmichael and Hamilton's *Black Power*, just what policies are called for. Nevertheless, the term designates a mood that is very important to understanding the contemporary scene. The background, the perspective, and the ambiguities well caught up in the statement by Christopher Lasch:

Black Power represents, among other things, a revival of black nationalism and therefore can-

[38] See, for example, *The New York Times*, May 14, 1971, pp. 1, 20.

[39] Joel D. Aberbach and Jack L. Walker, "The Meanings of Black Power: A Comparison of White and Black Interpretations of a Political Slogan," *American Political Science Review*, June, 1970, p. 367.

not be regarded simply as a response to recent events. Black Power has secularized the separatist impulse which has usually (though not always) manifested itself in religious forms. Without necessarily abandoning the myth of black people as a chosen people, the new-style nationalists have secularized the myth by identifying black people in America—whom many of them continue to regard as in some sense Negroes of the diaspora—not with "the Asian Black Nation and the tribe of Shabazz," as in Black Muslim theology, but with the contemporary struggle against colonialism in the Third World. Where earlier nationalist movements, both secular and religious, envisioned physical separation from America and reunion with Islam or with Africa, many of the younger nationalists propose to fight it out here in America, by revolutionary means if necessary, and to establish—what? a black America? an America in which black people can survive as a separate "nation"? an integrated America?[40]

These ambiguities in black power are not likely to be eliminated, but some among the various forms of its present statement are likely to emerge as the dominant ones, not so much because of its own inner development as a movement, as because of the setting created by American actions and policy.

Jewish Organizations in the Field of Intergroup Relations. There are dozens of Jewish organizations interested in intergroup relations, but perhaps the leading ones in this field are the American Jewish Congress, the Anti-Defamation League of B'nai B'rith, and the American Jewish Committee. The American Jewish Congress, founded in 1918, has a professional staff of 110. ". . . It is best known for activities designed to invoke legal sanctions against discrimination, including drafting legislation and participating in litigation affecting constitutional and legislative rights."[41] It is also interested in the investigation of intergroup tension and winning community support for its program.

The Anti-Defamation League, with a staff of 250, has a national office and 25 regional offices that work in coordination with other agencies on programs to reduce discrimination in communities. On the national level the League has sponsored scores of workshops, published a great deal of antiprejudice material, and developed an interest in most phases of intergroup relations. In 1959 it established a Department of Colleges and Universities to coordinate its work in institutions of higher education. The American Jewish Committee has emphasized educational work and is particularly prominent for its encouragement and sponsorship of research. Founded in 1906, it has the largest professional staff, 350, of the groups mentioned here.

A number of the Jewish agencies have joined together to form the National Community Relations Advisory Council in order better to coordinate their various programs and to undertake some common projects. The Council is composed of the American Jewish Congress, the Jewish Labor Committee, the Jewish War Veterans, the Union of American Hebrew Congregations, the Union of Orthodox Hebrew Congregations, the United Synagogue of America, and 35 state and local organizations. Total expenditure by the Council and its affiliated organizations, in 1969, was $15.3 million. "The purposes of the Jewish community relations field have been defined as the protection and enhancement of equal rights and equal opportunities and the fostering of conditions that contribute toward the vitality of Jewish living."[42] Various members of the NCRAC specialize on particular aspects of this total program. Indeed, there is some disagreement in emphasis, some competition for particular types of programs, for which various groups claim priority or special facilities. Despite such disagreements, the various groups contribute to common goals and cooperation continues on specific activities. The Jewish agencies have regarded the problem of discrimination as indivisible and have

[40] Christopher Lasch, *The Agony of the American Left*, Random House, 1969, pp. 128–129. See also Harold Cruse, *The Crisis of the Negro Intellectual*, Morrow, 1967, pp. 544–565.

[41] Joseph B. Robison, "Organizations Promoting Civil Rights and Liberties," *Annals*, May, 1951, p. 21.

[42] National Community Relations Advisory Council, *Joint Program Plan for Jewish Community Relations 1956–57*, 1956, p. 2.

participated in cases involving other minorities as well as those affecting Jews.[43]

The National Conference of Christians and Jews. Although the National Conference of Christians and Jews has been, from its founding in 1928, primarily concerned with the promotion of harmonious relations among members of different religious faiths, it has also been interested in other aspects of intergroup relations. It has worked on the community level through its 62 regional offices, and on the national level by promoting seminars, providing advanced training in intergroup relations, sponsoring Brotherhood Week, and encouraging research. The Conference is strictly an interfaith agency, with the aim of developing understanding, tolerance, and cooperation, but with no desire to eliminate differences among the faiths. Its methods, broadly speaking, are educational; more attention is given to the use of the mass media than perhaps is true of any other agency concerned with intergroup relations.[44]

Church Organizations and Intergroup Relations. In addition to the Jewish agencies and the NCCJ, there are many organizations among Protestants and Catholics that are devoted primarily to the reduction of prejudice and discrimination. These are too numerous even to list, but mention at least must be made of the existence of specialized intergroup agencies or staff members in other agencies among most of the large Protestant denominations (particularly the Methodist, Presbyterian, Episcopal, and United Church), several of the smaller denominations and sects (e.g., Unitarian-Universalist and Quaker), in the Catholic Church (National Catholic Welfare Conference, Social Action Department, and the National Catholic Conference for Interracial Justice), and in the National Council of Churches of Christ (Department of Racial and Cultural Relations).[45]

Mexican-American Civil Rights Organizations. Although there have been mutual benefit and culturally oriented associations in the Mexican-American community for many decades (La Alianza Hispano Americana was founded in 1894), it was not until after World War II that various political, economic, and civil rights causes became major objects of their attention. There are now dozens of such groups, local, regional, and national; we shall only illustrate the range of their interests.

Some of the groups are concerned primarily with political activity. After World War II, Mexican-American veterans organized the GI Forum, to encourage greater political interest and participation. The Political Association of Spanish-Speaking Americans (PASSO) in Texas and the Mexican-American Political Association (MAPA) in California are supported directly by only a small minority of the Chicanos in their regions, but are coming to be quite widely recognized. Until about 1965, most such political organizations emphasized their strong loyalty to the United States, even developing the "we were here first" theme to indicate that Mexican-Americans are old Americans. But more militant political movements are growing. The young Texas Chicanos, working for an independent political force, as in La Raza Unida (which has won several municipal offices in Texas) and the Mexican-American Youth Organization (MAYO), are calling for more radical changes. Assimilationist views are to some degree being replaced by emphasis on the Mexican heritage and by a desire to maintain and enrich the cultural unity of the barrio. If this trend continues, as we think it will, the political force of "brown power" will become a critical factor in the Southwest.[46]

Cesar Chavez and his National Farm

---

[43] Robison, *op. cit.*, pp. 20–23.

[44] See James Pitt, *Adventures in Brotherhood,* Farrar, Straus, 1955; and Everett R. Clinchy, *The Growth of Good Will: A Sketch of Protestant-Catholic-Jewish Relations,* National Conference of Christians and Jews, 1953.

[45] *Interracial News Service,* which was published bimonthly by the Department of Racial and Cultural

Relations, is a valuable source of information about church activity and other events in intergroup relations, up to 1965.

[46] See Leo Grebler, Joan W. Moore, and Ralph C. Guzman, *The Mexican-American People: The Nation's Second Largest Minority,* Free Press, 1970, chap. 22; *The New York Times,* Aug. 2, 1970, p. 1; and Mar. 14, 1971, p. 61; Armando Rendon, "La Raza—Today not Mañana," in John H. Burma (ed.), *Mexican-Americans in the United States,* Schenkman, 1970, pp. 307–324.

Workers Association is the best known of the Mexican-American groups that focus primarily on economic questions. His campaigns of "militant nonviolence" have won union recognition and some improvement of wages and working conditions for the fruit and vegetable pickers in the West. The frequently drawn parallel between Chavez and Martin Luther King is, we believe, a useful one, not only because of their common emphasis on Gandhian techniques, but also because of their similar charismatic, somewhat mystical quality of leadership. This, of course, is not for everyone, particularly those who have shifted toward more "nationalistic" goals; but Chavez' brand of militancy seems likely to continue to be the major appeal to those suffering serious economic discrimination.[47]

There are Mexican-American agencies emphasizing other aspects of the life and disprivileges of Chicanos in America, the National Council for Chicano Studies and the National Mexican-American Anti-Defamation Committee, for example. Some coordination among the many associations is developing, as in the Congress of Mexican American Unity, with hundreds of local organizations and clubs affiliated. The federal government is beginning to show more concern for the difficulties faced by the Mexican-American.[48] And in 1968, with a $2 million grant from the Ford Foundation there has been established the Mexican American Legal Defense and Education Fund, designed, as is the NAACP Legal Defense and Education Fund, to bring the resources of the law to bear on the discriminations suffered by Chicanos.

American Indian Organizations. Indians have been fighting and negotiating for their rights for nearly 500 years, but we cannot tell that important story here. Suffice it to say that they were pushed back into small enclaves, their population decimated (not quite literally, but from perhaps 800,000 down to 300,000), and opportunities either to live as Indians or in the larger society were seriously limited. Even after the "Indian Wars" were over, the land base on which Indians lived declined, from 146 million acres in 1897 to 56 million acres in 1970. Federal policy vacillated, but reached what some thought was a "final" stage in 1953, with the passage of the Termination Act. This was designed "to get the United States out of the Indian business," by permitting sale of reservation lands and developing various training and educational plans for individuals.[49]

1961 can be regarded as another important turning point in Indian affairs. Stimulated by the civil rights movement generally, the American Indian Chicago Conference brought representatives of 210 tribes together to draft a statement of principles and aims. There was, of course, a wide range of judgments, varying from an emphasis on detribalized assimilation to the belief that Indians are citizens of independent nations, not of the United States. But there was overwhelming support for the principle that decisions about the best course of action should be made by Indians. Most participants supported the position of the National Congress of American Indians,[50] that reforms could come from within the system by working with the Bureau of Indian Affairs, provided that it could be made into an instrument for the expression of Indian judgments and interests.

One of the products of the American Indian Chicago Conference was the organization of the National Indian Youth Council, a militant, intertribal organization. Confederations among Indian tribes go back, of course, to the seventeenth century (the

[47] See Peter Matthiessen, *Sal Si Puedes: Cesar Chavez and the New American Revolution*, Random House, 1970, for a somewhat uncritical but valuable account.

[48] See Inter-Agency Committee on Mexican American Affairs, *The Mexican American: A New Focus on Opportunity*, Government Printing Office, 1967.

[49] For various articles dealing with government policy and Indian-white relations, see George E. Simpson and J. Milton Yinger (eds.), "American Indians and American Life," *Annals*, May, 1957 (whole issue).

[50] This is the most important group working for Indian rights. The Association of American Indian Affairs, comprised mainly of Whites, supports a variety of educational and welfare activities through its American Indian Fund.

League of the Iroquois and perhaps some Pueblo intertribal organizations preceeded contact with Europeans), but tribal autonomy has been much the stronger force.

1961 also marked the beginning of change in government policy. President Kennedy halted termination and began to bring more Indians into the Bureau of Indian Affairs. It was not until 1966, however, that an Indian was named Commissioner, a policy that has continued; Louis Bruce, an Oglala Sioux, presently holds the office. By 1970, 13 of the 25 top administrative posts were held by Indians, and nearly 60 percent of the work force of 14,400 were Indian.[51] Such a large staff (one worker for every 50 Indians in the country) has, through the years, created dependence on the BIA at the same time that it has meant bureaucratic rigidity and what many regard as excessive governance of Indian affairs.

President Nixon has asked for the recall of the "termination resolution," which, although not much acted upon since 1960, is still the law; and has asked for extensive increase in aid to Indian education, health, and economic affairs. It is not yet clear how these requests will be translated into legislation and effective policy.

Further aspects of the current American Indian scene help to set the context within which present protest activities are developing. In 1946, Congress set up the Indians Claims Commission, in an effort to resolve the myriad of unresolved disputes over land and other issues that had accumulated through the decades. By 1970, $359 million had been awarded to various tribes. There were still 290 claims before the Commission, with an estimated value of $150 million, but the law set a termination date of April 10, 1972, which means that many issues will remain unresolved unless the life of the Commission is extended.[52] We should also note that perhaps one-third of America's 700,000 Indians now live off the reservations (in addition to the million or more with some Indian ancestry who are not regarded as Indian). Like many other migrant groups, a large proportion of them suffer from culture shock, from lack of necessary skills, from unfamiliarity with city life.[53]

Combine serious disprivilege and discrimination, a growing awareness of the larger society through service in the armed forces and work in the cities, a vacillating yet currently fairly favorable federal policy, a growing number of educated and middle-class leaders, a powerful and highly visible protest movement by black Americans, and one has the ingredients for a vigorous Indian protest movement. The National Congress of American Indians shows less and less readiness to accept policy laid down by "the great white father." Vine Deloria, Jr., former executive director of the NCAI, has written an angry attack on past and present policy and practice that points up the mood and the beliefs of the growing number of "nationalistic" Indians: Do not try to remake us in some foreign image.[54] Indians occupied Alcatraz Island for several months to dramatize their grievances, and held parts of the Mount Rushmore National Park, to protest what they regard as failure to settle land claims. These highly visible acts may lead us to overlook the high rates of infant mortality, the unemployment, the inadequate educational opportunities of Indians in more remote areas. But we expect an intensified civil rights and to some degree "nationalistic" movement among American Indians during the 1970s.

[53] See Theodore D. Graves, "The Personal Adjustment of Navajo Indian Migrants to Denver, Colorado," AA, Feb., 1970, pp. 35–54; Alan L. Sorkin, "Some Aspects of American Indian Migration," SF, Dec., 1969, pp. 243–250; Joan Ablon, "American Indian Relocation: Problems of Dependency and Management in the City," Phylon, Winter, 1965, pp. 362–371.

[54] See Vine Deloria, Jr., Custer Died for Your Sins, Macmillan, 1969; and Vine Deloria, Jr., We Talk, You Listen, Macmillan, 1970. See also Stuart Levine and Nancy O. Lurie (eds.), The American Indian Today, Penguin Books, 1970, especially the chapters by Shirley H. Witt, "Nationalistic Trends Among American Indians," pp. 93–127, and Robert K. Thomas, "Pan-Indianism," pp. 128–141, in addition to the Foreword and the Afterword by the editors.

[51] The Plain Dealer, Nov. 12, 1970, p. 6F; The New York Times, July 12, 1970, p. 3E. The budget of the BIA is over $350 million a year.

[52] See Nancy O. Lurie, "The Indian Claims Commission Act," Annals, May, 1957, pp. 56–70; The New York Times, Oct. 1, 1970, p. 4.

The American "Freedom Revolution"

Have these numerous protest organizations affected American society? Are the categorical lines of privilege and disprivileged that characterize a majority-minority stratification system being erased? Is America being transformed from a majority-minority society into an open-class society? We think that there are powerful evidences that this is happening—not, of course, without countercurrents. Indeed, somewhat paradoxically, both the strength of the protest movement since World War II and the strength of the resistance are signs that significant change is taking place. To explore that paradox requires that we examine briefly the general theory of revolution.

America has been facing the classic revolutionary situation: the slowing down or reversal of a fairly long period of steady improvement. It is well established that revolutions do not occur among those who are most poorly off; nor do they occur among those who are well off and hopeful of the future. Typically there has been a long period of improvement, a sharp rise in aspiration and expectation—and then frustration.[55] It is clear that between about 1940 and 1955, Negroes in America had experienced the most rapid rate of improvement of occupational status and income they had ever known. But in the mid-1950s they hit a plateau. Much of the slowing down, it should be noted, was relative to new objectives and hopes, not to fixed standards.[56] When a group is on the upswing, the gap between what one has and what one had is unimpressive. The gap between what one now has and the newly visible future is critical. It is for this reason that major societal transformations cannot proceed "with all deliberate speed." They move rapidly, or the society is thrown into turmoil. It is sometimes seen as paradoxical that protests occur at times when progress is being made, but such a view overlooks the way that the progress appears to the minority. Kenneth Clark shows this nicely when he remarks about the intensity of the riots just after the passage of a major Civil Rights Act: "The Civil Rights Act [1964] was so long coming it served merely to remind many Negroes of their continued rejected and second-class status."[57]

Whether judged by relative or absolute standards, the slowing down could, for a few years, be interpreted as a temporary lapse, due to the recession of 1958 or some other factor; but by 1963 it was apparent that the steady economic gains had stopped. We cannot explore the reasons fully in this volume. Doubtless these factors were involved: continuing automation, which hit particularly hard at jobs held by minority workers; the general sluggishness of the American economy, manifest in a slow rate of growth and persistent high unemployment; focus of American attention outward because of the problems and expenditures of war; and vigorous opposition to desegregation, the counterrevolution, precipitated by the Supreme Court school decision in 1954 and the legal changes that followed.

It is significant that the levelling off of Negro gains in the mid-1950s did not hit their educational improvement. Thus their qualifications, expectations, and aspirations continued to increase while their opportunities ceased to improve. This is one of the major reasons why Negro students have taken such a vital role in the protest movement. And once again, the theory of revolution helps us to understand the reasons. It has often been observed that students have been at the center of many revolutionary movements abroad. They make up, in many ways, the talented, trained, and ambitious; but as societies undergo severe strains, with no clear vision of what social structures are

[55] We cannot here develop this important branch of sociological theory. See James C. Davies, "Toward a Theory of Revolution," *ASR*, Feb., 1962, pp. 5–19; Lyford P. Edwards, *The Natural History of Revolution*, Univ. of Chicago Press, 1927; Crane Brinton, *Anatomy of Revolution*, Vintage Books, 1957; Raymond Tanter and Manus Midlarsky, "A Theory of Revolution," *JCR*, Sept. 1967, pp. 264–280.

[56] See Carl F. Grindstaff, "The Negro, Urbanization, and Relative Deprivation in the Deep South," *SP*, Winter, 1968, pp. 342–352.

[57] Kenneth Clark, *Dark Ghetto*, Harper & Row, 1965, p. 17.

going to be built, students are in grave doubts about the future. Will there be a place for them? In a world of doubt they propose to answer that question for themselves, by joining or leading the revolt.

The growing number of Negro college students see a different world from that of their parents. Their hopes for full participation in American society have grown rapidly; they have no lack of knowledge of the opportunities in that society; yet they graduate, in a large proportion of cases, into segregated jobs, work at levels of skill and income far below those of their white contemporaries, and face a situation in which their training is partly irrelevant to their placement.

It is testimony both to the good health and the good fortune of American society that the Negro protest has sought, mainly, to realize the democratic ideology, not to destroy it. There have been attacks on it of course—both the deflected, individual attack of demoralization and crime and some organized attack. Faith in the ability of the system to make major changes has been reduced. But to date, the dominant cry has been: "Stop being hypocrites." A hypocrite is one who has latent standards to which an opponent can appeal.

In what way are current developments a sign of the good health of American society? To answer this we must comment briefly on the definition and theory of revolution. Davies defines revolutions as ". . . violent civil disturbances that cause the displacement of one ruling group by another that has a broader popular basis for support."[58] This differs from most definitions only in making explicit the idea that a revolution presupposes a widening base of support. Presumably a change in ruling group that narrowed the base of support (power being held by a monopoly of coercion or by the aid of an ideology accepted by the majority) would be counterrevolutionary. Davies' conception fits the American scene quite closely. If the current civil rights movement continues to develop, we will see the displacement, in the halls of Congress, on the boards

of directors of American industry, in labor unions, on boards of education, etc., of persons who have made decisions in favor of middle- and upper-class white America, and to some degree lower-class white America, by persons who make decisions with the interests of white and black America in view. In this sense, we are in the midst of a revolution.

Of course we are led to wonder how violent is violent before we speak of a revolution. Dozens have been killed, hundreds injured, and thousands jailed in the United States, but surely the transition has been nonviolent, as revolutions go. This points up a significant difference between dramatic social changes in a democratic society—one open to currents of public opinion and protests and capable of the continuous process of adjustment called for by changing circumstances—and changes in closed societies. In democratic societies, revolutions are always partial; and they are never completed. We would say that the current civil rights struggle is part of America's *continuing revolution*. It is another stage in broadening the popular basis of support that is the essence of a democratic society. This may prove to be the greatest social invention of man—the creation of a type of social system in which continuous adjustments can be made without violent destruction of the whole structure. A society designed to permit a continuing revolution is one that can avoid the twin dangers of most revolutions: A new tyranny, if the revolt succeeds, or perpetual repression and terror if the counterrevolution succeeds. These twins are alive, but not very healthy, on the American scene today, embodied on the one hand in the more virulent forms of minority-group nationalism and on the other hand in the policies and aims of counterrevolutionaries for whom humanity does not extend past middle-class white Americans.[59] To picture what often happens

[58] Davies, *op. cit.*, p. 6.

[59] In general terms, counterrevolutionaries are persons or groups who possess power and status in the existing, but weakening social structure, and feel seriously threatened with loss, often supported by those who have always been status-hungry (the "poor whites"), who feel threatened with a perpetuation of status deprivation and loss of what little prestige they

when societies experience prolonged violent revolution, we need only imagine what kind of society would be organized by either of these two groups. This would be, however, only an exercise in imagination if the 1970s prove to be the decade of the American Revolution when the country declares its independence from "internal colonialism," if we may be oratorical about it.

"Internal colonialism" is often treated as a burden to the "colony," but a source of wealth and power to the dominant group. In our judgment, it is a burden to both, for reasons we have indicated at several points, although particular individuals profit greatly from their colonial advantages. The concept of an internal colony is an apt one if it is not taken too literally. Robert Blauner characterizes the colonization complex as one in which (1) the minority has been brought in by force; (2) its culture and social organization are seriously weakened by a policy ". . . which constrains, transforms, or destroys indigenous values, orientations, and ways of life"; (3) the colony is "managed and manipulated" by ethnic outsiders; and (4) the relationship is justified by racist doctrines.[60]

In the ghettos and barrios of America, the houses, the stores, the places of work are owned, in overwhelming proportion, by out-

siders. Police systems and schools are controlled by organizations in which the area residents have little power and from which, until recently, they were excluded substantially. It is going to be extremely difficult to find a way to harmonize the demands for community control with problems of financing, maintenance of individual mobility, reduction of stereotyping and enforced segregation, internal justice (not all ghetto residents agree with one another; not all of Harlem's landlords are white), and the like. It would compound our present tragedies if, in the name of community control, minority groups were to find themselves in control of cities, or large segments of cities, with wholly inadequate resources, faced by continued inmigration of newcomers lacking adequate training, and cut off from the larger community by reciprocal hostilities. Yet we believe that the demand for a substantial increase in community control to reduce the exploitation by outsiders is well founded. There is no doubt that "the poor pay more." The problem is to create a situation in which they, in fact, pay less, not to endorse a symbolic crusade that only promises such an outcome.

Such a situation, we believe, has several elements. The lack of any one of them may make it impossible to produce the compound we need:

1. A vastly increased range of opportunities for members of minorities to enter into the educational, job, housing, and other aspects of the larger system. Freedom, in our view, is the presence of good alternatives. These the ghetto dweller often lacks; and community control by itself will not furnish them.

2. A sharp increase in the ownership and control of houses, businesses, and shops by minority-group members in the areas where they live in substantial numbers and also fully representative participation in the agencies of the total community. This is not to support black capitalism, for example, in an ideological and separatist sense, but to support greatly increased opportunities for black businessmen.

3. A readiness on the part of the majority,

do have as members of a superior "caste." These are sometimes joined by the *nouveaux riches,* insecure in their new status and fearful that freshly won affluence will be swept away by further social change.

[60] See Robert Blauner, "Internal Colonialism and Ghetto Revolt," *SP,* Spring, 1969, pp. 393–408 for a valuable discussion. Harold Cruse may have been the first to use the idea of an internal colony, in a 1962 paper reprinted in *Rebellion or Revolution,* Morrow, 1968. Kenneth Clark wrote that "The dark ghettos are social, political, educational and—above all— economic colonies" (*op. cit.,* p. 11). And his book is a vivid account of the consequences of such colonial status. The concept of internal colonialism is central to the discussion of Carmichael and Hamilton, *op. cit.* And its full impact is carefully examined by Arnold Schuchter, *White Power/Black Freedom,* Beacon Press, 1968. For arguments against the use of the concept of "internal colonies," see Robert Fogelson, "Violence as Protest," in Robert Connery (ed.), *Urban Riots: Violence and Social Change,* Academy of Political Science, 1968, pp. 32–35; and Nathan Glazer, "Blacks and Ethnic Groups: The Difference, and the Political Difference it Makes," *SP,* Spring, 1971, pp. 444–461.

as Blauner suggests, to accept a fairly high level of confrontation, conflict, and disorder, for the colonized are not likely to accept fully the rules of the game—the very rules that they now perceive as having kept them down and out of the system. ("Accept" means here to treat them as "protests," as Turner uses that term, not as rebellion.) The alternative is probably a high level of repression that can only perpetuate existing inequities.

4. At the same time—and to point up the dilemmas of which every policy is a part—the average majority group member has a stake in stability. Whatever one may think of the importance of this value, those who hold it believe it is important, and will act on that belief. The alternative to recognizing it is probably a high level of coercion. "The Black militant movement is a threat to the orderly procedures by which bureaucracies and suburbs manage their existence, and I think today there are more people who feel a stake in conventional procedures than there are those who gain directly from racism."[61] Although Blauner gives this observation a negative interpretation, we see no reason not to regard it as simply another of the facts of the situation, not to be disregarded by the wise strategist. (There is an overwhelming tendency in the literature today to moralize about the behavior of majority-group members, while treating that of minorities naturalistically, that is, to seek for its causes. We find this no more satisfactory than the earlier reverse situation.)

We don't know what various compounds can be formed from these four elements, but we think that obtaining the proper "mix" between one and two, and between three and four is of the utmost importance in planning for social change into a nondiscriminatory society.

Varieties of "Sectarianism" Among Minority Groups

With our brief comments we have only given examples of the hundreds of groups now

[61] Blauner, *op. cit.*, p. 408.

concerned with intergroup relations and the general movement in which they participate. Perhaps we can draw these comments into focus by inquiring whether or not there is any pattern to the variety of minority-group organizations. We think there is such a pattern, and in discussing it we are brought back, in a somewhat different connection, to a topic raised in Chapters 1 and 7. Minority-group protest organizations can helpfully be compared with religious sects (indeed, in many cases, they can well be regarded as religious sects). They exhibit the same three fundamental ways of responding to deprivation: One can say that the system within which the deprivation is felt needs drastic overhauling, but that it is capable of reform and contains some possible allies; one can see the system as fundamentally incapable of being remade—it must therefore be replaced; or one can see the system as so evil and resistant to change that the best choice is to withdraw from it. Seldom does any individual take one of these positions in a pure form; the purposes and strategies of groups also typically represent a blend. Yet various of the groups we have discussed approach more or less closely to one of the type positions. Their relationships can be described in the form of a triangle, with the "pure types" labelled at the angles, and illustrative guesses noted from among American Negro groups.

Figure 10 / Strategic Responses to Discrimination

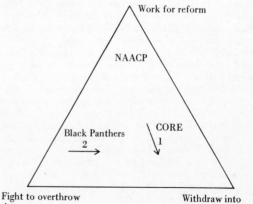

Work for reform

NAACP

Black Panthers
2 →

CORE
1 ↓

Fight to overthrow
the system

Withdraw into
own communities

Sources of "Sectarian" Strategies

Probable Strategy	Is the group optimistic about its own power to compete with the dominant group?	Is the group optimistic about the capacity of the prevailing system to change?
1. Fight for reform	yes	yes
2. Attack the system	yes	no
3. Work for separation	no	no

We lack systematic studies of the combinations of cultural, structural, and characterological conditions that incline an individual or group toward one or another of these choices. The answers given to two critical questions reflect, in our judgment, cultural training, the structure of opportunities, and individual motives and experiences. They can be put into a Guttman scale, as in the table above. If either variable changes, the possibilities and the consequences of the various strategies change. Thus if one's sense of power goes up, as it has in the United States for many members of minority groups, one moves along the plane from right to left in figure 10. If perception of the capacity of the system to change goes up, one moves along the plane from bottom to top. (It should be noted that perception of the capacity to change is not identical with the actual capacity to change, although they are closely related. Their separation is a fundamental fact in any social system, whether it be as a result of the fact that minority-group members fail to perceive new opportunities, or believe in opportunities not there.) If, after a period of rising hope, the sense of one's own power and of the system's change capacity decline, there is a movement toward the lower-right corner. Arrow 1 may designate what happened to CORE after 1964; and arrow 2 what happened to the Black Panthers after 1970.

Some groups and leaders stand, or attempt to stand, equidistant from the three angles. Or, more commonly, they take a nondoctrinaire position that says, in effect, that there is need for all three approaches. They say, with the Reverend Jesse Jackson that "no man can tell a man who is hurting how to holler." It is only by taking such a position that a minority group can get a shared strategy. Those who insist that there is only one way "to holler" emphasize the group's divisions.

Origins of the Civil Rights Movement

When did the current phase of the American Revolution begin? In a situation of "infinite regress" this question can be answered only dramatically, by picking a symbolically important event, not definitively. Some prefer to think of an ancient beginning—perhaps with the Jewish prophets of the eighth century B.C. or the Sermon on the Mount. Others go back to the eighteenth-century enlightenment and the American and French Revolutions. The Emancipation Proclamation a century ago is an apt choice. But some choose a recent event: The Supreme Court decision on school desegregation, May 17, 1954, or the December day in 1955 when a Negro lady in Montgomery got tired of moving on a bus to accommodate white passengers (in this instance to give her seat, according to the law and the instructions of the driver, to a white man), or February 1, 1960, when a group of Negro students in Greensboro, North Carolina, sat quietly at a lunch counter in a five-and-ten-cent store and asked to be served.

For present purposes we prefer to mark the beginning at about a generation ago. Ralph McGill said that desegregation, insofar as it is a southern process, began with the boll weevil. Lest we give the little devil too much credit, it should be remarked that his attack on cotton was most intense at the same time that a major depression was attacking the economy. Between the two, the one-crop system was dealt a serious blow. The federal government began to give greater encouragement to crop diversification, the mechanization of agriculture increased rapidly, an accelerated movement to urban areas was set in motion, and the pace of industrialization was quickened. Many an ardent segregationist, in fact, was a strong supporter of moves to encourage the location of industry in the South. Had he been an equally ardent student of social organization, he might have been curious about some of the unintended consequences. Urbanization, the beginning of unionization, the upgrading of some Negro workers, the migration of Yankees, the development of an urban middle class, the growing integration with the national economy—all of these factors disturbed the existing patterns. Although the South is still less urban than most other areas of the country, it has been urbanizing more than twice as rapidly as the rest of the nation since 1900.

The move to the cities has been accompanied by a rapid increase in industrial employment. On common indexes of industrial production, the South, since 1930, has increased at a rate about one-third faster than the rest of the nation. This increase, to be sure, is from a lower base; but the gap is being closed. Per capita income in the South was less than half the national average in 1930, but by 1950 it was two-thirds. Significantly for race relations, however, there has been little gain since 1950. The region with the largest black population is still the poorest region.[62]

Meanwhile, of course, there has been a substantial increase in the Negro population of the North and West, particularly in the largest urban centers. There has also been a significant gain in the Chicano, Puerto Rican, and Indian population living in the cities.

One does not need to accept the *gemeinschaft-gesellschaft* tradition in sociology to the full to recognize the enormous shift that takes place in intergroup relations when the setting is moved from farm or plantation or peasant village to the city. "The urban premium on freedom, impersonality, efficiency and profits, voluntary organizations, and participation by representation . . ."[63] destroys earlier accommodative patterns. There is a period of trial and error and inventiveness while the society works out modes of relationship appropriate to the new opportunities and new problems.

THE STRATEGY OF CHANGE

Thus a new context for intergroup relations has been created in the United States—and indeed throughout the world. We must be careful not to give our sole attention to the militant protest movements or the extensive legal changes, for they have been going on during a quiet revolution that has weakened the foundations of the earlier structures of relationship. The multiple forces at work—demographic, economic, international, religious, educational, and many others—have been remaking, drastically, views of the world held by minorities and, at the same time, they have significantly changed the structures within which intergroup relations occur.

With both hopes and power raised, it has been inevitable that minorities would protest the continuing patterns of discrimination and would seek to enlarge their gains. Much of the initiative has been shifted to the minorities. In discussing their differing levels of optimism, we noted the varying ways in which they bring pressure to bear on the discriminatory structure. It may be useful, however, to focus more directly on strategic questions, to try to discover the conditions that lead to one or another choice, and to estimate their consequences.

Nonviolent Resistance

When Mrs. Rosa Parks refused to give her seat to a white man on a Montgomery bus,

[62] See John C. McKinney and Linda Brookover Bourque, "The Changing South: National Incorporation of a Region," *ASR*, June, 1971, pp. 399–412.

[63] Hylan Lewis, "Innovations and Trends in the Contemporary Southern Community," *JSI*, 1954, First Quarter, p. 24.

she precipitated a series of events that have yet to run their course. In the months that followed, Negroes combined the strategy of economic boycott with a philosophy of nonviolent protest in a way that proved to be highly effective. The fact that they succeeded in winning nonsegregated seating on Montgomery buses, after many months of struggle, was less significant in the long run than the solidarity of purpose, the testing of method, the strengthening of self-respect, and the discovery of leadership that came from the dispute.

Under what conditions are such nonviolent protests likely to be effective? The most general factor is the extent to which potential opponents are divided or unified, both individually and collectively. If some are individually ambivalent, sharing values and goals with the protesters, while also holding contrary views, they are more likely to be persuaded by nonviolence. They may, indeed, not be ambivalent, but sympathize wholeheartedly with the protest, yet need an effective argument to disidentify with the dominant position of their own group.

"The principal virtue of nonviolence as a strategy is that it does not serve the opponent by unifying his force and intensifying his anger, as does an aggressive or violent act."[64] It is a critical question, therefore, how members of a minority envisage the dominant group. If they see no moderates when in fact there are some, they are unlikely to act in such a way as to exploit the resources available to nonviolent protests. They may see no moderates, of course, because there are none. But there are other reasons. Those who themselves have been violent—on whatever side—are unlikely to recognize moderation on the other side because it makes their own actions seem less reasonable or civilized. A different series of interactions characterizes some white activists and intellectuals today, as during most

times of crisis: For fear of being thought sentimental or unsympathetic to a just protest or insensitive to injustice, they describe a thoroughly racist society.[65] It is easier today to be categorically alienated than to look for evidence. One can be a hero in a minute by condemning all the bad guys. *But poor appraisal of the actual situation means poor strategy.* Sweeping generalizations may be emotionally simpler, but their effects are negative.

Applying this point of view to the Montgomery bus boycott as an illustration, we find several factors that contributed to its success. The supremacy of the Constitution in the American legal system left no doubt what the ultimate court decision would be. The interdependent economy of the city meant that white supporters of desegregation were ambivalent. The bus company needed Negro riders; and white women, many of them working for $75 a week (these were 1955 dollars), needed their Negro maids, whom they paid $20. The quiet technique of the Reverend Martin Luther King and his coworkers was ideally suited to win the support of moderates and weaken the

[64] James S. Coleman, "Race Relations and Social Change," in Irwin Katz and Patricia Gurin (eds.), *Race and the Social Sciences*, Basic Books, 1969, p. 316. There are valuable comments on the effectiveness of nonviolence scattered throughout *The Urban Guerrilla*, by Martin Oppenheimer, Quadrangle Books, 1969.

[65] There are scores of books and articles today dealing with the concept of "racism." It is not a new term—Ruth Benedict made significant use of it in her classic *Race: Science and Politics* (Modern Age, 1940) over 30 years ago—but it has recently come into prominence. In many ways it is a useful shorthand way of saying: a complex of discriminations and prejudices directed against an alleged inferior race. Nevertheless, we have made only minimal use of the term for two related reasons: Racism tends to be a "swearword," not an analytic term; as such, in most of its present uses, it freezes the mind and perpetuates a vocabulary of praise and blame that we think reduces our ability to understand—and therefore to reduce—intergroup hostilities and injustices. The second reason is closely related. Racism is often used as an explanation, rather than a description of a situation. "White racism is essentially responsible for the explosive mixture which has been accumulating in our cities since the end of World War II." (*Report of the National Advisory Commission on Civil Disorders*, Bantam Books, 1968, p. 10.) This does not take us very far. It is equivalent to saying that we are having a serious epidemic because many people have been infected by a virus. How does the virus work to cause the disease? Who is vulnerable, who immune? What situations harbor it? The tragedies associated with intergroup hostility are too severe to permit us the luxury of "medieval" explanations by naming or by lodging the cause in individual choice.

opposition, who were put in the position of extremists. In these circumstances, the restrained but insistent demand for equal services by the use of legal processes was effective.

What is the origin of this strategy of nonviolence? It has often been referred to as a Gandhian technique, and there is no doubt that the early leaders of CORE, SCLC, and others have been influenced by study of Gandhi and his work in South Africa and India.[66] This is an inadequate explanation, however, particularly of the alacrity with which nonviolent resistance was adopted by thousands of Negroes, young and old, North and South, lower class and middle class, most of whom doubtless knew Gandhi only as a remote historical figure. The total explanation would certainly be complex, but these factors are probably involved: Relatively powerless groups, who would inevitably be overcome in any open contest of force, have often found nonviolent resistance a way of maximizing their strength in dealing with an opponent who has some respect for law and a conscience. In a sense, this is a way of getting part of the dominant force over on the minority's side.[67] (This is a tactic, of course, in interpersonal as well as intergroup relations. We will leave it to the reader's memory to identify the conditions under which children employ it successfully.)

To this perhaps humanwide source of nonviolent resistance one must add the Christian tradition. It comes as a natural part of the cultural training of most Negroes to believe that they can achieve through suffering, that they should turn the other cheek, that the enemy can better be overcome by love than by force. When Negroes were virtually powerless, this religious tradition led to otherworldliness, accommodative attitudes, and repressed or deflected aggression. In the last decade, however, many Negroes have become militant. Vander Zanden suggests that the nonviolent resistance movement is an effort to mediate between the tradition of accommodation and the new militancy. The latter arouses guilt feelings that the nonviolent protests help to allay by their emphasis on suffering.[68]

Narrowing the sources of this movement further, we would note the American tradition as one of the essential ingredients. Half a century before Gandhi began his work, Henry David Thoreau was advising civil disobedience of laws that were an offense to one's conscience; and there was ample precedent for his advice (although the nonviolent quality gets lost) in the Boston Tea Party or the American Revolution itself. It is perhaps not too much of an exaggeration to say that there is a touch of the anarchist in every American: hateful laws and offensive authorities are not to be obeyed. This is both the glory and the problem of a free society.

In reply to a letter from eight Alabama ministers who expressed regret over the vigor of the protest against segregation in Birmingham, Martin Luther King wrote:

You express a great deal of anxiety over our willingness to break laws. . . . An unjust law is a code inflicted upon a minority which that minority had no part in enacting or creating . . . I submit that an individual who breaks a law that conscience tells him is unjust, and willingly accepts the penalty by staying in jail to arouse the conscience of the community over his injustice, is in reality expressing the very highest respect for law. We can never forget that everything Hitler did was 'legal' and everything the Hungarian freedom fighters did in Hungary was 'illegal.'[69]

This sounds as much like Patrick Henry as Gandhi. But more than that, in the course of his long letter, King cited, among others, the eighth-century prophets, Socrates, St. Paul, St. Thomas, Thomas Jefferson, Abraham Lincoln, Martin Buber, and Paul Tillich,

---

[66] See Bell, *op. cit.,* esp. chap. 3; and Thomas R. Frazier, "An Analysis of Nonviolent Coercion as Used by the Sit-In Movement," *Phylon,* Spring, 1968, pp. 27–40.

[67] For a discussion of its use in South Africa, see Leo Kuper, *Passive Resistance in South Africa,* Yale, 1957.

[68] James W. Vander Zanden, "The Non-Violent Resistance Movement Against Segregation," *AJS,* Mar., 1963, pp. 544–550.

[69] Letter from a Birmingham Jail," *Liberation,* June, 1963, pp. 12–13; this letter was reprinted also in *Atlantic Monthly,* Aug., 1963, pp. 78–88, and in *Progressive,* July, 1963, pp. 9–13.

not to mention Shadrach, Meshach, and Abednego. Such is the reach of the goals and strategy of freedom.

We shall not undertake to describe the wave of nonviolent protests that swept across the United States, particularly in the early years of the 1960s. There were thousands of boycotts, sit-ins, freedom rides, picketing, and mass rallies.[70] Some of these were designed to win a specific goal—to secure jobs or to open facilities from which nonwhites had been barred—others were primarily symbolic affirmations of the need for an open society. Boycotts by a minority group become effective when their buying power, for the particular firms involved, represents the difference between economic health and bankruptcy. This requires, of course, that the group be sufficiently well organized to focus their opposition, and the absence of such focus on the part of groups who oppose the boycott. Even in favorable circumstances, employers and merchants are likely to resist the pressure of boycotts even if they have no particular desire to discriminate and are do-

[70] These are not new strategies. Boycotts go back at least to the first of the century, and CORE began its sit-in movement in the early 1940s. But as a mass movement, such activities appeared only in the 1960s. For a sampling of studies, see August Meier and Elliott Rudwick, "The Boycott Movement against Jim Crow Streetcars in the South, 1900–1906," *Journal of American History*, Mar., 1969, pp. 756–775; Warren Eisenberg and Marvin Weisbrod, "Money Talks in the City of Brotherly Love," *Progressive*, Aug., 1963, pp. 20–23; Ray Shaw, in the *Wall Street Journal*, June 30, 1961, pp. 1, 10; Hannah Lees, "The Not-Buying Power of Philadelphia's Negroes," *Reporter*, May 11, 1961, pp. 33–35; Merrill Proudfoot, *Diary of a Sit-In*, Univ. of North Carolina Press, 1962; James Peck, *Freedom Ride*, Simon & Schuster, 1962; James Peck, *Cracking the Color Line*, CORE, no date; Louis Lomax, *The Negro Revolt*, Harper & Row, 1962, chaps. 10 and 11; "Freedom Rides," *New South* (whole issue), July–Aug., 1961; C. Eric Lincoln, "The Strategy of the Sit-in," *Reporter*, Jan. 6, 1961, pp. 2–23; Ruth Searles and J. Allen Williams, Jr., "Negro College Students' Participation in Sit-Ins," *SF*, Mar., 1962, pp. 215–220; Ralph McGill, *The South and the Southerner*, Little, Brown, 1963; Glenford Mitchell and William Peace III (eds.), *The Angry Black South*, Corinth Books, 1961; Martin Luther King, Jr., *Stride Toward Freedom: The Montgomery Story*, Harper & Row, 1958; Martin Luther King, Jr., *Strength to Love*, Harper & Row, 1963; "The Negro in America," *Newsweek*, July 29, 1963, pp. 15–34; Harold Isaacs, *The New World of Negro Americans*, John Day, 1963.

ing so more out of habit than necessity or conviction. They are likely to be unhappy about a further limitation of their freedom of action (much as they are uncomfortable about many union demands). They may not need new employees in the positions involved (if jobs are the goal of the boycott). Seniority provisions may interfere; union practices may oppose the change; minority-group members with the requisite skills and training may be difficult to find. Nevertheless, in numerous cases, boycotts have enlarged the range of jobs open to minority groups and improved their treatment by merchants.

Sit-ins and freedom rides involve a great deal of courage and self-discipline, for their purpose is to persuade people without violence to abide by a law that they have long been disregarding, usually with support from the dominant community and the police. These protests started with restaurants and lunch counters, and spread out to parks, libraries, art galleries, swimming pools, churches, and transportation facilities, all of which were substantially segregated in the South in 1960. There were wade-ins, read-ins, ride-ins, and pray-ins. Violence broke out in many cases, and many of the protesters were injured and thousands more were jailed. Several were killed. The total effect, nevertheless, was the desegregation of many public facilities, but more importantly, the dramatization of segregation and discrimination so vividly that they can never again be taken for granted in the United States.

Violent Resistance

Almost everybody admires at least one revolution—usually one distant in time if the person is comfortable and a contemporary one if he is not. The staunchest defenders of law and order recognize the role of coercion in human affairs; but they want the use of violent coercion limited to the official representatives of society. For those who deeply believe, however, that they suffer from that society—and at the hands of those representatives—such a restriction on the use of violence is unacceptable. Coercion is monopolized only under those rare conditions when the locus of legitimacy is unanimously agreed upon. Clearly that is not the situation in most societies today. Minorities in many places are saying: Why should we simply capitulate to *their* violence? It is less moral than our own.

We cannot discuss, here, the conditions under which such loss of legitimacy is likely to occur.[71] Briefly, it is the product of a cycle of causes: rising aspirations and a sharply increased sense of relative deprivation on the part of minorities; pressure against the system; reaction by the dominant group, some of it violent (violence may actually decrease, but it is more visible, and probably more "official," because the informal social control mechanisms prove to be inadequate); stronger pressure against the system, with supporting ideologies now justifying reciprocal violence (we are an internal colony, with every right to break free).

For the dominant group it is clear that violence is successful in maintaining allegiance only when it is used minimally. Greater use may maintain sullen and unwilling compliance, but not allegiance. A related principle applies to minorities: Minimal violence used to underline a neglected legitimacy may get support, or not arouse major retaliation. When the conflict is heightened, counterviolence is increased and it becomes more difficult to maintain a publicly accepted definition that the minority violence was an understandable (if unfortunate) protest.[72]

It is, of course, difficult to draw a line between violence and nonviolence. Is it violent to hurt a child personally, but nonviolent to support a system that causes the child to be malnourished as an infant, so that he does not fully develop, physically or mentally? Is it violent to smash the windows in a man's store and loot his shelves, but nonviolent to picket his business so that his economic loss is as great as it would have been had he been looted? Those who justify opposition to violence on moral grounds need to be certain they are not drawing a distinction without a difference.

Important as these moral questions are, the focus of our attention in this chapter is on strategy. In this light, a minority appropriately asks how the willingness or unwillingness to use violence increases the resources at its disposal and reduces the deficits. In a relatively open society the marshaling of resources is more dependent on the mutual trust within the minority than on their persuading or coercing the majority to make concessions. Effective action requires the *accumulation* of resources. Politically, this means the use of flexible and focused voting that can be brought to bear on particular issues and elections, rather than scattered and competitive politics that divides the minority vote. Economically, it means the building up, out of funds that are individually too small, of resources that jointly are adequate to accomplish a given purpose. Clifford Geertz describes the "revolving credit associations" that exist in many villages and towns of Southeast Asia and Africa. The associations are circles of friends and neighbors who make periodic contributions to a common fund. Each member, in an order determined by lot or by some prearranged method, has his turn in using the fund for some major purchase.[73]

Similar arrangements are not uncommon among minority communities in the United States and elsewhere. Chinese, Japanese, and Jews have been among those who have thus focused their resources. The Black Muslims accumulate collectively in a way that has permitted the founding of many businesses. Even the numbers racket can be looked upon as an incipient "rotating credit association;" but as Coleman notes, the return is so small as a proportion of the "investment" and the

---

[71] For a valuable series of studies of situations attesting to low "legitimacy" see Hugh D. Graham and Ted R. Gurr (eds.), *Violence in America: Historical and Comparative Perspectives*, Praeger, 1969. See also H. L. Nieburg, "Uses of Violence," *JCR*, Mar., 1963, pp. 43–54.

[72] See Robert M. Fogelson, "Violence as Protest," *op. cit.*; pp. 25–41.

[73] Cited by Coleman, *op. cit.*, p. 286, from Clifford Geertz, "The Rotating Credit Association: A 'Middle Rung' in Development," *Economic Development and Cultural Change*, April, 1962, pp. 241–263.

likelihood of winning so unpredictable, that the effect is to drain rather than aid the community.

What has this to do with the question of violence? Violence is an outward strategy. It is based on the assumption that coercing the majority is the primary need. Although it is sometimes justified as a source of minority community solidarity, it tends in fact to tear the fabric of trust on which community solidarity depends. Whenever a situation has developed in which discrimination by the majority has fallen off, and new procedures to take advantage of new openings are called for, violence deflects energy and wastes resources. It is one of the ironies of history that violence is most likely to erupt precisely when, and partly because, new opportunities are opening; and it may persist into the period when techniques for exploiting newly available opportunities are the chief need.

Interpretations of the impact of violence differ widely, not only because of differing moral premises, but also because the situation is extremely complex. One must be alert to long-run, and not only short-run, consequences, to all the unintended as well as to the intended effects. Among interpretations of the riots in American cities during the 1960s, for example, one finds such contrasting notions as these: Riots increase hatred, confirm prejudices; action to remedy grievances must not follow riots or it will appear that lawlessness and hostility are being rewarded. Yet others argue that desparately needed action seems to come only after a riot, which smashes complacency and exposes the problem as nothing else has been able to do. The assessment is difficult. It does seem clear that under some circumstances, riots are heard as a cry of pain. They may help to transform private trouble into a public issue, to use a theme developed by C. Wright Mills in another connection, by flooding the media of communication with the importance of the problem. Yet riots, in addition to the immediate losses and costs, tend to confirm mutual stereotypes, to increase segregation by speeding the flight of Whites to the suburbs, and to give the participants a sense they have struck a blow for freedom, when in fact they have only indicated the need for freedom, while leaving the basic difficulties intact.

We agree with B. L. R. Smith that extensive use of violence tends to spread through a society a "revolutionary myth" that has serious unanticipated, long-run costs.

The costs are partly visible in such things as an increased sense of fear in the community shared by whites and blacks alike, the greater salience of politics for people's lives in a society which has usually resisted the encroachments of political attitudes into the sphere of basic human relationships, and the prospect that, since the stakes of politics are higher, ruling elites in the future may seek to manage conflict by excessive resort to force. Violence begets more violence and ultimately will leave deep scars on the nation's image of itself, profoundly alter life styles, and change the temper of the American mind.[74]

Barrington Moore suggests that violence fails to work ". . . mainly when revolutionary rhetoric outruns the real possibilities inherent in a given historical situation,"[75] that is, when a group underestimates the opposition. We believe it also fails, in the sense that in entails great costs without concomitant gains, when it overestimates the opposition, when it fails to see possibilities that are available in a situation at much lower cost than that required by violence.

We are confronted, in the matter of violence, with an extremely sharp dilemma in any society that maintains serious barriers to full participation by some of its members. On the one hand, we are told by some that ". . . extremism on the left helps to undermine the democratic center and prepare the way for a takeover by the right . . ."; but also that ". . . by following what they call moderate and responsible policies those devoted to liberalism may become the hostages, and even agents, of repressive and reactionary trends."[76] A society cannot solve a dilemma of this kind. So long as the conditions

[74] B. L. R. Smith, "The Politics of Protest: How Effective is Violence," in Connery (ed.), *op. cit.*, p. 128.

[75] Barrington Moore, Jr. "Thoughts on Violence and Democracy," in *ibid.*, p. 6.

[76] *Ibid.*, p. 5. Moore is summarizing positions, not stating his own in these quotations.

that produce it exist, those seeking to reduce the deprivation and injustice suffered by minorities will be split strategically; some will sanction a mainly self-defeating violence and others will accept a mainly illiberal social system. The dilemma can be made to a greater or lesser degree irrelevant by undermining its causes, by using all the various strategies we have discussed to open up structures of opportunity. In our judgment, the level of violence is an index of relative success but is an inefficient strategy for bringing about that opening.[77]

CHANGING THE MINORITY-GROUP MEMBER

Our discussion of strategy has so far emphasized the task of removing special disprivileges faced by minority-group members. Where causes are cyclical, however, and mutually reenforcing, this is not sufficient. Built into the personality systems and group structures of minorities are some of the consequences of *past* discrimination. These may persist into situations that are less discriminatory, preventing the reduction of prejudice and lowering the possibilities that present opportunities will be exploited. Thus the responses of minority-group members to prejudice and discrimination frequently lend support to further hostility. One line of approach that strategy may take, therefore, is to discover ways of changing some of the responses of the minorities. Many comfortable people—including the relatively more comfortable members of the minorities themselves—too often emphasize this as *the* solution. Let the Negro improve himself, they say, and prejudice will disappear. When the Jew stops being Jewish, there will be no discrimination against him. If the immigrant will adopt American ways, no one will oppose him. This approach suffers from the double error of "bootstrap" thinking (demanding that minorities change many characteristics that are the *results* of prejudice

[77] For other references on violence, see footnote 30, chap. 7.

before the prejudice can be reduced) and a limited monocultural, homogeneous view of society that is probably not harmonious with the realities of the modern, complex world. There is, however, a small way in which this approach is useful, as part of a total strategy. To the prejudiced person, the characteristics and the responses of minority-group members are part of the total situation that seems to him to justify his action. If they can be changed, or his conception of them changed, he will perceive the situation differently.

The emphasis on self-improvement is greeted with derision by some minority-group members because it seems to place the responsibility for prejudice on the oppressed people. In our view "responsibility" for hostility, if one wants to use that term, must be located in the nature of man; but effective strategy may require attention to the best responses by members of the minorities.

In a time of sharp controversy this point is difficult to make. If members of the dominant group call attention to the behavior of minority-group members—whatever the cause —and the support that behavior gives to prejudice and discrimination, they are liable to criticism for blaming the victim for having the weaknesses that mistreatment has forced upon him. If one of the minority-group itself calls attention to the need for discipline and self-improvement, he runs the risk of being called an "Uncle Tom" or "Uncle Tomahawk," a traitor to the cause.

Nevertheless the point should be made, for there is great need for further study of the conditions that promote the perpetuation of minority subcultures and personality tendencies which prevent the entrance of minority-group members into the full range of community life even when barriers have been lowered. Perhaps recriminations can be avoided if one puts the issue, not in terms of a vocabulary of praise and blame, but in terms of cause and effect. One then asks a strategic question: To what degree is emphasis on changes in the motivation, values, behavior, and group structures of minorities effective as a complement to changes in patterns of dominant-group discrimination and segregation, in the effort to remove inequities? Or, perhaps more adequately, under what conditions is emphasis on minority-group changes most effective? There is little that one can say with confidence in answer to this question, but we would suggest that the further desegregation has proceeded the stronger should be the emphasis on minority change. We may be getting in some regions and in some aspects of American life to the place where a call for expanded opportunities meets an embarrassing shortage of persons qualified to use those opportunities.

Attention to minority tendencies is based on the interdependence of minority-majority patterns. The attainment of equality may demand not only the reduction of discrimination by those who are dominant, but a change in motivations by those who are suppressed. Minority-group norms and character structures are to some degree tuned to a discriminatory society; they reflect efforts to adjust to or deal with that society, for they are part of an interlocking system. When discrimination declines, minority-group members may not be ready to seize new opportunities fully. Protected islands may be demanded, or built (and perhaps are needed during a period of transition), and the system may still be blamed. If, however, this blame is poorly placed, if it does not identify the true situation, it will be an expensive luxury.

Following this line of argument, we are led into one of the great issues of social change: What force is powerful enough to transform men, to create individuals ready and able to respond effectively to a new world? Some argue, as we noted in an earlier chapter, that violence can do this, that it is, to repeat Sartre's words "man recreating himself." But this does not ask what he is recreating himself for. The Nazis were recreated and united "by the terrorism around us," just as Eldridge Cleaver remarked of "the most beautiful sight . . . leather jackets, black trousers . . . and each with a gun." Oppenheimer asks ". . . whether this therapeutic effect stems from violence or from the effect of struggling against oppression. . . ."[78] And Fanon, even as he exalts

violence, also notes its great psychic costs, for the individual, his family, and the total community.

Are there less costly ways to achieve necessary personal transformations? The power of some religious movements to "revitalize" their adherents has often been studied. (This is not necessarily in contradistinction to violence, it should be noted, since violence may be heightened by the belief that one is fighting for a sacred cause.) One of the critical elements in Max Weber's analysis of *The Protestant Ethic and the Spirit of Capitalism* was his belief that Calvinism drastically reorganized the motivations and perceptions of its adherents. David McClelland traces the "need for achievement" primarily to the family background wherein aspirations and values are taught. He sees that need as prerequisite to actual achievement, although other factors are involved.[79] It has been observed frequently that the Black Muslims have a great power to reorganize the motives and goals of their members.[80] Applying this thesis to race relations in the United States, without specifically religious connotations, it may be ". . . that the real benefit of the civil rights movement is the psychological change it has produced and is producing in those Negroes who are active in it."[81] A more drastic interpretation of this thesis gives it a group dimension, and perhaps takes us back to the question of violence. As Coleman describes this point of view: "Participation in revolutionary action transforms the previously apathetic masses by giving them a goal and the hope of achieving the goal."[82]

Whatever one may regard as the most effective method for achieving this goal, it is clear that some personality reorganization, not only of the majority-group member, but of the minority-group member as well is necessary as part of the process whereby majority-minority systems are transformed.

---

[78] Oppenheimer, *op. cit.*, p. 65.

[79] See Max Weber, *The Protestant Ethic and the Spirit of Capitalism*, George Allen and Unwin, 1930; David McClelland, *The Achieving Society*, Van Nostrand, 1961.

[80] C. Eric Lincoln, *The Black Muslims in America*, Beacon Press, 1961.

[81] James S. Coleman, *op. cit.*, p. 295.

[82] *Ibid.*, p. 294.

CONCLUSION

The freedom movement of the last few decades has brought inescapably to the white man's attention the plight and the demands of the nation's minorities. Probably more important, it has galvanized the minorities themselves into action, and has increased their self-respect and the sense that they can struggle with their difficult conditions with some chance of success. America can go on with her revolution, broadening the base of participation, or she can go through a long period of tension, conflict, and repression; but the relatively stable majority-minority system, with its great inequities, has been drastically modified.

This does not mean that new patterns will emerge smoothly, automatically, peacefully. The speed of change, the degree of conflict which accompanies it, the extent to which attitudes change along with behavior, depend upon the strategic skill of the contending groups and upon the way in which America deals with various problems before her that have nothing directly to do with majority-minority relations. Two of these problems are basic: international tensions and economic instability. Although disputes with other nations to some degree tend to reduce lines of separation within a country, there are also powerful forces on the other side: not only does a vast military budget deprive us of many of the resources with which we might deal with internal problems, but international tensions also give the bigot an opportunity for attacking minority groups as somehow threatening to the nation.

Economic questions are also of vital importance. There are 40 million persons in the United States who, by almost any definition, live in poverty. Two-thirds of them are white. In the last decade there has been a tendency for the economy to move up for the top 75 or 80 percent of the population, but to leave the 40 million behind. In most instances these are the untrained and the unskilled; their jobs are being sharply reduced by automation; many of them are caught in a vicious circle of low income—poor health—poor schools—low motivation that has become more difficult to escape because of changes in the economy. So long as the United States fails to deal successfully with this problem, she may open up opportunities for the trained talents among her minorities, but for most, lack of legal or customary obstacles will not be enough. So long as they are caught in poverty's vicious cycle they will not be able to take advantage of the opportunities now formally, and painfully, being opened to them.

Throughout this analysis we have emphasized the interactive and cumulative nature of the forces influencing intergroup relations. For purposes of discussion, it has frequently been necessary to isolate one aspect of the total pattern; but it would be a costly error to forget the total empirical scene, for that is what, in the last analysis, we want to understand and to control. The interlocking of the many factors that affect majority-minority relations greatly complicates the work of the student and of the social engineer. We have all too often tried to untangle this complexity by oversimplified theories and strategies. Williams emphasizes this point strongly:

. . . The known facts create a strong presumption that a main source of the persistence of intergroup hostility is precisely the interlocking and mutual reinforcement of cultural differences, other visible differences, realistic interests, deflected aggression, and other factors. In short, the most important questions may concern not the influence of particular factors but the way in which mutual reinforcement operates, and determination of the strategic factors in a plan for shifting the resultant pattern. In this connection, there is a definite possibility that the factors which are most important in producing hostility and conflict are by no means the same as those which are most important for control purposes. Thus, the roots of intergroup hostility may lie in the early socialization of children in the home. But this process is so inaccessible to direct external control that other, even seemingly far removed approaches may be more promising for immediate action.[83]

The problem can perhaps be illustrated by an analogy. What causes tuberculosis? It seems to be the interaction and accumulation of several factors: perhaps a hereditary predisposition, early environmental conditions

[83] Robin Williams, Jr., *The Reduction of Intergroup Tensions*, SSRC, 1947, pp. 41–42.

(diet and living quarters), general physical health, specific occupational hazards, contact with infected persons, and so on. To say that tuberculosis is "caused" by a hereditary predisposition or by poor general physical condition or some other factor is equivalent to saying that prejudice and discrimination are caused by personal insecurity or economic competition or some other one factor.

The analogy might also apply to the question of prevention or cure. Hereditary predisposition might be important in many cases of tuberculosis, but at the present time that is beyond our control. An effective campaign must be directed at the most vulnerable factors—perhaps the isolation of infected persons or the removal of specific occupational hazards, or a school program of examination and dietary supplements that greatly reduces the problem of persuading 50 million families to improve their diets or have regular examinations.

This distinction between the causal factors and the factors most vulnerable to strategic attack applies equally well to intergroup hostility. Some of the (frequently brilliant) analyses of the personality elements in prejudice leap too easily to strategic conclusions. As MacIver said:

Since policy measures can hardly hope to change the basic drives of human beings whereas they have some potency over social institutions and economic conditions the concentration of effort should be directed to the latter rather than to the former aspects of the discrimination complex. We doubt, for example, whether any serious gain can be made by highlighting the "scapegoat" element in discriminatory treatment. It need by no means be left out of the reckoning, but any advantage to be derived from the exposure of it will be at best quite subsidiary to a strategy the main assault of which must be delivered against less elusive and more controllable factors.[84]

The Need for Research. Only a small proportion of the time and energy spent in trying to improve intergroup relations is devoted to research—to analysis of the effectiveness of specific programs and to the study of the total causal complex; hence much of the

work may be inefficient or even harmful. In many areas of modern life, extensive research is considered indispensable. In industry, in medicine, in the development of military weapons, no important program is adopted before vast sums have been spent to develop the most efficient means. This approach is only beginning to be used in the analysis and control of human behavior. It is only in a partial sense that this is a "scientific age." A great many people, faced by the confusion and anxiety of modern life, have developed a prideful antiscientism when it comes to understanding human beings. The qualifications that science demands, the painstaking research, the refusal to declare unqualifiedly that this or that is true, regardless of conditions—these aspects of the scientific frame of mind seem to increase the anxiety of many people for they prevent the acceptance of easy, comforting answers to life's problems. We experience a "failure of nerve" when it comes to analyzing ourselves; we seek a way to "escape from freedom."

But the present authors firmly believe (this is a premise, not a conclusion) that the turning back to old formulas—traditional answers, unqualified nationalism, the seemingly self-confident declarations of the "practical" man—can only deepen our problems. In the field with which we are concerned we must demand of every proposition its methodological credentials: What is the evidence? What variables are involved? How were they controlled? How does this harmonize with, or contradict, existing theoretical positions? It may seem like tedious business to some—to others it is exciting adventure—but there is no easier way to understanding and control.

We share the belief that science should be relevant, and hope that this book expresses our support.[85] There is a serious danger, however, that the cry for relevance can carry us back to old antagonism and drastic swings of the pendulum unless it is accompanied by a matching belief: *Let relevance be scientific.* There's not much point in making very good time if we don't know where we are headed.

[84] MacIver, *The More Perfect Union*, p. 81.

[85] For several interesting papers on science and policy, see "Sociological Research and Public Policy," *American Sociologist* (whole issue), June, 1971.

Of the research that we do have in the area of intergroup relations a high proportion has been concerned with the causes of prejudice and discrimination, relatively little with strategies that are effective, in specific situations, in reducing them. There is great need for more of the latter. A large number of the studies have been of the pencil-and-paper variety; these must be supplemented by more studies of other kinds of behavior and of the relation between verbal and non-verbal responses in intergroup relations.

Science and Values. It is sometimes said that science cannot contribute to the solution of such moral problems as prejudice because its predictions are of the "if and when" variety; they tell us only what will happen when certain specified variables are controlled, not what will occur in a particular situation. True, science cannot make concrete predictions; it must state its predictions for specific situations in terms of probability limits, depending upon the degree to which certain variables are operative. Nevertheless, as we isolate more and more of the influencing factors and learn more about their interaction, we can greatly narrow the probability limits. We can classify situations into more and more homogeneous types on the basis of the variables involved, and thus come nearer to understanding specific situations.

The discouraging aspects of the concepts of interaction, of the vicious circle and the self-fulfilling prophecy, have led some to believe that science, in describing these processes, has deepened our pessimism and injured the will to action. But science does not say that these things are inevitable; it says they will occur if certain variables do not change.

The self-fulfilling prophecy, whereby fears are translated into reality, operates only in the absence of deliberate institutional controls. And it is only with the rejection of social fatalism implied in the notion of unchangeable human nature that the tragic circle of fear, social disaster, reinforced fear can be broken. . . .

Nor can widespread, even typical, failures in planning human relations between ethnic groups be cited as evidence for pessimism. In the world laboratory of the sociologist, as in the more secluded laboratories of the physicist and chemist, it is the successful experiment which is decisive and not the thousand-and-one failures which preceded it. More is learned from the single success than from the multiple failures. A single success proves it can be done. Thereafter, it is necessary only to learn what made it work.[86]

It is often said that social science is deterministic in the sense that it makes any human effort useless. Man behaves the way he does because of what he is. He is a product of heredity and environment; since his nature cannot be changed, nothing can be done. If this view is taken, one gives up or becomes either a cynic or a theologian.

This is not the sense, however, in which science is deterministic. Science does state that events have a natural pattern and that man is part of the natural world, a creature of law. *If* certain forces are operative, these will be the results. But it may well be (and it is at this point that science is deterministic, but not predeterministic) that an understanding of the nature of events is a new variable that changes the results. Natural laws indicate that if one eats certain kinds of food in excess and fails to brush his teeth, he is liable to tooth decay. *Knowledge of those facts is a new variable that may prevent that result.* The laws are still true—*if.* Knowledge can help to free us; it does not bind us to the inevitable *application* of the natural laws. It will not work fast. Parents may know, intellectually, the best way to deal with their children, yet be unable to apply this knowledge. Some specific acts are more subject to rational control—institutional processes that do not involve the emotions of individuals, for example. These can improve the second generation, which, in turn, can bring knowledge and action more closely into line; it can change a little more, creating a better situation for the next generation. Those who demand the millennium day after tomorrow will be frustrated by this slow process. But many may find in the promise of this difficult road a quiet confidence that modern man sorely needs.

[86] Robert K. Merton, *Social Theory and Social Structure*, Free Press, rev. ed., 1957, p. 436.

BIBLIOGRAPHY*

Auerbach, Joel D., and Jack L. Walker, "The Meanings of Black Power: A Comparison of White and Black Interpretations of a Political Slogan," *American Political Science Review*, June, 1970, pp. 367–388.

Ablon, Joan, "American Indian Relocation: Problems of Dependency and Management in the City," *Phylon*, Winter, 1965, pp. 362–371.

Abrams, Charles, *The City Is the Frontier*, Harper & Row, 1965.

Abrams, Charles, *Forbidden Neighbors*, Harper & Row, 1955.

Abrams, Charles, "The Housing Problem and the Negro," *Daedalus*, Winter, 1966, pp. 64–76.

Ackerman, Nathan W., and Marie Jahoda, *Anti-Semitism and Emotional Disorder: A Psychoanalytic Interpretation*, Harper & Row, 1950.

Adelson, Joseph, "A Study of Minority Group Authoritarianism," in Marshall Sklare (ed.), *The Jews*, Free Press, 1958, pp. 475–492.

Anti-Defamation League, *Law, Special Report 1*, 1970.

Adorno, T. W., Else Frenkel-Brunswik, D. J. Levinson, and R. N. Sanford, *The Authoritarian Personality*, Harper & Row, 1950.

Ahmann, Mathew (ed.), *Race: Challenge to Religion*, Regnery, 1963.

Alex, Nicholas, *Black in Blue: A Study of the Negro Policeman*, Meredith, 1969.

Alland, Alexander, Jr., " 'Possession' in a Revivalist Negro Church," *JSSR*, Spring, 1962, pp. 204–213.

Allen, Russell O., and Bernard Spilka, "Committed and Consensual Religion: A Specification of Religion-Prejudice Relationships," *JSSR*, Fall, 1967, pp. 191–206.

Allen, Vernon (ed.), "Ghetto Riots," *JSI*, Winter, 1970 (whole issue).

Allport, Gordon W., *The Nature of Prejudice*, Addison-Wesley, 1954.

Allport, Gordon W., *Personality and Social Encounter*, Beacon Press, 1960.

Allport, Gordon W., and Bernard M. Kramer, "Some Roots of Prejudice," *JP*, July, 1946, pp. 9–39.

Allport, Gordon W., and J. Michael Ross, "Personal Religious Orientation and Prejudice," *JPSP*, Jan., 1967, pp. 432–443.

Altshuler, Alan A., *Community Control: The Black Demand for Participation in Large American Cities*, Pegasus, 1970.

Alves, Pagel L., Jr., "The Urban Scene: Housing and Poverty," in Patricia W. Romero (ed.), *In Black America*, United, 1969, pp. 235–237.

American Council for Judaism, "Soviet Jews: An Investigation," *Issues*, Summer, 1968 (whole issue).

Amir, Yehuda, "Contact Hypothesis in Ethnic Relations," *Psychology Bulletin*, May, 1969, pp. 319–342.

Anderson, Thomas P., "Edouard Drumont and the Origins of Modern Anti-Semitism," *Catholic History Review*, Apr., 1967, pp. 28–42.

Andrews, Benny, "On Understanding Black Art," *The New York Times*, June 21, 1970, p. D21.

Angell, Robert C., "Preferences for Moral Norms in Three Problem Areas," *AJS*, May, 1962, pp. 650–660.

Antonovsky, Aaron, "The Social Meaning of Discrimination," *Phylon*, Spring, 1960, pp. 81–95.

Antonovsky, Aaron, "Toward a Refinement of the 'Marginal Man' Concept," *SF*, Oct., 1956, pp. 57–62.

Antonovsky, Aaron, and Melvin J. Lerner, "Occupational Aspirations of Lower Class Negro and White Youth," *SP*, Fall, 1959, pp. 132–138.

Aptheker, Herbert, *The Negro People in America*, International, 1946.

Arnez, Nancy Levi, and Clara B. Anthony, "Contemporary Negro Humor as Social Satire," *Phylon*, Winter, 1968, pp. 339–346.

Asher, Steven R., and Vernon L. Allen, "Racial Preference and Social Comparison Processes," *JSI*, Jan., 1969, pp. 157–166.

Aubery, Pierre, *Milieux Juifs de la France contemporaine*, Paris: Plon, 1962.

Axelrad, Sidney, "Negro and White Male Insti-

---

* In addition to the sources cited here, there are many references in the footnotes to books and articles that deal with the topics discussed in this volume. These can be located by use of the Index.

tutionalized Delinquents," *AJS*, May, 1952, pp. 569–574.

Bagley, Christopher, "Race Relations and Theories of Status Consistency," *Race*, Jan., 1970, pp. 267–288.

Bailey, Kenneth K., *Southern White Protestantism in the Twentieth Century*, Harper & Row, 1964.

Baldwin, James, *The Fire Next Time*, Dial Press, 1963.

Baldwin, James, *Nobody Knows My Name*, Dell, 1961.

Baldwin, James, *Notes of a Native Son*, Beacon Press, 1955.

Ball, Harry V., George E. Simpson, and Kiyoshi Ikeda, "Law and Social Change: Sumner Reconsidered," *AJS*, Mar., 1962, pp. 532–540.

Ball, Harry V., and Douglas S. Yamamura, "Ethnic Discrimination and the Marketplace: A Study of Landlords' Preferences in a Polyethnic Community," *ASR*, Oct., 1960, pp. 687–694.

Banfield, Edward C., *The Unheavenly City: The Nature and Future of Our Urban Crisis*, Little, Brown, 1968.

Banfield, Edward C., and Morton Grodzins, *Government and Housing in Metropolitan Areas*, McGraw-Hill, 1958.

Banton, Michael, *The Coloured Quarter*, Jonathan Cape, 1955.

Banton, Michael, *Race Relations*, Basic Books, 1967.

Banton, Michael, "What Do We Mean by 'Racism'?" *New Society*, Apr. 10, 1969, pp. 552 ff.

Barbour, Floyd B. (ed.), *The Black Power Revolt*, Porter Sargent, 1968.

Barker, Horace, "Open Housing: No Southern State Has Moved to Enforce This Law of the Land," *South Today*, Mar., 1971, pp. 4 ff.

Barron, Milton L., "A Content Analysis of Intergroup Humor," *ASR*, Feb., 1950, pp. 88–94.

Barron, Milton L., "The Incidence of Jewish Intermarriage in Europe and America," *ASR*, Feb., 1946, pp. 6–13.

Barron, Milton L. (ed.), *Minorities in a Changing World*, Knopf, 1967.

Barron, Milton L., *People Who Intermarry*, Syracuse Univ. Press, 1948.

Barron, Milton L., "Research on Intermarriage: A Survey of Accomplishments and Prospects," *AJS*, Nov., 1951, pp. 249–255.

Bass, Bernard M., "Authoritarianism or Acquiescence," *JASP*, Nov., 1955, pp. 616–623.

Bastide, Roger, and Pierre Van den Berghe, "Stereotypes, Norms and Interracial Behavior in Sao Paulo, Brazil," *ASR*, Dec., 1957, pp. 689–694.

Bayley, David H., and Harold Mendelsohn, *Minorities and the Police: Confrontation in America*, Free Press, 1969.

Bayton, James A., "The Racial Stereotypes of Negro College Students," *JASP*, Jan., 1941, pp. 97–102.

Beach, Waldo, "Storm Warnings from the South," *Christianity and Crisis*, Mar. 19, 1956, pp. 27–30.

Becker, Howard P., *Man in Reciprocity*, Praeger, 1956.

Bell, Inge Powell, *Core and the Strategy of Non-Violence*, Random House, 1968.

Bell, Robert R., "Lower Class Negro Mothers' Aspirations for Their Children," *SF*, May, 1965, pp. 493–495.

Bell, Robert R., *Marriage and Family Interaction*, Dorsey Press, rev. ed., 1967.

Belth, Nathan, and Morton Puner (eds.), *Prejudice and the Lively Arts*, ADL, 1963.

Benedict, Ruth, *Race: Science and Politics*, Modern Age Books, 1940.

Bennett, Lerone, Jr., "What's in a Name," *Ebony*, Nov., 1967, pp. 46–52, 54. Reprinted in Peter I. Rose (ed.), *Americans from Africa: Old Memories, New Moods*, Atherton Press, 1970, pp. 373–383.

Berger, Morroe, *Equality by Statute: The Revolution in Civil Rights*, Doubleday, 1967.

Berkowitz, Leonard, and James A. Green, "The Stimulus Qualities of the Scapegoat," *JASP*, Apr., 1962, pp. 293–301.

Berkowitz, Norman H., and George H. Wolkon, "A Forced Choice Form of the F Scale—Free of Acquiescent Response Set," *Sociometry*, Mar., 1964, pp. 54–65.

Bernard, Jessie, *Marriage and Family Among Negroes*, Prentice-Hall, 1966.

Berry, Brewton, *Almost White*, Macmillan, 1963.

Berry, Edwin C., and Walter W. Stafford, in Harold Baron (ed.), *The Racial Aspect of Urban Planning*, Chicago Urban League Research Report, 1968.

Besanceney, P. H., "On Reporting Rates of Intermarriage," *AJS*, May, 1965, pp. 717–721.

Bettelheim, Bruno, and Morris Janowitz, *Social Change and Prejudice*, Free Press, 1964.

Billingsley, Andrew, *Black Families in White America*, Prentice-Hall, 1968.

Black, Donald J., and Albert J. Reiss, Jr., "Police Control of Juveniles," *ASR*, Feb., 1970, pp. 63–77.

Blalock, Hubert M., Jr., *Toward a Theory of Minority-Group Relations*, Wiley, 1967.

Blauner, Robert, "Internal Colonialism and Ghetto Revolt," *SP*, Spring, 1969, pp. 393–408.

Blood, Robert O., *Marriage*, Free Press, 2nd ed., 1969.

Blood, Robert O., and Donald M. Wolfe, "Negro-White Differences in Blue-Collar Marriages in a Northern Metropolis," *SF*, Sept., 1969, pp. 59–64.

Bloom, Leonard, and Ruth Riemer, *Removal and Return: The Socio-Economic Effects of the War on Japanese Americans*, Univ. of California Press, 1949.

Bloom, Richard, Martin Whiteman, and Martin Deutsch, "Race and Social Class as Separate Factors Related to Social Environment," *AJS*, Jan., 1965, pp. 471–476.

Bloombaum, Milton, "The Conditions Underlying Race Riots as Portrayed by Multidimensional Scalogram Analysis: A Reanalysis of Lieberson and Silverman's Data," *ASR*, Feb., 1968, pp. 76–91.

Blue, John T., Jr., "Patterns of Racial Stratification: A Categoric Typology," *Phylon*, Winter, 1959, pp. 364–371.

Blumberg, Leonard, and Michael Lalli, "Little Ghettoes: A Study of Negroes in the Suburbs," *Phylon*, Summer, 1966, pp. 117–131.

Bock, Wilbur E., "The Decline of the Negro Clergy: Changes in Formal Religious Leadership in the United States in the Twentieth Century," *Phylon*, Spring, 1968, pp. 48–64.

Bock, Wilbur E., "Farmer's Daughter Effect: The Case of the Negro Female Professionals," *Phylon*, Spring, 1969, pp. 17–26.

Bogardus, Emory S., *Immigration and Race Attitudes*, Heath, 1928.

Bogardus, Emory S., "Race Reactions by Sex," *Sociology and Social Research*, July–Aug., 1959, pp. 439–441.

Bogardus, Emory S., "Racial Distance Changes in the United States During the Past Thirty Years," *Sociology and Social Research*, Nov.–Dec., 1958, pp. 127–135.

Bogardus, Emory S., "Racial Reactions by Regions," *Sociology and Social Research*, Mar.–Apr., 1959, pp. 286–290.

Bone, Robert A., *The Negro Novel in America*, Yale, 1958.

Bone, Robert A., "The Novels of James Baldwin," in Seymour L. Gross and John E. Hardy (eds.), *Images of the Negro in American Literature*, Univ. of Chicago Press, 1966, pp. 265 ff.

Bontemps, Arna (ed.), *American Negro Poetry*, Hill & Wang, 1963.

Bontemps, Arna, "The Negro Contribution to American Letters," in John F. Davis (ed.), *American Negro Reference Book*, Prentice-Hall, 1966, chap. 25.

Borrie, W. D., *et al.*, *The Cultural Integration of Immigrants*, United Nations Educational, Scientific and Cultural Organization (UNESCO), Paris, 1959.

Boskin, Joseph, *Urban Racial Violence in the Twentieth Century*, Glencoe, 1969.

Bossard, J. H. S., and E. S. Boll, *One Marriage Two Faiths*, Ronald Press, 1957.

Bowles, Samuel, "Towards Equality of Educational Opportunity," *HER*, Winter, 1968, pp. 91–97.

Boyd, William C., "Four Achievements of the Genetical Method in Physical Anthropology," *AA*, Apr., 1963, pp. 243–252.

Boyd, William C., *Genetics and the Races of Man*, Boston Univ. Press, 1958.

Brace, C. L., and M. F. Ashley Montagu, *Man's Evolution*, Macmillan, 1965.

Bracey, John H., Jr., August Meier, and Elliott Rudwick (eds.), *Black Nationalism in America*, Bobbs-Merrill, 1970.

Breed, Warren, "Group Structure and Resistance to Desegregation in the Deep South," *SP*, Summer, 1962, pp. 84–94.

Brimmer, Andrew, "Black Capitalism," *South Today*, Mar. 1970, p. 6.

Brody, Eugene B., "Color and Identity Conflict in Young Boys," *Psychiatry*, May, 1963, pp. 188–201.

Brody, Eugene B., "Social Conflict and Schizophrenic Behavior in Young Adult Negro Males," *Psychiatry*, Nov., 1961, pp. 337–346.

Broom, Leonard, and John I. Kitsuse, *The Managed Casualty: The Japanese-American Family in World War II*, Univ. of California Press, 1956.

Brophy, William, and Sophie Aberle (eds.), *The Indian: America's Unfinished Business*, Univ. of Oklahoma Press for The Fund for the Republic, 1966.

Brown, Claude, *Manchild in the Promised Land*, New American Library, 1965.

Brown, Clifton F., "Black Religion—1968," in Patricia W. Romero (ed.), *In Black America*, United, 1969, pp. 345–354.

Brown, Sterling A., "The Blues," *Phylon*, Fourth Quarter, 1952, pp. 286–292.

Brown, Sterling A., "Negro Character as Seen

by White Authors," *JNE*, Jan., 1933, pp. 180–201.

Brown, Sterling A., "Negro Folk Expression," *Phylon*, First Quarter, 1953, pp. 50–60.

Brown, Sterling A., *The Negro in American Fiction*, Associates in Negro Folk Education, 1937.

Brown, Sterling A., *Negro Poetry and Drama*, Associates in Negro Folk Education, 1937.

Brown, Sterling A., *Southern Road*, Harcourt Brace Jovanovich, 1932.

Brown, Sterling A., Arthur P. Davis, and Ulysses Lee (eds.), *The Negro Caravan*, Dryden Press, 1941.

Brunswick, Ann F., "What Generation Gap? A Comparison of Some Generational Differences among Blacks and Whites," *SP*, Winter, 1970, pp. 358–371.

Bugelski, B. R., "Assimilation Through Intermarriage," *SF*, Dec., 1961, pp. 148–153.

Bullough, Bonnie, *Social-Psychological Barriers to Housing Desegregation*, Univ. of Calif., Housing, Real Estate, and Urban Land Studies Program and the Center for Real Estate and Urban Economics, Special Report No. 2, 1969.

Burchinal, Lee B., and Loren E. Chancellor, "Survival Rates Among Religiously Homogamous and Interreligious Marriages," *SF*, May, 1963, pp. 353–362.

Burgess, M. Elaine, *Negro Leadership in a Southern City*, Univ. of North Carolina Press, 1962.

Burke, Peter J., "Scapegoating: An Alternative to Role Differentiation," *Sociometry*, June, 1969, pp. 159–168.

Burma, John H., "Humor as a Technique in Race Conflict," *ASR*, Dec., 1946, pp. 710–715.

Burma, John H., "Interethnic Marriage in Los Angeles, 1948–1959," *SF*, Dec., 1963, pp. 156–165.

Burma, John H. (ed.), *Mexican-Americans in the United States*, Schenkman, 1970.

Burma, John H., "Race Relations and Antidiscriminatory Legislation," *AJS*, Mar., 1951, pp. 416–423.

Burma, John H., "Research Note on the Measurement of Interracial Marriage," *AJS*, May, 1952, pp. 587–589.

Burns, Haywood, "Can a Black Man Get a Fair Trial in This Country?" *The New York Times Magazine*, July 12, 1970, pp. 46 ff.

Byrne, Donn, and Terry J. Wong, "Racial Prejudice, Interpersonal Attraction, and Assumed Dissimilarity of Attitudes," *JASP*, Oct., 1962, pp. 246–253.

Cahnman, Werner J. (ed.), *Intermarriage and Jewish Life*, Herzl Press, 1963.

Campbell, Angus, and Howard Schuman, *Supplemental Studies for the National Advisory Commission on Civil Disorders*, Government Printing Office, 1968.

Campbell, Ernest Q., "On Desegregation and Matters Sociological," *Phylon*, Summer, 1961, pp. 135–145.

Campbell, Ernest Q., "Moral Discomfort and Racial Segregation—An Examination of the Myrdal Hypothesis," *SF*, Mar., 1961, pp. 228–234.

Campbell, Ernest Q., "Negroes, Education, and the Southern States," *SF*, Mar., 1969, pp. 253–265.

Campbell, Ernest Q., and T. F. Pettigrew, *Christians in Racial Crisis. A Study of Little Rock's Ministry*, Public Affairs Press, 1959.

Campbell, Ernest Q., and T. F. Pettigrew, "Racial and Moral Crisis: The Role of Little Rock Ministers," *AJS*, Mar., 1959, pp. 509–516.

Canning, Ray R., and James M. Baker, "Effect of the Group on Authoritarian and Nonauthoritarian Persons," *AJS*, May, 1959, pp. 579–581.

Caplan, Eleanor K., and Eleanor P. Wolf, "Factors Affecting Racial Change in Two Middle Income Housing Areas," *Phylon*, Fall, 1960, pp. 225–233.

Caplovitz, David, and Candace Rogers, *Swastika 1960: The Epidemic of Anti-Semitic Vandalism in America*, ADL, 1961.

Carmichael, Stokely, "Power and Racism," in Floyd B. Barbour (ed.), *The Black Power Revolt*, Porter Sargent, 1968, pp. 61–71.

Carmichael, Stokely, and Charles V. Hamilton, "The Search for New Forms," in Sethard Fisher (ed.), *Power and the Black Community*, Random House, 1970.

Carnegie, Mary E., and Estelle M. Osborne, "Integration in Professional Nursing," *The Crisis*, Jan., 1962, pp. 5–9.

Carr, Leslie G., "The Srole Items and Acquiescence," *ASR*, Apr., 1971, pp. 287–293.

Carter, Lewis F., "Racial-Caste Hypogamy: A Sociological Myth?" *Phylon*, Winter, 1968, pp. 347–350.

Cash, W. J., *The Mind of the South*, Knopf, 1941.

Catrice, Paul, "L'Antisemitisme social français au Miroir de la Littérature des XIX° et XX° Siècles," *Revue de Psychologie des Peuples*, Sept., 1967, pp. 248–281.

Catton, William R., Jr., "The Functions and Dysfunctions of Ethnocentrism: A Theory," *SP*, Winter, 1960–1961, pp. 201–211.

Catton, William R., Jr., and Sung Chick Hong, "The Relation of Apparent Minority Ethnocentrism to Majority Antipathy," *ASR*, Apr., 1962, pp. 178–191.

Caudill, William, and George DeVos, "Achievement, Culture and Personality: The Case of the Japanese Americans, *AA*, Dec., 1956, pp. 1102–1126.

Cavan, Ruth Shonle, *The American Family*, Crowell, 1969.

Centers, Richard, and Bertram Raven, "Conjugal Power Structure: A Re-examination," *ASR*, Apr., 1971, pp. 264–278.

Chancellor, Loren E., and Thomas P. Monahan, "Religious Preference and Interreligious Mixtures in Marriages and Divorces in Iowa," *AJS*, Nov., 1955, pp. 233–239.

Chapman, Loren J., and Donald T. Campbell, "The Effect of Acquiescence Response-Set Upon Relationships Among the F Scale, Ethnocentrism, and Intelligence," *Sociometry*, June, 1959, pp. 153–161.

Chapman, Loren J., and Donald T. Campbell, "Response Set in the F Scale," *JASP*, Jan., 1957, pp. 129–132.

Chase, Philip H., "A Note on Projection," *Psychological Bulletin*, July, 1960, pp. 289–290.

Chein, Isidor, "Some Considerations in Combating Intergroup Prejudice," *Journal of Educational Sociology*, Mar., 1946, pp. 412–419.

Chein, Isidor, Morton Deutsch, Herbert Hyman, and Marie Jahoda (issue eds.), "Consistency and Inconsistency in Intergroup Relations," *JSI*, Third Quarter, 1949.

Cheng, C. K., and Douglas S. Yamamura, "Interracial Marriage and Divorce in Hawaii," *SF*, Oct., 1957, pp. 77–84.

Christie, Richard, and Peggy Cook, "A Guide to Published Literature Relating to the Authoritarian Personality Through 1956," *JP*, Apr., 1958, pp. 171–199.

Christie, Richard, Joan Havel, and Bernard Seidenberg, "Is the F Scale Irreversible?" *JASP*, Mar., 1958, pp. 143–159.

Christie, Richard, and Marie Jahoda (eds.), *Studies in the Scope and Method of "The Authoritarian Personality"*, Free Press, 1954.

Clark, Kenneth B., *Dark Ghetto: Dilemmas of Social Power*, Harper & Row, 1965.

Clark, Kenneth B., *Prejudice and Your Child*, Beacon Press, 1963.

Clark, Margaret, *Health in the Mexican-American Culture*, Univ. of California Press, 1959.

Claude, Inis L., Jr., *National Minorities. An International Problem*, Harvard, 1955.

Cleage, Albert B., Jr., *Black Messiah*, Sheed & Ward, 1968.

Cleaver, Eldridge, *Soul on Ice*, McGraw-Hill, 1968.

Clift, V. A., "Higher Education of Minority Groups in the United States," *JNE*, Summer, 1969, pp. 293 ff.

Cloud, Jonathan, and Graham M. Vaughan, "Using Balanced Scales to Control Acquiescence," *Sociometry*, June, 1970, pp. 193–202.

Cohen, Albert K., and Harold M. Hodges, Jr., "Characteristics of the Lower-Blue-Collar-Class," *SP*, Spring, 1963, pp. 303–334.

Cohen, Nathan (ed.), *The Los Angeles Riots: A Socio-Psychological Study*, Praeger, 1970.

Cohen, Oscar, "The Case for Benign Quotas in Housing," *Phylon*, Spring, 1960, pp. 20–29.

Cohen, Rosalie A., "Conceptual Styles, Culture Conflict, and Nonverbal Tests of Intelligence," *AA*, Oct., 1969, pp. 828–856.

Coleman, James S., "The Concept of Equality of Educational Opportunity," *HER*, Winter, 1968, pp. 22 ff.

Coleman, James S., "Race Relations and Social Change," in Irwin Katz and Patricia Gurin (eds.), *Race and the Social Sciences*, Basic Books, 1969, pp. 274–341.

Coleman, James S., Ernest Q. Campbell, Carol J. Hobson, James McPartland, Alexander M. Mood, Frederick D. Weinfeld, and Robert L. York, *Equality of Educational Opportunity*, U.S. Office of Education, 1966.

Coles, Robert, *Children of Crisis. A Study of Courage and Fear*, Little, Brown, 1967.

Coles, Robert, *The Desegregation of Southern Schools: A Psychiatric Study*, ADL and SRC, 1963.

Coles, Robert, *The Migrant Farmer*, SRC, 1965.

Collins, Sidney F., "The Social Position of White and 'Half-Caste' Women in Colored Groupings in Britain," *ASR*, Dec., 1951, pp. 796–802.

Comas, Juan, "Racial Myths," *The Race Question in Modern Science*, Morrow, for UNESCO, 1956, pp. 11–54.

Comas, Juan, " 'Scientific' Racism Again?" *CA*, October 1961, pp. 303–340.

Comer, James P., "The Social Power of the Negro," in Floyd B. Barbour (ed.), *The Black Power Revolt*, Porter Sargent, 1968, pp. 72–84.

Commission on Law and Social Action of the American Jewish Congress, *Report on Twenty Anti-Discrimination Agencies and the Laws They Administer*, Dec., 1961.

Cone, James H., "Black Consciousness and the Black Church: A Historical-Theological Interpretation," *Annals*, Jan., 1970, pp. 49–53.

Cone, James H., *Black Theology and Black Power*, Seabury Press, 1969.

Connery, Robert H. (ed.), *Urban Riots: Violence and Social Change*, Academy of Political Science, Columbia Univ., 1968.

Conot, Robert, *Rivers of Blood, Years of Darkness*, Bantam Books, 1967.

Cook, Mercer, and S. E. Henderson, *The Militant Black Writer*, Univ. of Wisconsin Press, 1969.

Cook, Stuart, and J. J. Woodmanse, "Dimensions of Verbal Racial Attitudes: Their Identification and Measurement," *JPSP*, Nov., 1967, pp. 240–250.

Coon, C. S., *The Origin of Races*, Knopf, 1962.

Coon, C. S., *The Races of Europe*, Macmillan, 1939.

Coon, C. S., S. M. Garn, and J. B. Birdsell, *Races*, Thomas, 1950.

Coon, C. S., with E. E. Hunt, Jr., *The Living Races of Man*, Knopf, 1965.

Cooper, Eunice, and Marie Jahoda, "The Evasion of Propaganda: How Prejudiced People Respond to Anti-Prejudice Propaganda," *JP*, Jan., 1947, pp. 15–25.

Coser, Lewis A., *Continuities in the Study of Social Conflict*, Free Press, 1967.

Coser, Lewis A., *The Functions of Social Conflict*, Free Press, 1954.

Coser, Lewis A., "Unanticipated Conservative Consequences of Liberal Theorizing," *SP*, Winter, 1969, pp. 263–272.

Cothran, Tilman C., and William Phillips, Jr., "Negro Leadership in a Crisis Situation," *Phylon*, Summer, 1961, pp. 107–118.

Couch, Arthur, and Kenneth Keniston, "Yeasayers and Naysayers: Agreeing Response Set as a Personality Variable," *JASP*, Mar., 1960, pp. 151–174.

Courlander, Harold, *Negro Folk Music U.S.A.*, Columbia, 1963.

Cousens, Frances R., *Public Civil Rights Agencies and Fair Employment*, Praeger, 1969.

Cowen, Emory L., Judah Landes, and Donald E. Schaet, "The Effects of Mild Frustration on the Expression of Prejudiced Attitudes," *JASP*, Jan., 1959, pp. 33–38.

Cox, Keith K., "Changes in Stereotyping of Negroes and Whites in Magazine Advertisements," *POQ*, Winter, 1969–1970, pp. 603–606.

Cox, Oliver C., *Caste, Class and Race: A Study in Social Dynamics*, Doubleday, 1948.

Crain, Robert L., "School Integration and Occupational Achievement of Negroes," *AJS*, Jan., 1970, pp. 593–606.

Cramer, M. Richard, Ernest Q. Campbell, and Charles E. Bowerman, *Social Factors in Educational Achievement and Aspirations Among Negro Adolescents: Vol. 1 Demographic Study; Vol. 2, Survey Study*, Institute for Research in Social Science Monographs, Univ. of North Carolina Press, 1966.

Crawford, Thomas J., and Murray Naditch, "Relative Deprivation, Powerlessness, and Militancy: The Psychology of Social Protest," *Psychiatry*, May, 1970, pp. 208–223.

Cronon, E. David, *Black Moses: The Story of Marcus Garvey and the Universal Negro Improvement Association*, Univ. of Wisconsin Press, 1955.

Cruse, Harold, *The Crisis of the Negro Intellectual*, Morrow, 1967.

Cruse, Harold, *Rebellion or Revolution*, Morrow, 1968.

Culver, Dwight W., *Negro Segregation in the Methodist Church*, Yale, 1953.

Current Anthropology, "More on 'Scientific' Racism," June 1962, pp. 284 ff.

Dahrendorf, Ralf, *Class and Class Conflict in Industrial Society*, Stanford, 1959.

Daniel, Johnnie, "Negro Political Behavior and Community Political and Socioeconomic Structural Factors," *SF*, Mar., 1969, pp. 274–280.

Daniel, V. E., "Ritual and Stratification in Chicago Negro Churches," *ASR*, June, 1942, pp. 352–361.

D'Antonio, William V., and Julian Samora, "Occupational Stratifications in Four Southwestern Communities," *SF*, Oct., 1962, pp. 17–25.

Davies, James C., "Toward a Theory of Revolution," *ASR*, Feb., 1962, pp. 5–19.

Davis, Allison W., and John Dollard, *Children of Bondage*, ACE, 1940.

Davis, Allison W., B. B. Gardner, and M. R. Gardner, *Deep South*, Univ. of Chicago Press, 1941.

Davis, Arthur P., "Integration and Race Literature," *Phylon*, Second Quarter, 1956, pp. 141–146.

Davis, Arthur P., "Jesse B. Semple: Negro American," *Phylon*, First Quarter, 1954, pp. 21–28.

Davis, John P., *The American Negro Reference Book*, Prentice-Hall, 1966.

Dean, John P., and Alex Rosen, *A Manual of Intergroup Relations*, Univ. of Chicago Press, 1955.

DeFleur, Melvin L., and Frank R. Westie, "The Interpretation of Interracial Situations," *SF*, Oct., 1959, pp. 17–23.

DeFleur, Melvin L., and Frank R. Westie, "Verbal Attitudes and Overt Acts: An Experiment on the Salience of Attitudes," *ASR*, Dec., 1958, pp. 667–673.

DeLorean, John Z., "The Problem," in William F. Haddad and G. Douglas Pugh (eds.), *Black Economic Development*, Prentice-Hall, 1969, pp. 10 ff.

Deloria, Vine, Jr., *Custer Died for Your Sins*, Macmillan, 1969.

Deloria, Vine, Jr., *We Talk, You Listen*, Macmillan, 1970.

De Mott, Benjamin, "Jewish Writers in America," *Commentary*, Feb., 1961, pp. 133 ff.

Dentler, Robert A., and Mary Ellen Warshauer, *Big City Dropouts and Illiterates*, Praeger, 1968.

Derbyshire, Robert, and Eugene Brody, "Social Distance and Identity Conflict in Negro College Students," *Sociology and Social Research*, Apr., 1964, pp. 301–314.

Deutsch, Martin, *Minority Group and Class Status as Related to Social and Personality Factors in Scholastic Achievement*, Society for Applied Anthropology, Monograph No. 2, 1960.

Deutsch, Martin, "Organizational and Conceptual Barriers to Social Change," *JSI*, Autumn, 1969, pp. 5–18.

Deutsch, Martin, "Trust, Trustworthiness, and the F Scale," *JASP*, Jan., 1960, pp. 138–141.

Deutsch, Martin, Irwin Katz, and Arthur R. Jensen (eds.), *Social Class, Race, and Psychological Development*, Holt, Rinehart & Winston, 1968.

Deutsch, Morton, and Mary Evans Collins, *Interracial Housing: A Psychological Evaluation of a Social Experiment*, Univ. of Minnesota Press, 1951.

Diab, Lutfy N., "Factors Affecting Studies of National Stereotypes," *JSP*, Feb., 1963, pp. 29–40.

Dickie-Clark, H. F., "The Marginal Situation: A Contribution to Marginality Theory," *SF*, Mar., 1966, pp. 363–370.

Dillingham, Harold C., and David F. Sly, "The Mechanical Cotton-Picker, Negro Migration, and the Integration Movement," *Human Organization*, Winter, 1966, pp. 346 ff.

Dizard, Jan E., "Black Identity, Social Class, and Black Power," *Psychiatry*, May, 1970, pp. 195–207.

Dobzhansky, Theodosius, *Mankind Evolving*, Yale, 1962.

Doddy, Hurley H., "The Status of the Negro Public College: A Statistical Summary," *JNE*, Summer, 1962, pp. 371–379.

Dodson, Dan W., "Can Intergroup Quotas Be Benign?" *JIR*, Autumn, 1960, pp. 12–17.

Dollard, John, *Caste and Class in a Southern Town*, Yale, 1937.

Dollard, John, "Hostility and Fear in Social Life," *SF*, Oct., 1938, pp. 15–26.

Dollard, John, Neal E. Miller, L. W. Doob, *et al.*, *Frustration and Aggression*, Yale, 1939.

Dover, Cedric, *American Negro Art*, New York Graphic Society, 1961.

Dozier, E. P., G. E. Simpson, and J. M. Yinger, "The Integration of Americans of Indian Descent," *Annals*, May, 1957, pp. 158–165.

Drake, St. Clair, and Horace R. Cayton, *Black Metropolis*, Harcourt Brace Jovanovich, 1945.

Dubey, Sumati N., "Blacks' Preference for Black Professionals, Businessmen, and Religious Leaders," *POQ*, Spring, 1970, pp. 113–116.

DuBois, W. E. B., *Black Reconstruction in America*, World, 1962.

Duncan, Beverly, and Otis D. Duncan, "Minorities and the Process of Stratification," *ASR*, June, 1968, pp. 356–364.

Duncan, Otis D., "Discrimination Against Negroes," *Annals*, May, 1967, pp. 85–103.

Duncan, Otis D., and Beverly Duncan, *The Negro Population of Chicago: A Study of Residential Succession*, Univ. of Chicago Press, 1957.

Dunn, L. C., *Heredity and Evolution in Human Populations*, Harvard, 1960.

Dunn, L. C. and Theodosius Dobzhansky, *Heredity, Race, and Society*, Penguin Books, 1952.

Dustin, David S., and Henry P. Davis, "Authoritarianism and Sanctioning Behavior," *JPSP*, June, 1967, pp. 222–224.

Duvall, Evelyn M., and Reuben Hill, *Being Married*, Heath, 1960.

Dworkin, Earl S., and Jay S. Efran, "The Angered: Their Susceptibility to Varieties of Humor," *SPSP*, June, 1967, pp. 233–236.

Edwards, G. Franklin, *The Negro Professional Class*, Free Press, 1959.

Edwards, Harry, *Black Students*, Free Press, 1970.

Egerton, John, "Almost All-White," *SER*, May, 1969, pp. 2–17.

Ehrlich, Howard, "Stereotyping and Negro-Jewish Stereotypes," *SF*, Dec., 1962, pp. 171–176.

Ehrlich, Howard, and G. Norman Van Tubergen,

"Exploring the Structure and Salience of Stereotypes," *JSP*, Vol. 83, 1971, pp. 113–127.

Eisenman, Russell, and Thomas F. Pettigrew, "Comments and Rejoinders," *JSI*, Autumn, 1969, pp. 199–206.

Elder, Glen H., Jr., "Group Orientations and Strategies in Racial Change," *SF*, June, 1970, pp. 445–461.

Elder, Glen H., Jr., "Racial Conflict and Learning," *Sociometry*, June, 1971, pp. 151–173.

Elkins, Stanley M., *Slavery: A Problem in American Institutional and Intellectual Life*, Univ. of Chicago Press, 1959.

Epps, Edgar G. (issue ed.), "Motivation and Academic Achievement of Negro Americans," *JSI*, Summer, 1969.

Epstein, Benjamin R., and Arnold Forster, *Some of My Best Friends*, Farrar, Straus & Giroux, 1962.

Epstein, Jason, "The Politics of School Decentralization," in Marilyn Gittel and Alan G. Hevesei (eds.), *The Politics of Urban Education*, Praeger, 1969, pp. 296–297.

Epstein, Ralph, and S. S. Komorita, "Childhood Prejudice as a Function of Parental Ethnocentrism, Punitiveness and Outgroup Characteristics," *JPSP*, March, 1966, pp. 259–264.

Erber, Ernest, *Jobs and Housing: A Study of Employment and Housing Opportunities in Suburban Areas of the New York Metropolitan Region*, National Committee Against Discrimination in Housing, 1970.

Erlich, Howard J., "The Swastika Epidemic of 1959–1960: Anti-Semitism and Community Characteristics," *SP*, Winter, 1962, pp. 264–272.

Essien-Udom, E. U., *Black Nationalism: A Search for Identity in America*, Univ. of Chicago Press, 1962.

Etzioni, Amitai, "The Ghetto—a Re-Evaluation," *SF*, Mar., 1959, pp. 255–262.

Fanon, Frantz, *The Wretched of the Earth*, Grove Press, 1963.

Faris, R. E. L., "Reflections on the Ability Dimension in Human Society," *ASR*, Dec., 1961, pp. 835–843.

Farley, Reynolds, "The Changing Distribution of Negroes Within Metropolitan Areas: The Emergence of Black Suburbs," *AJS*, Jan., 1970, pp. 512–529.

Farmer, James, *Freedom—When?* Random House, 1966.

Fauset, A. H., *Black Gods of the Metropolis*, Univ. of Penn. Press, 1944.

Fax, Elton C., "The American Negro Artist," in Patricia Romero (ed.), *In Black America, United*, 1969, pp. 273–292.

Fendrich, James M., "Perceived Reference Group Support: Racial Attitudes and Overt Behavior," *ASR*, Dec., 1967, pp. 960–970.

Fendrich, James M., "A Study of the Association among Verbal Attitudes, Commitment and Overt Behavior in Different Experimental Situations," *SF*, Mar., 1967, pp. 347–355.

Ferman, Louis A., *The Negro and Equal Employment Opportunities: A Review of Management Experiences in Twenty Companies*, Praeger, 1968.

Feshbach, Seymour, and Robert Singer, "The Effects of Personal and Shared Threats upon Social Prejudice," *JASP*, May, 1957, pp. 411–416.

Fichter, Joseph H., *Graduates of Predominantly Negro Colleges of 1964*, The National Institutes of Health, 1967.

Fine, Morris, and Milton Himmelfarb (eds.), *American Jewish Yearbook*, Vol. 71, American Jewish Committee and Jewish Publication Society of America, 1970.

Fineberg, S., *Punishment Without Crime*, Doubleday, 1949.

Finestone, Harold, "Cats, Kicks, and Color," *SP*, July, 1957, pp. 3–13.

Finkelstein, Louis (ed.), *The Jews, Their History, Culture, and Religion*, Harper & Row, 2 vols., 3rd ed., 1960.

Fischer, John H., "School Parks for Equal Opportunities," *JNE*, Summer, 1968, pp. 303 ff.

Fisher, Sethard (ed.), *Power and the Black Community*, Random House, 1970.

Fishman, Joshua A., "Childhood Indoctrination for Minority-Group Membership," *Daedalus*, Spring, 1961, pp. 329–349.

Fishman, Joshua A., "An Examination of the Process and Function of Social Stereotyping," *JSP*, Feb., 1956, pp. 27–64.

Fishman, Joshua A., "Moving to the Suburbs: Its Possible Impact on the Role of the Jewish Minority in American Community Life," *Phylon*, Summer, 1963, pp. 146–153.

Fitzpatrick, Joseph P., "Intermarriage of Puerto Ricans in New York City," *AJS*, Jan., 1966, pp. 395–406.

Flowerman, S. H., "Mass Propaganda in the War Against Bigotry," *JASP*, Oct., 1947, pp. 429–439.

Fogelson, Robert M., "Violence as Protest," in Robert H. Connery (ed.), *Urban Riots: Violence and Social Change*, Proceedings of the

Academy of Political Science, Columbia, 1968, pp. 25–41.

Foley, Eugene P., "The Negro Businessman," *Daedalus*, Winter, 1966, pp. 107–144.

Fong, Stanley L. M., "Assimilation of Chinese in America: Changes in Orientation and Social Perception," *AJS*, Nov., 1965, pp. 265–273.

Ford, Nick A., "Battle of the Books," *Phylon*, Summer, 1961, pp. 128 ff.

Forster, Arnold, and Benjamin R. Epstein, *Cross-Currents*, Doubleday, 1956.

Forward, John R., and Jay R. Williams, "Internal-External Control and Black Militancy," *JSI*, Winter, 1970, pp. 75–92.

Foy, Felician A. (ed.), *National Catholic Almanac*, 1962, St. Anthony's Guild, 1962.

Frady, Marshall, "God and Man in the South," *Atlantic*, Jan., 1967, pp. 37–42.

Franklin, J. H., *From Slavery to Freedom*, Knopf, 1948.

Franklin, Raymond S., "The Political Economy of Black Power," *SP*, Winter, 1969, pp. 286–301.

Frazier, E. Franklin, *Black Bourgeoisie*, Free Press, 1957.

Frazier, E. Franklin, *The Negro Church in America*, Schocken Books, 1963.

Frazier, E. Franklin, *The Negro Family in the United States*, Citadel Press, rev. and abr. ed., 1948.

Frazier, E. Franklin, *The Negro in the United States*, Macmillan, rev. ed., 1957.

Frazier, E. Franklin, *Negro Youth at the Crossways*, ACE, 1940.

Frazier, E. Franklin, *Race and Culture Contacts in the Modern World*, Knopf, 1957.

Frazier, E. Franklin, "Sociological Theory and Race Relations," *ASR*, June, 1947, pp. 265–271.

Frenkel-Brunswik, Else, and Nevitt R. Sanford, "Some Personality Factors in Anti-Semitism," *JP*, Oct., 1945, pp. 271–291.

Freyre, Gilberto, *The Mansions and the Shanties: The Making of Modern Brazil* (trans. by Harriet de Onís), Knopf, 1963.

Freyre, Gilberto, *The Masters and the Slaves* (trans. by Samuel Putnam), Knopf, 1946.

Friedmann, Georges, *The End of the Jewish People?* Doubleday, 1967.

Fuchs, Lawrence H., *The Political Behavior of American Jews*, Free Press, 1956.

Gaither, Edmund B., "A New Criticism Is Needed," *The New York Times*, June 21, 1970.

Galarza, Ernesto, Herman Gallegos, and Julian Samora, *Mexican-Americans in the Southwest*, McNally & Loftin, 1969.

Gans, Herbert J., "The Ghetto Rebellions and Urban Class Conflict," in R. H. Connery (ed.), *Urban Riots: Violence and Social Change*, Academy of Political Science, Columbia, 1968, pp. 42–51.

Gans, Herbert J., "The Origin and Growth of a Jewish Community in the Suburbs: A Study of the Jews of Park Forest," in Marshal Sklare (ed.), *The Jews: Social Patterns of an American Group*, Free Press, 1958, pp. 205–248.

Gans, Herbert J., *The Urban Villagers: Group and Class in the Life of Italian-Americans*, Free Press, 1962.

Garn, Stanley, *Human Races*, Thomas, 1961.

Garza, Joseph M., "Race, the Achievement Syndrome, and Perception of Opportunity," *Phylon*, Winter, 1969, pp. 338–354.

Gast, D., "Minority Americans in Children's Literature," *Elementary English*, Jan., 1967, pp. 12–23.

Genovese, Eugene D., "American Slaves and Their History," *The New York Review of Books*, Dec. 3, 1970, pp. 34–43.

Genovese, Eugene D., *The Political Economy of Slavery*, Pantheon, 1965.

Genovese, Eugene D., *The World the Slaveholders Made*, Pantheon, 1969.

Geschwender, James A., and Benjamin D. Singer, "Deprivation and the Detroit Riot," *SP*, Spring, 1970, pp. 457–462.

Geschwender, James A., "Negro Education: The False Faith," *Phylon*, Winter, 1968, pp. 371–379.

Gilbert, G. M., "Stereotype Persistence and Change Among College Students," *JASP*, Apr., 1951, pp. 245–254.

Ginzberg, Eli, *The Negro Potential*, Columbia, 1956.

Ginzberg, Eli, "Segregation and Manpower Waste," *Phylon*, Winter, 1960, pp. 311–316.

Ginzberg, Eli, and Dale L. Hiestand, "Employment Patterns of Negro Men and Women," in John P. Davis (ed.), *The American Negro Reference Book*, Prentice-Hall, 1966, pp. 229–231.

Gitelman, Zvi, "Soviet Jews vs. Other Minorities: Similarities and Differences in Their Treatment," *Issues*, Summer, 1968, pp. 10–19.

Gitell, Marilyn, "Community Control of Education," in Robert H. Connery (ed.), *Urban Riots: Violence and Social Change*, Academy of Political Science, 1968, pp. 60–71.

Gittell, Marilyn, and Alan G. Hevesi, *The Politics of Urban Education*, Praeger, 1969.

Glass, Ruth (assisted by Harold Pollins), *London's Newcomers: The West Indian Migrants*, Harvard, 1961.

Glazer, Nathan, *American Judaism*, Univ. of Chicago Press, 1957.

Glazer, Nathan, "Blacks and Ethnic Groups: The Difference, and the Political Difference It Makes," *SP*, Spring, 1971, pp. 444–461.

Glazer, Nathan, "Blacks, Jews, and the Intellectuals," *Commentary*, Apr., 1969, pp. 33–39.

Glazer, Nathan, "The Jewish Revival in America," *Commentary*, Dec., 1955, pp. 493–499, and Jan., 1956, pp. 17–24.

Glazer, Nathan, "Negroes and Jews: The New Challenge to Pluralism," *Commentary*, Dec., 1964, pp. 29–34.

Glazer, Nathan, *The Social Basis of American Communism*, Harcourt Brace Jovanovich, 1961.

Glazer, Nathan, and Davis McEntire (eds.), *Studies in Housing and Minority Groups*, Univ. of California Press, 1960.

Glazer, Nathan, and Daniel P. Moynihan, *Beyond the Melting Pot: The Negroes, Puerto Ricans, Jews, Italians and Irish of New York City*, MIT and Harvard, 1963.

Glenn, Norval D., "Occupational Benefits to Whites from the Subordination of Negroes," *ASR*, June, 1963, pp. 443–448.

Glenn, Norval D., "White Gains from Negro Subordination," *SP*, Spring, 1966, pp. 159–178.

Glickstein, Howard A., "Federal Programs and Minority Groups," *JNE*, Summer, 1969, pp. 303–314.

Glock, Charles Y., and Rodney Stark, *Christian Beliefs and Anti-Semitism*, Harper & Row, 1966.

Gloster, Hugh M., *Negro Voices in American Fiction*, Univ. of North Carolina Press, 1948.

Gloster, Hugh M., "Race and the Negro Writer," *Phylon*, Fourth Quarter, 1950, pp. 369–371.

Gobineau, Arthur de, *The Inequality of Human Races* (trans. by Adrian Collins), Putnam's, 1915.

Goldblatt, Harold, and Florence Cromien, "The Effective Social Reach of the Fair Housing Practices Law of the City of New York," *SP*, Spring, 1962, pp. 365–370.

Golding, Louis, *The Jewish Problem*, Penguin Books, 1938.

Goldman, Albert, "The Predicament of the Jewish Musician, *Commentary*, Feb., 1961, pp. 110 ff.

Goldstein, Sidney, and Calvin Goldscheider, *Jewish Americans*, Prentice-Hall, 1968.

Gomillion, C. G., "The Tuskegee Voting Story," *Freedomways*, Summer, 1962, pp. 236 ff.

Goodlad, John I., "Desegregating the Integrated School," in U.S. Civil Rights Commission, *Racial Isolation in the Public Schools*, 1967, pp. 268 ff.

Goodman, Mary Ellen, *Race Awareness in Young Children*, Collier Books, rev. ed., 1964.

Gordon, Albert I., *Intermarriage: Interfaith, Interracial, Interethnic*, Beacon Press, 1964.

Gordon, Albert I., *Jews in Suburbia*, Beacon Press, 1959.

Gordon, Albert I., *Jews in Transition*, Univ. of Minnesota Press, 1949.

Gordon, Edmund W., "Compensatory Education in the Equalization of Educational Opportunity," *JNE*, Summer, 1968, p. 270 ff.

Gordon, Milton M., *Assimilation in American Life*, Oxford, 1964.

Gordon, Milton M., "Assimilation in America: Theory and Reality," *Daedalus*, Spring, 1961, pp. 263–285.

Gottfried, Martin, "Is All Black Theater Beautiful? No," *The New York Times*, June 7, 1970, pp. D1, 3.

Graeber, Isacque, and S. H. Britt (eds.), *Jews in a Gentile World*, Macmillan, 1942.

Graham, Hugh D., and Ted R. Gurr (eds.), *Violence in America: Historical and Comparative Perspectives*, National Commission on the Causes and Prevention of Violence, 1969.

Graves, Theodore D., "The Personal Adjustment of Navajo Indian Migrants to Denver, Colorado," *AA*, Feb., 1970, pp. 35–54.

Grebler, Leo, Joan W. Moore, and Ralph C. Guzman, *Mexican-American People: The Nation's Second Largest Minority*, Free Press, 1970.

Greeley, Andrew M., "Religious Intermarriage in a Denominational Society," *AJS*, May, 1970, pp. 949–952.

Green, Edward, "Race, Social Status, and Criminal Arrest," *ASR*, June, 1970, pp. 476–490.

Greenberg, Herbert M., "The Development of the Integration Attitude Scale," *JSP*, June, 1961, pp. 103–109.

Greenberg, Jack, *Race Relations and American Law*, Columbia, 1959.

Greenblum, Joseph, and L. I. Pearlin, "Vertical Mobility and Prejudice," in Reinhard Bendix and S. M. Lipset (eds.), *Class, Status, and Power*, Free Press, 1953, pp. 480–491.

Greenwald, Herbert J. and Don B. Oppenheim,

"Reported Magnitude of Self-Misidentification Among Negro Children—an Artifact?" *JPSP*, Jan., 1968, pp. 49–52.

Greer, Scott, *Last Man in: Racial Access to Union Power*, Free Press, 1959.

Grier, Eunice, and George Grier, *Discrimination in Housing*, ADL, 1960.

Grier, Eunice, and George Grier, "Equality and Beyond: Housing Segregation in the Great Society," *Daedalus*, Winter, 1966, pp. 77–106.

Grier, Eunice, and George Grier, *Privately Developed Interracial Housing: An Analysis of Experience*, Univ. of California Press, 1960.

Grier, William H., and Price M. Cobbs, *Black Rage*, Basic Books, 1968.

Griffith, Beatrice, *American Me*, Houghton Mifflin, 1948.

Grimshaw, Allen D., *Racial Violence in the United States*, Aldine, 1969.

Grimshaw, Allen D., "Relationships Among Prejudice, Discrimination, Social Tension, and Social Violence," *JIR*, Autumn, 1961, pp. 302–310.

Grindstaff, Carl F., "The Negro, Urbanization, and Relative Deprivation in the Deep South," *SP*, Winter, 1968, pp. 342–352.

Grodzins, Morton, *The Loyal and the Disloyal: Social Boundaries of Patriotism and Treason*, Univ. of Chicago Press, 1956.

Grodzins, Morton, "Making Un-Americans," *AJS*, May, 1955, pp. 570–582.

Grodzins, Morton, *The Metropolitan Area As a Racial Problem*, Univ. of Pittsburgh Press, 1959.

Grossack, Martin M., "Group Belongingness Among Negroes," *JSP*, Feb., 1956, pp. 167–180.

Group for the Advancement of Psychiatry, Committee on Social Issues, *Psychiatric Aspects of School Desegregation*, Report no. 37, Group for the Advancement of Psychiatry, 1957.

Guilford, J. P., "Racial Preferences of a Thousand American University Students," *JSP*, May, 1931, pp. 179–204.

Gurin, Patricia, "Motivation and Aspirations of Southern Negro College Youth," *AJS*, Jan., 1970, pp. 607–631.

Gurin, Patricia, Gerald Gurin, Rosina C. Lao, and Muriel Beattie, "Internal-External Control in the Motivational Dynamics of Negro Youth," *JSI*, Summer, 1969, pp. 29–53.

Gurin, Patricia, and Daniel Katz, *Motivation and Aspiration in the Negro College*, Survey Research Center, Univ. of Michigan Press, 1966.

Hacker, Andrew, "The Violent Black Minority,"

The New York Times Magazine, June 2, 1970, pp. 67 ff.

Haddad, William F., and G. Douglas Pugh (eds.), *Black Economic Development*, Prentice-Hall, 1969.

Hadden, Jeffrey K., *The Gathering Storm in the Churches*, Doubleday, 1969.

Hadden, Jeffrey K., and Raymond C. Rymph, "Social Structure and Civil Rights Involvement: A Case Study of Protestant Ministers," *SF*, Sept., 1966, pp. 51–61.

Haimowitz, Morris L., and Natalie R. Haimowitz, "Reducing Ethnic Hostility Through Psychotherapy," *JSP*, May, 1950, pp. 231–241.

Halpern, Ben, "America Is Different," in Marshall Sklare (ed.), *The Jews: Social Patterns of an American Group*, Free Press, 1958, pp. 23–39.

Hamblin, Robert L., "The Dynamics of Racial Discrimination," *SP*, Fall, 1962, pp. 103–121.

Hamilton, Charles V., "An Advocate of Black Power Defines It," *The New York Times Magazine*, Apr. 14, 1968, pp. 79 ff.

Hamilton, Charles V., "Riots, Revolts and Relevant Response," in Floyd B. Barbour (ed.), *The Black Power Revolt*, Porter Sargent, 1968, pp. 171–178.

Handlin, Oscar (issue ed.), "Ethnic Groups in American Life," *Daedalus*, Spring, 1961.

Handlin, Oscar, *The Uprooted*, Little, Brown, 1951.

Hannerz, Ulf, *Soulside: Inquiries into Ghetto Culture and Community*, Columbia, 1969.

Harding, John, Harold Proshansky, Bernard Kutner, and Isidor Chein, "Prejudice and Ethnic Relations," in Gardner Lindzey and Elliot Aronson (eds.), *The Handbook of Social Psychology*, Addison-Wesley, Vol. 5, 1969, pp. 1–77.

Harding, Vincent, "Religion and Resistance among Ante-Bellum Negroes, 1800–1860," in August Meier and Elliott Rudwick (eds.), *The Making of Black America*, Atheneum, 1969, pp. 179–197.

Harris, Marvin, "Caste, Class, and Minority," *SF*, Mar., 1959, pp. 248–254.

Harris, Marvin, *Patterns of Race in the Americas*, Walker, 1964.

Harrison, Robert H., and Edward H. Kass, "MMPI Correlates of Negro Acculturations in a Northern City," *JPSP*, Nov., 1968, pp. 262–270.

Hartley, Eugene L., *Problems in Prejudice*, Kings' Crown Press, 1946.

Hawley, L. T., "The Negro's New Economic

Life," *Fortune*, Sept., 1956, pp. 128, 252, 254, 256, 258.

Haythorn, William, Arthur Couch, Donald Haefner, Peter Langham, and Launor F. Carter, "The Behavior of Authoritarian and Equalitarian Personalities in Groups," *HR*, Feb., 1956, pp. 57–74.

Heer, David M., "The Marital Status of Second-Generation Americans," *ASR*, Apr., 1961, pp. 233–239.

Heer, David M., "Negro-White Marriage in the United States," *Journal of Marriage and the Family*, Aug., 1966, pp. 265–273.

Heer, David M., "The Trend of Interfaith Marriages in Canada: 1952–1957," *ASR*, Apr., 1962, pp. 245–250.

Heiss, Jerold S., "Premarital Characteristics of the Religiously Intermarried in an Urban Area," *ASR*, Feb., 1960, pp. 47–55.

Heller, Ceila S., *Mexican American Youth: Forgotten Youth at the Crossroads*, Random House, 1966.

Helm, June (ed.), *Spanish Speaking People in the United States*, American Ethnological Society, Univ. of Washington Press, 1969.

Helper, Rose, *Racial Policies and Practices of Real Estate Brokers*, Univ. of Minnesota Press, 1969.

Henderson, Vivian W., "The Economic Imbalance: An Inquiry into the Economic Status of Negroes in the United States, 1935–1960," *JNE*, Winter, 1961, pp. 4–16.

Henshel, Anne-Marie, and Richard L. Henshel, "Black Studies Programs: Promise and Pitfalls," *JNE*, Fall, 1969, pp. 424 ff.

Hentoff, Nat, *The New Equality*, Viking, 1965.

Herskovits, M. J., *The Myth of the Negro Past*, Beacon Press, 1958.

Herskovits, M. J., "Who Are the Jews?" in Louis Finkelstein (ed.), *The Jews, Their History, Culture, and Religion*, Harper & Row, 3rd ed., 1960, vol. 2, pp. 1505 ff.

Hertzberg, Arthur, *The French Enlightenment and the Jews*, Columbia, 1968.

Higham, John, *Social Discrimination Against Jews in America, 1830–1930*, Reprinted from a publication of the American Jewish Historical Societies, Sept., 1957.

Hilberg, Paul, *The Destruction of the European Jews*, Quadrangle Books, 1961.

Hill, Herbert (ed.), *Anger, and Beyond*, Harper & Row, 1966.

Hill, Herbert, "Black Labor in the American Economy," in Patricia W. Romero (ed.), *In Black America*, United, 1969.

Hill, Herbert, "Patterns of Employment Discrimination," *The Crisis*, Mar., 1962, pp. 137–147.

Hill, Herbert, "Racial Discrimination in the Nation's Apprenticeship Training Programs," *Phylon*, Fall, 1962, pp. 215–224.

Hill, Herbert, "Racism Within Organized Labor," *JNE*, Spring, 1961, pp. 111 ff.

Hill, Herbert (ed.), *Soon, One Morning*, Knopf, 1963.

Hill, Samuel S., Jr., *Southern Churches in Crisis*, Holt, Rinehart & Winston, 1967.

Hirsh, Selma, *The Fears Men Live By*, Harper & Row, 1955.

Hitler, Adolf, *Mein Kampf*, Reynal and Hitchcock, 1940.

Hodge, Claire C., "The Negro Job Situation: Has It Improved?" *Monthly Labor Review*, Jan., 1969, p. 22.

Hodge, Robert W., and Donald J. Treiman, "Occupational Mobility and Attitudes Toward Negroes," *ASR*, Feb., 1966, pp. 93–102.

Hoetink, Harry, "Change in Prejudice: Some Notes on the Minority Problem, with References to the West Indies and Latin America," *Bijdragen*, No. 119, 1963, pp. 56–75.

Hofstetter, C. Richard, "Political Disengagement and the Death of Martin Luther King," *POQ*, Summer, 1969, pp. 174–179.

Hollingshead, August B., "Cultural Factors in the Selection of Marriage Mates," *ASR*, Oct., 1950, pp. 619–627.

Hooft, W. A. Visser 'T, *The Ecumenical Movement and the Racial Problem*, UNESCO, 1954.

Hooton, E. A., *Up from the Ape*, Macmillan, rev. ed., 1946.

Horowitz, Irving L., and Martin Liebowitz, "Social Deviance and Political Marginality: Toward a Redefinition of the Relation Between Sociology and Politics," *SP*, Winter, 1968, pp. 280–296.

Horowitz, Laura G., "A New College with a City View," *SER*, May, 1969, pp. 18–23.

Hough, Joseph C., Jr., *Black Power and White Protestants: A Christian Response to the New Negro Pluralism*, Oxford, 1968.

House, James S., and Robert D. Fischer, "Authoritarianism, Age and Black Militancy," *Sociometry*, June, 1971, pp. 174–197.

Howton, Louise G., "Genocide and the American Indian," in Bernard Rosenberg, Israel Gerver, and F. William Hooton (eds.), *Mass Society in Crisis*, Macmillan, 1971.

Hughes, Everett C., "Good People and Dirty Work," *SP*, Summer, 1962, pp. 3–11.

Hughes, Everett C., "Race Relations and the Sociological Imagination," *ASR*, Dec., 1963, pp. 879–890.

Hughes, Langston (ed.), *The Book of Negro Humor*, Dodd, Mead, 1965.

Hughes, Langston, *Fight for Freedom: The Story of the NAACP*, W. W. Norton, 1962.

Hughes, Langston (ed.), *New Negro Poets U.S.A.*, Univ. of Indiana Press, 1966.

Hulse, Frederick S., "Race as an Evolutionary Episode," *AA*, Oct., 1962, pp. 929–945.

Hunt, J. McVicker, "Environment, Development, and Scholastic Achievement," in *Social Class, Race, and Psychological Development*, Martin Deutsch, Irwin Katz, and Arthur R. Jensen (eds.), Holt, Rinehart & Winston, 1968, pp. 293–336.

Hutt, W. H., *The Economics of the Colour Bar: A Study of the Economic Origins of Racial Segregation in South Africa*, Deutsch, 1964.

Hyman, Herbert H., and John Shelton Reed, " 'Black Matriarchy' Reconsidered: Evidence from Secondary Analysis of Sample Surveys," *POQ*, Fall, 1969, pp. 346–354.

International Migration Review, "The Puerto Rican Experience on the United States Mainland," Spring, 1968 (whole issue).

Irelan, Lola M., Oliver C. Moles, and Robert M. O'Shea, "Ethnicity, Poverty, and Selected Attitudes: A Test of the 'Culture of Poverty' Hypothesis," *SF*, June, 1969, pp. 405–413.

Irons, Edward D., "Black Capitalism—1968," in Patricia W. Romero (ed.), *In Black America*, United, 1969, pp. 217–228.

Isaacs, Harold R., *The New World of Negro Americans*, John Day, 1963.

Jackson, Douglas N., S. J. Messick, and C. M. Solley, "How 'Rigid' Is the 'Authoritarian'?" *JASP*, Jan., 1957, pp. 137–140.

Jackson, Esther Merle, "The American Negro and the Image of the Absurd," *Phylon*, Winter, 1962, pp. 359–371.

Jaffe, A. J., Walter Adams, and Sandra G. Meyers, *Negro Higher Education in the 1960s*, Praeger, 1968.

Janowitz, Morris, and Dwaine Marvick, "Authoritarianism and Political Behavior," *POQ*, Summer, 1953, pp. 185–201.

Janowsky, Oscar I. (ed.), *The American Jew*, Harper & Row, 1942.

Janowsky, Oscar I, *Nationalities and National Minorities*, Macmillan, 1945.

Jeffries, Vincent, and H. Edward Ransford, "Interracial Social Contact and Middle-Class White Reactions to the Watts Riot," *SP*, Winter, 1969, pp. 312–324.

Jencks, Christopher, and David Riesman, "The American Negro College," *HER*, Winter, 1967, pp. 3–60.

Jensen, Arthur R., "Authoritarian Attitudes and Personality Maladjustment," *JASP*, May, 1957, pp. 303–311.

Jensen, Arthur R., "How Much Can We Boost IQ and Scholastic Achievement?" in *Environment, Heredity, and Intelligence*, *HER* Reprint Series No. 2, 1969.

Johnson, Charles S., *Growing Up in the Black Belt*, ACE, 1941.

Johnson, Charles, *The Negro College Graduate*, Univ. of North Carolina Press, 1938.

Johnson, Charles S., *Patterns of Negro Segregation*, Harper & Row, 1943.

Johnson, Guy B., "Personality in a White-Indian-Negro Community," *ASR*, Aug., 1939, pp. 516–523.

Johnson, Lawrence, and Wendell Smith, "Black Managers," in William F. Haddad and G. Douglas Pugh (eds.), *Black Economic Development*, Prentice-Hall, 1969.

Johnson, Norman J., "A Review of *Racial Politics and Practices of Real Estate Brokers* by Rose Helper," *ASR*, Feb., 1971, pp. 142–143.

Johnson, Robert, "Negro Reactions to Minority Group Status," in Milton L. Barron (ed.), *American Minorities*, Knopf, 1957, pp. 192–214.

Johnstone, Ronald L., "Negro Preachers Take Sides," *Review of Religious Research*, Fall, 1969, pp. 81–88.

Jones, LeRoi, *Black Magic: Collected Poetry, 1961–1967*, Bobbs-Merrill, 1969.

Jones, LeRoi, *Blues People*, Morrow, 1963.

Kallen, Horace M., *Cultural Pluralism and the American Idea*, Univ. of Pennsylvania Press, 1956.

Kantrowitz, Nathan, "Ethnic and Racial Segregation in the New York Metropolis, 1960," *AJS*, May, 1969, pp. 685–695.

Kardiner, Abram, and Lionel Ovesey, *The Mark of Oppression: A Psychological Study of the American Negro*, Norton, 1951.

Karlins, Marvin, Thomas L. Coffman, and Gary Walters, "On the Fading of Social Stereotypes: Studies in Three Generations of College Students," *JPSP*, Sept., 1969, pp. 1–16.

Katz, David, and Kenneth Braly, "Racial Stereotypes of One Hundred College Students," *JASP*, Oct.–Dec., 1933, pp. 280–290.

Katz, Jacob, *Exclusiveness and Tolerance: Studies in Jewish-Gentile Relations in Medieval and Modern Times*, Oxford, 1961.

Katz, Irwin, *Conflict and Harmony in an Adolescent Interracial Group*, New York Univ. Press, 1955.

Katz, Irwin, "A Critique of Personality Approaches to Negro Performance, with Research Suggestions," *JSI*, Summer, 1969, pp. 13–28.

Katz, Irwin, "Review of Evidence Relating to Effects of Desegregation on the Intellectual Performance of Negroes," *American Psychologist*, June, 1964, pp. 381–399.

Katz, Irwin, and Patricia Gurin (eds.), *Race and the Social Sciences*, Basic Books, 1969.

Katz, Irwin, Thomas Henchy, and Harvey Allen, "Effects of Race of Tester, Approval-Disapproval, and Need on Negro Children's Learning," *JPSP*, Jan., 1968, pp. 38–42.

Katz, Shlomo (ed.), *Negro and Jew: An Encounter in America*, Macmillan, 1967.

Kaufman, Walter C., "Status, Authoritarianism and Anti-Semitism," *AJS*, Jan., 1957, pp. 379–382.

Keech, William R., *The Impact of Negro Voting: The Role of the Vote in the Quest for Equality*, Rand McNally & Co., 1968.

Keil, Charles, *Urban Blues*, Univ. of Chicago Press, 1966.

Kelman, Herbert C., "A Social-Psychological Model of Political Legitimacy and Its Relevance to Black and White Student Protest Movements," *Psychiatry*, May, 1970, pp. 224–246.

Kendall, Patricia, *Conflict and Mood*, Free Press, 1954.

Kenkel, William F., *The Family in Perspective*, Appleton-Century-Crofts, 2nd ed., 1966.

Kennedy, Ruby Jo Reeves, "Single or Triple Melting-Pot? Intermarriage Trends in New Haven, 1870–1940," *AJS*, Jan., 1944, pp. 331–339.

Kephart, William M., *Racial Factors and Urban Law Enforcement*, Univ. of Pennsylvania Press, 1957.

Kerlinger, Fred, and Milton Rokeach, "The Factorial Nature of the F and D Scales, *JPSP*, Oct., 1966, pp. 391–399.

Killens, John O., "The Writer and Black Liberation," in Patricia W. Romero (ed.), *In Black America*, United, 1969, pp. 265–272.

Killian, Lewis M., *The Impossible Revolution: Black Power and the American Dream*, Random House, 1968.

Killian, Lewis M., and Charles M. Grigg, *Racial Crisis in America: Leadership in Conflict*, Prentice-Hall, 1964.

Killian, Lewis M., and Charles M. Grigg, "Urbanism, Race, and Anomia," *AJS*, May, 1961, pp. 661–665.

Killingsworth, Charles C., *Jobs and Income for Negroes*, Institute of Labor and Industrial Relations, Univ. of Michigan, 1968.

Killingsworth, Charles C., "Jobs and Income for Negroes," in Irwin Katz and Patricia Gurin (eds.), *Race and the Social Sciences*, 1969, pp. 194–273.

King, Martin Luther, Jr., "Letter from a Birmingham Jail," *Liberation*, June, 1963, pp. 10–16, 23.

King, Martin Luther, Jr., *Strength to Love*, Harper & Row, 1963.

King, Martin Luther, Jr., *Stride Toward Freedom: The Montgomery Story*, Harper & Row, 1958.

King, Martin Luther, Jr., *The Trumpet of Conscience*, Harper & Row, 1968.

King, Martin Luther, Jr., *Why We Can't Wait*, Harper & Row, 1963.

Kirscht, John P., and Ronald C. Dillehay, *Dimensions of Authoritarianism: A Review of Research and Theory*, Univ. of Kentucky Press, 1967.

Kitano, Harry H. L., *Japanese Americans: The Evolution of a Subculture*, Prentice-Hall, 1969.

Klineberg, Otto (ed.), *Characteristics of the American Negro*, Harper & Row, 1944.

Klineberg, Otto, "Life Is Fun in a Smiling, Fair-Skinned World," *Saturday Review*, Feb. 16, 1963, pp. 75–76.

Klineberg, Otto, "Race and Psychology," *The Race Question in Modern Science*, UNESCO, 1956, pp. 55–84.

Klineberg, Otto, *Social Psychology*, Holt, Rinehart & Winston, rev. ed., 1954.

Klineberg, Otto, *Tensions Affecting International Understanding*, SSRC, 1950.

Kluckhohn, Clyde, Henry A. Murray, and David Schneider (eds.), *Personality in Nature, Society, and Culture*, Knopf, 2nd ed., 1953.

Kohn, Melvin L., and Carmi Schooler, "Class, Occupation, and Orientation," *ASR*, Oct., 1969, pp. 659–678.

Kohn, Melvin L., and Robin M. Williams, Jr., "Situational Patterning in Intergroup Relations," *ASR*, Apr., 1956, pp. 164–174.

Konvitz, Milton R., *The Constitution and Civil Rights*, Columbia, 1946.

Konvitz, Milton R., and Theodore Leskes, *A Century of Civil Rights*, Columbia, 1961.

Kramer, Hilton, " 'Black Art' and Expedient Politics," *The New York Times*, June 7, 1970.

Kramer, Hilton, "Trying to Define 'Black Art': Must We Go Back to Social Realism?" *The New York Times,* May 31, 1970, p. D17.

Kramer, Judith R., *The American Minority Community,* Crowell, 1970.

Kramer, Judith R., and Seymour Leventman, *Children of the Gilded Ghetto,* Yale, 1961.

Krech, David, and Richard S. Crutchfield, *Theory and Problems of Social Psychology,* McGraw-Hill, 1948.

Kroeber, A. L., *Anthropology,* Harcourt Brace Jovanovich, rev. ed., 1948.

Krug, Mark M., "Freedom and Racial Equality: A Study of 'Revised' High School History Texts," *School Review,* May, 1970, pp. 297–354.

Kuritz, Hyman, "Integration on Negro College Campuses," *Phylon,* Second Quarter, 1967, pp. 125–126.

Kutner, Bernard, Carol Wilkins, and P. R. Yarrow, "Verbal Attitudes and Overt Behavior Involving Racial Prejudice," *JASP,* July, 1952, pp. 649–652.

Kvavaceus, William C. (ed.), *Negro Self-Concept: Implications for School and Citizenship,* McGraw-Hill, 1965.

LeFarge, John, *The Catholic Viewpoint on Race Relations,* Doubleday, 1956.

Lambert, Richard D., and Marvin Bressler, "The Sensitive-Area Complex: A Contribution to the Theory of Guided Culture Contact," *AJS,* May, 1955, pp. 583–592.

Lansing, John B., Charles Wade, and James M. Morgan, *New Homes and Poor People: A Study of Chains of Moves,* Institute of Social Research, Univ. of Michigan, 1969, pp. 68 ff.

Lasch, Christopher, *The Agony of the American Left,* Random House, 1969.

Laue, James H., "A Contemporary Revitalization Movement in American Race Relations: The 'Black Muslims,'" *SF,* Mar., 1964, pp. 315–323.

Laumann, Edward O. (ed.), *Social Stratification: Research and Theory for the 1970s,* Bobbs-Merrill, 1970.

Laumann, Edward O., "The Social Structure of Religious and Ethnoreligious Groups in a Metropolitan Community," *ASR,* Apr., 1969, pp. 182–197.

Laurenti, L., *Property Values and Race,* Univ. of California Press, 1960.

Lazarsfeld, Paul F., and Frank N. Stanton (eds.), *Communications Research, 1948–49,* Harper & Row, 1949.

Lecky, Robert S., and H. Elliott Wright, *Black*

Manifesto: Religion, Racism and Reparations, Sheed & Ward, 1970.

Lee, Rose Hum, *The Chinese in the United States of America,* Hong Kong Univ. Press, 1960.

Leeson, Jim, "Busing and Desegregation," *SER,* Nov., 1968, pp. 18 ff.

Lefton, Mark, "Race, Expressions, and Anomia," *SF,* Mar., 1968, pp. 347–352.

Leggett, John C., *Class, Race, and Labor: Working Class Consciousness in Detroit,* Oxford, 1968.

Lehrman, R. L., *Race, Evolution, and Mankind,* Basic Books, 1966.

Leighton, Alexander Hamilton, *The Governing of Men,* Princeton, 1945.

Lenski, Gerhard, *Power and Privilege: A Theory of Social Stratification,* McGraw-Hill, 1966.

Lenski, Gerhard, *The Religious Factor,* Doubleday, 1961.

Lenski, Gerhard, and John C. Leggett, "Caste, Class, and Deference in the Research Interview," *AJS,* Mar., 1960, pp. 463–467.

Levine, Stuart, and Nancy Lurie (eds.), *The American Indian Today,* Penguin Books, 1970.

Lewin, Kurt, *Resolving Social Conflicts,* Harper & Row, 1948.

Lewis, Hylan, *Blackways of Kent,* Univ. of North Carolina Press, 1955.

Lewis, Hylan, "Innovations and Trends in the Contemporary Southern Negro Community," *JSI,* 1954, Vol. 10, No. 1, pp. 19–27.

Lewis, Hylan, "'Tough' Aspects of Higher Education," *Phylon,* Fourth Quarter, 1949, pp. 359–361.

Lewis, Oscar, *Five Families: Mexican Case Studies in the Culture of Poverty,* Basic Books, 1959.

Lewis, Oscar, *La Vida: A Puerto Rican Family in the Culture of Poverty—San Juan and New York,* Random House, 1965.

Lewis, W. Arthur, "Black Power and the American University," *University: A Princeton Quarterly,* Spring, 1969, pp. 9 ff.

Lichtheim, George, "Socialism and the Jews," *Dissent,* July–Aug., 1968, pp. 314–342.

Lieberson, Stanley, "The Impact of Residential Segregation on Ethnic Assimilation," *SF,* Oct., 1961, pp. 52–57.

Lieberson, Stanley, "The Old-New Distinction and Immigrants in Australia," *ASR,* Aug., 1963, pp. 550–565.

Lieberson, Stanley, "A Societal Theory of Race and Ethnic Relations," *ASR,* Dec., 1961, pp. 902–910.

Lieberson, Stanley, "Suburbs and Ethnic Residential Patterns, *AJS*, May, 1962, pp. 673–681.

Lieberson, Stanley, and Arnold R. Silverman, "The Precipitants and Underlying Conditions of Race Riots," *ASR*, Dec., 1965, pp. 887–898.

Liebman, Charles S., "Orthodoxy in American Jewish Life," in Morris Fine and Milton Himmelfarb (eds.), *American Jewish Yearbook*, American Jewish Committee and Jewish Publication Society of America, 1965.

Liebow, Elliot, *Tally's Corner: A Study of Negro Streetcorner Men*, Little, Brown, 1967.

Lincoln, C. Eric, *The Black Muslims in America*, Beacon Press, 1961.

Lincoln, C. Eric (ed.), *Is Anybody Listening to Black America?* Seabury Press, 1968.

Lincoln, C. Eric, "The Relevance of Education for Black Americans," *JNE*, Summer, 1969, pp. 222 ff.

Lind, Andrew W. (ed.), *Race Relations in World Perspective*, Univ. of Hawaii Press, 1955.

Linn, Lawrence S., "Verbal Attitudes and Overt Behavior: A Study of Racial Discrimination," *SF*, Mar., 1965, pp. 353–364.

Linton, Ralph (ed.), *Acculturation in Seven American Indian Tribes*, Appleton-Century-Crofts, 1940.

Linton, Ralph, *The Science of Man in the World Crisis*, Columbia, 1945.

Lippitt, Ronald, and Marian Radke, "New Trends in the Investigation of Prejudice," *Annals*, Mar., 1946, pp. 167–176.

Lipset, Seymour M., "Democracy and Working-Class Authoritarianism," *ASR*, Aug. 1959, pp. 482–501.

Lipset, Seymour M., " 'The Socialism of Fools': The Left, the Jews, and Israel," ADL, 1969.

Lipsitz, Lewis, "Working-Class Authoritarianism: A Re-Evaluation," *ASR*, Feb., 1965, pp. 103–109.

Lipsky, Michael, *Protest in City Politics*, Rand McNally, 1970.

Lipsky, Michael, "Protest as a Political Resource," *American Political Science Review*, Dec., 1968, pp. 1144–1158.

Lockard, Duane, *Toward Equal Opportunity*, Macmillan, 1968.

Locke, Alain, *The Negro in Art: A Pictorial Record of the Negro Artists and of the Negro Theme in Art*, Associates in Negro Folk Education, 1940.

Locke, Alain, and B. J. Stern (eds.), *When Peoples Meet*, Hines, Hayden & Eldridge, rev. ed., 1946.

Locke, Harvey J., Georges Sabagh, and Mary

Margaret Thomas, "Interfaith Marriages," *SP*, Apr. 1957, pp. 329–333.

Loescher, F. S., *The Protestant Church and the Negro*, Association Press, 1948.

Lohman, J. D., and D. C. Reitzes, "Deliberately Organized Groups and Racial Behavior," *ASR*, June, 1954, pp. 342–344.

Lohman, J. D., and D. C. Reitzes, "Note on Race Relations in Mass Society," *AJS*, Nov., 1952, pp. 240–246.

Lomax, Louis E., "The American Negro's New Comedy Act," *Harper's*, June, 1961, pp. 41–46.

Lomax, Louis E., *The Negro Revolt*, Harper & Row, 1963.

Lowenthal, Leo, and Norbert Guterman, *Prophets of Deceit: A Study in the Techniques of the American Agitator*, Harper & Row, 1949.

Lowie, Robert H., *The German People*, Farrar, Straus & Giroux, 1945.

Lutterman, Kenneth G., and Russell Middleton, "Authoritarianism, Anomia, and Prejudice," *SF*, June, 1970, pp. 485–492.

Macartney, C. A., *National States and National Minorities*, Oxford, 1934.

Maccoby, Eleanor, Theodore M. Newcomb, and E. L. Hartley (eds.), *Readings in Social Psychology*, Holt, Rinehart & Winston, 3rd ed., 1958.

MacCrone, I. D., *Race Attitudes in South Africa*, Oxford, 1937.

MacCrone, I. D., "Reaction to Domination in a Colour-Caste Society: A Preliminary Study of the Race Attitudes of a Dominated Group," *JSP*, Aug., 1947, pp. 69–98.

MacGregor, Gordon, *Warriors Without Weapons*, Univ. of Chicago Press, 1946.

MacIver, R. M. (ed.), *Discrimination and National Welfare*, Institute for Religious and Social Studies, Harper & Row, 1949.

MacIver, R. M. (ed.), *Group Relationships and Group Antagonism*, Harper & Row, 1944.

MacIver, R. M., *The More Perfect Union*, Macmillan, 1948.

Mack, Raymond, and Richard Snyder, "The Analysis of Social Conflict—Toward an Overview and Synthesis," *JCR*, June, 1957, pp. 212–248.

MacKenzie, Barbara Kruger, "The Importance of Contact in Determining Attitudes Toward Negroes," *JASP*, Oct., 1948, pp. 417–441.

MacKinnon, William J., and Richard Centers, "Authoritarianism and Urban Stratification," *AJS*, May, 1956, pp. 610–620.

Maddox, James G., E. E. Liebhafsky, V. Henderson, and H. M. Hamlin, *The Advancing South:*

Manpower Prospects and Problems, Twentieth Century Fund, 1967.

Madsen, William, *Mexican-Americans of South Texas,* Holt, Rinehart & Winston, 1964.

Major, Clarence (ed.), *The New Black Poetry,* International, 1969.

Malcolm X, *The Autobiograph of Malcolm X,* Grove Press, 1966.

Malinowski, Bronislaw, *Myth in Primitive Society,* Norton, 1926.

Malof, Milton, and Albert J. Lott, "Ethnocentrism and the Acceptance of Negro Support in a Group Pressure Situation," *JASP,* Oct., 1962, pp. 254–258.

Mandel, William M., "Soviet Jewry Today," *Issues,* Summer, 1968, pp. 4–9.

Mangum, C. S., Jr., *The Legal Status of the Negro,* Univ. of North Carolina Press, 1940.

Mann, John H., "The Effects of Inter-Racial Contact on Sociometric Choices and Perceptions," *JSP,* Aug., 1959, pp. 143–152.

Maranell, Gary M., "An Examination of Some Religious and Political Attitude Correlates of Bigotry," *SF,* Mar., 1967, pp. 356–363.

Marcus, Lloyd, *The Treatment of Minorities in Secondary School Textbooks,* ADL, 1961.

Marshall, Gloria, "Racial Classification, Popular and Scientific," in M. Mead *et al.* (eds.), *Science and the Concept of Race,* Columbia, 1968.

Marshall, Thurgood, "The Rise and Collapse of 'The White Democratic Primary'," *JNE,* Summer, 1957, pp. 249–254.

Martin, James G., *The Tolerant Personality,* Wayne State Univ. Press, 1964.

Marx, Gary, *Protest and Prejudice,* Harper & Row, 1967.

Marx, Gary, "Religion: Opiate or Inspiration of Civil Rights Militancy Among Negroes?" *ASR,* Feb., 1967, pp. 64–72.

Mason, Philip, *Race Relations,* Oxford, 1970.

Masotti, Louis H., Jeffrey K. Hadden, Kenneth F. Seminatore, and Jerome Corsi, *A Time to Burn?: An Evaluation of the Present Crisis in Race Relations,* Rand McNally, 1970.

Massing, Paul W., *Rehearsal for Destruction: A Study of Political Anti-Semitism in Imperial Germany,* Harper & Row, 1949.

Mast, Robert, "Police-Ghetto Relations: Some Findings and a Proposal for Structural Change," *Race,* Apr., 1970, pp. 453–454.

Matthews, Donald R., and James W. Prothro, *Negroes and the New Southern Politics,* Harcourt Brace Jovanovich, 1966.

Matthiessen, Peter, *Sal Si Puedes—Escape if You Can: Cesar Chavez and the New American Revolution,* Random House, 1970.

Mayer, John E., *Jewish-Gentile Courtships,* Free Press, 1961.

Mayhew, Leon, *Law and Equal Opportunity: A Study of the Massachusetts Commission Against Discrimination,* Harvard, 1968.

Mays, Benjamin E., *Seeking to be Christian in Race Relations,* Friendship Press, 1957.

Mays, Benjamin E., "The Significance of the Negro Private and Church-Related College," *JNE,* Summer, 1960, pp. 251 ff.

Mays, Benjamin E., and J. W. Nicholson, *The Negro's Church,* Institute of Social and Religious Research, 1933.

McCall, George J., "Symbiosis: The Case of Hoodoo and the Numbers Racket," *SP,* Spring, 1963, pp. 361–371.

McClain, E., "Personality Characteristics of Negro College Students in the South," *JNE,* Summer, 1967, pp. 324 ff.

McClelland, D. C., *The Achieving Society,* Van Nostrand, 1961.

McClosky, Herbert, "Conservatism and Personality," *American Political Science Review,* Mar., 1958, pp. 27–45.

McCord, William, Joan McCord, and Alan Howard, "Early Familial Experiences and Bigotry," *ASR,* Oct., 1960, pp. 717–722.

McDill, Edward L., "Anomie, Authoritarianism, Prejudice, and Socio-economic Status: An Attempt at Clarification," *SF,* Mar., 1961, pp. 239–245.

McEntire, David, *Residence and Race,* Univ. of California Press, 1960.

McGill, Ralph, *The South and the Southerner,* Little, Brown, 1963.

McGrath, Earl J., *The Predominantly Negro Colleges and Universities in Transition,* Columbia, 1965.

McGraw, B. T., "The Housing Act of 1954 and Implications for Minorities," *Phylon,* Second Quarter, 1955, pp. 171 ff.

McKay, Claude, *Harlem Shadows,* Harcourt Brace Jovanovich, 1922.

McKee, James B., "Changing Patterns of Race and Housing: A Toledo Study," *SF,* Mar., 1963, pp. 253–260.

McKee, James B. "Community Power and Strategies in Race Relations," *SP,* Winter, 1958–1959, pp. 195–203.

McKinney, John C., and Linda B. Bourque, "The Changing South: National Incorporation of a Region," *ASR,* June, 1971, pp. 399–412.

McPartland, James, "The Relative Influence of School and of Classroom Desegregation on the Academic Achievement of Ninth Grade Negro Students," *JSI*, Summer, 1969, pp. 101–102.

McWilliams, Carey, *Brothers Under the Skin*, Little, Brown, rev. ed., 1951.

McWilliams, Carey, *A Mask for Privilege: Anti-Semitism in America*, Little, Brown, 1948.

McWilliams, Carey, *Prejudice—Japanese-Americans: Symbol of Racial Intolerance*, Little, Brown, 1944.

Meier, August, and Elliott M. Rudwick, *From Plantation to Ghetto*, Hill & Wang, 1966.

Meier, August, and Elliott M. Rudwick (eds.), *The Making of Black America: Essays in Negro Life and History*, Atheneum, 1969.

Meier, August, Elliott M. Rudwick, and Frances L. Broderick (eds.), *Black Protest Thought in the Twentieth Century*, Bobbs-Merrill, 2nd ed., 1971.

Merton, Robert K., *Social Theory and Social Structure*, Free Press, rev. ed., 1957.

Merton, Robert K., and Robert A. Nisbet (eds.), *Contemporary Social Problems*, Harcourt Brace Jovanovich, 2nd ed., 1966.

Metzger, L. Paul, "American Sociology and Black Assimilation: Conflicting Perspectives," *AJS*, Jan., 1971, pp. 627–647.

Meyer, Philip, "Aftermath of Martyrdom: Negro Militancy and Martin Luther King," *POQ*, Summer, 1969, pp. 160–173.

Middleton, Russell, "Alienation, Race, and Education," *ASR*, Dec., 1963, pp. 973–977.

Middleton, Russell, "Ethnic Prejudice and Susceptibility to Persuasion," *ASR*, Oct., 1960, pp. 679–686.

Middleton, Russell, and John Moland, "Humor in Negro and White Subcultures: A Study of Jokes Among University Students," *ASR*, Feb., 1959, pp. 61–69.

Middleton, Russell, and Snell Putney, "Religion, Normative Standards, and Behavior," *Sociometry*, June, 1962, pp. 141–152.

Miller, C. L., "The Publicly Supported Junior College," *JNE*, Summer, 1962, pp. 387–388.

Miller, J. Erroll, "The Negro in National Politics in 1968," in Patricia W. Romero (ed.), *In Black America*, United, 1969, pp. 3–40.

Miller, Kent S., "Psychological Characteristics of the Negro," in *The Negro in American Society*, Florida State Univ. Studies, No. 28, 1958, pp. 21–22 ff.

Miller, S. M., and Frank Riessman, "Working-Class Authoritarianism: A Critique of Lipset,"

British Journal of Sociology, Sept., 1961, pp. 263–276.

Miller, Walter B., "Lower Class Culture as a Generating Milieu of Gang Delinquency," *JSI*, Third Quarter, 1958, pp. 5–19.

Milner, Esther, "Some Hypotheses Concerning the Influence of Segregation on Negro Personality Development," *Psychiatry*, Aug., 1953, pp. 291–297.

Mittelbach, Frank G., and Joan W. Moore, "Ethnic Endogamy—The Case of Mexican Americans," *AJS*, July, 1968, pp. 50–62.

Mittnick, Leonard L., and Elliott McGinnies, "Influencing Ethnocentrism in Small Discussion Groups through a Film Communication," *JASP*, Jan., 1958, pp. 82–90.

Molotch, Harvey, "Racial Integration in a Transition Community," *ASR*, Dec., 1969, pp. 878–893.

Montagu, M. F. Ashley, "The Concept of Race," *AA*, Oct., 1962, pp. 919–928.

Montagu, M. F. Ashley, *The Idea of Race*, Nebraska, 1965.

Montagu, M. F. Ashley, *An Introduction to Physical Anthropology*, Thomas, 3rd ed., 1960.

Montagu, M. F. Ashley, *Man's Most Dangerous Myth: The Fallacy of Race*, World, 4th ed., 1964.

Montagu, M. F. Ashley, *Statement on Race*, Henry Schuman, 1951.

Moon, Henry Lee, *Balance of Power: The Negro Vote*, Doubleday, 1948.

Moore, Barrington, Jr., "Thoughts on Violence and Democracy," in Robert H. Connery (ed.), *Urban Riots: Violence and Change*, Academy of Political Science, Columbia Univ., 1968, pp. 1–12.

Morais, Herbert M., "Medicine and Health," in Patricia W. Romero (ed.), *In Black America*, United, 1969, pp. 365–378.

Morsell, J. A., "Racial Desegregation and Integration in Public Education," *JNE*, Summer, 1969, pp. 283 ff.

Moskos, Charles C., "Racial Integration in the Armed Forces," *AJS*, Sept., 1966, pp. 132–148.

Mourant, A. E., "Evolution, Genetics and Anthropology," *The Journal of the Royal Anthropological Institute of Great Britain and Ireland*, July–December 1961, pp. 159 ff.

Murray, Albert, "Something Different, Something More," in Herbert Hill (ed.), *Anger, and Beyond*, Harper & Row, 1966, pp. 116 ff.

Mussen, Paul H., "Some Personality and Social Factors Related to Changes in Children's Attitudes Toward Negroes," *JASP*, July, 1950, pp. 423–441.

Myrdal, Gunnar, with the assistance of Richard Sterner and Arnold Rose, *An American Dilemma: The Negro Problem and Modern Democracy*, 2 vols., Harper & Row, 1944.

Nash, Manning, "Race and the Ideology of Race," *CA*, June 1962, pp. 285–288.

National Commission on the Causes and Prevention of Violence, *To Establish Justice, to Insure Domestic Tranquility*, Government Printing Office, 1970.

National Committee Against Discrimination in Housing, *Trends in Housing*, Vol. 14, No. 4, Special Report 1, 1970.

Needler, Martin, "Hilter's Anti-Semitism: A Political Appraisal," *POQ*, Winter, 1960, pp. 665–669.

Nelson, Harold A., "The Defenders: A Case Study of an Informal Police Organization," *SP*, Fall, 1967, pp. 127–147.

Newcomb, Theodore M., "Autistic Hostility and Social Reality," *HR*, June, 1947, pp. 69–86.

Newcomb, Theodore M., "The Influence of Attitude Climate Upon Some Determinants of Information," *JASP*, July, 1946, pp. 291–302.

Newcomb, Theodore M., and Eugene L. Hartley, *Readings in Social Psychology*, Holt, Rinehart & Winston, 1947.

Nieburg, H. L., "Uses of Violence," *JCR*, Mar., 1963, pp. 43–54.

Noel, Donald L., "A Theory of the Origin of Ethnic Stratification," *SP*, Fall, 1968, pp. 157–172.

Northrup, Herbert R., *Organized Labor and the Negro*, Harper & Row, 1944.

Office of Policy Planning and Research, U.S. Department of Labor, *The Negro Family: The Case for National Action*, Mar., 1965.

Olsen, Marvin E., "Perceived Legitimacy of Social Protest Actions," *SP*, Winter, 1968, pp. 297–310.

Olsen, Marvin E., "Social and Political Participation of Blacks," *ASR*, Aug., 1970, pp. 682–697.

Olson, Bernhard E., *Faith and Prejudice*, Yale, 1963.

Oppenheimer, Martin, *The Urban Guerrilla*, Quadrangle Books, 1969.

Orum, Anthony M., "A Reappraisal of the Social and Political Participation of Negroes," *AJS*, July, 1966, pp. 32–46.

Padfield, H., and W. Martin, *Farmers, Workers, and Machines*, Arizona, 1965.

Padilla, Elena, *Up from Puerto Rico*, Columbia, 1958.

Parker, Seymour, and Robert J. Kleiner, "The Culture of Poverty: An Adjustive Dimension," *AA*, June, 1970, pp. 516–527.

Parker, Seymour, and Robert J. Kleiner, *Mental Illness in the Urban Negro Community*, Free Press, 1966.

Parkes, James W. *Antisemitism*, Valentine and Mitchell, 1963.

Parkes, James W., *An Enemy of the People: Antisemitism*, Penguin Books, 1946.

Parkes, James W., *The Jewish Problem in the Modern World*, Thornton Butterworth, 1939.

Parkman, Margaret A., and Jack Sawyer, "Dimensions of Ethnic Intermarriage in Hawaii," *ASR*, Aug., 1967, pp. 593–607.

Pasamanick, Benjamin, "Some Misconceptions Concerning Differences in the Racial Prevalence of Mental Disease," *American Journal of Orthopsychiatry*, Jan., 1963, pp. 72–86.

Patterson, Lindsay, "The Negro in the Performing Arts," in Patricia W. Romero (ed.), *In Black America*, United, 1969, pp. 305–316.

Patterson, Shelia, *Immigrants in Industry*, Oxford, 1968.

Peabody, Dean, "Attitude Content and Agreement Set in Scales of Authoritarianism, Dogmatism, Anti-Semitism and Economic Conservatism," *JASP*, July, 1961, pp. 1–11.

Peñalosa, Fernando, and Edward C. McDonagh, "Social Mobility in a Mexican-American Community," *SF*, June, 1966, pp. 498–505.

Peres, Yochanan, "Ethnic Relations in Israel," *AJS*, May, 1971, pp. 1021–1047.

Petersen, Ruth C., and L. L. Thurstone, *Motion Pictures and the Social Attitudes of Children*, Macmillan, 1933.

Petersen, William, "A General Typology of Migration," *ASR*, June, 1958, pp. 256–266.

Petersen, William, and David Matza (eds.), *Social Controversy*, Wadsworth, 1963.

Pettigrew, Thomas F. (issue ed.), "Desegregation Research in the North and South," *JSI*, Fourth Quarter, 1959.

Pettigrew, Thomas F., "Negro American Personality: Why Isn't More Known?" *JSI*, Apr., 1964, pp. 4–23.

Pettigrew, Thomas F., *A Profile of the Negro American*, Van Nostrand, 1964.

Pettigrew, Thomas F., "Racially Separate or Together?" *JSI*, Jan., 1969, pp. 43–69.

Pettigrew, Thomas F., "A Social Psychological View of the Predominantly Negro College," *JNE*, Summer, 1967, pp. 279–280.

Pettigrew, Thomas F., and Rosalind Barclay Spier, "The Ecological Structure of Negro Homicide," *AJS*, May, 1962, pp. 621–629.

Phillips, U. B., *American Negro Slavery*, Appleton-Century-Crofts, 1918.

Phillips, U. B., *Life and Labor in the Old South*, Little, Brown, 1929.

Phillips, U. B., "Slavery-United States," *Encyclopaedia of the Social Sciences*, Vol. 14, Macmillan, 1934.

Phillips, W. M., Jr., "The Boycott: A Negro Community in Conflict," *Phylon*, Spring, 1961, pp. 24–30.

Photiadis, John, and Jeanne Biggar, "Religiosity, Education, and Ethnic Distance," *AJS*, May, 1962, pp. 666–672.

Photiadis, John, and Arthur L. Johnson, "Orthodoxy, Church Participation, and Authoritarianism," *AJS*, Nov., 1963, pp. 244–248.

Pinkney, Alphonso, *The Committed: White Activists in the Civil Rights Movement*, College and Universities Press, 1968.

Pinson, Koppel, S. (ed.), *Essays on Antisemitism*, Conference on Jewish Relations, 1946.

Plant, James S., *Personality and the Culture Pattern*, Commonwealth Fund, 1937.

Podhoretz, Norman, "My Negro Problem—and Ours," *Commentary*, Feb., 1963, pp. 93–101.

Pollitt, Daniel H., "Equal Protection in Public Education: 1954–1961," *AAUPB*, Autumn, 1961, pp. 201–202.

Porter, James A., *Modern Negro Art*, Dryden Press, 1943.

Porter, John, "The Future of Upward Mobility," *ASR*, Feb., 1968, pp. 5–19.

Poussaint, Alvin F., and Carolyn O. Atkinson, "Negro Youth and Psychological Motivation," *JNE*, Summer, 1968, pp. 250 ff.

Powdermaker, Hortense, *After Freedom: A Cultural Study in the Deep South*, Viking, 1939.

Powdermaker, Hortense, "The Channeling of Negro Aggression By the Cultural Process," *AJS*, May, 1943, pp. 750–758.

The President's Committee on Civil Rights, *To Secure These Rights*, Simon & Schuster, 1947.

The President's Committee on Equality of Treatment and Opportunity in the Armed Services, *Freedom to Serve*, Government Printing Office, 1950.

Price, H. D., *The Negro and Southern Politics: A Chapter of Florida History*, New York Univ. Press, 1957.

Pulzer, P. G. J., *The Rise of Political Anti-Semitism in Germany and Austria*, Wiley, 1964.

Putnam, Carleton, *Race and Reality*, Public Affairs Press, 1967.

Putney, Snell, and Russell Middleton, "Rebellion, Conformity, and Parental Religious Ideologies," *Sociometry*, June, 1961, pp. 125–136.

Rainwater, Lee, "Crucible of Identity: The Negro Lower-Class Family," in Talcott Parsons and Kenneth B. Clark (eds.), *The Negro American*, Houghton, Mifflin, 1966, pp. 167–181.

Rainwater, Lee, "Open Letter on White Justice and the Riots," in Peter H. Rossi (ed.), *Ghetto Revolts*, Aldine, 1970, p. 71.

Rainwater, Lee, "The Problem of Lower Class Culture," *JSI*, Spring, 1970, pp. 133–148.

Rainwater, Lee, and William L. Yancey (eds.), *The Moynihan Report and the Politics of Controversy*, M.I.T., 1967.

Rapkin, Chester and William G. Grigsby, *The Demand for Housing in Racially Mixed Areas*, Univ. of California Press, 1960.

Record, C. Wilson, *The Negro and the Communist Party*, Univ. of North Carolina Press, 1951.

Record, C. Wilson, *Race and Radicalism: The NAACP and the Communist Party in Conflict*, Cornell, 1964.

Redding, J. Saunders, *On Being Negro in America*, Bobbs-Merrill, 1962.

Redding, J. Saunders, *To Make a Poet Black*, Univ. of North Carolina Press, 1939.

Reich, Donald R., "Schoolhouse Religion and the Supreme Court: A Report on Attitudes of Teachers and Principals on School Practices in Wisconsin and Ohio," *Journal of Legal Education*, Vol. 23, No. 1, 1971, pp. 123–143.

Reichmann, Eva G., *Hostage of Civilization: The Social Sources of National Socialist Anti-Semitism*, Beacon Press, 1951.

Reimers, David, *White Protestantism and the Negro*, Oxford, 1965.

Reiss, Ira L., "Premarital Sexual Permissiveness among Negroes and Whites," *ASR*, Oct., 1964, pp. 688–698.

Reitzes, Dietrich C., "Institutional Structure and Race Relations," *Phylon*, First Quarter, 1959, pp. 48–66.

Reitzes, Dietrich C., *Negroes and Medicine*, Harvard, 1958.

Report of the National Advisory Commission on Civil Rights, Bantam Books, 1968.

Rex, John, *Race Relations in Sociological Theory*, Weidenfeld & Nicolson, 1970.

Reynolds, Harry W., Jr., "What Do We Know About Our Experience with Relocation?" *JIR*, Autumn, 1961, pp. 342–354.

Rhyne, Edwin Hoffman, "Racial Prejudice and Personality Scales: An Alternative Approach," *SF*, Oct., 1962, pp. 44–53.

Ribich, Thomas I., *Education and Poverty*, The Brookings Institution, 1968.

Richmond, Anthony H., "Sociological and Psychological Explanations of Racial Prejudice: Some Light on the Controversy from Recent Researches in Britain," *Pacific Sociological Review*, Fall, 1961, pp. 63–68.

Riley, Clayton, "We Will Not Be 'A New Form of White Art in Blackface,'" *The New York Times*, June 14, 1970, pp. D1, 3.

Rinder, Irwin D., "Strangers in the Land: Social Relations in the Status Gap," *SP*, Winter, 1958–1959, pp. 253–260.

Rinder, Irwin D., "A Note on Humor as an Index of Minority Group Morale," *Phylon*, Summer, 1965, pp. 117–121.

Ringer, Benjamin B., *The Edge of Friendliness: A Study of Jewish-Gentile Relations*, Basic Books, 1967.

Roach, Jack L., and Orville R. Gursslin, "An Evaluation of the Concept 'Culture of Poverty,'" *SF*, Mar., 1967, pp. 383–392.

Roberts, A. H., and Milton Rokeach, "Anomie, Authoritarianism, and Prejudice: A Replication," *AJS*, Jan., 1956, pp. 355–358.

Rodman, Hyman, "The Lower-Class Value Stretch," *SF*, Dec., 1963, pp. 205–215.

Roen, Sheldon R., "Personality and Negro-White Intelligence," *JASP*, July, 1960, pp. 148–150.

Rogers, J. Overton, *Blues and Ballads of a Black Yankee*, Exposition Press, 1965.

Rohrer, John H., and Munro S. Edmonson (eds.), with Harold Lief, Daniel Thompson and William Thompson, co-authors, *The Eighth Generation: Cultures and Personalities of New Orleans Negroes*, Harper & Row, 1960.

Rohrer, Wayne C., *Black Profiles of White Americans*, Davis, 1970.

Rokeach, Milton, "Attitude Change and Behavioral Change," *POQ*, Winter, 1966–1967, pp. 529–550.

Rokeach, Milton, *Beliefs, Attitudes, and Values*, Jossey-Bass, 1968.

Rokeach, Milton, "Generalized Mental Rigidity as a Factor in Ethnocentrism," *JASP*, July, 1948, pp. 259–278.

Rokeach, Milton, *The Open and Closed Mind*, Basic Books, 1960.

Rokeach, Milton, "Political and Religious Dogmatism: An Alternate to the Authoritarian Personality," *Psychological Monographs*, 1956, Vol. 70, No. 18 (whole issue).

Rokeach, Milton, "I. Values Systems in Religion. II. Religious Values and Social Compassion," *Review of Religious Research*, Fall, 1969, pp. 3–39.

Romero, Patricia W. (ed.), *In Black America*, United, 1969.

Rorer, L. G., "The Great Response-Style Myth," *Psychological Bulletin*, March, 1965, pp. 129–156.

Rose, Arnold M., "Inconsistencies in Attitudes Toward Negro Housing," *SP*, Spring, 1961, pp. 287–292.

Rose, Arnold M., "Intergroup Relations vs. Prejudice: Pertinent Theory for the Study of Social Change," *SP*, Oct., 1956, pp. 173–176.

Rose, Arnold M., *The Negro's Morale*, Univ. of Minnesota Press, 1949.

Rose, Peter I. (ed.), *Americans from Africa: Old Memories, New Moods*, Atherton Press, 1970.

Rose, Peter I., (ed.), *Americans from Africa: Slavery and Its Aftermath*, Atherton Press, 1970.

Rose, Peter I., *The Ghetto and Beyond: Essays on Jewish Life in America*, Random House, 1969.

Rosen, Bernard C., *Adolescence and Religion*, Schenkman, 1965.

Rosen, Bernard C., "Race, Ethnicity, and the Achievement Syndrome," *ASR*, Feb., 1959, pp. 47–60.

Rosenberg, Stuart A., *The Search for Jewish Identity in America*, Doubleday, 1965.

Rosenblatt, Paul C., "Origins and Effects of Group Ethnocentrism and Nationalism," *JCR*, June, 1964, pp. 131–146.

Rosenthal, Erich, "Acculturation without Assimilation? The Jewish Community in Chicago, Illinois," *AJS*, Nov., 1960, pp. 275–288.

Rosenthal, Erich, "Jewish Intermarriage in Indiana," *American Jewish Yearbook*, Vol. 68, 1967, pp. 263 ff.

Rosenthal, Robert, and Lenore Jacobson, *Pygmalion in the Classroom*, Holt, Rinehart & Winston, 1968.

Ross, Malcolm, *All Manner of Men*, Reynal & Hitchcock, 1948.

Rossi, Peter H., "The Education of Failure or

the Failure of Education," *JNE*, Summer, 1969, pp. 332 ff.

Rossi, Peter H., *Ghetto Revolts*, Aldine, 1970.

Rothney, William B., "Racial, Ethnic and Income Factors in the Epidemiology of Neonatal Mortality," *ASR*, Aug., 1962, pp. 526 ff.

Rotter, J. B. "Generalized Expectancies for Internal versus External Control of Reinforcement," *Psychogical Monographs*, Vol. 80, No. 1, 1966.

Rowan, Carl T., *Go South to Sorrow*, Random House, 1957.

Roy, Prodipto, "The Measurement of Assimilation: The Spokane Indian," *AJS*, Mar., 1962, pp. 548–551.

Rubel, Arthur J., *Across the Tracks: Mexican-Americans in a Texas City*, Univ. of Texas Press, 1966.

Rubin, Irwin M., "Increased Self Acceptance: A Means of Reducing Prejudice," *JPSP*, Feb., 1967, pp. 233–238.

Rubin, Morton, *Plantation County*, Univ. of North Carolina Press, 1951.

Rubin, Morton, "Social and Cultural Change in the Plantation Area," *JSI*, First Quarter, 1954, pp. 28–35.

Rubin, Ronald I. (ed.), *The Unredeemed: Anti-Semitism in the Soviet Union*, Quadrangle Books, 1969.

Rudwick, Elliott M., *The Unequal Badge: Negro Policemen in the South*, SRC, 1962.

Rudwick, Elliott M., and August Meier, "Organizational Structure and Goal Succession: A Comparative Analysis of the NAACP and CORE, 1964–1968," *Social Science Quarterly*, June, 1970, pp. 9–24.

Rymph, Raymond C., and Jeffrey K. Hadden, "The Persistence of Regionalism in Racial Attitudes of Methodist Clergy," *SF*, Sept., 1970, pp. 41–50.

Rytina, Joan Huber, William H. Form, and John Pease, "Income and Stratification Ideology: Beliefs about the American Opportunity Structure," *AJS*, Jan., 1970, pp. 703–716.

Samora, Julian, *La Raza: Forgotten Americans*, Notre Dame, 1966.

Samuel, Maurice, *The Great Hatred*, Knopf, 1940.

Samuels, Howard J., "Compensatory Capitalism," in William F. Haddad and G. Douglas Pugh (eds.), *Black Economic Development*, Prentice-Hall, 1969.

Sartre, Jean-Paul, *Anti-Semite and Jew* (trans. by George J. Becker), Schocken Books, 1965.

Scanzoni, John H., *The Black Family in Modern Society*, Allyn & Bacon, 1971.

Schary, Dore, "The Mass Media and Prejudice," in Charles Y. Glock and Ellen Siegelman (eds.), *Prejudice U.S.A.*, Praeger, 1969.

Scheffler, Linda W., "What 70 SEEK Kids Taught Their Counselor," *The New York Times Magazine*, Nov. 16, 1969, pp. 54 ff.

Schermerhorn, Richard A., *Comparative Ethnic Relations: A Framework for Theory and Research*, Random House, 1970.

Schermerhorn, Richard A., "Minorities: European and American," *Phylon*, Second Quarter, 1959, pp. 179–185.

Schermerhorn, Richard A., *These Our People: Minorities in American Culture*, Heath, 1949.

Schmidt, Fred H., *Spanish Surnamed American Employment in the Southwest*, Government Printing Office for the Equal Employment Opportunity Commission, 1970.

Schmitt, Robert C., "Interracial Marriage and Occupational Status in Hawaii," *ASR*, Oct., 1963, pp. 809–810.

Schmitt, Robert C., and Robert A. Souza, "Interracial Households in Honolulu," *SP*, Winter, 1963, pp. 264–268.

Schnepp, G. J., and A. M. Yui, "Cultural and Marital Adjustment of Japanese War Brides," *AJS*, July, 1955, pp. 48–50.

Schuchter, Arnold, *White Power/Black Freedom*, Beacon Press, 1968.

Schuman, Howard, and Jean M. Converse, "The Effects of Black and White Interviewers on Black Responses in 1968," *POQ*, Spring, 1971, pp. 44–68.

Schuman, Howard, and Barry Gruenberg, "The Impact of City on Racial Attitudes," *AJS*, Sept., 1970, pp. 213–261.

Schuman, Howard, and John Harding, "Prejudice and the Norm of Rationality," *Sociometry*, Sept., 1964, pp. 353–371.

Seale, Bobby, *Seize the Time: The Story of the Black Panther Party*, Random House, 1970.

Seeman, Melvin, "Alienation and Social Learning in a Reformatory, *AJS*, Nov., 1963, pp. 270–283.

Seeman, Melvin, "On the Meaning of Alienation," *ASR*, Dec., 1959, pp. 783–791.

Selltiz, Claire, and S. W. Cook, "Factors Influencing Attitudes of Foreign Students Toward Their Host Countries," *JSI*, 1962, Vol. 18, No. 1, pp. 7–23.

Selznick, Gertrude J., and Stephen Steinberg, *The Tenacity of Prejudice: Anti-Semitism in Contemporary America*, Harper & Row, 1969.

Senior, Clarence, *Strangers—Then Neighbors*, Freedom Books, ADL, 1961.

Shapiro, H. L., "Race Mixture," *The Race Question in Modern Science*, Morrow, for UNESCO 1956.

Sharp, Harry, and Leo F. Schnore, "The Changing Color Composition of Metropolitan Areas," *Land Economics*, May, 1962, pp. 169–185.

Sherif, Muzafer, *In Common Predicament: Social Psychology of Intergroup Conflict and Cooperation*, Houghton Mifflin, 1966.

Sherif, Muzafer, O. J. Harvey, B. Jack White, William R. Hood, and Carolyn W. Sherif, *Intergroup Conflict and Cooperation: The Robbers Cave Experiment*, Univ. Book Exchange, Norman, Oklahoma, 1961.

Sherif, Muzafer, and Carolyn W. Sherif, *Groups in Harmony and Tension*, Harper & Row, 1953.

Sherman, C. Bezalel, *The Jew Within American Society: A Study in Ethnic Individuality*, Wayne State Univ. Press, 1961.

Shibutani, Tamotsu, and Kian M. Kwan, *Ethnic Stratification: A Comparative Approach*, Macmillan, 1965.

Shuey, Audrey M., *The Testing of Negro Intelligence*, Social Science Press, 2nd ed., 1966.

Shuval, Judith T., "Emerging Patterns of Ethnic Strain in Israel," *SF*, May, 1962, pp. 323–330.

Siegel, Bernard J., "Defensive Structuring and Environmental Stress," *AJS*, July, 1970, pp. 11–32.

Silberstein, Fred B., and Melvin Seeman, "Social Mobility and Prejudice," *AJS*, Nov., 1959, pp. 258–264.

Silverman, Julian, "Shamans and Acute Schizophrenia," *AA*, Feb., 1967, pp. 21–31.

Simmel, Georg, *Conflict*, Free Press, 1955.

Simmons, Ozzie G., "The Mutual Images and Expectations of Anglo-Americans and Mexican-Americans," *Daedalus*, Spring, 1961, pp. 286–299.

Simpson, George E., "Ethnic Groups, Social Mobility, and Power in Latin America," in Anthony Leeds (ed.), *Social Structure, Stratification, and Mobility*, Studies and Monographs, VIII, Pan American Union, 1967.

Simpson, George E., and J. Milton Yinger (issue eds.), "American Indians and American Life," ANNALS, May, 1957.

Singer, David L., "Aggression Arousal, Hostile Humor, Catharsis," *JPSP*, Jan., 1968, pp. 1–14.

Skala, Martin, "Inner-City Enterprises: Current

Experience," in William F. Haddad and G. Douglas Pugh (eds.), *Black Economic Development*, Prentice-Hall, 1969.

Sklare, Marshall, *Conservative Judaism*, Free Press, 1955.

Sklare, Marshall, "Intermarriage and the Jewish Future," *Commentary*, Apr., 1964, pp. 46–52.

Sklare, Marshall (ed.), *The Jews: Social Patterns of an American Group*, Free Press, 1958.

Sklare, Marshall, and Joseph Greenblum, *Jewish Identity on the Suburban Frontier: A Study of Group Survival in the Open Society*, Basic Books, 1967.

Sklare, Marshall, and Marc Vosk, *The Riverton Study: How Jews Look at Themselves and Their Neighbors*, American Jewish Committee, 1957.

Slater, Mariam K., "My Son the Doctor: Aspects of Mobility among American Jews," *ASR*, June, 1969, pp. 359–373.

Smith, Bradford, *Americans from Japan*, Lippincott, 1948.

Smith, Bruce L., "The Politics of Protest: How Effective Is Violence?" in Robert H. Connery (ed.), *Urban Riots: Violence and Social Change*, Proceedings of the Academy of Political Science, Columbia Univ., 1968, pp. 113–130.

Smith, Carole R., Lev Williams, and Richard H. Willis, "Race, Sex, and Belief as Determinants of Friendship Acceptance," *JPSP*, Feb., 1967, pp. 127–137.

Smith, Lillian, *Killers of the Dream*, Norton, 1949.

Smith, M. Brewster, "Opinions, Personality, and Political Behavior," *American Political Science Review*, Mar., 1958, pp. 1–17.

Snyder, Eldon E., and Joseph B. Perry, Jr., "Farm Employer Attitudes Toward Mexican-American Migrant Workers," *Rural Sociology*, June, 1970, pp. 244–252.

Solomon, Barbara Miller, *Ancestors and Immigrants*, Harvard, 1956.

Sorkin, Alan L., "Some Aspects of American Indian Migration," *SF*, Dec., 1969, pp. 243–250.

Southern Regional Council, *Desegregation in Higher Education*, Report L-23B, Feb., 13, 1963.

Sovern, Michael, *Legal Restraints on Racial Discrimination in Employment*, Twentieth Century Fund, 1966.

Spicer, Edward H., *Cycles of Conquest: The Impact of Spain, Mexico, and the United*

States on Indians of the Southwest, 1553–1960, Univ. of Arizona Press, 1962.

Spicer, Edward H., Asael T. Hansen, Katherine Luomala, and Markin K. Opler, *Impounded People: Japanese-Americans in the Relocation Centers*, Univ. of Arizona Press, 1969.

Spike, Robert W., *The Freedom Revolution and the Churches*, Association Press, 1965.

Spilerman, Seymour, "The Causes of Racial Disturbances: A Comparison of Alternative Explanations," *ASR*, Aug., 1970, pp. 627–649.

Spilka, Bernard, and J. F. Reynolds, "Religion and Prejudice: A Factor-Analytic Study," *Review of Religious Research*, Spring, 1965, pp. 163–168.

Sprey, Jetse, "Sex Differences in Occupational Choice Patterns Among Negro Adolescents," *SP*, Summer, 1962, pp. 11–23.

Sprole, Leo, "Social Integration and Certain Corollaries: An Exploratory Study," *ASR*, Dec., 1956, pp. 709–716.

Stampp, Kenneth M., *The Peculiar Institution: Slavery in the Ante-Bellum South*, Knopf, 1965.

Stanford University, Center for Latin American Studies, *The Mexican American: A Selected and Annotated Bibliography*, Stanford Univ. Press, 1969.

Steckler, G. A., "Authoritarian Ideology in Negro College Students," *JASP*, May, 1957, pp. 396–399.

Stein, David D., "The Influence of Belief Systems on Interpersonal Preference: A Validation of Rokeach's Theory of Prejudice," *Psychological Monographs: General and Applied*, Vol. 80, No. 8, 1966.

Stein, David D., Jane A. Hardyck, and M. Brewster Smith, "Race and Belief: An Open and Shut Case," *JPSP*, April, 1965, pp. 281–289.

Stein, Herman D., and John M. Martin, "'Swastika Offenders': Variations in Etiology, Behavior and Psycho-social Characteristics," *SP*, Summer, 1962, pp. 56–70.

Steiner, Ivan D., and Homer H. Johnson, "Authoritarianism and Conformity," *Sociometry*, Mar., 1963, pp. 21–34.

Steiner, Stan, *La Raza: The Mexican-Americans*, Harper & Row, 1970.

Steiner, Stan, *The New Indians*, Dell, 1968.

Stember, Charles Herbert, *Education and Attitude Change: The Effect of Schooling on Prejudice Against Minority Groups*, Institute of Human Relations Press, 1961.

Stember, Charles Herbert, *et al.*, *Jews in the Mind of America*, Basic Books, 1966.

Stephenson, Richard M., "Mobility Orientation and Stratification of 1,000 Ninth Graders," *ASR*, Apr., 1957, pp. 204–212.

Stewart, Don, and Thomas Hoult, "A Social-Psychological Theory of the Authoritarian Personality," *AJS*, Nov., 1959, pp. 274–279.

Stillman, Richard J., *Integration of the Negro in the Armed Forces*, Praeger, 1968.

Stinchcombe, Arthur L., Mary McDill, and Dollie Walker, "Is There a Racial Tipping Point in Changing Schools?" *JSI*, Jan., 1969, pp. 127–136.

Stoddard, Lothrop, *The Rising Tide of Color Against White World-Supremacy*, Scribner's, 1920.

Stone, Chuck, *Black Political Power in America*, Dell, rev. ed., 1970.

Stonequist, Everett V., *The Marginal Man: A Study in Personality and Culture Conflict*, Scribner's, 1937.

Stouffer, Samuel A., *Communism, Conformity, and Civil Liberties*, Doubleday, 1955.

Street, D., and J. C. Leggett, "Economic Deprivation and Extremism: A Study of Unemployed Negroes," *AJS*, July, 1961, pp. 53–57.

Street, James H., *The New Revolution in the Cotton Economy*, Univ. of North Carolina Press, 1957.

Strong, Donald S., *Organized Anti-Semitism in America: The Rise of Group Prejudice During the Decade 1930–40*, American Council on Public Affairs, 1941.

Strong, Donald S., *Negroes, Ballots, and Judges*, Alabama, 1968.

Stroup, Atlee, *Marriage and Family: A Developmental Approach*, Appleton-Century-Crofts, 1966.

Stryker, Sheldon, "Social Structure and Prejudice," *SP*, Spring, 1959, pp. 340–354.

Stuckert, Robert S., "The African Ancestry of the White American Population," *Ohio Journal of Science*, May, 1958, pp. 155–160.

Sullivan, Patrick L., and Joseph Adelson, "Ethnocentrism and Misanthropy," *JASP*, Apr., 1954, pp. 246–250.

Sutherland, Robert L., *Color, Class, and Personality*, ACE, 1942.

Sweat, Edward F., "State and Local Politics in 1968," in Patricia W. Romero (ed.), *In Black America*, United, 1969, pp. 133–146.

Taeuber, Karl E., "Negro Population and Housing: Demographic Aspects of a Social Accounting Scheme," in Irwin Katz and Patricia Gurin (eds.), *Race and the Social Sciences*, Basic Books, 1969.

Taeuber, Edward F., "The Problem of Residential Segregation," in Robert H. Connery (ed.), *Urban Riots: Violence and Social Change*, Proceedings of the Academy of Political Science, Columbia Univ., 1968, pp. 103–112.

Taeuber, Edward F., and Alma F. Taeuber, "Is the Negro an Immigrant Group?" *Integrated Education*, June, 1963, pp. 25–28. Reprinted in August Meier and Elliott Rudwick (eds.), *The Making of Black America*, Atheneum, Vol. 2, 1969, pp. 503–507.

Taeuber, Edward F., and Alma F. Taeuber, *Negroes in Cities*, Aldine, 1965.

Tajfel, Henry, "Cognitive Aspects of Prejudice," *JSI*, Autumn, 1969, pp. 79–97.

Tannenbaum, Frank, *Slave and Citizen: The Negro in the Americas*, Knopf, 1947.

Tanter, Raymond, and Manus Midlarsky, "A Theory of Revolution," *JCR*, Sept., 1967, pp. 264–280.

Tarter, Donald E., "Toward Prediction of Attitude-Action Discrepancy," *SF*, June, 1969, pp. 398–405.

TenBroek, Jacobus, Edward N. Barnhart, and Floyd W. Matson, *Prejudice, War, and the Constitution*, Univ. of California Press, 1954.

TenHouten, Warren D., "The Black Family: Myth and Reality," *Psychiatry*, May, 1970, pp. 145–173.

Thomas, John L., *The American Catholic Family*, Prentice-Hall, 1956.

Thomas, W. I., and Florian Znaniecki, *The Polish Peasant in Europe and America*, 2 vols., Knopf, 1927.

Thompson, Charles H., "Equality of Educational Opportunity," *JNE*, Summer, 1968, pp. 196–197.

Thompson, Charles H., "The Higher Education of Negro Americans, Prospects and Problems," *JNE*, Summer, 1967, p. 201.

Thompson, Charles H., "The Present Status of the Negro and Church-Related College," *JNE*, Summer, 1960, pp. 236–244.

Thompson, Daniel C., *The Negro Leadership Class*, Prentice-Hall, 1963.

Thompson, Daniel C., "Problems of Faculty Morale," *JNE*, Winter, 1960, pp. 38–46.

Thurow, Lester C., *Poverty and Discrimination*, Brookings Institution, 1969.

Tobin, James, "On Improving the Economic Status of the Negro," *Daedalus*, Fall, 1965, pp. 891–893.

Tomlinson, T. M., "Determinants of Black Politics: Riots and the Growth of Militancy," *Psychiatry*, May, 1970, pp. 247–264.

Traxler, Sister Margaret Ellen, "American Catholics and Negroes," *Phylon*, Winter, 1969, pp. 355–366.

Treiman, Donald J., "Status Discrepancy and Prejudice," *AJS*, May, 1966, pp. 651–664.

Triandis, Harry C., and Early E. Davis, "Race and Belief as Determinants of Behavioral Intentions," *JPSP*, Nov., 1965, pp. 715–725.

Triandis, Harry C., Earl E. Davis, and Shin-Ichi Takezawa, "Some Determinants of Social Distance among American, German, and Japanese Students," *JPSP*, Oct., 1965, pp. 540–551.

Triandis, Harry C., and W. D. Loh, "Race, Status, Quality of Spoken English, and Opinions About Civil Rights as Determinants of Interpersonal Attitudes," *JPSP*, April, 1966, pp. 468–472.

Triandis, Harry C., and Vasso Vassiliou, "Frequency of Contact and Stereotyping," *JPSP*, Nov., 1967, pp. 316–328.

Troldahl, Verling C., and Fredric A. Powell, "A Short-Form Dogmatism Scale for Use in Field Studies," *SF*, Dec., 1965, pp. 211–214.

Trubowitz, Julius, *Changing the Racial Attitudes of Children: The Effects of an Activity Group Program in New York City Schools*, Praeger, 1969.

Tuck, Ruth D., *Not with the Fist*, Harcourt Brace Jovanovich, 1946.

Tumin, Melvin M. (ed.), *Comparative Perspectives on Race Relations*, Little, Brown, 1969.

Tumin, Melvin M., *Race and Intelligence: A Scientific Evaluation*, ADL, 1963.

Turner, Ralph H., "The Public Perception of Protest," *ASR*, Dec., 1969, pp. 815–830.

Tyler, Lawrence L., "The Protestant Ethic Among the Black Muslims," *Phylon*, Spring, 1966, pp. 5–14.

Tynan, John, "Funk, Groove, and Soul," *Down Beat*, Nov., 24, 1960, pp. 18 ff.

U.S. Advisory Commission on Civil Disorders, *Report*, Bantam Books, 1968.

U.S. Army Western Defense Command and Fourth Army, *Japanese in the United States, Final Report: Japanese Evaluation from the West Coast*, Government Printing Office, 1943.

U.S. Bureau of the Census, "Consumer Income: 24 Million Americans—Poverty in the United States, 1969," *Current Population Reports*, Series P-60, No. 76, Dec. 16, 1970.

U.S. Bureau of the Census, "Religion Reported by the Civilian Population of the United States: March, 1957," *Current Population Reports*, Series P-20, No. 79, 1958.

U.S. Bureau of the Census, *The Social and Economic Status of Negroes in the United States*, 1969.

U.S. Commission on Civil Rights, *Civil Rights U.S.A., Housing in Washington, D.C.*, 1962.

U.S. Commission on Civil Rights, *Civil Rights, U.S.A., Public Schools North and West*, 1962.

U.S. Commission on Civil Rights, *Civil Rights, U.S.A., Public Schools Southern States*, 1962.

U.S. Commission on Civil Rights, *Civil Rights, U.S.A., Racial Isolation in the Public Schools*, 2 vols., 1967.

U.S. Commission on Civil Rights, *Report*, 1959.

U.S. Commission on Civil Rights, *Report, Education*, Book 2, 1961.

U.S. Commission on Civil Rights, *Report, Employment*, Book 3, 1961.

U.S. Commission on Civil Rights, *Report, Justice*, Book 5, 1961.

U.S. Commission on Civil Rights, *Report, Voting*, Book 1, 1961.

U.S. Committee for Refugees, *World Refugee Report*, 1970.

U.S. Department of Justice, *Report of the Commissioner of Immigration and Naturalization*, 1969.

U.S. Department of Labor, Office of Policy Planning and Research, *The Negro Family: The Case for National Action*, Mar., 1965.

U.S. Inter-Agency Committee on Mexican-American Affairs, *The Mexican American: A Guide to Materials Relating to Persons of of Mexican Heritage in the United States*, 1969.

Valentin, Hugo, *Antisemitism, Historically and Critically Examined* (trans. by A. G. Chater), Viking, 1936.

Valentine, Charles A., *Culture and Poverty*, Univ. of Chicago Press, 1968.

Valien, Preston, "Improving Programs in Graduate Education for Negroes," *JNE*, Summer, 1967, pp. 242–245.

Van Darn, H. G., "Antisemitismus ohne Juden," *Politische Studien*, Mar.–Apr., 1965, pp. 133–138.

van den Berghe, Pierre L., "The Dynamics of Racial Prejudice: An Ideal-Type Dichotomy," *SF*, Dec., 1958, pp. 138–141.

van den Berghe, Pierre L., *Race and Ethnicity: Essays in Comparative Sociology*, Basic Books, 1970.

van den Berghe, Pierre L., *Race and Racism: A Comparative Perspective*, Wiley, 1967.

van den Berghe, Pierre L., *South Africa: A Study in Conflict*, Wesleyan Univ. Press, 1965.

Vander Zanden, James W., "The Klan Revival," *AJS*, Mar., 1960, pp. 456–462.

Vander Zanden, James W., "The Non-Violent Resistance Movement Against Segregation," *AJS*, Mar., 1963, pp. 544–550.

Vazquez, H. I., "Puerto Rican Americans," *JNE*, Summer, 1969, pp. 247–254.

Wagley, Charles, "On the Concept of Social Race in the Americas," in D. B. Heath and R. N. Adams (eds.), *Contemporary Cultures and Societies of Latin America*, Random House, 1965.

Wagley, Charles (ed.), *Race and Class in Brazil*, UNESCO, 1952.

Wagley, Charles, and Marvin Harris, *Minorities in the New World*, Columbia, 1958.

Wallace, Anthony, F. C., "Revitalization Movements," *AA*, Apr., 1956, pp. 264–281.

Warner, Lyle G., and Melvin L. DeFleur, "Attitude as an Interactional Concept: Social Constraint and Social Distance as Intervening Variables Between Attitudes and Actions," *ASR*, Apr., 1969, pp. 153–169.

Warner, Lyle G., and Rutledge M. Dennis, "Prejudice Versus Discrimination: An Empirical Example and Theoretical Extension," *SF*, June, 1970, pp. 473–484.

Warner, W. L., B. H. Junker, and W. A. Adams, *Color and Human Nature: Negro Personality Development in a Northern City*, ACE, 1941.

Warren, Donald I., "Suburban Isolation and Race Tension: The Detroit Case," *SP*, Winter, 1970, pp. 324–339.

Washington, Joseph R., Jr., *Black and White Power Subreption*, Beacon Press, 1969.

Washington, Joseph R., Jr., *The Politics of God*, Beacon Press, 1967.

Watkins, Mel, "The Black Revolution in Books," *The New York Times Book Review*, Sept., 10, 1969, p. 8.

Weaver, Charles N., and Norval D. Glenn, "The Job Performance of Mexican-Americans," *Sociology and Social Research*, July, 1970, pp. 477–494.

Weaver, Robert, "Housing for Minority Families," *The Crisis*, Oct., 1966, pp. 425–426.

Weaver, Robert, *Negro Labor, A National Problem*, Harcourt Brace Jovanovich, 1946.

Weinberg, Martin S., and Colin J. Williams, "Disruption, Social Location and Interpretive Practices: The Case of Wayne, New Jersey," *ASR*, Apr., 1969, pp. 170–182.

Weinryb, Bernard, Trafford Maher, and Bernard Olson, "Intergroup Relations in Religious

Textbooks," *Religious Education*, Mar.–Apr., 1960, pp. 109–138.

Weiss, Walter, "An Examination of Attitude Toward Negroes," *JSP*, Oct., 1961, pp. 3–21.

West, E. H., "Progress Toward Equality of Opportunity in Elementary and Secondary Education," *JNE*, Summer, 1968, pp. 215–216.

Westie, Frank R., "The American Dilemma: An Empirical Test," *ASR*, Aug., 1965, pp. 527–538.

Westie, Frank R., "Negro-White Status Differentials and Social Distance," *ASR*, Oct., 1952, pp. 550–558.

Westie, Frank R., and Margaret L. Westie, "The Social-Distance Pyramid: Relationships Between Caste and Class," *AJS*, Sept., 1957, pp. 190–196.

Whitam, Frederick L., "Subdimensions of Religiosity and Race Prejudice," *Review of Religious Research*, Spring, 1962, pp. 166–174.

White, Ralph K., and Ronald Lippitt, *Autocracy and Democracy: An Experimental Inquiry*, Harper & Row, 1960.

White, Walter, *A Man Called White*, Viking, 1948.

Whitten, Norman E., and John F. Szwed. *Afro-American Anthropology*, Free Press, 1970.

Wicker, Allan W., "Attitudes versus Actions: The Relationship of Verbal and Overt Behavioral Responses to Attitude Objects," *JSI*, Autumn, 1969, pp. 41–78.

Wiley, Norbert F., "The Ethnic Mobility Trap and Stratification Theory," *SP*, Fall, 1967, pp. 147–159.

Williams, J. Allen, Jr., "Regional Differences in Authoritarianism," *SF*, Dec., 1966, pp. 273–277.

Williams, J. Allen, Jr. and Paul L. Wienir, "A Reexamination of Myrdal's Rank Order of Discriminations," *SP*, Spring, 1967, pp. 443–454.

Williams, Robert L., and Harry Byars, "The Effect of Academic Integration on the Self-Esteem of Southern Negro Students," *JSP*, Apr., 1970, pp. 183–188.

Williams, Robin M., Jr., *The Reduction of Intergroup Tensions*, SSRC, 1947.

Williams, Robin M., Jr., with John P. Dean and Edward A. Suchman, *Strangers Next Door*, Prentice-Hall, 1964.

Willie, Charles V. (ed.), *The Family Life of Black People*, Charles E. Merrill, 1970.

Wilner, Daniel M., Rosabelle P. Walkley, and Stuart W. Cook., *Human Relations in Interracial Housing*, Univ. of Minnesota Press, 1955.

Wilson, Cody, "Extrinsic Religious Values and Prejudice," *JASP*, Mar., 1960, pp. 286–291.

Wilson, James Q., "The Negro in Politics," *Daedalus*, Fall, 1965, pp. 949–973.

Wilson, James Q., *Negro Politics: The Search for Leadership*, Free Press, 1960.

Wilson, James Q., *Varieties of Police Behavior*, Harvard, 1968.

Wilson, Prince E., "Some Aspects of the Education of Black Americans, 1968," in Patricia W. Romero (ed.), *In Black America*, United, 1969.

Wirth, Louis, *The Ghetto*, Univ. of Chicago Press, 1928.

Wirth, Louis, "The Problem of Minority Groups," in Ralph Linton (ed.), *The Science of Man in the World Crisis*, Columbia, 1945, pp. 347–372.

Wolf, Eleanor P., "The Invasion-Succession Sequence as a Self-Fulfilling Prophecy," *JSI*, Vol. XIII, No. 4, 1957, pp. 7–20.

Wolfgang, Marvin E., and Bernard Cohen, *Crime and Race*, Institute of Human Relations Press, 1970.

Wood, James R., "Authority and Controversial Policy: The Churches and Civil Rights," *ASR*, Dec., 1970, pp. 1057–1069.

Wood, James R., and Mayer N. Zald, "Aspects of Racial Integration in the Methodist Church: Sources of Resistance to Organizational Policy," *SF*, Dec., 1966, pp. 255–265.

Woodward, C. Vann, *The Strange Career of Jim Crow*, Oxford, 1955.

Woofter, T. J., Jr., *Landlord and Tenant on the Cotton Plantation*, Division of Social Research, Works Progress Administration, 1936.

Works, Ernest, "Types of Racial Discrimination," *Phylon*, Fall, 1969, pp. 223–233.

Wright, Richard, *Black Boy*, Harper & Row, 1937.

Yarrow, Marian Radke (issue ed.), "Interpersonal Dynamics in a Desegregation Process," *JSI*, 1958, Vol. 14, No. 1, pp. 1–63.

Yinger, J. Milton, "Contraculture and Subculture," *ASR*, Oct., 1960, pp. 625–635.

Yinger, J. Milton, "On the Definition of Interfaith Marriage," *JSSR*, Spring, 1968, pp. 104–107.

Yinger, J. Milton, *A Minority Group in American Society*, McGraw-Hill, 1965.

Yinger, J. Milton, "Recent Developments in Minority and Race Relations," *Annals*, July, 1968, pp. 130–145.

Yinger, J. Milton, "A Research Note on Interfaith Marriage Statistics," *JSSR*, Spring, 1968, pp. 97–103.

Yinger, J. Milton, *The Scientific Study of Religion*, Macmillan, 1970.

Yinger, J. Milton, *Sociology Looks at Religion*, Macmillan, 1963.

Yinger, J. Milton, *Toward a Field Theory of Behavior*, McGraw-Hill, 1965.

Yinger, J. Milton, Kiyoshi Ikeda, and Frank Laycock, *Middle Start: Supportive Interventions for Higher Education Among Students of Disadvantaged Background*, U.S. Office of Education, Bureau of Research, Final Report for Project No. 5–0703, 1970.

Yinger, J. Milton, Kiyoshi Ikeda, and Frank Laycock, "Treating Matching as a Variable in a Sociological Experiment," *ASR*, Oct., 1967, pp. 801–812.

Yinger, J. Milton, and George E. Simpson, "The Integration of Americans of Mexican, Puerto Rican, and Oriental Descent," *Annals*, Mar., 1956, pp. 124–131.

Young, Kimball, *Social Psychology*, Appleton-Century-Crofts, 3rd ed., 1956.

Young, Whitney M., Jr., *To Be Equal*, McGraw-Hill, 1964.

Young, Whitney M., Jr., *Beyond Racism: Building an Open Society*, McGraw-Hill, 1969.

Young, Virginia Heyer, "Family and Childhood in a Southern Negro Community," *AA*, Apr., 1970, pp. 269–288.

Yuan, D. Y., "Chinatown and Beyond: The Chinese Population in Metropolitan New York," *Phylon*, Winter, 1966, pp. 321–332.

Zimmer, Basil G., "The Adjustment of Negroes in a Northern Industrial Community," *SP*, Spring, 1962, pp. 378–386.

INDEX OF NAMES

Aaron, Daniel, 298
Abate, Mario, 149
Aberbach, Joel D., 710
Aberle, Sophie, 112
Abernathy, Ralph, 705
Ablon, Joan, 714
Abrams, Charles, 435, 436, 438–440, 446
Ackerman, Nathan W., 26, 73, 74, 287, 288, 295, 296
Adams, Harold E., 639
Adams, R. N., 36
Adams, Romanzo, 142
Adams, W. A., 169
Adams, Walter, 583–586, 591, 593, 594, 607
Adelson, Joseph, 84, 197, 295
Adler, Cyrus, 279
Adorno, T. W., 78, 79, 96, 287, 660, 691
Ahmann, Mathew, 533, 534
Ailey, Alvin, 635
Alex, Nicholas, 454, 456, 457
Alexander II, 260
Alexander III, 260
Alexander, Charles, 9
Ali, Muhammad, 522
Ali, Noble Drew, 520, 521
Allen, James S., 128
Allen, Russell O., 529, 530
Allen, Vernon, 184, 193, 194, 218
Allport, Gordon, 65, 162, 289, 527–529, 673, 675, 695
Almond, Gabiel, 298
Altshuler, A. A., 353, 354, 358, 404, 410, 459, 573–575
Alves, Paget L., Jr., 441
Anderson, Marian, 635
Anderson, S. E., 623
Anderson, Thomas, 266
Andrews, Benny, 638
Angell, Robert, 82, 93, 133, 527, 534
Anisfield, Moshe, 295
Anthony, Clara B., 223
Anthony, Earl, 709
Anthony, P., 551
Antonovsky, Aaron, 28, 29, 178, 179, 185, 199
Aptheker, Herbert, 128, 136
Ardrey, Robert, 10, 76
Arendt, Hannah, 266
Armor, David, 193
Arnez, Nancy L., 223
Aronson, Elliot, 65, 692
Asher, Steven, 193, 194
Atkinson, Carolyn O., 571
Aubery, Pierre, 271
Axelrad, Sidney, 453
Axline, Virginia M., 695

Babchuk, Nicholas, 230
Badillo, Herman, 124
Bagley, Christopher, 187
Bailey, Kenneth K., 535
Baker, James, 83

Baldwin, James, 72, 73, 196, 252, 521, 525, 526, 617, 619, 622, 624, 626
Baldwin, James M., 167, 248
Ball, Harry V., 9, 450
Ball, Richard, 175
Banfield, Edward, 175
Banton, Michael, 11, 15, 34, 60, 144, 515
Barbour, Floyd B., 402, 403
Barker, Horace, 441
Barnett, Ross, 35
Barnhart, Edward N., 120
Barnicot, Nigel A., 40
Barron, M. L., 196, 223, 492, 497, 500, 504, 507, 511
Barthe, Richmond, 635
Bass, Bernard M., 84, 85
Bayley, David, 184
Bayton, J. A., 146, 148, 584, 591
Beach, Waldo, 535, 536
Beals, Ralph, 36
Beard, Charles A., 106, 273
Beard, Miriam, 258, 259
Beattie, Muriel, 179
Beck, Dorothy F., 695
Becker, Howard P., 191
Belafonte, Harry, 643
Bell, Inge P., 707, 722
Bell, Robert R., 464
Belth, N. C., 278, 279, 643–645
Bender, Eugene, 291
Bendix, Reinhard, 133, 286
Benedict, Ruth, 107, 109–111, 721
Benjamin, L., 99
Bennett, Fay, 317
Bennett, Lerone, 32
Benyon, E. D., 521
Berger, Milton, 695
Berger, Morroe, 418, 431–434, 450, 611
Berk, Richard, 411
Berkowitz, Leonard, 69, 85
Bernard, Jessie, 470–472
Berrien, F. Kenneth, 149
Berry, Brewton, 196, 497
Berry, Edwin C., 447
Bettelheim, Bruno, 132, 171, 284–286, 528, 692
Beverly, G., 132
Bienen, Henry, 218
Biggar, Jeanne, 82, 93, 530
Biggers, John, 636
Bilbo, Theodore, 276
Billingsley, Andrew, 376, 468–471, 473
Birch, Herman, 203
Birdsell, J. B., 45
Bismarck, Otto von, 110, 263
Bivens, B., 82
Black, Isabella, 10
Blalock, H. M., Jr., 11, 132, 134
Blatchford, Herbert, 189
Blauner, Robert, 717, 718
Blood, Robert O., 464, 506, 507, 514, 516

Bloom, B. S., 82
Bloom, Leonard, 120, 486, 543
Bloom, Richard, 166
Blue, John, Jr., 12
Blumenthal, Ralph, 386, 387
Blumer, Herbert, 7, 29, 697
Boas, Franz, 35, 50
Bock, E. Wilbur, 525
Bock, R. Darrell, 85
Boeke, J. H., 8
Boesel, David, 218, 411
Bogardus, Emory S., 144, 149, 150
Bogue, Donald J., 317, 475, 513
Boll, E. S., 493, 506, 508
Bond, H. M., 369, 375, 377, 546, 547
Bone, Robert A., 615, 617, 619, 624
Bontemps, A., 614, 616
Borhek, J. T., 198
Borrie, W. D., 125
Boskin, Joseph, 408
Bossard, J. H. S., 493, 506, 508
Boulainvilliers, Count de, 34, 109
Bourgue, Linda B., 720
Bourne, Randolph, 7
Bowen, Don R., 218
Bowles, Samuel, 337, 569
Boyd, William C., 41–43, 46, 53
Brace, C. L., 43, 45
Bracey, John H., Jr., 199, 215, 220, 519, 602
Braly, Kenneth, 145
Breed, Warren, 104, 697
Bressler, Marvin, 673
Briggs, William, 687
Brimmer, Andrew, 354, 361, 362, 380, 586
Brink, William, 291
Brinton, Crane, 715
Britt, S. H., 49, 255, 258, 298, 304, 307, 308, 543
Broderick, Francis L., 249, 704, 706, 707, 709
Brody, Eugene, 144, 146
Bronfenbrenner, Urie, 173
Brooke, Edward W., 6
Brookover, Wilbur, 99
Brooks, Gwendolyn, 615, 619, 621
Broom, Leonard, 66, 123, 187, 485
Brophy, William, 112
Brown, Claude, 222, 626
Brown, Clifton F., 374
Brown, Francis J., 485
Brown, H. Rap, 705
Brown, J. F., 307
Brown, John, 519
Brown, Roger W., 87
Brown, Sterling A., 612–618, 639, 640
Bruce, Louis, 714
Brunswick, Ann F., 169, 210, 228, 232
Brustein, Robert, 668

INDEX OF SUBJECTS